Bill Jacklin, *Sheep Meadow III*, 1990. Courtesy of Marlborough Gallery I

Bill Jacklin
Sheep Meadow III, 1990
Oil on canvas

Since moving to New York City in the mid-1980s, Bill Jacklin (1943-), a British figurative painter, has focused on the ambiguities in contemporary human experience. His talent lies in his ability to depict both the private world of individuals and the movement and power associated with groups of people. As we study this diverse gathering in New York's Central Park, we begin to see order in the world's constant flux. Similarly, social psychologists look for order in diversity—influences that make different individuals react in the same way under the same social circumstances.

Chapter 4 **The Self**	Chapter 5 **Perceiving Groups**	Chapter 6 **Social Identity**	Chapter 7 **Attitudes and Attitude Change**
We construct an impression of the self based on a multitude of cues.	We construct impressions of social groups based on our interactions with group members and what we learn from others.	We construct the self using our knowledge about our social groups.	We construct attitudes based on our beliefs and feelings about objects.
Our perceptions of other people and their reactions to us pervasively influence our self-concept and self-esteem.	These interactions and the things we learn are shaped by society and culture.	This construction process imports social influences into the very core of the self.	In this construction process, we draw heavily on information supplied by other people or by persuasive messages.
Perceiving that we control our environment helps mental well-being and physical health.			Attitudes help us master our environment and obtain rewards.
		Group memberships that we share with others are rewarding.	Attitudes also help us express our connectedness with groups or ideas we value.
Self-enhancing biases shape our self-concept and elevate self-esteem.		We positively value the groups to which we belong as well as our individual self.	
Once formed, the self-concept is resistant to change and well defended against threats.	Stereotypes perpetuate themselves by shaping both the way we think and the way we act.		
The self-concept and self-esteem depend on information and experiences that come readily to mind.			
	Stereotypes influence judgments made quickly with little thought and also judgments made by collecting further information.		Attitude change may result when we process persuasive messages superficially or when we think about them in more depth.

At&S + Behav.

Social Psychology

Social Psychology

Eliot R. Smith
Purdue University

Diane M. Mackie
University of California, Santa Barbara

Worth Publishers

To our parents
Curtis and Elaine Smith
and
Daniel and Joan Mackie

Social Psychology

Manufactured in the United States of America
Library of Congress Catalog Card Number: 94-60648
ISBN: 0–87901–719–8
Printing: 1 2 3 4—97 96 95

Development Editor: Phyllis Fisher
Design: Malcolm Grear Designers
Art Director: George Touloumes
Production Editor: Toni Ann Scaramuzzo
Production Supervisor: Barbara Anne Seixas
Layout: Matthew Dvorozniak
Photographs: June Lundborg Whitworth
Line art: Demetrios Zangos
Composition and separations: TSI Graphics, Inc.
Printing and binding: Von Hoffmann Press, Inc.

Also Available for Students
Alan Marks *Study Guide to accompany Social Psychology*
ISBN: 0–87901–749–X

Cover: Bill Jacklin, *Sheep Meadow III* (detail), 1990.
Courtesy of Marlborough Gallery Inc.
Illustration credits begin in the back of the book on page IC, and constitute an extension of the copyright page.

Worth Publishers
33 Irving Place
New York, NY 10003

About the Authors

Eliot R. Smith is Professor of Psychological Sciences at Purdue University. He received his BA and PhD from Harvard University. He has taught a wide range of undergraduate and graduate courses in social psychology at Purdue since 1982, and before that at the University of California, Riverside (1975–1982).

A distinguished researcher, his current interests center on person perception, stereotyping, and memory. Since 1992 he has chaired the Social and Group Processes research review committee of the U.S. National Institute of Mental Health. This experience, along with service as Associate Editor of the Attitudes and Social Cognition section of the *Journal of Personality and Social Psychology,* and as a member of the editorial boards of two major social psychology journals, has given him a broad view of the research being conducted in all areas of social psychology.

He is coauthor of two books, *Research Methods in Social Relations, 6th edition* (with Charles Judd and Louise Kidder) and *Beliefs about Inequality* (with James Kluegel), and author of more than 50 book chapters and articles.

Eliot and Pamela Smith are parents of two children—Miranda, an undergraduate at Indiana University, and Tom, an avid Boilermaker fan who shares his Dad's interest in music and sports.

Diane M. Mackie is Professor of Psychology at the University of California, Santa Barbara, where she has been honored with a 1994 Distinguished Teacher Award. She grew up in New Zealand, received her BA and MA at the University of Auckland, and then worked as a researcher for a year in Geneva. She received her PhD in social psychology from Princeton University in 1984.

The opportunities her education afforded her to become steeped in both the European and North American traditions of social psychology are evident in her research and in the integration of topics in this textbook. She is editor of *Affect, Cognition, and Stereotyping* (with David L. Hamilton) and author of about 50 articles and chapters on persuasion, social influence, and group and intergroup processes. Among her many honors are the Western Psychological Association's Outstanding Young Researcher Award in 1992 and the American Psychological Association's Young Psychologist Award 1989.

Dr. Mackie is Associate Editor of the *Personality and Social Psychology Bulletin* and a member of the editorial boards of other professional journals and of the grant review panels of the U.S. National Science Foundation and the Social Sciences and Humanities Research Council of Canada.

Contents in Brief

Social Psychology in Applied Settings

This brief index provides a ready reference to major application sections integrated within the chapters. Other shorter discussions of applied topics also appear throughout the book.

Business

Education

Environment

Health

Legal System

Media

Politics and Social Change

Sports

Contents

Preface

"No wise fish would go anywhere without a porpoise," claims *Alice in Wonderland*'s Mock Turtle. "Why, if a fish came to me, and told me he was going on a journey, I should say 'With what porpoise?'" Had the Mock Turtle asked us our purpose in undertaking this textbook-writing journey, the answer would have been simple. We wanted to convey to an undergraduate audience some of our excitement about and appreciation for the richness and variety of human social behavior by presenting social psychology in a conceptually integrated way. Both of us have felt frustration at textbooks that portray social behavior as a list of interesting but unrelated phenomena explained by numerous never-to-be-heard-from-again minitheories. We have felt disappointment when laboratory studies are presented in isolation from "real-world" settings—the courtroom, school, supermarket, or hospital—where "real" applications take place. And we have been concerned that the special nature of social psychology as the interface between the individual and the social world becomes lost in treatments that emphasize one of these two aspects over the other.

Our purpose, then, has been integration. Our goal is to present both social behavior and the science that studies it in a conceptually and thematically integrated way. We want to show students not just the wonderfully diverse *what* of social behavior but also the impressively orderly and organized *how* and *why* of it. Our pursuit of these goals is reflected in three ways of weaving together the content of this book.

Three Types of Integration

- *Integration of diverse topics through unifying principles.* Eight basic principles that apply to social behavior emerge and reemerge in the text. The two most fundamental are that people construct their social reality and that social influence pervades social life. In addition, we structure our discussion of people's interaction with their social world by introducing three overarching motivational principles and three processing principles that direct and determine thoughts, feelings, and actions. The powerful effects of these principles give coherence to our descriptions of research findings and theoretical approaches in every area of social psychology. By focusing on these core ideas, students can enhance their conceptual understanding of social psychology and can take away from the course knowledge that is applicable to their everyday lives.

- *Integration of the social and the cognitive.* Our discipline was founded—indeed broke away from its parent field of psychology—on the idea that people's behavior depends on their perceptions and interpretations of social situations. Recent research in social cognition has aimed at spelling out in detail the way these cognitive processes operate. But social psychologists are also aware that social motives, interpersonal relationships, and emotional attachments to group membership guide and direct everything people do. The intertwining of social and cognitive processes is the essential tension of human social behavior, and we have made it a central theme of our textbook. The theme is reflected in the social and cognitive nature of the unifying principles. It is reflected again in the research and theories we describe: we have made a special effort to bring together the contributions of both North American and European social psychologists, who have emphasized somewhat different aspects of the cognitive/social interface. Finally, it is mirrored in our special focus on cultural, ethnic, and national similarities and differences in social behavior.
- *Integration of basic science and applications.* Historically, social psychology has focused simultaneously on advancing theory and addressing important social problems. In our book we stress that the same underlying processes of social perception, social influence, and social relations operate in the experimental laboratory, in field research, and in people's everyday lives. In each chapter we describe the practical implications of the theory and research being discussed. There is a discussion of polygraph usage next to a section on nonverbal cues to deception, an overview of jury decision making in the chapter on group influence, a discussion of Pygmalion in the classroom as part of the presentation of self-fulfilling prophesies, and an account of subliminal advertising following the description of persuasion and counterargument. These applications should stimulate students to think about the breadth and generality of the underlying processes, reinforcing the idea that ours is an integrated field.

In formulating and pursuing these integrative goals we have been inspired by the example set by David Krech and Richard S. Crutchfield's famous 1948 social psychology text. Despite the huge differences between the social psychology of their day and ours, their approach and ours are similar in several key ways. Most fundamentally, Krech and Crutchfield also aimed at a systematic, integrated treatment. They also stressed the linkages between basic and applied research: "The basic guiding principle has been that a theoretically sound social psychology is also a practically valid and immediately useful social psychology" (p. vii). Finally, they emphasized the role of both social and cognitive processes in social behavior, drawing particularly on the most active area of cognitive psychology in their time: the study of perception. The ideas presented in the Krech and Crutchfield text had a profound influence on those who taught us social psychology and who instilled in us a passion for combining, intertwining, and integrating the social and the cognitive.

The impetus for an integrated treatment of social psychology is the same today as it was a generation ago. There is an esthetic pleasure in showing students how the diverse findings of our field fit together in an intellectually coherent way. As social psychologists who care deeply about our field, we take pride in demonstrating its growth as a science and the accumulation of knowledge about social behavior. The integrative enterprise also reveals the existence of a number of fascinating substantive areas still underresearched. For example, huge amounts of research have examined the impact of attitudes on behavior. Though the effect of *norms* on behavior is equally great—and arguably greater—only a scattering of existing studies address this relationship.

However, the most important benefits of integration are pedagogical: showing students social psychology as an integrated whole, rather than as a list of topics that happen to share a label, makes our field both *easier to understand* and *more applicable.* As the same few principles emerge again and again in diverse topics, they become a coherent organizing framework for particular findings and theories. Many recent reports and studies of science education support the integrated approach. They conclude that science is most effectively taught to students of all ages not by cramming them full of "facts" but by stressing integrative themes, presenting findings in their context, and showing theories together with their applications (Tobias, 1990; Celis, 1993). We believe our approach will enable students at every level of ability to succeed in the course and to take away ideas that will help them to understand themselves and others better throughout their lives.

Organization and Emphases of the Text

After two chapters that introduce the field of social psychology and the conceptual basis of its research methods, the remaining chapters are organized into three broad topic areas that build one on another: social perception, social influence, and social relations. Within each of these areas are four chapters, the first two dealing with individuals and the last two focusing on groups.

In terms of the book's integrative principles, the material on social perception naturally emphasizes the role of cognitive processes, but it continually reinforces the idea that all cognition is socially influenced—even such basic and personal ideas as what we think about ourselves. The section on social influence naturally focuses on the role of social processes, but it stresses that the effects of social processes are mediated through cognitive processes—as, for example, the amount of effort people devote to processing persuasive arguments. Finally, the section on social relations illustrates the manner in which social and cognitive processes are inextricably intertwined as they influence the ways we get to know and like other people, help or harm them, and cooperate or compete in groups. The book ends with a brief Epilogue summarizing the major themes and reflecting on some of their interrelationships and applications.

Although this organization seems to us to enhance the thematic presentation of concepts and topics, the integrated nature of the material allows instructors considerable flexibility in organizing their courses. The **Instructor's Resources** suggests several teaching sequences that emphasize different approaches to the material—without surrendering the advantages of integration. For example, those who wish to focus on the "social" before the "psychology" will find that the group chapters work as well before the individual chapters as after them. Those who believe that attitudes are the core topic in the field will find that the social influence section can easily precede the social perception chapters.

In keeping with our integrated approach, there are no separate chapters on "law," "business," or "education." Instead of relegating these interesting topics to the "back-of-the-bus," we have integrated applications of social psychological theories and research throughout the text. By so doing, we hope to reinforce and strengthen the idea that exactly the same processes studied by researchers in their labs operate in applied settings to produce socially significant effects. Further, we use a broad definition of "applied," considering not only major institutions like law and business but also such topics as media violence and aggression, social support and health, cooperation in solving environmental problems, "choking under pressure" in sports, conflicts in international relations, and the effectiveness of advertising. Sections focusing on applied topics are flagged by red arrows. For the convenience of instructors who wish to devote lecture time specifically to summing up the implications of social psychology for an applied area, and for students with a special interest in a particular area, we have supplied a topical index to applications on page vii.

Features to Enhance Learning

There are several special features to aid the student's learning.

- **Integrative Features.** Consistent with our generally integrative intentions, the text has no "boxes" or "special points of interest"—indeed, everything of interest is right there in the main text. The emergence and reemergence of the basic principles are noted by the repetition of key words or phrases designed to activate and reactivate these concepts in students' minds. At the end of each chapter, a themes table summarizes the most important applications of the basic principles—and these summaries are all brought together in a matrix printed in the endpapers. To further the idea that the same principles recur again and again, we provide margin references to related points in other chapters.

The end of the narrative of each chapter is devoted to Concluding Comments, our reflections on some larger issues raised by the chapter, on interrelations among chapters, or on special aspects of the way the principles play themselves out in the chapter.

- **Organizational Features.** Each chapter opens with an outline of the chapter's main headings, and an introduction to the key problems and topics to be discussed. In addition, each major section within the chapter begins with a short preview to give the reader an idea of what is coming. Such advance organizers provide a simple structure that helps students understand material as they read it for the first time. For example, by identifying the main ideas of the section, the preview allows students to focus their initial reading on grasping those ideas rather than becoming sidetracked by details. The innovative nature and placement of these preview sections resulted from class-testing a preliminary version of the book.

- **Graphical Features.** An important innovation is the end-of-chapter graphical overview, which summarizes the chapter with a conceptual map rather than a verbal summary. At a glance, it provides an overview of the main concepts of the chapter and their interrelations. Advocates of concept mapping and similar approaches have repeatedly found that graphical summaries of key concepts can greatly enhance learning (Ault, 1985; Briscoe & LaMaster, 1991). We hope that these will help students develop a coherent understanding of the way specific processes and their products fit together to constitute the big picture. Students who class-tested the manuscript have raved about these graphical overviews.

  In line with our emphasis on the principles that underlie the diversity of behavior, explanations are often supplemented by graphical flowcharts, representations of key processes that demonstrate how and why such behavior arises. Results from key studies are also shown in easy-to-understand bar charts.

- **Other Features.** A running glossary defines the most significant terms and concepts on the pages on which they are introduced. All entries are included in the glossary at the end of the book. Finally, besides the conceptual map and summary of key themes, the end of each chapter also features a verbal summary that includes the key terms, for review and reference.

Supplements That Accompany the Book

The **Instructor's Resources,** by Angela Lipsitz of Northern Kentucky University, provides extended outlines, lecture suggestions, "activities" for use in and out of class, classroom demonstrations, handouts, and lists of audiovisual materials for each chapter of the text. To help develop student appreciation of the integrated approach to social behavior, this manual includes coverage of how the basic principles are manifested in each chapter. It also offers suggestions for teaching the material in different sequences and for using the text to provide an extended focus on specific areas of application.

An extensive set of acetate **Transparencies** that includes integral flow charts and tables from the textbook is available upon request.

Rae Gilchrist of the University of Western Ontario has prepared the **Test Bank,** which includes 840 multiple-choice questions covering the material in each chapter. In addition to assessing factual knowledge, questions emphasize concept acquisition, understanding of underlying processes and principles, integration of material within the chapter, and application of chapter material to everyday situations. Worth Publishers provides both a printed **test bank** and **Computerized Test-Generation Systems** that use these questions as a database.

Alan Marks of Berry College in Georgia has written the excellent **Study Guide.** Blending humor with useful summaries and self-tests, the **Study Guide** will help students read for understanding and study for mastery as they focus on the textbook's central themes. It guides students as they learn and review, and it encourages them to extend their understanding by applying learned material to new situations and events—particularly those relevant to students with interests in business, education, law, and the health professions. Hypothetical situations and concept maps are included in each chapter. Thus the **Study Guide** benefits students who need help to learn, and it extends and deepens the understanding of all students.

Acknowledgments

As the Mock Turtle no doubt knew, it takes more than just a porpoise to allow wise fish to complete a journey. We owe thanks to many, many people who have helped us not just to make the journey but to become wise fish. First, our friends, students, and colleagues at the University of California, Santa Barbara, and at Purdue University have provided advice and social support—Arlene Asuncion, Don Carlston, Denise Driscoll, Alice Eagly, Kurt Frey, Faith Gleicher, Dave Hamilton, Janice Kelly, Stan Klein, and Fran Rosselli were particularly important to us. The many undergraduate students who participated in classroom tests of various drafts of the manuscript were also extremely helpful to us—even their occasional puzzled looks provided useful feedback. The all-engrossing process of writing a book always becomes an imposition on family, friends, and companions. We are grateful to Pamela Smith, Miranda Smith, and Tom Smith, and to Pamela Gibbons, Dave Hamilton, Steve Esky, and Russell Esky for putting up with us and giving us perspective on our work. We promise to be in a better mood from now on, to talk about something else every once in a while, and to stop trying to use them as examples until the next edition.

We have been lucky indeed to have had the talent and expertise of Worth Publishers behind us. We began with the conviction that a textbook taking an integrated approach to social psychology could now be written. We thank J. George Owen, good friend and incomparable next-door neighbor, for steering us toward Worth Publishers. The people at Worth—particularly Acquisitions Director Tom Gay and Managing Editor Anne Vinnicombe—liked our ideas and believed we could accomplish our goals. Others had warned us that publishers always try to make you write a book that differs from the one you set out to write. Our experience at Worth has been just the opposite: their efforts were aimed at maintaining the integrity of our original vision, and those efforts have improved and focused our vision enormously.

Our most ardent champion and trenchant critic through the entire process has been Phyllis Fisher, our developmental editor. She coordinated reviews, blue-penciled meandering sentences, pounced on flabby thoughts, and gave us wise advice. We benefited from far more than just her editorial skills: her extensive familiarity with social psychology and her uncommon good sense were also extremely important to us. She made this a much better book than it could possibly have been without her. Nancy Fleming ably assisted with line editing, and Toni Ann Scaramuzzo applied her powers of organization as production editor for the project. We also thank George Touloumes, the director of production; Dometrious Zangos, the designer and preparer of the artwork; Barbara Anne Seixas, the production supervisor for our text; and Matthew Dvorozniak, who did the layout.

Many of our colleagues and friends generously gave their time to review portions of this text. Among the reviewers, Alan Marks and John Skowronski were particularly important to us. Alan's comments on almost every chapter were invariably thoughtful and constructive, and when other reviewers made conflicting suggestions we often found ourselves asking, "What does Alan say?" John not only provided detailed reviews based on his own reading and class-testing but also made important suggestions that greatly improved the graphics and other elements of the book. We hope that Alan and John see how many of their ideas and suggestions have found their way into the text and that they realize how much we appreciate their help. To all those who reviewed various portions of the manuscript, and whose insightful comments have often gently shaped and smoothed the ideas we present here, our heartfelt thanks.

Judith Allen, *Drake University*
Scott T. Allison, *University of Richmond*
Galen V. Bodenhausen, *Michigan State University*
David S. Boninger, *University of California, Los Angeles*
Nyla R. Branscombe, *University of Kansas*
Donal E. Carlston, *Purdue University*
Ken DeBono, *Union College*
Jeffrey D. Fisher, *University of Connecticut*
Philip A. Fisher, *Portland VA Medical Center*

Christopher J. Frost, *Southwest Texas State University*
Frederick Gibbons, *Iowa State University*
Pamela Gibbons, *University of California, Santa Barbara*
Peter Glick, *Lawrence University*
Peter Gray, *Boston College*
Bryan Hendricks, *University of Wisconsin, Marathon Center*
Chester A. Insko, *University of North Carolina*
Dale Jorgenson, *California State University, Long Beach*
Charles M. Judd, *University of Colorado*
Martin F. Kaplan, *Northern Illinois University*
Janice R. Kelly, *Purdue University*
David A. Kenny, *University of Connecticut*
Norbert Kerr, *Michigan State University*
Mary E. Kite, *Ball State University*
William M. Klein, *Colby College*
George Koblyk, *Mohawk College*
Roderick Kramer, *Graduate School of Business, Stanford University*
John Levine, *University of Pittsburgh*
Patricia W. Linville, *Fuqua School of Business, Duke University*
Angela Lipsitz, *Northern Kentucky University*
Alan Marks, *Berry College*
Doug McCann, *York University*
Joseph E. McGrath, *University of Illinois, Urbana–Champaign*
Rowland S. Miller, *Sam Houston State University*
John B. Nezlek, *College of William and Mary*
James M. Olson, *University of Western Ontario*
Susan Opotow, *Teachers College, Columbia University*
Bernadette Park, *University of Colorado*
Richard E. Petty, *Ohio State University*
Mark Schaller, *University of Montana*
Jeff Simpson, *Texas A&M University*
Robert C. Sinclair, *University of Alberta*
John J. Skowronski, *Ohio State University*
Richard M. Sorrentino, *University of Western Ontario*
Garold Stasser, *Miami University (Ohio)*
Janice M. Steil, *Adelphi University*
Bill Swann, *University of Texas at Austin*
Daniel L. Wann, *Murray State University*
Michael A. Zárate, *University of Texas at El Paso*

Finally, we would like to thank each other for the many benefits of coauthorship. Through our collaboration on each section—and sometimes on each sentence—of the text, we believe we have accomplished a sort of integration through teamwork. We learned to respect and admire each other's different strengths and talents, to appreciate each other's different views of the field, and to blame each other when deadlines were missed! We also became much better friends in the process.

To the Student

As you begin your study of social psychology, you may be wondering what this field is all about, and how it relates to your own personal experiences. You are in for a treat, because it is a fascinating field that has much to do with you. Our goal in writing this book is to convey some of the excitement and satisfaction that comes with understanding more about your own and others' social behavior.

One of the reasons social psychology is so fascinating is that the limitless variety of social behavior we see around us every day can be understood as the effects of a few basic principles. Rather than asking you to memorize a large number of unrelated ideas, we have tried to write a book that makes those basic principles easy for you to *see, understand, remember,* and *apply* in your own life. We have sought to accomplish this by

- clearly *identifying* the most basic principles so that you can distinguish them from the many interesting (but less important) facts, studies, and comments;
- *illustrating* the way the basic principles apply to a wide range of situations, including research studies and people's everyday lives.

In our years of studying and teaching, we have found that certain ways of approaching written material can greatly facilitate learning. Based on that experience, we have included a number of features in each chapter to assist you. The basic premise underlying these features is that *effective studying and learning is an active process.* You won't get much out of this or any other textbook if you try to rush through a whole chapter rapidly and passively, the way you might approach a mystery novel. You should divide the chapter into chunks, read each chunk more than once, and reflect on what you have read. Here are some suggestions on how to do that.

- Start by reading the chapter title and looking at the outline of headings. Read the chapter introduction. Browse through the photos and read their captions. This process will give you a general overview of the chapter's content.
- Every chapter contains several major sections. Work on one section at a time, paying particular attention to the *previews,* a unique feature highlighted in yellow that offers a capsule survey of the information that follows. By giving you an idea of what is coming, the previews make it easier to understand the material the first time you read it. The previews will tell you the main ideas of the section to help you avoid getting bogged down in details or mistaking a subsidiary point for the key idea. When you encounter a *flowchart,* read and consider it carefully. It will show you how processes work together or will summarize the main points of a section.
- Keep alert for appearances of the basic principles. By focusing on these

core ideas, you will be able to build an integrated and coherent picture of social psychology's research findings and theories. To remind you of the basic principles, we use the same key words or phrases whenever an example of their operation arises.

- Follow up on the *margin references* whenever they interest you or if you are uncertain whether you remember an idea or argument. This feature is designed to remind you of related ideas elsewhere in the book and to point out similarities or parallels between chapters, helping you to link new material to what you already know.
- The important terms and concepts of the field are presented in **boldface** and are defined in the margins of the pages on which they appear. Psychologists use technical terms for precision in writing. Don't try to memorize their definitions on first reading; it is more important first to understand the gist of what you are reading. You will find it helpful, however, to learn these terms on second reading and to review them when studying for an exam. An alphabetical glossary of all terms and concepts, keyed to the page number on which the term first appears, is at the back of the book.
- After you finish studying each of the chapter's main sections, read the Concluding Comments and the Summary, and review the chapter's main themes, which are highlighted in a table at the end of the chapter. If anything in the Summary seems unfamiliar or unclear, reread the relevant section of the text.
- You're now ready to use the *graphical overview,* the conceptual map at the end of the chapter. This is a visual overview of the most important ideas in the chapter. The concepts are in colored boxes, and their interrelationships are indicated by lines and linking words. You'll find that checking your understanding of this map will help you not only to be clear about the big picture of the chapter's main points but also to review the content before exams. You may want to close the book and see if you can redraw the map as a final check of understanding.

Conceptual maps are a simple way of presenting and organizing a set of related ideas and information. Such maps are a useful tool that promotes active study. You'll have opportunities to engage in many kinds of active study in the excellent *Study Guide* prepared by Professor Alan Marks. It is intended to be used as you study the chapter initially, to help you focus on the key ideas and gain more complete understanding. You may be accustomed to using a study guide only as you review and prepare for an exam. This one will serve that purpose, of course, but it will be most helpful if you use it at each stage of your study.

Finally, we urge you to enjoy yourself. We think social psychology is fascinating and we hope that what you learn in this course will convince you of that, too.

A guide to the special features of this book

It is with great pride that we point out in the following pages some of the distinguishing characteristics of this thoughtful, innovative, user-friendly textbook. With authors Eliot Smith and Diane Mackie as their guides, students are presented with an introduction to social psychology that is broadly relevant and appealing but also readily comprehensible. A few basic themes serve to focus and order what can otherwise seem to the novice a confusing variety of unrelated topics. All explanations, analyses, and applied examples are presented within the context of this thematic framework. Supported with innovative pedagogy, this carefully wrought conceptual integration will do much to ensure that students retain the empowering insights of social psychology long after they have completed the course.

Worth Publishers

Unifying themes provide conceptual integration

The diversity of topics found in social psychology are conveyed through a small number of themes in this book. These themes are engagingly explained, with research studies and applied examples, and their relevance and applicability in a variety of contexts are repeatedly brought home—even in the photos and captions. Chapter themes are recapped at the end of the chapter, and those for the entire book are summarized inside the front and back covers.

Groups, Norms, and Conformity

Conformity to Group Norms
The Development of Social Norms
Public Versus Private Conformity

The Dual Functions of Norms: Mastery and Connectedness
Expecting Consensus
Whose Consensus?
The Dual Functions of Norms
Salience of Group Membership

How Groups Form Norms: Processes of Social Influence
Group Compromise: Taking the Middle Ground
Group Polarization: Going to Normative Extremes
Superficial Processing: Relying on Others' Positions
Systematic Processing: Attending to Both Positions and Arguments

Conformity Pressure: Undermining True Consensus
When Consensus Seeking Goes Awry
Consensus Seeking at Its Worst: Groupthink

Minority Influence: The Value of Dissent
Successful Minority Influence
Processes of Minority and Majority Influence

In August of 1990, scandal rocked the French political scene. At first the annual conference of the French Socialist party seemed a success, with well-attended talks and an enthusiastic reception for the party platform. Then, on the third day of the conference, some members of the audience mistakenly approached reporters to ask for their fee. In doing so, they revealed a gap between appearances and reality: a cabinet minister had hired students, unemployed actors, and day laborers to pose as an enthusiastic audience at the otherwise sparsely attended affair.

As you can imagine, the minister's deception sparked outrage and he was forced to resign in disgrace (Tempest, 1990). But what he may have lacked in political savvy, he made up as a keen observer of social behavior. The minister realized that people are profoundly influenced by others' reactions, and that salting an audience with a few noisy supporters can effectively sway the opinions of many other people.

The political sphere is not the only area in which other people's reactions affect the way we think and act. Consider, for example, the bursts of "audience" laughter blended into the sound tracks of TV comedies. When jokes and slapstick routines are accompanied by canned laughter, people find them funnier and laugh longer and harder (Fuller & Sheehy-Skeffington, 1974; Smyth & Fuller, 1972). Bartenders, street musicians, and collectors for charitable agencies use a similar ploy. They know that if they put dollar bills in their tip jars and collection boxes it will substantially increase the flow of contributions. All of these examples are forms of social influence, which affects every aspect of our lives. We revise our way of speaking to keep up with the status quo—abandoning old expressions and adopting new ones. (What ever happened to *groovy?* And where did *retro* come from?) We update our wardrobes periodically to include this year's most popular colors and to discard the outdated trousers from three years ago. Even our political ideas seem somehow to lean right or left in unison from time to time.

In spite of the frivolous fads that occasionally sweep over us, the impact of others' thoughts, feelings, and behavior is usually positive and appropriate. In fact, a basic premise of social life is that many heads are better than

Defining reality and defining identity
Group members—no matter what their age—soon come to share similar thoughts, experience similar emotions, and act in similar ways. The power of group norms rests on two important human motivations: to master our environment by seeing the world accurately and to achieve a sense of belonging and connectedness with others.

351

Chapter outlines help to organize students' first reading.

The chapter's key themes are recapped.

Chapter summaries follow the development of key ideas in the chapter.

Chapter 9 Themes

Construction of Reality
Individuals and groups construct consensus about what is true and good.

Pervasiveness of Social Influence
This construction process involves conformity and mutual influence among group members.

Striving for Mastery
Conformity helps us to hold valid opinions because the convergence of many opinions often means correctness.

Seeking Connectedness
Conformity helps us feel connected to and valued by other group members.

Conservatism
Positions supported by a majority in a group usually attract more supporters and do not readily change.

Superficiality Versus Depth
People process the opinions of other group members either in superficial ways or with careful consideration.

tion, like that of other social groups, is to seek consensus. Regardless of researchers' different theoretical perspectives, tests of theories and evaluations of information should ultimately converge on the same outcome. And reaching the same conclusion from different theoretical backgrounds, using different techniques, with different subjects, offers strong evidence for the validity of the shared conclusion. Such convergence increases our certainty that we are learning about a phenomenon that is real to all of us and independent of our preconceived views. All the norms and procedures of science are intended to promote systematic processing and the acceptance of positions based on the underlying evidence rather than on public conformity. This in turn means that minority influence should be maximized, allowing for the acceptance of new insights and innovations.

True consensus is achieved only when a variety of opinions are processed from multiple points of view and are accepted only after being proved valid by such processing. When we think about how consensus is forged, we can see that true consensus should be constantly undergoing revision. The current norm should be constantly open to new ideas that might challenge the status quo. We should listen to minority opinions, instead of closing our minds and finding comfort in majority support for our existing view. When new ideas become too threatening to the status quo, groups often try to expel the deviants from the group. But as we have seen, the expression and consideration of minority views is crucial to the development of reliable group norms. Thus it is important to nurture diverse and different voices in any group: the strength of a group's norms depends on their being forged from the consideration of many points of view.

Summary

Conformity to Group Norms Because people are profoundly influenced by others' ideas and actions, interaction causes the thoughts, feelings, and behaviors of members of **face-to-face groups** to become more alike. Whether a judgment task is clear-cut or ambiguous, individual members shift their views toward the group consensus to form a social norm. Norms reflect the group's generally accepted ways of thinking, feeling, and acting.

Conformity is the convergence of individual responses toward group norms. Conformity occurs for two reasons: because people believe that the group is right and because they want the group to accept and approve of them. Most of the time people engage in **private conformity**, adopting group norms as their own because they believe them to be correct and appropriate. Sometimes, however, people display **public conformity**, acting consistently with norms they do not privately accept.

The Dual Functions of Norms: Mastery and Connectedness Private conformity comes about because we expect to see the world in the same way similar others see it. In fact, we often assume that most other people share

394

Basic and applied science are integrated

A wealth of examples from the law, business, education, health, and other applied settings makes it abundantly clear that the same underlying processes operate in the laboratory, the field, and everyday life. A guide to the major discussions of applied topics is on page vii. Within the book, these are highlighted by ▶. Other applied discussions are integrated throughout the book.

Social Psychology in Applied Settings

This brief index provides a ready reference to major application sections integrated within the chapters. Other shorter discussions of applied topics also appear throughout the book.

▶ **Minority Influence in the Jury Room.** As we have seen, the expression and consideration of minority views can be vital to preventing groupthink and forming a valid consensus. And this principle has important implications for jury deliberations. In 1972, the U.S. Supreme Court ruled that states may allow juries to give verdicts that command only majority support, holding that there is neither legal nor historical basis for requiring unanimity. Unfortunately, this ruling makes it possible for a majority to ignore minority views. An initial majority would have no need to convince the minority to go along with its position, nor any strong reason to listen to the minority's arguments. Could loosening the requirement of unanimity weaken minority influence and perhaps even lessen the quality of jury decisions?

Turning minorities into majorities In the film "Twelve Angry Men," Henry Fonda (second in on far right) finds himself the lone juror voting for acquittal in a murder case. Fonda's character presents his minority view with such consistency and confidence that other members of the jury consider the evidence systematically—and eventually change their minds. In real jury rooms, establishing an alternate consensus and maintaining it with consistency and confidence are so difficult that minorities rarely win out over majorities.

To investigate these issues, Charlan Nemeth (1977) divided University of Virginia students into mock juries and asked them to reach a verdict about the guilt or innocence of a defendant charged with murder. Nemeth made sure that each group included some students who initially favored acquittal and others who favored conviction. Some of the juries were forced to deliberate until they reached a unanimous verdict, while others were allowed to bring in a verdict with only a two-thirds majority. The groups forced to consider and respond to minority points of view not only deliberated longer but also were more confident about their eventual decisions. Subjects recalled more of the evidence, suggesting that they had considered it more thoroughly than subjects in juries where unanimity was not required. Even more importantly, they were more likely to change their initial

Major coverage of applied topics are highlighted by ▶ and indexed on page vii.

Additional applied topics are discussed throughout the book, for example this discussion of jurors on page 380.

Consensus Without Acceptance: Public Conformity. The most dangerous threat to the ideal of consensus formation is public conformity, which we earlier defined as people's behaving consistently with norms that they do not privately accept as correct. When some of Asch's subjects went along with norms that they did not believe were correct, they were demonstrating public conformity. Motivated by the desire to avoid wrath or ridicule, these students followed the motto "go along to get along" (Deutsch & Gerard, 1955; Kelley, 1952), and their public conformity destroyed the reliability of the consensus.

Public conformity reflects people's recognition that groups dispense rewards to members who go along with the consensus and punish members who do not. People who disagree with other group members often anticipate negative reactions (Gerard & Rabbie, 1961), and their fears are well founded. When Stanley Schachter (1951) set up an experiment in which a confederate persistently disagreed with other group members, he found that the group first tried hard to win over the deviant. When this failed, the group ignored his views, assigned him to undesirable tasks, and suggested that he be excluded from the group.

Even jurors experience the pressure to conform. In the first trial of four White Los Angeles police officers accused of beating the Black motorist Rodney King, one juror went public to describe the extreme pressures she felt from other members of the jury. Bullied and ridiculed for her dissenting opinion by the majority who favored acquittal, and worn down by seven days of deliberation, she commented that other jurors' "eyes weren't open, and I said to God, 'If you could give me one more person on my side, I would know'" (*New York Times,* 1992b). Could any statement more clearly demonstrate Asch's finding that a single supporter helps people resist pressure from a majority? When another person changed positions and offered her support, the dissenting juror was able to deadlock the jury on a single charge against one officer despite acquittals on all other charges. Jurors have admitted capitulating under group pressure in other recent cases, including the convictions of boxer Mike Tyson and ex-Panamanian strongman Manuel Noriega (*New York Times,* 1992d).

Unfortunately, because public conformity brought about by fear, exhaustion, or the desire to please cannot easily be distinguished from real acceptance, it can influence others. When everyone publicly adheres to a norm that no one privately endorses, the situation is called *pluralistic ignorance.* Such ignorance abounds in many areas of daily life, even in the classroom. Have you ever been afraid to ask a question because the silence of your classmates led you to believe that everyone but you understands the teacher? Many of the other students undoubtedly were feeling exactly the same way but made the same false assumption you did (Miller & McFarland, 1987).

Pluralistic ignorance may also contribute to such significant social problems as widespread alcohol abuse on college campuses. One study supporting this idea reported that most students engaged in behaviors—such as excessive drinking or bringing liquor to parties—that suggested more

Innovative pedagogy facilitates learning

The book provides advance organizers, graphical summaries, and other pedagogical aids that help students to learn more, process it more deeply, and retain understanding of the key concepts of social psychology.

Concluding Comments reflect on the chapter's main issues and tie ideas together.

Concluding Comments

As you reflect on the evidence presented in this chapter, you may conclude that biases in impressions are pretty hard to overcome. Most of the time that is true. We get a lot of mileage out of the simple rule of thumb that behavior reflects personality. Yet we also know that human nature is more complicated than this rule would indicate. When accuracy is of the utmost importance, we attend fully, process carefully, and are rewarded with more accurate impressions of other people. But why is accurate person perception so likely to be the exception rather than the rule in our daily life? Why are simple rules of thumb, with all their possibilities of bias, usually more than adequate for our needs?

First, in many cases, our needs for accuracy in day-to-day person perception are modest. Correspondent inferences work perfectly well if our encounters with people are limited to particular situations or roles. For example, your assumption that the office bookkeeper is a quiet and restrained person on the basis of his office demeanor will not create problems if the office is the only place the two of you interact—though you might be surprised to see how he acts at a wild party. We can ignore people's specific individual qualities and still interact successfully with them if their behaviors are governed largely by the power of social situations and roles.

Second, people's behavior in particular situations often accurately reflects their personalities because they often choose the situations they are in. Suppose you watch someone telling jokes at a comedy try-out. Technically, it might be correct that her provocative, lively, and funny behaviors are called for by this situation. But since the would-be comedian *chose* the situation, it is probably reasonable to assume that she is a lively, funny person. Thus, a correspondent inference works just fine. If you want to find a Deadhead, you do not need to interpret subtle cues—just go to a Grateful Dead concert and look around.

Third, correspondent inferences are often accurate because other people offer us accurate cues to their true nature, at least as they themselves perceive it. As you will see in the next chapter, being perceived accurately by others is rewarding, and being misperceived is frustrating and uncomfortable. So the lover of baroque music might wear a J. S. Bach T-shirt to let us know. Even if the cues a new acquaintance offers do not ring quite true, it is often wise to go along for the ride, accepting rather than challenging the person. Certainly the interaction will go more smoothly if we save the other's face.

Thus, people's tendency to take others' behaviors or observable cues at face value can grease the wheels of social interaction, and this tendency usually lets us get along quite well. Still, going beyond first impressions to seek greater accuracy in person perception is sometimes important. In choosing a housemate, we want to predict a variety of compatible behaviors accurately on the basis of a few items of background information and a brief conversa-

Overview concept maps at the end of chapters highlight the big picture.

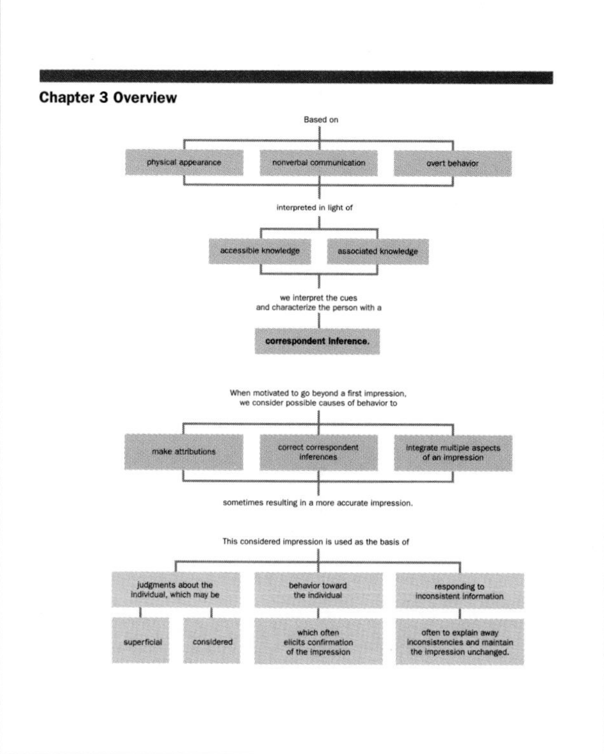
Chapter 3 Overview
Based on
physical appearance
nonverbal communication
overt behavior
interpreted in light of
accessible knowledge
associated knowledge
we interpret the cues and characterize the person with a
correspondent inference.
When motivated to go beyond a first impression, we consider possible causes of behavior to
make attributions
correct correspondent inferences
integrate multiple aspects of an impression
sometimes resulting in a more accurate impression.
This considered impression is used as the basis of
judgments about the individual, which may be
behavior toward the individual
responding to inconsistent information
superficial
considered
which often elicits confirmation of the impression
often to explain away inconsistencies and maintain the impression unchanged.

Flow charts within chapters clarify processes and emphasize relationships.

Our impression of the same individual may differ greatly from one situation to another because attributes that stand out in one context may go unnoticed in another. An attribute that is salient in its context may give rise to inferences that become part of our first impression of a person.

Figure 3.2 Salient cues dominate impressions

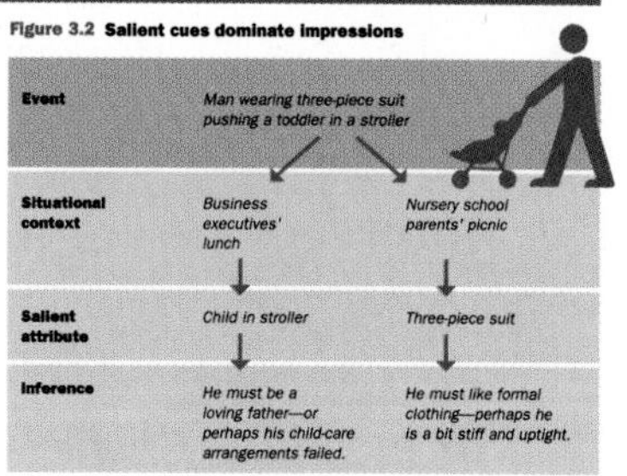
Event
Man wearing three-piece suit pushing a toddler in a stroller
Situational context
Business executives' lunch
Nursery school parents' picnic
Salient attribute
Child in stroller
Three-piece suit
Inference
He must be a loving father—or perhaps his child-care arrangements failed.
He must like formal clothing—perhaps he is a bit stiff and uptight.

Salience refers to a cue's ability to attract attention in its context. So you probably will not notice the tall person's coffee-drinking habits or the rude person's height if those characteristics do not depart much from the average. Of course, a cue that is unusual or unexpected in one context may be quite normal in another, as Figure 3.2 shows. The person who towered over everyone might be salient in the cafeteria but not on the basketball court, surrounded by equally tall team members. Thus, attributes that stand out in one context may be unnoticed in another. When we have information about a person's physical appearance, their nonverbal communication, and some of their behavior, those aspects that are salient are likely to grab our attention and provide the basis for first impressions.

Unusual and salient characteristics not only make a difference in impressions of others, but also help us define ourselves, as you will see in Chapter 4, pages 118 to 119.

Interpreting Cues

Cues have no meaning in themselves. Instead, they are interpreted in the light of a person's stored knowledge about people, behaviors, traits, and social situations. Stored knowledge that is linked to the cue itself or is easy to bring to mind is most likely to be used in interpreting cues.

We seem to leap effortlessly from the cues of appearance, body language, and behavior to the personality characteristics we believe they reflect. Yet none of the cues we use in perceiving people has much meaning in itself. No

salience The ability of a cue to attract attention in its context.

Margin cross-references remind students of the reappearance of basic principles and unifying themes.

Capsule previews, highlighted in yellow, introduce major sections and prepare students for focused reading.

Key terms are defined in a running glossary.

Social Psychology

What Is Social Psychology?

In the fall of 1951, Princeton University's undefeated football team played Dartmouth College in a particularly hard-fought game. The teams were long-term rivals, and the game started rough and went down hill. Before Princeton finally won, penalties punctuated the game, and fights left players on both sides with serious injuries. One month later, two social psychologists asked Princeton and Dartmouth undergraduates to view a film of the game (Hastorf & Cantril, 1954). The responses were astonishing. Princeton fans and Dartmouth supporters reported seeing events so differently that they might have been watching different games. Princeton students saw a constant barrage of Dartmouth violence and poor sportsmanship, with Princeton players occasionally retaliating in self-defense. Dartmouth students rated the teams as equally aggressive but saw their battered team's infractions as understandable responses to brutal Princeton attacks. One Dartmouth alumnus who watched the film saw so few Dartmouth violations that he concluded he had accidentally been sent an edited copy of the film.

Perhaps these findings are not really so astonishing if you consider that fans of opposing teams hardly ever agree on the impartiality of the umpiring. Similarly, partisan observers of political debates almost always proclaim their own candidate "the winner," and proud parents at the school music contest often disagree with the judges' decision. If the world is objectively "out there" for all to see, how can observers reach such different conclusions about what seems to be the same event? Why do we so often end up seeing exactly what we expected to see, and, if that is the case, how do we decide what "really" happened? Can the same innocent feelings of belonging that make us see our team, our candidate, or our child in such positive terms also produce biased judgments, unfair decisions, and unequal treatment of others?

Thirty years after Hastorf and Cantril's study, researchers at Vanderbilt University asked two groups of students to consider the difficult issue of whether convicted criminals should be given probation as an alternative to imprisonment (Axsom and others, 1987). One group of students had a special reason to be concerned with the issue: they had been led to believe that

Constructing reality What do you see in the image on the left? Do you like it? Human beings are constantly making judgments about all aspects of their environment. If you jumped to a quick conclusion, turn the page. You may be surprised!

the probation policy might soon be introduced in their area. For the other group, the issue was merely academic—the policy was not being considered for their community. The researchers told the two groups that, to help them make up their minds, they would hear a tape of a local candidate speaking in favor of the issue at a political rally. What the students were not told was that the researchers had actually prepared four quite different tapes. On one tape, the candidate put forward compelling evidence in support of probation while an enthusiastic audience warmly applauded his words. On a second, the same effective presentation elicited only scattered hisses, boos, and heckling from the audience. A third tape had the candidate giving rambling, specious, and disjointed arguments, which were met with enthusiastic applause from the audience. And on the fourth tape, the weak arguments were greeted by boos and hissing. Some students heard one of the four tapes.

When the researchers polled the students whose interest in the probation issue was merely academic, the impact of the audience's taped response was clear. These students adopted the candidate's position when the audience greeted it with enthusiasm and rejected it when the audience voiced disdain. A different pattern of responses emerged among students who expected the issue to affect their community. These students focused on the content of the speech. They were swayed if they heard the candidate give cogent arguments but remained unpersuaded if the arguments were weak—regardless of the applause or hisses of the taped audience.

Why were the reactions of other people so compelling to some students and so unimportant to others? Why did some participants "go with the flow" while others considered the issues carefully? Did some students care less than others about being right, or were all of the students trying to take different paths to the "truth?"

Although few of us are confronted by the same issue the Vanderbilt students faced, we are all bombarded by advertising campaigns, paid political messages, even the cajoling of friends and family. Consider the last time you were persuaded by one of these attempts. What approach was used by the person who persuaded you? Did that person present you with the hard facts, or did he or she play on your emotions? If you were told that "everyone else" had already joined the parade, would you be more likely to go along or more likely to rebel? Or would it depend on the issue?

Questions like these lure social psychologists into their labs every day in search of reliable answers. Social psychology offers a special perspective on human behavior, because the social aspects of human behavior can be both powerful and puzzling. Our goal in this book is to introduce you to some of the many questions social psychologists ask about social behavior, the ways they go about answering those questions, and the answers they have found. We hope that you will find these questions intriguing and that the often surprising answers will make you want to delve more deeply into issues you find interesting.

Our first step will be to provide a definition of *social psychology*—to chart out the territory we will be covering and to give you a glimpse of what

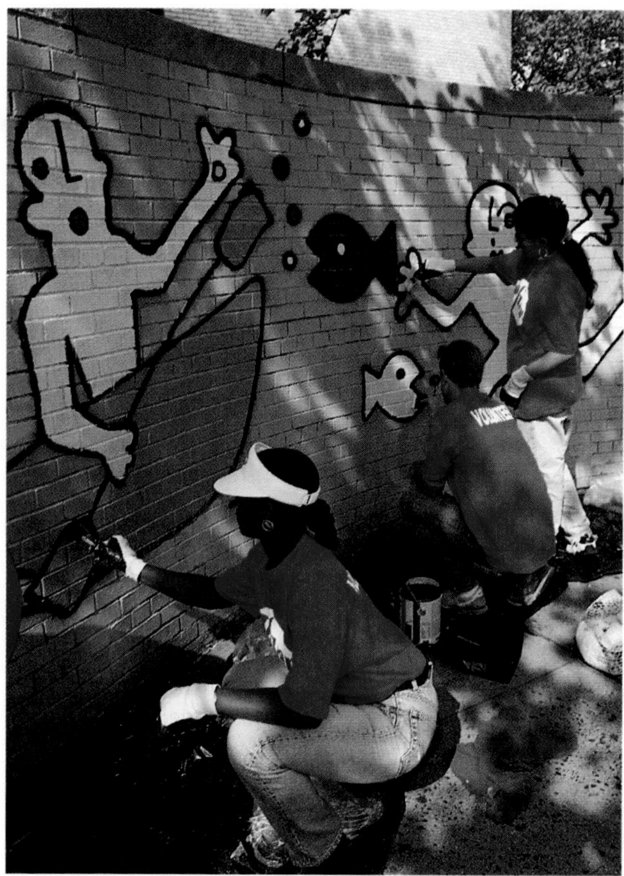

It's all a matter of interpretation Perhaps the fragment of New York Cares' wall mural seemed like graffiti to you, but its social context reveals it to be different. Like all social phenomena, graffiti can have many meanings: art, a prank, an act of vandalism, or even a political statement. It all depends on the perspective of the viewer and the social context.

makes that terrain so fascinating. We next describe how social psychology developed its special perspective on human behavior. Like other fields of human inquiry, contemporary social psychology is a product of its own history and of the history of the societies in which it developed. With a quick survey of the past behind us, we then map out the territory ahead. The final part of the chapter provides a sneak preview of the material we cover in the rest of this text. To help you find your way with confidence, we point out some signposts and landmarks to look for along the route.

A Definition of Social Psychology

Social psychology is the scientific study of the effects of social and cognitive processes on the way individuals perceive, influence, and relate to others. Notice that this definition states that social psychology is a science, that social psychologists are as keenly interested in underlying social and cognitive processes as they are in overt behavior, and that the central concern of social psychology is how people understand and interact with others. Let us consider each of these components in turn.

social psychology The scientific study of the effects of social and cognitive processes on the way individuals perceive, influence, and relate to others.

The Scientific Study . . .

This is a brief preview of the section that follows. For advice on how you can use it to improve your efficiency in studying the text, turn back to the "To the Student" section in the Preface.

Social psychologists, like other scientists, gather knowledge systematically, by means of scientific methods. These methods help to produce knowledge that is less subject to the biases and distortions that often characterize common-sense knowledge.

Of course, you have been studying social behavior all your life. We all use common sense and "street smarts" to make sense of the social world we inhabit because we all want to make good friends, reach mutually satisfying decisions, raise children properly, hire the best personnel, and live in peace and security rather than in conflict and fear. How does the social psychologist's approach differ from our everyday approaches? The answer is found in methods, not goals (Fletcher & Haig, 1990). Although scientific researchers and common-sense observers share many goals—both wish to understand, predict, and influence people's thoughts and behavior—their methods for achieving those goals differ greatly.

As common-sense observers, people often reach conclusions about social behavior haphazardly, based on their own or others' experiences. Therefore, common-sense knowledge is sometimes inconsistent, even contradictory. As scientists, on the other hand, social psychologists study social behavior systematically, seeking to avoid the misconceptions and distortions that so often afflict our common-sense knowledge. Of course, even scientific knowledge is not infallible. The history of science shows that many conclusions proposed as scientific truths are eventually overturned by new observations or new insights. But as you will see in Chapter 2, scientific conclusions are sounder and more resistant to challenge than common-sense knowledge because they are based on systematic methods of gathering information and are constructed with an awareness of the possibility of error.

. . . of the Effects of Social and Cognitive Processes

The physical presence of other people, the knowledge and opinions they pass on to us, and our feelings about the groups to which we belong all deeply influence us through social processes—whether we are with other people or alone. Our perceptions, memories, emotions, and motives also exert a pervasive influence on us through cognitive processes. Effects of social and cognitive processes are not separate; they are inextricably intertwined.

A first date, a classroom presentation, a job interview, a problem-solving session with co-workers—what do these situations have in common? Each is a situation in which others observe or interact with us, influencing our thoughts, feelings, and behavior. We try to make a good impression, to live up to the standards of the people we care about, to cooperate or compete with others as appropriate. These examples show the operation of social processes. **Social processes** are the ways in which our thoughts, feelings, and actions are affected by input from the people and groups around us: the groups to which we belong, our personal relationships, the teachings of our parents and cultures, and the pressures we experience from other people and groups.

Do not assume, however, that social processes affect us only when others are physically present. On the contrary, we are social creatures even when alone. Faced with an important decision, we often stop to think about the possible reactions of absent friends, relatives, or fellow group members—and these thoughts can also influence us. Even during many of our most private activities—studying, practicing a musical instrument, exercising, or showering alone—we are motivated by our concern for what others think of us. Think about the last time you rode an elevator in which you were the only passenger—we bet you faced the doors, just as you would have if other people had been physically present. In that elevator, and in many other situations, the influence of imagined others—your expectation of how they would react to you or your memory of how they have reacted in the past—was just as real as the effects of others who are physically present.

Cognitive processes are the ways in which our memories, perceptions, thoughts, emotions, and motives influence our understanding of the world and guide our actions. The effects of these processes are pervasive, for we act and react on the basis of what we *believe* the world is like. Social influences—as well as the nonsocial factors that shape our lives—exert their effects through our cognitive processes. The content of our thoughts, the goals toward which we strive, and the feelings we have about people and activities all reflect the influences of other people and our social surroundings.

Thus, social and cognitive processes are inextricably intertwined. To illustrate their intimate connections, consider the two basic ways in which people affect one another, as studied by social psychologists.

First, by studying the *individual in the group,* researchers gain insights into how people are affected by others who are physically present—offering friendly hugs or scornful glares, providing trustworthy information or trying to deceive, leading by example or waiting for someone to follow. In the physical presence of others, social processes obviously have influence—but their effects depend on how the person *interprets* them, and therefore on the operation of cognitive processes.

Second, by considering the *group in the individual,* social psychologists examine how people are affected by their knowledge about the beliefs, attitudes, and actions that are considered appropriate for them as members of their group. Because our group memberships become part of who we are, they influence us even when other group members are absent. Whether other supporters are present or not, we rise to the defense of our party's political platform and feel elated about our college team's victory. We react in this way because *our* party or *our* college has become a basic part of *our*

social processes The ways in which our thoughts, feelings, and actions are affected by input from the people and groups around us.

cognitive processes The ways our minds work: how our memories, perceptions, thoughts, emotions, and motives influence our understanding of the world and guide our actions.

The group in the individual Members of our group influence us even when they are nowhere near. Like this man (far right), most of us so thoroughly accept our group's beliefs, attitudes, and practices that they become part of the self and affect what we think, feel, and do—and even what we wear.

identity. Cognitive processes influence us when we are alone—but the nature of their effects depends on the social influences of other people and our group memberships.

. . . on the Way Individuals Perceive, Influence, and Relate to Others

> *Social psychology focuses on the way individuals' perceptions of, influence upon, and relations to others are affected by social and cognitive processes.*

Social psychology seeks to understand the social behavior of *individuals*—a focus that distinguishes it from sociology, political science, and other social sciences. The cognitive and social processes we have just described affect individuals as they perceive, influence, and relate to others. Consequently, these processes shape all forms of social behavior, including some that are significant concerns in today's world. Here are some examples of social behaviors that are important concerns and some questions social psychologists might ask about them.

- *Why do many marriages end in divorce?* A social psychologist might study divorce as an outcome of how individuals handle conflicts in their marriages. The research might focus on questions like the following: How do couples deal with events that put the relationship under stress? What alternatives to the relationship do they believe they have? What factors determine whether they storm angrily out of the house or kiss and make up after a fight? Whereas sociologists might study the effects of unemployment on divorce rates in a society, social psychologists might instead examine the ways that unemployment causes conflict and divorce by affecting how the partners think about their relationship or how they try to influence one another.

- *How do door-to-door salespeople sell products?* As a salesperson departed from your door, have you ever found yourself holding an item that you never wanted and wondering how you were manipulated into purchasing it? A social psychologist would be interested in knowing the processes through which people are induced to buy—for example, how a sales pitch expertly plays on the consumer's needs, desires, or feelings of guilt or obligation in order to make the sale. In contrast, an economist might study whether, for a certain product, newspaper advertisements or door-to-door sales techniques are more profitable.
- *What causes outbreaks of ethnic violence?* A historian or journalist might document the unique events that sparked a particular conflict. To the social psychologist, however, intergroup hostility stems from fundamental aspects of the relations among people and groups. These include both people's competition for concrete resources (like jobs and political clout) and people's attitudes, emotions, and actions toward their own and other social groups. Social psychologists would ask whether the ways people categorize individuals into groups, the stereotypes they form about others, their preferences for people "just like them," or their feelings of power or powerlessness contribute to intergroup hostility.

Social Psychology's Special Perspective

Understanding the effects of social and cognitive processes can help us to comprehend why people act the way they do, and that understanding may also help us to solve important social problems.

We have said that social psychologists focus on how social and cognitive processes affect the ways individuals perceive, influence, and interact with others. How does this special perspective actually help social psychologists understand social behavior? How can we use this approach as we try to understand and explain the complex social behaviors we encounter every day? To see the implications of our definition of social psychology, consider the questions social psychologists might ask about an incident that drew national attention and was widely reported in the media.

Every year U.S. Navy aviator "top guns" from around the country used to gather at the "Tailhook" convention—named for the piece of equipment that helps planes land on the deck of an aircraft carrier. In 1991 the convention was held at the Las Vegas Hilton. In the course of the revelry, some male aviators formed a drunken gauntlet along a hotel corridor and assaulted scores of women, including pilots, aides, and officers, as they tried to pass. When some of the women complained to their superior officers, the officers initially disbelieved the women and then apparently suppressed the accusations. Once the Tailhook incidents became public, however, journalists and commentators reported on these rather sensational events and analyzed their supposed antecedents at great length.

How would social psychologists try to understand and explain what happened? What kinds of issues would they explore concerning the intertwining social and cognitive processes that influenced the pilots' perceptions and actions? A social psychologist undertaking a study of these events might begin by posing the following questions.

1. *Given the heat of the moment, the excitement of the party activities, and the free flow of alcohol, did the pilots even notice that their behavior caused the women distress?* Studies have demonstrated that emotional arousal, rapid presentation of information, and mind-altering drugs—all part of the social environment at Tailhook—decrease the accuracy and detail with which people form impressions and make inferences.

2. *How did the actions of his companions influence each man's behavior?* Research shows that people often join others in behavior that they might condemn if they were acting alone. The fact that none of the other officers protested the women's treatment probably reduced the likelihood that any one man would come to the women's aid.

3. *Did the aviators believe their female counterparts "asked for it" by acting provocatively?* Researchers have found that when men and women engage in the same behaviors—drinking with colleagues, socializing with supervisors—people often interpret the behaviors quite differently.

4. *Did the officers harbor prejudices against women which led them to see their own female colleagues merely as representatives of a disliked outgroup?* Research shows that such feelings are common in intergroup situations and are exacerbated when there is conflict between groups. Indeed, the admiral who led the initial probe into the event was quoted as saying that the men "simply did not want women in the military" (*Newsweek,* 1992).

5. *Did the officers believe that their peer group—other naval aviators—would approve of the way they treated the women?* Studies of group influence suggest the answer is yes. People tend to conform to the standards of the groups with which they identify.

Understanding why people act the way they do in social situations helps us explain events in our own lives—that disastrous first date, the successful job interview, the loneliness of being the new kid on the block, the hesitation we feel before making a major decision. It also helps us understand the factors that contribute to the complex events of our times—the debate over abortion, ethnic unrest and civil war, the spread of the AIDS epidemic, the destruction of the global environment. And if we understand how people are influenced by social and cognitive processes, we can begin developing solutions for such pressing social problems. For example, knowing that shared beliefs about women or group pressures may have contributed to the Tailhook incident suggests that changing those beliefs or altering group standards might help to prevent recurrences. In fact, social psychological research has been instrumental in exposing workplace discrimination (Fiske and others, 1991) and recommending procedural changes to lessen biases in courtrooms and jury rooms (Kassin & Wrightsman, 1985). It has suggested policies to deal with violence and explicit sex in the media (Donnerstein & Linz, 1986) and to improve classroom environments for minorities and women (Steele, 1992). It has also been influential in finding ways to change perceptions of the risks of AIDS (Fisher & Fisher, 1992) and in developing programs to reduce international tensions (Lindskold, 1986). Thus the social psychological perspective invites us not only to understand but also to act on that understanding.

It's not easy being green As economic and population pressures threaten to destroy the quality of life on this planet, social psychologists have risen to the challenge. Contests like this, for example, in which the goal is to influence the young designers as well as those who view their posters, rest on the important social psychological finding that our actions can have a profound effect on our beliefs.

Historical Trends and Current Themes in Social Psychology

How did social psychology come to develop its particular point of view? Like any field of knowledge, social psychology is a product of its past. The current focus of its research reflects historical events of the twentieth century, changing societal concerns, and developments in other scientific fields, as well as changes in the topics social psychologists have explored and the techniques they have used in their research. This brief survey of the field's history can serve both as a context and as a partial explanation for where social psychology stands today.

Social Psychology Becomes an Empirical Science

Soon after the emergence of scientific psychology in the late nineteenth century, researchers began considering questions about social influences on human thought and action.

From the time of the ancient Greeks, the study of the human condition was considered to be the domain of philosophy. As social psychologists do today, early philosophers recognized the impact that other people can have on individual behavior. Plato, for example, speculated about the "crowd mind," arguing that even the wisest individuals, if assembled into a crowd, might be transformed into an irrational mob. Philosophers continued to theorize about the workings of the human mind—and still do—but the development of social psychology had to await the emergence of its parent discipline, the science of psychology. This new field was born in the late nineteenth century, when a few researchers in Germany, impressed by laboratory methods being used by physiologists, began to employ experimental techniques to understand mental processes like sensation, memory, and judgment.

The experimental investigation of social psychological issues began soon afterward, as researchers in North America, England, and France began the task of systematically measuring how behavior is influenced by the presence of others. A study published in 1898 by Norman Triplett is sometimes cited as the first research study in social psychology (Allport, 1954a). Triplett, having noticed that swimmers and cyclists performed better when competing against rivals than when practicing by themselves, wondered whether the presence of other people has a generally beneficial effect on performance. To find out, he asked schoolchildren to wind fishing line onto reels as quickly as possible, with and without others present. Sure enough, the children's performance improved in the presence of others. This interesting finding, however, appeared to contradict a conclusion that Max Ringelmann, a French agricultural engineer, had reached in an even earlier study conducted in the 1880s. Ringelmann found that when people work together to pull on a rope or push on a cart, they put less effort into the task than when they work alone (Ringelmann, 1913). Such apparently inconsistent findings help to explain why the study of group effects on performance still continues today. But we now know that Ringelmann and Triplett's results are not necessarily inconsistent. Researchers have concluded that the presence of others often facilitates performance when individual contributions are easily identified, but it reduces performance when people are "lost in a crowd."

We will have more to say about the resolution of these apparent inconsistencies in Chapter 13.

For the first social psychologists, this puzzle was just one among many questions about how people influence one another. They also tackled questions about how facial expressions and body movements signal people's feelings, how people conform to the suggestions of others, and the role that experimenters might play in influencing the outcomes of studies (Haines & Vaughan, 1979). The first two textbooks bearing the name *Social Psychology* appeared in 1908. One of these, by psychologist William McDougall, argued that all social behavior stems from innate tendencies or instincts, an idea that was popular in general psychology at the time. The other, by sociologist E. A. Ross, took up the theme that was soon to become social psychology's central concern: that people are heavily influenced by others, whether those others are physically present or not.

Social Psychology Splits from General Psychology over What Causes Behavior

> *Throughout much of the twentieth century, North American psychology was dominated by behaviorism, but social psychologists maintained an emphasis on the important effects of thoughts and feelings on behavior.*

Although it arrived on the coattails of general psychology, social psychology soon developed an identity distinct from that of its parent discipline. Beginning early in the twentieth century, North American psychology as a whole was dominated by the behaviorist viewpoint. This perspective, exemplified by the work of John B. Watson and B. F. Skinner, denied the scientific validity of explanations that invoke mental events like thoughts, feelings, and emotions. For radical behaviorists, a legitimate science of human activity could be based only on the study of observable behavior as influenced by observable environmental stimuli.

Most social psychologists, however, resisted the behaviorist view that thoughts and feelings had no place in scientific explanations. They accepted the behaviorists' argument that the ultimate goal of science is to explain behavior, but their studies showed that explanation was impossible without taking into account people's thoughts and feelings. Social psychologists learned that individuals often hold divergent views of, and react in different ways to, the same object or idea—be it capitalism, a political candidate, or a football game. Such findings could be explained only by differences in individuals' attitudes, personality traits, impressions of others, group identifications, and emotions (Allport, 1924). Behaviorists were certainly right in their belief that external stimuli can influence behavior. However, social psychologists maintained that the effect of any stimulus depends on how individuals and groups interpret it. Right from the start, then, social psychology was distinctive in its conviction that understanding and measuring people's perceptions, beliefs, and feelings is essential to understanding their overt behavior.

The Rise of Nazism Shapes the Development of Social Psychology

In the 1930s and 1940s, many European social psychologists fled to North America, where they had a major influence on the field's direction. Significant questions generated by the rise of Nazism and the Second World War shaped research interests during and after this period.

It has been said that the person who has had the most impact on the development of social psychology in North America is Adolf Hitler (Cartwright, 1979). Ironic though this observation is, it contains important elements of truth. In fact, both the events that precipitated the Second World War and the war itself made a dramatic and lasting impression on social psychology.

As Nazi domination spread across Europe in the 1930s, a number of psychologists fled their homelands to continue distinguished scientific careers in North America. This influx of researchers consolidated social psychology's special emphasis on how people interpret the world and how they are influenced by others. Most European researchers were trained not in the behaviorist tradition but in Gestalt theory, which took for granted the role cognitive processes play in our interpretations of the social world. Around the same time, researchers became increasingly impressed by anthropologists' accounts of the pervasiveness of cultural influences on people's thought and behavior. It fell to social psychologists to identify the mechanisms by which such influence occurred, and they soon developed techniques to perform realistic studies of complex social influences in the laboratory (Jones, 1985). Muzafer Sherif's elegant experiments (1936), for example, showed that a social group can influence even the perception and interpretation of physical reality, as you will see in Chapter 9 of this text.

The war's effect on social psychology went beyond adding a new cast of skilled researchers. Revelations of Nazi genocide led a horrified world to ask questions about the roots of prejudice (Adorno and others, 1950). How could people feel and act on such murderous hatred for Jews, Gypsies, homosexuals, and members of other groups? These questions still resonate today as the world contemplates "ethnic cleansing" in Bosnia; tribal wars in Armenia and Azerbaijan, South Africa, and elsewhere; and "gay bashing" in the streets of North American cities.

Conditions created by the Second World War also drew social psychologists into the search for solutions to immediate practical problems. With food in short supply and rationing in full swing, the U.S. government asked social psychologists how to convince civilians to change their eating habits—to eat less steak and more kidneys and liver, to drink more milk, and to feed their babies cod-liver oil and orange juice (Lewin, 1947). Social psychologists were also called on to help the military maintain troop morale, improve the performance of aircraft and tank crews (Stouffer and

Social influences on scientific concerns This German photograph from 1938 shows an advertisement for a special edition of *Der Stürmer* with the headline "Jews Are Criminals." Many of the social psychologists who fled Nazi-dominated Europe were horrified at the Nazis' success in swaying the public mind against the Jews. These concerns triggered lifelong efforts to understand the roots of prejudice, the causes of obedience, the power of propaganda, and other social issues.

others, 1949), and teach troops to resist enemy propaganda—and even to brush their teeth regularly (Hovland and others, 1953).

Social psychologists fell to applied research with a will, realizing that they would be able to develop and test general theories of behavior even as they solved practical problems. Kurt Lewin found that active participation in discussion groups—establishing new behavioral standards in a social context—was more effective in changing what women fed their families than passive listening to lectures on the topic. Lewin's findings are still successfully applied in support groups like Weight Watchers, Overeaters Anonymous, and many other organizations. Samuel Stouffer's research on American soldiers (1949) showed that morale depended more on the soldiers' interpretations of how they were doing than on how they were actually faring in relation to other enlisted men. Satisfaction with the rate of promotion, for example, was sometimes lower in units with higher-than-average promotion rates. Stouffer suggested that in these units the soldiers' expectations of promotion were high, setting them up for disappointment if others were promoted but they were not. The importance of comparisons with others and the resulting feelings of relative deprivation are still important topics in current social psychological research. And, though we may be amused by the assignment given to Carl Hovland of devising ways to persuade GIs to brush regularly, current theories of persuasion build on his original demonstrations that persuasive success depends on who delivers the message, who receives the message, and how the message is processed.

During this crucial period of research and theory building, the work of one social psychologist particularly embodied the themes that characterized the young discipline. Kurt Lewin, who was among the scientists who fled

Hitler's Europe, held that all behavior depends on the individual's *life space*, which he defined as a subjective map of the individual's current goals and his or her social environment (Lewin, 1936). Perhaps you can see how Lewin's ideas sum up two of social psychology's enduring themes: that people's subjective interpretation of reality is the key determinant of their beliefs and behaviors, and that social influences structure those interpretations and behavior. Lewin's work also reflected the close link between research aimed at understanding the underlying social and cognitive causes of behavior and research aimed at solving important social problems—a link that will receive considerable attention throughout this book. Lewin had a gift for conducting research that combined the testing of theories with the solving of problems. As he put it, "There is nothing so practical as a good theory" (1951, p. 169).

Growth and Integration

> *During the 1950s and 1960s, social psychology grew and flourished, moving toward an integrated theoretical understanding of social and cognitive processes and toward further applications of social psychological theory to important applied problems.*

Both basic and applied social psychology flourished during the prosperous 1950s and 1960s. Backed by expanding university enrollments and generous government grants, researchers addressed a great variety of topics central to understanding social behavior. Research contributions during this period laid the foundations of what we now know about self-esteem, prejudice and stereotyping, conformity, persuasion and attitude change, impression formation, interpersonal attraction and intimate relationships, and intergroup relations—all key topics within social psychology today.

By the 1970s, social psychology had developed a set of reliable and repeatable findings, a mark of scientific maturity. The time was ripe for both internal integration, the melding of various specific topic areas into broader explanations of behavior, and external integration, the meshing of social psychology with neighboring scientific fields and with significant social concerns. And so the movement toward integration began.

Integration of Cognitive and Social Processes. The study of cognitive processes became a natural framework for integration both within and outside social psychology. As the tight grip of behaviorism on North American psychology was finally broken, a cognitive revolution got under way (Neisser, 1967). Cognitive themes and theories swiftly gained attention in experimental, developmental, personality, and even clinical psychology. Of course, the cognitive revolution was no revolution for social psychology. Cognitive themes were familiar because their foundations had been laid decades earlier in Allport's, Sherif's, and Lewin's work in the 1930s and in Stouffer's and Hovland's studies in the 1940s. Concepts such as attitudes, norms, and beliefs, already common currency in social psychology, spread to new areas of study: personal relationships, aggression and altruism, stereotyping and discrimination. Thus, during the 1970s and 1980s, theoretical concerns and experimental methods converged as researchers in many areas of social psychology focused on the study of cognitive processes (Jones, 1985).

Concern with cognitive processes is only one side of the coin, however. Social psychologists have always been aware that social processes, including personal and group relationships and social influence, also impinge on everything people do. True, our behavior is a function of our perceptions and interpretations and our attitudes and beliefs—but those factors in turn are fundamentally shaped by our relationships to others, our thoughts about their reactions, and the group memberships that help us define who we are. Our understanding of the way social and cognitive processes work together to mold all social behavior has benefited from the increasing integration of North American social psychology with European social psychology, where the impact of social group memberships has long been a dominant theme (Tajfel, 1978; Doise, 1978; Moscovici, 1980). Today, researchers in all domains of social psychology are bringing the effects of cognitive and social processes together into explanations of people's experience and behavior.

Integration of Basic Science and Social Problems. Can technological advancement by itself offer solutions to such global threats as resource depletion, environmental pollution, war and ethnic conflict, and overpopulation? Many people believe the answer to that question is no. Solving such massive problems may depend on technological advances, but at a more fundamental level it will require profound changes in human behavior.

Social psychologists are attacking these and other crucial social problems, and this attack will require their best theoretical efforts. In this regard, social psychologists are lucky. Scientists in many other fields have to choose whether they will work on purely theoretical issues or apply their theoretical knowledge to practical problems. A materials scientist, for example, may seek to understand the nature of molecular bonds that produce stronger materials, but it is the engineer who will use the new materials to design an improved wind-turbine blade. Social psychologists do not have to make this kind of choice. It is difficult to think of a single area of social psychological research that does not have some application to significant social issues. Whether social psychologists are looking at close relationships or divorce, altruism or aggression, attitude change or the effectiveness of advertising, intergroup conflict or its resolution, they simultaneously address the basic theoretical questions that spur pure scientific curiosity and the important phenomena that affect our daily lives.

Traditionally, many psychologists have thought of basic and applied research as distinct, even opposite, areas, with applied research taking a distant second place to basic research. This stance is foreign to contemporary social psychology. Because virtually all social psychological research is relevant to significant social issues, it is simultaneously basic and applied. The same underlying social and cognitive processes operate wherever people perceive, influence, and interact with each other, both inside the research laboratory and outside it—in schools, factories, courtrooms, playgrounds, boardrooms, and neighborhoods. For this reason, as we describe theories and research areas throughout this text, we will also discuss their applied implications. As you will see, talented researchers are studying social psychological processes in many applied settings, with a particular focus on major issues relevant to health, education, law, the environment, and business. We have highlighted special section headings to help you locate particularly important applications to these and other areas.

1. *Health.* Good health is just a matter of good diet, regular exercise, and lucky genes, right? Wrong. The emotions we experience, the amount of stress we encounter in daily hassles, our ability to find love and acceptance in close relationships, and even the way we feel about ourselves can influence our bodies as well as our minds. When public health officials promote exercise and fight drug abuse, when hospitals allow patients more control over their treatments, and when support groups speed recovery from illness, addiction, and grief, social psychological processes play a part in producing sound minds in sound bodies.

2. *Education.* As teachers teach and students learn, more is being communicated than just Spanish and geography. Teachers' expectations can shape their pupils' self-esteem, self-confidence, and even their actual performance. Classroom activities can encourage competition or cooperation, and can eliminate or exacerbate ethnic and gender stereotypes. No wonder that for some the classroom is an open field of opportunity, whereas for others it is a minefield of adversity and disappointment.

3. *Law.* How do the police extract confessions? Do lie detectors really detect deception? Is a defendant in suit and tie more credible than one in

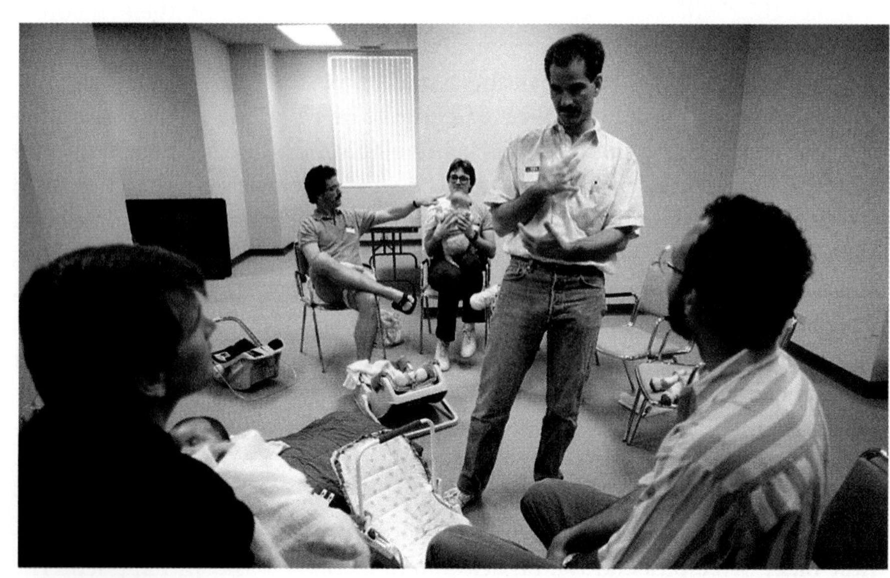

Bonding in Bootee Camp These dads are members of Bootee Camp, a mutual support group for new fathers founded in Irvine, California. Early social psychological research showed that participation in such groups is one of the most effective ways of changing attitudes and behaviors. Support groups now offer a helping hand to such widely diverse groups as recovering alcoholics and religious converts.

prison fatigues? How might leading questions and inadmissible evidence influence a juror's thinking? Does the minority opinion of a dissenting juror ever sway jury verdicts? From crime to conviction, social psychological processes are at work as police enforce laws, juries weigh evidence, and societies try to distribute justice.

4. *Environment.* Yields of Atlantic fisheries decline, Japanese commuters buy whiffs of oxygen from coin-operated machines in subways, and North American motorists waste hours in traffic jams. These human dimensions of environmental change are among those motivating social psychologists who are attempting to discover how individuals can be motivated to conserve energy or to recycle used materials. Others are working hard to determine the ways groups can be convinced to cooperate in harvesting renewable resources instead of overexploiting and destroying them.

5. *Business.* From advertising to sales techniques, to the pitfalls of managerial decision making, social psychological processes are the gears that drive the wheels of business. Consider, for example, the way effective leadership can mold diverse individuals into a smoothly functioning work team, while ineffective leadership generates only conflict, dissatisfaction, and low productivity.

In social psychology, the everyday world is not just a place to test discoveries made during laboratory research. Instead, social psychologists regard issues that are important outside the laboratory—ethnic conflict, the AIDS epidemic, rampant aggression, declining productivity, global interdependence—as both a source of theoretical ideas and a target for solutions (Rodin, 1985).

How the Approach of This Book Reflects an Integrative Perspective

Not surprisingly, given the way social psychology has developed, our conception of social psychology is an integrated one. In this text we share with you our view of social psychology as a field that integrates not only the cognitive and the social but also basic theory and applied research. Our basic theme is that all the diversity and richness of human social behavior can be understood in terms of a few fundamental social psychological processes. These processes flow from eight principles: two fundamental axioms, three motivational principles, and three processing principles.

As we describe specific topics like attraction, aggression, altruism, and attitude change, we will show you how all these forms of social behavior flow from the interaction of these same fundamental principles. At the same time, seeing these principles at work in different settings, producing apparently different forms of social behavior, will enhance your understanding of their meaning and implications. Here we can give you just a quick sketch of these basic principles and the processes that flow from them.

Two Fundamental Axioms of Social Psychology

Two fundamental axioms of social psychology are that people construct their own reality, and that social influences are pervasive.

Two fundamental axioms, or most important principles, integrate all the topics in this text. The first is that *people construct their own reality.* The second is that *social influence pervades all social life.*

Construction of Reality. At first glance, studying social behavior may seem to be an exercise in the obvious. As we go through our daily routines, we trust that we perceive the world around us as it is—that an objective reality exists "out there" for all to see. When we join friends to watch a ball game or to eat dinner in a restaurant, we assume that we all see the same game and hear the same enjoyable dinnertime conversation. When we meet someone new, we quickly form an impression of what he or she "is like." And when we see someone raise a fist, furrow a brow, or slump in a chair, we know what the behavior means because "actions speak louder than words." Because we assume that our impressions are accurate and true, we usually expect anyone else who meets the same person, goes on the same date, or sees the same action to share those impressions.

Who is this woman? Is Hillary Rodham Clinton a calculating manipulator or a victim of nasty gossip? A radical feminist lawyer or a cookie baking mom? Or is she none of these? The answer depends on who is doing the perceiving—conservative detractors, the liberal media, her family, or Clinton herself. What seems real to us is socially constructed and, like beauty, is in the eye of the beholder.

Every now and then, however, we are forced to think twice. Our usual lack of awareness of the extent to which we construct our own reality is overturned when we discover how different the reactions of others can be to the "same" social event. Try reminiscing with one of your parents about what happened on your first day of school, and you may discover that your memories of the details of that milestone in your lives are quite different. Or, if you are a sports fan, compare your recollection of an important game with the view of the opposing fans and see if you agree about what happened. At such times, we discover that we do not, in fact, share the same experience. A fist can be raised in intimidation or triumph, and a furrowed brow can indicate depression or concentration. What is real for each of us is a **construction of reality**, shaped in part by *cognitive processes*—the ways our minds work—and in part by *social processes*—input from others, who are either actually present or whose presence we imagine.

Cognitive processes operate as we piece together fragments of information, draw inferences from them, and try to weave them into a coherent whole. We hear a speaker deliver a series of arguments, note the audience's response, draw inferences about how others feel, and decide whether the message is worth our close consideration. In this sense, a person's view of the world is certainly in the eye—or the ear—of the beholder.

Social processes enable us to influence and be influenced by the views of others until we can agree about the nature of reality. Within the groups that are important to us, agreement is our touchstone for interpreting and responding to events. For example, most members of Western societies enjoy kissing, although the meaning of the kiss varies, depending on whom we kiss and how. But when the Thonga of southeast Africa first saw Europeans kissing, they were disgusted by what they regarded as "eating each other's saliva and dirt" (Hyde, 1979, p. 18). Whether we are Thonga cattle herders or North American college students, we tune in to others' interpretations—our parent's views about kisses or the cheers or boos of an audience listening to a speech—and we use those interpretations as the basis for our own responses. In this sense, a person's view of the world is at least in part a reflection seen in the eyes of others.

Pervasiveness of Social Influence. We could probably all agree that other people influence our public behavior and that our actions in turn can influence what others say and do. Having supporters at our back gives us just a bit more courage to speak out; face-to-face confrontations with detractors may frighten us into silence. Was this principle operating among the aviators at the Tailhook convention? Perhaps. Some may have joined in the debauched activities only after considerable goading or ridicule from their fellows.

Recall, however, what we noted earlier about even the imagined presence of others influencing us. Through the **pervasiveness of social influence,** other people have an effect on virtually all of our thoughts, feelings, and behavior, whether those others are physically present or not. Our thoughts about others' reactions and our identification with social groups mold our innermost perceptions, thoughts, feelings, motives, and even our sense of self. Do you proudly think of yourself as a Celtics fan, a member of your temple, a citizen of Canada? Our allegiances may be small scale, such as membership in families, teams, and committees, or large scale, including affiliations based on race, ethnicity, religion, gender, or the society and culture in which we live. But whether the group is large or small, our membership in it provides a frame and a filter through which we view social events. The Dartmouth-Princeton game had a particular meaning for students from each school, and a quite different meaning to people who felt no allegiance to either

construction of reality The axiom that each person's view of reality is a construction, shaped both by cognitive processes—the ways our minds work—and by social processes—input from others either actually present or imagined.

pervasiveness of social influence The axiom that other people influence virtually all of our thoughts, feelings, and behavior, whether those others are physically present or not.

team. And even among those on the same side, the game meant different things to the team members and their fans.

We sometimes experience social influence as social pressure, as when we encounter an aggressive salesperson or are berated for holding out on an otherwise unanimous jury. But social influence is most profound when it is least evident: when it shapes our most fundamental assumptions and beliefs about the world without our realizing it. The reactions of the Princeton and Dartmouth fans were certainly shaped and biased by their school allegiances, but were the fans aware of that influence? Probably not. We would not expect anyone to think, "I'd better interpret that tackle as vicious because my friends will reject me if I don't." Social influences have surrounded us since infancy, and it is therefore no surprise that we usually are unaware of their impact. Does the fish know it swims in water? The impetus we need to become aware of the impact of social influence often takes the form of a shift in perspective. Such shifts are familiar to all of us: a rebellious teenager becomes a parent and imposes a curfew on his own teenagers; a die-hard Braves fan moves from Atlanta to Toronto and joins with her new co-workers to support the Blue Jays. Throughout this text, you will see evidence of the powerful effect social influence has in molding the reality we construct for ourselves—and therefore our thoughts, feelings, and actions—whether we are together with others or alone with our thoughts.

Three Motivational Principles

As they construct reality and influence and are influenced by others, people have three basic motives: to strive for mastery, to seek connectedness with others, and to value themselves and others connected to them.

As individuals and groups construct reality while influencing and being influenced by others, they direct their thoughts, feelings, and behaviors toward three important goals.

People Strive for Mastery. **Striving for mastery** means that each of us tries to understand and predict events in the social world we inhabit in order to obtain many types of rewards. Achieving this mastery is an important incentive in our attempt to form and hold accurate opinions and beliefs about the world, because accurate beliefs can guide us to effective and satisfying actions. For example, if you want the last available part-time job at the campus bookstore, forming an accurate impression of the manager's needs and knowing yourself well enough to give a convincing account of your qualifications may help you get the job. Similarly, insightfully diagnosing business problems and successfully understanding students' and faculty members' needs may help you keep such a job. In many everyday decisions, individuals and groups choose to act in ways that appear likely to lead to the most rewarding results, guided by the most reliable and accurate information we can muster.

striving for mastery The motivational principle that people seek to understand and predict events in the social world in order to obtain rewards.

People Seek Connectedness. In seeking **connectedness**, each person attempts to create and maintain feelings of mutual support, liking, and acceptance from those they care about and value. For the men at Tailhook, shared feelings of disregard for women seemed in part to define what it means to be a Navy pilot. Apparently, conforming to group standards, even standards that have destructive consequences for people outside the group, fulfilled a need for belonging and connectedness. But the consequences are not always destructive. This same motive cements the relationships that bring joy and meaning to our lives, linking us to our teammates, families, friends, and lovers.

People Value "Me and Mine." The motivational principle of **valuing "me and mine"** means that we are motivated to see ourselves and anything or anyone connected to us—such as our families, teams, nations, or even possessions—in a positive light. Even people with life-threatening illnesses can maintain a positive view of themselves by comparing themselves with others who are even worse off. Our biased views of those who are connected to us often explain why members of different groups see the same events in very different ways. A Princeton fan may view the Dartmouth quarterback's broken leg as an accident—unfortunate, but all part of the game of football and certainly not something that reflects badly on the Princeton team. A Dartmouth supporter might blame the injury on a viciously dirty tackle, clear evidence that the Princeton team is incapable of good sportsmanship. Little wonder that these fans came away from the game with very different views of it—views that emphasized the positive characteristics of their own team and let them feel good about themselves.

Three Processing Principles

> *The operation of social and cognitive processes is described by three processing principles: established views are slow to change, accessible information has large effects, and processing is sometimes superficial and sometimes goes into great depth.*

In seeking rewards and connectedness and in valuing me and mine, people and groups gather and interpret information about the world in which they live. Three principles describe the cognitive and social processes that operate as we construct a picture of reality, influence other people, and are influenced by them.

Conservatism: Established Views Are Slow to Change. **Conservatism** is the principle that individuals' and groups' views of the world are slow to change and prone to perpetuate themselves. The Princeton supporters, convinced that their Tigers were the better team, interpreted what they saw through the filter of their beliefs. Their selective perceptions thus supported their views of reality—as did the influence of their group, the equally biased

seeking connectedness The motivational principle that people seek support, liking, and acceptance from the people and groups they care about and value.

valuing "me and mine" The motivational principle that people desire to see themselves, and other people and groups connected to themselves, in a positive light.

conservatism The processing principle that individuals' and groups' views of the world are slow to change and prone to perpetuate themselves.

Conservatism: What people think is slow to change Perhaps because she too was used to her fellow aviators' ideas about hard partying, Navy lieutenant Paula Coughlin (shown here) did not at first label what happened to her at the 1991 Tailhook Convention as sexual assault. Only when she described the incident to a Navy colleague who pointed out its seriousness did she file a formal complaint. The same process of conservatism may have led the Navy establishment, which at first refused to take complaints about the event seriously, to interpret the event in "boys will be boys" terms.

fans around them. Similarly, the Tailhook pilots, sure that women need not be taken seriously, treated them without respect—and their biased perceptions provided seeming justification for doing so. Examples of conservatism are almost endless—the first impressions we form of job applicants, the stereotypes we harbor about other groups, or preferences we nurture for the brand of peanut butter Mom always bought. In all these cases and more, the principle is the same: established knowledge tends to perpetuate itself. In the chapters to come you will see why prior beliefs, expectations, and preferences are so hard to change, and you will become more aware of the consequences of their resiliency and the enormous amount of effort needed to budge them at all.

Accessibility: Accessible Information Has Large Effects. **Accessibility** is the principle that the information that is most readily available also usually has the most impact on our thoughts, feelings, and behavior. Much of the time, our judgments and actions are based on only a tiny fraction of the possibly relevant information. From football games to political debates, every social situation provides an incredibly rich array of information—so rich that we could not consider all its details. Consequently, we are likely to consider, remember, and use only the most readily accessible information. In many situations, what comes most easily to mind is what we were already thinking. So, to return to the football example, Dartmouth stalwarts used their belief in their team's good sportsmanship as a basis for their judgments of what had happened. In other situations, we base our judgments on the information that is most easily noticed and interpreted. For many of the uninvolved students who listened to the probation speech, enthusiastic applause or disapproving whistles were sufficient basis for their poorly thought-out judgments.

Superficiality Versus Depth: People Can Process Superficially or in Depth. Much of the time, people seem to operate on automatic, putting little effort into forming a superficial picture of reality and relying heavily on whatever information is most accessible. But sometimes, particularly when we notice that events fail to match our expectations or when our important goals are threatened, we take the time and trouble to process information more extensively. These are examples of the principle of **superficiality versus depth.** Confronted with an opposing point of view—a view that clearly contradicted their own—students who cared about probation reconsidered their positions. They reviewed the arguments and based their opinions on the content of the speeches rather than on the circumstances of their presentation. Disagreement or rejection challenges not only our sense of mastery and understanding but also our feelings of connectedness, triggering anxiety and uncertainty. Threats to any of our important goals may motivate us to consider information in more depth and to think hard about our own beliefs and actions.

The interrelationships among the eight basic principles of social psychology are summarized in Figure 1.1.

accessibility The processing principle that the information that is most readily available generally has the most impact on thoughts, feelings, and behavior.

superficiality versus depth The processing principle that people ordinarily put little effort into dealing with information but at times are motivated to consider information in more depth.

Figure 1.1 Interrelations among the eight basic principles of social psychology

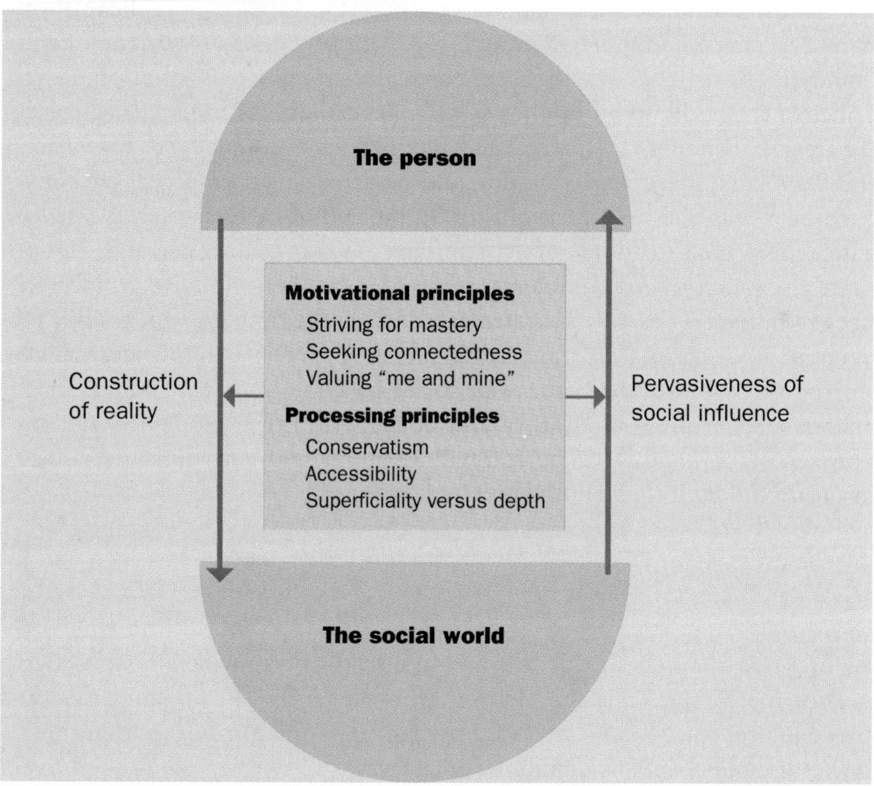

Two fundamental axioms link the individual person to the social world. Each person constructs his or her own picture of social reality, which then guides all thoughts, feelings, and actions. At the same time, the pervasiveness of social influence affects virtually all aspects of the person. Three motivational principles and three processing principles determine both the nature of the constructed reality and the nature of the social influence.

Good and Bad Outcomes

It would be wonderful if these cognitive and social processes we use to form our opinions and guide our behavior guaranteed accurate social thinking, positive social emotions, and successful social interaction. Unfortunately, this is not the case. As our examples demonstrate, the same processes that produce useful and valuable outcomes in some situations will produce misleading and destructive outcomes in others. Our ability to construct reality allows us to see our world as a coherent and meaningful place, but it also opens the door to bias and misinterpretation. Social influences sometimes provide us with safety in numbers, but they also may lead us like lambs to the slaughter. The drive for connectedness and the value we place on me and mine can give us the warm glow of belonging, but it can also prompt us to reject, devalue, and exclude others not in our chosen circle. Basing decisions on accessible information often produces extremely efficient decision making but sometimes leads to bad decisions. Even when we contemplate information as thoughtfully as possible, we are not always guaranteed an accurate decision. Sometimes the very act of thinking about things can slant our interpretations and introduce mistakes without our being aware of the problem.

Human behavior is not always as simple as it seems, but neither is it impenetrable to scientific inquiry or impossible to understand systematically. In fact, although social behavior is incredibly diverse, this diversity results from the operation of these same few processes. Thus, as you move from chapter to chapter in this text, watch for these processes at work. We offer some help by calling attention to particular applications of the general themes of the book. In addition, we make special efforts to present theories and research findings as interrelated sets of ideas—by placing cross-references to related ideas in the margin, and by providing a graphical overview of the key ideas and their relationships at the end of each chapter. We know that disconnected items of information are hard to remember and do not contribute much to a real *understanding* of social behavior. We would like you to see this text as an integrated story of (1) the fundamental social and cognitive processes that operate as human beings perceive, influence, and interact with others, and (2) the way social psychologists learn about these processes, both in the laboratory and in the world of everyday life. It is a fascinating story, and we hope you will learn much about yourself and others as you follow it through the text.

Plan of the Book

The first two chapters of this text are an introduction to social psychology, covering the "Why?" and the "How?" of our science. The remainder of the book explores the "What" of social psychology—the topic areas that make up the discipline. In this chapter we have tried to convey *why* social psychologists ask the questions they do. Chapter 2 tells more about *how* they seek answers.

- *Asking and Answering Research Questions.* Have we convinced you already that peoples' interpretive processes and social surroundings may bias what they know? Chapter 2 describes the logical checks and balances built into the structure of science that help researchers to guard against subjectivity and bias.

Chapters 3 through 14 explore *what* social psychologists study. Following our definition of social psychology, we deal in turn with how individuals perceive, influence, and relate to others. Within each of these three areas, the first two chapters deal with individuals and the last two focus on groups.

Chapters 3 through 6 focus on *social perception,* the way we come to know and understand the basic elements of our social world—both individuals and social groups.

- *Perceiving Individuals.* From fleeting impressions of passing strangers to the intimate familiarity of our best friend, Chapter 3 deals with knowing and understanding other people.

- *The Self.* What person is probably most important, most near and dear to each of us? Chapter 4 describes how we understand the self.
- *Perceiving Groups.* In Chapter 5, we investigate the beliefs and feelings people develop about social groups like working women, Russians, schoolteachers, or Muslims.
- *Social Identity.* Chapter 6 brings these topics together in a discussion of how we come to see ourselves *as* members of a social group—how a group can become part of the self.

Social influence is the impact each of us has on others, and it is the topic of Chapters 7 through 10. The elements of social psychology do not occur in isolation: each of us is constantly influencing and being influenced by others. Others affect us whether they are in our face—like an aggressive salesperson—or on our minds—even when we are alone.

- *Attitudes and Attitude Change.* Advertisements aim at our pocketbooks, political campaigns play on our fears, debates appeal to our reason. Do they change our minds? If so, how? Chapter 7 gives some answers to questions like these.
- *Attitudes and Behavior.* Under the right circumstances, attitudes both reflect and guide behaviors. Chapter 8 tells a tale of their mutual influence.
- *Groups, Norms, and Conformity.* A different kind of mutual influence is the focus of Chapter 9. Here we examine how groups reach agreement and why that agreement has such compelling effects on group members.
- *Norms and Behavior.* Chapter 10 describes the effects of groups on what people do, not just on what they think. Bringing all the chapters of this section together, we describe how attitudes and group influences combine to affect behavior.

In the final four chapters we concentrate on *social relations,* the bonds that link us one to another, as individuals and as groups. Whether we are bound by attraction or cooperation, or shackled by aggression and conflict, our relations with others can pull us together or drive us apart.

- *Liking and Loving.* Chapter 11 takes a close look at feelings of attraction to other people and the formation and development of close and loving relationships. We also review what social psychology can tell us about why relationships flourish or wither.
- *Helping and Hurting.* Dramatic incidents of selfless heroism or horrifying examples of senseless violence—why do they occur? Chapter 12 examines the conditions under which we help or hurt other people and our reasons for doing so.

- *Interaction and Interdependence.* Small groups—management committees, paramedic teams, juries, and others—do society's work. Chapter 13's topic is how we interact with others in small groups, and how groups cooperate to accomplish shared tasks.
- *Conflict and Conflict Resolution.* Who can watch the evening news without being struck by the many conflicts that pit group against group? In Chapter 14 we analyze the career of such conflicts: how they can arise, escalate, and, sometimes, be resolved.

The text ends with an Epilogue that summarizes the major themes and reflects on some of their interrelationships and applications.

As you read this book, we invite you to join us in seeing social psychological principles at work in people's actions and interactions. Seeing events around you in this framework is the first and most essential step toward *becoming* a social psychologist, having the fun of doing research both to advance our knowledge of how the principles work and to apply them to important problems. But you do not have to do research to use your new knowledge to understand why your friends act as they do, how other people influence you, or what accounts for group conflicts around the world. We hope you will come to appreciate both the usefulness and the excitement of social psychology, no matter what course your life might take.

Summary

A Definition of Social Psychology **Social psychology** is the scientific study of the effects of social and cognitive processes on the way individuals perceive, influence, and relate to others. Like other sciences, social psychology gathers knowledge systematically by means of scientific methods. These methods help produce knowledge that is less subject to the biases and distortions that often characterize common-sense knowledge.

The physical presence of other people, the knowledge and opinions that they pass on to us, and our feelings about the groups to which we belong all deeply influence us through **social processes**—whether we are with other people or alone. Our perceptions, memories, emotions, and motives also influence us through **cognitive processes.** Effects of social and cognitive processes are not separate; they are inextricably intertwined.

All types of social behavior, from personal relationships to persuasion to ethnic conflict around the globe, reflect the operation of social and cognitive processes. Understanding these processes can help us comprehend why people act the way they do, and it may also help to solve important social problems.

Historical Trends and Current Themes in Social Psychology Social psychology emerged soon after the beginning of scientific psychology in the late nineteenth century, when researchers began considering questions about social influences on human thought and action. Through much of the twentieth century, North American psychology was dominated by behaviorism, but social psychologists maintained an emphasis on the important effects of thoughts and feelings on behavior.

In the 1930s and 1940s, many European social psychologists fled to North America, where they had a major influence on the field's direction. Throughout this period, significant questions inspired by the rise of Nazism and the Second World War shaped research interests.

During the 1950s and 1960s, social psychology grew and flourished, moving toward an integrated theoretical understanding of social and cognitive processes and toward further applications of social psychological theory to important applied problems.

How the Approach of This Book Reflects an Integrative Perspective Social psychology is a field that integrates not only the cognitive and the social but also basic theory and applied research. All the diversity and richness of human social behavior can be understood in terms of social processes that flow from eight principles. Two fundamental axioms are that people **construct their own reality** and that **social influences are pervasive.** Three motivational principles are that as they construct reality and influence and are influenced by others, people **strive for mastery,** for understanding and control of their environment; **seek connectedness** with others; and **value "me and mine,"** both themselves and other people or groups connected to them. People's thoughts and actions are also influenced by three processing principles. One is **conservatism;** established views are slow to change. Another is **accessibility;** easily accessed information has large effects. The final principle is **superficiality versus depth;** people can process information superficially or in depth.

Plan of the Book This text has four main sections. Chapters 1 and 2 introduce social psychology and its typical research methods. Chapters 3 through 6 focus on social perception, the ways that people interpret and understand other people, themselves, and social groups. Chapters 7 through 10 deal with social influence, the ways that people and groups affect each other as they interact and communicate. Chapters 11 through 14 describe the social relations that lead people to help and hurt each other, form relationships, and work together in groups.

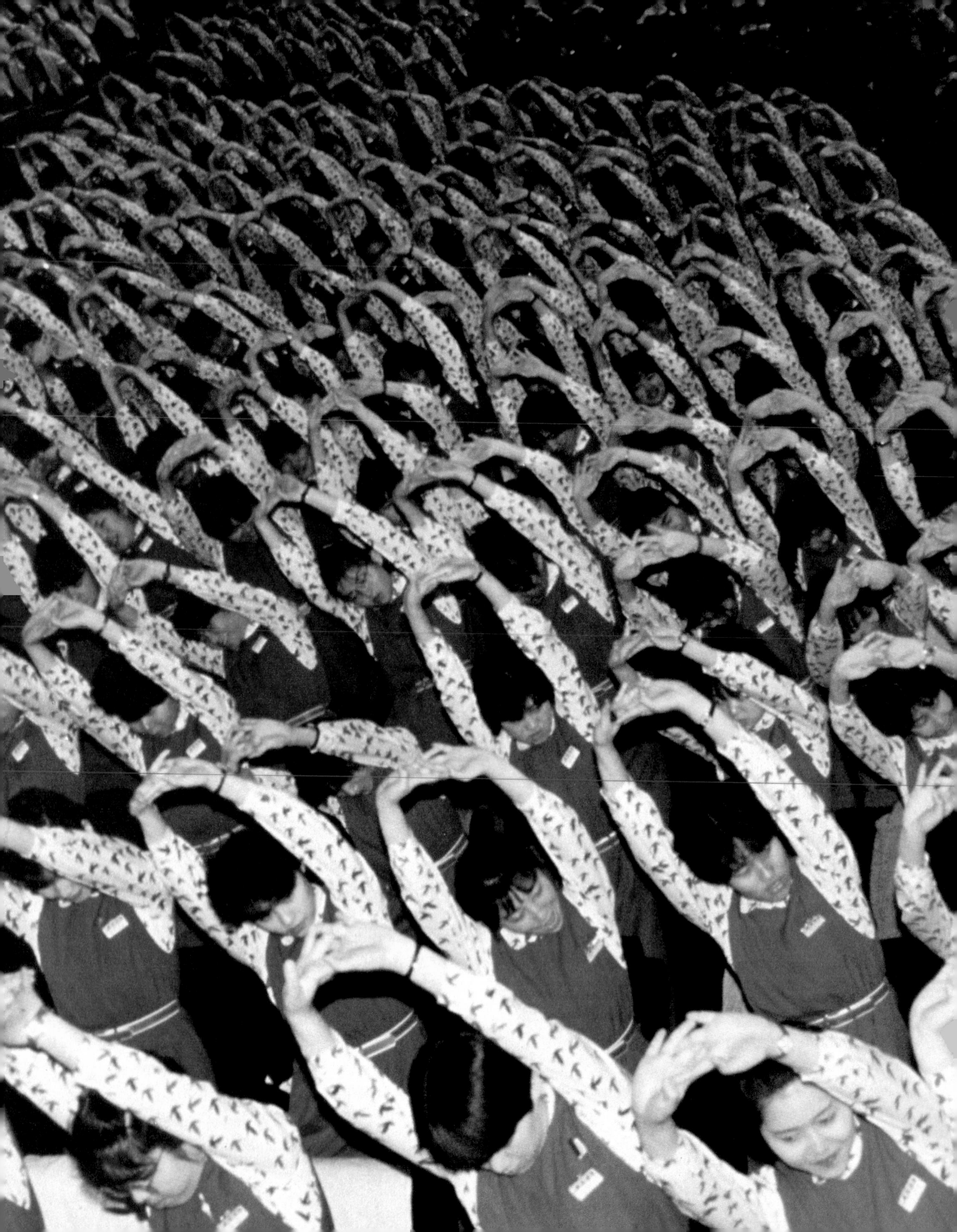

2

Asking and Answering Research Questions

Imagine winning the state lottery. Or receiving a promotion after only five months in your new position. Or getting a would-be buyer to meet your price on the sale of your used car. How do you think you would react to these events? Most people would anticipate feeling very happy. Now imagine finding out that you have a life-threatening illness, that you have worked at the same job for years and still have little hope of advancement, or that you got much less for your used car than you were hoping for. You probably would predict being unhappy about these outcomes. Social psychological research has shown, however, that these intuitively obvious conclusions are not always true. Lottery winners are soon no happier than the rest of us (Brickman and others, 1978). Those receiving rapid promotions are often more dissatisfied than people with less chance of advancement (Stouffer and others, 1949), and patients with serious illnesses often show remarkably good spirits (Wood and others, 1985). And it turns out that the money actually gained or lost in negotiation with others has little to do with people's satisfaction about the outcome (Loewenstein and others, 1989).

Most people find these research findings surprising. Common sense tells us that good outcomes make people feel happy, contented, and satisfied, and that negative events or failures will make us feel unhappy. But conclusions based on scientific research are not always the same as those we reach using everyday common sense. And when those conclusions differ, which should you trust: research findings or common sense? Are research findings really more dependable, trustworthy, or accurate than our everyday understanding of social behavior?

These kinds of questions are at the heart of this chapter. Social psychology is an *empirical science,* meaning that its theories and conclusions about social behavior rest on the results of research. Like other scientists, most social psychologists believe that scientific research methods produce answers that are more likely to be trustworthy and unbiased than those we arrive at through everyday common sense, hunches, and intuitions. Why? It is not that scientists are perfectly objective logicians like *Star Trek*'s Mr. Spock or Commander Data. On the contrary, scientists are human, too, and they are just as vulnerable as anyone else to preconceptions, prejudices, and wishful

Order in diversity: The regularities of human behavior During morning exercises at a Japanese company (shown at left), the workers blend together in a mosaic of stretching limbs. The goal of social psychological theory and research is the understanding of patterns in human behavior—the influences that make different individuals react in the same way under the same social psychological circumstances.

thinking. This is exactly why scientific methods are so important. Most people are unaware of the biases in their everyday thinking and knowledge, and they therefore fail to guard against them. But because scientists know that biases can distort their reasoning and their findings, they use research methods specifically designed to counter such slips in thinking.

Most of this chapter is dedicated to describing the lengths to which social psychologists go to try to keep their research free from bias and error. Their goal is reaching general conclusions about human social behavior which are as trustworthy as possible. Understanding the practical and logical steps researchers take to reach this goal will help you grasp *why* social psychologists do the sorts of research you will read about in this book. It will also be useful when you see research findings reported in newspapers and other popular media sources. You will better understand which studies should be taken seriously, and which fall short of their goal.

But good science is about more than just producing trustworthy and general results. Social psychological research is a human enterprise, in which people are both the investigators and the investigated. This situation inevitably raises issues of values and ethics. How should research participants be treated? Are there research questions that should not be pursued? Should the results of research be made known to everyone, no matter how they will use those results? No researcher can ignore these questions, and neither should any consumer of social psychological research. As you read this chapter and the rest of this text, we hope you will reflect on the values implicit in social psychologists' work and on how your own values guide your reactions to the topics and results discussed here. Clarifying ethical and value stands about research issues is just as important to good science as carefully following the rules of scientific methodology.

Research Questions and the Role of Theory

Research is almost always provoked by curiosity—the researcher's desire to know the answer to some question about events, ideas, and people. Some questions are provoked by unexpectedly negative or positive events. The brutality of ethnic warfare in the former Yugoslavia and the global outpouring of aid for African famine victims provoke questions about hatred and altruism. The fiery deaths of self-styled messiah David Koresh and his followers cause social psychologists, like other observers, to ask how patterns of obedience are established. And the way rescuers work together to help victims of earthquakes, floods, hurricanes, and fires stimulates researchers' curiosity about processes leading to cooperation. But research ideas also stem from questioning the mundane and the accepted—the everyday events that affect the lives of all of us. Why do women still earn much less than men for performing the same jobs? How good are people at judging others' character? How can city managers convince more motorists to carpool? Is breaking up really hard to do—even if you are the breaker upper rather than the broken-up-with?

Part of what makes a person choose to become a social psychologist is a healthy store of curiosity about why people act the way they do. Notice, however, that many of these questions go beyond mere curiosity. Many social psychologists try to explain and solve social problems that have a major impact on many people's lives: racial prejudice, gender discrimination, depletion of environmental resources, violence, unhealthy lifestyles, and depression. And although individual events and people may provoke their research questions, social psychologists are not interested merely in understanding *specific* events or *specific* individuals. They seek instead to discover general principles that explain the behavior of many people in many situations. From those principles will flow an understanding of why certain behaviors occur and under what conditions.

Research Questions and Scientific Theory

> *Social psychologists seek to develop scientific theories to provide explanations of social behavior. A scientific theory is a general statement about the causal relationships among abstract constructs.*

To conduct their research, social psychologists have to translate specific questions about individuals and events into general statements about social behavior. Consider, for example, some of the research referred to at the beginning of this chapter. One study interviewed women diagnosed with breast cancer and noted whether they compared themselves to others who were adjusting better or worse to the disease (Wood and others, 1985). In another study, business school students engaged in a mock negotiation learned whether their opponent was happy or sad about the outcome (Loewenstein and others, 1989). What was the point of these exercises? Were the researchers concerned only about the behavior of particular cancer patients, or about specific students involved in one set of negotiations? Not at all. The real goal of these studies was not to gauge the reactions of particular individuals in particular situations but rather to test a general social psychological *theory* about human behavior. In fact, all the research referred to in the introduction was designed to test some aspect of *social comparison theory*—the idea that people evaluate their abilities, opinions, and outcomes by comparing themselves to others (Festinger, 1954). All of our judgments about ourselves—as slow or smart, right or wrong, winners or losers—depend on our comparisons of our own abilities, attitudes, and outcomes with those of others.

Information gleaned from comparison with others has a major impact on what people think and how they feel about themselves, as described in Chapter 4, pages 118 to 119, and 133 to 134.

Theories provide general explanations for social behavior. More formally, a scientific **theory** satisfies three requirements:

- It is a statement about *constructs.*
- It describes *causal relations.*
- It is *general in scope,* although the range of generality differs for different theories.

theory A statement that satisfies three requirements: It is about constructs; it describes causal relations; and it is general in scope, although the range of generality differs for different theories.

Let us look more closely at each part of this definition.

1. *Theories are about constructs.* **Constructs** are abstract concepts. For example, "the knowledge of others' abilities and attitudes" and "the evaluation of one's own abilities and attitudes" are two constructs that are featured in social comparison theory. Each of these constructs is abstract in two senses:

- It cannot be directly observed. You cannot see knowledge or touch an evaluation.
- It is general. Neither of these two statements is concerned with particular individuals or particular reactions.

2. *Theories describe causal relations.* The most powerful theories describe causal relations among constructs. A theory states that a change in one construct (the cause) produces a corresponding change in another construct (the effect). Social comparison theory is a theory about cause and effect: our knowledge of other people's outcomes, performances, or opinions has a causal impact on how we evaluate our own outcomes, performances, or opinions.

Because they offer reasons to explain *why* events occur, theories that describe causal relations are very powerful. If we know that one state or event causes another, we can take practical steps to change behavior or solve problems. The knowledge that people evaluate their own abilities and attitudes by reference to those of other people, for example, could have a variety of practical applications. A city might decide to saturate the community with posters featuring the names and photos of residents who form car pools. Social comparison theory would predict that knowing that their neighbors are committed to car pooling might cause other residents to decide to share rides. Similarly, medical personnel who work with patients with treatable forms of an illness might encourage those patients to compare themselves with others who have more serious forms of the disease. Such a comparison might help patients to cope more effectively with their illness. Without research that shows the truly causal impact of comparisons between our own experiences and those of other people, these strategies might never be pursued.

3. *Theories are general in scope, although the range of generality differs for different theories.* Theories are intended to apply to many people in different times and settings. Social comparison theory, for example, is intended to be a very general statement about how all people evaluate many aspects of their life. And, indeed, judging one's own experience in the context of what happens to others does appear to be a general human characteristic, although reactions to the comparison may differ in different cultures (Moghaddam and others, 1993).

Other theories, however, have a more limited scope than social comparison theory. Perhaps they pertain only to males, or only to people raised in Eastern cultures. The more generally applicable a theory is, the more useful

constructs Abstract and general concepts that are used in theories and that are not directly observable.

it is because it will hold for many different kinds of people at different times and in diverse settings. Currently, however, little is known about just how broadly most social psychological theories do generalize (Bond, 1988; Smith & Bond, 1993). This important issue of the generality of theories is explored in more detail later in this chapter.

Testing Theories: From Theory to Research

Ultimately, good research is designed to test theories. This testing allows social psychologists to assess whether a theory offers a good explanation of human behavior. Theories can be evaluated only on the basis of *valid* research—research that is trustworthy because the researcher has taken pains to exclude bias and error. How can researchers be sure that their research is valid and that it provides evidence for or against theories? It turns out that valid research is guided by the three properties of theories just described (Cook & Campbell, 1979; Judd and others, 1991).

1. Because theories deal with *constructs*—abstract concepts—researchers have to be sure the specific observations they make in their studies are in fact relevant to those constructs.
2. Because theories describe *causal relations,* researchers have to be sure they know the causes of any changes in behavior they find in their studies.
3. Because theories *are intended to apply to many* types of people, times, and settings, researchers have to be sure that their results can generalize beyond the people, time, and setting of a particular study.

Research that meets these three criteria is said to have *construct validity, internal validity,* and *external validity.* As we shall see, all three of these criteria are essential links in the logical chain by which research supports theory. We now examine each of them in more detail.

Construct Validity: Assessing Constructs

> *To provide a valid test of a theory, research must have construct validity, which means that the independent and dependent variables used in the research must correspond to the intended theoretical constructs. Construct validity is endangered if subjects behave in ways they think are expected or are socially desirable. Researchers ensure construct validity by manipulating and measuring independent and dependent variables in many different ways.*

The researcher's first task is to make sure that the events that occur in the research setting actually correspond to the theoretical constructs under investigation. Although this is not always an easy task, if the researcher accomplishes it, the research will have **construct validity**.

Remember that cause and effect constructs in a theory are abstract concepts and therefore are not directly observable. Their presence or absence has to be inferred by *manipulating* (or varying) or *measuring* other events that are observable. Concrete manipulations or measurements of assumed causal factors are called **independent variables.** Concrete measurements of assumed effects are called **dependent variables.** The term *dependent* indicates that the experiment has been designed to see how this factor depends on the independent variable.

An example can help clarify these terms. Let's consider a theory called *realistic conflict theory* (Sherif and others, 1961). It states that hostility between social groups can be caused by direct competition for limited resources. Researchers have tried to study the abstract construct of "competition for limited resources" by manipulating concrete events in experiments. For example, they have offered teams of school boys prizes for their athletic performances, asked trios of managers to produce the "best" business plan, or promised one group of subjects pennies for points they won in competition with other groups. Each of these manipulations is intended to create competition for limited resources, which the theory suggests will cause another construct, "hostility between social groups," to vary. As measures of this construct, researchers have used dependent variables such as negative beliefs, insults, refusals to help, and acts of aggression that rival groups direct toward each other. If the concrete independent and dependent variables used in the research correspond to the intended theoretical constructs, the researchers will be able to draw valid conclusions about those constructs.

Competition for material and social resources is indeed a frequent cause of bitter intergroup hostilities, as you will see in Chapter 14.

Construct validity has two parts. First, independent and dependent variables must correspond to the *intended* construct, and, second, they must not correspond to *other* constructs. Let us consider them in relation to a study in which two teams of school boys were encouraged to compete in sporting events for trophies, badges, and pocket knives. The researchers measured the boys' mutual hostility by observing, among other things, what the groups said to each other and how they interacted (Sherif and others, 1961).

Does this study have construct validity? It does if the boys' opportunity to vie for prizes produced a significant change in the intended construct, "direct competition for limited resources" but in nothing else. Similarly, the construct validity of the study depends on the assumption that the number of insults hurled at the other team and the number of raids on each other's possessions really reflected intergroup hostility but nothing else.

As you will see in the pages that follow, much of the ingenuity in social psychological research goes into selecting and refining ways to manipulate and measure important theoretical constructs without manipulating or measuring other unintended constructs.

construct validity The extent to which the independent and dependent variables used in research correspond to the theoretical constructs under investigation.

independent variable A concrete manipulation or measurement of a construct that is thought to influence other constructs.

dependent variable A concrete measurement of a construct that is thought to be influenced by other constructs.

Threats to Construct Validity. Unfortunately, ensuring construct validity is a pretty tall order. Construct validity may be compromised in one of two ways. First, the *manipulations* that researchers intend to influence one construct may also influence others. Second, research *measures* may not really measure the construct they are supposed to measure.

How might a manipulation intended to affect the boys' competition for prizes also have other effects? One possibility is that encouraging the boys to compete in sporting events—the event intended to create competition—might have excited them or made them worry about failure. If this is true, construct validity is threatened because factors other than the intended construct might influence subjects' behavior.

The Rattlers and the Eagles These archival photographs show two groups at Sherif's experimental study. On the left, the boys compete in a tug of war. On the right, they cooperate to solve a problem with the water tank.

Another possibility is that the researchers' own behavior changed as they tried to manipulate the presence or absence of competition. What if the researchers had been calm and peaceable before the competition began but changed after it was under way—exhorting the boys to win, cheering their victories and scorning their defeats? The events that occurred in the research setting might then not correspond to the intended theoretical construct alone. The boys might have taken their cues not from the competition itself but from what the researchers seemed to expect. They may have been asking themselves, "What do they want me to do?"

Behaviors that are based on the subject's perceptions of the research purpose are said to be influenced by **demand characteristics**. Demand characteristics threaten construct validity because something other than the intended construct—such as the subjects' impression of what the researcher wants or expects—has been manipulated (Orne, 1962; Rosenthal, 1969). When research takes place in a strange and novel environment like the laboratory, people are remarkably sensitive to subtle cues that tell them how they are expected to act.

demand characteristics Cues in a research setting that lead participants to make inferences about what researchers expect or desire and that therefore bias how the participants act.

This effect was clearly demonstrated in a study in which subjects were asked to judge the degree of success or failure indicated by the expression on the faces of people in a series of photographs (Rosenthal & Fode, 1963). One group of subjects was guided through the study by a researcher who had been led to believe that the photos represented "successful" faces. The second group worked with a researcher led to believe the same photos showed faces of "failure." Both researchers followed identical procedures and gave their subjects identically worded instructions. Though subjects were told nothing about the photos, they obviously picked up clues about the expected responses from the researchers' subtle nonverbal behaviors. In each group, the subjects' evaluations of the photos corresponded exactly to the researcher's expectations. Because their responses reflected not only the intended construct (perceptions of the photos) but also demand characteristics (the responses the researcher seemed to expect), this study demonstrates how construct validity can be compromised.

To counteract demand characteristics, researchers often exercise an extra set of precautions with members of the research team who will have contact with subjects. These team members are prevented from knowing the responses expected from any particular subject, so that they cannot subtly and unintentionally communicate those expectations to the subject. In addition, as you will see later in this chapter, researchers often attempt to conceal the true purpose of their research from subjects and, in some cases, may even mislead subjects about the purpose.

Sally Forth

Reprinted with special permission of King Features Syndicate

Even if demand characteristics can be eliminated, a second threat to construct validity exists: the possibility that the dependent variable will not measure what it is intended to measure. For example, the number of insults aimed at each group may not have reflected the intended construct of intergroup hostility. The researchers unknowingly may have been measuring the boys' pent-up frustration or anger produced by high levels of arousal. An even more common problem for researchers trying to accurately measure constructs is **social desirability response bias**, people's tendency to act in ways that make them look good (Rosenberg, 1969). For example, a researcher measuring the construct of conscientiousness might ask the following questions: Are you a punctual person? Do you keep your promises? Do you carry your share of responsibilities in group projects? Most people's responses to such questions would reflect both their appraisal of their conscientiousness and a tendency to say good things about themselves. The researcher might think she is measuring conscientiousness, but she in fact also would be measuring people's desire to look good. Social psychologists must be constantly on guard against the threat of social desirability biases in their measurements. This is particularly true when they are interested in attitudes or behaviors that might meet with some social disapproval—such as stereotyping, prejudice, aggression, or unusual opinions or lifestyles.

Ensuring Construct Validity. Researchers take great pains to avoid compromising the construct validity of their studies. They do so by choosing their manipulations and measurements very carefully and by using multiple manipulations and measures.

1. *Using the best manipulation and measure for the purpose.* Researchers try very hard to choose manipulations and measurements that tap the construct under investigation but minimize other influences. A specific manipulation that seems to zero in on a particular construct and on no other will permit an especially effective test of a theory. Over the years researchers have developed effective and valid manipulations of a wide range of constructs including people's mood, anxiety level, or choices for social comparisons.

Measures used in research fall into a few distinct categories, each with its own strengths and weaknesses. For example, *self-report measures,* which rely on asking the individual about his or her thoughts, feelings, or behaviors, are probably the most easily available sources of information about beliefs, attitudes, and intentions. But they are also particularly susceptible to demand characteristics and social desirability biases—especially if the topic is a sensitive one. Thus, asking people overt questions about their racial prejudice is unlikely to produce answers with high construct validity (Crosby and others, 1980).

A researcher studying racial prejudice might decide, therefore, that a better technique for his particular study would be to use *observational measures:* to watch and record people's behavior. The researcher could watch, for example, how close a subject stood or sat next to a person of another race, and whether people participating in such intergroup interactions displayed relaxed smiles or nervous fidgeting. Observational measures often have good construct validity, particularly when subjects are unaware of being observed. Of course, if the research setting is public or if subjects know they are being observed, social desirability biases could still undermine construct validity.

Many researchers decide that performance measures are most appropri-

social desirability response bias People's tendency to act in ways that they believe others find acceptable and approve of.

Ensuring construct validity by getting real To ensure that subjects' reactions to manipulations are not contaminated by their beliefs about how they should act in a laboratory setting, social psychologists sometimes stage incidents in public settings to gauge people's "natural" reactions. Here a man pretends to verbally abuse a young woman. How might you react if you were a bystander at such an event?

ate for their goals. *Performance measures* ask subjects to perform some task as well as they can—for example, by answering questions as rapidly and accurately as possible or by recalling as much as they can about information presented earlier. A performance measure of prejudice might require subjects to read a complicated description of a character's successes and failures and then to recall everything they could from the story. If subjects recalled mostly successes when they believed the character was White but mostly failures if the character was African American, the researcher might conclude that the subjects were prejudiced against African Americans. Because people usually just try to perform as well as they can on such tasks, social desirability and demand characteristics tend to be less of a problem than they are with self-report or observational measures.

Like any good carpenter or chef, a social psychology researcher must choose the right manipulation and measurement tool for the job at hand. Manipulations and measures that prove to be particularly precise and effective ways of varying constructs often become quite popular in research, as ones with less construct validity fall by the wayside. But even the best available manipulation or measure might not by itself ensure construct validity.

2. *Using multiple manipulations and multiple measures*. Since different kinds of manipulations and measures have different strengths, the best way a researcher can ensure construct validity is to use multiple manipulations and multiple measures.

The use of multiple manipulations and multiple measures increases researchers' confidence in their findings. To understand why, imagine that you wanted to be sure your boss was in a good mood before you asked for time off. You check her expression for a smile and conclude she probably is feeling fine. Because you really are not sure, however, you check with a co-worker, who reports that your supervisor has been quite amiable. Still, you decide to see if she chooses to work out during her lunch hour—usually a pretty good sign of an upbeat mood. Each of these different means of gathering information has its own unique problems, but the accumulated evidence all points to the likelihood that your boss is feeling pretty chipper. You can see how your confidence in your reading of your supervisor's mood would grow with each converging piece of evidence, even though no single piece of evidence could be conclusive. When different manipulations and different measures produce the same results it works the same way: researchers can be reasonably confident that they are manipulating and measuring the intended construct and nothing else.

Now imagine for a moment that you are part of a research team trying to test the impact of positive or negative mood on helping. You have been asked to help choose among the manipulations and measures that have been proposed. (Funding and personnel are not problems; your budget is generous.) One team member has proposed manipulating the subjects' mood by exposing them to pleasant or putrid smells. Another has suggested providing them with bogus feedback of success or failure on a test of intelligence. Still others want subjects to watch amusing or sad movies, listen to upbeat or depressing music, or recall pleasant or sad events from their pasts. What all these manipulations have in common is the essential aspects of mood, and nothing else.

Similarly, a large number of suggestions have been made about ways to measure helping. One team member proposes asking subjects directly about their intentions to help. Another wants to count the number of spilled papers they retrieve or tally the dollars they are willing to donate to a worthy cause. A third suggests timing how long it takes subjects to come to another person's aid. These are diverse measures of willingness to help. Which manipulations and measures should you use? In this case, your best choice might be "all of the above." If you selected only one way to manipulate mood and one measure of helping, the results of your research might reflect unique aspects of those specific variables. By using diverse manipulations of mood and measures of helping, the likelihood is greater that the research results will reflect the intended constructs.

Internal Validity: Assessing Causal Relations

To provide a valid test of a theory, research must have internal validity so that observers can conclude that changes in the independent variable actually caused changes in the dependent variable. If the independent variable is measured rather than manipulated, the research may lack internal validity because many other unknown factors could affect the research results. Random assignment of subjects to groups, followed by manipulation of independent variables, will allow the researcher to draw stronger conclusions about cause and effect.

A good test of a theory provides solid evidence about cause and effect. Research has high **internal validity** if the researcher can confidently conclude that a change in the independent variable *caused* a change in the dependent variable. Whether or not such a conclusion can be drawn depends primarily on a study's *research design,* which specifies how different groups of subjects will be selected, treated, and measured. Research designs differ, and some offer a higher chance of internal validity than do others.

Threats to Internal Validity. The major threat to internal validity is that factors other than changes in the independent variable may have caused the observed changes in the dependent variable. Eliminating all such alternative factors is often very difficult, as you will see in the following example.

The conditions under which intergroup contact can undermine prejudice and help resolve intergroup conflict are described in Chapter 5, pages 204 to 205, and Chapter 14.

The *contact hypothesis* is a theory that states that casual, friendly contact with members of a different ethnic group can increase liking for that group (Allport, 1954a). Some obvious ways of testing this theory involve investigating the impact of important, naturally occurring, causal variables—such as contact with different groups in a neighborhood—on liking for those various groups. Rudolf Kalin and J. W. Berry (1982) did just that, using data from a public opinion survey. The survey asked what Canadians thought of English-speaking and French-speaking Canadians, Canadian Native Americans, and other Canadian citizens of German, Jewish, Italian, and Ukrainian descent. Kalin and Berry compared the survey data with information from the Canadian Census to establish which ethnic groups lived in the same neighborhoods with the various survey respondents. Their results showed that people who lived in areas with a relatively high percentage of a particular group liked that group more than did people who lived far away from members of that group. This study is an example of a **nonexperimental research** design, a design in which researchers simply measure both the independent variable (in this case, neighborhood ethnic composition) and the dependent variable (people's opinions of groups).

Unfortunately, nonexperimental designs are vulnerable to many threats to internal validity. Measurement of the independent variable does allow subjects to be classified into groups—such as those who live near many French-speaking Canadians and those who do not. However, the design does not control for the possibility that these groups of subjects may differ in many other unknown ways. As a result, even if the groups differ in the average favorability of their response toward some ethnic group, researchers cannot confidently state the cause of that difference. Although highly favorable responses may be due to the causal impact of frequent contact with the group in the subjects' neighborhood, other factors could also be the cause. Rather than contact causing liking, for example, liking may cause the contact. That is, people who hold more positive views of a group might choose to move into or remain in a neighborhood in which many members of that group live. Another explanation may be that people who live in a particular neighborhood share other personal characteristics—such as a particular type of social background—that influence both where they live and how they feel about ethnic diversity.

internal validity The extent to which it can be concluded that changes in the independent variable actually caused changes in the dependent variable in a research study.

nonexperimental research A research design in which both the independent and dependent variables are measured.

Yes, but is it internally valid? Many nonexperimental studies find that children who watch violent television are more aggressive than those who do not. Unfortunately, these designs lack internal validity. Their results cannot tell us whether watching violent TV causes aggression, or whether aggressive children prefer to watch violent TV. To establish the causal role of TV violence, social psychologists have turned to experimental research designs with high internal validity, as discussed in Chapter 12.

In a nonexperimental design it is always possible that people who differ on the intended independent variable may also differ in other unintended ways. Each additional difference offers an alternative explanation for any results found. And each alternative explanation for changes in the dependent variable threatens the internal validity of the research.

Ensuring Internal Validity. Given the vast number of differences that characterize humankind, is it possible to set up a research design that ensures that groups of people will differ only in the way the researcher intends? Amazingly, the answer is yes. This feat can be accomplished by using an **experimental research** design. Two aspects of experimental design are crucial in promoting validity: first, subjects are *randomly assigned* to experimental groups (sometimes called *conditions*); second, the independent variable is then *manipulated* rather than measured. Here is how these two aspects work.

First, researchers divide subjects into groups that are equivalent. To do so, they use a technique similar to a lottery or a flip of a coin to make the assignments. **Random assignment** gives every person who is a subject in an experiment exactly the same chance of ending up in any given experimental group. Random assignment of subjects is designed to ensure that the groups are approximately equivalent in every way. Suppose you started out with twenty people, ten men and ten women, and randomly divided them into two groups by flipping a coin for each person. Would it be likely that all of the women would end up in one group and all the men in the other? It could happen, but it is extremely unlikely; in fact, this outcome would occur less often than once in 500,000 times. Because the coin has the same chance of landing head-up each time it is flipped, every person has an equal chance of being assigned to the "heads" group. In the end, each group will probably have a roughly even number of males and females. The same logic applies to all attributes of the individuals who are being assigned—not only their gender but their age, eye color, friendliness, shoe size, and even other character-

experimental research A research design in which researchers randomly assign subjects to different groups and manipulate one or more independent variables.

random assignment The procedure of assigning subjects to different experimental groups so that every subject has exactly the same chance as every other subject of being in any given group.

istics the researcher would not think of or could not measure. So, on the average, random assignment creates groups that are approximately equivalent to one another before the manipulation is applied.

This sets the stage for the second important step in an experimental design: the researcher now manipulates the independent variable so that subjects in the different conditions are exposed to different treatments. Because the groups were expected to be equivalent to begin with, this procedure creates groups that differ *only* in terms of the independent variable. Having taken these precautions, the researcher then measures the dependent variable. It is now reasonable to conclude that any observed differences in the dependent variable were caused by the independent variable—simply because no other differences between the groups were expected to exist initially.

Donna Desforges and her associates (1991) chose an experimental design when they set out to test the contact hypothesis. These researchers randomly assigned some U.S. college students to work cooperatively with a person described as a former mental patient. (The "patient" was actually a *confederate,* a research assistant playing a specific role in the study.) Other subjects simply sat in the same room with the person. Subjects who interacted cooperatively with the individual came to hold more positive beliefs about former mental patients than did subjects who simply worked in the same room. We can be confident that the interaction caused this difference because the groups of subjects who received these two treatments were created by random assignment and therefore can be expected to be equivalent in every other way.

Experimental Versus Nonexperimental Research Designs. A researcher who wishes to test a theory may choose either an experimental or a nonexperimental design. In general, experimental designs offer higher internal validity and therefore permit stronger tests of the causal relations between constructs. If a nonexperimental study shows that the dependent variable changes when the independent variable changes, that result is certainly consistent with a causal theory. It does not provide strong support for the theory, however, because factors other than the independent variable could also be causing the observed pattern of results. Experimental designs provide stronger tests of theory because random assignment rules out virtually all alternative explanations.

Why, then, would a researcher ever use a nonexperimental design? There are many reasons. First, some theoretically important independent variables, like gender and ethnicity, cannot be varied. Second, for ethical reasons, researchers must not manipulate variables like subjects' relationships with their marriage partner, or their feelings of depression, or the degree of their ethnic prejudice. Finally, often research manipulations just cannot be as powerful as the variation in constructs found in everyday life. For example, no experimental study of the effects of television watching on aggression could faithfully reproduce the accumulated effect of watching four or more hours of television every day for a period of ten or twenty years.

Table 2.1 Advantages and disadvantages of nonexperimental and experimental designs

Type of validity	Nonexperimental design	Experimental design
Internal validity	*Low,* because the lack of random assignment and manipulation means that alternative explanations for results may be possible.	*High,* because random assignment and manipulation allow alternative causal explanations to be ruled out.
Construct validity	*High,* if powerful effects of real-life variables—including those that cannot practically or ethically be manipulated—can be studied in their natural contexts.	*Low,* when practical or ethical constraints render manipulations weak or artificial. *High,* when manipulations can adequately vary theoretically important constructs.

For all these reasons, researchers sometimes prefer using nonexperimental designs in their studies. Table 2.1 summarizes the advantages and disadvantages of experimental and nonexperimental designs.

External Validity: Assessing Generalizability

To provide a valid test of a theory, research must have external validity, meaning that its results can be generalized beyond the people, time, and setting of a particular study. Some theories are intended to apply to many different kinds of people and places, whereas others apply more narrowly. When a theory is intended to apply to a particular population and setting, external validity is ensured by conducting repeated studies using that population and setting. When a theory is intended to apply generally across different people, times, and places, external validity is ensured by conducting repeated tests of the theory in diverse populations, settings, and cultures.

A research study is usually conducted with a single type of subjects at a single time and place. Research has **external validity** if its results can be assumed to hold for other types of subjects, other times, or other places relevant to the theory.

The results of the study by Desforges and her associates, for example, offer support for the contact hypothesis. But would these results be found *only* if the subjects were North American college students, or *only* if the contact group was former mental patients? One of the important functions of research is to determine just how broadly theories generalize. As we have already pointed out, the more generalizable a theory is—the broader the spectrum of people whose behavior it explains—the more powerful it is. But not all theories claim to hold true for all people in all places (Cook & Campbell, 1979; Kruglanski, 1975). Some research aims at generalizing *to* specific people in a specific situation, whereas other research seeks to generalize more broadly *across* various kinds of people, times, and places.

external validity The extent to which research results can be generalized to other appropriate people, times, and settings.

Generalizing to Versus Generalizing Across People and Places. In some research, a specific target population and setting is the researcher's primary interest. Applied research, where the goal is to use scientific findings to solve immediate practical problems, often falls into this category. For example, researchers have long known that when people have a sense of control over their situation they cope better with stress. This knowledge raises a question that could have important practical applications. Could a sense of control help seriously ill patients cope better when they are hospitalized? A study that attempts to answer this question needs a specific and relevant population and setting. Only people with serious illnesses will do as subjects, and they must be studied in a hospital. Researchers need these specific subjects because hospitalization for a serious illness is so overwhelming an experience that such patients' reactions to being given a sense of control might differ from those of other people. The hospital setting is also necessary because it might introduce other psychological and social processes that overwhelm the effects of giving the patients a sense of psychological control. Thus, as the example shows, generalization *to* a target setting (a hospital) and particular subjects (patients) is safest when research is conducted in that setting with that kind of subject. In fact, giving hospitalized patients some control over their situation is now a widely used technique for helping them deal with stressful medical procedures (Pranulis and others, 1975).

Most research you will read about in this text does not attempt to generalize *to* a single, specific target population or setting. Instead, the research goal is usually a broader sort of generalization *across* various factors. Another way to state this is as a question: Does the research have implications for many types of people in various places at more than one period in time? Does it apply, for example, to women as well as men? To Israelis and Koreans, as well as North Americans? To people living in the year 2020 as well as those living today? A typical study is conducted with a limited number of subjects of a particular type—usually college students—in one location at one point in time. Few people would be interested in research results that had no broader applicability than to those subjects at that time and place. The key question therefore becomes, exactly what aspects of the research conclusions will successfully generalize?

Let us return to the example of the North American college students who engaged in a cooperative learning task in the laboratory with a person they believed was a former mental patient. These students came to hold more favorable beliefs about that particular group—former mental patients (Desforges and others, 1991). What generalization can be drawn from this finding, assuming it passes the tests of construct validity and internal validity? One could ask whether exactly the same finding would be obtained among Ethiopian college students, among Israeli sixth-graders, and among adults in Papua-New Guinea. But social psychological researchers rarely study subject populations as diverse as these. In any case, this is not precisely the right question to ask about generalizability. Whether the study's *specific findings* can be directly generalized is not the crucial issue.

Figure 2.1 Research results generalize through theories

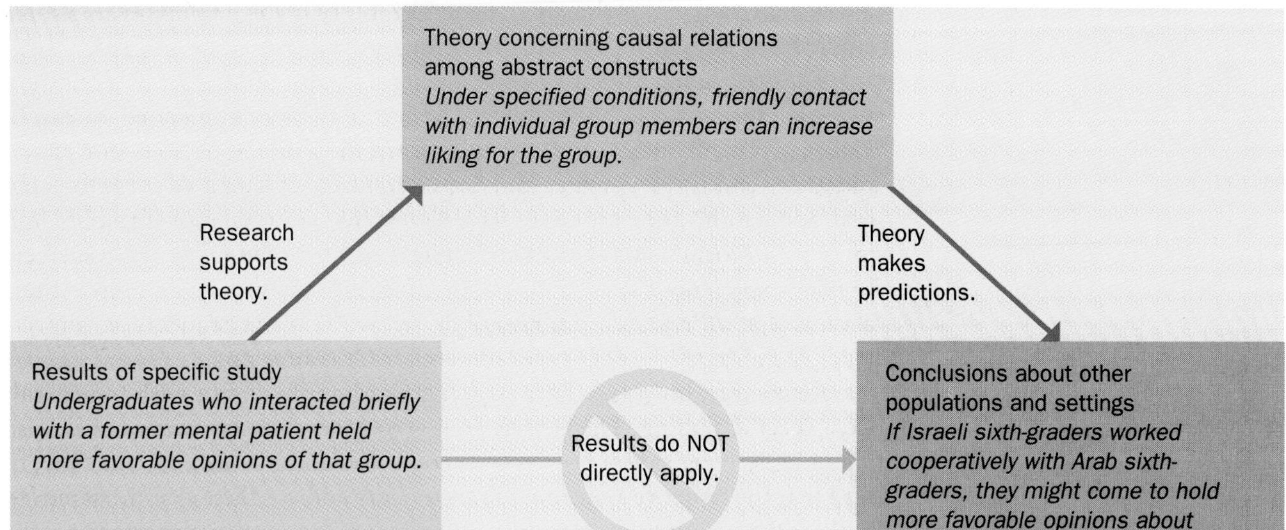

Most studies are conducted to test theories. The theory may then make predictions that apply to different people and places. The results of a particular study are not generalized *directly,* but they have implications for other people, times, and places to the extent that the results support a valid and general theory.

What is the appropriate generalization? To answer that question, we need to recall the fundamental reason why a study like that of Desforges and her associates is conducted. That study was not aimed at generalizing *to* some target population or setting. Nor was it intended to reveal some modestly interesting fact about people's opinions of former mental patients—that is, about the specific dependent variable used in the study. Instead, the goal was to test a *theory* regarding causal relations among abstract constructs and thereby lend support to that theory. In this case, the theory states that under specific conditions, friendly interaction with individual group members often causes changes in people's attitudes and beliefs about the group. And this theoretical level is the one at which generalization is to be expected. So we would not expect all kinds of people all around the world to hold the same views about former mental patients. We would, however, expect to find that similar processes of stereotype change are caused by friendly interaction with group members, at least until further research demonstrates limitations on generalizability.

Recall that we emphasized in Chapter 1 that you should seek to learn general principles about social psychology rather than the findings of a great many specific studies. In exactly the same way, researchers hope that the underlying principles, rather than the details of the findings, will generalize from one population and setting to other appropriate ones. Figure 2.1 illustrates this idea: the results of a study are not applied directly to another population or setting but are used to support a general theory, which in turn has implications for other people and places (Mook, 1980).

Threats to External Validity. Recall that if research has external validity, its results can be assumed to hold for other types of subjects, other times, or other places relevant to the theory. In other words, the results can be generalized. The two major threats to generalizability involve the types of *people* studied and the *setting* in which they are studied.

The first major threat to generalizability is using subjects who are unrepresentative of all the people to whom a theory is intended to apply. College students differ in many ways from the average person—for example, they tend to be younger and better educated. Compared with the general population, they probably have less stable close relationships, are still involved in forming new roles and images of themselves, and are less likely to have experienced serious illness, divorce, or parenthood. Can researchers assume that *all* research findings obtained with college students as subjects will generalize to all other types of people? Of course not.

Remember, however, that researchers ordinarily do not wish to generalize a specific finding. Their usual goal is to generalize a broader conclusion about underlying causal processes. So one would not expect, for example, to find that the issues responsible for arguments and conflict were the same for both college dating couples and older married couples. Nevertheless, the causal impact of arguments on the partners' satisfaction with their relationship might be similar for both kinds of couples. Or, to use another example, students may not have as many well-developed social roles as older people, but the process by which they form their self-views and the implications of the formation of those views on behavior may be the same for many diverse groups of people. Thus generalizing about causal explanations is more justifiable than generalizing about the content of thoughts and behavior.

The social psychological processes that are most likely to operate in similar ways among diverse groups of people are the most basic ones. These include the ways people respond to social influence from others, use the most accessible information, and seek mastery over their environment and connectedness with other people. As you will see in later chapters, these are the sorts of processes many social psychologists have investigated, using college students as subjects because they were easily accessible. Still, the only way to be really sure that research conclusions generalize is to repeat the research with different types of subjects because, as you will see, sometimes even conclusions about processes cannot be generalized.

The representativeness of subjects is just one factor that can limit generalizability. The second major factor is the setting in which the research is conducted. Each research setting, whether in the laboratory or outside it, has advantages and disadvantages that arise from its particular characteristics.

1. *The laboratory.* Most social psychological research is conducted in the laboratory because the researcher can control this setting. In the laboratory, the researcher can randomly assign subjects to different conditions, manipulate independent variables while keeping other factors constant, and measure dependent measures with high construct validity. The chief virtue of the

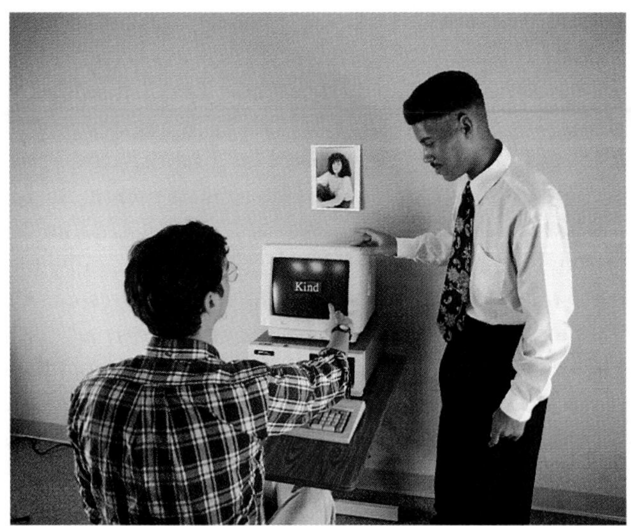

Experimental control in the laboratory A graduate student in Professor Uleman's social cognition laboratory at New York University delivers instructions to a subject in a study of how people make inferences about personality traits. Although the lab setting cannot reproduce all aspects of the judgments people make in everday life, it does allow experimenters complete control of independent variables and precise measurement of the dependent variables.

laboratory setting is that experimental designs with high internal validity are most easily implemented there.

But the lab also has a down side. One disadvantage is the short time span of most studies, which usually last no more than a few hours. Another is the somewhat artificial quality of many laboratory manipulations and measures. A researcher may, for example, ask subjects to donate to another student the points they earn in the experiment and then use the number of donated points as a measure of the concept of helping. A third disadvantage is that participating in research may itself elicit special motives. Demand characteristics and the social desirability bias are probably more likely to affect behavior in strange, novel settings like the laboratory than in more familiar, realistic settings of everyday life (Orne, 1962). This makes laboratory investigation of socially sensitive topics particularly difficult.

In addition, subjects in the laboratory probably pay much more attention to the information provided than they would in some other setting. In laboratory research on persuasion, for example, subjects read persuasive messages and their attitudes are measured: different kinds of messages can then be shown to be more or less effective in changing attitudes. But outside the laboratory people do not go around reading every persuasive communication they see. Do you read every political poster in your neighborhood? Or every ad for cold medicine in your bus or subway car? In everyday life outside the lab, the effectiveness of any persuasive message depends crucially on its ability to attract your attention so that it is read. Thus, when different processes operate in laboratory and nonlaboratory settings, theories supported by findings from the laboratory may not apply outside of it.

2. *Nonlaboratory settings.* The strengths and weaknesses of *field research* —research that takes place outside the laboratory—complement those of laboratory research. Field researchers can study the long-term effects of such variables as relationship development or public health campaigns.

They can measure concrete, powerful variables. For example, instead of counting the points students donate in experiments, they can count donations of blood as a measure of helping. Field researchers can also study the effects of major events such as an earthquake prediction, an alarming event that could not ethically or practically be reproduced in a laboratory. Thus, field research often has good construct validity—the variables used in the research correspond to the intended theoretical constructs. And if random assignment of subjects and manipulation of independent variables can be implemented in the field—in other words, if experimental procedures can be used—then research done in the field can also provide good internal validity. That is, the researcher can confidently conclude that the manipulations of the independent variables caused the change in the dependent variables. However, for practical reasons, carrying out experiments outside the laboratory is often very difficult. As a result, most field studies are nonexperimental in design.

Field research, whether experimental or nonexperimental, can have high external validity if it avoids triggering the special processes—such as a concern for social desirability—that can operate in the novel laboratory setting. However, you should not make the mistake of assuming that research conducted in the field always has more external validity than laboratory research. Diverse field settings, such as hospitals, airport departure lounges, and office cafeterias, also have characteristics that influence people's thoughts, motives, and actions in specific ways. Research conducted in one of these settings may or may not generalize to another—just as laboratory research may or may not generalize to a field setting.

Cultures and External Validity. People who have traveled in a country other than their own can testify that patterns of social behavior differ, and anthropologists' scientific observations confirm this conclusion. Since social psychology remains largely a North American and Western European phenomenon, do the research conclusions of social psychologists generalize across the world's societies and cultures? We can answer this question only by examining the specific set of research conclusions that we expect to generalize. Consider the observation that people tend to have certain expectations, or stereotypes, about what other social groups are like. Though the stereotypes that French and Australian subjects (for example) have of the English will probably be very different, the way the two groups of subjects develop those stereotypes and how they use them are likely to be very similar. Culture strongly dictates the *contents* of people's thoughts and actions. The processes by which those contents are developed and used, however, are more likely to be generalizable.

Sometimes both contents and processes can differ for members of different cultures. For example, members of Western cultures are particularly likely to think of themselves as separate from other people and to express their individuality in references to their uniqueness. In Eastern cultures like Japan, people tend to think of themselves as linked to others, and they express their individuality in references to their relationships to others

(Markus & Kitayama, 1991). The different content of their self-concepts leads to several differences in the ways Westerners and Easterners process information about the self, respond to social conflict and disagreement, and experience emotions. Any theory on these topics that has been formulated and tested in only one type of culture may not generalize to members of other cultures.

Ensuring External Validity. The keys to achieving external validity, then, depend on the underlying research purpose.

1. *If the goal is to generalize to some specific target population and setting, the subjects and setting must be representative of the target.* For example, if the goal is to see how assembly-line workers respond to changes in a supervisor's behavior, the most useful and appropriate study would be of assembly-line workers in their factory.

2. *If the goal is to generalize across people, places, and time periods, the best way to do so is to repeat the research in multiple settings and with multiple populations—including people from different cultures.* Most of the research you will read about in this text is concerned with generalizing across people and places. Ultimately, as social psychology adopts a more integrative perspective and becomes less bound by Western culture, two important consequences will follow. Cultural variables—such as East-West differences in self-conceptions—will be incorporated in theories so that cultural differences in social behavior can be explained rather than merely described. In addition, research will be performed in diverse cultural settings, so that such broadly integrative theories can be developed and tested. Indeed, social psychology is currently moving in these directions (Bond, 1988; Moghaddam and others, 1993; Smith & Bond, 1993). The following chapters report the results of cross-cultural research whenever it throws new light on our understanding of the social and cognitive processes that influence human behavior.

Cultural differences: When can research findings be generalized? In both of these photos, employees are shown taking advantage of corporate-sponsored exercise programs. How they exercise illustrates some of the differences between Western and Eastern cultures. Social psychologists—aware that not all research findings generalize across cultures—have started to explore cultural effects on many popular theories. These new findings are discussed throughout this book.

Table 2.2 Properties of theories and corresponding characteristics of the three forms of research validity				
Property of theory	**Corresponding type of validity**	**Threats to validity**	**Relevant aspects of research**	**Ideal research characteristics**
A theory deals with abstract constructs.	Construct validity: Observable variables used in research match the theoretical constructs.	Subjects may respond in socially desirable ways or act in accordance with perceived demands.	Measures and manipulations	Multiple measures; multiple manipulations
A theory proposes causal relations among constructs.	Internal validity: Relationship among observable variables is due to postulated causal process.	Alternative causal explanations may be possible.	Designs	Experimental designs
A theory is general in scope, although the range varies across theories.	External validity: Research results can be obtained with many types of people, times, and settings.	Findings may apply to only limited types of people, times, or settings.	Populations and settings	Multiple replications

Construct, internal, and external validity pertain to different aspects of the research process, are threatened by different factors, and are ensured by different types of strategies. Table 2.2 summarizes the most important characteristics of the three types of validity.

Evaluating Theories: The Bottom Line

> *Theories become generally accepted if the results of multiple valid studies show them to be superior to rival theories. Sometimes theories that seem to compete are in fact complementary explanations of events. Social psychological research cannot help but be influenced by researchers' personal beliefs and cultural values. However, the rigorous use of research methods is our best hope for excluding the biases and errors that characterize everyday thinking.*

Theories about social behavior ultimately stand or fall on the basis of how well they are supported by the results of valid research. As shown in Figure 2.2, the process involves a logical chain in which all three types of validity play a part. And just as a chain can be no stronger than its weakest link, each type of validity is crucial if research is to provide support for a theory.

Of course, no theory ultimately stands or falls on the basis of a single study. The results of any one study might have been influenced by simple mistakes by the researcher, the use of particular manipulations or measures, poor internal validity, special characteristics of the subjects, or even chance variation. Indeed, researchers' attempts to increase one form of validity (for example, internal) often decrease other forms (external or construct validity). Kalin and Berry's (1982) survey testing the contact hypothesis in the field had high construct and external validity, as it measured long-term and powerful intergroup contact in the general population. But as we pointed out, that study had low internal validity because many differences other than degree of contact might explain the results. In contrast, the test of the same theory in a laboratory setting by Desforges and others (1991) had high internal validity because they randomly assigned subjects to different levels of contact. But their study, in turn, had questionable construct and external validity, given the artificial nature of the laboratory cooperative learning task.

Figure 2.2 The role of research validity in supporting theory

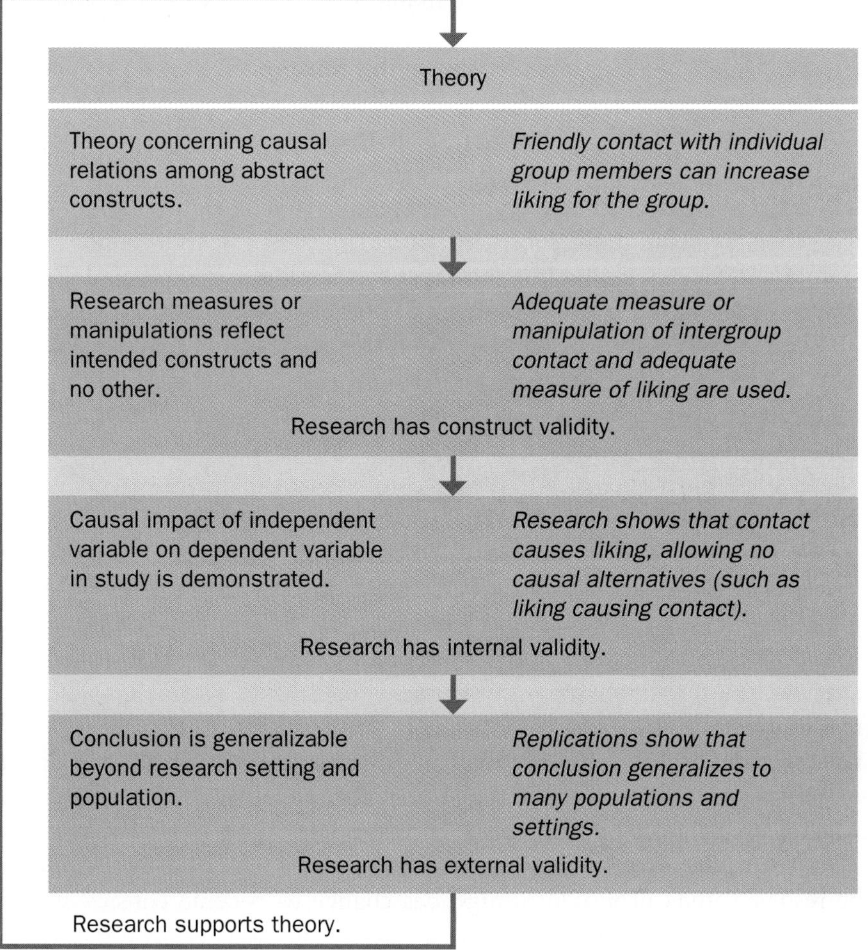

Theory
Theory concerning causal relations among abstract constructs.
Friendly contact with individual group members can increase liking for the group.
Research measures or manipulations reflect intended constructs and no other.
Adequate measure or manipulation of intergroup contact and adequate measure of liking are used.
Research has construct validity.
Causal impact of independent variable on dependent variable in study is demonstrated.
Research shows that contact causes liking, allowing no causal alternatives (such as liking causing contact).
Research has internal validity.
Conclusion is generalizable beyond research setting and population.
Replications show that conclusion generalizes to many populations and settings.
Research has external validity.
Research supports theory.

To test a theory, researchers must follow a logical chain. Only if the research has high construct validity, strong internal validity, and good external validity can the theory be supported with confidence. Any weak validity link breaks the inferential chain.

The Importance of Replication. Because no single study can be fully convincing by itself, researchers seek to **replicate**, or reproduce, the results of prior research. Indeed, scientists are required to disclose the procedures and methods of their studies so that other researchers can repeat the research. The most important replications produce the same results by using different manipulations of the theoretical constructs in different settings with different subject populations.

Because replications provide such convincing support for theories, social psychologists often compare the results of different tests of the same theory. They perform these comparisons using *meta-analysis,* a technique for systematically locating relevant studies and summarizing their results (Cooper, 1990; Rosenthal, 1991). Meta-analysis allows researchers to examine the generality of results across replications conducted by different researchers using diverse methods, settings, and subject populations. When many such studies all produce similar results, they provide stronger evidence for or against theories. Thus, for example, when studies as different as Kalin and Berry's survey and Desforges and her associates' laboratory tests showed the same result, we can have greater confidence that positive intergroup contact does indeed increase liking. Because replication is so important, you will often see more than one study or the results of a meta-analysis cited to support conclusions reported in this text.

Competition with Other Theories. The theories that social psychologists propose for explaining social events or processes sometimes compete with and contradict each other. Eventually, one theory may stand out among all the others as being more consistent with replicated research findings. This victory may be only temporary, however. Research in social psychology, like that in other sciences, is ongoing, and some psychologists may propose a new theory that is even better able to explain the research findings. For this reason scientists avoid applying the term *proven* to a theory. At best a theory is *generally accepted,* a phrase that points to the importance of scientific consensus—a judgment made by the community of scientists.

In some cases, theories that first compete to explain research findings turn out to provide complementary explanations. Consider, for example, the competition that took place in the 1960s and 1970s between two theories that sought to explain why attitudes often change to reflect people's behavior. In a series of studies, subjects were assigned the task of writing an essay supporting a position they initially opposed. Researchers demonstrated that after the subjects wrote the essay, their attitudes often became more similar to the view they had advocated in their writing (Linder and others, 1967; Goethals and others, 1979). To explain these changes, one group of psychologists—those who supported *cognitive dissonance theory*—argued that when people choose to act inconsistently (such as writing an essay they disagree with), the inconsistency creates psychological tension. The tension can be resolved, they proposed, if attitudes change to become consistent with

replication Conducting new studies in an effort to provide evidence for the same theoretically predicted relations found in prior research.

behavior (moving toward the stand taken in the essay). In contrast, proponents of *self-perception theory* suggested that such changes occurred merely because people observed their own behavior and inferred their attitudes from their behavior. "I agreed to write the supportive essay, therefore I suppose I must have a supportive attitude."

Peanuts

Although researchers conducted many studies and compared the predictions of the two theories, they were not able to settle the controversy. Cognitive dissonance theory and self-perception theory were each supported by some results, but neither theory gained general acceptance at the expense of the other. Finally, researchers Russell Fazio, Mark Zanna, and Joel Cooper (1977) noticed an interesting difference between the two sets of findings. Most successful tests of self-perception theory occurred when people behaved in ways not too inconsistent with their original attitudes. But the successful tests of cognitive dissonance theory seemed to be those in which people were induced to act in a way that absolutely opposed their initial convictions. This observation led Fazio, Zanna, and Cooper to suggest that the two theories offer a complementary understanding of the effect of behavior on attitudes. Perhaps self-perception processes operate to change attitudes when behavior is mildly different from initial attitudes. Cognitive dissonance processes, on the other hand, might kick in when behavior is so divergent from original attitudes that the discrepancy is upsetting. Further research confirmed their suggestions. Thus two theories that started out as seeming competitors now work together to provide a better understanding of the interplay between action and attitudes, as you will see in Chapter 8.

Getting the Bias Out. Perhaps you can see now why scientists prefer to believe well-supported theories, even when they conflict with common sense. The logic behind research methods is designed to exclude many biases and errors by maintaining concern with all three forms of validity.

1. *Concern for construct validity*—making sure that observable events are good measures of general constructs—helps researchers avoid incorrect interpretations of specific events. Consider, for example, a conversation in which a New Yorker has trouble communicating with a person from the deep South. New Yorkers tend to speak faster than people from other areas of the United States—particularly those from the South—and they leave shorter pauses between "turns" in the conversation (Tannen, 1990). If the New Yorker takes the difficulty of having a conversation with a Southerner as a sign that the Southerner is a bit slow-witted—rather than as a measure of different group standards for speech—an error of construct validity has occurred.

2. *Concern for internal validity*—being certain that one event causes another—makes it less likely that researchers will fall into the everyday trap of failing to consider alternative explanations. If you see a man fidgeting nervously, for example, you might assume that he is basically an anxious person. That assumption, however, does not take into account the fact that he is waiting to be called in for a job interview—a situation in which anyone is likely to feel nervous. Research needs to exclude such alternative explanations for behavior before citing a behavior as good evidence for or against a theory.

In fact, people often jump to the conclusion that behavior reflects personality, without looking for alternative explanations. You'll find out why in Chapter 3, pages 80 to 84.

3. *Concern for external validity*—being sure an observation can be generalized—makes it clear why we should not base conclusions about human nature on our own limited and possibly unrepresentative experience. For example, a visitor from Quebec may be brushed aside by a rude New Yorker who grabs the only available taxi during a downpour. If the Canadian concludes that none of the citizens of that city know how to behave, an error in external validity has been made. Such a broad generalization is hardly justified on the basis of one obnoxious individual, who may not be an unbiased sample of the entire population of New York City.

You should not assume, however, that scientists always successfully achieve their objective of excluding bias and error from their research methods. On the contrary, the scientific enterprise is *full* of judgment calls that open the door to such influences as researchers' personal attitudes and beliefs, cultural beliefs, family or educational background, scientific training, or religious, moral, and political views. Scientists, after all, are human beings and are no more able than anyone else to stand outside their culture and society and evaluate theories with a pure, detached rationality (Gould, 1978). They too tend to prefer theories that are consistent with their culture's generally accepted beliefs and values. For example, the 1935 *Handbook of Social Psychology* contained chapters on the "negro," the "red man," the "white man," and the "yellow man." The contents reflected the unquestioned assumptions of that time—assumptions that most people today would regard as offensively racist and sexist.

Feminist psychologists have pointed out cultural assumptions about women and men that have crept unnoticed into scientific practice (Sherif, 1979; Hare-Mustin & Marecek, 1988; Peplau & Conrad, 1989; McGrath and others, 1993). For example, in some areas of research, such as the study of achievement motivation, the conclusions have been based almost entirely on the responses of male subjects. Although deciding to limit the subject pool only to males may have allowed the researchers to avoid some complexities, other unwanted consequences may have resulted. For example, unique aspects of women's behavior may never be discovered if results from men are assumed to generalize to all humans. And even if such differences are discovered, they may be interpreted as mere deviations from the male "standard" rather than legitimate parts of the standard (Denmark and others, 1988).

Sylvia by Nicole Hollander

Nevertheless, their fundamental reliance on research findings has often enabled social psychologists to expose and overturn generally accepted myths and falsehoods. For example, many social psychologists participated in preparing a statement presented to the U.S. Supreme Court in the 1954 *Brown* v. *Board of Education* case. Challenging the prevailing acceptance of "separate but equal" education for Whites and Blacks, the statement summarized research evidence showing that racially segregated schools could never be equal. That statement contributed to the Court's landmark decision to overturn legally enforced school segregation (Klineberg, 1986). Science is a human enterprise with no guarantees of objectivity. Nevertheless, its research techniques are the best ways yet devised to limit the effects of bias.

The Role of Ethics and Values in Research

Social psychologists have a responsibility to live up to the standards of the scientific community. Scientists who abide by those standards do not falsify or misrepresent their procedures or data. They avoid personal attacks in scientific controversies, while engaging in full, no-holds-barred debates on theoretical and empirical issues. And they allocate credit fairly for scientific work. They do not plagiarize other scholars' work, and in publications they give credit to all who earned it by working on the research project. Good science depends on the integrity of each researcher, and serious violations of these rules of conduct are not tolerated.

But social psychology shares with the other social sciences a special obligation due to the fact that humans are both the investigators and the investigated. There are people filling out questionnaires as well as devising them, people exposed to independent variables as well as manipulating them, and people in front of the camera as well as at the controls. The inherently people-packed nature of the social sciences means that researchers often must grapple not only with research problems and scientific responsibility but also with issues of values and ethics. When designing and conducting studies that might provide answers to questions about human behavior, researchers must always ask whether the end justifies the means. Do the research results justify the experiences of the research participants? And when the results are in hand, another question arises. If those findings can easily be applied to society as a whole, will the results of research be used in a socially responsible way? The issues of fairness to research participants and of social responsibility are a special part of social psychologists' scientific training (Ethical Principles, 1992).

Do research ends justify means? In these photos of the Stanford prison experiment, a student assigned to the role of prisoner is undergoing public arrest and a group is being subjected to the humiliation of a head count. Although these experiences caused considerable pyschological distress, the results of the experiment provided important information about the sometimes frightening power of social roles and institutions. Such an experiment could not be conducted today, yet the same questions about research remain: Can the social significance of results justify studies in which subjects have unpleasant experiences? Can the same questions be asked in less potentially damaging ways? What do you think?

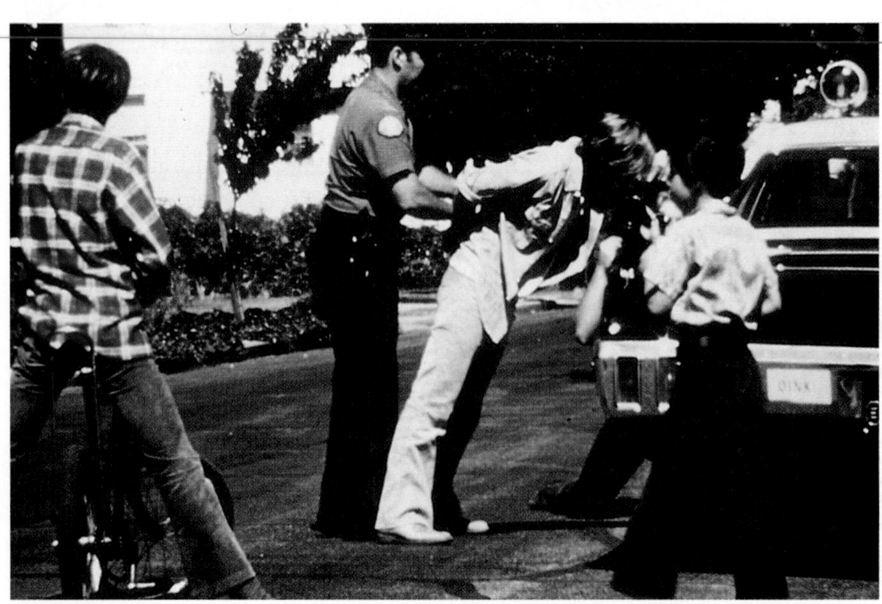

Being Fair to Subjects

Researchers seek to treat their subjects fairly, usually informing them about what they will experience in the study and obtaining their agreement to it in advance. However, to avoid biases when sensitive topics are investigated, researchers sometimes deceive subjects about various aspects of the study. If deception is used, subjects must be given information about research procedures and purposes at the conclusion of the study.

One of social psychology's best-known experiments began when Philip Zimbardo of Stanford University signed up male volunteers between 17 and 30 years of age to participate for pay in a study of "prison life" (Haney and others, 1973; Zimbardo and others, 1973). Some of the men were randomly assigned to be prison guards and others to be prisoners. The researchers arranged for the "prisoners" to be taken unexpectedly into custody by real police officers, fingerprinted, and taken to the "prison"—which had been set up, complete with barred cells, in the basement of the psychology building. Dressed in shapeless prison smocks and wearing ankle chains, the prisoners were at the mercy of any rules the "guards" cared to invent and enforce. As time passed, the cruelty and abusiveness of the guards and the passivity and dehumanization of the prisoners increased. The experiment soon went out of control: first one prisoner, then another, was released with depressive or psychotic symptoms. In the end, the entire experiment had to be terminated less than halfway through its planned duration.

Unexpected as they were, the results of the experiment led Zimbardo to conclude that the institutional roles of prisoner and guard caused the some-

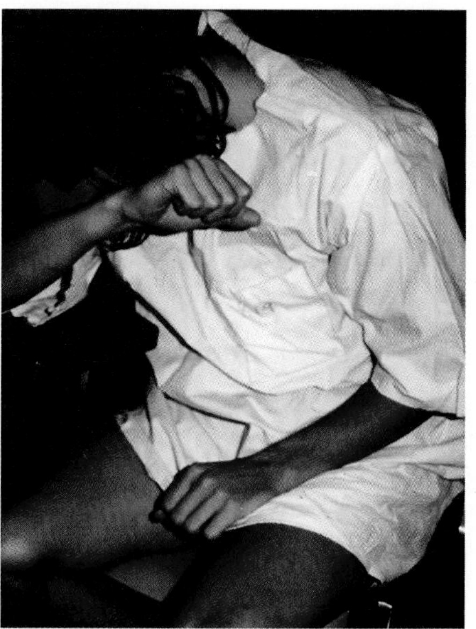

times shocking behaviors in his prison. The personalities of these initially normal, well-adjusted men did not produce the results. The finding was no doubt important; perhaps, by extension, the same conclusion applies to what happens daily inside actual prison walls. But did the results justify the research participants' experiences, which were far more difficult and exceedingly stressful than they expected on volunteering for the experiment? It is now generally agreed that the study violated a number of the special obligations psychologists have to their research subjects. For instance, the volunteers were given almost no details about the research project at the time they signed up.

Primary among those obligations, of course, is to avoid harming participants. Potential harm can come from several sources. Self-reports or observations may reveal things about subjects that they would not wish to have publicly known. In most studies, this threat is averted by keeping subjects' responses anonymous and unidentifiable. Another source of harm is that subjects can be upset or distressed by their participation in research, as they were in the Stanford prison study. Subjects may experience intense distress when they are involved in potentially doing harm, are required to make difficult decisions, or are placed in situations over which they have no control. They also may be upset by their own reactions to events, as the fake prison guards may have been when they so easily became brutal.

Research on topics as divergent as helping and stereotyping often causes distress when subjects later realize that their actions were socially undesirable. This poses a dilemma: social psychologists want their research to address important issues, but in the course of it some subjects may discover troubling information about themselves or others. How, then, can researchers ethically proceed with such studies? The answer is by obtaining subjects' **informed consent**. In response to legitimate concern over studies like the Stanford prison project, social psychologists must now help to protect research participants against the possibility of harm by telling them they can withdraw from a study without penalty at any time. And they must give any volunteer enough information about the research to allow them to make an informed decision about participating. "Without penalty" means that subjects (often college students) cannot be coerced into participating, and any rewards resulting from participation—such as earning course credit—must be made available in alternative ways. "Informed consent" does not mean subjects are told everything about the research. They do not need to know the specific theory being tested, the rationale for the procedures, or other technical details. They must, however, be informed about and consent to the experiences they will undergo—filling out personality questionnaires, watching a videotape of erotic scenes, participating in a group discussion, and so on. Subjects who know they are free to participate and know what will happen to them if they take part can freely choose to avoid any procedure they consider potentially harmful.

informed consent Consent voluntarily given by a research person who decides to participate in a study after being told what will be involved in participation.

The Use of Deception in Research. Because of the importance of informed consent, ethical questions arise when researchers use *deception* to keep subjects in the dark about various aspects of the research. Most instances of deception are relatively trivial. Subjects are often told in advance what they will experience during the study (for example, watching a brief video clip and filling out a questionnaire) without being told the exact purpose of the study or the details of the procedure until their participation is complete.

In other cases subjects are actually misled about what will happen to them. Charles Hardy and Bibb Latané constructed an elaborate ruse to compare people's efforts on a task when they thought they were working alone or with others. Participants were told the study concerned the effects of sensory deprivation on noise production. This explanation provided a rationale for having them wear earphones and blindfolds, which meant they had to rely on the researcher's word as to whether they were alone or with others. When told to yell and clap as loudly as they could, subjects made less noise when they thought a second person was performing with them, compared to when they thought they were working alone (Hardy & Latané, 1986). Although deception was involved, its consequences were rather minor.

This drop-off in individual effort often found in groups, called social loafing, is discussed in detail in Chapter 13.

Why do social psychologists engage in deceptive practices? The point is to combat demand characteristics and social desirability biases while gathering information about socially important topics. Think honestly about how you would act if a researcher told you "This study concerns the effects of racial prejudice on reactions to requests for help," or "We are testing the ways failure at an important task can affect people's self-esteem." Perhaps you and everyone else would refuse to take part; these topics then could never be studied. Even if you did agree to participate, how could you prevent your knowledge of the topic from affecting your responses? Perhaps you might try, with the best of intentions, to help confirm the researcher's expectations. Or you might act in the most socially acceptable way you could think of. Either of these reactions, which are responses to factors other than the researcher's intended causal construct, would invalidate the research findings.

Most social psychology researchers argue that such topics as helping, aggression, racial and gender prejudice, and conformity are so sensitive that deception is often necessary to produce valid results. Yet the use of deception frequently makes it impossible to obtain truly informed consent, and it runs counter to most peoples' ideas about honest and fair treatment of others. Once again the question arises: does the end justify the means? Most researchers are willing to use deception as a last resort when they judge the research topic to be highly important and when no other alternatives are feasible. Even then, they try to keep it to a minimum, and they inform subjects of the deception as soon as possible through **debriefing.** Debriefing has several goals.

debriefing Informing research participants—as soon as possible after the completion of their participation in research—about the purposes, procedures, and scientific value of the study, and discussing any questions participants may have.

- The subject can raise questions and concerns about the research, and the researcher can address them.
- The researcher can fully explain any necessary deception and apologize for it.
- The researcher and subject can discuss the overall purpose and methods of the study, thereby enhancing the educational value of research participation.
- The researcher can detect and deal with any possible negative, long-lasting effects of the research.

Because most of its goals are important even for research that does not involve deception, debriefing is now customary in most research. When deception is involved, however, debriefing is particularly important. If a subject has been led to believe that he or she has failed at an important task, for example, the deception must be carefully explained and every effort made to ensure that subjects leave the study feeling no worse than when they entered (Ross and others, 1975). In response to a heightened concern with ethical issues, the studies that social psychologists perform today usually have little potential for long-lasting harm. That was not always true in the past. The prison experiment researchers, for example, offered their subjects extensive debriefing, but you may wonder whether any after-the-fact explanations could fully eliminate lasting ill effects of such powerful experiences (Baumrind, 1964; Milgram, 1964). Fortunately, most research shows that debriefing can provide deceived subjects with more positive attitudes both about themselves and about research activities (Smith & Richardson, 1983; Thompson and others, 1980; Epstein and others, 1973). To do so, the debriefing must be thorough and professional, emphasize the importance of the research, and treat subjects with respect.

When it comes to making difficult decisions about the ethics of an experimental procedure, researchers are not forced to rely solely on their individual judgment. Since the middle 1970s, universities and other research institutions have established Institutional Review Boards. These committees, made up both of scientists and members of the community, review and approve research plans. They have the power to ask for changes in a plan or even to deny approval if they believe a study may harm subjects. Despite some researchers' initial fear that such an approval process would interfere with worthwhile research, it has worked smoothly in most instances. Today's greater ethical sensitivity, which was sparked largely by controversy over a few well-publicized studies like the Stanford prison study, does mean that some types of study can no longer be performed. Take a moment to think about how you, as a member of a review board, would weigh the social and scientific importance of the Stanford prison study against the undoubted stress it would cause to subjects.

Being Helpful to Society

Researchers have obligations as citizens and members of society to make choices about what topics to study and how their findings should be applied. Although social psychological research cannot decide moral or ethical questions, valid research can provide relevant evidence to inform individual and societal decision making about such issues.

Like every individual, each scientist has his or her own conception of responsibility to society and to humanity. Social psychologists have long focused on major social issues like poverty, prejudice, pollution, and peace because we believe that our discipline can contribute to solving these problems. As you read this book you will see some of the results of this research.

Of course, psychologists often disagree about social and political issues. In the area of research, these differences often show up as disagreements over how science can best serve society. For instance, one researcher who studies persuasion may firmly believe that advertising offers major economic benefits by informing consumers about available products and services. Another may believe just as firmly that advertising manipulates and exploits consumers, that it creates limitless desires for *this year's* model and encourages people to spend money on products they do not want or need. These two researchers would presumably also disagree on the appropriate application of social psychological research on persuasion. The first might act as a consultant, assisting companies that want to use the research to make their advertising more effective. The second might use the same research findings to develop ways to teach children to resist the lure of ads for faddish toys. And a third researcher might take a middle ground, endorsing the use of knowledge about the processes of persuasion as legitimate in public health campaigns to encourage healthier lifestyles but opposing their use in selling consumer products. These three views represent disagreements about how science can best serve society.

In practice, every researcher must come to her or his own conclusions about how research findings should be applied. Psychologists can refuse to participate in research they find morally objectionable and can encourage others to do the same. Some researchers, for example, question the benefit of conducting research designed to show gender or ethnic differences, especially in politically and legally sensitive areas like leadership potential or propensity for aggression.

Social psychology is an empirical science, and as such it is designed to answer empirical questions. Scientific research will not answer questions of morality and ethics—whether abortion is right or wrong, whether or when aggression is justified, or how much our individual freedoms should be curtailed by a government's concern for the population as a whole. Such issues must be decided by every individual—scientist and nonscientist alike—through the democratic political process. But we can hope that this process is informed by the results of valid scientific research where it is relevant. And that is the legitimate role of social psychological research. Although it cannot tell us whether abortion is right or wrong, it can tell us who has abortions and why, how women make such difficult decisions, how they adjust to the experience, and whether it has effects on their later emotions, attitudes, and behaviors. These are all issues that may enter into individuals' moral judgments.

Concluding Comments

Chapter 1 described how each of us, individually and as a member of social groups, constructs his or her own picture of reality. Scientists are no different from anybody else in this respect, even as they ply their trade. Relying on inference, deduction, and generalization, they draw on fragmentary, incomplete, and sometimes contradictory bits of research evidence to construct a coherent picture of reality. A scientific theory—a statement about unobservable causal relationships among abstract constructs—is intended to be such a picture.

Because scientific theories are invented rather than discovered, the scientific enterprise draws on the creativity and imagination of its practitioners. The greatest contributions Galileo, Newton, Darwin, and Einstein made were not new data; they were new conceptions of reality that organized and explained existing evidence. On a more mundane level, creativity is also a crucial ingredient in devising ways to test existing theories. A clever study, like a novel theory, is a product of creative imagination as well as disciplined hard work. As any social psychologist will tell you, this is one of the main reasons why doing research is fun.

Science is a human activity, which means it cannot be completely logical and unbiased. Just as scientists—like all humans—construct a version of reality based on bits and pieces of evidence, so are scientists—like all humans—subject to biases. Cultural values, political and religious views, and personal preferences may influence the problems that scientists choose to study and the theories they find congenial or abhorrent. Further, once a scientist creates or endorses a theory, it is likely to influence the way he or she evaluates research. Some studies may be uncritically applauded because their results support a "pet" theory, while less supportive studies are dismissed as methodologically flawed or inadequately generalizable. Still, the standards and procedures of science, especially its public nature and its emphasis on the possibility of bias, limit the effects of such biases. And the danger of bias recedes even further when a number of studies conducted by scientists with diverse theoretical orientations in various places converge to support a theory.

This text now turns from the "how we find out" of methods in social psychology to the "what we know" about social behavior. However, the transition is not as drastic as you might think. As Chapter 1 pointed out, all of us, scientists and nonscientists alike, are constantly constructing theories to help explain what we experience. As you will see throughout this text, these processes are at work when people watch a football game, read a political advertisement, or deal with conflict in a relationship. One of the most important applications of these processes occurs when we get to know someone, when we form impressions of what others are "really like." Just as scientists try to explain "the facts" theoretically, we all gather information about the social world around us and try to make sense of it. The information we gather and the way we put it together can have a dramatic impact on how we act and react to the others around us.

Summary

Research Questions and the Role of Theory Social psychologists seek to develop scientific theories to provide explanations for social behavior. A scientific **theory** is a statement about causal relationships among abstract **constructs**. It is general in scope, although the range of generality differs for different theories.

Testing Theories: From Theory to Research To provide a valid test of a theory, research must have three types of validity. **Construct validity** means that the **independent variables** and **dependent variables**—the concrete manipulations or measures used in the research—must correspond to the intended theoretical constructs. Construct validity is threatened by **demand characteristics** if subjects behave in ways they think are expected, or by the **social desirability response bias** if subjects act in ways they think are socially desirable. Researchers ensure construct validity by manipulating and measuring independent and dependent variables in many different ways.

To provide a valid test of a theory, research must also have **internal validity** so that observers can conclude that changes in the independent variable actually caused changes in the dependent variable. In **nonexperimental research** in which the independent variable is measured rather than manipulated, the research may lack internal validity because many other unknown causal factors could affect the research results. **Random assignment** of subjects to groups, followed by manipulation of independent variables, defines **experimental research**. Experiments allow researchers to draw stronger conclusions about cause and effect.

Finally, research must have **external validity**, meaning that its results can be generalized to other appropriate people, times, and settings. Some theories apply to many different kinds of people and places, whereas others

Chapter 2 Themes

Construction of Reality
Scientific theories are developed to summarize and explain observed patterns of behavior.

Pervasiveness of Social Influence
Scientists are influenced not only by the rules and customs of science but also by personal and cultural values and goals.

Striving for Mastery
Scientists attempt to understand and predict nature.

Conservatism
Once formulated, a scientific theory is hard to overturn by inconsistent evidence alone, unless a competing theory is available.

apply more narrowly. When a theory is intended to apply *to* a particular population and setting, external validity is ensured by conducting studies using that population and setting. When a theory is intended to apply more generally *across* different people, times, and settings, external validity is ensured by conducting **replications,** repeated tests of the theory in diverse populations, settings, and cultures.

Theories become generally accepted if the results of multiple valid studies show them to be superior to rival theories. Sometimes theories that seem to compete are in fact complementary explanations of events. Social psychological research cannot help but be influenced by researchers' personal beliefs and cultural values. However, striving to maximize all three forms of validity is our best hope for excluding the biases and errors that characterize everyday thinking.

The Role of Ethics and Values in Research Researchers seek to treat their subjects fairly, usually informing them about what they will experience in the study and obtaining their agreement to participate in advance, a procedure called **informed consent**. However, to avoid biases when sensitive topics are investigated, researchers sometimes deceive subjects about various aspects of the study. If deception is used, subjects must be given information about research procedures and purposes in a **debriefing** at the conclusion of the study.

Researchers have obligations as citizens and members of society to make choices about what topics to study and how their findings should be applied. Although social psychological research cannot decide moral or ethical questions, valid research can provide relevant evidence to inform individual and societal decision making about such issues.

The chart on the right is a graphical overview of the main concepts in this chapter and their interrelations. For advice on how to use this overview to help you review and understand this text, turn back to the Preface.

Chapter 2 Overview

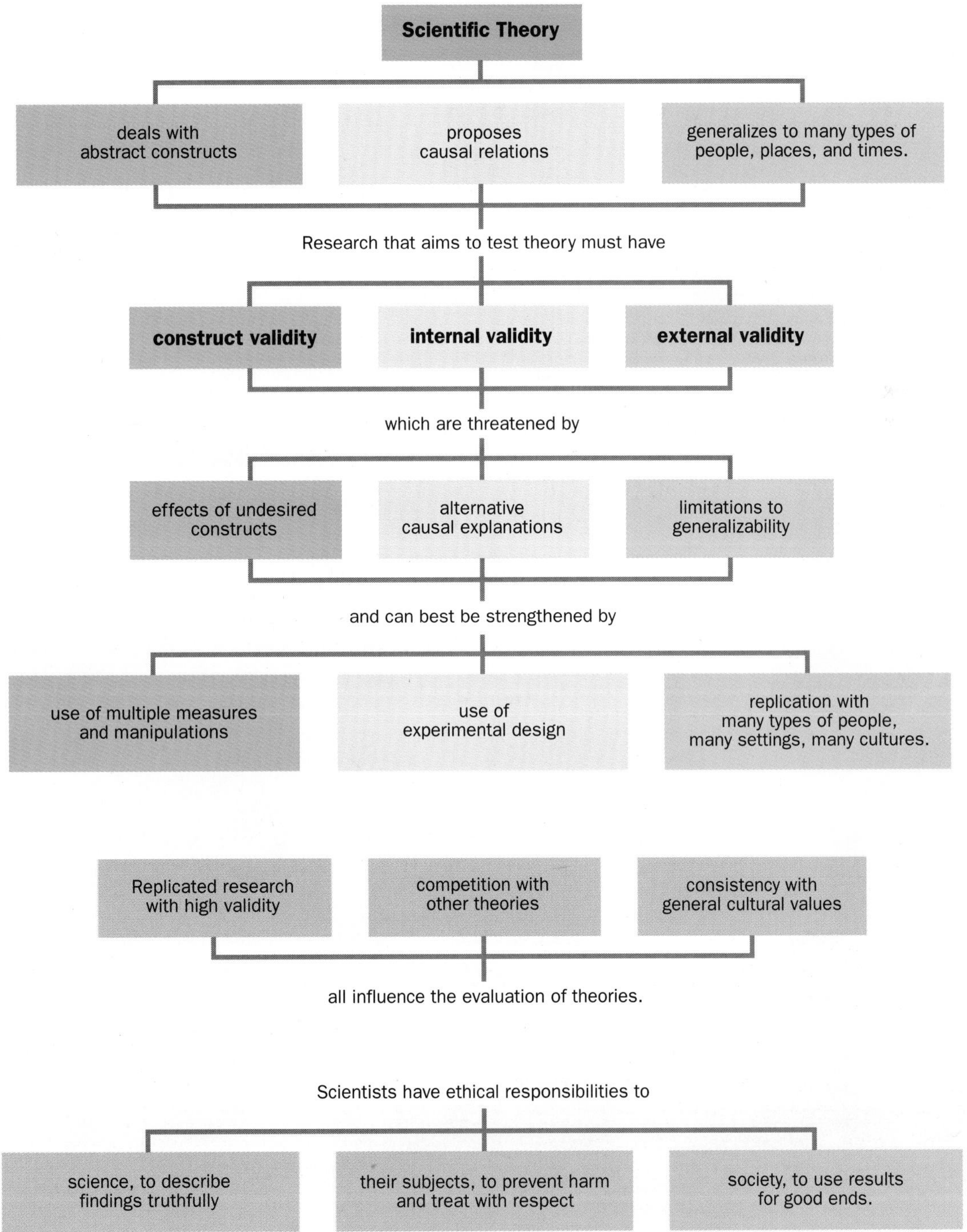

Scientific Theory
deals with abstract constructs
proposes causal relations
generalizes to many types of people, places, and times.
Research that aims to test theory must have
construct validity
internal validity
external validity
which are threatened by
effects of undesired constructs
alternative causal explanations
limitations to generalizability
and can best be strengthened by
use of multiple measures and manipulations
use of experimental design
replication with many types of people, many settings, many cultures.
Replicated research with high validity
competition with other theories
consistency with general cultural values
all influence the evaluation of theories.
Scientists have ethical responsibilities to
science, to describe findings truthfully
their subjects, to prevent harm and treat with respect
society, to use results for good ends.

Perceiving Individuals

If you woke one morning to discover you were a patient in a mental hospital, would anyone be able to tell that you were perfectly sane? A classic study by David Rosenhan (1973) suggests an answer to this question. He arranged for individuals with no emotional problems to be admitted to twelve different psychiatric hospitals. After gaining admission by saying they heard nonexistent voices, the individuals acted as normally as possible in the hospitals. In clinical interviews they honestly reported their personal backgrounds and experiences, although they did omit their connection with Rosenhan. Though their hospital stays averaged over two weeks, *not one* pseudopatient was detected as an impostor by the hospital staffs! Could it be that the psychologists and other staff members, expecting patients to be mentally ill, saw only what they expected to see? Their reactions call to mind the exchange between Alice and the Cheshire Cat in *Alice in Wonderland:*

> Said the Cat: "We're all mad here. I'm mad. You're mad."
> "How do you know I'm mad?" said Alice.
> "You must be," said the Cat, "or you wouldn't have come here."

Surely, though, the evidence of our everyday lives contradicts the findings of Rosenhan's study. As a student of social psychology, you probably are an interested observer of other people's behavior, and you probably believe that you do reasonably well at understanding other people and forming judgments about them. Indeed, research shows that in many situations, person perception can be quite accurate. For example, people can make fairly accurate judgments even about a stranger, assessing the person's poise, warmth, and sociability after just a few minutes of observation (Funder & Colvin, 1988). And even in the Rosenhan experiment, some people were making pretty good judgment calls. Although hospital staff members seemed blind to the psychological normality of the pseudopatients, other *patients* often suspected them of being sane.

What accounts for this puzzling mixture of accuracy and inaccuracy in our perceptions of other people? Why do we find some people so easy to understand and others so hard to read? This chapter explores the ways that

Forming impressions of others We are used to thinking of other people as having fixed personalities that we come to know. In fact, impressions of others are constructed. To see how his mother's influence affects the impression we might form of this well-dressed young man, turn the page.

people construct, maintain, and change their impressions of others. First, we describe how people rely on general knowledge plus some convenient rules of thumb to form impressions of strangers. Surprisingly, these judgments are often quite accurate—at least accurate enough to let people move smoothly through most everyday social encounters.

Sometimes, however, we need to go beyond snap judgments to form detailed impressions of others. Mental health workers must decide which patients are really ill, employers must decide which job applicants are right for their business needs, and teachers must decide which students know the material. And of course, all of us are constantly faced with decisions on whom to befriend, live with, or even marry. Does increased effort guarantee increased accuracy in impression formation? Not necessarily, because, as this chapter explains, our motives and expectations can slant our judgments. Although Juliet may spend a lot of time thinking about Romeo, you probably would ask someone else if you wanted an impartial picture of his personality. As you will see, once our minds are made up, we find it hard to see, let alone accept, evidence that contradicts our views.

Different cues, different boy Because we believe they reflect a person's character, the kind of cues we notice—physical appearance, body language, and behavior—help determine the impressions we form. The context of an after-school play date has a profound influence on these cues and allows us to form an entirely different view of this young man.

Of course, sometimes we have to face facts that are clearly inconsistent with our impressions. What happens then? Our discussion concludes with a description of the ways we can change impressions to accommodate contradictory evidence. How we handle inconsistency has important consequences for the accuracy of our impressions—and therefore for the success of our dealings with others.

Forming First Impressions: Cues, Interpretations, and Inferences

Try to answer a few questions about the people pictured in Figure 3.1. Which of these people is most likely to prefer Metallica to Mozart? Who would rather read the philosophical works of Jean-Paul Sartre than the latest Tom Clancy thriller? Who would prefer season tickets to the Metropolitan Opera, and who to the Oakland A's? You can probably answer such questions fairly readily and with some confidence. But how did you form the impressions that gave you your answers? The raw materials of first impressions are the way people look and how they act. However, these cues are informative only because we believe that appearance and behavior reflect personality characteristics, preferences, and lifestyles.

Our knowledge about people's characteristics and the ways they are related to one another is one type of **cognitive representation**—a term for a body of knowledge an individual has stored in his or her memory. We have cognitive representations of situations, people, and social groups. For example, our knowledge of what typically happens at a child's birthday party is a cognitive representation. Our impressions of specific individuals are cognitive representations, and so are our beliefs about members of particular occupations, nationalities, and ethnic groups. Because our stored knowledge

cognitive representation A body of knowledge that an individual has stored in memory.

Figure 3.1 What are your impressions of these people? Physical appearance offers many cues to people's personality and preferences, but these cues are interpreted through our *own* prior beliefs. Did you predict that the man on the left prefers Sartre? What might that say about your expectations of well-dressed, bearded men?

influences virtually all of our social beliefs and behaviors, descriptions of the effects of various types of cognitive representations appear throughout this text. This section, however, focuses on the knowledge that guides our first impressions of others: the aspects of a person's appearance and behavior that call particular representations to mind, and the kinds of personal characteristics that are associated with those aspects of a person's appearance and behavior.

The Raw Materials of First Impressions

> *Perceptions of other people begin with visible cues, including physical appearance, nonverbal communication, and overt behavior. Cues that stand out and attract attention in their context are particularly influential.*

Impressions from Physical Appearance. According to tennis star Andre Agassi, "Image is everything." It may not be everything to everyone, but physical appearance certainly influences our impressions of other people, as it probably influenced your reactions to the photo in Figure 3.1. After all, the way people look usually is our first and often our only cue to what they are like. Our ideas about the meaning of physical appearance are endless. An honest face elicits trust, whereas shifty eyes evoke suspicion. Blondes are sociable and fun-loving, but redheads are fiery and quick-tempered. People who wear glasses are scholarly and those with silvery hair are distinguished. Research evidence may not support these beliefs, but that does not stop people from relying on them when they meet a stranger.

Physical beauty, particularly a beautiful face, calls up a variety of positive expectations. Apparently people assume that "what is beautiful is good" (Dion and others, 1972) or, as the German poet and philosopher Johann Schiller wrote over a century ago, that "physical beauty is the sign of an interior beauty, a spiritual and moral beauty" (1882). We expect highly attractive people to be more interesting, warm, outgoing, and socially skilled than less attractive people (Eagly & Makhijani, 1991; Feingold, 1992). In fact, attractiveness exerts a surprisingly wide range of effects on other people. Research shows, for example, that strangers are more likely to give help to a physically attractive person than to one who is less attractive (Benson and others, 1976). In another study, when elementary school teachers were shown children's photos and report cards, the teachers rated the more attractive youngsters as possessing more intelligence and academic potential (Clifford, 1975). And apparently justice is not blind after all, for even in the courts attractive people fare better than unattractive people. More attractive defendants have lower bail set in misdemeanor cases (Downs & Lyons, 1991), and if they are convicted, they receive lighter prison sentences (Stewart, 1985).

Beauty is not the only physical characteristic that activates expectations about personality. For example, certain patterns of facial features can also function this way. Some people have *baby-faced* features—large, round eyes, high eyebrows, and a small chin. In studies conducted in both the United States and Korea, Diane Berry and Leslie McArthur found that baby-faced adult males were viewed as more naive, honest, kind, and warm than males of more mature facial appearance (Berry & McArthur, 1985; McArthur & Berry, 1987). A high-pitched fast voice and a youthful walking gait produce similar effects (Montepare & Zebrowitz-McArthur, 1987, 1988). People with baby faces even seem to view *themselves* as possessing relatively childlike psychological characteristics (Berry & Brownlow, 1989).

Physical Appearance in the Workplace. Do expectations triggered by physical appearance have an impact on our everyday work lives? Research shows that the answer is yes. One study compared physically attractive and unattractive job candidates and found that the attractive candidates were more likely to be hired by college students role-playing employment interviewers (Cash & Kilcullen, 1985). Another researcher found that newly hired professional men taller than 6 feet 2 inches received starting salaries 10 percent higher than those given to men under 6 feet (Knapp, 1978).

Attractiveness may be a mixed blessing for women in organizations, however. One study asked people to evaluate a fictitious assistant vice president of a corporation on the basis of a photo. Some subjects saw a photo of an attractive male; others saw a less attractive male. Still other subjects saw an attractive or unattractive female. The subjects rated the attractive male as higher in ability than the unattractive one, but the reverse was true for females (Heilman & Stopeck, 1985). Subjects appeared to believe that an attractive woman might have been promoted because of her appearance rather than her ability.

Impressions from Nonverbal Communication. Did your mother tell you that the proper way to greet people was to "stand up straight, look them in the eye, smile, and shake hands firmly"? If so, she knew how much information is communicated by facial expressions, eye contact, and body language. We like people who orient their body toward us—facing us directly, leaning toward us, nodding while we speak—and we believe that they like us (Mehrabian, 1972). People who make frequent eye contact are perceived as honest, straightforward, friendly, and likable (Kleinke and others, 1974), whereas those who avoid eye contact are seen as unfriendly, shifty, or perhaps shy (Zimbardo, 1977). Of course too much eye contact—staring—can be unpleasant and often signals anger or hostility (Ellsworth & Carlsmith, 1973).

Body language offers a special insight into people's moods and emotions (Ekman and others, 1972). In such diverse cultures as those of Germany, Hong Kong, Japan, Turkey, and the United States, people express sadness and happiness, fear and anger, surprise and disgust in similar bodily postures and facial expressions, and they interpret them in the same ways (Ekman and others, 1987). In fact, emotional expression is a kind of universal language. From culture to culture the same expression signals pretty much the same internal feeling even though there may be differences in *when* and *where* it is appropriate to feel and express the emotion (Ekman, 1973).

This does not mean, however, that all emotions are equally easy to read. For example, people can spot a single angry face in an array of happy faces more quickly and easily than they can see one happy face in a crowd of angry ones (Hansen & Hansen, 1988). Perhaps because anger can pose a threat, its facial signs seem to jump out at the viewer.

A flair for faking it The popularity of the pop duo Milli Vanilli, shown here in concert, plummeted after their manager revealed that they never sang a note on their best-selling debut album. Before the revelation, their lip-synching deception had proven almost impossible to detect. What clues might you look for to gauge the authenticity of a performance?

Detection of Deception. Have you ever wondered how people can be gullible enough to lose their savings to a con artist who has told them some outrageous lie? Or how an instructor could believe some far-fetched excuse spun by one of your classmates? Perhaps you told yourself that you could never be so easily deceived. Maybe not, but detecting lies is not easy.

Paul Ekman and Wallace Friesen (1974) suggest that liars often give themselves away with nonverbal cues, but those cues are not the ones we usually watch for. Most people look for evidence in a liar's face or words, when in fact these are what the liar can easily control (Ekman & Friesen, 1974; DePaulo and others, 1982). The best cues are a quivering or high-pitched tone of voice or restless movements of the hands and feet. People who pay attention to those cues are relatively successful at detecting deception.

Can people be trained to pay attention to the correct cues? To find out, Ekman and Maureen O'Sullivan (1991) compared four groups of professional deception detectors: police detectives and agents from the U.S. Customs Service, Central Intelligence Agency, and Secret Service. When asked to judge whether an individual shown on film was making true or false statements, the Secret Service agents outperformed all others. The other professional law-enforcement personnel were no better at detecting deception than untrained subjects who also saw the films. The researchers suggest that Secret Service agents' training, which includes scanning crowds to detect threats to the president and other high officials, may sensitize them to valid cues to deception.

The fact that people tend to use the wrong cues in assessing truthfulness may also account for a seemingly paradoxical finding: the less information people receive, the better they may be at detecting deception. For example, people can detect deception better when they see only the speaker's body on videotape than when they see both the body and face. Focusing on the easily controlled face apparently leads them astray (Zuckerman and others, 1981). Similarly, people who observe someone speaking usually pay most attention to the speaker's words and consequently are relatively poor at detecting the body's hints at deception. One study found that subjects who are distracted by a difficult cognitive task, which prevents them from giving full attention to the speaker's words, are better at detecting deception than subjects without any distraction (Gilbert & Krull, 1988).

Given the difficulty of detecting deception, perhaps it is not surprising that some people have looked for more mechanical means of exposing dishonesty.

Lie Detection in the Legal System. "Accused Embezzler Passes Lie Detector Test—Denies Any Wrongdoing." The "lie detector" in the headline is a polygraph, a device that measures signs of physiological arousal—such as rapid breathing, increased heart rate, and sweating—as the test taker answers questions. Because people cannot completely control them, these responses are assumed to reveal the extra stress and effort of lying. However, current research evidence suggests that polygraph examinations are not precise enough to warrant their widespread use. In one study, for example, polygraph examiners correctly detected 75 percent of guilty suspects, but they also declared guilty 37 percent of those who actually were innocent (Saxe and others, 1985; Lykken, 1985).

Nevertheless, polygraph tests continue to be widely used. Much of their apparent effectiveness may derive from superstitions about the device rather than from its inherent accuracy. Some criminal suspects who anticipate that their lies will be detected may decide to confess when confronted with a polygraph examination (Lykken, 1985). Similarly, some dishonest job seekers may avoid employers who screen applicants with the polygraph.

Impressions from Behavior. Physical appearance and nonverbal communication are important sources of information, but the most useful resource for developing an impression of another person is the individual's behavior. If you know that someone donates hours of free time working in a local food bank, you may reasonably conclude that the person is caring, altruistic, and philanthropic. If you find out that someone stole money from a cash register at work, you can probably assume he or she is dishonest. Like these examples, many behaviors are strongly linked to particular personality traits. Indeed, people are often advised to judge others by their deeds, not by their appearance or their words. (The processes by which people draw inferences from others' behaviors will be described in detail shortly.)

Which Cues Capture Attention? Imagine sitting in the cafeteria idly watching those around you. What cues might attract your attention? You might notice that one person makes loud and nasty comments to the clerk at the cash register, that another drinks three cups of coffee in quick succession, or that a third towers over all the other people in the room. Characteristics that are different stand out, and this is true for all kinds of characteristics, including behaviors such as making rude comments or physical cues like tallness.

Our impression of the same individual may differ greatly from one situation to another because attributes that stand out in one context may go unnoticed in another. An attribute that is salient in its context may give rise to inferences that become part of our first impression of a person.

Figure 3.2 Salient cues dominate impressions

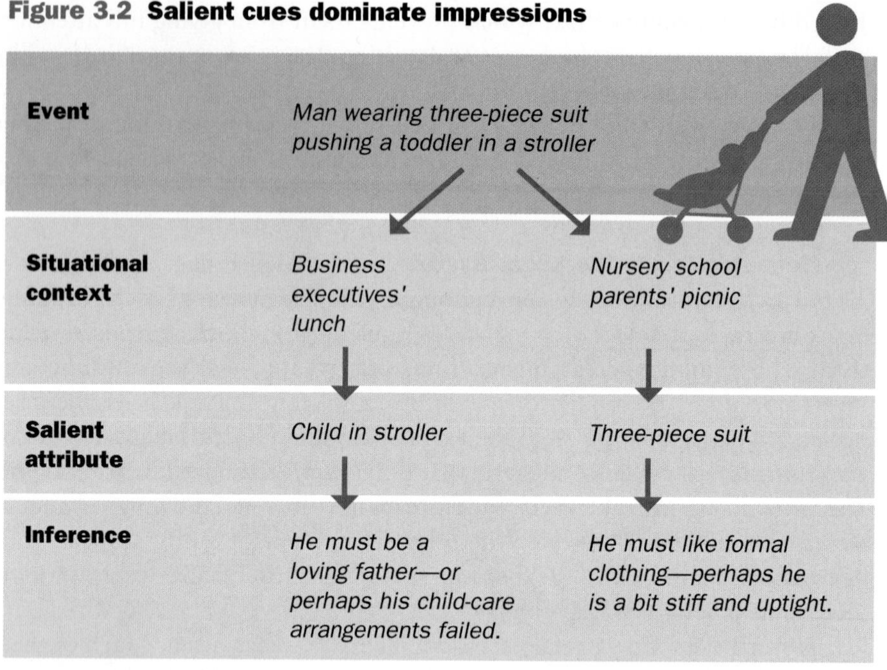

Salience refers to a cue's ability to attract attention in its context. So you probably will not notice the tall person's coffee-drinking habits or the rude person's height if those characteristics do not depart much from the average. Of course, a cue that is unusual or unexpected in one context may be quite normal in another, as Figure 3.2 shows. The person who towered over everyone might be salient in the cafeteria but not on the basketball court, surrounded by equally tall team members. Thus, attributes that stand out in one context may be unnoticed in another. When we have information about a person's physical appearance, their nonverbal communication, and some of their behavior, those aspects that are salient are likely to grab our attention and provide the basis for first impressions.

Unusual and salient characteristics not only make a difference in impressions of others, but also help us define ourselves, as you will see in Chapter 4, pages 118 to 119.

Interpreting Cues

Cues have no meaning in themselves. Instead, they are interpreted in the light of a person's stored knowledge about people, behaviors, traits, and social situations. Stored knowledge that is linked to the cue itself or is easy to bring to mind is most likely to be used in interpreting cues.

We seem to leap effortlessly from the cues of appearance, body language, and behavior to the personality characteristics we believe they reflect. Yet none of the cues we use in perceiving people has much meaning in itself. No

salience The ability of a cue to attract attention in its context.

behavior, appearance, gesture, or expression *directly* indicates a person's inner qualities. Instead, even our first impressions rely on rapid but seemingly effortless cognitive processes.

The first step in processing is interpreting the cues themselves—deciding whether a wrinkled brow reflects menace or puzzlement, or whether a lie is an act of deceit or of loyalty. Two crucial kinds of stored knowledge help us make these decisions: the associations we have already learned, and the thoughts that are currently in our mind.

The Role of Associations in Interpretation. On learning that a customer at the local convenience store was caught stealing money from the cash register, most people would immediately conclude that the person is dishonest. Why do we jump to that conclusion? The answer has to do with the strong link that exists between two cognitive representations. Our concept of stealing money is **associated**, or linked, to our knowledge about the trait of dishonesty. When we think about stealing, the associated trait of dishonesty is *activated*, or brought to mind. To understand why association is important, imagine a child's toy box containing a jumble of all kinds of toys, among them a paddle connected by a string to a rubber ball. If you pull the paddle out of the box—think of this as hearing about the behavior of stealing—you can be sure the ball—the associated trait of dishonesty—will soon follow.

Associations can arise from *similarity in meanings* between two cognitive representations—like the similarity between the concept of stealing and the concept of dishonesty. However, even unrelated ideas can become associated if they are repeatedly *thought about together*. Thus, Lennon and McCartney, honesty and George Washington, and cops and robbers have become associated concepts for most of us.

Once we form an association, it links the two cognitive representations just as the string links the paddle and ball. If either of the linked representations comes to mind, the other will usually come to mind also. Because of these patterns of stored associations, some cues are easier to interpret than others. For example, the act of turning in money found on the floor in a secluded part of the library stacks is so closely connected with our idea of honesty that we would be hard pressed to interpret the behavior in any other way. Similarly, superior performance in the decathlon immediately conjures up the idea of athleticism. However, the meaning of cues is not always so clear-cut.

The Role of Accessibility in Interpretation. Imagine discovering that someone you know had shared test answers with a classmate. How would you interpret that behavior? The act of sharing could reflect helpfulness or dishonesty, and you might have difficulty choosing one interpretation over the other. In such cases, we tend to rely on relevant information we currently have in mind. The **accessibility** of knowledge—the ease and speed with which it comes to mind and is used—exerts a powerful influence on the

association A link between two or more cognitive representations.

accessibility The ease and rapidity with which a cognitive representation comes to mind and is used.

A kiss is just a kiss Or is it? In fact, accessible knowledge influences the way in which any action is interpreted, and thus cultural ideas about appropriate behavior change the interpretation of the action. In North America a scene like this—in which Mikhail Gorbachev greets Erich Honecker at a celebration marking the 30th anniversary of East Berlin—might have an entirely different meaning.

interpretation of behavior or other cues. Going back to our toy-box metaphor, accessible toys are those near the top of the pile, while the less accessible ones are buried near the bottom.

The more accessible the knowledge, the more likely it is to come to mind automatically—without our consciously trying to retrieve it—and the more likely it is to guide our interpretation of cues (Higgins & King, 1981). Thus, someone whose ideas about helpfulness are highly accessible may interpret the act of sharing answers as a helpful act. Another person—perhaps an instructor for whom the concept of academic dishonesty is more accessible—might see the same behavior as dishonest, a quite different interpretation. Among the factors that influence the accessibility of knowledge are expectations, motives, moods, context, and recency and frequency of activation.

1. *Expectations.* When we expect something to occur, our thoughts about the anticipated outcome color our interpretation of what actually does happen. In a classic demonstration of the effects of expectations, Harold Kelley (1950) arranged for a guest instructor to conduct twenty-minute discussions in psychology courses. Before the guest's appearance, the students were given background information about the guest instructor. Though they were unaware of it, different students were given different background information. One group of students learned that the guest instructor was "a very warm person, industrious, critical, practical, and determined." The other group was informed that he was "a rather cold person, industrious, critical, practical, and determined." All students then had an extensive opportunity—twenty minutes—to observe the instructor's actual behavior during the discussion. They then rated his personality. The results clearly demonstrated the effects of expectation. Students who expected the instructor to be warm rated him as more considerate, informal, sociable, popular, good-natured, humorous, and humane than did those who expected a colder individual.

The effects of expectations on social perception are pervasive (Harris, 1991; Rosenthal, 1985). Supporters of opposing candidates in presidential debates expect that their own candidate will show statesmanlike behavior and leadership potential and will win the debate. And when the debate is over, each group of supporters is usually sure that they saw just that (Kinder & Sears, 1985). Doctors and nurses in psychiatric facilities expect disturbed behavior from their patients, and that is usually what they think they find. In David Rosenhan's study, one of the pseudopatients admitted to a psychiatric hospital told clinical interviewers he had a warm relationship with his wife, marred only by occasional angry exchanges. Filtered through the expectations of staff therapists who thought him mentally ill, the healthy relationship was seen in a new light. His written case history commented that "affective [emotional] stability is absent. . . . Attempts to control emotionality with his wife . . . are punctuated by angry outbursts" (Rosenhan, 1973, p. 253).

2. *Motives.* We often see not only what we expect to see but also what we *want* to see. Simply thinking about desired goals is enough to make cognitive representations of those goals accessible, and this in turn affects our interpretations of others' behavior. For example, people who want to act cooperatively are likely to interpret others' behavior as cooperative (Liebrand and others, 1986; Fincham & Bradbury, 1987). Similarly, people in conflict are quick to interpret their opponents' behaviors in the worst possible way. Recall, for example, the opposing fans' very different perceptions of the football game described in Chapter 1.

3. *Moods.* It sometimes happens to professors in college towns—the person serving the table turns out to be a student in one of last year's courses. When this happened to one of the authors of this text on a warm evening this past summer, the waiter served up more than a good meal. "Oh the course was great," the former student enthused in front of suitably impressed guests from out of town. "I was in history, but I decided to be a psych major after taking that course!" Does anything put one in a good mood faster than a compliment? Is anything a better guarantee of a great evening than being in a good mood? The conversation seemed particularly scintillating and witty that night; the guests' behavior was especially charming and generous; and even the parking attendant seemed friendly and gracious.

In fact, positive or negative moods have a well-documented impact on how we interpret behavior and, thus, on our reactions to others. People in a happy and cheerful mood see both their own and others' behavior through rose-colored glasses, assigning to all behavior more positive ratings than those given by people in neutral moods (Isen, 1987; Williamson & Clark, 1989). The converse is also often true—being in a blue mood sometimes gives everything a negative tinge.

Moods affect us this way because they make other positive or negative thoughts accessible, bringing them to the surface where they can influence our interpretations of behaviors. These accessibility effects help explain an interesting finding: the impact of negative mood is not as strong as the impact of positive mood. Positive mood is often strongly associated with many other positive pieces of information, which come to mind and help us interpret further information in an equally positive light. In contrast, negative moods are less consistently and tightly associated with other negative pieces of knowledge. The reason may be that when we are in a bad mood, we often try to think of good things to help ourselves feel better (Isen, 1984). When some careless motorist scrapes the fender of your parked car, your resulting bad mood may remind you of other disasters—or you may attempt to repair your mood by thinking about your upcoming promotion.

Figure 3.3 What is this woman feeling? Emotional expressions are some of the easiest signals for humans to understand. But before you come to a firm conclusion, turn the page.

4. *Context.* Sometimes the situation in which an ambiguous behavior occurs helps us interpret it. Look at the photo in Figure 3.3, for example. Are the tears streaming down the woman's face tears of joy or tears of sorrow?

The social context of interpretation Even our understanding of emotional expression is influenced by the social context. Now that you know that Greek hurdler Parakevi Patoulidou is "celebrating" her gold medal in the 1992 summer Olympics, her tears are clearly tears of exultant joy rather than anguish or sorrow.

Is the woman's face twisted in pain or expressing wry humor? Yaacov Trope found that people answer such questions in different ways, depending on what they know about the situation. Trope (1986) showed subjects photos of people wearing ambiguous facial expressions together with information about the context as in Figure 3.3. The same expression looked grief-stricken to subjects who were told the photographed person was attending a funeral but was interpreted as tearful laughter by subjects who thought the person was at a comedy performance.

5. *Recent activation.* A toy that a child has recently used can be found near the top of the toy chest. Similarly, a cognitive representation that has recently been brought to mind also remains accessible for a time (Wyer & Srull, 1989). Therefore, anything that brings an idea to mind—even coincidental or chance events—can make it accessible and influence our interpretations of behavior. Imagine walking down the street with a friend and noticing in passing a movie poster featuring Clint Eastwood in an aggressive pose. Could the poster increase the accessibility of your cognitive representations related to hostility and aggression? If so, might it influence your interpretations, leading you to see hostility in an ambiguous remark made by your friend when none was intended?

The answer to both these questions is yes. To demonstrate this effect,

Tory Higgins and his colleagues (1977) asked students to memorize several words. One group memorized words related to the positive trait *adventurous,* while another group learned words related to the negative trait *reckless.* This procedure was intended to activate students' stored knowledge about one or the other of these two traits, thereby making that knowledge accessible in the next step of the experiment. Then, in what students thought was an unrelated experiment, they read a description of "Donald," who had climbed Mount McKinley, gone white-water kayaking, and driven in a demolition derby. Later, the two groups were asked to describe Donald's activities. Their descriptions showed that the first group of subjects, for whom *adventurous* was accessible, saw Donald's behavior as daring, whereas those who had focused on words relating to *reckless* saw his behavior as foolhardy and rash. Correspondingly, the "adventurous" subjects evaluated Donald more positively than the "reckless" group.

Higgins and his colleagues wondered whether this effect would occur if *any* positive or negative word was made accessible. They used the same procedure with traits like *obedient* or *disrespectful,* but activating these traits had no effect on people's interpretations of Donald. People apparently do not use just any accessible cognitive representation to interpret information; rather, the accessible representation must be *applicable* to the information.

Activating a cognitive representation to increase its accessibility and make it more likely to be used is called *priming.* The effects of priming can be long-lasting and rather subtle. Concepts that have been primed can remain accessible and influence later interpretations for as long as twenty-four hours (Srull & Wyer, 1980). Their impact does not depend on people's awareness of the activation, as was demonstrated by a study that used priming with an interesting twist (Bargh & Pietromonaco, 1982). Some subjects were shown neutral words, while others saw words related to the trait of hostility. Then both groups read a description of a character's ambiguous behaviors. When the groups' responses were compared, those primed with the hostility-related words interpreted the behaviors as more hostile and aggressive. The interesting twist is that the presentation of the priming words was so brief—a mere flash on a computer screen—that the subjects could not say what the words were. Even when people are unable consciously to identify a word, encountering a stimulus can still make cognitive representations accessible and influence the interpretation of later information. Other similar studies have confirmed this remarkable finding (Niedenthal, 1990). So even if you just glimpse the Clint Eastwood poster out of the corner of your eye, it might make you interpret events as aggressive.

Chapter 7, especially pages 300 to 304, will discuss the thought-provoking possibility that our attitudes might similarly be influenced without our awareness.

6. *Frequent activation: Chronic accessibility.* What toys are usually found lying at the top of the toy box? The ones that get dragged out and played with every day. The same is true of thoughts. The frequent use of a cognitive representation over days, months, or years can make it *chronically accessible* (Bargh and others, 1986; Higgins, 1989). When this happens, people repeatedly use the same concepts in interpreting others' behavior. For exam-

ple, intelligence might always be important in one person's judgments, whereas friendliness or helpfulness might matter more to someone else. In fact, people can more easily recognize information relevant to their "favorite" traits and can remember it better than unrelated information (Bargh & Thein, 1985; Higgins and others, 1982). Imagine, for instance, that you observed someone performing many behaviors—greeting friends, going to a party, studying in the library, and working at a part-time job. If friendliness is chronically accessible for you, you would be more likely to notice and later remember the first two of these behaviors. Another observer for whom intelligence is a chronically accessible concept would more easily notice and remember the time the person spent in the library.

Chronic Accessibility and Mental Health. Recall that the more often people use particular concepts, the more likely those concepts are to come to mind again. Thus, individuals for whom particular traits are chronically accessible may see the world from only a single perspective. Sometimes the effect can be tragic. For instance, someone who is physically or emotionally abused for a long period—perhaps in childhood or in an abusive adult relationship—will have experienced threat and danger on a regular basis. As the concept of threat becomes chronically accessible, the abused person becomes particularly sensitive to interpersonal signals of threat. Soon even ambiguous behaviors by other people may be seen as threatening (Higgins, 1989). For example, the individual may interpret a mild critique of job performance as a total rejection, and this may trigger a strong emotional reaction. Highly accessible representations shape the way people interpret incoming information, and the abuse victim may literally see a severe attack in even the most constructive criticism. In therapy, such individuals must learn to become aware of and to overcome their automatic tendency to interpret other people and their actions in biased ways (Moretti & Shaw, 1989).

As you have seen in the last several pages, accessibility has many sources, and it works in many ways to alter the interpretation of a given behavior, as summarized in Figure 3.4. In fact, as you will see throughout this book, the principle of accessibility has implications for many of our thoughts and actions—not only for our impressions of others.

Characterizing the Behaving Person: Correspondent Inferences

People often assume that others have inner qualities that correspond to their observed behaviors. This assumption is frequently made even when external factors could have influenced the behaviors.

Sometimes off-the-cuff interpretations shaped by associations and accessible cognitive representations are enough for us. If we never expect to interact

Figure 3.4 Accessibility shapes inferences about behavior

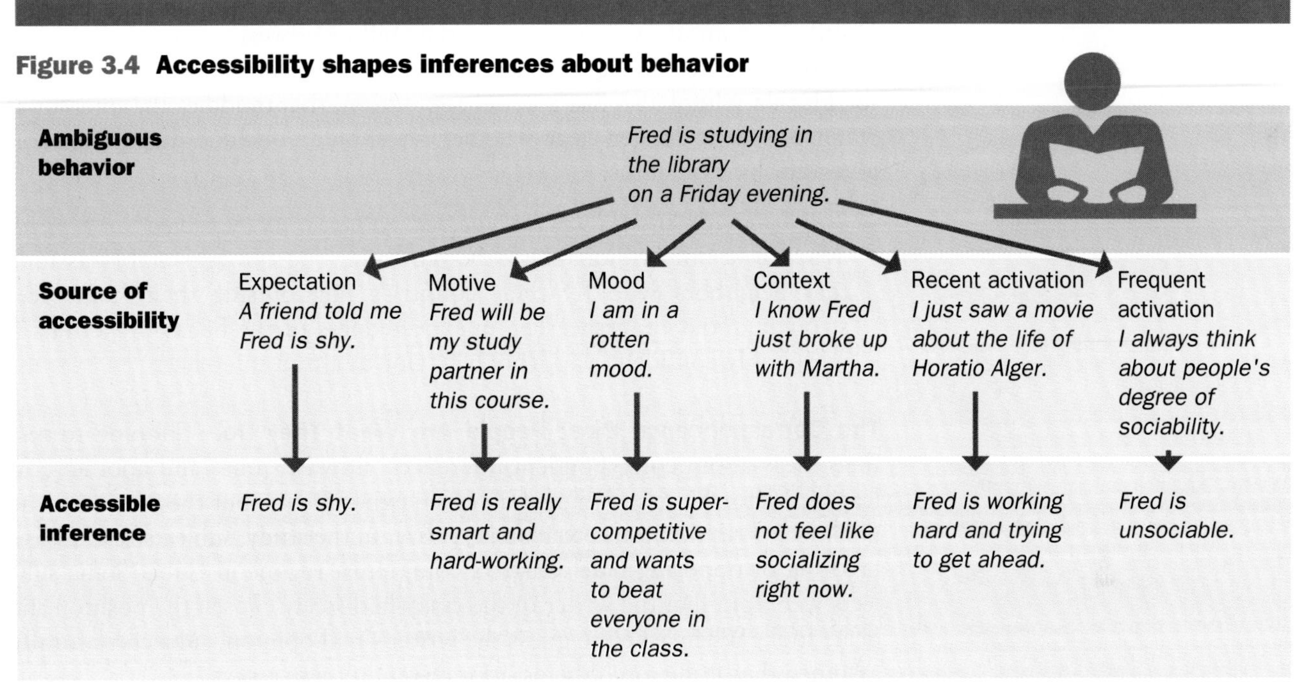

Ambiguous behavior
Fred is studying in the library on a Friday evening.
Source of accessibility
Expectation
A friend told me Fred is shy.
Motive
Fred will be my study partner in this course.
Mood
I am in a rotten mood.
Context
I know Fred just broke up with Martha.
Recent activation
I just saw a movie about the life of Horatio Alger.
Frequent activation
I always think about people's degree of sociability.
Accessible inference
Fred is shy.
Fred is really smart and hard-working.
Fred is super-competitive and wants to beat everyone in the class.
Fred does not feel like socializing right now.
Fred is working hard and trying to get ahead.
Fred is unsociable.

The same behavior can give rise to a variety of inferences, depending on what cognitive representations are accessible for the observer. Expectations, motives, and moods are just some of the many factors that can influence accessibility.

with a person again, we may not go beyond interpreting their behaviors. If circumstances require even a fairly superficial impression, however, we need to take a second step: applying our characterization of *behavior* to the behaving *person*. Does a menacing expression reveal a dangerous person? Does deceitful behavior imply that the person is untrustworthy? Characterizing someone as having a personality trait that corresponds to his or her behavior is called making a **correspondent inference**. When a correspondent inference follows the initial interpretation of a behavior, it completes a first impression—an initial cognitive representation of what the other person is like (Trope, 1986; Gilbert and others, 1988).

When Is a Correspondent Inference Justified? Edward Jones and Keith Davis (1965) spelled out three conditions under which making a correspondent inference is justified.

- *The individual must choose to perform the behavior.* No one should conclude that a child forced to write a pleasant thank-you note for an unloved birthday gift actually feels grateful.
- *The behavior must have few effects that distinguish it from other courses of action.* The fewer effects a behavior has that it does not share with other possible choices, the easier it is to decide which effect may have mo-

correspondent inference The process of characterizing someone as having a personality trait that corresponds to his or her observed behavior.

tivated the behavior. For example, if a person chooses a college in sunny Florida over an identical campus in the chilly Midwest, we would be justified in seeing the choice as reflecting a love of warm weather. However, if the Florida school also has a better reputation, that muddies the inferential waters—it is no longer clear whether we should conclude that the person loves sunshine or status.

- *The behavior should be unexpected rather than expected or typical.* When it is not fashionable to be patriotic, one can reasonably assume that neighbors who fly their country's flag outside their home feel strongly about the issue. The unexpectedness of the behavior permits a reasonably confident leap from behavior to a trait inference.

The Correspondence Bias: People Are What They Do. Hoping to test their ideas about correspondent inferences, Edward Jones and another colleague, Victor Harris, designed a classic experiment—but they found some unexpected results (Jones & Harris, 1967). In the study, subjects read essays favoring or opposing Fidel Castro's communist regime in Cuba. Some subjects were told that the writer of the essay had freely chosen the position she or he took. When asked to guess the writer's real opinion, subjects naturally assumed that it mirrored the position taken in these essays.

Other subjects learned that the writer was given no choice: the position had been assigned. You might expect these subjects to realize that a required

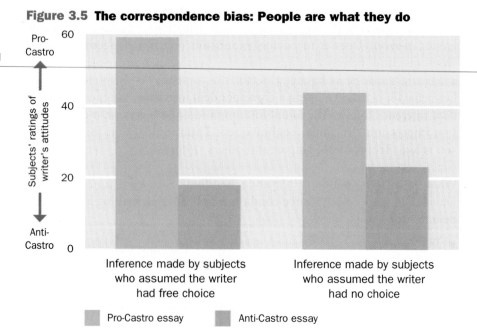

Figure 3.5 The correspondence bias: People are what they do

Subjects who read an essay and thought the writer had freely chosen the position were likely to infer that the writer's true position corresponded to that advocated in the essay (left bars). However, they were nearly as likely to make the same inference when they knew that the writer had no choice about the position (right). People often leap to the conclusion that behaviors reflect inner characteristics, when situational forces are truly responsible. (Based on Jones & Harris, 1967).

essay, like a dictated thank-you note, carries no information whatsoever about the writer's actual opinion. But they did not. Instead, like the subjects who thought the essay writer had a choice, the second group of subjects concluded that the writer actually held the views expressed in the essay, as Figure 3.5 shows. In other words, they made an unjustified correspondent inference when they inferred that the writer's opinion corresponded with the writer's behavior.

As Jones and Harris's study illustrates, correspondent inferences are sometimes justified and sometimes not justified. The tendency to draw correspondent inferences even when they are not justified, and even when other possible causes of the behavior exist, is known as the **correspondence bias.** Another term for the correspondence bias is *fundamental attribution error.* The correspondence bias has been demonstrated repeatedly, both inside and outside the social psychology laboratory (Jones, 1990). People tend to assume that the behaviors they observe must reflect the actors' inner characteristics even though other particular elements of the situation could explain those behaviors.

Correspondence Bias in the Workplace. The correspondence bias has serious implications for fairness in the workplace. If others see us as having personal characteristics that fit with our behaviors, we can be trapped by behaviors we are instructed to perform. Consider the results of an "employee interaction" study in which groups of five subjects were assigned in an obviously random way to two "manager" and three "clerk" positions (Humphrey, 1985). For a couple of hours, the managers made decisions, read documents, dictated letters to customers, and performed other varied and challenging tasks. Meanwhile the clerks filed papers, alphabetized cards, and filled out forms in triplicate, with little chance to make decisions or take initiative. When the participants rated each other at the end of the study, they did not recognize that the randomly assigned roles conveyed no information about their personal characteristics or abilities. Managers and clerks alike believed that managers were assertive and decisive, with real leadership potential. Even the *clerks* predicted that managers would be more successful than clerks in their real-life future careers.

When the correspondence bias occurs, roles define the person. Given this bias, how likely is it that even a highly competent secretary will ever be seen as having what it takes to be an effective manager?

How Associations Affect Correspondent Inferences. Because of their different patterns of associations with traits, some behaviors are more likely than others to lead to correspondent inferences. To illustrate this point, consider the question of whether a person is honest or dishonest. Most people would agree that a single theft is all it takes to trigger an inference that the thief is dishonest. In contrast, no single act is likely to cause most people to say that a person is indisputably honest. It takes a long period of consis-

correspondence bias The tendency to infer an actor's personal characteristics from observed behaviors even when the inference is unjustified because other possible causes of the behavior exist.

tently upright behavior to win a reputation for honesty (Skowronski & Carlston, 1989; Reeder & Brewer, 1979). The difference is due to patterns of associations between our cognitive representations of behaviors and traits. Dishonest behaviors are unambiguous; honest people do not commit dishonest acts. In contrast, honest behaviors are not good evidence because even dishonest people act honestly some of the time, in some situations, with some people. For this reason, as Figure 3.6 shows, an honest behavior could be associated with either the trait of honesty or the trait of dishonesty, leaving the observer unable to confidently draw any inference about a person who performs a single honest behavior. A dishonest behavior, however, is linked only to the trait of dishonesty, so the correspondent inference can readily be made.

Figure 3.6 shows a similar asymmetrical pattern of associations for *ability* traits. Poor performance on a test requiring intelligence or physical coordination may or may not be evidence of a lack of ability. But high performance sends a clear message because a person who lacks a high degree of intelligence or coordination could not be expected to perform above her or his level. Thus, a good performance can readily be interpreted as indicating high ability, while a poor performance is ambiguous and allows us to draw no inferences, at least not with any certainty.

Snap judgments about other people do not just "come to us"; we actively construct them. The construction follows the steps summarized in Figure 3.7, proceeding from initial cues to correspondent inferences.

If you see a single honest behavior, you cannot assume the actor is honest, but you can assume dishonesty from a single dishonest behavior. Dishonest behaviors are unambiguous because they are associated only with dishonest people, while honest behaviors may be performed by honest *or* dishonest people. Similarly, behaviors showing high levels of ability or intelligence are less ambiguous than behaviors showing lower levels. Consequently, high ability can be inferred more readily than low ability.

Figure 3.6 Associations and correspondent inferences

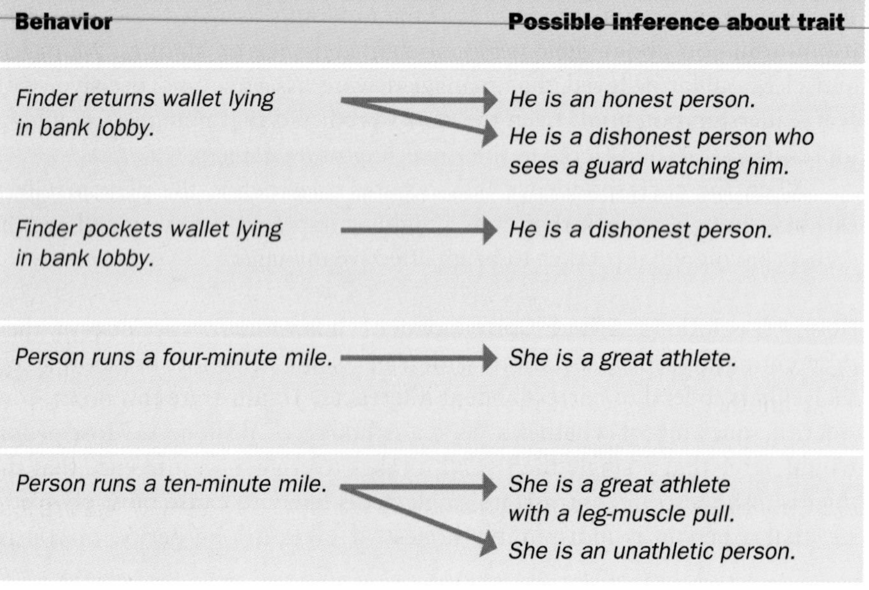

Figure 3.7 The processes involved in constructing a first impression

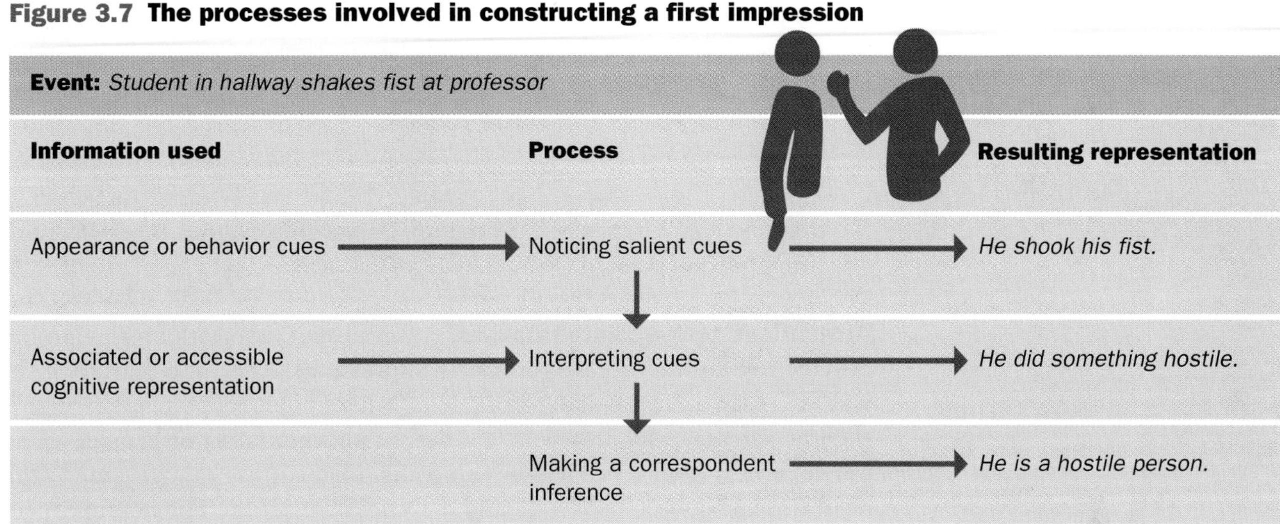

Although forming a first impression seems immediate and effortless, it involves processes of noticing salient cues, interpreting them, and making correspondent inferences about the person's characteristics.

Beyond First Impressions: Attribution and Integration

Think back to the last time someone paid you a particularly outrageous compliment. Did you buy it? Perhaps you took the compliment at face value and, drawing a correspondent inference, decided that the person had a particularly high opinion of you. Probably, however, you were not quite so naive. Astute observers know that people say and do things for many reasons—the desire to flatter others, the demands of social situations, or the wish to receive something in return. Because we know that actions do not always reflect the inner person, we sometimes try to avoid the correspondence bias, correcting our first impressions by considering other possible causes of behaviors (Gilbert and others, 1988).

In fact, making inferences about the causes of people's behaviors is central to our perception of other people. We make these **causal attributions**—judgments about the cause of a behavior or an event—as we try to figure out what another person is really like. Because real understanding of others seems to depend on knowing *why* they behave the way they do, causal attributions are an important part of going beyond superficial first impressions to form more complex and deeper understandings of others. Causal attributions also help us to combine the different things we learn about someone into a coherent overall picture.

causal attribution A judgment about the cause of a behavior or other event.

Sources of Attributions

To go beyond a first impression, people must engage in more extensive thought, particularly to arrive at explanations for behaviors. People are likely to consider potential causes that are linked to the behavior or are generally accessible, salient in context, or suggested by the pattern of available information.

We draw on many types of information as we think about others' actions and attempt to understand why they have occurred.

Attributions to Associated Causes. Recall that associations play an important role in the way we form first impressions. They also feature in the way we reach a deeper understanding of other people, but we use them in a slightly different way. In reaching a deeper understanding of people, we do not superficially link behaviors with traits. Instead, we are concerned with associations between behaviors and their possible *causes*. For example, people associate behaviors that are *actions* and those that are *experiences* with different types of causes (McArthur, 1972; Brown & Fish, 1983). Actions are seen as caused mostly by actors, as you will see if you were asked to complete the following sentence: "Romeo serenaded Juliet because . . ." Did you begin the next phrase with the word *he*? Perhaps you said something like, ". . . he wanted to win her heart." Experiences, however, are usually attributed to the *stimulus* rather than to the actor. So you would probably finish the sentence "Romeo loved Juliet because . . ." with a phrase beginning with the word *she*—". . . she had such admirable qualities."

Some behaviors are so closely associated with a particular situation that the causal role of the situation becomes obvious. We are most likely to see this causal role when we possess general knowledge about what is expected in a given situation, cognitively represented in a *script*. For example, undergraduates generally agree on the script for that familiar situation known as "dating." It includes such elements as "female greets male at the door," "they go to a movie," "male takes female home," "they kiss" (the element on which most subjects agree), and "they say good night and thank date" (Pryor & Merluzzi, 1985). People often learn scripts for unfamiliar situations by observing others. If your first Weight Watchers' meeting opens with everyone congratulating each other on how good they look, you can conclude that the situation demands these behaviors.

Scripts tell us what behaviors are normal and expected in given situations, and when an expected behavior occurs—such as wearing jeans and a funny T-shirt to a picnic—it can be attributed to situational pressures or demands. In contrast, behaviors that are unexpected, such as wearing the jeans and T-shirt to a formal dinner party, demand more attributional thought, and we may end up explaining them in terms of the personal characteristics of the actor.

Dressing for success Situational pressures are powerful influences on behavior. Apparently, for any self-respecting Democratic candidate in the 1988 presidential debates the power outfit of choice was a blue suit, white shirt, and red tie. For five points, can you name the candidate for whom it seems to have worked?

Attributions to Culturally Favored Causes. Of course, different people—for example, those from different cultures—associate behaviors with different types of causes. When Joan Miller (1984) looked at the way children and adults from the United States and India explained behaviors, she found striking cultural differences. Only adults from the United States were likely to attribute behavior to the actor's personality traits, or stable personality characteristics. Adults from India and children from both countries placed more emphasis on other characteristics of the actor, such as his or her roles and social relationships. The American children's explanations became more trait-based with increasing age, however, suggesting that they learned this pattern from their culture over time. Though the correspondence bias is universal, Miller's results make it clear that different cultures emphasize different types of personal characteristics. For example, in her study Americans explained examples of cheating and dishonesty on the basis of the actor's general traits, like competitiveness or selfishness. Indians explained similar behaviors as due to the individual's social roles or interpersonal relationships—such as the fact that the actor was unemployed and needed money, or that he had a history of conflict with his victim.

People in independent cultures, including the United States, tend to think in terms of traits, and those in interdependent cultures, such as India, emphasize roles and social relationships. This difference is also evident when people think about themselves, as you will see in *Chapter 4, especially pages 126 to 128.*

Attributions to Accessible Causes. The more accessible a potential cause, the more likely it is to be cited as an explanation of behavior. Thus, William Rholes and John Pryor (1982) reasoned, priming should influence people's causal attributions, just as it can affect their initial interpretations of behaviors. To test their hypothesis, the researchers first exposed subjects to words like *aviator* or *rug,* to make those concepts more accessible in memory. They then asked subjects to explain hypothetical events, such as

"The pilot liked the carpet." Subjects who had been primed with *aviator* attributed the behavior to the actor, while those who had seen *rug* attributed the behavior to the stimulus object. More accessible causes are more likely to be seen as responsible for an event.

Attributions to Salient Causes. The more noticeable or attention-getting a potential cause is the more likely it is to be used to explain behavior. And what is noticeable can depend literally on the perceiver's point of view. To demonstrate the impact of salience on attribution, Shelley Taylor and Susan Fiske (1975) arranged an experiment in which six student subjects watched a two-person conversation from three different viewing positions, as Figure 3.8 shows. When questioned about what they had seen, the subjects attributed a greater causal role to the person they were directly watching. They gave that person higher ratings for dominating the conversation and dictating its tone and outcome.

In this study, two people held a conversation as six others watched. The observers were seated so two could most easily see participant *A*, two faced participant *B*, and two could see both participants equally well. The results? The observers attributed a greater causal role to the participant they were directly watching than to the other participant. (Adapted from Taylor & Fiske, 1975, copyright © 1975 by the American Psychological Association. Adapted by permission.)

Figure 3.8 Salient causes dominate impressions

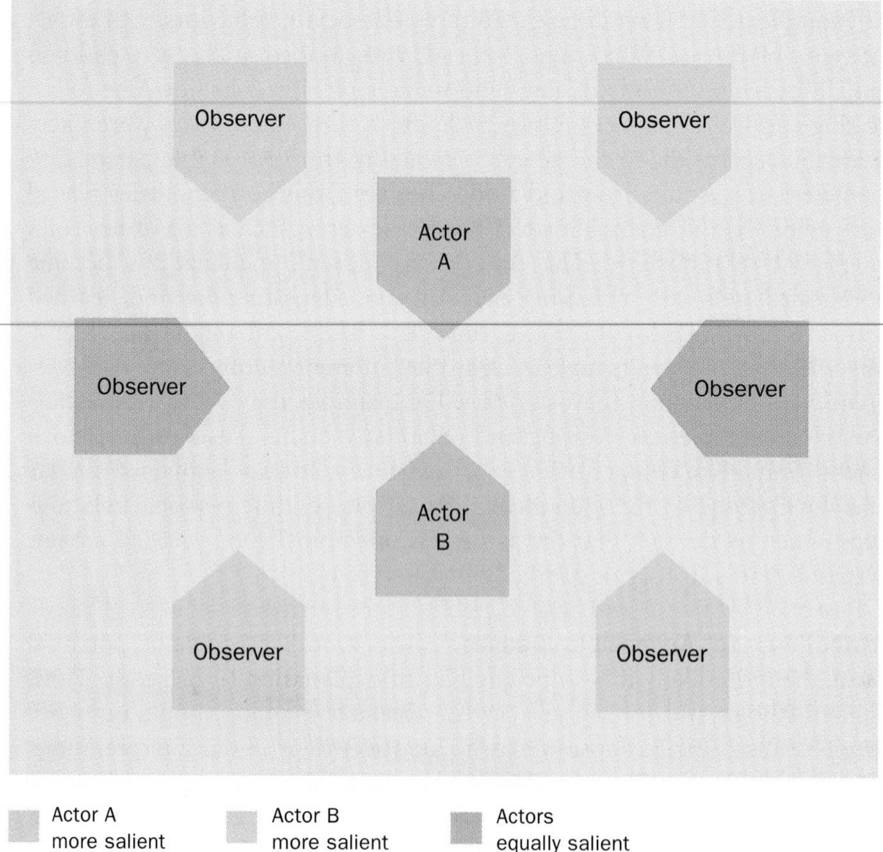

Salient features—whether they are people we are focusing on, bright colors, moving images, loud voices, or any other outstanding feature—can draw our attention, thereby turning a potential cause into the probable cause (McArthur & Post, 1977; Robinson & McArthur, 1982). Salience has these effects whether people make quick, relatively unthinking judgments or make an effort to think carefully and be accurate (Smith & Miller, 1979).

Consider the implications of these findings for courtroom proceedings. Imagine jurors watching a videotape of a suspect confessing while being interrogated by police. Was the confession voluntary—attributable to the suspect—or was it coerced—the result of pressure from the detectives? Salience can affect observers' answers to this question, as one study showed. Some observers saw a confession with the video camera focused on the suspect, and others saw the same interaction from a viewpoint that focused mainly on the interrogating detective. The first group judged the confession to be more voluntary and less coerced (Lassiter & Irvine, 1986). Is it any wonder that police agencies that are videotaping interrogations almost always focus the camera on the suspect?

Attributions Based on Covariation Information. Knowledge stored in the mind—cognitive representations that are activated by associations, accessibility, or salience—does not always provide ready answers to causal questions. If you see a graduate student flatter a professor (as graduate students do from time to time), a causal attribution may not immediately come to your mind. In such situations, people can try to ascertain the cause of the event by collecting *covariation information,* information about potential causal factors that are present when the event occurs and absent when it does not (Kelley, 1967).

Harold Kelley considered three major categories of possible causes of a social event like flattery (Kelley, 1967). First, he suggested, the behavior might be explained by something about the *actor*. Thus, the graduate student might be insecure about his standing in the department and might respond by flattering all professors frequently. Second, the behavior might be due to something about the *stimulus* of the behavior. Perhaps the professor is known to be susceptible to flattery. Third, the behavior might be caused by something about the *particular situation or circumstances*. Perhaps the graduate student plans to ask this professor for a letter of recommendation later in the day.

How do people decide which kind of attribution to make? Kelley argued that people look for the possible cause that *covaries* uniquely with the event. The one that is present when the behavior occurs and is absent when the behavior is absent wins the causal sweepstakes. For example, an observer would seek out *distinctiveness information* (whether the student flatters other people), *consensus information* (whether other people flatter the professor), and *consistency information* (whether the student flatters the professor under other circumstances).

You can probably guess some of the predictions that derive from Kelley's reasoning. Assume the professor, like a social magnet, seems to draw flattery from everyone, including even this rather reserved student who rarely flatters anyone. In that case, most people would conclude that something about the professor is causing the flattery. As you can see in Table 3.1, people would attribute the behavior to the stimulus. But imagine a different case. Perhaps the student flatters lots of people, most other people do not flatter the professor, and the student flatters her every time they meet. In that case, there is probably something special about the graduate student that explains the flattery. As you can also see in Table 3.1, given these pieces of information, most people would attribute the behavior to the actor. On the other hand, maybe the flattery occurred only today and did not occur last week, and few people in the history of the department have ever flattered this professor, who in fact is quite an unpleasant person. In this final case, most people would see the graduate student's behavior as due to some particular situation or circumstance (McArthur, 1972). Perhaps the student is, after all, about to request a letter of recommendation.

Table 3.1 Information about the presence or absence of potential causes influences attributions

Event *The graduate student flatters a professor.*

Situation A	Situation B	Situation C
High consensus *Almost everyone flatters this professor.*	Low consensus *Almost nobody flatters this professor.*	Low consensus *Almost nobody flatters this professor.*
High distinctiveness *The graduate student does not flatter anyone else.*	Low distinctiveness *The graduate student flatters almost everyone.*	High distinctiveness *The graduate student does not flatter anyone else.*
High consistency *The graduate student flatters this professor almost all the time.*	High consistency *The graduate student flatters this professor almost all the time.*	Low consistency *The graduate student does not flatter this professor on most occasions.*
↓	↓	↓
Attribution *Something about the professor (stimulus)*	Attribution *Something about the graduate student (person)*	Attribution *Something about the particular time or situation (circumstances)*

Correcting First Impressions

When external factors appear to have caused behavior, people may attempt to correct an initial inference about the actor's characteristics. This correction takes time and cognitive effort, however, so it often does not occur.

Attributional thinking may lead us to revise our initial correspondent inferences—that is, we may become less confident that the actor's inner characteristics correspond to his or her behavior. The term *discounting* refers to the process of reducing a belief in one potential cause of behavior—such as the flatterer's true opinion—because there is another viable cause—his need for a favor (Kelley, 1972). When you see your classmates sweating and biting their fingernails as they await the calculus exam, the association *anxiety* immediately springs to mind. You then may go on to draw a correspondent inference—to form a first impression that the students are nervous *people.* However, if you think about the circumstances in which the behavior is occurring—the looming examination—you might take a third step and correct your initial impression by discounting, concluding that the nail biters may not be such nervous Nellies after all.

This third step seems so logical and sensible that one might wonder why people so often fall prey to the correspondence bias, even when situational causes are quite obvious. The answer lies in the fact that the first two steps—labeling the behavior and characterizing the person—are relatively easy, but the third step—using causal reasoning to correct the impression—is difficult (Gilbert, 1991). In fact, the first two steps may occur automatically, without any conscious effort. In contrast, causal reasoning usually takes time and effort and, as we all can testify, things that take more time and effort often do not get done at all.

Daniel Gilbert and his colleagues (1988) have demonstrated that extra effort is required to discount an initial impression. In their experiment, subjects watched the visual portion of a videotaped interview of an obviously nervous woman. The topics with which she was supposed to be dealing were displayed as subtitles on the TV screen. One group of subjects believed the interview centered on such highly personal, anxiety-provoking topics as "My sexual fantasies" or "My most embarrassing moment." Another group thought she was discussing innocuous matters like "My favorite vacation." After seeing the interview, all subjects were asked to rate how anxious a person the woman was in general. A correspondent inference would suggest that because the woman showed signs of nervousness, she must be a nervous type. However, the researchers reasoned, subjects who knew of a situational cause for her anxiety—the personal topics—should engage in discounting. And, indeed, their ratings of her general level of anxiety were lower than those of the subjects who thought the topics were mundane.

Two additional groups of subjects in the experiment went through exactly the same procedure with one exception: the researchers required these subjects to memorize the topics the woman was supposed to be discussing.

Subjects who could focus their attention on their judgments rated a woman as a less anxious person when they knew she was discussing sensitive topics (left). In contrast, subjects who were distracted by an additional task failed to discount (right). Those who believed the topics were sensitive assigned approximately the same ratings as those assigned by subjects who believed the topics were innocuous. (Based on Gilbert and others, 1988.)

Figure 3.9 Correcting impressions is hard work

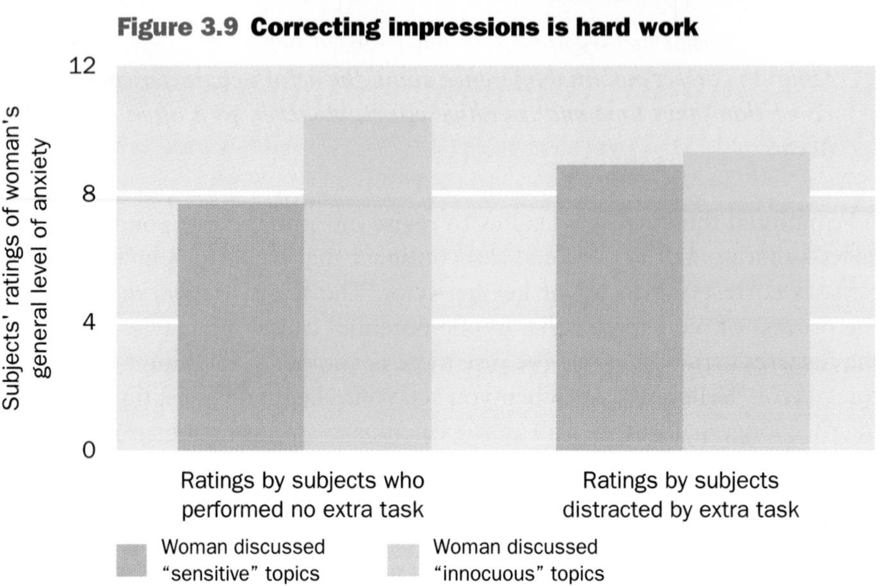

Gilbert and his colleagues predicted that this distracting activity would leave subjects with insufficient cognitive resources to engage in effortful discounting. As expected, the distracted subjects failed to discount their initial impressions. That is, they rated the woman as an anxious type even though they successfully memorized the anxiety-provoking topics (see Figure 3.9). Apparently, because the memory task absorbed some of their cognitive resources, they never went back to change their initial correspondent inferences—even though the role of situational factors, the anxiety-producing topics, was quite obvious. As this study shows, unless we are willing and able to process information systematically, the principle of conservatism applies: we stick with our first impressions.

All the typical demands of everyday interaction—trying to remember other people's names and faces, planning what we want to say, or working to create a good impression—also require considerable cognitive capacity. Thus, interaction itself may limit our ability to form accurate impressions of the people with whom we interact, leaving our impressions very much at the mercy of the behaviors we happen to see people perform first.

Putting It All Together: Forming Complex Impressions

One person's impression of another individual usually includes several characteristics. People may infer additional traits based on their knowledge or observations of the individual. The multiple components of an impression may become linked as people attempt to infer causal connections among them.

Our everyday encounters with other people are likely to reveal more about them than just a single characteristic. How, then, do we develop coherent overall impressions? Imagine being introduced to Paul at a city council meeting. As you chat, you find that in addition to his involvement in city politics, Paul sells salad dressing and popcorn, acts in movies, contributes to newspaper advertisements for political causes, writes to his congressional representative regularly, and drives race cars. How would you integrate all this information into an overall impression of Paul? We tend to form our overall impressions by inferring one trait from another and by integrating multiple characteristics.

Inferring One Trait from Another. We usually expect certain traits to go together. Knowing that an acquaintance is generous, for example, often leads us to expect that he will be warm as well. Our expectations about the relationships among traits are called *implicit personality theories* (Schneider, 1973). These theories guide the development and elaboration of complex impressions of others. For example, if you conclude that Paul is daring because he drives race cars, you might immediately conclude that he also is fearless or confident, because most people see these traits as closely related to the trait "daring" (Rosenberg and others, 1968). In general, people seem to think that most positive traits are related to each other and that negative traits form another distinct group. When people rely on their implicit personality theories, they may infer that a person has many positive qualities on the basis of a single good one, and they may expect a lot of negative characteristics if they learn about one bad quality. Learning that someone is pessimistic, most people would expect him or her to also be irritable, cold, vain, and finicky.

The general patterns of implicit personality theories are widely shared within a culture, but an individual may also make certain idiosyncratic trait inferences, depending on his or her own experiences (Smith & Zárate, 1992). For example, suppose you have a friend who is both exceptionally clumsy and quite reliable. If you meet someone else who is clumsy you might infer that this person is also reliable (Lewicki, 1985; Andersen & Cole, 1990). You would implicitly view these two traits as related because they are both included in your cognitive representation of your friend, even though they are not particularly close in most people's implicit personality theories.

Integrating Multiple Characteristics. As we observe or infer more and more characteristics of an individual, we try to organize what we know and infer causal relationships among our multiple pieces of knowledge. In this way, the overall impression becomes a complex and interlinked whole. Two types of processing contribute to this integration. The first forms clusters of similar behaviors; the second searches for causal links among behaviors and traits.

If you notice that several behaviors have similar trait implications, you may think about them together. This reflection, in turn, may result in the behaviors' becoming associated in your mind. For example, you may realize that Paul's behaviors of attending the council meeting, supporting the political ad campaign, and writing the letter to his congressional representative all reflect political activism. David Hamilton and his colleagues (Hamilton and others, 1980) suggest that behaviors that represent the same trait are linked into associated clusters in people's memory as people mentally *organize* their impressions of others. Supporting this idea, these researchers found that when people were asked to recall behaviors of a person they had earlier read about, they often recalled behaviors reflecting the same trait, one after the other.

The second type of processing that helps us make sense of a person's diverse behaviors and traits is creating causal links among them (Prentice, 1990; Park, 1986). You may know, for example, that tennis star John McEnroe wins a lot of matches and is quick-tempered. You might assume that McEnroe has a burning competitive drive that causes *both* his athletic successes *and* his outbursts of temper. You will then add this inference and these causal links to your impression of McEnroe, along with the behaviors and traits that led to them. These processes of inferring additional traits and linking multiple traits and behaviors into an integrated whole thus allow us to build impressions that are unified and coherent—not just lists of seemingly unrelated characteristics.

The Accuracy of Considered Impressions

Even considered impressions may not be completely accurate. When people devote extra thought to forming an impression, biases may still limit their accuracy, and the extra efforts may only confirm an existing positive or negative view. Unless people are aware of such biases in social perception, they are unlikely to try to correct them.

Just as going beyond a first impression to make attributions requires thought, so does integrating multiple behaviors and traits. What might motivate the expenditure of all this cognitive effort? And will the extra effort guarantee that considered impressions are unbiased, valid conceptions of what the person is really like?

Motivation to Be Accurate. Accuracy is one of the strongest motivations for working hard on forming an impression. Suppose you have a new acquaintance, Tom, and you want to bring him to a friend's party. You realize that your friend might hold you responsible if Tom turns out to be a bore. If it is important to be accurate because you will be held accountable, you will probably make an extra effort to gather information (Kruglanski & Freund, 1983). This effort sometimes allows us to overcome the effects of an initial expectation (Neuberg, 1989b).

Sometimes the motive for making an extra effort toward accurate perceptions of people is that we will have to work with them (Srull & Brand, 1983; Flink & Park, 1991). In one study, one group of subjects learned that they would have to cooperate on an upcoming task with a man who had been hospitalized for schizophrenia. Other subjects would meet the man but not work cooperatively with him (Neuberg & Fiske, 1987). The subjects then received an information sheet describing the man's personal background, hobbies, and so on. Those subjects who expected to cooperate with him spent more time reading about his personal characteristics and used that additional information in forming their impressions. In contrast, the other subjects spent less time reading about the man's attributes and formed an impression of the man that was based almost entirely on the schizophrenia diagnosis.

Suspicion about someone's motives may also cause us to think before leaping to a correspondent inference, as Steven Fein and his colleagues (1990) recently demonstrated. Students read a speech on a controversial issue that was supposedly the work of an applicant for a summer internship. One group of subjects was given two pieces of information about the applicant. They were told that the writer had freely chosen the side of the issue supported by the speech, and that the views given in the speech matched the position of the professor who would be evaluating the writer's application. Apparently inferring that the applicant might have been trying to curry favor, the subjects drew no inferences about the writer's personal position. In contrast, another group of subjects knew nothing about the professor's views but thought the writer had no choice in the position. This group fell prey to the correspondence bias—they inferred that the writer privately held the position espoused in the speech. Suspicion of ulterior motives evidently motivates people to think hard about the causes of behavior, which reduces their susceptibility to the correspondence bias.

Motivation to Form a Positive or Negative Impression. Extra efforts that people devote to processing information about others are not always in the service of accuracy. At times our hopes and desires guide our search for and our interpretation of facts (Kruglanski & Freund, 1983; Kunda, 1990). In one study, for example, subjects evaluated the trivia knowledge of a man whom they expected to be either their competitor or their partner in a contest. All subjects had watched him answer a few practice questions correctly. Subjects who expected to be the man's future partners rated his trivia ability higher than did those who expected to compete with him (Klein & Kunda, 1992). As this study shows, our approach is sometimes a lot like that of an attorney constructing the best possible case for a client. Rather than conducting an unbiased search, we hunt for evidence that supports our preferred conclusion. And because behavior is often ambiguous, we often easily find just what we are seeking. If the trivia player is to be our partner, we focus on how much knowledge his answers displayed; if we will have to compete with him, we instead emphasize how easy the practice questions were. When our search succeeds, we remain unaware of the biases in the search process and we blissfully forget that, had we searched with different goals, we might have unearthed a very different body of evidence.

Awareness of Bias. If we do become aware that our impressions may be inaccurate or biased, it may motivate us to devote extra effort to thinking about other people (Lombardi and others, 1987; Strack and others, 1989). Most of the time we remain blind to our biases, accepting the world we perceive at face value. We think that what we see is what actually is, because we are so good at constructing a coherent representation of reality. And we ordinarily get along well enough relying on our construction of reality (Fiske, 1993). But sometimes we compare notes with another person who sees things differently, and we realize that our views may be biased. Have you ever had a friend give a glowing description of someone you regarded as narrow-minded, hostile, and uncouth? Disagreement is often what motivates us to think hard to determine the truth—or at least to convince our-

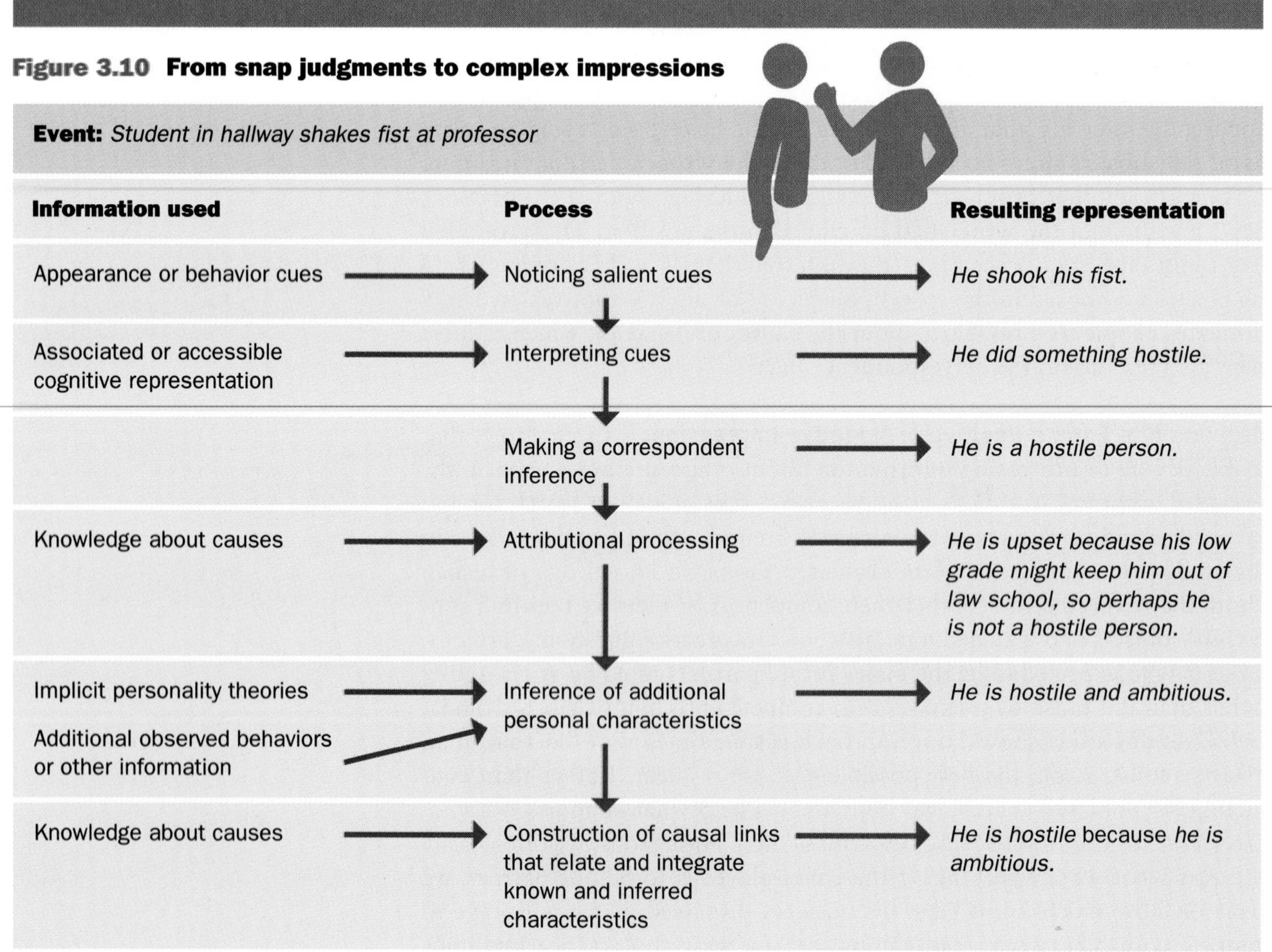

Event: Student in hallway shakes fist at professor
Information used
Process
Resulting representation
Appearance or behavior cues
Noticing salient cues
He shook his fist.
Associated or accessible cognitive representation
Interpreting cues
He did something hostile.
Making a correspondent inference
He is a hostile person.
Knowledge about causes
Attributional processing
He is upset because his low grade might keep him out of law school, so perhaps he is not a hostile person.
Implicit personality theories
Additional observed behaviors or other information
Inference of additional personal characteristics
He is hostile and ambitious.
Knowledge about causes
Construction of causal links that relate and integrate known and inferred characteristics
He is hostile because he is ambitious.

Figure 3.10 From snap judgments to complex impressions

selves that *other people's* interpretations and judgments, not our own, are biased. If disagreement never surfaces, however, we may feel quite satisfied with the impressions we form. We operate on the motto "If it ain't broke, don't fix it," and we generally do not even try to correct our impressions. Even when we do make the effort, a lack of time or cognitive resources may undermine our best intentions and leave us with considered impressions that are just as biased as our first impressions (Martin and others, 1990).

Figure 3.10 summarizes all the processes involved in impression formation, from noticing cues, to interpreting them, to inferring traits, to integrating multiple traits to form an overall impression. What is surprising is how little aware we usually are of all this processing. Our impressions of others seem to be formed immediately, rarely requiring much thought. But, in fact, this sense of immediacy actually reflects the unobtrusive efficiency with which our interpretive processes construct our picture of reality.

The Impact of Impressions: Using, Defending, and Changing Impressions

Once we have formed an impression of another person—whether it is a snap judgment or a thoughtful construction, and whether it is biased or accurate—we use it to guide our judgments and social interactions. Thus, once we have concluded that a popular singer is an exhibitionist or our next-door neighbor is a generous fellow, we trust that our interpretations represent objective reality. And even if these impressions are biased, they take on a reality as we act on them.

Impressions and Judgments

> *Once an impression is formed, it becomes a basis for judgments and behaviors. Sometimes judgments about others rest on simple, superficial processing; at other times people engage in extensive processing, attempting to put together the implications of all relevant information.*

Imagine that you need to find several housemates. As you interview a few candidates, you develop complex, well-articulated impressions of each of them. Whom should you pick? What aspects of your impressions will influence your decision? Sometimes only a single aspect of an impression really matters. If the only thing you care about is a compatible lifestyle (similar tastes in music, similar preferences for late hours), the happy-go-lucky night person may seem to be your best bet. If a shared interest in animal rights is your most important criterion, you certainly will not choose the woman in the fur coat. Often, however, more than one aspect of your impression seems important. You want someone with a compatible lifestyle and similar values, but you also want that person to be financially responsible—someone who will not stick you with bills for unpaid rent and telephone calls each month. How do we make judgments about others on the basis of our impressions of them?

Superficial Processing: Using a Single Attribute. Decisions based on a single accessible or salient characteristic require minimal effort and thought. You might pick the best-looking person who turns up to see your apartment or base your decision on some other equally obvious characteristic, ignoring all other considerations. Having to make a decision quickly or without full attention might force such **superficial processing** even if you would prefer a more systematic approach. Surprisingly, processes as simple as this underlie some remarkably important social judgments. For example, judges who set bail for criminal defendants have access to considerable information about the nature of the charges, the person's ties to the community, the history of drug use, and other similar facts. Yet one study found that judges disregard all but a single factor: the bail the prosecutor recommends (Ebbesen & Konecni, 1975).

Which Attribute Will Be Used? When people process quickly and superficially, they generally rely on their past judgments and inferences about an individual, rather than on the underlying evidence that led to those judgments in the first place (Carlston & Skowronski, 1986; Lingle & Ostrom, 1979). For example, on learning that your congressional representative takes conservative positions on several issues, you may form the judgment that she is a conservative. If a new issue, such as capital punishment, becomes a topic for political discussion, you probably will assume that she will take an equally conservative stand. If you make this assumption, you will be relying on your past judgment rather than on specific statements the representative may have made about capital punishment.

People tend to rely on their past judgments even if those judgments were made under circumstances that create bias. If a doting mother asked for an opinion of her rather ordinary son, most of us would find it difficult to describe him in anything except positive terms. Interestingly, giving such a slanted description can affect our later private impressions of the person (Sedikides, 1990; Higgins & McCann, 1984). Rather than thinking again about the evidence, people tend to draw on their previous description—forgetting or ignoring the fact that it was shaped by the demands of an audience.

People also prefer basing their judgments about others on what they know about the particular person, not on other potentially relevant information. While this preference may seem like simple common sense, it may shift the focus to nearly useless information and away from truly meaningful data. For instance, *base-rate* information—information about the frequency with which some characteristic or event occurs in a group of people—is often helpful in making judgments or predictions. Suppose you know that only 10 percent of all professors will let their students turn in pa-

superficial processing Relying on accessible information to make inferences or judgments, while expending little effort in processing.

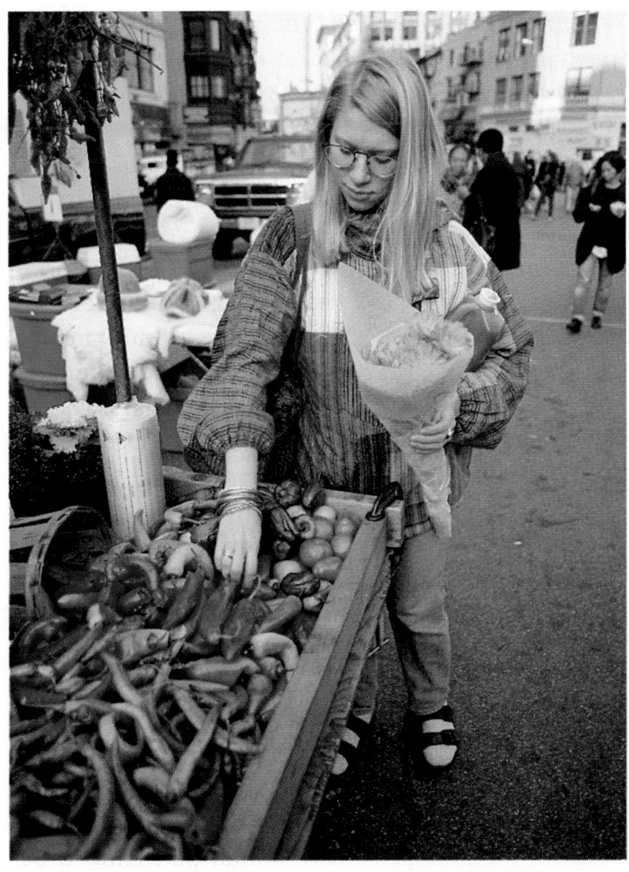

Is this young woman a vegetarian? Did you say, "Yes"? Are you aware that only a small percentage of the North American population are vegetarians? Research suggests that even if you knew that fact, it would not have influenced your estimate. Most of us fall prey to the base-rate fallacy: Our confidence in our theories about individuals has more impact on our judgments than information about what most other people are like.

pers after the due date. If you are asked to guess whether an unknown professor will accept overdue papers, you are likely to say the chance is 10 percent—appropriately using the base rate. However, if you know almost *anything* about the professor, such as the fact that he smiles pleasantly in class, you may confidently and incorrectly leap to the conclusion that the professor would be lenient about due dates. Our confidence in shaky theories about individual people, such as the theory linking a nice smile to a relaxed approach to deadlines, can keep us from appreciating the applicability of useful general information about groups of people (Kahneman & Tversky, 1973).

Only when people are powerfully reminded of the relevance of base-rate information do they use it appropriately in making judgments. For instance, base-rate information that suggests a causal explanation may be appreciated. If you were told that only 40 percent of students in one of your courses will pass the final exam, you would probably use that information in predicting whether an individual student would pass. In this context the base rate strongly suggests a causal interpretation: the exam is extremely difficult (Ginossar & Trope, 1987).

Extensive Processing: Integrating Multiple Factors. When we apply for jobs or loans, we all hope that those evaluating the application will process it with conscientiousness and depth, taking account of more than one of our characteristics. As noted earlier, when people know their decisions matter and when accuracy is extremely important to them, they often do carry out **systematic processing,** effortfully considering a wide range of relevant information (Neuberg & Fiske, 1987; Neuberg, 1989b).

One way of combining multiple factors is termed the *algebraic* approach. It is similar to the way an "ideal" consumer decides on an appliance or an automobile: examining the *Consumer Reports* table of product advantages and disadvantages and weighting each feature according to its importance for the particular decision (Anderson, 1981). For example, if you are considering someone as a potential date, you might assess the person in terms of a variety of individual qualities, some similar and some different from those you would consider for a potential study partner.

Alternatively, people may integrate multiple items of information in a less mechanical way. Instead of evaluating each attribute independently, people may attempt to fit the information together into a meaningful whole. In this integration process, one item may subtly change the meaning of others (Asch, 1946; Asch & Zukier, 1984). For example, suppose one person is described as intelligent and cold, and another as intelligent and warm. The very meaning of *intelligent* seems to differ in these two descriptions—connoting something like "calculating" or "sly" when combined with *cold,* but taking on the meaning of "wise" in the context of *warm*. When people use this *configural* approach to evaluate a person's multiple attributes, their overall judgment may depend on the particular way they combine the attributes. As mentioned earlier in this chapter, integrating multiple characteristics often involves causal reasoning, as when we infer that coldness leads people to use their intelligence in self-centered ways, making them seem calculating.

Defending Impressions

> *Impressions tend to resist change, partly because an initial impression can alter the interpretation of later information. As a result, impressions may even survive the discrediting of the information on which they were based. Impressions shape overt interaction as well as judgments. They often lead people to seek consistent information or even to elicit confirming actions from others.*

Once formed, our impressions of others can influence both our private judgments about those individuals and our interactions with them. As we obtain further information, we may slant our interpretations to maintain our impressions unchanged. And as we treat people in ways that reflect our existing impressions and expectations, we may produce in them the very behavior we expect to see. The principle of conservatism can be seen clearly here: once formed, our beliefs about other people tend to maintain themselves.

systematic processing Giving thorough, effortful consideration to a wide range of information relevant to a judgment.

Impressions Shape Interpretations. Suppose you are watching the quiz show *Jeopardy*. One contestant gives quick correct answers early in the show but cools off as the questions continue. The other contestant starts out with a series of wrong answers and then improves. By the first commercial break, they have an equal number of right and wrong answers. Which contestant seems more intelligent to you? If you are like most people, you will give the edge to the one who started strongly (Jones and others, 1968). Our initial impressions can set up an expectation that shapes our interpretations of later information—producing what is called a *primacy effect* (Asch, 1946). The primacy effect is one version of the principle of conservatism: initial impressions are slow to change and prone to perpetuate themselves.

In an illustration of the lasting effects of initial impressions, Bernadette Park (1986) arranged for small groups of strangers to meet together repeatedly over a seven-week period. After the first meeting, and periodically after that, participants wrote descriptions of one another. Week after week, first impressions dominated these profiles. The characteristics noted after the very first meeting turned up repeatedly, even though the first impressions were based on little information. Apparently initial impressions biased the subjects' interpretations of later behavior. Putting your best foot forward right from the start is much easier than trying to change opinions later.

Impressions Resist Rebuttal. Because our impressions can shape the interpretation of later information, their effects can persist even if the initial impression is discovered to be false. This distortion is called the *perseverance bias* (Lord and others, 1984). To investigate this bias, Lee Ross and his colleagues (1975) arranged for female students to observe others performing a "decision-making" task. Some observers received false feedback that made it appear that the decision maker performed quite well, getting 24 of 25 items correct. Others learned that the decision maker performed poorly,

First impressions are lasting impressions Massachusetts Senator Edward Kennedy's political connection and insider experience would seem to make him a likely candidate for U.S. president. But his chances of success may have been limited by lingering doubts about his behavior more than 20 years ago, when he left the scene of an accident in which a passenger was killed.

with only 10 correct items. The experimenter then revealed that the feedback had been randomly determined and had no relation to the decision maker's actual performance. However, even after the observers learned of this deception, their ratings of the decision maker's ability and their predictions of future performance still showed the effects of the now-discredited feedback. For example, observers who initially thought a decision maker had succeeded predicted that she would get an average of 19 items correct on a future trial; conversely, observers who initially saw failure predicted only 14.5 for the same decision maker. As this experiment shows, once beliefs have influenced our interpretation of other information, it is difficult to undo their effects completely if we later learn the beliefs are false (Gilbert & Osborne, 1989; Gilbert and others, 1990). No wonder that it is notoriously difficult to counteract rumors after they get started (Rosnow & Fine, 1976).

The most effective way to reduce or eliminate the perseverance bias is to explicitly consider the opposite possibility (Lord and others, 1984). Learning that the supposed 24 of 25 score was false had little effect on the observers in Ross's study. However, considering the possibility that the individual might have actually performed poorly could have reduced the bias.

Perseverance in the Courtroom. When legally inadmissible evidence is introduced in courtroom proceedings, it can be stricken from the official trial record. The judge may even instruct jurors to disregard it. Unfortunately, jurors cannot wipe the information from their minds as easily as the court reporter can expunge the record. In fact, research has found that inadmissible evidence does influence jurors' deliberations and verdicts (Thompson and others, 1981). The same is true of discredited evidence. In one mock-trial study, for example, one group of subjects saw minimal evidence against the defendant, and only 18 percent voted for conviction. A second group saw the same evidence plus an eyewitness identification of the defendant; in that group, 72 percent voted for conviction. A third group received all this information but then learned that the eyewitness was legally blind and was not wearing his glasses at the time he claimed to have seen the defendant. This discrediting information had virtually no impact, however. In the third group the conviction rate decreased only to 68 percent (Loftus, 1974). The perseverance bias means that, as in this example, information may have effects that persist even after the information is found to be false.

Selectively Seeking Impression-Consistent Behavior. Consider the fact that most of us are somewhat inconsistent in our behaviors—for instance, we may act shy at some times and outgoing at others. What would happen if someone expected you to be outgoing and attempted to test that belief? He or she might ask you leading questions about occasions when you were outgoing—for example, when you were the center of attention at a large party or particularly enjoyed a social gathering (Snyder & Swann, 1978). As you recounted such instances, the questioner's initial hypothesis would seem to be confirmed. But if the questions had focused on the times you felt shy and avoided other people, you would have been able to report on those equally well. Any hypothesis about another person could probably be confirmed if tested in this way.

Actually, people do not always ask biased or leading questions to test their beliefs about others. Given a choice, they often prefer questions that are *diagnostic*—questions whose answers will provide information about the truth or falsity of the hypothesis (Trope and others, 1984). For example, a diagnostic question to assess whether someone is outgoing could take the following form: "Would you rather attend a large party or have a quiet get-together with one or two close friends?" Unlike the earlier example, this question would not necessarily produce a false confirmation of an initial hypothesis. However, coming up with properly diagnostic questions is often difficult unless the questioner is aware of alternatives to the given hypothesis (Ginossar & Trope, 1987; Higgins & Bargh, 1987). As we have already seen, a strategy of "considering the opposite"—thinking about the possibility that the person might be quiet and retiring rather than outgoing—can reduce biases (Trope & Mackie, 1987).

Creating Impression-Consistent Behavior: The Self-Fulfilling Prophecy. Suppose you believe, for whatever reason, that people from the southern United States tend to be gracious and friendly. When you meet a Southerner, you will probably act warmly, and the person will naturally reciprocate (Snyder and others, 1977). You will probably end up liking the person, just as you thought you would. Of course, the outcome might be quite different if your initial expectation was that Southerners are hostile and unfriendly. As this example demonstrates, we do more than just ask other people about their behaviors. Our initial impressions may actually *create* corresponding behaviors. When a person's expectation about another causes that person to act in ways that confirm the expectation, the process is called a **self-fulfilling prophecy** (Merton, 1948; Darley & Fazio, 1980). Figure 3.11 portrays an example of this process.

self-fulfilling prophecy The process by which one person's expectations about another become reality by eliciting behaviors that confirm the expectations.

Figure 3.11 Expectations create confirmation: The self-fulfilling prophecy Once we have formed an impression of another person, our expectations often lead us to behave in ways that elicit expectation-confirming behaviors.

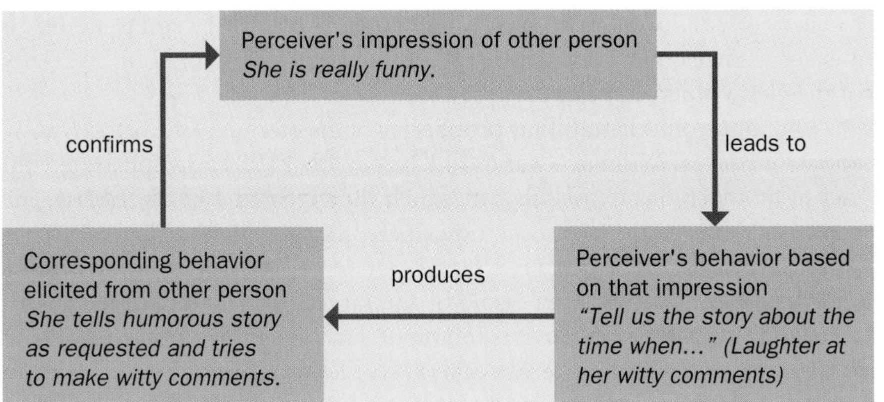

Of course, if people were aware of their influence on others, they might try to discount that influence to improve the accuracy of their impressions. Unfortunately, however, people sometimes fail to recognize even their clear and overt influences on others. To demonstrate this point, researchers set up an interview situation in which interviewers and interviewees read questions and answers from fixed scripts (Gilbert & Jones, 1986). The questions concerned politics; the prepared answers reflected a conservative or liberal viewpoint. The interviewer read each question and then pushed a "Liberal" or "Conservative" button, as specified by the script, to signal the answer the interviewee should read. Of course, by pushing the buttons, the interviewers themselves controlled the answers they heard. But did they recognize their own influence? No. They rated the interviewees as conservative when most of their answers were conservative, and liberal when most of the answers were liberal. It is surprisingly difficult for people to recognize the effects of their own actions on others, and without awareness we cannot correct our impressions to improve their validity.

Self-Fulfilling Prophecy in the Classroom. Self-fulfilling prophecies can operate anywhere—at home, on the job, and in the classroom. In studies pioneered by Robert Rosenthal and his colleagues, researchers gave schoolteachers the names of some pupils in their classes who were expected to "bloom" intellectually over the next few months (Rosenthal & Jacobson, 1968; Rosenthal, 1985). Actually, the students had been selected at random. Later in the school year all the students were tested. Multiple studies using this technique have shown that children identified as "bloomers" tend to perform better than their classmates—on objective tests, not just in the teachers' own estimation. The teachers' high expectations for these children are somehow translated into actual achievement over the course of a few months. The reason may be that teachers give students more attention and more challenging assignments when they expect them to perform at a high level (Cooper & Good, 1983). These types of teacher behaviors improve students' performance.

Limits on the Self-Fulfilling Prophecy. How vulnerable are we to the effects of other people's expectations, particularly those of people such as teachers or employers, who have some power over us? To some extent, the answer to that question is determined by our self-views and our awareness of the views others have of us.

One limit on self-fulfilling prophecies is the strength of our own views about ourselves. William Swann and Robin Ely (1984) demonstrated this fact in an ingenious experiment in which they created a conflict between a perceiver's expectations and the other person's own views. The researchers paired previously unacquainted female students, selecting one as a target and the other as a perceiver. Some of the targets were self-described introverts and others were extroverts. Some of each group had great confidence in their self-knowledge, whereas others were less confident. The perceiver in each pair was led to have the opposite expectation about the target—either with great confidence or with some tentativeness. Perceivers interviewed the targets three times, and then both women's impressions were assessed. Whose views exerted the most force? Most of the time, those of the target: perceivers usually changed their original impression to match the target's self-views. The effects of the self-fulfilling prophecy emerged only when the target initially had been uncertain about her self-views and the perceiver confidently believed the reverse. In such cases, the self-fulfilling prophecy influenced both the target's overt behavior and her self-views.

The second condition under which self-fulfilling prophecies are foiled is when targets are aware of the perceivers' expectations. If you met someone who expected you to be uncertain and naive, would you make a special effort to show your independence and sophistication? Many people would react just this way. Indeed, research shows that people who are aware of others' unfavorable expectations about them often succeed in disconfirming those expectations (Hilton & Darley, 1985).

Thus, the self-fulfilling prophecy particularly affects people who lack confidence in their own self-concepts or who are unaware of others' beliefs about them. Like the schoolchildren in Rosenthal's studies, these people are vulnerable to shaping by others' expectations. However, our confidence in our own self-views and our knowledge of other people's views can act as a shield, protecting us from the impact of others' expectations.

Dealing with Inconsistent Information

People sometimes encounter information that is clearly inconsistent with an impression. They may attempt to explain it away in various ways, or they may take it into account and assume that the other person has changed. Most of the time, however, people assume that others' personal characteristics are stable and enduring.

Consider the many mental tricks you may use to sustain your impression of another person. Believing that Albert is intelligent, you notice only his ground-breaking discoveries in science. When his behavior is ambiguous, you interpret it as being smart rather than stupid. Sometimes you seek out evidence of his intelligence, questioning him about his latest ideas on relativity rather than about the times he forgot where he parked his car. You may even create the opportunity for Albert to be smart by giving him his own lab, a supply of freshly sharpened pencils, a supercomputer, and all the coffee he can drink. Then, one day, Albert does something so remarkably stupid—so unambiguously inconsistent with your belief—that there can be no denying it. How would you handle this conflict? You could explain away this inconsistency, defending your original impression to the death. Or you could take account of the information in ways that make your impression of Albert more accurate.

Reconciling Inconsistencies. When we encounter inconsistent and contradictory information about someone, it challenges our sense of what that person is like. How would you react, for example, if one friend told you that a classmate is kind, and another friend said that the same person is hostile? When people in one study were presented with such potentially contradictory trait descriptions and asked to describe their impressions in their own words, they creatively integrated the seemingly inconsistent traits (Asch & Zukier, 1984). They decided, for example, that the person was hostile to most people but kind to family members, or that the person masked a hostile disposition with an appearance of kindness.

When people make the effort to reconcile inconsistent and contradictory information, it has several effects on cognitive processing and memory.

1. *People spend more time thinking about unexpected behaviors than about expected ones.* For example, if you read that your liberal state senator is fighting for a reduction in the minimum wage for young workers, you might pay extra attention, although you might quickly pass over more expected news of his support of several liberal causes (Belmore & Hubbard, 1987).

2. *People try to explain unexpected behaviors—to make sense of them.* Thus, you might begin to wonder *why* the senator supports reducing the minimum wage. Perhaps you will decide that he supports this measure because it will provide more jobs for the poor and disadvantaged, whose cause he generally favors. As we noted earlier, people are more likely to make causal attributions about unexpected events than about events that are normal and expected (Hastie, 1984).

3. *Extra processing improves people's ability to recall inconsistent behaviors.* The special attributional processing that we give to inconsistent behaviors may help us remember them better than the behaviors consistent with our expectations (Hastie & Kumar, 1979; Srull, 1981). In fact, any behaviors that people explain can be better recalled at a later time, compared with behaviors that people notice but do not explain (Hastie, 1984). This is true whether the behaviors are consistent or inconsistent with the person's expectations.

Reconciling inconsistent information takes as much cognitive effort as performing other types of attributional processing. People are likely to make this effort only under two conditions: they must be motivated to form or maintain a coherent impression, and they must have adequate time and processing resources to devote to the task (Srull and others, 1985). This means that reconciliation may not occur if someone is overwhelmed by time pressure or highly complex information about many people or many traits (Wyer and others, 1990; Hamilton and others, 1989).

Even when people make an effort at reconciliation, their impressions of others do not always change. Instead, the processing may be directed at explaining away the inconsistency. If unexpected behaviors can be attributed to situational factors, the initial impression can be maintained intact (Crocker and others, 1983). Thus, a battered woman might defend her impression that her abusive partner is basically a good person by attributing his occasional violence to external factors, such as the effects of alcohol or, sadly, even some behavior of her own.

Altering Impressions: Is Fundamental Change Possible? By now, you may be pretty pessimistic about the possibility of ever changing an established impression. Because so many processes tend to maintain our views, it is not surprising that even long weeks of interaction can leave people's initial impressions largely intact (Kenny, 1991; Park, 1986). Is fundamental change in impressions ever possible? Linda Silka's (1989) research offers some reason for optimism. Silka's subjects read the life history of a young woman who appeared, at least on the surface, to change greatly. Lany Tyler was a high school cheerleader who, although she initially failed to win admission to college, eventually obtained a Ph.D. and became a Princeton University professor of history. Subjects asked to write about how Lany had changed had no trouble identifying examples, noting that she changed "from the stereotypical 'social butterfly' to an intellectually geared individual" (p. 126). This finding suggests that when people are actively *looking* for change in an individual, they are able to perceive it. Indeed, faced with inconsistent information for which no situational explanations are obvious, people often make sense of the behaviors by assuming that the person's beliefs, attitudes, motivation, or ability has changed (Silka, 1989; Allison and others, 1993).

Other results of Silka's study are more sobering, however. Although subjects looking for change could find it, subjects told to search for stability and sameness in Lany's life had no trouble finding that either. One subject wrote, "A cheerleader and an Ivy League professor are two very different but both prestigious positions. I think this reveals Lany's need to feel as if she has achieved and even over time her need to be held in esteem by others never changed" (p. 125). Thus, we may end up seeing change only when the change is extreme, dramatic, and unambiguous, or when we specifically *expect* to find change. Expectations have a powerful impact on our impressions of others—whether we expect to see stability (as we usually do) or change.

Concluding Comments

As you reflect on the evidence presented in this chapter, you may conclude that biases in impressions are pretty hard to overcome. Most of the time that is true. We get a lot of mileage out of the simple rule of thumb that behavior reflects personality. Yet we also know that human nature is more complicated than this rule would indicate. When accuracy is of the utmost importance, we attend fully, process carefully, and are rewarded with more accurate impressions of other people. But why is accurate person perception so likely to be the exception rather than the rule in our daily life? Why are simple rules of thumb, with all their possibilities of bias, usually more than adequate for our needs?

First, in many cases, our needs for accuracy in day-to-day person perception are modest. Correspondent inferences work perfectly well if our encounters with people are limited to particular situations or roles. For example, your assumption that the office bookkeeper is a quiet and restrained person on the basis of his office demeanor will not create problems if the office is the only place the two of you interact—though you might be surprised to see how he acts at a wild party. We can ignore people's specific individual qualities and still interact successfully with them if their behaviors are governed largely by the power of social situations and roles.

Second, people's behavior in particular situations often accurately reflects their personalities because they often choose the situations they are in. Suppose you watch someone telling jokes at a comedy try-out. Technically, it might be correct that her provocative, lively, and funny behaviors are called for by this situation. But since the would-be comedian *chose* the situation, it is probably reasonable to assume that she is a lively, funny person. Thus, a correspondent inference works just fine. If you want to find a Deadhead, you do not need to interpret subtle cues—just go to a Grateful Dead concert and look around.

Third, correspondent inferences are often accurate because other people offer us accurate cues to their true nature, at least as they themselves perceive it. As you will see in the next chapter, being perceived accurately by others is rewarding, and being misperceived is frustrating and uncomfortable. So the lover of baroque music might wear a J. S. Bach T-shirt to let us know. Even if the cues a new acquaintance offers do not ring quite true, it is often wise to go along for the ride, accepting rather than challenging the person. Certainly the interaction will go more smoothly if we save the other's face.

Thus, people's tendency to take others' behaviors or observable cues at face value can grease the wheels of social interaction, and this tendency usually lets us get along quite well. Still, going beyond first impressions to seek greater accuracy in person perception is sometimes important. In choosing a housemate, we want to predict a variety of compatible behaviors accurately on the basis of a few items of background information and a brief conversation. In serving on a jury, we want to decide whether the defendant or the accuser is telling the truth.

In the final analysis, both accurate and inaccurate impressions flow from the same underlying *processes* that people use as they attempt to understand others. Therefore, it is these processes that social psychologists seek to understand. They include tapping our stored knowledge to make quick inferences about observed behaviors, thinking about the causes of behaviors or other events, integrating multiple items of information into a single judgment, and reconciling inconsistencies. People use these basic processes not only to understand other people, but also to understand other social objects. In the chapters that follow we will discuss how we perceive and interpret ourselves (Chapter 4), our own and other social groups (Chapter 5), consumer products and social issues (Chapter 7), our loved ones (Chapter 11), even our enemies (Chapter 14). Nothing in the nature of these processes necessarily leads to either accurate or inaccurate judgments. Accuracy depends more on the circumstances in which the processes are applied: the amount of useful information available, the applicability of the person's knowledge, the amount of effort the person is willing and able to put in, and whether the goal is to be accurate or to form a particular impression. Our perceptions of *all* social objects—including other people—are not determined solely by their observable characteristics. Instead, they also reflect our own individuality and uniqueness as perceivers: our motives and biases, our cognitive limitations, and the content and accessibility of our pre-existing knowledge.

Summary

Forming First Impressions: Cues, Interpretations, and Inferences. Perceptions of other people begin with visible cues, including physical appearance, nonverbal communication, and overt behavior. Cues that are **salient**—that stand out and attract attention in their context—are particularly influential.

These cues have no meaning in themselves, but are interpreted in the light of existing knowledge or **cognitive representations** about people, behaviors, traits, and social situations. A representation that is **associated** with the cue itself or is **accessible** and easy to bring to mind is most likely to be used in interpreting cues. Accessibility can stem from the person's expectations, motives, moods, the situational context, or from recent or frequent activation of the representation.

People often make **correspondent inferences**, assuming that others have inner qualities that correspond to their observed behaviors. In fact, people often make correspondent inferences even when situational causes actually account for behaviors, a pattern termed the **correspondence bias**.

Chapter 3 Themes

Construction of Reality
Our impressions of others are constructions based on our own selection and interpretation of cues.

Pervasive Social Influences
General knowledge shaped by our culture and past experiences enters into our impressions of others.

Striving for Mastery
Accurate understanding of others helps us deal successfully with them.

Conservatism
Once formed, an impression of another person tends to perpetuate itself by affecting our interpretations and our interactions.

Accessibility
The most salient cues and our most accessible knowledge contribute the most to our impressions.

Superficiality Versus Depth
Sometimes we are content with first impressions and snap judgments, but sometimes we strive to understand others more deeply.

Beyond First Impressions: Attribution and Integration. To go beyond a first impression, people must engage in more extensive thought, particularly to make **causal attributions** for behavior. People usually consider potential causes that are associated with the behavior, generally accessible, salient in context, or suggested by the pattern of available information.

When external factors appear to have caused behavior, people may attempt to correct their initial correspondent inference about the actor's characteristics. This correction takes time and cognitive effort, however, so it often does not occur.

An impression of another person usually includes several characteristics. People may infer additional traits based on their knowledge or observations of the individual. The multiple components of an impression may become linked as people attempt to infer causal connections among them.

Even considered impressions may not be completely accurate. When people devote extra thought to forming an impression, biases may still limit their accuracy, and the extra efforts may only confirm an existing positive or negative view. Unless people are aware of such biases in social perception, they are unlikely to try to correct them.

The Impact of Impressions: Using, Defending, and Changing Impressions. Once an impression is formed, it becomes a basis for judgments and behaviors. Sometimes judgments about others rest on simple, **superficial processing**; at other times, people engage in **systematic processing**, attempting to put together the implications of all relevant information.

Impressions tend to resist change, partly because an initial impression can alter the interpretation of later information. As a result, impressions may survive even the discrediting of the information on which they were based. Impressions shape overt interaction as well as judgments. They often lead people to seek consistent information or even to elicit confirming actions from others, creating a **self-fulfilling prophecy**.

Still, sometimes people encounter information that is clearly inconsistent with an impression. They may attempt to explain it away in various ways, or they may take it into account and assume that the other person has changed. Most of the time, however, people assume that others' personal characteristics are stable and enduring.

This chart on the right is a graphical overview of the main concepts in this chapter and their interrelations. For advice on how to use this overview to help you review and understand this text, turn back to the Preface.

Chapter 3 Overview

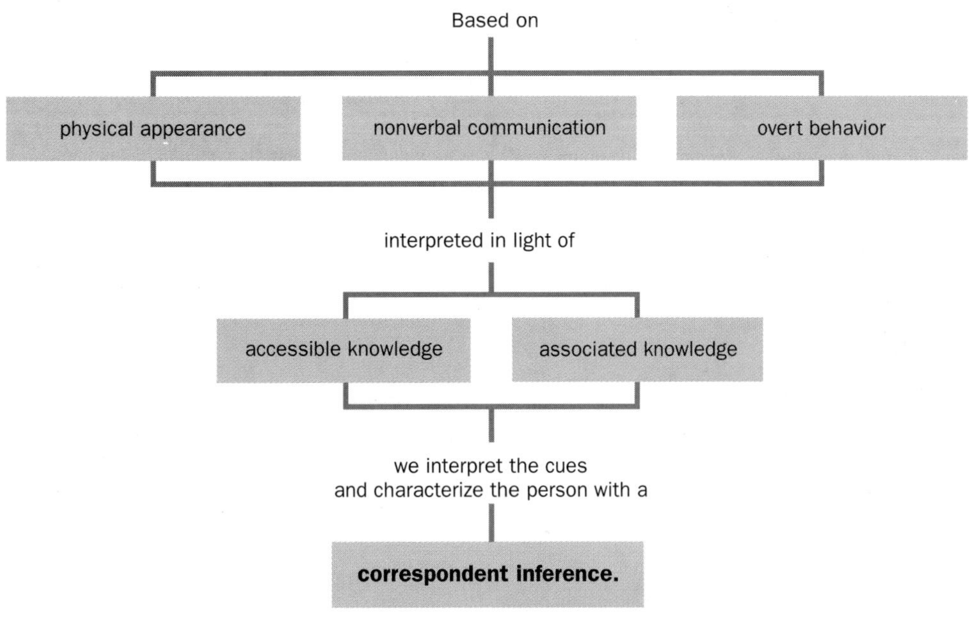

Based on
physical appearance
nonverbal communication
overt behavior
interpreted in light of
accessible knowledge
associated knowledge
we interpret the cues
and characterize the person with a
correspondent inference.

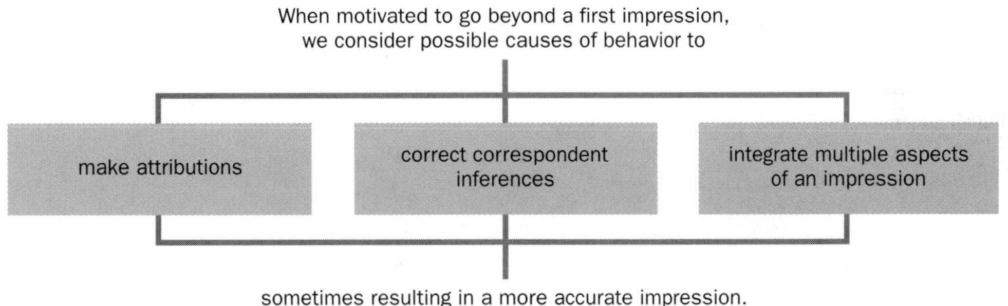

When motivated to go beyond a first impression,
we consider possible causes of behavior to
make attributions
correct correspondent inferences
integrate multiple aspects of an impression
sometimes resulting in a more accurate impression.

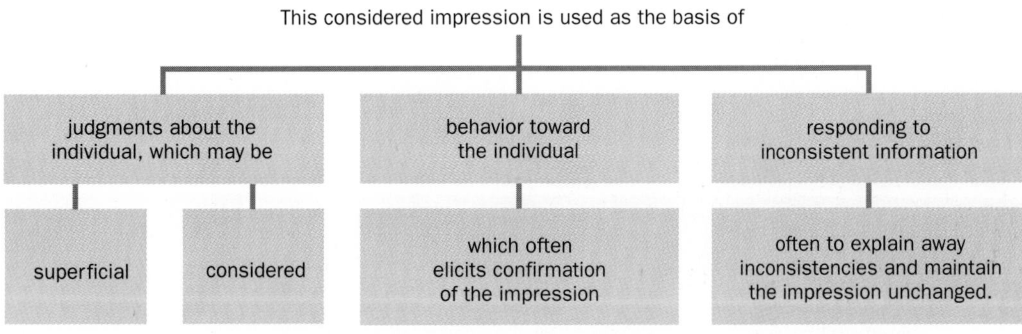

This considered impression is used as the basis of
judgments about the individual, which may be
behavior toward the individual
responding to inconsistent information
superficial
considered
which often elicits confirmation of the impression
often to explain away inconsistencies and maintain the impression unchanged.

4

The Self

Stroll past the popular psychology shelves in any bookstore, and you will be encouraged to *Celebrate Your Self, Be Your Best, Know Yourself,* and *Develop Your Potential.* You will be offered advice on *Making Peace with Yourself, Taking Control,* and *How to Raise Your Self-Esteem.* And you will find that you should be *Honoring the Self, Asserting Yourself, Healing Yourself,* and even *Talking to Yourself.* As these titles indicate, one of the most important life tasks you face is understanding who *you* are, discovering that special mix of qualities that, like your fingerprints, distinguishes you from others and makes you unique. What you think of yourself, how you feel about yourself, and the ways you choose to express yourself influence virtually all aspects of your life. In this chapter we examine the processes that help us not only to acquire accurate self-knowledge but also to protect and enhance that image we label "self."

What is this "self" anyway? Since ancient times philosophers have admonished, "Know thyself," for *the self is an object of knowledge.* You may be confident that you are shy or honest or intelligent or attractive. You may feel that, all things considered, you are a pretty decent human being. But how did you come to know these things about yourself? The first part of this chapter looks at the way you, we, and all other people form their impression of the self, how we come to know what we are like, and how we feel about ourselves. As you will see, the way we form impressions of the self is very similar to the way we perceive other people. However, we bring more biases to the process of self-perception. For most of us, the self-portraits we paint are colored by powerful motivational pressures to think well of ourselves.

The self has a second aspect as well: once established, *the self directs our thoughts, feelings, and behaviors.* Knowing ourselves to be honest, we welcome evidence that confirms our view and we resist information that contradicts it. Goals that are important to the self direct emotional responses to events. Valued accomplishments arouse pride and joy, while events that threaten or thwart us evoke the prick of fear or the sting of anger. And when we choose to coach Little League on the weekends or volunteer to lead tours through the art museum, our sense of self guides our behavior as we try to

Constructing the self The young man shown at the left has quite literally created an image of himself. Although our attempts are not usually this concrete, we are constantly engaged in efforts to construct an understanding of who we are and what we are like.

show others the kind of person we are. In the second section of the chapter we see the self in action, directing our interpretations and interactions with the social world.

In the final section of this chapter we consider what happens when our sense of self is challenged—when what happens is not what we planned, hoped for, or expected. Could you continue to think of yourself as intelligent if you received a failing grade in a major course? Will juggling a career and parenthood, fighting rush-hour traffic, or struggling to make ends meet be too much for you? How do people cope with sudden illness, the loss of a job, a house full of children becoming an empty nest? The last part of the chapter examines our attempts to cope with stresses, failures, and inconsistencies. As you will see, the way we defend ourselves against threats and disappointments influences not only our emotional well-being but also our physical health. In orchestrating our thoughts, feelings, and behaviors, in coordinating the person we see from the inside with the person others see from the outside, our sense of self becomes a special glue that holds body and soul together.

Constructing the Self-Concept: What We Know About Ourselves

A coherent self-impression has two components: the self-concept, what we know about ourselves, and self-esteem, how we feel about ourselves. Although these parts of our self seem as familiar and comfortable as a favorite pair of jeans, both in fact are constantly developing and changing as our experiences, life circumstances, and social surroundings change. No matter how well you believe you know yourself, you may be unable to predict your own response to a novel event, such as losing a job, or to a new role, like becoming a parent. Indeed, if complete self-understanding was easily attained, philosophers would not have to advise us to seek the self, therapists would not spend hours treating people, and bookstore self-help shelves would not be nearly so well stocked.

Sources of Self-Knowledge

People construct self-knowledge in much the same way that they form impressions of others—using similar types of information and similar interpretive processes. People often infer their own characteristics from their observed behaviors. They also use thoughts and feelings and other people's reactions to form opinions about themselves. Finally, people compare themselves to others to learn what characteristics make them unique.

self-concept The totality of an individual's knowledge about his or her personal qualities.

The **self-concept** is the sum of an individual's beliefs about his or her personal qualities. Having a self-concept requires having a self, of course, and research suggests that human babies start to recognize their own image in a mirror around the age of two (Lewis & Brooks-Gunn, 1979). But the development of a self-concept takes much longer. We piece together self-knowledge over time from our interpretations of many different kinds of information.

Drawing Inferences from Behavior. "How do I know what I think until I see what I say?" asked British author E. M. Forster. His tongue-in-cheek comment captures an important source of self-knowledge and the key idea of Darryl Bem's (1967) **self-perception theory**. At least when other sources of information are insufficient, we can learn things about ourselves by observing our own behavior. When we find ourselves yelling at the parking attendant and realize we are angry, or contemplate our church attendance and conclude we are religious, or take part in a community theater production and decide we are extroverted, self-perception processes are at work (Rhodewalt & Agustdottir, 1986; Salancik & Conway, 1975).

Even imagined behaviors can provide the raw materials for self-perception processes. Imagine for a moment doing various things to help preserve the environment—perhaps recycling aluminum cans or car pooling twice weekly. Try to picture yourself actually doing something like this. Do you now see yourself as a more environmentally aware person? Research suggests that imagining these behaviors might lead you to such a conclusion (Anderson & Godfrey, 1987). Of course, if you had been asked to imagine yourself taking thirty-minute showers or keeping the thermostat at eighty degrees in winter, you might have come to the opposite conclusion about yourself.

What explains these findings? Thinking about actual or imagined behavior increases the accessibility of related personal characteristics. Thus, you might imagine solving a puzzle and then reflect on your good spatial ability, recalling that you loved to play with puzzles as a child. As thoughts like these come to mind, they become the basis for a self-inference: "I am very good at solving puzzles." Interestingly, seeing the self as possessing relevant traits may improve not only your confidence, persistence, and effort but also your actual performance on the task (Campbell & Fairey, 1985).

Imagined Performances in Sports Training. Athletes and sports psychologists have put such findings to work in training routines that incorporate imagery. Visualization makes thoughts and feelings related to successful performance more accessible, which can improve actual performance (Murphy, 1990). For example, in one study runners were divided into two groups. One group was given strength training on an exercise bicycle; the other was not. Some members of each group were also instructed to imagine themselves sprint-racing (Van Gyn and others, 1990). Of course, sweating on the exercise cycles improved all the runners' performances, but those who also imagined themselves sprinting later obtained better race times

self-perception theory The theory that we make inferences about our personal characteristics on the basis of our overt behaviors when internal cues are weak or ambiguous.

Imagining can make it so As opera singer Marilyn Horne works through her vocal scores, she prepares with her mind as well as her body. And with good reason. Social psychological research has shown that imagining a performance can contribute to superior achievements.

than those who did not. In another study, imagining successful performances improved students' pistol-shooting scores (Hall & Hardy, 1991). As the Australian movie *Gallipoli* so vividly portrayed, however, imagining can affect performance off the playing field as well. In the film an aspiring sprinter follows his grandfather's advice as he prepares to compete. Before every race, the young man stares down the track, imagining his performance: "My legs are springs, steel springs. What are they going to do? They'll hurl me down the track. How fast can you run? As fast as a leopard! How fast are you going to run? As fast as a leopard!" Tragically, this same imagery later gives the young soldier the courage to charge in the face of enemy fire on the battlefields of Gallipoli.

Self-Perception of Motivation. Of course, we do not make snap judgments about ourselves willy-nilly. In fact, self-perception theory assumes that we draw inferences from our behavior only when internal cues are weak or ambiguous and when there are no compelling situational pressures present. So in the absence of strong internal feelings and compelling external pressures, people tend to view themselves as having qualities consistent with their past or present behavior (Chaiken & Baldwin, 1981; Fazio and others, 1981). However, if you had been having intense stomach pangs for several hours, you would not need to wolf down a sandwich to learn you were hungry. And it is unlikely that you would infer you were hungry because you observed yourself participating in an "Eat-athon" for charity.

In fact, people are most likely to draw inferences about themselves from behaviors that they see themselves as having freely chosen. Freely chosen behaviors are driven by *intrinsic motivation*—we are doing what we want to do rather than what we have to do. In contrast, when a behavior is performed as a means to some external end, it is governed by *extrinsic motivation,* and we often lose pleasure in performing it (Harackiewicz, 1979; Deci, 1971).

Ironically, then, providing external rewards often undermines intrinsic motivation, as Mark Lepper and his colleagues (1973) have demonstrated. Their subjects, three- to five-year-olds, were given an attractive new activity: drawing with colorful felt-tip markers. After drawing for six minutes, some children received a previously promised "Good Player" certificate, others unexpectedly received the same certificate, and still others received nothing. One to two weeks later, the markers were placed in the children's regular classroom, and the children were allowed to use them during their free time. The time each child spent playing with the markers was unobtrusively recorded as a measure of their intrinsic motivation.

The effect of the earlier rewards was clear. The children who had not been rewarded spent 16.7 percent of their free time drawing. The motivation of children who had received the unexpected reward also remained high: they drew for 18.1 percent of the time. In contrast, children who expected and received an award for playing with the markers used them for an average of only 8.6 percent of their free time. Their drop in motivation can be explained in terms of self-perception. Children who saw themselves drawing pictures when a reward had been promised must have concluded that they drew for the reward, not just for the pleasure of creating the picture. In contrast, drawing with no anticipation of reward led other youngsters to the conclusion that the activity must be interesting and enjoyable. External rewards can undermine intrinsic motivation, particularly when they are perceived as bribes that externally control behavior, rather than as bonuses that demonstrate competence (Deci, 1975).

Drawing Inferences from Thoughts and Feelings. No one knows you as well as you know yourself, right? Perhaps this is because our most significant clues to self-knowledge are our private reactions to the world: our thoughts and feelings. Even self-perception theory states that people draw inferences from their own behaviors only when internal cues—such as thoughts and feelings—are weak. These cues can tell us more about ourselves than our overt behavior does precisely because thoughts and feelings are less influenced by external pressures (Andersen & Ross, 1984). Attending your best friend's wedding may prompt you to act like the life of the party, but your inner feelings of envy and loss tell you more about yourself. One study underlines the importance of thoughts and feelings for self-knowledge (Andersen, 1984). Some observers in the study heard subjects talk about their thoughts and feelings in various everyday situations, while others heard subjects describe only their behaviors in those situations. The observers then wrote down their impressions. Observers who listened to descriptions of thoughts and feelings formed impressions that matched the subjects' own self-concept more accurately than the impressions recorded by observers who heard only about behaviors. This finding suggests that our thoughts and feelings can play a bigger role than behaviors in our inferences about what we are like.

Effects of Other People's Reactions. Other people's reactions also contribute to the development of the self-concept. In 1902, the sociologist Charles H. Cooley coined the phrase *the looking-glass self* to indicate that an important source of our self-knowledge is other people's reactions to us. These reactions serve as a kind of mirror, reflecting our image so that we, too, can see it (Felson, 1989). Parents coo over us. Peers belittle us. Relatives note with pleasure that we remind them of devout Aunt Agatha. Reactions like these tell us we are cute, unathletic, or religious.

One study supported the concept of the looking-glass self when it compared the behaviors of three groups of schoolchildren. Teachers and others repeatedly told some of the children that they *were* tidy. Children in another group were repeatedly instructed that they *should be* tidy, and the third group was not told anything special. The researchers then observed how much litter each group spread around. The tidiest youngsters were those in the first group. Labeled as tidy, they behaved accordingly, reflecting their new self-concept (Miller and others, 1975). This study demonstrates again the power of self-fulfilling prophecies. Other people's expectations influence both our behavior and our self-concept (Miller & Turnbull, 1986).

Chapter 3, pages 103 to 105, also described the way a perceiver's impression can shape others' behaviors.

A real standout People tend to describe themselves in terms of the characteristics that make them different from those around them. Thus, the little boy in the yellow T-shirt is probably quite conscious of his curly hair, which distinguishes him from all the members of his straight-haired family—even the dog!

Social Comparison. "President Will Be Old Enough To Be (GASP!) Me" read a *New York Times* headline reflecting some of the baby-boomer generation's reactions to the election of Bill Clinton to the U.S. presidency at age forty-six (Stanley, 1992). "Presidents have always been old guys with ropy necks," observed humorist Garrison Keillor, "and now suddenly . . . I'm one year older than the President." Why were some baby-boomers alarmed to find the Oval Office occupied by someone their own age? According to **social comparison theory**, the answer is that thoughts and feelings about the self often arise from comparisons between ourselves and others. This theory was initially proposed by Leon Festinger (1954), who assumed that people want to evaluate themselves accurately and that they therefore seek out *similar* others for comparison. If you as a moderately skilled player want to know how well you play chess, you can learn more by comparing your game with that of opponents with similar skills than by judging your game against those of chess masters or rank beginners. People of our own age or gender often become natural comparison points, just as President Clinton did for the forty-something generation.

By revealing what physical or social attributes distinguish us from familiar or similar others, social comparisons allow us to construct a sense of our own uniqueness. The attributes that distinguish us from most others often become defining features of the self. A left-hander is more likely to think of handedness, a personally distinguishing attribute, than is a right-handed person. Children writing self-descriptions are likely to mention characteristics, such as wearing glasses or being short, that mark them as unusual in their family or classroom (McGuire & McGuire, 1981; McGuire & Padawer-Singer, 1978). An interesting example of this search for distin-

social comparison theory The theory that people learn about and evaluate their personal qualities by comparing themselves to others.

Figure 4.1 Sources of self-knowledge

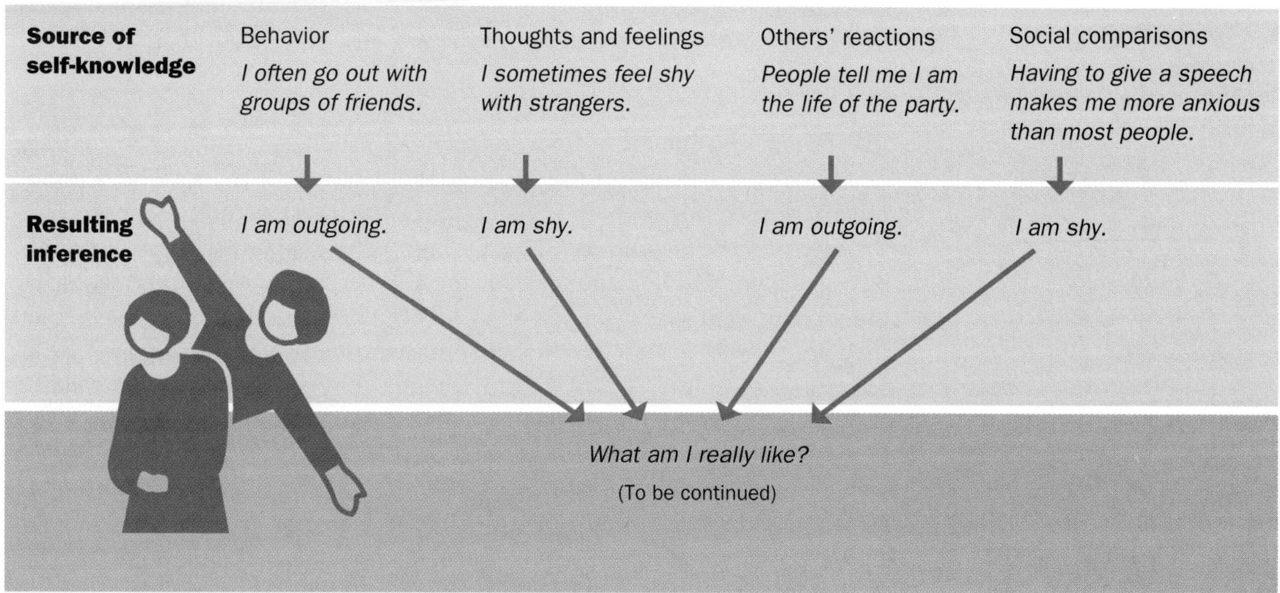

Because no one is totally consistent all the time, multiple sources of information about ourselves may lead to potentially conflicting inferences, which will eventually have to be integrated.

guishing attributes was reported by one of President Clinton's friends, who said she tried to keep in mind that "well, . . . at least Bill can't draw" (Stanley, 1992). In brief, by summarizing the ways in which we differ from others, social comparison permits us to construct a self-concept that gives each of us a strong sense of being unique and distinctive.

Figure 4.1 shows the many sources of self-knowledge. Note that social influences are pervasive even as we construct the self, learning what makes us unique.

Chapter 6 will deal with the aspects of self-knowledge, such as our membership in social groups, that we share in common with other people.

Self-Knowledge and Other-Knowledge: The Same or Different?

Despite the general similarity of the ways people learn about themselves and others, self-knowledge is richer and more detailed than knowledge about others. People can observe themselves in more situations and have better access to private thoughts and feelings. People also tend to explain their own and other people's behaviors differently, attributing their own actions to properties of the situation or the stimulus, while generally explaining others' actions by their personal characteristics. However, even people's explanations for their own behaviors may be inaccurate.

Most of the time, the cues we use to learn about ourselves are the same sorts of cues we use to learn about others. For instance, we draw inferences from our own thoughts, feelings, and behaviors, and we monitor the reactions of other people. Our reliance on similar sorts of cues creates important similarities between our knowledge about the self and others, but there are differences as well.

Differences in Amount of Knowledge. We usually have a greater quantity and variety of behavioral information about ourselves than we have about others. We see ourselves in a wider range of situations and for more time than we observe anyone else. This fact probably explains why we view ourselves as quite variable and unpredictable, whereas we view other people as more set in their ways (Baxter & Goldberg, 1987). Asked to state whether they are serious or carefree, for example, most people will describe themselves and those they know well by saying, "In-between," or "It depends." But they happily characterize those they know less well as closer to the extremes (Sande and others, 1988; Prentice, 1990).

Differences in Attribution. Because we have greater access to our own reactions, we are more aware of the impact people, places, and events have on us than of the impact they have on others. As a result, we may draw different inferences. Recall for a moment the last time you became really angry and yelled at someone, or even threw a punch. Why did you act the way you did? Try to answer the same question about the last person who acted aggressively toward you. Why did he or she do that?

If you are like most people, you probably answered these similar questions in very different ways. In explaining your own aggressive actions, you probably pointed to external factors, perhaps saying that the person you became angry with had been really annoying and provocative. Answering the same question about someone else, you probably cited that person's personal characteristics: he or she is just an aggressive type who boils over easily. Why the difference? People tend to attribute their own choices to situational factors but to make *correspondent inferences*—assumptions that behavior reflects personality characteristics—for others. Such **actor-observer differences in attributions** for behavior have been found repeatedly (Jones & Nisbett, 1972; Gioia & Sims, 1985). You can find a small sample of these differences by reading a few letters to Ann Landers in your local newspaper. Watch how people seeking advice tend to explain their own actions by citing external reasons, and to explain others' behaviors by describing those people's personal characteristics (Schoeneman & Rubanowitz, 1985).

Why are people so prone to these actor-observer differences in attribution? Differences in salience and assumed comparisons are two important factors.

actor-observer differences in attribution The tendency to attribute our own behaviors to situational causes while seeing others' acts as due to their inner characteristics.

1. *Whatever grabs our attention stands out as a likely causal culprit.* When we witness another person's behavior, that person is salient—he or she is the focus of attention and stands out against the back-

Actor-observer differences in attribution As perpetrator of the action, Phoenix Suns forward Charles Barkley would probably see this hard hit on Seattle Supersonics guard Gary Payton as caused by the rough-and-tumble competition of conference play-off action. Observers, however, might attribute such incidents to the actor's nature.

ground (Storms, 1973; Heider, 1958). In contrast, when we act, we literally look out at the world, so the *stimulus* or trigger for our action is the salient factor. You see the snake in the grass as causing your sudden jump, whereas a passerby focuses mainly on your startle response and concludes that you must be an easily frightened person.

2. *Causal culprits are chosen from line-ups, but the line-ups are different for the self and for others* (Kahneman & Miller, 1986; McGill, 1989). When asked why something occurred, people consider alternatives, but they consider different alternatives for the self and for others. For example, if someone asks you why you liked the latest Sue Grafton mystery, you will probably assume that the questioner means why you liked it *better than other books*. Obviously, then, it would be reasonable to cite the aspects of the novel that distinguish it from others. But if someone asks why a friend of yours liked the same book, you might assume that the questioner seeks to learn why this friend *among all other people* liked the book, and so you might cite some of your friend's unique personal characteristics (McGill, 1989). The difference in assumed comparisons for self and others produces very different answers (Wells & Gavanski, 1989).

Similarities in Accuracy. Although we know more about ourselves than about others, that knowledge is not always sufficient to let us make more *accurate* judgments about ourselves than about others. In fact, being the leading authority on the topic does not guarantee that we are always aware of why we think, feel, and act the way we do (Nisbett & Wilson, 1977). This limitation was demonstrated when subjects in one experiment were first rudely insulted by the experimenter and then asked to take some papers to either of two clerks who were sitting at different desks. Most subjects avoided approaching one clerk, who had a hairstyle similar to that of the obnoxious experimenter. Yet, when questioned, they indicated that they honestly had no idea that the unpleasant encounter had any impact on their choice between the clerks (Lewicki, 1986).

Even when people try hard to pinpoint the causes of their own behavior, they are not always accurate. Consider the efforts of fifty subjects who for five weeks kept diaries of their positive and negative moods and tried to identify the sources of those moods. Subjects stated, for example, whether the weather was sunny or wet and whether their mood coincided with Monday or a weekend day. Another group of subjects was simply asked to describe how these factors *generally* affect people's moods. Despite their efforts at self-analysis, the diary keepers' reports about the causes of their own moods were no more accurate than the blind guesses of people who did not know them (Wilson and others, 1982). Apparently, all the subjects relied on general causal theories—like the "fact" that rainy days and Mondays cause blue moods—even if they were explaining their own moods. Self-knowledge does not guarantee insight into our own unique actions and reactions: we often use our general knowledge about human behavior to interpret our own actions as well as the actions of others.

Multiple Selves

> *Because people see themselves in a wide range of situations and roles, self-knowledge is organized around multiple roles, activities, and relationships. People vary in the number and diversity of "selves" that they believe they possess.*

As information about the self accumulates from all these different sources, we soon become aware that many different "selves" inhabit our being. We begin to see that some of our behaviors, thoughts, and feelings depend on what we are doing and who our companions are (Markus & Wurf, 1987). For instance, most of us probably act and feel differently when we are working with our office mates—perhaps more responsibly and less playfully—than we do when we are with family and close friends. Social comparisons also vary from situation to situation. Someone who is one of the least polite people at work may be the most polite family member at home. Others' reactions also differ. Older relatives may view a forty-year-old medical doctor as a youngster, but his co-workers may see him as a mature leader in the field of transplant surgery.

Figure 4.2 Examples of self-concepts that are high and low in self-complexity

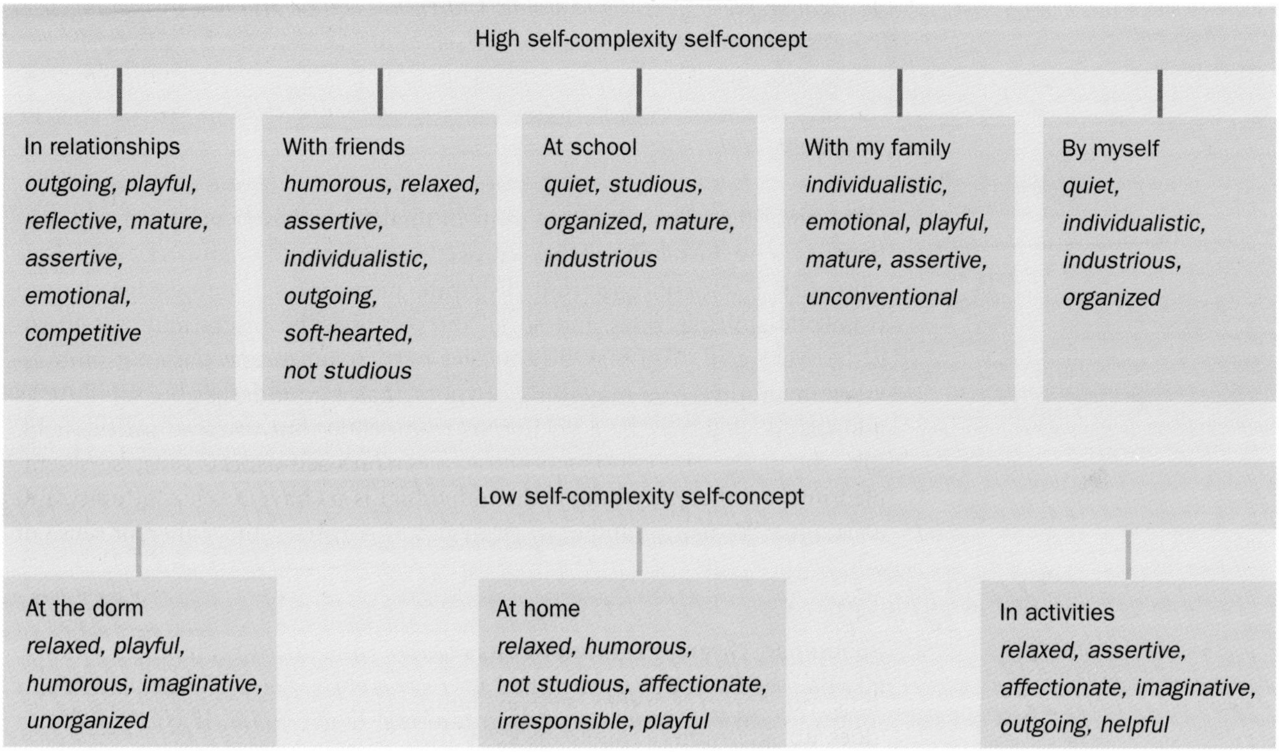

High self-complexity self-concept

In relationships	With friends	At school	With my family	By myself
outgoing, playful, reflective, mature, assertive, emotional, competitive	*humorous, relaxed, assertive, individualistic, outgoing, soft-hearted, not studious*	*quiet, studious, organized, mature, industrious*	*individualistic, emotional, playful, mature, assertive, unconventional*	*quiet, individualistic, industrious, organized*

Low self-complexity self-concept

At the dorm	At home	In activities
relaxed, playful, humorous, imaginative, unorganized	*relaxed, humorous, not studious, affectionate, irresponsible, playful*	*relaxed, assertive, affectionate, imaginative, outgoing, helpful*

The hypothetical individual at the top sees herself as having five self-aspects, characterized by relatively distinct sets of traits. The person at the bottom possesses only three self-aspects, with a greater degree of overlap: Note that some traits (like "relaxed" or "playful") are seen as applying to most or all self-aspects. (Adapted from Linville, 1987, p. 667.) Copyright © 1987 by the American Psychological Association. Adapted by permission.

How do we deal with all this varying and potentially confusing information? We organize it according to our various roles, activities, and relationships (James, 1890; Stryker, 1980; Carver & Scheier, 1981; Rogers, 1981). Thus, a woman might consider herself *studious* in academic situations, *hardworking* at the office, and *fun loving* when relaxing with a group of friends. Each of these different *self-aspects* summarizes what she believes she is like in a particular domain, role, or activity. Other self-aspects may reflect additional roles and activities such as sister, lover, chess player, or jogger (Hoelter, 1985).

People differ in **self-complexity**, or the number and diversity of the self-aspects that they develop for different situations, roles, or relationships. People with only a few, relatively similar, self-aspects are said to have low self-complexity, while people with many independent self-aspects are described as high in self-complexity (Linville, 1985). When college admissions committees look for "well-rounded" applicants, they are probably looking for individuals with high self-complexity. Such applicants might describe themselves not only in terms of their academic achievements but also as participants in other roles or activities: sports, volunteer work, school governance, art, or music. Examples of high and low self-complexity are shown in Figure 4.2. As you will see later, being high or low in self-complexity has implications for both mental and physical well-being.

self-complexity The number and diversity of the self-aspects that people develop for different roles, activities, and relationships.

Putting It All Together: Constructing a Coherent Self-Concept

People try to fit the diverse elements of self-knowledge together in a way that seems coherent and stable. Coherence can be attained by making accessible only limited facets of the self at any given time, by selectively remembering past acts, by explaining away inconsistencies, and by focusing on a few central traits. Cultures influence the type of coherence people seek.

Self-knowledge does not come to us in final form, neatly wrapped with ribbon and bow. Instead the label warns, "Some assembly required." When we construct a self-concept from disparate pieces of self-knowledge derived from our multiple roles and social interactions, the pieces may not fit together very well. You may be an eager participant in one class but unmotivated in another. You may think of yourself as a good father but a failure as a husband. You may be a vociferous team leader but reserved off the field. Like the pieces of a construction toy, a person's self-aspects must be assembled into a coherent whole if the individual is to have a sense of unity and constancy. We use a number of strategies to construct this coherent sense of self.

Coherence Through Limited Accessibility. Imagine for a moment a house in which every room is furnished in a different style: a country kitchen, a southwestern bedroom, a stately traditional living room. If you stood in a central hallway viewing all the rooms at once, the house would truly be a hodgepodge. But if you stepped into one room and closed the door, the decor would be coherent and the ambience comfortable. We often deal with inconsistencies among the various parts of our self-concept in the same way: we relax comfortably in one role because other inconsistent roles are out of sight and out of mind. What opens and closes the doorways between our several selves? Specific people and places are the keys. Recall that self-aspects are associated with specific individuals and situations; they are not thought about at other times. At work you may see yourself as logical, persistent, and authoritative, ignoring other traits (such as *fun loving* or *carefree*) that characterize your leisure-time self. Discomfort arises when situations activate inconsistent self-aspects at the same time, disrupting a coherent sense of the self. One author of this text recalls with dismay the times when breakdowns in child-care arrangements meant that he had to bring his toddler to class, simultaneously activating inconsistent aspects of his parent self and his professor self.

Coherence Through Selective Memory. As people think about their past, they reconstruct an autobiography that integrates their various self-aspects and characteristics (Gergen & Gergen, 1988; Bruner, 1986). For example, people whose behavior has changed from shy to outgoing may retrieve a biased set of autobiographical memories in which they were always outgoing (Ross & Conway, 1986). Reconstruction, like a totalitarian government's rewriting of history, deals with inconsistencies by erasing them (Greenwald, 1980). This strategy gives the person a sense of self that *feels* coherent over time, even if it fails to accurately record the facts of personal history. Michael Ross (1989) speculates that adults' frequent reminiscences (particularly to their misbehaving children) about their own praiseworthy, responsible childhood may be a product of reconstruction. As a responsible adult, it is easy to misremember one's child self as having been equally responsible and to forget incidents of childish carelessness.

Coherence Through Attribution. Would it surprise you to learn that your co-workers find you rather changeable—quiet and deferential one moment but bossy and domineering the next? If you are like most people, it probably would. You might reply that of course you are deferential when the boss is around, but when she is not, somebody has to get things organized. We explain our behaviors as reasonable responses to situations, so we are unlikely to see variations in our behavior as significant signs of instability. As pointed out earlier, most people attribute their own behavior to circumstances, not to stable, general personality traits. This tactic enables us to interpret our inconsistent behavior as a result of inconsistent circumstances, not of our inconsistent selves.

Coherence Through Selecting a Few Key Traits. People also construct a unified and enduring sense of self by noting a few core attributes that they believe characterize them uniquely among people and consistently across situations. These important and distinctive personal characteristics form the *self-schema* (plural: *schemata*) (Markus, 1977). Once a particular characteristic is incorporated into the self-schema, people notice and process information about it very efficiently. For example, people with a trait like *helpful* as part of the self-schema can answer questions like "Are you helpful?" more quickly than other individuals (Markus, 1977). People tend to see evidence for these core traits even in their most mundane behaviors, thereby reinforcing their sense of a stable and unitary self (Cantor & Kihlstrom, 1987). Thus, you might see confirmation for your view of yourself as helpful even in a trivial interaction like giving directions to a stranger on campus. And, as we will see, people are quick to reject feedback that is inconsistent with their self-schemata, thereby increasing their sense of consistency even further (Markus, 1977; Swann & Hill, 1982).

As we saw earlier, different sources often provide mixed information about the self. But Figure 4.3 illustrates several ways that people can construct a self-concept that is coherent and meaningful.

Figure 4.3 Reconciling inconsistencies: Forming a coherent self-concept

Source of self-knowledge	Behavior *I often go out with groups of friends.*	Thoughts and feelings *I sometimes feel shy with strangers.*	Others' reactions *People tell me I am the life of the party.*	Social comparison *Having to give a speech makes me more anxious than most people.*
Resulting inference	*I am outgoing.*	*I am shy.*	*I am outgoing.*	*I am shy.*
	What am I really like?			
Way of achieving coherence	Accessibility *With family, my feelings of being outgoing are most accessible.*	Selective memory *I only recall times when I was shy.*	Attribution *When I was outgoing, it was because the situation demanded it.*	Focus on key trait *Being outgoing is central and important to me.*
Resulting self-concept	*Outgoing self-concept*	*Shy self-concept*	*Shy self-concept*	*Outgoing self-concept*

We have several ways to reconcile inconsistencies in the process of forming a stable and coherent self-concept. Different people select different strategies from among these alternatives.

Coherence in Different Cultures. Imagine two recalcitrant four-year-olds, each steadfastly refusing to taste the carrots. "Just try them," coaxes one mother, "vegetables help you grow up big and strong. You want to be big and strong, don't you?" The other caregiver tries a different tactic: "Think of the poor farmer who grew the carrots so you could have them to eat. He will be so disappointed if you don't like them. Just a taste, to make the farmer happy!" Perhaps you recognize one or the other of these strategies. In fact, the first "you-oriented" approach is more often used by parents in cultures that emphasize individuality, whereas the second strategy reflects the "other-directed" concerns of community-oriented cultures. Do cultures with such different emphases also foster different conceptions of the self?

Although members of all cultures seek a coherent sense of the self,

Hazel Markus and Shinobu Kitayama (1991) have suggested that different cultures offer diverse visions of the ideal self. In many of the countries of North America and Western Europe, people tend to see the self as independent, separate from other people, and revealed primarily in inner thoughts and feelings. North American students writing self-descriptions tend to list general attributes that mark them as unique or distinctive individuals, such as "I am intelligent," or "I am musical"—the sort of characteristics that make up the self-schema.

In contrast, people in the interdependent cultures found in many parts of Asia, Africa, and South America tend to see the self as connected with others and revealed primarily in social roles and relationships. Students of Chinese cultural background are more likely than Westerners to define themselves in terms of attributes they share with others, such as "I am from Shanghai," or "I am Buddhist" (Trafimow and others, 1991). Because relationships with others are so important, many Asians seem to rely on self-aspects—their social roles and relationships with others—to define the self, not on self-schemata (Markus & Kitayama, 1991). As a result, unlike North Americans, Japanese people are reluctant to describe themselves in general terms unless the question specifies a particular role, relationship, or social context: "Describe yourself *as you are with your family* (or *in the workplace).*" Once a context is specified, they are willing to characterize themselves as optimistic or warm-hearted or as having some other general trait (Cousins, 1989). Table 4.1 shows some of the contrasts between independent and interdependent cultural views of the self.

Table 4.1 Some differences between construction of the self in independent and interdependent cultures

Feature	Independent culture	Interdependent culture
Definition of the self	Unique individual, separate from social context	Connected with others in mesh of social roles and relationships
Structure of the self	Unitary and stable, constant across situations and relationships	Fluid and variable, changing from one situation or relationship to another
Important features	Internal, private self (abilities, thoughts, feelings, traits)	External, public self (statuses, roles, relationships)
Significant task	Being unique Expressing yourself Promoting your own goals Being direct (saying what's on your mind)	Belonging, fitting in Acting appropriately Promoting group goals Being indirect (reading others' minds)

Source: Adapted by permission from "Culture and the self: Implications for cognition, emotion, and motivation," by H. Markus and S. Kitayama, *Psychological Review, 98,* p. 230. Copyright © 1991 by the American Psychological Association.

A match made by culture Many Western women may wonder at Masako Owado's choice of mate. The princess, shown here in an official wedding photo, gave up a brilliant diplomatic career and her legal existence as a person to marry Japan's Crown Prince Naruhito. From the point of view of Japanese culture with its valuing of connectedness to others and the greater good of the group, the choice may not have been so hard to understand.

Thus, cultures tell us much about the kinds of selves we "should" have (Markus & Kitayama, 1991). Independent societies like those found in Europe and North America emphasize independence, and people in those societies see themselves as unique, characterizing their individuality in traits represented by words such as *honest, responsible,* or *outgoing*. In contrast, in interdependent societies like Japan the emphasis is on fitting in; instead of general traits and characteristics, relationships with specific persons and groups are most important. Indeed, a Japanese person will experience social connections and obligations to others as the core of the self, even if those linkages conflict with his or her inner feelings. Japanese people who thought about themselves as most North Americans do and who acted accordingly would be considered at least antisocial, and perhaps even mentally ill. It is paradoxical that our seemingly most private possession—our sense of who we are—is so thoroughly molded by our cultural groups and by the people around us.

Constructing Self-Esteem: How We Feel About Ourselves

self-esteem An individual's positive or negative evaluation of himself or herself.

The self-concept is *what we think* about the self; **self-esteem**, the positive or negative evaluation of the self, is *how we feel* about it (Jones, 1990a). Self-esteem is reflected in people's agreement or disagreement with statements like "I feel I'm a person of worth," or "On the whole, I am satisfied with myself" (Rosenberg, 1965). And research suggests that, by and large, people feel pretty good about themselves. In fact, most people see themselves as above average—on almost everything.

Self-Enhancement: I Am the Greatest!

The overall evaluation of the self is greatly influenced by motivational pressures to think well of the self. These motivations color and bias many of our thoughts and feelings about the self.

Pick some traits—honesty, social sensitivity, and leadership, for example—and ask some people to rate themselves on each characteristic. You will probably find few people who rate themselves below average on any one (let alone on all) of these qualities. Researchers have found that most people rate themselves above average on a variety of characteristics—including things like managerial ability, driving skills, and health habits (Larwood & Whittaker, 1977; Svenson, 1981; Weinstein, 1987). This self-enhancing tendency has been termed the Lake Wobegon effect, after the humorist Garrison Keillor's mythical town where "all the children are above average." Of course, the vaguer the criteria for a characteristic, the easier it is for people to see themselves as above average. Thus, we are more likely to believe we are better than average in sensitivity, discipline, or sophistication than in punctuality—a trait easily measured against the clock (Dunning and others, 1989). For the same reason, people are more likely to estimate that they are above average on dimensions of morality than on dimensions of intellectual performance (Allison and others, 1989).

Not only do most people think they are doing just fine in the present, they also think their future is pretty rosy, too. They bolster that assumption with the belief that the qualities they possess are just the ones that will serve them well in the future. For example, people who see themselves as extremely intelligent but not very sociable believe that intellectual talents are the most important factor in future career success. People who think that they are only average in intelligence but that they have a special gift for getting along with others see things in just the opposite way: they believe being a "people person" will guarantee job success (Alloy & Ahrens, 1987; Kunda, 1987). No wonder, then, that when subjects in one study compared themselves with same-sex classmates, they saw themselves as more likely to own a home, travel to Europe, receive a good job offer before graduation, and live past the age of eighty. Maintaining this rosy glow, they also predicted that they would be less likely to have a drinking problem, attempt suicide, get fired, or even buy a car that turned out to be a lemon (Weinstein, 1980). Of course this illusion of invulnerability can have a down side. For example, a majority of sexually active female college students in another study saw themselves as uniquely unlikely to become pregnant, a belief that could easily interfere with their effective use of birth control (Burger & Burns, 1988). And people who believe that they are above average sometimes make risky decisions that ultimately increase their chances of failure (Klein & Kunda, in press).

Calvin and Hobbies by Bill Watterson

How do we manage to create and maintain such positive views of ourselves? Because people prefer to feel good about themselves—to value "me and mine"—they process information about the self in ways that favor a positive view. **Self-enhancing biases** sneak into the processes of gathering and interpreting information (Kunda, 1990). However, people do not think they are biased. In fact, most of us intend to gather objective evidence with which to evaluate ourselves. In the end, the impression of the self we develop is a lot like a TV docudrama: part truth and part fiction.

Sources of Self-Esteem

People evaluate the self on the basis of daily successes and failures, social comparisons with others, and comparisons with their own internal standards. Any of these sources of evaluation may be biased in the direction of elevating self-esteem. For example, people often seek areas of activity in which they can succeed, compare themselves with others who are worse off, and make biased estimates of how they measure up.

Just as many sources of information contribute to the self-concept, so we have many ways of evaluating the self. We tally our successes and failures, compare ourselves to others, and evaluate ourselves against internal standards.

The Pain but Mainly Gain of Personal Experiences. Remember how happy you felt the first time you beat your regular opponent at tennis? And how your image of yourself plunged on the day you broke up with your first love? Those experiences and others like them can raise or lower self-esteem at a moment's notice. Success and acceptance make us feel particularly good about ourselves, and failure, rejection, and loss can knock us to our knees. If people's experiences and thoughts about the self are mostly positive, they probably will have habitually high self-esteem. If their experiences are

self-enhancing bias Any tendency to gather or interpret information concerning the self in a way that leads to overly positive evaluations.

mainly negative, they may develop chronically low self-esteem. As you will see later, people with high and low self-esteem differ significantly in the ways they respond to and cope with all kinds of life experiences.

As we noted, however, self-enhancing biases color the impact of our experiences on self-esteem. Almost without thinking about it, most of us stack the deck so that life produces more gain and less pain.

- *We choose situations in which we can shine.* One of the authors of this text is a member of a choir and regularly chooses to sing in public; the other takes care to avoid embarrassment by putting a great distance between herself, choirs, and even occasional invitations to Karaoke nights. Most of us tend to abandon relationships that make us miserable, hobbies that fail to hold our interest, and careers that do not allow us to flourish. Our life choices often move us into domains that let us be all that we can be.
- *We interpret our experiences to give ourselves the benefit of the doubt.* Perhaps finishing the race is as good as winning; perhaps the woman who just turned down your invitation to a romantic dinner would be a better friend than a date. We often decide that the way things turn out for us is all for the best.
- *We inflate our contributions to joint efforts or projects.* In part, this bias may stem from the natural workings of memory. It is easy to remember one's own contributions to a joint project; the hours others worked are naturally less vivid. It is interesting, however, that people inflate their own contributions to a lesser extent when a project ends in failure (Ross & Sicoly, 1979). If overestimating were due only to the vividness of memory for one's actions, then the overestimate should occur to an equal extent when a project fails. Since it does not, we can infer that the tendency stems at least in part from a self-enhancing motive to overestimate one's positive contributions.

For all these reasons, then, most of us amass more positive experiences than negative ones, both in reality and in memory. As humorist Ashleigh Brilliant put it, "Let's be proud of who we are, regardless of the facts."

Personality Differences in the Impact of Experiences. Individuals differ both in the way they react to positive and negative events and in the impact such events have on their self-esteem. Patricia Linville's (1985) research demonstrated that the effect of positive and negative events is exaggerated for people who are low in self-complexity, who see themselves as having relatively few distinct self-aspects. Linville set up an opportunity for her subjects to experience success or failure. Compared with subjects with higher self-complexity, those with low self-complexity experienced more positive moods after success and more negative moods after failure, as Figure 4.4 shows. Those low in self-complexity also had larger changes in self-esteem after a success or failure experience.

In one study of the influence of self-complexity, success or failure had a marked impact on the mood of individuals who were low in self-complexity (left bars). Note, in contrast, the narrower range of good and bad feelings these events produced in individuals with high self-complexity (right bars). (Data from Linville, 1985.)

Figure 4.4 Self-complexity influences mood

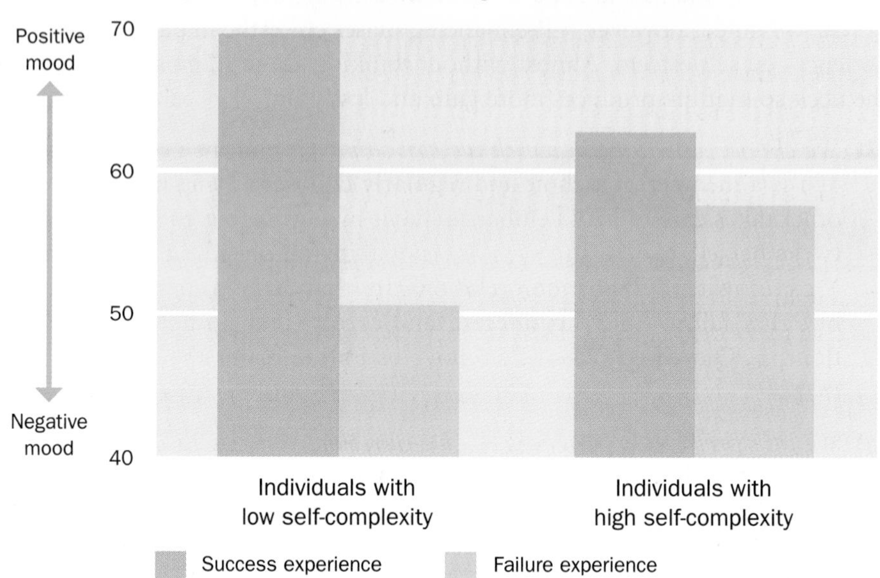

Why does high self-complexity protect people from swings in mood and self-esteem? Linville argues that a good or bad event, such as an argument or a reconciliation with a loved one, is likely to have a *direct* effect on only one or two self-aspects (one's view of oneself as a supportive confidant, for example, or as a family-oriented spouse). If people have many independent self-aspects, only a small portion of their self-concept will be affected by an event. Such people may reflect, "Well, I may be hopeless when it comes to romance, but at least I am still a good writer and a great basketball player." People with high self-complexity can also limit the damage by setting up positive events related to their different self-aspects. After a run-in with the boss, for example, they can arrange an outing with friends to go to the movies; a positive experience for the "friend self" can partially offset the negative event affecting the "work self" (Linville & Fischer, 1991). In contrast, a single positive or negative event will color a major portion of the self-concept of a person with relatively few self-aspects, and that person will therefore experience events relatively intensely. So when our lives go really well, we may benefit from having a relatively simple self-concept because our highs will be higher. But for most of us, life experience is a mix of good and bad events, and we probably should try not to "put all of [our] eggs in one cognitive basket" (Linville, 1985).

Constructing a relatively complex self-concept gives people a better chance of avoiding the devastating lows and maintaining a consistent, stable level of self-esteem. How can people increase self-complexity? According to Linville's (1987) research, the answer is not only to be involved in many social roles and activities but also to see the various roles and activities as involving somewhat different selves. Having numerous roles would not help much if you saw yourself as thinking, feeling, and acting in similar ways in each one. Instead, making distinctions between the different selves seems to be the key to maintaining stable moods and self-esteem against the vicissitudes of life.

Social Comparisons: Better or Worse Than Others? Self-esteem, like our self-concept, depends on social comparisons. Consider, for example, the plight of a young man who recently enrolled in college with a basketball scholarship. He is an athlete of above-average talent who is expected, in time, to make real contributions to the team. The problem is that his older brother, who played basketball for the same school two years earlier, was a major star and is now beginning a career as a professional. It seems inevitable that the young man will face comparisons with his older brother.

How might these comparisons influence the young man's self-esteem if his performance is not equal to his brother's accomplishments? Abraham Tesser's (1988) model of *self-evaluation maintenance* suggests two possible reactions. Both depend on the *closeness* of the other person—in this case, the fact that the star player was a brother rather than, for example, a cousin—and the *importance* of the attribute in question for the person—the centrality of being an athlete. If the young man does not have a big investment in his athletic abilities, he may react by feeling good because of the reflected glory of his brother's impressive successes. But if being a star player is an important and central part of the younger man's self-concept, his disappointment stemming from the comparison could overwhelm his pleasure in his brother's success. In fact, being outperformed by a sibling or close friend may be even more painful than being beaten by a stranger because the likelihood of social comparison is greater. Sometimes we want to bask in a loved one's reflected glory; at other times the glare of his or her achievement is just too painfully illuminating.

Chapter 6, pages 228 to 230, will discuss in more detail the ways in which connections with other people can help us feel good or bad about ourselves.

As the example illustrates, we are not always free to choose whom to compare ourselves with (Wood, 1989). Most of us have probably had the unfortunate experience of performing in public—at a track meet, speech contest, or piano recital—immediately after the local superstar turned in a superb performance. This kind of inescapable comparison can induce feelings of envy and resentment and can lower self-esteem (Salovey & Rodin, 1984; Tesser & Collins, 1988).

"Of course you're going to be depressed if you keep comparing yourself with successful people."

Biased Comparisons: Definitely Better Than Others. When people *can* choose social comparisons, they often attempt to avoid comparisons that make their abilities and traits look bad. One common tactic we employ is establishing distance between ourselves and those who are successful. We do this by either downplaying our similarities to them or backing off from our relationships with them (Tesser, 1988). Another form of protection involves *downward comparisons,* which allow us to compare ourselves with others who are in some way less fortunate or less successful. An average grade on the calculus final looks better in the light of the failing grades some students received. A not-so-exciting home life sure beats the hardships experienced by recently divorced friends. In fact, people who learn that they have some positive attribute tend to underestimate the number of others who share the same characteristic—a bias that fosters a sense of superiority (Goethals and others, 1991). Even when the situation is objectively pretty grim, it helps to know that life could be worse. Interviews with breast-cancer patients, for example, found that they compared themselves with others who were worse off—people whose disease was not responding to treatments, those who lacked social support, or those who contracted the disease at a comparatively young age (Taylor & Lobel, 1989). Buoyed by such comparisons, most cancer patients think they are better off than their peers (Taylor and others, 1986). Perhaps Helen Keller, who was both blind and deaf, put it best when she noted that comparing ourselves with others often demonstrates that we are among the privileged.

Evaluating the Self Against Internal Standards: Self-Guides. Do you know someone who despite her many accomplishments nevertheless feels she is a fake who will soon be caught, or some high achiever who is constantly worried that he does not measure up? If so, you realize that self-esteem is affected not only by what happens *to* us but also by what happens *inside* us. Even if most people describe our lives as successful, we may still feel we fail to measure up to the standards we set for ourselves. Tory Higgins (1987) calls the personal standards toward which we strive *self-guides.* Self-guides come in two flavors: the *ideal self* (the person we would like to be) and the *ought self* (the person we feel we should be) (Higgins, 1987; Markus & Nurius, 1986). Ideal self-guides include the traits that help you match your aspirations; ought self-guides include those that help you meet your obligations.

According to Higgins's **self-discrepancy theory**, the difference between who we think we actually are and our self-guides determines our emotional well-being. For example, a *self-discrepancy* could arise from a mismatch between a slender, athletic ideal self and a corpulent couch potato actual self, or between a virtuous, altruistic ought self and a selfish, greedy actual self. If you are like most people, you will not simply note the existence of such discrepancies matter-of-factly. On the contrary, your reactions will be emotional and negative (Strauman & Higgins, 1988; Higgins, 1987). However, the type of emotion a person experiences as a result of self-discrepancies will depend on whether the discrepancy involves the ideal or ought self, as

self-discrepancy theory The theory that people evaluate themselves against internal "ideal" and "ought" standards, producing specific emotional consequences.

Figure 4.5 Summary of self-discrepancy theory

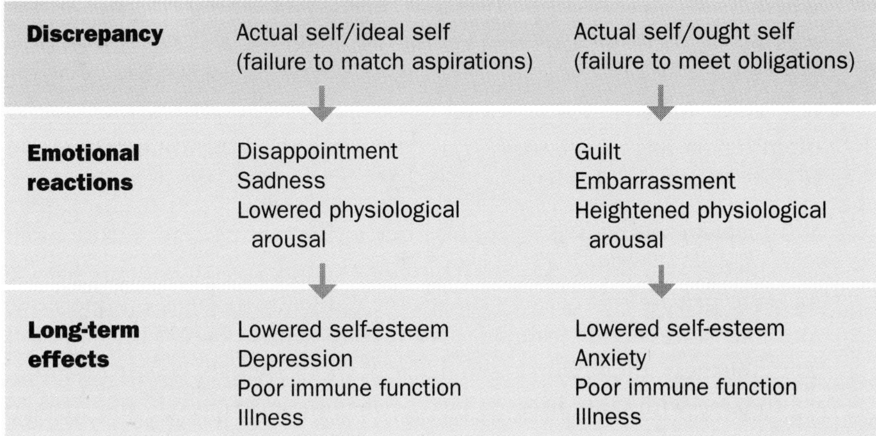

Discrepancy	Actual self/ideal self (failure to match aspirations)	Actual self/ought self (failure to meet obligations)
Emotional reactions	Disappointment Sadness Lowered physiological arousal	Guilt Embarrassment Heightened physiological arousal
Long-term effects	Lowered self-esteem Depression Poor immune function Illness	Lowered self-esteem Anxiety Poor immune function Illness

Discrepancies between the actual self and ideal or ought self-guides give rise to characteristic emotions. They also have long-term negative consequences that affect the body as well as the mind.

Figure 4.5 shows. A mismatch between actual and ideal selves leads to feelings of disappointment, dejection, and frustration. If you think slender people are attractive, you may feel sad because you are so different from the person you would like to be. On the other hand, a mismatch between actual and ought selves arouses guilt, embarrassment, and anxiety. Realizing that you took more than your share when you ought to have been more generous makes you feel ashamed. In extreme cases, self-discrepancies trigger negative emotions that can lead to a cycle of sadness and anxiety, lowered self-esteem, and even depression (Pyszczynski & Greenberg, 1987; Csikszentmihalyi & Figurski, 1982).

Regardless of whether a self-discrepancy involves an ideal or ought self, certain thoughts and situations can exaggerate our awareness of our shortcomings, and some people are generally highly aware of them.

1. *Self-focusing thoughts*. Thinking, however fleetingly, about people who represent our inner standards brings those standards to mind, as Mark Baldwin and his colleagues (1990) recently demonstrated. The researchers primed some of their subjects, who were Roman Catholic college students, by exposing them to a scowling photo of Pope John Paul II. As an experimental control, other subjects saw a similarly grim-faced photo of social psychologist Robert Zajonc, whose unfamiliar face would not be associated with any particular standards for these subjects. When later asked to evaluate themselves, the practicing Catholics who had seen the photo of the Pope felt worse about themselves, whereas subjects who saw Zajonc displayed no such reaction.

2. *Self-focusing situations*. Do you know someone who hates being photographed or having his or her voice recorded? The reason may be that these situations focus our attention inward on ourselves. Most of the time our thoughts are turned outward. However, talking about our-

selves, being scrutinized by an audience or a camera, even catching sight of ourselves in a mirror, can create **self-awareness,** directing our attention to our internal standards and heightening our awareness of whether we measure up to them. According to the *theory of self-awareness,* focusing attention on the self makes self-discrepancies obvious, which is why it is often unpleasant (Duval & Wicklund, 1972; Carver & Scheier, 1981). Research supports this proposition: people often report feeling relatively unhappy when thinking about themselves (Csikszentmihalyi & Figurski, 1982).

3. *Self-focusing individuals.* People differ in the tendency to devote attention to the self. Table 4.2 shows some examples of statements used to measure *private self-consciousness,* the tendency to focus on one's own internal states and feelings. Compared with people low in self-consciousness, those who are high are more likely to be aware of, and to try to cope with, any discrepancy between their actual self and their internalized standards (Carver & Scheier, 1981). This increased awareness means that negative self-related information leads to stronger feelings of distress and sadness (Scheier & Carver, 1977).

Table 4.2 Examples of items used to measure private self-consciousness

1. I'm always trying to figure myself out.
2. I reflect about myself a lot.
3. I never scrutinize myself.
4. I'm alert to changes in my mood.
5. I'm constantly examining my motives.

Note: A person who agrees with items like 1, 2, 4, and 5, and disagrees with item 3 and similar items is probably high in private self-consciousness. The actual scale contains many more than five items, so it can more accurately classify people as high or low in private self-consciousness.

Source: From "Public and private self-consciousness: Assessment and theory," by A. Fenigstein, M. F. Scheier, & A. H. Buss, *Journal of Consulting and Clinical Psychology, 43,* p. 524. Copyright © 1975 by American Psychological Association. Reprinted by permission.

Biased Estimates of How We Measure Up. But wait, you might be thinking, no one is perfect. Since we all live with self-discrepancies, why do we not feel terrible all the time? One reason is that we do not notice self-discrepancies when our personal standards are inaccessible. Certain thoughts, certain situations, and certain people can bring self-discrepancies to mind, but as day-to-day events unfold we usually do not dwell on how we are measuring up. And even when we do engage in self-analysis, we hardly ever gather all the relevant evidence. Unlike a good detective, we stop short of a thorough search. It is interesting that the most accessible evidence—the information that has the maximum impact—is frequently biased in our favor. What explains this self-enhancing bias?

self-awareness A state of heightened awareness of the self, including our internal standards and whether we measure up to them.

1. *The outcome determines the evidence.* Memories that come to mind most easily are those associated with the outcome being considered

(Kunda, 1990). If you are gauging your career success, your past achievements will come to mind more readily than your failed opportunities. As a result, you would conclude you have been pretty successful. Of course, if you had searched instead for career failures, you might have found some of those, too.

2. *We access successes, suppress failures.* Because it is pleasant to linger over our successes and not so comfortable to think about our failures, our positive memories will be retrieved more frequently than our negative memories, and therefore will become more accessible (Kunda, 1990).

Thus, as we try to pull together relevant evidence, most information we bring to the surface will probably suggest how good we are. In one demonstration of this self-enhancing bias in memory, students were led to believe that either extroversion or introversion was a desirable characteristic (Sanitioso and others, 1990). When all students then recalled relevant past behaviors, they described more memories of the sort they believed to be desirable. Success and failure do not have to be very important to bias our recall. People who were led to believe that brushing their teeth has negative effects on health remembered brushing their teeth less frequently in the past than others who thought brushing was a healthy practice (Ross and others, 1981).

All the self-enhancing biases summarized in Figure 4.6 help us construct a self-impression infused with a positive tilt and a rosy glow. As Oscar Wilde quipped, "To love oneself is the beginning of a life-long romance." We often avoid situations in which we do not perform well, refuse to com-

Figure 4.6 Events, self-evaluation, and self-enhancement

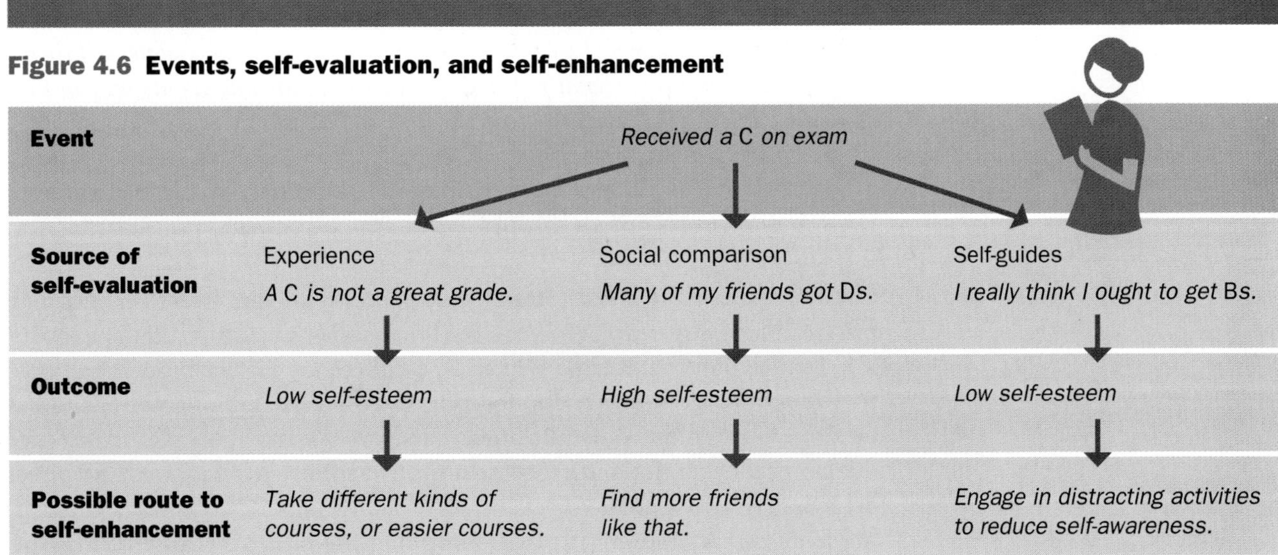
Event
Received a C on exam
Source of self-evaluation
Experience
A C is not a great grade.
Social comparison
Many of my friends got Ds.
Self-guides
I really think I ought to get Bs.
Outcome
Low self-esteem
High self-esteem
Low self-esteem
Possible route to self-enhancement
Take different kinds of courses, or easier courses.
Find more friends like that.
Engage in distracting activities to reduce self-awareness.

Many self-relevant events are neither intrinsically positive nor intrinsically negative. Instead, they must be interpreted and evaluated. The evaluation process may lead to increases or decreases in self-esteem, and it almost always leaves room for the operation of self-enhancing biases.

pare ourselves with more successful others, and fail to notice that we are not all that we could or should be. Even when our inadequacies become obvious, however, we are not without resources. Later in the chapter you will see that failures, inconsistencies, and shortcomings set off some of the self's best defense mechanisms.

Effects of the Self: Directing Emotion and Behavior

What a difference a self makes! Once we know what we think about ourselves, many things change. The familiar principle of conservatism comes into operation, and we become much less open to new information about the self. A young child might begin to think of himself as tidy after noticing that he picks up his room a few times, but once the self-concept is firmly established, people no longer have to make inferences from their behaviors to decide who they are (Klein & Loftus, 1993). In fact, most of the time inconsistent behaviors have little impact on firmly established self-knowledge (Chaiken & Baldwin, 1981; Fazio and others, 1981). Other people's reactions also play less of a role after self-knowledge becomes entrenched (Allen, 1988). Feedback inconsistent with an established self-concept is avoided, distrusted, or resisted—even if it is flattering (Markus, 1977; Swann & Read, 1981).

At the same time that self-knowledge becomes more resistant to change by new information, it starts to regulate many important aspects of our lives—particularly our emotions and our behavior.

The Self and Emotions: For Me or Against Me?

Emotions are sparked by interpretations of self-relevant events and their causes. Emotions signal the occurrence of significant events and motivate us to act in response—for example, to flee from danger. As they perform this function, emotions involve the whole self, body and mind: they activate facial expressions, physiological responses, subjective feelings, and overt behaviors.

Emotions mark the most meaningful moments of our lives. Feelings like pride, anxiety, joy, fear, or anger signal that something important is happening. Fear signals that a danger must be escaped, joy lets us know that a positive outcome should be celebrated. The intrusive quality of emotions forces us to pay attention to significant events, even as the positive or negative quality of the emotion indicates the nature of the event. Emotions also direct behavior toward a goal. For example, fear directs our efforts toward escaping from threat, and anger toward harming the target. Because of their intrusiveness, emotions often seem to "just happen," but as we shall see, they actually depend on the perceiver's interpretation of both the self and the external world.

Where Do Emotions Come From? Emotions are complex and multifaceted and involve the entire self—body and mind. When you feel angry, your heart pounds and blood rushes to your face. You want to strike out at the target of your anger. You believe deeply that he or she injured you without cause. Thoughts, feelings, bodily reactions, and desires for action are tied together in patterns that characterize different emotions. Which of these many components is primary in *causing* the emotion? Psychologists have offered different answers to this question over the years. A century ago, William James (1884) argued that sensations from the skin and muscles were the chief causes of the experience of emotion. A generation ago, Stanley Schachter and Jerome Singer (1962) identified emotion as the product of physiological arousal plus a belief concerning its cause.

The prevailing view today is that emotions are caused by cognitive appraisals of a self-relevant object or event (Arnold, 1960; Frijda, 1986; Roseman and others, 1990; Scherer, 1988; Weiner, 1985). A **cognitive appraisal** is an interpretation of an event, including both the causes of the event and how the event affects the self. Different appraisals of the same situation can produce different emotions, as is illustrated in Figure 4.7 for the everyday event of feeling hungry and finding the refrigerator empty. Two types of appraisals are particularly important in influencing emotions.

cognitive appraisal An individual's interpretation of a self-relevant event or situation that directs emotional responses and behavior.

Figure 4.7 Appraisals dictate emotional reaction to events

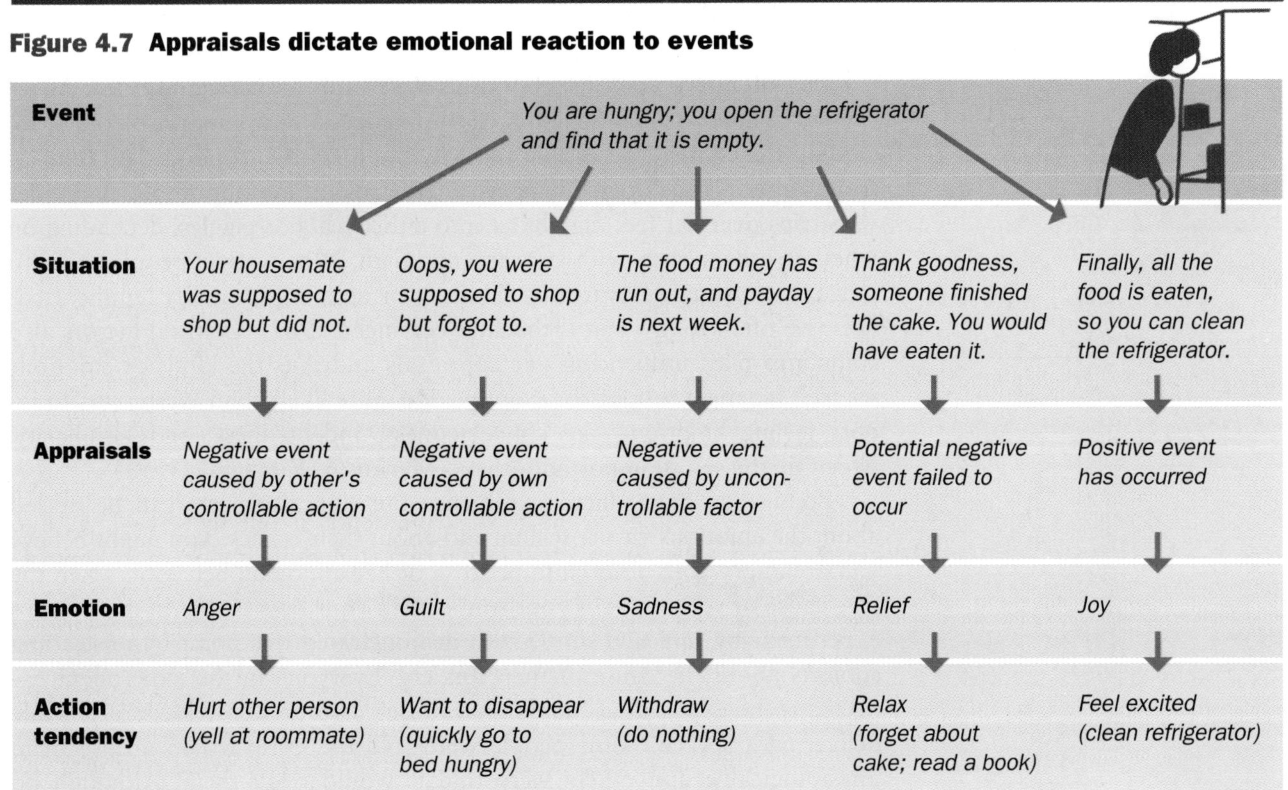
Situation	Your housemate was supposed to shop but did not.	Oops, you were supposed to shop but forgot to.	The food money has run out, and payday is next week.	Thank goodness, someone finished the cake. You would have eaten it.	Finally, all the food is eaten, so you can clean the refrigerator.
Appraisals	Negative event caused by other's controllable action	Negative event caused by own controllable action	Negative event caused by uncontrollable factor	Potential negative event failed to occur	Positive event has occurred
Emotion	Anger	Guilt	Sadness	Relief	Joy
Action tendency	Hurt other person (yell at roommate)	Want to disappear (quickly go to bed hungry)	Withdraw (do nothing)	Relax (forget about cake; read a book)	Feel excited (clean refrigerator)

Here are examples of different emotions and action tendencies arising from different appraisals of the same event—in this case, opening the refrigerator and finding that it is empty.

1. *Our appraisal of the event's positive or negative implications for the self.* Actions and events that we interpret as supportive of ourselves and our goals produce positive emotions such as joy, hope, and gratitude. If you were trying to lose ten pounds to fit into a new swimsuit but had just succumbed to the temptation of finishing off yesterday's chocolate cake, you might be happy to find an empty refrigerator. But how would you feel if the shelves were empty because the food money had run out and your paycheck was not due for another two days? You probably would be both angry and frightened by this event. Actions and events that threaten, frustrate, or repel us evoke negative emotions like fear, anger, and disgust.

2. *Our appraisal of the cause of the event.* Was someone to blame, or was the event beyond everyone's control? And did *you* bring about the event, or was someone else responsible? The emotions you feel and the actions you subsequently take will be quite different depending on your answer to those two questions. If you were unable to shop because you worked so many overtime hours that the stores closed before you could get to them, you will have one set of responses. But if your housemate simply failed to contribute his share of the grocery money or to do his share of the shopping chores, your feelings and actions will be quite different. Figure 4.7 shows how our appraisal of credit or blame affects emotions (Weiner, 1985).

Like all interpretations, appraisals are flexible, not cut and dried. As we saw in Chapter 3, many factors can influence how we appraise events, including the context, accessible thoughts, and transient moods. And, as always, other people's reactions play a large role in our appraisals. A toddler who trips over her feet may burst into either tears or giggles, depending on whether others gasp with concern or laugh. When other people seem to judge that a situation warrants calmness or dejection or goofy lightheartedness, we often follow suit (Schachter & Singer, 1962). Cultural factors also come into play, influencing our appraisals and thus the kinds of emotions we feel. Japanese people, for example, are more likely than Westerners to report feeling emotions like connectedness, indebtedness, and familiarity, which tie the self to important others (Markus & Kitayama, 1991).

Because so many factors influence our appraisals, we can be misled about the emotions we are feeling and about their causes. You might believe you are angry with your child because of her annoying behavior, when the true cause of your anger is your run-in with your boss earlier in the day. An experiment by James Olson (1990) demonstrated this point by misleading subjects about the cause of their anxiety. Everyone in the experiment expected to be exposed to "subliminal noise" as they were videotaped while delivering a speech. Some people were told the noise would arouse them physiologically, and others were told it would relax them. Although no noise was played, the subjects' beliefs about it still influenced their emotions. Those who thought the noise would arouse them rated themselves as less anxious and made fewer speech errors than those who expected to be more relaxed. Apparently those who expected arousal attributed their stage fright to the "noise," whereas those who expected relaxation had no such excuse. Thus, like other aspects of self-knowledge, the emotions we experience and our beliefs about their causes actually reflect our *appraisals*. And appraisals are often based on salient cues—conspicuous features, people, or events that may or may not correspond to true causes of our emotions (Reisenzein, 1983).

Changing Appraisals in Clinical Settings. The fact that emotions follow from appraisals allows each of us to maintain control—to take the emotional driver's seat. After all, if appraisals cause emotions, modifying those appraisals should enable us to control our emotions. And, in practice, this principle is a fundamental part of several systems of cognitive therapy (Beck, 1976; Ellis & Grieger, 1977). How might one go about making such changes? Perhaps if you feel extreme anxiety at making a speech or presentation before a group, you might assume that the *presence of the group*, something over which you have no control, causes your feelings. But stop and think. Are you always petrified by groups? How do you feel when you do not care what a group thinks of you? Then you probably would not be anxious. You might come to realize that your feelings actually flow from the *way you think about the group*, not from its simple presence (Foersterling, 1986). You can control those thoughts, and by doing so you can control the anxiety. Similarly, anger arises from the appraisal that someone has intentionally harmed you. Thus, to diminish anger, you could consider the possibility that the behavior was not controllable. Perhaps the poor fellow yelled at you because he has a low boiling point—he could not help himself. It is usually more productive to think of your emotions as deriving from your appraisals of the world, rather than as being directly caused by external events. Thinking "I feel angry because I am interpreting his harmful behaviors as intentional," rather than believing "He made me angry," puts you in charge.

Appraisals, Emotions, Bodily Responses: All Together Now. A pattern of appraisals not only causes emotional feelings but also affects many aspects of our body and mind. People in all cultures smile when they feel happy, frown when they feel sad, and wrinkle their brow when they feel angry (Ekman and others, 1987). Physiological systems come on line, revving us up or calming us down. We are motivated to act: to strike back in anger, escape in fear, or move closer in happiness. Some of these action tendencies, like attack and flight, appear to be universal and biologically determined. Other emotional behaviors are, of course, learned and differ from one culture to another (Frijda and others, 1989; Markus & Kitayama, 1991).

Emotions also affect thinking, focusing us on the content of our appraisals. Thus, in the grip of extreme rage you may be totally focused on the thought of how your antagonist mistreated you and how he deserves to have his lights punched out. Strong emotions of any sort, positive or negative, can create intense arousal that limits people's ability to pay attention to other events (Easterbrook, 1959).

All of these components—appraisals, bodily responses, subjective feelings, and emotionally driven behavior—become so associated that any one aspect can engage all the rest. If your heart is pounding, your face is contorted in a snarl, and your fists are tightly clenched, you are likely to feel anger, just as anger provokes those same responses. Because our inner feelings and outward expressions of emotion are so intertwined, bodily signs of emotion often intensify emotional feelings (Adelmann & Zajonc, 1989; Ekman, 1992). Fritz Strack and his colleagues (1988) ingeniously demonstrated this point by having subjects write with a pen either clenched tightly between their teeth or held loosely between pursed lips. These maneuvers force expressions resembling a smile and a scowl respectively, although subjects were unaware of this fact. (Try it yourself.) The experimenters then asked both groups to assign ratings to a series of cartoons, telling how funny they were. The subjects holding the pen between their teeth in a "smile" assigned higher ratings than did those holding the pen "scowlingly" between their lips.

If an emotional facial expression promotes emotional experience, it stands to reason that a neutral or inconsistent expression will reduce the intensity of the emotion. For example, if you avoid making facial expressions of disgust when looking at disgusting objects, your feelings of disgust will probably be reduced. The effects of facial expressions on emotional feelings are another example of self-perception theory: what we do often influences how we feel.

Actually, you may already have put the effects of expressions and behaviors on emotions to work for you. Have you ever been in a clutch situation and been terrified you would choke? Perhaps you were about to speak to a large audience. Did you take a couple of long deep breaths to calm yourself down or lock your face in a determined grin? If so, you were trying to take advantage of the way emotions often follow behavior and expressions. The old advice to "whistle past the graveyard" and your "keep on smiling" strategy both reflect the fact that we can lessen the effects of fear by acting cheerful while feeling afraid.

As Figure 4.8 shows, emotions tie together all aspects of body and soul, action and thought (Shaver and others, 1987; De Rivera, 1977).

The Self in Action: Self and Behavior

Sometimes people act in ways that express their true inner selves. At other times, people are concerned with shaping others' opinions in order to gain power, influence, or approval. But even behaviors intended for others' consumption may end up influencing people's private views of themselves.

Figure 4.8 Components of emotions

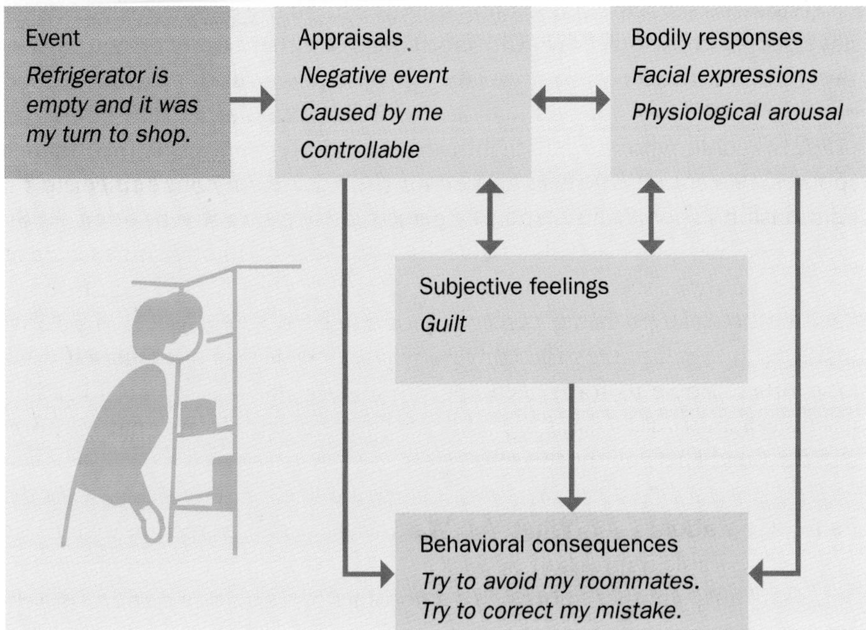

When events are appraised as self-relevant, the resulting emotion has many components: cognitive appraisals, physiological responses, and subjective feelings. Each component can affect the others, and all may contribute to emotionally driven behaviors.

Since her arrival on the music scene almost ten years ago, Madonna has changed her appearance frequently and dramatically. Yet from the days of her Marlene Dietrich look to the publication of her aptly titled book *Sex,* Madonna's every marketing, musical, and fashion move has conveyed the same message: a devil-may-care sexual independence. What motivates her behavior? Is she really an inherently sexual person whose fame allows her to express her true nature to her thousands of fans across the globe? Or is Madonna the consummate actress, carefully crafting her behavior to convey an impression she believes will buy her the greatest success in the marketplace?

If there is one domain where the impact of who we are and how we feel is dramatic, it is in our interactions with others. Like Madonna, we can act in ways that convey and reaffirm who we actually are or select our behaviors to convey particular impressions and achieve particular goals.

Self-Expression: I Am What I Am. When people engage in **self-expression** they attempt to convey their self-concept through their actions. Self-expression confirms and reinforces the individual's sense of self and also conveys it to other people. If you think of yourself as a committed animal rights activist, you may see many of your behaviors—volunteering at the Humane Society or campaigning to stop unnecessary cosmetics testing—as expressions and affirmations of that self-concept. Research shows that, if given a choice, most people prefer to enter social situations that allow them

self-expression A motive for choosing behaviors that are intended to reflect and express the self-concept.

to act in a way consistent with their self-concept (Snyder & Gangestad, 1982). Thus, an outgoing man may accept invitations to parties, or an organized woman may take a job that offers clearly structured tasks.

Our need for self-expression is so powerful that we sometimes prefer to have people know our flaws and shortcomings rather than perceive us positively and inaccurately. To illustrate just how powerful this motive can be, consider a study of married couples by William Swann and his colleagues (1992). People who viewed themselves negatively were asked about their spouses' perceptions of them and about their degree of commitment to the relationship. Those whose spouses perceived them negatively—that is, the same way they perceived themselves—were more committed to their marriages than those whose spouses viewed them positively. These individuals apparently preferred being perceived accurately to being seen in a positive light. Because self-expression conveys what we believe is our true self, it allows other people to form accurate impressions of what we are like. This permits them to treat us as we want to be treated—in ways that reinforce our existing beliefs about the self.

Self-Presentation: I Am What You Want Me to Be. Sometimes we try to create a desirable impression, whether we believe the impression is accurate or not. Thus, another motive for choosing particular behaviors is **self-presentation,** our efforts to shape other people's impressions of us in order to gain power, influence, or approval (Jones & Pittman, 1982; Tedeschi, 1981). Most people care about conveying a positive impression to others. After all, attracting a desirable date or impressing a job interviewer can have a real impact on the course of our lives. Even in less crucial situations, we usually want to show the world a face it can like, admire, and respect. In fact, *ingratiation,* trying to convey the impression we are likable, and *self-promotion,* trying to convey an impression of competence, are two of the most common goals of social interaction (Arkin, 1981; Jones & Wortman, 1973).

We all have had so much practice trying to win approval and respect that ingratiation and self-promotion should be easy. To be seen as likable, we go out of our way to help, to fit in with the other person's wishes, and to deliver charming compliments. To be seen as competent, we play up our strong points, mention our accomplishments, and display our knowledge. But self-presentation is fraught with potential pitfalls; taken too far, these qualities become blatant flattery or unseemly boasting. In one study that took place in India, a hypothetical character who discussed a possible promotion with his boss in an ingratiating fashion was rated as both less likable and less competent than a character who did not try to ingratiate (Pandey & Singh, 1986). And in another study, undergraduates instructed to draw attention to their accomplishments in a staged interaction not only failed to convey competence but were pegged as braggarts and disliked to boot (Godfrey and others, 1986). Simply injecting obvious self-praise willy-nilly

self-presentation A motive for choosing behaviors intended to create in observers a desired impression of the self.

into a conversation is an ineffective form of self-presentation. Far more acceptable tactics are discussing your strong points in response to others' comments or questions or having others do the bragging for you in letters of reference (Jones & Pittman, 1982; Holtgraves & Srull, 1989; Baumeister and others, 1989). Regardless of whether ingratiation or self-promotion is the goal, subtlety is undoubtedly the best policy. For advice on how to ingratiate yourself smoothly, look at Table 4.3.

Table 4.3. The self-presenter's handbook, lesson 1: How to make others like you without being obvious

Don't let others notice that you are conforming to their opinions. (Or, if you are going to try to get in someone's good books, keep it credible.)
- Disagree on trivial issues, agree on important ones.
- Be wishy-washy when you disagree, forceful when you agree.

Be modest (selectively).
- Make gentle fun of your standing on unimportant traits.
- Put yourself down in areas that don't make much difference.

Keep your need for others' approval under wraps.
- Don't conform or flatter someone in a situation where it is expected—for example, when talking to your boss just before annual raises are handed out.
- Use these tactics only when you really need to.
- Get others to do the self-presentation for you—for example, in letters of reference.

Bask in others' reflected glory if you can.
- Make casual references to connections with winners.
- Link yourself to losers only when it cannot be used against you.

Source: Adapted from *Interpersonal perception,* by E. E. Jones, 1990, San Francisco: Freeman, p. 184.

From Self to Behavior, and Back Again. Self-presentation can amount to a sort of "trying a self on for size," perhaps acting in a way that is consistent with an ideal "wanna-be" self (Baumeister, 1982). Adolescents, for example, may experiment with such selves as "rebel," "intellectual," or "environmental activist." These experiments can have lasting effects because self-presenters often end up influencing themselves just as much as their audience (Gergen, 1965; Schlenker, 1985; Jones and others, 1981). Actors, models, and other professional self-presenters may experience real problems, as Caprice Benedetti, a New York fashion model, pointed out. "Some days, I'm changing my face and changing my clothes 10 times. I'm elegant. I'm casual. I'm chic. I'm downtown. I'm sexy. I'm theatrical. I begin to wonder: Who am I? I'm 10 different people. Where's the real me? You have an identity crisis. Who is this?" (Kleinfield, 1993). Sorting out self-presentations from the self may be even more difficult as the performance becomes routine. We would do well to heed sociologist Erving Goffman's warning: choose your self-presentations carefully, for what starts out as a mask may become your face (Goffman, 1959).

Personality Differences in Behavior: Self-Monitoring. Although everyone engages in both self-expression and self-presentation, people show stable preferences for one or the other. This personality difference is called **self-monitoring** (Snyder, 1974). High self-monitors typically shape their behaviors to project the impression they think their current audience or situation demands. Low self-monitors behave in ways that express their internal attitudes and dispositions, and they therefore behave more consistently from audience to audience and situation to situation. You might like to answer the questions in Table 4.4 to see whether you tend to be high or low in self-monitoring.

Table 4.4. Examples of items used to measure self-monitoring

1. I have considered being an entertainer.
2. In a group of people I am rarely the center of attention.
3. I have trouble changing my behavior to suit different people and different situations.
4. I guess I put on a show to impress or entertain people.
5. I may deceive people by being friendly when I really dislike them.

Note: People who agree with items 1, 4, and 5 and disagree with items 2 and 3 are probably high in self-monitoring. The actual scale contains many more than five items, so it can more accurately classify people as high or low in self-monitoring.

Source: From "The self-monitoring of expressive behavior," by M. Snyder, 1974, *Journal of Personality and Social Psychology, 30,* p. 531.

The importance of personality differences in self-monitoring was demonstrated by a study of people's reactions to success or failure at a rather peculiar task: portraying themselves as corrupt and immoral individuals (Jones and others, 1990). In a simulated job interview, each subject pretended to be an ambitious, selfish person who would be suitable for a "cut-throat position in a dog-eat-dog environment." Some subjects learned that their act was convincing by overhearing comments like "He wouldn't mind selling his mother down the river." Others learned they had failed in their portrayals. High self-monitors felt better about themselves when they *succeeded* at the task, even though success meant convincing others that they were corrupt. Apparently creating an "appropriate" impression was more important than being true to who they really were. In contrast, low self-monitors felt better about themselves after *failing* at this task. They appear to prefer being seen as they truly are instead of successfully, even profitably, putting on a false face.

Once we have constructed a sense of self, we begin to use it to regulate many aspects of our lives. Our self-concept tends to resist change and to influence our thoughts, emotions, and behavior. Figure 4.9 summarizes some of the effects of the self.

self-monitoring A personality characteristic defined as the degree to which people are sensitive to the demands of social situations and shape their behaviors accordingly.

Figure 4.9 What a difference a self makes

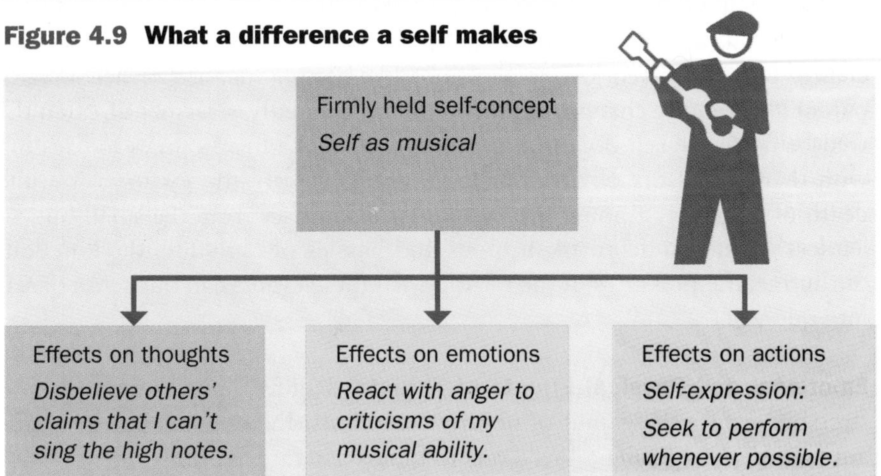
Firmly held self-concept
Self as musical
Effects on thoughts
Disbelieve others' claims that I can't sing the high notes.
Effects on emotions
React with anger to criticisms of my musical ability.
Effects on actions
Self-expression:
Seek to perform whenever possible.

Once formed, a person's self-concept influences his or her thoughts, feelings, and actions.

Defending the Self: Coping with Stresses, Inconsistencies, and Failures

Our sense of self is our most valued possession, and we certainly treat it that way. We use it continually, both as a guide for action and an aid in interpreting others' reactions to us. We keep it polished and in good repair as we enhance our self-esteem and present our best face to others. And, as we shall see, we strive to defend our sense of self against all comers. When events set off our security alarms, we may respond in two different ways. We may attempt to deal with what set off the alarm, or we may try to change the way it makes us feel.

Threats to the Well-Being of the Self

When threatened by external events or negative feedback, people must defend their sense of who and what they are. Major failures and disasters obviously threaten the self, but so do inconsistent information and daily hassles and stresses. Threats to the self affect not only emotional well-being but also physical health. The most damaging threats are those we appraise as uncontrollable.

Anything that contradicts our sense of who we are and how we feel can cause us to question our impression of the self. Three types of events pose especially significant threats. *Failures*—flubbing the driver's test, being passed over for promotion, ending a marriage in divorce—expose us to negative feedback about who we are and what we can do. *Inconsistencies*—illness in a usually healthy person, an empty nest for a full-time Mom—provide us with information that contradicts who and what we thought we were. Events do not have to be negative to be inconsistent. Because they change our lives, even joyous occasions like getting married or becoming a parent also require changes in the self-concept. Finally, *stressors* threaten the well-being of the self because they seem to exceed our resources for dealing with them. Stressors obviously include major crises—the loss of a job, the death of a spouse, a house fire. But stress also arises from the small but relentless grind-you-down frustrations and hassles of daily life, the boredom of routine, the pressures of the rat-race. All these events call our sense of self into question.

Emotional and Physical Effects of Threat. Failures, inconsistencies, and stressors arouse the gamut of negative emotions. Experiences like a serious auto accident or losing a loved one to illness activate the most intense emotions: terror, crushing depression. Such threats to the self do not affect our emotions alone. Research over the past twenty years has convinced even the sometimes-skeptical medical community that such events also contribute to physical illness. Major setbacks adversely affect our health, but so do even the everyday minor hassles—fighting with a best friend, receiving a parking ticket, having to wait in line at the bank. Threats to the self bring us down, tick us off, and also alter our immune responses, nervous-system activity, and blood pressure—the kinds of physiological changes that contribute to illness (O'Leary, 1990; Rodin & Salovey, 1989; Lazarus, 1984). For example, one study found that when people were reminded of significant self-discrepancies, levels of "natural killer" cell activity in their bloodstream decreased (Strauman and others, 1993). These immune-system cells are important in defending the body against viral infections and cancers.

It is the negative emotions we experience in response to threats that put physical health at risk. People who habitually respond to failures, setbacks, and stresses with negative emotions are the most likely to suffer physically (Watson & Pennebaker, 1989). One of the best-known examples of this finding is the Type A behavior pattern, which is associated with risks of heart disease in both men and women (Booth-Kewley & Friedman, 1987; Thoresen & Low, 1990). The Type A pattern includes ambitiousness, competitiveness, rapid speech style, hostility, and anger, but not all of these characteristics are harmful to health (Dembroski & Costa, 1987). Anger and hostility appear to be the most important risk factors (Booth-Kewley & Friedman, 1987). People who react with rage to everyday annoyances—such as noticing that the person before you in the ten-items-or-less line at the supermarket has eleven items in their shopping cart—may be at greatest risk from heart disease (Angier, 1990).

Threat and Appraisals of Control. We must respond to frustrations, shortcomings, hassles, disasters, or any event we appraise as a threat. By far the most threatening events, however, are those we judge to be out of our control (Rodin & Salovey, 1989). Think about how the issue of control might

Taking control to cope with lack of control Members of the kindergarten class at New York City's Public School 95 were caught in events outside their control on February 26, 1993. They were trapped on the observation deck of the World Trade Center after a bomb exploded 110 floors below. Perhaps some of their ability to cope grew from the control they were able to exercise: They began rehearsing for their spring show while waiting for rescue.

affect some of your own responses. Do you feel more comfortable driving a car or riding in an airplane? Most people choose driving even though flying is as much as ten times safer than driving, as measured in deaths per mile. This perverse response reflects our deep-seated preference for control. When our basic motive to master our environment is called into question, a vital part of our sense of self is threatened. Feeling that events are beyond one's control increases the likelihood of many kinds of negative outcomes, including worker "burnout" and the perception of overcrowding in dormitories and prisons (Paulus, 1988; Pines and others, 1981). For example, if you were assigned roommates in a dormitory suite, you would probably feel more crowded than if you roomed with the same number of individuals whom you had picked yourself. Not surprisingly, the anxiety and frustration that accompany lack of control take their toll on physical well-being. Uncontrollable stressful events are much more hazardous to health than controllable ones (Kiecolt-Glaser & Glaser, 1988; Frankenhaeuser & Johanssen, 1986; Fleming and others, 1987).

Control and Depression. Perhaps the most negative result of repeated experiences of lack of control is *learned helplessness* (Seligman, 1975; Abramson and others, 1978). Animals and humans that have endured uncontrollable outcomes often give up attempting to control their fate (Seligman & Maier, 1967). In one study in which people were exposed to inescapable bursts of noise, they later failed to protect themselves from noises they could easily have stopped (Hiroto, 1974). Learned helplessness can undermine people's efforts to master their situations. For example, people who work on insoluble problems or experience uncontrollable failures may give up trying, even in situations where their efforts might be of use. Part of the reason may be that repeated thoughts—such as "I can't do anything," or "My efforts are useless"—and the associated sad and hopeless emotions interfere with the thought processes that would help people actually gain control (Sedek & Kofta, 1990).

Findings such as these have led researchers to argue that appraisals of events as uncontrollable contribute to *clinical depression,* a psychological disorder characterized by negative moods, low self-esteem, pessimism, and a disruption of thinking, sleeping, eating, and activity patterns (Abramson and others, 1978). Figure 4.10 shows how the process works. A negative event or situation that occurs is appraised as both uncontrollable and laden with widespread implications for many areas of the person's life. The expectation of lack of control produces learned helplessness.

But other researchers argue that learned helplessness offers an incomplete explanation of depression. Their revised model suggests that depression is likely if global, enduring, uncontrollable events are also attributed to internal causes—that is, perceived to be "my fault" (Abramson and others, 1978). For instance, in explaining the break-up of a romantic relationship, a person might conclude that he is now and always will be completely and totally unlovable. This explanation robs him of control in his present situation and of any hope of finding a future loving relationship. Research shows that people who use a *depressive attributional style* are more likely than others to become depressed when things go wrong in their lives (Anderson and others, 1988; Nolen-Hoeksema and others, 1986).

Figure 4.10 Attributions, learned helplessness, and depression

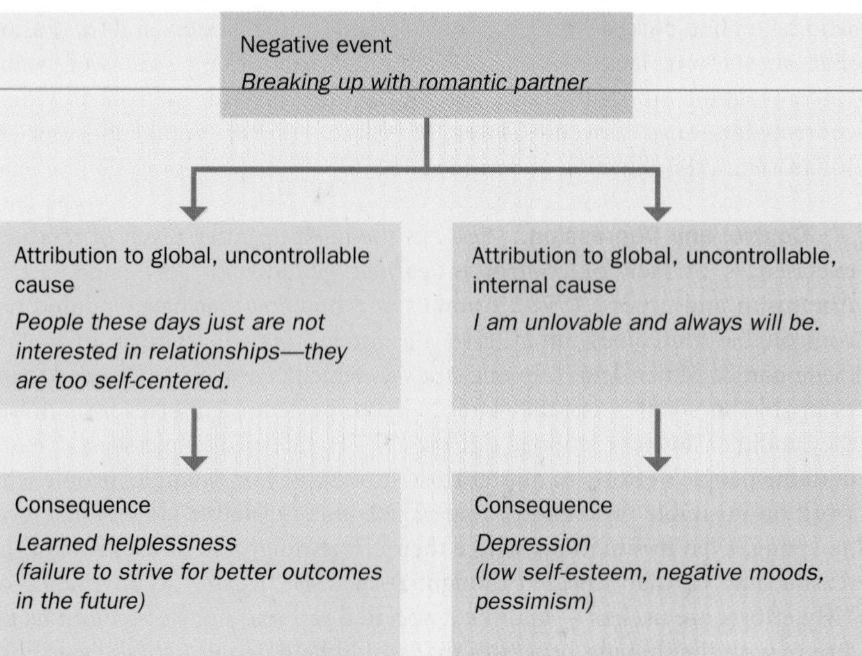

When a negative event is seen as due to a general and uncontrollable cause, people may give up and stop trying—a symptom of learned helplessness. Depression results when the cause of a negative event is seen not only as global and uncontrollable but also as internal.

Escaping from Threat: Emotion-Focused Coping

To defend against threats, people sometimes try to manage their emotional responses to threat—through escape, distraction, redefinition of an event's importance, or self-expression.

Though learned helplessness may keep people from doing anything about events that are appraised as threats to the self, people ordinarily respond with **coping strategies**—efforts to reduce the negative consequences produced by threatening events. In one common type of coping response, *emotion-focused coping,* people attempt to deal with the negative emotions associated with the event, perhaps by escaping or avoiding the threatening situation. Faced with family discord, for example, a person could ignore the problem or become immersed in some distracting hobby or activity. Other emotion-focused strategies include affirming success in a particular domain, downplaying the threat, and attempting to release stress-related emotional tension, often through prayer, meditation, self-expression, or talking about problems. How do these strategies of emotion-focused coping work?

Escaping from Threat: Shipping Out. When events conspire to bring home our failures and shortcomings, a common first impulse is to ship out rather than shape up. After all, escape mercifully terminates the painful awareness of inadequacies (Gibbons & Wicklund, 1972). Experimental evidence bears out the idea that people who have just fallen short of a personal standard will make a quick exit from the stressful situation—if they can. In one study, an experimenter told subjects that they had scored very well or very poorly on a test of intelligence and creativity and then asked them to wait five minutes for a second experimenter. For half of the subjects, the waiting room was equipped with a mirror and videocamera, both designed to induce self-awareness. Did the combination of embarrassing self-discrepancies (scoring poorly on the test) and self-awareness (finding oneself in front of mirror and camera) make escape look like the best option? Apparently so. The people who scored poorly and were told to wait in the specially equipped room left significantly sooner than did other subjects (Duval & Wicklund, 1972).

Ignoring Threat: Anything to Take My Mind Off It. Sometimes attempts to avoid painful self-knowledge and the pressures of uncontrollable events produce a new set of negative effects. People drink, take drugs, and engage in "just for kicks" risky behavior for many reasons, but sometimes these activities are attempts at blotting out the uncomfortable consequences of self-discrepancies and constant stress (Baumeister, 1991). For example, Jay Hull (1981) found that people really can "drown their sorrows" with alcohol: alcohol consumption reduces self-awareness.

Based on this finding, Hull and Robert Young (1983) reasoned that people who have experienced failure might use alcohol to escape from self-awareness, while people who had succeeded would not. To test this idea,

coping strategies Efforts undertaken to reduce negative consequences of self-threatening events.

Subjects who were high in self-consciousness and learned that they failed on a task drank more wine than students in the other three conditions—presumably to blot out painful awareness of their shortcoming. In contrast, successful students who were high in self-consciousness drank the least of any group. They probably wanted to avoid dulling their good feelings about themselves. (Data from Hull & Young, 1983.)

Figure 4.11 Effects of self-awareness on alcohol consumption

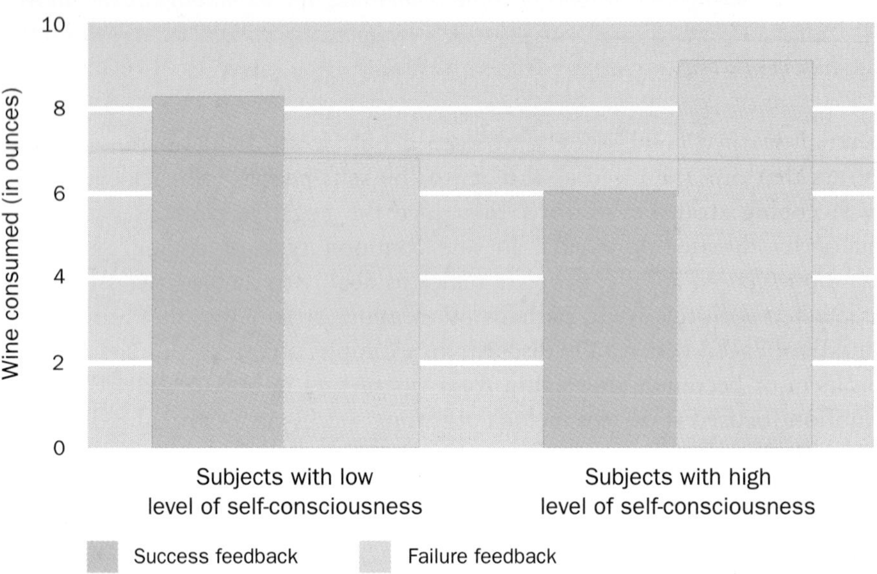

they selected students who were high or low in self-consciousness and gave them bogus success or failure feedback on intellectual tasks. They then offered them a chance to escape from their feelings, disguised as a wine-tasting task. The researchers subsequently measured the amount of wine consumed. As Figure 4.11 shows, the highly self-aware subjects who had experienced failure drank significantly more than those in the other three groups. Similarly, studies of alcohol use among high school students show that consumption is highest among those who are both high in self-consciousness and low in academic performance (Hull and others, 1986).

Of course, using alcohol to reduce self-awareness can create problems of its own. Alcohol consumption contributes to serious health risks. The short-term solace it may offer to people under stress is overshadowed by the role it plays in overall stress-related health damage.

Downplaying Threat: Accentuate the Positive, Eliminate the Negative. Fortunately, people have available more constructive strategies than drinking alcohol to help them cope with failures and shortcomings. One way to manage the negative consequences of poor performances is to downplay their importance. Faced with irrefutable evidence of our couch-potato behavior and our selfish motives, we may decide that slimness and generosity are not all they are cracked up to be. We may also downgrade their importance compared with areas in which we do excel, reasoning that those other areas of life are the ones that are *really* important (Lewicki, 1984). Research shows, for example, that the more highly skilled people are on dimensions like academic ability, social skills, or artistic ability, the more important they think those dimensions are (Pelham, 1991).

Reaffirming who we are, by expressing the personal characteristics we see as most important and value most highly, can also help us cope with failure, uncertainty, and stress (Steele, 1988). Shelley Taylor (1983) found that breast-cancer patients who were facing the possibility of death often expressed and reaffirmed what they regarded as their most basic self-aspects. Some individuals quit dead-end jobs, while others turned to writing poetry or reaffirmed significant relationships.

Protecting Self-Esteem in the Classroom. Downplaying the importance of domains in which we experience failure may bring benefits for self-esteem, but sometimes the costs are tremendous. Claude Steele (1992) has argued that high failure and dropout rates among African-American students are due at least in part to their need to protect themselves against the unremittingly negative feedback that many receive in school. Faced with teachers who expect them to fail, labeled as "at risk," and seeing their culture marginalized, some Black students may resist measuring themselves against the goals and values of an educational system that does not welcome them. One form of resistance can involve a change in self-concept, so that academic success is no longer important to self-esteem. Unfortunately, withdrawal of academic interest and effort sets off a self-fulfilling spiral of failure. As Steele puts it, this method of defending self-esteem, "like a pain-killing drug, . . . undoes [the] future as it relieves [the] vulnerability" (1992, p. 74).

Supporting Steele's views, research has shown that African-American college students' beliefs about the importance of academic achievement in their lives are strongly related to their grades—more strongly even than their level of academic preparation for college is related to grades (Nisbett and others, 1992, cited in Steele, 1992). This kind of self-esteem protection is undoubtedly a common cause of academic failure among students of all ethnic and socioeconomic backgrounds. During this period when many communities are examining ways to get the greatest payback for their education dollars, school systems might consider searching for new educational strategies that build opportunities for academic success into the curriculum. By exposing students to meaningful positive feedback, these strategies make an important contribution to students' self-esteem, and the result may be an increase in the value placed on academic achievement.

Working Through Threat: Talking It Out. "Sometimes I wonder how all those who do not write, compose, or paint can manage to escape the madness, the melancholia, the panic fear which is inherent in the human situation" (Greene, 1980, p. 285). As novelist Graham Greene realized, self-expression helps people cope emotionally. Even such simple forms of self-expression as talking about the feelings produced by threatening events can help overcome some of their emotional and physical costs (Bulman & Wortman, 1977; Tait & Silver, 1989).

James Pennebaker (1989) has championed the idea that bringing to the surface deeply buried stressful events can help alleviate some of their negative effects. In one dramatic illustration of this idea, he and his colleagues asked some students to write about personally traumatic life events that they had never before discussed, and they asked others to write about trivial topics (Pennebaker and others, 1988). On the four successive days of the experiment, the first group reexperienced extremely significant events in their lives, such as the sudden death of a sibling or an instance of childhood sexual abuse. Not surprisingly, they reported more negative feelings and more physical discomforts (headaches, muscle tension, pounding heart) at the time, compared with subjects who wrote about unimportant topics. However, physiological measures showed that immune-system functioning was superior among subjects in the first group. This boost in health persisted for six weeks, during which the trauma group visited the university health center less often than did the other subjects.

Of course, although these subjects benefited in the long run, the immediate impact of writing about traumatic events was negative. Before agreeing to participate in this study, subjects were warned that they might be asked to write about extremely upsetting events. In addition, researchers conducting studies of this type are always prepared to refer for counseling any subjects who become overly distressed.

Self-Expression and Coping with Unemployment. Another study of the effects of writing about traumatic events focused on people who had been laid off from professional jobs. They were assigned to write for twenty minutes on five successive days, either about their deepest feelings concerning the job loss or about their job-searching plans for the day. The result? This study found only small differences in physical health between the two groups. But eight months later, more than half of those who had written about their feelings had found full-time jobs, compared with less than 24 percent of those who had written only about their plans (DeAngelis, 1993). Writing about the trauma of job loss evidently helps people cope—and the concrete, practical results may include a better chance of finding a new job.

Traumatic events do, of course, harm the victim in many ways, and merely thinking and writing about the event cannot remove all its negative effects. But disclosure can at least help reduce the costs of suppressing and inhibiting painful thoughts, and it is often the first step toward appraising negative events differently (Horowitz, 1987). As you will see, reappraising events is one way to cope directly with problems.

Attacking Threat Head-On: Problem-Focused Coping

Sometimes people respond to threats directly, attempting to remove the negative event or situation itself. Possible strategies are reinterpreting evidence, making excuses, seeking to take control, or directly attacking the problem.

Focusing on the emotional responses produced by threats to the self can help us to feel good about ourselves, but sometimes we prefer tackling events head on. *Problem-focused* coping directs people's cognitive, emotional, and behavioral resources toward reinterpreting the event as nonthreatening—through biased evaluation processes—or physically removing the event.

Biased Evaluation: What Problem? As teachers, we have to tell you that we don't get many visits from students who got an *A* but think the test was unfair. Usually, it's those who do less well who think the test did not reveal their true abilities. When people receive any negative information—not just a bad test score—they may reject it out of hand or at least question its validity in order to dismiss any threat to the self. Thomas Pyszczynski and his colleagues (1985) studied this strategy in a laboratory experiment in which women took a test of "social sensitivity." Regardless of their actual performance, subjects were told either that they had done well or had performed poorly. They were then invited to read and evaluate two research reports, one supporting the validity of the social sensitivity test, the other questioning it. As you might have guessed, the subjects' evaluations of the two research reports were determined by their supposed scores on the test. Those who had "succeeded" thought the supporting study was the better of the two; those who had "failed" came to the opposite conclusion. This kind of biased evaluation of self-relevant information can help us cope with our failures and shortcomings: a threat redefined can be a threat defeated.

Making Excuses: It's Not My Problem. What happens when our worst fears are realized and we do fail a test, get caught out in a lie, or get pulled over for speeding on the expressway? Although we have all wished the earth would open up and swallow us under such circumstances, our usual recourse is to apologize, offer excuses, and try and pick up where we left off. Whenever an action ends in disaster and threatens our self-concept, a good excuse is worth its weight in gold.

Why are excuses so important? The answer has to do with *self-enhancing attributions* that distort people's explanations for successes and failures (Mullen & Riordan, 1988). Most people like to take credit for their successes and notable accomplishments and to attribute failure to external causes. A good grade on an exam reflects well on our intelligence and motivation, while a failing grade is surely due to poorly written test items, an emergency at home, a sudden bout of the flu, or even loud music playing down the hall (Miller & Ross, 1975). "I missed the appointment because my car broke down." "The dog ate my homework." "That old football injury got in my way." Yankee baseball star Yogi Berra was a master of the excuse, proclaiming, "I never blame myself when I'm not hitting. I just blame the bat and if it keeps up I change bats. . . . After all, if I know it isn't my fault that I'm not hitting, how can I get mad at myself?"

Self-Handicapping. A good excuse can be even more valuable if it is lined up before the performance: if we do fail, our defense is already in place. Charles Snyder and his colleagues found that people often use disclaimers like shyness, anxiety, ill health, or disruptive events when they anticipate failing at an important task (Snyder & Higgins, 1988; Snyder and others, 1985). Letting others think we are shy, sick, or under stress seems preferable to conveying the impression that we are unlikable or incompetent.

If verbal excuses help us save face, could the creation of actual barriers to successful performance do the same? Strange as it may seem, some people actually sabotage their own performance to provide an excuse for subsequent failure. The strategy is called *self-handicapping* (Berglas & Jones, 1978). To see how and why self-handicapping might work, imagine that you have been bragging for months about your chicken curry, and now your friends are finally coming over for dinner. It suddenly occurs to you that your culinary skills may not quite match those you have advertised. Is there any way out? One possibility is self-handicapping—you could intentionally arrange to run out of a crucial ingredient for the curry. In attributional terms, self-handicapping is a no-lose proposition: observers' impressions of your skill will be even more positive than they otherwise would be, regardless of the dinner's failure or success. If the curry is not so great, your reputation as a great cook will be saved as your friends blame the disaster on the missing ingredient rather than on your poor skills. If the dinner is wonderful anyway, your culinary expertise will appear even more impressive. But remember, you purchased this attributional benefit of self-handicapping at the cost of lowering your real probability of good performance: you chose probable failure rather than the attributional consequences of *possible* failure (Baumgardner & Brownlee, 1987).

Taking Control of the Problem. If external attributions usually help us to save face, what do you make of the following finding? In one survey of U.S. residents, people who regarded themselves as poor or economically struggling were questioned about their attributions for their situation and about their general emotional well-being. Poor people who believed they had had a fair chance to achieve felt more pride and joy and less guilt and disappointment about their lives than those who believed that external forces had held them back (Smith & Kluegel, 1982). That is, even when their outcomes are negative, people often feel better if they think they have control. Blaming external factors for failures might let you off the hook momentarily, but interpreting as *controllable* the forces that influence your life will put you back in charge for the long term.

Consider what happened, for example, when Ellen Langer and Judith Rodin decided to see what difference a small degree of control would make to the well-being of a sample of nursing-home residents (1976; Rodin & Langer, 1977). The daily routine in most nursing homes is highly regulated, and residents' ability to control their own lives is limited. Langer and Rodin

Figure 4.12 How increased control can affect well-being

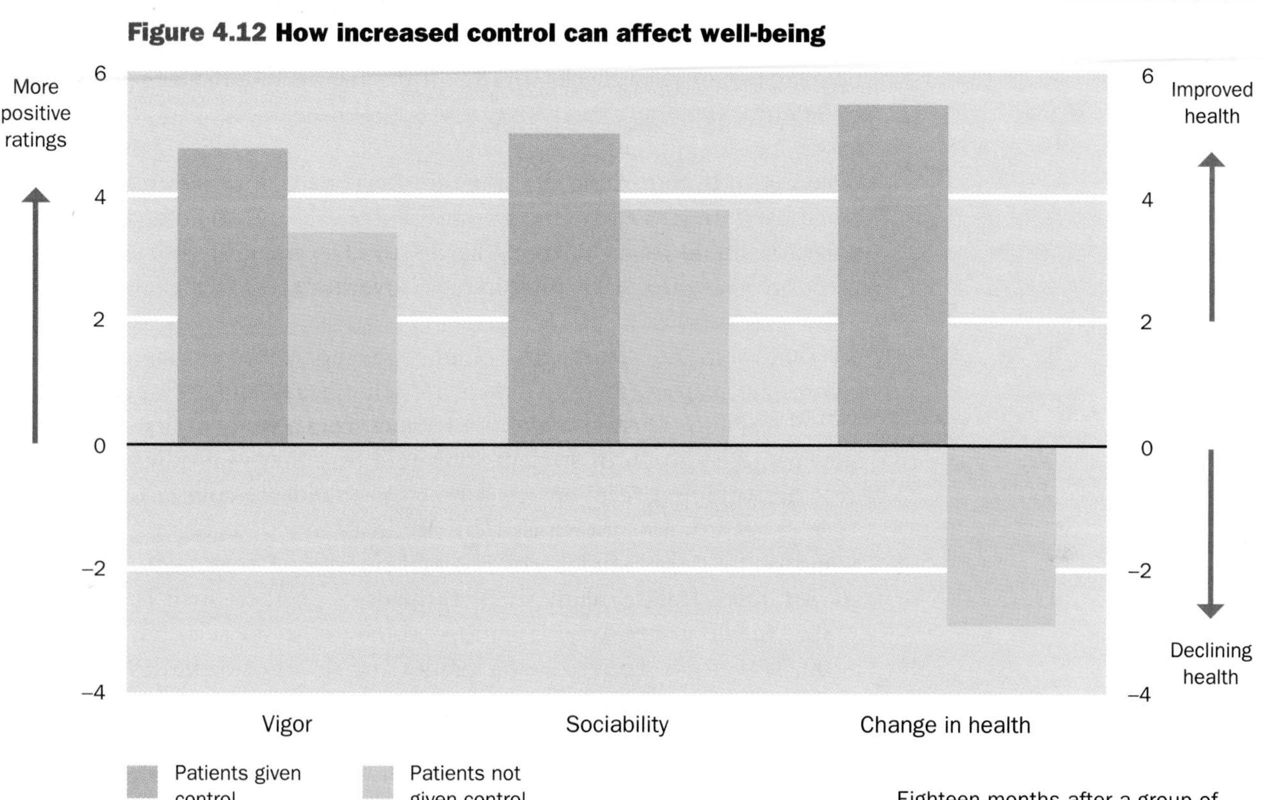

Eighteen months after a group of nursing-home residents were given increased control over small aspects of their daily lives, the staff rated them as more vigorous and more sociable than a comparison group of patients, as shown on the left scale. Correspondingly, control led to an improvement in physical health over the eighteen-month period, while the health of the comparison group had deteriorated, as shown on the right scale. (Data from Rodin & Langer, 1977.)

encouraged a randomly selected group of residents in one home to control such matters as the movies they chose to attend and the location of plants placed in their rooms. Compared with other residents who did not have these opportunities for control, the participants in the study felt better and remained healthier longer, as can be seen in Figure 4.12. In fact, eighteen months after the initial contact, only 15 percent of the group with increased control had died, compared with 30 percent of the comparison group. Feelings of control are so important that we attempt to exert control whenever we can (White, 1959). In fact, we often exaggerate the amount of control we possess, even in situations actually ruled by chance (Langer, 1975). For example, most people who play the state lottery prefer to pick their "lucky number," even though any number would have an equal chance of winning.

What can give people the feeling that they can control events in their lives? One crucial ingredient is their confidence in their ability to deal with a particular area, such as passing exams in psychology or successfully managing their social life. This confidence in our ability to produce the outcomes we desire is termed *self-efficacy* (Bandura, 1986). Self-efficacy is particularly strongly linked with the way people explain their *failures:* whether they explain them in terms of controllable or uncontrollable causes. If the bank bounces one of your checks for the third time this month and you explain it by saying "Oh, I just can't keep a checkbook balanced; I'm no good at finance," you are pointing to your supposed lack of ability—an uncontrollable cause. If you blame the situation on your lack of effort or attention, you are pointing to a potentially controllable cause. Such an explanation for a failure should lead you to try harder to keep track of your deposits and withdrawals, which may result in fewer overdraft fees in the future.

Control in the Classroom. Can people be trained to blame failures on controllable causes, thereby improving self-efficacy and even performance? One clue that the answer may be yes comes from a study of first-year college students. One group of students was told that first-year adjustment problems are common reactions to the new demands of college life, and that such problems are not caused by students' own inadequacies. Another group of first-year students was given no special treatment, presumably leaving them free to blame their difficulties on their own shortcomings. When the two groups were compared at the end of the school year, students in the first group received better grades and fewer of them dropped out of college (Wilson & Linville, 1982).

Training that increases feelings of control apparently works for elementary-school students, too. Children who are taught to view their failures as a consequence of either their lack of effort or their use of ineffective strategies—not the uncontrollable factor of low ability—improve in persistence and classroom performance (Dweck, 1986). And children who are given a sense of control over their own behavior are less aggressive than children whose every action is externally constrained (Ryan & Grolnick, 1986). This finding is particularly dramatic because it contradicts the usual assumption that externally imposed rewards and punishments are the best means of reducing aggression.

Edward Deci and Richard Ryan (1987) draw a number of lessons from studies like these. They argue that the unequal power inherent in the teacher-student relationship often robs students of a sense of control. Teacher-imposed rules, deadlines, and performance standards are all culprits in this theft. The result is that the pupils lose their intrinsic motivation to learn and school then holds no interest or enjoyment. If students are permitted to join in setting rules and exercising choices, both their outlook and their performance improve.

Solving the Problem: Rising to the Challenge. The negative feelings aroused by failures, self-discrepancies, and stress can have positive motivational consequences. We do not always ship out; sometimes we decide to shape up. When people believe they can successfully reduce self-

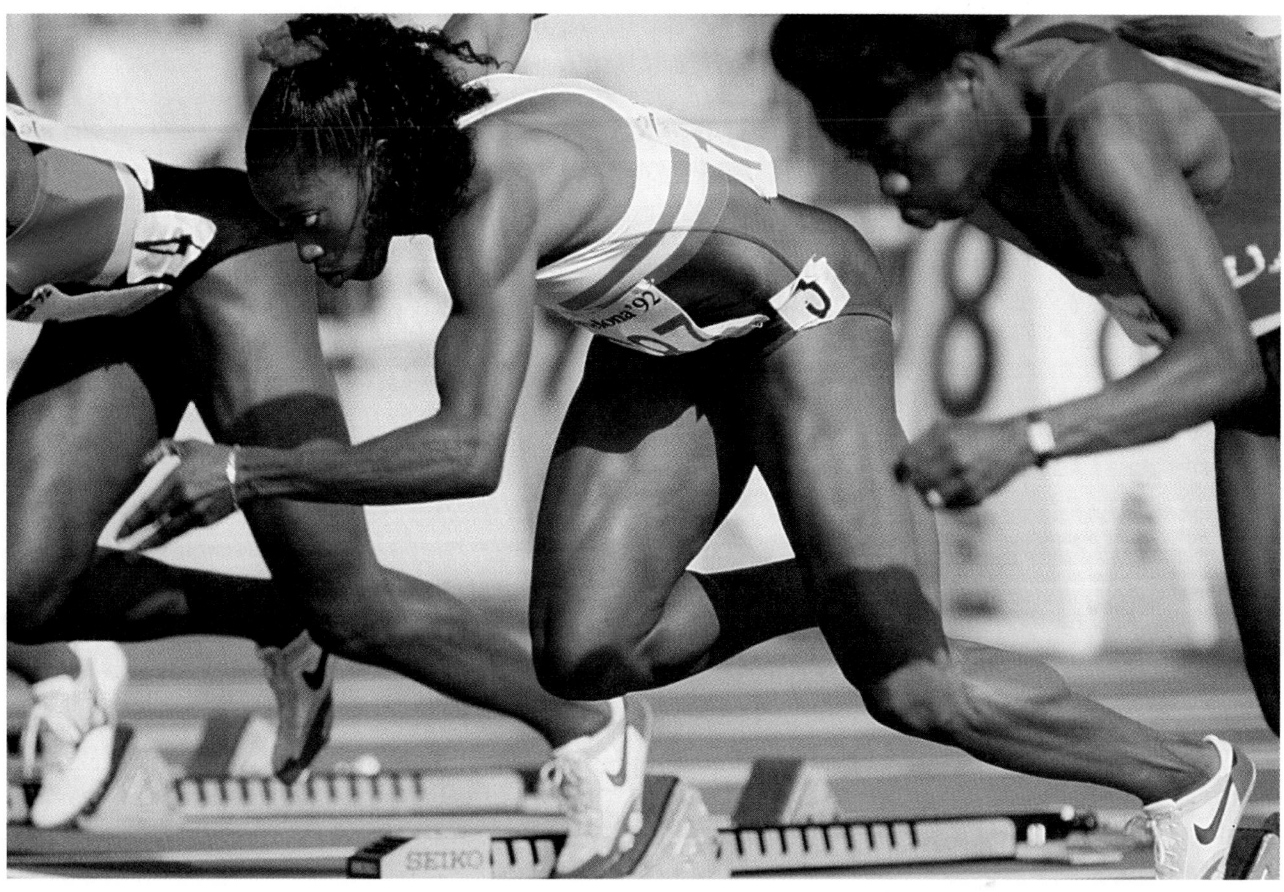

Rising to the challenge Only a year before she won an Olympic gold medal in the women's 100-meter sprint, Gail Devers couldn't walk. After a diagnosis of a thyroid condition provided an explanation for a variety of debilitating symptoms, Devers struggled to overcome their effects and get back into the kind of shape that allowed her to win this competitive race. Her friends and family credit her strong personality and the support of her trainer for the turnaround.

discrepancies, when they attribute their shortcomings to controllable forces, or when they see ways to master real-life problems, they often work to do so. Many residents of high-crime neighborhoods are dealing with their stress by fighting back—organizing neighborhood crime-watch networks, volunteering for safety patrols, and developing after-school activities for latch-key children. Many have successfully moved drug dealers out of their neighborhoods.

The painful nature of self-discrepancies can also motivate people to live up to their own ideals and self-guides. Self-awareness often makes people behave in ways consistent with their own personal values (Gibbons, 1978). Startled by being labeled as a couch potato, the former star quarterback might decide to substitute an hour of lifting weights for an hour of watching TV reruns. When we can attribute bad outcomes to controllable factors, we can activate strategies designed to change our performance. If you decide that your low grade was due to a lack of preparation rather than an inability to understand the material, setting up a regular study time may help you prepare for the next exam well in advance.

How to Cope?

The individual's resources as well as characteristics of the threatening situation dictate the best response to threats. No single type of response is always best, but many types of coping can help overcome the threat, preserve psychological well-being, and protect physical health.

As we have seen, there are many ways to cope with threats to the self. Both problem-focused and emotion-focused coping can improve psychological well-being and lessen the health damage caused by threatening events (Cohen, 1984; Kiecolt-Glaser and others, 1987). But which type works better? The answer depends on the threatened—the individual and the resources she or he brings to the situation—and also on the threat, particularly its controllability.

Personality Resources for Coping. Different people have different cognitive and emotional resources at their disposal to aid in coping. Recall that people with high self-complexity are better able to ride out a jolt to a specific self-aspect because their other self-aspects remain unthreatened. Self-esteem is also an important resource for coping with threats to the self. Those with high self-esteem roll out a formidable arsenal of weapons to defend against threats. For example, they fight negative feedback, setbacks, or stress with an aggressive use of self-enhancing biases and problem-focused coping (Epstein, 1992; Josephs and others, 1992; Brown, 1986). They compare themselves with others who are worse off and make self-enhancing attributions for their failures and shortcomings. A challenge to one aspect of the self-concept, such as interpersonal sensitivity, may be met with affirmation of another aspect: generosity, athletic prowess, or intellectual acumen (Steele, 1988). Finally, a strong sense of control lets people with high self-esteem tackle problems head-on. The successful use of this impressive array of self-enhancing biases and coping strategies restores and maintains high self-esteem so the whole cycle can begin again (Taylor & Brown, 1988). Like a reflection in a series of fun-house mirrors, high self-esteem leads to self-enhancement and successful coping, which restore high self-esteem, which triggers self-enhancement, and so on. No wonder, then, that people with high self-esteem respond to threat with far fewer emotional and physical symptoms than do those with low self-esteem (Brown & Smart, 1991).

If you have ever interacted with someone who has low self-esteem, however, you may have noticed a completely different set of reactions. Rather than predicting that the rain clouds will be followed by spring flowers, people with low self-esteem seem resigned to permanent flood conditions. Indeed, depressed people and those with low self-esteem are much less likely to self-enhance than others (Alloy & Abramson, 1979; Taylor & Brown, 1988). They make downward comparisons less often, remember more negative things about themselves, and assume they have less control over events.

Interestingly, however, the less positive and protective views of the world expressed by mildly depressed people are more accurate than those formed by the self-enhancing majority (Taylor & Brown, 1988). Researchers have coined the term *depressive realism* to capture the idea that mildly depressed people are more accurate self-evaluators and less enthusiastic self-enhancers than others. But despite their accuracy, these individuals see the world as a dangerous and threatening place.

So it is clear that everyday decisions—whether to apply for graduate school, try out for the band, or ask a popular classmate for a date—are very different proposals for different individuals, depending on their level of self-esteem. Great rewards might follow from taking these actions, but individuals with low self-esteem may be unable to take the risk because they are highly sensitive to the possibility of failure and embarrassment (Leary and others, 1986). "To the person high in self-esteem . . . the world is an oyster bed of opportunities to enhance themselves, but to the person low in self-esteem, it is a minefield that can humiliate and depress" (Josephs and others, 1992, p. 35). With fewer personal resources to fall back on, people with low self-esteem typically engage in denial, escape, or avoidance of threat (Epstein, 1992).

Controllability and Coping. The best way to cope depends on the characteristics of the threat as well as those of the threatened. The most important appraisal is of a threat's controllability. With controllable threats, problem-focused coping might be best. In contrast, escape, distraction, and other forms of emotion-focused coping may be the only effective ways to deal with uncontrollable threats and stressors (Folkman, 1984). Sometimes the best solution is trying both types of coping at once. When a romantic relationship breaks up, for example, the two newly alone individuals may be well advised to try both to meet new people (problem-focused attempts) and to immerse themselves in a new hobby or interest (emotion-focused activities).

Aid in fighting stress also comes from external sources. The presence of others who give support, advice, and assistance can help ward off the negative consequences of threat. We see how this happens in Chapter 11, pages 475 to 478.

Calvin and Hobbes by Bill Watterson

Figure 4.13 Ways of coping and their effects

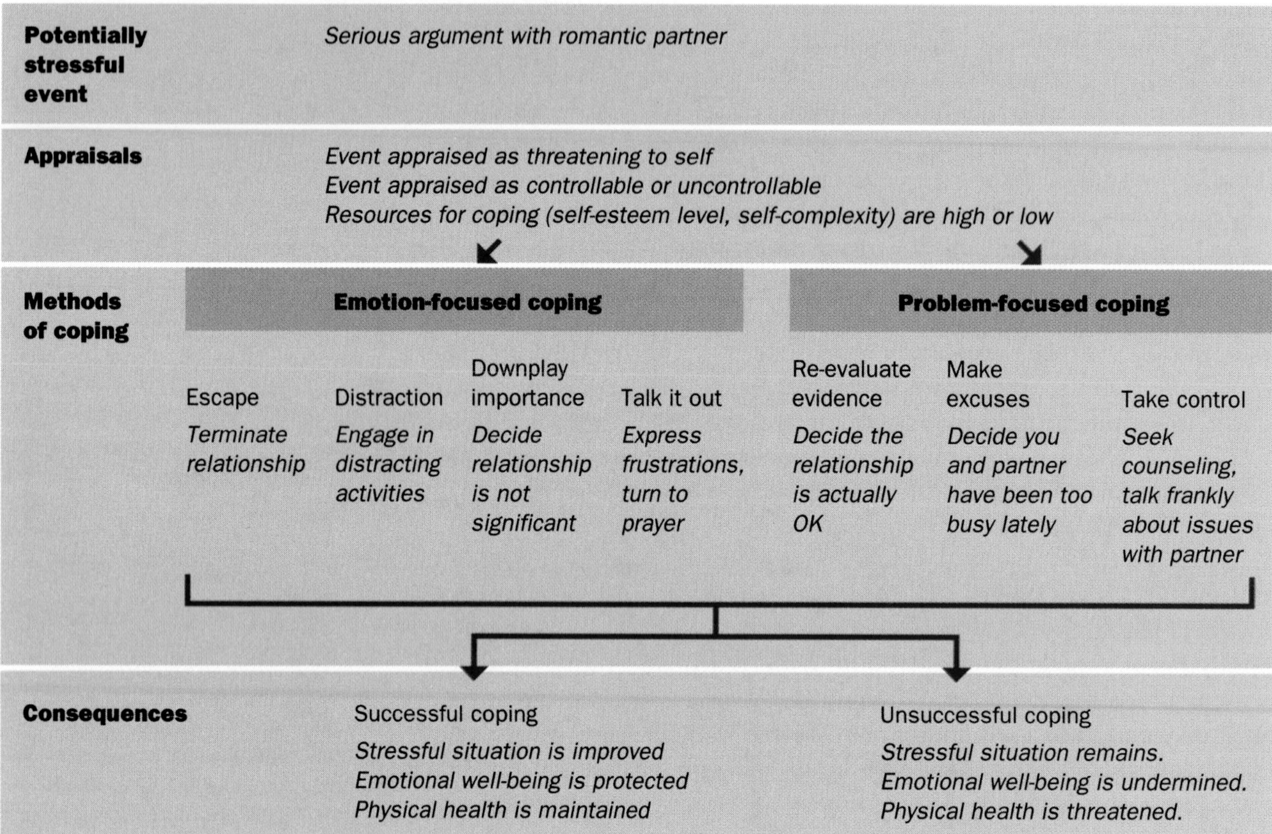
Potentially stressful event
Serious argument with romantic partner
Appraisals
Event appraised as threatening to self
Event appraised as controllable or uncontrollable
Resources for coping (self-esteem level, self-complexity) are high or low
Methods of coping
Emotion-focused coping
Problem-focused coping
Escape
Terminate relationship
Distraction
Engage in distracting activities
Downplay importance
Decide relationship is not significant
Talk it out
Express frustrations, turn to prayer
Re-evaluate evidence
Decide the relationship is actually OK
Make excuses
Decide you and partner have been too busy lately
Take control
Seek counseling, talk frankly about issues with partner
Consequences
Successful coping
Stressful situation is improved
Emotional well-being is protected
Physical health is maintained
Unsuccessful coping
Stressful situation remains.
Emotional well-being is undermined.
Physical health is threatened.

Appraisals of a self-threatening event—particularly of its controllability—and of one's coping resources influence the selection of coping strategies. Successful or unsuccessful coping may influence emotional well-being and physical health—as well as affecting the concrete stressful situation itself.

Costs and Benefits of Coping Strategies. Depending on their appraisals of the threat and of their own resources, people can choose among many possible coping strategies, as Figure 4.13 shows. Every style of coping, however, has costs as well as benefits. Avoidance can efficiently reduce the stress of short-term threats, but it does not help people anticipate and manage long-term problems (Suls & Fletcher, 1985). Problem-focused confrontation makes long-term stress reduction more likely, but it increases immediate distress (Miller & Mangan, 1983). Defending the self often presents us with dilemmas such as these (Wood, 1989; Taylor & Lobel, 1989).

Concluding Comments

We started the chapter by saying that one of the most important life tasks each of us faces is understanding both who we are and how we feel about ourselves. Philosophers have long admonished us to "know thyself," the first aspect of this important task. An accurate understanding of our individual abilities, preferences, and talents enables us to choose the partners, pastimes, and professions that suit us best. It lets us know where we fit in the world of others and provides a starting point in any attempt at change or improvement. But psychologists know that "know thyself" is not enough. Positive self-esteem is equally central in our lives. Viewing the self as both good and in control—even in exaggerated ways—protects our emotional and physical well-being as we cope with inconsistencies, failures, and stress. Whenever we think about the self, we are faced with two sometimes-conflicting motives: enhancing the self and accurately evaluating the self.

The dual needs for accurate self-knowledge and positive self-esteem play themselves out in a variety of ways that were evident throughout this chapter. Sometimes we seek accurate assessments of the self; at other times we engage in biased searches or interpretations to come up with self-enhancing information. Sometimes we compare ourselves with similar others and sometimes with others who are worse off than we are. Sometimes we choose our behaviors to accurately reflect the person we believe we are, but at other times we try to create a positive impression of ourselves. Even the ways we defend ourselves against such threats as negative feedback, obvious shortcomings, and large and small stressors provoke the same dilemma. The warm glow of positive thinking infuses us with strength to clear life's many hurdles, but escaping into a fantasy world of self-enhancement can just as easily set us up for a fall. Taking negative feedback at face value can help us to deal constructively with, and possibly to overcome, our failures and shortcomings. But it can also be painful.

Does this mean we are caught in a no-win situation, forced to make trade-offs between reality and illusion, happiness and depression? Are our choices limited to being eternal optimists, happy but out of touch, or hard realists, on top of the facts but miserable because of it? Fortunately, we have other options. The recipe for a healthy sense of self calls for both accurate self-knowledge and protective self-enhancement, in just the right amounts at just the right times. Weighing these ingredients may be the most important aspect of constructing and maintaining the self. The correct measure of self-enhancement keeps our spirits high and our body healthy, while a judicious amount of self-assessment keeps our goals realistic and our efforts focused in the best direction. A good dollop of self-evaluation tells us what we need to do, a splash of self-enhancement gives us the courage to do it.

Chapter 4 Themes

Construction of Reality
We construct an impression of the self, based on a multitude of cues.

Pervasiveness of Social Influence
Our perceptions of other people and their reactions to us pervasively influence our self-concept and self-esteem.

Striving for Mastery
Perceiving that we control our environment helps mental well-being and physical health.

Valuing Me and Mine
Self-enhancing biases shape our self-concept and elevate self-esteem.

Conservatism
Once formed, the self-concept is resistant to change and well defended against threats.

Accessibility
The self-concept and self-esteem depend on information and experiences that come readily to mind.

Summary

Constructing the Self-Concept: What We Know About Ourselves People construct the **self-concept** in much the same way that they form impressions of others—using similar types of information and similar interpretive processes. People often infer their own characteristics from their observed behaviors, as **self-perception theory** notes. They also use thoughts and feelings and other people's reactions to form opinions about themselves. Finally, according to **social comparison theory**, people compare themselves to others to learn what characteristics make them unique.

Despite the general similarity of the ways people learn about themselves and others, self-knowledge is richer and more detailed than knowledge about others. People can observe themselves in more situations and have better access to private thoughts and feelings. People also tend to explain their own and other people's behaviors differently, producing **actor-observer differences in attribution.** They attribute their own actions to properties of the situation or the stimulus, while explaining others' actions by their personal characteristics. However, even people's explanations for their own behaviors may be inaccurate.

Because people see themselves in a wide range of situations and roles, self-knowledge is organized around multiple self-aspects representing roles, activities, and relationships. People vary in **self-complexity**, the number and diversity of **"selves"** that they believe they possess.

People try to fit the diverse elements of self-knowledge together in a way that seems coherent and stable. Coherence can be attained by making accessible only limited facets of the self at any given time, by selectively remembering past acts, by explaining away inconsistencies, and by focusing on a few central traits. Cultures influence the ways in which people seek coherence.

Constructing Self-Esteem: How We Feel About Ourselves Self-esteem is greatly influenced by motivational pressures to think well of the self. These motivations color many of our thoughts and feelings about the self through **self-enhancing biases.**

People evaluate the self on the basis of daily successes and failures and through social comparisons with others. In addition, **self-discrepancy theory** holds that people compare themselves with their own internal standards. Any of these sources of evaluation may be biased toward elevating self-esteem. For example, people often seek areas of activity in which they can succeed, compare themselves with others who are worse off, and make biased estimates of how they measure up.

Although our thoughts are turned outward most of the time, some events create **self-awareness,** a state of heightened awareness of the self, including our internal standards and whether we measure up to them. Focusing attention on the self makes self-discrepancies obvious.

Effects of the Self: Directing Emotion and Behavior Once the self-concept is formed, it tends to resist change by new information and begins to regulate many aspects of our lives. Emotions are sparked by **cognitive appraisals** of self-relevant events and their causes. Emotions signal the occurrence of significant events and motivate us to act in response—for example, to flee from danger. As they perform this function, emotions involve the whole self, body and mind; they activate facial expressions, physiological responses, subjective feelings, and overt behaviors.

The self also directs behavior. Sometimes people engage in **self-expression**, acting in ways that express their true inner selves. At other times, people are concerned with **self-presentation**, attempting to shape others' opinions in order to gain power, influence, or approval. The personality variable **self-monitoring** reflects the degree to which people seek these two general goals. But even behaviors intended for others' consumption may end up influencing people's private views of themselves.

Defending the Self: Coping with Stresses, Inconsistencies, and Failures When threatened by external events or negative feedback, people must defend their sense of who and what they are. Major failures and disasters obviously threaten the self, but so do inconsistent information, daily hassles, and stresses. Threats to the self affect not only emotional well-being but also physical health. The most damaging threats are those we appraise as uncontrollable.

Faced with threats, people respond with **coping strategies**. Sometimes they try to manage their emotional responses to threat—through escape, distraction, redefinition of an event's importance, or self-expression. At other times, people respond to threats directly, trying to reduce the negative consequences of self-threatening events. Possible strategies are reinterpreting evidence, making excuses, seeking to take control, or directly attacking the problem.

The individual's resources, including self-esteem and self-complexity, as well as characteristics of the threatening situation, dictate the best response to threats. No single type of response is always best, but many types of coping can help overcome the threat, preserve psychological well-being, and protect physical health.

Chapter 4 Overview

Based on

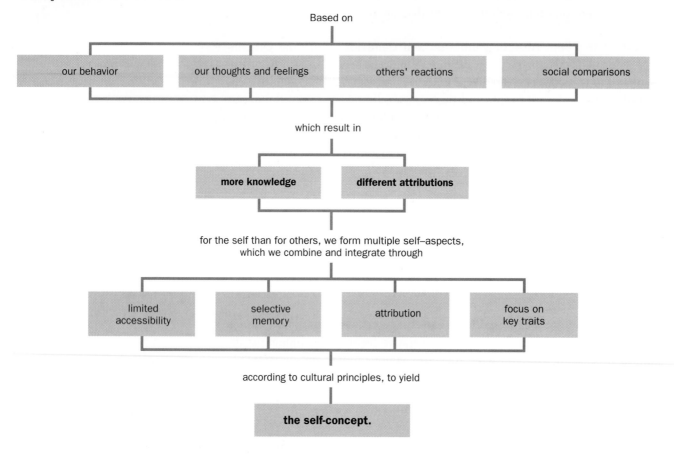

our behavior | our thoughts and feelings | others' reactions | social comparisons

which result in

more knowledge | **different attributions**

for the self than for others, we form multiple self–aspects, which we combine and integrate through

limited accessibility | selective memory | attribution | focus on key traits

according to cultural principles, to yield

the self-concept.

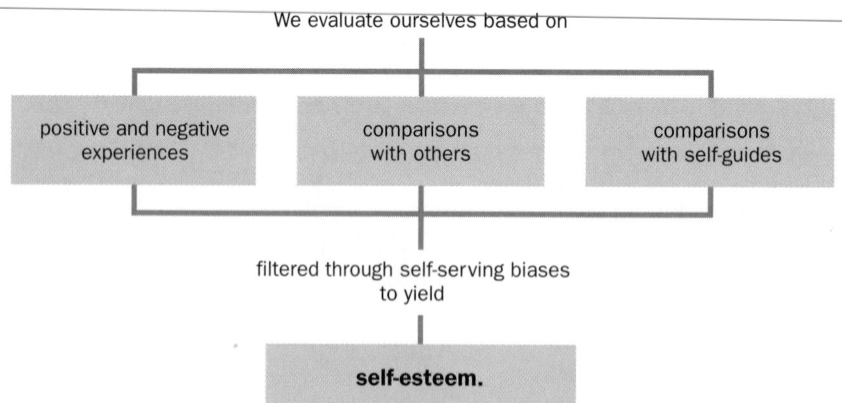

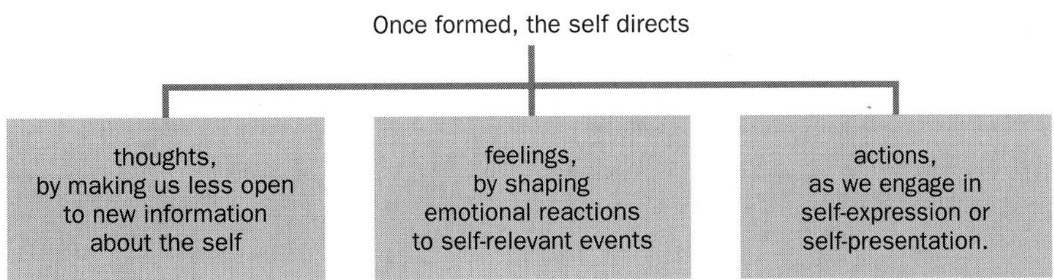
Once formed, the self directs
thoughts,
by making us less open
to new information
about the self
feelings,
by shaping
emotional reactions
to self-relevant events
actions,
as we engage in
self-expression or
self-presentation.

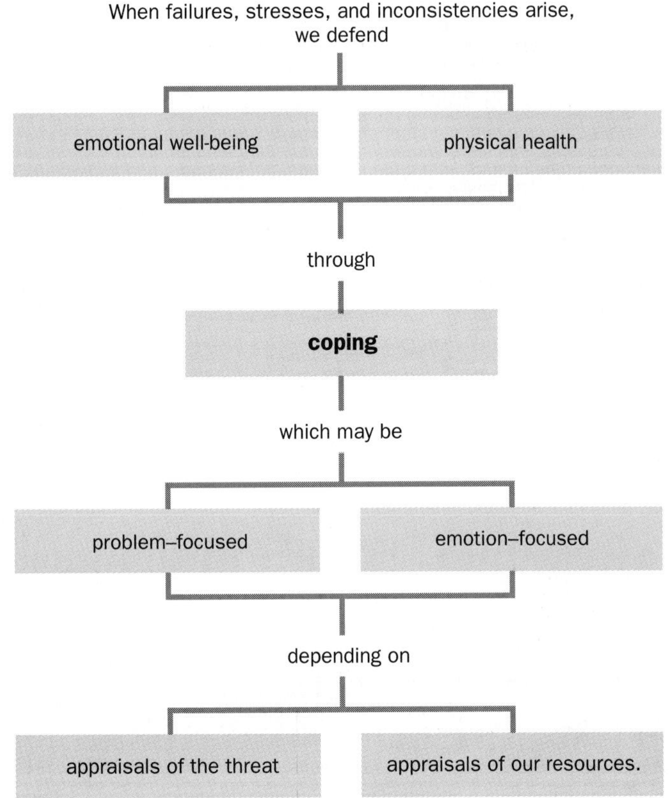
When failures, stresses, and inconsistencies arise,
we defend
emotional well-being
physical health
through
coping
which may be
problem–focused
emotion–focused
depending on
appraisals of the threat
appraisals of our resources.

GO BRAVES
BRAVES

5

Perceiving Groups

Cedric Holloway sat in his car outside the Great Western Bank in Tamarac, Florida, poring over the current interest rates for certificates of deposit and money market funds. Earlier in the day, the twenty-year-old chef's helper had visited the Great Western twice trying to decide how to invest the $1,000 he had saved. Suddenly his car was surrounded by sheriff's deputies, guns drawn. Holloway was ordered out of the car, handcuffed, and read his rights. Why? Because bank employees, suspicious that the young man was planning to rob their branch, had called the police. After forty-five minutes of questioning, the police accepted Holloway's explanation and released him (Williams, 1991).

Were the officers justified in suspecting that the man parked outside the Florida bank was a potential bank robber? Or was Holloway, an African American, approached, accused, and arrested because he was a victim of discrimination? The term **discrimination** refers to positive or negative behavior directed toward a social group and its members. Of course, people are usually concerned with negative behaviors—with discrimination *against* a specific group—but discrimination against one group inevitably amounts to discrimination in favor of others. For example, the South African system of apartheid—legally enforced segregation—victimized Blacks while preserving the power and wealth of the small White minority. Apartheid and many other forms of discrimination are outlawed in the United States, but many people still find themselves ill-treated because of their group memberships. Physical attacks, vandalism, harassment, and threats against Jewish Americans, African Americans, Japanese Americans, and gay men and lesbians have increased in recent years (Baker and others, 1991; Greer, 1991; Mydans, 1992). Economic discrimination victimizes women and people of color when they try to purchase a used car, rent or purchase a home, or negotiate a salary (Schmidt, 1990; Abrams, 1991; Goldin, 1990). And, as Cedric Holloway and most young African-American men are well aware, non-Whites' experiences with the criminal justice system differ substantially from those of most Whites (Bell, 1973; Silverstein, 1965).

Unfortunately, discrimination seems to be found everywhere around the globe. People of Korean descent living in Japan—even those whose families

Stereotypes and society It is easy to see the prejudice reflected in cross-burnings and massacres. But sometimes stereotypes are so embedded in cultural practice and are such a routine part of our thinking that it takes a special effort to see their powerful effects and their implications for our views of other social groups.

Cedric Holloway This young man's experience offers graphic evidence of the extent to which stereotypes can bias our perception of individuals.

have resided there for generations—are barred from voting and are required to carry alien registration cards at all times and to report their addresses to the government (Sterngold, 1992). French Canadians feel oppressed by the English-speaking majority; Canadian Mohawk Indians feel oppressed by French Canadians. Between 1988 and 1990 the number of racially motivated incidents of harassment or violence reported to the police in Britain jumped nearly 50 percent (Nelan, 1991). Turks and other foreigners living in Germany have been victims of verbal abuse, beatings, arson, and murder by neo-Nazis and teenage "skinheads." Tamils in Sri Lanka, Sikhs in India, and Blacks in South Africa have little access to adequate schooling, health care, or political power.

What leads one group of people to victimize another? Religious thinkers, political leaders, social scientists, and others have searched for an answer to this important question. Social psychologists believe that the underlying processes leading to discrimination usually include **prejudice**—the positive or negative evaluation of a social group and its members. Once again, people's concern is most often with negative evaluations, which range all the way from mild dislike to blind hatred. As you will see in the first part of this chapter, prejudice is complex and multifaceted, and its roots can be traced to cognitive and social processes that guide our every interaction with groups. So many processes contribute to prejudice, in fact, that we will need two chapters (Chapters 5 and 6) to tell the whole story.

In this chapter we start with the very basis of prejudice: the way people divide the world into social groups. We then consider the **stereotypes**, or impressions, that people form of groups by associating particular characteristics and emotions with particular groups (Hamilton, 1981; Eagly & Mladinic, 1989). The sometimes biased and often sketchy impressions we form of groups can permeate our thinking and become a basis for both prejudice and discrimination. For example, many White Americans associate African-American men with the characteristics of violence and criminal behavior. In Cedric Holloway's case, this stereotype was translated into prejudice—the mistaken evaluation of Holloway's motives—and discrimination—his mistreatment by bank employees and the police.

Is it possible to eliminate the stereotypical thinking that contributes to prejudice? Will a young African-American man ever just fade into the crowd of other bank customers, attracting no more and no less suspicion than they do? The answer is a cautious but optimistic yes. Stereotypes can be changed, though it does not happen easily. Initial impressions of groups, like first impressions of individuals, tend to have a lasting power. Established stereotypes often influence thoughts and behaviors in ways that make stereotypes resistant to modification. But as you will see in the final section of this chapter, the defenses protecting stereotypes from change can be breached under some conditions. Negative stereotypes can then be replaced by more favorable impressions, and prejudice can be replaced by more positive evaluations.

discrimination Any positive or negative behavior that is directed toward a social group and its members.

prejudice A positive or negative evaluation of a social group and its members.

stereotype A cognitive representation or impression of a social group that people form by associating particular characteristics and emotions with the group.

The Social and Cognitive Roots of Prejudice

It is discouragingly easy to find evidence of racism, sexism, and other "-isms" throughout the world—prejudice based on race, ethnicity, age, gender, religion, and sexual preference. For example, about half of all Americans polled believe that too many immigrants are entering the country from Asia and Latin America (*Newsweek,* 1990). Seventy-one percent of French citizens think that too many "foreigners" live in France, and 94 percent acknowledge that prejudice is "widespread." Citizens of Great Britain and Italy express similar feelings (Nelan, 1991). To explain these findings, we need to understand how prejudice arises and how groups become the target of everything from mild dislike to contemptuous hatred.

What Causes Prejudice?

Prejudice, the positive or negative evaluation of a social group and its members, has at times been viewed as the product of distorted thinking in a few troubled individuals. But both social and cognitive factors contribute to prejudice. One important source of prejudice is people's beliefs about a group's positive or negative characteristics.

Prejudice can be "hot" or "cold." Virulent hatred for other groups, such as that espoused by the Nazis or the Ku Klux Klan, is easy to recognize. It shows itself in burning crosses, campaigns of "ethnic cleansing," pogroms, and massacres. Unfortunately, the very obviousness of this type of bigotry and hatred may blind us to a more insidious type of prejudice based on the calm assumption that certain groups just "do not have what it takes" and should therefore be excluded from desirable positions, wealth, or power. This quieter, cooler form of prejudice is at work when sports-team owners profit from the performance of African-American athletes on the field but can never find a "qualified" African American for a front-office job. And it is present when construction unions maintain an all-male membership by restricting access to apprenticeship programs, or when real estate agents steer prospective home buyers to particular neighborhoods based on their race. Such discriminatory actions are carried out calmly, routinely, and without any of the familiar overt signs of bigotry. But even though no hooded robes or swastika armbands are anywhere in sight, very real harm is suffered by those on the receiving end.

Prejudice wears so many different faces that it is no wonder no single cause of prejudice has been found. Some of social psychologists' first systematic attempts to explain prejudice were triggered by the genocidal policies of the Nazi government during the Second World War (Ashmore & DelBoca, 1981). The extreme nature of that prejudice and discrimination seemed to call for equally extreme explanations.

The Authoritarian Personality Explanation. Drawing on the work of Sigmund Freud, researchers theorized that hatred of other groups is abnormal. In one influential study, Theodor Adorno and his colleagues (1950) argued that prejudice has its roots in the inner conflicts of those with *authoritarian personalities*—people who cannot accept their own hostility, believe uncritically in the legitimacy of authority, and see their own inadequacies in others. Thus, the theorists argued, prejudice protects these individuals from an awareness of their painful inner conflicts and self-doubts. To understand Adorno's position, imagine, for example, an authoritarian athletic coach who doubts his own abilities but is not consciously aware of those feelings. His response to a lost game might be to see his players as clumsy and incompetent and to heap blame on them for their loss.

There is something psychologically satisfying about the authoritarian personality explanation of prejudice. If prejudice is rooted in the mental and emotional deviance of certain individuals, it becomes the exception rather than the rule, a problem *other* people have. Despite its appeal, though, this explanation does not stand up against the accumulated evidence (Billig, 1976). Some individuals' extreme prejudice may in fact flow from deep inner conflicts, as Adorno described (Esses and others, 1993). Unfortunately, however, as the statistics cited at the beginning of the chapter suggest, prejudice seems to be the rule and not the exception. In fact, it is so pervasive that social psychologists have come to a more mundane, but also more consequential, conclusion: prejudice most often grows out of the same social and cognitive processes that affect all aspects of our lives.

Social Influences: A Primer for Prejudice. In both subtle and not-so-subtle ways, our social interactions and interrelations with others influence not only the way we divide the world into groups but also our thoughts and feelings about those groups. When the only women that male executives deal with are those in subordinate positions, the resulting patterns of social interaction contribute to prejudice by reinforcing views of women as dependent and unsuited for leadership positions. And when children learn bigotry from their parents or peers, they are following the example of these loved or respected others because of motives of connectedness and belonging—but the result is prejudice. Group membership itself can also dictate people's prejudice as people act out the wish to see their own groups as superior, a wish often satisfied by putting other groups down.

Cognitive Factors: A Nurturing and Sustaining Force. In part, prejudice is also a by-product of our perception of the world and our efforts to make sense of it. We deal with the social world by clumping together people who seem similar and by treating one member of a group the same as another. These tendencies promote perceptions of group differences, essential to the most virulent prejudices. And, of course, cognitive processes are not always unbiased. The way we think usually promotes our self-interest by supporting what helps us and opposing what hurts us. It is no coincidence that these processes protect the privileged position of "me and mine." Nor is it always just chance that we gather and interpret information in a way that seems destined to confirm, rather than overthrow, our established beliefs and prejudices.

These social and cognitive processes often build on one another to produce the many forms of prejudice we confront in our daily lives. A world divided into social groups provides a framework on which prejudice can be constructed. Impressions of groups, beliefs about their various qualities and the emotions they arouse, soon flesh out this framework. These impressions provide not only a basis for prejudice but also a justification for it. When voters dislike politicians because they believe them all to be corrupt and self-serving, stereotypes generate prejudice. When men hire women only for service positions because they have "nurturing" natures, stereotypes produce discrimination.

Social Identity. As we shall see later in this chapter and also in Chapter 6, people's impressions of groups are not the whole story behind prejudice; people can even be prejudiced against groups they know nothing about. The desire to see "me and mine" in a positive light can lead people to prefer their own groups and to feel anything from disdain and dislike to hatred and repulsion for outsiders. For example, some of the people who were suspicious of Cedric Holloway might simply have disliked African Americans—not because of any specific stereotype but because, for them, Blacks constitute an out-group whose very difference makes them suspect. Such feelings can be especially dangerous when one group has greater social or material resources than another and therefore also has the power to act on its prejudices. The way people's feelings about their own groups can lead to prejudice against members of other groups, and the factors that can escalate and intensify these reactions even further, are considered in detail in Chapter 6. As process builds upon process, the effects of stereotypic impressions and preferences for our own groups can work together and reinforce each other to produce malignant group hatred and appalling discrimination. Stereotypes can contribute to prejudice, but prejudice can also nourish stereotyping.

Conflicts between groups often intensify prejudice and discrimination. Chapter 14, pages 600 to 622, describes the often explosive consequences of intergroup conflict and competition.

Targets of Prejudice: Social Groups

> *Any group that shares a socially meaningful common characteristic can be a target for prejudice. Different cultures emphasize different types of groups, but race, religion, gender, age, social status, and cultural background are important dividing lines in many societies.*

Stereotypes, prejudice, discrimination—we have been talking about processes that depend on identifying people as members of social groups. But what is it that turns "people" into "members of social groups"? To be a target of prejudice, a **social group** needs only to be two or more people who

social group Two or more people who share some common characteristic that is socially meaningful for themselves or for others.

Multiple group memberships
Listening to the tour guide and snapping shots of landmarks, these people share the socially meaningful characteristics of "tourists." But several of them share memberships in other social groups. Thus, under different circumstances they could be categorized in terms of their ethnicity, gender, family membership, or age.

Members of some groups have much more in common than shared features. Interaction and shared goals also affect group members' beliefs, feelings, and behavior in important ways, as you will see in Chapters 9 and 13.

share some common characteristic that is socially meaningful for themselves or for others (Shaw, 1976; Tajfel & Turner, 1979; Turner, 1981a). The key phrase here is *socially meaningful*. People who share just any attribute—such as pedestrians who happen to be waiting in the same place to cross the same street—do not qualify as a social group. Categories of people who share socially meaningful attributes—college students, Quakers, the "working poor," white-collar criminals, environmentalists—are groups, however. In fact, individuals who believe they share socially significant attributes are a group even if others do not think of them that way. Likewise, people who are seen by others as sharing meaningful similarities are a group even if they themselves do not agree. Recent immigrants who see themselves as blending into their new culture are often disappointed when their new compatriots think of them as "foreigners." Social groups exist very much in the eyes of their beholders.

Socially meaningful characteristics, of course, can change from time to time and from culture to culture. If six Asian-American and Anglo-American men and women are discussing dating, they will probably think of themselves and each other primarily as members of the groups "men" or "women." If the topic shifts to race relations, however, the implicit lines of group membership will also probably shift. These six people may now see themselves and each other as members of racial groups.

Even though rapid changes in perception of group membership are possible, each society and culture generally emphasizes particular group distinctions. Contemporary North Americans considering the issues of stereotypes and prejudice are probably acutely aware of "racial" groups. Interestingly, the concept of "race" originated fairly recently (around the middle of the nineteenth century) as a pseudoscientific category used to provide a biological justification for socially determined differences in the treatment of different groups (Gould, 1981). Thus, race is largely a social concept with little, if any, biological meaning (Dobzhansky, 1973). For most of human history, religion has been the characteristic that elicited the most prejudice and discrimination, and it continues to hold that distinction in many parts of the modern world (Allport, 1954b, p. xi). In Lebanon, for example, the characteristic that matters is whether a person is Muslim or Christian; in Northern Ireland, Catholic or Protestant identity is what counts. In other places, however, cultural background is the trigger for prejudice. The Chinese, for example, have historically been prejudiced against the Japanese, the Japanese against the Koreans, and so on.

Social Categorization: Dividing the World into Social Groups

> *People identify individuals as members of social groups because they share socially meaningful features. Social categorization is helpful because it allows people to deal with others efficiently and appropriately. However, social categorization also exaggerates similarities within groups and differences between groups, and hence it forms the basis for stereotyping.*

"Doggie," says the 2-year-old, pointing to a horse. "Doggie," she says again as she spies a cat. This common mistake reflects an attempt at categorization, the process of recognizing individual objects as members of a category because they share certain features. Categorization is the process by which we group things or people, and it is an intrinsic part of the way we think about and try to understand the world. We know the elm in our backyard and the oak across the street are both trees because they share features that characterize deciduous trees. "Satisfaction" and "Hey Jude" go together because they are both classic rock-and-roll hits. In the same way, we divide the enormous number of individuals we meet into groups, lumping them together on the basis of their shared socially relevant features. Instead of individuals, they become men, women, Latinos, Whites, Jews, Japanese, elderly persons, single mothers, or blue-collar workers. **Social categorization** occurs when people are perceived as members of social groups rather than unique individuals. Gender, ethnicity, and age are obvious bases for social categorization, but they are not the only attributes we use. Name tags, uniforms, or tools of the trade, for example, help us categorize people by occupation, whereas accent and speech dialect may identify an individual's nationality, regional background, or social class.

social categorization The process of identifying individual people as members of a social group because they share certain features that are typical of the group.

Why does social categorization occur? It is, in fact, a useful, even essential tool—one that enables us to master our environment and function effectively in society (Taylor, 1981; Wilder, 1986). Think what you gain when you categorize the man standing by the library stacks as a librarian (Andersen & Klatsky, 1987; Bond & Brockett, 1987). First, you can infer that he will help you locate a book, check it out, and even keep the place quiet so you can study. That is, knowing that this individual is a member of the group "librarians" tells you he has many characteristics shared by members of that group, even if they are not immediately obvious. Second, categorization allows you to ignore unimportant information. You can focus on what is relevant—his knowledge of books and where they are kept—without having to notice the color of his suit or wonder about his political leanings, food preferences, or lifestyle. Social categorization saves you the effort of having to deal with all the unique aspects of every individual you meet, when they are irrelevant to your interaction. Thus, categorization has a dual purpose: it provides useful information that cannot immediately be perceived, and it allows us to ignore unnecessary information (Bruner, 1957).

However, as victims of prejudice and discrimination know well, categorization also has negative side effects. Social categorization makes all members of a group seem more similar to each other than they would be if they were not categorized (Tajfel & Wilkes, 1963; Tajfel and others, 1964). This is true whether people sort others into groups on the basis of real differences or of arbitrary and trivial characteristics. The librarian who breeds cocker spaniels and the librarian who writes movie scripts seem more similar if we focus only on their shared group membership as librarians. Because of this increased similarity, people often overestimate group members' uniformity and overlook their diversity (Allport, 1954b; Brigham, 1971; Wilder, 1981). Thus, we go from a world in which some professors are forgetful to one in which all professors are absentminded, and we move beyond the news that a majority of the voters have cast their ballots for a right-wing Republican to the idea that the electorate is uniformly conservative (Allison & Messick, 1985).

Social categorization also exaggerates differences between groups. Thinking about Steffi Graf and Pete Sampras as members of different gender or ethnic groups makes them seem more different than if we think of them both as world-champion tennis players. In fact, once we categorize people into groups, we become more aware of the characteristics that make one group different from another rather than of those that make them similar (Krueger & Rothbart, 1990). Anthropologists report that in the African country of Ruanda, for example, the slight average height difference between the Tutsi and the Hutu peoples is emphasized and exaggerated, as is the difference in dominance, a trait attributed to the taller Tutsi (Maquet, 1961). And in the United States, men are slightly more aggressive than women, yet our impressions of men and women vastly overestimate that small difference (Martin, 1987). Social categorization brings the world into sharper focus, but the exaggeration of similarities within groups and differences between groups is the price we pay for better resolution.

Forming Impressions of Groups: Establishing Stereotypes

You might have noticed that both the advantages and disadvantages of categorization spring from a single source: the fact that we associate certain characteristics with the social groups to which we assign people. Because we think "checks out books" characterizes "librarians," knowing that someone is a librarian allows us to infer that he will check out our reading selections. And because we associate "aggression" with the group "men," we tend to assume all men are aggressive. The characteristics that become associated with our social categorizations are thus of crucial importance to our impressions of groups, and they influence whether we are prejudiced for or against them. What kinds of characteristics are included in stereotypes? Where do these stereotypes come from?

The Content of Stereotypes

Many different kinds of characteristics are included in stereotypes, which can be positive or negative. Some stereotypes accurately reflect actual differences between groups, though in exaggerated form. Other stereotypes are completely inaccurate.

Stereotypes Include Many Types of Characteristics. Walter Lippmann, a journalist who introduced the current meaning of the term *stereotype* in 1922, saw stereotypes as "pictures in the head," simplified mental images of what groups look like and what they do. Stereotypes often do incorporate physical appearance, typical interests and goals, preferred activities and occupations, and similar characteristics (Andersen & Klatzky, 1987; Brewer, 1988; Deaux & Lewis, 1983, 1984). Yet they usually go well beyond what groups *look* like or *act* like. Stereotypes more often make statements about what groups *are* like: the personality traits group members are believed to share, and the emotions and feelings group members arouse in others.

Early research on stereotypes found that college students held well-developed beliefs about the traits characterizing various ethnic groups (Katz & Braly, 1933). Considerable social pressure now exists against the public expression of such beliefs, but stereotypes have not disappeared. Do you have a mental image of the "typical" college professor, accountant, or truck driver? Or, if you are an English Canadian, what is your view of French Canadians? Research suggests you may think of them as talkative, excitable, and proud (Gardner and others, 1988), whereas French Canadians may describe you as educated, dominant, and ambitious (Aboud & Taylor, 1971). Russians view men of Caucasian nationalities—Georgians, Armenians, and others from the mountainous Caucasus region—as brazen, flashy, criminally inclined, and likely to accost respectable women in the street (Bohlen, 1992). According to a recent study of three hundred U.S. communities, a majority of respondents believes that African Americans are less industrious, intelligent, and patriotic than White Americans—despite the dramatic overrepresentation of African Americans in the armed forces (*The New York Times,* 1991).

Gender stereotypes are held even more strongly and confidently than ethnic stereotypes (Jackman & Senter, 1981). Most people describe women as sensitive, warm, dependent, and people-oriented, whereas men are considered dominant, independent, task-oriented, and aggressive (Ashmore, 1981; Spence and others, 1985). In fact, these gender stereotypes are found in similar forms among adults and children in North and South America, Asia, Africa, Europe, and Australia (Williams & Best, 1982).

The personality traits included in group stereotypes often reflect the emotions that group members arouse in others. For example, observers may regard members of one group with feelings of disgust and repulsion, a second group with fear and apprehension, and yet a third with respect and admiration (Mackie & Hamilton, 1993). As a result, the first group may be labeled "disgusting," the second "hostile," and the third "admirable." As we will see shortly, our emotions can have important effects on our actual face-to-face interactions with members of stereotyped groups.

Even Positive Stereotypes Can Have Negative Consequences. As these examples make clear, stereotypes can include positive as well as negative characteristics. You may wonder, though, why we should be concerned with positive beliefs about groups—perhaps you think that only negative stereotypes have negative consequences. If so, consider the belief, widespread among White American college students, that Asian Americans are straight-*A* students. One problem with that stereotype is its implication that everyone in the group is the same, and, as Chapter 4 showed, people prefer to be thought of in terms of their unique personal characteristics.

A second problem created by positive stereotypes is that they may set unrealizably high standards, so that an Asian-American student who gets average grades may be regarded as particularly dull. Finally, positive stereotypes can create a backlash, as Harry Duh, a Stanford University biology major, discovered the day he dressed as a "typical Asian nerd." Duh, who walked around campus with a bulging backpack, hitched-up pants, and pocket calculator, was harassed by Whites and shunned by his embarrassed ethnic peers (*Santa Barbara News-Press,* 1992). North-American Jews face a similar backlash because many people believe that they are richer and more powerful than non-Jews and that their influence in society should be curtailed (Lewin, 1992).

The psychological consequences of stereotyping are overestimated uniformity and rigid expectations, and the social translation of those consequences is prejudice and discrimination. This connection warrants our continued concern with stereotypes, regardless of whether they are positive or negative.

Stereotypes Can Be Accurate or Inaccurate. Perhaps even more important than whether stereotypes are positive or negative, is the issue of whether they are accurate or inaccurate. No good yardstick is available for measuring the accuracy or inaccuracy of most stereotypes. There is no solid evidence, for example, on the relative frequency of Georgian men's propositions to female passers-by versus those of Russian men. In addition, many concepts included in common stereotypes—for example, "clannish," "lazy," or "dirty"—are so subjective as to be virtually meaningless.

Nevertheless, other aspects of stereotypes can be measured against "reality," and when they are, researchers find some to be accurate in direction if not in degree. This is not surprising since people often join together in clubs, political parties, professional associations, and other groups precisely because they share attitudes, feelings, and beliefs. This self-sorting process creates real group differences that may be reflected in stereotypes. Social customs also help create accurate stereotypes by prescribing what men and women, teenagers and retirees, and different racial groups can or should think, feel, and do. For example, as Table 5.1 shows, many gender stereotypes accurately describe the direction of differences between men's behavior and women's behavior, although in exaggerated form (Eagly, 1987; Martin, 1987).

Table 5.1 Do gender stereotypes reflect actual gender differences? Results from meta-analyses

Gender stereotypes	Differences identified by research
Aggressiveness: (male) aggressive (female) soft-hearted	Men are more aggressive than women overall. The difference is larger for physical than for psychological aggression, and in situations in which aggression may be dangerous.
Influenceability: (male) independent (female) submissive, dependent	Women are more influenceable than men. The difference is larger for influence exerted by a group than for persuasive messages, and larger when the topic is regarded as "masculine."
Emotionality: (male) strong, tough (female) affectionate, anxious, emotional, sensitive, sentimental	Women are more nonverbally expressive and more nonverbally sensitive than men are.
Leadership style: (male) autocratic, dominant (female) sensitive, emotional	As leaders, women are more democratic and men are more autocratic. The difference is larger in laboratory studies than in studies of leadership in real, ongoing organizations.

Sources: Stereotypes—Williams and Best (1982); Meta-analyses of research on gender differences—Eagly (1987), Eagly and Johnson (1990).

Yet stereotypes can also be *in*accurate. Consider an early study of Californians' stereotypes of Armenian Americans (LaPiere, 1936). The researcher compared official statistics on this small, segregated minority with popular stereotypes about their behavior. Whereas Californians claimed that Armenians were constantly in trouble with the law, records showed that only about 1.5 percent had arrest records, compared with about 6 percent of the rest of the population. Similarly, Californians believed Armenians were more likely to be on welfare than working. In fact, only 1 of every 500 Armenians had applied for welfare, while the proportion for all Californians was five times higher. Popular stereotypes of the 1990s are equally inaccurate. Common stereotypes about homosexuals include the notions that male homosexuals are effeminate, psychologically maladjusted, and attracted to young boys (Hyde, 1979; Zastrow, 1988). Research shows that male homosexuals are indistinguishable in appearance and mannerisms from heterosexuals (Tripp, 1975), that their responses on batteries of personality and psychological adjustment tests do not differ from those of heterosexuals (Hooker, 1957), and that homosexual child molesting is less common than its heterosexual counterpart (Robertson, 1980).

Finally, there is one sense in which every stereotype is inaccurate: when it is viewed as applying to *every* member of a group. Not every French Canadian is talkative; not every woman is emotional; not every Asian American is a straight-*A* student. So it is an error for anyone to confidently assume that an individual member of a group possesses all of the group's stereotypic qualities. Clearly, acting on inaccurate or exaggerated stereotypes has a tremendous potential for harm.

But whatever their content—positive characteristics or negative ones, accurate descriptions or inaccurate distortions—stereotypes are a very real part of our daily lives. Each of us could reel off dozens of well-known stereotypes. Used-car dealers cannot be trusted; the French are great lovers; men are adventurous; women are affectionate; people in their seventies cannot live alone. Where do these stereotypes come from? In most cases, we learn these things from interaction, either with members of the stereotyped group or with other people who tell us about the group.

Forming Stereotypes Through Personal Experience

> *Stereotypes learned through personal experience with group members may be biased because people pay attention to extremes or inaccurately perceive groups' characteristics. Social roles often shape group members' behaviors, but people attribute the behaviors to group members' inner characteristics. The emotions generated by interaction with groups can also become part of stereotypes about those groups.*

The world is getting smaller. In central Europe, boundaries between nations and peoples are suddenly permeable. The once-homogeneous populations of

Germany, France, and Italy are face to face with immigrants about whom they know little: Albanians, Mozambicans, Arabs, Namibians, and Turks. Changes in U.S. immigration patterns have created a similar situation. The new family moving into the apartment across the hall might be Vietnamese Hmong, the new student assigned to your section might be Lithuanian, and the new sales representative joining your company might be from El Salvador.

As people encounter groups for the first time, their interactions with the newcomers can become the basis of stereotypes. In the absence of other information, idiosyncratic experiences with only one or two Hmong, Lithuanians, or Salvadorans are used to construct a personal stereotype of the group. And even if people interact with more than one member of an unknown group with the genuine intention of forming an accurate, unbiased impression, the interactions themselves often generate exaggerated stereotypes (Rothbart and others, 1984). Why do firsthand observations of group members—seemingly the most trustworthy form of information—often lead to biased and exaggerated impressions of their groups?

People Notice Some Members More Than Others. Next time you are at a party, stand back a little and glance around the room. Whom are you most likely to notice, even in passing? The guest in the tuxedo, when everyone else is wearing blue jeans? Or the very tall woman standing over by the window? If these people stand out, it is because our attention is typically drawn to what is unusual, unexpected, or salient (McArthur, 1981). For this reason, distinctive individuals can have a disproportionate impact on the formation of group stereotypes, as Myron Rothbart and his colleagues (1978) demonstrated. One group of subjects in their experiment read a list of the actions of fifty men, ten of whom had committed nonviolent crimes. A second group of subjects read the same list, but the criminal actions of the ten men were violent and salient. The subjects were later asked how many men from each group had committed crimes. Compared with those exposed to the nonviolent crimes, subjects exposed to the violent crimes attributed more crimes to the group as a whole. The extensive fraud perpetrated by banker Charles Keating and the shocking revelations about television evangelist Jim Bakker may have attracted the same sort of attention. Many Americans may have formed more negative views of bankers and TV evangelists than they would have if they had heard about smaller transgressions.

Some Information Attracts More Attention Than Other Information. Even if a few extremes stand out, why do our impressions of groups remain unchanged when we encounter other group members whose appearance or actions are quite ordinary? One answer is that biases in processing lead us to form an association between unusual or distinctive characteristics and unusual or distinctive groups. These processes can operate even if we have no prior stereotype of a group: thus they can generate a stereotype more or less out of thin air.

Suppose you move to a new city and discover that the residents there classify themselves as Eastsiders or Westsiders, but you have no idea what characteristics are associated with these categories. As you read the "Police Blotter" column in the local newspaper, you notice that more Eastsiders than Westsiders are mentioned. Most members of each group are named for innocent reasons—such as reporting mysteriously broken car windows or cats stranded in trees—but about a third of each group are named as crime suspects. What impressions would you form of the two groups?

According to David Hamilton and Robert Gifford (1976) you might overestimate the incidence of crime among the Westsiders—the smaller group. Your overestimate would illustrate the creation of an *illusory correlation,* a perceived association between two characteristics that are not actually related. In a demonstration of the illusory correlation, Hamilton and Gifford asked subjects to read a series of sentences, each describing a desirable or undesirable behavior performed by a member of Group *A* or Group *B*. For both Group *A* and Group *B*, more desirable behaviors were reported than undesirable ones: the ratio was about two positive behaviors for every negative one. Overall, subjects saw more sentences about Group *A* than Group *B*. When subjects were asked their impressions of the groups, they liked Group *B* less. They had formed an illusory correlation by perceiving a link between the two relatively infrequent and distinctive characteristics: membership in the smaller group and undesirable behavior.

What explains this surprising bias in our perceptions of groups? Researchers have found that when something occurs infrequently, it becomes distinctive and people pay attention to it. When two distinctive characteristics occur *together*—as, for example, when a Group *B* member does something anti-social—they really stand out. These discrete behaviors may attract special attention when people encounter them (Hamilton & Sherman, 1989). Or they may have a disproportionate impact when people combine what they know into judgments about the groups (Smith, 1991). Either way, these doubly distinctive behaviors have the greatest impact on the impressions we form of groups.

Could these processes contribute to the formation of stereotypes outside the laboratory? They could, particularly when people have only limited encounters with a few members of a small or segregated group. Even if criminal acts are equally rare among members of a large group and those of a small group, observers may form an illusory correlation, judging the small group to be more criminal than the larger group. Remember the Californians' stereotypes of the unfortunate Armenians? Though only a small proportion of that minority group was involved in crime, observers tended to see Armenians as constantly running afoul of the law. Illusory correlation processes might also have been at work in the more recent development of negative stereotypes of Muslims. After the bombing of the World Trade Center in 1993, extensive media coverage was devoted to the arrest of militant Muslim cleric Sheik Omar Abdel-Rahmen and several of his followers. Although mercifully rare, such incidents of terrorism are exceedingly violent and thus particularly distinctive. And media portrayal of Muslims at the time was (and still is) quite infrequent. Processes of illusory correlation may thus have contributed to creating a false stereotype of Muslims as particularly prone to violence (Mashberg, 1993; Newell and others, 1986).

Social Roles Trigger Correspondence Biases. Regardless of how often we encounter a group, what we see the group doing has a big impact on our impressions. Yet even this kind of firsthand observation can lead to biased stereotypes when a group's social role limits the behavior that can be observed. Consider a new stereotype that the citizens of Moscow recently seem to have developed. In increasing numbers, farmers from the sunny lands of Azerbaijan, Georgia, Dagestan, and other regions of the Caucasus are setting up stalls in major Russian cities to sell fresh fruits, vegetables, chickens, and other goods that are scarce or unavailable in ordinary food stores. But far from welcoming this new source of food, Russians are turning against the Caucasians, resentful of their apparent prosperity and the high prices they charge. Russians have overturned Caucasians' stalls in the markets and scrawled slogans like "Russia for the Russians" on walls. One Russian woman commented, "In my view, frankly, they deserve to get beaten up.

The role maketh the man Did you look twice at this photo? If you did, it's probably because we usually see linebackers and wide receivers in more aggressive roles. Perhaps seeing this Dartmouth College ballet class (designed to improve football players' balance and flexibility) will lead to different correspondent inferences.

These southerners are so brazen that it gets to the point where an average Russian man can't take it anymore" (Bohlen, 1992).

This upsurge in prejudice based on stereotypes of the Caucasians as brazen and dishonest may involve social roles. Most Russians interact with Caucasians only in their social role of produce vendor, and the Caucasians' behavior is constrained by that occupational role. Because the Russians remain largely oblivious to the effects that the role has on the farmers' behavior, they form a stereotype that reflects the characteristics of the role. Of course, Russian vegetable buyers are not unique in this regard. Most of us form our impressions of doctors by watching a doctor care for us or for a loved one, or of ministers or rabbis by watching one perform a religious ceremony. Our stereotypes of particular groups typically reflect the social roles occupied by those groups (Campbell, 1967; Eagly, 1987). Consider the following facts.

- In the Middle Ages, money handling was one of very few occupations open to Jews, who soon came to be seen as excelling in this occupation for reasons of personality—because they were inherently "sharp" and "frugal." These same traits have been attributed to many other groups: the Chinese in Indonesia and Malaysia, Muslim merchants in eastern and southern Africa, Korean merchants in African-American neighborhoods, and now produce sellers from the Caucasus in Russia. What do these wildly diverse groups have in common? They all fill the same "middleman" economic niche in their societies (Pettigrew, 1968). Apparently the role produces the assumed personality characteristics, rather than the other way around.

- In virtually every society, the lowest socioeconomic group, regardless of its ethnicity, is seen as ignorant, lazy, loud, dirty, and carefree. In the United States this stereotype has been applied to a number of groups in the last century: first to poor Irish immigrants, then to the first wave of Italian immigrants, and more recently to Puerto Rican and Mexican Americans (Ross & Nisbett, 1990; Pettigrew, 1968). As the economic position of a group rises, stereotypes about them change and, like hand-me-down clothing, the lower-class stereotype is passed on to some new and less fortunate group.

- Stereotypes adapt rapidly as a group's roles change. Such changes are especially obvious in times of war or hardship, as we shall see in Chapter 14. As peace is replaced by war, the Germans become "Huns" and the Japanese "Japs." And as war is replaced by peace, German ruthlessness becomes German efficiency, and Japanese cunning becomes Japanese ingenuity. In the 1990s, trade tensions between the United States and Japan may once again be turning popular views of the Japanese in negative directions (Mydans, 1992).

As all these facts suggest, stereotypes do not reflect what groups are actually like. Instead, they reflect the roles groups play in society relative to the per-

Figure 5.1 Social roles shape stereotypes

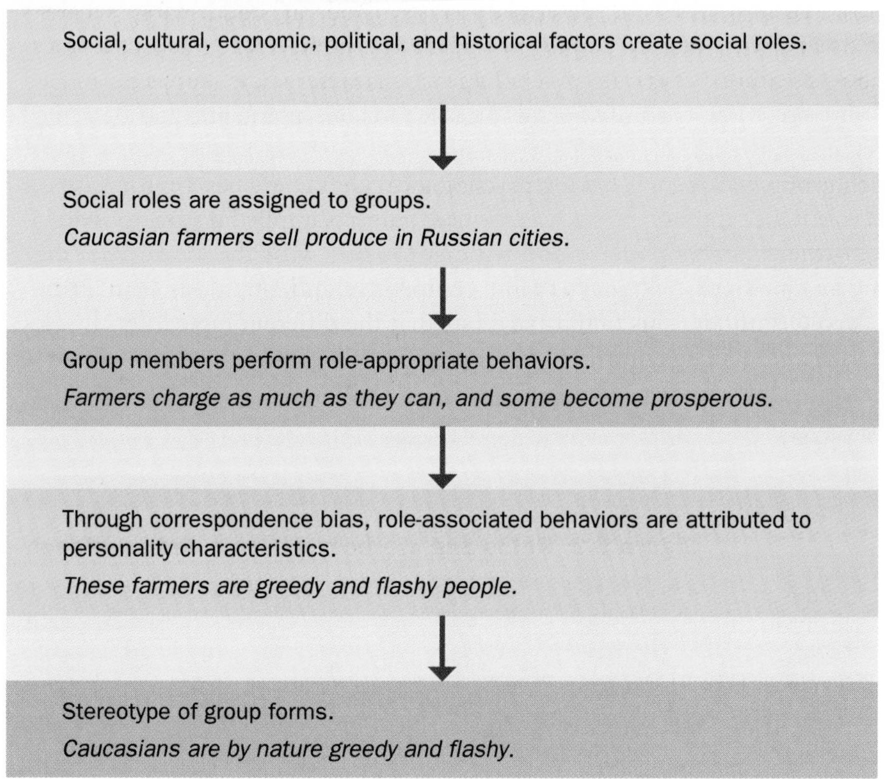

Social, cultural, economic, political, and historical factors create social roles.
Social roles are assigned to groups.
Caucasian farmers sell produce in Russian cities.
Group members perform role-appropriate behaviors.
Farmers charge as much as they can, and some become prosperous.
Through correspondence bias, role-associated behaviors are attributed to personality characteristics.
These farmers are greedy and flashy people.
Stereotype of group forms.
Caucasians are by nature greedy and flashy.

The roles allocated to a particular group influence group members' behavior. Based on that behavior, observers are likely to be influenced by correspondence bias—ignoring the effects of the roles and attributing the behavior to the group members' personality characteristics. These characteristics then become part of the stereotype of the group.

ceiver. The correspondence bias leads people to see behavior as reflecting others' inner dispositions, even if roles or situational contingencies truly cause the behavior. As can be seen in Figure 5.1, the outcome is the formation of a stereotype.

How and why people fall prey to the correspondence bias when making inferences was discussed in Chapter 3, pages 80 to 92.

Social Roles and Gender Stereotypes. Males' and females' differing social roles also contribute to gender stereotypes (Eagly, 1987). (Look back at Table 5.1 for some examples.) The process works like this. Virtually all societies assign men and women to somewhat different roles and occupations. In Western cultures, men are more often employed outside the home, while women are more likely to be responsible for home and family. Employee roles demand the kinds of traits—task-orientation, assertiveness, rationality—that characterize the traditional male stereotype. In contrast, the role of homemaker requires those qualities—sensitivity, warmth, gentleness—that characterize the female stereotype (Eagly & Steffen, 1984). Thus, if men and women tend to act in ways that are appropriate for their roles, observers who note those differences and fail to make allowances for the effects of roles may conclude that men are *by nature* task-oriented and women are interpersonally oriented.

A clever laboratory study by Curt Hoffman and Nancy Hurst (1990) demonstrated this process. Students read descriptions of fictitious groups of "Orinthians" and "Ackmians" who supposedly inhabit a distant planet. Most Orinthians were described as involved in child care, whereas Ackmians were mainly employed outside the home. When asked to guess these creatures' typical psychological characteristics, subjects judged Orinthians to be typically nurturant, affectionate, and gentle and described Ackmians as typically competitive and ambitious (see Figure 5.2). That is, each group was seen as having psychological characteristics appropriate for its role. Once the stereotype was formed, subjects applied it even to individual group members whose occupations clashed with the stereotype: they saw an employed Ackmian as more competitive and ambitious than an employed Orinthian. This finding suggests that the different typical social roles of men and women contribute to shaping earthly gender stereotypes.

Subjects viewed group members who performed their group's typical roles as possessing psychological characteristics appropriate for that role. They then generalized those characteristics to all group members. Thus, they saw an Ackmian engaged in child care as more assertive than an Orinthian city worker. (Based on Hoffman & Hurst, 1990.)

Figure 5.2 Roles and stereotypes on a distant planet

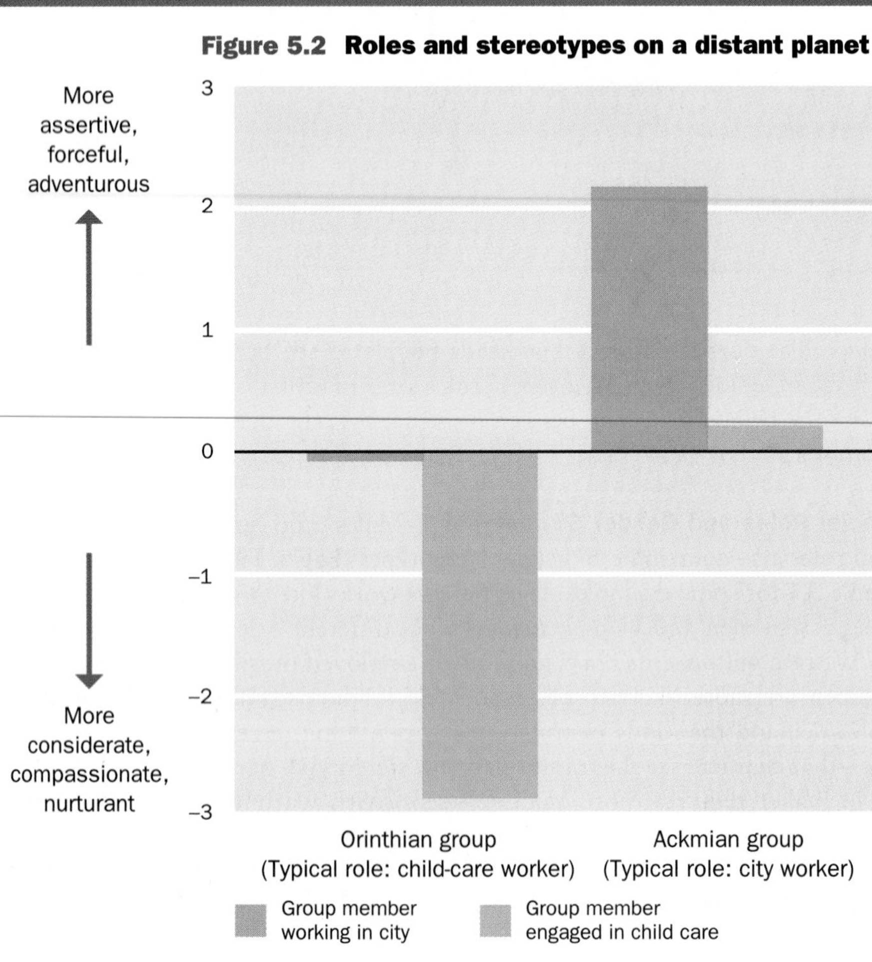

Interactions and Emotion. Roles are not the only things that shape and constrain people's interactions. Whenever people move outside their own group, they enter unknown social territory. This happens, for example, when people travel to a foreign country, rise from the blue-collar ranks to middle management, or encounter ethnic newcomers in their neighborhoods. Feelings of uncertainty and concern often arise when people interact with novel groups, and these feelings can influence the stereotypes people form.

Dutch adults described just these feelings when asked about their everyday dealings with Surinamers, Turks, and Moroccans, groups that recently have immigrated in large numbers to The Netherlands (Dijker, 1987). According to the respondents, interactions with these groups produced anxiety, and the interactions with Moroccans and Turks—the groups culturally most different from the native-born Dutch—also provoked feelings of irritation. North American college students responded the same way when asked to imagine what emotions they might experience in a casual conversation with someone of a different race (Vanman & Miller, 1993). The most frequently reported emotion was irritation, followed closely by dislike, apprehension, and anxiety. Other research shows that the presence of another man they know to be homosexual can make heterosexual men nervous and uncomfortable (Jackson & Sullivan, 1989).

Why are interactions across group lines so often tinged with arousal and anxiety? In intergroup interactions, ignorance is not bliss. For example, Walter Stephan and Cookie Stephan (1985) found that the less Asian Americans and Whites in Hawaii knew about each other's groups, the more anxious and irritated they felt when they met. The same researchers obtained similar results when they investigated interactions between Latinos and Whites in New Mexico. Not knowing what to do or say and not knowing how another person will react, usually creates awkwardness, frustration, and impatience. Yet with only 51 percent of Whites working with members of other races and only 47 percent socializing with members of other races outside of work, ignorance and unfamiliarity continue to be the rule (*Newsweek* Poll, 1991).

When even relatively benign cross-group interactions cause anxiety and irritation, imagine the strength of emotion that is generated when groups threaten one another, compete for scarce resources, and violate one another's values. Under these circumstances, powerful emotions become associated with group encounters, and anxiety, irritation, and awkwardness are soon overwhelmed by fear, anger, frustration, and revulsion.

More of the factors that increase the emotional intensity of prejudice become obvious in Chapter 6, pages 241 to 245, and Chapter 14, pages 618 to 619.

Of course, being ill at ease is hardly the majority's prerogative. On the contrary, finding oneself on alien social territory is both a more common and a more negative experience for minority group members than for majority group members (Lord & Saenz, 1985). Anyone stands out in such circumstances, and the smaller the minority, the more its members stand out (Mullen, 1987) and therefore the greater their discomfort.

One potential benefit of school desegregation is that it provides an increased range of informal contexts in which members of different groups can meet with ease. Unfortunately, however, desegregated classrooms often empty out into resegregated cafeterias and playgrounds, where members of the same group congregate to the exclusion of others (Schofield, 1978). Perhaps one reason for this voluntary self-segregation is people's desire to minimize the discomfort of being in different social surroundings: being constantly on one's guard can take its toll. In recent years, historically Black colleges have experienced a surge in applications from African-American students, including many of the nation's very best students who could attend any college they chose (Radin, 1992). The main reason seems to be the students' desire *not* to stand out as different, to be able to relax and focus on studies in an emotionally supportive environment. In the words of 50-year-old African-American insurance salesman Joseph Lattimore, "Being black in America is like being forced to wear ill-fitting shoes. . . . It's always uncomfortable but you've got to wear it because it's the only shoe you've got. Some people can bear the uncomfort more than others. Some people can block it from their minds, some can't" (Terkel, 1992, p. 136).

The emotions provoked by uncomfortable intergroup encounters may become an integral part of a stereotype. When group interaction is repeatedly accompanied by negative emotion, bad feelings are soon transferred to the group itself through the process of classical conditioning. **Classical conditioning** occurs when a person or object that has been repeatedly paired with a particular emotion begins itself to elicit the emotion. After several uncomfortable interactions, the emotions arising from the encounter become associated with the group—so that seeing group members, hearing the group mentioned, or even thinking about the group will itself reactivate the emotion. An individual who repeatedly experiences disgust, fear, or hatred in interactions with group members eventually will view the group as *intrinsically* disgusting, threatening, or loathsome.

Forming Stereotypes Through Social Learning

Social learning contributes to stereotypes. Stereotypes and discriminatory behavior are often accepted and endorsed as right and proper by members of a particular group. Group members learn such stereotypes from family, friends, and the media.

Personal encounters are not the only way we form impressions of groups. One White woman, for example, told a reporter that it angered her when Blacks "buy porterhouse steaks with food stamps, while we eat hamburgers." When questioned by the reporter, she admitted that she had never actually seen an African American using food stamps this way—she just knew that they did (Wilkerson, 1992). Examples like this suggest that stereotypes do not always depend on direct experience. They often come ready-made

classical conditioning The process by which a previously neutral object, after repeated pairings with an emotion or other response, comes to elicit that response.

and prepackaged, and we learn them in particular social, economic, cultural, religious, and political contexts.

Learning Stereotypes from Others. Parents, teachers, and peers offer us our first lessons about group differences. By age five, for example, most children have begun to develop clear-cut racial attitudes (Goodman, 1952; Rosenfield & Stephan, 1981). One White woman, raised in the southern part of the United States in the first half of this century, wrote, "I do not remember how or when, but by the time I had learned that God is love, . . . that all men are brothers with a common Father, I also knew that I was better than a Negro, that all black folks have their place and must be kept in it" (Smith, 1949, p. 18). Parents and teachers do not have to teach hate explicitly, although they sometimes do. Children can pick up stereotypes and prejudice simply by observing and imitating their elders—listening to disparaging group labels or derogatory jokes that elicit approving laughter, following family rules against playing with those "other" children. With experiences like this, no wonder that young children's ideas about racial groups are highly similar to those of their parents and friends (Epstein & Komorita, 1966; Stephan & Rosenfield, 1978; Patchen and others, 1977).

Parents' and teachers' words and deeds reflect **social norms**—generally accepted ways of thinking, feeling, or behaving that people in a group agree on and endorse as right and proper (Thibaut & Kelley, 1959). When stereotypes and prejudices are deeply embedded in the social norms of a culture, people learn them naturally as a part of growing up. In fact, those who adhere most closely to their culture's social norms also show the most prejudice (Pettigrew, 1958). A study of White U.S. soldiers during the Second World War, a time when military units were racially segregated, underscores the extent to which social norms can underlie prejudice. Asked whether their units should remain segregated, about 80 percent said yes, reflecting the current popular view. In contrast, fewer than half said they had personal objections to working in the same unit with African-American soldiers (Stouffer and others, 1949). Thus, nearly 40 percent who had no personal objections to working side-by-side with African Americans unquestioningly accepted the prejudiced norms. The power of norms is probably one reason that President Harry S Truman's postwar desegregation of the U.S. armed forces was accomplished relatively easily: accepting the new norms came to be a force for equality.

Learning Stereotypes from the Media. The expression of group norms in art, literature, drama, and film reflects and thus reinforces the stereotypes deeply ingrained in a culture. This pattern is found in today's rap music and other forms of confrontational art (Nields, 1991), but it also occurred in William Shakespeare's plays, written over 350 years ago. Othello is called "thick lips" because he is Black. Shylock is spat on because he is a Jew. Lady Macbeth wishes to be unsexed because women are weak. Richard III attributes his evil to his physical deformity, and King Lear is reviled because he is old.

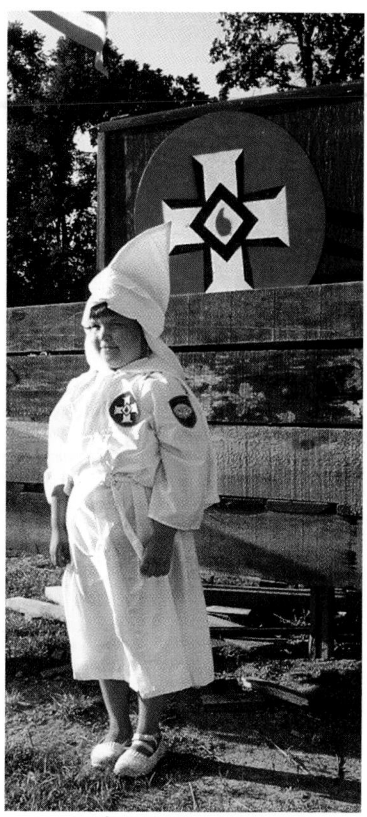

Learning stereotypes from those you love Children can learn stereotypes and prejudice by imitating those they trust and by conforming to the norms of the groups they belong to. This can happen long before they understand the consequences of such beliefs.

How norms form, and why we usually go along with our group's norms, are considered in detail in Chapters 9 and 10.

social norms Generally accepted ways of thinking, feeling, or behaving that people in a group agree on and endorse as right and proper.

Today's cultural medium of choice is television, of course. On an average day, North American children watch three hours of television, and during those hours children are receiving a mixed message. Prime-time television has, for example, reversed the traditional invisibility of people of color. In the 1977–1978 season, African Americans were appearing in 20 percent of prime-time advertisements and 59 percent of prime-time dramas (Weigel and others, 1980). *The Cosby Show,* portraying the family life of an African-American doctor and lawyer and their children, ranked as the most popular show in the United States for more than five years. The parents' occupations were no fluke. One study of television in the 1970s showed that in over 70 percent of cross-race interactions, African Americans held some position of authority (Weigel and others, 1980).

Stacked against some positive images on prime-time television, however, is the negative news coverage of African Americans' lives, often in stories focusing on violence and poverty. Without full awareness of the conditions that contribute to such outcomes, many viewers may associate such scenes exclusively with African Americans. In addition, African Americans remain nearly invisible in major national magazine ads, despite the fact that they make up 11 percent of all magazine readers. One study of advertisements appearing in twenty-seven national magazines between 1988 and 1991 found that only about 3 percent of the models were Black—and most of those were depicted as athletes, musicians, or objects of charity (Rothenberg, 1991).

Media portrayal of other ethnic groups is no better. Most Native American men are still portrayed as silent, passive, lazy, drunken, and immoral, and Native American women are shown as beautiful, loyal, and submissive (Trimble, 1988). Asian Americans appear only rarely and are likely to be depicted as cunning. Differences between Chinese, Japanese, and Koreans are minimized or ignored. Fewer than 1 percent of models in advertisements in national magazines are Asian American (Rothenberg, 1991). Latinos fare equally poorly. They are unlikely to be the central characters in story lines, and they are often portrayed as violent and unstable (Omi, 1989). Media stereotyping and underrepresentation send a strongly biased message (Rothenberg, 1991).

Gender Stereotypes and the Media. Recent media messages about women can be summed up in a single word: *contradictory.* On the one hand, television programming increasingly has portrayed women in realistic and counterstereotypic roles. The female characters of such popular series as *Family Ties; Cagney & Lacey; Murphy Brown; Murder, She Wrote; Sisters;* and *Designing Women* are competent, assertive, independent, and successful in their careers. However, in paid commercials women generally are cast in subordinate roles. They are seen being instructed by and focusing on men, and they are often portrayed as dreamlike, emotional, or ill (Courtney & Whipple, 1983).

But not all media images are as blatant as the eager woman receiving instructions on how to clean the toilet bowl. Some reinforce gender stereotypes in more subtle ways. After inspecting thousands of photographs appearing in news magazines in twelve different countries, Dane Archer and his colleagues (1983) reported that men's faces were much more likely to be portrayed prominently than were women's faces. A similar bias was found in women's magazines such as *Ms.* and *Good Housekeeping* (Nigra and others, 1988). One possible explanation for this curious difference is that it flows from a cultural concern with women's whole bodies. Women's bodies are more likely to be shown than are men's, reducing the relative prominence of their faces in photographs. Another possible factor is the traditional stereotype of the male as thoughtful and rational, traits often symbolized by shots of the head.

Regardless of the reason, the bias in portrayals has a subtle effect on perceptions. When Archer asked subjects to evaluate photos of male and female models, the subjects judged models with visually prominent heads and faces to be more intelligent and ambitious, regardless of gender (Archer and others, 1983).

Do such portrayals matter? The question is difficult to answer. One study shows, for instance, that adolescent girls who watch relatively traditional portrayals of female roles on television tend to believe in traditional gender stereotypes (Morgan, 1982). However, studies like this are nonexperimental and cannot demonstrate that watching television actually causes stereotypes. But experimental studies support the notion of a causal role for the media. Florence Geis and her colleagues (Geis and others, 1984; Jennings and others, 1980) showed college women one of two sets of television commercials. One set depicted men and women in traditional roles, with the woman playing an alluring and subordinate role. In the other set the roles were reversed, with the man shown as subordinate and seductive. The young women who watched the traditional commercials later expressed lower self-confidence, less independence, and fewer career aspirations than did those who watched the nontraditional commercials. If media portrayals can subtly influence viewers' thinking about themselves as men and women, it is undoubtedly true that they can similarly affect our thinking about members of other groups as well.

Forming Stereotypes That Justify Inequalities

> *The stereotypes prevalent in a society often serve to justify existing social inequalities. They do so by portraying groups as deserving their social roles and positions on the basis of their own characteristics.*

We have seen that people acquire stereotypes as they interact with members of other groups and as they learn the beliefs and norms prevalent in their own group. These two sources of information usually work together to reinforce each other and, ultimately, to reinforce the perception that members of different groups are naturally suited for the roles they play. Most cultures, for example, assign nurturing roles to women, so perceivers see women as "naturally" nurturing. In part, this perception is another instance of the correspondence bias—for, as people fail to realize that women's roles demand nurturing behaviors, they attribute the behaviors to women's personalities (Eagly, 1987). The stereotype that women are "naturally" suited to nurturing is further strengthened as people learn what society teaches about women. This stereotype soon becomes the basis for an inference with even more serious consequences. The belief that women have the right stuff to care for others then becomes a justification for retaining them in that role: they have the perfect qualifications. As this example illustrates, most stereotypes tend to justify groups' existing places and roles in society as right, natural, and inevitable (Jost & Banaji, 1993).

Every society maintains inequalities that benefit some groups and hurt others. Sunni Muslims rule Iraq and deny power to their more numerous Shi'ite counterparts. Mainland Chinese who fled the Communists in 1949 still dominate native Taiwanese. Enormous gaps in income and opportunity between men and women, and between most Whites and people of color persist in the United States. As stereotypes reflecting these differences have developed, they have justified and rationalized the underlying inequalities (Pettigrew, 1980). Historically, women and people of color have often been viewed in ways that justified their treatment—as childlike, unintelligent, and weak, and thus in need of direction and guidance (Hacker, 1951).

Why do we slide so quickly down the slope from behavior to stereotype to justification of inequality? One reason may be the widespread belief that the world is just and that people therefore deserve what they get and get what they deserve. This *just-world belief* (Lerner, 1980) leads people to blame victims for their misfortunes. This effect was demonstrated by one study in which subjects watched a woman apparently receive painful electric shocks (Lerner & Simmons, 1966). Did they react with sympathy toward this unfortunate victim? On the contrary, most derogated the victim, concluding that she must have done something to deserve her suffering. Rape victims, victims of spouse abuse, and people with AIDS often suffer the same fate (Carli & Leonard, 1989; Hunter & Ross, 1991), as do those whose social roles confine them to subordinate positions. Believing that groups' positions in society are somehow deserved, fitting, or justified lets us off the hook morally, as Martin Luther King observed so astutely:

> It seems to be a fact of life that human beings cannot continue to do wrong without eventually reaching out for some rationalization to clothe their acts in the garments of righteousness. And so, with the growth of slavery, men had to convince themselves that a system which was so economically profitable was morally justifiable. The attempt to give moral sanction to a profitable system gave birth to the doctrine of white supremacy (King, 1967, p. 72).

Blaming victims is a way to maintain our view of the world as understandable and controllable and of ourselves as good and deserving. It is comforting to believe that bad things happen only to bad people—that AIDS is a punishment for taking drugs or for a gay lifestyle, or that poor

Figure 5.3 Multiple sources of stereotypes

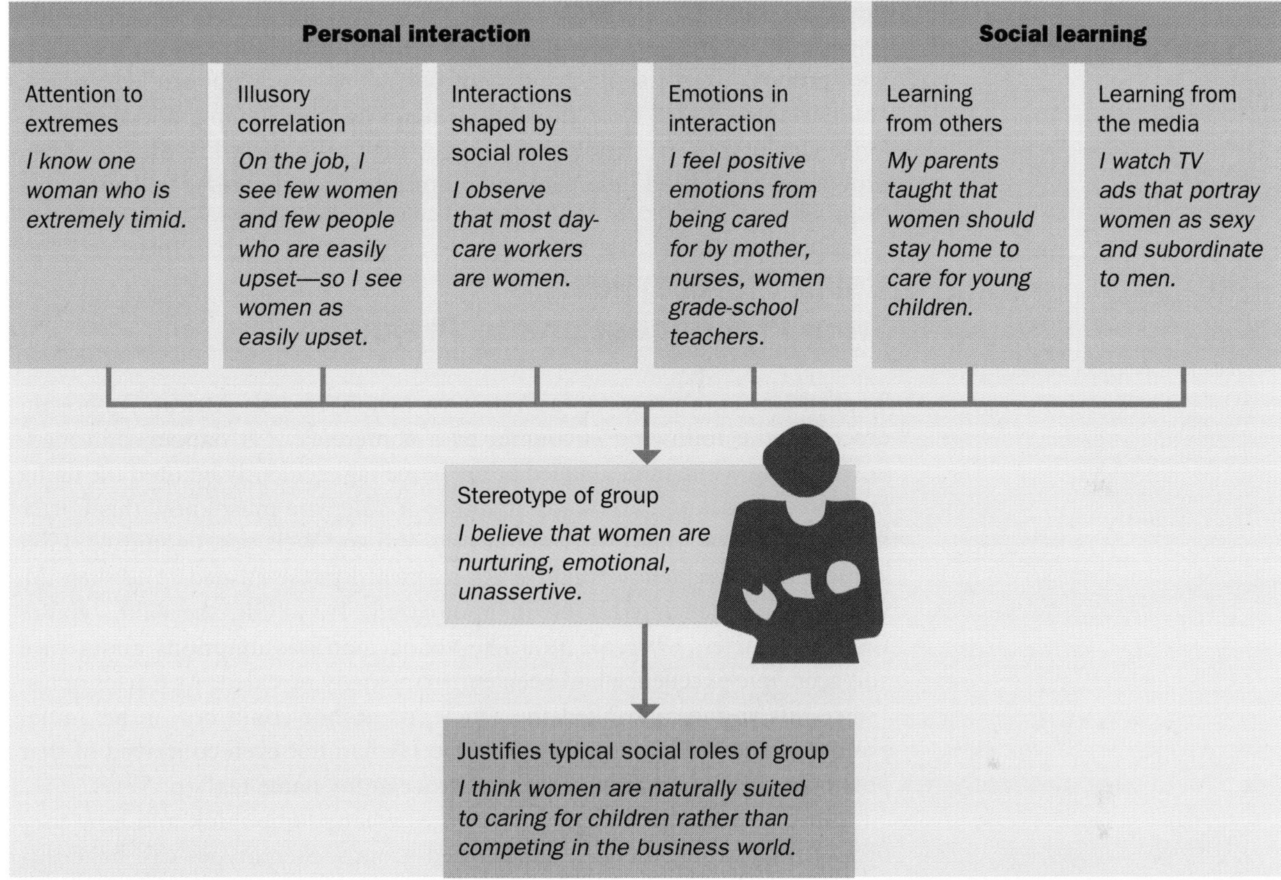

Personal interaction
Social learning
Attention to extremes
I know one woman who is extremely timid.
Illusory correlation
On the job, I see few women and few people who are easily upset—so I see women as easily upset.
Interactions shaped by social roles
I observe that most day-care workers are women.
Emotions in interaction
I feel positive emotions from being cared for by mother, nurses, women grade-school teachers.
Learning from others
My parents taught that women should stay home to care for young children.
Learning from the media
I watch TV ads that portray women as sexy and subordinate to men.
Stereotype of group
I believe that women are nurturing, emotional, unassertive.
Justifies typical social roles of group
I think women are naturally suited to caring for children rather than competing in the business world.

People's impressions of groups are formed by their personal interactions with group members and by what they learn from others. Multiple sources of information often converge to support a stereotype that justifies the social roles typically held by group members.

people are lazy and shiftless (Furnham & Gunter, 1984; Robinson & Bell, 1978). Indeed, two-thirds of White Americans believe that the reason African Americans generally have worse jobs, lower incomes, and poorer quality housing than Whites is that they lack the motivation to do better (Kluegel & Smith, 1986). Without beliefs that justify and rationalize inequalities, we would have to face the unsettling thought that bad things could easily happen to us.

Trait by trait, emotion by emotion, our personal experiences and the teachings of others help us construct a coherent impression of the social groups around us. As you can see in Figure 5.3, the information we weave together is a product both of our own personal interactions and of the influence of others. However, if group impressions were nothing more than neutral descriptions, it would be hard to imagine them provoking prejudice and discrimination. The content of stereotypes is far from neutral. When we think of men as aggressive, of immigrants as cliquish, or of Scots as thrifty, those terms have evaluative implications, whether positive or negative, mild or extreme. Moreover, stereotypes often incorporate emotions we associate with groups. We see some groups not only as hostile, stubborn, aggressive, and deviant but also as frightening, frustrating, threatening, and repulsive. Once stereotypes are firmly established, they take on a life of their own, provoking prejudiced judgments and directing discriminatory behavior.

Using Stereotypes: From Preconceptions to Prejudice

Stephen Carter, a professor at Yale Law School and an African American, described the following encounter at a conference. "A dapper, buttoned-down young white man glanced at my name tag, evidently ignored the name but noted the school, and said, 'If you're at Yale, you must know this Carter fellow who wrote that article about thus-and-so.' Well, yes, I admitted. I did know that Carter fellow slightly. An awkward pause ensued. And then the young man, realizing his error, apologized. . . . 'Oh,' he said, 'you're Carter'" (Carter, 1991, p. 56). The young man's assumptions about race and academic excellence had been embarrassingly revealed. As Carter notes, "since this young man liked the article, its author could not, in his initial evaluation, have been a person of color. He had not even conceived of that possibility, or he would have glanced twice at my name tag" (p. 57).

Once a stereotype exists, it influences what people think and how they behave toward members of stereotyped groups. Stereotypes can have this impact whether we are making snap judgments of others quickly and with minimal thought—like the young man at the conference—or making carefully considered judgments involving extensive processing of information.

What Activates Stereotypes?

> *Once established, a stereotype can be activated by obvious cues, use of group labels, or the presence of a group member, especially as a minority in a social situation. Some stereotypes are learned so well and used so often that their content comes to mind automatically.*

A stereotype can influence judgments or actions only if it first comes to mind. Does this happen frequently? You bet it does! The very first thing we notice about other people is often their group memberships, and once a category is activated, the associated stereotype comes to mind as well. In fact, some categories seem so important that we use them to classify people even when they appear irrelevant to the social context. Consider the first thing most people ask the parents of a newborn: Is it a girl or a boy? Regardless of the social context, perceivers almost always note general categories like gender, race, and age (Brewer, 1988; Stangor and others, 1992).

The more obvious and salient the cues to category membership, the more likely it is that the category and its related stereotypes will come to mind. Indeed, women with a highly feminine physical appearance and dress are perceived as also having highly feminine natures (Deaux & Lewis, 1984; Forsyth and others, 1985). The deliberate use of pejorative group labels, national nicknames, or ethnic slurs can bring stereotypes to mind at once (Greenberg & Pyszczynski, 1985).

A category often becomes particularly salient when only a single member of the group is present. Consider an increasingly common occurrence: a woman is hired as a member of a previously all-male work crew, or a single Puerto Rican student joins a class or seminar. Because of their salience, such solo appearances draw much more attention, and the extra attention usually leads to particularly stereotypic perceptions. A solo male seems more masculine and a solo female more feminine than they would in a more evenly split group (Taylor and others, 1978; Taylor, 1981). Field studies in work organizations have recorded the same effects (Kanter, 1977). "Token" integration of a workplace or other social setting—admitting a single member of a previously excluded group—can thus increase the likelihood of stereotyped thinking rather than decrease it.

The ease with which race, gender, age, and role categories come to mind often sets off a vicious cycle. The more a category is used, the more accessible it becomes; the more accessible it is, the more it is used (Higgins and others, 1985; Stangor and others, 1992). This means that a perceiver who has frequently used racial categories will be especially ready to categorize—and stereotype—others by race rather than by gender, occupation, or other groupings (Zárate & Smith, 1990). In fact, a stereotype sometimes becomes so well learned and so often used that it becomes an automatic source of prejudice. Suppose that beliefs associated with group membership were activated spontaneously whenever people perceived a cue linked to a social category—such as skin color, a male or female body type, or a wrinkled face or a baby face. These beliefs could then automatically lead to expectations about group members' characteristics. Just as the correspondence bias often leads us spontaneously to assume that someone's traits match his or her behavior, so stereotypic thinking can result in a spontaneous inference that group members have traits consistent with their group membership.

Evidence seems to support the view that stereotypes can be automatically activated. Recall that once a particular trait has come to mind, we use it to help us interpret ambiguous behavior. When the trait *aggressive* is accessible, for example, a playground shove or a sidewalk jostle is likely to be interpreted as a hostile act rather than a playful or clumsy gesture (Higgins and others, 1985). Patricia Devine (1989) used this finding to determine whether the prevalent stereotype of African Americans as aggressive could be activated automatically, without conscious intent. Devine asked White

Courtesy of COLORS Magazine

How is our understanding influenced by race? This is the provocative question asked by Italian clothing manufacturer Benetton in their company magazine. Their altered photos of Queen Elizabeth II and Arnold Schwartzenegger offer a graphic demonstration of the influence of stereotypes on our inferences.

In Chapter 3, page 79, we described evidence that words that could not be consciously read nevertheless could bring related beliefs to mind, without the subject's awareness.

subjects to watch flashes of light on a screen. The flashes—actually words traditionally associated with African-American stereotypes—were displayed so briefly that subjects could not consciously read or remember them. None of the words was related to aggression. Devine assumed that the words would nevertheless activate stereotype-related cognitive representations. Subjects then heard about a man's behaviors, such as returning merchandise and demanding money back immediately after making a purchase—acts that might or might not be aggressive. Subjects who had been primed with the stereotype-related words were more likely to interpret the ambiguous acts as aggressive than were subjects who had been primed with a list of nonstereotypic words. These results suggest that the priming that activated other aspects of the African-American stereotype automatically brought to mind the idea of aggression. Thus a reminder of group membership might bring stereotypical characteristics automatically and unintentionally to mind, producing prejudice without awareness.

Stereotypic Snap Judgments

Once activated, a stereotype can lead to snap judgments about the group member. These judgments are particularly likely when the perceiver lacks cognitive capacity or is in the grip of strong emotions.

Once activated, a stereotype can serve as a basis for making judgments or guiding action, and it may be the *only* basis if the perceiver is processing superficially. Thus, individuals identified as group members may be seen as possessing all the features associated with the group, while their unique personal characteristics are overlooked (Rodin, 1987; Rothbart & John, 1985). One of us had just such an experience while eating dinner with friends at a restaurant. The waiter introduced himself, described the specials, and recommended some wine. He was back later to take our orders and soon after delivered our meals. When she then realized that she needed extra silverware, she was dismayed to find that she could not identify the waiter. Having interacted with him only in terms of his "serving" qualities, she had no idea what he actually looked like.

Being treated only as an anonymous, interchangeable group member is a common experience for victims of stereotyping and prejudice. Like Cedric Holloway, many African Americans find that White store employees cannot see beyond a dark skin to recognize a potential customer. Debbie Allen, the actress, once entered a Beverly Hills jewelry store but found that the clerk would not show her any merchandise, assuming that no African American could afford what the store had to sell. To avoid such misperceptions, a 28-year-old New York lawyer reports that he always wears a jacket and tie when shopping, but even that is not always sufficient. He observed, "When I walk into a store, they don't see my Princeton undergraduate degree, my Harvard law degree, my associate law status. They see a black man" (Williams, 1991).

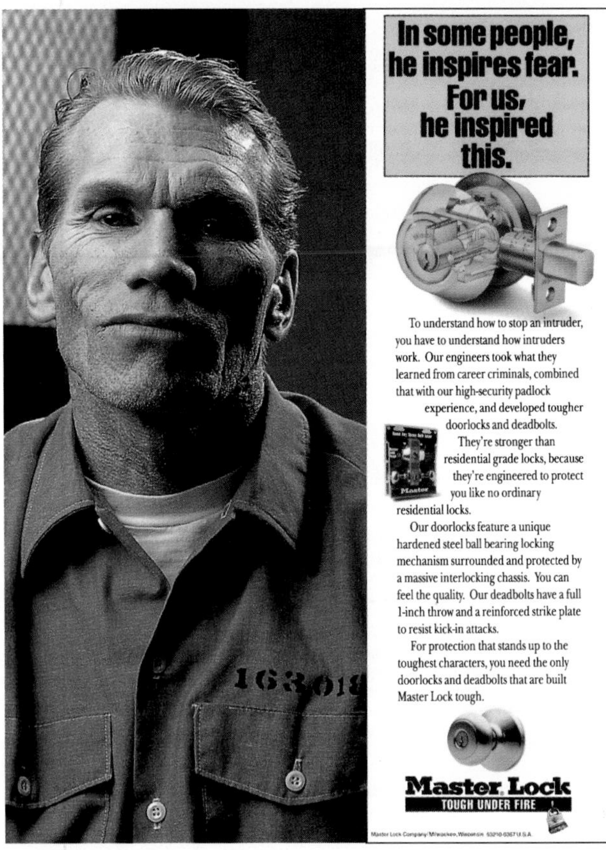

In some people, he inspires fear. For us, he inspired this.
To understand how to stop an intruder, you have to understand how intruders work. Our engineers took what they learned from career criminals, combined that with our high-security padlock experience, and developed tougher doorlocks and deadbolts.
They're stronger than residential grade locks, because they're engineered to protect you like no ordinary residential locks.
Our doorlocks feature a unique hardened steel ball bearing locking mechanism surrounded and protected by a massive interlocking chassis. You can feel the quality. Our deadbolts have a full 1-inch throw and a reinforced strike plate to resist kick-in attacks.
For protection that stands up to the toughest characters, you need the only doorlocks and deadbolts that are built Master Lock tough.
Master Lock
TOUGH UNDER FIRE
163018

Stereotypes at work This model's "hardened criminal" appearance is calculated to activate stereotype-consistent information. If "fear" makes our need for "maximum protection" salient and inspires us to head for the hardware store, the advertisement will have achieved its goal.

Less Capacity, More Stereotyping. The harder it is to make a judgment, the more likely we are to rely on stereotypes. When time constraints, complexity of information, or diminished cognitive capacity affects our decisions, we are prone to reach for the nearest stereotype.

For example, people who must make quick decisions about others are more likely to rely on stereotypes than are those who can take their time (Freund and others, 1985; Kruglanski & Freund, 1983). In one study, the less time subjects had, the more likely they were to rely on gender stereotypes in deciding among male and female job candidates (Bechtold and others, 1986). Police officers who must make snap judgments in life-threatening situations may base their decisions on the stereotypes that are most salient at that moment.

Lack of time is not the only factor that can render a decision difficult. Sometimes information is just too complex to process adequately. Under such circumstances, people may rely on stereotypes as their best bet for making the judgments, even if they have plenty of time and the consequences of their decisions are important. In one mock jury trial, for example, "jurors" based their decisions on their unfavorable stereotypes of the Latino defendant when the information relevant to making the judgment was complex. They did not show stereotypic biases when the information was presented in a simpler way (Bodenhausen & Lichtenstein, 1987).

Almost anything that diminishes an individual's cognitive capacity can also increase the impact of stereotypes on judgment. Are you a morning per-

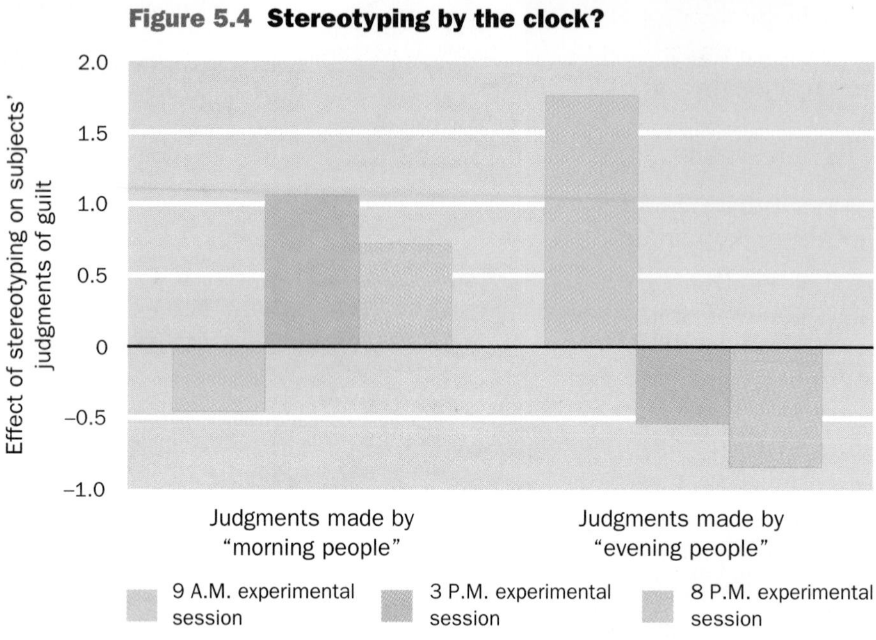

Figure 5.4 Stereotyping by the clock?

At people's nonpreferred times of day, they were more likely to fall back on ethnic stereotyping. For morning people, the stereotype of Latinos as aggressive had its greatest effect on their judgments of guilt in the afternoon and evening. For night owls, the effect of the stereotype was greatest in the morning. (Based on Bodenhausen, 1990.)

son or a night person? In either case, you probably realize that at certain times of day your thinking is not at its best. Galen Bodenhausen (1990) wondered whether time of day could have an impact on stereotyping. He used a questionnaire to measure whether subjects were "morning types" or "evening types" and then assigned them randomly to experimental sessions that met at 9 A.M., 3 P.M., or 8 P.M. Their task was to read several items of evidence about a fictitious character named either *Roberto Garcia* or *Robert Garner*, who was accused of assault. After reading the evidence, subjects were asked about Garcia/Garner's guilt. When subjects were scheduled for their worst times, they were more prone to rely on their stereotypic expectations that Latinos are aggressive and to assert that the Latino individual had committed the crime (see Figure 5.4). So morning people: beware of stereotyping others after lunch. And night people: watch what you think in the morning!

More Emotion, More Stereotyping. If the impact of stereotypes is magnified when decision making is difficult, what happens when emotions like anxiety, irritation, or anger cloud our judgment? If you suspect that stereotyping will get worse, you are right, as recent research shows (Mackie & Hamilton, 1993). By disrupting careful processing and short-circuiting attention, strong emotions increase our reliance on stereotypes (Dijker, 1987; Stephan & Stephan, 1984). For example, fear, anxiety, and sadness increase the impact of stereotypic expectations on perceptions of individual group members (Hamilton and others, 1993; Kim & Baron, 1988; Wilder & Shapiro, 1988), and they decrease recognition of differences among group members (Stroessner & Mackie, 1992). In one study of the effect of anger on stereotyping, students playing mock jurors were asked to decide the guilt or innocence of a defendant whom some believed to be a Latino and others thought was ethnically nondescript (Bodenhausen & Kramer, 1990). Subjects who were made to feel angry by an experimental manipulation before reading the evidence were more likely to deliver a guilty verdict against the Latino defendant than against the other defendant. In contrast, subjects who were not angered treated the two defendants the same.

Stereotypes and Considered Judgments

> *Even when people make considered judgments, established stereotypes exert an effect. People tend to look for stereotype-confirming, not disconfirming, evidence and to interpret ambiguous information as stereotype-consistent. People may even elicit stereotype-consistent information from others by the way they interact with them.*

We have seen that people often use stereotypes when they are in a hurry, when they make judgments without much thought, or when they are emotionally upset. Unfortunately, stereotypes also leave their mark even when people carefully consider their judgments. Stereotypes often guide our decisions because we believe they allow us to make valid judgments. If you need help in a store, identifying a store clerk—any store clerk—is the first step in getting that help. Similarly, if you are sick or injured, your physician stereotype helps you by indicating the type of person who can provide aid. People have two reasons for feeling confident that their stereotyped judgments are correct. First, any information that is consistent with expectations will tend to increase confidence that those expectations are correct. And, as you will see, stereotypes can bias the information people process, producing apparent consistency. Second, consensus creates confidence. A socially shared stereotype boosts our confidence by letting us know that other people agree with our beliefs and react in the same way we do.

In many situations, of course, confidence in a stereotype is not enough. We need to see beyond group membership and consider personal characteristics, reactions, or emotions. For example, in choosing an employee, competency is more important than gender, and in choosing a friend, shared tastes and preferences are more important than race. So in some situations—when the judgment is important and when we choose to devote attention to the task—we may try to go beyond group stereotypes and collect further information about people as individuals (Fiske & Neuberg, 1990; Hoffman, 1986; Rodin, 1987). Even when we collect additional information, however, stereotypes can subtly bias the way we see other people.

We discussed the conditions that lead people to go beyond their initial expectations to consider others as individuals in Chapter 3, pages 94 to 97.

Seeking Evidence to Confirm the Stereotype: Just Tell Me Where to Look. How do stereotypes distort our considered judgment of others' behaviors, reactions, and feelings? One source of bias is our stereotypic expectations: we tend to notice and remember what we expect to see. Recall from Chapter 3's discussion of person perception that when we carefully consider information about an individual, we pay special attention to unexpected information and remember it particularly well (Hastie & Kumar, 1979). In contrast, we rarely concern ourselves with unexpected information about social groups if the information fails to conform to our stereotypes. We instead tend to focus on what we expect to see. In one study demonstrating this point, subjects were led to expect certain characteristics from a group of men. One group of subjects expected the men to be intelligent; other subjects expected the group to be friendly (Rothbart and others, 1979). All subjects then read information about the men, including descriptions of friendly and unfriendly acts and intelligent and unintelligent behaviors. When later asked what they could recall, subjects tended to remember the behaviors that were consistent with their expectations. For example, subjects who expected the group to be intelligent were relatively more likely to recall that one group member had a 4.0 grade point average, while forgetting that another had failed a test.

The same perception processes operate outside the laboratory. When bias molds people's observations and memories so that they fit their stereotypes, the stereotypes grow even stronger (Rothbart & John, 1985; Wilder & Shapiro, 1984).

Interpreting Evidence to Fit the Stereotype: Well, If You Look at It That Way. The implications of a good deal of the information we gather are not immediately obvious. As Cedric Holloway sat in his car outside a bank, who could say whether he was pondering his financial future, planning a robbery, or merely taking a nap? When information is ambiguous, activation of a stereotype influences our interpretation of the behavior (or of the individual performing the behavior), making it seem consistent with the stereotype (Darley & Gross, 1983).

Think about how people judge others' looks. Facial features show tremendous variability in the placement of eyes, the width and expression of mouth, the location of wrinkles and smile lines, and the size of various features relative to one another. It is not at all clear what these features tell us about personality, though as we discussed in Chapter 3, people are sure they can tell a book from its cover. Activating a stereotype can guide people's interpretation of such ambiguous information, as one classic study demonstrated (Razran, 1950). In the study, subjects were asked to rate each of thirty photographs of ethnically ambiguous female faces on a wide range of different traits. The ratings showed little agreement in the subjects' judgments. Two months later, however, they repeated the task with the same photos, which were now labeled with names highly characteristic of one of several ethnic groups, such as *Amato* and *Colletto* or *O'Brien* and *Foley*. The subjects' new ratings were quite consistent: they reflected different sets of traits stereotypically associated with the various ethnic groups. The members of any particular group were seen as being alike and quite different from the other groups. Thus, once a stereotype was brought to the subjects' minds, the ambiguous facial features suddenly became good evidence for the presence of stereotype-consistent traits.

Andrew Sagar and Janet Schofield (1980) have shown that stereotypes can also influence the interpretation of ambiguous behavior. In their experiment schoolchildren were shown stick-figure drawings of children who were identified as African American or White, and each stick-child's behavior was described. For example, a picture of two students sitting one behind the other in a classroom was accompanied by the following description: "Mark was sitting at his desk, working on his social studies assignment, when David started poking him in the back with the eraser end of his pencil. Mark just kept on working. David kept poking him for a while and then he finally stopped." When David was African American, the children saw his behavior as more mean and threatening than when he was White. Thus the same behavior was interpreted differently depending on who the actor was and what stereotype his group membership evoked.

Stereotypes can similarly influence our interpretations of others' behavior in everyday situations, as an episode recounted to author Studs Terkel (1992) demonstrates. A White man described how his wife, driving down the street in an African-American neighborhood, noticed that the people on the street corners were all gesturing at her forcefully. Frightened, she closed the car windows and drove very determinedly through the area. Only after several blocks did she discover that she was going the wrong way on a one-way street and that the pedestrians had merely been trying to help her.

Thus, expectations stemming from a stereotype about a group can lead us to see exactly what we expect to see. To test this idea in the laboratory, David Hamilton and Terry Rose (1980) asked subjects to read a series of sentences giving a person's first name, occupation (accountant, doctor, or salesman), and two trait adjectives. Some of the trait adjectives were stereotypically associated with one of the three occupations but not with the other two. Each trait was used to describe each person exactly twice. A salesman and a doctor had an equal chance of being described as timid, and an accountant was just as likely to be described as outgoing as to be described as methodical. Although the traits actually were applied equally often to the different occupations, subjects overestimated the number of times stereotypical traits were associated with each occupation. They thought, for example, that they had seen accountants described as boring more often than they had seen doctors described as boring. The researchers concluded that subjects paid more attention to sentences with expectation-consistent traits, thought about them more, and thus remembered them better. These biases mean that once a stereotype is in place, people may falsely believe they see the stereotype confirmed in their actual encounters with group members. As Hamilton and Rose concluded, believing is seeing.

If stereotypes can bend our interpretation of behaviors in one direction or another, some group impressions may be almost impossible to counteract. If a group is reputed to be cunning, anything it does could be considered further evidence of a duplicitous nature. During the Second World War, former California governor Earl Warren regarded the *absence* of evidence of subversion among Japanese Americans as the most ominous sign that they were planning surprise attacks of sabotage.

Constraining Evidence to Fit the Stereotype: The Self-Fulfilling Prophecy. People not only seek out stereotype-consistent behavior, they may even elicit it. One of us observed just such a situation when he was in graduate school. Two of his fellow students who had co-authored a paper ran into the professor who had given them their assignment. The professor immediately engaged the male student co-author in conversation, spending several minutes complimenting him on the paper and discussing a few of its fine points. The woman student stood by, silently fuming. So did the observer, because he knew that the woman was by far the more talented student and suspected that three-quarters of the work on the paper was hers. Yet the professor, stereotypically assuming that the male student was the primary author, was holding a conversation that reinforced his opinion that the male student could talk intelligently on the topic while the female student had nothing to say.

When stereotypes lead us to act in ways that produce the very behaviors that confirm our expectations, the stereotype becomes a *self-fulfilling prophecy*. Recall from Chapter 3 that when people interact with someone about whom they hold a particular expectation, they often induce that person to confirm the expectation (Snyder and others, 1977). Similarly, people's actions often elicit information that confirms and maintains their stereotypes. When we ask women about their family and men about their job, our behavior produces responses that are likely to tell us what we already know.

Self-Fulfilling Prophecies in School. The self-fulfilling nature of stereotypes can set up a chain reaction in which not only the perceiver's beliefs but also the actual behavior of members of the stereotyped groups are affected (Word and others, 1974). In the classroom, the consequences can be devastating. For this reason, researchers have intensively studied the effects of teachers' expectations on student performance. Expectations may be based on social categorizations like gender, race, or social class, or on personal characteristics like physical attractiveness (Harris, 1991). When teachers' expectations for students are high, they tend to treat them with more warmth, teach them more material, and give them more chances to contribute to discussions and answer questions in class. These differences translate directly into differences in student achievement (Harris & Rosenthal, 1985). Such findings make it clear why we should be concerned about studies like one recently undertaken in a New York City suburb. That research indicated that teachers' expectations for African-American children are consistently lower than for White children, regardless of the children's actual abilities (Ross & Jackson, 1991). Similarly, a recent review shows that classroom teachers generally give more attention and encouragement to boys than to girls (Wellesley College Center for Research on Women, 1992).

Self-Fulfilling Prophecies at Work. Self-fulfilling prophecies operate in the workplace, too. An employer's preconceptions can predetermine the outcome of applications for job openings. For example, interviewers who

Figure 5.5 Stereotypes are self-perpetuating

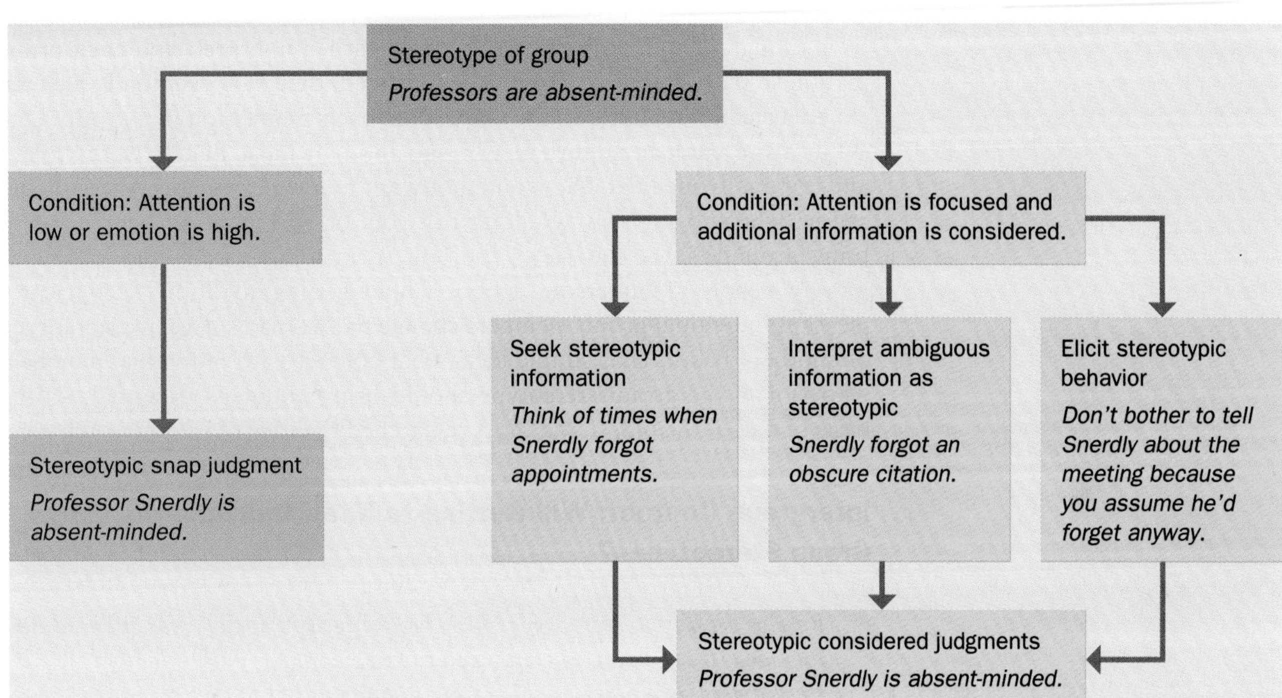

Whether people make snap judgments or attempt to process information more carefully, stereotypes shape their thoughts and action. In most cases, the result seems to confirm and perpetuate the stereotype.

believe that a particular candidate is not suitable for a position are likely to probe for negative information (Binning and others, 1988), whereas those with positive preconceptions tend to spend time gaining and giving positive information (Phillips & Dipboye, 1989). In one study, White subjects interviewed African-American or White applicants. When dealing with African Americans, they conducted briefer interviews and sat farther away, causing the applicants to react in a less confident and effective manner (Word and others, 1974). Self-fulfilling prophecies also restrict the opportunities of employees already on the job. Employers can generate confirmations of their stereotypes in a number of subtle ways. A supervisor who regularly interrupts his female subordinates is clearly communicating to them that their contributions are unimportant. A boss who delegates responsibilities to his female staff but then checks up on every detail is not only advertising his lack of confidence but also denying the women the opportunity to prove their competence.

No wonder then, that group stereotypes, like other cognitive representations, tend to perpetuate themselves and to be slow to change. When people process superficially, stereotypes alone can dictate their judgments. When people process more extensively, stereotypes influence what they see and how they interpret it. Either way, the outcome is likely to be a judgment consistent with the stereotype, as Figure 5.5 demonstrates.

Changing Stereotypes: Overcoming Bias to Reduce Prejudice

Even though people sometimes selectively gather, interpret, and elicit information so that their stereotypes are confirmed, they may eventually have an experience that unambiguously contradicts their impression of a group. One White store clerk in suburban Chicago thought most Blacks were violent and criminally inclined. She would not want to live next to any, she said, because "who's to say they wouldn't rob you, or what kind of people they'd bring around?" Yet she views the few African Americans she knows as "lovely people" (Wilkerson, 1992). Could getting to know such clearly pleasant individual group members change the woman's negative stereotype of another group? That simple idea—that contact with individual members who violate the group stereotype should bring about its downfall—is the basis of one of the oldest and most researched theories of stereotype change.

Intergroup Contact: Will Getting to Know Individuals Change Group Stereotypes?

> *Research on how stereotypes may be changed in society has focused on the idea that under specific conditions, contact with members of a stereotyped group may reduce stereotyping and prejudice.*

The **contact hypothesis** suggests that under certain conditions, direct contact between members of different groups can reduce intergroup stereotyping, prejudice, and discrimination (Allport, 1954b; Amir, 1969; Stephan, 1987). Consider, for example, the actions of a group of East Germans, who in late 1990 opened their doors to soldiers from the former Soviet army, occupiers of their homeland since the end of the Second World War. One family welcomed a 19-year-old private for the Christmas vacation with a home-

Climbing over stereotypes When members of Boston's Chiltern Mountain Club meet others on hiking trails, the pink triangles they wear attract a lot of attention. Apparently, few people expect to find gay men and lesbians hiking in the woods. The group members go camping, biking, kayaking, rock climbing, and sailing for the fun of it, but an added pleasure is the impact of their activities on stereotypes about gay people and how they socialize.

cooked meal, a little gift, and a tour of the city. "It's heart-to-heart contact, people to people. The old regime was based on suspicion and hatred. Now we can be friendly" (*Santa Barbara News Press,* 1990). The reasoning behind this impromptu test of the contact hypothesis was straightforward. East Berliners and Russian soldiers, socializing for the first time, hoped to exchange the kind of information that undermines stereotypic thinking, and in so doing they provided an impromptu test of the benefits of contact. Getting to know group members on a one-to-one-basis should make it obvious that they do not fit the group stereotype. In the face of this inconsistent information, common sense says that the stereotype should change.

Barriers to Stereotype Change: Is Contact Enough?

> *Even when people obtain information that is blatantly inconsistent with a stereotype, stereotypes may remain unchanged because people explain away the inconsistency, create a new category for exceptions to the rule, and see the behavior of unusual group members as being irrelevant to the group stereotype.*

Unfortunately, reality is not as straightforward as theory. Consider, for example, the high level of contact between men and women, police officers and gang members, former East Germans and their former West German counterparts. None of these contact situations has been a prejudice-reduction success story. The problem lies in the fact that contact in and of itself—even contact that contradicts a stereotype—may not undermine a stereotype (Allport, 1954b; Amir, 1969; Stephan, 1987). In fact, exposure to inconsistent information can trigger powerful stereotype-defense mechanisms that protect established stereotypes from change.

Explaining Away Inconsistent Information. Well-intentioned authors of uplifting stories for young people sometimes devise plots in which the hero holds a negative stereotype about Group *X*, meets an *X*, after some initial misunderstandings gets to know the *X* as a person, and finally decides the stereotype was wrong and *X's* are as likable as anybody else. The idea that a stereotype can be changed by a single inconsistent experience, a process called *conversion* (Rothbart, 1981), is appealing. But the plot somehow seems contrived. Does true conversion occur so easily?

One barrier to conversion is the fact that people often explain away information that fails to fit their expectations. Information that is in some way discrepant often makes us look hard for its causes, and thus makes it likely that we will find some "special circumstances" to explain it. If we interpret friendly and positive behaviors performed by a member of a disliked group as just the result of special circumstances, we will not accept the behaviors as a reflection of the actor's true nature (Crocker and others, 1983). Consider the responses of subjects asked to explain why a college student succeeded on an object recognition task (Deaux & Emswiller, 1974). When

contact hypothesis The theory that certain types of direct contact between members of hostile groups will reduce prejudice.

If it doesn't fit, explain it away In the male-dominated sport of bullfighting, women like Christina Sanchez are beginning to achieve some success. Does Sanchez (shown here in a practice session) have what it takes to become Spain's first female matador? For some of her male colleagues, the answer is no. They explain away her success, attributing it to the young bulls that Sanchez has fought so far. According to them, "Women can only handle so much animal."

the task involved recognizing "feminine" objects like a double boiler, subjects made the same attributions about a man or a woman who did well. However, when the task involved recognizing male objects such as an auto jack, the man's success was attributed to his ability, whereas the women's success was attributed to good luck. The subjects—both males and females—implicitly denied a woman credit for her success on the masculine task. This study is an example of a more general finding that women who succeed in a "man's world" are often viewed as highly motivated or very lucky, rather than as very able (Heilman & Stopeck, 1985). Encountering a few successful women—or "lovely" African Americans or polite Russian soldiers—generally will not change prejudiced observers' stereotypes.

Compartmentalizing Inconsistent Information. Even when inconsistent information is too plentiful to be explained away, people can still defend their stereotypes by resorting to specific **subtypes**—social categories that are narrower than broad groups like *men* or *Latinos*. For example, White people have different stereotypes for African-American subtypes, such as athletes, businessmen, and ghetto dwellers (Devine & Baker, 1991; Hamilton & Trolier, 1986). North Americans also categorize older citizens into some common subtypes, such as respected elder statesman, sweet grandmother, and inactive senior citizen (Brewer and others, 1981).

Although these differentiated categories permit the perceiver to formulate fine-grained expectations about different group members, they also protect stereotyped beliefs from change. If we place a group of people who are exceptions to the rule in a new category, the old rule can remain inviolate. White business executives who work alongside highly competent Black colleagues can form an "African-American businessman" subtype that allows them to maintain a more general belief that *most* African-American men cannot succeed in business (Rothbart & John, 1985; Weber & Crocker,

subtype A narrower and more specific social group that is included within a broad social group like men, women, Latinos, or Whites.

1983). In fact, the characteristics White people associate with African-American businessmen and athletes overlap very little with their stereotypes of African-American men in general and have no apparent impact on these general views (Devine & Baker, 1991; Rothbart & John, 1985). Similarly, we can maintain our view that outstanding physical feats are the province of the young if we compartmentalize stereotype-inconsistent older people in special subtypes. We merely create an exceptions-to-the-rule category for people like Nolan Ryan, who hurled his seventh no-hitter at age 44; George Foreman, who at age 42 took a much younger man to the limit in the boxing ring; and ninety-one-year-old Hulda Crooks, who recently climbed Mount Fujiama.

Compartmentalizing can protect stereotypes when, with the best of intentions, a group's cultural contributions are singled out separately from the mainstream. Claude Steele (1992) suggests, for example, that consigning the particulars of African-American life and culture to special days, weeks, or even months of the year sends the message that African-American contributions have no general value. By excluding these contributions from images of the American mainstream, these special occasions frustrate African Americans' desire to be seen as part of that mainstream.

Differentiating Atypical Group Members: Contrast Effects. Stereotype-inconsistent information can be defused in yet a third way. If we cannot explain away inconsistencies or create new subtypes, we may defend our stereotypes by seeing stereotype-disconfirming individuals as remarkable or exceptional people. When stereotypic expectations serve as a background against which individual group members are judged, people who do not behave as expected seem even more different, creating what is called a *contrast effect*. In one study, for example, researchers created stereotypes of patients in a mental hospital. They had subjects read statements, supposedly written by the hospital's patients, that revealed the patients as either severely disturbed or only mildly disturbed (Manis and others, 1988). Subjects then read statements by other patients who showed a moderate level of pathology. If subjects had been led to expect severe disturbance, they judged these new patients to be only mildly ill, whereas if they expected only mild disturbance, they thought the new patients were extremely ill. Similar processes probably explain why people's stereotypes of an employed woman are quite different from those for a "typical woman" and are very similar to their impression of an employed man. People apparently assume that employed women have actively chosen that role and that only the most ambitious and independent women—the ones most unlike the rest of their group—would so choose (Eagly & Steffen, 1984).

Through contrast effects, members who deviate from expectations for their group seem even more different from the rest of the group than they really are. As a result, others can easily decide that these unusual people are not true group members at all: their difference makes them exceptions to the rule. As such, they have little bearing on people's impressions of the group as a whole (Rasinski and others, 1985; Rothbart & John, 1985).

Overcoming Stereotype Defenses: The Kind of Contact That Works

Effective contact has to provide stereotype-inconsistent information that is repeated (so that it cannot be explained away), that involves many group members (so that subtyping is prevented), and that comes from typical group members (so that contrast will not occur). When these conditions exist, contact does reduce stereotypes and improve intergroup relations.

Given all the barriers to stereotype change, can contact ever alter our stereotypes and reduce prejudice? We have seen that contact by itself is not enough to bridge the gap of ignorance separating stereotypes from reality. The answer seems to lie in the kind of contact that occurs (Cook, 1985; Stephan, 1987). First of all, contact with members of a stereotyped group has to be direct and personal to be effective in changing stereotypes. If the contact is not relatively close and one-on-one, perceivers will have no chance to learn about the unique individual characteristics of the group members, and stereotypes will continue to dominate their impressions. No stereotype change is likely to occur under such circumstances (Brewer & Miller, 1984). However, not all in-depth, personal contacts will change stereotypes. To allow the kind of information exchange that undermines stereotypic thinking, contact situations must expose people to information that cannot be explained away, subtyped, or contrasted.

Repeated Inconsistency: An Antidote for "Explaining Away." One counterstereotypic act can easily be explained away. The sales manager who expects inferior performances from women might attribute a woman sales rep's single week of outstanding sales just to extra effort or sheer luck. However, if the strong performance continues week after week, these attributions become harder to support. When behavior remains stable over time and circumstances, attributions to the person are warranted. Thus, stereotype change requires counterstereotypic behaviors to be performed more than once or twice. Of course, this places a special burden on members of stereotyped groups. They cannot afford to perform poorly, even once, for fear that a failure will reinforce rather than change others' stereotypes (Steele, 1992).

Widespread Inconsistency: An Antidote for Subtyping. Even if the sales manager in the previous example changes his impression of that particular woman sales rep, he may still maintain his stereotype by simply compartmentalizing her as a member of a small subgroup of highly competent women. When inconsistent behaviors are performed by just a few individual group members, perceivers may create a subtype to insulate their general stereotype from change. To illustrate how this defense can be overcome, Reneé Weber and Jennifer Crocker (1983) gave people information about many behaviors performed by members of a group. Some subjects learned that just a few group members performed stereotype-inconsistent behaviors; the other members' actions were all in line with the stereotype. These subjects did not change their overall stereotype of the group, presumably because they categorized the few inconsistent individuals into a new subtype (Johnston & Hewstone, 1992). In contrast, other subjects who learned that the same number of inconsistent behaviors were spread out over a large number of group members were more likely to change their stereotype. In the latter case, the inconsistent individuals could not be considered a subtype: too many group members had unusual, counterstereotypic features.

Being Typical as Well as Inconsistent: An Antidote for Contrast Effects. People have other weapons besides subtypes to use in defense of their stereotypes. Recall that group members who violate the stereotype may simply be considered highly unusual individuals—so atypical that their characteristics have no impact on impressions of "typical" group members (Johnston & Hewstone, 1992). This defense can be overcome if individual stereotype violators provide strong and consistent reminders of their group membership. In one study, college students interacted with a confederate posing as a student from a rival college. The students initially disliked people from the other school, but this particular interaction was positive and friendly. The students' general beliefs about those attending the rival school, however, became more positive only if the confederate acted and dressed in ways perceived to be "typical" of the rival college (Wilder, 1984). If the confederate did not display such highly typical characteristics, the friendly interaction had no impact on subjects' general views about the other college.

This finding poses a dilemma for group members who wish to change others' negative stereotypes by being a positive example of their group. The very accomplishments and valued attributes that make you a *positive* example may make you less of an *example*—by making you less typical of the group in the eyes of an observer who holds negative stereotypes (Rothbart & John, 1985; Desforges and others, 1991). Indeed, any sort of extensive personal information about you, whether positive or negative, can make you seem less of a group member (Fein & Hilton, 1992). As others get to know you as an individual, they may fail to generalize their positive feelings about you to other members of your group. If your goal is stereotype change, therefore, you should forcefully remind others of your group membership, so that they cannot treat you as an exception to the rule.

The Effectiveness of Contact. When interaction involves the right kind of contact—contact that blocks explaining away, subtyping, and contrast effects—stereotypes can change. In one classic laboratory study, Stuart Cook (1971) hired people who were led to believe they were testing a management training exercise. The complex and involving task required them to create an imaginary railroad system. Teams of three had to work out profitable rates and schedules for several railroad lines carrying goods to and from ten cities. The research subjects were Whites, selected to be high in racial prejudice. Their two "co-workers" were experimental confederates, one African American and one White. During the twenty days of their employment, subjects had many opportunities for informal conversations with their co-workers during breaks.

This experience provided positive contacts that encouraged participants to get to know one another personally. Consistent with the contact hypothesis, the experience had dramatic positive effects on the participants' high levels of prejudice. One subject, for instance, said before the experiment that he would not want to attend an interracial party or church supper or have African Americans as dinner guests in his home. The contact changed his mind to the point where he would accept any of these relationships (Cook, 1985). Moreover, he came to support racial desegregation in general, which he had opposed at the outset.

Other laboratory research has demonstrated similar positive effects of intergroup contact. You may recall from Chapter 2, Donna Desforges and her associates (1991) set up a one-hour laboratory session in which subjects interacted with a confederate posing as a former mental patient, a member of a group about which the subjects had negative stereotypes. The contact was structured to be cooperative in nature, and as a result students came to like their partner. They also developed improved attitudes toward former mental patients.

Intergroup Contact in the Neighborhood. Finding that contact breaks down stereotypes in the controlled conditions of the laboratory is one thing, but can the right kind of contact break down prejudice in other settings, too? Several studies suggest that reductions in prejudice are associated with increased everyday contact.

The 1950s were a period of large-scale desegregation of public housing units in the United States, creating the conditions for research on the effects of living near members of other groups. Morton Deutsch and Mary Collins (1951) studied the responses of White families assigned to live alongside African-American families as well as Whites living in all-White buildings. When the groups were compared, those living in desegregated housing, and particularly those who lived closest to African-American families, had more positive feelings about African Americans. Such contact also dissolved stereotypes about the previously unknown group. Two Canadian researchers obtained similar results when they matched national survey data on prejudice with census information on the racial composition of residential neighborhoods (Kalin & Berry, 1982). People felt relatively positive about the groups that lived nearby—suggesting again that informal, everyday contact reduces prejudice. Thus the results of nonexperimental studies of contact in the neighborhood are consistent with experimental findings from the laboratory.

Chapter 2, pages 50 to 52, describes why replication of findings inside and outside the laboratory increases researchers' confidence that contact of the right kind does in fact reduce prejudice.

Many potential benefits of integrated neighborhoods are lost, however, if one ethnic group flees when members of other groups move in. A recent survey showed that only 31 percent of White adults live in a racially mixed neighborhood (Life, 1988). White flight from neighborhoods and schools during the 1960s and 1970s was fueled by fears that property values, school standards, and neighborhood services would plummet. In some areas, White flight became a self-fulfilling prophecy as public services and businesses exited with the former home owners.

Home owners who refuse to flee can learn firsthand that their stereotypes are false. One team of researchers, for example, interviewed White home owners in several suburban Connecticut neighborhoods during the year after the first African Americans moved into each area. The neighborhoods stayed mostly White, yet contact with just a few African-American residents was enough to have important effects. The old residents learned that their fears about untended houses and yards and declining property values were unfounded—in fact, property values did not differ from comparable suburbs that remained segregated. As the residents' stereotypes and initial fears were disconfirmed, their prejudice declined (Hamilton & Bishop, 1976). White Americans who remain in their homes, sharing the neighborhood with African-American residents, find many of their old preconceptions and prejudices challenged by their interactions with their new neighbors.

Overcoming Automatically Activated Stereotypes: The Will Provides the Way

People who consciously reject prejudice are able to overcome the effects of automatically activated stereotypes. They do so by devoting conscious thought to seeking disconfirming information and correcting their judgments.

The right kind of contact gives people ammunition that could blow some old stereotypes out of the water—crystal-clear evidence that the stereotypes are wrong. Yet we noted earlier that common and well-learned stereotypes can be activated automatically, so that any encounter with or reminder of the group brings all the stereotypic content to mind. If the content of stereotypes automatically comes to mind to influence our thoughts, feelings, and behaviors every time we encounter a group member, how can new things we learn through interaction ever make a difference? Once a category is activated, can people do anything to overcome its effects?

Fortunately, the answer seems to be yes. Recall that when subjects in one study were presented outside of their awareness with words that primed the cultural stereotype about African Americans, other aspects of the stereotype were automatically activated (Devine, 1989). Perhaps the most intriguing aspect of these findings was that the stereotype was automatically activated for all subjects equally—for those who were revealed by a separate questionnaire to be low in prejudice against African Americans and for those who were highly prejudiced. Thus even Whites who are not overtly prejudiced tend to automatically think of aggression when they encounter words related to the Black stereotype. If the stereotype is automatically activated in the same way for everyone, how could the low-prejudiced subjects maintain their relatively positive views of African Americans? Fortunately, even though negative stereotypic information may be activated whenever a particular category comes to mind—at the mere sight or sound of a group member—negative judgments about the group or its members are not inevitable. The activation of a category brings certain information to mind, but we do not have to rely on this information alone. Instead, people can make conscious efforts to look for the kind of individuating and inconsistent information that breaks down stereotypes.

Devine (1989) argues that this is exactly what genuinely nonprejudiced people do. She believes that everyone is affected by the negative content of early learned and deeply ingrained stereotypes, but that some people try to overcome their insidious consequences just as they might attempt to break any bad habit. This work is not easy, for it requires people to wrestle with inner conflicts between the negative stereotypes they have learned and the nonprejudiced views they also hold (Katz & Hass, 1988). A generation ago, Gordon Allport (1958, pp. 310–311) quoted two college students writing anonymously about their feelings about groups:

> Intellectually, I am firmly convinced that this prejudice against Italians is unjustified. And in my present behavior to Italian friends I try to lean over backwards to counteract the attitude. But it is remarkable how strong a hold it has on me.
>
> These prejudices make me feel narrow-minded and intolerant and therefore I try to be as pleasant as possible. I get so angry with myself for having such feelings, but somehow I do not seem to be able to quench them.

Like any thorough, detailed processing of available information, overcoming the effects of stereotypes requires both motivation and opportunity (Fiske & Neuberg, 1990). Nevertheless, nonprejudiced individuals make the effort, whereas prejudiced people do not even try to overcome the automatic effects of group stereotypes on their judgments. As we have seen before, stereotyping is easy, but processing people's unique individual characteristics takes more effort.

So what is the bottom line for changing stereotypes and reducing the prejudice that springs from them? Stereotype change is not easy, but it is possible. Although many factors conspire to keep stereotypes in place, exposure to the right kinds of information can eventually beat down the defense mechanisms that protect stereotypes from change. Even when old stereotypes are activated, people can choose to counter them with nonprejudiced thoughts, feelings, and behaviors. Figure 5.6 shows both the factors that make stereotypes resistant to change and the factors that can finally overcome that resistance. Although it is sometimes difficult to find situations that have all the necessary ingredients working together, contact of the right type can break down negative stereotypes and engender warm feelings of friendship with particular individuals. When this kind of contact is extensive and sustained, those positive feelings can become generalized to the group as a whole, changing stereotypes and reducing prejudice. Although stereotype change might be difficult, it surely is worth the effort.

Figure 5.6 Possible fates of stereotype-inconsistent information

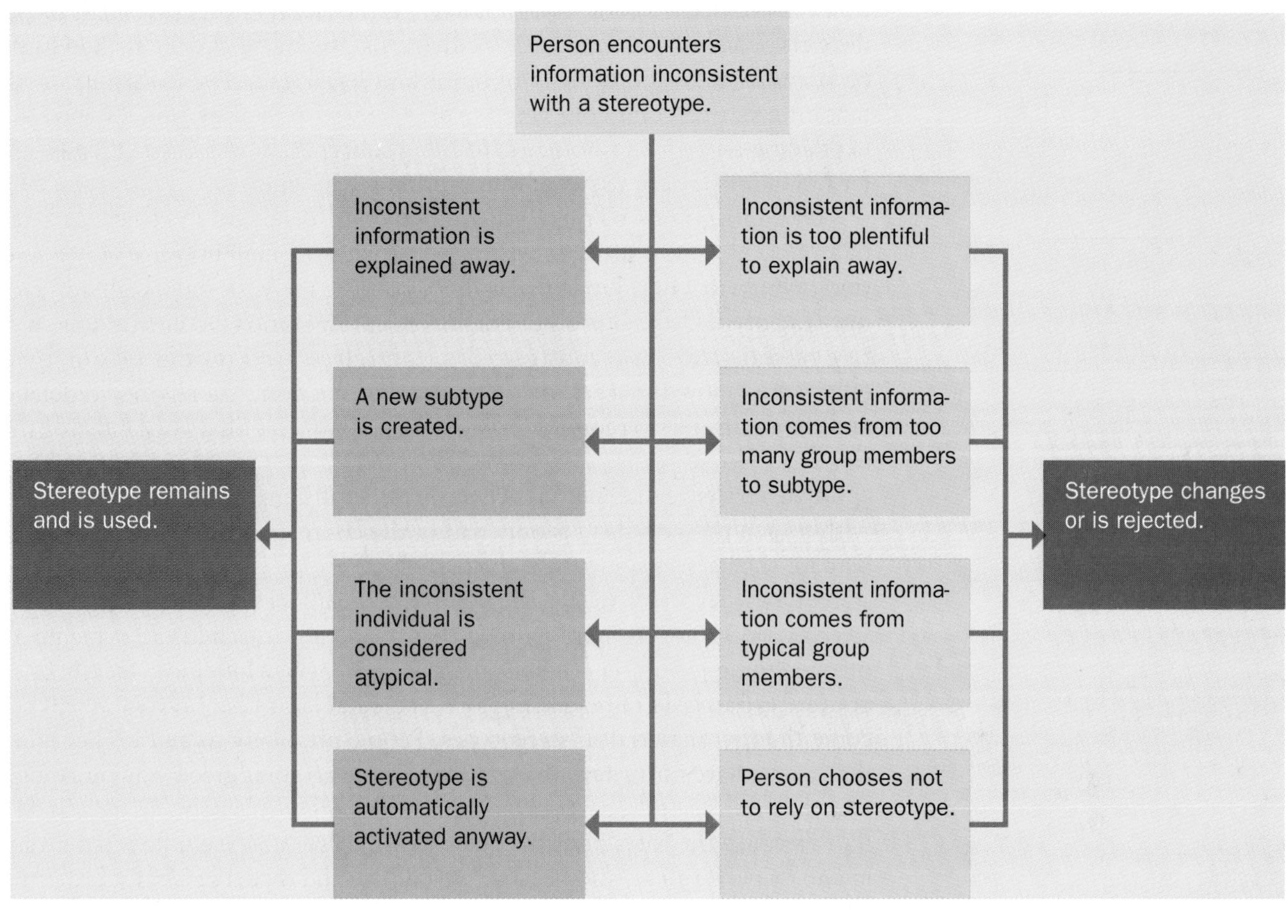

Inconsistent information will not always lead people to change or reject their stereotypes, because people have many ways to defend stereotypes against such information (shown on the left side of figure). However, these defenses can be overcome if the inconsistent information appears in the right patterns, or if the individual intentionally chooses not to rely on the stereotype (right side). In some circumstances, stereotypes can be changed.

Concluding Comments

One theme that has surfaced repeatedly in this book is that our social knowledge is slow to change and tends to perpetuate itself. Stereotypes offer perhaps the most dramatic illustration of this principle, for they perpetuate themselves in two different ways.

First, within each individual, the effects of stereotypes mean that believing is seeing. Stereotypes color our perceptions so that unclear or ambiguous events are quickly interpreted in line with the stereotype. If we think politicians are self-serving, we might decide that any action they take is made only for its publicity value. When we read in the newspaper that our member of Congress donated $100 to the local orphanage, for example, we then conclude that the donation was meant to attract media attention. Even when we try to think hard and process carefully, stereotypes shape the information we seek out, remember, and use to make judgments. We might question the politician about foreign junkets rather than efforts on behalf of the district, or we might remember incidents like bounced checks at the House bank rather than sponsorship of important legislation. Even when inconsistent information comes our way, we are likely to defend our stereotypes—by explaining away inconsistencies, forming subtypes, or contrasting a particular individual as a praiseworthy exception to the rule.

Of course, none of these self-fulfilling and defensive tendencies are intentional. No one consciously decides, "I want to maintain my biased and stereotypic view of politicians, so don't confuse me with the facts!" Instead, our stereotypes, like our other cognitive representations, constitute the picture of reality we have constructed for ourselves. And for this reason, their effects are below the level of our awareness. We don't usually *try* to defend and maintain our stereotypic beliefs—it just happens that way most of the time.

The pervasiveness and power of the self-fulfilling quality of stereotypes within each person's head is only half of the complete story: stereotypes perpetuate themselves and resist change in society as well. As we have seen, stereotypes generally reflect the roles society allocates to members of the stereotyped group. If more women than men care for children, if members of one ethnic group tend to be small shopkeepers while most members of another group hold unrewarding jobs as menial laborers, those roles will become the raw material of stereotypes. People are likely to end up believing that women are nurturant, that the first ethnic group is greedy and grasping, and that the second group is lazy and dirty. Stereotypes track social roles both because the roles limit the behaviors that we observe individual group members performing, and because the culture and media generally foster the idea that personal characteristics fit roles. Thus the circle is closed: because people believe groups are naturally suited for the roles they play, those beliefs become the justification for keeping the groups in those roles. Social change that would alter groups' roles is seen as a violation of the natural order of things, and it becomes morally wrong as well as impractical.

Thus stereotypes have self-fulfilling force not only in an individual's head but also in society. Because stereotypes operate on two levels, changing them will demand alterations not only in the way we think but also in the way we live. We need to consciously reflect on the extent to which social roles and other external constraints determine not only other people's actions but also our own. Equally, we need to interact with members of all groups in more varied contexts, to see them in more diverse roles, and to work toward change in social inequalities that are reflected in and rationalized by stereotypes.

Could changes like these allow us to retain the benefits of social categorization while eliminating the costs of stereotypes? We would still perceive groups, but we would know each group for its positive and valued characteristics. Perhaps all groups would respect and value all other groups, a goal that is implicit in the concept of multiculturalism. Unfortunately, another factor stands in the way of developing a society in which all groups are equally valued and respected: we all show strong preferences for the groups to which we belong. In Chapter 6 we consider the consequences of this preference for the way we think about and act toward others and ourselves.

Summary

The Social and Cognitive Roots of Prejudice **Discrimination,** or treatment of individuals based on their group memberships, and **prejudice,** evaluations of individuals and groups, are significant problems in the world today. Prejudice has at times been viewed as the product of distorted thinking in a few troubled individuals. But both social and cognitive factors contribute to prejudice. One important source is people's **stereotypes,** positive or negative beliefs about a group's characteristics.

Any **social group** that shares a socially meaningful common characteristic can be a target for prejudice. Different cultures emphasize different types of groups, but race, religion, gender, age, social status, and cultural background are important dividing lines in many societies. People identify individuals as members of social groups because they share socially meaningful features. This process of **social categorization** is helpful because it allows people to deal with others efficiently and appropriately. However, it also exaggerates similarities within groups and differences between groups, and hence it forms the basis for stereotyping.

Forming Impressions of Groups: Establishing Stereotypes Many different kinds of characteristics are included in stereotypes, which can be positive or negative. Some stereotypes accurately reflect actual differences between groups, though in exaggerated form. Other stereotypes are completely inaccurate.

Stereotypes can be learned through personal experiences with group members. However, these stereotypes may be biased because people pay attention to extremes or inaccurately perceive groups' characteristics. Social roles often shape group members' behaviors, but people attribute the behaviors to group members' inner characteristics. The emotions generated by interaction with groups can also become part of stereotypes about those groups, often as a result of **classical conditioning.**

Social learning also contributes to stereotypes. Stereotypes and discrimination are often accepted and endorsed as right and proper by members of a particular group, becoming **social norms**. Group members then learn these beliefs and behaviors from family, friends, and the media.

The stereotypes prevalent in a society often serve to justify existing social inequalities. They do so by portraying groups as deserving their social roles and positions on the basis of their own characteristics.

Chapter 5 Themes

Construction of Reality
We construct impressions of social groups based on our interactions with group members and what we learn from others.

Pervasiveness of Social Influence
These interactions and the things we learn are shaped by society and culture.

Conservatism
Stereotypes perpetuate themselves by shaping both the way we think and the way we act.

Superficiality Versus Depth
Stereotypes influence judgments made quickly with little thought and also judgments made by collecting further information.

Using Stereotypes: From Preconceptions to Prejudice Once established, a stereotype can be activated by obvious cues, use of group labels, or the presence of a group member, especially as a minority in a social situation. Some stereotypes are learned so well and used so often that their content comes to mind automatically.

Once activated, a stereotype can lead to snap judgments about the group member. These judgments are particularly likely when the perceiver lacks cognitive capacity or is in the grip of strong emotions.

Even when people make considered judgments, established stereotypes exert an effect. People tend to look for stereotype-confirming, not disconfirming, evidence and to interpret ambiguous information as stereotype-consistent. People may even elicit stereotype-consistent information from others by the way they interact with them.

Changing Stereotypes: Overcoming Bias to Reduce Prejudice Research on how stereotypes may be changed in society has focused on the **contact hypothesis,** the idea that under certain conditions, contact with members of a stereotyped group may reduce stereotyping and prejudice. Mere contact is not sufficient. Even when people obtain information that is blatantly inconsistent with a stereotype, stereotypes may remain unchanged because people explain away the inconsistency, create a new **subtype** for exceptions to the rule, and see the behavior of unusual group members as irrelevant to the group stereotype.

To be effective, contact has to provide stereotype-inconsistent information that is repeated (so it cannot be explained away), that involves many group members (so subtyping is prevented), and that comes from typical group members (so contrast will not occur). When these conditions exist, contact does reduce stereotypes and improve intergroup relations.

People who consciously reject prejudice are able to overcome the effects of automatically activated stereotypes. They do so by devoting conscious thought to seeking disconfirming information and correcting their judgments.

Chapter 5 Overview

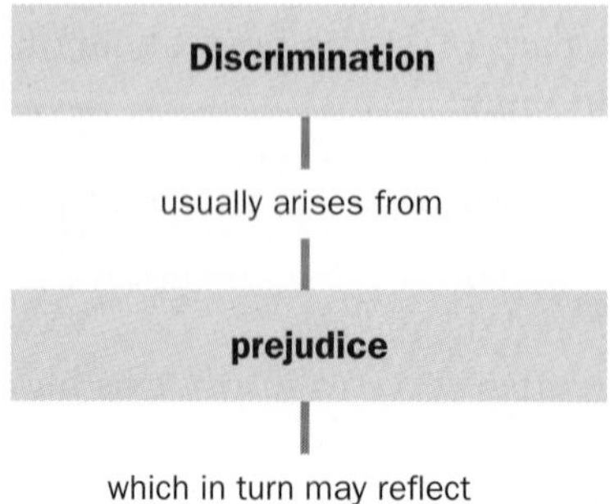
Discrimination
usually arises from
prejudice
which in turn may reflect

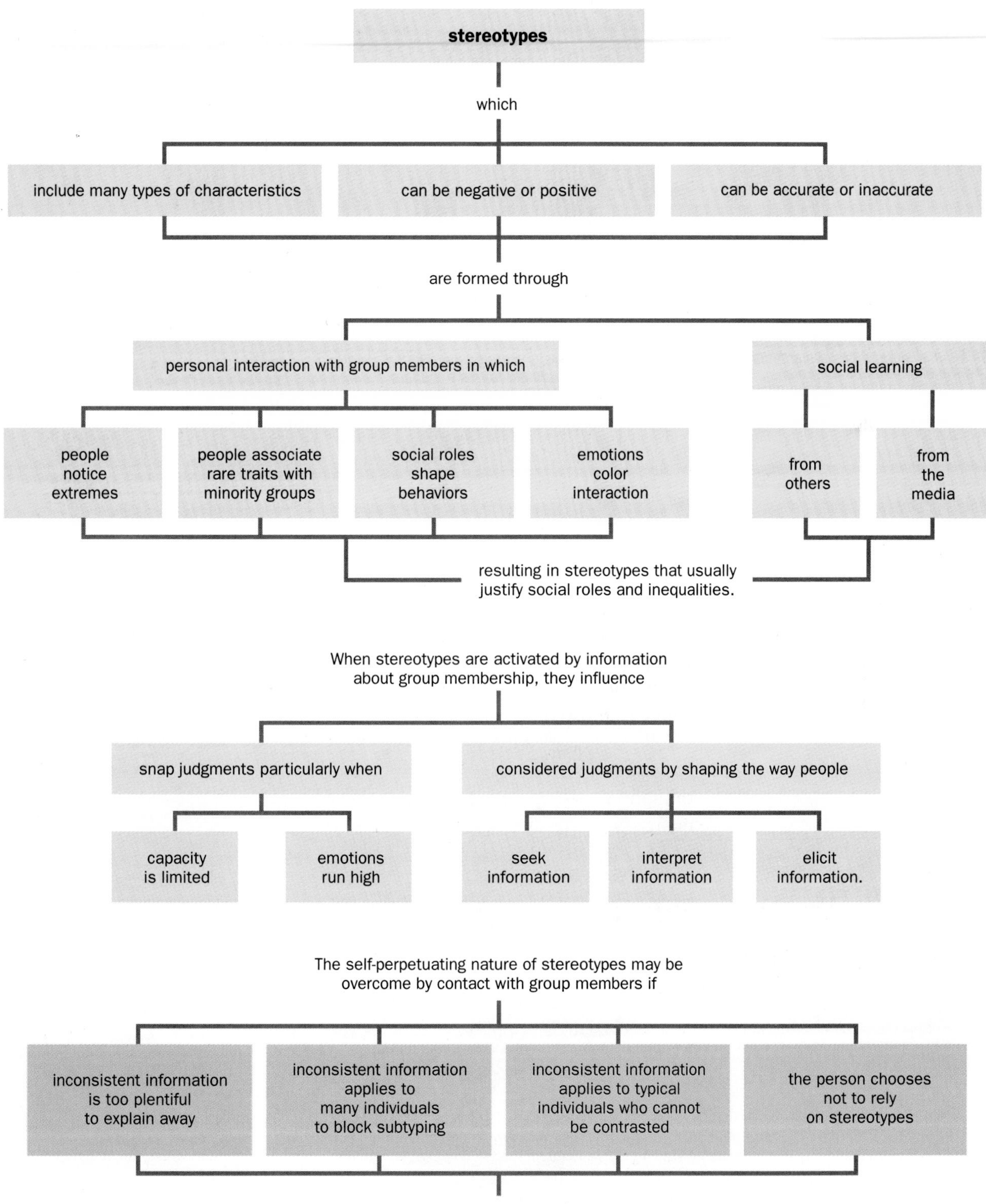
stereotypes
which
include many types of characteristics
can be negative or positive
can be accurate or inaccurate
are formed through
personal interaction with group members in which
social learning
people notice extremes
people associate rare traits with minority groups
social roles shape behaviors
emotions color interaction
from others
from the media
resulting in stereotypes that usually justify social roles and inequalities.
When stereotypes are activated by information about group membership, they influence
snap judgments particularly when
considered judgments by shaping the way people
capacity is limited
emotions run high
seek information
interpret information
elicit information.
The self-perpetuating nature of stereotypes may be overcome by contact with group members if
inconsistent information is too plentiful to explain away
inconsistent information applies to many individuals to block subtyping
inconsistent information applies to typical individuals who cannot be contrasted
the person chooses not to rely on stereotypes
resulting in changing or ignoring the stereotype.

PHIL BONDI
CHICAGO
DANIEL
KNOCK
KNOCK
KNOCK'IN ON HEAVENS' DOOR
Love You
RICK

6

Social Identity

Before reading any further, take a clean sheet of paper and write "I am . . ." in the left margin ten times. Now go back to the top of the page and complete the sentences. What descriptions come to mind? Who are you?

Some of your statements probably refer to individual traits, feelings, or behaviors, such as "I am outgoing," or "I am in a good mood," or "I am sitting in the library"—the types of self-related information we discussed in Chapter 4. Others probably reflect groups to which you belong: "I am Filipino," or "I am on the swim team," or "I am a woman." In fact, if you are like most people, you probably listed more groups than individual characteristics (Kuhn & McPartland, 1954). Why are ethnicity, team affiliation, gender, and other social categories so important? Like individual attributes, these memberships give us information about ourselves—what we do, what we think, and how we act—and thus help us define who we are (Mead, 1934; Hyman & Singer, 1968). Social psychologists use the term **social identity** to refer to those aspects of our self-concept that derive from our knowledge and feelings about the group memberships we share with others (Rosenberg, 1979; Tajfel, 1972). Social identity turns "I" into "we"; it extends the self out beyond the individual to include other members of our groups (Brewer, 1991).

Think about your responses to the "I am . . ." task. Being a Filipino, for example, influences the type of person you are, including many of your thoughts, feelings, and actions. As you made your list, you may have felt good or bad about yourself, depending on the group that came to mind. Our self-esteem also depends in large measure on how we and others feel about the groups we belong to. If we identify with the group, being part of the Filipino community or the swim team, being a woman or a member of any other group can boost or lower self-esteem. Group memberships are an essential part of the self.

Group membership can confer tremendous benefits. Groups give us a sense of belonging and worth, of being valued for who we are. They allow us to be part of something bigger than our individual selves. As group members, we can reap far more than we can sow individually, bask in the glow of achievements other than our own, and feel at home in a haven of similarity

Belonging defines the self Like an individual square sewn in memory of a loved one who died of AIDS, every individual has his or her place in the fabric of the group. Group belonging provides us with identity and with the connections to others that help define us. In contributing quilted squares and in paying their respects to what the quilt represents, people reaffirm their identification with their loved ones and their solidarity with their cause.

and understanding. A sense of group membership that connects us to others is the basis for our participation in social life. It even protects our mental well-being and physical health, as you will see in Chapter 11.

The many benefits of group belonging come at a cost, however. Because our self-esteem depends not only on our individual attributes and achievements but also on those of the group, we need to see our groups as attractive, valued, and successful. Unfortunately, valuing our own groups often entails preferring them over other groups. Regard, esteem, and liking for *in-groups*—groups to which we belong—are often coupled with disregard, derogation, and dislike for *out-groups*. As sociologist William Graham Sumner said long ago, "loyalty to the in-group, . . . [and] hatred and contempt for outsiders . . . all grow together" (1906, p. 13). From school rivalries to ethnic prejudice to national patriotism, both the exaltation of in-groups and the belittling of out-groups in part reflect people's need to secure a positive social identity.

These all-but-inseparable positive and negative sides of social identity will be explored throughout this chapter. The chapter first describes the way people come to view social groups as aspects of the self: how we learn what group memberships mean, and what factors conspire to make a particular membership significant at any given time. The chapter then turns to the consequences of placing ourselves and others in social categories. Once a group membership is activated, it affects the way we see and respond to ourselves and others. Shared group membership tends to make us view other in-group members as similar to ourselves and as likable, so we try to treat them justly and fairly. In contrast, we often respond to out-group members with indifference, dislike, and discrimination.

The chapter concludes with a discussion of the effects of belonging to a group that others look down upon. Being chubby or speaking with an accent are enough to evoke scorn in elementary-school classrooms and playgrounds. Being mentally ill, old, homeless, or on welfare can provoke dislike and avoidance among adults. Such negative group identities can take their toll, both on individuals and groups. But this outcome is not inevitable, and the chapter concludes by describing how people resist the implications of a negative identity and even work to change society's evaluation of their groups.

Categorizing Oneself as a Group Member

Some group memberships are so important that they become a basic part of our view of ourselves. Consider, for example, the experiences of a young woman who, when applying to a training program, faced these obstacles: she was warned to send her application by registered mail or it might be "lost." She almost missed her final interview when the notification letter mysteriously "disappeared." She faced hazing and isolation during four years of apprenticeship. But she made it. She is now a fully qualified and

social identity Those aspects of the self-concept that derive from an individual's knowledge and feelings about the group memberships he or she shares with others.

well-paid master electrician, respected by her male and female peers. If we had asked this woman to do the "I am . . ." task, her identity as a member of her craft would undoubtedly head the list. If someone's occupation, gender, or other group membership is important enough, it becomes incorporated into the person's social identity. The process of seeing oneself as a member of a group is known as **self-categorization** (Turner and others, 1987). If this term sounds familiar, it is because it is so similar to *social categorization,* the process we described in Chapter 5 as underlying the perception of social groups.

Although some group memberships are only fleetingly important—being part of the "red jerseys" team in a lunch-hour basketball game, for example—most group memberships are stable and enduring. Membership in gender and ethnic groups lasts a lifetime. Being a member of the Duran or the Jackson family, or being Muslim, Roman Catholic, or Buddhist, or being a Connecticut Yankee or a Southern Belle can be nearly as long-lasting. How do we learn these group labels, and how do we come to understand what characteristics are associated with those labels?

Learning About Our Groups

People learn about the groups to which they belong in the same ways that they learn the characteristics of other groups, through observation of other group members or from the culture.

We learn about our own groups in the same ways that we learn about other groups. Lessons come from parents, teachers, peers, and the media, but our most important lessons come from fellow group members and what they do. Consider your first job. What did it mean to become part of the team in the typing pool, on the factory floor, or in corporate headquarters? Whom did people ask for help when something went wrong? Did they joke around, or was the atmosphere pretty serious? Did they call the supervisor by her first name? Did they take pride in their work, or was it "just a job"? Probably you figured out what it meant to be an employee in your company primarily—maybe only—by watching others. Learning by watching others is particularly important when group membership is transitory and situation-bound. Today the "white jerseys" may be ball hogs, always looking for a chance to shoot; tomorrow they may be team-spirited and ready to pass the ball.

To review the kinds of information on which we base impressions of groups, see Chapter 5, especially pages 180 to 194.

What we observe other group members doing often depends on their cultural roles. In any society, members of a group may occupy particular roles that influence who they are. If you are an American woman, for example, you are three times more likely than a man to be a nurse, child-care worker, or social worker, and three times less likely to be a mechanic, engineer, or dentist (U.S. Census Bureau, 1986). This is true because occupations are not distributed randomly between men and women in this population.

self-categorization The process of seeing oneself as a member of a social group.

Does a group's assignment to certain roles and occupations have an impact on group members' views of themselves? The answer is a qualified yes. People may not make direct inferences about their own characteristics on the basis of role-constrained behaviors as readily as observers do. Still, roles affect the individuals who hold them because as people enact their roles, they acquire role-related skills and develop tendencies to behave in certain ways. These skills and tendencies in turn make those behaviors, and correspondent self-inferences, more likely. A woman's experiences raising young children may leave her better able to interpret nonverbal behaviors or to comfort people when they are distressed. A man's experiences with aggression—perhaps in military service or organized sports—may leave him with the belief that aggressive behaviors are often effective. Thus, performing a role based on gender or on membership in some other group can shape our future behaviors and, ultimately, our self-knowledge (Eagly, 1987).

By turning to Chapter 4, pages 120 to 121, you can remind yourself of the reasons for this actor-observer difference in attributions.

Welcome to who you are As this young Tewa girl performs the movements and gestures of the corn dances of the Santa Clara Pueblo Indians, she also learns what it means to be Tewa. So it is with every group. As socialization processes teach them history, traditions, and customs, young members absorb even deeper lessons: who they are and what their group stands for.

Accessibility of Group Memberships

Knowledge about group memberships may be activated by direct reminders, such as group labels; by the presence of out-group members; by being a minority; or by intergroup conflict. Group membership is particularly significant in some cultures and for some individuals.

No matter how extensive our knowledge about the characteristics of our groups, that knowledge will have little impact unless the group membership comes to mind. Imagine that you are a male midwestern feminist, or a female Canadian conservative. Perhaps you are also musically talented, nearsighted, and love Cajun food. Under what circumstances will your gender, politics, or other group memberships be more important than your individual attributes? And which group membership will matter? Researchers have found that a variety of social and cognitive factors conspire to make a particular group membership accessible. Let's look at some of these factors.

Direct Reminders of Membership. If someone calls you "Reverend," or "nerd," or "dumb jock," you are reminded directly and quite vividly about your social identity. Honorary titles or pejorative labels bring group membership home in a hurry (Charters & Newcomb, 1958; Billig & Tajfel, 1973). Often, however, the process is more subtle. Circumstances remind us of our similarities with others, and this activates knowledge of group membership. The mere presence of other in-group members can be a potent reminder (Doise & Sinclair, 1973; Wilder & Shapiro, 1991). Just hearing another New Zealand accent is enough to make one of the authors of this text "feel" like a New Zealander, and seeing someone in a Harvard T-shirt reminds the other author of his New England background. When group similarities are highlighted—as when a team wears uniforms or when members coordinate their actions for a common goal—membership and all it entails become even more accessible. This process is powerful enough to overcome important cross-cutting categorizations (Gaertner and others, 1990). So White and African-American football players are molded into a unified college team, and Republicans and Democrats coordinate their talents on a town planning committee.

Presence of Out-Group Members. The presence of out-group members can also be a forcible reminder of shared group membership, as one of the authors discovered at a recent conference. He was standing with a dozen or so social psychologists in a hallway between conference sessions, chatting over coffee. Suddenly three strangers walked by; their nametags identified them as members of an association of bank loan officers, attending their own conference in the same hotel. Their presence made us even more aware of what we social psychologists had in common. The fact that out-group members' presence emphasizes the importance of an in-group's social identity was also demonstrated in a study conducted in Belgium. Two groups of Belgian university students were asked to write descriptions of typical students of Belgian and North African origin. For one group, the experimenter who made this request was a North African; for the other, the experimenter was Belgian. The responses of the students who wrote in the presence of an out-group member, the North African experimenter, revealed greater identification with their in-group—Belgians (Marques and others, 1988). Apparently the presence of even a single out-group member is enough to increase the importance of in-group membership.

When outsiders are present, resourceful group members sometimes put their mouth where their membership is, using language to emphasize their identification with their group. For example, when French-speaking Canadians were confronted with English-speaking Canadians in one experiment, the French speakers either broadened their accents to indicate their usual use of their native language or switched to that language altogether (Bourhis and others, 1978). Ethnic languages are important sources of social identity, as attempts by French speakers in Canada, Catalans in Spain, and Welsh nationalists in Britain to preserve their languages all attest.

Being a Minority. If a few out-group members arriving on the scene can make in-group membership accessible, imagine the impact when they crowd in by the hundreds to outnumber the in-group. In Chapter 4 we noted that people are more likely to think of themselves in terms of individual characteristics that are unusual or distinctive in their social group (McGuire & Padawer-Singer, 1978). The same principle operates at the group level: people are more likely to think of themselves in terms of their memberships in smaller groups than in larger ones (Turnbull and others, 1990; Mullen, 1991; Taylor and others, 1978). Consider the results obtained when William McGuire and his colleagues (1979) asked grade-school children to talk for five minutes about themselves and carefully coded these self-descriptions. As can be seen in Figure 6.1, the researchers found that boys and

In this study, grade-school children spoke for five minutes in response to the instruction "Tell us about yourself." Notice that both boys and girls were more likely to mention their gender if their gender was a minority at home. (Based on McGuire and others, 1979.)

Figure 6.1 Being in the minority matters

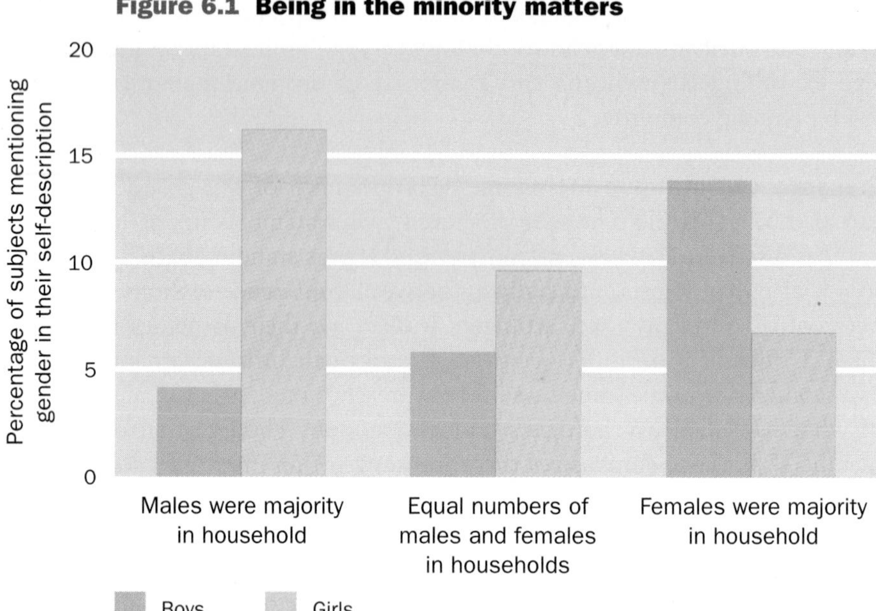

You may recall a similar point from Chapter 5, page 195: a solo member of a group tends to be perceived by observers in terms of that group membership.

girls from households where their gender was in the minority were more likely to mention gender than were children from households where their gender made up the majority. Similarly, children whose ethnic group constituted a minority at school were more likely to mention their ethnicity in informal self-descriptions than were children who were part of the ethnic majority (McGuire and others, 1978). As sociologist Joe Feagin commented, "Being White means never having to think about it. Being Black means having to think about it all the time. Black people are constantly reminded of it" (Benning & Bennett, 1992). Look back at your responses to the opening exercise. Did you list group memberships that make you different from most other people?

Chapter 14 will describe the famed "Robbers Cave" study, a vivid demonstration of the effects of intergroup conflict on group identification.

Conflict or Rivalry. Although all of these reminders can make a social identity accessible, probably the most potent factor that brings group membership to mind is conflict or rivalry between groups (Ryen & Kahn, 1975; Doise & Weinberger, 1973). Remember when your gym teacher used to arbitrarily split the class into two teams for a game? Did you find yourself cheering your teammates' accomplishments and jeering at your rivals? Even a news report of rivalry can remind us of group loyalties. In one study, exposure to a campus newspaper headline like "Humanities, Science Majors at Odds Over Core Program" was enough to increase the accessibility of students' identity as scientists or humanists (Price, 1989). Thus, conflict is perhaps the most powerful factor in making a group membership accessible.

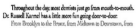

Throughout the day, most dentists just go from mouth-to-mouth. Dr. Russell Karmel has a little more fun going door-to-door.
From Brooklyn to the Bronx, from Midtown to Downtown, from Staten Island to Suffolk County, people who want dental care in their very own homes call on Russell Karmel, D.D.S.
Russell took to the streets a while back as a less expensive way to break into the crowded dental market of the Metropolitan New York area. (Instead of the overhead of a dental office, he has a reasonably low car payment.) It's a little unusual, Russell admits, to practice dentistry out of the back end of a car (so it's good to drive a car you really like), but it turns out there are a lot of people who just can't make it into a dentist's office—his phone never stops ringing.
Would Russell like to have a regular office someday? Sure. But for now, he carries everything he needs (X-ray machine, drill, suction, etc.—patients provide the chair) in the trunk of his Saturn coupe. Best of all, when he's done with someone's mouth, he doesn't just jump right into another. He jumps into 124 horses, sport-tuned suspension and a perfectly matched set of gear ratios—and the Long Island Expressway becomes his own personal Grand Prix. (He still has to obey the law, but at least he doesn't have to spend all day listening to elevator music.)
A Different Kind of Company. A Different Kind of Car.

A different kind of car, a different kind of car owner Sharing unusual characteristics can make those characteristics socially significant. Like owners of the distinctive Volkswagen "beetle" before them, Saturn owners have achieved group status: they find themselves honking at each other on the freeway and gathering in parking lots to discuss their cars.

Cultural Differences in the Importance of Group Membership. Group membership does not exist in a vacuum, of course, but has an importance that depends on the cultural context. Interdependent cultures like most in Asia, South America, and Africa foster and reinforce views of the self in group terms. People from these cultures tend to see themselves as members of larger groups or categories—perhaps as workers at a particular plant, graduates of a certain school, or inhabitants of a specific village. In such societies, family units are often multigenerational, and employment relationships may last a lifetime.

In contrast, people who live in the United States, Canada, Northern Europe, and other individualistic cultures are encouraged to think of themselves in comparatively idiosyncratic terms—for example, as tall, dark, and handsome. They tend to value freedom, personal enjoyment, and the achievement of individual goals, while viewing group memberships as temporary and changeable (Bellah and others, 1985). Members of these societies have high divorce rates and often seem comfortable switching churches or employers. Thus, cultural differences can affect whether people think of themselves more often as individuals or as members of groups, and by so doing, they can create corresponding differences in social behavior (Markus & Kitayama, 1991). But as we will see, even in individualistic cultures in which group memberships are seen as more fluid and less omnipresent, group memberships make a big difference to people's ways of thinking about themselves and those around them.

Personality Differences in Group Membership Importance. Every time you think of yourself as a group member—as, perhaps, a Texan, a Micmac, or a single mother—the mere thought increases the likelihood that you will think of yourself that way again. A group membership that is personally very significant—religious identification for a member of the clergy, party affiliation for a politician, or racial or ethnic group membership for a civil

Figure 6.2 Factors that make a social identity accessible

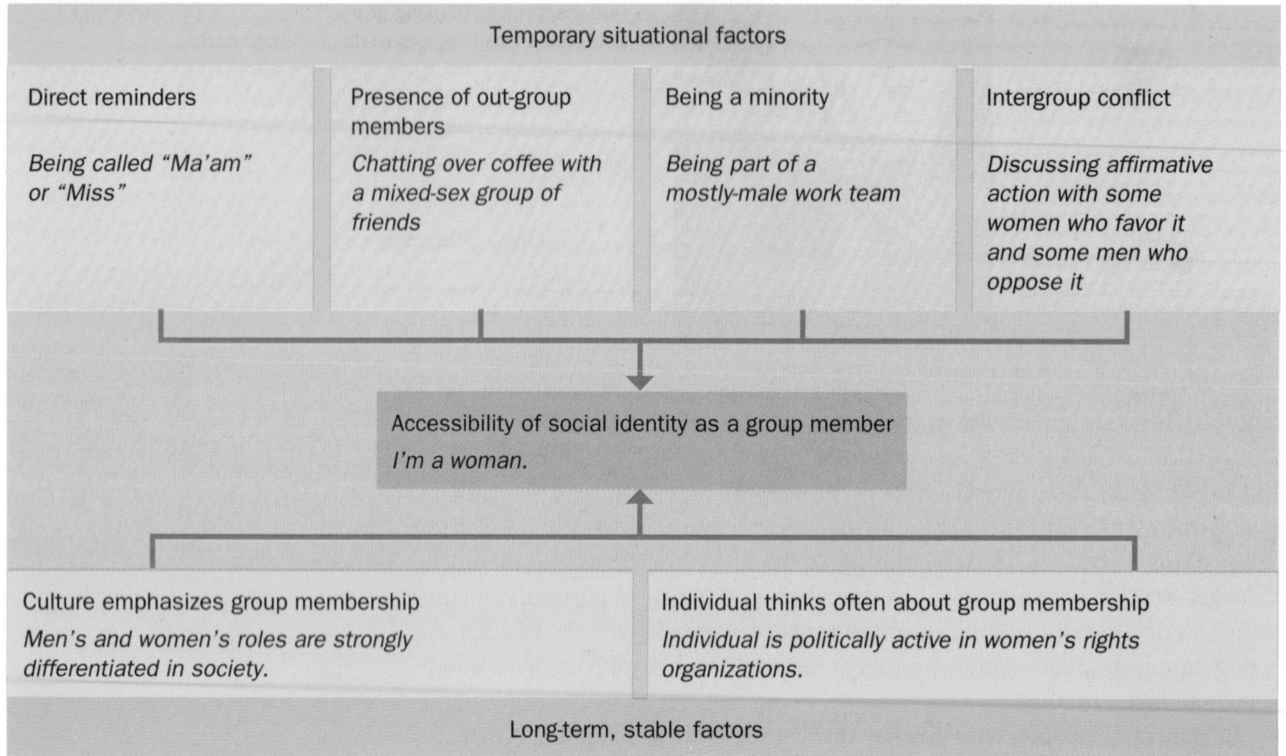

Many factors can increase the accessibility of a particular group membership. Not only obvious reminders, like group labels or intergroup conflict, but even relatively subtle factors like the presence of out-group members can activate our knowledge of group membership. A particular membership that is significant in the general culture or is personally important to an individual may be highly accessible virtually all the time.

rights leader—will be frequently activated and highly accessible. This accessibility produces reliable and predictable differences in the way each of us habitually sees ourselves and others. For example, people for whom gender is chronically important and accessible have "male" or "female" as part of their self-schemata (Bem, 1981). Accordingly, these individuals tend to perceive, and to react to, themselves and others in terms of gender rather than other social attributes (Frable, 1989). Most people move from one self-categorization to another and from seeing themselves as group members to seeing themselves as individuals. In contrast, some people who tend to think of themselves more consistently as men or women rather than as members of other categories may react to others primarily as males and females and may see every situation in terms of its implications for male-female relations.

Although most research has examined the effects of having gender as part of a self-schema, similar effects no doubt follow from other highly accessible group memberships. The chair of the Democratic National Committee probably thinks of politicians and policy positions primarily in terms of their identification with one of the two American political parties. Figure 6.2 summarizes all the factors that can make a social identity accessible.

To remind yourself of the consequences of having a particular trait as part of the self-schema, see Chapter 4, especially page 125.

Me, You, and Them: Effects of Social Categorization

Does it really make a difference if we see ourselves as Mexican-Americans, Californians, lefties, or libertarians? Aren't we pretty much the same people most of the time? And don't we see and treat in-group members and out-group members in pretty much the same way from one day to the next? By now you probably are not surprised to hear that the answer is no. When group memberships surface, they influence the way we see ourselves and others, making a huge difference in what we think, how we feel, and what we do.

"I" Becomes "We": Social Categorization and the Self

Activated knowledge about a group membership has multiple effects on people's self-concept and self-esteem. People tend to see themselves as typical group members. Group memberships also influence people's moods and self-esteem as they feel bad about their groups' failures or good about their successes.

Seeing Oneself as a Group Member. Seeing oneself as a group member means seeing oneself in stereotypic terms. Recall that when we stereotype members of other groups, we see them as possessing the typical characteristics that are believed to be associated with the group. The same processes operate when we see ourselves as group members. In fact, when a group membership is activated, we see ourselves as more typical of our group than we do under other circumstances (Turner and others, 1987). One experiment demonstrated this effect by having some students listen to a discussion in which one group presented pro-environmental attitudes. Some of the students were about to join the group voicing the positive attitudes, but others knew they would not be joining. The students who identified with the group rated themselves as higher in environmental awareness than did the other students who heard the same discussion (Mackie, 1986). In another study, students rated themselves and a student from a different university. Some subjects made the ratings alone, whereas others did so in the presence of an audience of in-group members—fellow students from their own school. The subjects who had an audience saw themselves and the out-group member as more typical representatives of their respective schools than did subjects who had no audience (Wilder & Shapiro, 1991). Evidently the in-group audience activated the students' own group identity, causing them to see both themselves and the other student in group-stereotypic terms.

When people see themselves as typical members of a group, this perception—just like any other aspect of the self-concept—directs their thoughts and actions. This process may be responsible for the finding that when labo-

Becoming what we are: The power of self-stereotyping When we belong to a group, we often come to see ourselves as embodying the very essence of our group memberships. In the movie "Glengarry Glen Ross," Alec Baldwin (left) plays the quintessential salesman, striving to represent everything that he deems important about his profession. His portrayal has great significance for people who work in sales.

ratory groups include men, women speak more tentatively than they do in all-female groups (Carli, 1990). The presence of men apparently makes the women's identity as females accessible, causing many of them to act in ways that they regard as typical of women, such as by avoiding assertive speech.

Accessibility of Gender Identity in the Classroom. If group memberships can affect people's behavior in a situation as transient as a research discussion group, what is the likely long-term impact of highly accessible gender roles? College enrollment statistics suggest that they may influence women's and men's career and educational choices. In coeducational schools, men tend to major in the hard sciences and mathematics, and women in the humanities and fine arts. These majors are consistent with traditional stereotypes of men and women, which a mixed-sex environment renders more accessible. In contrast, compared with their counterparts in coeducational schools, women in women's colleges are more likely to major in science or math, and men in men's colleges in the arts or humanities (Smith, 1977). For example, a study in the early 1980s found that Mount Holyoke College, a small women's college in western Massachusetts, had graduated more women who went on to obtain doctoral degrees in biology and chemistry than had any other college or university, regardless of size (Rossiter, 1982). Though many factors no doubt contribute to explaining outcomes like these, could the reduced salience of gender in single-sex schools reduce the impact of gender stereotypes on men's and women's choices of major?

Liking Ourselves: Social Identity and Self-Esteem. We have all experienced it: we feel great when our team wins. Chicagoans poured out onto the streets to celebrate the Bulls' "three-peat" victory in the 1993 NBA Finals. Spanish citizens cried with joy when Jordi Calafat and Francisco Sanchez took the dais to accept the gold medal in the 1992 Olympic 470-class yachting race. Why? We experience emotions on behalf of our groups because group memberships are a part of our social identity (Smith, 1993). When

Basking in reflected glory When we identify with a group, their emotional ups and downs become our own. Like these high school students, we are not only happy to join in a victory celebration, we are happy *because* our team has won.

good things happen to our team, our school, or our city, we feel good—about life and about ourselves.

Strivers for positive self-esteem that we are, we play up group memberships that make us feel good about ourselves (Tesser, 1988). Robert Cialdini and his co-workers (1976) investigated this tendency to **BIRG**, or *bask in the reflected glory* of a positive group identification, by counting "in-group" clothing worn on school days following football games. At seven universities they found that students wore more school sweatshirts, baseball caps, scarves, and pins if the football team won than if it lost.

You may recall from Chapter 4, pages 130 to 138, that, in the same way, people tend to play up the idiosyncratic characteristics they feel good about.

To test their hypothesis that a positive group membership can serve to raise self-esteem, Cialdini and his colleagues gave students a brief general-knowledge test and temporarily raised or lowered their self-esteem by manipulating the results. Some randomly selected students were told falsely that they had performed poorly on the test, and others were told that they had done well. The students were then asked, seemingly incidentally, to describe the outcome of a recent game. In their descriptions, the students who thought they had failed the test were more likely to associate themselves with winning teams (referring to them as "we") and to dissociate themselves from losing teams (referring to them as "they"), than were students who believed they had done well and whose self-esteem was intact. Thus, people BIRG (pronounced "burge") as a way of restoring positive self-regard, and they do so particularly when self-esteem is threatened.

Even a characteristic as arbitrary as a shared birth date can link individuals into a "group" so that the positive and negative characteristics of other group members affect self-esteem. Subjects in one study "incidentally" learned that they had the same birth date as another individual who was described either positively or negatively. Talking about themselves later, subjects who had experienced a personal failure tended to BIRG by mentioning the positively described, associated individual (Cialdini & De Nicholas, 1989). And one of us remembers feeling irrationally embarrassed when he first learned he shares a birthday with the former vice president Dan Quayle.

BIRG (bask in reflected glory) A way of boosting positive mood and self-esteem by identifying oneself with the accomplishments or good qualities of fellow in-group members.

Identifying with a group can help people feel good about themselves in another way, even if the group is not regarded as particularly positive. As we saw in Chapter 4, people generally like to see themselves as unique individuals, distinct from others. Yet they are also motivated to seek connectedness and similarity with others. Group membership can simultaneously satisfy both of these desires. Perceiving the differences between "our" group and other groups and seeing the similarity among members within "our" group can help us feel good about ourselves (Brewer, 1991). Though individual and cultural differences influence the relative strengths of these opposing motives, the best balance for most people most of the time involves membership in relatively small groups. By identifying with small groups, we neither see ourselves as completely unique nor identify with a group that is so large and inclusive that we are lost in it. This option provides the optimal balance between perceived uniqueness and separateness on the one hand, and similarity and connectedness on the other (Brewer, 1991).

Others Become "We": Social Categorization and the In-Group

When group membership is highly accessible, people see other in-group members as similar in their central group-linked characteristics. However, extensive personal interaction (when group membership is not activated) provides knowledge about their unique and diverse personal characteristics. People like fellow in-group members and tend to treat them in fair, humane, and altruistic ways, seeing in-group members as similar to themselves in their goals and interests.

An accessible group membership is not just an aspect of the individual self, like height or chess-playing ability. Instead, it is an aspect of *social* identity that links the individual to others, influencing the way the person thinks, feels, and acts toward other in-group members.

Perceiving Fellow In-Group Members. When we think about fellow in-group members, what is uppermost in our minds? When group membership is accessible, we think mostly about the features we believe we share with the group, thereby causing us to see other in-group members as similar to ourselves. In one demonstration of this effect, students were assigned to groups ostensibly on the basis of their artistic preferences. They were then asked to guess the extent to which other in-group members shared their own personal characteristics and preferences (Allen & Wilder, 1979). As expected, the students assumed that all members of the group would be very similar in art preferences. Surprisingly, they also thought that in-group members' interests, activities, and even their personality traits would match their own. Anything that increases the accessibility of group membership—engaging in competition with another group, for example—further enhances this assumed similarity (Miller & Brewer, 1986).

Although a highly accessible shared group membership leads us to focus on our similarities with other in-group members, we also manage to learn quite a lot about other in-group members' personal qualities—the things that make them unique as individuals. This awareness of specific, personal attributes develops as we interact with other members in a variety of contexts and situations (Turner and others, 1987). It is particularly acute when personal rather than group identities are most salient, as when a group of close friends chats together over dinner.

Knowing others' unique characteristics also helps us to find our own place in the group. As Chapter 4 noted, we tend to define our personal selves in terms of what makes us distinct from others (McGuire and others, 1978; Park & Rothbart, 1982). Among your fellow students you may be the serious one, the conservationist, the lover of country music. Of course, to make these differentiations you have to pay attention to the personality, passions, and preferences of your fellow in-group members. In doing so, you learn a lot about them—so much, in fact, that when group membership is not highly accessible, you are likely to see your group as quite diverse in characteristics *not* related to group membership (Park & Judd, 1990).

Liking In-Group Others: To Be Us Is to Be Lovable. Because they share our attributes, fellow in-group members become part of "me and mine" and so we like them—usually much more than we like out-group members. Asked to evaluate essays or creative solutions to problems, people treat their own group's work more generously than out-group products. They choose to interact with and to befriend members of their own rather than of another group (Brewer, 1979; Brewer & Silver, 1978). Even people assigned to groups on a trivial or random basis evaluate their own group as more positive and desirable than other groups, although of course the in-group bias is stronger when the groups are real and meaningful (Mullen and others, 1992).

Indeed, the very concept "we" seems to have positive connotations, as compared with the concept "they" (Perdue and others, 1990). People think that nonsense syllables (like *xeh*) that have been paired with the word *we* have more positive meanings than syllables paired with the word *they*. Subjects also respond more quickly to positive words that follow *we* than to those that follow *they*. Both of these findings suggest that the label *we* activates positive associations that affect the interpretation of other information. In a clever study of the consequences of these effects for intergroup behavior, subjects were asked to read a description of the task that they were to perform with other individuals. For one group of subjects, this task was described as "something *we* all have to do *our* best on;" for another group it was "something *they* have to do *their* best on." When asked to imagine the quality of the interaction and the likability of the other participants, subjects who had been exposed to the in-group pronouns had more positive expectations than those of subjects who had read out-group pronouns (Dovidio & Gaertner, 1993).

It may have occurred to you that attraction to other in-group members is somehow different from "ordinary" feelings of liking for another individual. After all, attraction usually depends on getting to know someone—on recognizing their desirable personal characteristics and your common interests. In contrast, attraction in group situations seems to depend merely on the knowledge of shared group membership (Turner and others, 1983). Indeed, people often prefer others who belong to their own group even if they would not be especially likable on the merits of their individual characteristics alone. This pattern has been observed in many types of groups, including work groups and an Australian football team (Hogg & Hardie, 1991; Hogg and others, 1993). In a sense, in-group members are liked not as individuals but as representatives of the liked group (Hogg, 1987).

This special kind of liking leads us to give fellow in-group members the benefit of the doubt when we make attributions about their behaviors. Unfortunately, we are not nearly so generous with out-group members (Islam & Hewstone, 1993). Consider the responses of Hindu office workers who were presented with descriptions of either a Hindu person or a Muslim person behaving in a socially desirable or undesirable way—for example, a shopkeeper being particularly generous or cheating a customer (Taylor & Jaggi, 1974). When the Hindu subjects explained the actor's behavior, they demonstrated *group-serving attributional biases*. That is, they attributed positive behavior by Hindus and negative actions by Muslims to enduring personality traits, in statements like "Hindus are generous" or "Muslims are basically cheats." Conversely, they attributed negative behavior by Hindus and positive behavior by Muslims to fleeting situational causes, such as "The Hindu cheated him because the man has been stealing from his store," or "The Muslim was generous because he thought the man worked for the authorities."

You might have noticed that the attributions we make about our groups are just like the self-enhancing attributions we make as individuals. To check the parallels for yourself, see Chapter 4, pages 130 to 138.

People everywhere make positively biased attributions for the behaviors of the in-group, but not for the out-group (Pettigrew, 1979). English schoolboys at private schools believe they and their comrades fail only because they do not try, but they think students in other schools fail because they are stupid (Hewstone and others, 1982). Similarly, employed people believe the unemployed are unwilling to work, whereas the unemployed blame their plight on external factors—"the breaking of trade unions by management," or "the economic downturn" (Furnham, 1982).

A recent study found in-group bias in the very language people use to describe others' actions. Anne Maass and her colleagues (1989) used cartoon drawings to examine how people describe positive actions by in-group and out-group members. Subjects produced relatively concrete and specific descriptions of out-group behavior, whereas the in-group descriptions were more abstract and general. If an out-group member comforted a lost child on a crowded street, subjects said "he *talked to* the child," or some similarly specific statement. The same action by an in-group member elicited "he *helped* or *cared for* the child." The researchers argue that the concreteness of the out-group descriptions implicitly casts the behaviors as ungeneralizable, one-of-a-kind instances, while the more abstract terms used for in-group actions emphasize the actor's positive general personality traits, such as helpfulness or caring.

Treating the In-Group Right: Justice and Altruism. If in-group members are lovable and similar to us, we will want to treat them as we ourselves would like to be treated. Indeed, people sometimes act in ways that seem to make no sense from the perspective of individual costs and benefits. Parents scrimp and save to leave an inheritance for their children. Soldiers sacrifice their lives for their comrades or their country. From the perspective of a social group, however, actions like these make a great deal of sense. Groups prosper when their members are willing to subordinate personal interests to the group and to help other members in times of need. This has been true since members of many early hunting societies shared the meat from large animals among the whole group (Fiske, 1992). When group memberships are uppermost in people's minds, they often act in these altruistic ways.

When people see the world through the lens of their group memberships, what is best for the group blurs together with what is best for the individual. "I" becomes "we," and the distinction between self-interest and group interest vanishes (Turner and others, 1987). This merging of perceived individual and group interests constitutes the psychological basis for fair and altruistic behavior. Almost a century ago Charles Darwin (1909) argued that morality derives originally "from the social instincts": actions are judged good or bad "solely as they obviously affect the welfare of the tribe." When people think of themselves as members of a family, community, ethnic group, or nation, they feel *like* and feel *for* fellow in-group members. As a result, treating those others with fairness and compassion—indeed, treating others as they themselves would like to be treated—becomes easy, natural, and the right thing to do (Deutsch, 1973, 1990; Staub, 1978; Struch & Schwartz, 1989).

It is this unification of self-interest and group-interest that makes altruistic and self-sacrificing behavior possible, as we will see in Chapter 12. It is also the basis of effective functioning of small interacting groups, a topic discussed in detail in Chapter 13.

An accessible group membership makes other in-group members part of "me and mine." As a result, shared group membership has dramatic effects on the way we think about, evaluate, and behave toward other members, as shown in Figure 6.3.

Figure 6.3 Social identity turns others into "we"

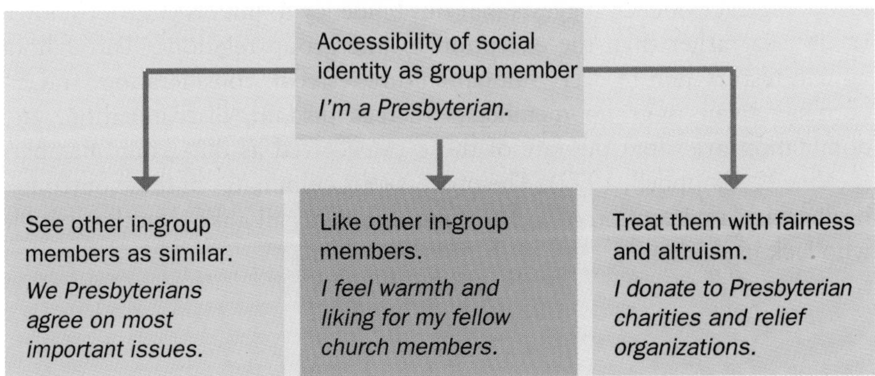
Accessibility of social identity as group member
I'm a Presbyterian.
See other in-group members as similar.
We Presbyterians agree on most important issues.
Like other in-group members.
I feel warmth and liking for my fellow church members.
Treat them with fairness and altruism.
I donate to Presbyterian charities and relief organizations.

When a shared group membership is accessible, it has positive effects on the way we see, evaluate, and treat other group members.

Others Become "They": Social Categorization and the Out-Group

People see out-groups as quite uniform and homogeneous. People also dislike, devalue, and discriminate against out-group members, depending on the extent to which they are seen as threatening the in-group. When the out-group is simply different it elicits mild dislike. When the out-group is seen as outdoing the in-group, this more serious threat results in resentment, dislike, and overt discrimination. Out-groups that are seen as severe threats to the in-group elicit murderous hatred, discrimination, aggression, or moral exclusion.

The comedian Emo Phillips describes a conversation with a suicidal man threatening to jump off a bridge:

> I said, "Are you a Christian or a Jew?" He said, "A Christian." I said, "Me too. Protestant or Catholic?" He said, "Protestant." I said, "Me too. What franchise?" He says "Baptist." I said, "Me too. Northern Baptist or Southern Baptist?" He says, "Northern Baptist." I said, "Me too. Northern Conservative Baptist or Northern Liberal Baptist?" He says, "Northern Conservative Baptist." I said, "Me too. Northern Conservative Fundamentalist Baptist or Northern Conservative Reformed Baptist?" He says, "Northern Conservative Fundamentalist Baptist." I said, "Me too. Northern Conservative Fundamentalist Baptist, Great Lakes Region, or Northern Conservative Fundamentalist Baptist, Eastern Region?" He says, "Northern Conservative Fundamentalist Baptist, Great Lakes Region." I said, "Me too. Northern Conservative Fundamentalist Baptist, Great Lakes Region, Council of 1879 or Northern Conservative Fundamentalist Baptist, Great Lakes Region, Council of 1912?" He says, "Northern Conservative Fundamentalist Baptist, Great Lakes Region, Council of 1912." I said, "Die, heretic!" and I pushed him over (cited in Hamilton & Mackie, 1990, p. 10).

Emo Phillips makes comic what more often is tragic: the tendency to hate and mistreat those who are not members of our in-group, regardless of how similar to us they may seem to outsiders. Just as feeling good about our groups often involves giving them the edge over others, bringing our group up in the world sometimes means putting others down. Unfortunately, anthropological evidence suggests that this tendency to put other groups down is the rule rather than the exception in intergroup relations. Throughout human history and in every human culture, esteem, consideration, and favoritism await in-group members, whereas disdain, discrimination, and domination are often the fate of those categorized as out-group members (LeVine & Campbell, 1972). The process that culminates in these outcomes begins with a perception of out-group members as all alike—faceless people who lack individuality.

Perceiving the Out-Group as Homogeneous: "They're All Alike!" One of us is an avid swimming fan. During the 1992 Olympics, she never missed the listing of the previous day's results in her local newspaper. There was something curious about those results, however. Consider the men's 100-meter butterfly final: "1. Pablo Morales, Santa Clara, California. 2. Rafal Szukala, Poland. 3. Anthony Nesty, Surinam." Or the women's 200-meter breaststroke final: "1. Kyoko Iwasaki, Japan. 2. Lin Li, China. 3. Anita Nall, Towson, Maryland." Can you figure out what caught her eye? In this California newspaper, U.S. medal winners were differentiated by state and hometown, whereas only the country was reported for non-U.S. competitors. Next time your local paper reports on an international sporting event, check to see how out-group members are described, compared with the in-group.

You should have no difficulty finding other examples of this **out-group homogeneity effect**—the tendency to perceive out-group members as "all the same" compared to the relatively more diverse in-group. People of European origin typically see the widely diverse groups of Native Americans as "all the same" while finding great diversity and variety among those of European descent. Brothers in one fraternity find members of other houses just as they expected them to be but do not think they themselves fit their own group's stereotype (Linville and others, 1989; Mullen & Hu, 1989). And a member of an Isla Vista, California, band recently explained, "Los Angeles bands are all homogeneous. Seattle bands all sound like Seattle bands. But Isla Vista music is more original. Bands here play all kinds of music!" (Lagerquist, 1992).

Thus the tendency to see out-groups as relatively homogeneous is quite widespread. What accounts for this out-group homogeneity effect?

1. *Familiarity: It's who you know.* One obvious explanation involves numbers: we usually know more in-group members than out-group members, and we are therefore more aware of their diversity. The more students you know on your campus, for example, the better your chances are of coming across a wide variety of individuals, such as the vegetarian gourmet cook, the athlete majoring in engineering, the ROTC cadet, and the antinuclear activist. No wonder the in-group seems more diverse than the students at another, less familiar college (Linville and others, 1989). But lack of familiarity with the out-group cannot be the whole story. In fact, even members of laboratory groups—who meet under carefully controlled conditions so that participants have equal information about their own and other groups—see their fellow members as more varied than members of other groups (Mackie and others, 1993; Judd & Park, 1988). In such cases, we must look for other processes that also contribute to the out-group homogeneity effect.

out-group homogeneity effect The tendency to see the out-group as relatively more homogeneous and less diverse than the in-group.

2. *It's not who you know, it's how you know.* Even if we interacted with the same number of in-group and out-group members, interactions with out-group members would be relatively more constrained. A person's very presence as an outsider may be enough to make the group close ranks and present a unified front. In fact, people's exposure to out-groups often takes place in settings where no individual interaction is even possible—for example, when students from a rival school attend a sports event en masse. In such settings one can easily gain the impression that out-group members are pretty much all alike. In contrast, in-group interactions are likely to be relatively more varied, relaxed, and informal (Rothbart and others, 1984). As a result, in-group members' unique roles, traits, and opinions can emerge, so members are seen in more differentiated terms.

3. *Future interaction: Tomorrow is another day—or not.* Even if you happen to strike up conversations with students from a rival school, what you learn will be limited by the realization that you probably will never encounter them again. You have no special reason to learn each individual's special characteristics and interests or even their names. In talking to your fellow students, however, you may expect to see them again tomorrow—perhaps in the bicycle repair shop, the statistics study group, or the coffee shop. You probably will pay attention to what they say and do, and you will make an effort to learn more about them. Expecting future interaction makes us try to form impressions of people as unique individuals rather than as members of a faceless crowd (Srull & Brand, 1983), and in-group members benefit much more than out-group members from this fact.

4. *Self differentiation: I am me and you are not.* Finally, as we stated earlier, people habitually focus on the personal characteristics that make them unique and different from others. Within the in-group, this means that we learn a lot about others' characteristics in the process of finding out what differentiates us from them. But we can feel unique and different from out-group members just by noting the group-defining characteristics, such as ethnicity, gender, nationality, or university affiliation (Turner and others, 1987). In a study demonstrating this effect, Bernadette Park and Myron Rothbart (1982) asked subjects to read brief newspaper stories about men and women. When the subjects later were asked to recall as much as they could about the protagonists, they remembered more personal details, such as occupation, about same-sex than about opposite-sex individuals (see Figure 6.4).

All of these factors usually operate together to make the out-group seem homogeneous, and unfortunately these factors perpetuate a vicious cycle. If we firmly believe "they're all alike," then we feel justified in generalizing from the actions of a single out-group member to the group as a whole (Quattrone & Jones, 1980). We may learn that one out-group member com-

Figure 6.4 It is easier to remember us than them

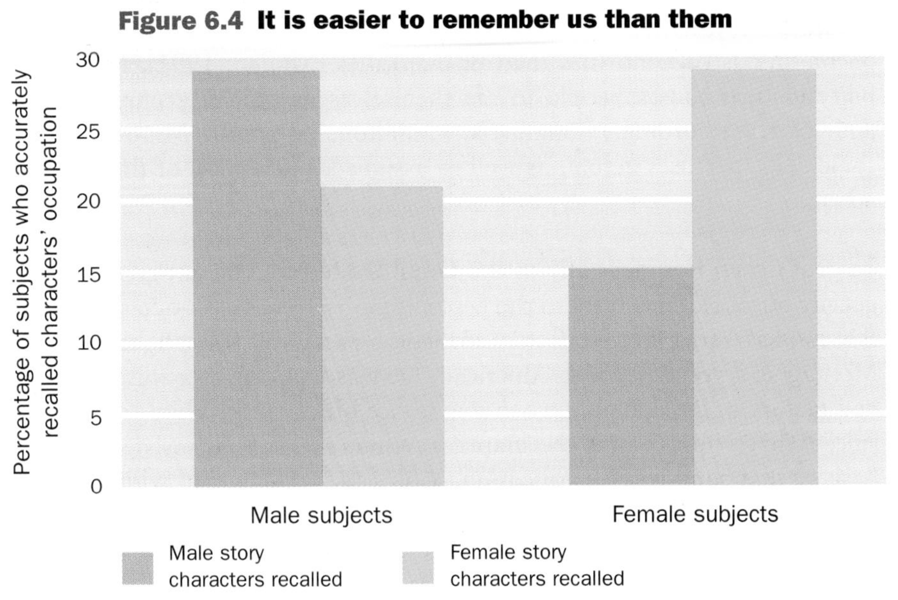

In this study, men and women were asked to read a "newspaper story" and, at a later time, to recall information about the main characters. As you can see, men more easily recalled the occupations of male characters, whereas women more easily recalled female characters' occupations. (Based on Park & Rothbart, 1982.)

mitted a crime and jump to the conclusion that they are all bad apples. But if an in-group member commits the same crime, we may shrug it off as the action of one bad person. Because our own group is so diverse, there are bound to be a few bad apples in the barrel: it does not mean everyone is bad. Of course, this reasoning makes the out-group look still more homogeneous. The Dutch philosopher Spinoza noticed this tendency three centuries ago, when he said, "If we have been affected with joy or sorrow by any one who belongs to a class or nation different from our own, . . . we shall not love or hate him merely, but the whole of the class or nation to which he belongs" (1677/1930, p. 161).

Although out-groups are usually perceived as more homogeneous than in-groups, there is an interesting exception to the rule. When the in-group is a minority group, it tends to be perceived as more homogeneous than the majority out-group, both by outsiders and by its own members (Simon & Brown, 1987; Brown & Smith, 1989). But even this exception can be explained by the same processes outlined earlier. People who belong to a small minority may know even more members of the majority out-group than members of their own small in-group. They often see majority individuals in a wide variety of roles and situations, and they can expect to interact with them as frequently as with members of their own small group—or even more frequently. And, if the majority commands more power and resources than the minority, minority group members may have to depend upon the majority and will have to be careful to treat individual majority group members in appropriate ways. For all these reasons, members of minority groups typically have strong reasons for recognizing fine distinctions among members of the majority group as well as among members of their own in-group. Finally, as we have already seen, group membership is more often on the minds of minorities than of majorities (Mullen, 1991). Its accessibility in turn causes people to see themselves as typical group members and to act accordingly (Simon & Hamilton, in press). Minority status sometimes increases actual, as well as assumed, uniformity of thought and action.

Out-Group Homogeneity in the Legal System. The out-group homogeneity effect extends even to the perception of physical characteristics, and this can have destructive effects. Consider, for example, the plight of Darryl Montague, a young African American. He was working as a shipping clerk at a factory in Philadelphia when two police officers asked him to step outside. "That's him! That's the man!" a White 17-year-old insisted. On the basis of that confident identification, Montague was charged with burglary. After spending fourteen months in prison because he could not make bail, Montague was eventually set free when a jury decided that the eyewitness identification would not hold up (Knight-Ridder, 1991).

Montague's false arrest and incarceration reflects an unfortunate instance of an effect called the *cross-race identification bias*. People can recognize the faces of members of their own ethnic group more easily than the faces of members of other groups (Bothwell and others, 1989; Anthony and others, 1992). Apparently members of other groups "all look alike." In one study, for example, Texas convenience store clerks were asked to identify three male customers—actually experimental confederates—who had stopped by to make a purchase earlier in the day. One confederate was African American, another was Mexican American, and the third was Anglo-American. The shop clerks—eighty-six of them in all—were also African American, Mexican American, and Anglo-American. As Figure 6.5 shows, the clerks made more accurate identifications of the customer belonging to their own group than they did of the customers from the other two groups (Platz & Hosch, 1988). As familiarity with a group grows, so too does identification accuracy (Goldstein & Chance, 1985). No wonder, then, that criminal defendants and their attorneys often question the accuracy of eyewitness identifications across ethnic group lines.

The tendency to see members of the out-group as all alike may in itself be relatively harmless, but it sets the stage for worse events. You need only look at any newspaper, turn on the television newscasts, or flip back to the examples in Chapter 5 to see ample evidence that groups treat other groups badly, in ways ranging from mild dislike and overt discrimination all the way to domination, exploitation, and massacre. As we will see, the way out-groups are treated depends on how much threat they seem to pose to the in-group.

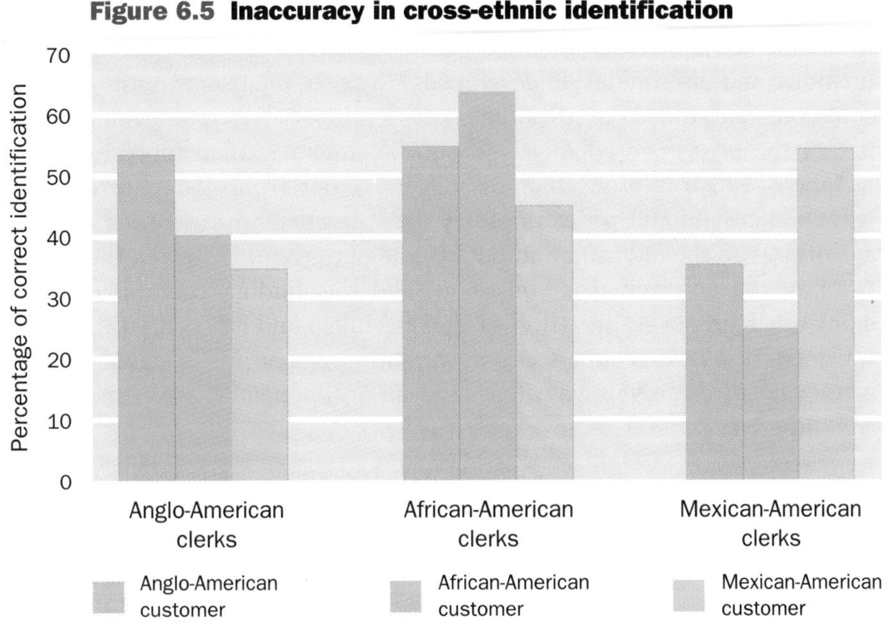

Convenience store clerks who were either Anglo American, African American, or Mexican American tried to identify customers that researchers had sent to visit their store earlier. The three customers also belonged to one of the three ethnic groups. As shown here, clerks were best able to identify customers from their own group. (Based on Platz & Hosch, 1988.)

Effects of Mere Categorization: They're Different, but We're Better. For any of the manifold examples of one group's maltreatment of another, commentators can offer multiple explanations, including forces stemming from negative stereotypes, mutual ignorance and fear, unjust distribution of resources, and a history of conflict. However, perhaps the most sobering body of social psychological research on the issue reaches a startling conclusion: explanations like these are not always necessary. Discrimination can occur when a dividing line simply creates two groups, even in the absence of these common sources of antagonism.

In one of the experiments that initially demonstrated this point, a number of English boys aged fourteen to sixteen were assigned either to Group *X* or to Group *W* on the basis of a coin toss (Billig & Tajfel, 1973). The groups had no defining characteristics, and members did not know what other individuals were in each group. There was no basis for in-group or out-group stereotypes, and the groups had no history of conflict or antagonism—indeed, no history at all. For all these reasons, this situation was appropriately labeled a **minimal intergroup situation**. After being assigned to a group, each boy was given the opportunity to distribute rewards worth a small amount of money to two other individuals. For example, he might be asked to divide, in any way he wanted, 15 points between two other boys, who were identified only as "Member number 49 of the *W* group" and "Member number 72 of the *X* group."

minimal intergroup situation A research situation in which people are categorized, on an arbitrary or trivial basis, into groups that have no history, no conflicts of interest, and no stereotypes.

The late European social psychologist Henri Tajfel had devised this procedure as a baseline for further comparisons. He planned to go beyond merely categorizing subjects into groups, and to add other ingredients—such as negative stereotypes or conflict over resources—one at a time until prejudice and discrimination developed. However, the results in the baseline situation confounded the researchers' expectations. Even in this minimal situation the boys favored their own group: they awarded more points to members of their in-group than to boys in the out-group. They were not always blatantly unfair; for example, of the 15 points, boys awarded an average of 8.08 to the in-group and 6.92 to the out-group. However, the bias in favor of the in-group was consistent, and this finding was replicated in many other similar studies (Brewer, 1979; Mullen and others, 1992). Simple categorization into groups seems to be sufficient reason for people to dispense valued rewards in ways that favor in-group members over those who are "different."

Discrimination and Social Identity. What explains the favoritism found in minimal intergroup situations? Were people simply seeking material gain for the in-group? Tajfel was not so sure. His further explorations of behavior in minimal intergroup situations revealed a startling tendency: subjects often favor the in-group over the out-group *even when doing so costs the in-group in absolute terms*. For example, Tajfel gave some of his subjects a choice between option *A*, which allocates 11 points to an in-group member and 7 to an out-group member, and option *B*, which gives 17 points to each. Many subjects preferred option *A*, which gave the in-group an edge over the out-group, even though choosing *A* instead of *B* cost the in-group 6 points (Tajfel and others, 1971). Other studies of minimal groups showed that members give their own group higher ratings on positive traits, evaluations of performance, and inferences of morality (Brewer, 1979). Apparently group members want to make their groups better, stronger, and more lovable in any way available to them.

These findings led Tajfel to propose that just as we strive to view our individual selves positively, we also want to view our social identities in positive terms. This idea was the basis for **social identity theory**, which argues that people's motivation to derive positive self-esteem from their group memberships is one driving force behind in-group bias. Preferring the in-group over the out-group becomes a way of expressing regard for the in-group, and it is therefore a way of feeling good about oneself. In fact, research shows that the opportunity to discriminate against an out-group does increase people's self-esteem (Lemyre & Smith, 1985).

social identity theory The theory that people's motivation to derive positive self-esteem from their group memberships is one driving force behind in-group bias.

Findings like these suggest that being categorized in one of two unknown groups constitutes a threat to most people. Consider the experimental situation from the subject's point of view. You are assigned to a totally meaningless group and referred to by a code number rather than by name. Your only possible source of identity is the in-group–out-group distinction,

and even the in-group cannot provide much of a positive identity because it is indistinguishable from the out-group. The results of one study demonstrated that this type of categorization can indeed be threatening. In the study, some subjects were categorized as member 16 of an unknown "Red group," while others were assigned the personal code number 16 but were not categorized. Those assigned to an unknown group were found to have lower self-esteem than the other subjects (Lemyre & Smith, 1985). The subjects' lost self-esteem was restored only by the opportunity to discriminate in favor of the in-group—to say, in effect, that the difference between the in-group and the out-group is that the in-group is *better*.

Effects of Perceived Disadvantage: They're Doing Better Than We Are So Let's Compete with Them. Threats to group status occur not only within the laboratory but also in the outside world of everyday life, where they have the same effect of triggering intergroup discrimination. When an in-group perceives an out-group to be higher in status, more powerful, more prosperous, or more favored by government programs, in-group members' feelings generally turn from mild dislike to stronger emotions. Anger, resentment, and support for overt discrimination against the out-group are frequent outcomes. Consider what happened, for example, when researchers asked members of high-status and low-status campus sororities to evaluate their own and other sororities (Crocker and others, 1987). Sorority members who knew that other students did not regard them highly showed a stronger bias against the out-group than did their higher-status sisters.

Similarly, when groups in society possess high status and sufficient power to protect that status, they can afford to be relatively charitable toward out-groups, showing a kind of benevolent paternalism (Lambert & Taylor, 1986). In contrast, Whites in the United States who regard their group as threatened by racial out-groups tend to oppose interracial marriage, affirmative action, the use of busing to desegregate schools, and welfare spending (Sears & Allen, 1984; Jones, 1992).

Even individuals who are not *personally* threatened may react strongly if they believe that their group is threatened. This effect is sometimes demonstrated in voting behavior. Consider one concrete reflection of Whites' level of prejudice against African Americans—their willingness to vote for African-American political candidates. Regardless of their *personal* economic standing, White voters who believe that Whites as a group are economically threatened by African Americans often refuse to support African-American candidates (Vanneman & Pettigrew, 1972; Bobo, 1983).

Effects of Extreme Threat: They Threaten Us So Let's Attack First. In a Houston parking lot, a gang of teenagers set upon Paul Broussard, a 27-year-old banker, and beat him to death. The attackers did not know Broussard personally, and they had no history of disagreement or conflict with him. Their only motive for this brutal crime was that Broussard was gay (Baker, 1991). What can explain this kind of hatred? Stereotypes can produce group prejudice, as we discussed in Chapter 5, and Broussard's attackers probably believed that gays have a variety of negative characteristics. But can stereotypes fully account for such murderous hatred?

When prejudice turns from dislike to extreme hatred, it usually reflects the perception that what "they" stand for threatens everything that "we" stand for. People can feel this way even if they do not see themselves as personally threatened. For example, Whites who feel that their group is threatened by African Americans' political gains in their city often resist busing to desegregate schools even if they themselves have no school-age children (Sears & Allen, 1984).

When people believe that their groups are threatened they usually respond in two interrelated ways. First, they exalt in-group symbols and values. Past or present group leaders, flags, slogans, and the group's historical accomplishments are glorified and cast in a totally positive light. Second, they belittle, hate, and attack the out-group they perceive as threatening. Hatred for outsiders that arises in connection with the exaltation of in-group symbols—directed against homosexuals, women, immigrants, or racial, ethnic, or religious groups—is termed **symbolic prejudice** (Kinder, 1986; Sears, 1988).

symbolic prejudice Hatred for out-groups that arises, together with the exaltation of in-group symbols, in response to perceived threat.

The effects of symbolic prejudice could be seen when the Communist regime in the former Yugoslavia began to fail. People of Serbian descent felt themselves threatened by Croatians and Muslims, though the groups had been living peacefully side by side. Following a strongly nationalist leader, Slobodan Milosevic, Serbians began proclaiming the historic rights of their people and remembering past martyrs and Serbian blood shed in many wars over the centuries. In actions that are chillingly reminiscent of Nazi atrocities, the Serbians then launched military campaigns aimed at "ethnic cleansing," creating a new, larger homeland by killing members of other groups or driving them from their homes and lands. In just one attack in 1992, heavy shelling drove out or killed three-quarters of the 120,000 inhabitants of the city of Mostar; in all, over 2 million people were made homeless refugees.

The exaltation of in-group values and symbols not only goes hand in hand with mistreatment of out-groups but also is used to justify it (Esses and others, 1993; Sears, 1988). In the eighteenth and nineteenth centuries, for example, some Christian leaders cited biblical passages as evidence that slavery was divinely sanctioned (Swartley, 1983). Of course, many of their contemporaries posed the opposite argument, that slavery contradicted the basic message of the Bible. Apologists for slavery took such arguments as assaults on in-group values, as Albert Taylor Bledsoe did in his defense of slavery in 1860: "The history of interpretation furnishes no examples of more willful and violent perversions of the sacred text than are to be found in the writings of the abolitionists. They seem to consider themselves above the scriptures. . . . They put themselves above the law of God" (Swartley, 1983, p. 49). Today, some people are using similar arguments to oppose antidiscrimination protection for homosexuals. When people perceive threats to their groups, esteem and reverence for in-group symbols are often accompanied by prejudice against out-groups—which is justified by reference to those very symbols.

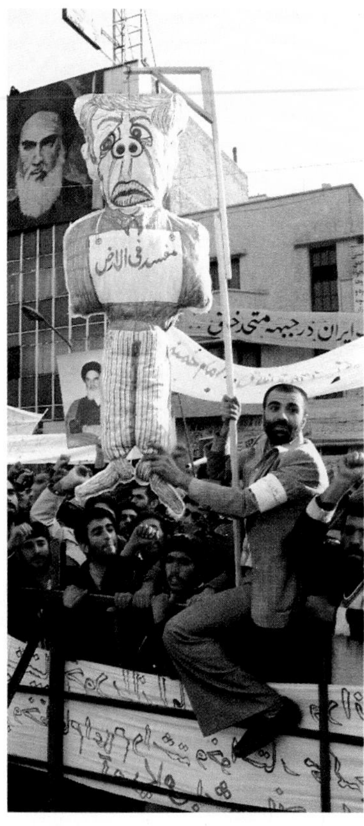

Symbolic prejudice Some of the most virulent intergroup hatred arises from reverence for an in-group's cherished values or from out-group threats to those values. During the administration of former U.S. president Jimmy Carter, he became a hated symbol for militantly anti-American Iranians. Here followers of the Ayatollah Khomeini hang him in effigy, while banners and posters extolling their leader adorn surrounding buildings.

As these examples indicate, wherever you see virulent hatred of out-groups and support for outright discrimination, you can *always* expect to find the perception that the out-groups pose extreme threats to the cherished in-group. James Ridgeway, author of a book on hate groups in the United States, described the manifestation of these feelings at a meeting with Ku Klux Klan (KKK) leaders:

> You could feel the hatred. In this delusional world, I realized, fear and hatred grew together: fear of a world that had left them behind, in which they could participate only marginally; hatred of the people they believed had caused them to lose out. . . . Everybody was after you. You were the only one left. Death was everywhere: figuratively, in terms of the White race perishing; and literally, as you fought, threatened, intimidated, and killed to "save" your people (Ridgeway, 1991, p. 5).

Moral Unconcern. Groups like the KKK, which carry discrimination to its extreme, view out-groups as fundamentally inferior to the in-group—subhuman and outside the domain in which the rules of morality apply (Opotow, 1990). History has recorded numerous instances in which slaves, women, racial and religious minorities, and enemies of the nation or ruling power have been viewed this way. In all these cases, the out-group was treated as fundamentally inferior to those who held power. This attitude has significant consequences because it allows us to suspend behaviors we usually consider both human and humane, such as helping others and treating them fairly and justly. These rules of justice and civility depend on seeing oneself and others as members of a community, and they therefore do not apply to out-group members (Tyler & Lind, 1990).

One important consequence of this attitude is **moral unconcern**—viewing out-group members as expendable or undeserving. Their suffering or victimization can be accepted with equanimity; it does not move us to empathy as the suffering of an in-group member would. For example, in 1971 a huge public outcry followed the deaths of four White, middle-class college students killed when National Guard troops fired on an anti-Vietnam War demonstration at Kent State University. Only days later, two African-American college students were shot and killed when police opened fire on a women's dormitory at Jackson State University in Mississippi—but this event received almost no notice from the media or the general public. Why did the deaths of innocent Whites trigger moral outrage while deaths of innocent Blacks did not?

Moral Unconcern in the Legal System. Examination of the U.S. legal system raises similar questions about moral unconcern. Studies of the imposition of the death penalty have repeatedly shown that it is racially biased. The bias is not the obvious one. In fact, African Americans and Whites who commit equivalent crimes are sentenced to death at about the same rates. But the race of the murder *victim* makes a big difference. One study found that Blacks who killed Whites in South Carolina were sentenced to die *forty times* more often than Blacks who killed other Blacks (Paternoster, 1983). Do these statistics indicate moral unconcern in the White-dominated U.S. criminal justice system? If murder victims are not members of the in-group, does the crime somehow become less monstrous?

Moral Exclusion. Moral unconcern for the fates of out-group members is essentially a passive response. Learning that out-group members are victimized or suffering, we pause briefly and then go about our business. However, **moral exclusion** is a more extreme stance in which out-group members are seen to be outside the boundary of moral principles. When members of relatively powerless groups are excluded from the scope of moral principles, the stage may be set for extreme intergroup oppression, massacre, or genocide (Opotow, 1990).

Moral exclusion can begin with symptoms that appear relatively benign, such as a belief in the in-group's moral superiority. The disease quickly spreads, however. In-group members may disparage the out-group, perhaps by labeling them as vermin, barbarians, or even germs "infecting" the pure in-group, or by dismissing their ability to experience human sentiments like pain or grief. Destructive actions against the out-group may be rationalized by the idea that "they brought it on themselves" or by self-justifying comparisons with horrible atrocities committed by others. The actions may be given euphemistic and misleading labels, like Hitler's genocidal "final solu-

moral unconcern The view that out-group members are expendable individuals whose suffering can be ignored.

moral exclusion The view that out-group members are outside the boundary of moral principles, often leading to their oppression, exploitation, or genocide.

Figure 6.6 Social identity turns others into "them"

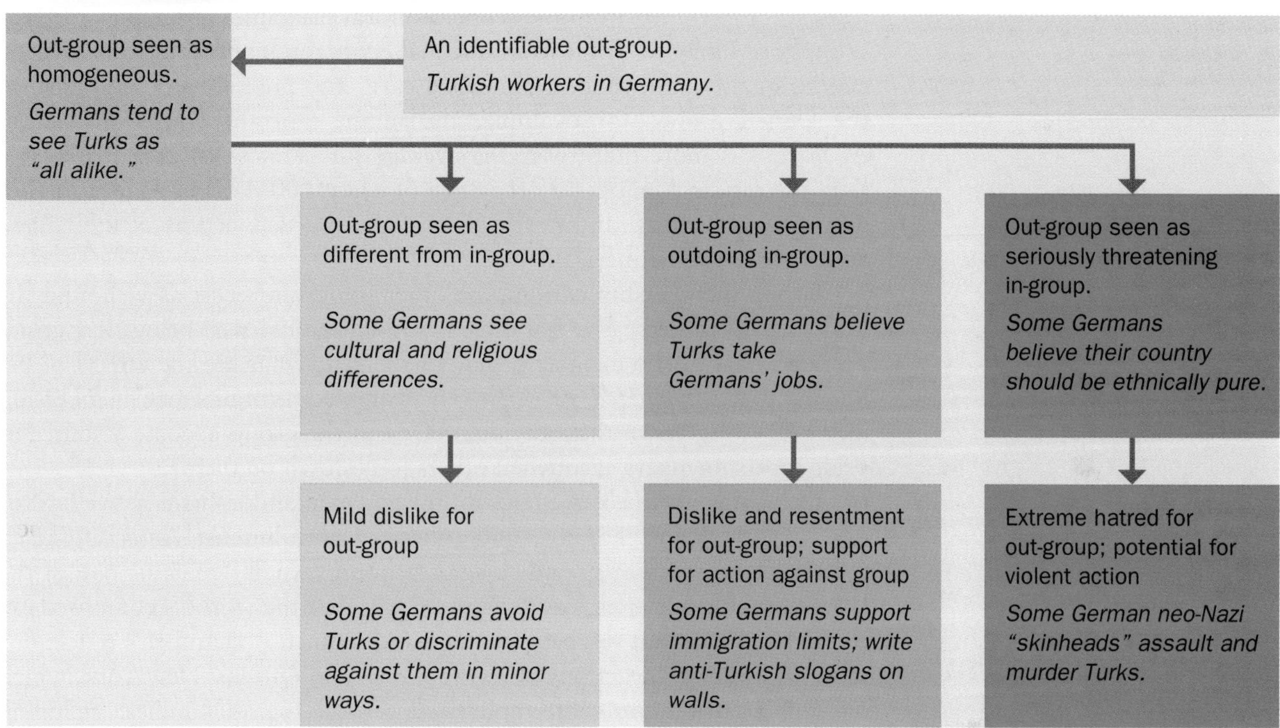

Out-group members tend to be seen as "all alike." In addition, they are often disliked and victimized by discrimination, depending on the magnitude of threat they are seen as posing to the in-group. Negative reactions may range from mild dislike, due to the simple perception of difference, to extreme hatred or even genocide when the in-group's very existence is believed to be threatened.

tion" or the Serbian "ethnic cleansing." Finally, group members reject personal responsibility for hateful or destructive acts by appealing to the in-group's welfare as a source of higher moral authority. These aspects of moral exclusion often play a role in the dynamics of intergroup conflict, which we will discuss in Chapter 14.

People's reactions to out-groups usually stop short of virulent hatred and moral exclusion. Still, as shown in Figure 6.6, the reactions, though they range from mild to intense, are always negative. Moreover, prejudice and discrimination against out-groups are found in all cultures (LeVine & Campbell, 1972), and they may be even stronger in the interdependent cultures of Asia and Africa than in Western independent cultures (Moghaddam and others, 1993; Hsu, 1983). Dislike, distrust, and discrimination seem to be intrinsic parts of the way people respond to out-groups: they are inextricably linked to the esteem and favor that in-groups enjoy.

When Group Memberships Are Negative

What are the costs of belonging to a group that is disliked, discriminated against, or excluded from the scope of moral principles? Members of these groups are likely to suffer from unequal economic opportunity, lack of access to quality education and medical care, and poor living conditions. In the United States, for example, the infant mortality rate for African Americans is more than twice the average for Whites—in fact, it is worse than the rate in Malaysia. Forty-three of every 100 African-American children live in poverty, and nearly half of the murder victims in the United States are African American.

Group membership can impose other important costs as well, and the price is paid in decreased self-esteem and emotional well-being. If a group becomes part of the member's view of the self, what are the effects of belonging to a *stigmatized,* or negatively evaluated, group? Does membership inevitably drag down the individual? Or can the group become a source of pride for its members even when others look down on them?

Questions like these are relevant for gay men and lesbians as well as for African Americans, Latinos, and others. The columnist Anna Quindlen (1992) has noted that prejudice against homosexuals "remains one of the last acceptable bigotries," as "children learn that the world is composed exclusively of love and sex between men and women." Quindlen's reflections were inspired by the actions of a school board in Queens, New York, which rejected a curriculum that emphasized respect for all families, including those headed by gay and lesbian parents. "Given statistical estimates, the board is telling 1 out of 10 kids that the life they will eventually lead is not

"A marked man, forever aware of the shadow of contempt that lay across my destiny and over my self-esteem" When Arthur Ashe died in 1993, he was hailed as a man of "integrity, honor, and humanity"—a man who was supremely self-confident and accomplished. Yet he attributed his drive to succeed and to right social wrongs at least in part to his membership in a stigmatized group. The battle to maintain self-esteem in the face of cultural devaluation is just part of the terrible cost of prejudice and discrimination.

part of the human program. Among their students are surely boys and girls who will discover they are gay and who, from their earliest years, will have learned that there is something wrong with that, and therefore with them. Learned it from classmates, from teachers. Worst of all, from their own mothers and fathers."

However, homosexuals are not alone in having to defend themselves against the negative implications of group membership. Most of us belong to one or more groups that society devalues and stigmatizes, at least in certain contexts—women, people of color, the elderly, recent immigrants, people with AIDS, the overweight, the disabled, the unemployed, the addicted—the list seems endless. If you cannot think of any negatively regarded groups that you belong to yourself, perhaps reading the questions in Table 6.1 will give you a sense of what others experience.

Table 6.1 Turning the tables: Questions implying that group membership is abnormal and devalued

1. What do you think caused your heterosexuality?
2. When and how did you decide you were a heterosexual?
3. Is it possible that heterosexuality is just a phase you may grow out of?
4. Is it possible your heterosexuality stems from a neurotic fear of others of the same sex?
5. If you've never slept with a person of the same sex, is it possible that all you need is a good same-sex lover?
6. To whom have you disclosed your heterosexual tendencies?
7. Why do heterosexuals feel compelled to seduce others into their lifestyle?
8. Why do you insist on flaunting your heterosexuality? Why can't you just be who you are and keep quiet about it?
9. Why do heterosexuals place so much emphasis on sex?
10. There seem to be very few happy heterosexuals. Techniques have been developed that might enable you to change. Have you considered aversion therapy?
11. Considering the menace of hunger and overpopulation, can the human race survive if everyone were heterosexual like yourself?
12. Despite social support of marriage, the divorce rate is still 50 percent. Why are there so few stable relationships among heterosexuals?

Note: This questionnaire has been used in sensitivity-training workshops to provoke discussion. Does it give you a sense of what it might feel like to belong to a group that most people dislike and regard as abnormal?

Source: From *Working It Out: The Newsletter for Gay and Lesbian Employment Issues.*

Because social group membership contributes so directly to individual self-identity, the stigma of belonging to a negatively regarded group can take its toll on the individual. Kenneth Clark, a distinguished social psychologist whose research contributed to the 1954 U.S. Supreme Court decision on school desegregation, commented, "Human beings . . . whose daily experience tells them that almost nowhere in society are they respected and granted the ordinary dignity and courtesy accorded to others, will, as a matter of course, begin to doubt their self worth" (Clark, 1965, p. 64).

This is not the first time we have seen that feeling bad about oneself can produce symptoms of depression. Look back at Chapter 4, pages 148 to 150.

Clark was right to be worried, for feelings about group membership do have a major impact on the emotional and physical well-being of members of stigmatized groups. One group of researchers measured African-American and White students' personal self-esteem, their feelings about their group memberships, and symptoms of depression (Luhtanen & Crocker, 1992). For Whites, low personal self-esteem was the key factor that increased the risk of depression. For African Americans, in contrast, *collective self-esteem*—positive or negative feelings about group membership—was more strongly related to depression than was personal self-esteem (Luhtanen and others, 1991). That is, among African-American students with similar levels of individual self-esteem, those who were less proud and happy about their group membership were more likely to be depressed. Writers like Malcolm X (1966) have eloquently described their struggles in coming to terms with their ethnic identity, integrating group membership into a positive overall sense of self.

Wouldn't you expect that belonging to a group that many people look down on, despise, and discriminate against would bring *you* down? Then consider this puzzle: individual members of many stigmatized groups, including African Americans, people with developmental disabilities, and people who are facially disfigured, have self-esteem that is just as high as that of individuals who are not members of these groups (Crocker & Major, 1989). Clearly, at least some members of negatively regarded groups can defend and enhance their self-esteem. How are they able to value themselves in a society that devalues their groups?

Defending Individual Self-Esteem

Belonging to a group that is disliked and discriminated against by others can have a major impact on the individual. But this experience does not inevitably lead to lowered self-esteem, because people can attribute negative reactions to others' prejudice or make most of their social comparisons against fellow in-group members.

Using Attributions to Advantage. An African American described a common dilemma to a White reporter. "If you go into a restaurant and get totally lousy service, you know it's for one reason. They do totally lousy service. I go into a restaurant and I get totally lousy service, I don't know why. . . . Is it because we're black or is it because . . . it's a bad service person?" (Duke & Morin, 1992). When a member of a devalued group is treated badly, attributional ambiguity is created: the treatment might have been due to group membership. The same uncertainty arises in more significant form when group members are rejected for jobs, promotions, or bank loans. People in these situations are likely to attribute others' behavior to their group membership.

One clever experiment demonstrated that people often see another person's behavior as a response to a stigma—even when the stigma could not possibly have had any effect (Kleck & Strenta, 1980). Subjects were made up to look as if they had a large and disfiguring facial scar, which they examined in a mirror before the experimenter applied "moisturizer." Without the subjects' knowledge, the moisturizer they thought would "set their make-up" in fact removed the scar. Subjects then spent several minutes with a second person to assess the effects of the disfigurement on social interaction. Subjects who falsely believed they were disfigured thought their scar had a tremendous effect on how they were treated, even though their partners were of course unaware of the stigma. People who permanently belong to stigmatized groups, like the African-American restaurant patron, always have group membership accessible as a potential explanation for the way others treat them.

Of course, attributing reversals to others' prejudice against one's group can protect self-esteem against the negative psychological effects of failure (Crocker & Major, 1989). However, the strategy, like many of the self-enhancing biases described in Chapter 4, also carries a cost. First, negative feedback is sometimes realistic, and discounting it can prevent accurate self-assessment and self-improvement. Second, the strategy may breed a sense of hopelessness and a loss of control: if one always expects to be treated as a group member, no personal action will make any difference. Third, attributing other people's reactions to group membership can destroy trust in positive feedback. Are praise and promotions signs of respect and admiration for one's accomplishments, or are they due to sympathy, pity, and resigned affirmative action? Research suggests that members of stigmatized groups are likely to suspect the latter—to discount positive feedback and attribute honors and accomplishments to others' efforts to appear unprejudiced. Unfortunately, these cynical views are sometimes right. Leaning over backwards to avoid seeming prejudiced, people can inflate their evaluations of members of disliked out-groups compared to their ratings of in-group members who turn in the same performance (Crocker and others, 1991).

One study demonstrates both the costs and benefits of this attributional strategy. African-American students participated in a "study of friendship development" with a White same-sex evaluator. Some subjects believed the evaluator seated in the next room could see them (the blinds on a window between the two rooms were up), while others knew the evaluator could not see them (the blinds were down). After exchanging self-description forms with the partner, subjects received either a very favorable or very unfavorable response that was supposedly from the partner but was actually prepared by the researchers. African-American students who received negative feedback were more likely to attribute the evaluation to prejudice—thereby protecting their self-esteem—when the blinds were up than when the blinds were down. However, they also distrusted the evaluator's positive response when they thought it might reflect leaning over backward. A positive response increased the African-American students' self-esteem when they could not be seen, but actually *decreased* it when they could be seen (Crocker and others, 1991). Belonging to a stigmatized group can be a buffer against the chill of negative feedback, but it also barricades you from the warm pleasure usually derived from positive feedback.

Attributional Ambiguity in the Workplace. Not knowing how to interpret feedback can create serious workplace problems for people with disabilities, women, and other groups. For example, if a few wheelchair users are hired at a typical business, they draw more than their fair share of attention. Like members of other groups, they may feel that their every move is scrutinized and that their behavior reflects not only on themselves but on all people with disabilities (Pettigrew & Martin, 1987).

In some cases, an employee may suspect that he or she is a *token*—a single group member hired in order to avoid more thoroughgoing change. Consider the dilemma this suspicion creates: in these circumstances, people find it hard to trust feedback because outcomes seem to be determined by group membership. For example, women managers who believe they were hired because of their gender show lower organizational commitment and job satisfaction and higher role stress than women who believe they were hired for their abilities (Chacko, 1982).

In an experimental demonstration of this effect, one group of men and women were told that they were selected for a leadership role because they had scored well on leadership potential tests. Another group learned that they had been selected because the experimenter "needed more" of their gender in leadership positions (Heilman and others, 1987). Later, the subjects learned that they had either succeeded or failed on the leadership task. As can be seen in Figure 6.7, women selected on the basis of gender rather than merit devalued their own leadership ability, regardless of whether they performed well or poorly as leaders. The women in this condition also reported less interest in continuing as leaders. In contrast, men did not show such self-doubts, whether they believed their selection reflected merit or gender-based preference. Members of groups that are typically devalued and discriminated against—women in this case—are the most likely to interpret feedback as reflecting their group membership rather than individual accomplishment.

Making the Most of Intragroup Comparisons. Chapter 4 showed that social comparisons are an important source of self-evaluation. Thus, is it any wonder that a female middle manager in a large firm might choose to think of herself as "one of the highest-ranking women here at Acme Corporation" rather than to compare herself to the male members of top corporate management? This kind of in-group comparison is also typical of ethnic groups. One study found that African-American schoolchildren who compared themselves mainly with other African Americans had higher self-esteem than those who compared themselves with White children (Rosenberg &

Figure 6.7 Preferential treatment can lead to self-doubt among women

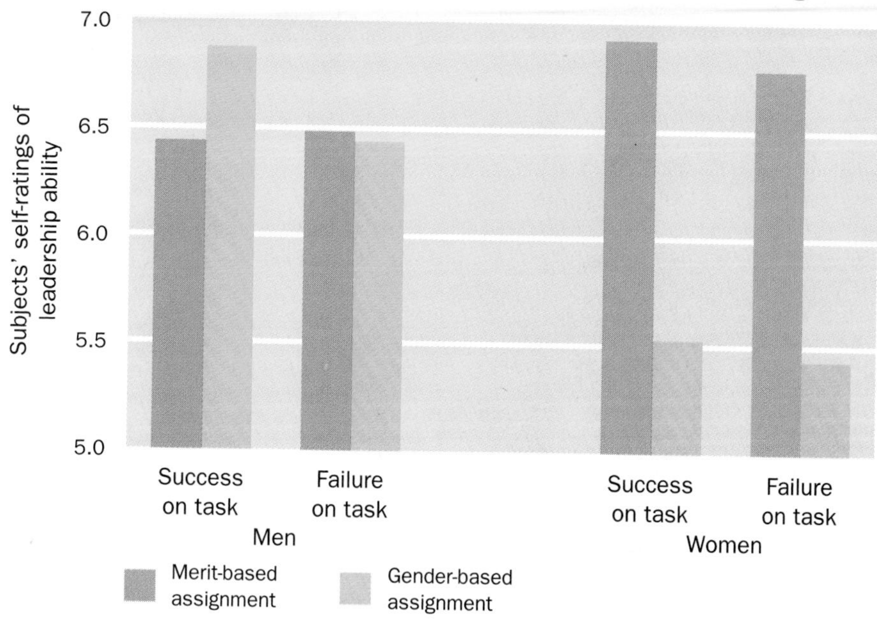

Men or women were led to believe that they were chosen as leaders either on the basis of merit or through gender-based preferential treatment. They were then told that they either succeeded or failed on a leadership task. When male subjects rated their own leadership ability, as the left bars show, their ratings were about equal in all conditions. However, women who thought that they had been chosen on the basis of gender doubted their own leadership ability— whether they had succeeded or failed. (Based on Heilman and others, 1987.)

Simmons, 1971). Intragroup comparisons not only boost self-esteem by showing us that we are better off than some others, they also remind us of in-group members who are doing particularly well—even if we are not. When given the opportunity to choose others for comparisons, schoolchildren from low-status groups in both New Zealand and the United States often name other in-group members who are high performers in the social, academic, or athletic domains (Aboud, 1976; Mackie, 1984).

Women's Self-Esteem: What's Special About Gender? We now have a partial solution to the puzzle posed earlier: members of many stigmatized groups, such as people with disabilities, can use several strategies to maintain levels of self-esteem equal to that of the dominant group—in this case, Whites. However, another puzzle remains. Even though they also can use all of the strategies we have discussed, women seem to have lower self-esteem than men (Skaalvik, 1986; Freiberg, 1991). The gender gap in self-esteem initially arises in adolescence, when teachers and other adults often discourage girls from academic pursuits while giving boys more attention and more challenging assignments in class.

The self-esteem difference has real consequences: girls are much more likely than boys to lower their career aspirations, feeling that they are "not smart enough" to fulfill their dreams (Freiberg, 1991). These findings remind us that psychological strategies of self-esteem defense are not always

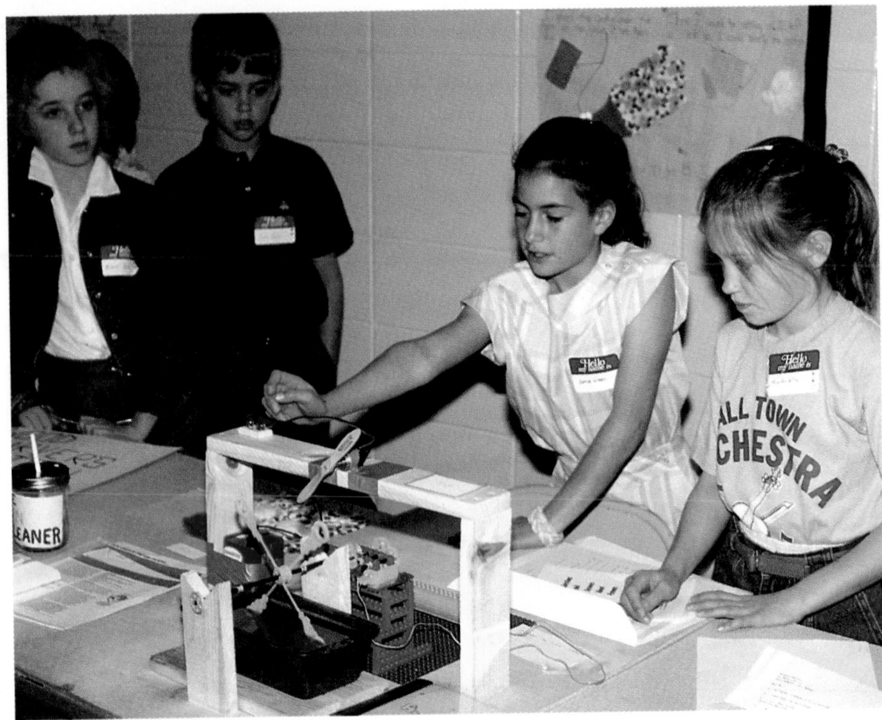

Making adolescence harder than it has to be Young girls like these are as interested in science and math as their male peers. But by adolescence differential treatment by adults has begun to take its toll on self-esteem. Reacting to their teachers' belief that they are not good enough or smart enough to do the very things at which they excelled in elementary school, young women begin to doubt their own abilities and to see some career choices, especially in math and science, as out of reach.

sufficient when teachers and other powerful people behave differently toward students from different groups. The findings also suggest that the same strategies may not work equally well for all groups. Why is gender different from other important group memberships? One reason may be that gender roles are learned extremely early in life and are reinforced by parents and peers. As a result, both men and women usually place a high value on behaving in accordance with these roles and may see gender as a more central aspect of the self than other group memberships (Fiske & Stevens, 1993).

Social Mobility: Escaping Negative Group Membership

If self-protective strategies are insufficient, people can attempt to escape from membership in a negatively regarded group. They can psychologically disidentify with the group, for example, by playing down group memberships that reflect badly on them or by regarding themselves as atypical group members. Another option is to dissociate—to escape physically, by "passing" or keeping group membership hidden "in the closet."

When strategies intended to buffer self-esteem against the implications of negative group membership prove ineffective, people may turn to more long-term solutions involving either social mobility or social change (Tajfel

& Turner, 1979). **Social mobility** is a strategy involving individual escape from membership in a negative group, either through disidentification—creating a psychological distance between oneself and the group—or through dissociation—physically escaping the group. Social mobility frees the individual from many of the costs of group membership and leaves the group's situation as a whole unchanged in the short run. Social change, in contrast, involves efforts to improve society's evaluation of the entire group.

Disidentification: Putting the Group at a Psychological Distance. Social mobility can be purely psychological, as when people *disidentify,* or minimize their personal connections to the group. One strategy is to avoid reminders of membership in a stigmatized group, as a laboratory study demonstrated (Snyder and others, 1986). Subjects participated in a group problem-solving session and each group received success feedback, failure feedback, or no feedback at all. The experimenter then announced that subjects could take home team badges that advertised their group membership. Would team performance influence pride of membership? Apparently so. Over half of the members of groups that succeeded or received no feedback took badges home. But only 9 percent of those on a losing team welcomed the opportunity to announce their membership in it.

People can also disidentify from a group by publicly criticizing and devaluing an in-group member's poor performance. This reaction, termed *cutting off reflected failure,* or **CORF**ing, makes it clear that the critic regards the poor performance as unrepresentative of the group. For example, imagine that you (a law student) have to evaluate speeches given by a fellow law student and by a philosophy student. If the law student's speech was third-rate, your self-categorization with him would put you in an uncomfortable situation. Under these circumstances, you might be inclined to CORF—to downgrade the in-group speaker, rating her even more negatively than an out-group member who performed equally poorly. By doing so, you will make it clear that this in-group member's performance is not representative of your group. Marques and Yzerbyt (1988) obtained exactly this pattern of results. People rated successful in-group members higher, and poorly performing in-group members lower, compared with out-group members. When the previously cheering fans turn to booing and hissing the home team's losses with even more enthusiasm, perhaps part of their motivation is to psychologically distance themselves from poor performance (Branscombe and others, 1993).

Yet a third way of disidentifying is to consider *oneself* to be an exception rather than a typical group member. For example, many women acknowledge that women in general are discriminated against but insist that discrimination does not affect them personally (Crosby and others, 1989). The same pattern of beliefs is found among many other groups, including French-speakers in Quebec and immigrants to Canada from Haiti and India (Taylor and others, 1990). Of course, there could be many reasons for this belief, and it is certainly possible that some individual group members are fortunate enough to escape discrimination personally. However, the belief is

social mobility The strategy of individual escape, either physical or psychological, from a group held in low esteem.

CORF (cut off reflected failure) The act of criticizing or distancing oneself from an in-group member who is viewed negatively.

held most often by those who identify least strongly with their groups, suggesting that the belief serves, at least in part, as a psychological distancing mechanism (Crosby and others, 1989).

Individuals who see themselves as exceptions within their group may focus on another of their many group memberships as a sphere in which to achieve. For example, women can disidentify with their gender-based group by focusing on a career-based group. They can exercise social mobility by seeking to move up in pay, status, and power in their careers. One female graduate of the Air Force Academy, who pilots TR-1 spy planes for a living, told an interviewer that she does not think of herself as a "pioneer" for women in the military—she is "just doing her job" (Kantrowitz, 1991). Perhaps she regards herself as an Air Force officer first and a woman second. Many women in similar situations believe that to win acceptance they have to act just like their male co-workers. One study, for example, found that many female police officers try to act particularly tough and aggressive, explicitly taking on the police officer role rather than following the female gender stereotype (Martin, 1982).

As increasing numbers of women overcome stereotypes and discrimination to enter previously male-dominated occupations, their actions may, over time, alter societal stereotypes of women. Recall that the roles typically held by group members are often reflected in stereotypes of the group (Eagly, 1987). Accordingly, individual social mobility in large enough doses can lead to social change, a topic we return to shortly.

Dissociation: Putting the Group at a Physical Distance. Whereas disidentifying takes place in the mind, dissociating involves actual escape from a disadvantaged group or concealment of group membership. This form of social mobility occurs, for example, when immigrants cast off their cultural and linguistic heritage and become indistinguishable members of a new nationality. Gays or lesbians who are "in the closet" are concealing their group membership. A related strategy of some historical importance is "passing," a pattern in which light-skinned individuals of African-American ancestry adopted a White identity, or American Jews adopted anglicized names and the customs of Gentile society (Lewin, 1948).

How successful is escape as a solution to membership in a negatively evaluated group? The answer seems to be that it is a mixed blessing. The individual does reap some personal benefits, such as freedom from discrimination, but for some, these benefits may be outweighed by the strategy's potential costs. New members of a group often suffer the isolation of not being thought quite the same as those "born to it." In addition, concealing group membership can be lonely and dangerous. The heartache of having to join in the laughter at anti-gay or racist jokes might be surpassed only by anxiety at being "outed." Finally, those who conceal their group membership give up opportunities to influence others' thinking about their group. U.S. Representative Barney Frank kept his homosexuality secret when he was first elected to Congress. He recalls that when he lobbied his colleagues on gay issues, "they would say 'Ah, you're right. But you know, it's not that important.' The pain gay people felt was unknown. We were hiding it from them. How the hell are they supposed to know when we were making damn sure they didn't?" (Schmalz, 1992).

Disidentification and dissociation are not viable options for many group members, leaving them only the option to turn and fight. Instead of separating from the group, either psychologically or physically, group members can directly attack society's negative evaluation of their group. Their aim is a change in social identity through concrete social change.

Social Change: Changing the Intergroup Context

Sometimes group members attempt to change society's evaluation of their in-group. They may redefine group characteristics in positive terms, engage in direct intergroup conflict or struggle, or seek to overturn the in-group–out-group distinction altogether.

Strikes, protest marches, and struggles in the courts and legislatures to outlaw discrimination are familiar tactics of the civil rights movement in the United States. These tactics reflect a social change strategy of confronting and challenging the hierarchy of group domination. **Social change** refers to the strategy of improving the overall societal situation of a group held in low esteem. Social change is preferred by people who identify strongly with their group and see themselves as typical members. Rather than changing only their personal situation, they wish to, and believe they can, change the way society regards their group as a whole (Tajfel & Turner, 1979). The main tactics employed by these determined group members are social creativity, social competition, and recategorization.

Social Creativity. When faced with a negative identity on one dimension, groups can introduce and emphasize alternative dimensions on which the in-group is superior. A group of French boys at a summer camp showed this kind of *social creativity* when they found themselves in a hut-building contest with another team that had better construction materials (Lemaine, 1974). Realizing their inability to construct a large and sturdy structure, they created an elaborate garden around their mediocre cabin and asked the judges to consider them the garden-building winners. By introducing a new dimension of competition, the group maintained its superiority and distinctiveness. Similarly, players on the last-place team in a competitive ice hockey league cannot make a claim on skill and competitiveness, but they may be able to think of themselves as "cleaner" and more sportsmanlike than other teams. For one team, adopting this belief served to maintain the players' self-esteem, even though it seemed to correspond very little with reality—for observers and coaches viewed the last-place team as one of the "dirtiest" in the league (Lalonde, 1992).

social change The strategy of improving the overall societal situation of a group held in low esteem.

Some women show similar social creativity by accepting society's definition of femininity and seeking a positive group identity through its distinctive positive characteristics. For example, they may emphasize dimensions of achievement that they view as specifically feminine, such as nurturing or peacemaking. This cultural feminism does not directly challenge social definitions of gender roles, but it does proclaim the value of feminine qualities and strengthen collective self-esteem. Along the same lines, a gay pride movement has emerged, with an emphasis on celebrating the accomplishments of gays and lesbians, particularly in artistic and cultural fields. "Black is beautiful!" was one ethnic group's statement that distinctive characteristics that have been derogated by the majority—such as skin color, language, or cultural heritage—can be redefined as a source of pride (Bourhis and others, 1978).

Social Competition. Sometimes groups attempt to build in-group solidarity, oppose domination by the out-group, and improve the relative position, status, power, and resources of the in-group. When they do so, they are engaging in *social competition* by directly seeking to change the conditions that lead to their disadvantaged status. In experimental contexts, this is the strategy reflected by in-group bias, when a member gives the in-group an edge over the out-group by allocating his or her group more resources, evaluating in-group products more positively, and judging the in-group to be morally and socially superior. Groups engage in these strategies when they believe they can make a difference and improve their situation (Tajfel & Turner, 1979). But what looks like opportunity for advancement to disadvantaged groups often appears as threat to a dominant group. Earlier, we saw that favored groups respond with increased levels of prejudice and discrimination against out-groups when they see those groups as threats. Thus, social competition strategies are likely to provoke a backlash from powerful groups.

Social competition strategies take many forms. They include the strategy of radical feminism (e.g., Kate Millett, 1970) and the pressure for racial self-sufficiency and separatism advocated by the Nation of Islam. Everywhere in society lobbies and advocacy organizations seek social changes that will benefit particular groups. The American Association of Retired Persons and Gray Panthers mobilize efforts on behalf of seniors. Groups such as the Coalition of Citizens with Disabilities and Mainstream, Inc. lead "wheelchair rebellions." Radical gay and lesbian groups such as Queer Nation actively combat gay bashing, anti-gay prejudice, and negative portrayals of homosexuals in the media while lobbying for open and equal opportunities for their groups. Individuals as well as organizations can engage in social competition strategies, for example by creating informal associations of group members aimed at community building and mutual support. Individuals can also speak out against stereotypes, prejudice, and discrimination whenever they encounter them—in ethnic slurs, sexist jokes, or "old boy" hiring practices in organizations.

Recategorization: Changing the Definition of In-Group. Social change can also come through transcending group categorizations. In any business organization, for example, some of the senior staff and some of the junior staff will be male and some will be female. Thus, some individuals who are out-group members on one dimension will be in-group members on another; the categorizations by professional status and gender cut across each other. What impact does *cross-categorization* have on in-group bias? To find out, one experimenter set up groups in which out-group members on one dimension were in-group members on another dimension. When such a cross-categorization was introduced, intergroup discrimination against members of partially overlapping in-groups was greatly reduced (Vanbeselaere, 1991). This technique cannot completely wipe out discrimination, however. The male senior staffers may expand their in-group to include senior females or junior males, bestowing on them the many benefits of in-group membership. In this sense, cross-categorization also produces recategorization, but the female junior staff remain outside even the redrawn group boundaries.

Thus, perhaps the best way to transcend group antipathies is to form new inclusive in-groups from which esteem and identity can be derived (Feshbach & Singer, 1957; Turner, 1981b). Laboratory demonstrations using minimal groups have confirmed that a blurring of boundaries can coalesce groups into one larger overarching structure, thereby reducing bias and discrimination. Samuel Gaertner and his colleagues (1989) found, for example, that intergroup relations were improved when members of two subgroups were placed at alternating seats around a table and when they gave the joint group a new and separate name.

The idea that "we're all in this together" can help outside the lab as well. Currently, for example, many men's groups argue that traditional gender roles damage men by forcing them to suppress their feelings, by emphasizing aggression and achievement, and by devaluing emotional sharing and intimacy, particularly with other men (Pleck, 1981). Like many women's organizations, these men's groups support concrete social changes—such as women taking equal places with men in business and political life—that in time will alter traditional definitions of gender roles. Working together for such shared goals can lead to a redefinition of men and women as members of a common group with shared interests and values (Miller & Brewer, 1986). Recategorization could mean that we will not need to take refuge in moral unconcern over the sufferings of outsiders, because there will be no outsiders.

These recategorization strategies are important weapons in the fight against intergroup conflict. We discuss their implications for reducing conflict in Chapter 14, pages 634 to 635.

One Goal, Many Strategies

No one approach is always best for dealing with a negatively evaluated group membership, just as no single coping strategy is uniformly the best way to handle threats to the individual self.

Figure 6.8 How can I value myself when others devalue my group?

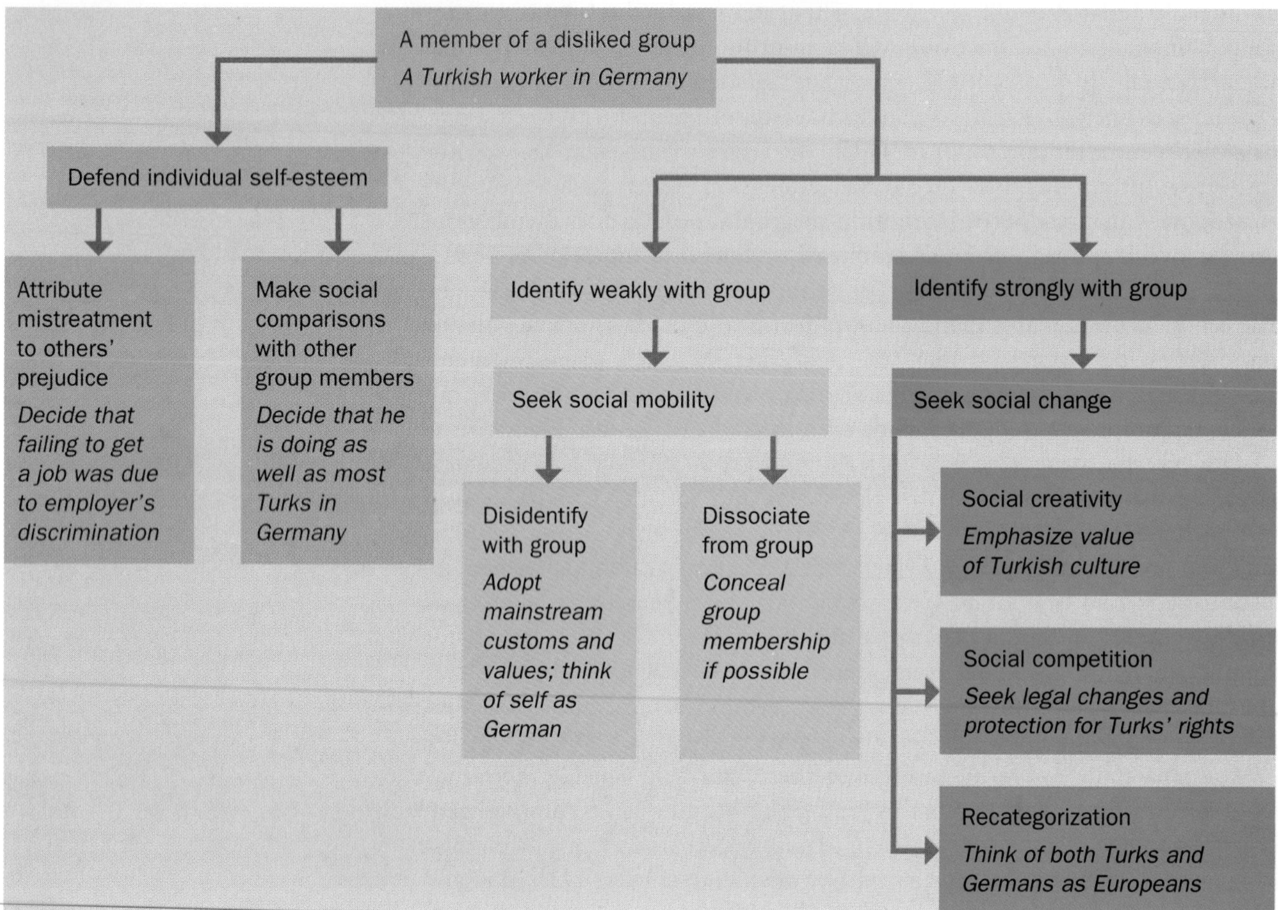

Members of groups that suffer dislike and discrimination try to defend their individual self-esteem. In addition, they may seek escape from their group through social mobility or seek to improve the whole group's situation through social change, depending on the strength of their identification with the group.

As you can see in Figure 6.8, there is more than one way to cope with the threat to social identity posed by negative group memberships. No one way is always better or worse than others; like the strategies for coping with threats to the individual self that were described in Chapter 4, the effectiveness of each method depends on many factors. The size of a group, the resources its members control, the ease or difficulty of concealing group membership, and the personal significance of group membership for each individual will all influence how people respond.

At times, multiple forces push and pull people in different directions. For example, many African Americans feel a fundamental tension between the desire to maintain in-group solidarity and the desire for individual advancement in White-dominated society. Deep, often emotional disagreements have sprung up between advocates of various strategies. It seems to some that "in order to be accepted by Whites they must give up everything that is Black; that if they played basketball before they now have to play golf" (Williams, 1991). Yet those who seek professional advancement sometimes "fear that if you are successful you will be too alienated from Black people," according to Cornel West, a Princeton University professor (Cary, 1992). When Clarence Thomas, an African-American lawyer, reached the pinnacle of his profession by being nominated to the U.S. Supreme Court, many activist groups opposed him on the grounds that his strongly conservative views did not reflect mainstream opinions among African Americans. The different strategies of social mobility and social change often contradict each other. Nevertheless, all aim at improving the group's situation and any one of them may be appropriate for a particular individual or group, given the unique social situation.

In thinking about the ways in which people cope with *being* a likable member of a devalued group, you may have noticed some similarities with the ways in which people deal with *meeting* a likable member of a disliked group (discussed in Chapter 5). These parallels, detailed in Table 6.2, are no accident. They reflect the fundamental principle that group memberships influence our thoughts and feelings about individual group members, whether the individual is someone else or the self.

Table 6.2 Three types of responses to a likable member of a disliked group

Response	*Knowing* a likable member of a disliked group	*Being* a likable member of a disliked group
See the individual as unrepresentative of the group; separate beliefs about the group from beliefs about the individual.	Exclude the individual from the group by seeing him or her as a special type of the general category (*subtyping*) or by seeing him or her as extremely different from typical category members (*contrasting*).	Remove the self from group, either psychologically by downplaying group membership as an aspect of the self (*disidentification*) or physically by escaping from or concealing group membership (*dissociation*).
See the individual as representative of the group; use beliefs about the individual to modify beliefs about the group.	See the likable individual as a typical group member, improving the evaluation of the group (*stereotype change*).	Attempt to make society's evaluation of the group more positive (*social change*). Interpret the group and its history, culture, and other distinctive aspects in positive terms (*social creativity*) or struggle to change the group's generally low status and power in society (*social competition*).
Change the lines of social categorization.	Merge the out-group into a larger in-group.	Expand the in-group to include former out-groups.

Concluding Comments

Social identity is central to every aspect of social behavior, just as this chapter occupies a central place in this text. As you think back on the concept of social identity, notice how intertwined are people's knowledge about groups, their conceptions of themselves, and their impressions of others. The fact that you *are* a group member means that the ways you perceive your own and other groups will fundamentally affect the ways you perceive other individuals and yourself. Not only do we see ourselves in group terms and act in accordance with in-group standards and norms, but as in-groups become part of the self, we think about our groups in many of the same ways that we think about ourselves as individuals. For example, various biases lead us to view not only ourselves but also our groups through rose-colored glasses.

Social identities anchor us in the social world by connecting us to other people—people whom we otherwise might have little reason to trust, to like, or even to know at all. Because relationships are encouraged and even made possible by our assumptions about what we have in common, group belonging and identification provide a truly social basis for thinking, feeling, and acting. Thus, understanding group membership is vital for understanding many aspects of social behavior. As you will see in later chapters, our beliefs, opinions, and behavior, our close and loving relationships with other individuals, and the ways we act in face-to-face groups depend crucially on the ways we accept and identify with in-groups. No wonder, then, that we often feel lost and adrift when we lose important social identities—as when we are expelled or fired—or when our social identities are threatened—for example, when we experience discrimination and realize that others devalue our group. We may still be the individuals we always were, but important parts of our whole selves have been damaged or have disappeared because our place in the social world is lost or threatened.

Negative views of out-groups sprout from the same roots as people's positive views of themselves and their own kind. The biased stereotypes of groups that were discussed in Chapter 5 are only part of the underpinnings of prejudice and discrimination. Disregard and maltreatment of others are supported by our social and psychological investment in our own groups as well. When group membership is most important, out-group members are only faceless outsiders; their individual identities are of little concern to us. We see "them" as all the same and as totally different from us in their goals, values, and beliefs. As we will see, this way of thinking is an important basis for both aggression and intergroup conflict.

Perhaps understanding how group membership can contribute to hurtful and destructive human behavior will help provide solutions to some of these problems by redefining in-groups and out-groups. Whether the effects of social identity are good or bad, the fundamental fact remains that our sense of self extends beyond our skin to encompass some people and exclude others, and this fact has powerful implications for how we see and treat others and ourselves.

Summary

Categorizing Oneself as a Group Member Group memberships can turn into a **social identity** when they become a significant part of a person's self-concept through the process of **self-categorization.** People learn about many aspects of the groups to which they belong in the same ways that they learn the characteristics of other groups: through observation of other group members or from the culture.

Knowledge about group memberships may be activated by direct reminders, such as group labels; by the presence of out-group members; by being a minority; or by intergroup conflict. Group membership is particularly significant in some cultures and for some individuals, who tend to see the world in terms of that group membership.

Me, You, and Them: Effects of Social Categorization Activated knowledge about a group membership has multiple effects on people's self-concept and self-esteem. People tend to see themselves as typical group members. Group membership also influences people's moods and self-esteem, as they feel bad about their group's failures or **BIRG**—bask in reflected glory—when their group succeeds.

When group membership is highly accessible, people see other in-group members as similar in their central group-linked characteristics. However, extensive personal interaction (when group membership is not activated) provides knowledge about their unique and diverse personal characteristics. People like in-group members and tend to treat them in fair, humane, and altruistic ways because people see them as similar to themselves in their goals and interests.

In contrast, the **out-group homogeneity effect** means that people see out-groups as quite uniform and homogeneous. People also dislike, devalue, and discriminate against out-group members, depending on the extent to which they are seen as threatening the in-group. When the out-group is simply different it elicits mild dislike. This effect can be demonstrated even in the **minimal intergroup situation,** in which mere categorization results in mild discrimination against the out-group. According to **social identity theory,** people respond in this way to being categorized to derive self-esteem from their in-group membership.

When the out-group is seen as outdoing the in-group, this more serious threat results in resentment, dislike, and overt discrimination. Out-groups that are seen as severe threats to the in-group elicit **symbolic prejudice,** which often goes hand in hand with murderous hatred, discrimination, and

Chapter 6 Themes

Construction of Reality
We construct the self using our knowledge about our social groups.

Pervasiveness of Social Influence
This construction process imports social influences into the very core of the self.

Seeking Connectedness
Group memberships that we share with others are rewarding.

Valuing Me and Mine
We positively value the groups to which we belong as well as our individual self.

aggression. When the out-group is viewed as fundamentally inferior to the in-group, the rules of justice and civility are suspended and **moral unconcern** and, in more extreme cases, **moral exclusion** result.

When Group Memberships Are Negative Membership in a group that others dislike or discriminate against can harm individuals in many concrete ways. However, this experience does not inevitably lead to lowered self-esteem, because people can attribute negative reactions to others' prejudice or can make most of their social comparisons against fellow in-group members.

If these strategies are insufficient to protect individual self-esteem, people can use **social mobility** strategies, attempting to escape their membership in a group held in low esteem. They can psychologically disidentify with the group, for example, by playing down group membership or by regarding themselves as atypical group members. **CORF**ing—cutting off reflected failure—is one way to distance oneself from a negatively regarded group membership. Another option is to dissociate—to escape physically, by "passing" or keeping group membership hidden "in the closet."

Sometimes group members adopt **social change** strategies, attempting to alter society's evaluation of their in-group. They may redefine group characteristics in positive terms, engage in direct intergroup conflict or struggle, or seek to overturn the in-group–out-group distinction altogether. No one approach is always best for dealing with a negatively regarded group membership, just as no single coping strategy is uniformly the best way to handle threats to the individual self.

Chapter 6 Overview

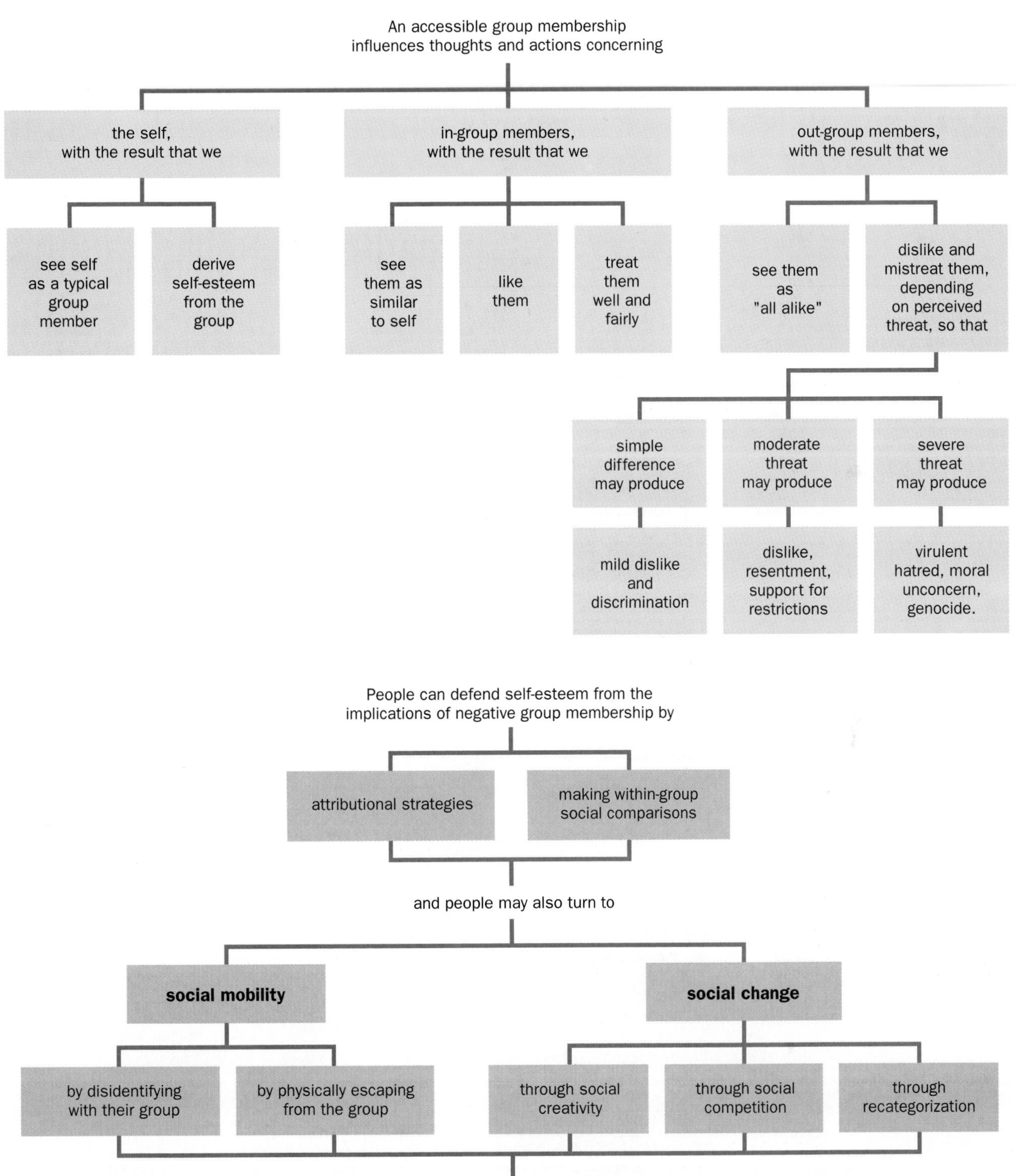

An accessible group membership
influences thoughts and actions concerning
the self,
with the result that we
in-group members,
with the result that we
out-group members,
with the result that we
see self as a typical group member
derive self-esteem from the group
see them as similar to self
like them
treat them well and fairly
see them as "all alike"
dislike and mistreat them, depending on perceived threat, so that
simple difference may produce
moderate threat may produce
severe threat may produce
mild dislike and discrimination
dislike, resentment, support for restrictions
virulent hatred, moral unconcern, genocide.
People can defend self-esteem from the
implications of negative group membership by
attributional strategies
making within-group social comparisons
and people may also turn to
social mobility
social change
by disidentifying with their group
by physically escaping from the group
through social creativity
through social competition
through recategorization
depending on the individual's and group's situation and resources.

THE JORDACHE LO
A&S
W 34 ST
SAUSAGES
FRANKFURTER
FRANKFURTER
BEEF

7

Attitudes and Attitude Change

What do the following events have in common? Basketball superstar Magic Johnson announces he is infected with the AIDS virus and becomes a national spokesperson for the fight against the disease. U.S. presidential candidate Ross Perot buys prime television time to take his economic recovery plan to the people. A cigarette manufacturer launches a major advertising campaign featuring cartoon character Joe Camel, who quickly becomes more familiar to children than the Disney character Mickey Mouse. Religious groups seek converts on street corners, scientists dispute evidence for a well-established theory, and friends argue over the best place to buy snow tires.

In all of these cases, a person or a group is trying to develop, maintain, or change the attitudes of others. Whether as initiators or targets of such efforts, each of us participates in this form of social influence every day. Because attitude formation and change exercise such a pervasive influence on our everyday social life, they have been one of social psychology's central concerns since the discipline began. Both this chapter and the next focus on the development, maintenance, and change of attitudes and on the impact attitudes have on what we think, feel, and do.

This chapter begins by asking what attitudes are and where they come from, why we form attitudes, and what kinds of information form the building blocks of attitudes. Understanding the what and why of attitudes opens the way to thinking about how attitudes come to be developed, maintained, and changed. This is the domain of **persuasion,** the process by which attitudes are formed, reinforced, or changed by communications. As you will see, persuasive communications can be direct or subtle, frightening or funny, intriguingly innovative or boringly repetitious. They may appeal to emotions or to cold logic. They can support our best interests or someone else's goals. Regardless of what they say or how they say it, persuasive communications attempt to provide information that will make a lasting change in our attitudes.

But what makes some persuasive messages effective while others fail to change our minds? To answer this question we have to explore the way people process persuasive communications. As you will see in the second and third sections of the chapter, how carefully we consider persuasive informa-

Preferences and pocketbooks Attempts to develop, reinforce, and change attitudes toward objects, ideas, actions, and events are a pervasive aspect of our daily lives. In the competition for our preferences and our pocketbooks, what makes one appeal forceful and another futile?

tion is the key to attitude formation, maintenance, and change. Careful thinking plays a central role in persuasion whether others try to change our attitudes by feeding us facts or by playing on our feelings. Responding thoughtfully to persuasive communications can also make the difference between being at their mercy and resisting their appeals. As you will see in the final section of the chapter, despite the sophistication of many of the techniques used to influence us, whether we are persuaded or not depends largely on us. Chapter 8 will build on this chapter by describing the relations between attitudes and behavior. After all, the main reason people try to persuade us is the hope of ultimately influencing our actions.

Attitudes and Their Origins

Do you agree with laws that ban smoking on airplanes? Do you think that brand-name products are superior to generic ones? Was the message of the liberal or the conservative candidate more convincing in the last political campaign? Should women in the military be allowed to serve in combat? The answers people give to these kinds of questions reflect their attitudes. An **attitude** is any cognitive representation that summarizes our evaluation of an *attitude object*—the self, other people, things, actions, events, or ideas (McGuire, 1985; Ostrom, 1969; Zanna & Rempel, 1988). Because our evaluations of attitude objects can be favorable, neutral, or unfavorable, attitudes are said to have a positive, neutral, or negative *direction*. And, just as they differ in direction, attitudes also differ in *intensity*, reflecting whether the evaluation is weak or strong.

People can—and do—hold attitudes about just about anything. We have already discussed some of these different attitudes: attitudes about other individuals in Chapter 3, attitudes about ourselves in Chapter 4, and attitudes toward our own and other groups in Chapters 5 and 6. Although Chapters 7 and 8 focus on attitudes about objects, issues, events, ideas, and actions, these discussions can also be applied to evaluations of other people, social groups, and ourselves. As you will see, although the content of our various cognitive representations may be different, the ways in which they are formed, maintained, used, and changed are startlingly similar.

Measuring Attitudes

Social psychologists measure attitudes in a variety of ways. They may directly ask people about their evaluations or directly observe people's overt behavior. Or they may use indirect measures, such as assessments of physiological responses.

Unlike physical objects that can be weighed, watched, or observed under microscopes, attitudes cannot be measured directly. *Expressions* of attitudes, however, can be measured, either directly or indirectly.

persuasion The process of forming, reinforcing, or changing attitudes by communication.

attitude A cognitive representation that summarizes an individual's evaluation of a particular person, group, thing, action, or idea.

Direct Measures: Self-Reports and Direct Observations. The most straightforward approach to attitude measurement is simply to ask people to give *self-reports*—to say what they think. Consumer surveys, political polls, most attitude change research, and even our daily exchange of opinions with friends and family are forms of self-reports. In our day-to-day conversations, we rely on people's words, tone of voice, and body language to tell us the direction and intensity of their attitudes. In their research, social psychologists use attitude scales to assess direction and intensity of people's views because these scales provide precise and reliable information (Dawes & Smith, 1985). An *attitude scale* is a series of questions that ask people how strongly they agree or disagree, favor or oppose, or like or dislike any attitude object. Respondents choose among options that range from an extreme negative evaluation through a neutral point to an extreme positive evaluation.

Because people's attitudes are often reflected in their behaviors, social psychologists also use *observations* of behavior to gauge attitudes. For example, they might observe whether people will volunteer to stuff envelopes for a campaign to save the Spotted Owl, and how many envelopes they are willing to stuff (Deci, 1975; Wilson & Dunn, 1986). A particular choice—volunteering to work for a cause or refusing to participate—is assumed to reflect the direction of the person's attitude. The amount of behavior—the number of envelopes actually stuffed—is the indicator of attitudinal intensity.

Self-report techniques and observational measures depend on people's honesty, and most of the time people say what they think and act on their convictions. Unfortunately (as everyone who has held an unpopular view knows) people also want to make a good impression. Nobody wants to appear ignorant, prejudiced, or out of step. Most of us also like to tell others what we think they want to hear and to show them what we think they want to see. These motives may lead people to be less than honest in reporting or acting on their attitudes, especially when the issue is a sensitive one (Campbell, 1963).

The social desirability response bias, and the methods researchers use to avoid it, were initially discussed in Chapter 2, pages 37 to 39.

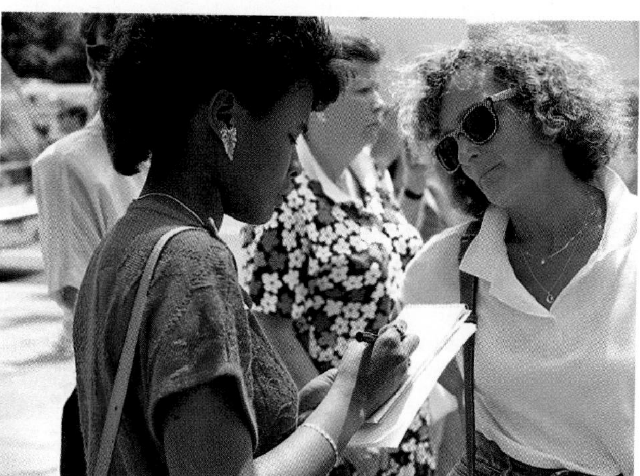

Tell us what you think Like this interviewer, most social psychologists measure attitudes using self-report techniques—a method that relies on people expressing the intensity and direction of their opinions openly and honestly.

Indirect Measures. Social psychologists have developed a number of techniques to get around people's desire to look good. Anonymity is the rule in almost all laboratory research on attitudes, so participants need not fear being publicly identified with a particular attitude. Another approach involves measures that subtly reveal attitudes without the subjects' knowledge. In one clever technique, subjects are quizzed about obscure events in the lives of important public figures (Hammond, 1948; Pratkanis, 1989). One question, for example, asked students to give their "best guess" about which of the following statements was true: "Ronald Reagan maintained an *A* average at Eureka College" or "Ronald Reagan never achieved above a *C* average." Because subjects were unlikely to know which statement was accurate, the researcher expected their attitudes to guide their best guesses. And he was right: students with positive attitudes about Reagan tended to give him *A*'s, whereas those who did not like Reagan picked the lower average.

Researchers have also attempted to increase the honesty of answers about sensitive attitude issues by using the *bogus pipeline,* a device that causes subjects to believe their physiological reactions are being measured. When subjects are attached to this device, they fear that dishonest responses will be detected and therefore are presumed to answer questions honestly. This technique has been used successfully to study stereotyping and prejudice, and it also helps researchers get straight answers about issues such as attitudes toward drug and alcohol use and safe-sex practices (Quigley-Fernandez & Tedeschi, 1978; Wech and others, 1989). You may recall from Chapter 3 that the mere threat of a lie detector test, even if it never actually takes place, can increase people's honesty about sensitive topics (Jamieson & Zanna, 1983).

Of course, bogus pipeline techniques do not provide any real physiological measure of reactions to attitude objects, such as an assessment of heart rate or perspiration. But such measures would not be particularly useful in attitude research anyway. The problem is that heart rate and perspiration levels might increase in response to either a positive or a negative event—at the thought of either winning the state lottery or discovering your car had been stolen. Thus, although these physiological measures give some indication of the intensity of the person's response, they would provide no clue about the direction of the attitude.

John Cacioppo and Richard Petty have developed a physiological measurement technique that gets around this difficulty, permitting precise measurements of both the intensity and direction of attitudes (Cacioppo and others, 1986). Their technique relies on facial electromyography (EMG), which measures the electrical activity of muscles. When people are experiencing happiness or sadness, different muscle groups in the face contract. These contractions become obvious when the corners of the mouth lift in a smile or the brow furrows in a frown. Such muscle activity occurs, however, even when changes cannot be seen with the naked eye. This is where technology steps in—EMG can measure muscle activity, as shown in Figure 7.1. In one demonstration of their technique, Cacioppo and Petty (1979)

Figure 7.1 Facial electromyograph (EMG): An indirect measure of attitudes

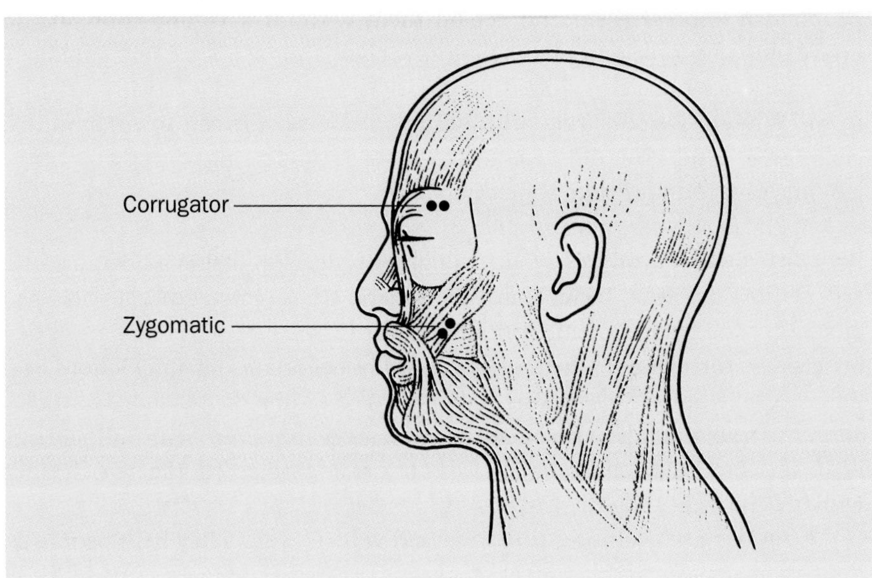

When people react positively to an attitude object, activity in the zygomatic muscles increases, whereas negative responses are accompanied by increased activity in the corrugator muscles. Although this activity cannot be observed with the naked eye, it can be measured by electrodes placed at the indicated positions. (Adapted from Petty & Cacioppo, 1986, p. 42.)

recorded male subjects' facial muscle activity as they listened to a speech that either supported or opposed their views on alcohol possession or dorm visitations. EMG revealed a pattern of muscle activity consistent with the direction and intensity of subjects' views. Students who agreed with the speech showed increased activity in the muscles associated with smiling, even though observers could catch no glimpse of these subtle changes in the students' faces. Those who opposed the speech, however, showed more activity in the brow muscles associated with frowning, again despite the fact that these changes were not visible to the naked eye.

Using EMG is obviously impossible without lots of equipment, a carefully controlled environment, an expert experimenter, and very cooperative subjects. When performed properly, however, this technique holds the promise of accurately revealing both the direction and intensity of an attitude.

Attitude Formation: Why and How?

People form attitudes because they are useful in mastering the social environment and in expressing important connections with others. Attitudes are assembled from three types of information: beliefs about the object's positive or negative characteristics, feelings and emotions about the object, and information about past and current actions toward the object. Once an attitude has been formed, it becomes closely linked to knowledge about the object.

What is your opinion of Bill Clinton? How do you feel about your hometown? We expect that you can answer these questions without much thought. Many attitudes are so well established and so frequently used that people can express them and act on them without a second thought. But even familiar people and places that now elicit almost a knee-jerk evaluative response were once confronted for the first time. Where do attitudes come from? Why do we construct attitudes toward almost every object in our social world? And how do we come to favor one idea and resist another, to like one object and dislike something else?

Why Attitudes Form. Not surprisingly, we develop attitudes because they are useful to us (Katz, 1960; Smith and others, 1956). First, attitudes help people master the environment. Attitudes toward chocolate ice cream and calculus classes, for example, help us successfully negotiate our interactions with these attitude objects, devouring the first and avoiding the second. This *object appraisal function* (also known as the *knowledge function*) of attitudes orients us to the important characteristics of an attitude object so that we can deal with it effectively and efficiently.

We encountered attitudes that serve the value-expressive or social identity function in Chapter 6, pages 242 to 243. Value-expressive attitudes are so centrally tied to our definitions of ourselves and our groups that any threat to them becomes a threat to the self and to the group.

Attitudes are useful to us in a second way as well. They help people express their real selves, voice their convictions, show what they stand for, and affirm their significant relationships. This *social identity function* (or *value-expressive function*) of attitudes helps people gain and maintain connectedness with others. Attitudes like a belief in the value of hard work, or equal opportunity, or worship help us define who we are.

These two important functions of attitudes are not mutually exclusive. Many attitudes serve both object appraisal and social identity functions, although not necessarily to the same degree. Attitudes toward practical objects like a new hot water heater or a down vest, for example, may serve the purpose of object appraisal much more than that of social identity. Attitudes about religious practices, a cherished memento from childhood, or the animal rights movement, on the other hand, are probably more expressive of a person's identity (Shavitt, 1990).

The Building Blocks of Attitudes. Some positive and negative evaluative tendencies are inborn. One of them is a preference for pleasure over pain (Tesser, 1993). Most attitudes, however, are learned. As people learn about an attitude object (either by interacting with it or by hearing about it from friends, family, teachers, or the media), they build a cognitive representation of the object. This representation includes cognitive, affective, and behavioral information associated with the object.

1. *Cognitive information is what people know about an attitude object—the facts and beliefs they have about it.* Perhaps the surgeon general's report has convinced you that cigarette smoking causes disease. This belief constitutes cognitive information about this attitude object, cigarette smoking.

2. *Affective information consists of how people feel about the object—the feelings and emotions the attitude object arouses.* Experiencing nausea or anger when you are in a smoky closed area qualifies as affective information associated with cigarette smoking.

3. *Behavioral information comprises knowledge about people's past, present, or future interactions with the attitude object.* The fact that you do not smoke constitutes behavioral information consistent with a negative attitude toward cigarette smoking.

Putting It All Together. How do attitudes emerge from all the varying information that accumulates about attitude objects? Like jurors, we seem to be swayed by the weight of the evidence, forming attitudes that are consistent with most of what we know, feel, and experience (Feather, 1969; Rosenberg, 1956). Consistency is a powerful force in human thinking—the presence of positive information about an attitude object typically results in a positive attitude, as Figure 7.2 suggests (Festinger, 1957; Heider, 1944). Similarly, the presence of negative beliefs, feelings, or behaviors produces a negative attitude.

Figure 7.2 Attitude formation and measurement

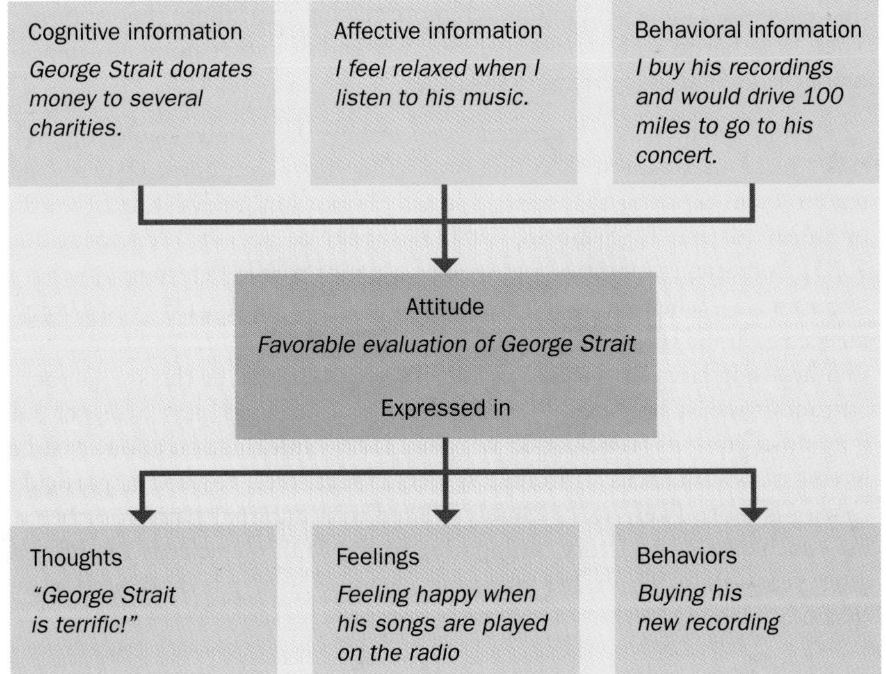

If you learn that George Strait donates money to several charities, feel relaxed when you listen to his music, and know that you would drive over one hundred miles to see him in concert, you are likely to form a positive attitude toward the popular country singer. The attitude in turn will influence thoughts, feelings, and observable behaviors. Researchers draw on these effects to measure the underlying attitude.

Of course the different pieces of information that accumulate do not always imply a consistent evaluation of an attitude object. Most people know arguments on both sides of major social issues, such as immigration control, the death penalty, and environmental management (Pratkanis, 1984; Judd & Kulik, 1980). Having evaluatively mixed beliefs and feelings toward particular attitude objects is also a common experience. For example, you might think blood drives are an excellent idea at the same time that you feel nauseated at the sight of a hypodermic needle (Chaiken & Baldwin, 1981; Breckler & Wiggins, 1989). With inconsistent information pulling us in both directions, why don't most people form middle-of-the-road, wishy-washy attitudes? The answer is that a variety of mechanisms work to help us avoid or resolve those inconsistencies.

1. *Our information base is usually lopsided.* Sometimes we avoid inconsistencies by collecting one-sided information. Because people usually share the same opinions held by their family and friends, day-to-day interactions provide a one-sided view of the issues. If everyone in your home, club, and church group is a liberal Democrat, for example, you will hear a great deal of support for the liberal point of view. Another source of one-sided information is set in motion by our initial reactions to people, places, and things. If, for example, a family's first encounter with a new neighbor is negative, they may adopt an avoidance strategy, preventing any changes in the lopsidedly negative information they have gathered.

Attitudes themselves can play a part in resolving inconsistencies because they influence the type of information we pay attention to or remember. When we think about a particular attitude, the arguments and information that support it come to mind much more readily than those that oppose it. Thus, whether in reality or in memory, we tend to gather more information on one side of an issue than on the other.

2. *All information is not created equal.* People do not give equal weight to every piece of available information as they form attitudes. Instead, they tend to focus on items that seem especially important, relevant, trustworthy, or salient (Ajzen & Fishbein, 1980; Fishbein & Ajzen, 1975; McGuire, 1985). Sometimes cognitive factors play a major role in determining what is important, as when we weigh the advantages of a large yard versus convenience to public transportation in choosing an apartment. And under emotion-arousing circumstances, affective information may be the key factor. In attitudes toward donating blood, for example, feelings play a bigger role than do cognitions (Breckler & Wiggins, 1989). Information about past behavior also influences attitudes. A person's attitude toward a particular charity is more likely to be closely related to a habitual pattern of behavior—such as a past history of donating to the Multiple Sclerosis Fund year after year—than his or her one-time response to a televised fund raiser (Fazio & Zanna, 1981).

3. *Accessible information determines attitudes.* Accessible information—information that comes most easily to mind or that grabs our attention—can dominate an attitude judgment. In one demonstration of this point, researchers deliberately planted conservative or liberal ideas in subjects' minds and then looked at the impact of these ideas on their judgments (Tourangeau & Rasinski, 1988). The subjects, Chicago women, were divided into two groups. The women in one group were first asked their opinions about conservative issues, like the value of hard work. The other group was asked to respond to liberal issues, like government's responsibility for the plight of the poor. Both groups were then encouraged to present their own views on social spending. Sixty-two percent of the respondents primed with conservative values stated that the government spent too much money on social programs. In contrast, only 46 percent of the respondents primed with liberal values expressed similar beliefs. Why the difference? The information made accessible by the earlier questions—thoughts supporting liberal or conservative values—tipped subjects' attitudes in the liberal or the conservative direction.

Information that is accessible because it is perceptually salient also exerts a strong effect on attitude judgments. Our preferences for and evaluations of our favorite foods probably relate much more to their obvious sensory appeal than to their hidden nutritional benefits. Thus, whatever is uppermost in our minds at the time can determine our attitude.

Although these processes all help to make our attitudinal database more consistent, we still might have to combine many pieces of information into a single evaluation. People seem to employ two strategies to achieve this. In the first, we weight each piece of information according to its value and importance and then combine them algebraically, either by adding them all up or by taking their average (Anderson, 1981; Fishbein & Azjen, 1975). In the other approach, we try to configure the information into a meaningful whole, letting each piece influence the others rather than evaluating each item independently. Regardless of which strategy people use, the end product is an attitude that acts as an evaluative summary of accessible information about the attitude object.

These algebraic and configural approaches to integrating information were first discussed as ways we make judgments about individuals based on our impressions of them. *See Chapter 3, page 100.*

Linking Attitudes to Their Objects. Once an attitude that summarizes relevant and important information about an attitude object has developed, it takes on a life of its own. The attitude becomes part of our cognitive representation of the object, just like other pieces of information, as can be seen in Figure 7.3. Further, if we think frequently about our attitude toward the object, the link becomes closer and stronger, and the attitude comes to mind automatically whenever we think about the object. For example, we do not just think about Bill Clinton, but about a president we respect or disparage. We do not just think about our hometown, but about a small town we love

People form attitudes based on cognitive, affective, and behavioral information about an attitude object. Once the attitude is formed, it too becomes associated with the mental representation of the attitude object, as shown in the center panel. If the attitude is repeatedly activated, perhaps because the person encounters the object frequently, the attitude's link to the object will be strengthened (bottom panel). As a result, the attitude is more likely to be retrieved and used whenever the attitude object is encountered.

Figure 7.3 Linking an attitude to the object

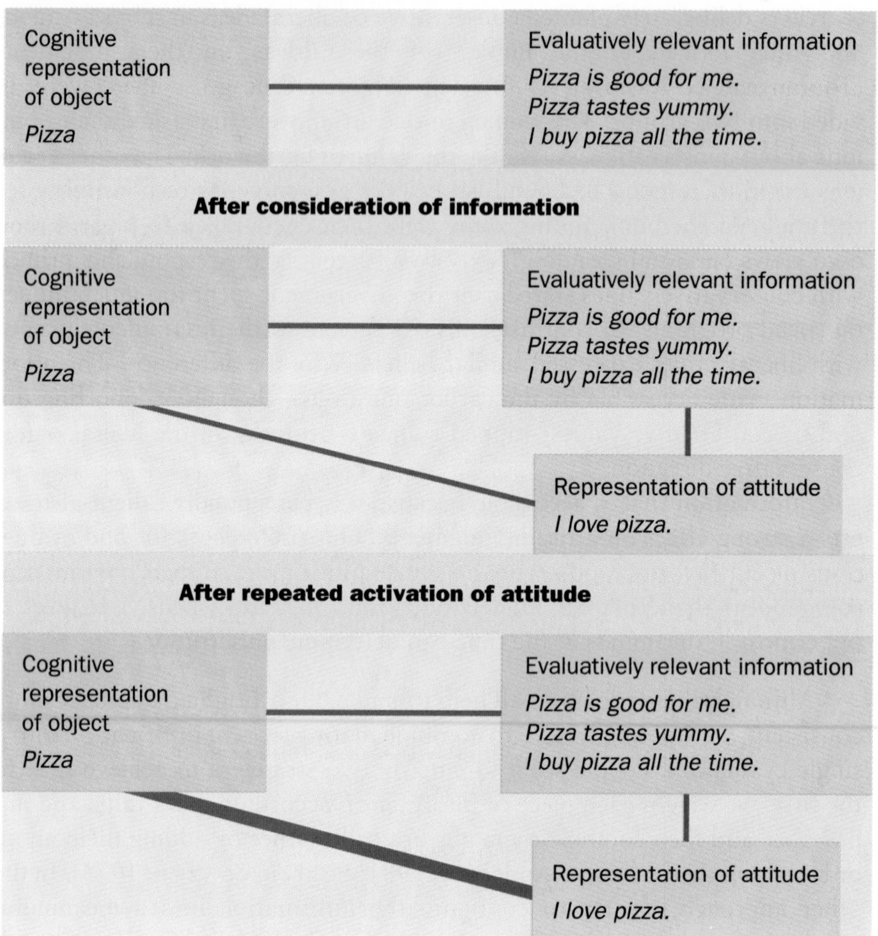

or despise. Thus our attitude becomes a short-hand substitute for what we know and how we feel about the attitude object. When people ask us what we think of country singer George Strait, our attitude tells us "We like him," without our having to think about the cognitions, feelings, and behaviors that initially generated our reaction (Lingle & Ostrom, 1979).

From Snap Judgments to Considered Opinions: Superficial and Systematic Routes to Persuasion

Although we form attitudes because they are useful to us, other people also find our attitudes useful. In the marketplace, the political arena, the classroom—wherever you go—you will find people trying to influence you to develop new attitudes or change old ones. And if positive beliefs, feelings, or behaviors produce positive attitudes, and negative beliefs, feelings, and behaviors produce negative attitudes, the persuader's task should be quite straightforward. To ensure that you will love their product, scorn drug use, or support prayer in schools, all they need to do is provide you with important cognitive, affective, or behavioral information consistent with the attitude they want you to develop. Right? Actually, it's not that simple. These ideas are at the root of almost all theories of attitude formation and change, and they also are the core of most persuasion techniques. But persuasion does not occur automatically. How carefully the receiver considers the communication can determine its success or failure.

Like the proverbial horse that can be led to water but cannot be convinced to drink, people can be provided with information but cannot always be convinced to think—or at least not to think deeply. And the way people process information can determine whether a persuasive effort will be effective. Shelly Chaiken (1980, 1987) and Richard Petty and John Cacioppo (1981, 1986) have argued that people deal with information about attitude objects in two different ways: they scan it somewhat superficially, or they consider it systematically. When people engage in *superficial processing,* they rely on accessible or salient information to make rather simple inferences about the attitude object. When people engage in *systematic processing,* they go beyond simple cues and also consider the strength of the arguments and their implications for the evaluation of the attitude object. As we shall see, both kinds of processing—superficial and systematic—can change attitudes, but they do so in very different ways.

These two types of processing should sound familiar, because superficial and systematic processing also come into play when we make judgments about other individuals (Chapter 3, pages 97 to 100) and about members of groups (Chapter 5, pages 196 to 203).

Superficial Processing: Persuasion Shortcuts

When people do not give persuasive communications much thought, various superficial aspects of the message can lead to attitude change. For example, people may agree with experts, with long messages, or with messages that use statistics.

When you thumb absentmindedly through a magazine, you pay very little attention to the actual words on the printed page. Nevertheless, despite the superficiality of your processing, some information is getting through. You may notice the beautiful people using a product, the amount of evidence that supports an advertising claim, or the irritating or pleasant photos in an advertisement. Such simple pieces of information can act as **persuasion heuristics**, which are rules of thumb that allow people to decide whether they like or dislike an object without having to consider information about it in any depth (Chaiken, 1980, 1987). Because superficial processors substitute these casual rules of thumb for careful processing, Petty and Cacioppo (1981, 1986) describe them as taking a *peripheral route to persuasion.*

persuasion heuristic A simple rule that allows people to evaluate an object based on superficial cues.

The Far Side by Gary Larson

Dog Endorsements

The Expertise Heuristic: Agreeing with Those Who Know. "Life on other solar systems is entirely possible!" Imagine that this sentence had caught your attention as you flipped through the television channels on a Sunday afternoon. You soon discover the source of the intriguing statement is a talk-show guest, a farmer who claims he has been taken for multiple rides on a spaceship. Would you nod in agreement or snort with derision? Imagine now that you had heard this same sentence from Dr. Carl Sagan, professor of astronomy and space science at Cornell University and creator of the television series, *Cosmos*. Would your reaction be different?

Research suggests that it would. Because communicators with excellent credentials usually offer cogent arguments, people often develop a simple rule: experts know what they are talking about. Once they have learned the *expertise heuristic,* people tend to accept the validity of a claim on the basis of *who* says it, instead of carefully analyzing *what* is said (Hovland & Weiss, 1951; Maddux & Rogers, 1980; Sternthal and others, 1978).

Why is Carl Sagan an expert source while the space-traveling farmer is not? To be credible, communicators must be competent. *Competence* refers to proof of the communicator's accomplishment or status in a particular field. When an ad features Jimmy Connors in action on the tennis court, a robed judge banging a gavel in a wood-paneled courtroom, or a stethescope-bedecked doctor writing prescriptions, its creators are hoping to capitalize on the expertise heuristic. One early demonstration of this simple rule of thumb compared the persuasive powers of a judge and a drug dealer (Kelman & Hovland, 1953). Subjects were told that one or the other had recommended relatively lenient treatment of a juvenile delinquent. As you might expect, they found the judge more persuasive than the drug dealer.

Occupation is not the only cue that leads us to invoke the expertise heuristic. The image of competence also seems to be created by rapid delivery. Although the fast-talking politician or salesperson might not seem an obvious source of valid information, research findings indicate that fast talkers are impressive. As long as people can understand the gist of a message, the faster the message is delivered, the more expert, objective, intelligent, and knowledgeable the communicator is seen to be (MacLachlan & Siegel, 1980; Miller and others, 1976). In fact, running television ads at 120 percent of their normal speed can increase the persuasiveness of weak commercials (Moore and others, 1986).

What enhances fast talkers' credibility is their apparent confidence. Although research has shown that fast talkers are no more sure of their facts than are people who speak slowly, jurors and judges often put more stock in confident testimony (Wells & Murray, 1984). Witnesses who speak without hesitation—a quality likely to be true of men's speech—are trusted more than those who hesitate, qualify, and soften their speech style—as women often do (Erickson and others, 1978; Lee & Ofshe, 1981).

People rely on expert communicators not only to know the facts but also to tell the truth (Eagly and others, 1978). Thus, after competence, *trustworthiness* is the most important characteristic a credible communicator can have. That is why communicators sometimes earn persuasion points by presenting both sides of an issue; the strategy makes them seem well informed and fair minded (Jones & Brehm, 1970). Trustworthiness is also the goal when advertisers arrange for their audience to "sit in on" or "overhear" product testimonials and "slice of life" endorsements. If the communication seems to happen by accident, rather than being tailored specifically for their ears, the casual observer is likely to think it is true and to be influenced by it (Walster & Festinger, 1962).

Of course, we are likely to be taken in by these ploys only if we are processing very minimally. If we devote even a little more attention to the communication, we might be prompted to ask *why* a particular source is advocating a particular position (Eagly and others, 1981). Such attributional processing can undermine a communicator's apparent trustworthiness. Imagine, for example, that an advertisement for Nike footwear prompts you to wonder why Michael Jordan endorses the product. Does Jordan promote Nikes because of the quality of the product? Could it be that this particular kind of sneaker is so terrific that Jordan cannot help but recommend it? Making a *stimulus attribution*—deciding that Jordan endorses Nike because the shoes are so good—produces persuasion (Eagly and others, 1978). If the advocate seems to have ulterior motives, however, people become suspicious. If they recognize that Jordan—or any other celebrity endorser—is well paid for an endorsement, they may find the ad less persuasive: maybe it's the money talking, not the quality of the shoes. Attributional processing may explain why people are particularly impressed when communicators seem to speak or act against their own best interests (Knight & Weiss, 1980). We would probably be persuaded if we learned that Michael Jordan owns stock in a competitive footwear company but feels compelled to recommend Nike because of its quality.

Attributional processing is concerned with discovering the causes for behavior, as you might recall from Chapter 3, pages 85 to 90.

The Message-Length Heuristic: Length Equals Strength. Just as the qualities of the communicator serve as rules of thumb when people are processing superficially, so the form of the persuasive appeal can lure people into changing their attitudes without giving them much thought. Perhaps you have noticed that longer campaign speeches seem more convincing than briefer ones. Such observations might produce a simple *message-length heuristic:* the longer the message, the more valid it appears to be. Ads that pointedly number "the twenty-five best reasons" to prefer a product are trying to invoke this heuristic. Table 7.1 describes another persuasion technique that encourages people to rely on the sheer number of arguments supporting a particular position.

Of course, quantity does not always mean quality and the focus on numbers can blind us to the inadequacy of the reasoning. Imagine the following scenario. You are waiting in line at the photocopy machine when you are approached by someone wanting to cut ahead of you. Her request is relatively small—she wants to make only five copies. Would you find her simple request persuasive? About 60 percent of students waiting in line to use the copy machine at the City University of New York (CUNY) did so (Langer and others, 1978). Now imagine that the would-be line cutter not

Table 7.1 Length equals strength: The Ben Franklin close

A *close* is a persuasive technique that "closes a deal." A salesperson using the Ben Franklin close would begin with a story like this:

> As you know, Ben Franklin has always been considered one of the wisest men America has ever had. Whenever he felt himself in a situation where he couldn't quite make up his mind, he felt pretty much as you do now. If it was the right thing, he wanted to be sure he did it. If it was the wrong thing, he wanted to be just as sure that he avoided it. Isn't that about the way you feel?
>
> So here's what he would do to arrive at a decision. He would take a clean sheet of paper and draw a line down the middle, like this. On one side of the line he would list all the reasons why he should make a "yes" decision and on the other side of the line he would list all the reasons against making this decision. When he was through, he would count the reasons that he was able to tally on each side, and his decision was made for him. Why don't we try it here and see what happens?

As the customer attempts to come up with reasons for buying the product, the salesperson helps suggest and list reasons. When it comes to producing reasons for the other side, however, the salesperson leaves the customer to work alone. Often it will be difficult for one person to generate more reasons than two people can. With the sheet of paper showing more reasons "for" than "against," the customer can be influenced by the message-length heuristic.

Source: Adapted with permission of Lexington Books, an imprint of Macmillan Publishing Company, from J. Jacoby (1984). Some social psychological perspectives on closing. In J. Jacoby & C. S. Craig (Eds.), *Personal selling* (pp. 73–92). Copyright © 1984 by Lexington Books.

only made the same request but also explained that she was in a rush. Would this legitimate argument in favor of letting her go ahead be even more persuasive? If you say yes, you agree with the CUNY students, 94 percent of whom agreed to the request when given a good reason.

These findings suggest that the quality of a message increases persuasiveness, but is that always the case? If people are processing heuristically—relying on whether the request is long or not, for example—maybe anything that *sounds like* an argument or reason will do. In fact, other people were approached by the woman with a request and an empty explanation that only sounded like a reason: "Excuse me, I have five pages. May I use the Xerox machine, because I have to make some copies?" Of these subjects, 93 percent agreed to let her go ahead! When people rely on the message-length heuristic, a longer message—even a single argument longer—seems compelling, no matter what it says (Petty & Cacioppo, 1984). As you will see later, however, when a request is large enough to provoke more extensive processing—for example, if the person had to make fifty copies instead of five—people will think more carefully about the reason.

Other superficial aspects of a message can also act as heuristics. Many people are strong believers in the "you get what you pay for" heuristic—when items like perfume, wine, and jewelry are sold for higher prices, we think they are of better quality (McConnell, 1968; Peterson, 1977). And many people are particularly impressed by speeches or advertisements that contain numbers, graphs, or equations, perhaps because they convey an air of scientific objectivity (Chaiken, 1987). Perhaps this explains why candidates often bring statistics when they take their platform to the people. Ross Perot was a master of this tactic during the 1992 presidential campaign, taking bar graphs and pie charts to his primetime television audience.

Most of the time, using persuasion heuristics is quite an effective strategy for dealing with messages we encounter. Experts usually know what they are talking about, and a long message often yields more relevant information than a short one. After all, the usefulness of these cues led people to develop the heuristics in the first place. Sometimes, however, superficial processing of a persuasive communication may not provide enough convincing information. Or we may want to know more about the attitude object than superficial processing provides. Under these circumstances we move into high gear, and we process information in depth.

Systematic Processing of Persuasive Communications

Sometimes people do carefully consider the content of arguments presented in a persuasive communication. When people pay attention to a message, understand its content, and react favorably to it, persuasion may occur. Change resulting from such careful consideration lasts longer than change produced by superficial processing.

When people process systematically, they cease relying solely on persuasion cues and begin considering additional kinds of evidence relevant to a communication. They make an effort to look beyond the superficial aspects of the communication and to evaluate the quality of the arguments made. How does this increase in thought affect persuasion?

Processing Arguments: The Central Route to Persuasion. Thoroughgoing systematic processing involves paying particular attention to the strength and quality of the arguments (Chaiken, 1980, 1987; Petty & Cacioppo, 1981, 1986). Because thinking carefully about the content of the message is so important in systematic processing, Petty and Cacioppo (1981, 1986) have called it the *central route to persuasion*. Over the years, researchers have gained considerable knowledge about the steps involved in systematic processing and how they influence persuasion (McGuire, 1969).

1. *Attending to the message.* In one popular French commercial for an all-purpose adhesive, the glue is applied to the soles of the announcer's shoes, and he is hung upside down from the ceiling. In a recent North American ad, a mid-size truck is pushed off a suspension bridge to dangle on a bungee cord. The reason advertisers go to such lengths is that they realize that getting the audience's attention is the first crucial step in bringing about persuasion, a fact Carl Hovland and his colleagues at Yale University recognized long ago (1949, 1953). It's also a step that is

easier said than done. Because people are bombarded by so many persuasive messages—more than three thousand a day by some estimates—most messages receive at best a superficial once-over. Professional persuaders know that, if they are to keep their candidate in the spotlight or make their product's packaging stand out from the rest, they must quickly snare the audience's attention, giving them a reason to watch and listen. As David Ogilvy concluded from his years of advertising experience, "People screen out a lot of commercials because they start with something dull. When you advertise fire extinguishers, open with the fire" (Ogilvy, 1983, p. 111).

2. *Comprehending the message.* Although getting the audience's attention is a critical first step in communicating, attention does not always guarantee comprehension. Reading or hearing an argument does not mean we understand it. For example, television advertisers, who have both vision and sound to work with, are able to make their ads more attention grabbing than messages delivered on radio or in print (Andreoli & Worchel, 1978). Nevertheless, audiences are more persuaded by appeals they see in print than by those they watch on television (McGuire, 1985). Research indicates, in fact, that much of the persuasive information aimed at us goes right over our heads. In one survey, for example, consumer psychologist Jacob Jacoby and his colleagues (1980) found that adult subjects misunderstood 30 to 40 percent of the information presented in thirty-second television segments. Comprehension of printed magazine ads and articles is somewhat better (Chaiken & Eagly, 1976), which perhaps explains why they have more effect on attitudes. But even here, misunderstandings are still quite frequent (Jacoby & Hoyer, 1989). So the golden rule for most media persuasion is: keep it simple.

3. *Reacting to message content.* People do not just soak up information; they react to it, sometimes favorably and sometimes unfavorably. Whether the persuasive communication is President Clinton's speech advocating his new economic program or your roommate's pitch to borrow your car, you will do more than just listen to it if it has engaged your attention and you understand it. You will think about whether you agree or disagree with the persuader's arguments. Favorable reactions might include merely registering agreement ("investing in the future sounds good to me"), or developing the supportive information even further ("yes, well, Sara really is a very careful driver"). Negative reactions may range from simply disagreeing with some point ("Oh, pleeease!") to developing a detailed set of counterarguments. The process of generating such favorable and unfavorable evaluative reactions to the content of a message is called **elaboration.** When people process systematically, the elaborations they generate in response to the content of the message play a key role in persuasion.

elaboration The generation of favorable or unfavorable reactions to the content of a message.

4. *Accepting the message.* If a systematically processed message stimulates favorable elaborations, it will be persuasive. If the arguments evoke unfavorable reactions, the message will fail to persuade (Greenwald, 1968; Petty and others, 1981). Thus people's *reactions* to the content of the message can be even more important than the content itself. Modern research has confirmed what philosophers have long suspected: as Blaise Pascal put it, "People are generally better persuaded by the reasons which they have themselves discovered."

If carefully processed arguments provoke positive elaborations, the more arguments there are, the more attitude change there will be. By the same token, greater numbers of carefully processed specious arguments will produce more negative responses than would result from only a few silly arguments. To assess the impact of systematic thinking about strong and weak arguments on persuasion, one study presented students with different numbers of arguments in favor of instituting comprehensive examinations for graduating seniors—a popular attitude issue in persuasion research (Petty & Cacioppo, 1984). Strong arguments—ones that typically prompt favorable elaborations—in this experiment included statements like the following: "Graduate schools and law and medical schools are beginning to show clear and significant preferences for students who received their undergraduate degrees from institutions with comprehensive exams." Weak arguments, which typically elicit unfavorable elaborations, included such statements as, "Graduate students have always had to take a comprehensive exam in their major area before receiving their degrees, and it is only fair that undergraduates should have to take them also." Some students heard three weak arguments, and others heard nine weak arguments. A third group heard three strong arguments and a fourth group nine strong ones. All students then gave their own opinion on the comprehensive exams issue. The results indicated that when subjects were processing systematically, they found three strong arguments persuasive and nine even more so. In contrast, a few weak arguments were unimpressive, and many weak arguments were a real turn-off. When communicators attempt to influence us with really bad arguments, we may even respond by moving in a direction opposite the one intended. This change is called a *boomerang effect.*

Compelling arguments aren't always provided for us, but persuasion can still occur when just thinking about an attitude issue brings more and more relevant evidence and arguments to mind. When this happens, merely thinking about the issue can lead to favorable or unfavorable evaluations of the information we consider, which in turn produce either more persuasion or a boomerang effect (Tesser, 1978)

The Benefits of Central Route Processing. When attitudes change because information is carefully attended, comprehended, and elaborated, all this mental work helps write the resulting attitudes almost indelibly in mem-

Systematic processing might stop this child's suffering The effectiveness of this ad is enhanced because it encourages systematic processing. The photo draws our attention to the easy-to-understand arguments, while the questions provoke active elaboration of message content. Systematically processed appeals usually result in attitudes that persist over time and resist further attempts to change them.

ory (Chaiken, 1980; Petty and others, 1986). In fact, the new attitudes become so firmly fixed that they are little affected by the passage of time or the presentation of new material (Cook & Flay, 1978; Chaiken, 1980). Compared with attitudes that change through heuristic processing, systematically altered attitudes are both persistent and resistant (Haugtvedt & Petty, 1992).

The fact that attitude change following superficial processing is more fleeting than that produced by systematic processing helps explain a finding that baffled persuasion researchers for years. When persuasive communications are attributed to credible or noncredible sources—to *The New York Times* versus *The National Enquirer,* for example—the heuristic effect is immediate: credible sources produce persuasion and noncredible sources do not. If the new attitudes are measured at a later time, however, this difference sometimes disappears. The attitude change induced by a message from the expert source may decrease over time, whereas reactions to a message from a nonexpert source may become more positive. In fact, over time, the impact of the message delivered by the noncredible source increases (Hovland and others, 1949; Hovland & Weiss, 1951). This delayed increase in persuasiveness is called the *sleeper effect.* The explanation of this surprising finding appears to be that attitude change produced by different aspects of the message has different life expectancies. It can be demonstrated by an example.

Imagine that, over coffee in the lunch room, Bob from the mailroom excitedly tries to convince the personnel manager that the company should change long-distance telephone carriers. The manager carefully considers the arguments, but thinks that Bob is a source with low credibility: relying on the expertise heuristic, he dismisses the idea out of hand. Some weeks later, however, the issue of the company's long-distance service comes up at the manager's division meeting. Because people do not give much thought to the source of a message, information about the persuasive communicator quickly disappears, along with any heuristic attitude change based on it (Kelman & Hovland, 1953). So the manager is unlikely to remember that it was Bob who recommended changing companies, and thus he has no immediate heuristic reason to dismiss the idea. At the same time, he can still recall the content of Bob's arguments, and the content of the message is persuasive. As the systematically processed arguments continue to have their effect and are no longer undermined by their noncredible origin, a sleeper effect occurs: the manager comes to see that changing phone companies is a good idea.

Of course, a sleeper effect can occur only if people process the content of the persuasive message systematically; if they do not, the impact of the message content cannot outlast the effect of the source (Gruder and others, 1978; Greenwald and others, 1986; Pratkanis and others, 1988). Thus, the reason originally rejected messages from a noncredible source can show a sleeper effect is that source-induced heuristic change fades earlier than argument-produced systematic attitude change.

Superficial and Systematic Processing: Which Strategy, When?

People process messages systematically only when they have both the motivation and the cognitive capacity to do so. The importance and self-relevance of the message determines motivation. Cognitive capacity is available when people have adequate ability, relevant knowledge, and the opportunity to concentrate.

So what is the best strategy if you want to change someone's mind about something? Whether you are addressing your constituents, launching a new business, or trying to get your family to adopt a sensible diet, any strategy that evokes systematic processing seems to be the best bet for both persuader and persuadee. For the persuader, systematic processing guarantees long-term and resistant attitude change: once you have won their minds, you are going to be able to keep their allegiance. For the consumer of persuasive communications, careful processing ensures more valid and useful attitudes. When we are systematically processing, we are unlikely to be persuaded by the commencement speaker's long-winded but hackneyed advice on how to succeed, or by the expert endorser's smooth pitch for a dubious product.

Why, then, don't people process systematically all the time? Unfortunately, there is a catch. The attending, comprehending, and elaborating that characterize systematic processing do not come easily—they require a substantial investment of effort and processing capacity. In fact, whether communications are processed superficially or systematically depends on two factors: people's motivation and their cognitive capacity to think carefully about the content of the message.

How Motivation Influences Systematic Processing. Goals and motives play an important role in how we approach persuasive communications. Imagine the plight of a small company's purchasing manager who has been given the responsibility of selecting and purchasing new computer equipment to be used for product design. The decision is a crucial one: the company needs to upgrade to stay competitive, but if it goes over budget it could be the last straw for a business hit hard by the recession. This is the manager's first real test as purchasing manager, and her reputation of mixing technical smarts with an eye for a bargain is on the line. How will she decide which product line uses her company's money most effectively? She probably will react as we all do. When it's important that we form accurate evaluations, and when the attitudes and opinions we form reflect directly on us, systematic processing is our greatest ally.

1. *The importance of being accurate.* When we are being held accountable for our preferences and are concerned about making the correct decision, the knowledge function of attitudes will predominate, and issues of accu-

racy will be central. The product manager will need solid evidence to justify her choice of computer system, because others will hold her accountable. She may also fear that if she chooses a faulty piece of equipment, the costs of being incorrect could be severe. Compared with people who have no one to answer to, accountable message processors and those anxious to avoid being wrong will process persuasive communications more thoroughly, think more about the information, and be more concerned with integrating new information as it comes to light (Kruglanski, 1988; Tetlock, 1983, 1985).

Accuracy concerns can also be triggered when the evidence seems mixed. Imagine that you have been looking forward to seeing a newly released movie and you discover that your local paper has panned it. Siskel and Ebert also give it two "thumbs down," and you decide not to see it. But then one of your friends says it is the best movie he has seen in a long time. Now your confidence in your judgment wavers, and you start looking for new input. Perhaps you ask your friend about the plot and characters, or you seek out several additional reviews. When persuasive communications advocate inconsistent positions, as they do in this example, people move from casual to careful processing. People are motivated to undertake a detailed analysis of all aspects of the communication when they encounter arguments that do not fit or conclusions that do not follow (Maheswaran & Chaiken, 1991; Chaiken and others, 1989; Festinger, 1954).

2. *The importance of self-relevance.* An old Chinese proverb says, "Tell me and I'll forget; involve me and I'll understand." People's tendency to carefully process personally relevant information is nothing new. When information is relevant to something that affects us, we want to know all about it. The product manager, for example, knows her decision will affect more than the company's bottom line. With her own reputation at stake, she will be motivated to pay careful attention to the information presented by the competing system manufacturers.

In a demonstration of the influence of self-relevance on persuasion, researchers asked groups of students to listen to a speech advocating a comprehensive exam requirement for graduation (Petty and others, 1981). Some groups heard a speech composed of strong and valid arguments for the exams, while other groups were given rather weak and silly arguments. Some groups were led to believe the speech had been delivered by an expert communicator—a Princeton University professor of education—whereas others were told the source was a nonexpert—a local high school junior "interested" in such issues. The most important manipulation was one of self-relevance. Some groups of subjects were told the exam would be implemented at their own school, which meant that they personally would be affected. Other groups were told the exams were planned for another institution, and thus they were personally less relevant. Perhaps you can guess how this manipulation of relevance influenced subjects' reactions. Those who thought the plan would not affect them processed the communication superficially. Relying on the expertise heuristic, they responded favorably to

You may recall similar findings from a study we discussed early in Chapter 1, pages 1 to 2, on the issue of parole for convicted criminals.

Figure 7.4 Effects of motivation on message processing

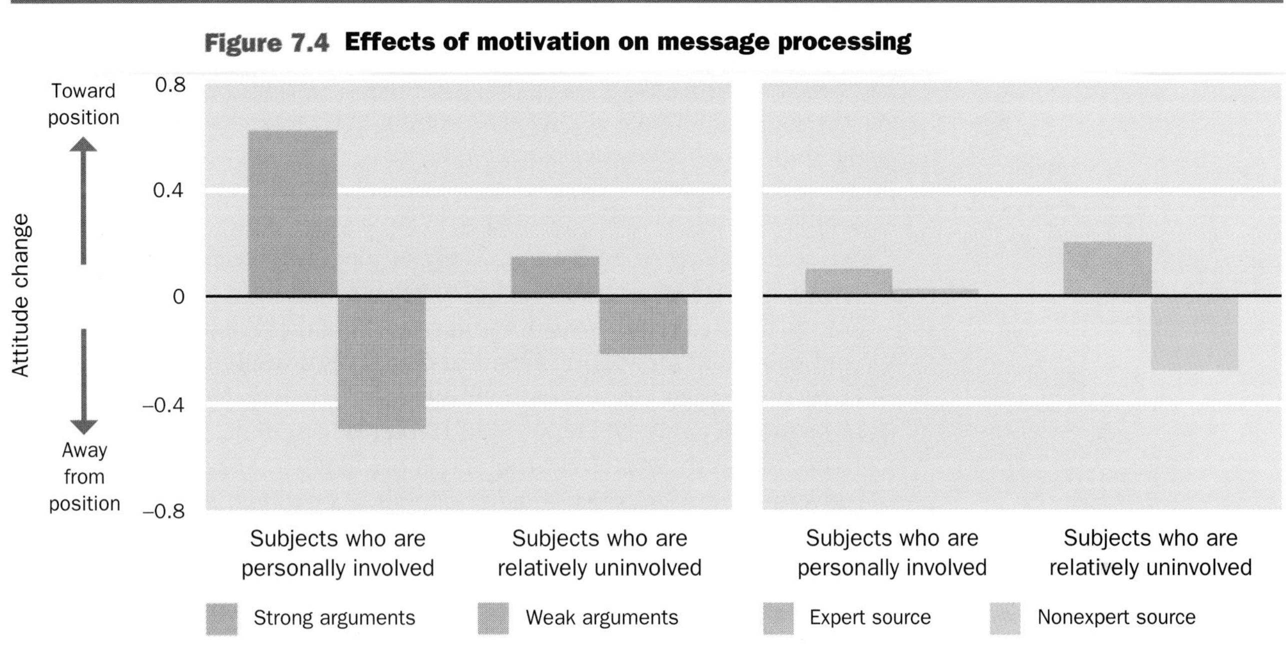

In this study, some subjects were highly involved in the issue and others were uninvolved. They heard strong or weak arguments, presented by an expert or nonexpert source. Notice that the strength of the arguments made more difference to highly involved subjects (graph on left). In contrast, the expertise of the source had more influence on the less involved subjects (graph on right). (Data from Petty and others, 1981.)

the expert communicator and unfavorably to the nonexpert, regardless of the message's content. As you can see in Figure 7.4, however, the message had quite a different impact on students who thought the exam proposal would affect them personally. These students were motivated to pay careful attention to the quality of the arguments. This systematic processing led them to accept strong and compelling arguments and to reject weak and specious ones, regardless of who espoused them.

Just as personal relevance can move people away from reliance on the expertise heuristic, it can also undermine dependence on other heuristics. The quality of a product becomes more important than the fame of the endorser when consumers think they may actually receive the product. And short but powerful messages are more convincing than long but empty ones when people are personally involved in an issue (Petty and others, 1983; Petty & Cacioppo, 1984).

Capacity Factors That Influence Systematic Processing. Even when we are highly motivated, we may encounter obstacles to systematic processing. Imagine the product manager spreading the dozen or so computer brochures out on her desk. Each describes different product lines in different ways; each computer system offers different features for different prices. Will she be able to understand and evaluate every claim? Even when people want to process systematically, they are not always able to do so.

1. *The ability to process.* Sometimes, people just do not have the mental resources to take in and evaluate all the available information. This is

particularly true when, as in the product manager's case, the information is technical, there is too much of it, or it has multiple dimensions on which alternatives differ (Janis & Rife, 1959). Even the most motivated processor of persuasive communications occasionally has difficulty understanding all the complex and rapidly presented information offered in print, radio, and television commercials.

Children are at even more of a disadvantage in this area. Young children often have enough ability to understand a message but lack the critical capacity to evaluate it. Many of them trust television to tell the truth, and they do not always know when programs stop and advertisements begin. They know the brand names and their jingles but they cannot remember the specific details of the ad. As a result, they are particularly prone to fall for the inducements served up with Saturday morning television (Palmer & Dorr, 1980; Liebert & Sprafkin, 1988). Children who frequently watch television are more likely to like, ask for, and eat advertised snacks, cereals, and fast foods. As children learn to evaluate information critically, they become less easily persuaded. And, as you will see later, parents can help develop, both in themselves and in their children, the critical thinking skills necessary to evaluate persuasive appeals.

2. *The knowledge to evaluate.* As she pores over the first of the many technical brochures, the product manager thanks her lucky stars for the extra computer know-how she picked up on the job. Without it, she might not be able to feel so confident about evaluating the manufacturers' claims. The more we know about a particular topic, the more expertly and systematically we can evaluate persuasive communications about it. Expertise makes material easier to understand and permits us to see through weak or incorrect arguments. Wendy Wood demonstrated this point in research comparing people's informed and uninformed reactions to an anticonservation appeal. She found that knowledgeable subjects were able to generate more counterarguments and consequently were less persuaded than those who knew little about environmental issues (Wood, 1982; Wood and others, 1985). Making a tough product purchasing decision is a lot easier when we have the necessary background knowledge to evaluate the sales pitches.

3. *The opportunity to concentrate.* No matter how motivated or expert we are, our ability to process systematically is diminished if we cannot concentrate. Ready and willing to understand and evaluate all the relevant material, our hapless manager is suddenly interrupted by the phone. As she hangs up, a co-worker stops by wanting to discuss a purchase order. Then her boss reminds her that the departmental meeting begins in an hour. These continual distractions, as you undoubtedly know from your own experience, will reduce her ability to process information carefully.

By reducing our critical ability, distractions can decrease the effectiveness of strongly persuasive communications because we are not able to elaborate them favorably. To make matters worse, distraction exerts the opposite effect on weak communications. It makes weak communications more persuasive because it reduces people's cognitive capacity, thereby making it difficult for them to counter flawed arguments or demolish shaky logic (Petty and others, 1976). And because of this reduced ability to process message content carefully, people rely more on various superficial strategies. Distracted subjects, for example, use the expertise heuristic: they are more impressed by a credible source than are their nondistracted counterparts (Kiesler & Mathog, 1968; Baron and others, 1973). No wonder the old advertising motto recommends "If you have nothing to say, distract them!"

Personality Differences in Responses to Persuasive Communications. Although motivation and ability to process persuasive communications often depend on the situation, individuals also differ in how willing and able they are to process systematically. One such difference seems to be how much people enjoy thinking itself. People differ, for example, in the degree to which they enjoy puzzling over difficult problems, resolving inconsistencies, and searching for the right answers. Those who enjoy such activities are said to have high *need for cognition* (Cohen, 1957; Cacioppo & Petty, 1982). This need is indicated by people's answers to items like the ones in Table 7.2.

Research has found that individuals with a high need for cognition are more likely than others to put time and effort into processing persuasive communications. In one study demonstrating this point, subjects read a strongly or weakly argued editorial. The higher their need for cognition, the more likely they were to respond favorably to strong arguments and to be unmoved by weak ones (Cacioppo and others, 1983). As you might expect, people with a low need for cognition are relatively more responsive to heuristic cues, like the expertise of a communicator (Cacioppo & Petty, 1984).

Another kind of personality difference influences the sorts of messages that people find personally relevant. For example, because high self-monitors are so conscious of how others evaluate them, they zero in on

Table 7.2 The Need for Cognition Scale: Sample items

1. I find satisfaction in deliberating hard for long hours.
2. Learning new ways to think doesn't excite me very much.
3. I like tasks that require little thought once I've learned them.
4. I would prefer complex to simple problems.
5. The notion of thinking abstractly is appealing to me.
6. More often than not, more thinking just leads to more errors.

Note: These are sample items from the Need for Cognition Scale, which assesses how much people enjoy engaging in effortful cognitive activities. People who agree with items 1, 4, and 5 and disagree with items 2, 3, and 6 would be regarded as high in need for cognition. The actual scale used in research contains many more than six items, so it can more accurately classify people as high or low in need for cognition.

Source: From "The need for cognition" by J. T. Cacioppo & R. E. Petty, 1982, *Journal of Personality and Social Psychology, 42,* pp. 116–131.

Figure 7.5 "Quality counts" versus "Image is everything": Self-monitoring and persuasion

High and low self-monitors evaluated consumer products advertised in quality-oriented or image-oriented magazine ads. High self-monitors preferred the product depicted in image-oriented ads, whereas low self-monitors favored the product featured in the quality-oriented ads. (Data from Snyder & DeBono, 1985.)

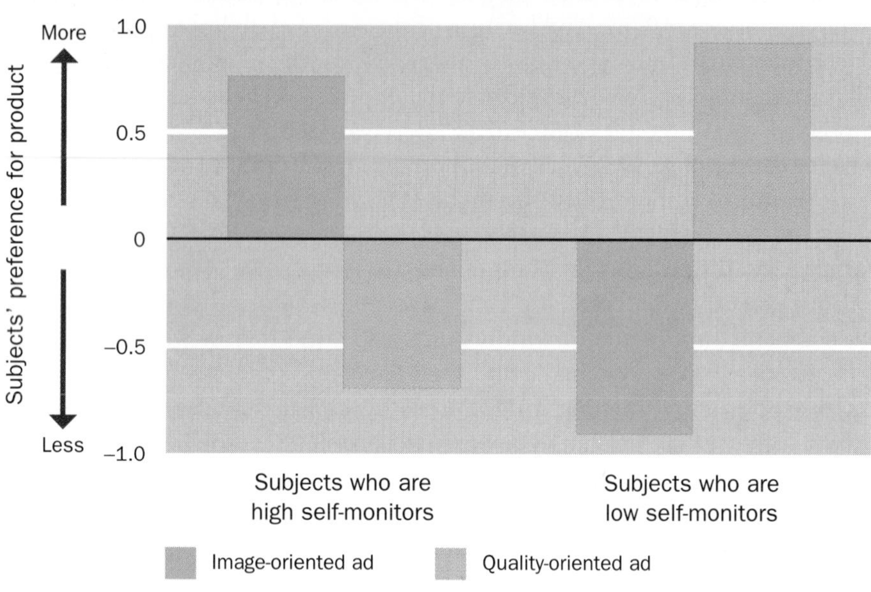

To remind yourself of other characteristics of typical high and low self-monitors, reread Chapter 4, page 146.

image-focused appeals, whereas low self-monitors care more about how they personally react to objects. Mark Snyder and Kenneth DeBono (1985) demonstrated the difference self-monitoring could make in a study that compared reactions to ads for instant coffee. The image-oriented slogan said, "Make a chilly night a cozy evening with Irish Mocha Mint." The quality-oriented ad proclaimed, "Irish Mocha Mint: A delicious blend of three great flavors—coffee, chocolate, and mint." The results of the study appear in Figure 7.5. As the researchers expected, high self-monitors preferred the coffee when it was advertised by image. They also said they would be willing to pay more for it. In contrast, low self-monitors favored the product when the ad featured quality. Both groups paid more attention to and spent much longer processing advertisements that matched their goals (DeBono, 1987; DeBono & Harnish, 1988).

In many situations, of course, differences among individuals in motivation and knowledge go hand in hand to determine how extensively a particular message will be processed and how great its impact will be. For example, when students with a legalistic bent are more persuaded by legalistic arguments than by other evidence, both the motivating force of self-relevance and the ability factor of extra background knowledge are probably at work (Cacioppo and others, 1982).

Cultural Differences in Persuasion. Like personality differences, cultural differences also influence the effectiveness of persuasive appeals. As we first pointed out in Chapter 4, independent cultures, like those found in North America, tend to emphasize individualism, whereas interdependent cultures, such as those found in Asia, are more concerned with group harmony and belongingness. It's not surprising, then, that persuaders in different cultures rely on different kinds of appeals. After examining the advertisements in popular American and Korean magazines, Sang-Pil Han and Sharon Shavitt (1993) concluded that American ads appealed more to individual benefits, personal success, and independence. These ads used slogans like "The art of being unique," or "You, only better," or "A leader among leaders." In contrast, Korean advertisements emphasized group benefits, interpersonal harmony, and family integrity. Slogans like "We have a way of bringing people together," "Sharing is beautiful," and "We devote ourselves to our contractors" were more typical in Korean ads. The cultural differences were also reflected in judgments of the persuasiveness of the advertisements, as the results of a second study demonstrated. American subjects tended to find individually oriented ads more persuasive than family- or group-oriented ads. Judgments made by Korean subjects reversed this pattern.

In summary, both motivation—which is highest when a message taps into values that are important for an individual or a culture—and capacity—which depends on knowledge and freedom from distraction—are prerequisites for systematic processing. Perhaps you can see now why most persuasive communications are processed superficially. As Figure 7.6 shows, the kind of careful message processing that produces long-term attitude change depends on both motivation and capacity.

Figure 7.6 Conditions for systematic processing

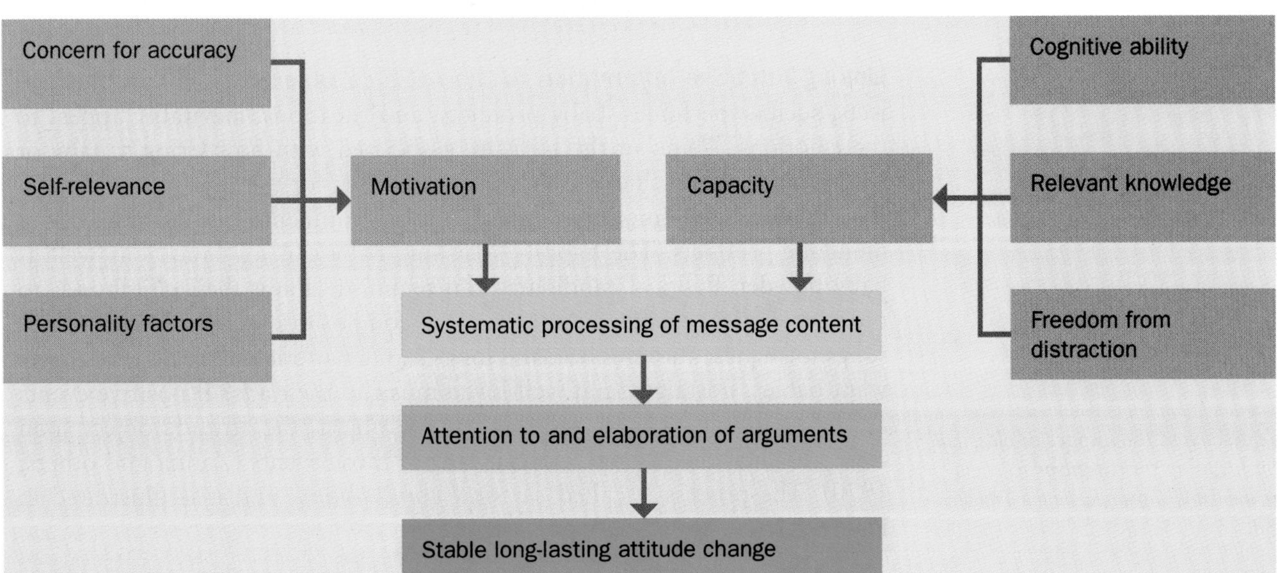

When people have both motivation and capacity, they are likely to process persuasive messages systematically by elaborating the arguments, and the result is enduring attitude change.

The Persuasive Power of Emotion: Superficial and Systematic Processing of Affective Information

"Reach out and touch someone." "Mazda: It just feels right." "It's a new day in America . . ." These advertising slogans and political catch phrases are not designed to provide facts about attitude objects. Instead they are *emotional appeals,* communications designed to produce feelings that in turn influence attitudes. Just as cognitive information can be used to change attitudes, affective information can also be used to persuade. And, just as beliefs can influence our attitudes in either a superficial or systematic way, feelings, moods, and emotions can color attitudes formed with either a little or a lot of thought.

Emotional Shortcuts: If It Feels Right, Do It

Emotional appeals often persuade through superficial processing. Emotions associated with attitude objects, or positive feelings evoked by an attractive source, pleasant music, or some other cause, may contribute to persuasion when people are not processing in depth.

Emotional reactions are often knee-jerk reactions, and professional persuaders use them to change our attitudes when our critical thinking defenses are down. An attitude object may evoke feelings of nostalgia, sentimentality, disgust, or fear. A communicator may convey boyish charm or sinister foreboding. A persuasive setting may feature inviting smells and cheerful music or glaring lights and uncomfortable temperatures. All of these tactics can influence the attitudes we form.

Linking Affective Information to the Attitude Object. Some attitude objects, such as perfumes, baby products, and vacations, inevitably appeal to the emotions. Think of the pleasure associated with powdering a baby or lying on a sun-drenched beach. No wonder ads for these products play on our emotions. But emotional appeals can also influence our attitudes about mundane products. The happily splashing baby can sell faucets as well as baby powder. Political candidates can reminisce about their childhoods to promote policy changes. And classical compositions can become theme songs for wines, automobiles, and long-lasting batteries. Why do advertisers want babies, nostalgia, and well-loved music in their ads? If positive events are repeatedly associated with an attitude object, the attitude object soon comes to elicit the feelings associated with those events (Zanna and others, 1970). The process is called *classical conditioning,* and it is illustrated in Figure 7.7.

We discussed the impact of classical conditioning on reactions to social groups in Chapter 5, pages 187 to 188.

Figure 7.7 Classical conditioning and attitude formation

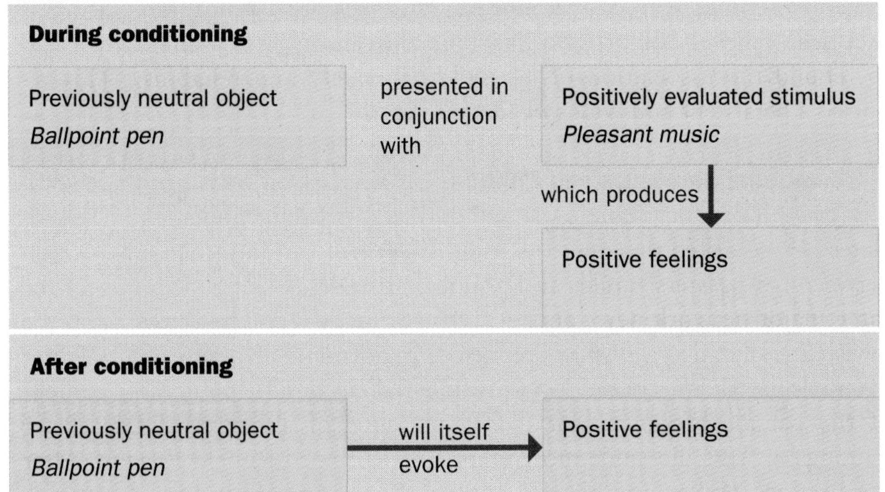

Suppose that people encounter a neutral object in conjunction with a stimulus that they evaluate positively or negatively. After this happens a few times, the feelings produced by the stimulus become associated with the object, resulting in the formation of an attitude.

Emotional Shortcuts in Marketing. Classical conditioning is the backbone of the "soft sell": "It sets off the product as something pretty wonderful by draping around it as many . . . pleasant associations as possible" (Martineau, 1957, pp. 13–14). Perhaps classical conditioning explains the popularity of the business lunch and the fund-raising dinner; associating a sales pitch or an appeal for a donation with good food may well increase its persuasiveness. One early experiment supports this idea. Students who snacked on peanuts and soft drinks expressed more agreement with controversial issues than did those who were not given the snacks (Janis and others, 1965).

Music may have the same effect. Popular songs evoke a special set of emotions and memories, and associating an attitude object with them capitalizes on classical conditioning to boost evaluations (Galizio & Hendrick, 1972). In one study that gauged the effect of popular music on product attitudes, students in a management class watched what they believed to be an ad agency's pilot version of an advertisement for a ballpoint pen (Gorn, 1982). The ad offered minimal information about the pen, but it was accompanied in one condition by popular rock-and-roll music and in the other by classical Indian music, which pretesting showed the students disliked. When subjects were later allowed to choose a pen as a reward for their participation in the study, they were much more likely to choose the pen that had been accompanied by the popular rock-and-roll music. Encouraging customers to rely on their emotional reactions rather than thinking carefully about the product can boost evaluations—and sales.

Of course, classical conditioning works the same way when negative events are associated with an attitude object. When several people died after someone tampered with bottles of Tylenol, the painkiller became associated in people's minds with danger and death. To restore Tylenol's reputation as "the pain reliever doctors and hospitals trust most," its manufacturers had to rebuild the association of Tylenol with safety and reliability. This required a persistent and widespread campaign.

Emotional Shortcuts and Politics. If association with a positive stimulus can sell products, can it also sell politicians? Brian Mullen and his associates (1986) asked this question after discovering an intriguing connection between newscasters' smiles and political attitudes. Using videotapes of the three major network news anchors, the researchers counted how often the newscasters smiled as they reported on Ronald Reagan and Walter Mondale, candidates in the 1984 presidential election. Although the content of the commentary was not biased in favor of either candidate, Peter Jennings of ABC did smile more when he mentioned Ronald Reagan. After the election, Mullen and his colleagues polled voters around the country to find out what news program they watched and how they voted. The results showed that the percentage of ABC viewers who had voted for Reagan was higher than that of CBS or NBC viewers. Could Jennings's smile actually have helped Reagan win? Because the study had a nonexperimental design, it was impossible to pinpoint the direction of the influence. Watching Jennings might have increased support for Reagan, but it was also possible that Reagan supporters watched Jennings because they noticed he liked their candidate.

To try to determine the direction of the influence, Carolyn Copper (1991) performed an experimental study in which subjects were randomly assigned to watch one of three versions of a simulated news broadcast. Each program included the same special report on the views of hypothetical Democratic and Republican congressional candidates, but the timing of the newscaster's smiles was varied. Smiles occurred when the announcer mentioned either the Republican candidate or the Democratic candidate or neither candidate. Subjects—self-identified as Republicans or Democrats—watched one version of the newscast and then rated the newscaster and both candidates. Regardless of the newscaster's facial expression, subjects preferred candidates from their own party. But the newscaster's smile did make a difference. First, it affected subjects' evaluations of the newscaster himself. Subjects liked him more if he smiled while mentioning their candidate, suggesting that partisan Reagan supporters might well have watched Jennings because he seemed to like their candidate. Second, smiling had a small effect on degree of preference for a candidate. Subjects liked the opposition candidate more and their own candidate less if the newscaster smiled while reporting on the opposition candidate.

The Attractiveness Heuristic: Agreeing with Those We Like. If a pleasant smile can be persuasive, imagine the power of an attractive face or a winning personality. Advertisements often pair an attitude object with a popular and attractive figure, betting that someone who turns our heads can also change our minds. These communicators make no claim to expertise; so why are they persuasive? Dale Carnegie, author of *How to Win Friends and Influence People,* knew the answer. Attractive people are likable people, and we often agree with people we like (Benson and others, 1976; Chaiken, 1987; Insko, 1981) and believe that people we like are right (Byrne, 1971). No wonder that Roger Ailes, adviser to both the Reagan and Bush presidential campaigns, calls likability a persuasive "magic bullet." "If you could master one element of personal communication that is more powerful than anything . . . it is the quality of being likable. . . . If your audience likes you, they'll forgive just about everything else." (1988, p. 81).

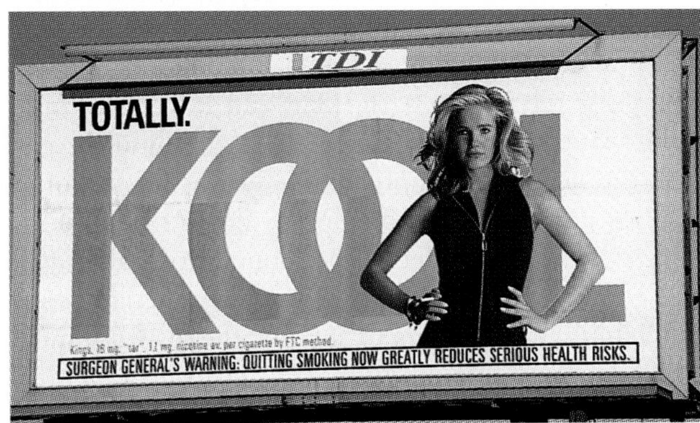

The attractiveness heuristic Perhaps cigarette advertisers hope that the persuasive power of attractive sources like this one will forestall careful processing of the Surgeon General's warning!

This isn't the only advantage that attractive people have over the rest of the population. See Chapter 3, page 70, and Chapter 11, pages 450 to 452.

Research demonstrates that attractive people do get their way more easily. One study, for example, showed that attractive people are more persuasive than those who are less attractive (Chaiken, 1979). The researcher arranged for male and female college students to solicit signatures for a petition asking the university to stop serving meat at breakfast and lunch. Attractive communicators obtained signatures from 41 percent of the students they approached, compared with a 32 percent success rate for those who were less attractive. So attractiveness serves as a persuasion cue: if Joe Montana likes Isotoner gloves, or Paula Abdul drinks Diet Coke, consumers will want to buy those products—at least that is the hope of the advertiser.

When advertisers use attractive communicators, they usually make them the most prominent feature of the appeal. Does the focus on a communicator's attractiveness increase our reliance on the attractiveness heuristic? Apparently so. Suzanne Pallak (1983) showed two groups of women the same article, which urged donations in support of the arts. One group also saw a vivid color photo of an attractive man who had supposedly written the article. Other students saw only a blurred photocopy of the man's photograph. Although the arguments were exactly the same, subjects for whom the communicator's attractiveness was made salient were much more persuaded than were subjects for whom the man's appearance was not so obvious.

Feelings as Heuristic Cues: If I Feel Good, I Must Like It. The business lunch and an attractive source have a lot in common. Not only do we like them (and thus whatever is associated with them), but they also make *us* feel good. And when people evaluate a persuasive appeal superficially, they often get their own feelings mixed up with the attitude object itself. That is, they like whatever they evaluate when they are feeling good and dislike whatever they evaluate when they are feeling bad.

Norbert Schwarz and Jerry Clore (1983, 1988) have explained such findings by suggesting that when people are processing superficially, they rely on the "How do I feel about it?" heuristic. When the attitude object actually elicits the feelings—for example, when being with a date makes you feel good or sky-diving makes you feel sick—the use of this shortcut makes sense. Sometimes, however, our feelings exist quite independently of a persuasive appeal or an attitude object. We just feel good—perhaps because the sun is shining, the memories are sweet, the music is upbeat, or we just received a compliment. Or we feel bad—maybe a friend is ill or we failed a test. Under these circumstances, relying on a shortcut can lead us astray. Consider, for example, this cautionary tale. Researchers in Illinois conducted a telephone poll on the need for comprehensive exams for seniors, calling some students on sunny days and some on gloomy days (Sinclair and others, 1991). Regardless of whether the caller offered sound or weak arguments for the proposal, the good weather group, who were assumed to be in a good mood, were more likely than the others to support the institution of exams.

So it is clear that the "How do I feel about it?" cue can be very powerful when people are engaged in superficial thinking. Students evaluate their lives more positively when interviewed on sunny upbeat days than they do on rainy downbeat days. Uninterested listeners are more accepting of persuasive messages when they are happy than when they are not happy. And pleasant music influences consumers' product preferences when choice has no real consequence. But all these effects disappear when subjects engage in thoughtful consideration of issues and objects (Petty and others, 1993; Gorn, 1982; Schwarz & Clore, 1983). Like other heuristics, the "How do I feel about it?" heuristic loses much of its power when we think carefully about the situation.

Positive Affect and Systematic Processing

> *Positive feelings can interfere with people's motivation and their ability to process persuasive messages systematically. This in turn lowers the effectiveness of strong arguments and increases the persuasiveness of weak arguments.*

An Alabama company recently published a brochure describing its line of school rings. The brochure suggested ways that children could persuade their parents to buy them a ring—including waiting until the parents were in a good mood before making their pitch ("Flier on school jewelry," 1993). Is this sound advice about persuasion? If you are like nine out of every ten students in our classes, you'll answer that question with a yes. Popular belief and professional practices based on them suggest that a person in a good mood is particularly easy to persuade. But research does not always support this belief.

Feeling Good but Not Always Thinking Straight. The evidence linking good mood and persuasiveness is quite mixed. We have already seen that when people base their evaluations on emotions, positive feelings will produce positive attitudes. And if thinking about arguments while in a good mood makes you evaluate them favorably, a good mood could increase persuasion (Petty and others, 1993). Other studies indicate, however, that a positive mood makes persuasion *less* likely to occur. What explains these differences?

Part of the answer is that people in a good mood are less likely than others to process the contents of persuasive appeals systematically. This in turn makes the use of other heuristic cues more likely. Consider what happened, for example, when some students unexpectedly won a dollar in a lottery—a pleasant event that raised their spirits—while others simply answered questions about lotteries (Worth & Mackie, 1987). All subjects then read and evaluated a speech about acid rain supposedly delivered by a delegate to an environmental conference. Whereas subjects in a neutral mood accepted strong arguments and rejected weak ones, happy subjects were equally impressed by weak and strong arguments. They also fell prey to the expertise heuristic, agreeing with a message delivered by a prestigious source and ignoring an appeal from a disreputable communicator.

This finding demonstrates the relationship between positive mood and persuasion. Since being in a good mood often decreases careful systematic processing, a happy person is more likely to succumb to an expert or attractive source, a long or "scientific looking" message, or other heuristic cues. Someone in a good mood is also less likely to see through weak arguments and to counter flawed assumptions. Even the mood itself can act as a cue, so happiness can deliver a doubly persuasive whammy. At the same time, rational arguments may have little impact on the happy person. Thus if you want to persuade your parents that you need a school ring, tailor your arguments to their mood. If your arguments are weak, pick a day when their spirits are high. But if you have compelling arguments to offer, wait until they are in a neutral mood when you can count on their careful attention.

Motivational and Capacity Consequences of Positive Mood. What is it about feeling good that leads to superficial processing? The answer has to do with the impact of mood states on motivation and cognitive capacity. When people feel good, they may not want anything to interfere with their good spirits—not even the effort of careful thought (Isen & Levin, 1972; Mischel and others, 1973). Or they may see no need to process carefully: their good mood tells them that everything they are doing is working just fine. They may feel so confident that their off-hand conclusions seem perfectly adequate (Johnson & Tversky, 1983; Schwarz and others, 1991; Martin and others, 1993).

When people feel good they also find it hard to concentrate. Think about the last time something wonderful happened to you. Did you turn it over and over in your mind? Some research suggests that a good mood might reduce systematic processing because people's minds are full of other thoughts. In demonstrating this point, researchers have given happy subjects extra time to process arguments (Mackie & Worth, 1989) and have helped them focus on key aspects of the message (Bless and others, 1990). Both of these strategies made it easier for happy people to evaluate persuasive communications. The reason is that the subjects' processing task is simplified when the information can be dealt with more slowly and the important points are highlighted.

Negative Emotions and Persuasion: Make Me Worry, Make Me Agree

> *Using negative emotions like fear to bring about persuasion can be complex. In the right dosage, fear and anxiety can motivate people to process, but an excess of these emotions can drain cognitive capacity and motivation, undermining systematic processing.*

"I hate milk! If you make me drink it, I'll hate you too!" Aha! One of our young nephews had realized the power of association, and he was using the insight to enhance his persuasive best. But when it came to using negative emotions to persuade, the psychologist had the upper hand. Knowing that fear is one of the most potent persuasion weapons around, she did what many frustrated child minders had done before. She told him that if people do not drink their milk, their bones will become weak and breakable—so they won't be able to play sports. It's amazing how hearing about such misfortunes can change a young boy's attitude about milk.

Fear Appeals in Advertising. Fear is by far the most common negative emotion that aunts, uncles, and other influence agents exploit. When advertisements remind us that body odor, bad breath, or dandruff could make us social pariahs, they are playing on our fears. When politicians tell us that their opponent is soft on crime or in the pocket of special-interest groups, they are using "fear and smear" scaremongering to garner votes. Many public health campaigns also use scare tactics in the hope of reducing dangerous behaviors like sunbathing and drinking before driving. One of the most extensive public health campaigns in recent years was launched in California in 1987. Using the proceeds from increased cigarette taxes, the state initiated an aggressive antismoking media campaign, including ads like the following. In the first scene a beautiful baby boy, held by a joyous parent, is introduced: "Ronald Marion Guest, III; 8 pounds, 10 ounces." A second baby is just as bouncingly beautiful: "Brittany Lauren Whitlow; 8 pounds, 2 ounces." A third grins contentedly at her obviously proud father: "Christina Ingram; 8 pounds, 6 ounces." A fourth baby lies screaming in an incubator, crisscrossed by tubes and bandages: "Michael David Eliot; 2 pounds, 2 ounces, and two packs a day." The ad closes with a simple message: "If you're pregnant, don't smoke."

The California campaign certainly seems to have worked. Since the ads were introduced, the percentage of adults who smoke has dropped 17 percent in California, compared with 8 percent in the rest of the United States (Cowley, 1991). Of course, not all the programs initiated by the state used scare tactics to bring home the reality of lung disease, birth defects, and cancer. And the extent to which the scare tactics produced the drop in smoking is uncertain. But the question remains: Can people be frightened into accepting a persuasive message? To answer this question, researchers have compared reactions to messages that invoke different degrees of anxiety. In one of the earliest studies of the effects of fear, the idea that people could be scared into agreement did not fare well (Janis & Feshbach, 1953). In that study, one group of students received graphic personalized warnings of the dangers posed by lack of dental hygiene. For example, tooth decay was said to lead to "secondary infections and diseases such as arthritic paralysis, kidney damage, or total blindness." This message provoked intense fear but little change in attitudes. In fact, it was less effective than the mildly fear-inducing appeal seen by other students. Did this mean that fear was an ineffective persuasion weapon?

Anxiety and Systematic Processing. In explaining the results of this study, Carl Hovland and his colleagues (1953) focused on the amount of fear that a persuasive message elicits. Foreshadowing what social psychologists now know to be true, they argued that the level of fear influences motivation and ability to process a message, and this in turn influences attitude change.

What *does* it take to stop drunk driving? Persuasive communications that provoke anxiety and fear—that show, for example, the appalling consequences of drunk driving—are often very effective. Research suggests, however, that this message would have been even more persuasive if it made clear how such negative outcomes could be avoided: don't drink and drive!

1. *The anxiety-motivation connection.* Hovland and his colleagues believed that a negative emotional appeal is persuasive only when the threat arouses enough—but not too much—fear. If a message does not arouse any anxiety, it can be ignored as irrelevant. If there is just the right amount of anxiety, people will pay attention in the hope that the anxiety-provoking event can be eliminated. For a fear appeal to be motivating, the audience must also be convinced that the threatened negative consequences will happen, and will happen to them (Leventhal, 1970; Rogers & Mewborn, 1976). To illustrate this point, Dawn Wilson and her colleagues (1987, 1988) arranged for doctors to send their patients mild or relatively frightening letters encouraging them to quit smoking. Of the patients receiving mild letters pointing out the benefits of quitting, only 8 percent tried to stop. Of patients receiving letters that pointed out that if they kept smoking *they* would die, 30 percent tried to quit. Efforts to promote seat-belt usage tell the same story. Appeals that show the mangled bodies of unprotected accident victims and send the message that "this could happen to *you*" are much more effective than less graphic messages (Rogers & Mewborn, 1976; Rogers and others, 1978).

Messages provoking too much fear, however, will turn off audiences. If people feel overwhelmed or unable to escape, they may respond with avoidance by belittling, denying, contradicting, or ignoring the threatening information (Janis & Terwilliger, 1962). This kind of reaction is called *defensive avoidance.* To overcome defensive avoidance a message must contain clear information on how to avoid the danger. Thus, the most effective fear-inducing messages are those that incorporate reassuring instructions on how to eliminate the anxiety (Hovland and others, 1953; Robberson & Rogers, 1988; Rogers, 1983). One study, for example, looked at responses to fear-inducing messages about preventing tetanus. The messages varied—some aroused high fear, some moderate fear, and others no fear at all. In addition, some contained specific instructions about where to get an inoculation and others did not (Leventhal and others, 1965). The high-fear messages inspired more positive attitudes toward getting shots than did the low-fear or no-fear messages. But attitudes aside, only some of the messages led to real action. People who received messages that both aroused fear and included specific information about how to obtain a shot were more likely than other subjects to respond by getting a tetanus inoculation.

2. *The anxiety-ability connection.* As their fear increases in intensity, people find it harder and harder to concentrate on message content and to evaluate it. In fact, high levels of stress impair performance on complex cognitive tasks like systematic processing (Darke, 1988). Christopher Jepson and Shelly Chaiken (1990), for example, found that how carefully a message is processed depends on how much the target fears its contents. Their subjects were college students who varied in their level of fear of cancer. The message, which advocated regular cancer check-ups, contained a number of reasoning errors. Very fearful subjects showed several signs of superficial processing. They detected fewer errors, recalled less of the message, and

responded with fewer elaborations of message content than did subjects with little fear. These responses occurred even though there was no sign that subjects were *avoiding* the message. In contrast, relatively unfearful readers processed the message carefully.

The bottom line? Fear works, but only in the right dosage and in the right combination. Fear has to be motivating without being debilitating. It works only if the threatened outcome is believable, and if the recommended change is both attainable and certain to bring relief. It takes just the right mixture to get people to increase seat-belt use, decrease smoking, get cancer check-ups, and drink that milk. In fact, both positive and negative emotions can increase or interfere with persuasion, under different circumstances, as Figure 7.8 shows.

Figure 7.8 Emotions can increase persuasion or interfere with it

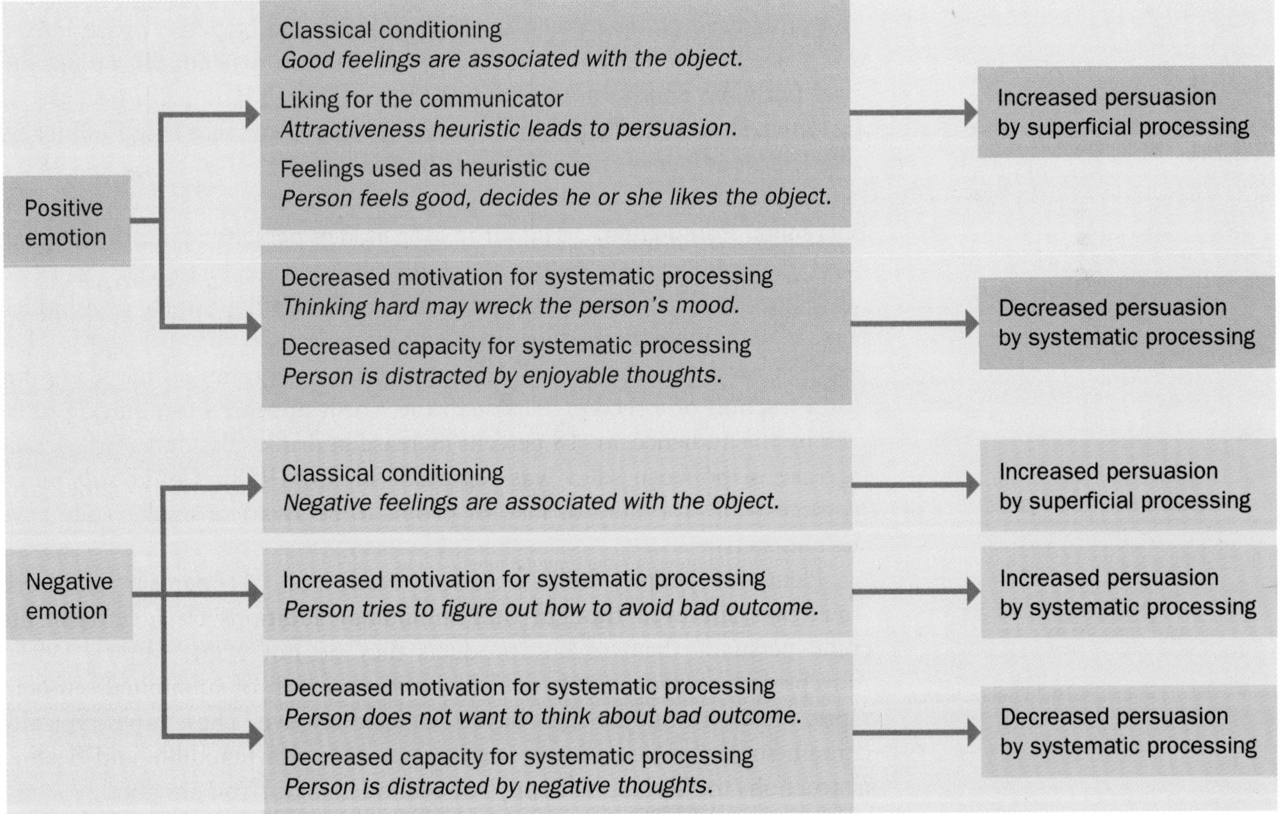

Both positive and negative emotions can set many different processes in motion. Depending on the particular circumstances and whether the person is processing superficially or systematically, the result may be increased or decreased persuasion.

Defending Attitudes: Resisting Persuasion

In the summer of 1990, the rock band Judas Priest went on trial, accused of embedding the hidden message "Do it" in the sound track of one of their songs. At issue was whether this alleged planted message could have contributed to the suicide deaths of two young men, both big fans of the band's music. Eventually, the group and its music company were cleared of any wrongdoing, but the trial itself and the issues it dealt with raised some of the public's worst fears about persuasion. Are we completely at the mercy of the mysterious forces of persuasion? Can we be persuaded without even knowing it?

Fighting Back: Awareness Is Half the Battle

People often seek to resist persuasion, and one of their best weapons is awareness. Though stimuli that are not consciously perceived can influence attitudes in laboratory settings, there are several reasons why they might have less influence on our everyday behavior.

You cannot fight a tiger you cannot see, says the old Nepalese proverb. And it is true that we cannot directly fight persuasion attempts if we are not aware of them and do not know what we are fighting. But just because we are often open to potential influences does not mean that those influences will determine our attitudes or our behavior.

Subliminal Persuasion. The furor over hidden persuasive messages began more than thirty years before the Judas Priest trial. In the fall of 1957, moviegoers in Fort Lee, New Jersey, became unwitting targets of a hidden persuasion campaign. As they sat watching a feature film, the words "Eat popcorn" and "Drink Coca Cola" appeared several times on the screen for just a fraction of a second. Although the words appeared too quickly to be seen by the audience, an 18 percent increase in drink sales and a 50 percent increase in popcorn sales was reported (Brean, 1958). Could *subliminal messages,* ones too faint or fast for people to be aware of them, really have such impact?

Plenty of people think so. In a recent poll, 61 percent of North Americans surveyed thought that subliminal additions to advertisements could persuade them to buy products they do not want (Muller, 1991). Entrepreneurs have recently sold $50 million worth of subliminal self-help tapes, mostly to middle-class buyers under forty-five. These tapes typically contain soothing New Age music interspersed with inaudible and fleeting instructions to "Relax, be happy" or reminders like "You are good, you are capable, you are calm." Inmates at Utah's South Point Prison reportedly listen to subliminal tapes designed to quell criminal impulses. Members of the Texas Rangers' pitching staff use custom-made cassettes to increase their

B.C. by johnny hart

By permission of Johnny Hart and Creators Syndicate, Inc.

on-the-mound confidence. Security personnel are also apparently convinced of the technique's effectiveness: the canned music piped into department stores in your area may well contain such subaudible messages as "I am honest. I will not steal" (Natale, 1988).

Research indicates that our evaluations can be influenced by stimuli that do not make it into our conscious awareness (Uleman & Bargh, 1989). Repeated exposure to a stimulus, for example, tends to increase people's liking for it. This **mere exposure effect** (Zajonc, 1968) occurs even if people are unaware of whether or how often they have seen the stimulus before. This point has been demonstrated in studies that ask subjects to identify stimuli that have been presented subliminally to them previously. Although they are unable to identify the stimuli, they nevertheless prefer those they have seen more often (Bornstein and others, 1987; Kunst-Wilson & Zajonc, 1980). As we saw in Chapter 3, subliminal presentation of different trait words can influence the way people interpret and evaluate ambiguous behavior; it can also influence the evaluation of attitude objects (Herr and others, 1983).

Even if we are unaware of the source of influence, evaluations changed by subliminal influence might translate into behavior, as they apparently did in one study. Researchers arranged for subjects to participate with two experimental confederates in making what was supposed to be a series of group decisions. The confederates had been instructed to disagree on most of the judgments, leaving the real subject in the uncomfortable position of casting the tie-breaking vote by siding with one of the two confederates. Subjects in a control condition agreed with each confederate about half the time. But a different pattern emerged among subjects in the experimental condition. They formed coalitions with one confederate much more often than with the other. The reason is that these subjects had been subliminally exposed to photographs of one of the confederates during a slide show prior to the discussion. Although they were not aware of their exposure to the photos, the subjects were more likely to side with this "familiar" face during the discussions (Bornstein and others, 1987).

mere exposure effect People's tendency to evaluate objects they have seen before more positively than they evaluate comparable novel objects.

How Subliminal Influence Can Be Resisted. Although some evidence suggests that we may be vulnerable to subliminal manipulation of our attitudes, the research itself raises questions about this possibility. First, in laboratory studies of subliminal effects, researchers require subjects to focus closely on the region in which subliminal stimuli are presented. In the normal confusion of everyday environments, such narrow focusing is unlikely, and so the messages probably would not receive even minimal processing.

Second, subliminal effects are obtained with a limited range of stimuli. Humans are more likely to encode pictures, especially faces, with little attention than to similarly encode words. So although pictures of buckets of popcorn and cups of soda might be effective stimuli, it is much less likely that the words "Eat popcorn" would have any impact. Some researchers have suggested, in fact, that the results of the original study could not be replicated, and they have serious doubts about the original findings (Weir, 1984). Research on the way we process sounds offers additional evidence that we are not so vulnerable. Because sounds that are heard simultaneously blend together, it is highly unlikely that humans are capable of decoding verbal subliminal messages.

This point is supported by carefully controlled studies of the effectiveness of self-help tapes. For example, one comparison of different subliminal tapes showed that their effect depended not on their content but on what subjects expected to hear (Greenwald and others, 1991). In this study, subjects listened every day for five weeks to a tape with a subliminal message designed either to improve memory or to boost self-esteem. The researchers introduced an interesting twist, however, when they reversed the labels on half of the tapes. This meant that half the subjects listening to a self-esteem tape thought they were improving memory and half the subjects listening to a memory tape thought they were improving self-esteem. Objective measures were taken at the end of the five week period. Although all subjects' memory scores had improved slightly, the content of the subliminal tapes made no difference in memory, as shown in Figure 7.9, or self-esteem. But subjects' self-ratings did not reflect these findings. Subjects thought their memory or self-esteem had improved if they had listened to an appropriately labeled tape—even though in half the cases, the label was wrong.

Expectancies obviously have powerful influences on social behavior, as we have already seen in earlier chapters. But subliminal tapes have no persuasive power to brainwash listeners without their knowing it. And if sounds presented just below the threshold of awareness are ineffective, it is certainly not possible that messages recorded backwards or at high speed can influence attitudes or behavior (Merikle, 1988). Since such stimuli would be impossible to interpret even if they were presented above the threshold of conscious awareness, how could they possibly be effective when presented subliminally?

There is a third line of evidence against the power of subliminal stimuli to determine our attitudes and behavior, and it is perhaps the most important of all. Even if subliminal stimuli have a potential impact on our atti-

Figure 7.9 Subliminal self-help: Fact or fantasy?

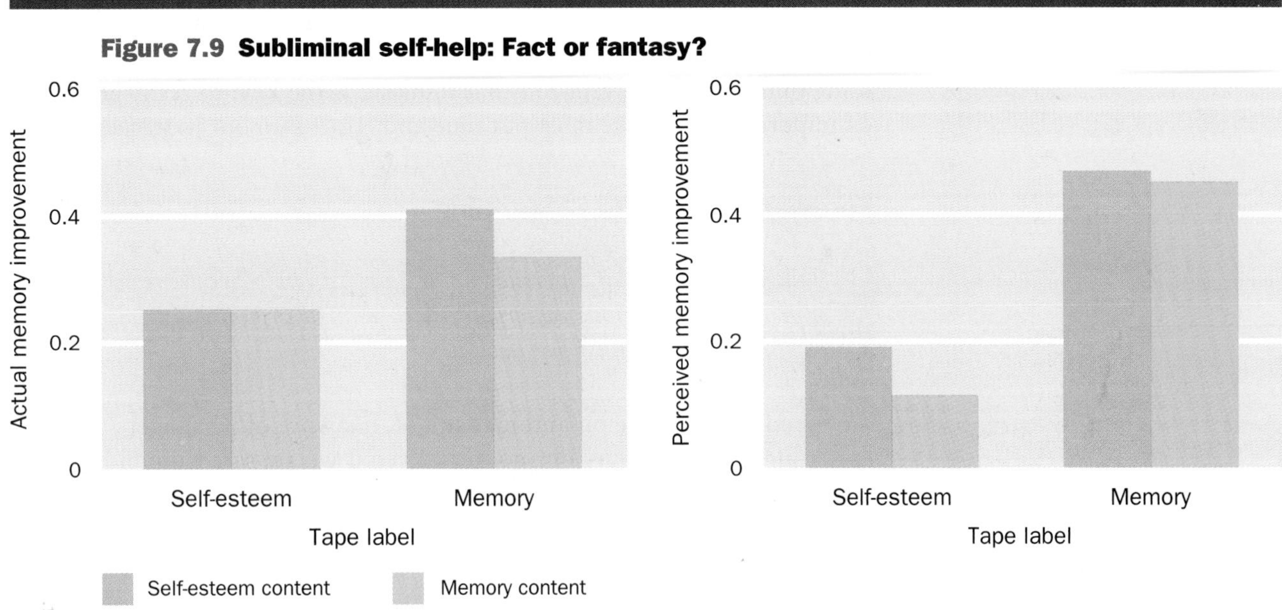

In this study subjects listened for five weeks to self-help tapes that were sold to improve either self-esteem or memory. Labels on half the tapes were switched so that half the people who were actually listening to a memory tape thought they were listening to a self-esteem tape, and vice versa. The results showed that actual memory scores (left-hand graph) and subjects' ratings of their memory abilities (right-hand graph) both improved when subjects *thought* they were listening to memory improvement tapes, regardless of the content of the tapes. (Data from Greenwald and others, 1991)

tudes, this potential is quickly nipped in the bud when conscious processing takes place (Bargh, 1989; Murphy & Zajonc, 1993). What we *know* to be true erases any "vague feeling" we might have. Although we might be influenced by information outside of awareness, its influence is diminished as soon as we know what we saw or heard (Martin, 1986; Martin and others, 1990). Consider the mere exposure effect, for example. When we are unaware of our exposure, the more we see something, the more we like it. But when we are conscious of the fact that we are seeing the same stimulus over and over again, no increase in liking is found (Bornstein and others, 1990).

The fact that conscious processing dominates subliminal influences means that what we *want* to do is much more powerful than any "hidden urges" we might experience. Consider what happened when subjects who were generally high or low in competitiveness were exposed to words related to competitiveness (*mean, hostile,* and *cutthroat,* for example) or to neutral words, without their awareness of it (Neuberg, 1989a). Playing a game later, the competitive subjects exposed to the competitive words acted more aggressively than did competitive subjects exposed to the neutral words. But the more important finding was that noncompetitive subjects were uninfluenced by mere exposure to the aggressive words.

Such results show that conscious processing typically overrides the impact of subliminal events. That in turn means that it is unlikely that subliminal influence can make us do anything we do not want to do, as long as some thinking is involved. But that thinking is the key: to resist persuasion on important issues, we must put time and effort into our judgments.

Forewarning Means Forearming

Being forewarned of a persuasion attempt can help people resist persuasion. Having previous experience with related arguments is also a successful defense against persuasion.

We spend a lot of time on automatic pilot, unaware of persuaders' attempts to fill our heads or empty our pockets. Even if we are safe from hidden messages, can we resist this constant bombardment of out-in-the-open appeals—most of which are irrelevant to our goals and needs? Considered thought is once again our best defense. When people expect to be the target of persuasion, they marshal arguments to mount a good defense (Kiesler & Kiesler, 1964; Petty & Cacioppo, 1977, 1979). For example, Hiromi Fukada (1986) exposed two groups of subjects to a persuasive message. One group had been warned that a persuasive attempt would take place; the other group did not receive the warning. A comparison of the two groups' reactions to the message showed that those who were warned were able to counter the persuasive claims with arguments of their own and, not surprisingly, were less persuaded than the other group. Other studies also indicate that the more time people have to prepare a defense of their views, the more successfully they resist persuasion (Freedman & Sears, 1965).

Inoculation: Practice Can Be the Best Medicine. Do we have to wait for a warning, or can we protect ourselves in advance against persuasive arguments? William McGuire (1964) has suggested that the most effective way to resist persuasion is to rehearse counterarguments. He draws an analogy to medical inoculations that stimulate the body's defenses by exposing the person to weak doses of an infection. According to McGuire, immunity to arguments can be obtained in the same way. The strategy seems to work, as was demonstrated when a team of researchers tackled the difficult issue of preventing smoking among young teenagers. Knowing that peer pressure often initiates first-time smoking, these researchers had older students "inoculate" younger ones against typical peer-pressure tactics (McAlister and others, 1980). In a series of sessions in the seventh and again in the eighth grade, the younger students learned to resist pressures to smoke with such counterarguments as "I'd be a real chicken if I smoked just to impress you." When the research team followed the students' progress over the next few years, they found that the inoculated students were much less likely to begin smoking than were a similar group of seventh graders who had received no

Figure 7.10 Inoculating teenagers against smoking

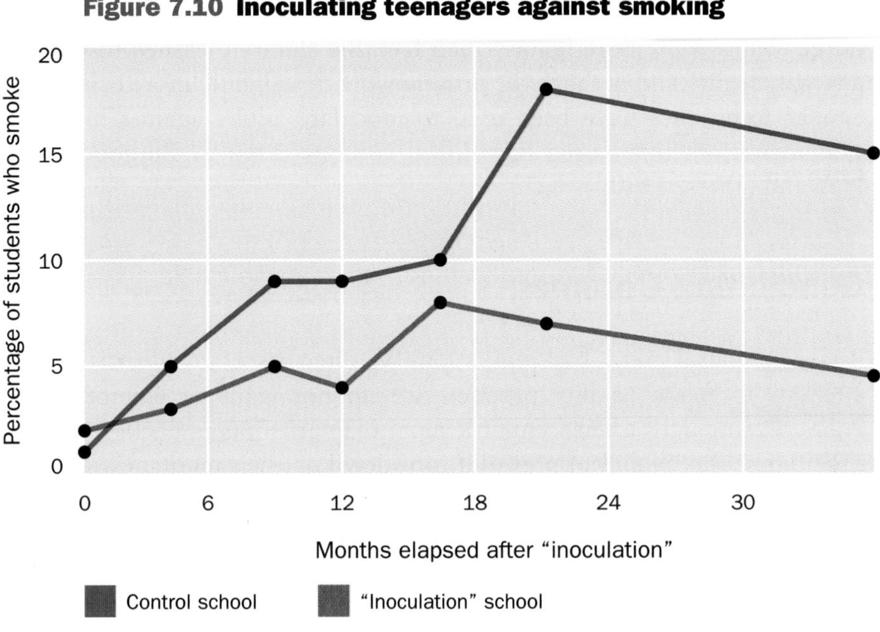

In this study, seventh- and eighth-graders were "inoculated" by older students who gave them practice in resisting prosmoking arguments that peers might use. Compared with students in another school who did not receive this treatment, the inoculated students were much less likely to smoke by the ninth grade. (Data from McAlister and others, 1980; Telch and others, 1981.)

training in resistance, as can be seen in Figure 7.10. Other research has confirmed that inoculation techniques are quite effective in reducing teenage smoking (Flay and others, 1985; Hirschman & Leventhal, 1989).

Inoculation and Advertising Effectiveness. Messages that give us practice in warding off opposing opinions have an added advantage: they strengthen our existing views (Kiesler, 1971; Batson, 1975). Advertisers are well aware of the effectiveness of this strategy. Refuting the claims of the competition and demonstrating one's own superiority is common advertising practice (Belch, 1981; Wilke & Farris, 1975). In an ad for laundry bleach, Vivid is compared to Clorox, and the advertiser performs a demonstration meant to show that Vivid gets whites even whiter. "Inoculation" ads are also more effective in overcoming people's objections to various safety-promoting behaviors. For example, although driver's-side airbags that inflate on impact reduce automobile injuries, campaigns to promote them are often stymied by people's fears of potential malfunctions or of unintended injuries caused by the bags' sudden inflation. Ads that allay people's fears about such dangers will be much more successful than ads that merely tout the devices' advantages (Szybillo & Heslin, 1973).

Can inoculation help four- to eight-year-old couch potatoes resist the advertisements on Saturday morning television? Norma Feshbach (1980) thought so. Feshbach gave small groups of elementary-school children in Los Angeles lessons on how to deal with the claims made in the barrage of

Saturday morning commercials. They listened to the claims and then discussed them. They played with the toys and found that they often could not make them do what the ads said they could. When they realized that some of the claims were more fantasy than fact, the children learned to view the advertisements (and perhaps the programs) with a slightly more cynical eye. Similar techniques have been used to inoculate adults against the smear campaigns sometimes used in political contests (Pfau & Burgoon, 1988; Pfau and others, 1990).

Concluding Comments

Persuasion has a pretty bad reputation. We often associate advertising with attempts to make us buy products we do not want or cannot afford. Political campaigns often seem little more than attempts to package and sell candidates who might not prevail if considered on their merits. Classic literature like George Orwell's *1984* warns us that by controlling information and playing on feelings, totalitarian governments may even persuade their citizens that the history they remember never really happened. Nowhere is concern about persuasion more obvious than in the public's fear that subliminal stimuli might influence us against our will.

Realizing that persuaders do not always have our best interests at heart is healthy: it pays to remember we can be misled. And it helps if we know what we are up against. The citizens of ancient Greece and Rome were schooled in the art—and artifice—of argumentation. But most of today's citizens, unless they take classes in social psychology or communication, are taught little about the different ways in which attitude change can come about. Perhaps the most important lesson to be learned from the research discussed in this chapter is that influence does not have to be something that others do to us: whether we are persuaded or not lies largely in our own hands, or at least in our own heads.

When we do not care or cannot cope with persuasive messages, we may well be influenced by emotional appeals, celebrity endorsements, and the use of complicated statistics. Of course, such simple cues and rules work pretty well most of the time. But sometimes circumstances demand careful evaluation of the communication. When we are motivated by concerns about mastery and connectedness, we pay attention, try to make sense of the information presented to us, and think it through carefully. This kind of careful thinking, responding, and reacting can help a persuasion attempt to flourish or let it wither away. Just as careful thought can flesh out a first impression into a coherent and balanced view of another individual, or take us beyond stereotypes and prejudices to more individualized conceptions of groups and their members, so careful thinking can prove a persuasion cue wrong and show a tear-jerker to be nothing more than a manipulative tug on the heart-strings. Because *our* knowledge, attention, and careful processing determines whether our attitudes will change, it is important to remember that we quite literally persuade ourselves.

Realizing our role in attitude change enables us to view persuasion as an empowering process rather than an overpowering one. In ancient Greece, the Sophists believed that persuasion was needed to lay bare the advantages and disadvantages of any object, and Aristotle argued that persuasion was needed to ensure that everyone came to see what was true and good. Persuasion does not have to involve deception, confusion, and trickery. The same processes that sometimes sell us inferior products and disreputable politicians are also at work when charitable organizations raise money for good causes, when public service messages improve the population's health, and when parents pass their values along to a new generation. And if we react to important appeals in an open but critical way, persuasion can be used to inform rather than confuse and to broaden rather than restrict our appreciation of attitude objects.

Summary

Attitudes and Their Origins Social psychologists measure people's **attitudes** in a variety of ways. They may directly ask people about their evaluations or directly observe people's overt behavior. Or they may use indirect measures, such as assessments of physiological responses.

People form attitudes because they are useful in mastering the social environment and in expressing important connections with others. Attitudes are assembled from three types of information: beliefs about the object's positive or negative characteristics, feelings and emotions about the objects, and information about past and current actions toward the object. Once an attitude has been formed, it becomes closely linked to knowledge about the object.

From Snap Judgments to Considered Opinions: Superficial and Systematic Routes to Persuasion When people are targets of **persuasion**, they sometimes do not give persuasive communications much thought. In this case, various superficial aspects of the message can lead to attitude change. For example, people may use **persuasion heuristics** that lead them to agree with experts, with long messages, or with messages that use statistics.

Sometimes people do carefully consider the content of arguments presented in a persuasive communication. When people pay attention to a message, understand its content, and **elaborate** or respond to it in a favorable way, persuasion may occur. Change resulting from such careful consideration lasts longer than change produced by superficial processing.

People process messages systematically only when they have both the motivation and the cognitive capacity to do so. The importance and self-relevance of the message determines motivation. Cognitive capacity is available when people have adequate ability, relevant knowledge, and the opportunity to concentrate.

Chapter 7 Themes

Construction of Reality
We construct attitudes based on our beliefs and feelings about objects.

Pervasiveness of Social Influence
In this construction process, we draw heavily on information supplied by other people or by persuasive messages.

Striving for Mastery
Attitudes help us master our environment and obtain rewards.

Seeking Connectedness
Attitudes also help us express our connectedness with groups or ideas we value.

Superficiality Versus Depth
Attitude change may result when we process persuasive messages superficially or when we think about them in more depth.

The Persuasive Power of Emotion: Superficial and Systematic Processing of Affective Information Emotional appeals often persuade through superficial processing. Emotions associated with attitude objects, or positive feelings evoked by an attractive source, pleasant music, or some other cause, may contribute to persuasion when people are not processing in depth.

Positive feelings can interfere with people's motivation and their ability to process persuasive messages systematically. This in turn lowers the effectiveness of strong arguments and increases the persuasiveness of weak arguments.

Using negative emotions like fear to bring about persuasion can be complex. In the right dosage, fear and anxiety can motivate people to process, but an excess of these emotions can interfere with cognitive capacity and motivation and undermine systematic processing.

Defending Attitudes: Resisting Persuasion People often seek to resist persuasion, and one of their best weapons is awareness. Though stimuli that are not consciously perceived can influence attitudes in laboratory settings, in everyday life people are unlikely to focus on subliminal stimuli or to act on vague feelings when decisions are important.

Being forewarned of a persuasion attempt can help people resist persuasion. Having previous experience with related arguments is also a successful defense against persuasion.

Chapter 7 Overview

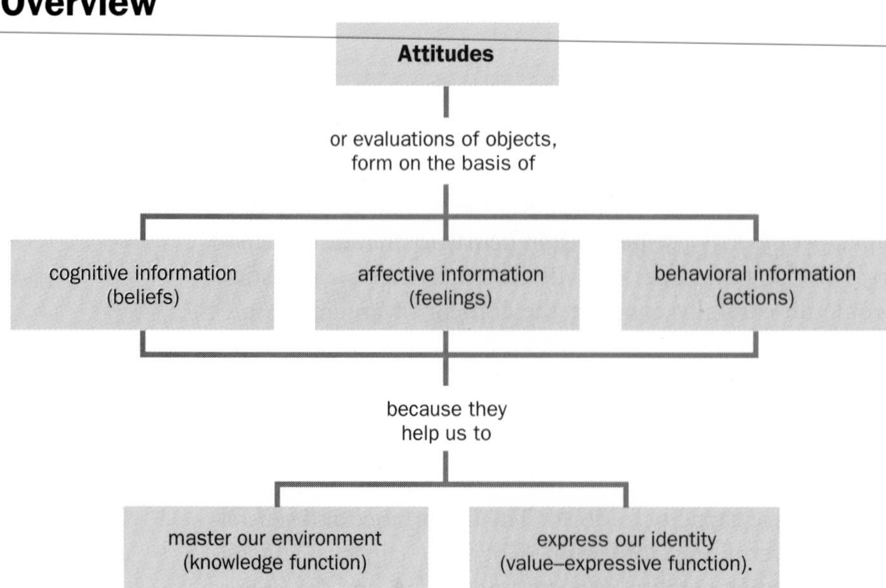

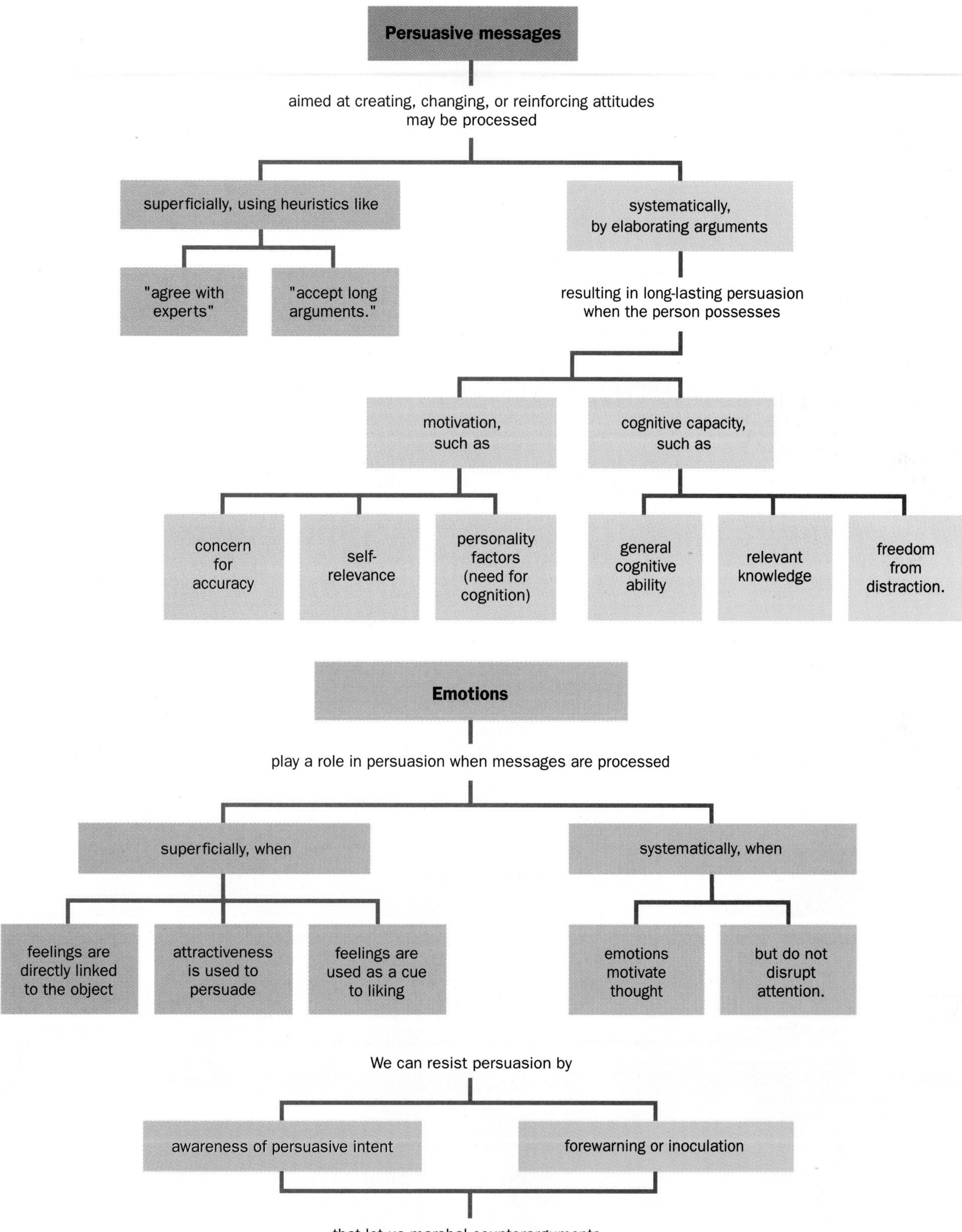
Persuasive messages
aimed at creating, changing, or reinforcing attitudes
may be processed
superficially, using heuristics like
"agree with experts"
"accept long arguments."
systematically, by elaborating arguments
resulting in long-lasting persuasion when the person possesses
motivation, such as
concern for accuracy
self-relevance
personality factors (need for cognition)
cognitive capacity, such as
general cognitive ability
relevant knowledge
freedom from distraction.
Emotions
play a role in persuasion when messages are processed
superficially, when
feelings are directly linked to the object
attractiveness is used to persuade
feelings are used as a cue to liking
systematically, when
emotions motivate thought
but do not disrupt attention.
We can resist persuasion by
awareness of persuasive intent
forewarning or inoculation
that let us marshal counterarguments.

Inch by Inch,
Row by Row
SAVE The
Whale
Peace.

8

Attitudes and Behavior

Most of us assume that what we think or feel on the inside influences what we do on the outside—that attitudes influence behavior. We take for granted that our political views affect our choice of candidate, our food preferences influence our selections at the supermarket, and our personal likes and dislikes dictate our choice of friends. Social psychology provides considerable evidence for this view. As pointed out in previous chapters, our impressions of others have an impact on a variety of behaviors—on whom we hire or fire, acquit or convict, treat as healthy or mentally ill. Similarly, our attitudes toward our own and other groups can determine whether we treat an individual with fairness or subject that person to discrimination.

Although the link is far from straightforward, attitudes and behaviors are quite predictably related, and for two very good reasons. The first is that *actions influence attitudes*—given the right conditions, our actions can change our attitudes. Collecting cans for recycling can help develop caring attitudes toward environmental conservation; donating some loose change to a panhandler can generate positive attitudes toward the homeless. In the first part of this chapter, we will consider two different ways in which attitudes are formed by behavior. Sometimes people notice what they are doing, make simple inferences about it, and bring their attitudes into line with their actions. At other times—for example, when their behavior has more serious consequences—people work hard to justify or rationalize their actions, and this too can result in attitude change. Thus, when our attitudes are changed by our actions, it's not surprising that actions and attitudes go hand in hand.

The second reason attitudes and behaviors are predictably related is that *attitudes influence actions.* You may recall this process from earlier chapters: our attitudes change how we look at attitude objects, and this in turn changes how we act toward them. Seeing their team as the most talented, the fans turn out for every game. Noticing only the immigrant's differences, the bigot refuses to hire him. Focusing on their children's positive qualities, the doting parents indulge their foibles and pamper them. The process by which our attitudes trigger action sometimes happens in an almost knee-jerk fashion, with very little forethought. On other occasions, the process is more deliberate. When this happens, our attitudes produce intentions to act

Actions and attitudes Pro-conservation attitudes may prompt actions like the one shown here, but the influence can also flow in the other direction. The act of decorating a sidewalk at an Earth Day celebration can strengthen or even create positive attitudes toward the environment.

in particular ways, and much time, effort, and thought is exerted to make good on our intentions. The means by which attitudes shape and direct behavior is the topic of the second part of the chapter.

To say that attitudes and behaviors are predictably related does not mean, however, they will always be in lockstep. We do sometimes act against our personal convictions. We raid the children's Halloween candy when we mean to diet. We watch action movies although we hate media violence. We buy trucks for our nephews and dolls for our nieces despite our long-standing opposition to gender stereotypes. We act in these contradictory ways because attitudes are only one of several factors that can affect behavior. Sometimes the impact of attitudes is weakened or even overwhelmed by particular circumstances and particular situations. One of the most powerful reasons attitudes are sometimes unrelated to behaviors is that action is often determined by social norms, shared standards of appropriate behavior. In fact, the impact that norms exert on behavior is so important that we will cover that topic in its own chapter, Chapter 10.

Attitudes have a much more potent effect on behavior when people's concerns about norms are weak or when normative pressures are absent. But even then, attitudes do not always affect behaviors. What has to happen for attitudes to play a role in guiding behavior? When will their influence be enhanced or undermined? These questions, which have important implications for attitudes and behaviors in clinical, business, and educational settings, are addressed in the final section of this chapter.

Changing Attitudes with Actions

Have you ever found yourself in a brand new role? Perhaps you were appointed office coordinator for the United Fund pledge drive or elected president of a student organization. A new position demands new actions, new ways of interacting with people, and these new actions soon spawn new attitudes. When Seymour Lieberman (1956) followed the careers of male factory workers, he found just such a change. Workers promoted to foremen soon showed increased sympathy for management's viewpoint; in contrast, those newly elected to union offices adopted more hard-line union positions. Lieberman's findings show the tremendous impact of career choices: careers can dictate conduct, which in turn can determine character. Even playing a part can change attitudes. For example, subjects acting the role of U.S. advisers in negotiation games often shift toward hard-line pro-American positions (Trost and others, 1989). If such transitory roles can exert this influence, it's no wonder that "taking on" the personalities of the roles they play is an occupational hazard for some actors and actresses (Magnusson, 1981). Actor Leonard Nimoy, portrayer of the coolly logical Vulcan on the series *Star Trek,* was even prompted to write a book proclaiming, *I Am Not Spock*. Apparently novelist George Eliot was correct: "Our deeds determine us as much as we determine our deeds."

The effects of behavior on attitudes are not limited to the job arena. Almost any kind of action can influence attitudes (White, 1971). People end up liking those they help (Blanchard & Cook, 1976) and disliking those they hurt (Davis & Jones, 1960; Glass, 1964). Even saying something that another person wants to hear can be enough to change an attitude. In one study demonstrating this point, subjects were asked to describe a man to someone who supposedly either liked or disliked him (Higgins & Rholes, 1978). When subjects believed the listener liked the man, they said more good things about him than when they thought the listener did not like him. These statements also colored the subjects' own attitudes. Subjects who had given glowing descriptions ended up liking the man better than those who had described him less favorably. (Now that you know this, you might be tempted to improve your professor's opinion of you by asking her to write you a strong letter of recommendation!)

As these studies illustrate, behavior can be an important part of the information on which we base our attitudes. Just as novel beliefs and feelings can change our opinions about an attitude object (Chapter 7), so too can new actions contribute to new attitudes. How does information about our actions exert an influence on our attitudes? By now you probably will not be surprised to learn that it is a matter of processing. Recall from Chapter 7 that we process persuasive communications either superficially or systematically, depending on their importance and self-relevance. We process information about our own behavior the same way. Sometimes people take what they do at face value and make simple action-to-attitude inferences. Under other circumstances, especially if the behavior has serious consequences, people move to a deeper consideration of the implications of their actions.

Action across attitude gaps These women are guests at an "intergenerational prom" held in a New York nursing home. Choosing to engage in such friendly interactions may help change the attitudes of both participants, reducing one dimension of "the generation gap."

Self-Perception: Inferring Attitudes from Behavior

Behavior is an important part of the information on which people base attitudes. If behaviors change, attitudes can also change. When people process superficially, they infer their attitudes by observing their own behaviors and the situations in which the behaviors occur. At such times, people often infer the presence of an attitude consistent with their behavior.

At the most superficial level of processing, people make straightforward inferences from action to attitude. Consider, for example, an ingenious study by Gary Wells and Richard Petty (1980) that demonstrated how simple gestures affect attitudes. Shaking the head from side to side is a near-universal gesture of rejection, one that may originally have signaled refusal of food (watch a toddler refusing vegetables sometime). In contrast, nodding one's head typically signals agreement. To see if subjects would infer their attitudes from such head movements, the researchers led them to believe they were testing the sound quality of stereo headphones during jogging or bike riding. To simulate jogging, some subjects were asked to move their heads up and down; to simulate bicycling, others moved their heads from side to side. These actions were carried out as they listened through headphones to an editorial, ostensibly broadcast from the campus radio station, that advocated increases or decreases in college tuition. As you can see in Figure 8.1, the gestures had an impact. Head nodders were relatively supportive of the position advocated in the broadcast, whereas head shakers opposed the position.

Chapter 4 (pages 115 to 117) described this process at work as people infer their own personal characteristics, like traits and dispositions, from their actions.

Self-Perception Theory. Darryl Bem's *theory of self-perception* (1972) explains such findings by suggesting that people infer their attitudes by observing their own behaviors and the situations in which those actions occur. You may have experienced self-perception processes yourself. Have you ever contemplated your growing collection of Bob Marley cassettes and suddenly realized you have developed a taste for reggae? Or, noting that you are spending more and more time at the gym, have you realized that you are committed to the benefits of regular exercise?

Researchers have mimicked such situations experimentally by asking subjects to focus on particular aspects of their previous behavior and then measuring their attitudes. In one study, for example, Gerald Salancik and Mary Conway (1975) used questions about the frequency of religious observance to draw subjects' attention to their own performance or lack of performance of religious behaviors. One group of subjects was asked questions that prompted them to reflect on the many religiously oriented behaviors they had performed, such as attending a house of worship or occasionally reading a religious publication. Another group of subjects were asked questions that led them to think about the many times they had failed to act in a

Figure 8.1 Head movements and opinions: Inferring attitudes from actions

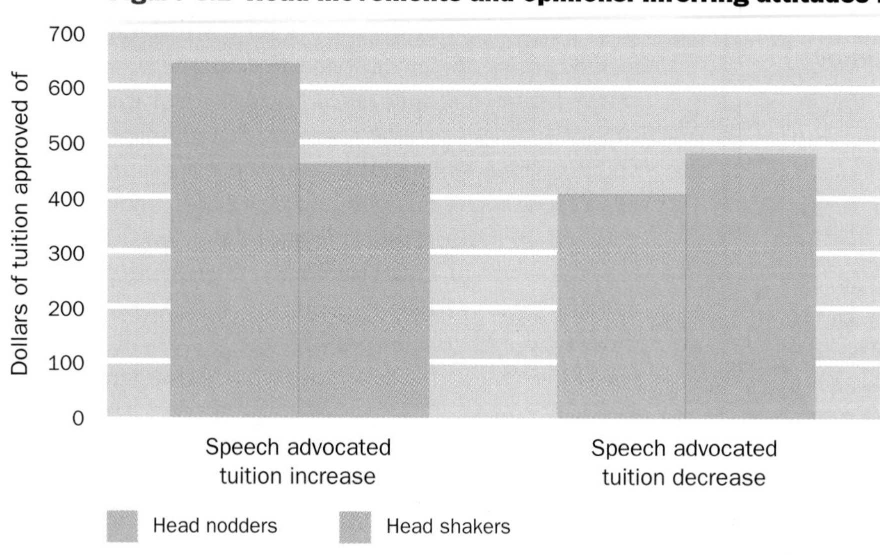

In this study, subjects nodded their heads up and down or shook them from side to side while listening to a speech calling for raised or lowered tuition. As you can see, their gestures influenced their attitudes. The nodders (green bars) were more supportive of the position taken in the message than the shakers (purple bars). (Data from Wells & Petty, 1980.)

religious way—failure to attend services regularly, to pray every day, and so forth. The researchers then asked subjects about their attitudes toward religion. Those who had reflected on their performance of religious behaviors reported favorable attitudes toward religion, whereas those who had been made aware of their failure to act did not. As predicted by self-perception theory, subjects inferred their attitudes from the kinds of behaviors they reviewed.

Advertisers and sales personnel have been quick to take advantage of the connection between behavior and attitude change. They sponsor slogan-writing contests that induce thousands of people to spend hours describing the benefits of particular products. They offer free samples, often counting on people to conclude that they must like the product—why else would they have agreed to use it? They offer their products to game shows, assuming that having contestants compete avidly for their goods will make those products seem valuable. Sales personnel are content with a small purchase from their customer, knowing that one small commitment to a product will often result in larger and larger sales. Thus, the simple process of self-perception has become a popular—and effective—social influence technique.

The Foot-in-the-Door Technique: Would You Mind Doing Me a Small Favor?

A particularly clever ploy that takes advantage of people's tendency to judge their own behavior at face value is called the **foot-in-the-door technique.** As the name implies, this social influence technique reflects the tactics of door-to-door salespeople who literally need to get a foot in the customer's door. It

foot-in-the-door technique A technique for increasing compliance with a large request by first asking people to go along with a smaller request.

The Far Side by Gary Larson

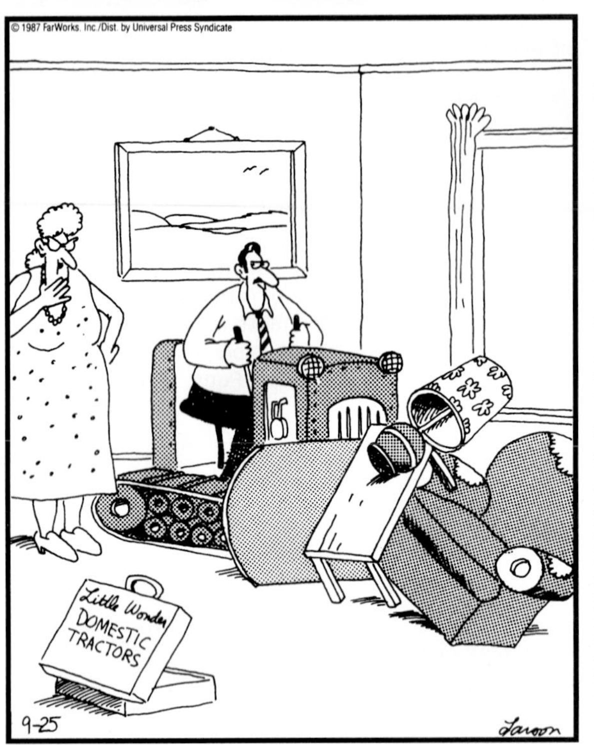

Darren's heart quickened: Once inside the home, and once the demonstration was in full swing, a sale was inevitable.

involves getting people to perform a small act consistent with an intended goal—an act that opens the way for further influence. Jonathan Freedman and Scott Fraser (1966) demonstrated the technique's effectiveness when they approached female householders in California and asked them to sign a petition supporting safe driving. Nearly all complied. Then, about two weeks later, they contacted the same group of women, and some who had never been approached before, with a big request: Would they agree to let the experimenters place a large, ugly "Drive Safely" sign in their front yards? The rate of agreement among those who had gone along with the first small request was three times that of those who had not received the first request.

How does the foot-in-the-door technique work? Why would a relatively inconsequential act of signing a petition translate into a costly commitment to obscuring one's house behind an unattractive billboard? The answer is that performance of the initial behavior triggers self-perception processes, and the presence of an action-consistent attitude is inferred. This new attitude then makes agreement with the second request more likely, but only if all the conditions are right. Research suggests that two conditions are crucial if the foot-in-the-door technique is to influence attitudes.

- *Performing the initial request must be meaningful.* Initial requests cannot be trivial. They have to be large enough to allow people to draw an inference about their support for a particular cause. Sometimes the person using the foot-in-the-door technique may find it necessary to draw the inference for the target. In one study, people who donated to a charity after a first request were explicitly told "you are the kind of person who supports charitable causes." This group of donors was much more likely to give a second generous donation than were donors whose first gift was received without comment (Kraut, 1973).

  If the initial request is significant enough, however, the target person will probably draw the inference unassisted. The more people agree to do themselves, the greater the chance that they will see their actions as evidence of their support of the cause. So actually signing a petition is more effective than merely expressing interest; completing a form as if one were placing an order works better than agreeing to consider a product. Of course, initial requests cannot be so large that people will refuse them. In this case, self-perception processes can boomerang and work against further change. If people view their refusal as evidence that they oppose the cause, the stage will be set for further refusals of future requests (DeJong, 1979).

- *Performing the initial request must seem purely voluntary.* As we saw in Chapter 4, people are quick to see their own behavior as determined by environmental forces. Not surprisingly, this tendency undermines the operation of self-perception processes. If attending religious services or donating to a cause is forced on you by parental insistence or your need for a tax shelter, you are unlikely to make the inference that you indeed have attitudes consistent with your actions (DeJong, 1979). You may recognize some irony here. Although we are used to thinking that we like what we are rewarded for, it is often the case that behaviors undertaken for external rewards fail to translate into internal preferences. Only when the initial choice seems ours alone—rather than being attributable to the reward—are we likely to infer we must hold an action-consistent attitude.

You may recall another example of inferences being more important than actual rewards from our discussion of intrinsic motivation in Chapter 4, pages 116 to 117.

Self-Perception Processes and Charitable Giving. With its ability to turn small commitments into large convictions, the foot-in-the-door technique is particularly helpful to those trying to solicit charitable donations of time, money, and effort. One study demonstrated how well this strategy can work for a good cause. The researcher called one group of residents of Bloomington, Indiana, and asked them if—hypothetically—they would volunteer to spend three hours collecting for the American Cancer Society (ACS). Three days later, a second experimenter called the same people and actually requested help for ACS. More than 31 percent of those responding to the earlier request agreed to help. Compared with the 4 percent of a similar group of townspeople who were willing to help when approached directly, this represented an increase of more than 700 percent in the volunteer rate (Sherman, 1980). In a similar study of donors in Israel, 92 percent of those who signed a petition supporting recreational facilities for the handicapped donated money to the cause when contacted two weeks later, compared with a rate of 53 percent among people who had not made the earlier commitment (Schwarzwald and others, 1983). The impact of the foot-in-the-door technique was again demonstrated when people who had made an appointment to give blood were induced to give a verbal restatement of their commitment simply by being asked "We'll count on seeing you then, OK?" The show-up rate for the group increased from the usual 62 percent to 81 percent (Lipsitz and others, 1989). When commitments affect self-perception, small public-spirited behaviors produce staunch public-minded volunteers.

Action-to-Attitude Inferences and Superficial Processing. Although action-to-attitude inferences seem to be made quite easily, in fact we are not constantly at the mercy of the wily persuaders who coax us to change our attitudes. Action-to-attitude inferences are made only when people process superficially. When actions have implications for attitudes that are important or self-relevant—factors that make people process systematically—self-perception processes do not operate (Bem, 1963). This difference was demonstrated in a study in which researchers led students to think about some small anti-environmental actions they had performed. Students who were initially uncommitted on the issue did indeed infer that they opposed conservation. But students with well-established pro-environmental attitudes did not infer a new attitude merely because they were asked to focus on some attitude-inconsistent past behaviors (Chaiken & Baldwin, 1981).

Indeed, simple action-to-attitude inferences are made only if the consequences are not particularly serious. To demonstrate this point, one researcher compared women's "gut reactions" to pictures of men under two circumstances: one group of women expected to meet one of the men whereas the other group did not (Taylor, 1975). As she viewed each photo, each woman received fake feedback allegedly revealing her physiological reaction to each man: the feedback falsely indicated that the subject's heart beat faster when she viewed some photos but not others. When asked to evaluate the men, the women who did not anticipate meeting them used their supposed reactions to infer their attitudes—they reported liking the men that seemingly "made their hearts beat faster." But the women for whom the ratings had real consequences—those who thought they would meet the man they rated most favorably—were unwilling to base their evaluations on their physiological responses alone.

As these studies show, action-to-attitude inferences are likely only when people are thinking rather superficially about their behavior. When behavior has serious implications, of course, people tend to think much more systematically. Just as high motivation increases systematic processing of persuasive communications, high stakes also cause us to think much more carefully about the implications of our behavior. This does not mean that behavior that is inconsistent with important implications never influences our attitudes, however. Even when people are processing quite extensively, the knowledge that they acted inconsistently can nevertheless result in changed attitudes.

Cognitive Dissonance: Changing Attitudes to Justify Behavior

> *When freely chosen actions violate important or self-relevant attitudes, the inconsistency produces an uncomfortable state of tension and arousal, which can motivate people to change their attitudes to make them consistent with their behavior. Because this kind of attitude change involves extensive processing, it is often long-lasting.*

In their daily lives, people's actions may contradict attitudes that are important to them and that have long-term consequences for them. Consider the following examples.

- During the Korean War, many U.S. soldiers were interned in Chinese communist prisoner-of-war camps. Trained to provide nothing but their name, rank, and serial number, these men went to their captivity fiercely opposed to the communist way of life. Nevertheless, some of them eventually authored lists of "problems with America," informed on fellow prisoners, and performed other small but significant acts of cooperation with the enemy.
- Results of a national survey in 1987 showed that 90 percent of U.S. adults believed that smoking increases one's chance of heart disease, lung cancer, and premature death (Shopland & Brown, 1987). Yet during the same time period, 33 percent of U.S. males and 28 percent of U.S. females continued to smoke, and the number of male and female smokers was increasing.

When such contradictions surface, people do not unthinkingly accept their actions as indications of their underlying attitudes. Instead, they reflect deeply on their behavior. Does this careful thinking prevent their actions from having any impact on their attitudes? On the contrary. There is often dramatic evidence of attitude change. For example, many soldiers returning from Chinese prisoner-of-war camps had changed their opinion of communism enough to believe that, while it might not work in North America, communism "is a good thing for Asia" (Segal, 1954; Schein, 1956). Let's see why.

The Theory of Cognitive Dissonance. In 1957 Leon Festinger, a brilliant young social psychologist, argued that when people become aware that their attitudes, thoughts, and beliefs ("cognitions") are inconsistent with one another, this realization brings with it an uncomfortable state of tension called **cognitive dissonance.** Cognitive dissonance often follows when behavior conflicts with a prior attitude: when, for example, people love their country but cooperate with its enemies, or they smoke while believing that smoking causes illness. According to Festinger, inconsistency alone is enough to cause dissonance. More recently, however, others have argued that the connection is more complex than Festinger's view. These researchers emphasize that only important and self-relevant inconsistencies—actions that compromise moral integrity or threaten a positive sense of self—have the potential to arouse dissonance (Baumeister, 1982; Steele, 1988; Steele and others, 1993).

Festinger did more than just suggest that inconsistencies cause discomfort. He also offered a bold new proposal: that people's motivation to reduce the unpleasant side effects of inconsistency often produces attitude change. According to cognitive dissonance theory, tensions caused by differences between important actions and attitudes are often reduced by adjustments we make to our thinking, not to our behavior.

In the three decades following Festinger's proposal, literally hundreds of experiments provided evidence for the existence and effects of dissonance.

cognitive dissonance An unpleasant state caused by people's awareness of inconsistency among various beliefs or attitudes.

Social psychologists were particularly fascinated with dissonance theory's explanation of how actions changed attitudes. Drawing together thirty years of dissonance research, Joel Cooper and Russell Fazio (1984) mapped out the processing steps involved in such situations. According to the accumulated research, four steps are necessary if discrepant acts are to produce dissonance and then attitude change. If any step fails to occur, no attitude change will follow.

1. *The individual must realize that the attitude-discrepant action has negative consequences.* Actions that produce negative consequences, or even the possibility of negative outcomes, create the potential for dissonance arousal (Cooper & Brehm, 1971; Scher & Cooper, 1989). If the action has no effects, we feel no uncomfortable tension between word and deed. Thus, reflecting on the reasons why communism may be better than capitalism and then dismissing those ideas will not cause dissonance because no harm was done. But we may feel tension if we know that the list of reasons might be used to persuade other prisoners, for example. Attitude-discrepant behavior that produces an unwanted or aversive outcome is the first step on the road to dissonance arousal (Goethals and others, 1979).

2. *The individual must take personal responsibility for the action.* Dissonance is aroused only when an internal attribution is made—when we perceive ourselves as having freely decided to engage in the attitude-discrepant behavior. When we are coerced by severe threat or driven by large rewards, we can attribute the action to an external cause, which will forestall dissonance arousal. If, for example, the Chinese had used torture to force cooperation, the prisoners' collaborative behavior would not have aroused dissonance. But instead of using coercion, the captors offered very small prizes for participation in "essay-writing contests," which the prisoners were free to refuse to enter. Laboratory research has confirmed the effectiveness of these tactics. Students *asked* to write an essay inconsistent with their personal beliefs about free speech experienced considerable dissonance, whereas others *required* to write the essay or promised large rewards for doing so showed no signs of dissonance arousal (Linder and others, 1967).

Dilbert by Scott Adams

3. *The individual must experience physiological arousal.* Just as Festinger suggested, dissonance seems to be experienced as an uncomfortable state of physiological arousal. Robert Croyle and Joel Cooper (1983) measured this arousal by attaching electrodes to subjects' fingers while the subjects participated in an essay-writing study. One group of subjects was asked to write essays that were consistent with their personal opinions (proattitudinal) and another group wrote essays that were not consistent with their attitudes (counterattitudinal). The experimenter told these subjects that it was their choice, but that it would greatly facilitate the research if they would agree to write the requested essays. Virtually all subjects complied with the request. Two other groups of subjects were simply told to write proattitudinal or counterattitudinal essays. The researchers expected dissonance to be aroused only when subjects freely chose to engage in attitude-discrepant behavior—when they were asked to write a counterattitudinal essay. The results confirmed their hypotheses. Only subjects who saw themselves as freely choosing to write counterattitudinal essays showed increases in physiological arousal. Other research using psychophysiological techniques has confirmed that dissonance is experienced as a feeling of unpleasant arousal (Elkin & Leippe, 1986; Losch & Cacioppo, 1990). If any of the wartime prisoners realized they had written anti-American essays of their own free will, they undoubtedly felt quite upset.

4. *The individual must attribute the arousal to the action.* Cognitive dissonance does not occur simply because people feel aroused. They must attribute that arousal to the inconsistency between their attitudes and their actions (Cooper & Fazio, 1984). This point has been demonstrated by studies in which people were tricked into believing that the discomfort they felt was due to something else—fluorescent lights that malfunctioned, a pill they ingested, electric shocks they were anticipating, or prism goggles they were required to wear (Cooper and others, 1978; Fazio and others, 1977; Pittman, 1975; Losch & Cacioppo, 1990). In such cases, the discomfort has no implications for the inconsistencies between attitudes and actions. But when people correctly attribute their discomfort to the inconsistency between attitude and action, their attention is focused on that inconsistency.

Just as people are motivated to eliminate uncomfortable physiological states like hunger and thirst, they want to reduce the discomfort of dissonance. When attitudes and behaviors are uncomfortably inconsistent, something has to change. Because freely chosen behavior and its negative consequences are hard to take back or deny, we can restore consistency most easily by changing our attitude. Unable to take back or deny the evidence of their small acts of collaboration, some American prisoners of war came to see things more and more from their Chinese captors' point of view. In fact, when the war was over, twenty-one prisoners who were given permission to return to the United States chose to remain in China. It is only when attitudes are brought into line with actions that dissonance is finally eliminated.

For dissonance to result in physiological arousal and ultimately in attitude change, four steps must occur.

Figure 8.2 Four steps to dissonance

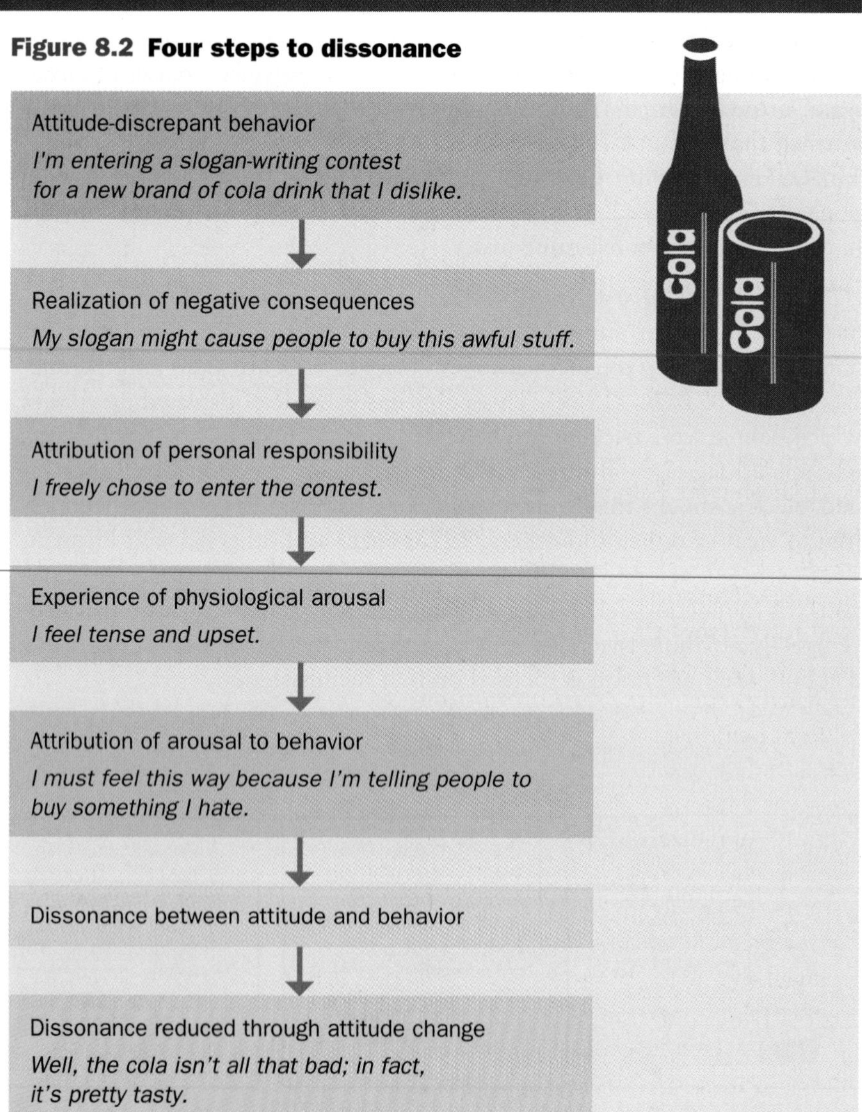
Attitude-discrepant behavior
I'm entering a slogan-writing contest for a new brand of cola drink that I dislike.
Realization of negative consequences
My slogan might cause people to buy this awful stuff.
Attribution of personal responsibility
I freely chose to enter the contest.
Experience of physiological arousal
I feel tense and upset.
Attribution of arousal to behavior
I must feel this way because I'm telling people to buy something I hate.
Dissonance between attitude and behavior
Dissonance reduced through attitude change
Well, the cola isn't all that bad; in fact, it's pretty tasty.
Cola
Cola

This whole process of dissonance arousal and its eventual reduction through attitude change is summarized in Figure 8.2.

In certain circumstances, then, people who behave in an attitude-discrepant way change their attitudes to conform to their actions. Dissonance theory provides a simple explanation for a wide variety of situations in which such changes occur. Its implications for attitude change have been developed in classrooms and clinics and on sales floors. In the next three sections, we explore three classic research areas that reflect the wide range of situations in which dissonance processes literally help people persuade themselves.

Justifying Attitude-Discrepant Behavior: I Have My Reasons! Imagine that you are a subject in a very boring experiment. For what seems like hours you perform meaningless and repetitive tasks. First, the experimenter gives you a pegboard containing forty-eight square pegs and asks you to give them a quarter turn to the left, a quarter turn back to the right, a quarter turn to the left again, back to the right, and so on, again and again. Just as you are sure you will die of boredom, you are instructed to change tasks. But the next task is no better—now you are instructed to remove pegs from the board, put them back, take them off, put them back on. Finally (mercifully) the experiment is over. But just as you are about to leave, the experimenter requests your help. A graduate student assistant who was supposed to motivate subjects in a different condition of the experiment has not arrived on time. Will you fill in, and tell the next subject how much you enjoyed the experiment? The experimenter even offers to pay you $1 for doing so.

If you agree, the classic conditions for dissonance have been set up. An attitude-discrepant behavior (lying about the experiment) with potentially negative consequences (the next subject's unrealistic expectations about the study) has been performed with insufficient external justification (the payment of $1). Thus dissonance will be aroused, and you will probably change your attitude about the experiment.

According to dissonance theory, attitude change is the most likely outcome when there is *insufficient justification*—when people perform an attitude-discrepant behavior for a small reward. Behavior is justified and dissonance is eliminated because the attitude about the task ("After all, the experiment did have scientific merit, it was a challenge rather than a bore") changes to match the behavior ("And that's what I told the next subject"). In their classic study of just such a situation, Festinger and J. Merrill Carlsmith (1959) confirmed this prediction. As you can see in Figure 8.3, control subjects who were not asked to mislead the next subject rated the experimental task as pretty boring. So did subjects paid $20 to lie about the experimental task: they had plenty of external justification for what they said to the next subject. In contrast, those who agreed to mislead others for the insufficient justification of a single dollar reduced dissonance by changing their attitudes.

All subjects in this classic study performed an exceedingly boring task. However, only those who freely chose to lie by saying the task was enjoyable for an insufficient reward (middle bar) reduced dissonance by bringing their attitudes into line with the lie. (Data from Festinger & Carlsmith, 1959.)

Figure 8.3 It must have been as interesting as I said: Justifying attitude-discrepant behavior

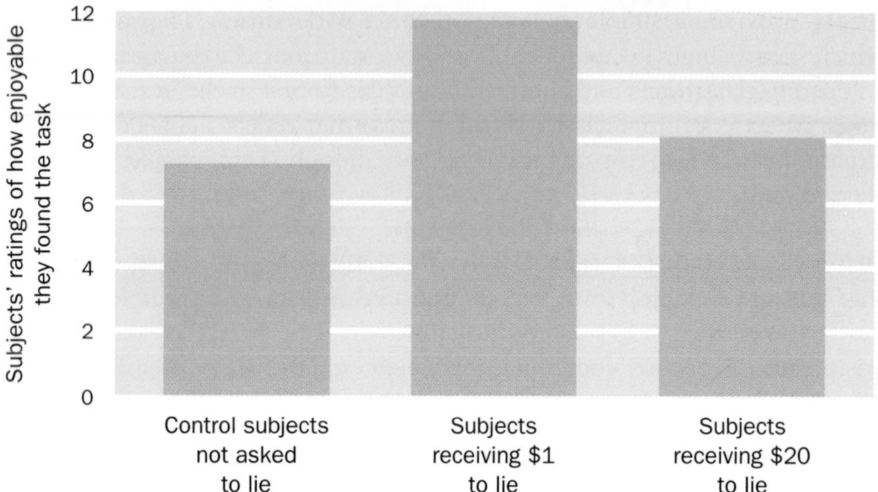

Just as a small reward is insufficient justification for attitude-discrepant behavior, so a small punishment is *insufficient deterrence* for attitude-discrepant *nonbehavior.* Dissonance theory predicts that when a threatened punishment is mild, people will change their attitudes to convince themselves that they do not want to act, and research bears out this prediction. In one study, four-year-old children were threatened with severe or mild punishment if they played with an attractive robot toy (Aronson & Carlsmith, 1963). When given freedom to play with any toy in the experimenter's absence, all children avoided the forbidden toy. However, when asked to evaluate the toys, only the children faced with mild punishment justified their avoidance by denigrating the toy. Children given the severe warning still liked it. If you can get someone to resist temptation with just a little threat, dissonance processes might fool them into thinking they really were not tempted at all.

Justifying Effort: I Suffered for It, So I Like It. Perhaps you have a friend who seems to get caught up in bad relationships. If so, you may have noticed that as the relationship worsens, your friend makes even more sacrifices, and as the partner grows more hurtful, your friend becomes more committed. Why do people sometimes come to like what they suffer for? Cognitive dissonance provides an explanation: people change their attitudes to justify their suffering. Members of groups who undergo severe initiation rituals value their groups more highly than those accepted without initiation

(Aronson & Mills, 1959). Subjects prefer difficult experimental tasks they perform for rude instructors to those they perform for personable ones (Rosenfeld and others, 1984).

Suffering is not the only kind of "work" that requires justification. Almost any kind of effort can result in dissonance-reducing attitude change. Danny Axsom and Joel Cooper (1985) demonstrated the practical benefits of this *effort-justification effect* in a clever study involving overweight female subjects. Some of these individuals, all of whom had volunteered in response to a newspaper advertisement, worked on difficult and effortful perceptual and auditory tasks during a three-week training period on weight reduction; others performed relatively easy and pleasant versions of the same tasks during the weekly sessions. Nothing was done in either of these conditions to explicitly encourage subjects to diet, although all were encouraged to keep track of what they ate and were weighed regularly. Six months later, participants were contacted again and reweighed. Results showed that the high-effort group had lost an average of 8.55 pounds, compared with only .07 pounds for the low-effort group. This difference was found again when participants reported their weight one year later. Perhaps the subjects justified the difficulty of the tasks they agreed to do by deciding that weight loss was important to them. Other research confirms the idea that the more you put into something—whether in time, money, pain, or effort—the more you like it (Wicklund & Brehm, 1976).

Justifying Decisions: Of Course I Was Right! Every difficult decision we make—to return to work or to stay at home with our children, to major in science or in the humanities, to expand our business into a new district or to consolidate local gains—has advantages and drawbacks. Whenever we make decisions we give up some things in order to gain others. By definition then, decisions involve dissonance. When people give up options freely, they experience *decisional dissonance*—tension between the alternative they have chosen and all the attractive features of the alternatives they have given up. According to dissonance theory, people try to reduce such tension by strengthening their positive evaluations of the chosen option and disparaging the unchosen alternative.

To show this process at work, Jack Brehm (1956) asked female students to evaluate several small appliances as part of a supposed study of consumer preferences. After they rated a toaster, a coffee pot, a radio, and other products, the subjects were allowed to choose one product in payment for their participation. Some subjects had a chance to choose between two products they had found almost equally desirable—a dissonance-invoking dilemma. After receiving their chosen product and completing some other tasks, the women were asked to evaluate all the products again. Their ratings offered strong support for dissonance theory: subjects now evaluated the product they had chosen much more positively than the item they rejected.

Dissonance processes help people in a variety of decision-making situations convince themselves that what they did was right. Racetrack patrons are much more confident about their chances of winning *after* laying their money down than they are *before* doing so (Knox & Inkster, 1968; Younger and others, 1977). And voters leaving the polling booth are more positive about the candidate they support than are voters entering it (Frenkel & Doob, 1976; Regan & Kilduff, 1988).

The Processing Payoff: Dissonance Creates Persistent Attitudes. The effort to justify inconsistent behavior prompts people to consider many arguments they might otherwise have ignored. In fact, the information marshaled in the justification process is one source of the new behavior-consistent attitude (Greenwald, 1968). In one study, for example, young women who smoked were encouraged to act out the part of a fellow smoker who had been diagnosed with cancer—a role that was highly inconsistent and uncomfortable (Janis & Mann, 1965). Playing the role required them to concentrate on and build a strong set of arguments against smoking. The arguments soon overwhelmed their prior attitudes; when contacted more than eighteen months later, they were smoking much less (Mann & Janis, 1968). Chinese prison officials used a similar approach to stabilize the new anti-American attitudes of Korean prisoners of war. Those who agreed with their Chinese captors' suggestion that the United States was not perfect were asked to indicate some of the reasons this was true and then to discuss those reasons in more depth, expanding on or defending them. At each stage, the men had to work harder to generate information inconsistent with their original attitudes—information that then helped bolster their new views about communism (Schein, 1956).

Given the extensive processing of information required to reduce dissonance, it is no surprise that attitude change brought about by dissonance reduction can be long-lasting. As we saw in Chapter 7, the more carefully information is processed, the longer the resulting attitude change will last. Carefully considering the justifications for one's initially inconsistent behavior has the same impact. Arguments are marshaled, new evidence is generated, action is rationalized, and challenges are successfully countered. All of these processes help solidify the new behavior-consistent attitude and inoculate it against further change. Recall that subjects in the weight-loss experiment described earlier—who must have spent considerable time and effort justifying their participation in the difficult training tasks—were still showing signs of changed attitudes more than a year later (Axsom & Cooper, 1985).

Attitude change brought about by dissonance processes can be just as powerful outside the laboratory as in it. In the United States, young men were randomly assigned lottery numbers in the 1969 military draft, and those who received low numbers were the first to be called up. Men who

At last—the dissonance diet! Do these succulent sausages look good to you? If the answer is no, you may have been influenced by recent campaigns designed to cut cholesterol consumption. Information about the health consequences of eating high-fat foods can trigger the unpleasant arousal associated with dissonance. And one way to reduce such dissonance is to alter one's attitude, turning former favorites into something quite unappetizing.

committed themselves to military service through the ROTC program could ordinarily avoid being sent to Vietnam, where most draftees ended up. Barry Staw (1974) took advantage of this naturally occurring "experiment" by tracking the attitudes of men who joined ROTC before being assigned their lottery numbers. Staw predicted that ROTC enrollees who subsequently received low numbers—which, if they had not enrolled, would have resulted in their being among the first to be drafted and sent to Vietnam—would feel justified in their decision to enroll in ROTC. Men who received high numbers probably would have escaped the draft even if they had not joined ROTC, and so had less justification for joining—classic dissonance-producing conditions. Sure enough, the high-number ROTC men apparently engaged in considerable processing aimed at reducing dissonance and restoring cognitive consistency. Over a year later, these men liked ROTC better and performed better in it than those with low draft numbers.

Dissonance Processes and Resisting Media Influence. The same dissonance-reduction processes have helped children resist the effects of violence-ridden Saturday morning television, as Rowell Huesmann and his colleagues (1983) demonstrated. The first time they tried to teach children to be critical of television violence, the researchers used lectures and demonstrations. These strategies had no effect on the children: neither their attitudes nor their behavior changed. But when the researchers put the power of dissonance to work, the outcome was quite different. They persuaded the children to "volunteer" to make a videotape to help "other kids" who had been "fooled by television" or who had "got into trouble for imitating what they saw on TV." In acting out antitelevision messages for no reward, the children had to justify attitudes inconsistent with their own behavior, a process that apparently helped them persuade themselves. Although they continued to watch as much television as the control subjects did, they reported a change in attitude: they were less interested in violent television and less impressed by it. Their behavior changed as well. While the control subjects became increasingly aggressive, the experimental children did not. For these children, watching no longer meant doing.

Alternatives to Attitude Change. You may have noticed that many experimental tests of dissonance theory set up situations in which attitude change is the only avenue by which cognitive consistency can be reestablished. Festinger (1957) was the first to point out, however, that people can reduce dissonance in other ways if they have the opportunity. Imagine that you have just broken a month-long diet by eating an entire bag of chocolate chip cookies. Rather than changing your prodieting attitude, you could dissipate dissonance at any point in the four steps of the arousal and reduction process. One strategy would be to minimize the negative consequences of the behavior: "A few cookies won't make any difference." As an alternative, you might try minimizing personal responsibility: "The cookies were a gift, not eating them would be rude." Or you could attribute your arousal to something other than your inconsistent behavior: "This diet is making me feel grouchy," thereby feeling no need to reestablish consistency between word and deed.

Measures taken to reduce the uncomfortable tensions of arousal can sometimes be harmful. Claude Steele and his colleagues (1981) have demonstrated that people may reduce dissonance by using alcohol. These researchers induced students to write an essay favoring a big tuition increase—an action clearly inconsistent with their attitudes. Displaying the usual dissonance-induced attitude change, subjects became more supportive of the fee hike, except in one condition. Right after writing the essay, some students participated in a "taste-test" in which they drank beer or vodka. These subjects showed none of the usual signs of dissonance and failed to change their attitudes. The researchers believe that drinking alcohol eliminated the unpleasant tension of dissonance, so attitude change never occurred. Their conclusion was that alcohol and drug use may become habitual and health-damaging ways in which some people avoid or reduce the tension cognitive dissonance creates in their lives (Steele, 1988; Steele & Southwick, 1985).

You may recall a similar point from Chapter 4, pages 151 to 152: some people seem to drink alcohol to reduce the awareness of unpleasant discrepancies between their current selves and their ideal or ought selves.

Fortunately, a more constructive avenue of reduction is often available. Because the actions and attitudes that trigger dissonance are usually important or self-relevant, people can reduce the uncomfortable tension associated with such inconsistencies by reaffirming their positive sense of self-worth and integrity (Steele & Liu, 1983; Dietrich & Berkowitz, 1989; Schlenker, 1982). Perhaps offering people who have just committed an attitude-discrepant act the opportunity to say: "Hey, I really am a good person, you know" could eliminate attitude change.

Researchers have tested this idea by giving people the chance to donate money, offer help, or reaffirm important values and self-identities just after they acted in ways inconsistent with their attitudes. As subjects in one study, for example, researchers recruited college students, some of whom were science majors and some of whom were not (Steele, 1988). All subjects were asked to rate ten popular record albums, and they then were given the choice of keeping either their fifth- or sixth-ranked album—a classic decisional-dissonance situation. Subjects were then asked to prepare for a second experiment, in which about half of the subjects would be required to don white lab coats. Then came a surprise task—everyone was asked to rate all the albums again. Consistent with dissonance theory, most subjects reduced the dissonance created by making their earlier difficult choice by evaluating their chosen record more highly than the one they had not chosen. But different results were found for one particular group of students, the science majors who had been asked to wear lab coats—a symbol of their values and training. Science students given this opportunity to reaffirm their positive self-identity showed no signs of the usual dissonance-induced attitude change (Steele & Liu, 1983; Tesser & Cornell, 1991). The potential distress aroused by performing actions inconsistent with a positive view of ourselves can often be dissolved by an act that underscores our sense of identity.

Figure 8.4 shows the entire sequence of steps by which dissonance arousal leads to attitude change—and the alternative processes that can either block the arousal of dissonance or reduce dissonance through self-affirmation rather than attitude change. As you can see, behavior that is inconsistent with attitudes can lead to many outcomes, not only to attitude change.

As we have seen, behaviors can have an impact on attitudes whether we engage in superficial processing or extensive processing. When actions are relatively trivial—when they do not violate cherished self-images or important attitudes—we infer our changed attitudes with little or no effort. In

Figure 8.4 Alternatives to dissonance and attitude change

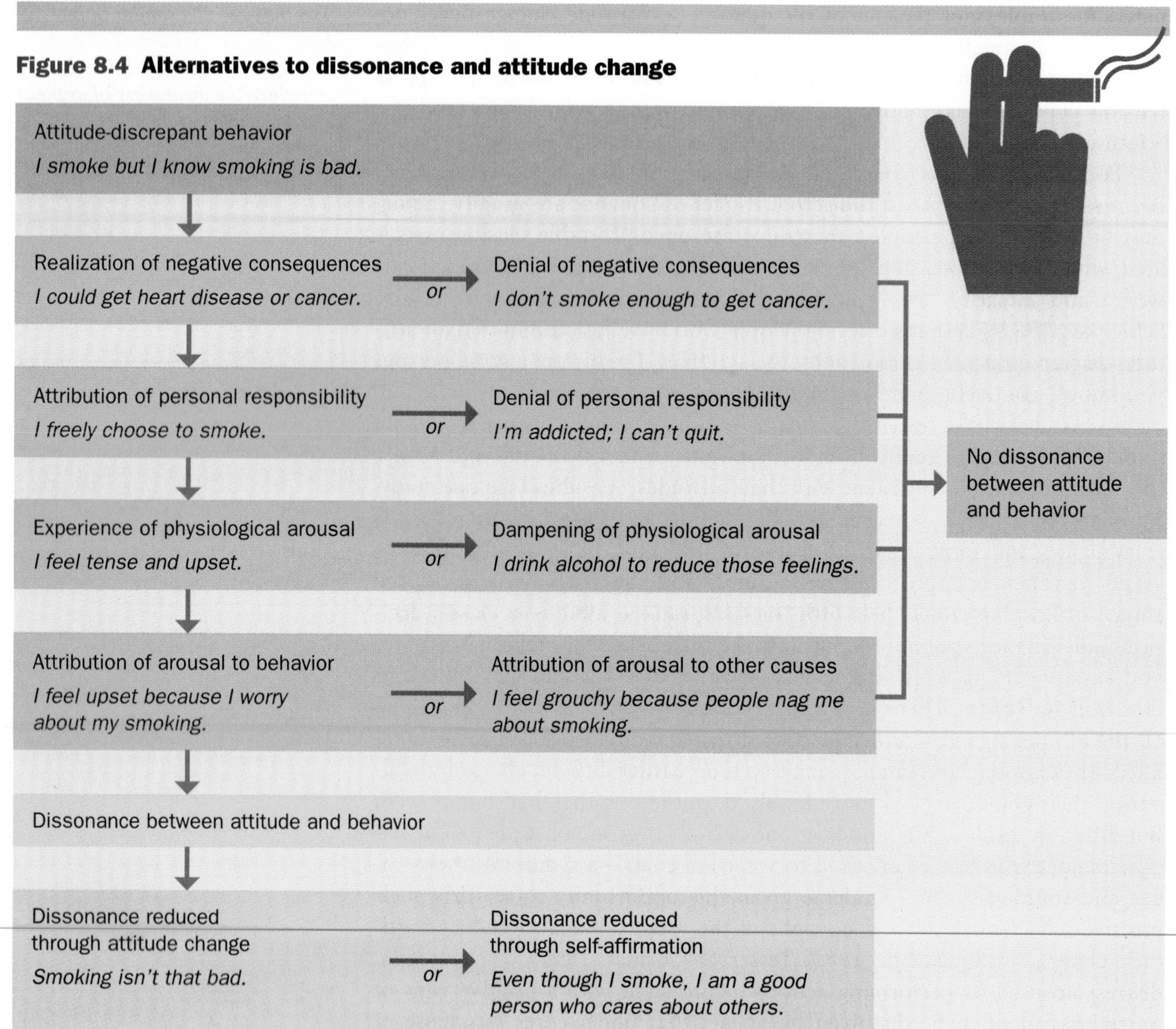
Attitude-discrepant behavior
I smoke but I know smoking is bad.
Realization of negative consequences
I could get heart disease or cancer.
or
Denial of negative consequences
I don't smoke enough to get cancer.
Attribution of personal responsibility
I freely choose to smoke.
or
Denial of personal responsibility
I'm addicted; I can't quit.
Experience of physiological arousal
I feel tense and upset.
or
Dampening of physiological arousal
I drink alcohol to reduce those feelings.
Attribution of arousal to behavior
I feel upset because I worry about my smoking.
or
Attribution of arousal to other causes
I feel grouchy because people nag me about smoking.
No dissonance between attitude and behavior
Dissonance between attitude and behavior
Dissonance reduced through attitude change
Smoking isn't that bad.
or
Dissonance reduced through self-affirmation
Even though I smoke, I am a good person who cares about others.

An attitude-discrepant behavior may lead to dissonance arousal, through the four steps described earlier in the chapter. However, at each step alternatives exist that will block the arousal of dissonance. Even if dissonance is aroused, it can be reduced by self-affirmation as well as by attitude change.

contrast, attitude-discrepant actions that have important implications may prompt lots of thinking as we work to change our attitudes in the service of dissonance reduction (Fazio and others, 1977). Both these routes provide means by which behaviors (as well as the thoughts and feelings discussed in Chapter 7) determine our attitudes. Once attitudes are well-established, however, they in turn start to influence what people do.

Guiding Actions with Attitudes

"Attitudes determine for each individual what he [or she] will do" wrote Gordon Allport more than half a century ago (Allport, 1935, p. 806). This basic tenet of social psychology—that attitudes direct behavior—is the driving force behind decades of research on how attitudes can be formed and changed. After all, if attitudes guide actions, then knowing something about people's attitudes permits the prediction of behavior. And if attitudes guide actions, changing attitudes—about ourselves, others, objects, events, and issues—permits behavioral change. The patient with a more positive self-view will treat herself with greater dignity, the convert to a religion will act on the teachings of the faith, and the duly impressed customer will follow through and buy the latest TV, computer, or pick-up truck.

Research has provided a lot of evidence to justify these optimistic statements. Attitudes often do go hand in hand with behaviors. Knowing who likes ice cream lets us guess pretty accurately which of our friends will turn up at the local Baskin-Robbins. Attitudes toward politicians closely predict voting (Schuman & Johnson, 1976). Attitudes about social drinking dictate how much wine, beer, and spirits people are likely to consume (Kahle & Berman, 1979). Pregnant women's attitudes about breastfeeding versus bottle feeding accurately foretell how their babies will be fed at six weeks of age (Manstead and others, 1983; Manstead and others, 1984).

Perhaps because we so often assume that attitudes and behavior go hand in hand, we are jolted when they seem glaringly inconsistent. Consider a recent political example. In the fall of 1992, the *Washington Post* reported detailed charges of sexual harassment against Oregon Senator Robert Packwood by women who worked for or with him. In and of itself, the senator's alleged behavior was distressing. But for many people, the most unsettling aspect of the charges was the contradiction between the senator's actions and his avowed attitudes. Packwood's support for abortion rights, family leave, and gender equality is a matter of public record. He was seen as genuinely supportive of women's attempts to succeed professionally. How could someone who supported unprecedented advances *for* women be accused of making unwanted advances *toward* them?

In their laboratory studies, researchers have found many such inconsistencies between attitude and action—in fact, they've found inconsistencies almost as often as they've found consistencies. One early study, for example, found large discrepancies between college students' attitudes about cheating and their actual behavior (Corey, 1937). Having ascertained their attitudes toward cheating, researchers gave students an opportunity to cheat by asking them to grade their own tests. Actually, the true-false tests had already been graded, so the difference between the real grade and the one students reported could be used as an index of cheating. Under these tempting circumstances, many students did in fact cheat. More important from a theoretical point of view, however, was the absence of a relationship between students' attitudes about cheating and their actual cheating. Those who were strongly opposed to cheating were just as likely to cheat as those who were not so opposed. In the years that followed, so many studies documented similar inconsistencies between attitudes and behavior that some social psychologists suggested that attitudes do not seem to influence behavior at all and that the concept of attitudes should be abandoned altogether (Wicker, 1969).

This was clearly an overreaction. As we noted earlier in the chapter, many studies have demonstrated that attitudes are powerful predictors of behavior. But the challenge did cause social psychologists to think carefully about the role of attitudes in eliciting, modifying, and inhibiting behavior. Rather than asking "Do attitudes guide behavior?" (to which the answer seemed to be, "Sometimes"), researchers began asking "How do attitudes guide behavior?" By understanding *how* behavior was influenced by attitudes, they hoped to learn *when* attitudes would influence behavior. This change in tactics led to new findings about the processes by which attitudes translate themselves into action.

How Attitudes Guide Behavior

Established attitudes can sometimes guide behaviors in a very direct way. Attitudes bias perceptions, thereby making attitude-consistent information about objects, people, and events more obvious and attitude-consistent behavior more likely. Attitudes also influence behavior in a more considered way by prompting intentions to act in certain ways. Intentions in turn can trigger planning that makes attitude-consistent behavior more likely.

Have you ever argued with someone whose mind is made up—perhaps a friend who is sure that her candidate is best, or a parent who is convinced that he knows what's right for you? If you have had this common experience, you know that people with established opinions seem to see the world in only one way. Even more obviously, they are committed to acting on their opinions, as candidate preferences are transformed into dedicated campaigning and firm child-rearing attitudes turn into a refusal to let you borrow the family car. Social psychologists have asked just what it is about attitudes that produces this increase in attitude-behavior consistency. Their answers suggest that attitudes are linked to behaviors in two different ways. Sometimes attitudes seem to trigger consistent behaviors quite directly, with little or no intervening thought. On other occasions, however, attitudes influence behaviors only after extensive and deliberate consideration of intentions.

Attitudes Guide Behaviors Without Much Thought. Sometimes attitude-behavior connections seem to occur without any effortful thought. Consider, for example, the way subjects responded to the opportunity to choose five small snacks (such as a Mounds candy bar, Dentyne gum, a packet of raisins) as payment for participation in an experiment (Fazio and others, 1992). Earlier in the session, subjects had indicated whether they liked or disliked a large number of products, including the target snacks. Subjects who held well-formed attitudes about the snacks (as indicated by the speed of their responses) were much more likely to make choices consistent with their attitudes than were the subjects who were uncertain of their likes and dislikes (as indicated by their slow responses). Attitudes guided action quite directly: preferred snacks were chosen and less-favored snacks were left on the table. What is it about the presence of an attitude that can guide behavior in this automatic fashion?

1. *Attitudes focus attention: Tell me where to look.* In the summer of 1973 the U.S. Senate Judiciary Committee held a series of hearings to investigate illegal activities during then-President Richard Nixon's reelection campaign. Media reports of the so-called Watergate investigation were generally unfavorable to Nixon, who subsequently resigned. Researchers who interviewed members of the public before, during, and after the hearings discovered an intriguing pattern of behavior. Although those who had voted for Nixon's opponent eagerly followed the media coverage, Nixon supporters avoided news about the hearings whenever they could (Sweeney & Gruber, 1984). Not surprisingly, both groups maintained their original opinions about the two men. Researchers now know that this is a common outcome: attitudes tend to narrow people's focus of attention, orienting them to information that is most in line with what they already believe and away from evidence that contradicts it (Fazio, 1986; Frey, 1986). In fact, like blinders on a horse, our attitudes seem to guide our attention toward consistent evidence and away from inconsistent information.

2. *Attitudes bias interpretation: Tell me what to see.* Attitudes not only selectively focus attention, they also affect the interpretation of information. They do so by creating a bias in favor of supporting information. First, information that is close to an established attitude is often seen as resembling the attitude exactly, a process called *assimilation.* So if a newspaper article ranked your school or college as the second most prestigious in the state, you might in fact see this as further confirmation of your view that yours is the best college around. On the other hand, information that is quite discrepant with your view—perhaps the article ranked your institution way down on the list—is often seen as even more inconsistent with the attitude than it actually is, a process called *contrast.* As you will see, such discrepant information is usually rejected out of hand as totally invalid.

Attitudes also bias interpretation in a second way. People's well-entrenched views seem to lead them to distort ambiguous evidence so that their original attitudes are supported. For example, Charles Lord and his colleagues (1979) showed two supposed research studies to Stanford undergraduates who supported or opposed capital punishment. One study provided evidence that capital punishment deters crime—a position consistent with an attitude supporting the death penalty. The second study contradicted the first and confirmed the views of the death penalty opponents. Both studies had several strong points but also some obvious weaknesses. As can be seen in Figure 8.5, both the supporters and the opponents of capital punishment judged whichever study was consistent with their own views to be much more convincing than the other one. And while reading the same body of conflicting information, the two groups not only reached different conclusions but also increased their disagreement with each other. Supporters of the death penalty now believed even more strongly in capital punishment, whereas its opponents were even more firmly opposed. Rather than moderating a well-established opinion, exposure to mixed or ambiguous information can intensify it, making it even more extreme. Whenever established attitudes come to mind, they affect what we attend and how we interpret it. As a result, we see a world of evidence to support our views.

We have seen before that well-established views influence our thoughts and behaviors in ways that confirm those views. In Chapter 3, pages 100 to 107, for example, we described why first impressions can be so lasting, and in Chapter 5, pages 196 to 203, why stereotypes are so persistent.

Sometimes, then, our attitudes bias our perceptions (Fazio, 1986, 1990). This process increases the likelihood that behavior consistent with the attitude will be elicited in a rather straightforward way. If attitudes bias perceptions of attitude objects, a favorable attitude makes the positive qualities of the object more obvious. If a negative attitude comes to mind, however, the object's unfavorable attributes are most salient. For those who love ice cream, the sight of a large bowl of it brings to mind its delicious flavor and smooth creamy taste. Those who dislike it are likely to think of its many calories and high fat content. If people then respond to the qualities of the objects that are most salient to them, attitude-consistent behaviors are likely to follow (Eagly & Chaiken, 1993). Focusing on flavor and taste will prob-

Figure 8.5 Established attitudes guide interpretation of attitude-relevant information

Undergraduates who supported or opposed the death penalty evaluated two studies whose results supported or undermined the idea that the death penalty has a deterrent effect. Both the supporters and opponents of capital punishment judged the study consistent with their views to be more convincing than the other study. (Data from Lord, Ross, & Lepper, 1979.)

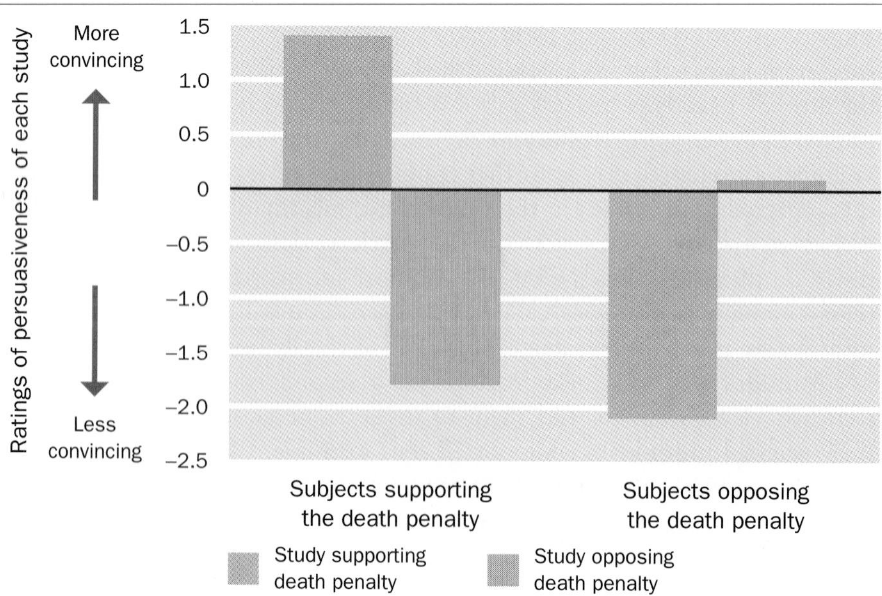

Calvin and Hobbes by Bill Watterson

ably lead to spoon wielding; focusing on calories and fat makes backing firmly away from the table more likely.

In sum, attitudes about objects can directly influence actions. Attitudes direct our attention to particular aspects of an object and influence our interpretations of the object. As a result, attitude-consistent behavior is more likely, and people can act on their attitudes in a relatively straightforward manner. At other times, however, attitudes play a role in a more complex sequence of action-producing events.

Attitudes Guide Behavior Through Considered Intentions. Attitudes can also guide behavior in a much more considered and thoughtful way. When people deliberately attempt to make their behavior consistent with their attitudes, they usually put considerable effort into forming intentions to act in a particular way (Ajzen & Fishbein, 1980). For example, if your old clunker keeps breaking down and you have formed a positive attitude toward buying a new car, you may thoughtfully consider a great deal of information as you form an intention to act.

Once intentions are in place, they are the single most important predictor of actual behavior (Fishbein & Azjen, 1975). This is the central idea of the *theory of reasoned action,* which argues that attitudes—together with social norms, as we discuss in Chapter 10—are an important source of intentions, which in turn produce behavior. Thus, knowing a person's intentions—whether to buy a new car within the next year or to finish a term paper by Friday—gives us the best chance of accurately predicting the person's future behavior—purchasing the car or completing the assignment. Indeed, intentions to act have been found to be good predictors of a wide variety of important social behavior, including donating blood, voting, using family planning techniques, attending church, eating out, practicing dental hygiene, having an abortion, smoking cigarettes, and participating in on-the-job training (Sheppard and others, 1988).

Intentions help translate attitudes into behavior by bringing to mind all we know about performing the intended behavior (Sternberg, 1990). Intentions can range from the very general to the very specific, and the level at which we think about our intentions determines the kind of information about potential behaviors that will be activated (Wegner & Vallacher, 1986). For example, a very general intention—"Time to lose some weight!"—brings to mind various options by which this intention can be carried out, such as cutting back on fats and sugars, signing up for a weight-loss program, or taking an aerobics class. But a very specific intention—"I intend to reduce my fat intake to no more than 30 percent of my daily calories"—is likely to activate corresponding specific behavioral information focused on fat reduction: "Eat more fruits and grains." Forming more specific intentions often helps us carry out desired behaviors because more specific behavioral options come to mind, but broad intentions allow us more flexibility (Vallacher & Wegner, 1987).

Once intentions have been formed and relevant behavioral information has been activated, the next step is planning (Miller and others, 1960). Each behavioral option that comes to mind might be weighed and considered until the optimal way of carrying through on the intention is selected. Even quite specific and mundane intentions—like picking up milk at the convenience store on the way home—require the selection and planning of a number of intermediate steps. Imagine how much more complicated it might be to carry through on an intention like reducing fat intake to 30 percent of daily calories. Successful execution of the intention might entail finding out which foods contain fat, learning to prepare meals without fat, dealing with cravings for fatty foods, and so forth.

With intentions in place, behavioral knowledge activated, and plans selected, we are ready to carry out intended behavior if an opportunity presents itself. Of course, once we start acting, our actions may or may not accomplish our intention. Social psychologists have found that people monitor their behavior against their intention: if the behavior seems to reduce the gap between the present state and the desired state, the behavior continues until the goal is attained. If, on the other hand, the action seems ineffective, it may be increased in intensity, replaced by a new plan, or eventually abandoned altogether (Carver & Scheier, 1990; Gollwitzer, 1990).

By influencing intentions, then, attitudes can guide attitude-consistent behavior in a more considered and thoughtful way. This does not mean that attitudes, intentions, and plans are deliberately formed anew each time you enter a new situation (Ajzen & Fishbein, 1980). An intention, and a plan to carry it out, may have been formed quite deliberately and systematically at some time in the past and might pop into mind almost automatically whenever a relevant attitude object or particular situation is confronted. A patriotic attitude, for example, may at one point have led to the conscious intention of saluting the national flag whenever it passes by in a parade, but that

Figure 8.6 Direct and indirect routes from attitude to behavior

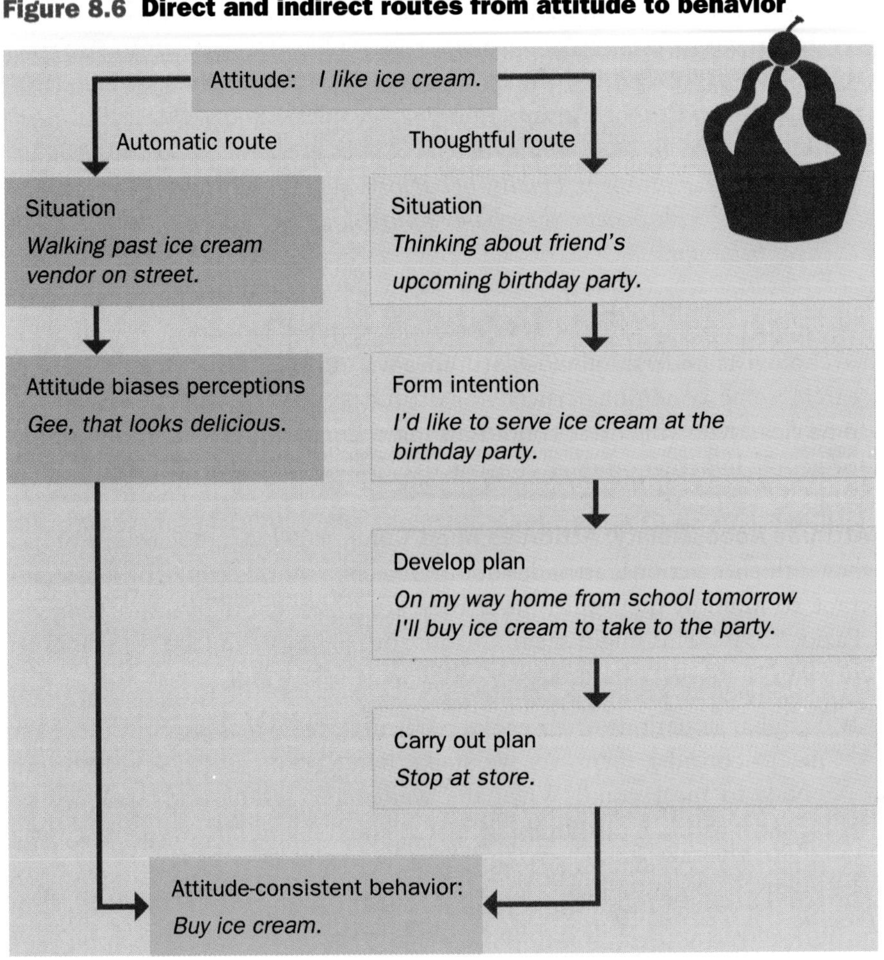

Attitudes can influence behavior relatively automatically by influencing people's immediate perceptions. At other times, the effect of attitudes on behavior occurs with more thought, when people plan and carry out intentions that result in attitude-consistent behavior.

behavior may now, after many repetitions, be performed virtually without thought.

Circumstances undoubtedly have a big impact on whether attitudes influence behavior in a relatively direct manner or through the more thoughtful process of intention formation and planning—the two routes shown in Figure 8.6. It is probably obvious that thinking about attitudes in relation to intentions, and about intentions in relation to behavior, requires a lot more effort and concentration than responding in a knee-jerk fashion to salient features of an attitude object. In fact, the motivation and opportunity to engage in such thinking dictates the route by which attitudes affect behavior (Fazio, 1990). When careful consideration is not possible because immediate action is necessary, or when your choice will have no serious consequences, behavior may follow quite straightforwardly from how the attitude object is viewed. When the stakes are high and extensive thinking is possible, however, attitudes may influence behavior through their impact on intentions.

When Do Attitudes Influence Action?

If attitudes are to guide actions, attitudes must be readily accessible, appropriate to the intended behavior, and useful. Attitudes can be made accessible by deliberate thought, self-awareness, or frequent use. Only attitudes specific to a particular behavior will be able to guide that behavior. Attitudes are more likely to guide behavior when they offer an adequate solution to a problem. Finally, behavior is more likely to reflect attitudes if people both believe they have control and actually do have control over behavior.

Answering the question of *how* attitudes guide actions has helped social psychologists understand *when* attitudes will do so. During the course of research, some conditions crucial for attitudes' impact on actions have become clear. Knowing these conditions may help design interventions that assist people in acting on their constructive and socially useful attitudes.

Attitude Accessibility: Attitudes Must Come to Mind. Regardless of how they influence actions, attitudes about objects, events, people, or ideas must come to mind at the right time if they are to have any effect on behavior (Fazio, 1990). This might seem obvious, but behavior in fact sometimes occurs independently of attitudes. Consider the following.

- Familiar situations often evoke particular behaviors without our pausing to consider them. As we shake hands, we automatically murmur "Nice to meet you." When the waiter asks about the meal, we say "Fine," without a second thought. Habits are behaviors that are triggered in particular situations so automatically that people "find themselves" in the middle of acting before they realize they have acted (Triandis, 1977, 1980). Experienced drivers who often travel the same route, for example, may not remember consciously deciding where to turn or when to slow down, and smokers often notice they are smoking but do not recall having decided to smoke or lighting the cigarette (Ikard and others, 1969).

- Behavior is sometimes maintained by rewards or punishments that overwhelm attitudes. Attempts are frequently made to override or circumvent unhelpful attitudes by directly influencing behavior. When employees' low morale and poor work attitudes lead to tardiness, absenteeism, and declining sales, managers may make rewards contingent on appropriate performance, and behavior often turns around fast (Luthans and others, 1981). Most big commercial firms offer vacations and other incentives to top sales personnel. Most parents reward their children with praise, and many city councils increase compliance with water conservation by offering rebates for limiting water use. Under all these conditions, behavior is triggered by environmental rewards and punishments, and attitudes may never be activated.

- *Social norms*—those socially agreed-upon rules about accepted ways of thinking, feeling, and acting—often determine social behavior despite personal attitudes. Smokers do not light up in their children's classrooms or their parents' sick rooms, even if they are feeling anxious. Party givers do not turn friends away from their door even if their guests bring along people they actively dislike. Social norms play such an important role in influencing thoughts, feelings, and behavior that we consider their impact in more detail in Chapters 9 and 10.

How, then, do attitudes get to be part of the equation? Behavior is responsive to attitudes only if attitudes come to mind at the appropriate time. This can be achieved in a number of different ways.

1. *Deliberately making attitudes accessible.* Attitudes can be brought to mind by a deliberate effort, so that taking a few minutes to think about an appropriate attitude increases its impact on behavior. Mark Snyder and William Swann (1976) demonstrated this idea in a study of attitudes toward affirmative action employment policies. Two weeks after their attitudes were assessed, undergraduate men served as jurors in mock sex-discrimination trials. Some of the men were given "a few minutes to organize your thoughts and views on the affirmative action issue" before hearing the case, whereas others were not. Only subjects who were first induced to bring their attitude to mind reached verdicts consistent with their attitudes. And, as other researchers have found, even overhearing someone else discussing an issue is enough to make attitudes come to mind, and thus to increase the impact they have on behavior (Borgida & Campbell, 1982).

Of course, people do not always recognize the relevance of a particular attitude (Snyder, 1982). In these cases, being reminded of the relationship of an attitude to the task at hand can increase the attitude's impact on behavior. To demonstrate this point, Snyder and Deborah Kendzierski (1982) set up another mock trial, also of a sex-discrimination case, in which jurors were or were not reminded of their own attitudes before coming to a verdict. One group of mock jurors was encouraged to think about their views on affirmative action before being presented with the case. Another group of subjects was not only encouraged to review their attitudes but was specifically informed that the issue of affirmative action—and thus their attitudes toward it—were relevant to the case they were about to hear. A third group received no reminder at all. Compared with the third group, the subjects in the two groups that received reminders reached verdicts that were more consistent with their prior attitudes. In addition, the subjects explicitly reminded that their attitudes were relevant to the judgment at hand showed even greater consistency between attitude and verdict than did the subjects who were merely encouraged to think about their attitudes.

The opposite result—decreased consistency between attitude and behavior—may occur when people are led to deliberate about something *other* than the relevant attitude right before making a behavioral choice. Imagine, for example, that you had always loved posters of Georgia O'Keefe's prints because the vivid colors made you feel so cheerful. If allowed to choose a poster to take home as a reward for participation in an experiment, your positive attitude would probably guide you to pick an O'Keefe. But what if right before you made the choice, you were required to analyze your thoughts or beliefs about the poster—to focus on its artistic merit or its fit with the color scheme in your living room, rather than just your attitude? Thinking about something other than the relevant attitude might disrupt the attitude-behavior link. In one experiment that tested this idea, one group of subjects was asked to analyze their thoughts about various art posters. Compared with subjects who were not required to analyze their thoughts, they were more likely to take home a poster they originally had not liked—and they also were more likely to regret their choice later (Wilson and others, 1993; Millar & Tesser, 1986). When the relevant attitude is not uppermost in the actor's mind at the time action is called for, its impact on behavior is reduced.

Similar effects of self-awareness on behavior were discussed in Chapter 4, pages 158 to 159. Recall also that certain individuals tend to be more in tune with their inner convictions and to act on them more frequently.

2. *Making attitudes accessible through self-awareness.* Making people *self-aware* also makes it more likely that important attitudes will come to mind. When people hear their own voices, see themselves unexpectedly in a shop window or store mirror, stand in front of an audience, or become the center of attention in a group, they are reminded of the extent to which they measure up to their convictions and standards (Duval & Wicklund, 1972; Gibbons, 1978).

Reflecting on our better selves
Situations that make us self-aware bring to mind attitudes relevant to that situation. Retailers capitalize on this fact of social life with mirrored walls and alcoves designed to remind customers of their attitudes about honesty and thus to reduce shoplifting.

Does such a reminder promote attitude-behavior consistency? In a further exploration of the conditions under which college students give in to the urge to improve a test score, Edward Diener and Mark Wallbom (1976) looked at the impact of self-awareness on the temptation to cheat. Their subjects were given anagrams to solve and told that the timed task was a test of intelligence. Left alone in the exam room (but observed through a one-way mirror), 71 percent of the students worked on after hearing a bell that indicated the time was up. When other subjects carried out the same task either in front of a large mirror or while listening to their own tape-recorded voices, only 7 percent cheated. Next time you notice the mirrored walls and alcoves of a large department store, consider the possibility that their presence provides shoppers with opportunities to become momentarily self-aware, particularly about their attitudes about honesty.

3. *Frequently used attitudes are accessible.* The more often attitudes are deliberately brought to mind and reflected upon, the more likely they are to produce consistent behavior (Fazio and others, 1982). It's not surprising, then, that attitudes built up by interaction, practice, and experience with attitude objects are also likely to direct consistent behavior (Fazio & Zanna, 1981). This is why well-established and frequently used political attitudes are much more likely to predict voting (Kallgren & Wood, 1986) than are less well-established and less frequently used attitudes. Similarly, environmental and racial attitudes that are well established are good predictors of ecological behavior and discrimination (Krosnick, 1988; Davidson and others, 1985).

4. *Making attitudes accessible automatically.* Using an attitude a lot makes it more potent because the attitude becomes more accessible (Fazio and others, 1982). And it becomes more accessible because use strengthens the link between the attitude and its appropriate attitude object. The more closely and strongly representations of attitudes and attitude objects are linked, the more likely it is that the attitude will come to mind whenever the attitude object is encountered.

If you have forgotten what we mean by the link between an attitude object and the attitude associated with it, refer to Figure 7.3 on page 274 for a quick refresher.

If the link between attitude and object becomes strong enough, attitudes can pop into mind spontaneously whenever the attitude object is present (Fazio, 1989; Fiske & Pavelchak, 1986; Bargh and others, 1992). Many factors can lead to the strengthening of attitude-object links. Some such connections might have genetic components to help us take immediate action whenever we perceive a dangerous stimulus (Tesser, 1993; Frijda and others, 1989). Others are built up through constant activation, deliberation, discussion, and action. Regardless of how the links between attitudes and their attitude objects are formed, attitudes that are automatically activated are much more likely to exert a spontaneous influence on behavior than are attitudes that must be deliberately called to mind (Fazio & Zanna, 1981).

Attitude Accessibility in Clinical Settings. Research on the attitude-behavior link has practical implications for dealing with bad habits like nail biting or overeating. People can gain attitudinal control over these destructive impulses, but only with tremendous effort. To do so, attitudes must be deliberately activated over and over again in high-risk situations (McFall, 1977). Every time you bite your finger nails when you feel put on the spot, or grab a candy bar as you pass a vending machine, you have to take a few moments to organize your thoughts and views and bring those important attitudes to mind. Former smokers, drinkers, and drug users face an even tougher battle. The first smoke, hit, or drink taken by smokers, heroin addicts, and alcoholics who "fall off the wagon" usually happens in a high-risk situation, like a bar, in which the habitual behavior previously occurred (Hunt and others, 1979). Because developing and activating appropriate attitudes can be hard at first, programs attempting to break such old habits often recommend that addicts initially avoid the triggering situation.

Of course, good habits can be learned and strengthened by activating attitudes over and over again. If you want to bring your behavior into line with your new pro-environmental views or eliminate your tendency to form stereotyped judgments, focusing for a few moments on the relevant attitudes before you act will increase the chances that those worthy attitudes will guide your behavior (Devine & Monteith, 1993). With lots of practice, positive attitudes can become so firmly attached to their attitude objects that they come spontaneously to mind, bringing the appropriate behavior with them. Seat-belt use becomes much more likely when people, because of repeatedly performing the behavior in a given situation, automatically reach for the belt as they sit down in the vehicle.

Attitude Compatibility: The Right Attitude Must Come to Mind. For an attitude to guide behavior, the right attitude must come to mind at the right time. Acting according to attitudes would be a lot easier if life were simple and a single attitude were relevant to each attitude object. Alas, that is rarely the case. Think about the issue of environmental conservation. You may favor conservation as a general principle, but that is not your only environmental attitude. You probably have several related and increasingly specific attitudes toward implementation—toward downsizing landfills, using recycled aluminum cans versus glass or plastic bottles, or cutting down on automobile emissions. It isn't enough if just any vaguely related attitude comes to mind when we contemplate action—how we feel about glass bottles is irrelevant at the gas pump. Only an attitude appropriate and relevant for a particular behavior can be expected to influence that behavior.

Several studies have demonstrated the importance of the appropriate attitude coming to mind if it is to influence behavior. When researchers tried to predict whether women would use birth-control pills during a two-year period, they found that the women's specific attitudes about *using* the pills were better predictors than their attitudes toward birth control in general (Davidson & Jaccard, 1979). Consistent with this finding is the discovery that attitudes about birth control in general are better predictors of whether *any* form of birth control will be used than are questions about a specific method (Ajzen & Fishbein, 1977). Whether you want to improve health habits, change environmental practices, or increase support for worthy causes, it is important to bring the relevant attitude to mind.

Research by Charles Lord and his colleagues (1984) makes a similar point. These researchers asked male undergraduates whether they would be willing to show a hypothetical transferring student, John B., around the Princeton campus. John was identified (ostensibly by a counseling psychologist at his current school) as being gay. Would subjects' attitudes about gays influence their willingness to spend time with John? The researchers hypothesized that this would be true only if John matched the students' expectations about typical gay men. To test this idea, subjects were asked to read a description of John that either closely matched or largely disconfirmed their stereotype. When John B.'s description matched students' preconceptions, their attitudes (whether positive or negative) toward gays were highly correlated with their willingness to interact with him. Subjects acted in line with their attitudes. When John did not appear to match the preconception, their attitudes had no impact, suggesting that only relevant attitudes can be expected to guide behavior.

Attitude Functionality: Attitudes Provide the Easiest Route to a Decision. Why are we so ready to act on relevant and accessible attitudes? One reason is that much of the time deciding what to do is not easy. The amount of information about where to go to graduate school, which vacation to take, or whom to befriend is overwhelming. When understanding and evaluating all the behavioral options is difficult, or a decision is needed quickly, we may welcome a decisional shortcut. Under these conditions, attitudes that easily come to mind have an advantage in guiding how we react because they offer a handy evaluative summary of the attitude object. Perhaps this is why attitudes are more likely to influence decisions when evidence is ambiguous and people are under time pressure than when a leisurely choice between clear-cut options is possible (Liberman and others, 1988). Internal pressures such as excitement, anxiety, and distress also make it more likely that people will rely on their attitudes when making decisions (Suedfeld & Tetlock, 1977; Tetlock, 1985).

Recall a similar finding from Chapter 5: people are more likely to rely on stereotypes and make discriminatory judgments when they are overwhelmed with information or under the pressure of a deadline.

Finally, reliance on well-established attitudes can make decisions easier. Researchers recently demonstrated this effect by giving subjects a series of trials in which they had just four seconds to look at a pair of abstract paintings and select the picture they preferred (Fazio and others, 1992). Individuals who had previously had a chance to inspect each painting and decide how much they liked it—in other words, those with established attitudes—found the task easy. Another group of subjects had also seen the paintings previously but had been asked to identify each painting's primary color rather than to form an attitude. These subjects found the four-second choice difficult and stressful.

When Even Attitudes Are Not Enough. For a useful and relevant attitude to guide behavior, of course, more is required than having it come to mind. People do not act on attitudes if they believe performance of the behavior is beyond their control (Liska, 1984). Perceptions of *personal control*—whether people feel capable of action—thus have a big influence on attitude-consistent intentions and behavior. When people perceive that they can control their behavior, attitudes can become highly effective in mobilizing and sustaining effective action. A sense of control has been shown to facilitate effective weight loss (Sheppard and others, 1988), performance of breast self-examinations (Alagna & Reddy, 1984), and the expectation and achievement of success at stopping smoking (Eiser & Sutton, 1977; Eiser and others, 1985). In contrast, overeaters who believe obesity is due to hormonal factors, smokers who attribute their behavior to addiction, and drivers who believe being in a car wreck is a matter of fate have no reason to follow through on even a relevant attitude and therefore do not do so (Ajzen & Madden, 1986; Bandura, 1982; Eiser & van der Pligt, 1986; Ronis & Kaiser, 1989). Such findings led Icek Ajzen (1991) to propose that perceptions of choice work along with attitudes to produce the intentions that then drive or derail attitude-consistent behavior.

The impact of perceiving control over one's actions will be discussed further in Chapter 10, pages 440 to 441.

Of course, even when our attitudes are positive, our intentions are firm, and we perceive ourselves to be in control, unforeseen circumstances or lack of ability can prevent us from following through on behavior. A would-be voter who cannot get transportation to the polls cannot translate his political attitudes into action. Many useful and much-wanted consumer products are so expensive that desire cannot be translated into ownership. And even if we *believe* we have control, we sometimes just do not have enough *actual* control to carry through on our attitudes and intentions. This is particularly true when attitude-consistent behavior requires social interaction—when we need other people to help us act on our attitudes. An uncooperative spouse may sabotage the best-laid plans to discipline the children. An old-fashioned boss may squash attempts to introduce parental-leave policy in a company. Intentions to conserve energy and lower utility bills may be sabotaged by family members who leave on lights and open windows in air-conditioned rooms. Although attitudes are personal, we often need interpersonal cooperation to carry through on them.

No wonder, then, that it's a long step from saying to doing. Whether we are deciding what to eat for breakfast or whether to join the armed forces, a behavioral decision, like all judgments large and small, depends on the information that goes into it. Attitudes are an important element in the behavioral equation, but they are seldom the only source of information relevant to action. As Figure 8.7 shows, attitudes are most likely to influence actions when the attitude comes to mind, when the attitude is appropriate, when it provides the easiest route to a decision, and when attitude-consistent behavior is not constrained in any other way. When we understand how attitudes influence behaviors, we come to see some of the complexities involved in getting attitudes to influence behavior in everyday situations.

Figure 8.7 When do attitudes guide behavior?

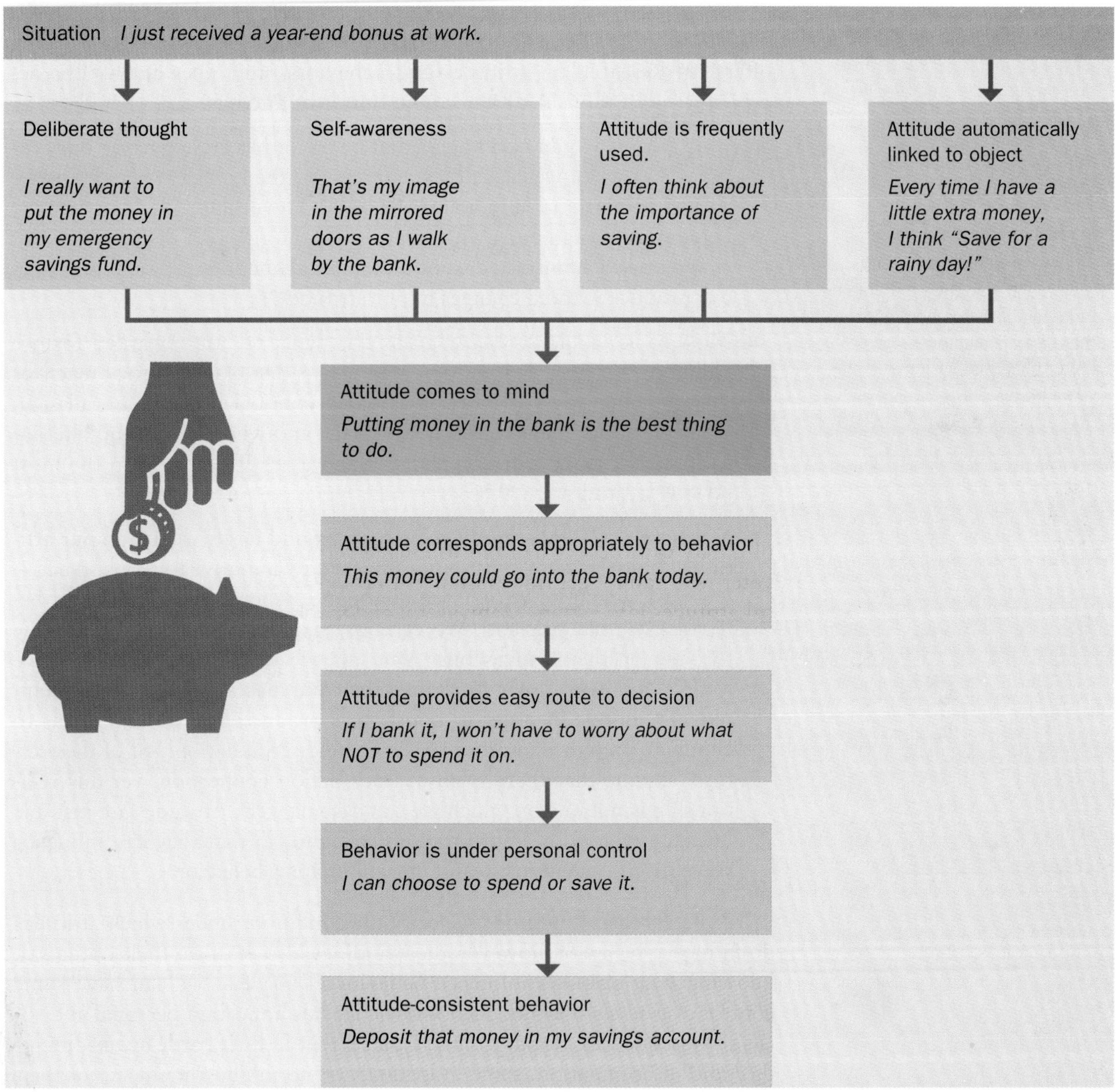
Situation *I just received a year-end bonus at work.*
Deliberate thought
I really want to put the money in my emergency savings fund.
Self-awareness
That's my image in the mirrored doors as I walk by the bank.
Attitude is frequently used.
I often think about the importance of saving.
Attitude automatically linked to object
Every time I have a little extra money, I think "Save for a rainy day!"
Attitude comes to mind
Putting money in the bank is the best thing to do.
Attitude corresponds appropriately to behavior
This money could go into the bank today.
Attitude provides easy route to decision
If I bank it, I won't have to worry about what NOT to spend it on.
Behavior is under personal control
I can choose to spend or save it.
Attitude-consistent behavior
Deposit that money in my savings account.

For attitudes to guide behavior, several processes must occur. Most important, the attitude must come to mind, either intentionally or automatically. If an attitude that comes to mind also meets the additional conditions shown, attitude-consistent behavior is a likely result.

Chapter 8 Themes

Construction of Reality

Our actions are guided by the attitudes we have constructed toward the world.

Pervasiveness of Social Influence

Both our attitudes and our behavior are shaped by other people and by our social surroundings.

Accessibility

Attitudes can guide behavior only when they come to mind.

Superficiality Versus Depth

The effect of behavior on attitudes, and also the effect of attitudes on behavior, can reflect either superficial processing or more thoughtful systematic processing.

Concluding Comments

A greater understanding of how our inner selves fit with our outer selves—of how behaviors can shape attitudes and attitudes can shape behaviors—is one of the most significant contributions that social psychological research offers us. Research on attitudes and behaviors often goes against the accepted wisdom. Consider these counterintuitive findings.

- Most people would *never* guess that behavior has an impact on our attitudes. Yet when we casually give money to the homeless person on the corner, or murmur support for the boss's unworkable plan, we may be helping to change our own opinions. As the research discussed in this chapter has demonstrated, subtle situational and interpersonal pressures can produce marked changes in our attitudes.
- Most of us would *probably* guess that what we are rewarded for, we will come to like. Yet self-perception and dissonance theory teach us that sometimes less is more. It is when external rewards are missing, when we suffer pains to reach our goals, and when we give up alternatives with many positive benefits, that we are likely to form the most positive attitudes.
- Most of us would *certainly* guess that, by and large, we act on our attitudes. Much of human activity is marked by a motive for consistency—why else would we experience dissonance when our attitudes and behaviors are inconsistent? We certainly expect other people to follow through on their convictions. After all, we work hard to change customers' minds in order to change their purchases. We try to raise employees' morale in order to boost their productivity; we take pains to eliminate prejudice in order to eliminate discrimination. All of these efforts assume that there is an attitude-action connection, yet this relationship is not one on which we can casually rely. Attitudes are just one of many factors that have to come to mind so that they can influence perceptions, intentions, plans, and, ultimately, behavior.

As researchers continue to specify the conditions under which attitudes do influence behavior, however, their findings also reaffirm their optimism: knowing *how* attitudes influence behavior means that we can have some control over *when* they do. Such knowledge has important personal and societal consequences. Recall from Chapter 5 that in their battle against prejudice and discrimination, some individuals try to inhibit the impact of their initial responses and consciously bring to bear more egalitarian attitudes. Similar processes could be involved when managers evaluate workers' performance and when jury panelists form impressions on which they acquit or convict defendants. The research described in this chapter suggests ways both to suppress the influence of some attitudes and to increase the influence of others. When we want attitudes to be potent, they must come to mind readily, be related to the behavioral options at hand, and provide an adequate solution to the behavioral dilemma. Weak connections between attitude and object, competition from other attitudes, and a lack of control over the desired behavior will all reduce the impact of attitudes on behaviors.

So, of course, does opposition from social norms. Social norms often conflict with people's personal inclinations. Yet information about others' standards of appropriateness is vital for effective social functioning—so vital that these standards often override personal attitudes to determine social behavior. The development of social norms and the impact they have on behavior are the focus of the next two chapters.

Summary

Changing Attitudes with Actions Behavior is an important part of the information on which people base attitudes. If behaviors change, attitudes can also change. When people process superficially, they infer their attitudes by observing their own behaviors and the situations in which the behaviors occur. At such times, people often infer the presence of an attitude that is consistent with their behavior. For example, in the **foot-in-the-door technique** people who are induced to comply with a small request come to view themselves as having corresponding attitudes. If they are later faced with a larger request from the same source, they are more likely to grant it than are people who never received the initial request.

When freely chosen actions violate important or self-relevant attitudes, the inconsistency produces an uncomfortable state of tension and arousal, termed **cognitive dissonance.** This can motivate people to change their attitudes to make them consistent with their behavior, to value highly what they have worked hard for, and to emphasize the positive aspects of options they have chosen. Because this kind of attitude change involves extensive processing, it is often long lasting.

Guiding Actions with Attitudes Established attitudes can sometimes guide behaviors in a very direct way. Attitudes bias perceptions, thereby making attitude-consistent information about objects, people, and events more obvious and making attitude-consistent behavior more likely. Attitudes also influence behavior in a more considered way by prompting intentions to act in certain ways. Intentions in turn can trigger planning, which makes attitude-consistent behavior more likely.

If attitudes are to guide actions, they must be readily accessible, appropriate to the intended behavior, and useful. Attitudes can be made accessible by deliberate thought, self-awareness, or frequent use. Only attitudes that are specific to a particular behavior and that offer an adequate solution to a problem are likely to guide behavior. Finally, behavior is more likely to reflect attitudes if people both believe they have control and actually do have control over their behavior.

Chapter 8 Overview

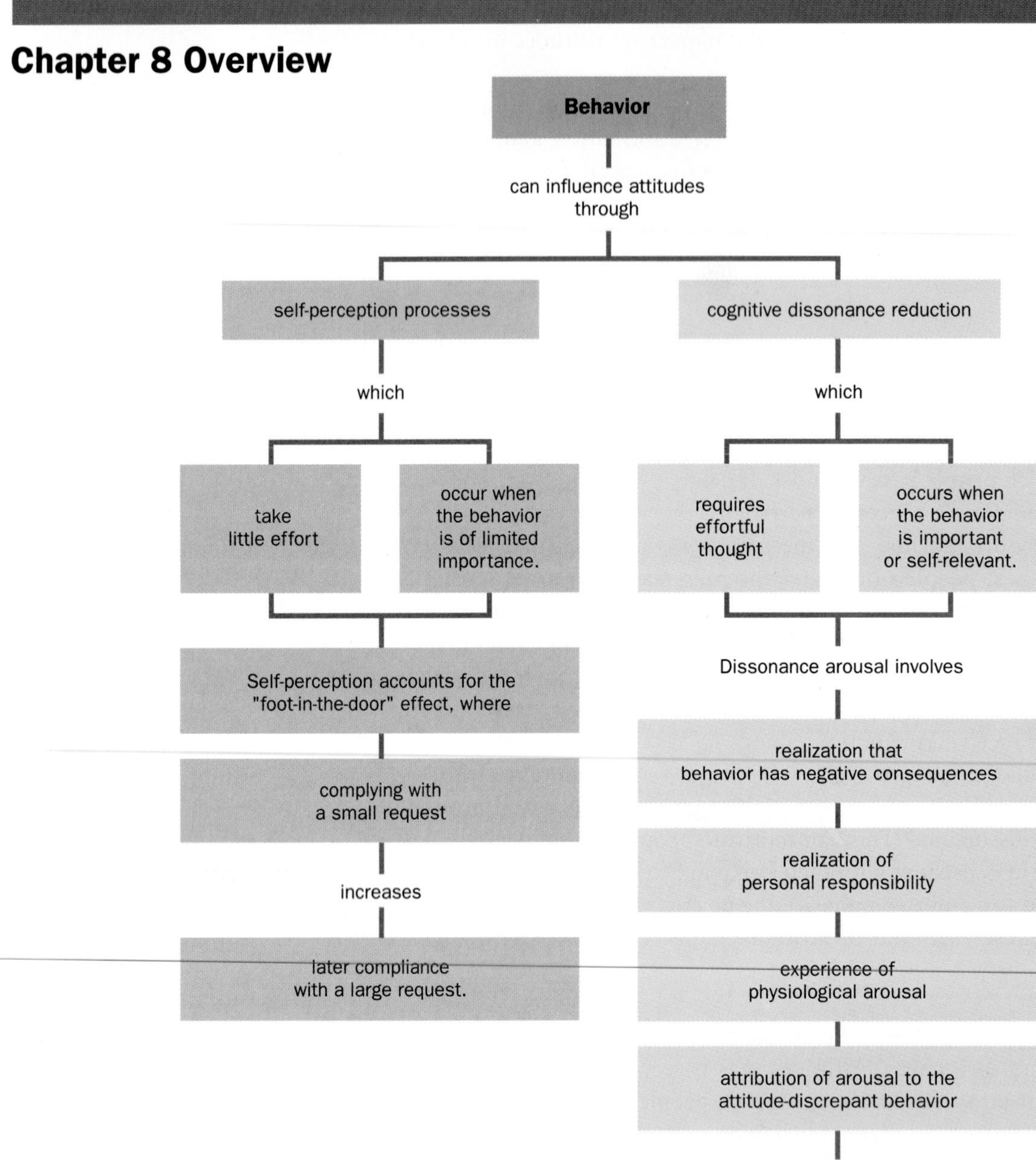

Behavior
can influence attitudes through
self-perception processes
cognitive dissonance reduction
which
which
take little effort
occur when the behavior is of limited importance.
requires effortful thought
occurs when the behavior is important or self-relevant.
Self-perception accounts for the "foot-in-the-door" effect, where
complying with a small request
increases
later compliance with a large request.
Dissonance arousal involves
realization that behavior has negative consequences
realization of personal responsibility
experience of physiological arousal
attribution of arousal to the attitude-discrepant behavior
and can be reduced by attitude change that is usually long lasting.

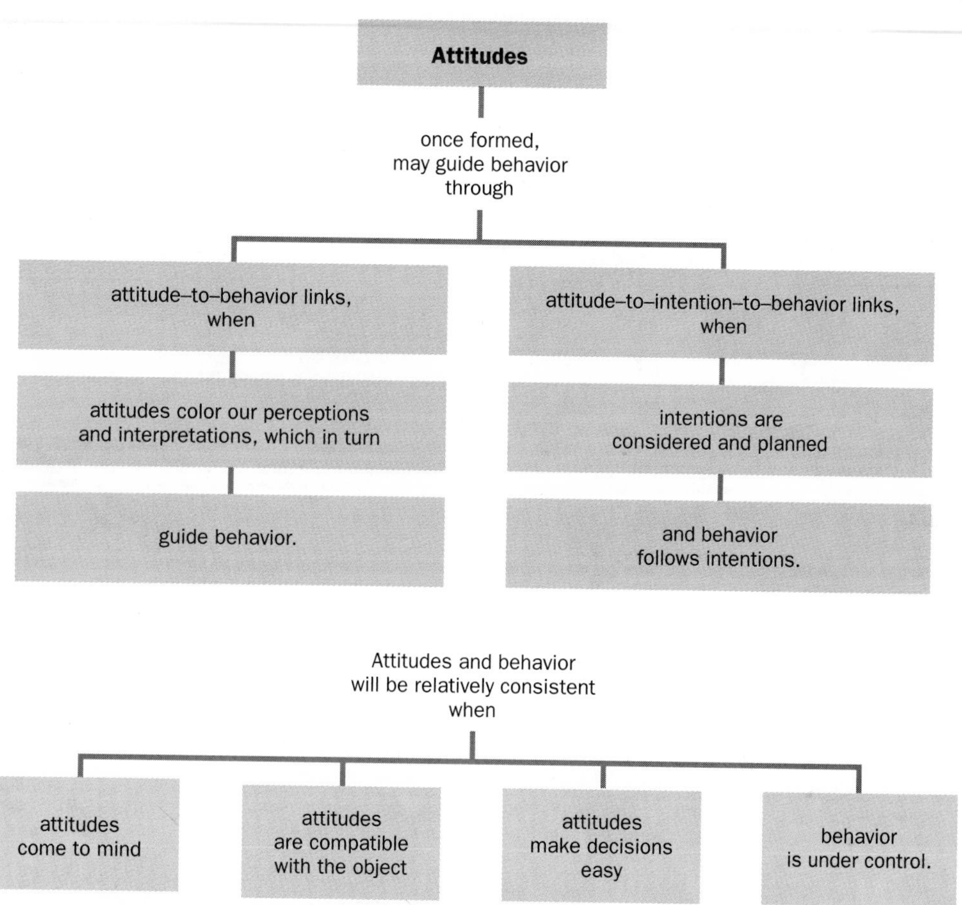
Attitudes
once formed,
may guide behavior
through
attitude–to–behavior links,
when
attitudes color our perceptions
and interpretations, which in turn
guide behavior.
attitude–to–intention–to–behavior links,
when
intentions are
considered and planned
and behavior
follows intentions.
Attitudes and behavior
will be relatively consistent
when
attitudes
come to mind
attitudes
are compatible
with the object
attitudes
make decisions
easy
behavior
is under control.

9

Groups, Norms, and Conformity

In August of 1990, scandal rocked the French political scene. At first the annual conference of the French Socialist party seemed a success, with well-attended talks and an enthusiastic reception for the party platform. Then, on the third day of the conference, some members of the audience mistakenly approached reporters to ask for their fee. In doing so, they revealed a gap between appearances and reality: a cabinet minister had hired students, unemployed actors, and day laborers to pose as an enthusiastic audience at the otherwise sparsely attended affair.

As you can imagine, the minister's deception sparked outrage and he was forced to resign in disgrace (Tempest, 1990). But what he may have lacked in political savvy, he made up as a keen observer of social behavior. The minister realized that people are profoundly influenced by others' reactions, and that salting an audience with a few noisy supporters can effectively sway the opinions of many other people.

The political sphere is not the only area in which other people's reactions affect the way we think and act. Consider, for example, the bursts of "audience" laughter blended into the sound tracks of TV comedies. When jokes and slapstick routines are accompanied by canned laughter, people find them funnier and laugh longer and harder (Fuller & Sheehy-Skeffington, 1974; Smyth & Fuller, 1972). Bartenders, street musicians, and collectors for charitable agencies use a similar ploy. They know that if they put dollar bills in their tip jars and collection boxes it will substantially increase the flow of contributions. All of these examples are forms of social influence, which affects every aspect of our lives. We revise our way of speaking to keep up with the status quo—abandoning old expressions and adopting new ones. (What ever happened to *groovy?* And where did *retro* come from?) We update our wardrobes periodically to include this year's most popular colors and to discard the outdated trousers from three years ago. Even our political ideas seem somehow to lean right or left in unison from time to time.

In spite of the frivolous fads that occasionally sweep over us, the impact of others' thoughts, feelings, and behavior is usually positive and appropriate. In fact, a basic premise of social life is that many heads are better than

Defining reality and defining identity Group members—no matter what their age—soon come to share similar thoughts, experience similar emotions, and act in similar ways. The power of group norms rests on two important human motivations: to master our environment by seeing the world accurately and to achieve a sense of belonging and connectedness with others.

one. We rely on juries to decide the fate of people accused of crimes. We trust boards of directors to run schools, businesses, and charitable organizations. We use community standards—what's accepted by a majority of people in the community—to define what is obscene. These arrangements reflect our trust that collective wisdom will emerge from the mutual interaction and influence of multiple individuals in a group.

Sometimes, however, our willingness to go along with other people's beliefs, opinions, or actions has a negative consequence. If the enthusiasm of the French minister's "hired hands" had been more influential than the content of the party leaders' speeches, the real Socialists would have been led astray. Failing to ask questions in lectures because nobody else does, littering highways and forests because others leave their garbage behind, and taking part in a riot are all examples of situations in which taking cues from others can be personally or socially destructive.

When groups interact closely to perform tasks, their feelings and behaviors can change quite markedly, as you will see again in Chapter 13.

Questions about how others shape our perceptions, feelings, attitudes, and actions have interested social psychologists for decades. And, not surprisingly, they have found that the groups to which people belong have a pervasive and far-reaching impact. Remember that *social groups* are made up of people who share socially relevant characteristics or features. But members of **face-to-face groups,** because they interact and influence each other directly, share more than important characteristics like gender, age, or an interest in the environment. Thus, the members of such groups can affect one another's thoughts, feelings, and behaviors dramatically. In this chapter we explore the processes that occur when groups of individuals interact with one another to reach agreement and exercise influence over one another. We begin by considering two related questions: *why* do groups seek to reach consensus, or agreement, and *why* do people accept influence from others? You will see that part of the answer to these questions is that people want to *understand and master* their social worlds—to see things the right way, hold correct opinions, and do the right thing. People also want to be *connected* to others, to be liked and valued by those whose opinions they respect. Forming and endorsing a group consensus usually accomplishes both of those goals.

We then turn to the question of *how* agreement is reached. For example, how are the differing opinions of twelve individual jury members forged into a verdict that all can accept? How are the jurors' individual views represented in the final group decision? As you will see, the processes of social influence are reciprocal. Individuals contribute their views to the group consensus, and the consensus influences each individual's views. When the group process is at its most effective, the final consensus incorporates multiple views and reflects the best available evidence.

face-to-face group Two or more individuals who interact and influence each other.

Mere agreement does not guarantee a positive outcome, however. Sometimes groups reach agreements that reflect neither careful consideration of information nor openness to divergent opinions. When groups make such decisions and act on them, the consequences can be disastrous. Poor business decisions can lead to bankruptcy. The wrong choice by a flight crew can cause an airplane crash. An ill-considered jury verdict can free the guilty or convict the innocent. In the final section we consider how such negative outcomes can be avoided. If groups foster rather than squelch dissent, they often reach agreements that are worthy guides for their members' thoughts, feelings, and beliefs.

Conformity to Group Norms

The Development of Social Norms

Because people are profoundly influenced by others' ideas and actions, interaction causes group members' thoughts, feelings, and behaviors to become more alike. Whether a judgment task is clear-cut or ambiguous, individual members' views converge to form a social norm. Norms reflect the group's generally accepted way of thinking, feeling, or acting.

When people interact in a group, their thoughts, emotions, and actions tend to converge, becoming more and more alike until they are identical, or nearly so. Consider, for example, Muzafer Sherif's (1936) classic demonstration of a group's power to affect its members' beliefs. Subjects in Sherif's experiment first sat alone in a totally dark room and focused on a single point of light. As they watched, the light seemed to jump erratically and then disappear. Seconds later they again saw the light appear, move, and disappear.

One group's norms are another group's deviance Behavior that one group deems appropriate may seem quite strange and unusual when seen through the filter of another group's norms. Are there norms in your society that might be violated by the very "normal" manner in which these Moroccan citizens interact?

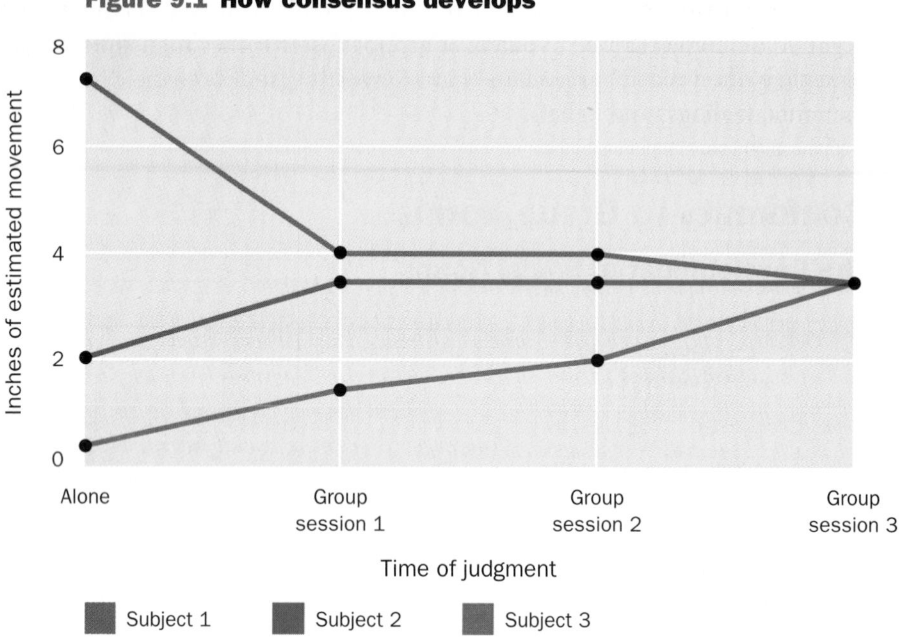

These three typical individuals in Muzafer Sherif's experiment entered the group with varied views about the apparent movement of the light, as indicated by their initial judgments. Note how their estimates in the group sessions gradually converged until they were identical. (Data from Sherif, 1936.)

Each time the light appeared, subjects had to estimate how far it moved. In fact the light did not move at all. Because a dark room provides no points of reference, a stationary point of light appears to careen in a jagged circle, an optical illusion called the *autokinetic effect.*

Given the ambiguity of the situation, it is not surprising that the participants' original distance estimates differed, ranging from an inch or so to nearly a foot. These numbers changed dramatically, however, when subjects returned to the lab during the following few days to judge the light's movement, this time as members of a three-person group. As they heard one another's estimates of the light's movement, group members' responses began to converge until they were nearly identical (see Figure 9.1). And these shared estimates had lasting power: as much as a year later, these subjects continued to use the common response when judging the light in the absence of other group members (Rohrer and others, 1954).

In coming to this collective opinion, or consensus, group members established a social norm about the movement of the light. As you may recall from Chapter 5, a *social norm* is a generally accepted way of thinking, feeling, or behaving that people in a group agree on and endorse as right and proper (Thibaut & Kelley, 1959). A social norm is what you may refer to as "tradition," "public opinion," "the way we do things," "fashion," or "a well-known fact." Social norms are similar to attitudes in that both are cognitive representations of appropriate ways of thinking, feeling, and acting in response to social objects and events. But whereas attitudes represent an *individual's* positive or negative evaluations, norms reflect *group* evaluations of what is true or false, appropriate or inappropriate. Thus, for example, a parent's love for his or her children is an attitude, whereas the idea that parents should love their offspring is a social norm. Social norms that form as a consensus emerges can range from the trivial (such as what a group finds funny) to the profound (a group's standards of morality). And, as Sherif's experiment shows, social norms can heavily influence our interpretation of events as basic as perception.

You may be thinking that Sherif stacked the deck in favor of social influence and against individual independence. After all, the experimental situation was highly ambiguous. Subjects could not measure the light's movement, and they received no feedback about right and wrong answers. Under these conditions, what else could the participants do but rely on the responses of others? But these very features—high ambiguity, no physical means of testing reality, and no one right answer—characterize many important questions people must answer in their lives outside the laboratory. For example, what is an acceptable risk in building a nuclear power plant, designing an infant's car seat, or testing for rat hairs in baby food? Is short-term corporate profit the proper yardstick for measuring an automobile manufacturer's success, or should long-term effects on the environment and on customer loyalty be considered? In all these cases, the agreement among *social* sources of information defines the appropriate answer.

Do groups still influence people when a decision is not ambiguous, when physical and other nonsocial sources of information are available? Surprisingly, the answer is yes. Solomon Asch (1951, 1955) provided one of the earliest and most convincing demonstrations of this point, although at the time he did not intend to do so. The suggestibility of Sherif's subjects disturbed Asch, and he hypothesized that when a judgment task is unambiguous, social influence would be eliminated.

Imagine being a subject in Asch's experiment. Along with eight others, you are shown two cards marked with lines like those in Figure 9.2. A single

Figure 9.2 Asch's line judgment task

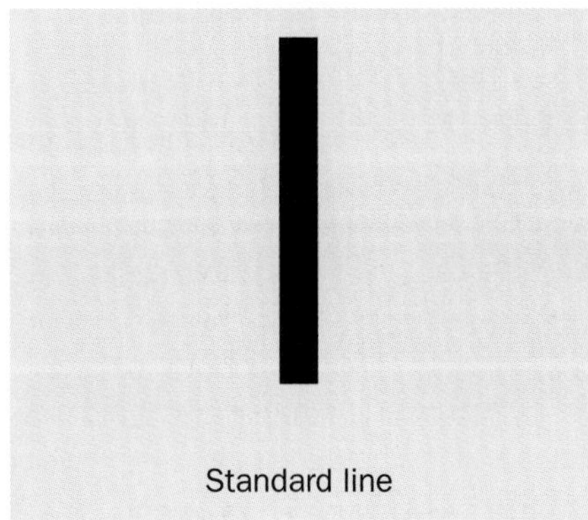

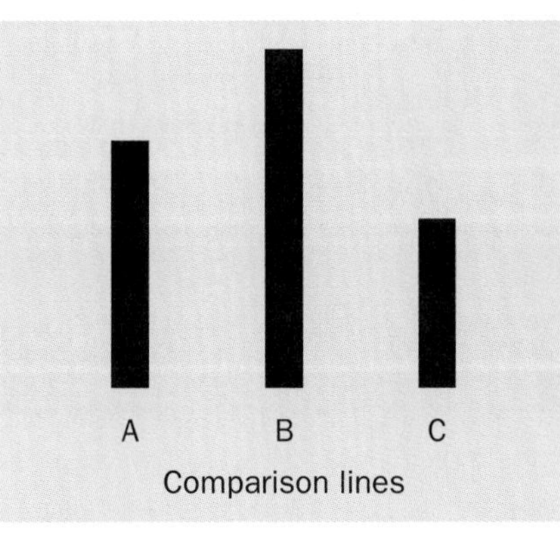

Subjects had to decide which comparison line—*A*, *B*, or *C*—was identical to the standard line for eighteen different sets of lines. On certain trials, confederates agreed on obviously wrong answers—in this case, *A* or *C*. Subjects conformed to this incorrect consensus about a third of the time. (Adapted from Asch, 1955.)

straight line, called the standard line, appears on one card, and three comparison lines of different lengths appear on the other. Your task is to state out loud which of the three lines is the same length as the standard line. For each of eighteen different sets of lines, group members will answer in order of seating, and you are next to last. The task seems simple: the test lines clearly differ from one another, and for the first few trials everyone agrees on the correct line. But on the next trial, all of the other subjects, each responding in turn, agree unanimously on an obviously wrong answer. Now it's your turn to respond. Faced with a conflict between the evidence of your senses and the opinions of your peers, how do you respond?

As you can probably guess, the other "subjects" in Asch's experiments were confederates coached to make incorrect responses on certain trials. On twelve of the eighteen experimental trials, the confederates unanimously agreed on a wrong answer, responding together that either a shorter or a longer line matched the standard line. Despite the ease of the task, the confederates' wrong answers had a considerable impact on the real subjects' responses, and they also produced a good deal of anxiety. Three-quarters of the subjects echoed the confederates' choice on at least one trial, and half agreed with an obviously wrong answer on six or more trials. Only a hardy 25 percent stood up for what their eyes were telling them on all twelve of the critical trials. Why did so many subjects yield? When questioned later, some subjects who went along with the group told Asch they felt bewildered and were concerned about looking ridiculous. Others said they quite literally "couldn't believe their eyes" and assumed that the group was correct. Even those who remained independent reported discomfort and were still looking for ways to reconcile their judgments with those of the majority when the experiment ended.

Huh? Why don't we agree? It's not hard to identify the real subject in this photograph from one of Solomon Asch's original experiments on conformity. Faced unexpectedly with unanimous disagreement from the rest of the group, participant Number 6 peers anxiously at the line matching task. What powerful social influences might make him accept the group norm over the evidence of his senses?

The essential results of Sherif's and Asch's studies—that people are influenced by and often adopt the opinions of other group members—have been replicated many times, both in the United States and in other countries and cultures (Matsuda, 1985; Chandra, 1973). But Sherif's and Asch's findings on the powerful impact of others' reactions are also demonstrated daily as groups all around us make decisions. Members of boards of trustees debate and decide on school policy. Union representatives hammer out an agreement on a management offer. Groups of friends negotiate about where to have dinner. Whether the judgment task is clear-cut or ambiguous, whether the group is large or small, whether prior opinions are held with more or less conviction, group members typically offer, exchange, and accept various points of view until consensus evolves.

Public Versus Private Conformity

Conformity is the convergence of individual responses toward group norms. Conformity occurs for two important reasons: because people believe that the group is right and because they want the group to accept and approve of them. Most of the time people adopt group norms as their own, believing them to be correct and appropriate. Sometimes, however, people publicly conform to norms they do not privately accept.

The convergence of individuals' thoughts, feelings, and behavior toward a group norm is called **conformity** (Allen, 1965; Kiesler & Kiesler, 1969). Most of the time, this tendency to let other people's reactions and responses guide our own occurs because we privately accept the group's view, believing it to be both a correct and an appropriate model for our own position. When people are truly persuaded that the group is right, and when they willingly accept group norms as their own beliefs, **private conformity** occurs. Sherif's subjects who adopted their group's standard for the movement of the light—even though there was no pressure to do so—provide an example of private conformity.

Sometimes, however, conformity occurs because we feel we have no choice but to go along with group norms. When people respond to real or imagined pressure and behave consistently with group norms that they do not privately accept as correct, **public conformity,** or *compliance,* occurs. Public conformity produces only a surface change: people pretend to go along with the group norm in what they say or do, but privately they do not think the group is right. People publicly conform because they fear ridicule, rejection, incarceration, or worse. Those of Asch's subjects who reluctantly accepted the incorrect majority view to avoid seeming ridiculous were publicly conforming, as are political dissidents who survive by paying lip service to the party line even though they do not agree with it.

conformity The convergence of individuals' thoughts, feelings, or behavior toward a group norm.

private conformity Private acceptance of group norms.

public conformity Overt behavior consistent with group norms that are not privately accepted.

Conformity and Culture. Do Sherif's and Asch's subjects seem spineless to you? Perhaps because North American culture puts such a high value on individual autonomy, both public and private conformity have come to have negative overtones for many of us. This cultural viewpoint, which pits the individual against the group, contrasts with the ideas of interdependent cultures such as those found in India or Japan. In interdependent cultures, individuals see themselves as an integral part of the group and view conformity as a kind of social glue (Markus & Kitayama, 1991). It is not surprising, then, that when studies like Sherif's and Asch's are replicated in interdependent cultures—with Fijians, Lebanese, Japanese, and Zimbabwean Bantus, for example—the degree of conformity to group norms is usually higher than in individualistic cultures (Smith & Bond, 1993).

But even individualistic North Americans are less autonomous and more subject to group influence than they would like to believe. Of course, blatant group efforts to change opinions or behavior may result in mere public conformity, a possibility we discuss in detail later in this chapter. But this kind of heavy-handed group pressure is far less prevalent—and far less effective—than the powerful and subtle influence of privately accepted group norms. Because we usually see our groups as valid and valued sources of knowledge about the world, we privately conform to their norms without even realizing that we are doing so, as you will see in the next section.

The Dual Functions of Norms: Mastery and Connectedness

Why do we conform to others' views at all? Consider this puzzle. Even as the twenty-first century is about to dawn, large groups of people in North America—for example, Hasidic Jews and the Amish—maintain the beliefs, customs, and style of dress of their ancestors in nineteenth-century Europe. Why do they—and we—accept the norms of some groups and not of others?

Expecting Consensus

> *Private conformity comes about because we expect to see the world the same way similar others see it. In fact, we often assume that most other people share our own opinions and preferences.*

The key factor in our conformity to norms is our *expectation of agreement.* We usually expect other people to see the world the same way we do. After all, we believe in the reality we construct, so we expect other people to support our perception of that reality. In fact, people tend to overestimate the extent to which others agree with their views of the world, a phenomenon called the **false consensus effect** (Mullen and others, 1985; Gilovich, 1990). To see the effect in action, ask a number of people to tell you whether they prefer 1960s music to 1980s music, and to estimate the percentage of other people who share their preference. Your respondents—no matter which opinion they express—will probably guess that most people agree with them. People generally see their own preferences as reasonable responses to the world, and so assume that any "reasonable" person will share them. (After all, who wouldn't choose the Beatles over Whitney Houston?)

When other group members share our views, their agreement fulfills our need for mastery of the world—it increases our confidence that we see things the right way, hold correct opinions, and do the right thing (Deutsch & Gerard, 1955; Jones & Gerard, 1967). Because we depend on others to define and endorse the ideas, values, and expectations that are the basis for the smooth operation of the social system, their agreement also strengthens our feelings of connectedness with those whose opinions we respect. Thus forming and endorsing a group consensus usually accomplishes the goals of mastery and of connectedness. In contrast, disagreeing with a consensus threatens these important goals and therefore leaves us uncertain and vulnerable to social influence.

Consensus in the Marketplace. Advertisers, market specialists, and campaign managers have been quick to use the idea that people rely on others' views and often adopt others' behaviors. Slice-of-life interviews—the hidden camera recording family breakfasts with Eggo waffles, the testimonial from the school teacher with the Excedrin headache—provide us with models of people "just like us" who are solving problems and improving their lives. Slogans such as "Everyone's changing to . . . ," "Be a part of the move to . . . ," and "More people bought . . . than all other brands combined" inform us about the thoughts, actions, and purchases of others with whom we can identify.

A similar message is conveyed by headlines that shout "Only two left at this price!" or "Get yours now while supplies last!" Such inducements are meant to convey how desirable, and thus how scarce, these products are. If they are disappearing fast, it must be because other people want them. Are these appeals to consensus information successful? Apparently so. In one demonstration of the effects of scarcity, Stephen Worchel and his colleagues (1975) asked students to taste-test a variety of chocolate chip cookies. Cookies chosen from a nearly empty jar received higher ratings than cookies from a full jar. And putting their money where their mouths were, students were willing to pay more for the scarce cookies. A second experiment showed that consensus increased preferences for scarce cookies even further. Some student testers were told that the cookies were scarce because they had been so popular with other participants; others were told the scarcity was due to a mistake by the experimenter. Subjects liked the popular cookies even more than the accidentally scarce cookies.

false consensus effect The tendency to overestimate others' agreement with one's own opinions, characteristics, and behaviors.

Whose Consensus?

> *People expect to agree with those who share attributes relevant to the judgment at hand. Agreeing with such a group ensures that people are in contact with a common reality and gives them the feeling of being valued. These goals are particularly important in close-knit groups, thus increasing conformity.*

Do you expect to agree with everyone about everything? Of course not. Rather, if you need support for a decision or evaluation, you turn to the people you believe are an appropriate source of information for the particular judgment (Moscovici, 1976; Turner, 1982; Turner and others, 1987). These people are called a **reference group.** The type of reference group you turn to will depend on whether the task is intellective or judgmental.

Intellective Tasks. Tasks that usually have one verifiably correct solution—like visual judgments, mathematical problems, or general knowledge questions—are called *intellective tasks.* The solutions require physical judgments or statements of fact. If the task involves visual judgments, for example—as Sherif's and Asch's experimental tasks did—people expect to agree with most other people who have reasonably good eyesight. Because many people have the knowledge and skills to verify the solutions to intellective tasks, most other people can serve as a reference group, and the expectation that most others will agree on such judgments is very strong (Insko and others, 1983; Kaplan & Miller, 1987).

"How would you like me to answer that question? As a member of my ethnic group, educational class, income group, or religious category?"

Judgmental Tasks. Of course, not all questions involve physical judgments or statements of fact. Some tasks require decisions about social and personal issues—ranging from big questions, like whether spending for social welfare should be cut back, to small ones, like which movie a couple should see. The people we accept as an appropriate source of information for such decisions are those who share similar values, attitudes, and relationships, for these are value-laden questions, or *judgmental tasks.* In such cases, people usually expect to agree with peers, family, and others who share their tastes and pastimes (Goethals & Nelson, 1973). If the judgmental task involves politics, morality, or social justice, our lifelong membership in national, ethnic, religious, or political groups can provide a ready-made reference group, whether we are French Canadians, Southern Baptists, or Democrats. In contrast, we do not expect to agree with people we dislike or with out-group members (Sherman and others, 1984).

Group Cohesiveness and the Influence of Group Norms. Any group with which we identify can act as a reference group. Recall that people sometimes think of themselves as group members even when a researcher brings together an ad hoc collection of strangers—a group only in the minimal sense of knowing that they have been placed together for some reason. However, the more characteristics group members share and the more each member identifies with the group, the greater the reference group's impact. Groups whose members are tightly knit and identify strongly with the group are said to be highly *cohesive:* many factors act like glue to keep them together (Cartwright & Zander, 1960). The more cohesive the group, the greater the expectation of agreement, and the greater the influence of group norms.

To remind yourself of how membership in even a minimal group can affect our thoughts and actions, see Chapter 6, especially pages 239 to 241.

The Dual Functions of Norms

Agreeing with a reference group not only assures people that they are in contact with a common reality but also gives them the feeling of being valued. Although particular circumstances can make one goal more important than the other, usually agreement with a group of similar others simultaneously fulfills the motives for both mastery and connectedness.

Norms Provide Reality Insurance. Reference group norms are important because we need other people to help us construct an appropriate view of reality. Other people's reactions tell us what the world is like. Imagine, for example, that you made both an apple pie and a peach pie for a family get-together. If everyone came back for seconds on the peach pie but there were no repeats on the apple, it would be natural to infer that your peach pie was a success but your apple was not as good as usual. When everyone prefers peach, we make the attribution that the characteristics of the pie itself, rather than any idiosyncrasy of the eaters, determine its positive reception. Consensus similarly affects our attributions about other aspects of reality. Knowing that others share our views increases our feelings of mastery, our confidence that our opinions are correct, and our resistance to persuasion (Crano and others, 1988). When conformity to group norms satisfies our needs for mastery because we believe those norms to be correct, the group has *informational influence.*

Some of the most convincing demonstrations of the importance of a consensus for influencing individuals' views of reality come from variations in Asch's experimental procedure. When Asch increased or decreased the number of confederates who agreed on the incorrect line judgment, he found that the amount of influence the group exerted increased as the size of

reference group Those people accepted as an appropriate source of information for a judgment because they share the attributes relevant for making that judgment.

Amassing a consensus of three people around an obviously incorrect answer caused considerable conformity among real subjects in this variation on Asch's procedure. Once the consensus was established, however, adding to it did not make much difference. A unanimous group of fifteen confederates caused no more conformity than a unanimous group of three. (Data from Asch, 1955.)

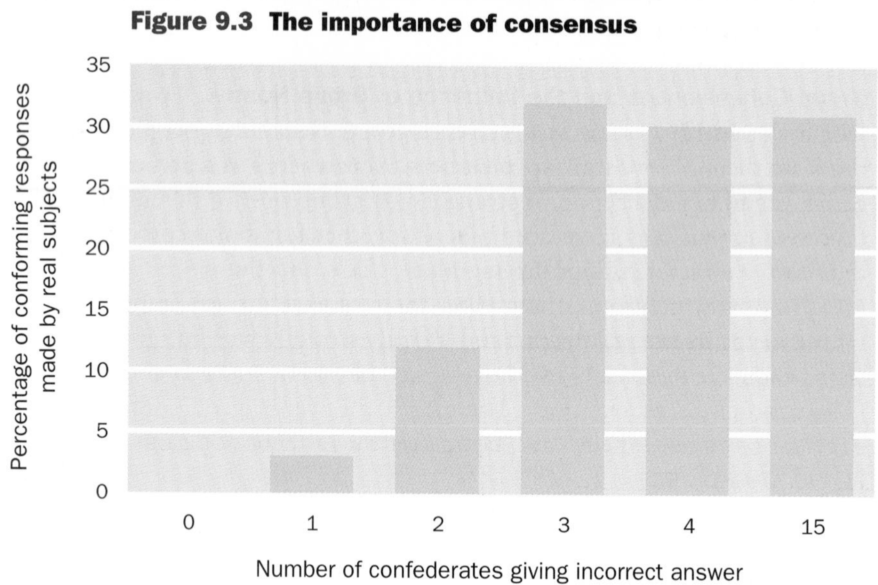

the group increased—but only up to a point. As you can see in Figure 9.3, an incorrect answer given by one person had very little effect. Two confederates elicited some conformity, but a consensus among three confederates led subjects to agree with their obviously incorrect answer about 33 percent of the time. Adding more than three confederates, however, did not lead to further increases in conformity. Once an adequate consensus has formed, adding to the size of that consensus apparently has no further effect (Insko and others, 1983).

If consensus exerts such an important influence on an individual's views, breaking the consensus should undermine the group's influence. To test this idea, Asch arranged for one of the confederates to agree with the real subject. He found that the presence of an ally dramatically decreased subjects' conformity. This was true even when the dissenter gave a different incorrect answer or dropped out after a few responses (Allen & Bragg, 1965; Allen & Wilder 1972). When there is no longer a consensus about reality, the group norm loses its power to persuade.

Why were Asch's subjects so responsive to the majority's views? For that matter, why are most people so dependent on group norms for reality insurance? First, consensus diminishes the possibility of individual error. One person can easily see things incorrectly, make the wrong decision, or come to a false conclusion, but multiple others are unlikely to do so (Allen, 1965, 1975; Asch, 1951). Second, consensus involves replication—different people come to the same conclusion after reviewing the evidence—and that replication is reassuring. As an old Spanish proverb says, "If three people call you an ass, put on a bridle!" If different people take different paths to the same conclusion, it is likely to be valid (Kelley, 1967; Festinger, 1950). Even in science—the ideal of an objective domain of knowledge—validity emerges only from replication and agreement among individuals with scientific training and knowledge.

The role of consensus in the process by which scientists seek validity is discussed in Chapter 2, especially pages 52 to 55.

It is just because we depend so much on agreement with others who are similarly qualified to make a judgment that disagreement causes surprise, confusion, and, eventually, uncertainty and self-doubt (Asch, 1956). Disagreement undermines our confidence in our view of reality. Finding themselves in the situation of Asch's subjects, most people would be anxious and unsure and would begin to doubt their own perceptions and to consider the group consensus as possibly correct. Thus, there is a potential for informational influence whenever people find themselves at odds with others with whom they expect to agree. Under these conditions, agreeing with the group consensus helps reconfirm our perception of reality.

Norms Give Us Feelings of Connectedness. In many religious communities, children who have reached an appropriate age go through some kind of ceremony, such as the Christian First Communion, the Jewish Bar or Bat Mitzvah, or the Hindu Sacred Thread ceremony. After these rituals, they are considered ready to participate fully in the rites of their community. The new members learn, through formal instruction or by observing others, how to speak, what thoughts and feelings are appropriate, and how to act. Knowing and following these standards allows them to take their place and fulfill their roles in the group. They experience a proud sense of belonging, as full members of their religious community.

All for one and one for all The more closely knit the group and the more strongly individuals value their membership, the more powerful the effect of group norms. Here Army recruits learn "the Army way." Developing total devotion to group norms is part of their training so that individual members won't forget their role or desert their group in times of danger.

What people gradually learn in such situations are group norms. By adopting such norms, we demonstrate our commitment and connections to our new associates and our pride in "who we are." When we conform in order to attain a positive social identity and become valued members of a group we care about—that is, to satisfy our needs for connectedness—the group exerts *normative influence.*

The desire to be a valued member of a group is so strong that people adopt group norms whenever they identify with a group. For example, when discussing cases together, mock jurors are much more likely to uphold the norm "innocent until proven guilty" (MacCoun & Kerr, 1988) than they are when they judge the same cases alone (Tindale & Davis, 1983). Groups, whether enduring or transitory, reward conformity to their norms: those who endorse the norms most strongly are often admired as more intelligent, competent, confident, and sincere (Eisenger & Mills, 1968; Levinger & Schneider, 1969). So, just as disagreement undermines our confidence that we view reality correctly, being out of step with group norms undermines the secure social identity we derive from belonging to a group. And just as moving toward the group consensus helps reconfirm our perception of reality, conforming to group norms helps reconfirm our sense of identity.

Mastery, Connectedness, or Both? Groups usually have both an informational and a normative function: we adopt group norms not only because we think they reflect reality but also because we want to express our identity with groups we value (Kelman, 1961). But depending on the circumstances, the balance may be tipped toward one function or the other. Among those circumstances, two of the most important are type of task and the way individual group members weight the two functions.

1. *When the need for mastery prevails.* The need for mastery takes precedence over the need for connectedness when a group is faced with an intellective task—a task that has one verifiably correct answer. For example, a town planning committee may be asked to recommend the most cost-efficient purchase of a fleet of buses to buy. After purchase price, reliability, maintenance requirements, and fuel efficiency have all been weighed, one manufacturer's product will probably be a "best buy." When groups are engaged in intellective tasks, with their focus on facts and information, reaching a valid consensus is the top priority. In these circumstances, the reality-testing function of conformity is particularly important (Kaplan & Miller, 1987; Stasser & Stewart, 1992).

2. *When the need for connectedness prevails.* In value-laden judgmental tasks, the identity functions of conformity become more salient (Kaplan & Miller, 1987). Consider what is involved when a committee must decide among foreign-made and domestically produced buses. The group task now involves economic patriotism as well as cost effectiveness. Expressing connectedness may be more important than establishing mastery when coming to a decision.

The connectedness function of consensus may also prevail for group members who consider it to be especially important. Because of their typical roles in our culture, women tend to be more attentive to social relationships and interpersonal feelings than men (Eagly, 1987). Therefore the connectedness function of norms may be more salient for women than for men. Women may see consensus as a way to facilitate interaction among group members and to create positive feelings of identity. Research does suggest that women are more easily influenced than men are, particularly in face-to-face interactions. This finding may reflect women's greater concern with the connectedness functions of group agreement (Becker, 1986; Eagly & Carli, 1981).

As you will see in Chapter 13, pages 579 to 581, female leaders are more likely to involve all group members in group decisions, perhaps because the connectedness aspects of group agreement seem so important to them.

Although the motive for mastery or connectedness prevails in some situations, agreement with a group of similar others usually fulfills both motives simultaneously. It assures us that we are in contact with reality. It also expresses and solidifies a rewarding group identification, helping us to be liked and accepted by those whose opinions we care about. In fact, the reality-seeking and identity-seeking motivations for conformity work together most of the time.

Group Norms in Clinical Settings. People seeking support and personal change often use the power of group norms to help them achieve their goal. People frequently choose this path when coping with a serious illness, the death of a loved one, or a substance-abuse or weight-control problem. Support and self-help groups are voluntary groups whose members meet to discuss their thoughts and feelings, share their problems, and develop ways of coping on a day-to-day basis (Forsyth, 1990). Alcoholics Anonymous (with more than one million members worldwide), WeightWatchers, and Parents Without Partners all use the power of group norms to change group members' perceptions and, frequently, their behaviors. One study randomly assigned overweight women to either of two treatment programs: one group received step-by-step instructions on exercise and diet, and the other group attended self-help meetings. Later, the women's diet progress was compared. Researchers found that those in the self-help groups not only were more optimistic about losing weight and more motivated to do so but also were more likely to act on their positive attitudes: they consumed less fat and exercised more. These changed attitudes and behaviors translated into an average weight loss of nine pounds for those in the self-help groups, compared with less than one pound for the others (Jason and others, 1991). Another study evaluated the effectiveness of an AIDS education program designed for people under treatment for drug addiction. Compared with a matched control group that received no specific treatment, people who attended support groups had more positive attitudes toward condom use and actually used condoms more often (Magura and others, 1991).

Self-help groups work so effectively for reasons that should now sound familiar. As members conform to the group norms, they obtain both a sense of mastery and a feeling of connectedness to valued others. As they share information, recount their personal histories, and explain their particular experiences, participants can learn many concrete, useful lessons. Among these are how others cope with their problems, what programs and resources are available to group members, and why people with their particular problem feel the way they do. At the same time, groups give members a feeling of being valued. The group offers comradeship in the recognition that all members are fighting a common battle. And it offers support in the opportunity to express emotions freely with no fear of rejection. Individual successes are cheered, and failures are accepted with sympathetic understanding (Yalom, 1985). Can you think of ways to use the power of group norms to support other types of constructive personal and social change?

Salience of Group Membership

> *The tendency to conform is strongest when group membership is highly accessible, such as when other group members are present. But the physical presence of others is not necessary for conformity.*

Maybe you have noticed how enthusiastically delegates to party conventions support the platform, or how wildly new converts at a revival meeting embrace the group's creed. The reason for their special conviction is that both kinds of motivations—mastering reality and expressing connectedness with others—are activated when individuals become aware of their group membership.

One of the factors that makes us most aware of our groups, of course, is the physical presence of other members. Being around others who are like us highlights all the features we share in common, thus making very salient the group's role as a reference group for testing reality. At the same time, all those cues to group membership bring identity and connectedness concerns to mind. The double motivational whammy of being in the presence of other group members in turn increases conformity to group norms (Crutchfield, 1955; Reid, 1983; Skinner & Stephenson, 1987).

The physical presence of group members can affect our perceptions of ourselves and others. Many of these effects were discussed in Chapter 6, pages 227 to 245.

This finding—that people agree more with the group in public than in private—is often interpreted as meaning that groups produce only public conformity, not private conformity. However, the evidence does not support this claim. Substantial conformity to group norms occurs even in private (Allen, 1965; Deutsch & Gerard, 1955; Insko and others, 1983). After all, the Republican delegate's belief in free enterprise does not disappear when she comes home from the convention; the new convert's faith does not falter just because the revival meeting ends. And remember that subjects in Sherif's study used the group norm as their personal standard as much as one year later, when they were asked to judge the light movements in the absence of other group members. The presence of others is not a necessary precondi-

Figure 9.4 Motives behind private conformity

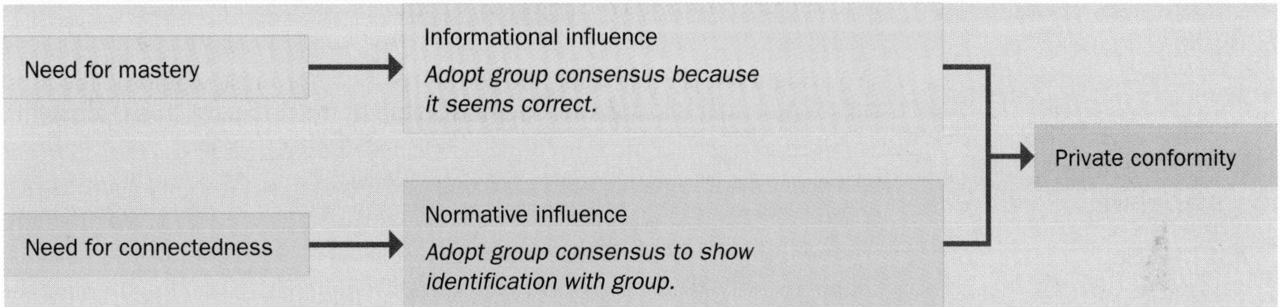

People adopt a group consensus as their own private belief because they wish both to hold correct opinions and to show their identification with a group they value and respect. These two processes are termed *informational influence* and *normative influence.*

tion either for group membership to be salient or for conformity to group norms to occur. Conformity occurs because the group is in the individual—as a social identity that is part of the self—as well as because the individual is in the group.

The formation and transmission of group norms is one of the most powerful examples of how we work together with others to socially construct a shared view of reality. As can be seen in Figure 9.4, the needs of mastery and connectedness guide our reactions to informational and normative influence from the group as we try to reach consensus on a multitude of judgments and decisions.

How Groups Form Norms: Processes of Social Influence

Every year in early spring, admissions committees in hundreds of colleges and universities across the country gather to discuss the current crop of applicants. In institutions like ours, roundtable discussions determine who will be invited to join the freshman class in the fall and who will be sent an "I'm sorry to inform you" letter. As members of the admissions committee meet and talk together, each contributes some of his or her views and ideas to the group, and each hears what others think and how they react. Gradually the group forms a consensus, agreeing on who should be accepted and who will be rejected. In these groups and others, the group norms forged from this kind of give and take sometimes reflect a middle-of-the-road consensus. But the merging of individual arguments can also move the consensus away from the center and toward the extreme.

Group Compromise: Taking the Middle Ground

When group members are initially split on an issue, group discussion usually results in convergence on a more moderate position.

You might expect that a middle-of-the-road compromise would be the most likely outcome when people share their views. For example, just as Sherif's subjects converged on a middling estimate of how far the light moved in the darkened room, people with extremely positive or negative evaluations of a particular candidate might move toward more moderate views. Surprisingly, though, this outcome is rare in group discussions. Such compromise usually happens only when a group's views are evenly split, with roughly half the members supporting an issue and half opposing it (Burnstein & Vinokur, 1977; Wetherell, 1987).

When group discussion does produce a compromise, the position reflected in the final group norm is more moderate than the initial views of its individual members—an effect called *depolarization.* The convergence of estimates by the subjects in Sherif's study demonstrate depolarization. Look back at Figure 9.1 and you will see that each group member moves toward a moderate group norm near the average of the members' initial opinions. The same pattern can be seen when an admissions application initially elicits an equal number of supporters and opponents. Opinions will converge toward a moderate position, which may or may not be good enough to gain admission for the would-be student.

Group Polarization: Going to Normative Extremes

When a majority of group members initially favor one side of the issue, discussion usually moves the group to an even more extreme position.

An even division of opinion is a rare phenomenon in group decision making. More commonly, a majority of group members initially favor a particular point of view. One large-scale study of jury proceedings, for example, found that a majority initially favored acquittal or conviction in all but 10 of 225 trials studied (Kalven & Zeisel, 1966). Why do groups initially lean in one direction or another? Often their views are influenced by the weight of the evidence. A student with good academic preparation and well-rounded extracurricular activities will appeal to the majority of admissions committee members, for example. And frequently the initial point of view actually defines the group. Individual members of the local Sierra Club probably joined because they favor conservation and thus share similar opinions on the spotted owl. Similarly, members of a neighborhood watch committee might share views about local law enforcement.

What kind of final consensus can we expect when most members of a group initially share an opinion? If you participate in admissions discussions long enough, you begin to notice a reliable pattern. Imagine that a candidate with some potential is being discussed. Someone points out her solid but not startling academic credentials. Another notes that her GPA improved over her high school years, even as she took on extracurricular activities. A third mentions that the candidate is on his "accept" list, at which point a fourth chips in with "Uh huh, I gave her a high rating, too." A particularly strong letter of recommendation is reread, and the group agrees enthusiastically on acceptance: the candidate is excellent. At first merely a person with potential, the candidate is now a superior applicant. And, of course, movement in the opposite direction can also happen. When the majority of committee members lean toward rejection, talking about credentials seems only to doom the candidate further. In the context of group discussion, the good get better and the bad get worse.

The first to notice this unexpected effect of group discussion was a young graduate student named James Stoner (1961). Stoner asked business school students to respond to a series of fictitious "choice dilemmas," in which they had to decide between a cautious course of action with a small potential benefit and a risky option with a large payoff. For example, imagine having to decide between staying in a job that offers security and moderate yearly raises and taking a better-paying job with a new firm that could go out of business in a year or two. Stoner found that when people work together in groups on this kind of problem, they opt for more risky actions than when they make decisions alone. This finding was originally called the *risky shift.*

Surprisingly, Stoner's results had little to do with the perception of risk. Other researchers soon demonstrated that if most people initially prefer a cautious line of action, group discussion produces a more cautious outcome. Similar patterns of group shifts emerged under a variety of circumstances. For example, if most members of a group initially are racially prejudiced, group interaction and discussion tends to increase their prejudice. If most members initially are not prejudiced, then group discussion shifts them further in the direction of egalitarian views (Myers & Bishop, 1971). Findings such as these have led to the conclusion that the various shifts are part of a general phenomenon, group polarization. **Group polarization** occurs when the initial preferences of the group become more extreme following group interaction (Moscovici & Zavalloni, 1969).

Polarization in the Jury Room. Group polarization can operate whenever like-minded individuals interact. In one demonstration of its impact on jury deliberation, David Myers and Martin Kaplan (1976) asked mock juries made up of U.S. college students to assess the guilt of defendants in traffic felony cases. The researchers manipulated the strength of the evidence, so that in some groups a majority initially favored conviction, whereas in others a majority initially favored acquittal. In the proconviction groups, discussion increased the likelihood that the defendant would be found guilty. In the proacquittal groups the reverse occurred. Similar results were found in a study of Japanese students serving as mock jurors (Isozaki, 1984).

group polarization The exaggeration during group interaction of a group's initial position or preference.

Group polarization When people who share views on an issue interact, their belief in their cause is often strengthened. Joining others who share their experiences with cancer has radicalized the attitudes of some women participants in grass-roots projects working for health-care reforms.

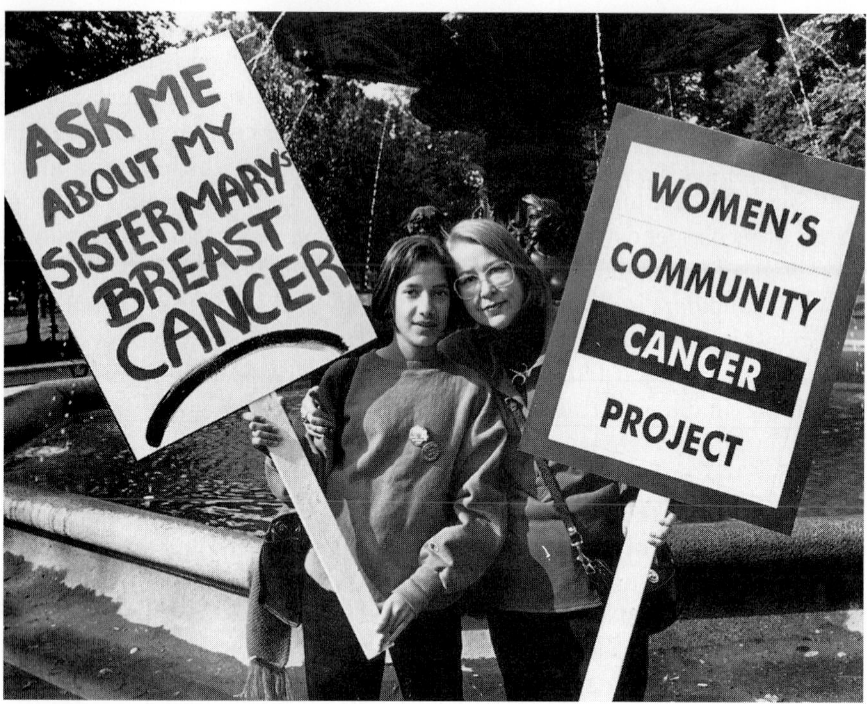

Research confirms that group polarization takes place among real jurors deciding real cases. In their survey of jury decisions, Kalven and Zeisel (1966) found that in 209 of 215 cases, the final outcome favored the position of the initial majority. The authors of the study offer an interesting metaphor for the impact of group discussion: "The deliberation process might be likened to what the developer does for an exposed film: it brings out the picture" (p. 489). This is a far cry from the compromise, middle-of-the-road, or depolarized position we might intuitively expect groups to adopt.

How do social psychologists explain group polarization? By now you may not be surprised to learn that the answer has to do with how deeply information is processed. We have seen that when people make judgments or decisions about other people or their messages, they sometimes use simple rules of thumb and at other times think deeply about the alternatives. Both superficial and systematic processing also characterize our reaction to information about others' opinions in group interaction. Sometimes we notice where others stand and go along with the majority without worrying about their reasons. If, for example, you and some friends are choosing a restaurant and you do not particularly care what you eat, you may pay no attention to claims about the quality of the food and service and simply throw your support behind the majority. But if you are in a situation in which your decision will matter a great deal—as a member of an admissions committee or a jury—you probably will consider more than just the other members' positions. You will also want to understand their reasons, evidence, and arguments. But even then you may not be immune to the persuasive effects of the majority's viewpoint. Group polarization can occur regardless of whether we are processing systematically or superficially.

Superficial Processing: Relying on Others' Positions

> *When people process superficially, merely relying on others' positions can produce polarization. Under these conditions, the majority consensus in the group is seen as reflecting reality and as defining what good group members are like. This viewpoint gives the majority position a persuasive advantage.*

Polarization can occur even when a very limited amount of information is available—for example, when people know only *what* others think but not *why* they came to their conclusions (Baron & Roper, 1976). The polarization that occurs in these situations usually reflects people's reliance on a ready-made consensus to help them master the social environment and meet needs for connectedness.

The Consensus Heuristic: Looking for Reality. Agreeing with a consensus fulfills people's desire for mastery of their social world—their desire to hold the correct views and do the right things. Because people believe that a consensus reflects reality, group consensus is sometimes used as a *heuristic cue*—a simple rule that allows people to make judgments and decisions they believe to be valid. The rule is straightforward: if most people think something is correct, then it probably is. Like other cues, the consensus heuristic can come into play almost automatically when people are not thinking too hard.

In one laboratory demonstration of the power of the consensus heuristic, students listened to strong or weak arguments that were presented in a speech supporting probation as an alternative to imprisonment (Axsom and others, 1987). During the presentation, one group of subjects heard several bouts of loud clapping and cheers from the audience listening to the speech; another group of subjects heard only scattered applause and occasional jeering. Some subjects in each of the two groups were told that the new probation policies would not affect them personally. As a result, these listeners were less involved and less attentive, and they were also very much influenced by the apparent consensus. When others cheered, these subjects agreed with the probation policy, even if the arguments were weak. When others jeered, they disagreed with the policy, even if the arguments were strong.

You may recall that this experiment was cited in Chapter 1, page 1, as an interesting example of social-psychological research.

If you now recall the anecdote about the French cabinet minister from the beginning of this chapter, you will appreciate just how well he understood social psychology, if not politics. He knew that audience members who devoted no real effort to evaluating the Socialist party platform would

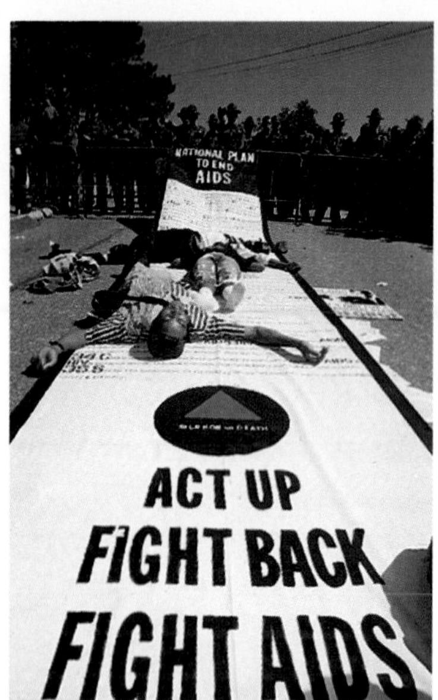

Act up acts up Because people pay more attention to extreme and unusual positions, the activities of radical groups like Act Up make the norms of all gay support groups seem more extreme. This may contribute to a polarization of attitudes in those sympathetic to gay rights and open the way for wider support for more "moderate" demands, like faster drug testing.

be persuaded by, and would then adopt, the apparent consensus of the paid supporters who applauded so noisily. And when undecided or dissenting members of a group adopt the majority consensus—whether apparent or real—the group's average position moves toward the extreme, and the result is group polarization.

Consensus and Connectedness: "Being the Best You Can Be." Another factor that leads groups toward polarization is peoples' desire to be the best possible members of their group. Because people see group norms as embodying the essence of the group, they demonstrate group identity by not only adhering to these norms but also exaggerating them.

Any group member who values his or her group membership naturally wants to represent the group ideal (Codol, 1975). In fact, most members of cohesive groups think of themselves not as average but as superior representatives of their groups (Myers & Lamm, 1976). Thus, for example, most business executives think of themselves as more ethical than the average executive, and most editors think their grasp of grammar is better than that of their average colleague. However, others' views may not support the opinions we hold of ourselves. Sometimes hearing what others think reveals that we are not as much above average as we thought we were. This realization may in turn prompt a speedy adoption of a more extreme position so that we can again become above average on important dimensions within the group (Singleton, 1979). As more and more group members adopt this strategy, the group norm grows more extreme.

Even when others' positions are all we know, our desire for mastery and our wish to be valued by important others make us want to agree with—and even go beyond—the majority's view. Group members who hold the minority position shift to adopt the majority consensus. Members of the majority may move even farther toward the extreme. Together, these two processes make group polarization a likely outcome as the average position in the group grows more extreme.

Systematic Processing: Attending to Both Positions and Arguments

When people process systematically, both positions and evidence work together to produce polarization. Majority arguments are more numerous, receive more discussion, seem more compelling, and are presented more persuasively. All these factors give majority views a persuasive advantage.

When decisions are important or affect the group directly, group decision makers move their processing into high gear. They consider not just the preferences of others but also their supporting *arguments and evidence.* If you suspect that such systematic processing can also cause group polarization, you are right.

In the lively interchange that characterizes most group discussions, preferences and the arguments for those preferences are aired simultaneously. Imagine, for example, that you are a jury member listening to another juror argue, "Well, if the defendant was at work, as his foreman testified, he could not possibly have arrived home before 6:30, and the doctors said that the victim was already dead by then." Although this statement reviews relevant evidence, it also reveals the juror's opinion. If, instead of laying out her position, the juror had merely voiced her opinion that the defendant was innocent, you might also have been able to figure out the unstated arguments supporting that view. When a jury or another group is deeply engaged in resolving a dilemma, both *what* other group members believe and *why* they believe it become important considerations. The resulting attention given *both* arguments and positions operates as a lever that moves the group toward the extreme, and once again group polarization is the outcome (Mackie, 1986). Although group members are engaging in systematic processing, the arguments supporting the position initially favored by the majority gain an even more persuasive edge than the arguments favoring the minority position. Several forces join together to produce this remarkable outcome.

1. *Majority arguments are more numerous.* The greater the number of people who hold a particular viewpoint, the more numerous the arguments favoring that position are likely to be. Imagine a situation in which your philanthropy committee is planning a fund raiser. Since most members favor a silent auction, more people speak in favor of that activity and give more evidence supporting it than in favor of any other activity. Not surprisingly, the effect of hearing this lopsided set of appeals—particularly the novel and compelling ones—is to further strengthen group members' views. This in turn produces polarization. The idea that initial preferences exert a bias on the kind of arguments discussed and that this bias pushes the group toward the extreme is called the *persuasive arguments explanation* of group polarization. The degree of polarization depends on the novelty and quality of the evidence. When group members hear persuasive arguments that they had not previously considered, they move toward the majority position and the group norm becomes more extreme (Hinsz & Davis, 1984).

2. *Majority arguments get more discussion.* Arguments endorsed by more than one group member are much more likely to be discussed than ideas endorsed by only a single person. In one demonstration of this effect, Garold Stasser and his colleagues (1989) asked students to read different sets of information about candidates for president of a student body. Some information was given to all members of the group, but other information was given to just one person. When the group met to evaluate the candidates, they discussed 46 percent of the shared information but only 18 percent of the unshared information. This bias remained even after the researchers structured the discussion, instituting rules that instructed the group to discuss *all* the facts available to them. In fact, this instruction resulted in an even more in-

tense focus on the shared information (see Figure 9.5). Group members apparently believe that the information on which they all agree is the information most relevant to the issue under discussion. This tendency is particularly strong with judgmental rather than intellective tasks (Stasser & Stewart, 1992). The bias toward discussing shared rather than individually held information is bound to strengthen the majority's case—after all, by definition majority arguments are shared viewpoints, whereas minority arguments are likely to be unique dissenting views. As the biased discussion confirms the majority position and convinces some minority members, the group norm becomes more extreme.

3. *Majority arguments seem more compelling.* When several people make the same argument, it has extra impact. Thus, for example, three different people voicing an identical argument are more persuasive than a single person who repeats the same argument three times (Harkins & Petty, 1983). This bias reflects the tendency of people to pay particular attention to replication—the fact that different people with different perspectives reach the same conclusion is particularly compelling. Consistent with this finding is the fact that people rate as more persuasive the arguments with which they think "most people" agree: if most people buy the argument, it must be a good one (McLachlan, 1986; Singleton, 1979). And what constitutes "most people"? A majority, of course! Thus, the arguments put forward by a majority in a group discussion seem particularly persuasive, and their influence moves the group further toward the extreme.

Figure 9.5 Let's talk about something we all know

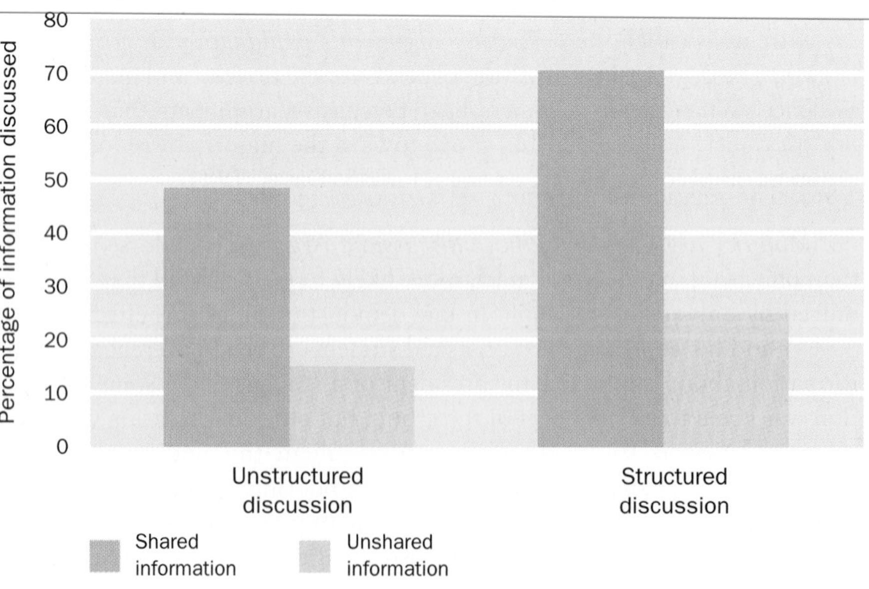

Subjects asked to evaluate candidates were much more likely to discuss information that everyone in the group shared than they were to discuss information known to only one member of the group. When rules were instituted to structure the discussion, the shared information was even *more* likely to be discussed. (Data from Stasser and others, 1989.)

Figure 9.6 Why a consensus is influential: Processes underlying group polarization

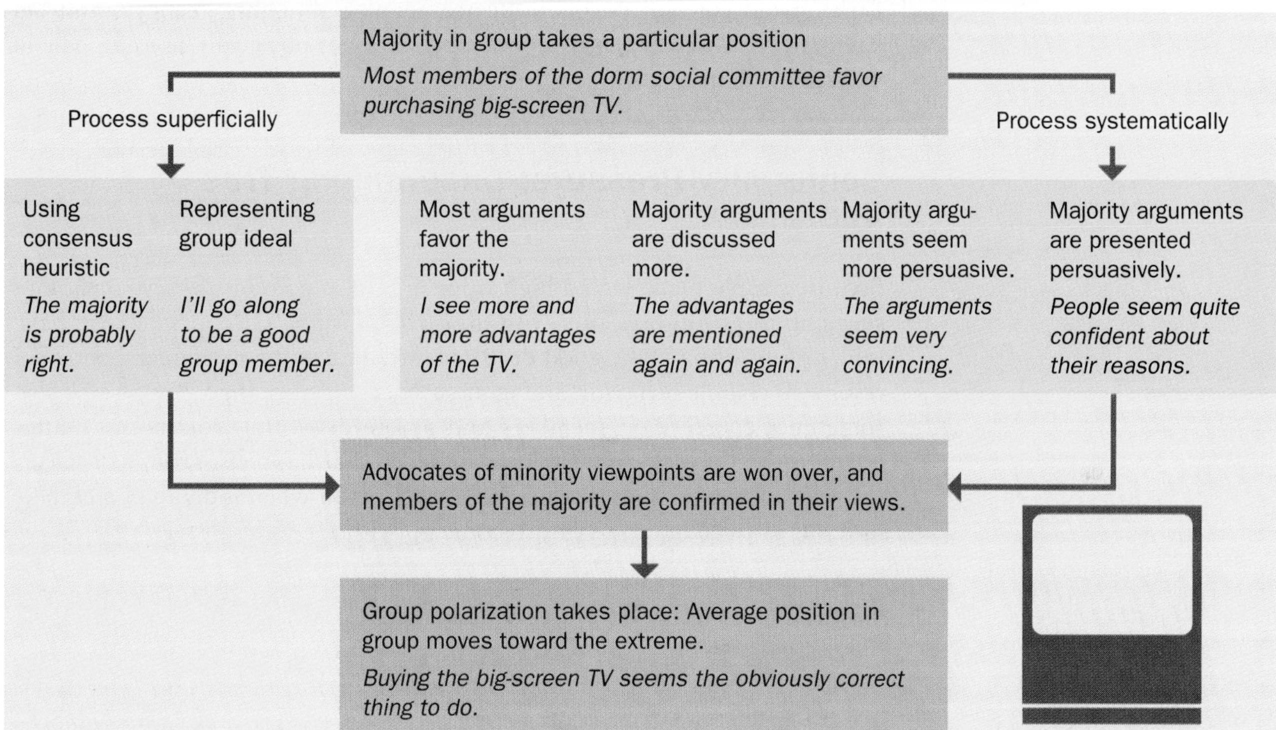
Majority in group takes a particular position
Most members of the dorm social committee favor purchasing big-screen TV.
Process superficially
Process systematically
Using consensus heuristic
The majority is probably right.
Representing group ideal
I'll go along to be a good group member.
Most arguments favor the majority.
I see more and more advantages of the TV.
Majority arguments are discussed more.
The advantages are mentioned again and again.
Majority arguments seem more persuasive.
The arguments seem very convincing.
Majority arguments are presented persuasively.
People seem quite confident about their reasons.
Advocates of minority viewpoints are won over, and members of the majority are confirmed in their views.
Group polarization takes place: Average position in group moves toward the extreme.
Buying the big-screen TV seems the obviously correct thing to do.

When a majority in a group initially leans in a particular direction, their consensus tends to influence others in a variety of ways—whether the group members process superficially or think about the issues in more depth. As the majority position attracts converts from the other side and majority members find their beliefs further strengthened and reinforced, the group's average position moves in the direction favored by the majority initially. Group polarization has occurred.

4. *Majority arguments are presented more compellingly.* One study found that group members, especially males, use a less cautious and more argumentative style of advocacy when they are members of the majority than when they are in the minority (Kerr and others, 1987). Perhaps this explains why other group members see those expressing the majority opinion as more confident and intelligent than those who disagree with it (McLachlan, 1986). The relative effectiveness of majority members' presentations may give the faction's arguments both a qualitative and a quantitative advantage. The result once again is that the majority seems more compelling, it wins more converts to its cause, and group polarization takes place.

In summary, when group members engage in systematic processing, the existence of consensus makes majority arguments more persuasive, and this persuasive advantage in turn strengthens the consensus. As members of the minority jump onto the majority bandwagon, majority members move toward even more extreme views, and polarization is the inevitable consequence. The process is summarized in Figure 9.6. As you may recall from our discussions of attitudes in Chapter 7, systematic processing is even more likely to produce private acceptance and lasting change than is superficial processing. Group norms formed through systematic processing have the same capacity to produce private acceptance and enduring change. Consequently, group norms influence people's thoughts, feelings, and behaviors even when other group members are not physically present, as you will see in Chapter 10.

Conformity Pressure: Undermining True Consensus

Because people place such a high value on group consensus they sometimes succumb to group pressure, with disastrous results. Of course, as we have said, groups often make good decisions, strengthen their members' personal resolve to change behavior, and ignite needed social change. But groups also sometimes coerce their members and ignore dissenting voices—no matter how worthy these opinions might be. When that happens, group consensus can lead to invalid and unreliable decisions, even when individual members have the knowledge and skills to come up with the right answer.

When Consensus Seeking Goes Awry

Consensus can only be relied on as valid when consensus is achieved in the right way. A consensus cannot be trusted if it arises from unthinking reliance on others' positions, contamination by shared biases, or public conformity. Such a consensus offers only the illusion of unanimity.

A decision is not necessarily valid merely because it is based on a consensus. Consider the decision to market the drug Thalidomide, which caused tragic birth defects; or the production of the flawed Hubble space telescope; or the 1980 plan to rescue the American hostages in Teheran, which ended with helicopter crashes in the Iranian desert. All these decisions depended in large part on group input, but all had serious flaws. Were they perhaps marred by faulty consensus seeking? As you will see, if a consensus is to provide trustworthy information about reality, the consensus has to be achieved in the right way.

Consensus Without Consideration: Unthinking Reliance on Consensus. If we use a rule of thumb to assess available information, we can be influenced by an unreliable or even a manipulated consensus. In 1990 key members of the U.S. Senate may have fallen prey to a manipulated consensus when they squashed legislation designed to reduce fuel inefficiency, air pollution, and dependency on foreign oil. This surprising action apparently represented legislators' views that "the people" did not want such changes.

Senators had received thousands of letters opposing the bill, and they relied on this consensus when deciding how to vote. If they had processed information more carefully, they might have realized that corporate consultants had orchestrated the apparent consensus (Waldman, 1991).

The influence of a manipulated consensus has been demonstrated in numerous studies, ranging from research that measured the effect of staged audience reactions on acceptance of persuasive communications (Axsom and others, 1987) to studies of the effects of canned laughter on reactions to bad jokes (Nosanchuk & Lightstone, 1974). Group members who unthinkingly go along with an apparent consensus are often led astray.

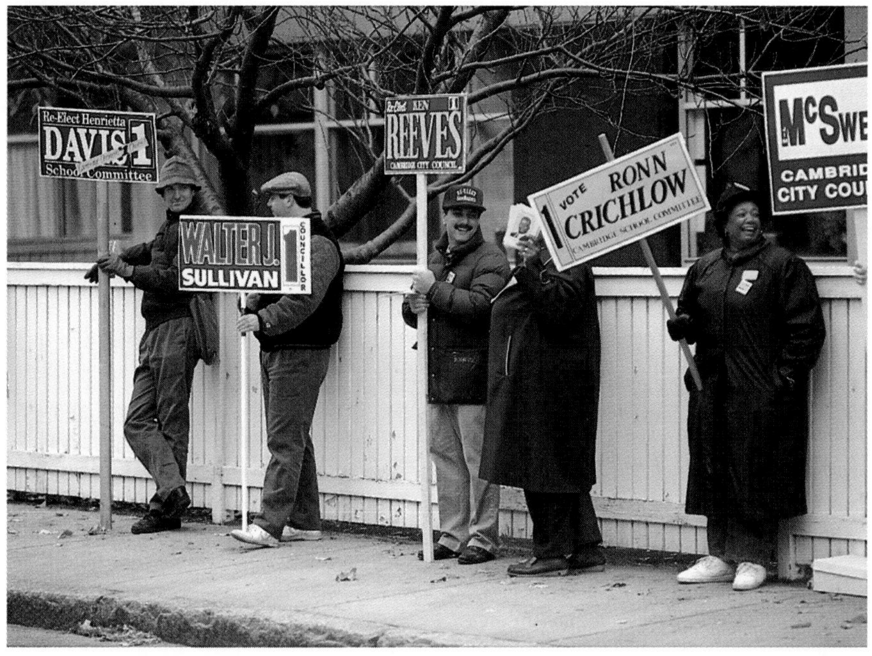

Unthinking reliance on apparent consensus Why are these people advertising their political preferences? Their presence on street corners and outside polling booths is intended to convince voters that their candidate has wide support. The potential power of the consensus heuristic is undermined, however, by the variety of candidates represented: apparently, there is no true consensus about who should be elected.

Consensus Without Independence: Contamination. The idea that a consensus provides reality insurance rests on an assumption: we believe we can trust the consensus because multiple individuals, who considered the evidence independently and from diverse perspectives, have eventually reached the same conclusion. Although we acknowledge that one person might be influenced by a particular bias, it seems unlikely that so many people with so many different perspectives will all make the same mistake.

Because of the importance of this assumption, people are often on the lookout for shared biases that might contaminate group decisions. In one study, for example, subjects trying to decide a mock court case watched the videotaped views of six people before giving their own opinions about the defendant's guilt or innocence. Some subjects heard the people on the tape described as two "groups" of three; other subjects believed they were hearing six independent individuals. The opinions of the taped speakers had less effect on the decisions of subjects who believed them to be two groups than they did on the other subjects (Wilder, 1977). Why? Perhaps the subjects feared contamination, thinking that the groups of speakers might have shared a bias or influenced each other. Consistent with this interpretation, another study showed that the mere perception that a group of confederates was a committee reduced their influence on subjects' opinions. The confederates' views were persuasive only when it was made clear that the committee members represented diverse perspectives—that their individual views had not been contaminated by undue influence or a shared bias (Harkins & Petty, 1987).

You may sense a contradiction here. On the one hand, we trust a consensus when independent and separate individuals endorse it; the convergence of their differing perspectives on the same position confirms the validity of that position. On the other hand, as you may recall from the discussion earlier in this chapter, we really expect to agree only with those who share our characteristics. If we disagree with people who are different from us, it is easy to write them off as confused, ignorant, or just plain wrong.

How can these contradictory statements be reconciled? We seem simultaneously to demand that group members be different and independent (so their consensus indicates validity) and similar and in accord (so they remain members of the in-group). In fact, simultaneous similarity and difference is just what we need. We need others to be *similar* to us in terms of the features relevant to making the judgment so that agreement with them will tell us about reality. But we need them to be *different* from us in every other possible way so that no other shared feature can be responsible for biasing everyone's judgment (Gorenflo & Crano, 1989).

This simultaneous similarity and difference is just what makes in-groups so much more persuasive than out-groups (Mackie and others, 1990). People usually see members of their own group as similar on characteristics that define the group but as variable and different in other ways. Thus an English major might see other English majors as sharing an appreciation for language and a love of literature, but interacting with them would reveal that they differ greatly in terms of hobbies, political views, food preferences, and so forth. In contrast, people see out-group members as all alike: to English majors, those dance majors all seem the same.

To refresh your memory about the reasons people see in-groups as more diverse than out-groups, review Chapter 6, pages 235 to 238.

David Wilder (1990) devised a clever experiment to demonstrate that this perception of simultaneous similarity and difference helped in-groups to be more persuasive than out-groups. Subjects listened to an audiotape of some in-group and some out-group members presenting their views on an issue. As the tape played each speaker's comments, subjects viewed a slide of that speaker's face. Then the researcher played a tape of each person's arguments again and asked subjects to match each speaker's picture with his or her arguments. Subjects also indicated how much they agreed with the views expressed by the group they had listened to.

The results showed that subjects could accurately match in-group members' faces to their arguments: they seemed able to keep track of each in-group member as a distinct and separate individual making distinct and separate arguments. In contrast, subjects could not distinguish among the out-group members and their arguments. Although they might remember that a particular point had been made by an out-group member, they had no idea which speaker had made the point. These different perceptions of in-group and out-group members translated into very different amounts of influence. Subjects saw in-group members as distinct individuals putting forward independent arguments and were persuaded by their consensus. They seemed to lump out-group members together, seeing them as faceless figures droning the party line over and over again. No wonder, then, that they found the out-group's views unpersuasive. As Figure 9.7 illustrates, thinking of the in-group as simultaneously similar and diverse makes their individual views seem independent and in turn renders their shared consensus persuasive. In contrast, the sameness of the out-group heightens the perception that their views might be contaminated, and it decreases their ability to exert influence.

Figure 9.7 How in-groups become more persuasive than out-groups

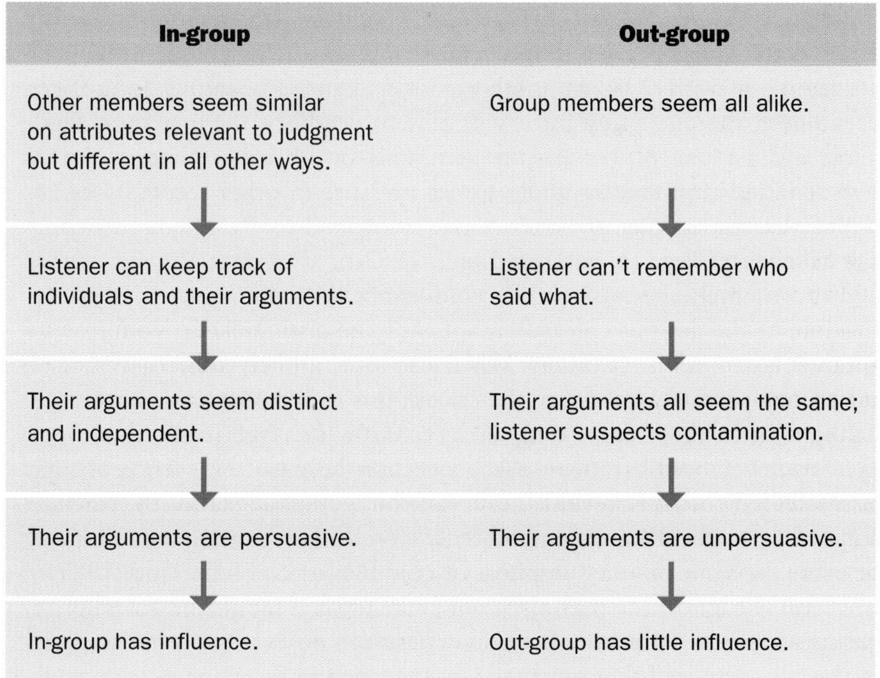

In-group
Out-group
Other members seem similar on attributes relevant to judgment but different in all other ways.
Group members seem all alike.
Listener can keep track of individuals and their arguments.
Listener can't remember who said what.
Their arguments seem distinct and independent.
Their arguments all seem the same; listener suspects contamination.
Their arguments are persuasive.
Their arguments are unpersuasive.
In-group has influence.
Out-group has little influence.

In-groups offer simultaneous similarity and difference. They are viewed as similar on attributes that are crucial for the judgment but as diverse in other ways. As a result, in-groups are more persuasive than out-groups.

Consensus Without Acceptance: Public Conformity. The most dangerous threat to the ideal of consensus formation is public conformity, which we earlier defined as people's behaving consistently with norms that they do not privately accept as correct. When some of Asch's subjects went along with norms that they did not believe were correct, they were demonstrating public conformity. Motivated by the desire to avoid wrath or ridicule, these students followed the motto "go along to get along" (Deutsch & Gerard, 1955; Kelley, 1952), and their public conformity destroyed the reliability of the consensus.

Public conformity reflects people's recognition that groups dispense rewards to members who go along with the consensus and punish members who do not. People who disagree with other group members often anticipate negative reactions (Gerard & Rabbie, 1961), and their fears are well founded. When Stanley Schachter (1951) set up an experiment in which a confederate persistently disagreed with other group members, he found that the group first tried hard to win over the deviant. When this failed, the group ignored his views, assigned him to undesirable tasks, and suggested that he be excluded from the group.

Even jurors experience the pressure to conform. In the first trial of four White Los Angeles police officers accused of beating the Black motorist Rodney King, one juror went public to describe the extreme pressures she felt from other members of the jury. Bullied and ridiculed for her dissenting opinion by the majority who favored acquittal, and worn down by seven days of deliberation, she commented that other jurors' "eyes weren't open, and I said to God, 'If you could give me one more person on my side, I would know'" (*New York Times,* 1992b). Could any statement more clearly demonstrate Asch's finding that a single supporter helps people resist pressure from a majority? When another person changed positions and offered her support, the dissenting juror was able to deadlock the jury on a single charge against one officer despite acquittals on all other charges. Jurors have admitted capitulating under group pressure in other recent cases, including the convictions of boxer Mike Tyson and ex-Panamanian strongman Manuel Noriega (*New York Times,* 1992d).

Unfortunately, because public conformity brought about by fear, exhaustion, or the desire to please cannot easily be distinguished from real acceptance, it can influence others. When everyone publicly adheres to a norm that no one privately endorses, the situation is called *pluralistic ignorance.* Such ignorance abounds in many areas of daily life, even in the classroom. Have you ever been afraid to ask a question because the silence of your classmates led you to believe that everyone but you understands the teacher? Many of the other students undoubtedly were feeling exactly the same way but made the same false assumption you did (Miller & McFarland, 1987).

Pluralistic ignorance may also contribute to such significant social problems as widespread alcohol abuse on college campuses. One study supporting this idea reported that most students engaged in behaviors—such as excessive drinking or bringing liquor to parties—that suggested more acceptance of alcohol use than they actually felt. As a result, most students believed that their peers were more comfortable with heavy drinking than the peers actually were (Prentice & Miller, 1993). The evidence indicated that everyone was drinking more than they actually wanted to because they thought that everyone else approved of that behavior! If students had discussed their real opinions on this issue, the impression that "everyone" accepts alcohol abuse might have been dispelled. Positive changes in actual behavior might also have followed.

Consensus Seeking at Its Worst: Groupthink

> *When groups become more concerned with reaching consensus than with how they reach consensus, actions based on their norms can be disastrous. Groupthink can be avoided when minority as well as majority viewpoints are considered.*

The Florida weather was unusually chilly on January 28, 1986, as the space shuttle *Challenger* was launched with a crew of seven including schoolteacher Christa McAuliffe. Seventy-three seconds after liftoff, a fiery explosion caused by the failure of a rubber O-ring in a booster rocket killed everyone on board and set back the U.S. space program for years. Investigations proved that the accident had not been an unforeseeable freak event. Indeed, only hours before launch, engineers from the company that built the booster rocket had urgently warned the National Aeronautics and Space Administration decision team that extremely cold temperatures might cause the O-ring to fail. Yet NASA proceeded with the launch—a tragic error that graphically displayed many of the ways that group consensus can go wrong (Esser & Lindoerfer, 1989).

Causes of Groupthink. Consensus formation is most likely to go awry when a group of like-minded individuals are working under pressure to make decisions. Under these conditions, merely reaching agreement becomes more important than how agreement is achieved, and decisions often arise out of pluralistic ignorance. In a pressured situation, group members may selectively withhold information on the minority side, suppress independent thinking, and try to force public conformity. All these tactics are attempts to preserve the group's cohesiveness and their sense that their decisions are valid, and all may result in group norms that are ill-considered, impractical, and unrealistic. Irving Janis (1972) coined the term **groupthink** for this kind of consensus formation, in which an almost fanatical pursuit of cohesion and unanimity undermines the reliability of consensus with potentially disastrous consequences.

Aware that U.S. presidents and their groups of advisers sometimes make ill-advised policy decisions, Janis (1972, 1982) analyzed decision making by Franklin D. Roosevelt and his advisers prior to Pearl Harbor, by John F. Kennedy and his advisers prior to the invasion of the Bay of Pigs in Cuba,

groupthink Group decision making that is impaired by the drive to reach consensus regardless of how the consensus is formed.

and by Richard M. Nixon and his advisers prior to their decision to cover up their responsibility for the Watergate break-in. In each situation, Janis discovered overpowering pressure for conformity, and the suppression of independent-minded dissent.

A presidential commission investigating the *Challenger* disaster found that NASA's decision making also was flawed by an emphasis on agreement rather than dissent—the essence of groupthink (Presidential Commission, 1986). The *Challenger* mission took place in the context of declining public and congressional support for NASA projects. In response, NASA officials sought to recapture the public's imagination and show that NASA was back on track with a series of missions carrying "ordinary" men and women into space.

How does groupthink operate? Three key processes undermine the guarantees that consensus usually offers.

1. *Consensus is achieved without considering all the available information.* Because reaching consensus is all that counts and pressures for agreement are so strong, group members devise multiple ways to avoid exposure to dissenting information. Doubting members engage in *self-censorship,* voluntarily suppressing their doubts and criticisms. Occasionally a *mindguard* emerges—someone who shields group members from unwelcome information that might destroy their confidence in the consensus. With only supporting evidence and ideas available, *collective rationalization* takes over. The group engages in justifying and bolstering its decision, strengthening consensus rather than testing it.

In the *Challenger case,* the engineers concerned about the potential failure of O-rings in cold weather were not allowed to present their doubts to those higher up the chain of command (Esser & Lindoerfer, 1989). They were asked to prove absolutely that the booster would not work—which, of course, was impossible. In the end, self-appointed mindguards shielded the top NASA decision makers from any knowledge of the engineers' reservations.

2. *Consensus is contaminated because members' views are not independent.* Groups whose members share similar backgrounds and similar points of view are most likely to fall prey to groupthink. Despite this danger, such groups often isolate themselves from outside influences and different perspectives, thereby making it more likely that shared biases will corrupt their decision making. Janis points out that mindguards often approach group members in private and squash their expression of dissatisfaction, sometimes by appeals to "think like an in-group member." At one point in the *Challenger* decision-making process, a top executive did just that: declaring that "a management decision" had to be made, he appealed to his engineering vice president to "take off his engineering hat and put on his management hat." In other words, the vice president was being told to think as management thought and to come to the management decision, rather than considering the issue from the engineering—or any other—point of view.

3. *Consensus is achieved through public conformity rather than private acceptance.* When groupthink operates, conformity pressure is often intense. Tolerance for any kind of disagreement is low, and dissenters are harshly brought into line or "cut out of the loop." Janis has shown that faulty consensus processes often start with voice votes among members, which permits powerful and respected members of the group to state their opinions before discussion takes place. If a majority of the group falls into line, any dissenter is then faced with a situation very much like that of Asch's subjects in the line-matching task. As the presidential commission noted, the NASA decision team was publicly polled in the final launch decision meeting, while the corporate executives, who knew of the engineers' concerns, listened. In turn, each team member recommended launch. In the face of such apparent consensus, the executives said only that they could not give an unqualified "go" (Presidential Commission, 1986). Unfortunately, this was not interpreted as a strong vote against the mission, and the launch proceeded.

As can be seen in Figure 9.8, these groupthink processes produce an illusion of unanimity, rather than a true consensus. Everyone thinks that everyone else accepts the group position. The apparent consensus in turn

Figure 9.8 Groupthink undermines the validity of consensus

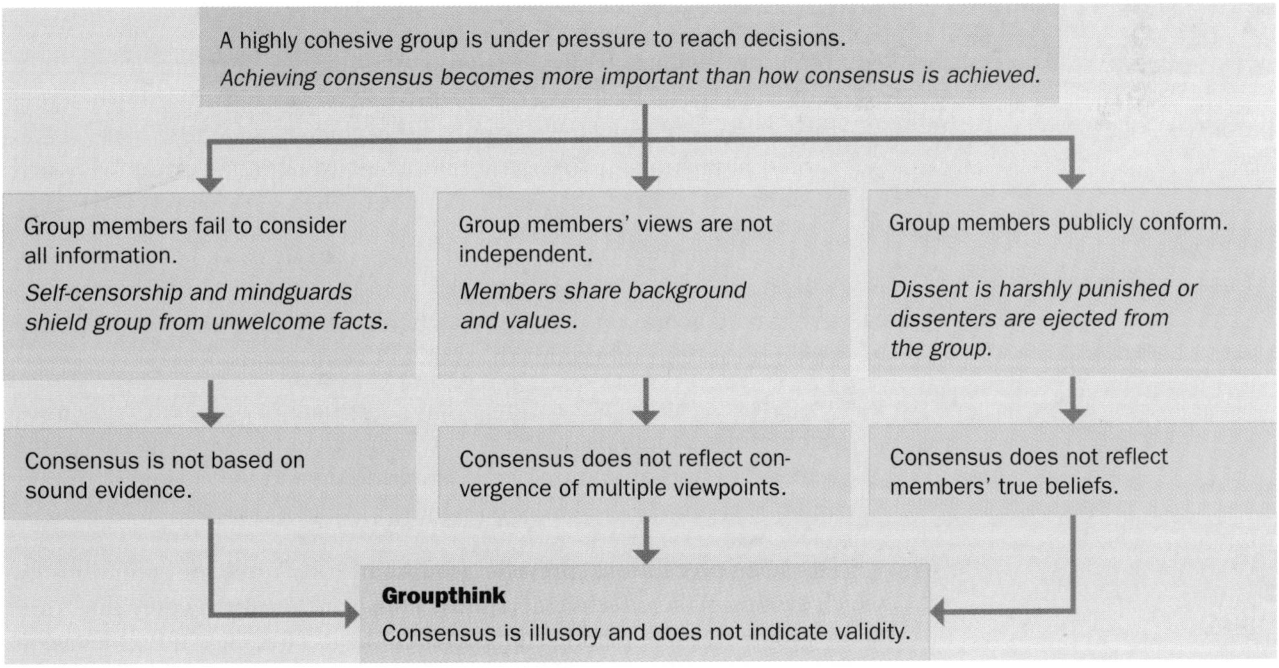

A highly cohesive group is under pressure to reach decisions.
Achieving consensus becomes more important than how consensus is achieved.

Group members fail to consider all information.
Self-censorship and mindguards shield group from unwelcome facts.

Group members' views are not independent.
Members share background and values.

Group members publicly conform.
Dissent is harshly punished or dissenters are ejected from the group.

Consensus is not based on sound evidence.

Consensus does not reflect convergence of multiple viewpoints.

Consensus does not reflect members' true beliefs.

Groupthink
Consensus is illusory and does not indicate validity.

For consensus to indicate correctness, it has to be attained in the right way. Groupthink produces a biased consensus that may be out of touch with reality.

validates the group's judgment: "all reasonable people" would have reached the same conclusion. Thus, the group perceives itself as invulnerable, moral, superior, and capable of doing no wrong—when in fact, the process producing consensus has gone horribly awry. Relevant information has not been processed, shared biases have produced contamination, and a group decision that should be based in fact actually reflects fantasy. In the case of the *Challenger* launch, the consequences of fantasy were fatal.

Blondie

Remedies for Groupthink How can the dangers of groupthink be combated? Janis (1982) recommends that groups take the following precautions.

1. To ensure adequate consideration of alternatives, open inquiry and dissent must be actively encouraged. Yea-sayers eager to rubber-stamp their superiors' preferences must be excluded, and devil's advocates should be appointed to ensure that weaknesses in the group's favored position are pointed out and that opposing views are heard.
2. To avoid contamination by shared biases, outsiders can be brought in to validate the group's decisions. Different groups with different perspectives could work simultaneously on the same problem, or the group could break into subgroups that take different points of view.
3. To reduce conformity pressures that contribute to apparent consensus, public votes should be the exception rather than the rule. The role of the leader should be minimized, and self-criticism and the voicing of doubts and objections should be encouraged.

Do such precautions prevent groupthink? By studying situations in which groups make effective decisions, Janis concluded that they do. After faulty group decision making culminated in the ill-fated Bay of Pigs invasion of Cuba in 1961, President Kennedy changed the way his team of advisers made policy recommendations. First, he insisted on full discussion of the pros and cons of each possible course of action, encouraging the expression of niggling doubts and skeptical dissent. In fact, he unofficially appointed his brother, Attorney General Robert Kennedy, as devil's advocate for the group. Robert Kennedy's job was to challenge the group's decisions, point out possible flaws in their reasoning, and find fault with their conclusions. Second, to avoid contamination from shared biases, the president arranged for his advisers to meet in two separate subgroups. Disagreement between the groups was taken as a signal that one group's thinking might be faulty or that more than one solution to a problem might be viable. At the very least, having two solutions to consider often provoked a lively debate and ensured that as many views as possible were put on the table. Finally, President Kennedy dropped his former practice of stating his personal preferences at the beginning of a meeting; instead, he withheld them until others had aired their own views. At times he even insisted that the group meet without him to ensure that public conformity to his views could not contribute to an illusion of unanimity.

When a new foreign policy crisis developed in October 1962, the new practices were in place. In response to the discovery of Soviet missile-launching sites in Cuba, Kennedy's Executive Committee met for five days, debating possible responses. Finally, after considering and rejecting many alternatives, after consulting with experts, after second-guessing themselves every step of the way, the committee recommended a blockade of Cuban ports, which opened the way for a resolution of the conflict. Eventually, the Soviets agreed to dismantle the missile bases in return for a U.S. promise not to invade Cuba.

Janis's solutions to the groupthink problem and the practices successfully instituted by President Kennedy after the Bay of Pigs misadventure are designed to ensure that minority views are given their due. Both men knew that the expression and consideration of minority views is crucial to the process of social influence.

Minority Influence: The Value of Dissent

Consider the obvious idea that the earth travels around the sun. What we now consider "obvious" was once the scandalous heresy of a single scientist, Galileo. Similarly, the norm that women should have the right to vote and own property was once championed by only a few hardy women and fewer men. Despite the strength of majorities, minority opinions sometimes win the day.

Successful Minority Influence

Minority views can sway the majority. To be influential, the minority must offer an alternative consensus, remain consistent, strike the right balance between similarity and difference from the majority, and promote systematic processing.

Minority viewpoints can alter the consensus reached in a group. But to achieve their victories and convince the majority to reconsider, minorities must turn the processes of social influence to their own advantage.

Offering an Alternative Consensus. Just as a majority's power lies in its command of consensus, the main source of a minority's power is its potential to *undermine* consensus and to promote an alternative consensus. Because group members expect to agree, a minority can exert influence by undermining confidence in the correctness of the consensus (Asch, 1956; Moscovici, 1980). Sometimes the exceptional credentials or charisma of a single person like Galileo or Martin Luther King may be able to sway others to the cause. But most of the time a lone dissenter has little impact on the group. To make the majority sit up and take notice, the alternative consensus must be shared by more than one person and presented in such a way that the majority takes it seriously.

- *Minorities are most powerful when they agree among themselves.* Do you remember the California juror quoted earlier, who prayed for just "one more person on my side" (*The New York Times,* 1992a)? Just as Asch found that influence began when groups of two formed and that groups of three or four had maximal influence, so researchers have shown that minority factions of three or four are more influential than a lone dissenter in mock juries (Tindale and others, 1990). The agreement of multiple group members on a single position apparently signals that the position is a viable alternative (Moscovici & Lage, 1976; Nemeth and others, 1977).
- *Minorities are most powerful when their consensus is more than a one-time affair.* Through the early summer of 1992, independent U.S. presidential candidate Ross Perot attracted many supporters—more supporters than either major-party candidate, according to many public opinion polls. But after withdrawing from the race and then reentering close to Election Day, Perot never recaptured his support and he finished a distant third. The decline in Perot's political fortunes was probably caused in part by his inconsistency—entering the race, then withdrawing, then entering again. Research indicates that because majorities are hardly ever swayed immediately, a minority must remain loyal to its consensus over time (Moscovici, 1980; Nemeth & Wachtler, 1983).

Many researchers have demonstrated that behavioral consistency is essential in giving a minority clout. The first to do so were Serge Moscovici and his colleagues (1969), who devised a mirror image of Asch's line-matching task. They asked groups of four subjects and two confederates to judge the color of a series of unambiguously blue slides. When the confederates insisted on all 36 trials that the slides were green, a small but significant number of subjects joined them in this error. However, when the minority wavered, calling the slides green on only 24 of the 36 trials, they had no influence on the majority. Other researchers have found that consistent minorities can influence others in mock jury deliberations (Nemeth & Wachtler, 1974), and in discussions of such social issues as feminism, the death penalty, and homosexuality (Paichelier, 1976; Maass & Clark, 1983; Maass and others, 1982). Consistency is important because it conveys commitment to the viability of an alternative position. Taken too far, however, the minority's consistency may be interpreted as rigidity or intractability, and their influence rapidly declines (Mugny, 1975; Mugny & Papastamous, 1980).

When a minority successfully challenges the majority view, the dissent can extend beyond the single immediate issue, pushing majority group members to be more open minded in the future. In fact, seeing a minority express opposition in one situation might even give majority members the courage of their convictions in other situations. One study looked at the effects of hearing a minority point of view on people's later ability to resist conformity pressure (Nemeth & Chiles, 1988). Subjects made color perception judgments in the presence of a confederate who made dissenting judgments—calling a blue slide green—all the time, some of the time, or not at all. Subjects later participated in a study like the Asch line-matching task, in which the majority agreed on an obviously incorrect response. Up against this unanimous majority, subjects who had not been exposed to any prior dissent conformed to the majority 70 percent of the time. But those who had viewed minority dissent in an earlier experiment were much more likely to hold out for the correct response. In fact, as can be seen in Figure 9.9, the more consistent the earlier observed dissent had been, the less subjects tended to conform to the group norm.

Figure 9.9 Learning independence from dissent

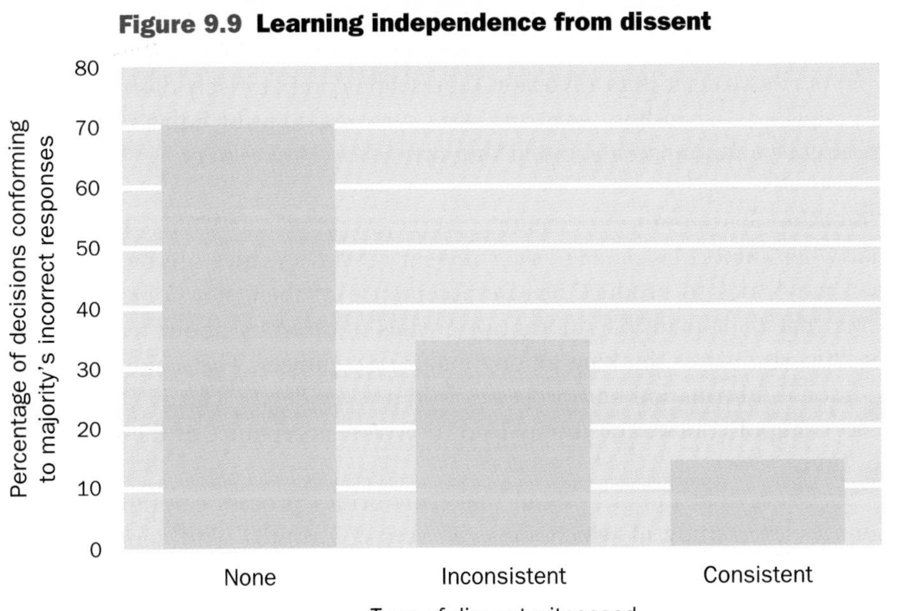

In the presence of confederates who made unanimous but obviously incorrect judgments on a line-matching task, subjects who had not been exposed to a dissenting minority in a previous study conformed 70 percent of the time. But those who had previously witnessed minority dissent conformed much less often. The more consistent the earlier dissent had been, the more independence subjects showed. (Data from Nemeth & Chiles, 1988.)

Being Different, but Not Too Different. Advocates of minority views face a dilemma. To influence the majority viewpoint, they must offer a consensus that clearly differs from the majority position. At the same time, however, dissenters will not be heard if they are perceived as too different from the majority and therefore not part of the in-group, or if they are judged to be lacking in the qualifications for making the judgment (Turner, 1991). Indeed, dissenters often are ignored, disliked, and rejected (Levine, 1980; Mugny, 1982). How can minorities successfully navigate this fine line? According to John Turner (1982) and Edwin Hollander (1958, 1985), the minority first has to establish itself as a credible part of the in-group, perhaps by agreeing with the group on important issues. Then other group members will show respect for their views on other issues—even deviations from the party line. Research confirms that members who first agree and then dissent are more persuasive than those who challenge the group immediately (Bray and others, 1982; Lortie-Lusier, 1987). As Hollander describes it, the dissenters must first build up "points," or *idiosyncrasy credits,* before they can spend them.

Representing Diversity. Recall that a majority consensus loses some of its power if group members share a common bias. Minority influence is similarly reduced if the minority viewpoint seems contaminated. *Double minorities*—those who hold a viewpoint different from that of the majority and who differ from the majority in an *obvious* way—are at a particular disadvantage. When gay advocates lobby for affirmative action laws or mothers petition their employers for child-care facilities, opponents can too easily dismiss their claims. Why? Because the claimants' shared attribute—sexual orientation, motherhood, or other group characteristics—can be portrayed as a factor that may bias the claimants' views and raise questions about their self-interest (Mugny & Papastamous, 1980). In such cases, the majority may assume that the minority viewpoint is invalid. The viewpoint will seem much stronger if its advocates represent a comparatively diverse group of people—as when both gays and nongays campaign for unbiased hiring, or parents and nonparents join in supporting day-care centers.

Chapter 7, page 227, described the attributional processes that weaken the impact of arguments when they seem to be governed by the source's self-interest.

Promoting Systematic Processing. Serge Moscovici (1980) has suggested that when minorities manage their dissent effectively, they are more likely than majorities to produce private acceptance of their viewpoint. He believes that their plausible alternative creates uncertainty about reality and that this stimulates thinking among majority members. The majority seeks additional information and processes it in greater depth. This is systematic processing, of course, and it may lead to private acceptance of the minority position.

Evidence that minorities can make majorities process carefully comes from a clever study in which subjects were confronted with confederates who were either a majority or a minority in each experimental session (Nemeth and others, 1990). The real subjects and the confederates listened

Figure 9.10 Minority consistency encourages systematic processing

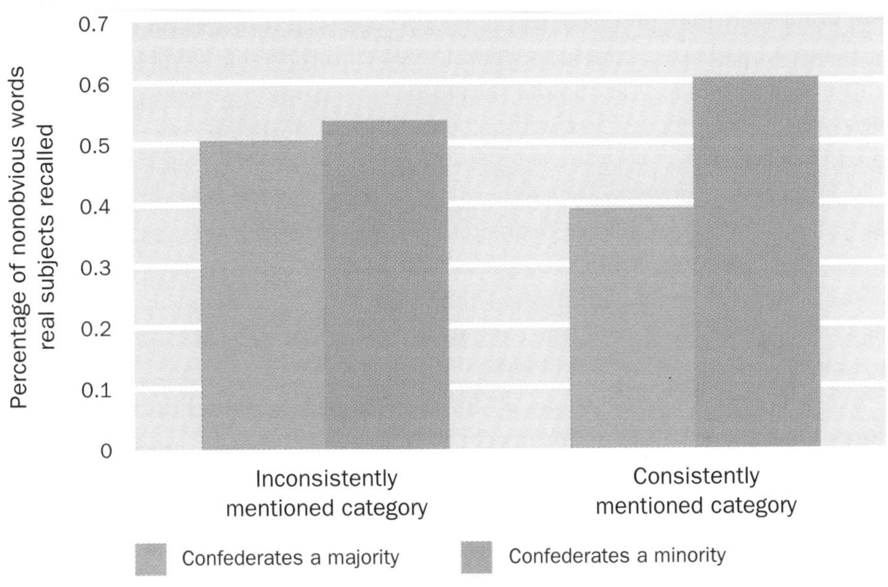

In this study, researchers used confederates who gave nonobvious answers in a series of three trials. When a minority rather than a majority mentioned a nonobvious category of words on a list, subjects could more easily recall the words at a later time—suggesting that they thought about them more thoroughly. Recall was particularly good when the minority consistently mentioned the nonobvious category on all three lists, rather than on only one. (Data from Nemeth and others, 1990.)

to three lists of words. After hearing each list, they took turns naming a category represented by some words on the list. For example, if the list contained many names of birds and a few names of fruit, "birds" was the obvious response and was usually named by the real subjects. The confederates, however, did not name the obvious categories. In some conditions, the rigged majority of confederates named the less obvious fruit category, whereas in other conditions the rigged minority named it. The consistency with which the confederates responded with the unusual category name was also varied. In some conditions, the nonobvious category was mentioned only once, and in others it was mentioned consistently on all three trials. At a later time, the real subjects were asked to recall words from all the lists. The results showed that they could recall more words from lists in which a minority rather than a majority mentioned the nonobvious category, suggesting that exposure to a minority point of view had made them process those words more carefully (see Figure 9.10). Recall was particularly good when the minority consistently mentioned the nonobvious category on all three trials, suggesting that a consistent minority was the most likely to make subjects process systematically.

Minority Influence in the Workplace. The tradeoff between quick decisions achieved by falling into line behind the majority and high-quality decisions attained by careful consideration of multiple viewpoints is also important in business and industry. In fact, the benefits of minority viewpoints for decision making may mean that the changing demographics of the U.S. work force could have a positive impact on business's bottom line. By 1995, it is estimated that more than 60 percent of women will be working outside the home and that minority ethnic group representation in the labor force will exceed 14 percent. Including employees who represent diverse age, race, cultural, and gender viewpoints should be one of the best ways of creating decision-making teams that will consider diverse positions and reach high-quality decisions.

Does this strategy work? According to management consultant Robert Lattimer, "diverse employee teams tend to outperform homogeneous teams of any composition. Managers tell us that homogeneous groups may reach consensus more quickly, but often they are not as successful in generating new ideas or solving problems, because their collective perspective is narrower" (Williams, 1992). In other words, diversity encourages systematic processing and sound decisions. From Burger King to Avon Products, many corporations are applying this insight to take advantage of—not just grudgingly accept—the changing composition of the U.S. work force.

Processes of Minority and Majority Influence

By and large, majorities and minorities influence others by the same processes. They can elicit public as well as private conformity, encourage systematic processing of the evidence, and offer positive social identities.

Does the fact that minorities can provoke systematic processing mean that majority and minority influence occur through fundamentally different processes? Serge Moscovici (1980) thinks so. He argues that minorities induce a process of validation, in which group members carefully process information to try to understand *why* dissenters hold their particular views. In fact, he argues, calling attention to their logical arguments is the dissenters' only recourse because they cannot offer either the validity-ensuring or the identity-confirming benefits of majority positions. In contrast, majority arguments induce a relatively superficial comparison process because people generally want to go along with the crowd, at least in public (Moscovici & Personnaz, 1980; Mugny, 1982). According to Moscovici, listeners focus on *what* majority members say, so that they can quickly comply and earn the rewards of being highly regarded members of the team. Thus minorities bring about private conformity, whereas majorities generate public conformity.

How are we to evaluate Moscovici's arguments? First, majority positions and arguments, as well as minority views, can be both extensively processed and privately accepted (Mackie, 1987; Baker & Petty, 1994)—we have already described research demonstrating this point. Second, it is easy to find examples of situations in which minorities, like majorities, elicit mere public conformity. Majorities may control rewards, but minorities can dispense punishments. One need only listen to the screaming 4-year-old who decides that the family will *not* go to the restaurant or the politician who filibusters far into the night to delay a vote on a bill. So both majorities and minorities can produce public and private conformity.

Third, although majorities offer group members positive identities as good team players, not everybody wants to be a member of the establishment team. A minority identity of deviance and rebellion can also be appealing. Can you imagine circumstances in which you might prefer a deviant image to a staid, conservative, respectable one? When being avant garde, innovative, or socially progressive is important, minority opinions offer a positive identity and minorities have a relatively strong influence (Nemeth, 1986; Paichelier, 1976).

Thus, although Moscovici's ideas have generated new ways of thinking about majority and minority influence, he may have overstated the differences between the processes underlying the two forms of influence (Kruglanski & Mackie, 1990; Latané & Wolf, 1981). By and large, majorities and minorities achieve influence by pulling the same levers. Both can elicit mere public compliance, as well as private conformity; both can induce people to process information about their positions and their arguments; and both can offer the rewards of positive self-images, whether that image is of a solid team member or a free-thinking innovator. In fact, as can be seen in Figure 9.11, minorities are influential when their dissent offers a consensus, avoids contamination, and triggers private acceptance—the same processes by which all groups achieve influence.

Figure 9.11 Minorities use consensus to attain influence

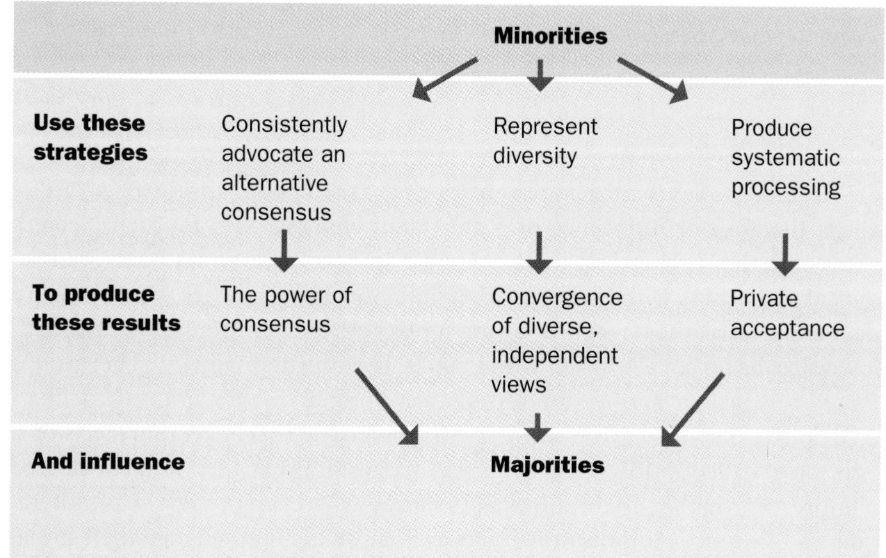

Minorities as well as majorities can influence others when they offer a consensus that represents the convergence of diverse views and is built on the systematic processing of relevant evidence.

Minority Influence in the Jury Room. As we have seen, the expression and consideration of minority views can be vital to preventing groupthink and forming a valid consensus. And this principle has important implications for jury deliberations. In 1972, the U.S. Supreme Court ruled that states may allow juries to give verdicts that command only majority support, holding that there is neither legal nor historical basis for requiring unanimity. Unfortunately, this ruling makes it possible for a majority to ignore minority views. An initial majority would have no need to convince the minority to go along with its position, nor any strong reason to listen to the minority's arguments. Could loosening the requirement of unanimity weaken minority influence and perhaps even lessen the quality of jury decisions?

Turning minorities into majorities In the film "Twelve Angry Men," Henry Fonda (second in on far right) finds himself the lone juror voting for acquittal in a murder case. Fonda's character presents his minority view with such consistency and confidence that other members of the jury consider the evidence systematically—and eventually change their minds. In real jury rooms, establishing an alternate consensus and maintaining it with consistency and confidence are so difficult that minorities rarely win out over majorities.

To investigate these issues, Charlan Nemeth (1977) divided University of Virginia students into mock juries and asked them to reach a verdict about the guilt or innocence of a defendant charged with murder. Nemeth made sure that each group included some students who initially favored acquittal and others who favored conviction. Some of the juries were forced to deliberate until they reached a unanimous verdict, while others were allowed to bring in a verdict with only a two-thirds majority. The groups forced to consider and respond to minority points of view not only deliberated longer but also were more confident about their eventual decisions. Subjects recalled more of the evidence, suggesting that they had considered it more thoroughly than subjects in juries where unanimity was not required. Even more importantly, they were more likely to change their initial views on the case than were members of groups allowed to bring in a two-thirds majority opinion. Similar results were found when more than eight hundred Massachusetts citizens recruited from the jury rolls participated in mock jury discussions after watching a videotaped trial (Hastie and others, 1983). When unanimity was not required, jurors usually terminated their deliberations as soon as they reached the required majority.

These findings suggest that loosening the unanimity requirement does weaken minority influence and may reduce the quality of a jury's deliberations. Of course, it is possible that the participants in these studies, aware that they were involved in research, acted differently than jurors in a real trial. Perhaps real jurors, knowing that their judgments would affect the lives of real people, would give careful consideration to each juror's point of view even if a unanimity rule did not force them to do so. The authors of the Supreme Court decision assumed that they would. Still, it appears that a unanimity rule both increases the likelihood that minority views will contribute to the final group consensus and improves the quality of group consensus formation.

Concluding Comments

Among the most important characteristics of group interaction are the formation, transmission, change, and reformation of group norms. When group members interact, they offer opinions and arguments and listen to others voicing their views, until finally a consensus emerges. Individuals are highly motivated to have their beliefs, feelings, and actions reflect reality. When participating in a discussion with similar others who share the same information, they fully expect to agree with one another. When such agreement fails to materialize, people are puzzled, distressed, and uncertain. Thus social dissent opens the way for social influence.

This view of group influence makes clear that both social and cognitive processes confer validity on group norms. The social process is the give-and-take interaction that occurs as the group works out a consensus. The cognitive process is the independent evaluation of information carried out by each group member. Maximal validity—maximal certainty about our view of reality—depends on both processes.

In many important ways, scientists are engaged in a reality-construction enterprise that is just like everyone's day-to-day attempts to understand social and physical reality. Recall our discussion of scientific method in Chapter 2. Just as people try to construct social reality by forging agreement with fellow group members, social psychologists use many of the same strategies to ascertain the truth about social behavior. Every individual researcher has his or her own personal biases that—despite all efforts to be objective—might influence research strategies, results, and interpretations.

Scientists often come to an experimental test as partisan adherents of a favorite theory. How to discover the truth? The scientific community's solu-

Chapter 9 Themes

Construction of Reality
Individuals and groups construct consensus about what is true and good.

Pervasiveness of Social Influence
This construction process involves conformity and mutual influence among group members.

Striving for Mastery
Conformity helps us to hold valid opinions because the convergence of many opinions often means correctness.

Seeking Connectedness
Conformity helps us feel connected to and valued by other group members.

Conservatism
Positions supported by a majority in a group usually attract more supporters and do not readily change.

Superficiality Versus Depth
People process the opinions of other group members either in superficial ways or with careful consideration.

tion, like that of other social groups, is to seek consensus. Regardless of researchers' different theoretical perspectives, tests of theories and evaluations of information should ultimately converge on the same outcome. And reaching the same conclusion from different theoretical backgrounds, using different techniques, with different subjects, offers strong evidence for the validity of the shared conclusion. Such convergence increases our certainty that we are learning about a phenomenon that is real to all of us and independent of our preconceived views. All the norms and procedures of science are intended to promote systematic processing and the acceptance of positions based on the underlying evidence rather than on public conformity. This in turn means that minority influence should be maximized, allowing for the acceptance of new insights and innovations.

True consensus is achieved only when a variety of opinions are processed from multiple points of view and are accepted only after being proved valid by such processing. When we think about how consensus is forged, we can see that true consensus should be constantly undergoing revision. The current norm should be constantly open to new ideas that might challenge the status quo. We should listen to minority opinions, instead of closing our minds and finding comfort in majority support for our existing view. When new ideas become too threatening to the status quo, groups often try to expel the deviants from the group. But as we have seen, the expression and consideration of minority views is crucial to the development of reliable group norms. Thus it is important to nurture diverse and different voices in any group: the strength of a group's norms depends on their being forged from the consideration of many points of view.

Summary

Conformity to Group Norms Because people are profoundly influenced by others' ideas and actions, interaction causes the thoughts, feelings, and behaviors of members of **face-to-face groups** to become more alike. Whether a judgment task is clear-cut or ambiguous, individual members shift their views toward the group consensus to form a social norm. Norms reflect the group's generally accepted ways of thinking, feeling, and acting.

Conformity is the convergence of individual responses toward group norms. Conformity occurs for two reasons: because people believe that the group is right and because they want the group to accept and approve of them. Most of the time people engage in **private conformity**, adopting group norms as their own because they believe them to be correct and appropriate. Sometimes, however, people display **public conformity,** acting consistently with norms they do not privately accept.

The Dual Functions of Norms: Mastery and Connectedness Private conformity comes about because we expect to see the world in the same way similar others see it. In fact, we often assume that most other people share our opinions and preferences, a tendency known as the **false consensus** effect.

People particularly expect to agree with those who share attributes relevant to the judgment at hand. Agreeing with such a **reference group** both ensures that people are in contact with a common reality and gives them the feeling of being valued. These goals are particularly important in close-knit, cohesive groups. Although particular circumstances can make one goal more important than the other, usually agreement with a group of similar others fulfills the motives for both mastery and connectedness simultaneously.

The tendency to conform is strongest when group membership is highly accessible, as when other group members are present. But the physical presence of others is not necessary for conformity to occur.

How Groups Form Norms: Processes of Social Influence When group members are initially split on an issue, group discussion results in convergence on a moderate position. But when a majority of group members initially favor one side of the issue, discussion usually results in **group polarization** as the group moves to an even more extreme position.

When people process superficially, merely relying on others' positions can produce polarization. Under these conditions, the majority consensus in the group is seen as reflecting reality and as defining what good group members are like. This viewpoint gives the majority position a persuasive advantage.

When people process systematically, both members' positions and their arguments and evidence work together to produce polarization. Majority arguments are more numerous, receive more discussion, seem more compelling, and are presented more persuasively. All these factors give majority views a persuasive advantage, thus pushing the group toward the extreme.

Conformity Pressure: Undermining True Consensus Consensus can only be relied on as valid when the consensus is achieved in the right way. A consensus cannot be trusted if it arises from unthinking reliance on others' positions, on contamination by shared biases, or on public conformity. Such a consensus offers only the illusion of unanimity. When groups become more concerned with reaching consensus than with how they reach consensus, actions based on their norms can be disastrous. Groupthink can be avoided when both minority and majority viewpoints are considered.

Minority Influence: The Value of Dissent Minority views sometimes can sway the majority. To be influential, the minority must offer an alternative consensus, remain consistent, strike the right balance between similarity with and difference from the majority, and promote systematic processing.

By and large, majorities and minorities influence others by the same processes. They can elicit public as well as private conformity, encourage systematic processing of their arguments, and offer positive social identities.

Chapter 9 Overview

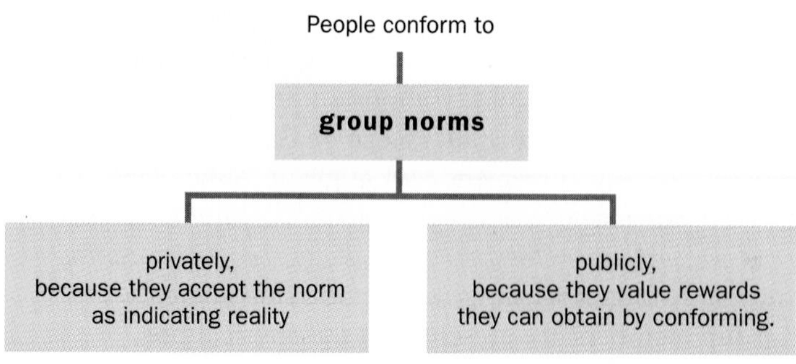
People conform to
group norms
privately,
because they accept the norm
as indicating reality
publicly,
because they value rewards
they can obtain by conforming.

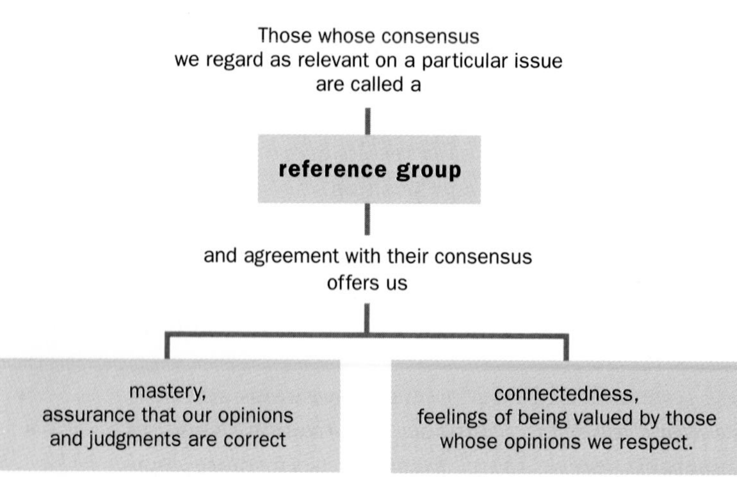
Those whose consensus
we regard as relevant on a particular issue
are called a
reference group
and agreement with their consensus
offers us
mastery,
assurance that our opinions
and judgments are correct
connectedness,
feelings of being valued by those
whose opinions we respect.

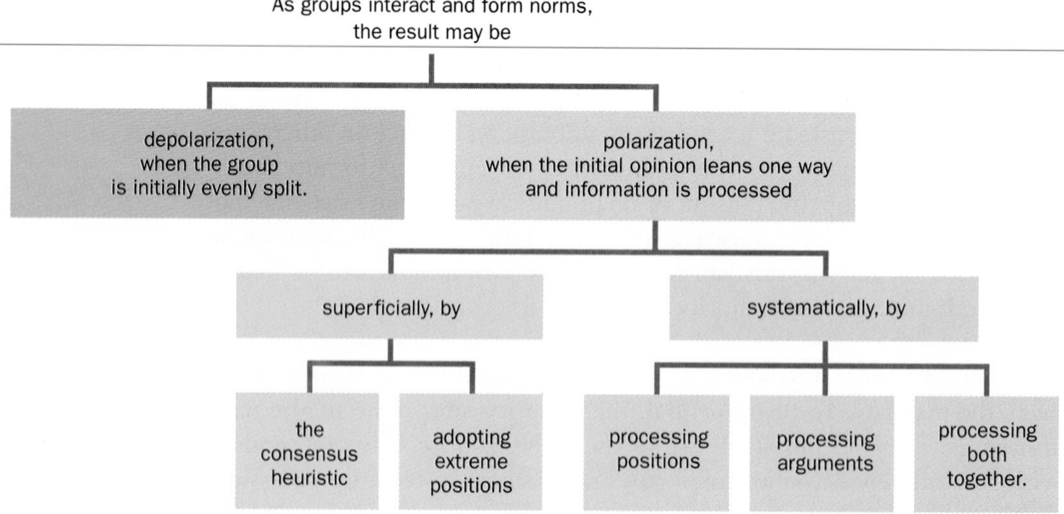
As groups interact and form norms,
the result may be
depolarization,
when the group
is initially evenly split.
polarization,
when the initial opinion leans one way
and information is processed
superficially, by
systematically, by
the
consensus
heuristic
adopting
extreme
positions
processing
positions
processing
arguments
processing
both
together.

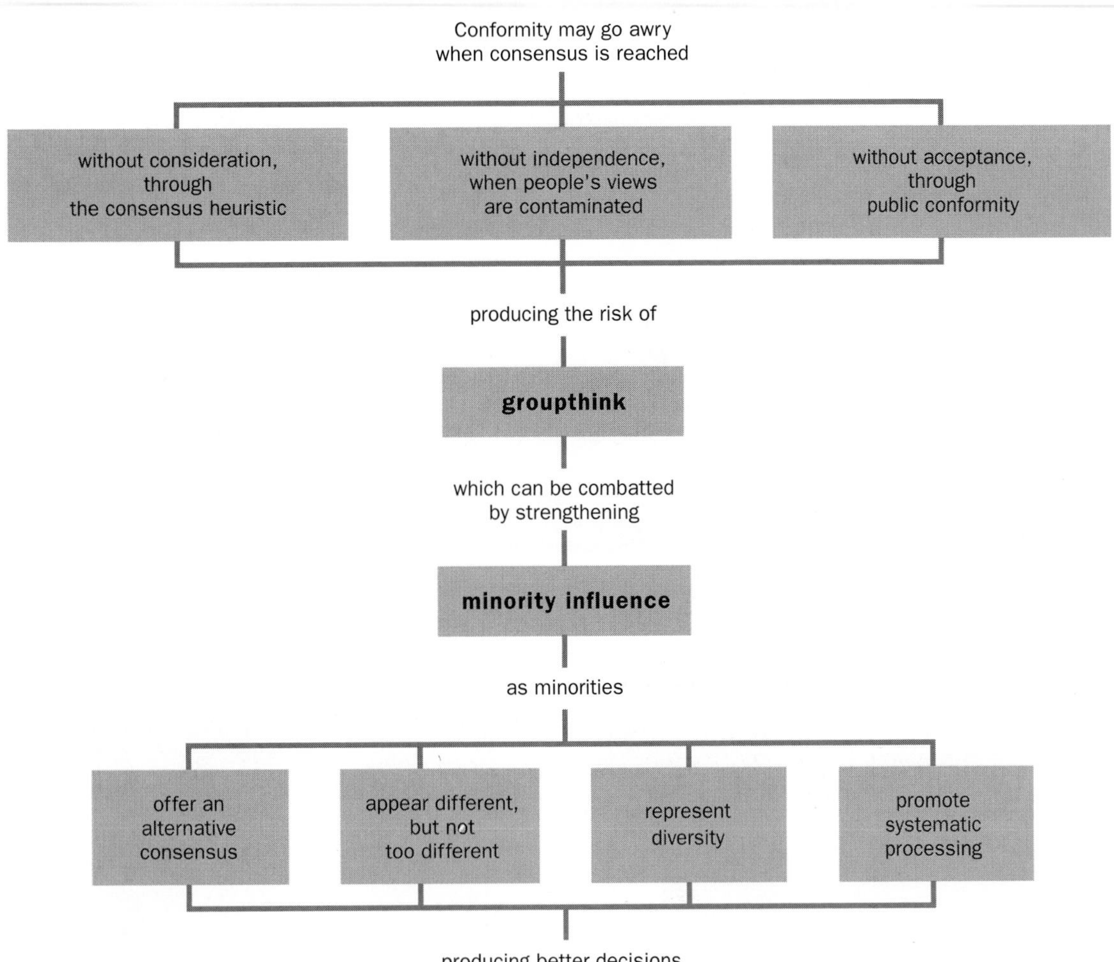
Conformity may go awry
when consensus is reached
without consideration,
through
the consensus heuristic
without independence,
when people's views
are contaminated
without acceptance,
through
public conformity
producing the risk of
groupthink
which can be combatted
by strengthening
minority influence
as minorities
offer an
alternative
consensus
appear different,
but not
too different
represent
diversity
promote
systematic
processing
producing better decisions.

POLICE
POLICE
POLICE
POLICE

10

Norms and Behavior

"I meant what I said and I said what I meant. An elephant's faithful, one hundred percent." With these words Horton the Elephant, the hero of the Dr. Seuss children's classic *Horton Hatches the Egg,* reminds himself of his promise to help Mayzie Bird hatch her egg. Mayzie takes off for Florida, abandoning both the egg and Horton, but Horton, one hundred percent faithful, sits on the egg for a whole year.

Like most children's books, *Horton Hatches the Egg* has a moral as well as a good story line. Horton keeps his end of the bargain, even though Mayzie shamelessly takes advantage of him. In life, as in story land, we usually fulfill our obligations, return favors to those who help us, and obey authority—even when such actions are personally costly or harmful. How are we to understand these important aspects of human interaction? Not surprisingly, the answer involves social norms. Through the processes we described in Chapter 9, all human groups establish and teach *social norms*—generally accepted ways of thinking, feeling, and behaving that people agree on and endorse as right and proper. Social norms reflect a group's view of the world, itself, and others, and they have a powerful effect on almost all aspects of our behavior. Of course, groups create laws and sanctions—systems of reward and punishment—to enforce appropriate standards of behavior among their members. But as you will see in the first part of this chapter, norms are powerful precisely because they usually control group members' behavior without any kind of outside enforcement. For most of us, norms are so well learned and privately accepted that when a norm is activated its standards automatically govern our behavior. Thus, most of the time people do what the social customs and conventions of their group prescribe because they *want* to, not because they *have* to.

Some of the most powerful norms reflect deeply held beliefs about how members of a group should treat one another. Norms about reciprocity dictate that people should repay others' kindnesses or favors. Norms about interpersonal commitment direct us to keep our word, stand by our promises, and be trustworthy and reliable. Norms about obedience command us to obey those to whom society has given legitimate authority. Because norms like reciprocity, commitment, and obedience are so important in regulating

Norms are powerful Acceptance of social norms can elicit obedience to legitimate authority, and also make it possible to band together in protest.

human interaction, we discuss them in detail in three major sections of the chapter.

What happens when others exploit our tendency to follow our groups' rules? Like Horton, we may find ourselves in trouble. If an opponent makes a meaningless concession, our impulse to reciprocate can trap us into giving up something of real value. Salespeople sometimes use this trick to entice us into unintended commitments. And throughout history malevolent authorities have used norms to make people act obediently in the service of great evil. Hitler's death camps, Stalin's secret police, and Argentinean dictators' death squads were all institutions that would have been unable to function without the norm of obedience.

If norms have such power, can people successfully rebel against them? We saw in Chapter 9 that considering diverse points of view can sometimes change group norms—even norms that are fully accepted and widely endorsed. The same strategy of careful thinking can help us resist inappropriate attempts to use norms against us. Because we are subject to a variety of norms that offer sometimes contradictory suggestions about how we should act, every influence situation is open to interpretation. By understanding how norms influence our actions, by questioning the norms that others assume *should* guide our behavior, and by deliberately considering which norms apply to each situation, people can successfully resist normative pressure.

Of course, norms are not the only cognitive structure that helps guide behavior. As you may recall from Chapter 8, attitudes also have a potent influence on what we do. As you will see in the final section of this chapter, norms and attitudes usually operate together to guide behavior. Because so many of our attitudes are a product of our memberships in groups, these attitudes rarely conflict with norms. Sometimes, however, norms and attitudes suggest different courses of action, and then the outcome depends on which of them comes to mind more easily. Whether or not an employee "blows the whistle" on a company's illegal actions or a young man challenges the government's authority to draft him into the military will depend on the mix of social norms and personal attitudes that are brought to bear in the situation. To understand how all these forces affect our actions, however, we have to begin at the beginning. How do norms influence our behavior, and why do they have such a powerful effect on what we do?

Norms: Effective Guides for Social Behavior

Kurt Lewin (1943) was one of the first social psychologists to demonstrate the powerful effect of group norms on behavior. During the Second World War, traditional cuts of meat like steaks and chops were scarce and, when available, were very expensive. To keep the civilian population healthy, the U.S. government wanted people to consume more liver, kidneys, and other unfamiliar organ meats. Commendable as this goal was, U.S. citizens found it hard to swallow at the dinner table. Pamphlets extolling the nutritional value of these meats, newspaper stories appealing to patriotism, even public lectures by expert nutritionists had little impact on well-entrenched food-buying and eating habits. Lewin believed that changes in such habits could be accomplished only by changing the prevailing norms governing what was appropriate to eat. To test this idea, he brought homemakers together in small groups to discuss in depth such questions as how to cook the new cuts and how to overcome family members' resistance. In the course of these discussions, group members' willingness to try the new foods increased, and this produced a shift in norms. A follow-up survey showed that over 30 percent of the discussion group members actually tried the unusual foods, compared with only 3 percent of homemakers who listened to a lecture advocating the same course of action but had no idea how other people in the audience would react. Norms had an impact that information alone could not achieve. How do norms come to influence behavior, and why are they so effective?

How Norms Guide Behavior

> *Norms must be brought to mind before they can guide behavior. They can be activated by deliberate reminders or by subtle cues, such as observations of other people's behavior.*

No norm, attitude, or other cognitive representation can influence behavior unless it comes to mind. Norms, like attitudes, can be activated either by deliberate reminders or by subtle cues. Deliberate reminders of appropriate norms are all around us. The sign in the library requests "Quiet, please." The reluctant child is instructed "Do as you're told!" And the announcer at the baseball game states, "Please rise for the playing of the national anthem." Not surprisingly, this direct approach pays off in norm-based behavior. In one demonstration of this effect, Robert Cialdini and his colleagues (1990) placed handbills on the windshields of cars parked at their campus library. Some handbills activated antilittering norms in a straightforward way, announcing, "April Is Keep Arizona Beautiful Month. Please Do Not Litter." Others delivered a message irrelevant to littering: "April Is Arizona's Fine Arts Month. Please Visit Your Local Art Museum." Unobtrusive observers counted (and we hope picked up) the handbills thrown to the ground. Twenty-five percent of those receiving the irrelevant message discarded it before getting into the car, compared with only 10 percent of those receiving the direct reminder about antilittering norms.

Although deliberate reminders effectively bring norms to mind, our behavior is usually influenced less directly. More often, people, places, or proceedings provide subtle cues that activate norms, which in turn guide behavior. The silence of others in libraries and in churches keeps our own voices hushed; the raucous cheering of basketball and football fans lets us know it's fine to yell. We slow down at the sight of flashing lights and pull over at the sound of a siren. The first few notes of the national anthem bring us to our feet, and the dimming of lights at a concert settles us down.

Norms and the Environment. Most of us have had the experience of having someone drop trash on the floor or the ground near us. When this happens, probably the first things that spring to mind are norms about such actions: is littering acceptable behavior or not? Direct reminders—like a sign posting the fines for littering—offer an easy guide, but your surroundings may also offer clues about the prevailing norm. Heaps of discarded trash suggest that other people have found it acceptable to litter, whereas a pristine environment implies norms against such behavior. Researchers have found that people are more likely to litter in messy environments than in surroundings that are clean and free of trash (Krauss and others, 1978). And the more salient the reminder of the norm is, the greater its impact will be.

One study demonstrating this point placed subjects in one of two settings: one was littered, the other was clean (Cialdini and others, 1990). The researchers found that more subjects littered the dirty environment than the clean one. These actions are evidence that prevailing norms have a big impact on behavior. For other subjects in the same environments, researchers drew attention to the norms regarding littering by having a confederate walk by and drop a piece of trash. Subjects who saw the confederate litter the clean environment littered even less than the subjects in the same environment with no confederate. In contrast, the confederate's littering made subjects throw even more trash into the dirty environment (see Figure 10.1).

Figure 10.1 Effect of activated norms on littering

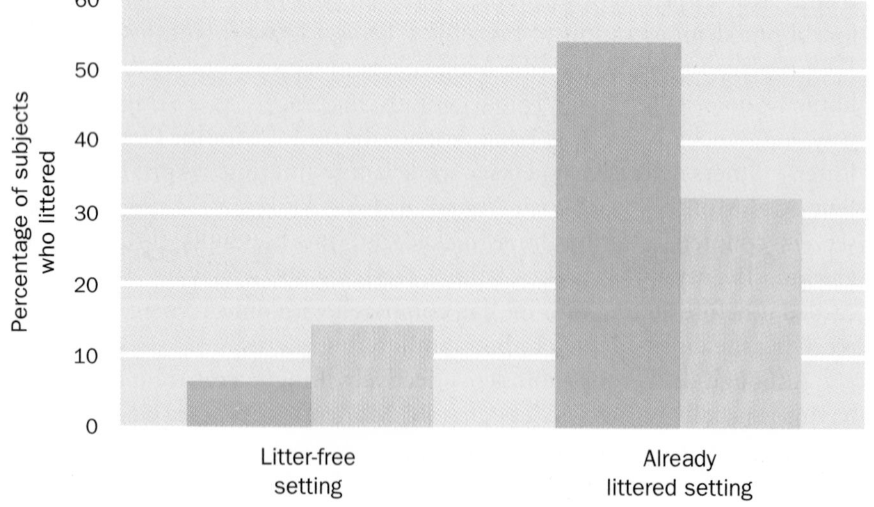

In this study, people littered least when they observed someone sullying a clean environment, and they littered most when they saw trash being thrown into an already dirty environment. Researchers explain this paradox in terms of norm accessibility: the litterer's behavior called attention to the prevailing norm, whether cleanliness or messiness, and the norm in turn influenced behavior. (Data from Cialdini and others, 1990.)

Evidently, the confederate's behavior made the norm implied by the state of the environment—whether neatness or messiness—even more accessible, and in doing so, it increased behavior consistent with the norm.

In a second study by the same researchers, making the norms accessible in a different way had the same impact. In this study, observers compared behavior in three environments: one was completely clean, one was marred by a single piece of trash, and one was covered with litter. As you might expect, subjects littered relatively little in the clean environment and a great deal in the already spoiled environment. But the single piece of trash seemed to make people really think about the prevailing antilittering norm, which in turn led them to litter even less than when the environment was completely clean.

Could it be that a single act of littering is the best prevention for littering? Although seeing a person litter a clean environment does make us more aware of antilittering norms, Cialdini and his associates are not advocating preventive littering. Clean environments stay clean for long periods, and when one person finally drops something, littering becomes even less likely. So starting with a perfectly clean environment is the best way to ensure maximum impact of antilittering norms on behavior. As the researchers note, it's about time the concept of norms was recycled to help clean up the environment.

Why Norms Guide Behavior So Effectively

Norms are sometimes enforced by rewards and punishments. More often, however, people follow norms because they seem right, because they are endorsed by the behavior of other group members, because they are frequently activated, and because they offer solutions to problems.

Why do we resist the impulse to litter a clean environment, especially when littering is probably easier than using a waste basket or recycling? And why should anyone return a favor? After all, accepting benefits from others and never giving anything back can be highly profitable, at least in the short run. Why do people adhere to social norms at all?

Enforcement: Do It, or Else. The most obvious reason we conform to social norms is that groups sometimes use a carrot-and-stick approach—rewards and punishments—to motivate people to adhere to group standards. Norms are important, often vital, to the smooth functioning of groups, and groups take quite seriously their need to identify and stop norm violators. In fact, people are better at detecting violations of social norms than they are at detecting violations of logic (Cosmides, 1989). You soon notice the colleague who never puts money into the office coffee fund while you dutifully pay for your daily mug of java.

Groups handle norm violations by embodying their norms in legal statutes—by specifying behaviors that are legitimate and those that are not.

Society takes this action not only out of concern for any particular wronged individual but to reinforce the importance of the norm to the group as a whole. And, as we saw in Chapter 9, groups often attempt to maintain conformity to social norms by withdrawing social acceptance and support from norm violators. Bucking social convention can be both a lonely and a painful activity.

Using rewards and punishments may be the most obvious way groups can establish and maintain norm-consistent behavior, but it is also the least effective. First, the carrot-and-stick approach may produce public compliance, but it is less likely to bring about private acceptance of norms. When those who are merely complying publicly with group norms escape group surveillance, watch out! Second, no society can afford enough monitors to enforce all appropriate norms on all its citizens all of the time—to say nothing of the problem of who will monitor the monitors.

Internalization: It's Right, So I Do It. Although rewards and punishments are effective, behavior often matches norms for a much more powerful reason: most norms are internalized and they seem right. People accept group consensus as truly reflecting reality, and norm-based actions are a way of maintaining a shared reality and expressing group identity. As any parent can testify, it takes considerable time and effort to teach new group members which behaviors are appropriate, and why. Children are taught to ask before they borrow someone else's property, to show respect toward people in authority, and a seemingly endless list of other do's and don't's. Luckily for parents, rules that benefit the group usually benefit the individual, which makes persuasion a lot easier. The new North American immigrant in England, for example, accepts with little resistance the norm that he must drive on the left side of the road to avoid injuring himself and others. Of course, the individual benefits of social rules are not always so immediately clear. Nevertheless, these norms—the norm of obedience for example, or the norm of social responsibility—become deeply ingrained through the process of socialization. Part of the process of learning what it means to be a group member is accepting and following group norms. Adhering to such norms not only feels like the right and proper thing to do but also makes people feel respected by others whose opinions they value.

Consensus and Support: You're Doing It, So I'll Do It Too. Because other members of our groups endorse the same norms, their presence promotes rather than interferes with normative behavior. Remember from Chapter 8 that our intentions to act in line with our attitudes are sometimes undermined by others who do not share our convictions. We may intend to be cooperative but a persistently aggressive opponent may make it difficult to carry out that intention. Some activities inherently require the participation of others, and almost any behavior can be undermined if others actively oppose it. With normative behaviors, this is not a problem—those around you are likely to be openly supportive, either because they share the same set of norms or because they are likely to be engaged in the same behaviors themselves. All of your fellow Sierra Club members will clean up the campsite before leaving, and they expect similar behavior from you.

Frequent Activation: Something Made Me Think About It, So I Do It. As we interact with other members of our group, we are often reminded of its norms. The more often a cognitive representation comes to mind, the more impact it can have on behavior. No wonder, then, that norms influence a lot of behavior: because norms are associated with groups, any reminders of belonging to the group can bring its norms to mind. The presence of fellow group members, hearing the group's language or seeing its symbols, and even the presence of out-group members can activate group norms and increase norm-consistent behavior. Put the average college sophomore in team colors by the side of classmates on a seat in a basketball arena, for example, and watch for behavioral signs of increased school spirit! And note what happens when the opposition team takes the court! Because people are so often reminded of their group memberships by choice or circumstance, norms have lots of opportunities to influence behavior.

Action Heuristics: I Do It Because It Makes My Life Easier. Like other cognitive representations, norms help us make decisions or decide on actions when the relevant information is very complicated or our emotions are running very high. If deciding how to distribute resources is particularly difficult, for example, people might rely on the norm of equality—"everyone gets an equal share"—to come to a decision without further thought. Even in the hubbub of the Fourth of July barbecue, six adults will understand that if each takes one of the six ears of corn, the food will be shared equally (Allison & Messick, 1990).

The Influence of Norms in the Workplace. Aware of the effectiveness of norms in guiding behavior, social psychologists were quick to realize that permitting groups to establish their own norms might help solve a familiar workplace dilemma—how to introduce changes in production procedures without loss of productivity, lowered morale, or outright hostility from workers. In one experiment demonstrating this point, researchers compared workers' responses to three different ways of introducing changes into production routines. The setting was a small rural pajama factory that employed women on a piecework basis (Coch & French, 1948). Pieceworkers are paid a set rate per unit of work they finish, so a change in production routines can seriously affect their income. Women in the control group were merely informed about the new procedures and the corresponding change in their item-by-item pay rates. Quite predictably, they reacted with dismay: productivity dropped dramatically and turnover increased. Women in a second group were told why the changes were being made, and they were al-

Group norms in the workplace Kurt Lewin argued long ago that letting work groups establish their own norms would increase both productivity and morale. Such practices are now common in Japanese and Scandinavian workplaces, and in the U.S. factories where Saturn cars are made. This relatively new company builds production and sales teams that maintain high group cohesion and high product quality.

lowed to choose group representatives who learned the new techniques and then taught them to others. Group representation helped: morale stayed high and productivity, after an initial decline, returned to original levels. A third group received the same explanation as the second, but responsibility for implementing the changes was delegated differently. Every worker became a "special operator," charged with figuring out the best ways to make the changes in production. The results in this total participation condition were dramatic. Morale stayed high, and the initial drop in productivity lasted only a day. After that, productivity climbed steadily until it was 15 percent higher than before the changes were introduced.

Although American industry did not immediately embrace U.S. social psychologists' insights into how productivity could be increased, other countries used the approach with great success. Participative decision making flourished in Japan, where workers were given a voice in making decisions that management traditionally had made. For more than forty years, Japanese workers have routinely participated in *quality circles*—small groups of people who engage in similar work and meet regularly on company time to discuss improvements in the production process and the work environment. Swedish automobile manufacturers instituted similar procedures. Workers at Volvo and Saab, for example, have long been organized into cooperative work units that make important decisions about the group's working conditions and assignments. Such changes have been credited with these nations' ability to produce large numbers of high-quality products very efficiently.

Almost fifty years after the pajama factory experiment, North American industry is rediscovering worker participation in norm formation. Anecdotal evidence for its success abounds: Blue Cross of Washington and Alaska report improved service to customers as a result of employee input, and Hertz Rent-a-Car agents in Oklahoma can produce information about car availability 27 seconds sooner because of an employee-initiated change in procedures (Marks, 1986).

Helping establish norms for one's own group appears to have the same dramatic effect in today's high-technology workplace that it had in a pajama factory in the 1940s. One study of machine operators in a U.S. factory showed that members of quality circles were more productive and less often absent than workers in a comparison group (Marks and others, 1986). In fact, as you can see in Figure 10.2, participants' productivity got better and better during the two-year study. This study used a nonexperimental design—workers could not be randomly assigned to quality circle or comparison conditions, so some threats to internal validity cannot be ruled out. However, as Figure 10.2 shows, the two groups had very similar productivity levels before the quality circles were introduced, raising our confidence that the differences observed later were due to participation in the new work organization.

Permitting groups to establish their own norms can have behavioral effects that continue even after people have left the group. Consciousness-raising and self-help groups have long made use of these techniques to help their members establish new norms of social awareness and healthful living. Factories, businesses, and corporations are also beginning to reap the benefits of allowing employees to establish their own high standards of quality. These techniques might be used with equal success in other social areas. For example, at the neighborhood level, norms involving conservation and recycling might be established and made effective in similar ways. Standards of curiosity and respect for learning might be reinforced in classrooms if students were given a more participatory role in establishing norms for classroom behavior. As social and environmental problems escalate, such techniques could help produce much needed change.

Figure 10.2 Group norms can affect workplace productivity

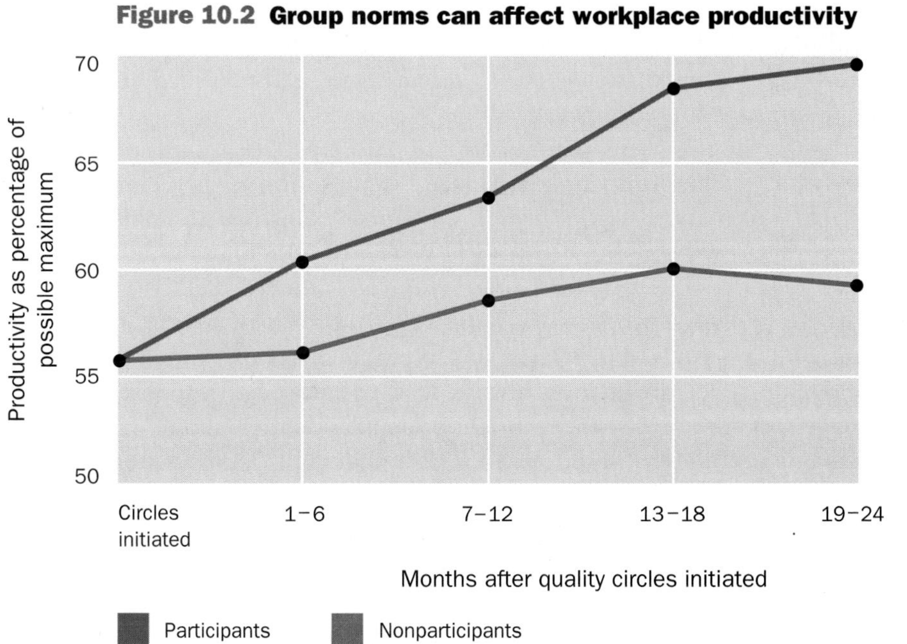

In this study of machine operators in a U.S. factory, some workers helped establish norms for their own group by participating in quality circles. Compared with those who did not participate, members of the quality circles showed superior productivity over the two years of the study. (Data from Marks and others, 1986.)

Deindividuation: When Norms Overwhelm

When individuals feel anonymous and lost in a group, their behavior is likely to be guided by group norms alone. The result can be either antisocial or prosocial behavior, depending on what norms are currently accessible.

Deindividuation: group norms and nothing but group norms When group membership dominates people's thinking, a likely outcome is blind conformity to in-group norms. For these (largely) British fans at a 1983 European Cup match, in-group colors and symbols and competition with another group so exaggerated their sense of group belonging that team support turned from partisan to violent. Soon after this photo was taken, they attacked Italian fans, and 41 people were killed.

Group norms do not always produce socially responsible behavior. Consider groups of British "soccer hooligans," for example, who have developed norms of extreme partisan support, violence against opposing fans, and vandalism following team victories. Such behavior is often triggered when groups of fans congregate, and it reaches fever pitch when one group of fans, decked out in the team colors and waving team flags, confronts equally fanatical supporters of other teams. The fact that violent behavior such as this often occurs in such group settings made early observers speculate that being in a crowd changes the rules of human behavior, making it less rational, more volatile, and often more violent (LeBon, 1908).

Some researchers have argued that crowds have this effect because they promote anonymity and the feeling that normative standards of conduct do not apply (Festinger and others, 1952). Some evidence supports the idea that crowds make antisocial behavior easier. In one study, for example, Philip Zimbardo (1970) had college students dress in identical overalls and hoods that concealed their faces. He assumed this anonymity would produce a state of *deindividuation,* or the feeling that one's personal and individual identity has become lost in the crowd. Compared to other students who wore normal clothing, whose faces were visible, and who wore name tags, the deindividuated students delivered stronger electric shocks to another student. Obviously, being anonymous and unidentifiable—wearing a hood or mask, being concealed by darkness, or melting into the crowd—makes it less likely that someone will be arrested and punished for vandalism, looting, assault, or arson.

Note that this view assumes that for most people group norms elicit merely public conformity or compliance—that as soon as surveillance is impossible, normative behavior ceases. Of course, being just an unidentifiable face in the crowd could undermine the power of even internalized norms if it also reduced self-awareness, and this in turn reduced the accessibility of internal standards for behavior (Diener, 1980). By this reasoning, deindividuation will always lead to socially unacceptable behavior.

But does deindividuation always lead to antisocial responses? If the crowd turns into a rock-throwing mob, deindividuation should cause people to join in. But what if the crowd is rushing to pull victims out of the rubble after an earthquake? Will deindividuation stop people from engaging in this altruistic activity, as early research suggested? Not according to Steven Reicher (1987). Reicher argues that rather than *reducing* self-awareness, being part of a crowd increases people's tendencies to see themselves as group members. Furthermore, he believes that being anonymous and indistinguishable *increases* feelings of shared group membership still further.

Under these conditions, group norms become maximally accessible; the only thing group members think about are what the other group members around them are thinking, saying, and doing.

Chapter 4, pages 134 to 136, described how self-awareness increases the accessibility of behavioral standards, or "self-guides," and thereby increases people's tendency to act in accordance with those standards.

Far from arguing that deindividuation frees people from normative constraints, this view suggests that deindividuation increases the power of group norms over behavior: people, acting purely as group members, end up thinking and doing what the group does. In this view, then, deindividuation would increase rather than decrease the tendency of individual members to join in any kind of group behavior, whether that behavior is tearing down goal posts or rescuing earthquake victims.

Research evidence supports this group-centered view of deindividuation. Consider, for example, the results of a study that varied the accessible norms in a situation in which people's anonymity was also manipulated (Johnson & Downing, 1979). Some groups of subjects in this study dressed in robes and hoods designed to activate negative associations, such as thoughts about the disguises worn by the Ku Klux Klan or the hoods worn by executioners. Other groups of subjects dressed in nurses' uniforms, outfits that activated positive associations with helping and caring. In addition, some groups of executioner and helper subjects were anonymous—their outfit covered their face—whereas others were identifiable. All subjects had to decide the level of shock to deliver to another person for failing a task. As can be seen in Figure 10.3, anonymous subjects in the Klanlike costume delivered higher levels of shock than those who were identifiable, replicating Zimbardo's findings with hooded subjects. But the anonymous subjects in nurses' uniforms delivered *lower* levels of shock when they were unidentifiable than when their faces and name tags were visible.

Figure 10.3 Deindividuation makes people act in accordance with accessible group norms

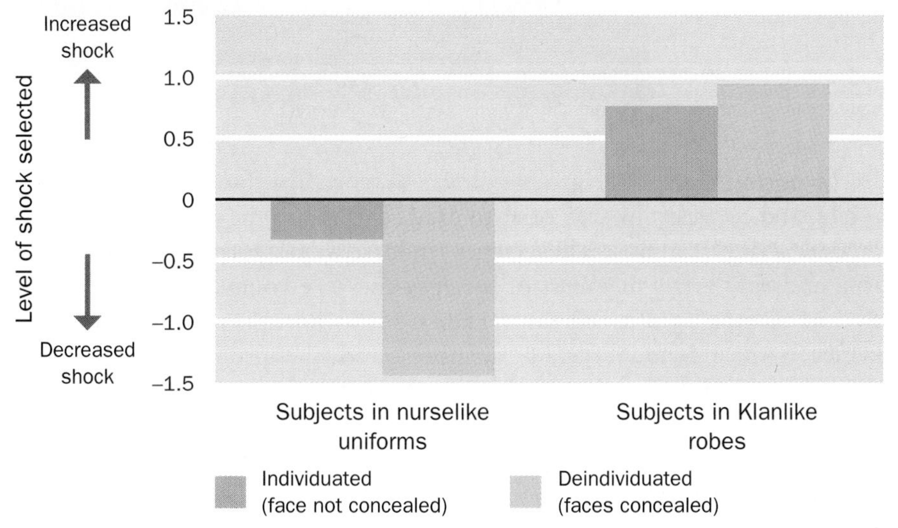

Subjects in this experiment could increase or decrease the levels of shock by 1, 2, or 3 units. When dressed in nurselike uniforms, subjects selected lower levels of shock, and deindividuation magnified this tendency. In contrast, subjects dressed in Klanlike robes tended to increase shock levels, and deindividuation increased this tendency still further. Deindividuation does not always lead to antisocial behavior, but it does make people more likely to follow currently salient norms. (Data from Johnson & Downing, 1979.)

These findings suggest that deindividuation does not universally "free" people to follow their "basic" antisocial impulses. Instead, deindividuation makes people act in accordance with whatever long-term or transitory group identification is accessible at the time—a member of a looting mob, a Manchester United soccer supporter, a KKK member, or even a nurse.

The Norm of Reciprocity: Treating Others as They Treat You

One boy, two apples. A younger boy, no apples. The older boy offers to share his windfall. When the younger child takes the bigger apple, the first protests, "Why did you take the big one?" "Which one would you have taken?" asks the younger boy innocently. "The smaller one, of course," replies the older boy. "Well then, you got what you wanted!" This is the stuff of children's arguments, but it is also an important lesson in social norms. The older child was outraged not because of the size of his treat, but because his companion broke a social rule. Didn't the younger boy know that when one person gives something away, the beneficiary is supposed to reciprocate—and return the favor? Instead of responding to his companion's generosity by choosing the smaller apple, the younger boy took advantage of it, thereby violating the norm of social reciprocity.

Teaching the norm of reciprocity Because it benefits the group and its members, the norm of reciprocity is often an explicit part of group socialization. These youngsters are learning the value that their group places on cooperative exchanges of ideas, feelings, and communications.

The **norm of social reciprocity** directs us to return to others the goods, services, and concessions they offer to us. According to the sociologist Alvin Gouldner (1960), almost all societies endorse some form of reciprocity norm, and only a few members of society—the very young, the sick, or the old—are exempt from it. The universality of this norm is not surprising; it benefits both individual group members and the group as a whole. Individuals gain because the norm helps ensure fairness: any resources they share will be returned by others. The group benefits because reciprocity strengthens the bonds that hold it together, building trust and commitment among its members.

norm of social reciprocity The shared view that we are obligated to return to others the goods, services, and concessions they offer to us.

Returning Favors

One of the most prevalent social norms directs us to return to others goods, services, and concessions that they offer to us. This norm can sometimes be activated to our disadvantage.

The offering of some valued resource triggers the norm of reciprocity, which directs us to give something in return. This means we are obliged to return gifts, favors, and compliments, even if they are unsolicited.

Consider the power of a small, unsolicited favor to increase compliance, as demonstrated by one laboratory study (Regan, 1971). As each male subject settled to his supposed task of making aesthetic judgments, he was joined by a confederate who was trained to be particularly friendly or rather rude. In one condition, the confederate returned from a break with two bottles of cola and offered one to the subject; in another condition he returned empty-handed. The confederate later asked the subjects to purchase some 25-cent raffle tickets. As you can see from Figure 10.4, subjects bought the most raffle tickets when the confederate had done them an unsolicited favor—even though at the time a bottle of cola cost much less than the 25-cent ticket. Notice also that the norm of reciprocity was so strong that it prevailed even when the confederate was unlikable. In fact, the power of the norm of reciprocity is so great that people even feel compelled to return the favors of a stranger who has been forced to help them out (Goranson & Berkowitz, 1966).

Salespeople, market managers, and survey researchers are well aware of the power of unsolicited gifts. When was the last time you received a free sample of a product through the mail, were offered a free aerobics session at

Figure 10.4 Banking on the norm of reciprocity

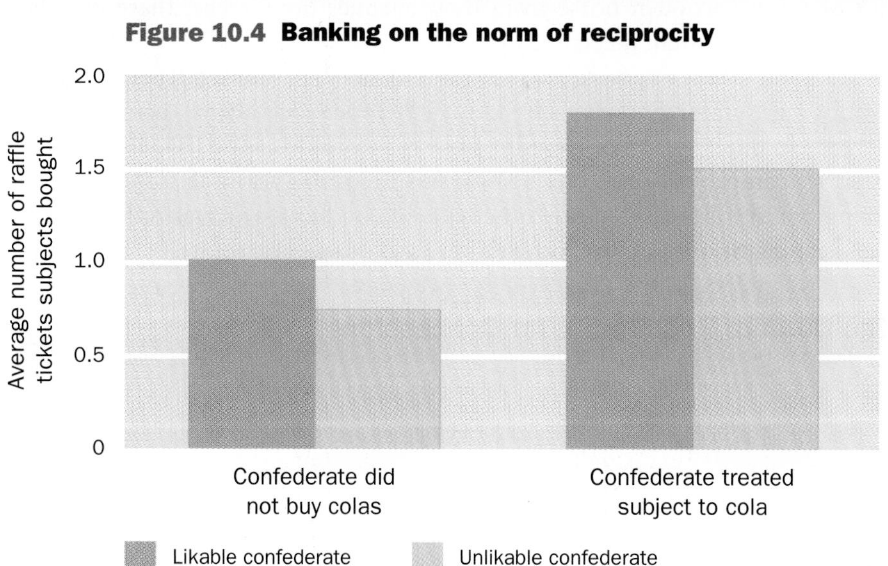

In this experiment, some subjects were treated to a bottle of cola by a likable or an unlikable confederate. Later, the confederate tried to sell subjects raffle tickets. Subjects who had received the unsolicited favor from the confederate bought more raffle tickets, even though they cost more than the drinks. They honored the norm of reciprocity—returning favors, goods, and services that others offered them—even when they did not like the confederate much. As these results show, honoring the norm of reciprocity can sometimes lead to returning a favor more valuable than the one received. (Data from Regan, 1971.)

a newly opened health club, or were sent a dollar as an incentive to fill out a long questionnaire? These techniques activate the feeling that you should do something in return: buy the product, enroll at the health club, or complete and return the questionnaire. And the technique seems to work. Door-to-door sales increase when households receive products to try for a day or two without charge. When a salesperson eventually follows up with a call, customers typically buy as many as half the products they have sampled (Cialdini, 1984). Sending a dollar bill along with a survey questionnaire increases the number of people who complete it from about 25 percent to over 50 percent (May, 1976). The norm of reciprocity works in the supermarket, too. The feeling that you are obliged to buy several packets of frozen waffles after accepting a delicious sample morsel—complete with whipped cream—keeps products moving briskly (Packard, 1971).

The prize for effective use of the reciprocity norm, however, probably should go to the members of the Hare Krishna religious sect (Cialdini, 1993). With their shaved heads and orange robes, they stand out from the crowd as they put the norm of reciprocity to work in airports and other public places. They present each passerby with a flower or other small item. It is a gift, they say, and cannot be returned, but a small donation would be welcome. Caught by the norm of reciprocity, most people find it very difficult to accept the flower with thanks and merely walk away. As a result, donations roll in, dollar by dollar. The value of the reciprocal gesture far exceeds the value of the original gift—a single flower. Like the subjects in Regan's study who bought raffle tickets that cost more than the bottle of cola they were given, people trying to live up to the norm of reciprocity sometimes return a favor more valuable than the one received. This is most likely to occur when the means for reciprocation are restricted. (Accepting a flower puts you "in debt"; the debt can be "repaid" only with a donation.) Thus, by activating the norm in our heads, others can subtly pressure us to do the things they want. As the Trojans discovered when they accepted the gift of a large wooden horse from their enemies the Greeks, there may be more to that gift than meets the eye.

Adhering to the norm of reciprocity can have other negative effects as well. As you will see in Chapter 14, page 162, responding to insult or injury with an "eye for an eye" can escalate intergroup violence.

Despite these sometimes less-than-beneficial consequences, social groups must maintain reciprocity norms. Without such norms, people might never help one another or develop close relationships. And, as you will see later, we can protect ourselves against misuse of the norm of reciprocity by trying not to follow it—or any other rule of conduct—without reflecting on the meaning of our action.

The Norm of Reciprocity for Concessions

Concessions are also supposed to be reciprocated. This can leave us vulnerable when influencers make concessions following our refusal to comply with a large demand—we feel obligated to make a concession in return. Because people believe in the norm of reciprocity, behaviors based on these concessions often persist over time.

The Door-in-the-Face Technique. One day a young man of about fourteen, casually dressed but cleanly scrubbed, appeared at the front door of one of the authors. He informed her that he represented a national service organization dedicated to helping local high school youths resist the temptations of easily available drugs and alcohol. The plan was to get local householders to "adopt" a youth—him. For one month he would spend ten hours a week cleaning, gardening, or performing other household chores in return for an hourly wage—$4—which would be paid to the organization. She would adopt him to help America's youth, wouldn't she?

Not that she didn't want to support America's youth, but working full time and on a tight budget, she was used to doing her own cleaning and gardening. "Well," she started weakly, "I'm not home all day, and I'm not sure . . . I'm really not sure . . . No, I don't think I can do that."

"Well, Ma'am," the young man replied, "we are offering householders like yourself an alternative way to help. If you can't help us out on the adoption program, a donation would be acceptable."

"Just a minute, I'll get my purse," she responded, feeling relieved that she had avoided having someone come to her house every day for a month. Then, as the young man walked away with her check for $20, the light dawned—she had been the target of the door-in-the-face technique. The young man had expertly manipulated social norms to increase the likelihood of her making a donation.

The **door-in-the-face technique** consists of making a large request and following its refusal with a concession that invokes the norm of reciprocity (Cialdini and others, 1975). The ploy gets its name from the fact that the requester wants the door to be slammed so that he or she can retreat from the initial request. In fact, the first request is always much greater than requesters actually want, leaving room for them to back down, thereby putting pressure on the other person to reciprocate with a concession.

The door-in-the-face technique is extremely effective. In one investigation of the technique, researchers asked two groups of students to volunteer for a worthy cause (Cialdini and others, 1975). The researchers approached some students—the control group—as they walked across campus and asked if they would be willing to accompany a group of teenage delinquents on a two-hour trip to the local zoo. Not surprisingly, the idea of spending several hours with an unspecified number of potentially uncooperative teenagers had little appeal, and only 17 percent agreed. Other students were first asked to spend *two years* serving as personal counselors to juvenile delinquents. When all refused this long-term commitment, the request was downgraded to the two-hour zoo trip. This technique induced 51 percent of the subjects to agree, more than three times the number in the control group.

The door-in-the-face technique will activate the norm of reciprocity only if three conditions exist (Cialdini and others, 1975). First, the initial request must be large enough that it is sure to be refused but not so large that it will breed resentment or suspicion. Second, the target must be given the chance to compromise by *refusing* the initial request and complying with the

door-in-the-face technique A technique in which the influencer makes an initial request so large that it will be rejected, and follows it with a smaller request that looks like a concession, making it more likely that the other person will concede in turn.

second request. Finally, the second request must be related to the first request and come from the same person, who must be seen as making a personal concession (Mowen & Cialdini, 1980; Schwarzwald and others, 1979).

Once it is clear that the requester has made a concession, the target is on the spot. The sense that the other person is really giving something up makes the target of the request worry—am I acting appropriately? Am I creating a negative impression? How can I make up for it? Agreeing to the second request gives the target an opportunity to repair a damaged sense of self (Pendleton & Bateson, 1979; Steele, 1975). When targets believe that a compromise has been made and that agreeing to it is the best way to restore self-respect, the door-in-the-face technique can be a powerful tool in closing a deal.

Calvin and Hobbes by Bill Watterson

Reciprocity of Concessions on the Salesfloor. Merchandise managers count on the norm of reciprocity when they offer discounts or special deals. They expect customers who have been given 10 or 15 percent off the price of a sweater or who have accepted a free child's toy with every hamburger to respond by buying more sweaters and more hamburgers. Their expectations are usually rewarded. Two favorite methods retailers use to activate the norm of reciprocity for concessions are the "that's-not-all" technique and the strategy of selling the top of the line.

1. *The that's-not-all technique.* In this ploy, the requester starts with an inflated price and then shifts to a better deal without even waiting for a refusal. The concession technique of immediately offering a discount or bonus has been called the *that's-not-all technique.* And it is effective, as Jerry Burger (1986) showed. He set up a table at a bake sale and offered cupcakes at $1.25 each—a price he immediately reduced to one dollar.

Buyers bought more cupcakes when they thought they were getting a bargain than they did when the cupcakes were simply sold for $1.00 with no previous "markdown." Burger achieved similar success when he "sweetened the pot" by offering a free cookie with every cupcake. In both cases, the seller offered the buyer a little more, and the norm of reciprocity for concessions helped clinch the sale.

2. *Selling the top of the line.* Retailers also use a concession technique called "*selling the top of the line.*" A salesperson using this strategy tries to interest the customer in the most expensive model of a product and then, if the sale is not made, directs the customer to the next-cheaper item. As the salesperson gives up trying to sell the preferred product, the consumer reciprocates by spending more than he or she intended. Does the technique work? Cialdini (1984) cites an excerpt from *Consumer Reports* that suggests that the answer is yes:

> If you were a billiard-table dealer, which would you advertise—the $329 model or the $3,000 model? The chances are you would promote the low-priced item and hope to trade the customer up when he comes to buy. But G. Warren Kelley, new business promotion manager at Brunswick, says you would be wrong [and] has actual sales figures from a representative store. . . . During the first week, customers . . . were shown the low end of the line . . . and then encouraged to consider more expensive models. . . . The average table sale that week was $550. . . . However during the second week customers . . . were led instantly to a $3,000 table, regardless of what they wanted to see . . . and then allowed to shop the rest of the line. . . . The result . . . was an average sale of over $1,000 (Cialdini, 1984, p. 58).

From the door-in-the-face technique, through the that's-not-all technique, to selling the top of the line, all these influence strategies rely on the same principles. Regardless of whether it is a smaller request, a special deal, or lowered expectations, people presented with a concession are nudged by the norm of reciprocity to respond with a concession of their own.

Long-Term Benefits of Reciprocating Concessions. Do targets shifted from large to small requests resent being the victim of such an approach? Far from it. For example, people who comply with the door-in-the-face technique are more likely to carry out the agreed-on behaviors than are those who make the same commitment without refusing a prior request. In one study in which the commitment involved two hours of work without pay in a community mental health agency, 85 percent of those in the door-in-the-face group actually reported for duty, compared with only 50 percent of the volunteers from the control group (Miller and others, 1976). Similar results were found in a study of participation in a blood drive (Cialdini & Ascani, 1976). A heightened sense of having acted consistently with the norm of reciprocity apparently moves people to complete the agreed-on behavior. Once again, privately accepted norms have a powerful effect on actual behavior.

The Norm of Social Commitment: Keeping Your Promises

"A man—or woman—is only as good as his or her word." "Don't make promises you cannot keep." "Put your money where your mouth is." These nuggets of folk wisdom reflect a key component of social life: the **norm of social commitment.** This norm requires us to stand by our agreements and fulfill our obligations. If your friend agrees to save your seat while you buy popcorn, she is obligated to protect it from encroachment. If you agree to subscribe to the Sunday paper, you must pay the delivery person when he or she comes to collect. Social contracts help ensure that members of a group or society behave in socially acceptable ways.

One study demonstrated the lengths to which people will go to maintain a commitment (Moriarty, 1975). The scene was a crowded New York beach. In one condition, the researcher made an explicit social contract with neighboring sunbathers: he asked them to keep an eye on his radio while he was away for a short time. In the control condition, the researcher only interacted socially with his neighbors; he asked them for the time before leaving. A few minutes later, a confederate pretended to steal the radio. Did the norm of social commitment affect behavior? Indeed it did. Ninety-five percent of the people who agreed to watch the radio tried to stop the thief, with some even running after the thief to retrieve it. In contrast, only 20 percent of the uncommitted bystanders bothered to intervene. In a replication of the study, a pocketbook was left for a few minutes in a booth at a fast-food restaurant, with similar results. The bystanders who helped were those who had made a prior commitment to do so.

Like the norm of reciprocity, norms governing commitment allow groups and societies to function effectively. Group members can trust one another, agreements can be long-lasting rather than fleeting, and future planning can be based on other people's stated intentions. Indeed, social commitment can help us stay on a chosen course even when we are subject to influences that lead us astray. But the norm of commitment, like the norm of reciprocity, can also be used to entrap us if we follow it unthinkingly. Like poor old Horton, who was exploited by Mayzie Bird, we can end up tending someone else's nest instead of our own.

The Low-Ball Technique

> *The obligation to honor agreements can make people vulnerable to influence when they make a deal and then find out there are hidden costs. People usually stick to the deal even though it has changed for the worse.*

norm of social commitment The shared view that people are required to honor their agreements and obligations.

Our tendency to honor interpersonal commitments, and the corresponding expectation that others will honor their commitments to us, are so ingrained that we stand by agreements even when the deal has changed to our disadvantage. Imagine the following scenario. An acquaintance asks if you will help her move her few belongings to a small apartment in your neighborhood on Saturday morning. You agree, but when you turn up, you find that she has a new plan. She is now moving into a house with one of her friends in a new location across town, so each trip will take about two hours. And the deal seems to include collecting her friend's belongings and helping her move in as well. Suddenly, a couple of hours work on a Saturday morning has turned into a mammoth moving experience that will probably take all day. Like Horton the Elephant, you have been "low-balled." **Low-balling** occurs when an influencer secures an agreement with a request but then increases the size of that request by revealing hidden costs. How will you respond in such a situation?

If the findings of social psychological research are any indication, you will probably spend the day helping your acquaintance move. In one study demonstrating the low-ball technique, experimenters phoned students and asked them to participate in an experiment for extra credit. Some subjects were told the bad news up front: the experiment was to start at 7:00 A.M. Knowing that, only 31 percent were willing to participate. Other subjects were low-balled: they were first asked to make a commitment to participate, and those who agreed were then told about the early starting time. Yet 56 percent of these students agreed to participate, a significantly higher percentage than found among those who were told about the time up front. Having made a deal, the students were reluctant to break the commitment, even though the deal had changed (Cialdini and others, 1978).

Long-Term Commitment: Why Do People Stay the Course?

People stick by their commitments for several reasons. They feel obligated, and being inconsistent makes them feel uncomfortable. They also add new thoughts, feelings, and behaviors to help support and bolster their action.

The power of the low-ball technique can influence behavior over the long term as well as in the short run. Consider the way in which Michael Pallak and his colleagues (1980) used low-balling to encourage energy conservation. After finding that merely asking families to conserve natural gas had no impact on their fuel use, these researchers offered an incentive to produce the desired commitment to saving fuel. The deal was that families who saved fuel would get their names in the paper as energy-conscious, public-minded citizens. It worked. In the very first month, each family saved an average of 422 cubic feet of natural gas. Then came the low ball. The researchers withdrew the incentive, sending a letter to each family saying it would be impossible to publish their names. Was the commitment strong enough to keep the families saving without the incentive? Apparently so. The researchers found that during the following three months the families continued to conserve at the original rate or an even better one.

low-ball technique A technique in which the influencer secures agreement with a request but then increases the cost of honoring the commitment.

Several processes conspire to make people stick by their commitments even when a deal has changed.

1. *Fulfilling social contracts.* We initially fall for the low-ball technique because we feel an obligation to fulfill our social commitments. The importance of this obligation can be seen in the effectiveness of a particular variant on the low-ball strategy, which is common practice among dealers of new and used cars. It is often the case that the customer and salesperson make an excellent deal, only to have "the boss" raise the price significantly. Despite the additional charges, most customers stick by their commitment to buy. In fact, low-balled victims are often very apologetic to salespeople for even considering backing out of a deal whose terms have changed (Cialdini, 1984).

   One reason this particular ploy is successful is that it cleverly sustains the customer-salesperson relationship, and the obligations that go with it. Having an outsider—"the boss," "management," "my supervisor"—be responsible for overturning the agreement maintains the customer's feelings of social obligation to the salesperson—after all, it's not the salesperson's fault the deal is changing. Committed to the original arrangement, the hapless buyers feel honor bound to fulfill their social contracts.

2. *Reducing inconsistencies.* What drives us to make good on a contract that now favors the other party? Apparently our own thoughts and feelings do so. We may know that the deal is weakened. We may even want to back out of an obligation. But we carry through because we have difficulty reconciling such behavior with our sense of being trustworthy and reliable members of society. Even though it might be wise to walk away from a deal that is now less desirable, the discrepancy between our past commitment to the deal and our withdrawal from it creates an uncomfortable arousal—*cognitive dissonance,* which you will recognize from Chapter 8. If we cannot reduce the discrepancy by revoking or reinterpreting the original commitment, we grit our teeth and seek to reduce the dissonance. Fulfilling the commitment helps, especially if the medicine can be made sweeter. Cognitive bolstering serves as the sweetener.

3. *Cognitive bolstering.* When *cognitive bolstering* occurs, the original commitment is strengthened by the addition of supportive new thoughts, feelings, and behaviors. First, people think of all the possible benefits the new behavior or product could provide. Even though its price has gone up, the new car will make vacations much easier, and we can save money on groceries by shopping at the supermarket instead of the convenience store. Second, people start to think of the object as their own (it's my first car and it's new, shiny, and attractive), which gives it special value and makes it harder to give up when the deal changes

(Beggan, 1992). Third, actually performing the behavior or interacting with the object offers additional rewards. Perhaps there are unexpected savings on gas, or the latest model's reduced pollution makes people feel they are helping clean up the environment. As these bolstering processes go to work, many other new thoughts, feelings, and behaviors come to support the original course of action.

Sales personnel are quick to provide opportunities for these bolstering processes to kick in. After the original commitment to buy, for example, the client may be allowed to try the new car out for the weekend. Taking relatives and friends out for a drive makes potential ownership a matter of public record, draws attention to the car's many benefits, and increases feelings of ownership, all of which make the customer's commitment to the car even stronger. Sales personnel refer to this kind of tactic as *the puppy dog close:* most people who spend time with a puppy find it hard to return it to the pet store.

The way these processes work together to bind people to a deal even though it changes are illustrated in Figure 10.5. At first, buying the car

Figure 10.5 Cognitive bolstering and maintaining commitment

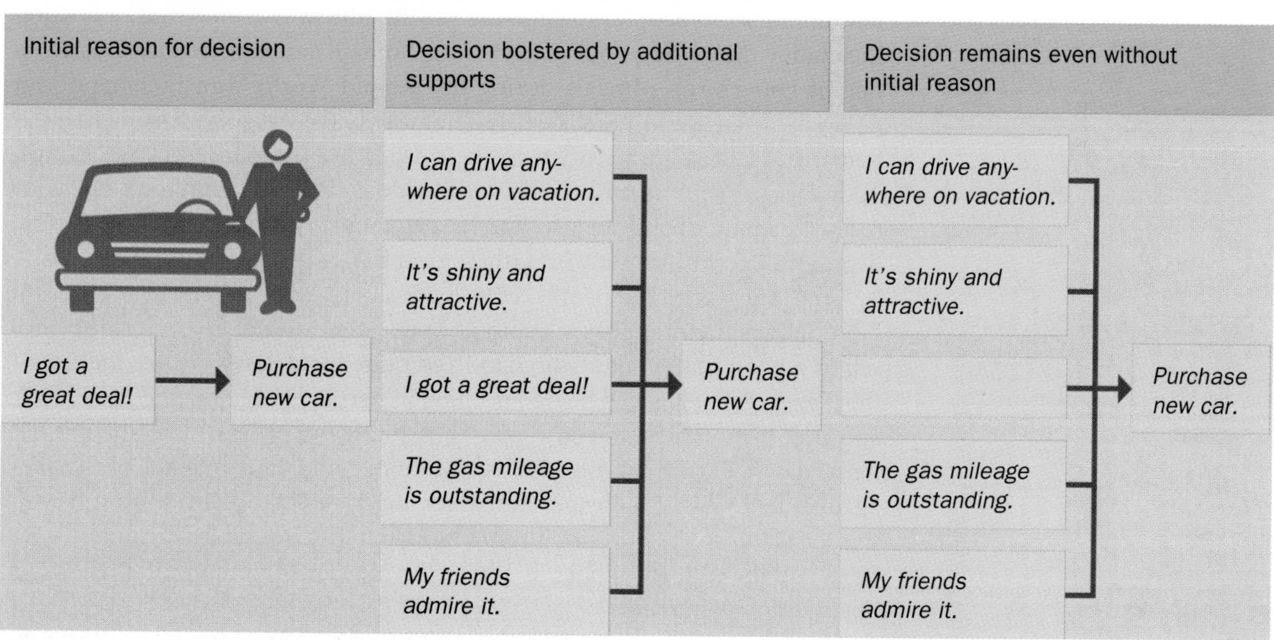

The original decision to purchase a new car may have been based mainly on the great deal the salesperson offered (left panel). Given time, the customer generates several additional reasons that also support the decision, as shown in the middle panel. When the customer is low-balled, these other reasons may sustain the decision, even after the initial reason vanishes.

depends purely on the great price the salesperson offers. But soon, many other reasons to stay the course come into being. With all these new cognitions, feelings, and actions supporting the new behavior, changing the original deal and removing the original incentive makes little difference. Just as the householders deprived of the opportunity for publicity found many other reasons to justify their continued energy conservation, so the customer now sees many reasons other than the original sales price which justify buying the new car.

Thus, the norm of social commitment, like the norm of reciprocity, is intended to foster group cohesion and support, but it can sometimes serve antisocial ends. We can reap the benefits of conservation as our heating bills decline, or we can suffer the consequences when we pay more than we need to for a new car. This double-edged quality is an inherent attribute of social norms, as it is of other cognitive representations, such as stereotypes and biased self-perceptions. But perhaps nowhere is the tension between possible societal good and the potential for harm more salient than in the case of the norm we discuss next—the norm of obedience to authority.

The Norm of Obedience: Submitting to Authority

For millions of people around the world, the war-crimes trial of Adolf Eichmann raised deep questions about human nature (Arendt, 1965). As one of Hitler's top officials during the Second World War, Eichmann sent millions of European Jews, Gypsies, homosexuals, Communists, mental patients, and Christian Scientists to their death in Nazi concentration camps. To his Israeli captors and to the worldwide audience, Eichmann's behavior seemed incomprehensibly evil. Surely such monstrous behavior reflects total depravity, extreme cruelty, or pathological hatred.

Yet, like countless people who have slaughtered others in the line of "duty," Eichmann appeared quite normal, even boring. He described himself as a good family man who had lived quite blamelessly before the rise of the Nazi regime. He said he had nothing in particular against the Jews. Over and over again, he claimed he was "just following orders." Eichmann's defense did not save his life—he was found guilty and hanged for crimes against the Jewish people and humanity. But genocidal policies are still with us today, and so the questions about human nature raised by Eichmann's actions and his trial still linger. Is torture or murder something that any of us might do on command?

Among those fascinated by the trial was the North American social psychologist Stanley Milgram. A firm believer in cultural differences, Milgram doubted that behavior like Eichmann's could occur in cultures where rugged individualism and independence were valued. He believed that members of such cultures would resist group pressure to obey orders, especially if those orders meant that someone else would get hurt. Once he had finalized the procedures for a control condition—a situation in which subjects were merely instructed to harm another without any group pressure to do so—Milgram planned to test his hypotheses about conformity and obedience in many different countries. But the startling responses of subjects in this control condition put Milgram's plans on hold. Understanding when and why people obeyed authority, even if doing so harmed others, became Milgram's main concern, and his findings became perhaps the best known and most controversial in social psychology.

Milgram's Studies of Obedience

In one of the best-known experiments in psychology, people obeyed orders to deliver shocks to an unwilling and clearly suffering victim. They obeyed these orders even though they were not forced to do so.

Using advertisements in a New Haven, Connecticut, newspaper, Milgram recruited men from all walks of life to participate in his experiment in return for a small payment. When each volunteer arrived in the laboratory on the Yale University campus, he was introduced to a middle-aged man, a confederate pretending to be another subject. The experimenter explained that the purpose of the study was to demonstrate the effects of punishment on learning, and he said that one of the participants would serve as teacher and the other as learner for the session. A rigged drawing assigned the real subject to the role of teacher. His job was to teach the pupil word pairs and to punish any incorrect response by delivering an electric shock to the pupil's wrist. As the teacher watched, the pupil was strapped without protest into a chair in an adjoining room and electrodes were taped to his wrist. To "test the equipment," the experimenter gave the teacher a low-voltage shock, enabling him to experience the small, mildly unpleasant, feeling that the learner would be subjected to in the early stages of the experiment.

The victim in Milgram's experiment In a simple experiment with powerful implications, Stanley Milgram studied obedience by asking subjects acting as "teachers" to deliver electric shocks to a "learner," shown here being fitted with electrodes and strapped into a chair. The results of the experiment demonstrated the often startling power of widely accepted social norms on behavior.

Back in the experimental room, the experimenter explained the operation of the equipment. To deliver a shock, the teacher merely had to flick one of the switches on the shock generator. There were thirty switches, in 15-volt increments ranging from 15 volts (labeled "slight shock") to 450 volts (ominously marked only with *XXX*). The teacher was to start with the lowest level of shock and move to the next higher level with each mistake. The shocks may be "painful," the experimenter said, "but do not cause permanent tissue damage." The experimenter stood beside the teacher as the experiment began.

The pupil's initial mistakes were met with only low levels of shock. But as incorrect responses mounted, so did the voltage. Soon, grunts of pain came from the pupil's room, but he continued trying to learn the word pairs.

Obedience rules Even when the learner's pain and distress were obvious, teachers often went along with the experimenter's implacable demands that they continue giving shocks. Why did so many people obey?

At this stage, the teachers typically showed visible signs of distress and tried to stop the experiment. But the experimenter was unrelenting, repeating only that the teacher must continue. Finally, at the 300-volt level, the learner pounded on the wall in protest and refused to answer further questions. Most teachers sighed with relief at this point, believing the experiment was over. Instead, the experimenter announced that silence was to be considered an incorrect answer and punished. Teachers' protests were met with the response: "The experiment requires that you continue." As the shocks increased and the learner pounded ever more feebly on the wall, the experimenter urged the teacher onward, saying, "You have no choice, you must go on." Finally, even the pounding stopped. Anguished teachers typically raised the possibility of injury, but the experimenter never wavered, insisting, "The responsibility is mine. Please continue."

As is now widely known, most of the subjects did continue. In one study, 68 percent of the subjects delivered shocks all the way to the 450-volt level (Milgram, 1963). Far from demonstrating that ordinary people would resist the dictates of authority, the experiment showed the opposite. The results astounded scientists and nonscientists alike. When Milgram described his experimental procedure to middle-class adults, college students, and psychiatrists, most guessed that only a few people in a thousand would obey the experimenter to the end. Yet more than two-thirds of the subjects agreed to perform actions they found repulsive.

Reasons for Obedience

The destructive obedience of Milgram's subjects was not due to personality defects, hard-hearted unconcern about the victim, or suspicion that the experiment was rigged. Instead, many subjects felt compelled by social norms to obey the experimenter.

Why did so many people obey? Were Milgram's subjects particularly heartless individuals, hardened urbanites too calloused to care for others? Could the subjects have seen through the deception and realized that no shocks were actually delivered? These explanations seem implausible in the face of the reactions of the subjects themselves. Milgram's teachers experienced extraordinary distress as the experiment progressed. They trembled, pleaded to be allowed to stop, muttered to themselves, stuttered when they spoke, laughed nervously, dug their nails into their flesh, and offered to take the learner's place. Clearly, they fully believed that the shocks were real, and they cared deeply about the learner's suffering.

In fact, the potential harm to the hapless subjects in Milgram's experiments attracted severe ethical criticism when the results were published (Baumrind, 1964). The critics first pointed to the subjects' severe distress, asking whether the trauma of the experience could have lasting aftereffects—effects that could not be dissipated by a postexperimental debriefing. They also raised questions about the debriefing itself. What would be the effect on subjects of realizing that they had been thoroughly hoaxed and that they were capable of committing great harm under instructions? Critics questioned whether these insights might decrease the subjects' trust in others or their self-esteem (Baumrind, 1964; Schlenker & Forsyth, 1977).

The nature and purpose of debriefing and informed consent were discussed in Chapter 2, pages 58 to 60.

Milgram (1964; 1977) responded by arguing that the debriefing was carefully and sensitively conducted. Subjects appeared greatly relieved (rather than upset) upon realizing the true nature of the experiment, and they came to believe the research purpose was worthwhile. In a follow-up questionnaire sent to subjects some months after their participation, 84 percent reported positive feelings about their participation, 15 percent reported neutral feelings, and only 1.3 percent described negative feelings. Despite these seemingly reassuring findings, the distress experienced by Milgram's subjects was one impetus for the introduction of "informed consent" procedures in psychological experimentation. Subjects must now be given enough information about an experiment so that they can make an informed decision about participation.

The fact that Milgram's subjects felt so badly about the punishments they believed they were inflicting makes it unlikely that they obeyed because they were cruel or heartless. Nor can their behavior be explained by their status as adult males in one particular society. Milgram's procedure has since been replicated in several different countries with women as well as men, and children as well as adults, in the role of teacher (Shanab & Yahra, 1977, 1978; Askenasy, 1978; Meeus & Raaijmakers, 1986). Most subjects expressed considerable distress at what they were asked to do, yet most also continued to obey.

If high levels of obedience cannot be attributed to the subjects' character, could it be a consequence of the nature of the experimental setting itself? Perhaps people who feel that obedience is appropriate in a protected laboratory environment would never dream of carrying out harmful orders in settings outside the laboratory. Unfortunately, obedience to authority occurs with potentially destructive consequences in many other settings.

Obedience in Medical Settings. In most medical settings, unquestioning obedience to the physician is the normal state of affairs. No one overrules the doctor—not the patient, not nurses, not interns, and certainly not other staff members. Doctors have been accused of attempting to maintain this power differential by insisting on giving the orders even when nurses know more about the case than they do (Ashley, 1976; Stein, 1967). What happens, then, when doctors make mistakes? Does anyone question them?

To find out, researchers looked at nurses' responses when a "doctor" gave an unreasonable order (Hofling and others, 1966). The "physician" phoned twenty-two different nurses' stations at different hospitals, identifying himself as a physician at the hospital. He instructed the nurse, who was alone at the station, to deliver twenty milligrams of the drug Astrogen to a specific patient. Such an instruction violated hospital policy in several ways. Prescriptions were supposed to be given in person, not over the phone. The drug had not been cleared for use on the particular ward. The requested dosage was twice the maximum listed on the container. Finally, the "doctor" giving the order was unknown to the nurse. Despite all these red flags, all but one of the nurses immediately prepared to obey. The norm of obedience overpowered their considerable medical training. No wonder that a report by the U.S. Health Care Financing Administration (1982) showed a 12 percent average daily error rate in medication instructions in U.S. hospitals. Many researchers attribute such problems largely to the unquestioning deference to authority that doctors demand and nurses accept (Davis & Cohen, 1981).

The Power of Social Norms. If neither the characteristics of subjects nor aspects of the setting can explain the obedience Milgram found, what does? In an attempt to find out why so many people continued to obey the experimenter and deliver painful shocks, Milgram systematically manipulated various features of the interactions among experimenter, teacher, and pupil. As he observed the responses of his subjects, he became increasingly convinced that the explanation lay in the power of the social situation to invoke obedience (Milgram, 1963, 1974). Two important aspects of the experimental procedure worked in tandem to produce obedience. First, the situation activated the norm of obedience—and only the norm of obedience—as an appropriate guide for behavior. Second, when the subjects began to obey, the gradual step-by-step nature of their compliance with the experimenter's escalating requests kept them in line.

The Norm of Obedience to Authority

The obligation to obey a legitimate authority figure had a powerful effect on behavior in Milgram's experiment. Conditions that decreased the accessibility of the obedience norm or increased attention to other norms (such as social responsibility) also decreased obedience.

The norm that was activated in Milgram's laboratory was the **norm of obedience to authority**—the shared view that people should obey commands given by a person with legitimate authority. "Legitimate" and "authority" are important parts of this definition. *Legitimacy* derives from the group: the group endows the authority figure with the might and right to give orders, and the group assigns to its members the responsibility of obeying. *Authority* derives from status, not from any particular person. When a private salutes a major in the army, for example, he or she is saluting the senior officer's rank, a gesture symbolizing the authority the major holds over the private.

norm of obedience to authority The shared view that people should obey those with legitimate authority.

Obedience to authority is sometimes enforced, as when military courts stand ready to enforce obedience to authoritative orders. Most often, however, obedience is motivated by private feelings of obligation, as it was in the case of the Milgram experiment. The experimenter represented legitimate authority, and his presence activated the norm of obedience—that is, subjects believed the experimenter had the legitimate right to tell them what to do, and that they had an equal duty to obey him. Several of Milgram's experimental variations support this explanation.

Authority Must Be Legitimate. In one experiment, Milgram put a confederate posing as a subject in the experimenter's role. The experimenter then left the room. With the authority figure gone, the results were dramatically different from those in the original experiment. Teachers now ignored the confederate and refused to deliver the shocks. When the confederate feigned disgust and tried to deliver the shocks himself, the teachers protested vigorously. Some went so far as to unplug the shock generator so it could not be used. Similar results were found in a Dutch study of obedience in which subjects were ordered to harass an applicant being tested for an important job. In a control condition in which the experimenter was absent, not a single subject obeyed. But when the experimenter was present and ordered subjects to follow instructions, 92 percent succeeded in ruining the candidate's chances of getting the job (Meeus & Raaijmakers, 1986).

In these experiments, the authority figure was easy to recognize, as is the case in many real-life situations. Medical doctors wear white lab coats and sling stethoscopes around their necks; police, firefighters, and paramedics wear uniforms and identification badges. These symbols are usually enough to activate the norm of obedience to authority. In one experiment demonstrating the power of a uniform, a "stranger"—actually an experimental confederate—asked passersby on a busy city street to comply with an unusual request: for example, to pick up garbage or move to the other side of a bus-stop sign (Bickman, 1974). Half the time, the stranger wore ordinary clothes; the rest of the time he wore a security guard's uniform. Clothes made the authority figure: many more people did his bidding when he was dressed in a uniform than when he wore street clothes. To test the limits of the power of an authority figure, the stranger approached passersby, pointed to a man about fifty feet away, demanded that they give him a dime for a parking meter, and then turned and *walked away.* Despite the fact that he was out of sight, 92 percent of the pedestrians followed his orders when he was wearing a uniform, compared with 49 percent when he was wearing street clothes.

It should not come as a surprise that Milgram's experimenter wore a white lab coat, embodying the authority of the expert research scientist pursuing knowledge. Whether by presence or by uniform, the more salient the authority figure, the more likely people are to obey, as can be seen in Figure 10.6.

By changing experimental conditions to make the norm of obedience more or less accessible, Milgram showed the power of the norm on behavior. In the laboratory, in the presence of the authoritative experimenter, fully 65 percent of men and women followed his orders. But in conditions that reduced the salience of the norm—such as a less "official" location, or a nonlegitimate authority giving orders, or the absence of any authority figure—obedience was reduced. (Data from Milgram, 1974.)

Figure 10.6 Conditions for obedience

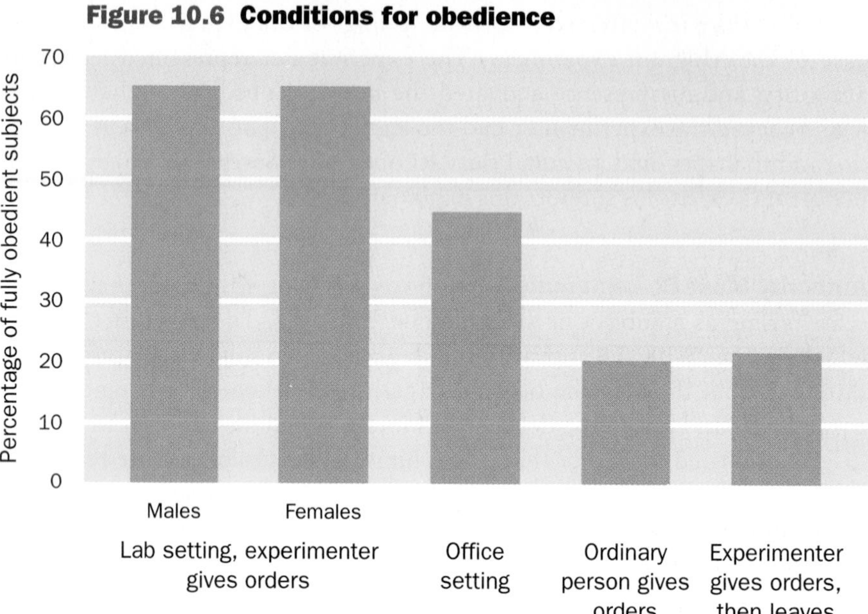

Authority Must Accept Responsibility. Recall that when some of the "teachers" in Milgram's experiments had qualms about continuing, the experimenter reminded them that he took full responsibility, and this was enough to maintain obedience. When all responsibility is ceded to the authority, people enter what Milgram called *the agentic state*—that is, they see themselves as merely the agent of the authority figure, part of the unthinking technical apparatus of obedience. They ignore the possibility that they could or should control their own behavior. In fact, the assumption of responsibility is crucial to the power of the authority figure. Obedience drops off when subjects believe that they, not the authority, are responsible for their actions (Tilker, 1970).

Individuals differ in the extent to which they abdicate responsibility when faced with orders from an authority figure. Some individuals believe that citizens owe legitimate authorities unquestioning obedience if society is to function effectively: these individuals deny that subordinates have responsibility for the effects of orders they carry out. In contrast, other people believe that individuals never give up their right to be responsible for their own behavior (Kelman & Lawrence, 1972). Table 10.1 shows some of the kinds of statements these two types of people endorse. The idea that individuals always maintain the right and duty to refuse an illegal order is part of the military code of conduct: although soldiers are ordinarily expected to obey superior orders, they are required to resist orders that are "manifestly illegal" or that a reasonable person would have known to be illegal (Department of the Army, 1956).

Table 10.1 Individual differences in assertion of responsibility.

1. I feel obligated to protest both vigorously and publicly if the government does something that is morally wrong.
2. If you have doubts about an official order, the best thing is to do what is required of you, so you will stay out of trouble.
3. The most valuable contribution a citizen can make is to maintain an active and questioning approach toward government policies.
4. One reason for supporting the U.S. government is that anarchy will result if there are too many critics.

NOTE: People differ in the extent to which they believe that individuals maintain personal responsibility when an authority figure orders them to do something. Responsibility asserters tend to agree with items like 1 and 3 and to disagree with items like 2 and 4. In contrast, responsibility deniers agree with items such as 2 and 4 and disagree with 1 and 3. Many more than four items would be used in a real test of such differences.

Source: From *Crimes of obedience: Toward a social psychology of authority and responsibility* by H. C. Kelman & V. L. Hamilton, 1989, New Haven, CT: Yale University Press.

The Norm of Obedience Must Be Accessible. As fully socialized members of society, Milgram's subjects initially accepted without question their obligation to administer mild shocks. But when events took a turn for the worse, many subjects began to express concern about the victim and about their role in his suffering. As we saw in Chapter 9, such uncertainty usually causes people to question current interpretations of reality and the norms based on them. But the experimenter quashed the teachers' protests, focusing implacably on the norm of legitimate authority. His escalating prompts—"You must continue," "The experiment requires that you continue," "You have no choice"—made obedience seem an appropriate response to the situation. His calm confidence in the face of both the subjects' indecision and the learner's apparent suffering further reinforced the idea that obedience was typical, normal, and expected behavior. By insisting on only one interpretation of the situation, the experimenter focused the subjects exclusively on the norm of obedience. With no social support for alternative interpretations of events, most subjects soon fell into line, following the experimenter's directions. As you will soon see, social support can make a difference in resisting normative pressures to obey.

Other Norms Must Be Less Accessible. When you think about how distressed the teachers felt, even as they obeyed, it becomes clear that these people were experiencing a normative conflict. Milgram may have been playing on their commitment to the norm of obedience, but they could not have been unaware of the *norm of social responsibility,* which exhorts us to help, not harm, others—especially those in need. In fact, Milgram deliberately provoked the conflict when, for example, he had the pupil cry out and bang on the wall in distress. Knowing that they should have gone to the pupil's aid, teachers agonized over the appropriate behavior. In most of the experimental variations, Milgram tipped the balance in favor of the norm of obedience.

Figure 10.7 Undermining obedience by making incompatible norms salient

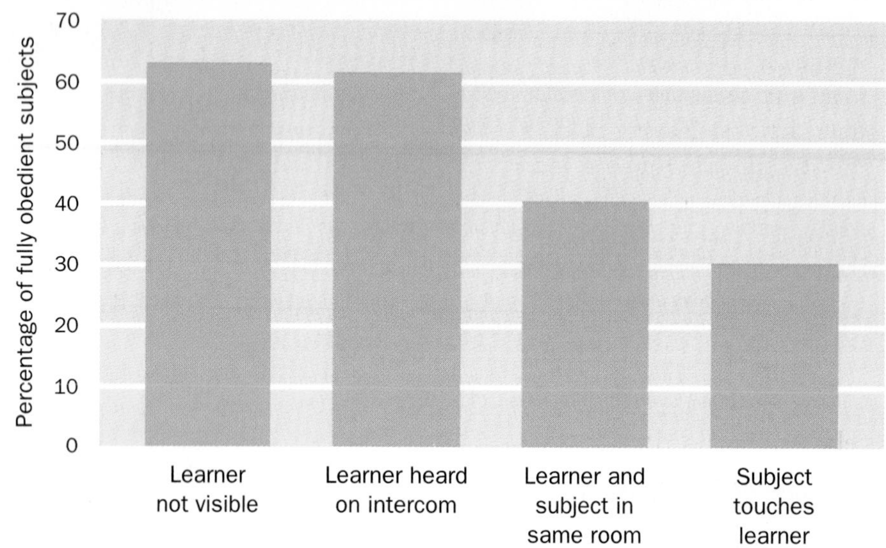

The norm governing obedience to legitimate authority held tremendous sway in Milgram's experimental situation. But it was not the only norm brought into play in the situation. When experimental variations focused subjects' attention on the suffering of the learner, the norm of social responsibility—our obligation to give aid to those who need it—reduced the level of obedience. (Data from Milgram, 1974.)

Wondering what would happen if alternative norms were made accessible, Milgram reduced the physical distance between the teacher and the pupil. He reasoned that this would increase the accessibility of the norm of social responsibility as the pupil's suffering was brought "up close and personal" (see Figure 10.7). And it did. When the learner and the subject were in the same room, only 40 percent of subjects obeyed. As Milgram gradually brought teacher and pupil closer together, the pupil's suffering became less avoidable and obedience decreased.

Milgram's experiment mimicked life: it is easier to drop a bomb from a plane than to kill a person with a bayonet, and it is easier to shuffle papers decreeing a death than to actually torture or kill someone (Silver & Geller, 1978). The same Eichmann who sat in his office dispassionately consigning people to their deaths reportedly was sickened when he was actually forced to tour the concentration camps.

Escalation and Entrapment: From the Acceptable to the Unthinkable, Gradually

> *Once obedience began, it became self-reinforcing. People justified their own behavior, and blamed the victim for their actions.*

As powerful as the norm of obedience to authority is, it does not fully explain the destructive behavior of Milgram's subjects. The gradually escalating sequential nature of the teacher's task also helped bind the subjects to continuing obedience. The process worked like this. First, the norm of social commitment was used against the subjects—they were low-balled. They unwittingly committed to a course of action that initially seemed quite benign: the shocks were quite weak and were intended to improve learning. Subjects did not know that the learner would make so many mistakes that the shocks would become very strong. Second, the subjects' initial compliance confirmed in their own minds the experimenter's right and authority to direct their actions. Having acknowledged the experimenter as a legitimate authority, subjects found it increasingly more difficult to refuse his gradually escalating demands. Third, subjects' initial obedience to the early small requests left them with no legitimate basis to refuse the larger requests. When the command to give a 45-volt shock has been obeyed, why should a command to give a 60-volt shock be disobeyed? At what point does the unobjectionable become the unacceptable?

Finally, as their behavior became more and more destructive, subjects experienced a state of *cognitive dissonance*. They undoubtedly saw themselves as kind, caring, decent people, as most of us view ourselves. But as the inconsistency between their self-concept and their actual harmful behavior increased, they must also have experienced an unpleasant arousal and an increasing motivation to reduce that arousal. With little hope of reconciling these inconsistencies through self-deception—the harmful nature of their actions was quite clear—subjects were motivated to provide other justifications for their behavior. They may have focused on the positive implications of being a reliable and obedient agent, on the superior knowledge and wisdom of the experimenter, or even on the idea that the learner somehow deserved to be punished for his slow-wittedness and frequent errors. Unfortunately, of course, any of these efforts at reconciliation would have maintained the subjects' tendency to obey. In fact, derogating the victim is a common means of reducing dissonance about one's role in a victim's suffering.

To remind yourself of the nature and consequences of cognitive dissonance, refer to Chapter 8, pages 318 to 330.

Blaming the Victim. As we saw in Chapter 4, people tend to attribute their own behavior to situational factors, especially if they behave badly. In fact, individuals who obey harmful orders sometimes react with anger, dislike, and hostility toward the authority figure that directed their behavior (Johnson & Ewens, 1971). However, people are less likely to react against the authority when they accept obedience as legitimate. More probable, and far more chilling in its consequences, is the response of *blaming the victim.* The tendency to blame victims stems from a widely held "belief in a just world," the idea that the universe is a just and orderly place where people "get what they deserve" (Lerner, 1980). If something bad happens, the victim must have "asked for it," provoked it, or brought it on in some way (Lerner & Miller, 1978). Of course, such beliefs are designed to protect the believer: if the world is not a just place, anyone could fall victim to the cruel twists of fate.

The nature and origins of just-world beliefs were discussed in Chapter 5, pages 191 to 194.

The tendency to blame the victim seems strongest when we ourselves are the instrument of another person's pain. Indeed, Milgram reported that many of his subjects, after delivering the maximum amount of shock, cruelly criticized the pupil with comments like "He was so stupid and stubborn, he deserved to get shocked." As Milgram noted, "Once having acted against the victim, these subjects found it necessary to view him as an unworthy individual whose punishment was made inevitable by his own deficiencies of intellect and character" (1974, p. 10). Blaming the victim may be the most potentially dangerous consequence of carrying out destructive orders. As it occurs, the target—once an innocent victim harmed only reluctantly—becomes a person deserving of abuse.

From Experimental Obedience to Social Atrocities

Outside the laboratory, norms like the obligation to obey orders are often reinforced by intergroup hatred and hostility. In these instances, obedience becomes destructive, and norms are used to justify inhumane treatment.

Although his research was provoked by the horrors of the Holocaust, Milgram's findings offer no simple shortcut to understanding atrocities committed in the name of obedience. His research, and many subsequent studies, confirm the powerful effects that norms can have on our behavior and their potential for eliciting antisocial acts. Two important contributors to real atrocities like the Holocaust are beliefs about the importance of au-

Atrocities also happen at home A young woman grieves over the body of one of four Kent State students killed in May 1970 when Ohio National Guardsmen fired on a group of demonstrators. In the social upheaval of the time, irreconcilable differences seemed to separate supporters of the establishment and those protesting against it, adding a context of intergroup hostility to the potentially destructive power of obedience.

thority and adherence to the norms of commitment, which can gradually escalate behavior. But they are by no means a complete explanation of such atrocities. Many social psychological processes combine to produce the kind of destructive obedience that characterized the Nazi extermination of Jews, the ethnic cleansing policies in Bosnia and Serbia, and the My Lai massacre ordered by U.S. commanders in the Vietnam War.

Why, for example, don't the norms that lead us to help and protect other human beings overcome other norms during such dark moments in human history? At least part of the answer lies in the processes of intergroup hostility. Massacres, atrocities, torture, and extermination often take place in a context of virulent hatred and intergroup hostility. This hatred leads to moral exclusion, in which the out-group victims are so dehumanized that norms like social reciprocity, responsibility, and commitment no longer seem to apply—their usual protections and the aggressor's usual inhibitions fall by the wayside. In a world where "ethnic cleansing" and "genetic purity" become justifications for acts of savagery, repression, and brutality, we must be especially vigilant about the purposes for which obedience is used.

Chapter 6, especially pages 239 to 245, described the often appalling consequences of intergroup hostility, particularly when an out-group is morally excluded.

Normative Trade-Offs: The Pluses and Minuses of Obedience

Like all norms, the obligation to obey authority figures can be used for good or evil purposes.

Although the norm of obedience can be exploited for great evil, acceptance of legitimate authority is essential for the optimal functioning of society. Almost every group, whether an informal group of friends or a complex society, develops roles and functions that give some members authority over others. Imagine what would happen if people made individual and independent decisions about which side of the road they would drive on or whether they would pay taxes to establish a system of justice. As Milgram points out, obeying legitimate authority has many advantages for every individual.

Perhaps the most important lesson we can take away from Milgram's studies is just how hard it is to resist the power of deeply ingrained and widely shared norms. Indeed, his findings make clear the often unexpected and unanticipated power of social situations. Obedience works well most of the time and, for that reason, resisting authority is very difficult. Neither Milgram himself, nor any of those who read descriptions of his studies, had any glimmer of the degree of obedience he would find. You may find it difficult to imagine that under similar circumstances you could act the same way Milgram's subjects did. Yet the social psychological processes invoked in this situation—activation of the norm of obedience, exclusion of other norms that might guide behavior, gradual commitment to a particular course of behavior, and justification of it—proved to be an overpowering combination.

Rebellion and Resistance: Fighting Back

An ad appearing in the newspapers of a small southeastern Michigan town sought paid participants for "market research involving group discussion of community standards" (Gamson and others, 1982). Those who responded met in groups of nine with the representatives of Manufacturer's Human Relations Consultants, Inc. (MHRC) at a local Holiday Inn. The coordinator, a young man in a business suit, explained that MHRC was conducting research for a major oil company involved in legal action against the manager of a local gas station. To give the court a picture of "community standards"—what local people believed to be right and wrong—MHRC would videotape the group while it discussed various issues relevant to the case. After signing a consent form and being paid for their participation, subjects learned that the oil company had terminated the manager because he was living with a woman to whom he was not married. The company claimed that this behavior offended community standards. For his part, the manager stated that his private life was none of the company's business, and that the company had sent investigators after him because he had criticized their pricing policies in a televised interview. After starting the video camera, the coordinator instructed the group to discuss the manager's behavior and then left the room for five minutes.

When the coordinator returned, he stopped the camera and gave the group a second discussion topic: would they be reluctant to do business with the manager because of his lifestyle? This time, he asked three of the nine group members to take a stand against the manager's behavior. Two more filming sessions followed: in the first, three additional people were asked to criticize the manager's behavior, and in the last, all nine of the participants were asked to take a stand against the manager. Participants were then given an affidavit to sign, permitting MHRC to edit the videotape and use it in court. Only then were participants free to leave. As you may have guessed by now, this was a research study, conducted by William Gamson and his colleagues.

How do you think participants responded? On the basis of Milgram's findings, we might expect the subjects to obey the researchers' instructions about what to discuss and what position to take. But they didn't. Only one of the thirty-three groups of subjects in the study allowed the procedure to be completed. In all the other cases, group members challenged the coordinator's authority to make them act in a blatantly unfair and potentially harmful manner. Rather than attacking the manager as instructed, some participants remained silent during the videotaping sessions. When they were not openly defying the coordinator—refusing to participate or to sign the final affidavit—they were arguing with him, calling into question the rationale and justification for the procedure. In twenty-five of the thirty-three groups, a majority of members refused to sign the final affidavit. Nine groups threatened action against MHRC, such as publicizing the abuse in the local newspaper. Even in the eight groups in which most people signed, participants refused to cooperate with some parts of the procedure.

Why were the participants in this study able to take a stand, while Milgram's subjects seemed unable to resist the norm of obedience to authority? By examining how groups that rebelled differed from those that did not, Gamson and his colleagues found that three processes—reactance, systematic processing, and using norms against norms—led to counterresistance rather than capitulation.

Reactance: Enough Is Enough

> *People can resist being manipulated by norms. People fight against threats to freedom of action when norms are not privately accepted or seen as appropriate.*

Look at the *Calvin and Hobbes* cartoon on this page! If you've just done so, you've seen Calvin illustrate reactance. But if you decided you would just keep reading for a while before looking at the cartoon, then you just demonstrated reactance yourself. People often respond to attempts to limit their choice with **reactance,** a desire to restore threatened freedom of action (Brehm, 1966). Reactance is common when people lose the opportunity to choose goods, services, or products. Banning a book or a recording in one part of the country ensures record-breaking sales elsewhere; reports that a movie is censored abroad is a sure-fire boost to domestic box office receipts. And every parent knows that the best strategy is sometimes "reverse psychology": telling children to stay in the house when you really want them to choose to go outside to play.

Calvin and Hobbes by Bill Watterson

Heavy-handed social pressure often raises the red flag of reactance. It certainly did so in the MHRC study. Some individuals, feeling that their behavioral freedom was being threatened, simply walked out of the experiment. Reactance also explains people's anger when they feel unfairly be-

reactance The motive to protect or restore a threatened sense of behavioral freedom.

holden to someone else—unsolicited favors make it difficult to refuse to do something in return. In fact, some people avoid accepting favors from others, simply to ward off the possibility that someone will try to "cash in" on reciprocity (Eisenberger and others, 1987; Greenberg & Westcott, 1983). And, like Calvin and the MHRC participants, people often choose to do just the opposite of what they are requested if they feel their personal freedoms are being restricted by orders or influence.

Why do people respond with reactance to a simple request but not to an order to shock another person? The answer has to do with perceptions of legitimacy of authority. When normative pressure is perceived to be inappropriate or illegitimate, reactance is triggered. In Milgram's experiments, the experimenter was perceived to be a legitimate authority. In the MHRC study, however, some participants disputed the market consultant's right to tell them what they should say and do. In such cases, reactance eventually pushes us to resist and say "Enough is enough."

Unfortunately, however, reactance is unlikely to help with resistance to norms that we accept as legitimate and appropriate in the situation. We privately accept most norms that are used against us—even when they are used with a heavy hand. We acknowledge their appropriateness and relevance to be applied in the situation. The subjects in Milgram's study struggled because norms they endorsed and accepted were applied in a way that seemed legitimate—at least at first. If a norm is seen as right and proper, its imposition is not seen as an infringement on our freedom. Such norms bypass the reactance aroused by inappropriate threats to our freedom.

Systematic Processing: Thinking Things Through

One of the best defenses against normative pressure is to think things through to make sure that a proffered norm is actually applicable.

By now you may not be surprised to learn that thinking is one of your best defenses against normative pressure. During the breaks in which the experimenter left the room, the participants in the MHRC study were given the opportunity to step back from the situation and consider what was going on, and many of them realized that unfair normative pressures were being applied. Thinking things through is not always easy, of course. Situations involving normative pressure often create anxiety and stress, and as anxiety mounts, we may be unable to think clearly. To avoid undue pressure, it's often a good idea to try to give yourself a "cooling off" period before you make a commitment, reciprocate a favor, or obey an order. Even then, vigilance is important. The following strategies can help you fend off unfair normative pressure.

1. *Question how norms are being used.* Recognizing how norms operate and how they can be used against you is a good starting point. When you realize that a norm is being used against you, it loses its power (Cialdini,

1993). In fact, explicitly drawing attention to the other side's questionable tactics helps prevent their recurrence (Fisher & Ury, 1981). So if you believe you are being low-balled, let the culprit know you understand the tactic. By doing so, you may embarrass the other person and encourage forthright negotiation. Even more important, you will free yourself from forced feelings of obligation. Realizing that "the boss's" change in the terms of a sale is part of a low-ball plan frees you from the norm of social commitment: the agreement the salesperson made with you was just part of a strategy, not an honest deal. Questioning the way a norm is being used is also a good tactic when you are feeling obligated as much by the norm of obedience as by the person giving orders. At that point, try considering whether this norm is being used appropriately or not. In fact, the now-widespread knowledge about the results of Milgram's obedience studies may decrease the proportion of people who would obey if similar studies could be carried out today (Sherman, 1980). Thus, the very knowledge of how people are effectively influenced by norms is also the most effective defense against that influence.

2. *Question claims about relationships.* You do not need to automatically accept another person's claim regarding his or her relationship with you. A good defense is questioning that claim. Does the person giving orders really have the authority to command you? Maybe not. Is the salesperson really your ally and advocate, fighting against an intractable "boss" who won't approve the deal? Probably not. And make sure that you are both abiding by the same rules of normative behavior. As part of the low-ball tactic, the salesperson often claims to be unable to make the deal without consulting the boss. This setup means that you have the power to make concessions, but the other person does not. As the old saying goes, "What's mine is mine; what's yours is negotiable!" In cases like this, insist on dealing directly with the person who can make a binding agreement (Fisher & Ury, 1981).

3. *Question others' views of the situation.* One of the most important lessons that social psychology can teach is that all situations are open to multiple interpretations. Your definition of what happened may be just as valid as the other person's. Did she really do you a favor? Do you really owe one in return? Don't automatically accept her version of "the facts"; instead, suggest that all assertions be objectively and independently verified before they become part of "the deal." And before buying into someone else's view of how you should behave, consider all the norms and attitudes that might be relevant. Balance such norms as obedience and social commitment against social responsibility.

The willingness of participants in the MHRC study to question others' views of the situation was central to their successful resistance. The coordinator brought two norms to bear on group members: the norm of obedience to legitimate authority and the norm of social commitment. If group members accepted the coordinator's legitimacy and their commitment to participate, they were likely to comply. But if they reinterpreted the coordinator's authority as illegitimate—after all, they were being asked to lie in taped testimony to be shown in court—they were likely to resist. As one participant put it, "I mean, we signed something that said, 'Yes, we're being taped,' but we didn't sign something that said, 'Yes, we're being taped to display something—an opinion—that we may not [agree] with.'" And when the coordinator invoked the norm of commitment, arguing that participants had contractual obligations to fulfill, the groups who rebelled asserted the norm of social responsibility—their obligation to protect the manager.

Remember from Chapter 9 that the best group norms grow out of consideration of multiple points of view. If your interpretation of a situation differs from the one being presented, suggest some alternatives. Others may agree with you, or, at the very least, the person trying to influence the group will have to defend his or her interpretation. The sooner you offer an alternative the better, because the longer you buy into the other person's definition of the situation, the harder it will be to resist (Gamson and others, 1982). Recall how the series of gradually escalating obedient responses quickly entrapped Milgram's subjects.

Using Norms Against Norms

Another effective defense is to use norms against norms—to forge or exploit an alternative consensus that a different course of behavior is the appropriate one.

As you may have noticed, the participants in the MHRC study had potential allies in their resistance, whereas Milgram's subjects had to grapple with the experimenter's orders all alone. The presence of others and the opportunity this affords to form and affirm group norms of resistance is the most crucial factor in creating rebellion. In every MHRC group in which discussion produced a consensus against compliance, group resistance to the coordinator followed. The coordinator's absence during taping sessions gave the group an opportunity to air their doubts and to find out that others felt the same way they did. To help build and strengthen the norm of resistance, participants stressed their shared views and bolstered their solidarity by referring to the group as "we." Consider, for example, the following interaction, when the coordinator applied pressure for agreement, and a group member responded, explicitly addressing him in the name of the group.

> *Coordinator:* Apparently you didn't understand. It's necessary for you to talk as if you actually are a member of the community who's offended . . .
>
> *Member:* I think you didn't understand it. We do understand it and we don't want to go on record, even pretending that we agree with what we're saying. We don't. All three of us feel the same way. I think every one of us feels that way here (Gamson and others, 1982, p. 102).

Group support for alternative interpretations of a situation allows members to break free from the power of inappropriate norms in a wide range of situations. In fact, when Milgram provided his otherwise solitary subjects with an ally, obedience was dramatically reduced. The shared disobedience apparently constituted a consensus that the norm of obedience did not apply.

Studies outside the laboratory have also confirmed that group consensus and social support are crucial to successful rebellion. In a replication of the study in which nurses were given false prescription orders, for example, only two of eighteen nurses were willing to follow an inappropriate instruction from a doctor—if they were allowed to talk to other nurses first (Rank & Jacobsen, 1977; Redfern, 1979). And group consensus was responsible for one of the few successful protests against the totalitarian policies of the Nazis. In 1943, two thousand Jewish men and women married to Aryan Germans were incarcerated in an administrative center in the heart of Berlin. An angry group of spouses, mostly women, soon gathered outside the building on the Rosenstrasse, crying out for the prisoners' release. Despite periodic threats of gunfire from armed guards, the group staged the protest day and night for a week, as the crowd grew ever larger. Where individual dissent was impossible, participants reported feeling a deep sense of solidarity and group determination in their protest. Incredibly, the prisoners were finally released when Joseph Goebbels decided that the simplest way to deal with the rebellion was to give in to the obvious will of the masses. At a time when individuals were executed for offenses as minor as telling an anti-Nazi joke, only a collective undertaking had any chance of success (Stoltzfus, 1992). As the historian Michael Walzer observed: "Disobedience . . . is always a collective act" (Walzer, 1970, p. 4).

"Disobedience . . . is always a collective act" Both the demonstrators who erected a "Liberty or Death" banner in Tiananmen Square in 1989 and the striking students whom they supported showed an extraordinary capacity to question the accepted norms of their society. Finding safety and encouragement in solidarity with others who share their beliefs, Chinese dissidents continue to protest the human rights record of their government.

To remind yourself of the nature and causes of groupthink, glance back at Chapter 9, pages 381 to 385. And to see how minority influence can help prevent these problems, look back at pages 385 to 392 of that chapter.

In terms of cause and cure, destructive obedience is like groupthink. In each case a natural and usually beneficial process—obedience to authority or conformity to a majority—goes awry. You may recall that the way to prevent or cure groupthink is to create conditions that enhance minority influence, especially the presentation of alternatives that promote careful, systematic processing of information. In the same way, the key to the prevention or cure of destructive obedience lies in creating alternatives—in particular, in forming or reaffirming a more appropriate and applicable group norm. Perhaps this is what Thomas Jefferson had in mind when he reminded James Madison that "a little rebellion, now and then, is a good thing, and as necessary in the political world as storms in the physical."

Putting It All Together: Multiple Guides for Behavior

Most of the behaviors that social psychologists study are voluntary—that is, people can decide whether to perform them. Of course, we sometimes lack the resources, ability, information, knowledge, or opportunity to do what we want to do (Ajzen & Madden, 1986). Usually, however, behavior is shaped by the way people define situations and by social influence exerted by others. Thus, how situations are perceived—both by the individual and by his or her groups—is enormously influential in determining what behaviors occur. In Chapter 8, we saw how and why individual attitudes—summary evaluations of how a person thinks, feels, and acts toward an attitude object—influence behavior. In this chapter, we have seen how social norms—shared ideas about appropriate ways to think, feel, and act—can exert a powerful effect on behavior. Each of these concepts tells only half the potential story, however. The full story is that attitudes and norms, although they sometimes operate individually to direct behavior, can work together to exert a combined influence on our actions.

Both Attitudes and Norms Influence Behavior

Attitudes and norms often work together to influence behavior, either by triggering behavior directly or by combining to influence intentions to act, which in turn direct behavior. People's perception of control over the behavior is also an important influence on intentions and, thus, on behavior.

To understand the complexity of influences on human social behavior, we need to keep in mind that attitudes and norms can combine to influence behavior by two different routes. They may trigger behavior directly and almost automatically, or they may operate indirectly, by influencing our intentions to act.

The Direct Route. Attitudes and norms can guide behavior rather simply and directly, especially when we do not give matters much systematic thought. At such times, activated attitudes may affect our perceptions of attitude objects, and activated norms may serve as decision heuristics. Together, the attitudes and norms can color our perceptions and influence our behavior in an immediate and automatic way. For example, a person who holds a negative attitude toward an out-group member may be more aware of the out-group member's hostility-provoking characteristics. At the same time, a norm that says "protect the in-group" may be activated, and the attitude and norm together may lead directly to aggressive behavior. Attitudes and norms are especially likely to affect behavior directly when the resources and motivation to process deeply are not available. As Figure 10.8 illustrates, behavior may then follow quite simply and without much thought.

Figure 10.8 Attitudes and norms affect behavior automatically

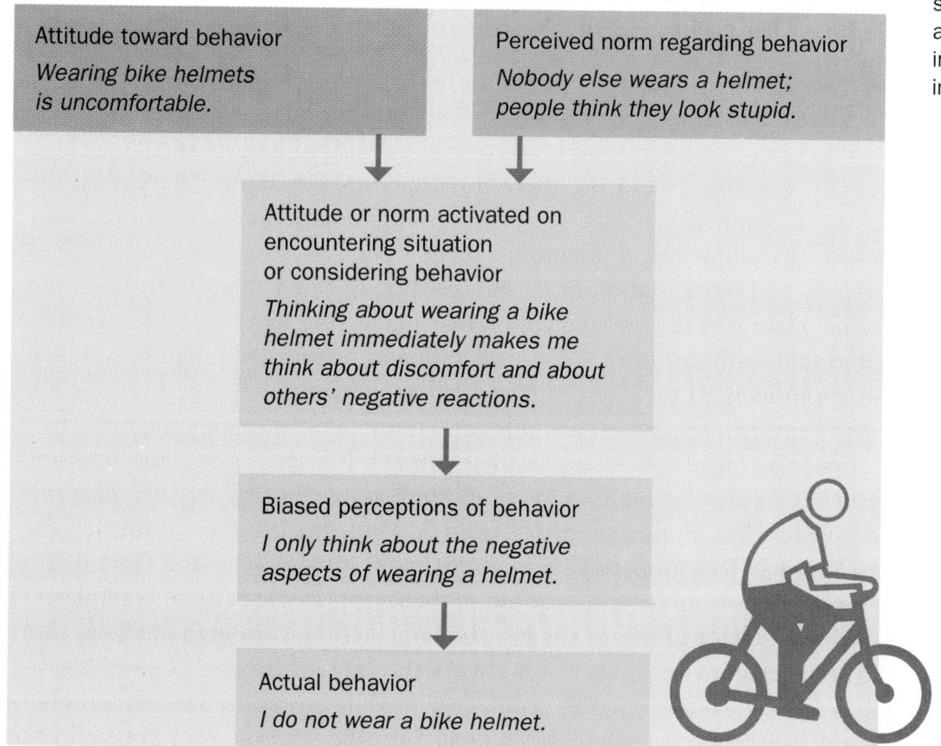
Attitude toward behavior
Wearing bike helmets is uncomfortable.
Perceived norm regarding behavior
Nobody else wears a helmet; people think they look stupid.
Attitude or norm activated on encountering situation or considering behavior
Thinking about wearing a bike helmet immediately makes me think about discomfort and about others' negative reactions.
Biased perceptions of behavior
I only think about the negative aspects of wearing a helmet.
Actual behavior
I do not wear a bike helmet.

When we do not give matters much systematic thought, both attitudes and norms can color our perceptions, influencing behavior in a relatively immediate and automatic way.

The Indirect Route. Sometimes attitudes and norms combine with other factors in a much more deliberate way as we form our intentions to act and then try to follow through on these intentions. The idea that multiple influences combine in this way to guide behavior is central to the **theory of planned behavior** (Ajzen & Fishbein, 1977, 1980). Like the theory of reasoned action described in Chapter 8, the theory of planned behavior suggests that people tend to act in line with their intentions. According to the theory of planned behavior, intentions are a function of three factors: attitudes about the behavior, social norms relevant to the behavior, and perceptions of control over the behavior.

Let us look at each of these factors in turn, using an example. If an expectant mother believes that breastfeeding will protect her baby from disease, and if she feels happy about such closeness with her infant or has nursed previous children successfully, her *attitude* toward breastfeeding is likely to be positive. Social norms have their influence because people wonder what significant reference groups, such as close friends, co-workers, experts, and family, would like or expect to see happen in this situation. If, for example, the mother knows that both her sisters chose to nurse their babies, and if most of her friends also have chosen to do so, she will perceive *social norms* as supporting breastfeeding. Finally, the theory of planned behavior suggests that people explicitly take into account their perceived control over behavior: a sense of control is necessary before positive attitudes and supportive norms translate into action. Only if a woman has confidence in her ability to nurse her baby successfully, and thus perceives herself as having *control* over breastfeeding, will she form the intention to do so.

In Chapter 4, pages 156 to 159, we saw that a sense of control and mastery was an important component of a healthy sense of self. Here we see it is an important prerequisite to effective functioning in the world.

Figure 10.9 illustrates the way behavior is influenced by attitudes, perceived norms, and perceptions of control associated with particular behaviors. By carefully measuring these three factors, researchers have used the theory of planned behavior to predict occupational choice, consumer purchasing decisions, blood donations, dietary changes, attendance at religious services, and participation in psychotherapy. In one study of attitudes and norms relating to the use of alcohol, marijuana, and hard drugs, researchers found that both attitudes and norms influenced students' intentions, which in turn influenced their self-reported behavior (Bentler & Speckart, 1979). Consistent with the theory, attitudes and norms influence only the behaviors that people consider to be under their control. If a smoker sees his behavior as due to an uncontrollable addiction, for example, norms and attitudes will have little effect on the behavior (Ajzen & Madden, 1986; Bandura, 1977).

You may have noticed that in discussing both the direct and more deliberate impact of norms and attitude on behavior, we have used examples in which attitudes and norms suggest the same action. Although attitudes and norms often converge, this is not always the case, of course. Milgram's subjects obviously *hated* what they did, even as they bowed to the norm of obedience. You may earnestly desire a quiet Saturday afternoon by yourself but nevertheless fulfill your social commitment to help your friend move. How do we behave when attitudes and norms are at odds?

theory of planned behavior The theory that attitudes, perceived social norms, and perceived control combine to influence behavior.

Figure 10.9 Attitudes and norms affect deliberately planned behavior

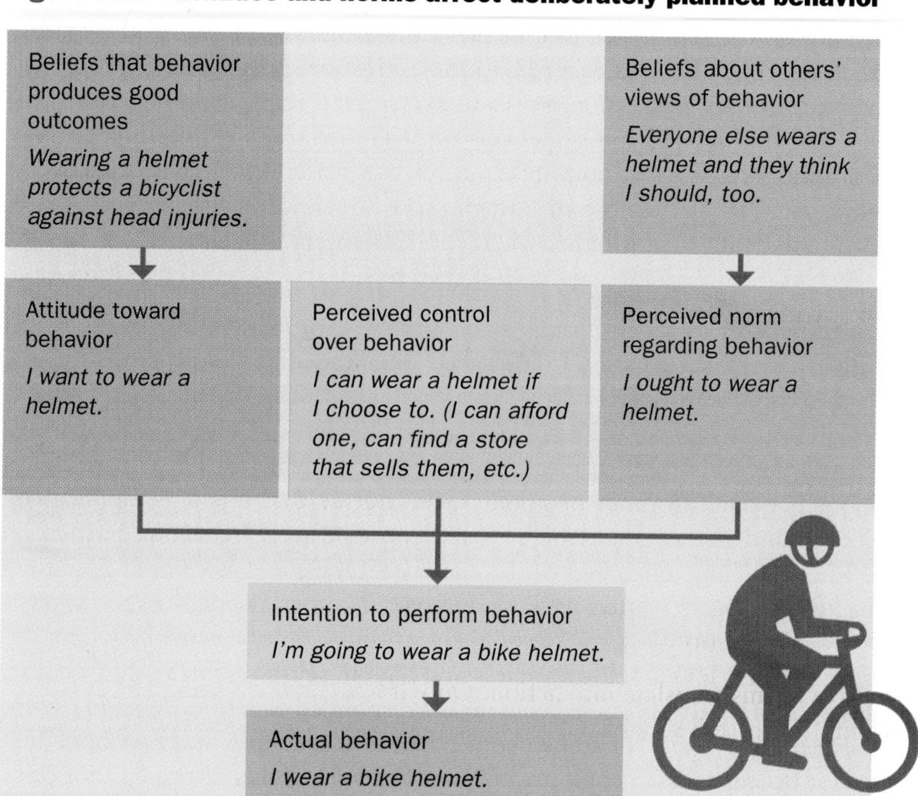

According to the theory of planned behavior, people's attitudes, perceived norms, and their perception of their own control combine to produce a considered intention to act. This intention, in turn, guides behavior. (Based on Ajzen & Fishbein, 1977, 1980.)

When Attitudes and Norms Conflict: Accessibility Determines Influence

Whether attitudes or norms have more influence on behavior depends on their relative accessibility for a particular behavior, in a particular situation, and for a particular person.

Norms, like attitudes, can guide behavior only if they are activated. When a relevant attitude is very accessible, it comes to mind easily, and behavior falls in line with it, as we saw in Chapter 8. And, as the research described in this chapter has demonstrated, this fundamental principle applies to norms as well: activated norms have a powerful influence on behavior. When attitudes and norms disagree, their impact on behavior—whether direct or indirect—depends on their relative accessibility: whichever is more accessible will have the greater influence on behavior. And the relative accessibility of attitudes and norms depends on a number of different factors.

1. *The behavior in question.* Behaviors differ in the extent to which they are governed by norms and attitudes. In general, normative concerns are more likely to influence behaviors that are performed in public, involve others, and are crucial to the well-being of the group. Most groups, for example, have rules about safeguarding food and water, protecting others' property, controlling aggression and sex, exchanging social resources, keeping social commitments, and respecting authority (Maccoby, 1980). Individual attitudes tend to have more influence over private, individual behaviors—what color car we choose to buy, the way we shave in the privacy of our own bathrooms, and whether we have a strawberry or a chocolate malt.

2. *The person in question.* Individuals differ in the extent to which they are responsive to social norms versus private attitudes. In one study, Lynn Miller and Joseph Grush (1986) asked 226 students about their attitudes, their perception of social norms, and their actual behaviors at school. These researchers also had their subjects complete self-consciousness and self-monitoring scales, which measure the extent to which students care more about personal attitudes or about social norms that might be applicable. They found that students high in self-consciousness (reflecting particular sensitivity to and awareness of their own attitudes) and low in self-monitoring (indicating a relative lack of interest in other people's expectations) showed high consistency between their attitudes and their behavior. In contrast, subjects low in self-awareness and high in self-monitoring showed just the opposite pattern: their behavior corresponded much more highly with social norms. Thus, for some people, attitudes are more likely to guide behavior because these people are constantly aware of their attitudes. For others, social norms are uppermost in their minds and tend to guide their behavior.

3. *The situation in question.* Situational factors can also determine whether norms or attitudes prevail. For example, one study showed that accessibility is a function of who is watching your behavior (Froming and others, 1982). Students completed a questionnaire twice, first giving their own attitudes toward punishment and then indicating what they thought their peers thought—that is, what they perceived as the relevant social norms. Later in the term, they participated as "teachers" in a learning experiment similar to Milgram's, in which they believed they were delivering short electric shocks to a failing "pupil." There were three conditions in the experiment. Some subjects delivered the shocks in front of a mirror, some before an audience of their classmates, and others before an audience of advanced psychology students. In the presence of their own image in the mirror—which increases self-awareness and activates people's private attitudes—the subjects' behavior was relatively consistent with their attitudes. But in the presence of the audiences, their behavior was more consistent with norms.

Neither attitudes nor norms predominate for all behaviors, for all people, in all situations. Whether their impact is direct or indirect, relevant attitudes can limit or modify the powerful influence of norms on behavior.

Similarly, norms that are activated and considered can restrict or change individual attitudes being expressed in behavior. In our daily lives, multiple social norms and a variety of personal attitudes contribute to how we perceive a given set of circumstances and, thus, to the way we behave. Will an employee blow the whistle on his company's illegal dumping of chemical waste? Will a young mother nurse her baby or use bottled formula? Will a soldier carry out orders she suspects are illegal? When the behavior is perceived as controllable, the answer will depend on the particular mix of norms and attitudes that are brought to mind as each individual interprets his or her situation.

Concluding Comments

Social psychology has always aimed at understanding the intricate interplay between social thoughts, social feelings, and social behavior. One thing that makes achieving such a goal difficult is the incredible diversity of human behavior. On the one hand are behaviors like stepping on the brake when the traffic light turns red—behaviors so automatic that they take no conscious thought. On the other hand are decisions about choosing a particular college or voting for a particular candidate—behaviors that require an agonizingly careful scrutiny of available information. As we hope you have seen in this and the three previous chapters, the differences between these two types of behaviors are more apparent than real. It is easy to see how cognitive processes and social influences contribute to the kinds of carefully reasoned actions that follow the consideration of a variety of relevant attitudes and norms. But even automatic behaviors are influenced by the way we and others interpret and define social situations. You won't stop at the traffic signal unless you recognize the red light and interpret its meaning appropriately. And how you interpret the red light is governed to a large degree by social conventions and norms: must you stay motionless until the light changes to green or can you turn right if the way is clear? Even your knowledge that the color red means "stop" is a cultural norm. Like carefully considered behaviors, apparently automatic actions are also influenced by both cognitive and social processes. Whether automatic or carefully thought through, then, all behavior is susceptible to the same principle of accessibility: the more readily the relevant attitude or norm comes to mind, the more impact it will have on behavior.

Although norms and attitudes affect behavior in the same ways, norms have a slight edge over attitudes. Indeed, if you think about it, you will probably be surprised to find how much more often you do what you think you *should* do rather than what you *want* to do. Part of the impact of norms comes from the fact that they are group-based, and thus the presence of group members is a cue that activates them. And because norms come from the group, norm-consistent behavior is likely to be supported and rewarded,

Construction of Reality
Every situation can be interpreted in multiple ways, making different norms applicable.

Pervasiveness of Social Influence
Social norms influence our actions, even when we are not physically in the group.

Striving for Mastery
Following norms helps us to obtain rewards from others.

Seeking Connectedness
Following norms helps us to feel like good group members.

Accessibility
Increasing the accessibility of norms increases their impact on behavior.

Superficiality Versus Depth
Resisting the effects of norms sometimes requires extensive thought.

rather than undermined. Although norm-consistent behavior can be maintained by threats or rejection, the pressure to conform usually comes from the inside—from our acceptance of group norms as the right and proper way to think, feel, and act. Thus, we construct a world of right and wrong, good and bad, that is reflected in the norms and attitudes we develop and maintain. Effective social influence really stems from the ability to create and then make accessible cognitive structures that make desired behavior more likely to occur.

Summary

Norms: Effective Guides for Social Behavior Norms must be brought to mind before they can guide behavior. They can be activated by deliberate reminders or by subtle cues, such as observations of other people's behavior. Norms are sometimes enforced by rewards and punishments. More often, however, people follow norms because they seem right, because they are endorsed by the behavior of other group members, because they are frequently activated, and because they offer solutions to problems.

When individuals feel anonymous and lost in a group, their behavior is likely to be guided by group norms alone. The result can be either antisocial or prosocial behavior, depending on the norms that are currently accessible.

The Norm of Reciprocity: Treating Others as They Treat You The **norm of social reciprocity** directs us to return to others goods, services, and concessions similar to those they offer to us. This norm can sometimes be activated to our disadvantage when people give us small favors to induce us to return something of greater value.

Concessions made during negotiations are also supposed to be reciprocated. This can leave us vulnerable when influencers use the **door-in-the-face technique**, making a concession following our refusal to comply with a large demand. We feel obligated to make a concession in return. Because people believe in the norm of reciprocity, behaviors based on these concessions often persist over time.

The Norm of Social Commitment: Keeping Your Promises The **norm of social commitment** directs us to honor our agreements. It can make people vulnerable through the **low-ball technique**, when they make a deal and then discover there are hidden costs. People usually stick to the deal even though it has changed for the worse.

People stand by their commitments for several reasons. They feel obligated to do so, and being inconsistent makes them uncomfortable. They also add new thoughts, feelings, and behaviors to help support and bolster their action.

The Norm of Obedience: Submitting to Authority In one of the best-known experiments in psychology, people obeyed orders to deliver shocks to an unwilling victim who was clearly suffering. They obeyed these orders even though they were not forced to do so. The destructive obedience of Stanley Milgram's subjects was not due to personality defects, hard-hearted unconcern about the victim, or suspicion that the experiment was rigged. Instead, many subjects felt compelled by social norms to obey the experimenter.

The obligation to obey a legitimate authority figure had a powerful effect on behavior in Milgram's experiment. Conditions that decreased the accessibility of the **norm of obedience to authority** or increased attention to other norms (such as social responsibility) also decreased obedience. Once obedience began, it became self-reinforcing. People justified their own behavior and blamed the victim for their actions.

Outside the laboratory, norms like the obligation to obey orders are often reinforced by intergroup hatred and hostility. In these instances, obedience becomes destructive and norms are used to justify inhumane treatment and moral exclusion. Like all norms, the obligation to obey authority figures can be used for good or evil purposes.

Rebellion and Resistance: Fighting Back People can resist being manipulated by norms. People display **reactance** by fighting against threats to their freedom of action when they do not privately accept norms or when they believe they are inappropriate.

One of the best defenses against normative pressure is to think things through to make sure that a proffered norm is actually applicable. Another effective defense is to use norms against norms—to forge or exploit an alternative consensus that a different course of behavior is the appropriate one.

Putting It All Together: Multiple Guides for Behavior Attitudes and norms often work together to influence behavior, either by triggering behavior directly or by combining to influence intentions to act, which in turn direct behavior. According to the **theory of planned behavior,** people's perception of control over the behavior is also an important influence on intentions and, thus, on behavior.

When attitudes and norms disagree, their influence on behavior will depend on their relative accessibility for a particular behavior, in a particular situation, and for a particular person.

Chapter 10 Overview

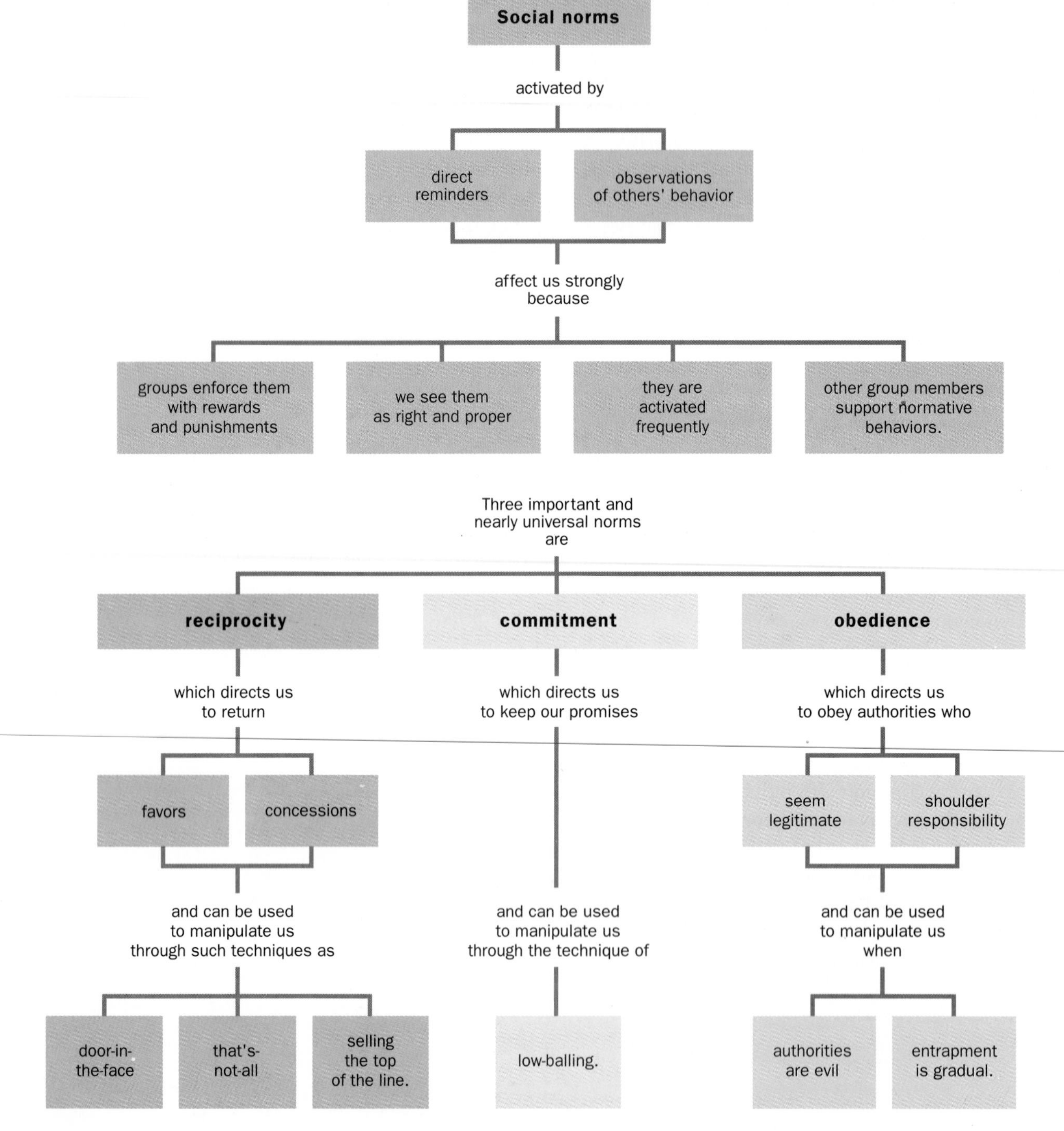

Social norms
activated by
direct reminders
observations of others' behavior
affect us strongly because
groups enforce them with rewards and punishments
we see them as right and proper
they are activated frequently
other group members support normative behaviors.
Three important and nearly universal norms are
reciprocity
commitment
obedience
which directs us to return
which directs us to keep our promises
which directs us to obey authorities who
favors
concessions
seem legitimate
shoulder responsibility
and can be used to manipulate us through such techniques as
and can be used to manipulate us through the technique of
and can be used to manipulate us when
door-in-the-face
that's-not-all
selling the top of the line.
low-balling.
authorities are evil
entrapment is gradual.

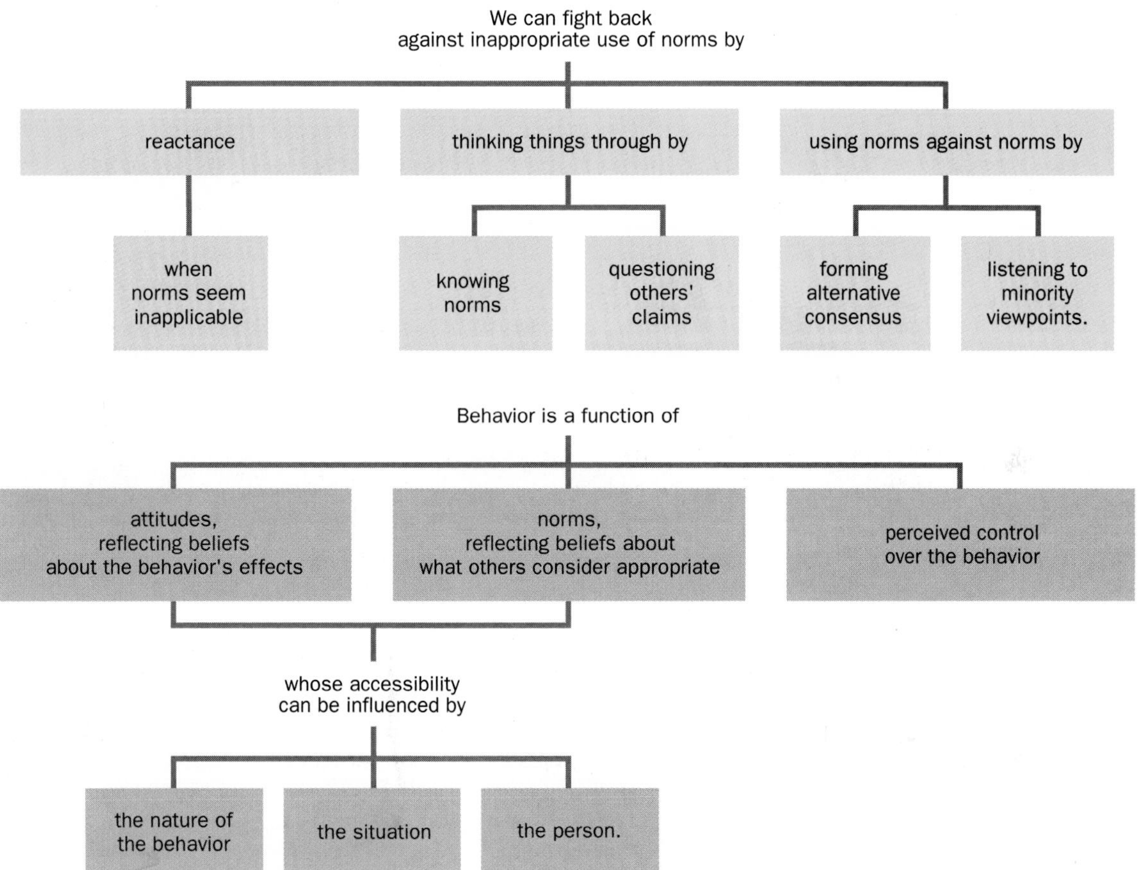

We can fight back
against inappropriate use of norms by
reactance
thinking things through by
using norms against norms by
when
norms seem
inapplicable
knowing
norms
questioning
others'
claims
forming
alternative
consensus
listening to
minority
viewpoints.
Behavior is a function of
attitudes,
reflecting beliefs
about the behavior's effects
norms,
reflecting beliefs about
what others consider appropriate
perceived control
over the behavior
whose accessibility
can be influenced by
the nature of
the behavior
the situation
the person.

11

Liking and Loving

Most people in the United States rate a happy marriage and a good family life as two of the most important elements of their lives. And they have good reasons for doing so—research findings suggest that good relationships with other people can make us healthy as well as happy. Consider the following findings:

- People who are happily married have immune systems that ward off infections more effectively than those of people in troubled marriages (Kiecolt-Glaser and others, 1987).
- The more college roommates like each other, the fewer colds and flu outbreaks they suffer (Goleman, 1992).
- The chances of surviving for more than one year after a heart attack are more than twice as high among elderly men and women who can count on two or more people for emotional support than among those who do not have this support (Berkman and others, 1992).

No wonder, then, that people's feelings about their relationships have a bigger impact on their overall satisfaction with their lives than does their job, income, community, or even physical health (Campbell and others, 1976). In fact, close relationships are so important to people's well-being that the end of a relationship can be psychologically and physically devastating (Weiss, 1976; Stroebe & Stroebe, 1986).

In this chapter we describe how our relationships with others develop and change over time. We begin by looking at the factors that spark initial attraction between people and motivate them to try to know each other better. You will see that once two people begin interacting on a regular basis—chatting on the phone and sharing meals and other activities—feelings of attraction based on personal characteristics become less important than feelings about the relationship and about what each partner gets out of it.

As two people's lives become interlinked and each comes to know the other more deeply, casual acquaintanceship is transformed into close friendship. Just as a group can become part of the self, so does the partner in a close relationship. And just as group norms influence what we do, the part-

Human connections The sense of belonging that friendship, romance, marriage, and family give us is vital not only for mental well-being, but also for physical health.

ner's thoughts, feelings, and behavior influence our own. Each partner responds directly to the other's joys and sorrows, and each in turn feels deeply known, understood, and accepted by the other. These elements of caring and psychological intimacy characterize many kinds of loving relationships—between best friends, parents and children, romantic partners, and spouses. Sexual feelings, like hot peppers in an antipasto salad, are powerful additional ingredients that spice some relationships.

Of course, conflicts eventually arise in any relationship. When they are dealt with constructively, relationships can endure and deepen over the years. If conflict leads to a breakup, however, the pain is swift and sure. In the final section of the chapter we consider the causes of problems in relationships and the ways people deal with them.

Initial Attraction

Newly arrived in a strange city or a freshman dorm, you look at the strangers around you and wonder, "Who will be my friends?" How do we form new connections and turn nodding acquaintances into pals and partners? In cultures that emphasize voluntary relationships instead of lifelong, unchangeable group memberships, the first step in getting to know a stranger is often sparked by feelings of *attraction* or liking (Moghaddam and others, 1993). As mysterious as attraction seems, it follows rules: people are usually drawn to those they find physically attractive and to those with whom they interact frequently.

Physical Attractiveness

> *The formation of a relationship is often spurred by feelings of attraction, or liking for another person. Attraction to strangers is strongly influenced by perceptions of physical attractiveness; these perceptions are shaped by cultural and individual differences.*

Everyone likes to look at beautiful people. Julia Roberts, Kevin Costner, Denzel Washington, and Gong Li are movie stars because of their good looks as well as their acting talents. Thinking about people like these suggests that physical attractiveness is a characteristic that some lucky people just *have*. But this is a misconception. For one thing, members of different cultures differ greatly in the physical characteristics they consider attractive. When anthropologists surveyed more than two hundred non-Western societies, they could not find a single characteristic that was considered attractive everywhere (Ford & Beach, 1951). For example, some societies value slimness in women, while others consider plumpness more attractive. Even within twentieth-century North America, major shifts in standards of physical beauty have been documented (Banner, 1983). Thus, definitions of physical attractiveness are culturally shaped.

Even among members of the same culture, attractiveness seems to be as much in the eye of the beholder as in the characteristics of the person being observed. Studies have demonstrated that the observer's liking for a person can influence perceptions of physical attractiveness. In one study, for example, men and women looked at a photo of a woman, read information about her personality traits, and then judged her physical attractiveness. Those who read that her personality was likable judged her to be more attractive than those who learned that she was dislikable (Owens & Ford, 1978). Interestingly, in this and another study (Klentz and others, 1987), the same manipulation had no effect on people's judgments of a man's physical attractiveness. Liking, at least liking a woman, will help you see the other person's beauty.

Beauty is in the eye of the beholder What is considered attractive differs across cultures and within the same culture across time—beauty is indeed in the eye of the beholder. How would you be greeted if you or your partner dressed for an important occasion in this turn-of-the-century high fashion?

Effects of Physical Attractiveness. Whatever its source, physical beauty is an important element in people's attraction to strangers. In a classic study, Elaine Walster and her colleagues (1966) randomly matched college students for an evening of talking and dancing. The researchers unobtrusively rated each student's attractiveness and social skills, and they also obtained their grades and their scores on intelligence and personality tests. After the evening ended, the researchers asked the students how satisfied they were with their dates. The partner's physical attractiveness was by far the most important influence on both men's and women's satisfaction. It also strongly influenced the likelihood of the men's contacting their partners to seek another date. None of the other variables measured in this study—intelligence, social skills, or personality differences—had a similar influence on liking for the partner.

Well, you may say, even if physical attractiveness is important to college students seeking dates, does it have more general effects? The answer is yes. When people evaluate fictitious "job applicants" for positions (Cash and others, 1977) or hear mock-trial evidence against a criminal defendant (Kulka & Kessler, 1978), more attractive applicants or defendants fare better than their less attractive counterparts. Even young children prefer their physically attractive peers, while regarding unattractive youngsters as unfriendly and aggressive (Dion & Berscheid, 1974). Clearly, physical beauty has a pervasive influence on our perceptions and evaluations of other people, even when dating and romance are not at issue.

One obvious reason we enjoy the company of beautiful people is the sheer esthetic pleasure we obtain from looking at them. However, that is not the only reason. In Chapter 3 we described the common belief that attractive people are warm, friendly, and socially confident (Eagly and others, 1991). This assumption may have some basis in reality, as a study by Mark Snyder and his colleagues (1977) illustrated. These researchers showed male college students a photo of a woman with whom they would supposedly have a telephone conversation. The photos were rigged: one group of students saw an image of a highly attractive woman; others saw a woman who was less attractive. Each subject then held an actual conversation with a female subject who knew nothing of this ruse. When other students later listened to tape

The ways our interactions with people can cause them to become what we expect them to be—creating a self-fulfilling prophecy—were detailed in Chapter 3, pages 103 to 105.

recordings of the two sides of the conversation, they found that the men's behavior varied, depending on which photo they had seen. Men who thought the partner was a very attractive woman acted more sociable, interesting, warm, and outgoing than those who thought she was less attractive. The women responded to these different conversational patterns: those whose partners thought they were attractive also acted more sociable, animated, and confident. The results of this study suggest that when we think people are attractive, we interact with them in a way that brings out the best in them. Thus, attractive people are liked not only because we enjoy looking at them, but also because we expect and elicit desirable behavior from them.

Who Cares About Physical Attractiveness? Physical attractiveness is not equally important to everyone. Among both men and women, high self-monitors—who care about acting in socially appropriate ways and fitting in with situational demands—place an especially high value on physical attractiveness in their partners. In contrast, low self-monitors are likely to seek partners with desirable personality traits and other inner qualities (Snyder and others, 1985). This personality difference influences not only the way people select dating partners but also the way they choose among "job applicants": high self-monitors pay more attention to physical attractiveness and low self-monitors attend more to the applicant's personality (Snyder and others, 1988).

Gender seems also to play a role. In general, men attach more importance to physical attractiveness than women do (Feingold, 1990). In "lonely hearts" personal columns, for example, more men than women specify that they are looking for attractive romantic partners. This concern for physical attractiveness is a characteristic *of men* as perceivers rather than a preference *about women* as partners. One source of evidence for this statement is a study of gay and lesbian advertising for partners. The gay men tended to specify attractiveness as a desired trait in a partner, whereas the lesbian women did not (Deaux & Hanna, 1984).

Positive Interaction

People are attracted to those with whom they have positive interactions. Interaction helps people master the world, and it also helps people find connectedness. In addition, interaction leads to simple familiarity, which increases liking. Similarity also increases attraction—by making positive interaction more likely, by suggesting that the other person likes the individual in return, and by validating the individual's beliefs and attitudes.

Most of us like the people we work with every day, regardless of their physical attractiveness. We also like the people who share our backgrounds, tastes, attitudes, and values. Why do we usually like people we frequently interact with and people who are similar to us?

Interaction Spells Liking . . . Most of the Time. Suppose you have a new job, and you are assigned a desk near another worker. As the days pass, your neighbor shows you the ropes and you begin eating lunch together. You will probably end up liking this person better than your other co-workers, a pattern suggested by a clever study by Chester Insko and Midge Wilson (1977). In this study, small groups of three students, either three men or three women, sat facing each other in a triangular pattern. Two of the three held a get-acquainted conversation for 5 to 15 minutes while the third person silently observed. Then one of that pair had a similar conversation with the third person. Finally, each student reported how much he or she liked the other two members of the group. Although everyone obtained exactly the same information about everyone else (because the observer always heard the conversation between the other two), participants preferred group members with whom they had actively interacted. They liked them more, thought them more similar to themselves, and thought that their interaction partner liked them better in return.

Studies outside the laboratory confirm that people who interact frequently—even if they are thrown together by sheer chance—tend to like each other. A classic study of residents in a married-student housing complex found that friendships tended to form among those who lived near one another (Festinger and others, 1950). The most popular residents were those whose apartments were located near the stairs or close to the mailbox area, where they had extra opportunities to interact with others. College roommates also tend to like each other, even if they do not initially share the kinds of characteristics that usually lead to attraction (Newcomb, 1961). Proximity leads to friendship even in the classroom. One study found that police trainees who were alphabetically assigned to classrooms and seats tended to form friendships with classmates whose names were in their part of the alphabet (Segal, 1974).

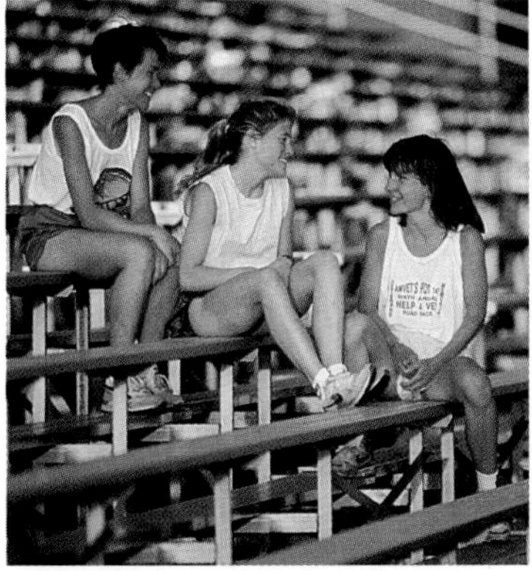

The closeness of connectedness Relationships need not involve romantic feelings to provide us with feelings of connectedness. More commonly we gain support, closeness, and a sense of identity from those with whom we share enjoyable activities or intimate revelations.

Why Interaction Increases Liking. We saw in Chapters 6 and 9 that people enjoy belonging to valued in-groups for two basic reasons. Our groups can help us master the world—to grasp reality and obtain individual rewards—as others cooperate with us, validate our beliefs and attitudes, and aid us in seeing the world correctly. Groups also help us enjoy a sense of connectedness and belonging. The same reasons usually make interaction with other people enjoyable—and therefore lead us to like those people (Bakan, 1966; McAdams, 1985; Cantor & Malley, 1991).

1. *Interacting with others helps us master the world.* If you stop to think about why you enjoy being with other people, your first reason will probably be that it's often just plain interesting and fun. Debating politics far into the night, cheering together at sports events, sharing what you know in joint study sessions are activities that meet our personal needs in many ways. Some are obvious: the study session may help improve test grades. Others are not quite so obvious. Discussing a personal worry with a close friend can help us understand and cope with trying circumstances and with our

own reactions to them. Thus, particularly when we are under stress, we seek to compare our own feelings and reactions with those of other people so that we can better understand ourselves (Schachter, 1959; Rofé, 1984). Similarly, when we feel uncertain of our opinions and beliefs, we may seek out others to test the validity of our views (Wheeler, 1974). When interacting with someone is rewarding for us in any of these ways, the result is the same: we tend to like the person.

2. *Interacting with others helps us find connectedness.* Interacting with another person who treats us with warmth, acceptance, and respect can confirm our sense of being connected to others (McAdams & Bryant, 1987). This sense of relatedness and attachment to the other person is another important reward of interaction—one that, as we shall see, increases in importance as relationships deepen.

The effects of mere exposure on liking were first discussed in Chapter 7, pages 300 to 301.

3. *Familiar others seem likable.* A third reason for liking people we frequently interact with is simple familiarity—the *mere exposure effect* (Bornstein and others, 1987). In fact, even when no actual interaction takes place, familiarity has positive effects, as Richard Moreland and Scott Beach (1992) demonstrated. They arranged for four women to attend varying numbers of sessions of a large college lecture course. The women sat quietly and took notes without interacting with any of the students. At the end of the semester, students in the course viewed slides of the women and answered questions about their reactions to them. The students thought the women they had seen more often were more interesting, attractive, warm, and intelligent than the women who had attended fewer sessions. The students thought they would like the more familiar women better and would enjoy spending time with them. Finally, they also thought that these women were more similar to them. The research suggests that even in the absence of interaction, familiarity can lead to both liking and perceived similarity. All

Figure 11.1 Interaction leads to attraction

Interacting with someone increases attraction to that person through three different processes.

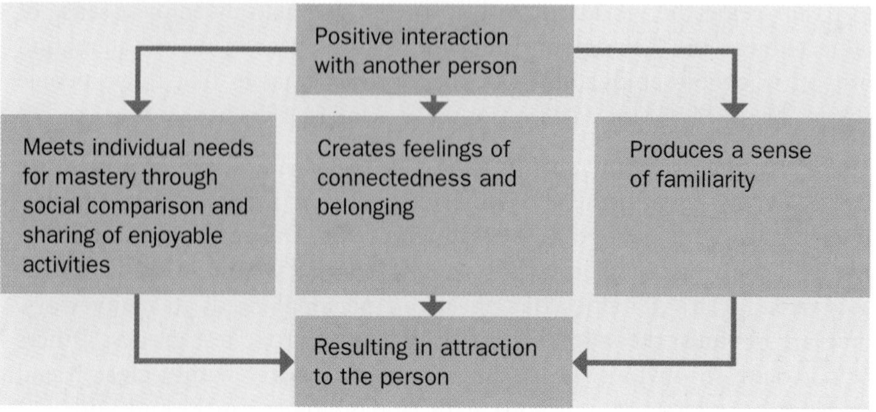

three of these reasons mean that we tend to like people we interact with a lot, as Figure 11.1 suggests.

Positive or Negative Interaction? At this point you may be remembering a particularly obnoxious roommate or next-door neighbor and thinking that interaction certainly does *not* always lead to liking. If so, you're right—when interaction fails to meet our needs or even harms us, it will lead to dislike. More interaction just spells more annoyance if you have to spend time with someone who holds offensive political views, cracks sexist jokes, or is just plain rude and ornery. Research supports this common-sense idea. When asked to name the people they most disliked, subjects in one study named individuals who lived near them (Ebbesen and others, 1976). Fortunately, most people seem to be more likable than annoying, so interaction more often leads to attraction than to repulsion (Rosenbaum, 1986).

The importance of positive interaction for attraction suggests one piece of practical advice: if you want to be liked, try to be fun to be with. In a recent study by Douglas Kenrick and his colleagues (1993), college students rated the criteria they would use to select a partner for a date. Along with physical attractiveness, the students gave the highest ratings to characteristics like *emotionally stable, easygoing, friendly, exciting,* and *good sense of humor*—in fact, women rated these personal characteristics higher than physical attractiveness. Even for a relationship as superficial as a single date, people do not simply seek out physically attractive partners; rather, they search for partners whose personal characteristics are likely to make interaction enjoyable.

Birds of a Feather: Liking Similar Others. Because you interact frequently with your nearby co-worker, and because her advice is so useful, you probably will end up liking her. However, as you get to know other people in the office over the next few months, you may identify someone who seems to be more similar to you—more "your type." This person may support the same candidate in the local election, share your love of bluegrass music, and come from the part of the country you call home. You probably will end up liking this person, too, for similarity breeds attraction (Newcomb, 1961). Though we all have heard that, like the north and south poles of magnets, "opposites attract," research shows this is not true for people (Berscheid & Walster, 1978). Similarity leads to attraction for three main reasons.

1. *We tend to interact with people who are similar to us.* "Birds of a feather flock together" is one of those old sayings that often holds true: people tend to interact with similar others. For example, pairs of best friends in high school and members of dating couples in college tend to be similar on many variables, including age, religion, race, and social class (Kandel, 1978; Hill and others, 1976). Shared interests obviously create opportunities for interaction: academically motivated students meet others of their kind at the library, fanatical golfers find their like at the golf course, and environmen-

talists find one another at Sierra Club meetings. Similarity also makes it more likely that the interaction will be positive. You will have no problem finding topics of common interest to discuss with fellow Sierra Club members, and you won't argue about whether to save the endangered spotted owl. Similarity, like proximity, thus increases opportunities for positive interaction—which, as we just saw, spells liking.

2. *We assume that similar others will like us.* If we know that someone is similar to us, we usually assume that person will like us (Aronson & Worchel, 1966). And being liked by someone is one of the strongest reasons for liking that person (Condon & Crano, 1988). Think about it: you may have an elderly uncle who dotes on you or a friend who obviously enjoys your company. Even if these people are very different from you in virtually every way, don't you like them in return?

3. *Similar others validate our beliefs and attitudes.* One of the earliest lines of research on attraction showed that people like similar others even before they have met them. Subjects in studies conducted by Donn Byrne (1971) were given a questionnaire concerning social and political attitudes supposedly completed by another student. The closer the stranger's attitudes were to their own, the more the subjects liked the unknown individual. You may think it strange to study attraction without having people meet other real people, but consider the ways in which the research situation mirrors real life. If you, a political liberal, were new in town and wanted to make friends, you might avoid the Conservative Club and show up at the Liberal League meeting. You would do so because you expect to find people with attitudes similar to your own—and thus likable people—among the Liberal League members.

Viewing our own characteristics as desirable and other self-serving biases were introduced in Chapter 4, pages 128 to 138.

The reason we like people with attitudes and beliefs similar to our own is that we tend to view our own characteristics as desirable. Thus we believe that those who share them have the *right* attitudes (LaPrelle and others, 1990). If you favor affirmative action, you will probably like other people who share that attitude—not just because they agree with you but because their attitude suggests an appropriate concern for the disadvantaged in society. Other people's support for your views is rewarding because it validates your own opinions (Byrne, 1971).

In summary, if two people are similar they are more likely to have positive interactions, to believe that they are liked in return, and to reinforce each other's attitudes and beliefs. For all these reasons, similarity tends to create attraction.

Liking, Similarity, and Interaction: Mutually Reinforcing Processes

Similarity, liking, and interaction all tend to influence one another. As a result, relationships tend to deepen and intensify over time.

As Figure 11.2 shows, interaction, liking, and similarity are all tied together in our everyday lives (Insko and others, 1973).

- Similarity encourages interaction, and when people interact, they discover more similarities. For instance, getting-acquainted conversations tend to involve a search for common friends, activities, or interests (Insko & Wilson, 1977).
- Interaction creates liking, and liking leads to more interaction because we seek out the company of those we enjoy. Further, the fact that two people spend time together suggests that each finds the other likable and enjoyable. And knowing that someone likes you is a powerful reason for being attracted to them: it boosts self-esteem and demonstrates your value as a person (Insko and others, 1973). Even in the absence of interaction, familiarity can cause liking as well as perceived similarity (Moreland & Beach, 1992; Insko & Wilson, 1977).
- Similarity and liking also go together. We like those who are similar to us, we think those we like *are* similar to us, and we assume that people who are similar to us will like *us* (Condon & Crano, 1988).

Each of these three factors—similarity, liking, and interaction—can cause increases in all the others. Thus a relationship initially may be sparked by chance proximity, by perceptions of similarity, or by transitory feelings of attraction that lead to an initial encounter. But once it gets going, all three factors come into play, and the relationship will tend to progress into fuller form.

Figure 11.2 The mutually reinforcing effects of interaction, similarity, and liking

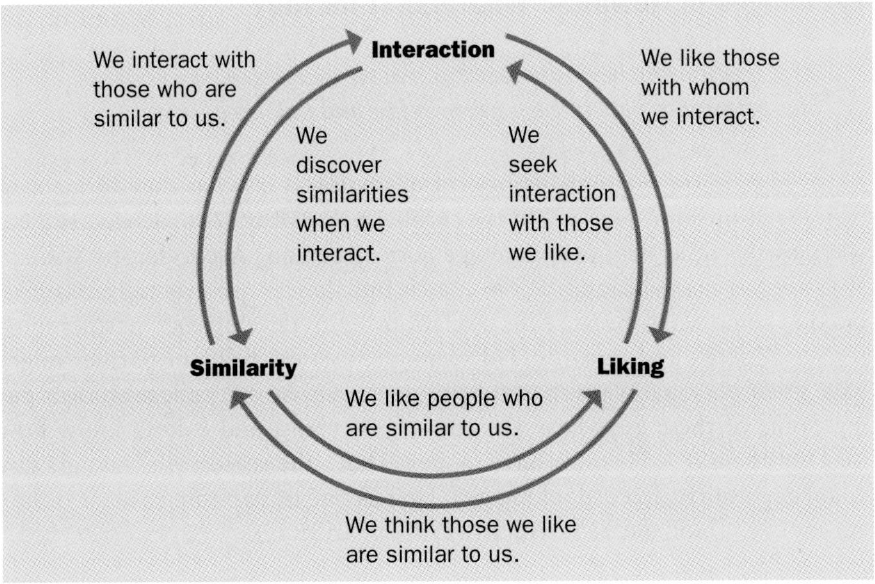

Interaction, similarity, and liking all tend to influence one another. Thus, if any one of these factors starts a relationship, the other two will tend to contribute to a self-sustaining spiral of friendship.

Relationship Development

If a group of strangers shares a few minutes of conversation, what kind of feelings about each other do you think they will have? Not surprisingly, almost everyone will find a few individuals especially attractive or friendly. Some people will also have idiosyncratic preferences: Erica may be especially attracted to people with red hair, and Jeff may find Joe's sense of humor objectionable. On such short acquaintance, however, the factors that make Jeff dislike Joe will have little to do with Joe's feelings about Jeff.

If the same people interacted for weeks, months, or years, the patterns would be very different (Kenny, in press). Although particularly attractive and friendly people may still be quite popular, preferences will mostly reflect the unique history of the interactions between specific pairs of individuals. Erica may like Jeff because he shares her passion for science-fiction novels, even though Jeff is not particularly popular with others. People's feelings will probably also be mutual. If Erica likes Jeff, Jeff will also like Erica. Patterns like this demonstrate the existence of *relationships*. As relationships develop, purely individual characteristics like physical attractiveness, which are central causes of attraction among strangers, become much less important.

What turns strangers into friends? The answer involves both of the key motives we have already discussed: the need to master the social environment and the need for connectedness with others (Cantor & Malley, 1991). Relationships develop through interactions that fulfill these two needs. Partners exchange rewards, helping each other find individual satisfactions, and they exchange self-disclosures, getting to know each other in increasingly intimate ways.

Exchanges of Rewards: What's in It for Me?

As a relationship begins to develop, the partners exchange rewards. They also attempt to benefit each other in fair and balanced ways.

Most of us know a couple who seem mismatched in what they brought to their relationship: one might be brilliant, wealthy, or socially skilled, whereas the other is just an average sort of person. According to William Walster and his colleagues (1978), such imbalances are generally compensated in some way—because for a relationship to develop *each* partner must receive benefits and rewards. For example, the less brilliant partner might have great personal warmth and helpfulness. Or, as one college student put it: "Some of these guys have the cutest girlfriends, and I don't know how they got them. . . . He must have money. That's the reason why an ugly guy could get a fairly decent-looking girl. He has one of two things: a car or he's got money" (Holland & Eisenhart, 1990, p. 153).

norm of equity The shared view that demands that the rewards obtained by the partners in a relationship should be proportional to their inputs.

"That's Just Not Fair!" The college student just quoted recognized an important factor in the health of relationships—exchanges of rewards usually follow the **norm of equity,** by creating a balance between each partner's inputs and rewards (Adams, 1965). For example, two people working on a joint project or investing in a business usually expect to split the resulting benefits in proportion to their contributions. Equitable relationships may seem awfully materialistic, but research suggests that they are as important to our personal lives as to our business lives (Walster and others, 1978). If you feel you are making the major contribution to a relationship, the norm of equity demands that you should receive more benefits than your less-burdened partner.

Equitable relationships tend to be happy ones. For example, college students' satisfaction with roommates they have known for a few months depends on their perceptions of how equitable the relationship is (Berg, 1984). Inequity creates not only dissatisfaction but other negative emotions as well. Being *underbenefited*—receiving fewer rewards than you think you should—may lead to anger, resentment, and a sense of deprivation (Walster and others, 1978). Being *overbenefited* may result in guilt. An underbenefited partner may demand increased benefits or a reduced workload or may even leave the relationship—a possibility discussed more fully later in this chapter.

However, people respond in different ways to inequity. Women are more uncomfortable about being overbenefited in relationships, and men more distressed by underbenefit (Hatfield and others, 1985). Men seem to care more about the rewards they receive from a relationship, whereas women are more oriented to their partner's welfare and the state of the relationship as a whole. In addition, cross-cultural research shows that equity is generally less important for members of interdependent cultures than in independent cultures (Fiske, 1991). One study demonstrating this point compared couples from The Netherlands and the United States (Van Yperen & Buunk, 1991). Although the U.S. couples were most satisfied if they felt their relationships were equitable, no similar pattern was found among the Dutch couples.

Calvin and Hobbes
by Bill Watterson

Reprinted with Permission.

Self-Disclosure

Relationship development also includes exchanges of self-disclosures as the partners come to know each other better. Self-disclosures increase liking and offer opportunities for sympathetic, supportive responses.

"I really like the Red Sox." "I can't believe how much money I just spent on groceries." Relatively impersonal topics like these are the kinds of things you might discuss with acquaintances. On the other hand, "My alcoholic father used to beat me," or "I don't know if I'm smart enough to make it in grad school" are the kinds of intimate disclosures we usually share only with close and trusted friends. Self-disclosures include facts about one's life and situation, as well as inner thoughts, feelings, and emotions (Morton, 1978). Both the depth of self-disclosure—the level of intimacy of the information—and the breadth—the range of topics—increase as a relationship develops (Altman & Taylor, 1973; Rubin and others, 1980).

Effects of Self-Disclosure. Disclosing something about yourself makes both strangers and friends like you more (Sprecher, 1987; Archer and others, 1980). This fact probably explains why salespeople often tell their customers cute stories about their kids. It may also explain why people who readily express their feelings nonverbally are liked more than less expressive individuals (Friedman and others, 1988). But self-disclosure can go too far: those who disclose more than is appropriate for the intimacy level of the relationship make others uncomfortable and are not well liked (Wortman and others, 1976).

You may recall our discussion of other implications of the norm of reciprocity from Chapter 10, pages 410 to 415.

When people are entrusted with a self-disclosure, the norm of reciprocity prescribes that they should respond in kind. For example, when someone describes sad personal experiences to you, you might recount similar events from your own life. Thus self-disclosures, like rewards, are often exchanged in a relationship as people try to maintain equity, or balance (Archer, 1980). This is particularly true in the early stages of acquaintance, as one experiment demonstrated. When subjects were asked to respond to a stranger's note with one of their own, the topic they wrote about tended to match the level of intimacy in their correspondent's note (Derlega and others, 1976).

People do not always respond in kind to self-disclosures, however. Nor do we want them to. Indeed, when we talk about our bad experiences, shortcomings, or anxieties, we usually expect to receive empathy, support, and acceptance in return (Reis & Shaver, 1988). Good friends often respond in just this way, saying things like, "That must have been terrible for you." A listener who responds with sympathetic concern to an intimate self-disclosure is liked better than one who simply reciprocates with a self-disclosure (Berg & Archer, 1980). As confidences elicit sympathy and support, self-disclosure leads to *self-validation,* the warm feeling of being truly known and accepted by the listener.

Self-disclosures bring other benefits besides self-validation to a relationship. Coordinating mutual activities is easier when each partner knows something of the other's abilities and preferences. And deeper mutual understanding lets each partner meet the other's needs more easily. Self-disclosure also signals trust, because in a particular relationship we may disclose things that we would not want the whole world to know.

There is a strong gender difference in the intimacy level of self-disclosure, as there is in so many other aspects of relationships. Women self-disclose more than men, particularly by revealing their feelings and emo-

Figure 11.3 Gender and the intimacy of interaction

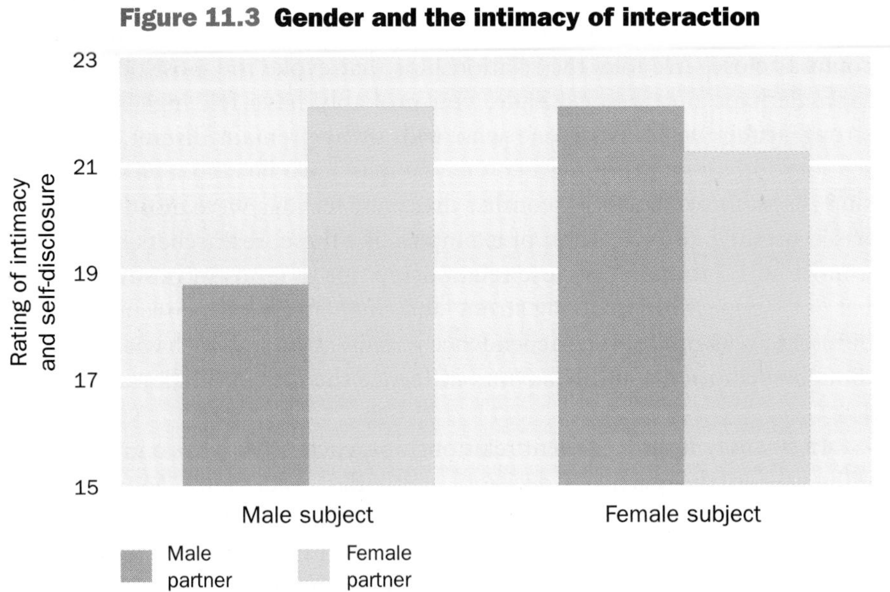

In this study, college students filled out brief questionnaires rating the intimacy of all their social interactions within a given time period. As the figure shows, interactions involving a female subject or a male subject and a female partner—that is, any interaction that involved a female participant—tended to be more intimate and self-disclosing than interactions between two males. (Data from Reis, 1986.)

tions (Morton, 1978; Dindia & Allen, 1992). As Figure 11.3 shows, the difference is largest in same-sex friendships: women disclose much more to other women than men do to other men (Reis, 1986). When men do engage in self-disclosure early in a heterosexual relationship, it can be part of an effort to make the relationship more intimate (Derlega and others, 1985). In contrast, women's disclosures seem to reflect their existing feelings about the relationship, rather than their intention to move toward greater intimacy (Adams & Shea, 1981).

In summary, as partners interact over time, their *individual* characteristics—the key causes of initial feelings of attraction—decline in importance. Instead, the course of the relationship comes to depend on the way the partners treat each other. As they equitably exchange rewards, they feel good about themselves and each other. As they share intimate information, they grow in mutual understanding, demonstrate trust, and give and obtain support and self-validation. Each partner's liking for the other now depends on the way the exchanges of rewards and self-disclosures operate in the relationship. If the processes continue smoothly, casual friendship may be transformed into a close relationship. And, paradoxically, psychological closeness transforms the nature of the two processes that produced closeness in the first place.

Close Relationships

Of your hundreds of relationships with other people, only a handful truly count as close. Are they the relationships that evoke the most positive feelings? Perhaps not. For example, you probably have felt high regard and strong attraction for someone who will always remain distant, such as a school football star or a teacher. Or you may have been in a close relationship that was so filled with conflict that your feelings were mostly negative. Based on their consideration of examples like these, researchers have found it most useful to define a **close relationship** not in terms of positive feelings but as a connection involving strong and frequent interdependence in many different areas of life. **Interdependence** is a situation in which each partner's thoughts, emotions, and behaviors influence the other's (Kelley and others, 1983).

When people are interdependent with the other members of a face-to-face group, it has many types of effects on their behavior, as we describe in Chapter 13, pages 563 to 585.

In strongly interdependent relationships, each person has a great deal of influence on the partner's decisions, activities, and plans. Moreover, the partners usually spend a lot of time alone together, and they share a number of different activities. According to a study by Ellen Berscheid and her colleagues (1989), relationships with these characteristics tend to endure over time. Moreover, relationship closeness is a better predictor of how long the relationship will last than is either the couple's positive feelings for each other or their subjective feelings of closeness.

When people deeply influence each other and spend a lot of time in each other's company doing a variety of different things, are we talking about love? Trying to define *love* may be a fool's game, and indeed most researchers have avoided doing so (Shaver & Hazan, 1988). Nevertheless, two intrepid researchers—Arthur Aron and Elaine Aron—have defined *love* as "the set of thoughts, feelings, and actions that are associated with a desire to enter or maintain a close relationship with a specific person" (1991, p. 26). This formal definition emphasizes the desire for closeness—that is, interdependence—and, like our everyday use of the word *love,* covers relationships with kin and close friends as well as romantic partners. That is, a close relationship can involve the secure, trusting attachment of *companionate love* or the intense sexual arousal of *romantic love* (Hatfield, 1988).

Research on Close Relationships

> *By necessity, most research on close relationships uses nonexperimental designs that leave some ambiguity about causal relations among variables. Research has also focused on the voluntary and potentially temporary relationships—particularly heterosexual romantic relationships—that are most important in Western independent cultures.*

close relationship A relationship involving strong and frequent interdependence in many domains of life.

interdependence A situation in which each person's thoughts, emotions, and behaviors influence those of other people.

As you read this section of the chapter, you will notice that most research on close relationships uses nonexperimental designs. For obvious reasons, people cannot be randomly assigned to have high or low levels of variables like commitment to their partners, nor can relationships be randomly assigned to last for years or break up quickly. The impracticality of random assignment rules out experimental designs and weakens conclusions about the direction of cause and effect. For example, researchers have found that the frequency of sexual intercourse is higher among couples who are generally satisfied with their relationship. This observation may mean that sexual activity increases relationship satisfaction—but it could also mean that couples who are generally satisfied with their relationship tend to have intercourse more often. Researchers are sometimes able to overcome such ambiguities by studying relationships over time, which may allow them to determine the order in which processes occur.

Relationships in Cultural Perspective. Existing research on relationships has another characteristic that becomes clear if we consider relationships from a cross-cultural perspective. Most research—even studies of processes common to all types of close relationships, such as how people handle conflicts—has focused on romantic relationships. This focus on voluntary and often temporary relationships fits well with the general characteristics of Western independent cultures (Moghaddam and others, 1993). It also reflects an easily available pool of research subjects: dating college students and married couples. Researchers have largely neglected relationships that are permanent and unchosen, such as ties to kin and other social groups, which in interdependent cultures are even more important than dyadic (two-person) romantic connections (Moghaddam and others, 1993). Nonromantic close friendships and homosexual romantic relationships have also received very little attention, even though available evidence suggests that homosexual and heterosexual romantic relationships are much more alike than different (Kurdek, 1991; Leigh, 1989).

Because all close relationships share certain basic properties, we consider those common processes before discussing what is special about romantic and sexual relationships.

Close Relationships Incorporate the Partner in One's Self

As a relationship develops, it may evolve into a close relationship, with extensive interaction and strong mutual influence. A desire for closeness with a particular other person seems to correspond to what people generally mean by "love." In a close relationship, the partner is incorporated into the self, just as a meaningful social group membership can be part of one's identity.

In the give-and-take that marks a close relationship, partners learn a lot about each other: she can repair her car, he once cheated on an important exam. As each partner becomes increasingly familiar with intimate and var-

The differences that usually exist between knowledge of the self and knowledge of another person were described in Chapter 4, pages 119 to 122.

ied information about the other, something important happens: the differences that typically exist between self-knowledge and knowledge about the partner are erased. Consider some of the self-other differences that melt away in a close relationship.

1. *People know what they think and feel but are usually unaware of others' thoughts and feelings.* Self-disclosure and extensive interaction, however, give a person access to his or her partner's inner life. In a close relationship, people often have the sense that they know just what their partners are thinking.
2. *People perceive themselves in a wide range of situations, whereas their opportunities to observe others are relatively restricted.* The shared intimacy of a close relationship changes that, as each partner learns about almost every aspect of the other person's life.
3. *People have a different perspective on themselves (as actors) than on others (as observers).* In a close relationship, self-disclosure allows each partner to share the other person's perspective and to know the reasons behind the other person's behaviors and preferences.
4. *People can control their own actions but not those of other people.* Interdependence in a close relationship narrows this gap, as each partner tries to shape his or her own behavior to take into consideration the other person's wishes.

As the differences between the cognitive representations of the self and the partner are reduced or eliminated, knowledge of the partner becomes more like self-knowledge. If Romeo wrote a description of Juliet, for example, he would probably include descriptions of her private thoughts, feelings, and reactions, and he would discuss how she responds to different situations (Prentice, 1990). Contrast this with how people usually describe unfamiliar others—by including little information about thoughts and feelings and assuming that the person behaves consistently across situations.

As the boundaries between self and other break down, the partner becomes part of the psychological self. People use *we* to refer to themselves and the partner, just as they do with an in-group with which they identify. In one study demonstrating the linkage of partner and self, people were asked to fill out three separate questionnaires in which they rated 90 trait words, like *dominant* or *anxious*. In the first questionnaire, subjects stated whether these words described themselves; in the second, whether the words described their spouses; and in the third, whether they described the actor Bill Cosby. Later, the subjects again rated whether each of the 90 terms described themselves, while the researchers recorded the amount of time they took to respond to each item. The researchers then compared the speed of responding and the number of "errors" (changes from the subject's earlier response) for those traits on which subjects thought they were similar to their spouses and for those traits on which subjects thought they differed from their spouses. Subjects were slower in responding and made almost twice as many errors on the traits where they thought they differed from their spouses (Aron and others, 1991). The researchers concluded that people's representations of themselves and their spouses are so intertwined that the connection can lead to confusion—or at least slow down someone's ability to decide, for instance, that he is not assertive when his wife is. No such pattern was evident when self-ratings and ratings of the stranger, Bill Cosby, were compared.

In a close relationship, therefore, the partner—whether a best friend, parent, or romantic partner—becomes part of each person's self-concept. Self-definition as a member of the twosome, and the support and validation provided by the partner, become important to the person's identity, just as a significant group membership becomes important. The merging of two identities means that the two engines that drive the development of casual relationships—the equitable exchange of rewards and the increase of mutual knowledge stemming from reciprocal self-disclosure—begin to lose steam. As this happens, the linkage of partner to self changes the ways in which we meet our basic needs within a close relationship.

To remind yourself of how a group can similarly become part of the self, refer to Chapter 6, pages 227 to 230.

Transformations in Exchange

The psychological linkage of the partner to the self alters the way partners exchange rewards. In a close relationship, partners do not reward each other to obtain rewards in return. Rather, they do so to show affection and because they want to make the partner happy.

Why would you do a favor for a close friend? Certainly not because you expect the favor to be repaid. In close relationships, the exchange of rewards has a different meaning from the equitable exchange found in more casual relationships. People want to show that they care for the other, and they want to make their partner happy because that makes *them* feel good.

Attributions in Close Relationships: It's the Thought That Counts. Your six-year-old son or your younger brother gives you a wonderful Christmas present: a lumpy pottery bowl he fashioned and painted himself in art class in school. The bowl is downright ugly and you don't have any idea what you will do with it. We bet, though, that you will still enjoy it because you appreciate the feelings behind the gift. In close relationships, it's the thought that counts. The ways the partners treat each other become less important than the *feelings and intentions* that those acts convey—just as the youngster's gift indicates his high regard for you (Kelley, 1979). The principle holds true on the negative side as well. A relatively minor sin like arriving late for a date, which might be shrugged off by a mere acquaintance, may be seen as indicating a lack of commitment to a close relationship and may precipitate a major crisis in the relationship.

Fortunately, attributions in close relationships are generally biased in a positive direction. As we saw in Chapter 4, our attributions for our own behaviors are often self-serving, and because a close relationship partner is part of "me and mine," the same self-serving biases apply to the partner. We inflate the significance of our partner's positive behaviors, linking them to his or her sterling qualities or loving feelings: "How much he must care about me!" We minimize the partner's negative behaviors, explaining them away as due to situational causes like a bad day at work or minor failings like a poor memory (Fletcher & Fincham, 1991).

Crock

Reprinted with Special Permission of North America Syndicate.

Dealing with Interdependence. Caring about the partner's feelings—wanting to make him or her feel good—can complicate decisions about what to do. Suppose, for example, you have a yen to take in a classic *Star Wars* film on a Friday night. If your partner prefers the latest *Terminator* epic, you have to consider that preference as well as your own in deciding on the evening's entertainment. We typically solve minor coordination problems like this many times each day, usually without even seeing them as problems. We do so because the nature of exchange is transformed in a close relationship (Kelley, 1979; Walster and others, 1978). Instead of giving in to the partner's preferences and expecting reciprocation in the future, people directly respond to their partners' wishes. After all, if your partner is part of yourself, his or her needs and desires become indistinguishable from your own.

In a study demonstrating this point, subjects allocated various amounts of money between themselves and another person (Aron and others, 1991). As Figure 11.4 shows, people gave themselves considerably more than they gave to a stranger. When the other person was their best friend, however, they gave the friend slightly more than they gave themselves. The experimenters told some subjects that the money would be sent to the friend with a note explaining the subject's role, while other subjects' friends would receive the money and an explanation that did not mention the subject's name. The pattern of generosity to the friend was the same in both cases, in-

Figure 11.4 Treating a best friend like the self

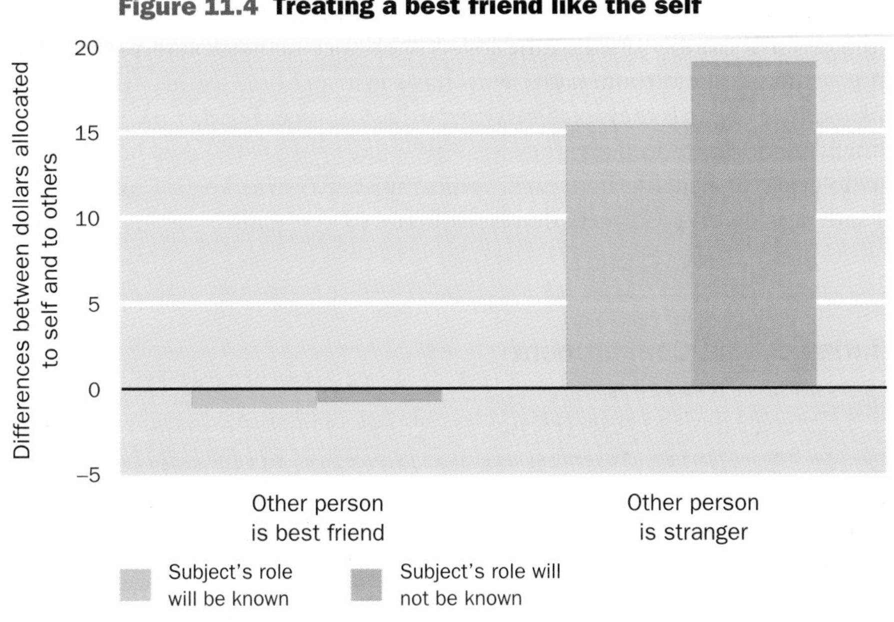

In this study, subjects were given a sum of money to divide between themselves and another person. As the left bars show, when the other person was their best friend, the subjects gave that person slightly more than they gave themselves—regardless of whether the friend would know of their role in the allocation. In contrast, when the other person was a stranger, the right bars show that subjects gave considerably more to themselves than to that person. (Data from Aron and others, 1991.)

dicating that the generosity was not motivated simply by people's desire to avoid upsetting their friends. Rather, people really want to benefit a close friend as much as they want to benefit themselves. Indeed, one's best friend is part of "me and mine."

Closeness in a relationship thus alters not only the *results* of the distribution of rewards but also the *reasons* for distributing them (Clark & Mills, 1979). In a casual relationship, termed an **exchange relationship,** people exchange benefits to preserve equity—they give to their partner in order to receive in return. In contrast, close friends or others who have **communal relationships** are directly concerned for each other's welfare, and they provide benefits to demonstrate that they care. For this reason, equity becomes less important as a relationship becomes close (Cate & Lloyd, 1988; Aron and others, 1991). One researcher interviewed homeowners whose friends had pitched in, usually without any payment, to help them build their homes. Though this level of inequity would be unthinkable in a relationship that was not close, the homeowners believed that the experience had strengthened their friendship (O'Connell, 1984). Of course, relationships cannot be completely one sided. People expect their partners to be responsive, and consistent failure to reciprocate benefits would raise questions about the person's commitment and caring.

As the distribution of rewards changes, so do the types of benefits the partners bestow on each other. Material rewards are typically exchanged in

exchange relationship A relationship in which people exchange rewards following the principle of equity.

communal relationship A relationship in which people reward their partner out of direct concern and to show caring.

relationships that are not close, whereas love and emotional support are more often the coin of close relationships (Hays, 1984; Lloyd and others, 1982). And the more deeply the partners know one another, the more finely the rewards can be tuned to the loved one's specific needs and preferences. For example, new roommates who have just met seek equity in the total amount of rewards they exchange, regardless of type. But as time passes and their relationship deepens, they are more likely to give each other the specific types of benefits that each values most. Roberta helps Carmen with math homework; Carmen drives Roberta to the mall or a movie (Berg, 1984).

Intimacy and Commitment

Ongoing processes of self-disclosure and sympathetic support lead to feelings of trust, closeness, and acceptance. As closeness increases, the partners feel a growing sense of commitment to each other. They trust that they can rely on the partner to fulfill their needs, and they hope and plan for the continuation of the relationship into the future.

Just as closeness transforms the processes underlying the exchange of rewards, it also fundamentally changes the partners' feelings for each other. A sense of intimacy grows, and the partners' commitment to each other deepens.

Psychological Intimacy. Perhaps the most important component of close relationships is **intimacy**, or psychological closeness (Sternberg, 1986; Hatfield, 1988). If asked about your feelings toward your closest friends or family members, you probably would use words like *caring, warmth,* and *acceptance.* These feelings are displayed in mutual understanding and support, a desire to help the partner and to share possessions and time, and a sense of happiness when the partner is present (Sternberg & Grajek, 1984). Intimacy develops slowly over time and is nourished by interactions involving self-disclosure, support, and validation (Altman & Taylor, 1973; Clark & Taraban, 1991). This is why it is difficult to imagine a truly intimate relationship springing up between two people "at first sight"—no matter how strong their mutual attraction might be.

Let's consider the dynamics of self-disclosure and response in a close relationship. Arriving home in the evening, you tell your partner, "My computer crashed today and then the boss chewed me out because some important files got lost. Sometimes I wonder how much longer I can handle this job." Instead of simply reciprocating with another self-disclosure, your partner is likely to try to convey acceptance, acknowledgment, and understanding (Derlega and others, 1976). Such interactions let you feel known and

intimacy Psychological closeness in a relationship, involving extensive self-disclosure and mutual feelings of understanding, caring, and acceptance.

validated (Berg & Archer, 1980), and they may give you the strength to go back to work the next day and face your temperamental hard disk and curmudgeonly boss. These feelings of warmth, acceptance, and connectedness are so important to people that psychological intimacy is perhaps the most central reward of a close relationship (Reis & Shaver, 1988). As the partner becomes part of self, the partner's esteem for you becomes just like your own self-esteem. You feel good when your partner likes you. Thus one of the best ways to keep a relationship happy is consistent communication of positive feelings (Byrne & Murnen, 1988). Of course, your partner knows you love him or her, but it still helps to say so repeatedly, with kind words or touches or eye contact and with phone calls or gifts.

Intimacy also brings danger. Exposing our deepest thoughts and feelings takes trust and courage, for intimate partners are uniquely able to hurt us. One woman, for example, suffered in isolation for a long time as her marriage fell apart; then, finally, she decided to confide everything in her sister (Hatfield & Rapson, 1993). The sister angrily attacked her, arguing that even contemplating divorce was a sin and that she was being selfish and would destroy her husband's and child's lives. As this woman discovered, intimacy is hard work, and when it is used against us it can be very painful. True intimacy requires us not only to communicate our feelings honestly but also to accept ourselves—and our partners—for what they are, warts and all. The price is sometimes heavy, but the rewards of closeness, affection, and acceptance are worth it.

Commitment. Intimacy may draw people closer, but it is commitment that holds a relationship together over time. **Commitment** consists of all the combined forces that keep people working to promote and maintain their partnership. Caryl Rusbult (1983) argues that commitment involves both feelings and actions.

Committed partners feel comfortable relying on each other for intimacy, advice, and support (Kobak & Hazan, 1991). Each believes that the other is trustworthy, responsive, and available when needed, and that his or her support can bring comfort in times of distress. Commitment also involves action: it affects people's intentions, desires, and plans for the future. Being committed means, for instance, wanting the relationship to last for a long time. The two aspects of commitment—trusting acceptance of interdependence with the partner and the desire to maintain the relationship—usually go together (Rusbult, 1983; Sternberg, 1986).

As Figure 11.5 shows, one key factor that creates and maintains commitment to a relationship is personal *satisfaction* with the relationship—recognition of the rewards it brings. Relationships offer many rewards, including the opportunity to make intimate self-disclosures, express sexuality, experience emotional involvement, find companionship for enjoyable activities, and feel secure, worthy, and validated (Drigotas & Rusbult, 1992).

commitment The combined forces that hold the partners together in an enduring relationship.

Figure 11.5 Factors influencing commitment to a relationship

Rewards from relationship
I enjoy being with her—she helps me feel good when I'm low.
Potential rewards from alternative relationships
I don't like dating around; no one else is so appealing.
Investments that would be lost if relationship ended
We have lots of mutual friends; it would be hard to break up our tape collection.
Costs of leaving relationship
Parting would involve lots of tears; I'd hate to have to tell our friends we broke up.
Satisfaction with relationship
Barriers to leaving relationship
Commitment to relationship
I am comfortable relying on her; I want the relationship to last a long time.

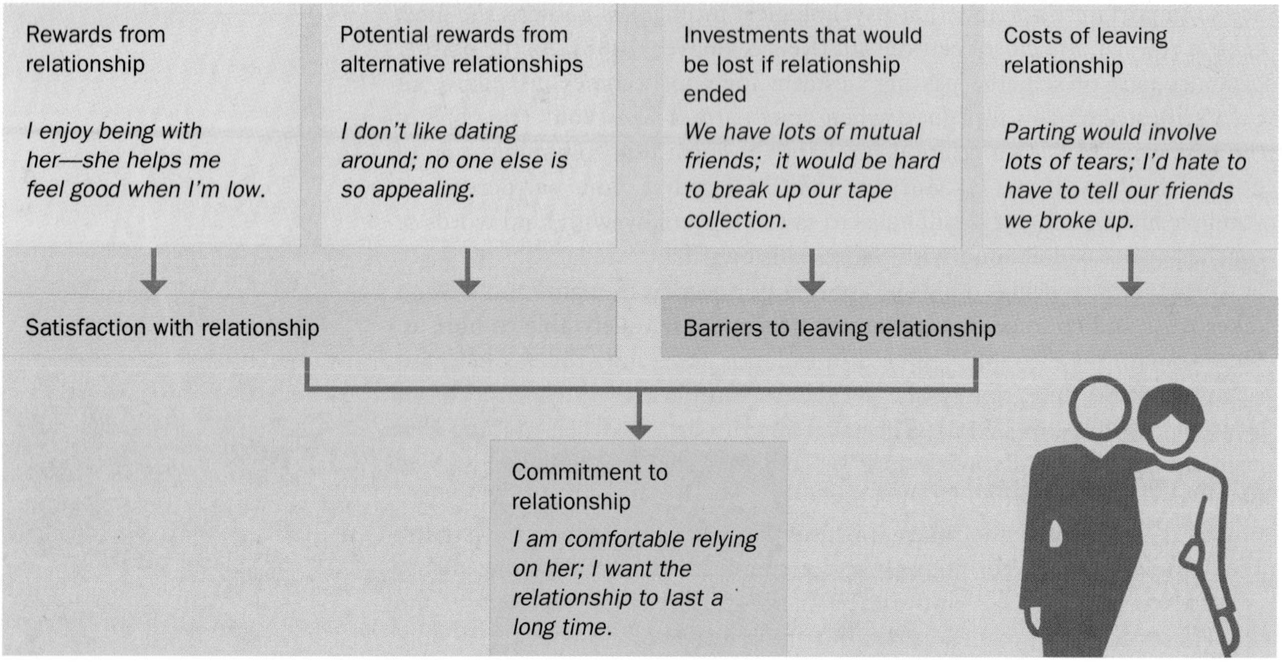

Commitment depends on satisfaction with the relationship relative to its potential alternatives. Commitment is also strengthened by perceived barriers to leaving the relationship. (Based on Rusbult, 1983.)

People evaluate these outcomes not in absolute terms but by comparing them with the rewards they believe would be available in alternative relationships—a standard termed the *comparison level for alternatives* (Thibaut & Kelley, 1959). If you see your relationship as offering unique rewards that you think would be unavailable from other relationships, you are likely to be strongly committed to it.

Negative forces can be as important as positive ones in maintaining commitment. Psychological or financial factors often pose barriers to leaving a relationship (Rusbult, 1983). For example, people contemplating divorce face the embarrassment of having to admit to friends that the relationship failed, and they must cope with the financial, emotional, and legal difficulties of breaking up a home and family. They also confront the loss of their investments of time, energy, and self-disclosures that they have made in the relationship. They may even lose mutual friends or treasured possessions. Barriers like these can help maintain a relationship even if satisfaction is low (Sternberg, 1986).

Commitment usually grows slowly as a relationship continues. As the partners' intimacy increases, they are likely to derive increasing satisfaction from the relationship, and they begin to perceive alternative relationships as less desirable and less available. In fact, compared with those who are dating casually, heterosexual college students who are committed to a dating relationship tend to see opposite-sex others as physically less attractive (Simpson and others, 1990). Needless to say, this means that they also see their partner as relatively more attractive. For all these reasons, longer-lasting relationships usually involve stronger feelings of commitment and are less likely to break up (Simpson, 1987).

Types of People, Types of Relationships

People differ in the ways they approach close relationships. Securely attached individuals are comfortable relying on the partner for support and acceptance. Avoidant individuals fear reliance on others, and anxious individuals worry that the partner will not be available and responsive. Different relationships also involve different combinations of intimacy, commitment, and passion. Finally, gender plays a role. Men usually emphasize the individual rewards that a relationship provides; women are more inclined to value intimacy and relationship closeness for itself.

In a committed close relationship, psychological intimacy allows caring partners to share self-disclosures and to comfort and support each other. However, some people are more comfortable than others with intimacy, trust, and reliance on a partner.

Attachment Styles. Imagine that a close friend has invited you to dinner at an elegant restaurant where the tab for dinner for two can easily exceed $100. How would you respond?

Most people will find this question difficult to answer. Your response will probably depend on several factors. You will examine your knowledge about your friend as an individual, of course. But your answer will also draw on your general beliefs about the self, other people, and the nature of relationships (Fletcher & Fincham, 1991; Surra & Bohman, 1991). These beliefs in turn are likely to be influenced by experiences in earlier relationships (Hazan & Shaver, 1987). Like all social perception, people's perceptions and evaluations of their relationships are influenced by their previous experiences and knowledge (Baldwin, 1992). Perhaps, for example, your mother often gave you expensive toys and clothing when you were a child but used these treats to create guilt feelings by which she later manipulated you. If so, you might be quite wary of accepting your friend's offer of an expensive dinner.

The many ways in which our prior knowledge influences our perceptions and interpretations are described in Chapter 3, pages 74 to 80.

Drawing on earlier research examining infants' patterns of attachment to their mothers (Ainsworth and others, 1978), Cindy Hazan and Philip Shaver (1987) theorized that adults' basic beliefs about self and others might affect the way they experience love and closeness. They used questionnaires with statements like the ones shown in Table 11.1 to classify college students into one of three attachment styles. Their studies demonstrated that **attachment styles** are related to many aspects of the students' love relationships (Shaver and others, 1988). *Securely attached* students, about 55 percent of those in their study, were the most likely to feel happiness and trust in their relationships and the least likely to fear closeness. Those categorized as *avoidant* (about 25 percent) feared closeness and were less accepting of their partners than were students in the other groups. Finally, the 20 percent of students classed as *anxious* were most prone to emotional extremes: compared with others, they felt more jealousy and passion and a greater desire for merging with the partner. As the table shows, the three groups also held different basic beliefs about self and others. For example, securely attached students were most likely to agree that "I am easier to get

Table 11.1 An example of statements measuring attachment styles in adult close relationships.

Self-description	Attachment style	Basic beliefs about self, others, and love
I find it relatively easy to get close to others and am comfortable depending on them and having them depend on me. I don't often worry about being abandoned or about someone getting too close to me.	Secure	I am likable. Other people are generally good-hearted. Romantic love can last.
I am somewhat uncomfortable being close to others; I find it difficult to trust them completely, difficult to allow myself to depend on them. I am nervous when anyone gets too close, and often, love partners want me to be more intimate than I feel comfortable being.	Avoidant	I am not particularly easy to get to know. It's rare to find somebody you can really fall in love with. Romantic love rarely lasts.
I find that others are reluctant to get as close as I would like. I often worry that my partner doesn't really love me or won't want to stay with me. I want to merge completely with another person, and this desire sometimes scares people away.	Anxious	I have many self-doubts. I am not particularly easy to get to know. Few people are as willing as I am to commit themselves to a relationship. It's easy to fall in love.

Source: "Love as attachment: The integration of three behavioral systems" by P. Shaver, C. Hazan, & D. Bradshaw, in R. Sternberg & M. Barnes (Eds.), *The psychology of love* (pp. 80–82), 1988, New Haven, CT: Yale University Press. Reprinted with permission.

attachment styles People's basic securely attached, avoidant, or anxious orientation toward others in close relationships.

to know than most people" and that "people are generally well-intentioned and good-hearted."

Do attachment styles have concrete, visible effects on the way close partners give and receive support? A fascinating study of dating couples by Jeffry Simpson and his colleagues (1992) examined this question. After the members of each couple completed questionnaires about their attachment styles, the two were separated. The woman was led to a waiting room where the researchers deliberately frightened her. They warned her that she would soon undergo "experimental procedures that arouse considerable anxiety and distress" and showed her a darkened room resembling an isolation chamber, filled with complex electronic equipment. The man, unaware of his partner's experience, was then brought into the waiting room. Without their knowledge, the couple's ensuing interaction was videotaped for five minutes.

People with different attachment styles showed distinct variations in their patterns of seeking and giving support, and the strongest differences were found between the securely attached and avoidant categories. Among securely attached women, extremely upset subjects sought more support from their partners than did the less frightened subjects. In contrast, among avoidant women, extremely upset subjects actually sought *less* support than did their less frightened counterparts. Almost one-fifth of the women, mostly those classified as avoidant, failed even to mention the stressful event to their partners.

The men's attachment styles also influenced the amount of support that was offered. Securely attached men tended to offer more support to a partner who displayed more fear than to a partner who was less frightened. But among avoidant men, a different pattern emerged: the more fear a woman displayed, the less support she was offered.

Regardless of their attachment styles, *all* the women in this upsetting situation were calmed if their partners made supportive comments. However, the avoidant women tended not to ask for, and the avoidant men tended not to offer, this potentially effective interaction.

The findings from this study suggest that basic beliefs about self and others, as reflected in attachment styles, influence both people's trust in their partners' support and their willingness to offer support in stressful situations. Securely attached partners, who turn toward one another for comfort, probably derive increased satisfaction from their relationship in the long term and probably achieve greater interdependence. Conversely, avoidant individuals' reluctance to seek or offer support may be a barrier to both interdependence and the rewards of psychological intimacy. As a result of these processes, attachment styles pervasively influence the ways people experience love. In general, securely attached people are highest in self-esteem and in happiness with their love relationships, and anxious people are lowest in both (Collins & Read, 1990; Simpson, 1990). As you will see later in the chapter, attachment styles also affect the way people handle conflict within close relationships.

According to Robert Sternberg's theory, seven types of love emerge from the various combinations of three basic ingredients. This figure shows the label Sternberg has given to each type, together with a brief description. (Adapted from Sternberg, 1986.)

Figure 11.6 A triangular theory of love

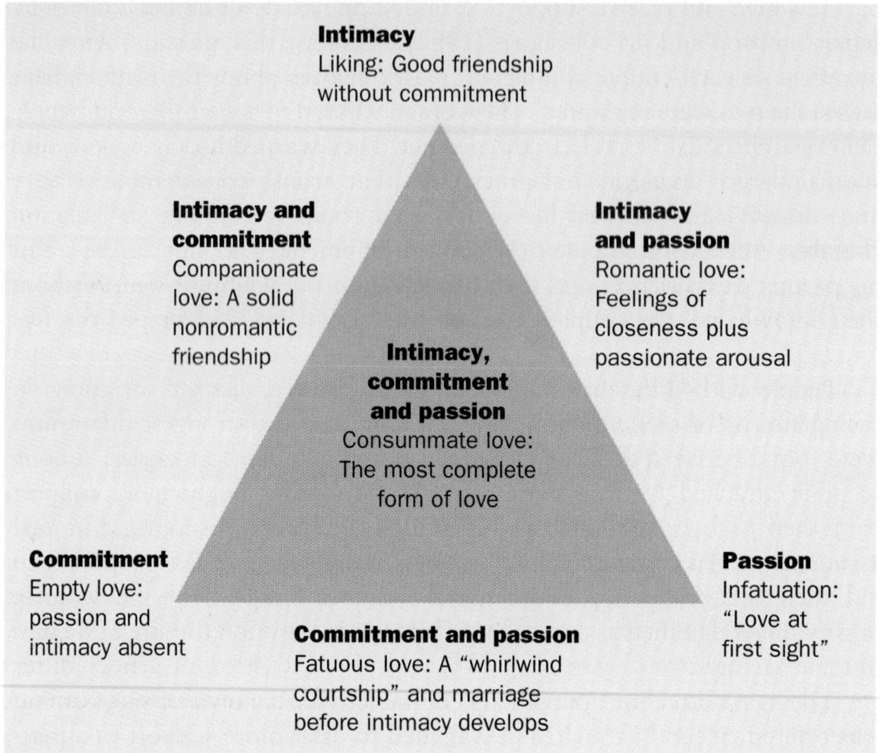
Intimacy
Liking: Good friendship without commitment
Intimacy and commitment
Companionate love: A solid nonromantic friendship
Intimacy and passion
Romantic love: Feelings of closeness plus passionate arousal
Intimacy, commitment and passion
Consummate love: The most complete form of love
Commitment
Empty love: passion and intimacy absent
Passion
Infatuation: "Love at first sight"
Commitment and passion
Fatuous love: A "whirlwind courtship" and marriage before intimacy develops

Triangular Theory of Love. Other researchers have also pursued the insight that people experience love in many different ways. Robert Sternberg (1986) has focused on three primary components—intimacy, passion, and commitment—which combine in different ways to form seven types of love (see Figure 11.6). For example, intimacy plus commitment equals a solid nonromantic friendship. Passion alone characterizes a sudden infatuation that arises outside a committed or psychologically intimate relationship. Of course, most actual relationships involve various blends of these three processes and fall somewhere between these pure types. But the variety of types of love reminds us that the nature of loving feelings can change over time and that they often differ from one person to another. In a close relationship, it is important to try to understand and appreciate the way your partner loves you, which may be different from the way you love him or her.

Gender Differences in Relationships. It may come as no surprise that men and women often approach close relationships differently. Women's close relationships, particularly with same-sex friends, tend to be more intimate than men's (Reis and others, 1985). This difference in intimacy is just one aspect of a more general principle: men and women place different emphases on the various rewards that relationships offer (Wright, 1982; Tannen, 1990). Men prefer participating in enjoyable activities with their partners, and women generally prefer intimacy and sharing feelings.

In one study demonstrating the impact of these differences on heterosexual relationships, Catherine Surra and Molly Longstreth (1990) questioned dating couples about activities that have to be performed together (like love making or intimate talks about the relationship). Not surprisingly, they found that when the partners' preferences for activities differed, those activities were often the focus of conflicts. In general, the men in their sample were more likely than the women to prefer sexual activity, and the women were more likely than the men to prefer intimate discussions about feelings and other activities aimed at strengthening the relationship. The study found that the way the partners dealt with such conflicts influenced both the activities they shared and how much they enjoyed them. The time devoted to these activities was usually controlled by the partner who enjoyed the activity less. For example, the less a man liked relationship-maintenance activities, the less the couple tended to engage in them.

The sources of satisfaction with the relationship also differed for men and women. The men's satisfaction depended on the way the couple spent their time: the more time the men spent participating with their partners in activities they enjoyed, the happier they were. In contrast, women were satisfied when the couple successfully avoided arguments and conflict. We have seen this pattern earlier in this chapter in the discussion of gender differences in relation to inequity. Men care more about the rewards they can obtain from interacting with the partner. Women care more about the relationship itself; they are happiest when the relationship is going well (Kelley, 1979; Wright, 1982).

Effects of Relationships

Relationships affect virtually all aspects of our lives, including physical health. Support from others can improve both physical and mental health and well-being, and the most crucial component of social support appears to be intimacy and acceptance. Because women's relationships are more intimate than men's, relationships with women tend to be more valuable for health than relationships with men.

In Chapter 4 we described research showing that the way we think about ourselves influences our feelings, our behaviors, and even our physical health. Relationships also affect these aspects of our lives because a partner in a close relationship becomes part of ourself.

Intimacy, Social Support, and Health. The medical community was initially puzzled by research showing that **social support**—coping resources provided by significant others—can influence physical health as well as psychological well-being. The findings are now beyond dispute. For example,

social support Emotional and physical coping resources provided by other people.

people with cancer and other diseases who participate in support groups of fellow sufferers can obviously expect to receive comfort, reassurance, information, and advice. It may surprise you to learn that they also have more effective immune-system responses and tend to live longer than patients without such support (Goleman, 1990). One British study demonstrating this point focused on women with advanced breast cancer. Women who received the best available medical care and also attended support groups lived twice as long—an average of 37 months—as women who received the same excellent medical treatment but had no group support. The results of another study of more than six thousand California residents, shown in Figure 11.7, suggest that social support has a marked impact on people's overall death rate (Berkman & Syme, 1979). A meta-analysis of over fifty such studies demonstrates that the effects of social support on physical health are pervasive, but they are strongest under two conditions: when the person receiving the support is a woman, and when the support is provided by family and friends rather than by strangers (Schwarzer & Leppin, 1989).

How does social support produce these striking benefits? Other people do provide practical help—from offering advice about problems to running errands for the patient. However, these concrete forms of assistance do not by themselves translate into the benefits of social support. Instead, social support offers opportunities for self-disclosure, companionship, and enjoyable interactions, and these seem to account for most of its benefits (Rook, 1987; Sarason and others, 1987; Wills, 1991). In the best of times, psychological intimacy helps us avoid loneliness and find happiness and satisfac-

Figure 11.7 Social support and physical health

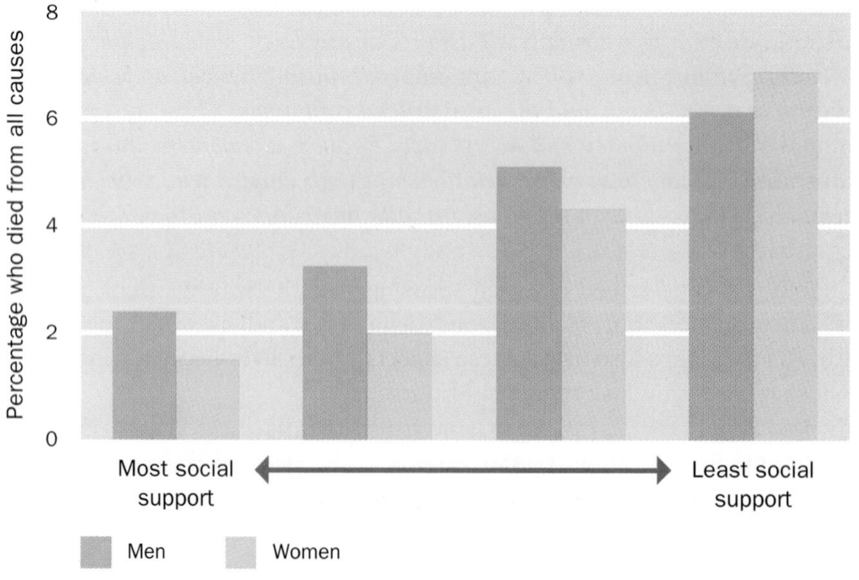

Researchers questioned over 6,000 California residents about their social support. Nine years later, they calculated the death rate from all causes for individuals who initially had been categorized as having various levels of social support. This graph shows the rates for people aged 30 to 49, though findings were similar for other age groups. As you can see, both men and women who initially had higher levels of social support had lower death rates. (Data from Berkman & Syme, 1979.)

tion (Wheeler and others, 1983; McAdams & Vaillant, 1982; Reis and others, 1985). In bad times, it becomes even more important. For example, the opportunity to disclose traumatic events to people who care and sympathize improves people's mental and physical health (Pennebaker, 1990).

Social support and health Researchers now know that supportive relationships can be just as important to good physical health as medical treatment and healthy living. When Esperanza Rolon, a member of the Retired Senior Volunteer Program (right), visits with this resident of a local nursing home, the benefits of their relationship flow both ways.

In general, married people are more likely to have a psychologically intimate relationship than unmarried people, although, as we will see, there are some exceptions to this generalization. The benefits of psychological intimacy mean, therefore, that marriage usually improves people's well-being, particularly men's, making them happier and more satisfied with their lives than unmarried people are (Veroff and others, 1981). Again, happiness translates into health. In one study, married men aged 45 to 64 had just one-half the death rate of unmarried men, even after other influences on health like income, smoking, drinking, and obesity were taken into account (Angier, 1990). Remember, though, that it is psychological intimacy, not marriage itself, that produces these benefits. Troubled marriages may bring distress rather than support (Rook & Pietromonaco, 1987), and many people, particularly women, find social support and intimacy in close friendships or nonmarital romantic relationships.

Gender and Social Support. In her recent book *You Just Don't Understand,* Deborah Tannen (1990, p. 49) describes a woman who was upset about a scar left visible on her body by an operation. Here are the responses she obtained from two different people:

A: "I know. It's like your body has been violated."
B: "You can have plastic surgery to cover up the scar."

Did you guess that response *A* came from a woman and *B* from a man? Women are more likely than men to respond to someone's negative feelings with understanding and acceptance—to reassure the speaker that it's all right to feel bad, perhaps by sharing an account of a time when they had similar feelings. Men are more likely than women to take the initial disclosure as a complaint about a problem and to offer helpful advice on solving it. Tannen points out that women and men often misunderstand each other's approaches. A woman may feel that a problem-solving response belittles her feelings by failing to deal with them directly. In this particular episode, the woman was upset because she felt that *B* (her husband) *wanted* her to have plastic surgery, and that suggesting a solution meant that he was unconcerned about her current emotional state.

But men may be equally troubled by a woman's typical responses. When a woman responds to a man's concerns by saying, "I know, sometimes I feel the same way," the man may feel that she is denying the uniqueness of his feelings and failing to contribute to a solution. Miscommunication might be less likely if each gender recognized the other's needs.

Emotional support is more helpful than problem solving to people who are ill or under stress (Rook, 1987). Since women are more likely to offer emotional support, it follows that people should feel healthier and happier after interacting with women than they do after interacting with men. Research confirms that, for both male and female college students, everyday interaction with women is a more effective safeguard against loneliness than is interaction with men (Reis, 1986). Similarly, men seem to benefit more from marriage than women do, and, when a spouse dies, men are at greater risk for depression and physical illness than women are (Bernard, 1973; Reis, 1986).

Of course, this gender difference in psychological intimacy is a matter of preference rather than ability (Reis and others, 1985). Both men and women are able to engage in intimate, meaningful interaction and to provide emotional support. All people, regardless of gender, fare better psychologically and physically when they interact with close others in a psychologically and emotionally intimate way.

Love and Work. Relationship troubles can interfere with a person's ability to concentrate on work, and the other side of this coin is that strong relationships can be a real benefit in the workplace. When Cindy Hazan and Philip Shaver (1990) investigated the impact of attachment styles on people's orientations toward work, they found that securely attached people value both love and work and are generally satisfied with their work and their co-workers. In contrast, avoidant individuals may immerse themselves in work to avoid dealing with other people—they may work late, for example, rather than confronting relationship problems. But although they may spend more hours in the workplace, avoidant individuals tend to be less satisfied with their work. Anxiously attached people also operate at a disadvantage. They fear rejection for low performance, enjoy their work less than others do, and may have difficulties concentrating on work unless they see it as an opportunity to gain love and respect from others. Thus, not only are close relationships central to our lives, but they also exert a powerful influence over specific aspects of our lives, such as our physical health and careers.

Romantic Love and Sexuality

Romeo and Juliet, Rhett Butler and Scarlett O'Hara, Richard Gere and Cindy Crawford—famous lovers of legend, lore, and the mass media feed our ideas about romance. Though high divorce rates suggest that many people fail to find the romance they seek, the ideal itself still influences how we act in relationships and how we feel about them. What is the mysterious force we call *romantic love* or *passion*? And how is it tied up with our ideas about sexuality and about marriage?

Passionate Feelings

> *Some relationships involve passionate feelings and emotions. Passionate emotions can arise quickly and are closely linked to sexual desires and behavior.*

"I want my partner—physically, emotionally, mentally." "Sometimes I feel I can't control my thoughts; they are obsessively on my partner." "I eagerly look for signs indicating my partner's desire for me." These are items from the Passionate Love Scale, which was developed by Elaine Hatfield (1988). They suggest that *passionate love* involves, in addition to sexual feelings, a sense of intense longing for the partner, euphoric feelings of fulfillment and ecstasy when the relationship goes well, and anxiety and despair when it does not (Hatfield, 1988; Hatfield and Rapson, 1993). Other components of love—commitment, trust, intimacy, and attachment—are relatively quiet. When people talk about passionate or romantic feelings, they use words like *stormy, roller coaster, head-over-heels,* and *obsession.*

Sometimes we realize that the object of our hopeless adoration is someone totally unsuitable, a person we don't know very well or even like very much. As Ellen Berscheid (1988) has noted, the intransigent independence of passionate feelings from the other components of love "can be testified to by anyone who has earnestly desired to be in love with another, often because the other *is* so likable, or because they *do* have all those qualities one desires (or ought to desire) in a mate, or because it would please one's parents, friends, or the other person; one can like the other so hard one's nose bleeds, but that—still—does not, and seemingly cannot, cause the liking state to be transcended and romantic love to appear" (p. 369).

Views on the mysterious and powerful force of passion differ from culture to culture. Most North Americans believe that romantic love is natural, desirable, and necessary for marriage (Simpson and others, 1986). However, most Chinese words for love have negative connotations: *infatuation, unrequited love, sorrow* (Hatfield & Rapson, 1993). In China, more pragmatic attributes (like a high income) are viewed as desirable characteristics in a marriage partner; romantic love is viewed with some suspicion, as illicit and socially disruptive (Dion & Dion, 1988).

To remind yourself of how emotions are linked to beliefs or appraisals and to action tendencies, turn to Chapter 4, pages 138 to 146.

Passion *is* disruptive, as many other emotions are. And, like all emotions, passion is linked to a set of beliefs about the beloved and motivations for specific types of action. The beliefs often idealize the partner: "For me, my partner is the perfect romantic partner" is another item from the Passionate Love Scale. The desired actions include sexual union and other types of closeness and contact with the beloved, such as touching or sustained eye contact.

Like all emotions—and like a roller coaster—passion has its peaks and valleys. When couples proclaim that they fell in love "at first sight," you can be sure that passion rather than commitment or intimacy is what they are describing. In fact, people often view passion as something that happens *to* them—as though they were struck by Cupid's arrow. Perhaps this helps explain why individuals who believe that external forces drive their lives are more likely to experience passionate love than are people who think they control their own fate (Dion & Dion, 1988).

The intense and sudden onset of passion at the beginning of a relationship is not surprising when you consider how important physical attractiveness is to initial attraction (Sternberg, 1986). However, after drawing people together, passion tends to fade as the relationship matures (Sternberg, 1988). The components of intimacy and commitment develop more slowly but become more important over time, giving a long-term close partnership quite a different character from the turbulent and frenzied feelings of its beginning.

Sometimes the excited feelings we identify as passion have nothing to do with the beloved but arise from other causes. As we saw in Chapter 4, people cannot always accurately identify the causes of their emotional arousal. For this reason, anything that causes arousal can influence passionate feelings. A few minutes of exercise or a hilarious Steve Martin comedy routine, for instance, can intensify passionate feelings toward attractive others (Zuckerman, 1979; White and others, 1981). The fact that arousal from external sources can intensify passionate feelings may explain the fact that, as we mentioned earlier, individuals with an anxious attachment style are more likely than others to fall head-over-heels in love, to experience obsessive preoccupation with the beloved, and to feel the emotional highs and lows that are characteristic of passion (Shaver and others, 1988). Similarly, adoles-

Calvin and Hobbes by Bill Watterson

cents who are highly anxious are particularly likely to experience passionate love (Hatfield and others, 1989). Parents sometimes unwittingly intensify this process by interfering with a teenager's passionate attachment to an "unsuitable" partner. When this happens, the "Romeo and Juliet effect," characterized by feelings of anger and struggles to overcome parental disapproval, may actually intensify passionate feelings about the partner (Driscoll and others, 1972).

Sometimes arousal from external sources is mistakenly attributed to passionate feelings. But in most ordinary circumstances, this is not the case. What, then, is the source of the arousal that underlies and strengthens passion? Ellen Berscheid, who has been studying love for almost two decades, answered this question by saying, "If forced against a brick wall to face a firing squad who would shoot if not given the correct answer, I would whisper 'It's about 90 percent sexual desire as yet not sated'" (1988, p. 373).

Sexual Attitudes and Behavior

People's attitudes about sex differ widely, depending in part on gender and personality differences. Some people see sex as an enjoyable activity even outside of a committed relationship; others see it as an expression of intimacy and commitment to the partner.

Do you think sexual activity is appropriate between people who like each other, even if they have not known each other very long? Between individuals who have a committed relationship but are not married? Between people of the same gender? Between a married person and someone other than his or her spouse? Does your opinion change depending on the kind of sexual activity—intercourse versus kissing and fondling, for example?

Researchers have asked such questions in surveys of the U.S. general public and of U.S. college students. As Table 11.2 shows, most people approve of sexual activity in a committed heterosexual relationship between unmarried people. Indeed, premarital intercourse seems to be very common: one study of teenagers found that about 75 percent of men and 60 percent of women had engaged in sexual intercourse, before age 18 on the average

Table 11.2 Sexual attitudes and behaviors: Survey results

Subjects	Statement	Percentage agreeing Male	Percentage agreeing Female
	Premarital sex		
General public	A man and woman having sex relations before marriage is wrong only sometimes or not wrong at all.	69	58
College freshmen	A couple should live together for some time before deciding to get married.	58	47
College freshmen	If two people really like each other, it's all right for them to have sex even if they've known each other only a very short time.	66	39
	Extramarital sex		
General public	A married person having sexual relations with someone other than the married partner is wrong only sometimes or not wrong at all.	12	6
	Same-gender sex		
General public	Sexual relations between two adults of the same sex are wrong only sometimes or not wrong at all.	15	22
College freshmen	It is important to have laws prohibiting homosexual relations.	62	45

Sources: Data from "Report: The sexual revolution?" by T. W. Smith, 1990, *Public Opinion Quarterly, 54,* 415–435; and *The American freshman: National norms for fall 1987* by A. W. Astin, K. C. Green, W. S. Korn, & M. Schalit, 1987, Los Angeles, CA: Higher Education Research Institute, University of California at Los Angeles. Reprinted with permission.

(DeLamater & MacCorquodale, 1979). Attitudes toward other types of sex outside of marriage are more negative. A great majority of the public sees extramarital sex as wrong, though some researchers estimate that about half of married adults have had extramarital affairs (Blumstein & Schwartz, 1983). And gay and lesbian sexual activity is viewed almost as negatively. Contrary to the image of college students as sexually permissive, many students advocate laws against homosexual activities. Still, recent estimates agree that around one in five men has had at least one homosexual encounter in his lifetime, and about 7 percent of men engage in homosexual acts as adults (Fay and others, 1989). Studies agree that the proportions for women are somewhat lower. None of these figures can be taken as valid for all time and all sorts of people, however. Patterns of sexual attitudes and behavior have been changing rapidly in recent decades, and the changes may be accelerating in the age of AIDS (Hatfield & Rapson, 1993).

Opinions are sharply divided on whether it's all right for unmarried people to engage in sex when they have known each other for a very short time. About two-thirds of college men and one-third of women approve. Since the 1950s and 1960s, men's and women's attitudes toward sex have converged somewhat as both moved toward a somewhat more permissive stance, but differences like this one still remain (Hendrick and others, 1985; Oliver & Hyde, 1993). Because of women's comparatively conservative stance, they tend to control the actual level of sexual intimacy in a relationship. That is, the traditional roles of males as initiators and females as gatekeepers apparently still hold (Surra & Longstreth, 1990).

Personality Differences in Sexual Attitudes. Although we have been discussing overall differences between men and women, the sexual attitudes and behaviors of individuals within each gender differ in systematic ways. Some people have what is termed a *restricted sociosexual orientation*: they seek closeness and commitment in a relationship before engaging in sex (Simpson & Gangestad, 1991). Individuals with an *unrestricted sociosexual orientation,* in contrast, have relatively permissive attitudes toward sex without commitment. When the two types are compared, unrestricted individuals report having had more "one-night stands" in the past, foresee having more sex partners in the future, and are more likely to maintain sexual relationships with more than one partner. Their relationships also involve less commitment, less love, and less psychological intimacy (Simpson & Gangestad, 1991). Perhaps as a result, unrestricted individuals' romantic relationships tend to break up relatively quickly (Simpson, 1987).

These findings suggest that people attach many different meanings to sexual activity. Some see it as an enjoyable activity even outside of a committed relationship. Others see it as an expression of their intimacy and commitment to the partner. Because sexual activity has so many meanings, open communication about it is extremely important in a relationship. If one partner thinks sex is just good fun and the other assumes it means commitment, serious conflicts are bound to result. But what are the actual effects of sexual activity on a relationship? Does it, for example, strengthen a dating relationship, making it psychologically more intimate, or can it become a focus of conflict capable of driving the couple apart? Because sexual activity can be interpreted in so many different ways, its impact on relationship processes will also vary, depending on the individuals and their relationship.

Sex in the Context of a Relationship

> *Like other mutually enjoyable activities, sexual activity can strengthen a relationship. But it can also be a focus of conflict.*

Some research shows that sexual intimacy is associated with increased satisfaction with the relationship. For instance, Jeffry Simpson (1987) studied the stability of relationships among dating couples who were not having sexual intercourse and among dating couples who were. He found that couples having intercourse were more likely to stay together over the course of three months.

However, over a longer time period, the story is not so clear. Anne Peplau and her colleagues (1977) compared dating couples who had sexual intercourse within a month of their first date; those who had intercourse later, an average of six months after starting to date; and those who had never had intercourse. The early-sex couples had more liberal sexual attitudes and engaged in sexual relations more often than the later-sex couples, and the women reported more sexual satisfaction. In contrast, the later-sex couples seemed to enjoy more emotional and psychological intimacy. They were more likely to say they were in love, they felt closer to their partners, and they were more likely to predict that they would marry the partner. Despite these differences, the two groups were equally satisfied with the relationships—and so were the couples in the study who had never had intercourse. Two years after the initial study, couples in all three groups reported similar outcomes: about 46 percent of the couples in all three groups had broken up, 34 percent were still dating, and 20 percent had married each other. Thus, neither the timing of sex nor the relative emphasis on psychological intimacy seemed to strongly affect the future of these dating relationships.

Love ain't what it used to be To face the growing complexity of relationships in the 1990s, these students participate in a contemporary sex education workshop at their school. By learning about the biological, psychological, and social aspects of relationships, they gain the knowledge and the skills to help them make wise choices.

Satisfaction with sex is closely tied to relationship satisfaction among married couples (Reiss & Lee, 1988). One study, which compared happily married couples and troubled couples who had sought marital counseling, found that the happily married couples had sex more frequently (Birchler & Webb, 1977). This pattern was not unique to sexual activity, however: these couples did *many things* together more frequently, including participating in sports and social events. The more rewarding and mutually enjoyable the activities in a relationship, the warmer the partners' feelings are likely to be. Conversely, when a couple is dissatisfied with sex or other major components of the relationship, satisfaction with the relationship is also likely to decline.

The reasons for sexual dissatisfaction tend to differ for women and men. Women become dissatisfied if they see their sexual relationships as lacking warmth, love, and caring, whereas men who are dissatisfied want more frequent and varied sexual activity (Hatfield, 1982; Hatfield and others, 1989). This gender difference, like other differences in sexual attitudes and behaviors, seems to diminish among older adults (Sprague &

Quadagno, 1989; Oliver & Hyde, 1993). The degree of sexual satisfaction, however, need not decline with age. Although the frequency of sexual activity is lower among older adults than among younger adults, one study interviewed healthy adults ranging in age from 80 to over 100 and found that most were still sexually active (Bretschneider & McCoy, 1988, p. 125).

People enjoy many types of activities with their partners. So why is sex such a unique and appropriate expression of love and intimacy in a close relationship? At least part of the answer is that sex uniquely combines the two fundamental processes that motivate people to form and maintain close relationships in the first place: mutual pleasure and enjoyment, and intimate self-disclosure (Reiss, 1986). These processes—giving and receiving pleasure, and knowing and being known—both flow from and reinforce the psychological integration of partner with self, which is the underlying truth of an intimate relationship (Aron & Aron, 1991).

When Relationships Go Wrong

In the course of most relationships, periods of calm are interspersed with troubled times. When problems do develop, all the processes that helped the relationship bloom appear to go into reverse, speeding up the decline. Partners no longer seem to enjoy doing things together. Their attributions for each others' behaviors become more negative. Instead of intimate self-disclosures, they exchange angry words and bitter complaints, which lead to arguments and fights. Understanding the processes of relationship development and maintenance can also help us comprehend how relationships run aground at the very start or slowly deteriorate into conflict and breakup.

Unrequited Love

When loving feelings are not mutual, both parties feel the pain. The situation may be worse for the target of unwanted affection.

So far we have been focusing on relationships that are equitable, balanced, and mutual, but some of the most difficult relationship problems arise when love is not reciprocated. Roy Baumeister and Sara Wotman (1992) have found that there is pain on both sides in such a relationship, as you may know from your own experience. Of course, the rejected lover suffers the pangs of heartbreak and lost self-esteem. However, because this person often blindly maintains loving and hopeful feelings, he or she ultimately may have some positive memories of the episode, along with the disappointment. For the rejector, the picture is more thoroughly negative. Although self-esteem initially may be bolstered by the rejected lover's obvious adoration, any benefits to self-esteem are often quickly supplanted by feelings of guilt, irritation, and even rage. Trying to be polite to the suitor may only raise false hopes.

Research indicates that more than half of all college women may have experienced daily letters and late-night phone calls from rejected suitors (Jason and others, 1984). For those who must deal with a would-be lover, Elaine Hatfield and Richard Rapson (1993) recommend using what they term the "zombie" approach. When interaction is unavoidable, be polite and brief. Display no emotion, negative or positive, that might reward the pursuer—remember, emotional self-expression is a type of intimacy.

Seeds of Trouble

> *Interdependence inevitably leads to disagreements and problems, but their impact on the relationship depends on how the couple handles them. Conflict becomes more serious when attributions for the partner's behavior become negatively rather than positively biased, when the partners' commitment to the relationship weakens, and when the partners are anxiously or avoidantly attached.*

In fairy tales, the characters find true love and live happily ever after. Not so in real life, where interdependence inevitably breeds conflicts and the key issue is how couples handle them. If conflict is diffused by relationship-maintenance activities such as talking about feelings and discussing the state of the relationship, loving feelings will not diminish. This pattern is typical in the early stages of a relationship (Cate & Lloyd, 1988). In a declining relationship, however, the pattern changes. In such relationships, couples who experience conflict do *not* spend more time on relationship maintenance, and they *do* feel less love. Not surprisingly, this pattern indicates that when conflicts are left to fester they will ultimately create negative feelings. How does trouble start, and what resources help people handle conflict constructively and avoid relationship meltdown?

Interdependence and Conflict. Perhaps you recall a time in your own life when a partner changed—maybe the person lost interest in an activity you had previously enjoyed together or had a falling out with a mutual friend. Because of the interdependence in a close relationship, the change in your partner probably affected you as well. Personal change, illness, or disability can reduce one partner's willingness or ability to meet the other's needs. As one or both find that they derive fewer rewards from the relationship, their satisfaction and commitment eventually decline (Rusbult, 1983; Drigotas & Rusbult, 1992).

External factors can also place stresses on relationships. If one person's job or family responsibilities increase, the resulting demands leave less time and energy for the partner. The birth of a couple's first child is a common source of stress for this reason—children bring their parents love and joy, but they also typically reduce marital satisfaction (Belsky, 1990).

Social norms can also create stress, by dictating that one partner should perform a particular task regardless of individual preferences or abilities,

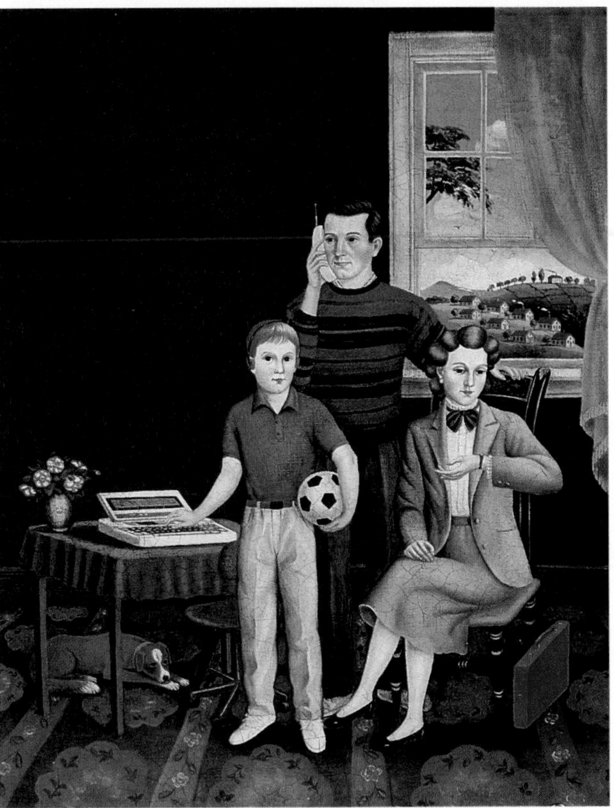

Families ain't what they used to be Modern families face stressors that are different from those of previous generations. How do pressures faced by this typical family of the 1950s differ from those faced by a high tech two-career family of the 1990s?

often creating conflict. For example, women in heterosexual couples are generally expected to perform the bulk of the housekeeping chores, even if they also work at a paying job outside the home (Atkinson & Huston, 1984; Biernat & Wortman, 1991). This holds true whether the couple is unmarried or married (Denmark and others, 1985). The imbalance in household responsibility is reinforced by economic factors. Women are paid on average only about two-thirds as much as men for full-time, year-round work (Goldin, 1990), which tends to force men into the "breadwinner" role. Conflicts about who does what—such as how to share responsibility for housework—are among the most important causes of breakups of both married and unmarried heterosexual relationships (Blumstein & Schwartz, 1983; Nettles & Loevinger, 1983).

A wide range of issues can spark relationship conflicts (Gottman, 1979). Leslie Baxter (1986), who asked people who had just ended dating relationships to write about the reasons for the breakups, found several common themes.

- *Desire for autonomy,* or problems in dealing with interdependence, was cited by 27 percent of men and 44 percent of women.
- *Dissimilarity* was almost equally important for men (27 percent) and women (32 percent).
- *Lack of support,* or the feeling that the partner undermined rather than enhanced self-esteem, was less important for men (19 percent) than for women (33 percent).

- *Lack of openness and intimacy* was also a bigger problem for women, named by 8 percent of men and 31 percent of women.
- *Absence of romance or passion*—feeling that "the magic has gone"—was an issue for more men (19 percent) than women (3 percent).

Issues like these sow the seeds of conflict as one or both partners come to feel that their needs are not being met (Peterson, 1983).

Attribution: You Did It Because You Don't Love Me. Even in the happiest of relationships, one partner's actions will occasionally annoy or frustrate the other. Minor annoyances do not have major consequences in most close relationships because attributions about the partner are positively biased (Fletcher & Fincham, 1991). However, if this pattern is reversed—if the partners are unhappy and attributions are negatively biased—trouble lies ahead.

To investigate the role of attributions, researchers asked happy and unhappy married couples to read brief descriptions of positive or negative behaviors, imagine that their spouse had performed the behavior, and provide an explanation for it (Fincham & O'Leary, 1983). Happy partners offered benign attributions, viewing positive behaviors as reflecting the partner's likable dispositions and seeing negative behaviors as inadvertent minor mistakes. Unhappy partners showed the opposite bias, viewing the partner's actions with great suspicion. They attributed positive behaviors to aspects of the situation or other external forces, and they attributed negative acts to the partner's bad intentions or unlikable personality. They might think, "My partner is acting nice only because other people are around, not because she loves me," or "I don't care if he did have a bad day at work—this constant criticism is typical of someone as meanspirited and selfish as he is." A shift toward negative attributions often precedes other indications of marital conflict, suggesting that attributions are a basic cause of relationship dissatisfaction (Bradbury & Fincham, 1990).

Commitment. When a couple is in conflict, their level of commitment becomes a crucial influence on their behavior. In fact, commitment is the best predictor of whether a person will remain in the relationship or leave (Rusbult, 1983). Strong feelings of commitment can motivate people to overlook their partners' flaws, to communicate about their needs, even to change their own behaviors in ways that help the relationship (Rusbult and others, 1991). As you might imagine, dating couples who perform more of these constructive behaviors are more likely to stay together than couples who perform fewer of them (Berg & McQuinn, 1986).

Even strong commitment can break down under stress, however. Because satisfaction with the relationship is so crucial to promoting and maintaining the partnership, the partners may begin to perceive alternatives as more attractive when a relationship declines, and accumulated investments may no longer seem to be important barriers to leaving.

Unfortunately, this process feeds on itself: as you begin to view others as potential partners, those others note your potential availability and may in turn begin to pay you more attention. The comparison level against which you assess the benefits of this relationship thus starts to change—in other words, you will have a growing sense that the grass might be greener on the other side of the relationship fence.

Attachment Styles. Handling conflicts is one of the many important aspects of relationships that is affected by people's attachment styles. Securely attached people generally have high levels of love, commitment, and satisfaction, which allow them to behave constructively when conflict arises (Simpson, 1990; Kobak & Hazan, 1991). They easily overlook a partner's faults or change their own behavior. In contrast, those with avoidant or anxious attachment styles tend to deal with conflict in less constructive ways—with outbursts of negative emotion, for example (Levy & Davis, 1988).

Conflict Processes

As satisfactions from the relationship decline, commitment may break down. The partners' responses to negative behaviors become destructive rather than constructive when commitment is weak. Under these circumstances, a negative action often is answered in kind, and conflict can spiral out of control as jealousy mounts and intimacy declines.

Communicating About Conflict. When we fight with those we love, the bad feelings can linger or be dispelled by efforts at better communication. Rusbult and her colleagues (1991) investigated couples' patterns of *accommodation,* the processes of responding to a negative action by the partner. Constructive accommodations are actions that help maintain the relationship, including actively discussing problems, seeking changes in behavior, or loyally waiting for the situation to improve. In contrast, destructive responses, such as screaming at the partner or refusing to spend time together actively endanger the relationship. A couple's patterns of accommodation—particularly the absence of negative responses rather than the presence of positive ones—influences relationship satisfaction. Constructive accommodation is more likely when people are committed to the relationship.

Some evidence indicates that women accommodate more constructively than men do (Rusbult and others, 1991). This finding is consistent with women's general tendency to be comparatively open about their thoughts and concerns about relationships. Men are less likely to talk about how they feel and are more apt to express their unhappiness in nonverbal signs of coldness and distance (Tannen, 1990; Levenson & Gottman, 1985). Like other gender differences, these communication patterns can provide a rich soil for the seeds of misunderstanding. She may view his silence as rejection, signaling declining intimacy and commitment. He may view her openness about her thoughts and feelings as threatening, without realizing that she may verbalize fleeting negative thoughts without any intent of giving them great importance. If men and women realize that they view communication differently, they can make adjustments and lessen misunderstandings.

Unfortunately, misunderstandings and misinterpretations of a partner's goals and feelings are common when couples argue. And the more troubled the relationship, the more prone the partners are to misunderstanding each other—though it is interesting that they have no similar difficulty in interpreting the feelings and intentions of strangers (Noller & Ruzzene, 1991). When distressed couples misunderstand each other, negative biases in their interpretations may escalate conflict.

To demonstrate this process, one researcher asked one member of a couple to read descriptions of everyday situations, such as, "You and your husband are sitting alone on a winter evening. You feel cold." (Noller, 1980). The woman was asked to imagine that she wanted to know if her husband felt cold, too, and to say, "I'm cold, aren't you?" Based on her verbal and nonverbal messages, the husband then had to guess at the woman's intention, choosing among such alternatives as, "You wonder if only you are cold or if I am cold, too," or "You think I am being inconsiderate in not having turned up the heat by now, and you want me to turn it up right away." In distressed couples, husbands were more likely to pick negative alternatives—even when the intended message was neutral or positive.

Negative attributions and unwillingness to accommodate constructively can release a vicious cycle of conflict, as each partner responds to the other's destructive behavior with an equally destructive reaction (Noller & Ruzzene, 1991). In a conversation, happy couples are likely to nod and smile at each other, to make eye contact, and to agree, whereas unhappy couples sneer, scowl, and shout, reciprocating each other's negative acts (Gottman and others, 1976). Ending such a cycle requires trust and the willingness to inhibit angry, hurtful impulses. Once a couple has raised their voices and exchanged insults, they find it very difficult to proceed immediately to a calm, logical approach to problem-solving (Peterson, 1979). The first step must be *emotional* reconciliation, which usually has two aspects. They must put the problem in perspective ("It's not important enough to fight about"), and one partner must accept some blame for the conflict ("I guess I was wrong to do that, and I'll try to fix it"). In relatively mild conflicts, the man most often tries to deflect negative feelings. However, when feelings run highest, men seem less likely to do this, leaving responsibility for deescalation to women (Hatfield & Rapson, 1993). If the partner accepts this "peace offering" and makes a conciliatory move in return, anger can diminish and the parties can begin cooperating to solve the problem.

Similar processes are involved in the reduction of large-scale intergroup conflict, as we will see in Chapter 14, pages 625 to 630.

Handling Conflicts in Everyday Life. Research on relationship conflicts suggests two constructive approaches to reducing your own conflicts.

- Try to avoid generalizing about the partner; instead, focus on discussing concrete actions. By doing so, you will help keep the problem in perspective and also avoid the tendency to become embroiled in arguments over negatively biased attributions. A conflict that has escalated from the behavioral level of "You did this" to the attributional level of "You always . . . ," "You never . . . ," or "You are such a . . ." becomes almost irresolvable (Peterson, 1983).

You may recall that attributing problems to global and stable causes can also lead to trouble of another sort. It is a recipe for learned helplessness and depression, as we discussed in Chapter 4, pages 149 to 150.

- Try to communicate about your feelings, perhaps with the words *I feel.* Contrast these statements: "You always leave the house so messy," versus "I feel upset when I see things left lying around the house." The first is accusatory and is likely to lead to pointless argument that avoids the real issue—"I don't *always* . . . ," or "It is not messy!" or "You sometimes leave messes, too." The "I feel" statement avoids these reactions because it may not trigger defensiveness and it cannot really be contradicted—the partner is not likely to deny that the speaker feels upset. Most important, the statement focuses both partners' attention on the real problem, which is negative feelings. Because it correctly attributes the feelings to the person and not to the external situation, "I feel" invites appropriately focused problem solving (Gottman and others, 1976).

Jealousy. When real or imagined rivals appear on the scene, most people experience a twinge of jealousy. This familiar negative emotion may be especially strong if a person feels inadequate in the relationship or distrusts the partner's commitment (White, 1981). Any sign of the partner's interest in other people may seem to be a dress rehearsal for impending rejection and the end of the relationship.

Breaking up partnerships, breaking up self Jealousy, declining intimacy, conflict: these processes come into play if the relationship goes sour. Because the partner becomes part of the self in close relationships, the losses suffered can have detrimental effects on the health and well-being of both partners.

Feelings of depression, anxiety, and anger may accompany jealousy. The depression and anxiety arise from the threatened loss of the valued relationship. Thus, they are similar to the feelings that would be aroused by other possible sources of loss, such as a life-threatening illness. Anger, in contrast, is due to the loss of self-esteem from being rejected by the partner in favor of someone else (Mathes and others, 1985). As you might expect, jealous feelings are more common among people whose attachment style is anxious and are less common among securely attached people (Collins & Read, 1990).

Extreme jealousy can be profoundly destructive, particularly when an individual feels that his or her self-worth is completely dependent on the relationship. The rage and anger that can arise when a threat to the relationship is interpreted as a fundamental threat to self-esteem can lead even to suicide and murder. Jealousy is estimated to be a factor in as many as one-quarter of all homicides (Salovey & Rodin, 1989).

Declining Intimacy. As conflicts escalate and commitment declines, the partners may spend less time together and become less open about their inner feelings. One important reason feelings are not shared is that many of them are likely to be negative. The growing distance diminishes the relationship's level of intimacy and, because intimacy is one of the most important rewards a relationship can offer, it speeds a downward spiral of dissatisfaction. Although the relationship may continue to satisfy needs for sociability or for sex, it no longer provides the feelings of self-validation and acceptance that spring from deeply intimate partnerships. In fact, low levels of intimacy, reflected in limited self-disclosure and low levels of attachment and love, characterize relationships that are destined for disintegration (Hill and others, 1976; Hendrick and others, 1988).

Relationship Conflict and Social Problems. Several significant social problems have their ultimate roots in conflicts in intimate relationships. Violence among intimates, particularly against women, is extremely common. One study found that 25 percent of all violent crimes against women are committed by family members or people they have dated, compared with just 4 percent of violent crimes against men (Lewin, 1991). And one in five women who was assaulted by a male relationship partner reported being the victim of a series of similar crimes.

Severe conflict in families can lead not only to violence but also to psychological problems for children. Recent large-scale studies of children in the United States and Britain examined the negative effects commonly attributed to parental divorce (Cherlin and others, 1991). Like other research, these studies found that children of divorced parents displayed more behavior problems and had lower school achievement than children from intact families. However, these researchers found that the problems usually appeared *before the parents separated.* Thus, these problems are not due to the trauma of divorce itself, as so many people assume, but to conditions within intact but troubled families. As these examples indicate, the immediate costs of ending a conflict-filled relationship are sometimes easier to bear than the costs of perpetuating it.

Breakup and Aftermath

If a relationship breaks up, each partner usually blames the other for the general decline in satisfaction. Individuals cope more effectively if they feel they controlled the final separation. After the end of a close relationship, loneliness and other negative feelings are common, even when the relationship involved more conflicts than satisfying interactions. But loneliness, an emotion that occurs when needs for intimacy and connectedness are not being met, can be overcome by finding close friendships and not only by romantic partners.

The Breakup: Your Fault, My Decision. Finally, a relationship may reach the breaking point. In dating couples as well as marriages, women terminate heterosexual relationships more often than men do (Hill and others, 1976; Gray & Silver, 1990). As you may recall, women are more distressed than men by relationship conflict, and that fact may explain why they more often pull the plug (Surra & Longstreth, 1990). But no matter who delivers the final word, the end of a relationship is often a lengthy and complex process, with repeated episodes of conflict and reconciliation (Cate & Lloyd, 1988). Each partner may feel victimized by the other, and their perceptions of responsibility for the relationship's decline may differ markedly. One study of divorced couples showed, not surprisingly, that each spouse primarily blamed the other for the decline of the relationship (Gray & Silver, 1990). However, the partners who felt that they controlled the separation coped more effectively with it. In dealing with the death of a relationship, as in so many other stressful events, feelings of psychological control are a key resource.

After the Breakup: Grief and Distress for Two. Most of us have been observers or participants in the breakup of more than one relationship and have seen first-hand that the psychological consequences of breaking up can vary. One sample of student couples found that the more depressed, lonely, and unhappy one partner felt after the breakup, the less the other partner did (Hill and others, 1976). Evidently being the "breaker-upper" feels different from being the "broken-up-with." But whatever your role, because close relationships are so psychologically important, the experience of ending a relationship is inevitably more negative than positive. If the partners cared deeply and helped each other in many ways, grief and distress are bound to occur. Such feelings arise even if the relationship's rewards were taken for granted before the breakup or if the interactions in the relationship were mostly negative (Berscheid, 1983; Simpson, 1987). Only when partners drift apart over time, so that the relationship lacks much intimacy and interdependence, are strong negative emotions likely to be absent.

The cognitive and emotional consequences of the end of a close relationship can be long-lasting. People may reflect often and intensively on why the relationship ended, as they do concerning other important negative events (Harvey and others, 1978). Because failures of relationships often leave the partners baffled about what went wrong, the search for causes may become somewhat obsessive as the person repeatedly reviews past events. Feelings of control—for example, knowing that you decided to end the relationship, or believing that you understand what happened—may influence the course of this stage (Clark & Collins, 1993). And understanding the causes of a relationship's end is an important learning experience that is likely to increase the chances of success in future relationships.

Till Death Do Us Part. Some close relationships are ended by death rather than breakup. The death of a spouse is generally regarded as the most stressful major life event (McCrae & Costa, 1988). It is also a particularly common one: almost half of the population will experience it. The first year or two following the death of a spouse are marked by serious threats to mental and physical health (Hansson and others, 1988). Most people eventually make it through this period and recover their previous levels of physical and mental functioning, but a minority fail to recover, even after several years. The most serious problems are likely to befall those whose spouse died unexpectedly and who believe that they have little control over their future (Stroebe and others, 1988)—a belief that may cripple their ability to cope effectively. Social support from friends, self-help groups, or professional counselors can help the bereaved cope. Social support can offer some of the rewards—such as opportunities to express inner feelings and to receive understanding and acceptance—that were part of the vanished relationship (Vachon and others, 1982).

Chapter 4, pages 148 to 150, described how perceived control helps people cope with stressful events.

Loneliness. No matter what terminates a close relationship—death, conflict, or simple geographical separation—the end usually brings loneliness. Lonely people feel distress, desperation, boredom, and depression. They may even view themselves as unattractive or unlovable (Rubenstein and others, 1979). Feeling lonely is not the same as being alone—sometimes you can feel loneliest in the middle of a crowd. Rather, *loneliness* is an emotion arising from unmet needs for affection and self-validation from a psychologically intimate relationship (Shaver & Hazan, 1985). Intense feelings of loneliness are common not only after the end of a relationship but also when people move to a new area and are separated from their existing close relationships.

The most effective responses to loneliness include trying to find new ways to meet people and making something valuable out of solitude—learning a new skill or hobby, studying or working, or listening to music (Rook & Peplau, 1982). More negative reactions include dwelling on your bad qualities, or even drinking and drug use. A study of college students by Carolyn Cutrona (1982) found that those who thought about loneliness as arising from transitory, potentially controllable causes most easily overcame it. Students who saw their loneliness as resulting from stable, negative personal qualities—such as unattractiveness or shyness—were more likely to remain lonely for long periods of time.

Cutrona also found that lonely people who downplayed the importance of friendship and thought that only a romantic relationship could help them had a more difficult time. Perhaps this is because friends are easier to find than "that perfect someone." After all, as we have seen in this chapter, a close friendship can meet our needs for self-validation and psychological intimacy (Rook & Peplau, 1982). These—rather than the sexual expression found in a romantic relationship—are the key to most of the benefits of relationships.

Concluding Comments

In concluding the chapter, we turn from conflict, breakup, and loneliness to something more positive: relationships that survive the challenges of time. Two factors are common to strong relationships in which the partners maintain and increase their love.

1. *The relationship satisfies many of the partners' individual needs.* Other people benefit us in many ways—as companions for leisure activities, as sources of social comparisons that help us understand ourselves, and as sources of validation for our beliefs and opinions. These rewards are most likely to be found when the partners are similar in their needs and desires, and when they reward each other to show love and caring.
2. *The relationship provides the partners with a sense of relatedness and connectedness.* As we indicated in Chapter 6, belonging to a group can give people the sense that they have a special place in the social world and that others value their thoughts, feelings, and behaviors—their very presence. As you have seen, intimacy and self-disclosure in a close relationship with another individual can also fulfill this need.

The dual motives to seek individual satisfaction and interdependent relatedness run as two parallel threads throughout many of the topics we have discussed in this chapter.

- Relationship development proceeds through the exchange of rewards as the partners satisfy each others' needs, and through the exchange of self-disclosures as the partners build the intimate linkage of partner to self.
- Gifts given and favors performed in a relationship have a dual meaning. The concrete act may be pleasant and rewarding in itself. The underlying messages of love and relatedness that each partner sends the other by kind and thoughtful acts become equally crucial.
- Gender differences in relationships reflect the dual motives of individual satisfaction and interdependent relatedness. Men generally emphasize rewards, such as participating in enjoyable activities with the partner, and women often care more about intimacy, the self-disclosure of feelings and intimate talks.

- Sexual behavior is particularly appropriate as an expression of relationship closeness because it fits with both motives: it is enjoyable and intimately self-disclosing.

The combination of these two powerful motives—the fact that at their best, close relationships can both help us find ourselves as individuals and find connection to valued others—makes relationships the most important components of our lives. As Charles Darwin wrote long ago (cited in Gould, 1991, p. 401), "Talk of fame, honor, pleasure, wealth, all are dirt compared to affection."

Summary

Initial Attraction The formation of a relationship is often spurred by feelings of attraction or liking for another person. Attraction to strangers is strongly influenced by perceptions of physical attractiveness. These perceptions are shaped by cultural and individual differences.

People are also attracted to those with whom they have positive interactions. Interaction helps people to master the world and to find connectedness with others. In addition, interaction leads to simple familiarity, which increases liking.

Similarity also increases attraction—by making positive interaction more likely, by suggesting that the other person likes the individual in return, and by validating the individual's beliefs and attitudes.

Thus, similarity, liking, and interaction all tend to cause one another. As a result, relationships tend to deepen and intensify over time.

Relationship Development As a relationship begins to develop, the partners exchange rewards, and they attempt to benefit each other in fair and balanced ways, following the **norm of equity.** Relationship development also includes exchanges of self-disclosures as the partners come to know each other better. Self-disclosures increase liking and offer opportunities for sympathetic, supportive responses.

As the partners interact frequently and exchange rewards and self-disclosures, simple attraction and individual factors such as physical attractiveness become less important. Instead, the nature of the interaction between the partners becomes crucial, and each partner's liking for the other tends to be reciprocated.

Close Relationships A **close relationship** is one marked by strong and frequent **interdependence** that affects many different areas of the partners' lives. A desire for closeness with a particular person seems to correspond to what people generally mean by "love." By necessity, most research on close relationships uses nonexperimental designs that leave some ambiguity about causal relations among variables. Research has also focused on the voluntary and potentially temporary relationships—particularly heterosexual romantic relationships—that are most important in Western independent cultures.

Many processes are common to all types of close relationships, not just romantic ones. In a close relationship, the partner is incorporated in the self, just as a meaningful social group membership can be incorporated. The psychological linkage of the partner to the self alters the way the partners exchange rewards. In an **exchange relationship** that is not close, partners reward each other to obtain rewards in return. In contrast, in close relationships and other **communal relationships,** the partners reward each other to show affection and because they want to make each other happy.

Ongoing processes of self-disclosure and sympathetic support lead to psychological **intimacy,** marked by feelings of trust, closeness, and acceptance. As closeness increases, the partners feel a growing sense of **commitment** to each other. They trust that they can rely on the partner to fulfill their needs, and they hope and plan for the continuation of the relationship into the future.

Attachment styles describe differences in the ways people approach close relationships. Securely attached individuals are comfortable relying on the partner for support and acceptance. Avoidant individuals fear reliance on others, and anxious individuals worry that the partner will not be available and responsive. Relationships also differ in the way they combine intimacy, commitment, and passion. Finally, gender plays a role. Men usually place more emphasis on the individual rewards that a relationship provides; women are more inclined to value intimacy and relationship closeness for itself.

Relationships affect virtually all aspects of our lives, including physical health. **Social support** from others can improve both physical and mental health and well-being, and the most crucial components of social support appear to be intimacy and acceptance. Because women's relationships are more intimate than men's, relationships with women tend to be more beneficial for health than are relationships with men.

Romantic Love and Sexuality Some relationships involve passionate feelings and emotions. Passionate emotions can arise quickly and are closely linked to sexual desires and behavior. People's attitudes about sex differ widely, depending in part on gender and personality differences. Some people see sex as an enjoyable activity even outside of a committed relationship; others see it as an expression of intimacy and commitment to the partner. Like other mutually enjoyable activities, sexual activity can strengthen a relationship. But it can also be a focus of conflict.

When Relationships Go Wrong When loving feelings are not mutual, both parties feel the pain. The situation may even be worse for the target of unwanted affection.

In any relationship, interdependence inevitably leads to disagreements and problems, but their impact on the relationship depends on how the cou-

Chapter 11 Themes

Pervasiveness of Social Influence
In a close relationship, the partner becomes part of the self, influencing all aspects of thoughts, feelings, and behavior.

Striving for Mastery
Relationships with others help us obtain rewards and individual satisfactions.

Seeking Connectedness
Relationships with others help give us feelings of connectedness and belonging.

Valuing Me and Mine
We are biased to view relationship partners favorably when they become part of the self.

ple handles them. Conflict becomes more serious when attributions for the partner's behavior become negatively rather than positively biased, when the partners' commitment to the relationship weakens, and when the partners are anxiously or avoidantly attached.

As satisfactions from the relationship decline, commitment may break down. The partners' responses to negative behaviors become destructive rather than constructive when commitment is weak. Under these circumstances, a negative action often is answered in kind, and conflict can spiral out of control as jealousy mounts and intimacy declines.

If a relationship breaks up, each partner usually blames the other for the general decline in satisfaction. Individuals cope more effectively if they feel they controlled the final separation, however. After the end of a close relationship, loneliness and other negative feelings are common, even when the relationship involved more conflicts than satisfying interactions. But loneliness, an emotion that occurs when needs for intimacy and connectedness are not being met, can be overcome by finding close friendships and not only by romantic partnerships.

Chapter 11 Overview

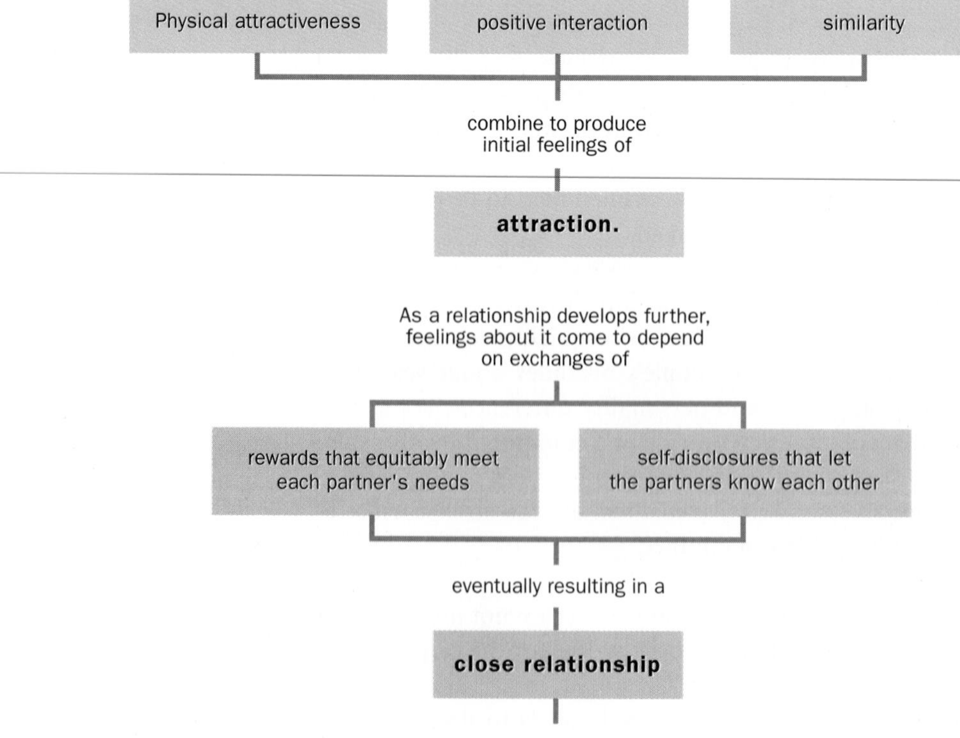

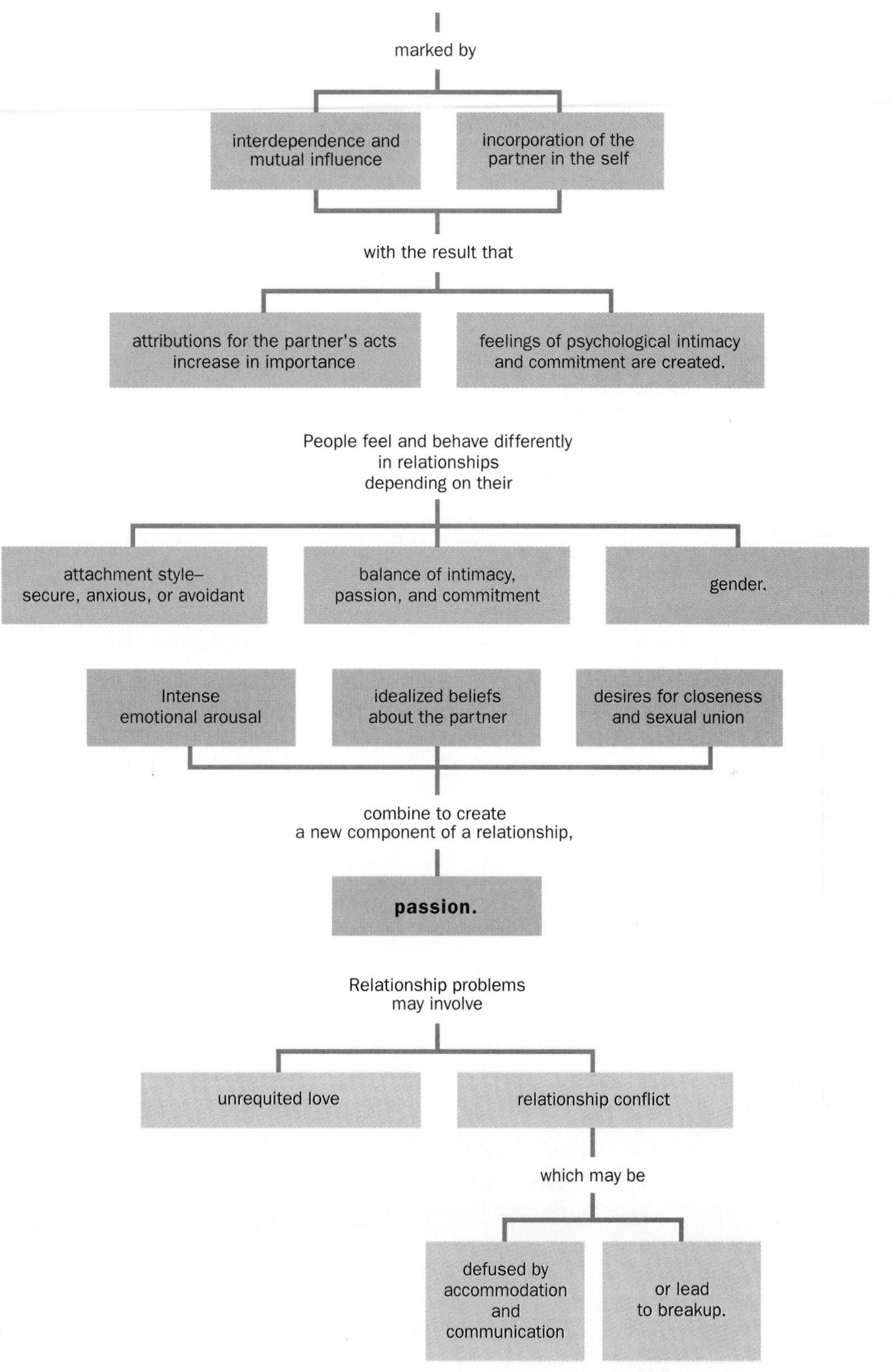
marked by
interdependence and mutual influence
incorporation of the partner in the self
with the result that
attributions for the partner's acts increase in importance
feelings of psychological intimacy and commitment are created.
People feel and behave differently in relationships depending on their
attachment style–secure, anxious, or avoidant
balance of intimacy, passion, and commitment
gender.
Intense emotional arousal
idealized beliefs about the partner
desires for closeness and sexual union
combine to create a new component of a relationship,
passion.
Relationship problems may involve
unrequited love
relationship conflict
which may be
defused by accommodation and communication
or lead to breakup.

12

Helping and Hurting

By 1942 the extermination of Jews living in Nazi-occupied Europe was in full swing. Although most people living under Nazi rule were unwilling or unable to take action, a few risked their lives to aid strangers. One was Anna Siniate, a scholar and librarian at Vilna University in Lithuania. As the scope of Nazi genocide became clear, she wrote, "I was ashamed that I was not a Jew myself. I had to do something" (Friedman, 1978, p. 22). What she decided to do was fraught with danger. Claiming she had to recover valuable books borrowed by Jewish students, Siniate persuaded the German authorities to let her enter the sealed Vilna ghetto. In trip after trip she smuggled out letters and diaries and smuggled in food and weapons. As the situation grew more desperate, she bribed guards to let out a few Jewish children. But the Gestapo were watching her, and she was arrested and sentenced to death. Her life was spared only because her university intervened. She was sent to a concentration camp in France, where she remained until the war's end (Friedman, 1978).

Contrast these acts of self-sacrifice with the following events that took place in late 1990. As nineteen-year-old Herman Everett and two friends were walking down a New York City street, a stranger approached them and demanded Everett's stylish jacket. The three friends ignored the mugger: with three against one, they thought, what could he do? What he did was pull out a gun and fire, missing Everett but killing twenty-year-old Bernard Richardson and wounding their other companion. Everett later reflected, "I think the reason he shot was he felt we disrespected him. Initially, I don't think he wanted to kill us. He just wanted to prove something to us" (Terry, 1991).

Siniate's self-sacrificing acts of helping and the mugger's violent acts of aggression are opposite extremes of human behavior. In this chapter we examine what social psychologists have discovered about helping, the positive end of this range, and about hurting, the negative extreme. We consider them together here because they are in many ways parallel: both can be understood in terms of the ways people interpret social situations and the motives and norms that move them to act. Here are a few parallels.

Healing the hurting Ironically, aggression often provides the opportunity for altruism. Here a man uses his shirt to wipe blood from the face of another man injured at an anti-Ku Klux Klan rally. The injured man's presence at the rally helps to heal the wounds of racism, while his helper heals the physical aftermath of the violence. As this chapter makes clear, aggression and altruism are often tied together by the same social psychological processes.

- *Both helping and hurting, like all other forms of social behavior, are driven by people's perceptions and interpretations.* Depending on how we perceive and interpret the person and situation, we may rush to help a man collapsed on the subway steps or shout at him in anger for blocking our way.
- *Both helping and hurting sometimes bring concrete rewards.* People sometimes help others because they want to gain something from it, just as the young mugger hoped his aggressive acts would win him a new jacket. Helping others for the sake of personal gain or social approval is an ancient idea: the Bible (Matthew 6:1-2) comments on hypocrites who gave to the poor but had trumpets blown to make sure that people would notice their generosity.
- *Both helping and hurting follow examples set by others.* Marian Wright Edelman, founder of the Children's Defense Fund, reports, "I was taught by my parents that life is about service—that service is the rent you pay for living. . . . They taught by precept and example." (*Newsweek*, 1992). Unfortunately, society also provides plenty of models of violence and aggression, not only in the media but also in all-too-real life in the streets.
- *Both helping and hurting are regulated by social norms.* Norms frequently encourage helping and restrain aggression, but sometimes they push us in the opposite direction. This happens when we "mind our own business" and ignore the sounds of a domestic dispute in the apartment next door, or when we "stand up for our rights" and fight over what we interpret as disrespect.

In addition to exploring the parallels between these seemingly opposite forms of social behavior in this chapter, we also consider practical questions: what are the social consequences of helping and hurting, and how can we promote the first and reduce the second? Before we turn to these questions, however, we need to know exactly what we are dealing with. Thus, we start with some formal definitions and then ponder a deeper question: are the tendencies to help or to harm inherently, inevitably, and unchangeably part of being human?

Helping, Hurting, and Human Nature

What Makes Behavior Aggressive or Altruistic?

> *A person's intention to help or to hurt someone else defines whether behavior is prosocial or aggressive. Both helping and hurting can be done for their own sake or to further some other goal.*

A wide variety of everyday behavior is labeled "aggressive" or "altruistic," but what do the terms really mean? Is it sensible to call a fast-talking salesperson or a defensive tackle aggressive? Is a restaurant owner who underwrites a public radio station altruistic? For social psychologists, the answers to these questions depend not on the outcome—help or harm—but on the actor's motive. And motives can be quite complex.

Consider the following situation: you are leaving the library with a companion you admire and someone collecting money for a homeless shelter approaches you for a donation. You respond by writing a check for ten dollars. You intended to help the homeless, but you also wanted to impress your companion with your generosity. Because this behavior involves an *intention* to help it is an example of **prosocial behavior.** But is it also altruism? No, because **altruism** refers to behavior intended to help someone else without gaining personal rewards. Some people argue that pure altruism does not exist—that helping is always selfishly motivated in one way or another. We discuss this intriguing issue later in the chapter.

Motive, or intent, is the key to defining aggression, too. **Aggression** is behavior intended to hurt someone. Accidentally injuring someone in a football game is not aggression, but cursing out the referee is. Even doing nothing at all—intentionally failing to warn a rival of impending danger—could be aggressive. Aggression, like helping, has its pure and not-so-pure forms. When harm is done simply for harm's sake—as when one person, enraged by an insult or slur, strikes out blindly at the provoker—it is called *emotional aggression.* When the harm is in the service of some further goal, as when a rival spreads false rumors in the hope of getting your job, it is called *instrumental aggression.*

Origins of Altruism and Aggression

> *Humans have evolved the capacity to act prosocially or aggressively. But this does not mean that either type of behavior is inevitable. Like other social behaviors, prosocial and aggressive behaviors depend on perceptions and interpretations of other people and situations, and on accessible desires and norms.*

As you read about Anna Siniate's heroic self-sacrifice and about the senseless murder of Bernard Richardson, perhaps you had a flicker of doubt about whether social psychology can really explain such extreme forms of behavior. Are altruism and aggression really driven by beliefs, emotions, interpretations, and norms, or are our tendencies to help or harm built into our very genetic makeup? And if these tendencies are part of our biological inheritance, does that make them both inevitable and uncontrollable?

The Image of the "Beast Within." Konrad Lorenz (1966) and other scientists studying animal behavior have offered one answer to these questions—an answer popularized by writers like Robert Ardrey (1966). Their view-

prosocial behavior Behavior intended to help someone else.

altruism Behavior intended to help someone else without any prospect of personal rewards for the helper.

aggression Behavior intended to harm someone else.

The beast within and the best within The much larger male baboon ruthlessly dominates the females in its group, suggesting the "natural" aggressiveness of our biological inheritance. The female ground squirrel attempts to alert her kin with a warning-call when she spots a predator, suggesting an equally "natural" basis for our prosocial behavior. Such contradictory examples show that neither altruism nor aggression is inherent or inevitable.

point, which could be called the "beast within" image (Klama, 1988), holds that evolution has shaped humans to be fundamentally and unalterably selfish. According to this view, "survival of the fittest" has meant survival of the *meanest,* in both senses of the word: miserly and cruel. Of course, these writers acknowledge that humans are capable of kindness and even altruism. But they view altruism as mainly the product of cultural teachings, people learning to "do unto others as you would have them do unto you." From this perspective, culture might at best add a thin veneer of civilization and channel our aggressive impulses, but it can never eliminate or replace them. No matter how fashionable the fur coat, the beast within still roars.

The Image of the "Best Within." Lorenz's viewpoint has rather pessimistic implications for human society. If aggression is a fundamental human tendency, interpersonal conflict and intergroup warfare are all but inevitable (Eibl-Eibesfeldt, 1979). However, we can take heart, for modern evolutionary psychology recognizes that altruism can also be part of our "basic" human nature. Altruism as well as aggression could have been selected in the course of human evolution because it, too, can promote survival. It does so in several ways.

1. *Altruistic individuals help their relatives, who also share their genes* (Hamilton, 1964). For example, female ground squirrels often cry out in alarm when they notice a predator, and this behavior is more likely when they are living with close kin than when they are with unrelated animals (Sherman, 1977). Making noise is riskier than hiding quietly, but if the alarm saves the lives of offspring, brothers, sisters, nieces, and nephews, then the squirrel's genes will survive to the next generation. Like ground squirrels, humans tend to offer more help to kin than to nonkin. For example, cross-cultural studies show that a child whose mother has died or is incapable of child rearing is most likely to be adopted by those who share the child's genes—grandmothers, aunts, and other relatives (Kurland, 1979).

2. *Altruistic individuals are often repaid in kind.* This type of reciprocal helping can evolve in species where individuals have the ability to remember other individuals who helped them in the past—or failed to do so (Trivers, 1971). Reciprocal helping is found not only among humans but also within other species. As we noted in Chapter 10, we often feel compelled to repay favors to those who have helped us. When helping engenders pay-back helping, those who help have a better chance of survival.

3. *The human capacity for empathy promotes altruism.* Our ability to *empathize,* or to identify with others' emotions, also motivates altruism. Responding to others' indications of delight or distress creates social bonds, encouraging the provision of help to those in need (Buck & Ginsburg, 1991). Even in very young children, empathy for others' suffering can promote helping (Hoffman, 1981; Eisenberg & Fabes, 1991).

4. *Following group norms can promote survival.* Nobel prize winner Herbert Simon (1990) argues that the tendency to follow norms, which he terms *docility,* is itself the product of evolution. Individuals who learn and follow their group's norms probably have a survival advantage because they can draw on others' knowledge about how to cope effectively with the physical and social world. The tendency to follow norms could therefore have been a trait favored in the process of natural selection during the course of human evolution. Many norms regulate aggression and altruism by telling people how to help or hurt others as well as when such responses are appropriate (Caporael & Brewer, 1991). In North American culture, for example, people learn that the way to offer help to a person lying unconscious on the sidewalk is either to apply first aid or to phone for an ambulance. They also learn that help is regarded as more appropriate when the victim is ill than when he or she is drunk.

Is "Biological" the Same as Inevitable? Perhaps we can agree that humans have evolved the capacity not only for aggression but also for altruism. But it does not follow that aggression or altruism is inevitable simply because it is part of our biological makeup (Oyama, 1991). Anthropologists have learned that human behavior—including aggression and altruism—varies tremendously from culture to culture. Some peoples are warlike, and others are peaceable. Some are cooperative, and others individualistic (Fiske, 1991). For example, members of different cultures respond very differently to an insult or provocation. In Western societies most people feel angry and want to strike back (Carlson & Miller, 1988). However, in many Asian cultures, like those of Japan or China, people prefer to withdraw or conform to the other's wishes in order to avoid conflict (Triandis and others, 1988).

To understand how culture can shape the expression of even strong, biologically based motives, think about hunger, which is felt by all people everywhere. Experiencing hunger does not inevitably lead to eating. Unsocialized infants may get away with stuffing into their mouths any food within reach, but adults in most societies must satisfy their hunger in less direct ways. The ways we experience hunger, the items we define as food, and the ways we act when hungry are all strongly influenced by norms, and thus by our groups and culture.

Is "Natural" Behavior "Right" Behavior? Finally, we should beware of regarding angry or hurtful behaviors as *right* because they are "natural" (Alexander, 1987). Concepts of right and wrong do not apply to the natural world, for the capacity to think about morality and to act in ways we consider right or wrong are products—perhaps the most significant products—of the human mind. We may decide altruism is morally right and aggression is morally wrong, but this decision cannot be based merely on our biological capacity for such behavior. As we struggle to make decisions about right and wrong and to act on them in our everyday lives, we are influenced by the same cognitive processes and the same social forces that have played such a big role in every other form of social behavior discussed in this text. These are the social psychological questions that will be our concern in this chapter: What motivates people to help or harm others in particular situations? How do beliefs and emotions enter into the process? And how do people respond to the social influences and cultural norms governing their treatment of one another?

Helping Others

Take a moment to think about helping others. You may form an image of everyday situations, such as helping a neighbor shovel out after a heavy snowfall, or an image of a more dramatic response, as when a passerby dives fearlessly into a river to rescue a drowning person. In their research on helping, social psychologists have studied both kinds of behavior. In laboratory studies, for instance, they have asked subjects to aid others who are working on boring and repetitive tasks (Berkowitz & Daniels, 1963) or to volunteer to take the place of someone scheduled to receive painful electric shocks (Batson and others, 1981). In the field, researchers have investigated whether passengers in an elevator will help someone pick up handfuls of spilled pencils (Latané & Dabbs, 1975), what circumstances affect responses to staged emergencies (Cramer and others, 1988), and why people donate blood and organs (Piliavin and others, 1982). The variety of research approaches means that researchers' conclusions about prosocial behavior often have high construct validity and good generalizability.

The reason the use of multiple measures contributes to construct validity—researchers' confidence that they are successfully assessing the concepts of interest—was detailed in Chapter 2, pages 38 to 39.

These conclusions indicate that whether people are responding to an emergency or making a long-term commitment, helping behavior is affected by what people *want* to do and what they think they *ought* to do. To begin to understand how these factors affect helping, let's consider an everyday opportunity to help that could confront any of us.

A friend of ours, walking in her Boston neighborhood early on a winter Sunday morning, noticed a car stopped by the roadside. She could hear fruitless attempts to start the motor but could not see the driver clearly. As the only person on the street, she felt a responsibility to help, but as she glanced repeatedly at the car, the driver did nothing—did not roll down the window, or wave, or gesture for help. Feeling uncertain, our friend decided to walk on and check things out on her return. A little later, from a distance, she saw a man go up to the car and tap on the window. The driver rolled it down, and then the man and the driver—a woman—walked off together, apparently to call for help.

Imagine the many questions that ran through our friend's mind as she thought about whether to help. Was there really a problem? Who was the driver of the car? Why did he or she not make eye contact? Was it inappropriate to help—perhaps the driver would be offended by interference rather than grateful for assistance? Might it even be dangerous to offer help—what if the apparent need for help were just a ruse? Resolving the potentially conflicting implications of many factors like these can be agonizingly difficult. Depending on who needs help and why, people may *want* to help—either because helping promises rewards or because they feel empathy with the victim. Norms also influence the decision to help. Sometimes people *feel they ought to* help because it is the right thing to do, but at other times norms discourage helping by mandating that we should mind our own business or leave others to sort out their own problems.

You may recognize that these two factors are the same ones—attitudes and norms—that were described as influencing all our social behavior in Chapter 10, pages 438 to 440.

Unfortunately, multiple motives often pull people in different directions. Helping has potential costs as well as rewards, and conflicts between competing impulses and desires have to be resolved before a decision to help is made. Sometimes people take so long to do so that, like our friend, they lose the opportunity to help. Regardless of where this decision process ends up, however, it always starts in the same place: noticing a need for help.

Perceptions of the Person in Need

Help is influenced first by perceptions of the victim's need, deservingness, and similarity to the potential helper. People are more likely to help similar others and those they see as deserving because they believe these individuals are not responsible for their own need.

Noticing a Need. Imagine walking through the quiet neighborhood early in the morning and hearing the motorist's repeated attempts to start the stranded car. Now imagine jostling your way down a busy city street, trying to tune out the roar of traffic and the honking of taxicabs. The driver of a car stopped by the sidewalk is trying in vain to start the motor. Where the first person's need is easy to notice, the second person's may not be. Becoming aware of a need is usually the first step in the helping chain of events (Darley & Latané, 1968), and busy or noisy surroundings reduce the likelihood of noticing that someone needs help (Korte and others, 1975).

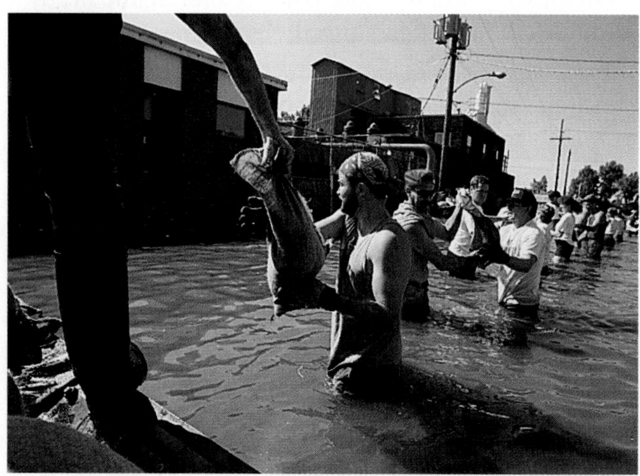

Lending a helping hand When flooding forced the Missouri River above its banks, whole communities turned out to try to help their neighbors. Here volunteer sandbaggers fight to save the small town of Parkville, Missouri, from the floodwaters—a valiant attempt that in the end proved futile.

No doubt this is one reason people are more likely to help others in quiet, rural areas than in large cities (Eisenberg, 1991).

Some people are better able than others to see a need for help. People who feel happy seem to pay more attention to others around them and are more likely to notice others' needs than are sad people (Schaller & Cialdini, 1990). No wonder, then, that positive thinking often translates into positive actions. In a study demonstrating this point, researchers put one group of subjects in a good mood by telling them they had succeeded on a task, whereas subjects in another group were put in a bad mood when they learned they had failed the task (Isen & Levin, 1972). When a nearby confederate then dropped a stack of books, happy subjects were more likely to help than unhappy subjects. Happy subjects also remembered much more about the confederate and her actions. Because happy people's attention is turned outward, they are more attuned to others' need for help.

But what happens when we do notice the stranded motorist, the panhandler asking for change on a street corner, or the person slumped in a doorway? Under what conditions are we likely to offer help? The answer seems to depend on two factors—deservingness and similarity.

Deservingness. Helping depends on whether we think help is *deserved.* And deservingness depends on the attributions we make about *controllability.* If we think people are in need "through no fault of their own" (an uncontrollable cause), we are motivated to help. If, on the other hand, we perceive people as having "brought it on themselves" (a controllable cause), we think they do not deserve help and we probably will not offer it (Schmidt & Weiner, 1988; Reisenzein, 1986). Perhaps this explains why people who believe that opportunity for economic advancement is open to all—and thus see poverty as the result of a lack of effort—are likely to oppose governmental programs to help those in need (Kluegel & Smith, 1986). Similarly, people who believed Iraq deserved the most responsibility for starting the 1991 Persian Gulf war were the least likely to advocate providing reconstruction aid to Iraq (Skitka and others, 1991).

Similarity. In deciding to help, we also take note of how similar the needy person is to us. Not surprisingly, similar others usually end up receiving the most help (Dovidio and others, 1991). Similarity creates feelings of connectedness between people—feelings of shared group membership and liking—which in turn increase helping. Most obviously, people usually are more willing to help friends than to help strangers (Schoenrade and others, 1986). In interdependent countries, where the in-group is even more important, this tendency is even stronger than in individualistic Western cultures. For example, compared with North American subjects, Chinese and Japanese subjects offer more help to in-group members than to out-group members (Bond, 1988).

Helping does not depend on long-term relationships, however. During elections, for example, passersby tend to be more helpful to their own can-

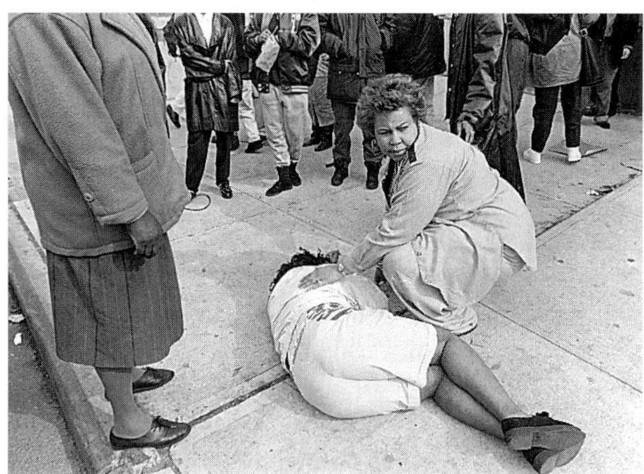

Who gets help from whom? Similarity is a good predictor of who will stop to help and who will walk by. Similarity creates feelings of shared group membership and liking, which, in turn, increase helping. Our special treatment of in-group members reflects the high value we place on "me and mine."

didate's workers than to those of the opposing candidate (Karabenick and others, 1973). Even a minimal social connection between two individuals can turn a bystander into a likely helper. One study found that people who had given their name to a researcher, made eye contact with her, or joined her in a trivial conversation were more likely to help her at a later time than were strangers (Solomon and others, 1981).

Wanting to Help: Costs and Rewards of Helping

Help may be motivated by perceived rewards or deterred by perceived costs or risks. These rewards and costs can be emotional: people sometimes help as a way of alleviating their own distress over the victim's suffering.

When we see someone in need, we may want to help, or we may just want to leave the scene as quickly as possible. The desire to help often depends on our *perceptions of the consequences of helping*—on its potential rewards and costs. As you will see, many different forms of cost and reward can inspire helping or stop it cold in its tracks.

The Consequences of Helping. As several men in business suits stood watching, a twenty-four-year-old woman dove into the Chicago River to rescue someone who had fallen in. Later she reported, "One guy said, 'I have an appointment. I can't get my suit wet'" (*Newsweek,* 1990b). The cost of a ruined suit or a missed appointment seems trivial next to the possibility of saving a life, but it may deter helping. For example, subjects in one study who thought they were a little late for their appointment with the experimenter were less likely to stop and assist an apparently ill confederate than were those who thought they had plenty of time (Darley & Batson, 1973). The costs of helping can be many and varied: lost time, effort, embarrassment, money, social disapproval, or physical danger. Even when the need is clear and the victim seems deserving, people may not help if the costs appear too high.

The potential helper's abilities also influence the cost of helping. Jumping into a river to rescue someone if you are not a strong swimmer could lead to two drownings instead of one. After all, the first rule of lifesaving is "Don't become a victim yourself." But the more helping skills a person has, the lower the costs of helping. People with relevant abilities or training, such as those with water-rescue or first-aid skills, are more likely to offer direct help (Cramer and others, 1988). Perhaps someone with mechanical skills, confident of his or her ability to start a balky engine, would have offered help more quickly to the stranded motorist we described earlier. Of course, training increases not only the likelihood of helping but also its effectiveness. One study staged a bleeding emergency and found that people with Red Cross training tended to give direct aid to the victim by applying pressure to the wound (Shotland & Heinold, 1985). Untrained individuals were equally likely to *try* to help in this obvious emergency—they phoned for an ambulance—but in the situation staged by the researchers this indirect help probably would not have saved the victim.

The importance of perceived ability to help may explain Alice Eagly and Maureen Crowley's (1986) finding that men are more likely to help than women are. This conclusion is based on a meta-analysis of the research literature, which includes a large number of studies of bystander intervention in emergencies. Indeed, Eagly and Crowley found that men perceive themselves as better able to help in most of the situations examined in research, such as assisting a motorist with a disabled car or carrying someone to safety—tasks requiring technical skills or physical strength. Thus, the observed gender differences in helping probably reflect the types of helping that researchers have chosen to study. Other research shows that anyone (male or female) who sees himself or herself as independent, forceful, and dominant can have the confidence to help in emergency situations (Senneker & Hendrick, 1983).

Emotional Rewards of Helping: Doing Good to Feel Better. The up side of helping is its many rewards. These benefits are often quite concrete: the gratitude of the victim, a reciprocal offer of help, the cheers of a crowd of onlookers, or the thrill of making the evening news. Altruism pays—sometimes quite literally, as a young boy discovered when he recently made headlines by returning a wallet containing a large sum of money. After the owner failed to give the youngster a reward, townspeople chipped in and contributed more than $10,000. More often, though, helping is its own reward: we feel good about ourselves because we helped others. Such internal rewards can be even more powerful motivators of helping than external rewards are.

Because helping makes us feel good, people sometimes help others in order to keep their own spirits high (Isen, 1970). In one study, for example, subjects who had been made to feel happy when they "happened" to find some money were asked to help the experimenter by reading a series of upbeat statements or depressing ones (Isen & Simmonds, 1978). Compared with people in a neutral mood, happy subjects were more willing to read the positive sentences—and thereby stay in a good mood—but they were less willing to read the negative sentences that might have made them feel blue. Thus, people who want to stay in a good mood may be particularly prone to good works, but only to the kinds of good works that prolong their good feelings.

Since helping others makes us feel good about ourselves, we may help as a way of escaping from a bad mood. For this reason, guilty people are often helpful people. The most successful donation collector for the entire international network of Save the Children agencies works the pavement on Saturdays outside a local supermarket near one of us. As each shopper tries to maneuver past him, the collector waves pictures of needy recipients and reminds us of how little these children have, saying, "You don't know how lucky you are!" Inducing guilt works, as it also does in experimental studies of helping. In these studies, researchers induce subjects to break little rules or to tell little lies, and they then give them the opportunity to make up for their sins by helping. In one study, for example, some subjects were induced to lie about having received advance information about a test. After taking the test, all participants were offered the chance to help the experimenter on another project. Those who had not lied donated just two minutes of their time, whereas the guilt-ridden subjects spent an average of sixty-three minutes making up for their hidden transgression (McMillen & Austin, 1971). A clever field study of guilt makes the same point. In that study, Roman Catholics were solicited for donations to a worthy cause either on their way into confession or on their way out (Harris and others, 1975). It is not hard to guess that those about to confess contributed more than those who had just confessed their sins.

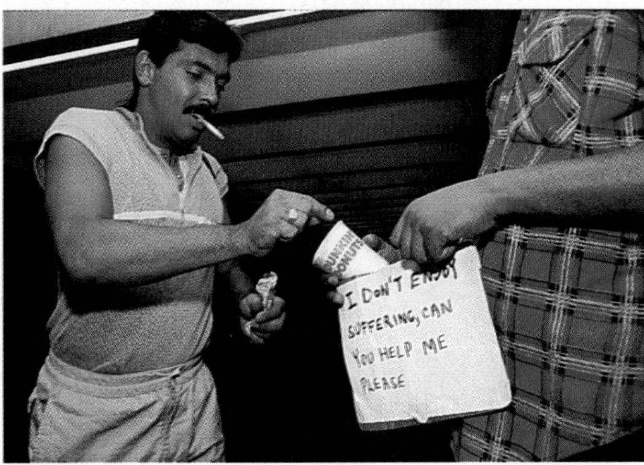

Guilt and giving Seeing other people suffer can be unpleasant and doing something to remove that unpleasantness—by donating money to someone less fortunate than ourselves, for example—can be nearly as rewarding for the giver as for the recipient.

These examples may remind you of a finding discussed in Chapters 4, pages 152 to 153, and 8, pages 328 to 330. When people's self-concept is threatened by stressors or inconsistent actions, they respond eagerly to opportunities to reaffirm their self-worth.

Guilt is not the only negative emotion that can increase our tendency to act charitably. If you had just found out that you received a bad grade, had a falling out with a friend, or lost your address book, would you be more or less likely to help a stranger requesting aid? Most research indicates you would help more (Cialdini and others, 1973; Cialdini & Kenrick, 1976). Apparently we are more willing to help because helping distracts us or reduces feelings like guilt, sadness, or disappointment. People know that helping makes them feel better, so those who want to feel better often offer their help.

A study by Robert Cialdini and his colleagues (Cialdini and others, 1973) clearly demonstrated people's tendency to help in order to make themselves feel better. The researchers made one group of subjects feel guilty about upsetting a stack of computer cards, while another group was not made to feel bad. But then the researchers added an interesting twist: they gave some of the guilty subjects a compliment and others an unexpected payment for being in the experiment. The remaining guilty subjects received nothing. The unexpected rewards were designed to put some of the guilty subjects back in a good mood. When all subjects were then asked to do a favor, guilty subjects were more likely to help than were nonguilty ones—unless they had received a compliment or cash. Thus, doing a favor or receiving external rewards seemed to be equally useful in helping people feel better.

Figure 12.1 Multiple effects of mood on helping

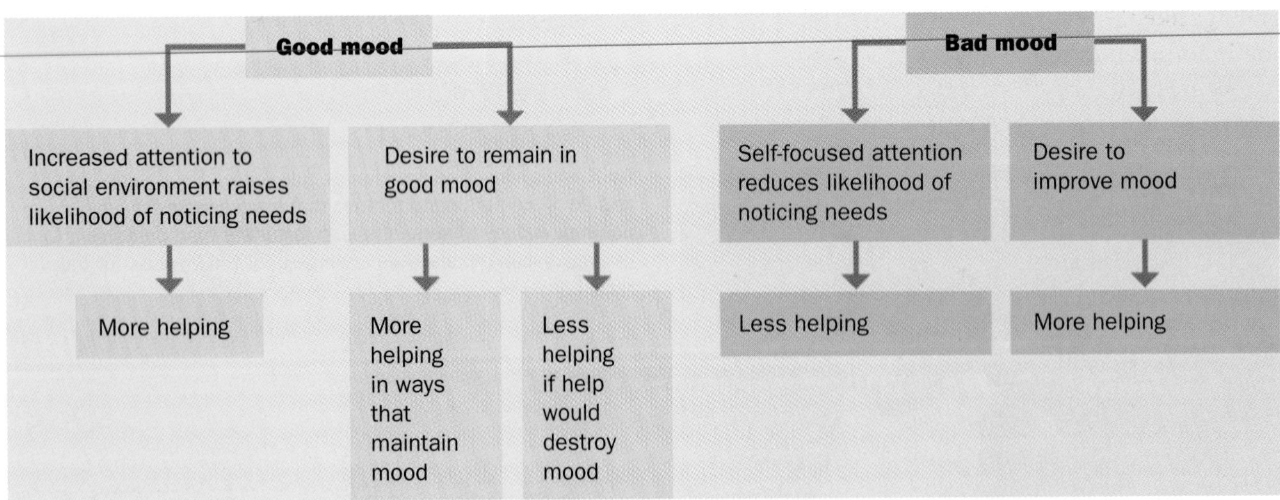

The effects of a positive or a negative mood on helping vary because they occur through several different processes. Both positive and negative moods have the ability to increase or decrease helping, depending on the circumstances.

There is, however, an exception to the rule that people who are feeling bad are likely to help. We cannot feel better by helping others if we do not notice that they need help. Unfortunately, those who experience deep depression and profound grief seem to disengage from the social world as self-absorption replaces social concern (Carlson & Miller, 1987). This self-focused attention may blind people to opportunities to lift their spirits by helping.

To demonstrate this negative effect, researchers in one study asked subjects to imagine in vivid detail that their best friend of the opposite sex was dying of cancer (Thompson and others, 1980). The researchers' instructions focused some subjects' attention on their own worry and grief, their own loss, and their own sadness. Others were told to focus on their friend—on his or her fear, uncertainty, and pain. Even though everyone felt equally sad, the two groups showed a decided difference in the way they reacted to an opportunity to help. Only 25 percent of the self-focused students responded to the researcher's request for help on an unrelated research project. In contrast, there was an 83 percent rate of volunteering among subjects who focused on their friend. If grief turns our thoughts inward, it may prevent us from using helping as an avenue to a better mood.

Thus emotions can produce both positive outcomes (increasing helping) and negative outcomes (decreasing helping). For a summary of the effects of mood on helping, see Figure 12.1.

Does True Altruism Exist? The Role of Empathy

People are often motivated by a feeling of empathy to relieve a victim's need, regardless of personal rewards and costs.

Findings like those just described raise an intriguing question. If people help simply to maintain their own positive feelings or to relieve their own negative feelings, doesn't that mean that most helping is self-interested rather than truly altruistic? The **negative-state relief model** of helping asserts that most helping occurs for exactly that reason (Schaller & Cialdini, 1988). According to this model, most people hate to watch others suffer. As a result, their help is not designed to aid the victim but instead to reduce their own distress. Certainly the finding that guilty or unhappy people may help in an effort to feel better is consistent with the negative-state relief model. The model also explains the opposite kind of behavior: why people sometimes choose to walk away from those in need. "Out of sight, out of mind" may be the easiest maxim to reduce negative feelings under these conditions. Distressed by the sight of starving refugees on a TV news program, we may write a check to a relief agency or we may simply switch channels. Research indicates that even the anticipation of a distracting experience—such as watching a comedy film, for example—is enough to reduce people's helpfulness (Schaller & Cialdini, 1988).

negative-state relief model The theory that people help others in order to reduce their own feelings of distress caused by the victim's suffering.

Do people help others only to reduce their own distress, as the negative-state relief model states, or is true altruism possible? Daniel Batson and his colleagues believe that true altruism does exist, and they have conducted a number of clever studies that attempt to demonstrate it. Imagine that you are a subject who has just arrived in their research laboratory. You learn that a second subject, Elaine, will be receiving mild electric shocks as she performs a task in another room. Your job will be to observe her performance through a window. As you watch, Elaine (who is, of course, a research confederate) is hooked up to some equipment and the shocks apparently begin. Obviously upset after two shocks, she asks for a glass of water and tells the experimenter that she's been frightened of electricity ever since a childhood accident when she was thrown by a horse into an electric fence. The experimenter hesitates. Perhaps Elaine should not continue. The experiment could be canceled . . . or perhaps you, the observer, would be willing to trade places with Elaine and take the remaining shocks for her? If you were the real subject in this experiment, would you suffer for someone else?

Batson and his colleagues (1981), who designed this scenario, expected subjects' responses to depend on how they reacted emotionally to the victim's plight and on how easy it was to escape from the situation. Their **empathy-altruism model** suggests that when people see someone in trouble they may experience either of two different types of emotions—*personal distress,* including alarm, anxiety, and fear, or *empathic concern,* including sympathy, compassion, and tenderness. Personal distress motivates either egoistic helping, which is aimed at reducing the observer's own negative feelings, or escape, just as the negative-state relief model predicts. In contrast, feelings of empathic concern lead to altruistic behavior: helping designed to relieve the victim's suffering. People who are motivated by feelings of empathic concern will help even if they could easily escape from the situation.

To test these ideas, the researchers manipulated subjects' emotional responses to the situation and their ease of escape. They told half the subjects that Elaine's personal values and interests were very similar to their own. Because similarity usually increases empathy, this information was designed to increase empathic concern—that is, to lead these subjects to empathize with Elaine. The other half of the subjects were told that she was quite different from them. To vary ease of escape, researchers told half the subjects that they would be required to observe two shocks. When Elaine became upset after the second shock, these subjects knew they could simply leave when the experimenter asked them to change places with her. The other half of the subjects were told they would have to watch Elaine go through a series of ten shocks.

empathy-altruism model The theory that concern for the victim's suffering motivates people to help others even though there is no reward.

As Figure 12.2 shows, the results of the experiment were consistent with the empathy-altruism model. The helping decisions of subjects who did not feel empathy depended on the ease with which they could escape the situation. Among those who could not escape—who knew they had to watch all ten shocks—a high percentage volunteered to take Elaine's place, presum-

Figure 12.2 Does altruism exist?

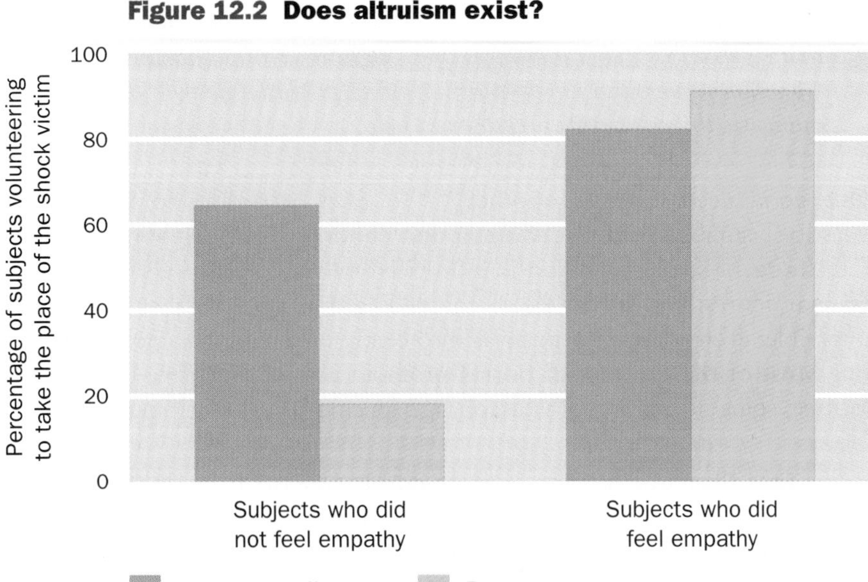

For subjects who did not empathize with Elaine, helping was a matter of avoiding personal distress. When escape was difficult—when subjects could not simply leave the experiment—most volunteered to receive shocks in Elaine's place. But when an easy escape was available, most of the low-empathy subjects left Elaine to suffer alone. In contrast, almost all those who empathized with Elaine volunteered to help her, regardless of the ease of escape. Their help must have been motivated by a focus on Elaine's feelings rather than by a desire to reduce their own distress. (Data from Batson and others, 1981.)

ably to avoid the distress of watching her suffer. However, the pattern was reversed for their low-empathy peers who could walk out the door. Most took advantage of the escape hatch, leaving Elaine to suffer out of their view. In contrast, subjects who empathized with Elaine helped altruistically, and they did so even when escape was easy. Most offered to stay and take the shocks for her.

A good deal of evidence now supports the idea that helping can be motivated by a true concern for and identification with the victim (Toi & Batson, 1982; Batson and others, 1988, 1991; Dovidio and others, 1990; Fiske, 1991). These results contradict the notion that maximizing personal rewards and minimizing personal costs motivate most helpful actions. This finding fits with what we already know—that when people identify with and feel connected to another individual or group they are as concerned about the welfare of those others as they are about their own. Thus, fellow feeling—empathy—increases people's *desire* to help.

Fellow feeling also identifies others as people to whom our shared standards of appropriate behavior apply, so it should not surprise you to learn that empathy contributes to people's feelings of *obligation* to help others. The empathic feelings make our common humanity salient, which in turn activates norms that often prescribe helping. The mirror image of this process is that when we fail to empathize with those whom we see as dissimilar from us, we may morally exclude them, placing them outside the range of applicability of norms and moral standards.

Chapters 6 (pages 227 to 233) and 11 (pages 463 to 465) described how groups and individuals can become part of "me and mine," so that we care for them as for ourselves.

Feeling One Ought to Help: Norms and Helping

People sometimes help because social norms, their own standards, or others' behaviors make them feel they ought to. Not all norms promote helping, however, and the presence of other potential helpers sometimes diminishes the normative pressures to help.

The norms of helping Norms such as social responsibility, reciprocity, and social commitment often play a role in motivating helping behavior. When thousands of people—old and young, healthy and sick—turn out for walkathons to help raise money for charitable causes, the decision to participate is influenced by social norms as well as personal desires.

"One good deed deserves another." "To each according to his need." "Charity begins at home." "Women and children first!" Helping, like all other forms of social behavior, is influenced by social norms as well as by personal desires. Norms can be so compelling that ignoring them is almost impossible, even when they push us into costly or dangerous courses of action. Most of the time social norms promote acts of altruism, but, as we shall see, some norms actually discourage specific types of helping.

Norms That Promote Helping. Most norms support helping as the right and proper thing to do, so helping usually increases when those norms become accessible. That certainly is true of the norms most likely to dictate helping: the norms of reciprocity, distribution, and social responsibility.

1. The *norm of reciprocity* requires us to return the benefits that others provide to us. We often help because we have been helped before or because we expect to be helped in the future (Gross & Latané, 1974). One of us has a cousin, a volunteer firefighter, who recently experienced the inescapable nature of the reciprocity norm when, as a member of the rescue crew, he arrived at the scene of a serious car crash. The crew found a badly injured victim trapped in the wreckage and recognized one of their fellow volunteers. As they struggled to extract him, the victim talked about the fires they had fought together. "When he talked about the other calls," the cousin said, "I thought about all the times we'd helped each other out. I knew we had to get him out alive. He'd have done it for me."

2. *Norms of distribution* dictate how resources should be divided among members of a group. One relevant norm is *equity,* which directs us to allocate rewards fairly in proportion to people's contributions. Motivated by their conceptions of fairness and equity, people who believe that they have more than their fair share often give valued resources to others or take less than they could (Mikula, 1980). Equity is often replaced by the norm of *communal sharing* in close relationships and cohesive groups (Clark & Mills, 1979; Fiske, 1991). This norm requires all members of a group to freely share resources with all other members without concern for differences in contributions, as, for example, when family members and friends sit down to share a meal together.

Chapter 11, pages 466 to 468, described the differences between relationships in which equitable exchanges are expected and those in which communal sharing is appropriate.

3. *The norm of social responsibility* dictates that we must help those who are unable to help themselves (Berkowitz, 1972). This norm often operates in close relationships when, for example, people care for children, parents, or close friends who are dependent on them (Berkowitz & Daniels, 1963).

But this norm also operates in society at large, suggesting that those more able to take care of themselves have a duty and obligation to assist others who cannot—the old, young, sick, or helpless. It is the norm that charities and relief agencies often play on when they remind average North Americans that "you don't know how lucky you are." However, the range of applicability of this norm differs widely in different cultures. Among the Moose people of West Africa, for example, even the most valuable resources, such as land, or water in time of drought, are shared freely with anyone who asks for them (Fiske, 1991). Similarly, people's feelings of obligation to strangers are stronger in India than in the United States (Miller and others, 1990).

This material may remind you of the discussion in Chapter 10, pages 400 to 410, of how effectively accessible norms can guide all forms of social behavior.

Though most people accept these norms as moral obligations, individuals differ in the extent to which they routinely incorporate them in their daily lives. As Shalom Schwartz (1977) pointed out, some individuals have strong *personal* feelings of obligation that lead them to help others in unusual, costly, or dangerous ways. These people who follow prosocial norms and help in situations in which others turn away often were deeply influenced by personal examples. Studies indicate that heroic helpers, such as the civil rights workers who fought segregation in the U.S. South during the 1960s and the Gentiles who sheltered Jews from the Nazis, often identify strongly with a parent who exemplified norms of concern for others (Oliner & Oliner, 1988; Rosenhan, 1970). Religious teachings can also make a difference: among both college students and the general public, religiously committed individuals are more prone to give time and money to help the needy than are the less committed (Benson and others, 1980; Colasanto, 1989).

Such personal standards are examples of the self-guides we discussed in Chapter 4, pages 134 to 136.

Norms That Inhibit Helping: Mind Your Own Business. Conservative estimates suggest that in the United States alone, at least 2 million young children, half of all adolescents, and as many as 2.5 million elderly people are the targets of physical violence from family members (Gelles & Cornell, 1985; Straus & Gelles, 1986). Given the power and variety of norms that promote care and concern for others, what accounts for these shocking statistics?

Part of the answer stems from norms themselves. Not all norms are prosocial: some specify that intervening to help is socially inappropriate. The *norm of family privacy,* for example, makes people reluctant to intervene when they observe family violence, whether that violence involves a mother angrily slapping her child in a supermarket aisle, a man verbally abusing his wife on the street, or an adult caretaker impatiently shaking an aging or forgetful parent. To demonstrate this point, Lance Shotland and Margaret Straw (1976) staged an attack by a man on a woman in front of male and female bystanders. Half the bystanders heard the victim say, "I don't know you!" The other half heard her say, "I don't know why I ever married you!" Fully 65 percent of the bystanders tried to prevent the stranger's assault, compared with only 19 percent who intervened in the marital dispute. People are often reluctant to intervene in a family affair because they think the wife will be embarrassed and upset by such intervention, and that the husband will turn on the would-be helper. Perhaps an increased awareness of and sensitivity to spousal abuse and date rape will gradually change this norm.

Norms restraining intervention in family violence can inhibit bystander intervention even when a stranger is the perpetrator. Over two-thirds of subjects shown a silent film of a man attacking a woman assumed that the attacker and the victim were dates, lovers, or spouses, though nothing in the film supported that conclusion (Shotland & Straw, 1976). As a "dispute" is mentally transformed into a "domestic dispute," the norms most salient to a bystander may be "that's family business" so "mind your own business," not the norm of social responsibility.

Activating Norms. Relevant norms have power over our behavior only when they are made accessible. Consider the image of a three-year-old, screaming, kicking, and struggling as a teenager half-carries, half-drags him down the street. How are we to know if we are watching maternal discipline, or the incompetence of an inept baby-sitter, or a kidnapping in progress? Situations in which people need help—particularly emergency situations—are both confusing and ambiguous. Helping is unlikely in these situations unless some relevant norm is activated. The usual ways norms are activated are through direct reminders, models, and self-awareness.

1. *Direct reminders.* "Save this child," the magazine ad bluntly demands, and some readers reach for their checkbooks. "You don't know how lucky you are," chides the collector outside the supermarket, and donations rise. Direct reminders are the surest way to activate norms and obligations, increasing their effects on our behavior. When one group of researchers sought ways to increase the money contributed to worthy causes, they found that a direct reminder of the appropriateness of giving—"We've already received contributions ranging from a penny up"—produced donations at double the frequency found in a control condition (Cialdini & Schroeder, 1976). Sometimes norms are so frequently mentioned they are just "in the air." During the Christmas season, for example, we are constantly being reminded of the value of love and charity. No wonder that many charitable organizations run "Christmas Cheer" campaigns to increase the public's generosity to their causes.

2. *Models.* When direct reminders are lacking, norms are often activated by the actions of others. Whenever we are faced with ambiguous situations, we rely on others for information that helps us understand what is happening and gives us clues about what we should do. If one person rushes to help a crying child, many more may also do so. The first person serves as a *model,* or example, implicitly defining helping as an appropriate response (Staub, 1978) and therefore encouraging others to do likewise.

In his **social learning theory**, Albert Bandura (1977b) argued that we learn much of our social behavior by watching and imitating others. Watching prosocial models should therefore promote helping. In one field study of the effect of imitation on helping, researchers stationed a motorist with an apparently disabled car at the side of the road while observers tallied whether other drivers stopped to help or zoomed on past. Drivers who recently had seen another motorist helping out with a disabled car—an incident also staged by the researchers—were more likely to offer aid than were drivers who had not had the opportunity to see an altruistic model (Bryan & Test, 1967).

Models can also inhibit helping. If people notice that bystanders and passersby are unresponsive, that observation reduces the likelihood that they will help (Smith and others, 1973). In fact, people sometimes fail to act because of *audience inhibition*—the fear of appearing foolish in front of others (Latané and others, 1981). The extent to which this fear affects our behavior is another reflection of the power of social norms: we feel free to act the way other people—models—are acting, but we are reluctant to be seen doing something that nobody else is doing. In an emergency, though, somebody has to be brave enough to be the first to run or call out for help.

3. *Self-awareness.* Self-awareness brings personal or group standards to the surface and increases their impact on behavior. Reflecting on the type of person you are increases self-awareness and, if you generally see yourself as a helpful person, can also increase helping (Batson and others, 1987; Piliavin and others, 1982). Externally caused self-awareness has the same effects. In one study demonstrating this point, women who had just seen their own image on a television monitor were more likely than others to volunteer their time and money to a needy cause (Duval and others, 1979). In another study, passersby who had just had their picture taken were more likely than other passersby to help when an experimenter staged a small accident nearby (Hoover and others, 1983).

Deactivating Norms: Diffusion of Responsibility. Just as some factors can activate helping norms, others can reduce normative pressures and interfere with helping. An event that took place on the streets of Queens, New York, early one March morning in 1964 riveted the attention of social psychologists and the general public alike on just such factors (Latané & Darley, 1970).

The facts of the case are straightforward and brutal. As Kitty Genovese returned home from work on that early March morning, she was attacked outside of her apartment building. Bleeding from multiple stab wounds, Genovese managed to stagger to a street corner where she called for help. As lights in the surrounding apartments went on, her assailant returned and stabbed her again. Over half an hour after the attack began, Kitty Genovese finally died. Investigations showed that at least thirty-eight people heard her cries for help or saw part of the attack. Why didn't any of them help?

social learning theory The theory that much social behavior is learned through observing and imitating others.

To those who pondered the question, it was clear that the onlookers knew that something was happening and realized that the situation was an emergency. Nearby residents heard the screams and switched on their lights; some looked out their windows. Onlookers initially may have wondered if the dispute was between a husband and wife, but Kitty Genovese herself made clear the seriousness of the situation with her screams: "My God, he stabbed me. Please help me, please help, I'm dying, I'm dying."

Although press reports castigated the indifference of Genovese's neighbors, two social psychologists, John Darley and Bibb Latané (1968), were not so sure. They suspected that the source of the neighbors' passivity lay in the presence of other onlookers, which influenced their decisions about whether helping was their responsibility or not. Darley and Latané decided to study this aspect of the helping situation in the laboratory.

THE FAR SIDE By GARY LARSON

Crossing the village, Mowaka is overpowered by army ants. (Later, bystanders were all quoted as saying they were horrified, but "didn't want to get involved.")

The subjects in Darley and Latané's study thought they had signed up to participate in a group discussion about problems of college life. Supposedly to minimize embarrassment and to guarantee anonymity, they were seated in intercom-equipped cubicles. Each person was told that his or her microphone would be turned on for two minutes, giving that individual a chance to talk while the other group members—but not the experimenter—listened. In reality, all of this was stage management, and the "other group members" were voices on a tape recording. Only one real subject participated at any given time, but each of them believed that one, two, or five other group members were also present.

Then came the emergency. The subjects heard one of the "group members," who had previously mentioned a susceptibility to epileptic seizures, suddenly begin to have a seizure. With increasing difficulty he asked for help and then lapsed into silence. As Figure 12.3 shows, the subjects' reactions depended on whether they believed other people were also hearing the plea for help. The more participants the subjects believed were present, the less likely they were to help and the longer they delayed before seeking aid. Of those who thought that five others were present, only 62 percent ever came to the victim's aid. Do not assume, however, that the passive subjects did not care about what was happening. Most were in the grip of anxiety and indecision, caught between behaving inappropriately by helping and behaving inappropriately by not helping.

Darley and Latané concluded that the number of participants in the group made a difference because when other people are present, responsibility is divided and each person feels less responsible for helping than he or she would when alone. This **diffusion of responsibility** explanation has been supported by additional studies showing that people who are alone when they notice an emergency feel that it is their personal responsibility to get involved, whereas far fewer do so when many other people are present (Schwartz & Gottlieb, 1980).

diffusion of responsibility A reduction in the normative pressure to help others that each individual feels when other potential helpers are also present.

Thus when other potential helpers are present some special factor is generally needed to provoke an individual to help. People who tend to help under these conditions are those who hold leadership responsibility or who

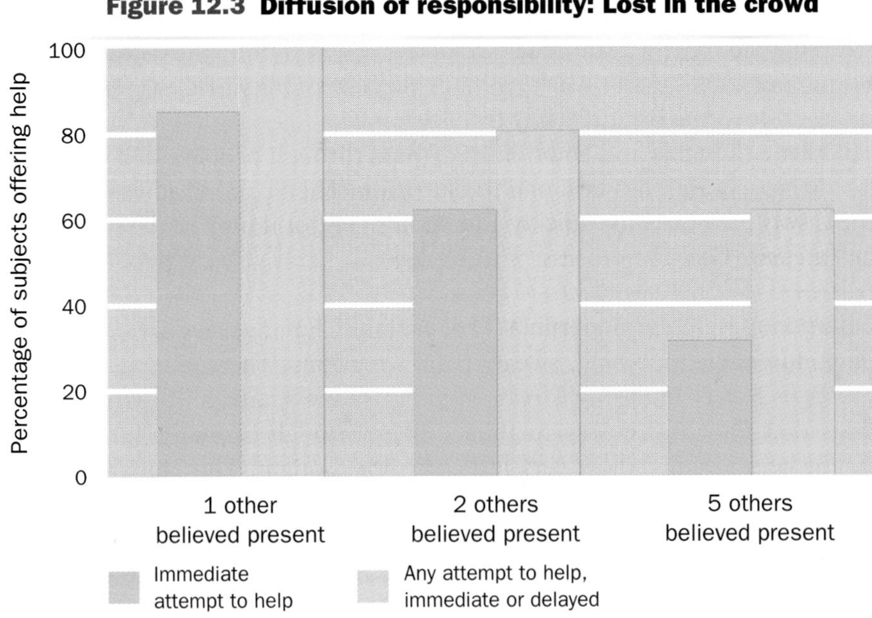

Figure 12.3 Diffusion of responsibility: Lost in the crowd

In this experiment, subjects heard another subject having a "seizure" in what they believed was a group of two, three, or six subjects. (They actually heard recordings of other voices.) The more people subjects believed to be present, the less likely the real subjects were to help. (Data from Darley & Latané, 1968.)

have been especially designated as the person who should help (Baumeister and others, 1988). We saw an instance of this kind of helping in Chapter 10 in the research study in which a confederate asked bystanders on a crowded beach to "watch my things." You may recall that 95 percent of the appointed helpers intervened when the confederate's radio was subsequently "stolen," compared with only 20 percent of bystanders who were not asked to be responsible (Moriarty, 1975).

Putting It All Together: Resolving Inner Conflicts

When our desires and norms conflict, we may consider the various factors superficially or think them through extensively before acting to help or not. Emotions can play a role in this process, for strong emotion disrupts extensive processing. When helping is a considered decision, though, it can result in a long-term commitment.

Sometimes deciding whether or not to help is relatively easy, but more often we experience conflict over what to do. We may desperately want to come to the aid of a mugging victim but fear the risks and costs to ourselves. We want to intervene when a child is spanked in the supermarket but feel that our intrusion into a "family affair" would be inappropriate. Recall our Boston pedestrian who struggled with her feelings of responsibility to help the stranded motorist but in the end decided it might be too dangerous. The impact of attitudes and norms always depends on their relative accessibility (Carver, 1975; Wegner & Schaefer, 1978). In fact, just before setting out on her walk, our friend had read in the morning newspaper about a passerby who stopped to help a stranded motorist and was shot by the motorist when his jumper cables didn't work. Perhaps the accessibility of these thoughts of danger tipped the balance away from helping.

Many thoughts and emotions may pass through people's minds as they size up the victim, the need, and the situation. The final decision to act or to turn away may be made quickly and impulsively, or it may be the product of an extensive decision process.

Emergency Helping: Superficial Processing. Emergencies are heart-stopping, adrenaline-pumping, sweaty-palm situations. The suffering of others causes us to feel anguish, distress, empathy, sadness, and guilt—strong emotions that limit our ability to think things through carefully. In addition, emergencies usually allow very little time for thought. This combination of arousal, emotions, and split-second timing usually leads people to respond to emergencies quickly and impulsively. That was certainly the case for an onlooker who witnessed an Air Florida jet crash into the ice-covered waters of the Potomac River in January 1982. As the onlooker watched, a U.S. Park Service helicopter attempted to drag a flight attendant from the freezing water, but she fell off the lifeline, plummeting back into the river. Without hesitation, the onlooker threw off his boots and coat and dived in to rescue her. "It's something I never thought [about] . . . somebody had to go into the water," he said later (Clines, 1982). When time for reflection is limited, people act on the basis of the most accessible motives or norms. In this case, the onlooker's empathy for the victim or his feelings of social responsibility outweighed his thoughts about his own discomfort and danger.

Long-Term Helping: Systematic Processing. Of course, instant help is not always needed, and helping norms or motives are not always readily accessible. Under such circumstances, a would-be rescuer may give careful and even agonized consideration to the available information. He or she may reflect on the victim's need, then on the possible cost and danger, and finally on feelings of personal responsibility and ability to help. Extensive thought can even reverse an initial quick reaction. When a Dutch couple with four children were asked to shelter a Jewish infant from the Nazis, they immediately rejected the idea. "This is going too far," they said. "We have given money to support and hide Jews—but we don't need a Jewish kid in the house" (Oliner & Oliner, 1988, p. 69). Reflection, however, produced a change of heart. By the next morning, they had come up with a scheme to save the infant. The wife, for example, planned to pretend to be pregnant for a time to allay neighbors' suspicions about the sudden appearance of a new child.

As we have pointed out many times, decisions based on extensive thought produce long-lasting commitments that are not easily changed. When people repeatedly help others, they come to see themselves as helpful and altruistic, and these self-perceptions reinforce further helping. Perhaps this process explains why people who give blood a few times become regular blood donors (Piliavin and others, 1982). Repeated helping also builds perceptions of *self-efficacy,* the sense that one's actions are effective and meaningful. Self-efficacy increases the likelihood that helpful attitudes and norms will be translated into helpful actions (Ajzen & Madden, 1986; Bandura, 1982).

Helping in the AIDS Epidemic. Society could scarcely function without volunteers. In 1989, nearly 100 million U.S. citizens performed irreplaceable services valued at $170 billion (Gallup, 1990). They worked, for example, as candy stripers in hospitals, teachers' aides in classrooms, stockers in church food pantries, tax-return preparers for the elderly, and volunteer firefighters. A new area of service drew many volunteers over the past decade as the AIDS epidemic left many of its victims in urgent need of help. The wave of volunteers who responded provide emotional support and do household chores for people with AIDS, staff counseling centers and hotlines, care for infants born with AIDS, and lobby the government on AIDS-related issues.

Like most volunteer activities, these forms of helping usually involve considerable time, trouble, and financial cost to the helper. Helping people with AIDS also involves the special emotional costs of confronting personal tragedy, illness, and death. Why do people get involved? According to Mark Snyder and Allen Omoto (1992), who have conducted a national survey of active AIDS volunteers, the reasons vary from individual to individual. Some are motivated by personal feelings of obligation to help others. Others seek personal growth in skills and understanding. Still others have community-centered concerns, such as feelings of obligation to the gay community. And some simply want to feel better about themselves. Regardless of the reasons, however, people who become involved reach their decisions after lengthy consideration.

AIDS volunteers illustrate that, as we have noted throughout this chapter, many different motives and norms can spur helping. One interesting finding in Snyder and Omoto's research is that volunteers who expressed the seemingly more "selfish" desires for self-esteem and personal growth were more likely to stick with their service over the course of a year than were those driven by the seemingly more "humanitarian" motives. The researchers note that "good, and perhaps romanticized, intentions related to humanitarian concern simply may not be strong enough to sustain volunteers faced with . . . tough realities and personal costs. . . . Therefore, volunteer organizations . . . may want to remind volunteers of the personal rewards of their work rather than underscoring how volunteer efforts benefit clients and society" (p. 115). Knowing that the long-term volunteers tended to express self-related motives for helping should not diminish our admiration for them. It is praiseworthy to be the type of person whose self-esteem and sense of self-worth are strengthened by helping others.

Perceptions of the person in need and of the helping situation influence people's desire to help or to refrain from helping. The desire to help (or not) will depend in part on an assessment of the rewards and costs involved in helping and on feelings of empathy with the victim. Perceptions of the person and situation also activate norms and influence feelings of obligation to help. Depending on how potential conflicts are resolved, the decision may be to offer help or to withhold it.

Figure 12.4 Multiple factors influence helping

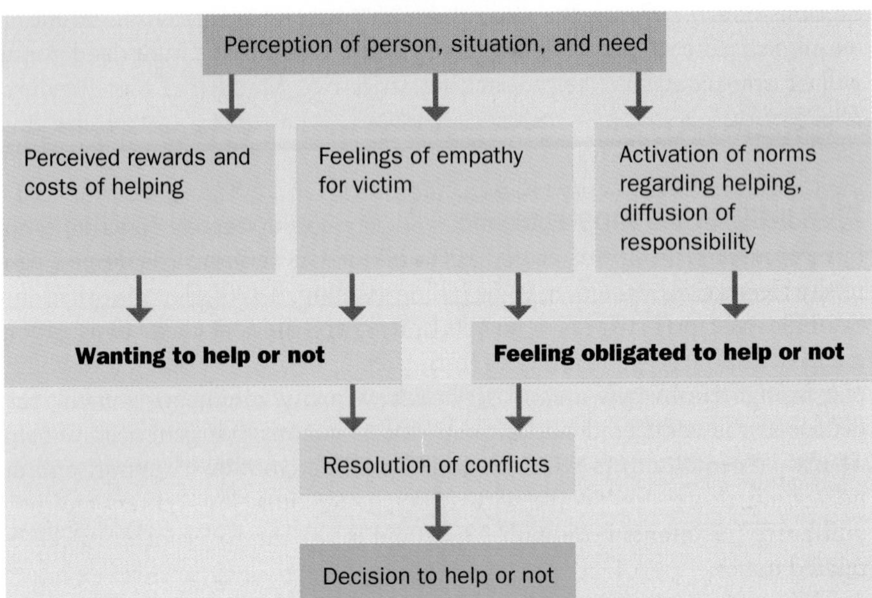

By now you can see how many factors contribute to a decision to help. The process begins when the individual notices that help is needed. If the potential rewards outweigh the costs of helping, if feelings of empathy with the victim's suffering are present, or if appropriate norms are activated, the *desire* to help or the feeling that one *ought* to help may be aroused. Although norms and attitudes often go hand in hand, desires and feelings of obligation sometimes conflict and have to be reconciled. This process may involve extensive thought or—when cognitive capacity is low, time is short, or emotional arousal is high—a quick snap judgment. The impact of these processes is illustrated in Figure 12.4.

As this figure shows, individual processes and social forces together make helping more or less likely. When personal motivation is missing, models, norms, and the urgent requirements of the situation may help us put our best foot forward. Still, we are not at the mercy of social factors. Given time for thought, we can intentionally bring to mind our own personal standards and use them to help guide our actions.

Help That Helps; Help That Hurts

A person who receives help may perceive it as a positive act of caring or as a negative threat to self-esteem. If people cannot reciprocate, they may resent the unequal power relationship between helper and helped.

Helpers usually feel good about themselves (Millar and others, 1988). But will the person receiving the help have equally good feelings? That will depend on the recipient's need and on how being helped affects their self-esteem. Help that relieves physical suffering or mental anguish is always welcome. Help that creates a positive relationship between helper and helped is welcome, too. If this relationship exists, helpers feel protective and proud of the person they rescued, and those who have been helped feel gratitude. The television show *Unsolved Mysteries* has a special segment on people's searches for someone who helped them long ago—an individual who extended a hand when they were down, nursed them through a long illness, or had faith in them when others did not. The beneficiaries usually just want to say thank you.

However, receiving help can also make people feel that they owe a favor, and that can be a problem for someone who is unable to reciprocate (Gross & Latané, 1974). People who cannot return a favor may resent the help and dislike the helper (Fisher and others, 1982). Helping produces this reaction because it sends a mixed message. The positive message of caring also has negative undertones: "I am more powerful, more able, more in control than you are—you need my help." The beneficiary is left to wonder, "Do they think I'm worthy of help and encouragement? Or do they think I couldn't make it without special treatment?"

Jeffrey Fisher and Arie Nadler (Fisher and others, 1982; Nadler & Fisher, 1986) call these opposing messages the self-supportive and the self-threatening aspects of receiving help. If recipients of help feel supported, they respond with gratitude. If the help seems threatening to their self-esteem, they dislike the helper and may refuse future help. Perhaps this mixed message explains a familiar stereotype about gender differences in seeking help: men would rather get lost than ask for directions, whereas women don't mind asking for a bit of help. Deborah Tannen (1990) argues that men generally are more sensitive to the status implications of requesting and receiving help, whereas women are more attuned to the positive relationship help can create.

Increasing Prosocial Behavior in Society

Helping in society can be increased by making needs clear, fostering a helpful self-concept in others, promoting identification and empathy, teaching and activating helping norms, and focusing responsibility rather than diffusing it.

For social psychologists, understanding helping behavior is both theoretically interesting and a very practical concern. Helping is essential to group life and social functioning, and research can offer insights into how we can increase both the giving of help and our chances of receiving it when we are in need.

1. *Reduce ambiguity: Make the need clear.* If you are injured in a fall, don't rely on the fact that passersby can see that you are bleeding. You can increase your chances of receiving aid by making your need obvious, by shouting, "Help me," for example (Clark & Word, 1972). Studies of why people report crimes have demonstrated the benefits of making it very clear that help is needed (Bickman, 1979; Bickman & Rosenbaum, 1977). Subjects in these studies witnessed a staged shoplifting, which an experimental confederate interpreted for one group of subjects by commenting, "Say, look at her. She's shoplifting. She put that in her purse." The confederate remained silent in the presence of the other group. Subjects who had the event interpreted for them were more likely to report the crime than those who did not.

2. *Foster a helpful self-concept in others.* One way to encourage people's generosity is to foster a helpful self-concept, so motivation is internal rather than external. Daniel Batson and his colleagues have shown that people doing good deeds for their own sake rather than for external rewards are likely to see themselves as genuinely altruistic people and to get hooked on helping (Batson and others, 1978; Batson and others, 1987). In their experiment, comments by a confederate led some subjects to attribute a helpful act to external factors: "I guess we have no choice." Others were guided toward attributing the act to their own compassion by comments like, "The guy really needed help." Later the researchers asked all subjects to help on an unrelated task. The percentage of "compassionate" subjects who volunteered was more than double that found in the other group. Similarly, people often make their initial donations of blood because of inducements and incentives, but after multiple donations they come to view themselves as giving and generous people. People who think of themselves as helpful are likely to help again (Piliavin and others, 1982).

3. *Promote identification with those who need help.* Whether the need is sudden and critical or chronic and long-term, a feeling of similarity with the person in need breeds empathy and increases willingness to help. This principle—that we help similar others as if we were helping ourselves—works with kin, friends, and in-groups. Perhaps this is why religious faith can be such a powerful motivator for giving (Colasanto, 1989). The language of sacred texts—"love your neighbor," "children of Allah," and the "human family"—remind us of our similarities with all humankind, increasing empathy and helping.

4. *Teach norms that support helping behavior.* Families and schools can reinforce norms supporting social responsibility and prosocial behavior both by explicit teaching and by personal examples or models (Rushton, 1975). Research on the impact of the media on behavior confirms that seeing promotes doing (Johnston & Ettema, 1986). In one study, preschoolers who watched episodes of the television program *Mr. Rogers' Neighborhood* were more helpful than children who saw neutral or aggressive programs (Stein

& Friedrich, 1972). Models like the heroic rescuers portrayed on *Rescue 911* can increase the accessibility of norms supporting helping. They also demonstrate possible ways to help and make clear the positive consequences of helping (Krebs, 1970).

5. *Activate helping norms.* Social norms that support helping have to be brought to mind before they can guide behavior. In an emergency situation, directions like "that small child needs help" or "that elderly man needs a coat" can activate norms of social responsibility to the young, the old, and the weak. In one condition of Bickman's crime-reporting study, the observer commented, "We saw the shoplifting. We should report it." Activating the norm boosted reporting of the incident to store management (Bickman, 1979; Bickman & Rosenbaum, 1977).

6. *Focus responsibility.* Directions that activate norms are not particularly useful if they are broadcast to the world at large. Focusing responsibility on specific people makes normative pressures to help more insistent—just as diffusing responsibility among many people lessens each one's feelings of obligation to help. To get help, therefore, make it clear that you want help from a particular person (Moriarty, 1975). If you are lying bleeding in the street, an even better strategy than shouting, "Help me!" would focus on a particular individual and give them a specific responsibility for helping: "You there in the red jacket! Help me now!"

Exemplifying norms of concern Although all members of a society subscribe to norms of social responsibility and helpfulness, not everyone follows through with altruistic behavior. Former President Jimmy Carter, seen here helping to construct affordable housing as a member of Habitat for Humanity, is one of those who does. Individuals with strong feelings of personal obligation not only help others directly, but also serve as role models who might encourage others to help.

The diversity of these recommendations reflects the large number of factors that can influence helping. Helping is a microcosm of human behavior. It begins with a series of judgments influenced by what we see and who we are, by our groups and our norms, and by what we think and how we feel. It culminates in action. Although these processes can lead to helping, however, they also can lead to aggression. As we pointed out at the beginning of this chapter, altruism and aggression seem to be opposite extremes of human behavior, but they are in many ways parallel. In the rest of the chapter we explore the power of perceptions, interpretations, emotions, identity, and connectedness as they foster or thwart the opposite of altruism: aggressive behavior.

Aggression

The young mugger who killed Bernard Richardson while trying to steal Herman Everett's jacket aggressed in two different ways. Threatening harm and demanding the jacket were instances of *instrumental aggression,* aggression used as a means to an end. The shooting of two people in an outburst of rage was *emotional aggression,* aggression as an end in itself. Aggression always involves the intention to harm someone. The route from intention to action is a long one, however, and it is posted with cognitive and social signs that can either check our aggressive impulses or hurry us along the path.

What factors motivate one person to hurt another? How do norms regulate aggression? How can aggression be reduced? Social psychologists have tried to answer these and other questions in their research on aggression.

Aggression in everyday life is, unfortunately, easy to observe. Researchers have watched as schoolchildren push, shove, and punch each other on the playground, as professional sports teams cross the boundary from rough play to violence, and as urban street gangs fight over territory and bragging rights. Some researchers have even used official records of violent crimes to test hypotheses about aggression.

Studying aggression in the laboratory is much more difficult than observing it elsewhere. For ethical reasons, researchers cannot set up situations in which people actually harm one another. In addition, adult subjects have reservations about aggressing in a research setting where they know they are being observed. As a result, most laboratory researchers either have studied children or have relied on a few somewhat cumbersome techniques in studies of adult subjects. In the most frequently used procedure, developed by Arnold Buss (1961), subjects are told they and another subject will be participating in a study of the effects of punishment on learning. A rigged drawing assigns the subject to the "teacher" role, and the other subject, actually a confederate, is given the role of "learner." The teacher is instructed to deliver electric shocks to punish the learner for wrong answers. The intensity and duration of the shocks selected by the teacher on the "aggression machine" serve as measures of aggression. The learner, of course, never actually receives any shocks.

You may recall from Chapter 10, pages 421 to 422, that Stanley Milgram used a version of this method for his famous study of obedience to authority.

Measures like these have been criticized as lacking construct validity because they may fail to adequately reflect the concept that researchers intend. Do they really measure aggression? What if subjects deliver the shocks not with the intent to harm—the definition of aggression—but because they believe the shocks will facilitate learning? In response to such questions, researchers have demonstrated that people who are highly aggressive outside the laboratory also give the most shocks with the shock machine, indicating that the laboratory measure possesses some construct validity (Carlson and others, 1989; Berkowitz & Donnerstein, 1982). The heavy reliance on a limited range of laboratory measures weakens the generalizability of the findings, however. And it is interesting to note the almost complete absence of research on one common, everyday form of aggression, verbal assaults such as insults, curses, and ethnic slurs. These, too, are delivered with the intent to harm. As we all realized as children, sticks and stones may break our bones, but names can also hurt us.

Despite the difficulties researchers face in investigating aggression, a number of clear patterns emerge from their studies. As you will see, many of these patterns appear consistently across different types of research, in the lab and in the field. To describe these patterns and to explain when and why people aggress, we must again begin at the beginning. Aggression, like helping, is usually set off by perceptions and interpretations of some event or situation.

What Triggers Aggression?

> *Some aggression is triggered by potential rewards and is suppressed by perceived costs or risks. Sometimes, however, perceived provocation produces anger, which can set off aggression regardless of the consequences.*

A situation that appears to offer opportunity for gain makes instrumental aggression look tempting. Likewise, perceived provocation often sets off emotional aggression. Of course, what looks like an opportunity for gain to one person may not even be noticed by another. And behavior that is a red flag to one person may not bother someone else. Thus aggression, like so many other behaviors, depends on the individual's perceptions and interpretations of other people, their behavior, and the situations in which behavior occurs.

Instrumental Aggression: Counting Costs and Rewards. Instrumental aggression occurs when people see an opportunity for gain—an unarmed young man wearing a trendy jacket, or a bank computer system with an unprotected password, or an opponent blocking the goal as the referee looks the other way. Those adept at instrumental aggression become particularly good at sensing appropriate opportunities—the experienced purse snatcher can spot the victims who are least able to resist effectively, and the schoolyard bully seems to zero in on smaller, weaker children. Cues that signal opportunities for gain are like billboards proclaiming: "Aggression pays."

When aggression pays, it becomes more likely (Patterson and others, 1967; Bandura, 1973). Perhaps it's no surprise, then, that children who believe aggression will lead to rewards or will prevent other kids from hurting them are the most aggressive in school (Perry and others, 1986). Nor is it surprising that teenage hockey players whose fathers applaud rough play are the most physically aggressive on the team (Ennis & Zanna, 1990). Conversely, when rewards are withdrawn, instrumental aggression usually subsides. Getting tough on terrorists—refusing to bargain with hijackers, hostage takers, and kidnappers—requires a heart of stone, but it eliminates the instrumental value of their tactics (Rubin, 1987). Even the threat of punishment can deter instrumental aggression, if the threat is believed (Baron, 1983a; Zillmann, 1979).

If instrumental aggression depends on the perceptions of rewards and costs, what factors influence those perceptions?

1. *Personal abilities.* Just as an ability to help increases helping, an ability to hurt increases aggression. Children who think aggression is easy, or who have used it successfully to gain rewards in the past, are more likely to use it again (Perry and others, 1986; Patterson and others, 1967).

2. *Gender differences.* Aggression is usually easier and less risky for men than for women, so men find it more rewarding and less costly. In a meta-analysis of the research literature, Alice Eagly (1987) found that

men are generally more likely to aggress than women, and this finding applies to both physical and verbal aggression. Eagly suggests that one reason for these differences is that men see aggression as less dangerous than women do.

3. *The impact of models.* Models also influence perceptions of rewards and costs by showing us just when and how aggression can be successful. When the partisan chants of the home crowd at a basketball game disrupt a visiting team's performance, others see that verbal aggression works, and they are likely to give it a try themselves at the next game. Of course, the verbal aggression strategy may backfire. A particularly vulgar chant may draw technical fouls that give the other team the edge, teaching that this particular form of aggression does not pay. Consistent with social learning theory, viewers of television violence are more likely to copy an aggressive act immediately if it is portrayed as successful than they are if it is punished (Bandura, 1973). However, the long-term effects of models are not as straightforward as the immediate effects. Even if observers see the aggression punished, they may learn the model's behavior and imitate it later when punishment seems less likely. So what people learn from models can go underground, only to surface when the observer is angry or wants his or her way.

   Nonviolence can be modeled, too. Just as aggressive models can increase aggression, nonaggressive models can decrease it. Models who walk away from provocation or who talk things out offer a quick how-to course in arriving at peaceable solutions. They teach others that aggression is not the only way to handle conflict (Baron & Kepner, 1970; Donnerstein & Donnerstein, 1976).

Emotional Aggression: Response to Provocation. Unlike instrumental aggression, emotional aggression is not motivated by the calculus of gain and loss. The main motivator of emotional aggression is the sheer desire to hurt the other person (Baron, 1971). In fact, like those who engage in altruistic helping based on empathy, people in the throes of emotional aggression are often insensitive to external costs and rewards. Propelled by "blind" fury, they seem immune even to the threat of punishment (Baron, 1983a). The shooting of Bernard Richardson, one tragic example of emotional aggression, was prompted by the gunman's anger over perceived disrespect. Although the events that provoke angry feelings and impulses toward emotional aggression sometimes seem almost random, the perception of provocation is a critical starting point in each case. Let's examine the factors that influence perceptions of provocation.

1. *Perceived intention to harm.* The act of inflicting pain is not by itself usually perceived as provocation. Accidents and painful medical treatments are unlikely to provoke retaliation because we do not perceive them as actions intended to harm us. Even a hard football tackle will

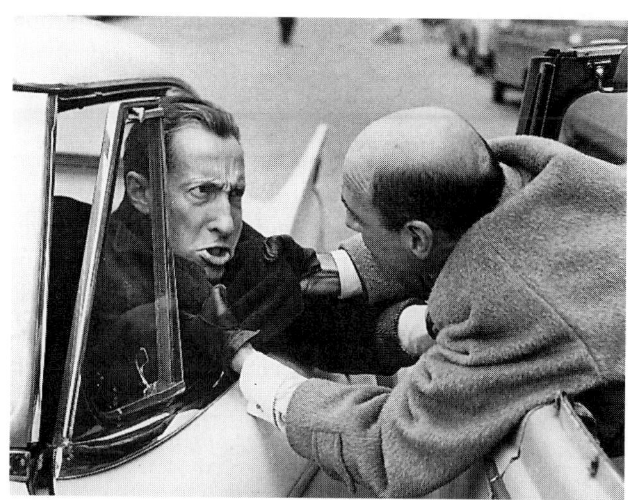

Emotional aggression The anger triggered by a perceived provocation—such as inconsiderate driving—is a springboard to violence. Propelled by a desire to retaliate, the angered are often immune to the costs of such violence. Instrumental aggression and angry aggression are thus influenced by different social psychological processes.

not spark aggression unless it is viewed as deliberately rough or meant to cause injury. Perceived intention is what transforms "just part of the game" into provocation (Greenwell & Dengerink, 1973; Geen, 1990). And when the provocation is seen as deliberate, retaliation is right behind (Ohbuchi & Kambara, 1985).

2. *Perceived controllability.* Sometimes even intentional harm can be forgiven if it can be justified or excused. You may excuse a person who hurts you if you believe the behavior was not under his or her control. If someone "couldn't help himself," striking out at you in the "heat of the moment" or in a state of anxiety or distraction, you probably will feel less pressure to retaliate than if the person's action is premeditated. To demonstrate people's reactions to such excuses, researchers arranged for an obnoxious experimenter to deliberately insult subjects. Subjects who were warned in advance that the experimenter was extremely anxious about an upcoming exam reacted with much less anger than those who had no warning (Zillmann & Cantor, 1976).

3. *Personality differences in perceptions of provocation.* Because provocation depends on interpretations of intent, an action that leaves some people unconcerned may move others to anger and retaliation. Chronically aggressive people are generally apt to interpret ambiguous acts as intentional provocations, and this perceptual bias is quite pronounced in aggressive children (Dodge & Crick, 1990). These children may interpret unintentional collisions on the playground as deliberate acts of aggression and may then retaliate, possibly starting a cycle of violence. Although this perceptual bias has a strong role in emotional aggression, it has no impact on acts of instrumental aggression, such as bullying a younger child out of his lunch money (Dodge & Coie, 1987). Findings such as this support the belief that emotional aggression and instrumental aggression involve quite distinct psychological processes.

Beyond Provocation: Emotional Aggression and Negative Emotion. Agitated by a loss, soccer fans riot using stadium seat covers and planks from police barricades to assault the opposing fans. Frustrated by failure, a schoolboy continually picks on smaller children, even though it leads to rejection from his peers (Price & Dodge, 1989). As events like these demonstrate, emotional aggression is not limited to striking back at a provoker. In fact, one of the most influential early theories of aggression, *frustration-aggression theory*, held that any frustration—defined as the blocking of an important goal—inevitably triggers aggression (Dollard and others, 1939). The aggression will not necessarily be directed against the source of the frustration, however, especially if that source is powerful. Instead, the theory held, aggression can be displaced to safer targets. Parents who frustrate one another may take out their aggression on their child, who in turn may pull the cat's tail.

Early research evidence supported frustration-aggression theory, but critiques and conflicting data soon started to accumulate (Miller, 1941). For example, many factors other than frustration were shown to trigger aggression (Buss, 1961). More recently, Leonard Berkowitz (1989) outlined a model that neatly accounts for the original evidence linking frustration and aggression. According to Berkowitz, *any* negative feelings can set off aggression. Such feelings include not only frustration and anger but also pain, fear, and irritation. As Berkowitz (1993) put it, "We're nasty when we feel bad."

Berkowitz seems to be right. We now know that a variety of conditions that create negative feelings—unpleasant heat or painful cold, stressful noises, crowding, even noxious odors and air pollution—can trigger aggression (Geen, 1990; Berkowitz, 1989). The relationship between heat and aggression, for example, has been established in both field and laboratory studies (Baron, 1972; Rule and others, 1987). Examination of weather and crime records reveals that when the outdoor temperature is high, there is an increase in the incidence of violent crimes, including murder and rape (Anderson, 1987). Figure 12.5 shows an instance of an increase in rapes and murders in Houston, Texas, when the temperature climbed above ninety degrees. The statistics on the numbers of crimes not involving emotional aggression (robbery and arson) during the same period showed no relationship to temperature.

Although negative feelings can lead to aggression, people do not necessarily understand why they are feeling upset. Even though the source of their irritability is discomfort related to a heat wave, for example, they may attribute their feelings to some highly noticeable event. Dolf Zillmann (1971, 1978) explored the implications of this idea for aggression. Zillmann's *excitation-transfer theory* suggests that if an individual is aroused for irrelevant reasons and then encounters a provocation, he or she may assume that the arousal stems from anger. The combination of preexisting arousal, plus anger generated by the provocation, may increase the likelihood of aggression. Consistent with this idea is the finding that arousal produced by strenuous exercise, such as pedaling an exercise bike or climbing stairs, can increase aggression against a provoker (Zillmann and others, 1972).

Figure 12.5 Negative feelings increase aggression: Temperature and violent crime

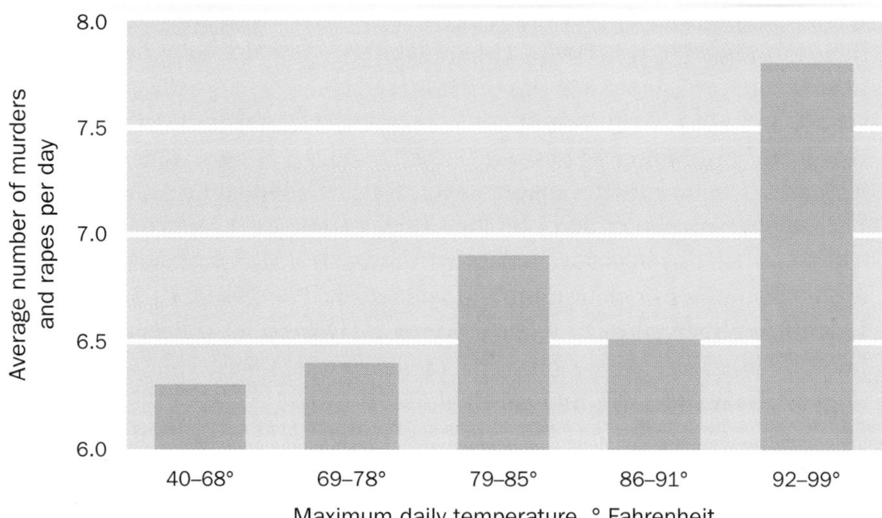

Between 1980 and 1982, researchers counted murders and rapes reported in a daily newspaper column based on police statistics. They compared these figures with the maximum daily temperatures as reported in official weather records. Results show that the highest numbers of aggressive crimes were committed on the hottest days. This pattern may reflect the impact of heat-related discomfort on the tendency toward emotional aggression. (Data from Anderson & Anderson, 1984.)

You may be wondering whether the opposite could also be true. If arousal, even arousal caused by a provocation, is attributed to a state *incompatible* with aggression, will aggression be reduced? Research says yes. One study arranged for subjects to receive electric shocks delivered by a confederate. Some of the subjects were led to believe that their arousal was due to a drug or to sexually arousing reading material. These misled subjects became less angry than subjects who correctly attributed their arousal to the shocks (Geen and others, 1972). Less anger meant less aggression: subjects who thought their arousal was drug-induced or sexual in nature gave the confederates fewer and less intense shocks in return. These findings confirm that the individual's interpretation of the arousal, not the true source of the arousal, dictates the person's emotional response. When we interpret our arousal as a response to a provocation, we may find ourselves striking out in an act of emotional aggression.

Norms Promoting and Restraining Aggression

Social norms can either promote or restrain aggression. They can be activated by the behavior of models witnessed in person or in the media. Norms that limit aggression apply with special force to aggression against similar others or in-group members.

Because aggression is a potentially destructive force, virtually all societies and groups have norms that regulate it. This does not mean that all norms operate to squelch aggression. As you will see, group norms often promote aggressive behavior rather than restrain it.

Norms of Aggression. According to one Chicago teenager, the code of the streets includes "Never, ever, disrespect anybody." The reason? Norms in the teenager's neighborhood dictate violent responses to disrespect. "People won't fistfight. . . . They'd shoot me, step over my dead body and go about their business" (Terry, 1993). Urban gangs are not the only groups whose norms support aggression (Klein, 1969; Reicher, 1987). When aggressive school-age boys are more popular than less aggressive boys, schoolboy norms are promoting aggression (Price & Dodge, 1989). When corporate managers fix prices and violate patent and copyright laws, their actions reflect a business norm that condones any action in the pursuit of profit. These business strategies, together with fraud and tax evasion, have caused more economic loss than theft and vandalism (President's Commission on Law Enforcement, 1967). When it comes to aggression, you cannot judge a book by its cover: aggression seems to wear a three-piece suit as easily as it does expensive sneakers and gang colors.

Cultural Differences in Aggressive Norms. Norms that promote aggression sometimes infect entire societies. In 1987, the United States suffered one of the highest homicide rates in the world for young men between the ages of 15 and 24: 22 per 100,000 (Howard, 1990). Among twenty-one industrial nations, no other country had a rate even one-fourth as high as that. Israel's rate was 3.7, despite ongoing armed conflict in that country, and Japan and the major nations of Western Europe have rates below 1.5 per 100,000 young men. Sadly, several prevalent norms in mainstream U.S. culture promote aggression.

1. *The right to bear firearms and to use them.* In the United States, this right is viewed not only as the right to resist tyrannical government, as foreseen in the U.S. Constitution, but as a response to perceived threats to home or hearth. Many people in the United States believe it is appropriate for a householder to shoot an intruder in his or her home, and some states have passed laws explicitly providing immunity from prosecution in such situations. In one recent tragic case, an American homeowner shot and killed a Japanese exchange student who mistakenly approached his house while looking for a Halloween party. When an American jury acquitted the man of manslaughter charges, the Japanese public—who have very different norms regarding gun use—was appalled. American public opinion even favors a tough line with petty criminals: in one case, a judge in Marion, Indiana, congratulated a defendant who shot and crippled a purse snatcher, saying, "My thanks, sir, for having tried to do something to help the problems in this country" (*Newsweek*, 1990a).

2. *The norm of male aggression.* In comparison with men in Northern European countries, men in the United States and in Southern European countries are much more admiring of "toughness" and "machismo" (Block, 1973). We need only remember presidential hopeful Michael

Dukakis trying to look tough as he perched uncomfortably atop a tank or think of President Ronald Reagan's pride in his "ranch-hand toughness" to see how important tough and manly images are to the American voting public (Halberstam, 1972).

3. *The norm of family privacy.* The old saying that a man's home is his castle is a symbol of the way private homes are considered to be havens, safe from public intrusion. The norm of family privacy insulates life inside the home, and it exempts family life from public standards of behavior. By so doing, this norm often increases violence in the nuclear family home (Sherman & Berk, 1984; Berk & Newton, 1985). Social norms also condone aggression between parents and children that would not be tolerated between strangers. Imagine the quick action that would be taken if a restaurant owner slapped a customer's child for not eating his or her vegetables! Norms supporting traditional family power structures, though they are gradually changing, may also encourage violence against women and children (Straus and others, 1980).

Models of Aggression. Not only the cultural backdrop but also other people's actions offer clues to the norms appropriate in a situation. As we stated earlier in this chapter, models who demonstrate the appropriateness of nonviolent solutions to conflict can reduce aggression. Unfortunately, aggressive models not only show people ways to aggress but also send the message that their response is right, correct, and acceptable, and others soon imitate them (Bandura and others, 1963, 1961). For example, at many sporting events, violence among fans is often preceded by aggressive play on the field (Goldstein, 1982).

Consider the role of models in one recent event. The 1992 acquittal of four police officers who had been videotaped beating the African-American motorist Rodney King touched off three days of rioting in Los Angeles. The riots escalated after initial incidents were shown on local television. A young man identified only as J.B. commented, "I was watching TV, and they were

Models of aggression We are exposed to aggression directly and indirectly. What might the observers of this confrontation between a Desert Storm victory celebrant and a peace activist learn about whether aggression is appropriate and useful in settling disputes? And how will audiences react to seeing the event in their newspapers or on their television screens?

saying, 'Not guilty. Not guilty.' An hour later I saw these guys . . . beating up the guy in the truck. They're the ones that got it started off. I said, 'OK, I'm down with that. If that's how they're going to do it, we're going to do it too'" (Mydans, 1992).

Laboratory studies confirm the powerful impact that models have on aggressive behavior. Compared with those who have watched an innocuous film, people who have watched a highly aggressive film of a boxing match give other subjects stronger shocks on Buss's "aggression machine" (Bushman & Geen, 1990). Exposure to aggressive models makes violent behavior seem more appropriate because it stimulates aggressive thoughts and feelings (Bargh & Gollwitzer, in press). It also makes people interpret ambiguous behaviors as more hostile, making retaliation to perceived provocations more likely (Carver and others, 1983).

Tragically, people often encounter aggressive models in their own homes. Children of abusive parents learn at an early age that aggression is both appropriate and acceptable. Indeed, until recently, surveys in the United States indicated that public opinion supported the physical punishment of children as legitimate and necessary (Gelles, 1972). Yet in the home as elsewhere, violent acts teach violent norms. People who abuse their children or spouses tend to have been on the receiving end of child abuse themselves (Sugarman & Hotaling, 1989; Straus and others, 1980).

Aggressive Models in the Media. Even children from peaceful homes are exposed to an enormous amount of violence because of the amount of time they spend watching television. On average, children in the United States watch 3.5 hours of TV each day, and during that time they see an average of 33 acts of violence (Heymann, 1989). Prime-time TV averages five violent acts per hour, whereas Saturday morning cartoons average twenty (Gerbner and others, 1986). Does aggressive media content really stimulate viewers' aggression? Researchers have conducted four types of studies—each with its own strengths and weaknesses—to answer this question.

1. *Nonexperimental studies* measure both television-viewing habits and aggression in a single group of people. For instance, after asking 141 parents how much television their kindergarten-age children watched, researchers visited the classrooms to observe the children's aggressive behavior at play (Singer & Singer, 1981). The children who viewed the most TV violence also behaved the most aggressively. This design is strong in external validity because it assessed both TV viewing and aggression in natural contexts. However, it is weak on internal validity: this study does not show that TV viewing *causes* aggression. Other causal relationships could lead to the same pattern of results. For example, parental neglect could both make children aggressive and cause them to spend a lot of time watching TV.

2. *Experiments* randomly assign subjects to watch different amounts or kinds of television. A classic field experiment randomly assigned incar-

cerated delinquent boys at three sites in the United States and Belgium to view aggressive films or nonaggressive films every evening for a week (Parke and others, 1977). The young men's aggressive behavior was observed both before and after the "film week." In all three locations, boys who saw aggressive films committed more physical attacks than those who viewed neutral films. We can conclude that film viewing *caused* aggression because of the high internal validity of the experimental design. However, like most experiments, this one was relatively short term, examining the effects of only one week of viewing. Another weakness of this study is that it cannot reveal whether viewing violent television might increase the aggressiveness of people who are not institutionalized male delinquents.

3. *Longitudinal studies* try to answer the "which comes first?" question about aggression and violent television. Longitudinal studies assess people's television viewing and aggressiveness over a long period of time to attempt to determine which variable causes the other. One ambitious study, which followed a group of subjects for twenty-two years, found that the more TV violence they had watched at age 8, the more likely they were to have been convicted for violent crimes by age 30 (Huesmann, 1986). These findings were confirmed in a three-year multination study in the United States, Finland, Israel, and Poland (Huesmann & Eron, 1986). Though time-consuming and costly to carry out, longitudinal research has important strengths: the variables can be measured in natural settings and strong causal conclusions can be drawn.

4. *Archival data analyses* have been used to support and confirm the consistent conclusions of the other three types of studies. In one rather alarming series of studies, sociologist David Phillips (1983) analyzed public records of death certificates to investigate the effects of media violence on aggression. His findings are striking: in the days following the broadcast of eighteen different heavyweight boxing matches that were nationally televised in the United States, homicide deaths rose, with a peak occurring on the third day after the fight. Phillips even found evidence that murders of White males increased in the days after a White heavyweight fighter was defeated, and murders of African-American males increased following the defeat of an African-American fighter. Just as viewing a violent film in the lab increases the level of shocks that people give others (Carver and others, 1983), viewing a boxing match on TV appears to increase the chance that a real-life disagreement will escalate into a fight or even a homicide.

A simple conclusion can be drawn from all these different studies: aggressive media content can increase viewers' aggressive behavior (Liebert & Sprafkin, 1988; Hearold, 1986). Perhaps even more ominously, the effect seems to have a long life. Studies indicate that, over the long term, witnessing violence dulls our perceptions and numbs our reactions, eventually leading to indifference and cynicism. For example, boys who watch a great deal of violence on television are not aroused by viewing a brutal boxing match (Cline and others, 1973). And frequent viewers of "slasher" movies are relatively unconcerned about violence toward women (Donnerstein and others, 1987). In fact, according to Thomas Redecki, research director for the National Coalition on Television Violence, "The horror themes . . . have become commonplace. As we consume more violence, we become more desensitized. People no longer consider *Nightmare on Elm Street* or *Friday the 13th* violent. They've seen worse" (Kennedy, 1991). Habitual exposure to violence gives people a Teflon coating—what ought to be upsetting slides right off.

Norms Restraining Aggression. Of course, not all models and norms foster aggression. Most societies try to maintain and teach some norms that limit and inhibit violence. "Pick on someone your own size" is a norm that, like many other norms, forbids aggression against the weak and helpless. And although "an eye for an eye, a tooth for a tooth" seems to be a formula for revenge, its original purpose was to prevent retaliation from spiraling out of control.

Some groups have developed norms that effectively counteract violence. Anthropological reports indicate that among the Inuit of the Arctic, the Pygmies of Africa, and the Zuni and Blackfoot peoples of North America, controversy and conflict are avoided, physical violence is rare, and war is nonexistent (Gorer, 1986). Japanese social norms also dictate that it is often better to yield than fight, as reflected in the expression *Makeru ga kachi*—"to lose is to win" (Alcock and others, 1988; Triandis and others, 1988).

Norms are usually most effective in limiting aggression against other in-group members. Thus, similarity reduces aggression, and it does so for two reasons. First, as we saw earlier in this chapter, perceived similarity breeds empathy, and fellow feeling is incompatible with aggression (Miller & Eisenberg, 1988). Second, the norms of most groups proscribe or strictly control aggression within the group so that cohesion can be maintained and group goals achieved. In-group members are protected by a norm that appears to warn, "Don't hurt me—I'm one of *us*."

Unfortunately, this protection from aggression does not extend to outsiders. For example, White subjects interpret a shove as much more aggressive if an African-American does the shoving rather than another White (Duncan, 1976). The readiness to take offense at the behavior of an out-group member suggests that people will react more aggressively to provocation by an out-group member than by an in-group member—a suggestion confirmed by research evidence. In one study of intergroup aggression using the typical shock paradigm, White subjects were paired with either an African-American or a White confederate trained to treat the subjects in an insulting or neutral manner (Rogers & Prentice-Dunn, 1981). When the interaction was neutral, subjects gave lower levels of shock to the African-American confederate than to the White—perhaps "leaning over backward" to show they were not prejudiced. But when the confederate had insulted and provoked them, subjects delivered more intense shocks to the African American.

When out-group members can be seen as totally unlike the in-group, aggression against them becomes much easier. Members of disliked out-groups are often dehumanized and morally excluded—considered outside the boundaries within which normative restraints apply. Norms that restrict violence against other in-group members, who are regarded as fully human, offer no protection to despised out-groups perceived as "subhumans," "worms," or "vermin" (Staub, 1990; Bandura, 1990).

Some of the other chilling consequences of moral exclusion of out-group members were described in Chapter 6, pages 242 to 245, and will come up again in Chapter 14, pages 620 to 622.

Given these findings about similarity and the protectiveness of in-group membership, the high rate of violence within families may seem particularly puzzling. After all, the family seems to be the ultimate in-group. But in this case, in-group membership is not protection enough. Family members have other features that make them tragically frequent targets. Perhaps the most obvious is simply that they are there: they are easily accessible. Differences in size and power also make weaker family members less able to retaliate. Finally, a coalition of norms place a protective shield around family violence. Norms of privacy make it unlikely that such aggression will be punished, and other norms may even offer imagined justification for "discipline" or "keeping the family under control." When these factors stack up on one side of the equation, the protective power of similarity is often overwhelmed.

Activating and Deactivating Norms. Because norms are rooted in group memberships, the presence of other group members can make norms more accessible. For example, in the presence of an audience that supports punishment, subjects give more "educational" shocks than they do when the audience opposes punishment (Froming and others, 1982). Sometimes, in fact, the presence of the group can overwhelm all other considerations. In the state of deindividuation (Zimbardo, 1969), which we described in Chapter 10, people become "faceless" members of their group, responsive only to that group's norms. If the group riots, the individual will probably be carried along heedless of the consequences, contributing to the sometimes extreme violence of rioting prisoners, hooligan soccer fans, and lynch mobs (Reicher, 1987). Remember, however, that if the group acts in a benevolent fashion, the individual is also likely to be caught up in good works.

Of course, even in the group's presence, some people are chronically more aware than others of normative constraints on aggression, and they are therefore more responsive to violations of norms restraining aggression. Apparently this is another domain in which gender makes a difference: women are more likely to feel guilt or anxiety about aggression than men are (Eagly, 1987). Such emotions give people an incentive to restore their behavior to a more appropriate track. No doubt women's sensitivity to norm violation is another reason—besides differences in physical size and strength—they are less aggressive than men.

Putting It All Together: When Desires and Obligations Conflict

Aggression may result from either superficial or extensive thought. Powerful cues often increase aggression spontaneously, whereas thinking carefully can reduce aggression. Many factors interfere with the ability to process information thoroughly, usually increasing the likelihood of aggression.

When desires and norms conflict—when you really want to smack someone, but you know it would be wrong—how are such inner conflicts resolved? When people are processing superficially, any salient aspect of the environment or accessible attitude or norm "wins": whatever grabs our attention most easily has the greatest impact on our behavior. Direct reminders, the salience of costs or rewards, or the behavior of models all affect accessibility, and thus help determine whether particular attitudes and norms will guide behavior. Situational cues such as these can sometimes trigger aggressive behavior with very little thought.

Superficial Processing: Cues for Violence, Cues for Peace. Violent objects breed violent thoughts. For most of us, guns, knives, and even clenched fists are strongly associated with the idea of aggression (Huesmann & Eron, 1984). If seeing a weapon cues thoughts of aggression, this in turn should make aggressive behavior more likely—and so it does, in an outcome termed the *weapons effect* (Berkowitz & LePage, 1967; Carlson and others, 1990). In one nonlaboratory study of this effect, Charles Turner and his associates set up a booth at a campus carnival and invited students to throw sponges at a target person. Passersby threw more sponges when they could see a rifle that had been placed nearby than when no rifle was present (Turner and others, 1977). Weapons and other aggressive cues increase aggression even when people are calm, but the effect is strongest for people who are already aroused and angered (Berkowitz, 1993). The mugger who shot Bernard Richardson carried a gun. That gun not only made the mugger's aggression more deadly, it may also have made aggression more likely in the first place. The National Rifle Association, an organization that has long opposed any form of gun control, argues that guns don't kill, people do. But the evidence suggests otherwise. As Leonard Berkowitz (1965) put it, "The finger pulls the trigger, but the trigger may also be pulling the finger."

Cues for violence These children are playing "terrorist" with ski-masks and squirt guns. Unless they have been exposed to terrorism directly, their behavior is most likely modeled on and encouraged by media depictions of such incidents. In addition, research suggests that the presence of violent cues—masks, guns—increases aggressive impulses, even in play.

Most of us associate weapons with violent behavior, but our personal histories can change even neutral objects into aggression cues. The sight of a longtime rival or the logo of a business competitor may become aggression cues for particular people. Even relatively brief exposure can turn a once-neutral stimulus into an effective cue for aggression, as a study conducted in Poland illustrated. One group of men repeatedly viewed the color yellow in association with cigarettes—a positive cue for them because they were smokers. Another group viewed the same color paired with electric shocks. Later, the men were required to punish someone else in the presence of yellow or another color. Men who had experienced yellow linked to painful shocks were more aggressive in the presence of that color than were the men for whom yellow brought positive thoughts to mind (Leyens & Fraczek, 1983). Evidently, a previously neutral color can become an effective cue for aggression.

Fortunately, cues can also decrease aggression. A kind and gentle response, the presence of an infant, and even laughter in a tense situation can cue thoughts and feelings that are incompatible with aggression (Berkowitz, 1984). Even normally aggression-producing cues such as guns can decrease aggression if they provoke fear, anxiety, or disgust, as they do for many people (Baron, 1983b). In fact, all of the factors that make desires and norms more accessible—models, reminders of group membership, self-awareness, and situational cues—can push us either toward or away from aggression, depending on the particular motives and norms they call into service.

Aggressive Cues in the Sports Arena. Can learned cues increase athletes' aggression toward one another? Mark Frank and Thomas Gilovich (1988) think so. They hypothesized that in many Western countries, cultural associations may cause black uniforms to act as cues to thoughts of aggression and death, thereby encouraging aggressive behavior. To test this hypothesis, they looked at the relationship between uniform color and penalties incurred by professional hockey and football players. Sure enough, from the Pittsburgh Steelers to the Philadelphia Flyers, teams wearing black uniforms were penalized more often over seventeen playing seasons than were teams wearing other colors. In fact, when a team changed to black uniforms during the course of its season, as the Pittsburgh Penguins did, their penalties increased. The uniform cue seems to influence both those wearing the uniforms (the teams become more aggressive) and those watching them (referees call more penalties against them). To replicate these effects in the laboratory, Frank and Gilovich formed groups of three college men and told them they could choose the game they wanted to play against another group of students. Each group was given either black or white "uniform" tops to wear over their regular clothing. Teams decked out in black were more likely than teams in white to choose "dart gun duel" or "chicken fights" over the less aggressive "block stacking" or "golf putting contest" games.

Systematic Processing: Thinking Things Through. When people have the time and capacity to consider deeply, they can intentionally try to activate the most appropriate, rather than the most accessible, cognitive structures. Given the opportunity, they can come up with alternatives to violence—talking over a conflict, weighing the costs and benefits of retaliation, compromising on a solution, realizing that an apparent provocation may have been accidental. But these things take time and effort, precious resources that people do not always have. Unfortunately, a variety of factors can limit people's motivation and ability to engage in complex thinking (Zillmann, 1982).

1. *Personality differences in social reasoning ability.* Although everyone's social reasoning ability improves as they grow older, there are differences among individuals in aggression that are relatively consistent across situations and over time (Olweus, 1979; Krebs & Miller, 1985). One of the main

reasons for this consistency is that some people are better able than others to think through a provoking situation and to come up with peaceful alternatives. Children with less ability to think of nonaggressive responses in social situations tend to be more aggressive than other children who can suggest more alternatives (Huesmann and others, 1987; Dodge & Crick, 1990). This difference becomes even more pronounced as life grows more complicated. As tasks become more challenging or as interaction becomes more structured, social and cognitive skills are strained to their limits. Aggressive children are then even more likely to turn to violence (Wright & Mischel, 1987; Dodge and others, 1986).

Sadly, there is evidence that the physical and emotional trauma of child abuse may diminish a child's ability to interpret social cues correctly and to generate imaginative responses to conflict situations (Dodge and others, 1990). These deficits in turn increase the child's own tendency to turn to aggression, which may be one important reason why abused children sometimes grow up to perpetuate abuse against their own spouses or children (Sugarman & Hotaling, 1989).

2. *Strong emotions.* Strong emotions can reduce people's capacity to process information carefully, as we have seen many times throughout this text. Thus, aggressive boys' tendency to see any bump or jostle as an act of aggression is magnified when they are very anxious (Dodge & Somberg, 1987). Because strong emotions often accompany conflict, they temporarily interfere with careful processing just when it is most needed.

3. *Alcohol use.* You may not be surprised to learn that drinking and violence often coincide (Bushman & Cooper, 1990). Alcohol is a factor in almost two-thirds of homicides and in one-third of rapes, burglaries, and assaults (Wolfgang & Strohm, 1956; Desmond, 1987). The statistics are less surprising, though no less shocking, when you realize that alcohol reduces people's capacity to process a wide range of information. Perceiving a restricted range of cues, a person under the influence of alcohol is likely to base his or her actions on whatever is most immediately obvious (Steele & Josephs, 1990). So alcohol by itself does not invariably lead to violence—people sometimes become jolly or weepy when they drink if they happen to focus on cues that push them in those directions. However, alcohol plus anger or threat is a surefire recipe for aggression (Taylor and others, 1976). In addition to reducing our capacity to process a wide range of cues, alcohol exerts a second and equally dangerous influence. It lessens people's concern for factors that ordinarily restrain aggression: the potential costs and dangers of aggressive acts, the social norms that constrain aggression, and the cues that ordinarily inhibit aggression, such as expressions of pain from the victim (Schmutte & Taylor, 1980).

At this point you may be thinking that just about *anything* can cause aggression—feeling too hot or cold, being with annoying peers, drinking beer, watching a violent movie, or even wearing black clothing. It is true that

A perceived provocation in a particular situation may spur desires to aggress or may activate norms that either favor or restrict aggression. The way the person resolves potentially conflicting desires and norms will determine whether aggression occurs.

Figure 12.6 Multiple factors influence aggression

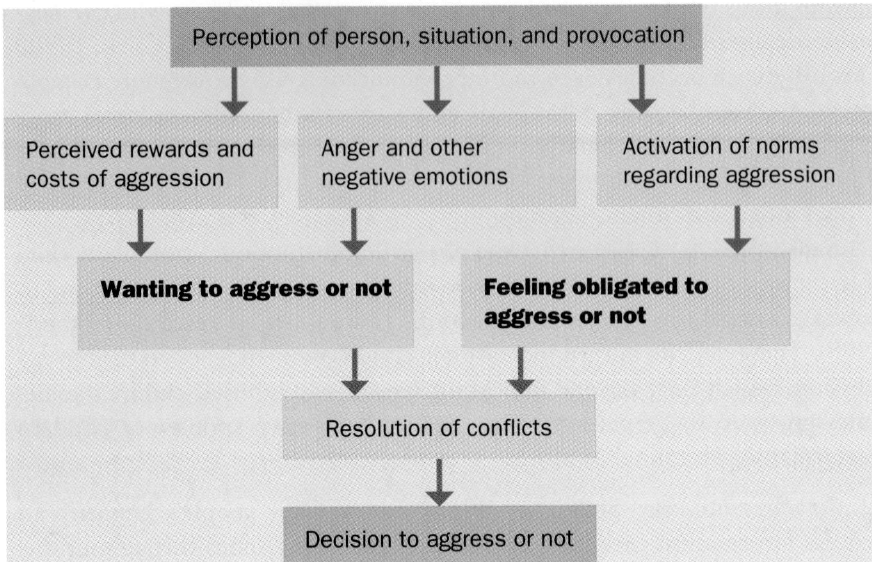

many different factors can push us in the direction of aggression, but all their effects can be understood in terms of the underlying processes shown in Figure 12.6. The process begins with perceptions of the person, situation, and provocation. The *desire* to hurt increases when potential rewards outweigh potential costs or when anger and other negative emotions are present. The desire to aggress does not always dictate action, however, because social norms and the actions of others also play a major role in initiating or restraining aggression. Violent models can show that violence is rewarded, offer evidence that aggression is normatively acceptable, and serve as a cue that makes aggressive thoughts and feelings more accessible. No wonder aggressive models are so potent in producing further aggression and that those aiming at reducing aggression in society have criticized the media for presenting so many aggressive models for public consumption.

But norms and models can also have a pacifying effect—if they are nonviolent and if they are brought to mind. This is one reason reconciling attitudes, norms, and cues that promote or oppose aggression is so important. Unfortunately, this requires time, effort, and ability, resources that might not be available when needed. Strong negative emotions like anger not only motivate aggression directly (Frijda and others, 1989), they also diminish people's capacity to think things through and to formulate nonaggressive responses to conflicts.

Effects of Aggression

For the victim, the effects of violence go far beyond physical injury or loss. The perpetrator of violence is also affected, sometimes in ways that make further aggression more likely.

Effects on the Victim. Victims of violent aggression, who are assaulted, beaten, raped, or robbed, experience pain beyond their obvious physical wounds (Bard & Sangrey, 1979). Victims feel violated, ashamed, and unable to trust others or to feel safe. Physical wounds may heal and insurance may help with financial losses, but emotional trauma cannot be so easily remedied. Many crime victims feel that for them, life will never be the same. Feelings of victimization are frequently compounded by the criminal justice system, which has sometimes failed to treat crime victims with respect, compassion, and sympathy (President's Task Force, 1982; Kelly, 1990). Victims frequently feel that others blame them for their own victimization, and they may even blame themselves. Psychological treatment for crime victims often involves professional counseling, combined with social support from others who have shared similar experiences (Siegel, 1983).

In fact others often do blame victims, for reasons described in Chapter 10, pages 429 to 430.

Effects on the Aggressor. Aggression also hurts the aggressor. First, committing one aggressive act makes another one more likely (Geen & Quanty, 1977), and repeated aggressive acts produce aggressive personalities. This finding contradicts Sigmund Freud's "catharsis" hypothesis, which presumed that aggression releases pressure built up by an inner drive. If the catharsis hypothesis were correct, an aggressive act that "blows off steam" would make further aggression less likely. This is not the case. Aggressive children, especially boys, tend to become aggressive adults, with more criminal convictions, drunk-driving convictions, traffic violations, and higher self-reports of aggression than their peers (Huesmann and others, 1987).

Aggression hurts the aggressor in a second way. Individuals who were more aggressive as children also have lower levels of intellectual achievement at age 30 (Huesmann and others, 1987). Researchers have concluded that childhood aggressiveness may reduce both the opportunity and the ability to learn. They reason that teachers and classmates may avoid these children and that they may be frequently suspended from school. The negative effects of consistent aggressive behavior in childhood, then, can last for decades (Moskowitz & Schwartzman, 1989).

Third, aggression can be detrimental even to physical health. Anger and hostility—the constant companions of aggressive behavior—increase the risk of major health problems, including coronary heart disease (Dembroski & Costa, 1987). And, finally, just as observing violence gradually desensitizes television viewers, continual violence also desensitizes its perpetrators. Serial murderers like Ted Bundy and Jeffrey Dahmer reportedly became less and less disturbed by their killings. The gang members who are unmoved by accidental killings of innocent bystanders, the torturers and executioners who are immune to their victims' suffering, and the carjackers who can throw an infant in a car seat from a speeding vehicle all demonstrate the frightening power of violence to dull the most human responses to need, pain, and death.

Reducing Aggression in Society

Aggression may be reduced when people think critically, teach and activate norms against aggression, minimize cues for aggression and the effects of media violence, and learn to identify with others instead of distancing and dehumanizing them.

What can be done to stop the rising flood of violence? Let's start with what we know. Certain events seem to provoke and escalate aggression. Some examples are interpreting accidents as provocations, ignoring the long-term consequences of violence for its short-term rewards, and failing to reflect on norms that restrain aggression. Our very ability to make this list offers some hope: our knowledge about the causes of aggression can now be recruited against violence.

1. *Interpret, and interpret again.* When you feel provoked, think about the other person's intentions: perhaps he or she did not mean the action the way you took it. Kenneth Dodge's research shows that children who have problems processing social cues display a bias in their reactions to ambiguous harmful actions—they tend to automatically react to them as intentionally hostile and, as a result, they act more aggressively in retaliation. But while their immediate reactions display this bias, their more considered reactions do not (Dodge & Newman, 1981). We can all learn from this finding. When a situation looks like a cause for angry retaliation or an opportunity for advantage through violence, we should try to see it in a different light before we respond.

2. *Teach norms against aggression.* By explicit teaching and personal example, anyone can develop norms against hurting others. Many of the norms and practices that encourage altruism are incompatible with aggression. Thus, teaching and modeling the norms of social responsibility, justice, and protection of the weak, young, old, and sick can help to reduce aggressive behavior. Demonstrations that a society means what it says may be even more impressive. Swedish toy manufacturers recently decided to discontinue the production of war toys, arguing that playing at war only teaches children to solve problems through aggression.

3. *Promote identification with others.* Aggression is easiest when victims are distanced and dehumanized. For example, portrayals of aggression against women, whether sexually explicit or not, dehumanize women and

increase the probability of their victimization (Linz and others, 1987; Donnerstein and others, 1987). It is tempting to place one's enemies outside the realm of human sympathy, eliminating normative and moral restraints against violence. To avoid this temptation we need to intentionally reflect on their humanity and thus on the things they share with us. Similarity is a barrier to violence.

This may seem to be a lofty ideal, but research suggests that it really is possible. Norma Feshbach and Seymour Feshbach (1982) trained elementary-school children to put themselves in other children's shoes, to recognize others' feelings, and to try to share their emotions. Compared with children in control groups, the children who engaged in this empathy training were much less aggressive in everyday playground activities. Empathy is fellow feeling, and fellow feeling is incompatible with aggression (Miller & Eisenberg, 1988).

4. *Minimize cues for aggression.* Some cues activate aggressive thoughts and feelings. We live in a society that believes that the ready availability of weapons deters violence, but the evidence suggests just the opposite. One study showed, for example, that motorists stopped by police officers acted more aggressively when the officers carried a holstered pistol than when they did not (Boyanowsky & Griffiths, 1982). The evidence suggests that when firearms are unavailable, violence not only is less deadly but also less likely. When Jamaica implemented strict gun control and censored gun scenes from television and movies beginning in 1974, robbery and shooting rates dropped dramatically (Diener & Crandall, 1979). When Washington, D.C., passed a handgun-control law, the numbers of homicides and suicides involving guns decreased substantially. Apparently those who are inclined to murder do not simply pick up a knife or a lead pipe if no gun is handy. The nation's capital experienced no offsetting increase in other methods of murder or suicide (Loftin and others, 1991).

5. *Limit the effects of media violence.* The effects of media violence on viewer aggression pose an obvious question: what should be done about it? In the United States, broadcasters are constitutionally protected from government censorship. Of course, broadcasters want an audience, and audience feedback can make or break a show. There may always be some demand for violent programming, but research indicates that viewer education can help limit its effects.

As part of a three-year longitudinal study in the United States, Ronald Huesmann and others (1983) randomly selected two groups of children, both of whom watched a lot of violent television. One group received no special treatment; the other group was given special training intended to limit the effects of viewing violent programs. Over a period of six to eight weeks, children receiving the training were encouraged to meet in small groups and discuss how unrealistic TV violence was, and how the TV characters could have solved their problems without violence. The discussions encouraged the formation of group norms favoring nonviolent solutions to interpersonal conflicts. In addition to their group meetings, the children were asked to write a short essay on one of two topics: "How television is not like real life" or "Is it bad for a kid to watch too much television?" They then observed themselves and their classmates reading their essays on videotape.

Dissonance reduction also contributed to the effects of this treatment, as we described in Chapter 8, page 328.

The children in the training group showed a reduced level of aggression, as compared with that found in the control group. Moreover, in follow-up observations the children's aggression was found to be less strongly related to their viewing of TV violence, suggesting that the training successfully broke the causal connection between viewing habits and aggressive behavior. Could similar programs be used more broadly to inoculate viewers against the negative effects of violent models?

6. *Think critically.* Take the time to think the situation through one more time. Many abuse prevention agencies recommend an age-old remedy to reduce violence: Stop and count to ten. This brief time-out can cool hot emotions and let personal standards and normative prohibitions against violence come back to mind. Careful consideration of the situation will probably reveal better solutions than senseless violence. We would all benefit from refusing to let emotion or alcohol interfere with thinking the situation through before we act.

Concluding Comments

We framed this chapter around the idea that many of the same factors lead us to help or hurt others. Examine Table 12.1 to see some of the parallels for yourself.

Finally, let us return to the moral issues that become so salient when one reflects on Anna Siniate or the teenage gunman described in the opening pages of this chapter. The big moral questions are easy to spot when we deal with altruism and aggression, but the behaviors we have been considering here are not unique in having strong moral implications. Almost all social behavior involves matters of right and wrong, including how people handle conflicts in close relationships (Chapter 11), whether they obey or disobey destructive authorities (Chapter 10), whether they stand up for their views or suppress doubts and go along with a majority in a case of "groupthink" (Chapter 9), and many other areas. At the heart of all these different behaviors lie the issues of responsibility and choice.

Like other behaviors, helping and hurting take many forms and are open to multiple interpretations. Most people might agree that aggression in self-defense is acceptable, for example, and that helping someone sometimes preserves their dependence on the helper over the long term. Yet the research discussed in this and other chapters teaches us that whenever we feel justified in taking some action, we would do well to examine our motives

Table 12.1 Factors that influence prosocial behavior or aggression

Type of parallel	Prosocial behavior	Aggression
Underlying motives	Sometimes people help others purely for the rewards it brings them: gratitude, fame, a warm feeling, or help in return.	Sometimes aggression is purely instrumental—motivated by the benefits people believe will flow from violence or exploitation.
	People often help others because they empathize with them. Empathy can lead to helping without regard for the consequences.	Emotional aggression is based on strong feelings aroused by a provocation. Anger can lead people to ignore the potential consequences of aggression.
	Norms—like the norm of social responsibility or the norm "mind your own business"—can either encourage or discourage helping.	Norms—like the norm of standing up for one's rights or the norm "pick on someone your own size"—can either encourage or restrain aggression.
Perceptions of person and situation	Empathy depends on seeing the victim's plight as uncontrollable and is more likely when the victim is an in-group member.	Anger depends on seeing the provocation as controllable and is more likely when the provoker is an out-group member.
	In an ambiguous helping situation, people may look to others to seek consensus about whether helping is an appropriate response. If others help, they also help.	In an ambiguous situation, people may look to others to seek consensus about whether aggression is appropriate. If others aggress, they also aggress.
How information is processed	The multiple, potentially conflicting thoughts cued by helping situations may be given much or little consideration. If strong emotions are aroused in an emergency, probably only the most salient factor(s) will be important. But when time and cognitive capacity are available, more factors can receive attention.	The multiple, potentially conflicting thoughts cued by an aggression situation may be given much or little consideration. If strong emotions are aroused by a provocation, probably only the most salient factor(s) will be important. But when time and cognitive capacity are available, more factors can receive attention.
	The time and ability to think things through can increase prosocial behavior, by increasing empathy and responsiveness to prosocial norms.	Factors that limit cognitive capacity—alcohol consumption, strong emotions or stressors—generally increase the likelihood of aggression.

one more time. Aggression in self-defense can be morally just, but the claim of self-defense is often a mask for self-interest. Failure to help others can be proper when the competing demands on our time and resources are truly more important, but "importance" often turns out to be nothing but personal convenience. In cases like these, it is important to try to consider multiple options and to avoid self-serving biases. As Chapter 9 discussed, seeking consensus from others often helps us see situations clearly. When we cannot consult with others and are unable to integrate different viewpoints—as is the case in emergency helping situations—we can still try to bring the most appropriate thoughts to mind. We sometimes need to focus actively on attitudes and norms that encourage us to do the right thing rather than let ourselves be carried along by self-interest or apathy.

Chapter 12 Themes

Construction of Reality
Our interpretations, not actual needs or provocations, influence helping and hurting.

Pervasiveness of Social Influence
Helping and hurting are affected by social norms and attitudes.

Striving for Mastery
We often treat others in ways that bring us rewards.

Seeking Connectedness
Altruistic helping often reflects common group membership.

Valuing Me and Mine
We treat in-group members with kindness, but we are more likely to aggress against the out-group.

Accessibility
The accessibility of norms can increase their impact on actions.

Superficiality Versus Depth
In-depth processing can promote long-term helping and alternatives to aggression.

And like other social behaviors, altruism and aggression are influenced by many factors that make their occurrence more or less likely. For example, people are more prone to aggress when they see other people acting aggressively. But these effects do not remove the individual's responsibility for his or her own actions. To say that the presence of models in violent films can excuse acts of street violence is to devalue the many young men and women who live in equally desperate conditions, witness the same models, yet do not act aggressively. Each of us can choose how we act, and each of us is responsible for our actions.

It is in this sense that social behavior always bears witness to our priorities. Anna Siniate empathized with the Jews of Vilna and believed she ought to help them. Many others no doubt felt the same. But unlike most others, Anna put that feeling above considerations of personal convenience and safety and actually translated her good intentions into action. The young gunman's actions also were motivated by his priorities. He desired material goods and was enraged at those who showed him disrespect. Many people have felt the same. But he put those desires above the social norms that restrain most of us from violent aggression.

Summary

Helping, Hurting, and Human Nature A person's intention to help or to hurt someone else defines an act as **prosocial behavior** or as **aggression.** Both helping and hurting can be done for their own sake or to further some other goal. **Altruism** is behavior intended to help someone else without the prospect of personal rewards for the helper.

Humans have evolved the capacity to act prosocially or aggressively. But this does not mean that either type of behavior is inevitable. Like other social behaviors, prosocial and aggressive behaviors depend on perceptions and interpretations of other people and situations and on accessible desires and norms.

Helping Others Helping is influenced by multiple factors including attitudes (desires to help or not) and norms (feelings of obligation to help or not). These factors are influenced first by perceptions of the victim's need, deservingness, and similarity to the potential helper. People are more likely to help similar others and those they see as deserving; they do so because they believe these individuals are not responsible for their own need.

Help may be motivated by perceived rewards or deterred by perceived costs or risks. These rewards and costs can be emotional: people sometimes help as a way of alleviating their own distress over the victim's suffering.

According to the **negative-state relief model,** this is the reason behind even seemingly altruistic helping. But according to the **empathy-altruism model,** people can be motivated by a feeling of empathy to relieve a victim's need, regardless of personal rewards and costs.

People sometimes help because social norms, their own standards, or others' behaviors cause them to feel they should help. **Social learning theory** emphasizes the impact of models on our own behavior. Not all norms promote helping, however, and the presence of other potential helpers sometimes leads to **diffusion of responsibility,** diminishing normative pressures to help.

When our desires and norms conflict, we may consider the various factors superficially or think them through extensively before we act. Emotions can play a role in this process, for strong emotion disrupts extensive processing. When helping is a considered decision it can result in a long-term commitment.

A person who receives help may perceive it as a positive act of caring or as a negative threat to self-esteem. If people cannot reciprocate, they may resent the unequal power relationship between helper and helped.

Helping in society can be increased by making needs clear, fostering a helpful self-concept in others, promoting identification and empathy, teaching and activating helping norms, and focusing responsibility rather than diffusing it.

Aggression Instrumental aggression is triggered by potential rewards and is suppressed by perceived costs or risks. Sometimes, however, perceived provocation produces anger, which can set off emotional aggression regardless of the consequences.

Social norms may promote or restrain aggression. They can be activated by the behavior of models witnessed in person or in the media. Norms that limit aggression apply with special force to aggression against similar others or in-group members.

Aggression may result from either superficial or extensive thought. Powerful cues such as weapons often increase aggression spontaneously, whereas thinking carefully can reduce aggression. Many factors interfere with the ability to process information thoroughly, usually increasing the likelihood of aggression.

For the victim, the effects of violence go far beyond physical injury or loss. The perpetrator of violence is also affected, sometimes in ways that make further aggression more likely.

Aggression may be reduced when people think critically, teach and activate norms against aggression, minimize cues for aggression and the effects of media violence, and learn to identify with others instead of distancing and dehumanizing them.

Chapter 12 Overview

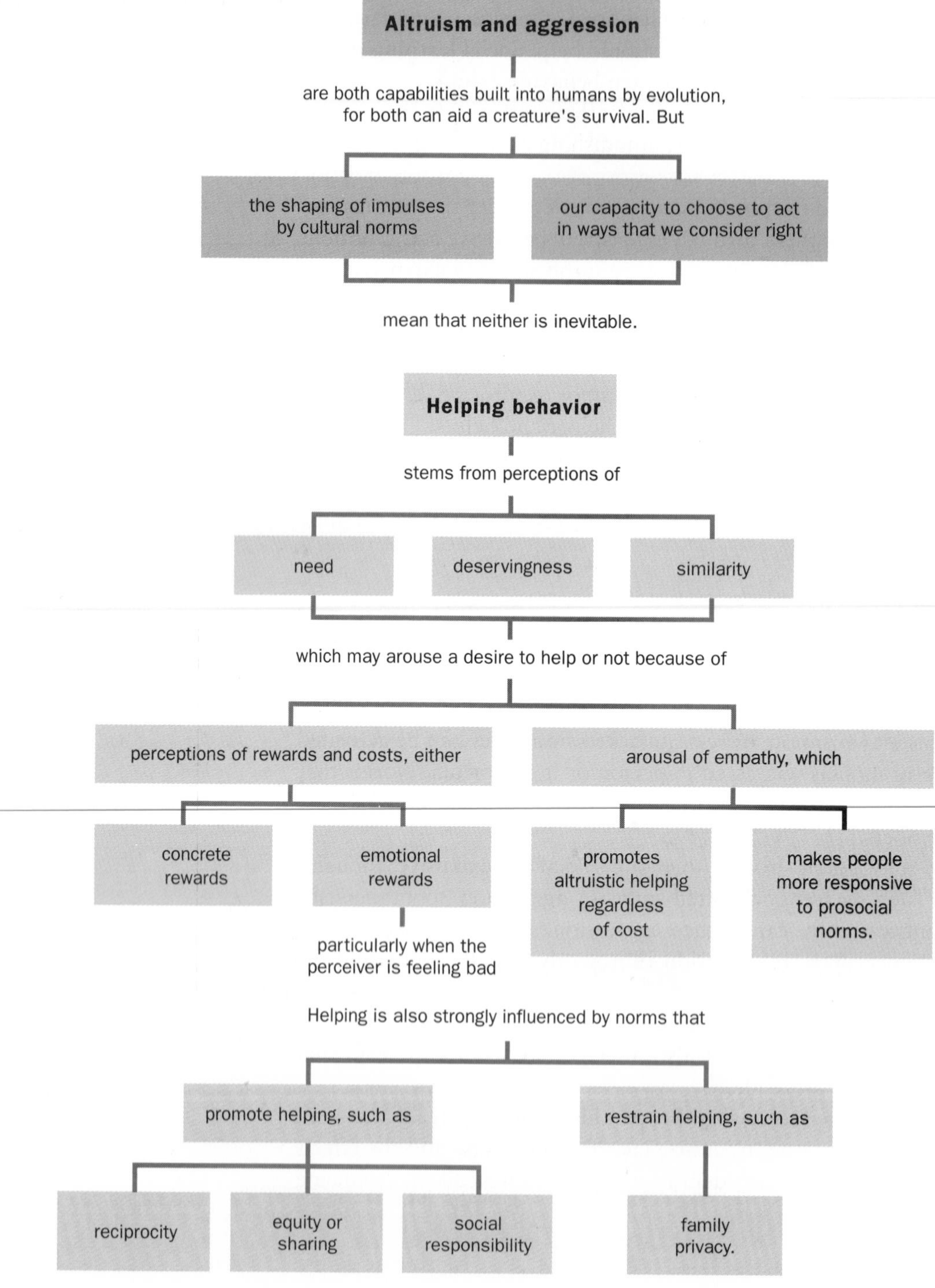

Altruism and aggression
are both capabilities built into humans by evolution, for both can aid a creature's survival. But
the shaping of impulses by cultural norms
our capacity to choose to act in ways that we consider right
mean that neither is inevitable.
Helping behavior
stems from perceptions of
need
deservingness
similarity
which may arouse a desire to help or not because of
perceptions of rewards and costs, either
arousal of empathy, which
concrete rewards
emotional rewards
promotes altruistic helping regardless of cost
makes people more responsive to prosocial norms.
particularly when the perceiver is feeling bad
Helping is also strongly influenced by norms that
promote helping, such as
restrain helping, such as
reciprocity
equity or sharing
social responsibility
family privacy.

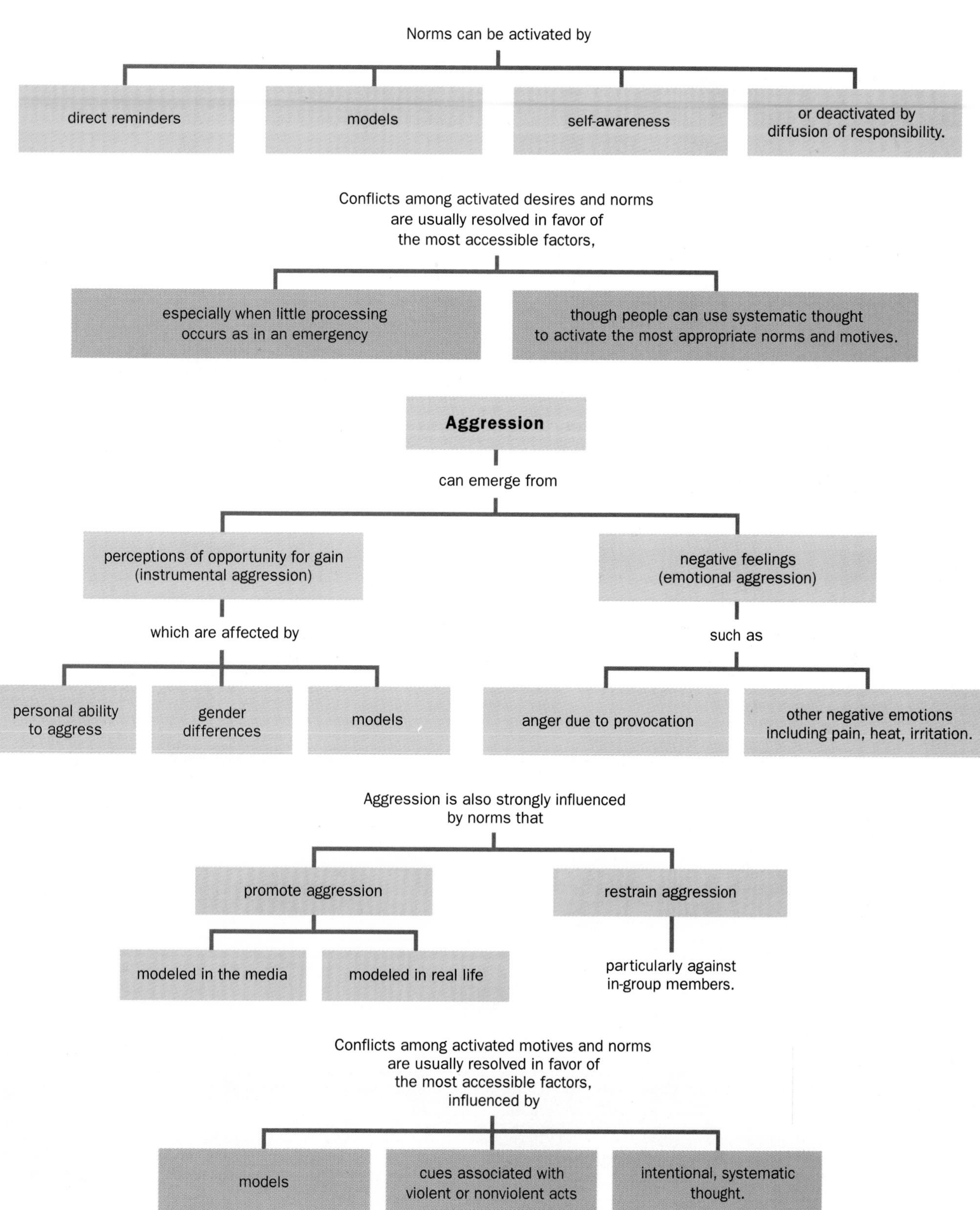

Norms can be activated by
direct reminders
models
self-awareness
or deactivated by diffusion of responsibility.
Conflicts among activated desires and norms are usually resolved in favor of the most accessible factors,
especially when little processing occurs as in an emergency
though people can use systematic thought to activate the most appropriate norms and motives.
Aggression
can emerge from
perceptions of opportunity for gain (instrumental aggression)
negative feelings (emotional aggression)
which are affected by
personal ability to aggress
gender differences
models
such as
anger due to provocation
other negative emotions including pain, heat, irritation.
Aggression is also strongly influenced by norms that
promote aggression
restrain aggression
modeled in the media
modeled in real life
particularly against in-group members.
Conflicts among activated motives and norms are usually resolved in favor of the most accessible factors, influenced by
models
cues associated with violent or nonviolent acts
intentional, systematic thought.

13

Interaction and Interdependence

The name *Harley-Davidson* was synonymous with *motorcycle* in the United States until high-quality, low-priced Japanese bikes suddenly flooded the market in the late 1970s, catching the U.S. company off guard. Harley-Davidson at that time was a poorly run organization. Its management and employees were often at odds, its product quality was low, and its workers were unmotivated. These problems were reflected in its sales, which soon dropped to only 4 percent of the U.S. market.

The challenges Harley-Davidson faced two decades ago are now widespread throughout the airline, trucking, banking, automobile, electronics, and heavy manufacturing industries. As costs escalate and competition stiffens, industries are realizing that achieving the dual goals of high performance and a motivated and enthusiastic work force are more important than ever before.

These critical issues of efficiency and morale are not confined to the workplace, however. They characterize any group of people who interact for some shared purpose and rely on one another to accomplish common goals. Our goal in this chapter is to understand the consequences of interaction and interdependence for behaviors, especially in group settings. To some extent, this topic has been woven throughout the earlier chapters. In Chapter 9, for example, we looked at the way juries and other groups make decisions. But decision making is often only a first step. Like the people at Harley-Davidson, most groups *act* on their decisions as they win or lose games, manufacture products, regulate work flow through an office, build roads, fight fires, undertake rescues, and treat patients. When people put their heads together—and their muscle and drive—their individual efforts are sometimes multiplied in astonishing ways, and the group can achieve goals far beyond the reach of any one member. The NASA group that put a man on the moon, the Apple Computer, Inc., team that marketed the first successful personal computer, and the legions of volunteers who staff the United Way are just a few examples of the remarkable achievements of group action. Of course, as Harley-Davidson's woes make clear, if a group is

The pervasiveness of interdependence These urban gardeners seem to be working independently on their plots, but such an endeavor involves considerable interdependence. Gardeners rely on one another not only to develop the resource, but also to deal with the weeds that spread from plot to plot, and even to maximize each small garden's yield. Similar kinds of interdependence mark most human tasks.

poorly organized or some of its members slack off, the efforts of hard-working members can be wasted.

Because the outcomes of group action are often strikingly different from the inputs of individual members—and sometimes very different from what is desired and intended—early theorists concluded that the behavior of a group has almost nothing to do with the individual characteristics of its members (Durkheim, 1898; LeBon, 1908). Rather, they argued, people lose their individuality in a group and, swept uncontrollably along by the crowd, they have no mind of their own. Although contemporary social scientists do not agree that individuals give up their autonomy to the group, they do recognize that being part of a group affects individual behavior in distinctive and sometimes dramatic ways. We saw in several earlier chapters that membership in groups defined by shared, socially significant features can influence people's thoughts, feelings, and behavior. The effects are even greater when people not only share a group identification but also interact with each other and are *interdependent*—relying on other members' actions as well as their own for material and social rewards.

Groups differ in the degree of interaction and interdependence they share. At one extreme is the **collective,** a number of people who, like passengers on an airplane, are physically in the same place but only minimally interdependent. At the other end of the continuum are *face-to-face groups* like the decision-making groups we discussed in Chapter 9. Members of face-to-face groups not only share socially relevant features but also interact with and rely on each other to achieve specific goals. Like the NASA and Apple teams, they share values and coordinate their efforts to get things done. Their attempts to reach their goals are marked by intense communication and extensive interaction. The group's success often depends on just how well its leaders and members can manage the problems of interdependence. Indeed, the eventual rebuilding and success of Harley-Davidson was due in large part to its managers' ability to improve *both* production efficiency and worker satisfaction simultaneously (Willis, 1986).

Although interdependence is a defining characteristic of face-to-face groups, it is not exclusive to them. Members of larger groups can also be dependent on one another. The requirements of our continuing survival on planet Earth make all humans mutually interdependent. Each of us is affected when someone—perhaps halfway across the globe—decides to destroy a rain forest or dump nuclear waste in the ocean. This chapter concludes with a discussion of the problems that groups of *any* size face when interdependence pits individual interests against long-term group interests. As you will see, many of the same principles that influence people's behavior in face-to-face groups apply to interdependence on a larger scale, and the same factors that help small groups work better may help solve global social dilemmas.

collective A number of people who are in the same place but have minimal direct interaction and minimal interdependence.

Social Facilitation: The Effects of Minimal Interdependence

Imagine that as you jog along your usual route, you catch up with another jogger who runs alongside you for a couple of blocks. You greet each other with a friendly nod and perhaps check out each other's brand of running shoe, but otherwise you have no contact before you go your separate ways. A block later, you pass by a half-dozen people gathered on a front porch, and they look up and follow your progress down the street. Although your contact with your fellow jogger and your momentary audience is minimal, their mere presence can influence your behavior in quite predictable ways.

Social Facilitation: Improvement and Impairment

> *The mere presence of others can produce arousal, either because they are highly evaluative or because they are distracting. Arousal improves performance of easy, well-learned behaviors, which helps with some tasks but hinders others.*

If you are like most people, your running time in the presence of others will be slightly faster than when you are alone (Worringham & Messick, 1983). This facilitating effect of other people on individual performance may seem familiar. In our Chapter 1 discussion of the history of social psychology, we described Norman Triplett's (1898) observation that children winding line onto fishing reels worked more quickly when in the presence of others than

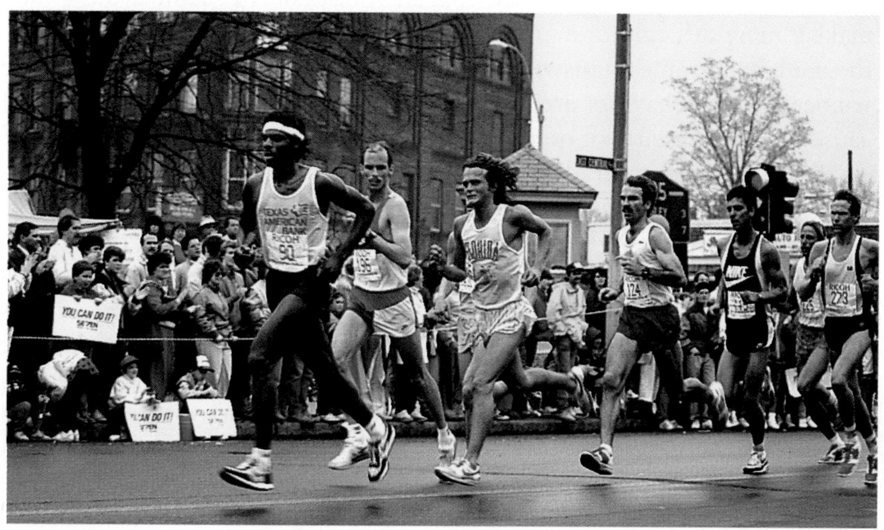

Presence and performance Perhaps the marathoner checking out the competition is aware of the dramatic effects of the presence of others. When the responses necessary for success are well-learned and highly accessible, others' presence can trigger superior performance.

when they were alone. Other research confirms the idea that the presence of others improves performance on a variety of simple tasks, from running to solving easy arithmetic problems (Guerin, 1986).

Is having others around always helpful? You may answer no if you can remember standing in the glare of the footlights desperately trying to remember your lines or stumbling through a complicated cheerleading routine before a crowd. And your answer would be correct, for research also shows that the presence of others can interfere with performance. On complicated and difficult tasks—from mazes to math problems to a newly learned tennis serve—our performance declines when others are present (Guerin, 1986; Bond & Titus, 1983). How can the presence of others both help and hurt performance?

Explaining Social Facilitation. In 1965, Robert Zajonc proposed an explanation of these apparently contradictory reactions to the presence of others. According to Zajonc, the **social facilitation** effect occurs because the presence of others increases an individual's level of arousal, which in turn makes some behaviors easier and others more difficult. Arousal facilitates the performance of behaviors that are very accessible because they are simple, well-learned, and highly practiced (often termed *dominant responses*) and it inhibits the performance of behaviors that are complex or new (*nondominant responses*). Accessibility should be a familiar concept by now. You may recall that accessible thoughts and feelings are more likely to come to mind than are less accessible ones; similarly, accessible behaviors are more likely to be performed than are less accessible ones. Thus, the arousal caused by an audience may help a jogger to run faster, an entrant in a math contest to ace the easy problems, and a professional performer like Bonnie Raitt to shine in her well-learned concert routines. That same arousal may make it more difficult for a novice skier to complete a difficult course, or for the math contestant to answer the tough final questions that will select the winner. When behaviors are complicated or not well learned, the arousal caused by the presence of others will detract from their performance.

Because of the contradictory effects of arousal, the presence of an audience can even affect two people in quite opposite ways when they are performing the same task. For example, expert pool players—for whom good shots are highly accessible responses—performed better when an interested audience was close by than when they thought no one was watching. In contrast, poor players—for whom miscues were most accessible—succeeded on fewer shots when others watched (Michaels and others, 1982). Zajonc's idea that other people cause arousal, and that arousal improves simple tasks but interferes with difficult tasks, makes sense of these findings and has been confirmed by most subsequent research (Guerin, 1986; Bond & Titus, 1983).

social facilitation The finding that in the presence of others highly accessible responses become more likely and less accessible responses become less likely.

Of course, these findings leave one question unanswered: why does the presence of others lead to arousal? Zajonc (1965) believed that humans and other animals have an innate tendency to be aroused by other members of their species. But, why should they arouse us? Subsequent research points to two underlying causes: evaluation apprehension and distraction-conflict (Geen, 1991).

Evaluation Apprehension. Most of the time, we want other people to value, include, and like us. In fact, our sense of self-esteem depends as much on what others think of us as on what we think of ourselves. For these reasons, we may worry about whether onlookers are judging us in some way. As you jog past people, for example, you may suddenly be concerned about whether you look out of shape, and you may pull in your stomach and step up your pace. Recent research has confirmed that the presence of others who can judge us produces *evaluation apprehension* (Rosenberg, 1969) and that this apprehension changes our performance in the way predicted by social facilitation theory. One study, for example, demonstrated that apprehension can improve performance on simple aspects of a task and hinder it on complex aspects of the same task. Scott Bartis and his colleagues (1988) asked groups of subjects to generate a variety of uses for a knife. Some subjects were given the simple task of coming up with as many uses as possible. Others had the relatively challenging task of being as creative as possible. In each group, some subjects believed the experimenter would evaluate their individual performance and others knew their responses would go into a common pool (where they could not be individually evaluated). As Figure 13.1 illustrates, the possibility of evaluation increased output on the simple task, and it decreased output on the intellectually more difficult task.

Figure 13.1 Effects of evaluation apprehension on simple and complex aspects of a task

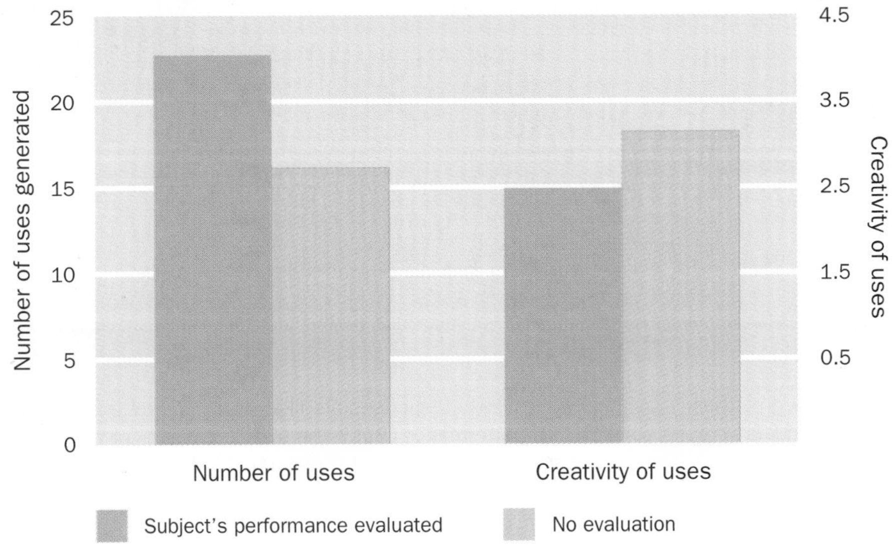

Some subjects (purple bars) knew their individual task performance would be evaluated by the experimenter, while others (tan bars) did not expect individual evaluations. When the task was fairly simple—generating as many suggestions as possible for ways to use a knife—evaluation improved performance, as shown by the bars on the left. However, when subjects were given a much harder task—being as creative as possible in devising uses for the knife—evaluation had the opposite effect; it decreased their creativity (see scale on the right). (Data from Bartis and others, 1988.)

No wonder, then, that if you expect to succeed at a task (because it is easy, or it involves an accessible response, or you have succeeded at this task in the past), you will do better when you are observed, while the opposite is true if you expect to fail (Sanna & Shotland, 1990). Other researchers have provided evidence that evaluation, not mere presence, is the critical factor that affects behavior. For example, the presence of actively supportive, nonevaluative observers—humans or even pets—neither provokes arousal nor interferes with performance (Allen and others, 1991).

Distraction-Conflict. The presence of others can also affect our performance by creating *distraction*—by causing us to think about others, to react to them, or to monitor what they are doing, thereby deflecting attention from the task at hand (Guerin, 1986; Baron, 1986). Researchers in one study, for example, had a person sit behind the subject in a location in which he or she could not possibly monitor the subject's performance. The presence of this person nevertheless improved the subject's performance on easy tasks and interfered with it on difficult ones (Schmitt and others, 1986). Such effects have also been found in nonhuman species. For example, centipedes run faster down a glass tube when other centipedes are placed in neighboring tubes than when the additional tubes are empty (Hosey and others, 1985). The centipedes presumably are not concerned about evaluation by the other centipedes. The effect seems to stem from distraction by the presence of others, affecting task performances.

Figure 13.2 The role of arousal in social facilitation

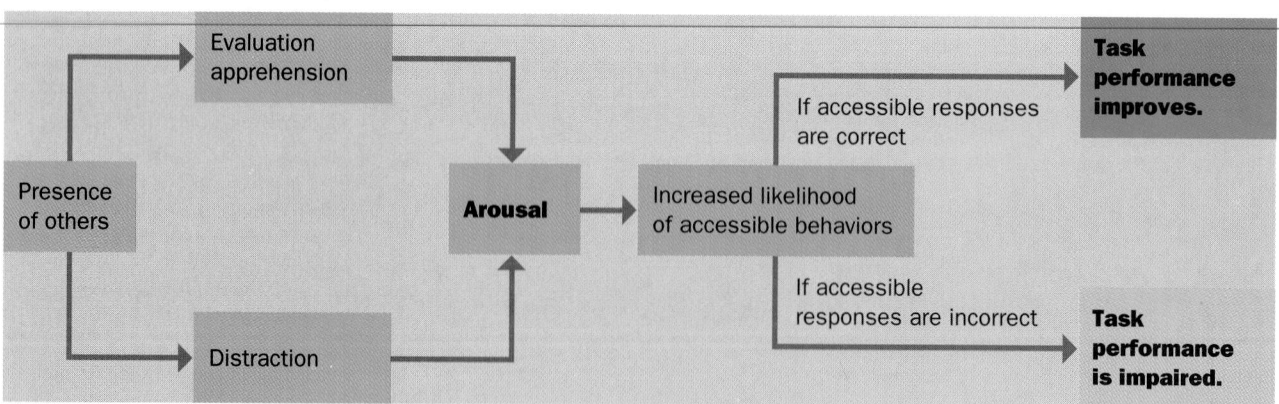

The presence of others can produce arousal, through either evaluation apprehension or simple distraction. Arousal increases the likelihood that people will perform the most accessible actions. With a simple or well-practiced task, highly accessible responses are likely to be correct and arousal improves performance. But if the task is complex or novel, accessible responses will not help much and arousal will impair task performance.

It is easy to understand why distraction could interfere with difficult tasks, but why would it improve performance on simple tasks? The answer seems to be that as our impulses to do two different things at once—concentrating on the task and reacting to others—start to conflict with each other, we become agitated and aroused (Geen, 1991). This arousal, like that caused by evaluation apprehension, can then improve performance on simple tasks and interfere with it on difficult ones. Figure 13.2 shows how the presence of others—even those with whom we do not interact—can make us worry about evaluation or can distract us.

Everyone has to perform in the presence of others from time to time—perhaps delivering an oral report in class or demonstrating a product to a new client. One way to avoid the disruptive effects of an audience is to make sure that your accessible responses—the ones most likely to be activated by arousal—are those that help you to perform the task. You can make the appropriate responses accessible by repeatedly practicing the task (Zajonc & Sales, 1966), and then arousal will work for you. Practice has the additional benefit of giving you self-confidence, so that you will not fear the audience's evaluation (Sanna & Shotland, 1990). It can also make your performance less vulnerable to distraction. Just as you can bike the familiar route from school to home without your other thoughts getting in the way, practiced responses run from start to finish and resist interference.

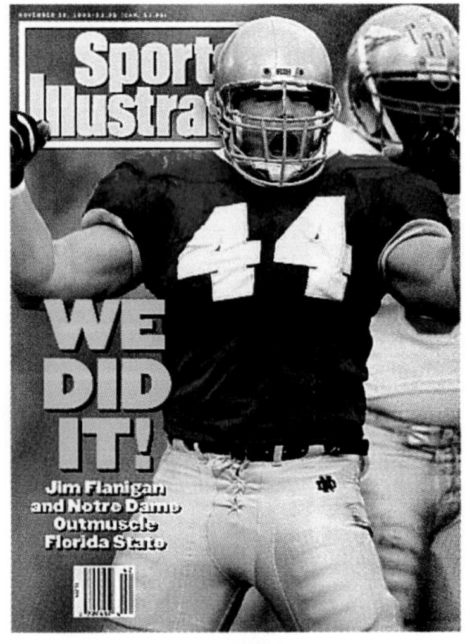

It's tough at the top Superstitious sports fans have named it the SI jinx: almost as soon as *Sports Illustrated* touts a Number 1 team with a cover story, the team is unceremoniously defeated. With a victory over supposedly invincible Florida State and an unbeaten record, Notre Dame gained Number 1 ranking, only to be beaten 41–39 by Boston College one week later. In fact, social psychological processes may contribute to the so-called jinx. High expectations from passionately partisan fans can sometimes cause a team to perform poorly under pressure.

Choking Under Pressure: Social Facilitation in the Sports Arena. In the final seconds of the men's basketball championship game in the 1993 National Collegiate Athletic Association tournament, University of Michigan and University of North Carolina were locked in a close battle. The crowd in the packed arena was on its feet and the noise was ear shattering. When his team suddenly had difficulty moving the ball up the court, the star Michigan player did what years of coaching, experience, and practice had made the accessible response in such a situation: he called for a time-out. Unfortunately, his team had used up all their allotted time-outs, and Michigan was assessed a technical penalty from which it never recovered.

The combined effects of evaluation apprehension and distraction are perhaps most powerful in the sports arena, where athletes must perform at their very best in front of demanding and noisy audiences. Social psychologists Roy Baumeister and Carolin Showers (1986) have studied these effects and have found that sports teams often perform more poorly in crucial championship games played at home than in noncrucial games. Why does the home court advantage turn into the championship choke? Baumeister and Showers found that one important reason is the vocal presence of the highly evaluative crowd of partisan fans. Distracted from their normal game and worried about disappointing their fans, athletes fall short of the peak performances required by championship games. Ironically, the crowd's high expectations sometimes contribute to a sad and sudden end to their team's championship dreams.

Crowding: The Presence of Lots of Others

Crowding is another source of arousal that can improve performance on easy tasks and disrupt performance on difficult ones. However, the effects of crowding depend on people's interpretation of the situation and on their sense of control.

Being packed into a rush-hour subway car or into a standing-room-only auditorium is a forcible reminder of how strongly—and negatively—we can be affected by the presence of other people. Researchers studying the effects of crowding in college dormitories found that when three students are assigned to a room designed for two, both their sense of contentment and their grades decline (Karlin and others, 1979). Crowding can even be life threatening: prisoners confined in crowded jail cells have higher death rates than those in more spacious facilities (McCain and others, 1980).

As you might have guessed, crowding has these negative effects because being crowded, like having an audience, is arousing. The arousal occurs for the same reasons: crowds create many opportunities for evaluation and distraction. One study found, for example, that ten strangers who were crammed into an 8-by-12-foot room had higher blood pressure and greater increases in other physiological indicators of arousal than did other subjects occupying a larger room (Evans, 1979). Like the arousal produced by an audience, arousal induced by crowding can energize effort, thereby improving performance on simple tasks and impairing performance on complex tasks (Hillery & Fugita, 1975; Paulus and others, 1976).

Crowding and the Urban Environment. Most social behavior—such as cooperating with others, helping those in need, and resolving conflicts—is complex. Since crowds can interfere with the performance of complex tasks, many people have suggested that living in a crowded city may disrupt social behavior. Crowding is a popular scapegoat for society's ills. It has been blamed for the superficial and transitory relationships of modern life and for deviant behavior, mental illness, and poor physical health (Simmel, 1950). Although social life undoubtedly is affected by the size and density of community populations, the evidence for crowding's negative role is far from conclusive. Social beings are very adaptable. Cognitive and social factors can help us buffer the arousal caused by crowding and thus limit its debilitating effects.

These beneficial effects of perceived control should not surprise you, given our discussion in Chapter 4, pages 148 to 150, of the many ways a sense of control acts as a buffer against stressful events.

The sense of psychological control seems to be a key factor in counteracting the negative effects of crowding. In one study of people working under crowded conditions, some subjects were given an "escape button" to press if they needed to leave the situation (Sherrod, 1974). Although the subjects never actually pressed the button, knowing they could control their situation helped these subjects perform better than those who had no control. Another study packed people into an elevator to find out who would feel the least stressed. Not surprisingly, that person was usually the individid-

Cultures define crowding Although research findings have long suggested that crowding triggers antisocial and unhealthful behavior, cross-cultural research indicates that responses to crowding depend on a culture's norms regarding appropriate behavior. How would you react to the extreme crowding experienced by these Tokyo commuters, who literally have to be pushed into the trains by attendants?

ual standing by the control panel (Rodin and others, 1978). Similarly, a study in India found that residents in crowded housing who saw themselves as having control over their environment fared better than others (Ruback & Pandey, 1991). The presence of others—especially crowds of others—arouses us, but our behavior depends on how we interpret that arousal, and particularly on whether their presence diminishes our feelings of control.

Performance in Face-to-Face Groups: Maximizing Interdependence

If the minimal influence of other members of a collective can influence our behavior, consider how much more potent is the effect of a face-to-face group. Members of such groups—families, flight crews, dance troupes, PTA groups, rock and roll bands, federal commissions, and others—are highly interdependent. They are **socially interdependent** because they rely on one another for feelings of connectedness and positive emotional outcomes, such as respect, caring, and positive social identity. They are **task interdependent** because their mastery of material outcomes depends on working together to perform some collective task—a successful flight, the negotiation of teachers' contracts, or the design of a new health-care plan. Large or small, all face-to-face groups are characterized by some combination of social and task interdependence (Forsyth, 1990).

All face-to-face groups also have goals and purposes (Forsyth, 1990). For businesses, the group goal is profit; for university faculties, it is the production of new knowledge and well-rounded graduates; for boards of directors, it is a well-administered organization. Depending on their goals, groups demand different amounts of social or task interdependence. Social interdependence is particularly important to some groups, like families and close friends, which value their members just because they are members. Of course, these groups also are frequently task interdependent, as when they

social interdependence Reliance on other members of the group for feelings of connectedness, social and emotional rewards, and a positive social identity.

task interdependence Reliance on other members of a group for mastery of material outcomes that arise from the group's task.

care for the yard, balance the budget, or organize vacations. Other groups, such as those found in most work settings, often exist for a specific purpose, so task interdependence is their defining feature. But as we all know, roles, status hierarchies, and friendships are inevitable in work settings, which means that work groups are also socially interdependent.

Indeed, every group faces the challenge of successfully managing both forms of interdependence in the process of achieving high levels of productivity and positive relationships with other group members. Managing these two forms of interdependence is a challenge because they sometimes conflict. Fostering task interdependence, for example, can interfere with feeling good about being in the group, as when parents prohibit horseplay in an effort to keep children focused on their share of Saturday house cleaning. Social interdependence can similarly detract from task performance if office workers socialize so much that work falls behind schedule. To understand how such problems arise and how they can be solved, we need to look at what happens as groups come together and work toward their goals. Although our examples will be work groups, the same processes operate in all groups acting together to produce something.

Stages of Group Development: Coming Together, Falling Apart

Face-to-face groups usually go through different stages of formation, conflict, development, performance, and dissolution as they try to develop an identity and reach their goals.

In 1981, the Ashland Corporation, a manufacturer of air conditioners, convened a special task group. The team, composed of a team leader, "team advisers," and several production line employees, was asked to turn a huge, empty factory building into a functioning production line for a new series of compressors. The team had to select, order, and arrange for the installation of production machinery. It also was responsible for organizing and training the production-line workers in a way that maximized their efficiency and maintained extremely high quality standards. As the group began to work toward its goals over a period of months, it confronted a series of problems and challenges, which in turn influenced the group's structure and operation. These changes were not unique to the Ashland team. All groups—whether short-term, ad-hoc groups that form to solve isolated problems or long-term groups that might take years to reach their goals—go through different stages of development (Eisenstat, 1990; Tuckman, 1965; Moreland & Levine, 1988). Although some groups go through all five of the stages described here, many others skip some steps, return to and repeat earlier ones, or dissolve before they ever reach the later stages (Gersick, 1990).

1. *Forming.* In the initial stage of group development, members try to get to know each other, to find out what makes the group tick, and to see if they will fit in. If successful, this period of orientation enables each individual to

see the self as a member of the group and the group as part of the self. The Ashland team had several strengths in this stage: frequent interaction, social and task interdependence, a developing feeling of attraction to the group and its members, and a belief in the group's uniqueness (Moreland, 1987). Managers ensured that a sense of identity would form by giving group members time to get acquainted and by stressing the special nature of their task—a task that could not be completed without everyone's full cooperation. In a short time, individual members had made the transition to a common group identity and were referring to the group as "we."

2. *Storming.* Conflict is often evident in the second stage and disagreements can be intense and emotional (Bales and others, 1979; Tuckman, 1965). At this point, members know each other, but they have no means of resolving genuine disagreements about the problems of interdependence. For the Ashland team, one conflict centered around a new leader's peering-over-the-shoulder style of management, which team members interpreted as a lack of confidence in their competence. Group members also clashed over priorities as production workers demanded training while trainers were absorbed in other matters. This particular conflict left the trainers feeling swamped and the workers feeling neglected (Eisenstat, 1990).

Deciding on group goals and the best ways to meet them is a common source of conflict at this stage, as members with different views jockey for position and coalitions and subgroups form among people with similar interests or agendas. Conflict may die down when a majority forms and persuades the group to adopt its views. Sometimes, however, a minority dissenting opinion prevails. One person may have radical ideas that the majority initially resists but eventually adopts. In fact, many companies deliberately build in protection for "screwball" ideas, so that "storming" works to keep them on the cutting edge. In a classic case of persistent and effective dissent, a market researcher at Compaq Computer Corporation persuaded management to disregard surveys that predicted a limited market for a briefcase-size laptop computer. Many companies would not have been swayed by the dissent of a single person, but Compaq reaped big benefits because it managed conflict well and preserved minority influence (Kotkin, 1986).

Recall from Chapter 9, pages 385 to 390, that the best group decisions are made when a group considers as many dissenting and different perspectives as possible before reaching a consensus.

3. *Norming.* If the group survives the storming stage, harmony and unity usually emerge as consensus, cohesion, and a positive group identity develop. Because members have internalized the group norms, overt social influence, with its high potential for conflict, is less necessary. Most members tend to be highly satisfied with the group and to agree about the group's purpose and the power and responsibilities of individual members. The Ashland team reached this stage as the deadline for shipping the first compressors drew near and team members realized that the plant's reputation rode on meeting the deadline with high-quality products. The group's purpose was finally clear, and everyone accepted the goal. As one worker put it, "Then everyone jelled together. . . . Nobody said no, everybody said yes. . . . It was smooth, and people [were] in a good mood" (Eisenstat, 1990).

4. *Performing.* With norms established, the group moves into the performance stage. In groups in which storming produces high-quality ideas and norming results in high productivity standards (Mayo, 1933), the performance stage is characterized by smooth management and high efficiency. Members cooperate to solve problems, make decisions, and generate output. They handle disagreements productively and exert social influence to achieve group goals. At this stage of the Ashland group's development, employees who had completed their regular tasks helped their less experienced co-workers rather than taking it easy. People worked long hours and operated as a team. As one worker commented, "I surprise myself. . . . We work as one, not as separate individuals." As the initial shipments of the new compressors received extremely high ratings on quality tests, the new Ashland plant was declared a success. News that the factory could proceed to full production reinforced the team members' feeling that they had done a terrific job (Eisenstat, 1990).

5. *Adjourning.* Most groups—especially ad hoc groups put together for a specific purpose—eventually reach the end of their life span, the adjourning stage. Some, like the new-factory team at Ashland, know from the outset that their lifetime is limited. Others dissolve because they have accomplished their goals. Still others fall apart when members lose interest, move away, or flee conflict (Rusbult, 1983; Thibaut & Kelly, 1959). The dissolution of a cohesive group can be stressful for members if group identification has taken place, because loss of the group entails a change in social identity. Members lose the benefits of others' skills and contributions and the security of others' support and companionship. When cohesion and interaction are particularly intense, the psychological impact of the adjourning of a group can be similar to that of a breakup of a close relationship, leaving the same feelings of grief and loneliness. Group members can prevent some of this stress if they prepare themselves for the adjournment by reducing group

Table 13.1 Stages of group development

Stage	Major processes	Characteristics
Forming	*Orientation:* Exchange of information, task exploration, identification of similarities	Tentative, polite interactions; self-disclosure
Storming	*Conflict:* Disagreement over procedures, attempted social influence	Criticism of ideas, hostility, polarization, coalition formation
Norming	*Cohesion:* Formation of consensus, growth of cohesion and unity, establishment of roles and norms	Agreement on procedures, increased positive group identity
Performing	*Performance:* Goal-focused efforts, task orientation	Decision making, problem solving, cooperation
Adjourning	*Dissolution:* Termination of roles, completion of tasks, reduction of interdependence	Disintegration and withdrawal, emotionality, regret

Source: From *Group Dynamics* by D. R. Forsyth. Copyright © 1990 by Brooks/Cole Publishing Co. Adapted by permission.

cohesion, stressing individual independence, and searching for new groups to join (Mayadas & Glasser, 1985).

Table 13.1 summarizes these five typical stages of group development, along with the processes that characterize each stage.

Getting the Job Done: Group Performance

To achieve their performance goals, groups must maintain their motivation and avoid problems of coordination. Developing a common social identity helps to avoid such problems by promoting cohesion and conformity to group performance norms.

For most groups, performing is the crucial stage because the work of the group must be accomplished during this period. Whether the group carries through with a flawless performance or collapses into disarray will depend on the kinds of tasks it faces, the quality of the group effort, and the resources available for reaching goals and repairing damage.

Forms of Task Interdependence. According to Ivan Steiner (1972), group tasks differ in terms of the type of interdependence they require. With *additive tasks,* the potential performance of the group is approximately equal to the sum of the performances of the individual members and is generally better than any one member's performance. A tug-of-war is an additive task, as is typing in an office pool or joining others to push a stalled car out of an intersection. In additive tasks, individual effort is the key because the final outcome is roughly proportional to the number of individuals contributing and how much they give (Littlepage, 1991). But coordination is also important: one person's tugs on the rope when all the others are resting will not ensure tug-of-war victory.

In *disjunctive tasks,* a group's performance is expected to be as good as the performance of its best individual member (Laughlin and others, 1991). When one of a group of "idea people" comes up with a terrific concept for a new ad campaign and everyone else recognizes its merit, the task is disjunctive. In this case, interdependence means that the outcome will be a function of the skills and talents of the group members. Thus, education or training of individual members can improve group performance, as can the selection of members with the right mix of skills (Hackman, 1987). Coordination is important, too, because other members have to be careful not to get in the way of any individual member who can complete the task (Littlepage, 1991; Diehl & Stroebe, 1991).

Conjunctive tasks depend on every member's playing his or her part. In this case, the group's performance is only as good as the performance of its worst member. Groups of mountain climbers, relay racers, or assembly-line teams are engaged in conjunctive tasks: their slowest member determines whether and how quickly they achieve their goal. If three students agree that

Many hands make light work, or too many cooks spoil the broth? Most complex tasks require multiple forms of interdependence. Here master chefs and their assistants coordinate their actions to ensure that ingredients are combined in the right way and at the right time, that each dish has the appropriate accompaniments, and that a single table's orders are ready at the same time. In this kitchen at least, many hands ensure that the broth is not spoiled.

one will do the research for a report, a second will write it, and the third will deliver it in class, their grade will depend on how well each of them performs his or her part of the task. Coordination is very important in conjunctive tasks, so the group has to organize its members' activities. If coordination failed so that two people did the research and nobody wrote the presentation, the total task would remain undone.

Most tasks are *complex tasks,* which consist of subtasks that involve all forms of interdependence. In playing football, for example, some tasks are disjunctive (any of several players can block the opposing defensive end) whereas others are conjunctive (the quarterback must throw the pass and the receiver must catch it). Of course, the more complicated the task is, the greater the need for planning and coordination will be to ensure that members' skills and efforts are appropriately allocated. And the more complicated the task, the greater the opportunity will be for the group's performance to multiply and surpass any possible effort by a single individual. At the same time, unfortunately, putting individuals' efforts together in complicated group tasks also provides many opportunities for things to go wrong.

Gains and Losses in Group Performance. "Two heads are better than one," and that certainly is one reason so much work is performed by groups. Groups do perform many tasks better than an individual could. Groups can multiply individual effort, provide a variety of skills that no one person possesses, and work together to complete tasks in parallel, rather than serial, fashion. Perhaps each Amish farmer has all the skills necessary to build a barn alone, but when all the members of his community pool their skills, labor, and enthusiasm, barns are raised in a day or two. The advantages of group effort are also evident on many cognitive tasks. For example, groups solve puzzles more quickly than individuals do (Laughlin, 1980). And their collective memory is also better: when asked to watch a videotape portraying a police interrogation, groups of subjects offered more accurate and detailed accounts of the event than those of individuals who worked alone (Clark and others, 1990).

But if two heads are better than one, are they twice as good? Some research has evaluated the popular technique known as *brainstorming*, in which a group of people tries to generate a large number of ideas without criticizing or evaluating them, at least initially. The premise is that one person's idea, even if wild and unworkable, may be built on and improved by other group members (Osborn, 1953). The evidence indicates that brainstorming groups usually come up with fewer ideas and ideas of poorer quality than those produced by the same number of individuals working separately (Diehl & Stroebe, 1991). When people perform poorly on group tasks, the cause is often a loss of either motivation or coordination among group members.

1. *Decreased motivation: Social loafing.* Sometimes the experience of working in a group leads people to slack off—to put less effort into the task than they would if working alone. As we noted in Chapter 1, this loss of motivation, termed **social loafing,** was first studied by Max Ringelmann, a French agricultural engineer who was interested in group performance on very simple additive tasks (Kravitz & Martin, 1986). Over a hundred years later, Ringelmann's early insights have been confirmed by laboratory experiments. In the study of social loafing illustrated in Figure 13.3, for example, college students were told to clap and cheer as loudly as they could. The amount of sound generated by each student's efforts decreased as the size of the group increased. Individual efforts seem quite literally to get lost in the crowd, and the degree of loss is substantial. In this study, an individual in a group of six made less than half the noise he or she made when clapping alone.

social loafing The tendency to exert less effort on a task when an individual's efforts are an unidentifiable part of a group than when the same task is performed alone.

Figure 13.3 Social loafing: Many hands make light work

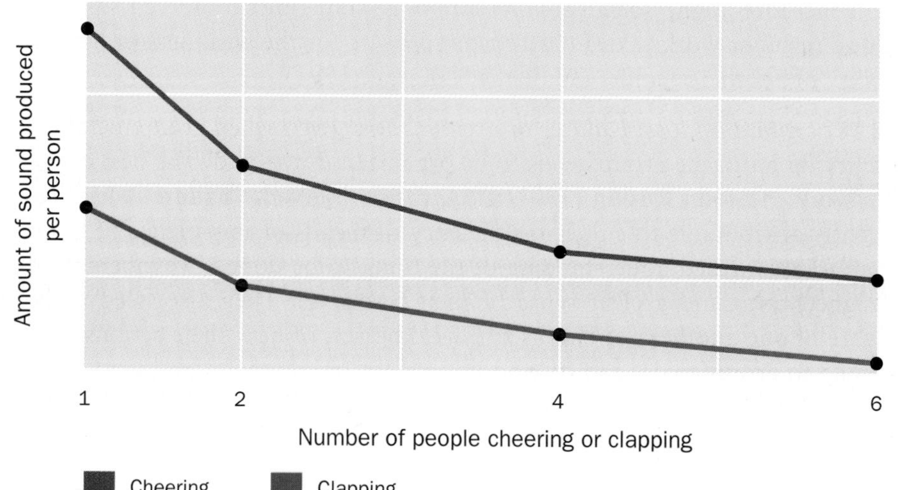

In this experiment, college students were told to clap or cheer as loudly as they could. Note that the noise produced by each person decreased as the number of people clapping or cheering together increased. Social loafing is most likely to occur if the task is unchallenging, if individual performances cannot be monitored, or if the individual's contribution to the group is dispensable. (Data from Latané and others, 1979.)

Social loafing is not restricted to simple motor tasks. When performance on cognitive tasks was measured, participants in three-person brainstorming groups generated only 75 percent as many uses for a common object as they did when working alone. And working in their groups, they made more than twice as many errors on a "vigilance" task of detecting brief flashes on a computer screen than they did when working alone (Harkins & Szymanski, 1989). Sharing responsibility can reduce effort on many kinds of tasks (Karau & Williams, 1993).

Why do people loaf on group tasks? To some extent, the nature of the task itself is a factor. Research indicates that social loafing occurs less often when tasks are interesting and involving (Brickner and others, 1986). But interdependence also plays a role. For example, when interdependence is minimal and individual roles are unimportant—as when the crowd rises to sing the national anthem before a baseball game begins—it is easy to let others pick up the slack (Karau & Williams, 1993; Kerr & Bruun, 1983). In contrast, social loafing is reduced when individual contributions are essential for success (Weldon & Mustari, 1988) or group members know their individual contributions can be monitored (Williams and others, 1981; Zaccaro, 1984). Not surprisingly, people are also less likely to slack off when there is a clear standard against which the group's performance can be measured (Harkins & Szymanski, 1989) and when they can be sure that others are not taking it easy (Kerr & Bruun, 1983).

People's orientation toward the group also influences the tendency to loaf. For example, women and members of interdependent cultures, who tend to be more group-oriented than men and people from individualistic cultures, are less likely to engage in social loafing (Karau & Williams, 1993).

As these findings indicate, to loaf or not to loaf seems to depend on both task and social interdependence. When individual performance makes an important or interesting difference to task performance, social loafing declines. And when an individual's performance can receive either praise or condemnation, social loafing declines. In fact, when task and social interdependence are high, *social compensation* is sometimes observed, as one group member works extra hard to compensate for the weakness or lack of ability of another member (Williams & Karau, 1991).

2. *Coordination loss: Failures of organization.* Even when group members are trying hard, the group needs to be organized if it is to do the best possible work. As John Ruskin (1907/1963, p. 1) observed, "Failure is less frequently attributable to either insufficiency of means or impatience of labor than to a confused understanding of the thing to be done." Members need assigned roles and a clear sense of their resources. They also need to be aware of one another's strengths and weaknesses, of how their actions contribute to group goals, and of who has a right to command and who has a duty to obey. Group performance suffers when group members leave crucial tasks undone, duplicate others' efforts, compete for personal resources and

status, or get in each others' way—literally or figuratively. Interference caused by other group members' efforts appears to be a major reason for the inferior performance of groups on brainstorming tasks. Listening to others talk may distract group members from thinking up superior ideas or may even cause them to forget some ideas before they can be expressed (Diehl & Stroebe, 1991; Stroebe & Diehl, 1991). Perhaps group brainstorming would be more successful if the group observed a moment of silence every few minutes to permit members to think without distraction.

Poor Coordination in the Workplace. Poor coordination on group tasks can be disastrous given the wrong circumstances. Consider, for example, the life-and-death responsibilities cockpit crews have on commercial airliners. If these small groups fail to work well together, the results could be tragic in an emergency. An investigation of one crash found that the pilot failed to pay attention to the copilot's repeated but timid comments that the takeoff was not proceeding normally. In another incident, a flight engineer manually silenced a noisy alarm, leaving the pilot with the impression that it was a false warning (Foushee, 1984).

Beetle Bailey

Reprinted with special permission of King Features Syndicate.

Airlines typically select pilots and copilots almost exclusively for their outstanding individual skills and knowledge, paying little attention to their interpersonal or communication skills. Unfortunately, research evidence indicates that successful performance of the flight crew may depend more on their coordination than on the skill of the individual group members (Lanzetta & Roby, 1960; Foushee & Manos, 1981). One study of a major airline's flight crews, using a realistic flight simulator, demonstrated this point (Harper and others, 1971). The researchers found that about 25 percent of the simulated flights crashed because the copilot failed to take control of the aircraft when the captain faked a collapse during a final landing approach.

Cures for Group Performance Losses. Loss of motivation and failures of coordination and communication can undermine a group's ability to achieve its goals and can frustrate individual members as well. Nipping such problems in the bud seems a wise step for any organization, and available research evidence indicates that one particularly successful strategy is making group membership a positive part of members' social identity.

Organizations often try to achieve this goal by selling the "corporate culture," the set of values, beliefs, understandings and norms shared by members of the organization (Levine & Moreland, 1991). To build a sense of group identity and cohesion, organizations create slogans and symbols, develop and distribute literature describing the principles that embody the company's ideals and goals, and introduce rituals, ceremonies and awards. For example, the J.C. Penney department stores sell their employees on "The Penney Idea," a list of guiding principles that set out the company's values and what it means to be a member. In sports, teams have uniforms, mascots, and "Most Valuable Player" awards to promote players' cohesiveness and dedication to their teammates (Hogg & Abrams, 1988). All of these tactics are designed to give group members a strong sense of shared social identity. U.S. Secretary of Labor Robert Reich says he uses a simple test when he visits organizations: he asks front-line workers to talk about their companies. "If the answers I get back describe the company in terms of 'they' or 'them,' I know it's one kind of company. If the answers include words such as 'we' or 'us,' I know it's another kind" (*Globe and Mail,* 1993).

But even if corporate culture makes people feel good, can it help reach the organization's goals? The answer is yes. Building positive social interdependence often helps solve some of the problems of task interdependence (Mackie & Goethals, 1987). Organizations sell the corporate culture because it encourages group cohesion, and group cohesion is a strong remedy for many of the motivational and coordination losses that can render groups ineffective.

1. *Cohesive groups encourage cooperation.* Cohesive groups foster cooperation in the service of group goals, rather than competition for individual ones (Turner, 1987). Cooperation leads to positive feelings among group members and helps them work together to achieve group goals (Sherif, 1966; Deutsch, 1949; Gaertner and others, 1990). For example, those who identify with a cohesive group are more likely to participate in and contribute to group activities than are members of noncohesive groups (Brawley and others, 1988). In sports like volleyball and baseball, cohesive teams are usually winning teams (Bird, 1977), suggesting that cohesion does promote cooperation and coordination.

One practical way to promote group goals is to make personal rewards clearly contingent on group rewards. For example, students in "cooperative classrooms" work together to help each other learn and are graded on the basis of the entire group's performance, whereas students' grades in "competitive classrooms" are based on comparisons between group members. In the classroom as in the laboratory, mutual cooperation leads to positive feelings: compared with members of competitive groups, cooperative group members generally like each other better—and they learn more. A meta-analysis of over one hundred studies concluded that cooperative learning results in better classroom performance than is found in either competitive or individualistic situations (Johnson and others, 1981).

The effects of cooperative learning on reducing intergroup conflict will be described in Chapter 14, page 632.

Employers sometimes adopt a similar reward arrangement—a contingent pay system in which employees receive bonuses only when certain group goals (such as production levels) are met. One study of 66 Fortune 500 firms compared compensation packages among low-performing organizations and high-performing companies. The study found that the companies with high performance records had packages that emphasized teamwork rather than individual competition (Schuster, 1985). These employers endorse the claim of W. Edwards Deming, the guru of managing for quality, that rewarding individual performance "annihilates long-term planning, builds fear, demolishes teamwork, and nourishes rivalry and politics" (Gabor, 1992). Indeed, General Motors Corporation's Cadillac Division, which adopted team-based rewards in 1989, credits them for the major turnaround that had propelled Cadillac to a top-ranking place in customer satisfaction among American cars by 1991.

2. *Cohesive groups exercise social influence.* A sense of group belonging usually helps members form norms about the group's goals and its strategies for accomplishing those goals. Once consensus has been reached, those who identify with the group are likely to adhere to its norms (McGrath, 1984), and new members quickly absorb the group's "way of doing things" (Levine & Moreland, 1991). If a group is cohesive and has a high-performance norm, its members will be highly productive (Keller, 1986). Of course, if group norms block performance, productivity will be low (Roethlisberger & Dickson, 1939). In a demonstration of this point, researchers surveying

The ways in which groups form a consensus were described more thoroughly in Chapter 9, pages 353 to 357. The ways in which these group norms influence group members' action was the topic of Chapter 10, especially pages 400 to 407.

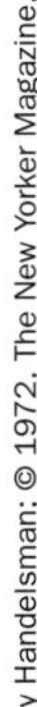

"Well, heck! If all you smart cookies agree, who am I to dissent?"

more than two hundred work groups found that job performance was related to group norms, which in turn were related to the labor-management climate (Seashore, 1954). Hostile management styles were associated with low-performance norms, and in these conditions, cohesive groups were less productive than noncohesive groups. Norms of high productivity tended to be found when management was supportive, and in these cases cohesive groups were the best performers. Experimental results confirm these findings (Schachter and others, 1951). What a cohesive group decides, group members usually do.

Reaching consensus also means the group no longer needs to spend time repeatedly renegotiating the issues. Members know what the group is set up to do and they know how to do it. These norms help both to eradicate motivation loss and to aid group coordination (Hackman, 1987). Consider, for example, the effect of norms on the goal of preparing a community meal. If the group has not reached a consensus, members may feel they have a right to work on the task they enjoy most, no one will do the dirty work, and there will be no dinner. Group norms, however, can specify that all the jobs must be done, that certain members have the right or obligation to do specific tasks, and that the tasks should be performed at certain times and in specific ways. Given these conditions, the community meal should proceed on schedule because when group norms match task demands, groups operate more smoothly.

3. *Cohesive groups attract and hold valued members.* When tasks are difficult, rewards are few, and conflict is frequent, potentially productive group members may slack off or drop out altogether. Member turnover can lessen a group's chances of achieving its goals, and it also often represents the loss of a huge investment in training and skill development. Shared social identity acts as a counterforce by boosting people's liking for the group, their satisfaction with belonging, and their morale (O'Reilly & Caldwell, 1985). You may recall that members of groups—even groups formed on the basis of arbitrary categorizations—tend to hold in-group members in higher esteem than out-group members (Hogg, 1987). This tendency is even stronger in cohesive face-to-face groups. Japanese businesses often see group cohesion as one way to keep their workers productive and happy. They are famous for their efforts to ensure that employee morale is high and that performance is rewarded. Companies foster friendships between members; sponsor picnics, parties, and sports teams; and promise long-term employment. Company-sponsored computer dating services even encourage employees to marry within the company. Their efforts no doubt contribute to the fact that Japanese workers seldom change companies.

To review the many ways in which membership in a social group increases preference for in-group over out-group members, see Chapter 6, pages 230 to 233.

Social identity can be such a powerful tool that it sometimes holds groups together when no material benefits are forthcoming. For example, groups with strong social identity often preserve (or even strengthen) their cohesion even when they lose or fail at important tasks (Brawley and others,

1987; Taylor and others, 1983). This occurred during the closing stages of the Second World War when units of the German army, outnumbered, undersupplied, and with no chance of victory, continued to fight against all odds. They did so not because they believed deeply in Nazi ideology but because they were motivated by group loyalty forged by shared identity (Shils & Janowitz, 1948). Studies of U.S. soldiers in Europe and Vietnam tell a similar story of social interdependence motivating performance (Stouffer and others, 1949; Moskos, 1969).

We have seen that group performance can suffer from two basic types of problems. The first occurs when members stop trying or drop out because they do not care about group goals or are unwilling to waste their efforts while others slack off. These motivational losses are often remedied when people cooperate and identify with group goals, as shown in Figure 13.4. The second problem arises when members try hard but cannot coordinate their efforts effectively because communication is poor or members interfere with each other. These coordination losses may be remedied when people identify with the group and follow its norms, at least when those norms favor high productivity. The best available remedies for *both* motivational and coordination losses stem from group cohesion. When group membership gives people a positive social identity, they are likely to take the group's goals as their own and to follow its norms in their behavior.

Figure 13.4 Group productivity: Problems and remedies

Source of productivity loss in groups	Motivation loss *Individuals diminish personal efforts, engage in social loafing.*	Coordination loss *Individuals interfere with each others' actions. Individuals fail to communicate effectively about group tasks.*
Remedy for productivity loss in groups	Cooperation: Individuals work toward group goals. *Individuals maintain efforts even when contributions are not identifiable.*	Consensus: Individuals agree on goals and strategies *Individuals follow group norms. If norms are appropriate, high productivity results.*
Contribution of group cohesion to remedy	Individuals adopt group goals as their own.	Group exercises social influence over individuals.

Group productivity declines when individual members do not try hard to accomplish group goals—for example, when they engage in social loafing—or when the members' efforts are poorly coordinated. Group cohesion can help remedy both of these problems by encouraging individuals to cooperate for group goals and to follow the group consensus on goals and ways of achieving those goals.

Leadership

Effective leaders enhance task performance and maintain social interdependence. Sometimes, however, stereotypical thinking prevents the most effective leaders from emerging in groups.

Whose job is it to make sure task interdependence and social interdependence intermesh smoothly? As former U.S. president Dwight D. Eisenhower once wrote, "Leadership is the ability to decide what is to be done, and then to get others to want to do it." Leaders are crucial to the attainment of group goals. In fact, **leadership** can be defined formally as a process in which group members are permitted to influence and motivate others to help attain group goals (Forsyth, 1990). Notice that in this definition the group grants the leader his or her power; as we noted in Chapter 10, legitimate authority works because the group accepts and agrees with it. The definition does not specify the route to power: leaders may be appointed by an outside authority, elected, or simply emerge as a group interacts. Leaders may or may not be effective, but before we explore that aspect of leadership, let's examine what leaders do.

What Do Leaders Do? Think back to the last time you worked on a group project. Did someone take on the job of asking for suggestions, coordinating the group's actions, and making the major decisions? In other words, did the group have a leader? It is difficult for a group of three or more to function effectively for any length of time unless someone takes that role. Because leadership is so important, if nobody is elected or appointed, a leader will often emerge from the group.

Early studies of interaction in small groups found that groups often develop two leaders—a task leader and a socioemotional leader. These researchers argued that the task leader makes the decisions that are translated into actual group performance. This individual typically makes task-focused comments, talks more than other members, and often addresses comments to the group as a whole rather than to individual members (Bales, 1953). As group size increases, the task leader's control of the conversation also increases (McGrath, 1984).

According to early research, a second individual—typically a person who talks more than anyone else except the task leader—becomes the group's socioemotional leader. Most of this person's contributions are aimed at soothing feelings, maintaining harmony, and encouraging participation. This presumed division of authority reflected the culture of the period in which this research was done. Researchers saw it as a "natural" and nearly universal pattern (Bales & Slater, 1955)—after all, weren't families composed of husbands who exercised task leadership and wives who provided socioemotional support?

Reevaluation of these findings suggests that the pattern of separate task

leadership A process in which group members are permitted to influence and motivate others to help attain group goals.

and socioemotional leaders is not truly universal (Burke, 1967). Leader behavior does tend to fall into two general categories, often labeled *initiating structure* (IS) and *consideration* (C) (Stogdill, 1963). IS behaviors, which include characteristics such as "lets group members know what is expected of them" and "decides what will be done and how it shall be done," have an obvious task focus. In contrast, C behaviors include items like "is friendly and approachable," "treats all group members as equals," and "does not act without consulting the group," characteristics related to the social interdependence of the group.

It seems clear that groups require both social and task leadership. Both functions are vital to effective group functioning, and they account for most of what leaders do (Mintzberg, 1980). But it is not equally clear that a group requires two separate leaders. One person may be quite capable of leading the group to task completion and simultaneously taking care of the group's psychological well-being.

Leadership Effectiveness: Person or Situation? Effective leaders can make or break countries, businesses, organizations, religions, clubs, sports teams, and even families. It is not surprising, then, that literally thousands of studies have tried to understand why some leaders have the capacity to inspire followers and others do not. When one considers the lives of Mohandas Gandhi, John F. Kennedy, Golda Meir, or Martin Luther King, Jr., there is a strong temptation to attribute their influence to their unique personal attributes. This tendency may be one more example of the correspondence bias at work, leading us to attribute behavior to individual traits rather than to situational demands.

In fact, early researchers on leadership had little success in identifying personality traits that characterized effective leaders. These studies revealed that the same person could be an effective leader in one context (for example, in a cockpit crew) but ineffective in another (such as a service organization). When researchers examined the relationship of leader behaviors to group outcomes, they found that giving socioemotional support consistently helped improve group morale. However, task-focused leader behaviors did *not* consistently improve group task performance (Vroom, 1976). This suggests that leadership effectiveness stems less from who the leader is or what he or she does than from the characteristics of the situation in which leadership is needed.

This insight about the importance of the situation was developed by Fred Fiedler (1964) in his *contingency model of leadership,* which is based on two assumptions. First, leaders differ, especially in their personal characteristics: some are task-oriented and others care more about relationships. Second, leadership situations also differ, especially in the amount of control leaders have over group outcomes. The key aspect of contingency theory is its "matching" proposition: to maximize leadership effectiveness, the leader's style should match the type of leadership demanded by the situa-

Figure 13.5 Leadership situations, leadership styles, and effectiveness

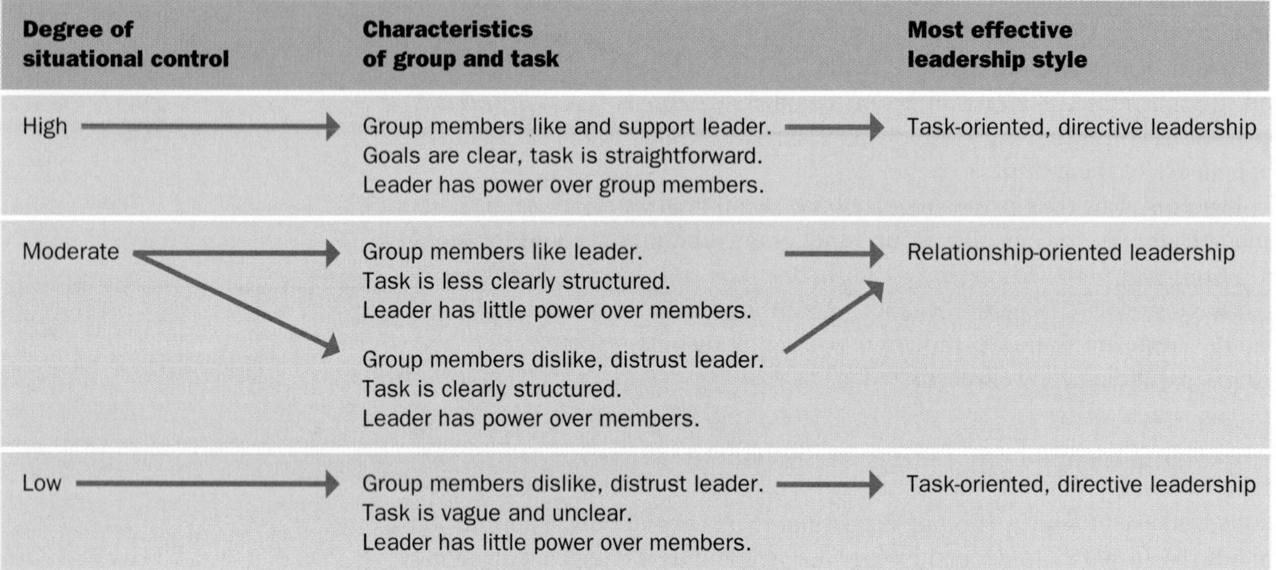

According to the contingency model of leadership, the most effective leadership style depends on the leader's and group's situation. When the situation allows high control, a directive and task-oriented leader can be most effective. The same leadership style also works well when conflict and ambiguity are extremely high, producing low control. In contrast, when either an unclear task or uncooperative group members produce moderate situational control, leaders are most effective when they adopt a relationship-oriented style to motivate group members toward task goals.

tion, as Figure 13.5 shows. When the group task requires lots of interpersonal interaction, a socioemotional leader may be most effective. When the group takes on a difficult and complex task, group performance may be maximized by a task-oriented leader. In situations in which leaders have either very high or very low levels of control, task-oriented leaders produce better performance. In contrast, relationship-oriented leaders are most effective where the leader has moderate control. The effectiveness of matching leader to task has been supported by a number of studies that have looked at such diverse groups as military units and basketball teams (Strube & Garcia, 1981).

Although some specific tasks may be best matched by a task-focused or relationship-oriented leader, most complex tasks require both leadership styles. In terms of group success, the leader's skill at handling one particular type of task may be less important than his or her ability to balance the two crucial elements of leadership as tasks and situations change (Hersey & Blanchard, 1982). In fact, the essence of good leadership may be the flexibility to adjust the mix of social and task motivation that a group needs in a particular situation. A group that first fails to understand instructions but then becomes overconfident may need a task leader initially and a relationship leader in the later stage.

If groups always need to have the problems of task and social interdependence solved, why isn't a person who is high in both relationship and task concern the best leader for every situation (Blake & Mouton, 1980)? Most of the time, this is true. The most effective supervisors in settings as diverse as banks, factories, coal mines, and government offices are in fact those who score well in both task and social leadership (Smith & Tayeb, 1989; Bass, 1985). But depending on the particular group and task, certain kinds of leadership behaviors may be unnecessary (Kerr & Jermier, 1978). For example, a skilled and experienced group working on a straightforward problem has little need for instructions on how to perform the task. An effective leader for this group will work to maintain positive feelings, group cohesion, and, therefore, motivation. In contrast, the leader of a cohesive unit may not need to worry about the interpersonal climate; in this situation, group effectiveness can be increased primarily by pushing task performance. In short, leadership is about the flexible exercise of social influence—given a particular group performing a particular task, a good leader simultaneously maximizes both successful task performance and positive social identity.

Do Groups Choose Effective Leaders? Contingency theories make it clear that groups should choose leaders whose styles match the demands of the situation. Like so many other social decision makers, however, groups do not always base their judgments on all the available information, and superficial thinking sometimes seems to rule the day. For example, laboratory studies show that group members who talk a lot tend to be viewed as leaders (Sorrentino & Field, 1986). Groups do need guidance, so choosing a talker is not necessarily a bad idea. Unfortunately, groups seem to base their decision more on *how much* is said rather than on the *quality* of what is said, and this is not the best basis for optimal leader selection (Hollander, 1985).

Groups also rely on stereotypes when picking leaders. For example, most people overestimate the importance of task-oriented thinking and give little weight to the socioemotional component of leadership. As a result, they are not very good at identifying truly effective leaders (Levine & Moreland, 1991; Eagly & Karau, 1991). For example, they are likely to think individuals who show a Type A behavior pattern (which includes a dynamic, task-focused interaction style) are more competent leaders than other people. However, groups with Type A leaders often perform more poorly (Strube and others, 1989), perhaps because groups often require socioemotional guidance as well.

Stereotypic thinking may help explain the preponderance of White males in leadership positions in business, government, religious, and military institutions. If people believe competence and assertiveness are associated with leadership and that males are competent and assertive, they may turn to males for leadership (Lord and others, 1986). Thus, the expectation that males make good leaders creates a self-fulfilling prophecy in which males assume most leadership roles. A wealth of research data support this point. For example, a meta-analysis has summarized 75 laboratory studies of mixed-sex informal groups that were allowed to interact without an appointed leader. When the group members later rated who acted as leaders, men were seen as playing leadership roles more often than women were (Eagly & Karau, 1991). Groups turn to women only when their tasks require extensive social interaction—as, for example, in consensus-seeking tasks or negotiations (Wood, 1987).

Sylvia

Stereotypes also limit ethnic minorities' chances of rising to leadership positions. When a Los Angeles Dodger executive commented in 1987 that African Americans "may not have some of the necessities" to be head coaches or executives, his remarks brought swift condemnation and vows of renewed efforts to recruit African-American coaches and executives. Nevertheless, the upper management levels of most professional sports in the United States are still relatively unintegrated. Football is one of the worst offenders: African Americans make up 60 percent of the players but only 7 percent of the head coaches. In baseball, 18 percent of the players are African American versus only 8 percent of the managers. Even team owners admit that lingering stereotypes bear some of the blame for this situation (Hammer, 1992).

Are groups hurting themselves by using such stereotypes to choose their leaders? Little research has examined ethnic differences, but meta-analyses of research on gender differences in leader effectiveness permit a partial answer to this question. The meta-analyses have looked at three related leadership qualities.

- *Who holds the group together?* On this issue, women leaders beat men hands down (Eagly and others, 1992). Both groups and individual group members are happier when their boss is a woman. One reason may be that, at least in laboratory groups, women leaders show more concern with morale and encourage more participation in decision making than men do (Eagly & Johnson, 1990).
- *Who gets the job done?* Studies of leaders in organizations find that, in general, women perform just as well as men on objective measures of leadership effectiveness. However, the type of organization makes a sub-

stantial difference. In business, educational, and government organizations, women leaders slightly outperform men on the average. In contrast, in the military men are much more effective leaders than women (Eagly & Karau, 1994).

- *Who do people think make good leaders in research?* Research in which a fixed set of leader behaviors—acted out by confederates or described in writing—is ascribed to either a man or a woman, subjects tend to rate female leaders as less effective than males who do exactly the same things (Eagly and others, 1992). Evidently, many people still doubt women's ability to lead, perhaps because women do not match their stereotype of a leader (Hollander, 1985).

When research findings like those just discussed reveal the reality beyond the stereotypes, the power of stereotypic thinking to obstruct the selection of the best leader for the job becomes clear. Perhaps this is why so many of us have worked for an incompetent boss, an unlikable coach, or a disorganized chairperson at some point in our lives. One study shows that at least 60 percent of workers say that dealing with their supervisor is the most stressful aspect of their job (Freiberg, 1991). Given the central role leaders play in coordinating both task and social interdependence in groups, perhaps it is time that stereotypical thinking about leadership went the way of the dinosaur.

Group Communication

> *High productivity and high morale can be achieved only through communication. Groups use both formal and informal channels to make sure communication is effective.*

Regardless of who leads and what the group's task is, leaders and groups have one primary weapon in the struggle to achieve high task efficiency while maintaining cohesion: communication. No wonder, then, that as group members share and exchange information, most of the talk is about getting the job done and feeling good while doing it (Bales, 1953).

The balance between such task-focused and socioemotional communications is crucial if a group is to be effective (McGrath, 1984). If a group's performance suffers because of ineffective strategies or inadequate skills, the group must seek task-focused remedies, such as repeated instructions, new directions, or reminders of goals (Schachter, 1951). When low cohesion produces poor performance, remedies must have a socioemotional focus, aimed at increasing positive interpersonal relationships and group identification. Over time, groups learn to alternate between a series of instrumental communications ("No, you do it *this* way") and a cluster of socioemotional ones ("Yes, you're doing a great job"), nursing along both task and social interdependence (Bales, 1953). Efficiency and morale depend on it.

Figure 13.6 Communication networks for social influence

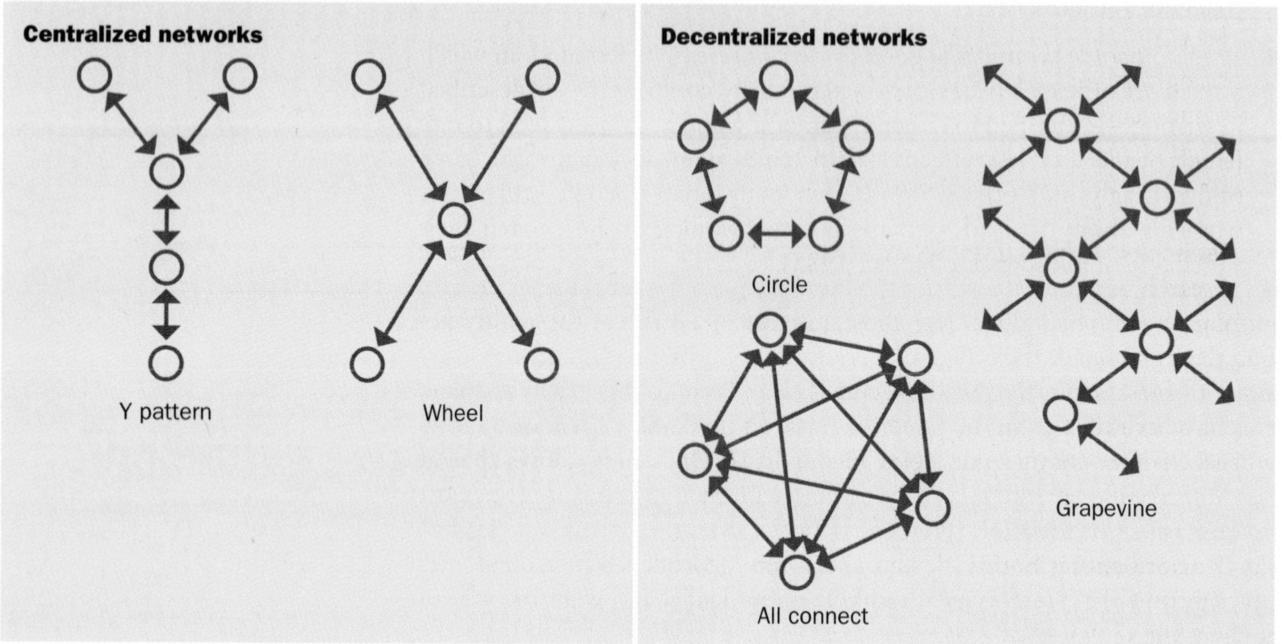

A group's success in accomplishing its tasks and the good feeling that its members have in working together depend on the group's ability to transmit task-focused and socioemotional messages. In communication networks, most communication must pass through a single individual. In decentralized networks, individuals can communicate more freely with one another. Performance on simple tasks is faster and more accurate when networks are centralized, but performance on complex tasks benefits from decentralized communication. (Adapted from Shaw, 1954 and Davis & Newstrom, 1985.)

How well task-focused and socioemotional messages permeate an organization depends on its *communication networks*—the typical patterns in which messages are transmitted. In a centralized communication network, one person is the focus of all problem solving and decision making. The wheel and *Y* patterns shown in Figure 13.6 are typical centralized networks. A university in which department heads take their cases for new teaching facilities to a dean, who decides priorities and allocates resources, has a centralized communication network that fits the wheel pattern. In a decentralized network, individuals can communicate freely with one another. For example, a university in which department heads meet together to discuss their needs and vote on the allocation of resources is an all-connect decentralized network, as shown in Figure 13.6. Laboratory experiments have demonstrated that groups with centralized structures usually solve simple problems faster than groups using other structures. As members gather information, the central person is in a position to coordinate it and quickly make a correct decision. But when problems are complicated, a central individual may find the information and responsibilities overwhelming. In these situations, decentralized networks, in which communication can flow more freely, are more likely to produce accurate decisions. Business groups solving research and development problems and planning sales strategies thrive on decentralized networks (Tushman, 1978; Shaw, 1954).

When formal routes of communication do not serve the group's needs, group members may rely on the grapevine. The grapevine is an informal person-to-person network linking members in all directions. Group members use the grapevine to fill in gaps in information and to deal with uncertainty. Although not officially sanctioned by groups, the grapevine can be surprisingly accurate and useful. One study showed that about 80 percent of grapevine items were work-related rather than personal, and that from 70 to 90 percent of the details passed through the grapevine were accurate (Simmonds, 1985; Davis & Newstrom, 1985)!

Technology and Communication. You may have noticed that most of the research on networks was carried out before computers and video revolutionized communication. In many modern organizations, the telephone, fax, electronic mail, and video conferences are displacing face-to-face interaction for brainstorming and resolving conflicts. Not surprisingly, the new technologies influence both how tasks are completed and how group members feel as they complete them.

Technology-mediated communication—information sharing that occurs via television or electronic mail—can be remarkably efficient at getting the job done. If you are sending a memo or leaving a message, you probably will get right to the point. Thus, because they emphasize the task-relevant features of the interaction, telephone calls and electronic mail tend to lead to good performance on simple tasks.

There is also evidence that computer-mediated group decision making may be less vulnerable to problems like the premature consensus of groupthink and biases that polarize majority views. In one comparison of three-member groups of university administrators reaching decisions, group polarization was less likely after computer-mediated discussion than when the groups met face-to-face (McGuire and others, 1987). In another study, the electronically linked groups took longer to reach consensus and made more unconventional decisions (Kiesler & Sproull, 1992).

One reason technologically-mediated communication allows groups to avoid decision-making pitfalls is that it seems to promote more equal participation among members. When groups meet face to face, high-status members typically dominate the discussion (Williams, 1977; Rutter & Robinson, 1981). This was certainly the case when researchers arranged for university students of different statuses to make decisions together: high-status members took up most of the "air time." When the same groups made comparable decisions using electronic mail, however, status inequalities in participation were reduced (Dubrovsky and others, 1991). If everyone participates, the group has a better chance of maximizing the potential of all its members to get the job done right.

You may remember from Chapter 9, pages 372 to 376, that majority views typically dominate group discussion and determine group decisions.

Of course, groups do not focus solely on getting their job done. Like traditional channels of communication, electronic communication is used as much for socializing as for sharing task-related information. And because

This is a typical finding, as Chapter 10, pages 403 to 407, discussed. People who contribute to group norms are greatly influenced by them.

more people can participate in group-related activities through the electronic networks, group members are likely to feel better about the group and their place in it. The use of new communication technologies can thus make a difference to group cohesiveness and commitment. One survey of city government employees found that the level of commitment to the organization was higher among employees who used computer mail and electronic bulletin boards than among those who used more traditional and status-dominated forms of communication (Huff and others, 1989). Of course, these findings are nonexperimental, but they do suggest that the opportunity to participate actively in group communication increases group commitment.

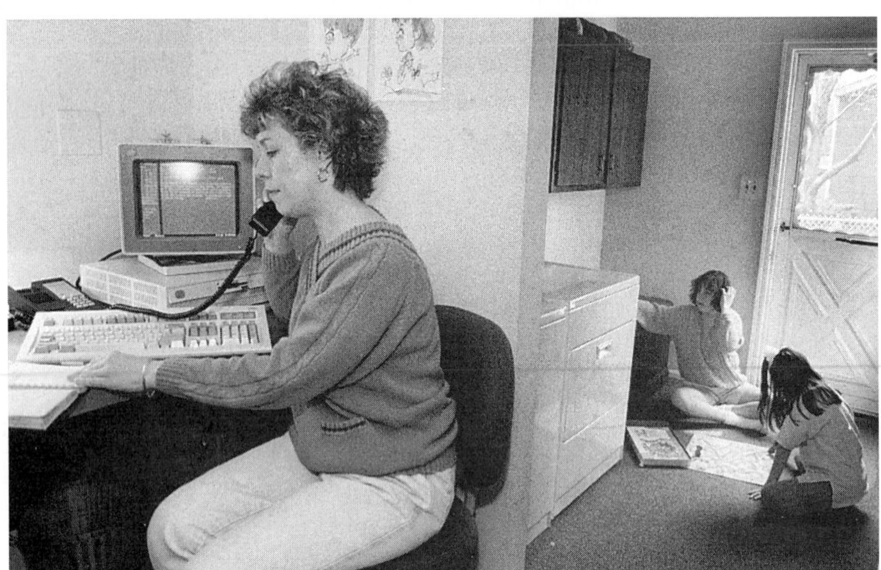

The new home office To cut costs, reduce commuting, and enable working parents to stay at home with their children, some companies have initiated telecommuting. Employees keep in touch with colleagues and with clients using computers, telephones, fax machines, and electronic mail. Research shows that such forms of communication often aid the performance of simple tasks by smoothing task interdependence and coordination. Although home workers profit from fewer interruptions from fellow workers, they do lose the benefits of social interdependence, which can maintain high morale and help solve complex problems.

Despite some of the advantages of high-tech communication channels, some aspects of communication are still achieved most effectively in face-to-face interaction. The emotional ties that develop from actual interaction seem more likely to encourage the growth of feelings of group solidarity. People working in small groups are happier and more satisfied with their work than are those working alone. The opportunity to read nonverbal cues like approval and disapproval or tension and relief also gives face-to-face interaction an advantage in solving complex interpersonal problems. And face-to-face communication still seems most effective in negotiation and conflict-resolution situations (Rutter & Robinson, 1981).

As technologies change, groups incorporate those changes into their communication patterns. Nevertheless, although the means of communicating are new, the end remains the same: effective task performance and the maintenance of group morale. From the family to the board of directors, from the hobbyist club to the office staff, we spend much of our lives in groups, trying to get something done. Coordinating actions and feelings is not easy, and groups are sometimes derailed by loafing members, lack of direction, or infighting. But when responsive leadership and appropriate communication channels help keep everyone and everything on track, groups succeed where no single individual could.

Social Dilemmas: Interdependence That Pits Individuals Against the Group

We are used to thinking that interdependence is a problem that assembly workers, sports teams, laboratory groups, and even families face. We rarely reflect on the fact that almost every aspect of our lives, even our long-term survival, also depends on actions taken by others—others we may never see. Consider the growing problem of air pollution, for example. Individuals use heat and air conditioning, drive sporty automobiles with powerful engines, and buy convenience products manufactured from petroleum. From a single person's point of view, such behavior may make sense. As a society, however, our appetite for fossil-fuel energy—in industry, transportation, and housing—is pumping millions of tons of carbon dioxide into the atmosphere each year. This process produces global warming through the so-called greenhouse effect and may result in worldwide damage to agricultural productivity, changes in global weather patterns, and large increases in the level of oceans (Stern, 1992). Other people's actions and our own are interdependent and have dramatic implications for every aspect of our lives.

One of the most fascinating aspects of this form of interdependence is the irony of the situation. If people do what makes sense from their *individual* points of view, the result is disaster for everyone. This form of interdependence is a **social dilemma**: a situation in which individual group members acting to benefit themselves bring harm to the group as a whole. We have already discussed one type of social dilemma in this chapter: social loafing, which occurs when individuals benefit by taking it easy—damaging the group's performance if everyone does likewise. But social dilemmas take many forms and can affect large groups as well as face-to-face groups. If every fishing vessel catches as many fish as possible there soon will be no fish for anyone; if we all watch public television without contributing to its support, public television stations will soon go off the air. Although social life is always characterized by tensions between individual and group goals, social dilemmas are an increasing concern when populations begin to outpace resources.

social dilemma A form of interdependence in which the most rewarding short-term action for each individual will, if chosen by all individuals, produce a long-term negative outcome for the entire group.

Types of Social Dilemmas

In some of the most important interdependent situations, the rewards for each individual conflict directly with the best outcome for the group. This can happen when people use a shared or commonly maintained resource.

What happens when self-interest clashes with group goals? Is there a way to short-circuit the negative effects of social dilemmas or to avoid such conflicts altogether? To answer these questions, social psychologists have set up laboratory situations that maintain the central feature of real-world social dilemmas: they pit individual goals against group interests. Although these studies never mimic all the complexities of actual large-scale dilemmas, they can offer insights into the social-psychological processes that create and defuse different kinds of social dilemmas. Interestingly, their results show that many of the same processes that influence action and interaction in face-to-face groups are also at work in larger groups.

Replenishable Resource Dilemmas. Replenishable resource dilemmas involve conflicts about the consumption of renewable resources, such as the world's rain forests or the populations of ocean fish. Individuals benefit personally by harvesting some of the resource. If enough of the resource is left untouched, it can reproduce and replenish itself so that harvesting can continue indefinitely. If too much of the resource is taken, however, reproduction cannot replenish the stock and the resource disappears.

To study this type of situation in the laboratory, individual subjects take many turns "harvesting" a group resource for individual profit. For example, subjects are told that a certain number of fish remain in a shared fishing spot. Each subject then decides how many he or she will take from the common resource pool. After everyone has made a decision, the total harvest is subtracted and the pool is allowed to replenish itself through reproduction, increasing by a set amount—for example, by 10 percent—before the next trial. The same process continues for many trials (Messick and others, 1983).

Consider the rewards and costs each participant faces in such a situation (see Figure 13.7). If the individual uses the resource, each fish taken from the pool translates into personal profit, and the more fish, the greater the profit. This is true regardless of whether other people also use the resource. If the individual decides to take fewer fish, others may continue to overfish, so a cautious participant could end up with reduced profit and still lose the resource. As Figure 13.7 indicates, the individual is better off using the resource than not using it—regardless of what others do. From a purely individual viewpoint, the logic of the situation dictates taking more fish.

Public Goods Dilemmas. Another type of social dilemma arises over how public goods should be acquired or supported. A *public good* is one that has

Figure 13.7 Possible outcomes in a replenishable-resource dilemma

Individual's action	Use resource *Catch as many fish as possible.*	Do not use resource *Take the season off.*
Result if others use the resource	Short-term profit; resource is soon depleted.	No profit; resource is depleted anyway.
Result if others refrain from using the resource	Short-term profit; resource is not depleted.	No profit; resource is not depleted.

Consider the possible outcomes faced by the owner of a fishing vessel when the catch is declining. No matter what others do, personal interests dictate using the resource. However, since exactly the same pressures will make all the other resource users act similarly, the resource will soon be depleted.

to be provided for everybody or nobody; it cannot be given to some and withheld from others. Unpolluted air, a strong national defense system, and public broadcasting stations are all public goods. Because a public good is available to all, *free riders* are tempted to use it without paying for it.

To illustrate the underlying dilemma, consider the situation faced by participants in an experiment by Linda Caporael and her colleagues (1989). The researchers gave $5 to each person in a group of seven subjects. The subjects were told that they would each receive a $10 reward—the public good—if at least four of them anonymously returned their $5 to the experimenter. If fewer than four people donated, however, no reward would be provided, and those who had donated their $5 would forfeit the money. Clearly, if every person donates, everyone ends up with $10. But is this really in the individual's best interest? How would you reason if you were presented with this dilemma? After all, if you donate but nobody else does, you lose your $5 and no public good is provided. Once again, your best individual bet seems to be free riding while hoping everyone else will be a better citizen than you are. By holding onto your $5 and collecting the bonus, you could even walk away with $15. The kicker is, of course, that if everyone follows this entirely sensible course of action, no one will contribute and no one will have the benefit of the public good—all will be worse off than they could have been.

Behavior in Social Dilemmas. Faced with such dilemmas, most people quite rationally—but disastrously—follow their individual interests. Almost every subject faced with a resource dilemma decides to harvest as much as possible, even though the resource is rapidly depleted (Messick and others, 1983). This decision is especially likely when people cannot accurately estimate the size of the resource pool; under these conditions, people take more for themselves and believe that others will do the same (Budescu and others,

1990). Of course, thinking that others will follow their own self-interest or actually seeing them do so provides selfish models, which might in turn encourage behavior that is even more socially irresponsible. And continuing to sacrifice when others are taking a free ride may make you feel like a sucker (Kerr & Bruun, 1983). This may help explain why the presence of selfish models makes people slow to respond constructively to a resource dilemma even when they realize the resource is being depleted (Messick and others, 1983).

These laboratory findings reflect behavior in the real world—New England fishermen, for example, are finding that their operations have so depleted the once abundant offshore schools that their total catch is now less than half that of a decade ago. Although their livelihood is now endangered, they cannot seem to agree on a solution to their dilemma (*New York Times,* 1992a).

Plenty of fish in the sea? These fishermen used to land up to 50,000 pounds of fish in a three-day trip along the coast of New England. Now it takes five or six days to bring in half as much. As fish are harvested faster than they can be replenished by reproduction, a resource dilemma is created. How will the fishing industry act? Should fishing boats continue to harvest as much as they can individually? If they do, what will happen when the resource runs out? Are there alternative solutions?

In public-goods dilemmas, as in resource-depletion dilemmas, self-interest usually wins the day. For example, only about 50 percent of the participants in Caporael's study made $5 donations, and as a result only a few experimental groups collected the bonus. To find out why, researchers looked at two possible motivations: the fear of wasting the donation and the greedy desire for profit (Rapoport & Eshed-Levy, 1989). To eliminate the influence of fear, researchers told some experimental groups that they would return the donated money if fewer than four subjects made donations. To neutralize greed, they warned other groups that if the $10 bonus was earned, no participant could leave with more than $10. Only eliminating greed increased the number of donations (Caporael and others, 1989). Thus, greed—not fear—seems to be the most important reason for most people's failure to contribute to the common good.

Cultural or gender differences may also be a factor in people's response to social dilemmas. We might expect to find more cooperation from women and from members of interdependent, group-oriented cultures. A meta-analysis of research on social loafing dilemmas generally supported both of these predictions (Karau & Williams, 1993). In studies of other types of dilemmas, some research found that Chinese students and manager trainees were more cooperative than their individualistic U.S. counterparts (Earley, 1989; Gabrenya and others, 1985). The limited amount of cross-cultural research is not altogether consistent, however. One researcher found that U.S. students were more trusting and more cooperative than Japanese students (Yamagishi, 1988).

Personality differences also influence behavior in social dilemmas. Compared with people who like to compete, individuals who generally prefer to cooperate make resource pools last longer (McClintock & Liebrand, 1988; Liebrand & Van Run, 1985). Findings like this give social psychologists something to think about: if cooperation overcomes the negative effects of social dilemmas, how can more people be encouraged to cooperate more of the time?

Solving Social Dilemmas

> *One proposed solution to social dilemmas involves restructuring the task to change people's actual outcomes. Another attempts to change the way people think about their outcomes, highlighting social interdependence to increase shared identity and commitment to group goals and norms.*

Research has suggested two kinds of solutions for social dilemmas (Messick & Brewer, 1983; Kerr, 1992). The first tries to change the structure of the dilemma so that task interdependence changes. The second attempts to focus on social interdependence to change the way people think about social dilemmas.

Using Task Interdependence to Solve Social Dilemmas. In this approach, authorities impose laws or regulations so that individual payoffs are changed and the dilemma is eliminated. Although each individual's outcome still depends on other people's behavior, everyone's behavior is regulated, so the nature of task interdependence is changed. A standard solution to a public-goods dilemma, for instance, is to levy taxes, perhaps to pay for a city park or a new bridge: if everyone benefits, everyone should pay. In a resource-depletion dilemma, solutions usually involve setting quotas so that users cannot deplete the resource. International fishery commissions, for example, restrict the size of the annual catch for different species of fish.

Unfortunately, structural solutions generate many problems as they try to solve others. First, structural solutions are impossible unless some person or organization has the authority to impose them. Experimenters can easily set sanctions in laboratory game playing, and groups sometimes elect leaders to decide each member's share (Samuelson and others, 1984). But who has the accepted authority to regulate use and misuse of the world's atmosphere or the proliferation of biological weapons? People rarely request authority to regulate the use of a valuable resource before it is threatened with extinction (Sato, 1987). Another problem with structural solutions is that they are often met with resistance. Even though New England fishermen are finding there aren't plenty more fish in the sea, they are resisting new regulations that would limit their catch and allow the fish to regenerate (*New York Times,* 1992a).

A final problem is that resistance necessitates a bureaucracy for monitoring compliance, and successful enforcement cannot be guaranteed (Yamagishi, 1986). Despite the existence of stiff penalties and routine inspection, many firms continue to routinely pollute the soil, water, and air. Unless people willingly accept restraints on their behavior, structural solutions seem inadequate ways of coping with many of our most intractable global dilemmas.

Social Interdependence and Social Dilemmas. Social solutions to dilemmas change the way individuals think about their choices without changing the actual payoffs (Lynn & Oldenquist, 1986). Solving social dilemmas requires cooperation—agreeing to cut one's consumption of resources, chipping in to pay for resources others can use, caring about others' outcomes as if they were your own. Cooperation in turn requires that individual goals and group goals coincide so that individuals can see that serving the group interest is in their own best interest. When group members take this view, the social dilemma disappears (Messick, 1974; Kramer & Brewer, 1984).

One way to get individuals to adopt group goals as their own is make group membership a salient part of an individual's social identity. When links to others are uppermost in people's minds, three changes usually take place. First, they give priority to the greater good of the group (Caporael and others, 1989). Contributing to a common good and other similar behaviors, which may appear foolish or naive from an individual point of view, seem loyal, trustworthy, and generous from the perspective of the group (Tetlock, 1989). Similarly, actions like free riding, which may seem clever and sensible to the individual, may be viewed as despicable and treacherous by the group.

The second change that occurs when the group thinks and works together as one is that people are more likely to assume other group members will also be helping, not hurting, the group effort. No group member need worry that others will be free riding while he or she exercises self-control, and no group member will take a free ride while others act responsibly (Caporael and others, 1989). In fact, when Caporael and her colleagues questioned the people who contributed in their experimental groups, these subjects said that they thought most other subjects would also contribute. Acting as you expect others to act—which also implies trusting others to act the same way as you do—lets the entire group share the fruits of cooperation.

The third change that occurs is that internalized norms about cooperation become salient and group norms become good guides for individual action. Subjects who thought that most others would also contribute must have realized that they could keep their own $5 and collect the bonus earned by others' contributions. Nevertheless, these individuals chose to follow what they saw as a group norm of contributing. The norm of commitment can have such a powerful effect that subjects who vow to cooperate during group discussion later carry through on this promise, even if they know their behavior is unlikely to solve the dilemma (Kerr & Kaufman-Gilliland, 1993).

Other examples of the power of the norm of social commitment on behavior were described in Chapter 10, pages 417 to 420.

Because of these changes, shared group identity can increase cooperative behavior in social dilemmas. In a study demonstrating this point, Marilynn Brewer and Roderick Kramer (1986) created a laboratory situation in which individuals were faced with a social dilemma. Subjects sat in individual cubicles with computer displays, but they were led to believe they were part of either a small eight-member group or a large thirty-two-member group. In addition, some people in each condition were encouraged to develop group identification and some were not. The manipulation was subtle: some subjects were simply told that their payment for participation would be decided for the group as a whole, rather than for separate individuals. Sharing this common fate was enough to change their behavior, significantly lowering the amount of resources they drew from the common pool when given the opportunity.

Identification with a group can be so complete as to totally submerge individual identity and interests, as when a parent rushes into a burning house to save a child, or a soldier dies in defense of his or her comrades. Of course, people do not need to identify with the group at such extreme levels to tolerate the minor inconveniences involved in conserving resources. Simply identifying others as worthy of social cooperation may provide adequate motivation for such behavior.

Creating Identification with Others to Solve Social Dilemmas. How can society encourage the powerful effects of connectedness with others to help solve social dilemmas? We have already seen that organizations stress corporate culture to give their employees a positive group identity; school spirit serves the same function in the classroom. What helps people develop the sense of community that lets them identify with others who use common resources or depend on the same public goods?

1. *Communication among group members.* Laboratory studies have repeatedly demonstrated that when members of a group are allowed to discuss a dilemma before making their decisions, cooperation is enhanced (Orbell and others, 1988). For example, only 47 percent of subjects in one study donated to a public good when no discussion was permitted, but when discussion was allowed, the figure rose to 84 percent (Caporael and others, 1989). As they talked with one another, group members worked on

forming consensus around a norm for appropriate behavior, defining the meaning of deviance from the norm, and making promises to stick to the norm. These discussions made them feel more connected, but they also committed them to promises of cooperation and sharing (Kerr & Kaufman-Gilliland, 1993). The limited possibilities for communication may help to explain why big groups often have a tougher time solving social dilemmas than smaller groups do (Brewer & Kramer, 1986). When it comes to solving social dilemmas, small is beautiful (Edney, 1980).

2. *Equality of opportunities and outcomes among group members.* If all group members use the same amount of a resource, that level of consumption becomes a norm for group members (Messick and others, 1983). But just as equality of resource use fosters a sense of community, inequality promotes self-interest. It does so by reducing people's certainty about others' behaviors, weakening conformity pressures, diminishing personal efficacy, and making people wonder if they are being exploited. On a global scale, inequality is a major roadblock to solving current problems of pollution and resource depletion (Simons, 1992). The poorer nations wonder why environmental considerations should require them to use fewer resources than those used by the already developed nations. Why should they give up the promise of prosperity when the developed nations literally took the quick and dirty route to wealth?

3. *Accessibility of group norms.* Keeping the value of acting in the group's best interest uppermost in everyone's mind gives this norm the best chance of guiding behavior. To demonstrate this point, some subjects in one experiment listened to others talk about the value of group cooperation: "Maybe I could have gotten more if I was greedy, but I just couldn't do it. If I'm in a group, I'm going to try to do what helps the group, not just myself" (Sattler & Kerr, 1991, p. 760). Compared with subjects who had not heard this message, these subjects took a smaller share for themselves when they later participated in a social dilemma problem.

4. *Linking individual efforts to the group good.* If people are given feedback that shows that their actions are effective, even on a small scale, they conserve more. Being able to see the effects of seemingly trivial actions like turning off unneeded lights or emptying wash water on flowerbeds apparently creates a sense that personal actions do matter (Seligman and others, 1981). Believing that their efforts make a difference makes people feel good and gives them a sense of psychological control. It also increases the likelihood that they will act on their attitudes and norms—whether that means installing flow-restricted showerheads, subscribing to public television, or gathering signatures on petitions to halt their nation's development of nuclear weapons. A person who hears "Because you donated your share, the company was able to raise over $5,000," learns how his or her action is magnified by the size of the group. The more responsible members feel for group success, the more likely they are to solve social dilemmas (Kerr, 1992).

Figure 13.8 Social dilemmas: Problems and remedies

Problems in solving social dilemmas	Motivation problems *Individuals seek personal rewards, undermining group benefits.*	Coordination problems *Individuals are unaware of others' choices. Individuals cannot trust others to cooperate.*
Remedies for social dilemmas	Task interdependence solutions: Change incentives for individuals. *Individuals seeking personal rewards now benefit group.* Social interdependence solutions: Individuals identify with group norms. *Individuals seek to act in ways that benefit the group.*	Social interdependence solutions: Individuals agree on appropriate actions. *Individuals assume others will cooperate.* Social interdependence solutions: Individuals follow group norms. *Norm of commitment keeps individuals cooperating.*
Contribution of group cohesion to remedy	Individuals adopt group goals as their own.	Group exercises social influence over individuals.

Social dilemmas worsen when individuals seek to serve their own interests in opposition to group interests, and when individuals are unable to coordinate their actions to solve general problems.

The rapid destruction of the global environment is not so much a failure of technology as it is a failure to solve large-scale social dilemmas. These dilemmas are perhaps most easily observed when humans exploit renewable natural resources such as fish populations and energy sources, but they are equally critical when people exhaust abstract "resources" like the earth's ability to eliminate pollution and recycle wastes. For example, biological and physical processes can absorb only limited amounts of emitted carbon dioxide and other "greenhouse" gases. Because humans are producing so much more than that amount, the composition of the atmosphere is changing, leading many geoscientists to predict massive global climate changes (Stern, 1992).

Unfortunately, groups that are interdependent with respect to the global environment are often enormous in size, have little in common, do not communicate, and are notably unequal in resource usage. These factors will make it difficult to create the sense of common group membership that may be the best hope of solving such dilemmas. A sense of personal efficacy is also hard to attain when environmental problems are global in scale.

In the very near future, however, we will all have to learn to identify with larger groups. Our current state of global interdependence is historically recent, and our sense of common purpose has not caught up with our mutual dependence. We have yet to learn that our choices—as individuals and as nations—have implications beyond our private well-being and our national interest. As Figure 13.8 shows, when people feel they are part of a community they tend to act more cooperatively, valuing group goals above individual ones and following group norms for appropriate actions. The future of our human group may depend on whether we can create and maintain that shared feeling of belonging.

Concluding Comments

Social life centers on groups, so by understanding how they work we can better understand ourselves as social beings. This chapter begins by considering the *individual in the group*—performing as a single person but affected by the physical presence of others. It ends with the *group in the individual*—the thoughts and feelings about the meaning of group membership that affect our behavior even when others are not physically present.

Interdependence, the sharing of common experiences and of a common fate, weaves these threads together. Most discussions of group interaction focus on task interdependence—on the need to coordinate individual skills, roles, and effort so that group tasks can be successfully completed. This is certainly the focus that drives human-engineering approaches to personnel management, organizational behavior, and management science. Our message in this chapter is slightly different. Task interdependence is important, of course, but social interdependence may be even more important. Our need for a shared understanding of the social world and of our place in it and our concern for being positively evaluated manifest themselves in almost every aspect of our social behavior.

The impact of social interdependence and the desire for group membership has been evident since the earliest research on group interaction and leadership. During much of that research, however, investigators viewed these social influences mainly as an impediment to the successful and efficient completion of group tasks. Thus, the social rewards of group membership and the development of group norms were seen as elements that interfered with the goals of production. Social psychological considerations offer a different point of view. Far from working against effective task interdependence, social interdependence can exert a positive influence on group behavior. Social, not technological, solutions may be our best bet for eliminating many apparently task-related problems—such as failures of coordination, social loafing, resource depletion, and low productivity. A positive social identity can provide the consensus, cohesion, and cooperation needed to get the job done.

However, we must add a word of caution here. As Chapter 6 made clear, cohesion and cooperation within the in-group often come at the cost of antagonism and hostility toward out-groups. And as Chapter 9 pointed out, a highly cohesive group can be so intent on feeling good about itself that its decisions and actions are vulnerable to groupthink. Thus, as we have argued before, the optimal solution is always one of balance. The sales group needs enough cohesion to keep morale high and attention focused on their sales goals, but not so much that they are in constant conflict with the production team. The local school board needs enough group identity to maintain its members' enthusiasm about solving the district's problems, but not so much that they make unrealistic and ill-advised decisions. We are all interdependent at many different levels. Even the most cohesive sales team will fail if the production team turns out too few products. Even the most innovative school board will be deadlocked if parent groups and teachers' unions refuse to cooperate.

Nowhere is this large-scale interdependence more obvious than in our common need to solve problems of global depletion of resources. We know that a shared group identity promotes both positive feelings *and* effective performance. Emphasizing what we have in common and focusing on pulling for, rather than against, one another may be our best chance of solving the problems that threaten us all.

Summary

Social Facilitation: The Effects of Minimal Interdependence In a **collective**, the mere presence of others can produce arousal, either because those others are highly evaluative or because they are distracting. Arousal improves the performance of easy, well-learned behaviors, which helps with some tasks but hinders others. This pattern is termed **social facilitation.**

Crowding is another source of arousal that can improve performance on easy tasks and disrupt performance on difficult ones. However, the effects of crowding depend on people's interpretation of the situation and on their sense of control.

Performance in Face-to-Face Groups: Maximizing Interdependence The members of face-to-face groups interact with one another and also share both **task interdependence** and **social interdependence.** Face-to-face groups usually go through different stages of formation, conflict, development, performance, and dissolution as they try to develop a shared identity and reach their goals.

To achieve their performance goals, groups must maintain their motivation and avoid problems of coordination. For example, groups must ensure that their members work hard and avoid **social loafing.** By promoting cohesion and conformity to group performance norms, a common social identity helps to avert such problems.

Effective **leadership** enhances task performance and maintains social interdependence. Sometimes, however, stereotypical thinking prevents the most effective leaders from emerging in groups.

Chapter 13 Themes

Pervasiveness of Social Influence
Being part of a collective or being interdependent in face-to-face or larger groups pervasively affects our thoughts and behavior.

Striving for Mastery
Behavior in groups is often motivated by the desire for rewards.

Seeking Connectedness
Behavior in groups is often motivated by the desire to display group identification.

Valuing Me and Mine
When we value group membership, we frequently seek to act in the group's interest.

High productivity and high morale can be maintained only through communication. Groups use both formal and informal channels to ensure effective communication.

Social Dilemmas: Interdependence That Pits Individuals Against the Group Among some of the most important interdependence situations are **social dilemmas,** situations in which the rewards for each individual conflict directly with the best outcome for the group. They can happen when people use a shared or commonly maintained resource.

One proposed solution to social dilemmas is restructuring the task to change people's actual outcomes. Another attempts to change the way people think about their outcomes, highlighting social interdependence to increase shared identity and commitment to group goals and norms.

Chapter 13 Overview

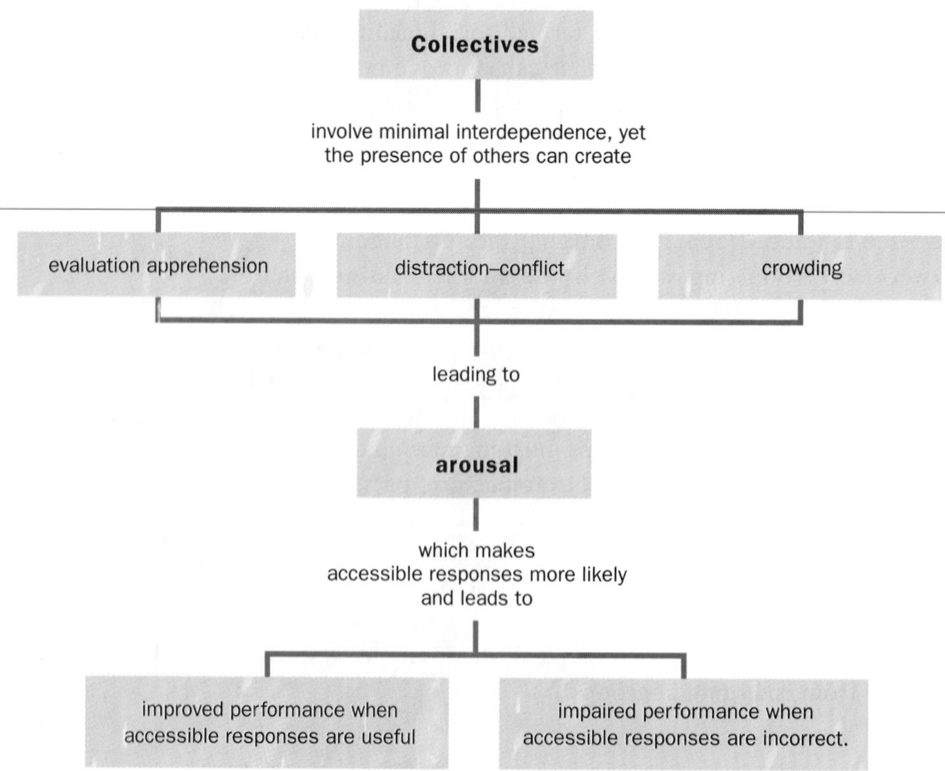

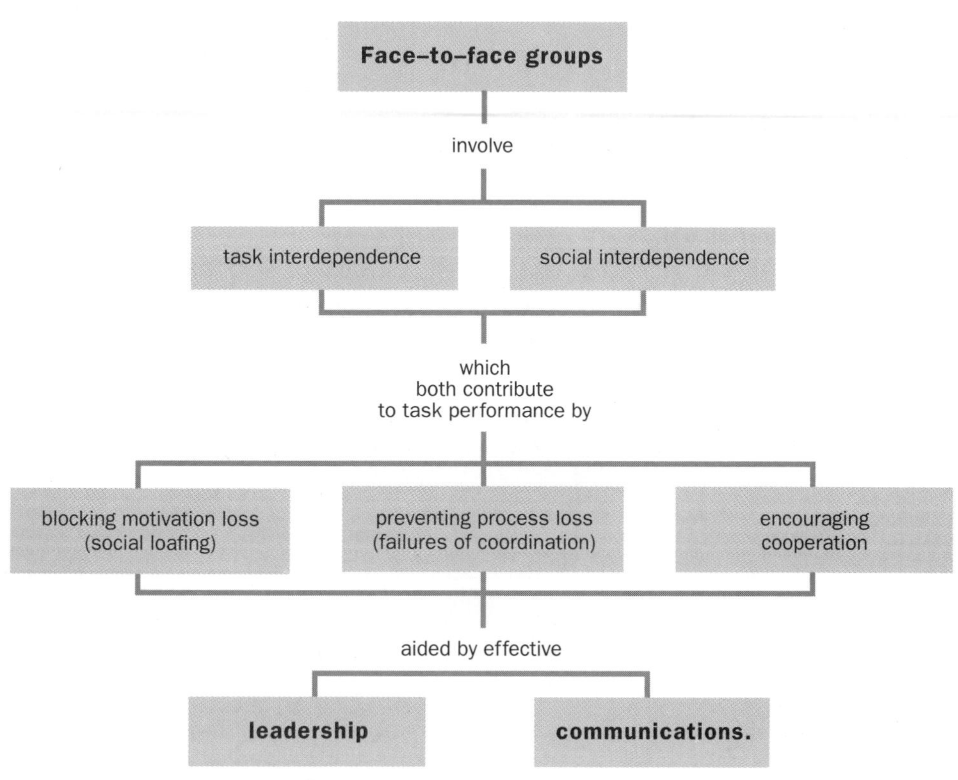
Face-to-face groups
involve
task interdependence
social interdependence
which both contribute to task performance by
blocking motivation loss (social loafing)
preventing process loss (failures of coordination)
encouraging cooperation
aided by effective
leadership
communications.

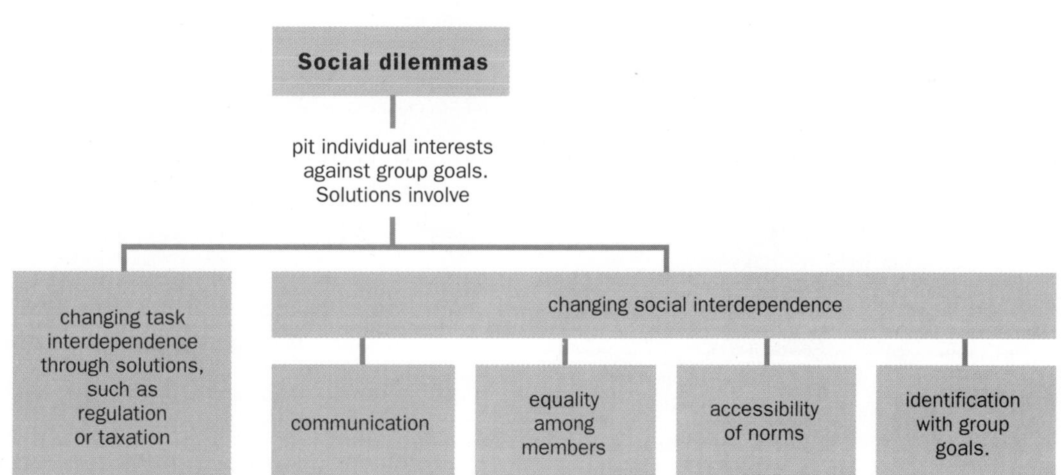
Social dilemmas
pit individual interests against group goals. Solutions involve
changing task interdependence through solutions, such as regulation or taxation
changing social interdependence
communication
equality among members
accessibility of norms
identification with group goals.

14

Conflict and Conflict Resolution

On June 19, 1954, two groups of eleven-year-old boys tumbled out of buses to start summer camp in the Sans Bois mountains near Oklahoma City, Oklahoma. Robbers Cave State Park—named for the hideout of the notorious outlaw Jesse James—offered a 200-acre site with fishing, swimming, canoeing, hiking, and the usual camp games and sports. The new arrivals were ordinary White, middle-class boys with no record of school, psychological, or behavioral problems. They had nothing on their minds except high hopes for a fun-filled three-week vacation.

The camp was more than it seemed, however. Without the boys' knowledge, their parents had agreed to let them participate in a field study of intergroup conflict set up by Muzafer Sherif and his colleagues—a study that came to be known as the Robbers Cave experiment (Sherif and others, 1961). The boys did not know that the camp counselors and directors were social psychologists and research assistants. Nor, at first, did members of each group know that another group was sharing the campsite.

During the first week, as they took part in separate activities designed to promote group cohesion, each group developed norms and leaders. They gave themselves names—the Eagles and the Rattlers—and each group designed a flag. Toward the end of the week, the groups discovered each other. Seeing "those guys" using "our ball field" and "our hiking trails" sparked demands for a competition. The staff was only too pleased to arrange a four-day tournament including baseball, tug-of-war, a treasure hunt, and other events. The experimenters even promised the winners a fancy trophy, shiny badges, and four-bladed pocketknives. Both groups practiced hard, cheered their teammates, and roundly booed and insulted the competition. Hostilities escalated as the tournament progressed, culminating in a flag burning when the Eagles lost the tug-of-war.

The Eagles ultimately won the tournament, collecting the trophy and the coveted pocketknives. But while they were taking a celebratory swim, the Rattlers raided their cabins and stole the prizes. The rivalry had turned into full-blown war, and the staff was kept busy silencing name calling, breaking up fist fights, and cleaning up after cabin raids and food fights.

Connections in the midst of conflict Amidst the rubble of war-torn Beirut, a Christian bride and a Muslim groom start their life together. Their situation raises questions both about the genesis of intergroup conflict and its resolution—the central topics of this chapter. How do conflicts between groups arise, and why do they sometimes erupt into bloodshed and warfare? What are the prospects for resolving such conflicts? How can group differences be resolved, and can individual members of very different groups—like this young married couple—ever hope to live in peace?

The experiment had transformed twenty-two perfectly normal boys into two gangs of brawling troublemakers, full of hostility and intent on exacting revenge for every real or imagined slight.

As you may have guessed, Sherif and his colleagues set up this situation to understand how intergroup hostilities develop and how they can be resolved. This is not a trivial issue: in the half-century since the end of the Second World War, more than one hundred wars have raged. Unrest and hostility mar not only international relations but also interactions between ethnic, political, and religious groups. Intergroup hostility also frequently occurs between groups with different economic interests as firms compete for market share, departments vie for a larger piece of the company budget, and labor and management clash over wages and hours (Walton and others, 1969).

Although every struggle has a unique history of causal events and group goals, they all have much in common with the intergroup hostilities that developed at Robbers Cave. In this chapter we consider the social psychological processes that characterize many of these group-conflict situations. We begin by looking at group competition for material and social resources as the genesis of group rivalry. We then examine the ways social and cognitive processes conspire to fan the flames of discord into full-blown conflict. Finally, we consider social psychological strategies to help reduce conflict between groups. We believe that understanding the dynamics of intergroup conflict can tell us how it can be resolved, just as understanding the processes that contribute to prejudice or aggression can suggest ways to reduce those problems. As you will see, the goal of reducing intergroup conflict goes well beyond merely stopping open hostilities and suppressing mutual antagonism. Genuinely peaceful intergroup relations are most attainable when conflict is resolved in ways that benefit all involved parties.

The Genesis of Intergroup Conflict

Conflict is a perceived incompatibility of goals: what one party wants, the other party sees as harmful to its interests. When groups perceive one another's goals as incompatible, it's easy to blame the other group when something goes wrong. When the factory falls short of its production quota, management finds fault with the workers, while folks on the shop floor blame a short-sighted management team. Conflict between groups is acted out in many forums—televised messages to concerned parties, protracted litigation in courtrooms, and bloody battles in war zones. Whether the conflict is between Coke and Pepsi, labor and management, or Armenia and Azerbaijan, the parties try to contradict, belittle, defy, or frustrate the opponent and to extend and protect their own group interests. The conflict at the heart of these disputes frequently focuses on control of material resources and social rewards.

conflict The perceived incompatibility of goals between two or more parties.

Sources of Intergroup Conflict: The Battle for Riches and Respect

Most conflict stems from competition for valued material resources or for social rewards like respect and esteem. People use social comparisons to determine acceptable levels of resources.

The most frequent source of conflict is **competition,** in which two or more parties' interests are directly opposed: each group's gains must come at others' expense. Competition is particularly likely when valued resources are limited and only one group can own or control them.

Realistic Conflict Theory: Getting the Goods. In the conflict between the Eagles and the Rattlers, each group defended its swimming and playing territory, stole the other's prized possessions, and engaged in athletic competition spiced by the knowledge that only the winners would receive new pocketknives. The resulting dramatic escalation of hostilities provided good evidence for **realistic conflict theory,** which argues that intergroup conflict arises from competition among groups for scarce but valued material resources (Campbell, 1965; Levine & Campbell, 1972; Sherif, 1966).

Laboratory research has confirmed that competition for scarce resources sours intergroup relations. In one study, for example, two groups of students at a time worked on tasks such as recommending a therapy program for a troubled adolescent or creating an advertising slogan for a new brand of toothpaste (Taylor & Moriarty, 1987). To set up a cooperative or competitive environment, researchers gave different instructions to the subjects in different conditions. To create a cooperative environment, researchers told some subjects that the proposals from the two groups would be combined to produce the best solution, and that both groups would be rewarded. In the competitive condition, subjects heard that only one group—the one that came up with the best idea—would receive a reward. The findings were consistent with predictions from realistic conflict theory. Compared with the cooperative groups, the competitive groups liked in-group members better and disliked out-group members more (see Figure 14.1).

As the Rattlers and Eagles demonstrated, group competition can quickly escalate from dislike into hostility (Horwitz & Rabbie, 1982; Rappaport & Bornstein, 1987). Indeed, competition for real resources—such as land, jobs, or natural resources—has been implicated as one cause of the many conflicts that pit nation against nation and ethnic group against ethnic group (Gurr, 1970; Brewer & Campbell, 1976; Streufert & Streufert, 1986). When countries battle over the right to control strategic waterways or land rich in oil and minerals, realistic competition is probably at the root of the conflict.

competition A type of interdependence in which one party's gains result from another party's losses.

realistic conflict theory The theory that intergroup hostility arises from competition among groups for scarce but valued material resources.

Two groups of subjects either competed against one another or cooperated for rewards. Compared with the cooperators, those who competed liked their fellow in-group members better and disliked out-group members more. (Data from Taylor and Moriarty, 1987.)

Figure 14.1 Competition increases solidarity and intergroup hostility

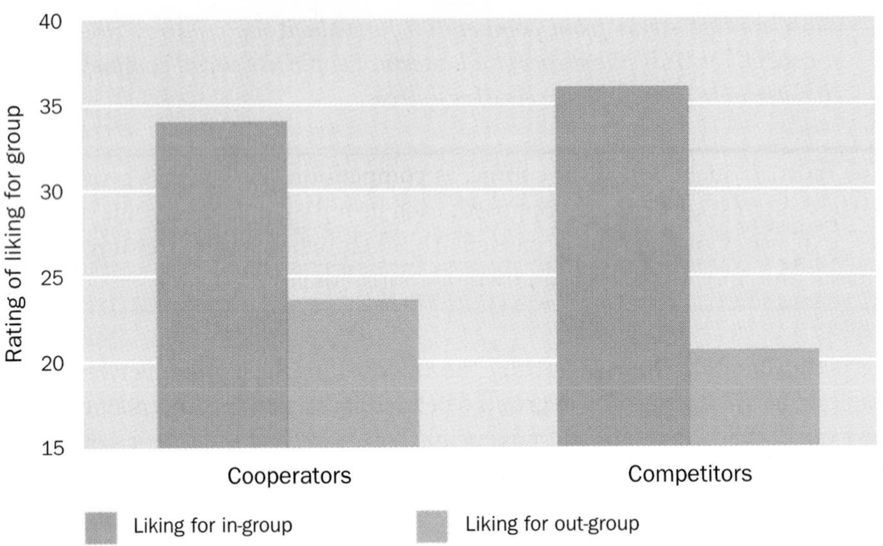

Realistic Conflict in the Workplace. Realistic conflict also rears its head when economic hard times create competition over dwindling resources, particularly jobs. Often this competition flares between ethnic groups (Olzak & Nagel, 1986). In the United States, for example, almost every group of immigrants has viewed the subsequent wave of newcomers as a threat to its share of the economic spoils and has tried to exclude them. When this happens, the discriminated-against frequently become the discriminators.

For example, in 1877, Irish workers—long-time targets of bitter opposition by Anglo-Saxon laborers—formed the Workingmen's Party to exclude Chinese immigrants who were competing with the Irish for jobs (Boswell, 1986). And the process continues, though the ethnic groups are different. Recent outbreaks of violence between African-American and Latino groups in Washington, D.C., and in New York reflect perceived competition over a diminishing supply of jobs. In Florida, impoverished Puerto Rican Americans compete against Haitians and African Americans for public housing and unskilled jobs—a situation worsened by the recession of the early 1990s. The 1992 Los Angeles riots included attacks on Korean-American store owners, a group African Americans sometimes perceive as having unfairly bypassed them on the climb up the economic ladder. In the aftermath of the riots, local dissatisfaction over the relative numbers of government grants awarded to White, Black, Hispanic, and Asian-American construction firms slowed the rebuilding process. When rewards are too few to be enjoyed by all, perceived competition for economic survival fuels intergroup hostilities (Hepworth & West, 1988).

Social Competition: Getting a Little Respect. If groups fought only over material resources, intergroup conflict might be more easily resolved. After all, groups could learn to solve their problems of task interdependence. They could make do with a little less, resources could be more equally distributed, and more goods could be produced—all of which might help groups live side by side in relative satisfaction. Unfortunately, social interdependence can also cause conflicts, when competition occurs over social goods—respect, esteem, and "bragging rights." And this is as true for adults as it is for small boys (Katz, 1965; Tajfel & Turner, 1979).

Consider a series of studies in which two groups of corporate executives attending a training program were assigned problem-solving tasks (Blake & Mouton, 1979, 1984). Researchers told the executives that experts would evaluate each team's performance, but they never mentioned competition nor did they promise concrete rewards for performance. Nevertheless, the experience of being divided into groups and anticipating evaluation was apparently enough to produce conflict. In a virtual replay of the Eagles-Rattlers scenario, team spirit soared and intergroup antagonism rose as group members huddled together during breaks and meals to plan strategies, analyze successful performances, and even hold pep rallies. In one version of the experiment, researchers asked representatives from each group to meet to evaluate the groups' products. These meetings almost always resulted in a deadlock, with each representative insisting his or her own group's work was best. When a neutral judge broke the deadlock, the losing team accused him of bias and incompetence. At one point the researchers had to break off the experiment to calm tempers and restore order.

What drives competition when no material resources whatever are at stake? If you think the answer has something to do with social identity, you're right. You may recall that people's desire to see their own groups as better than other groups can lead to intergroup prejudice. The same process can also contribute to outright conflict. People can even identify with groups formed on the basis of an arbitrary toss of a coin: they don't need to interact with other group members or even to know them, and they don't need to feel their access to material resources is at risk. Research indicates that members of such "minimal groups" nevertheless act as if they were at odds with other groups, treating them in ways that fuel conflict. They downgrade the out-group's products, dislike out-group members as individuals, and discriminate against the out-group in allocating rewards (Brewer, 1979; Turner, 1980). Thus, people's strivings for positive social identity may plant the seeds of intergroup conflict.

Social identity theory and studies that demonstrate people's readiness to identify even with arbitrary, transient groups were discussed in Chapter 6, especially pages 228 to 230.

Relative Deprivation: When Is Enough Enough? Perhaps conflict is understandable when material resources and respect are scarce. But even when this is not the case—when people seem to have adequate resources—they often continue to compete. Apparently once people have the basic necessities of life, few objective standards determine what resources are adequate and so they turn to comparisons with others. This idea is central to **relative**

deprivation theory, which suggests that social comparison, not objective reality, determines how satisfied or dissatisfied people are with what they have (Stouffer and others, 1949; Crosby, 1976; Bernstein & Crosby, 1980). It's not hard to see how this idea might apply in real life. If you had just bought a shiny new Chevrolet, you probably would feel pretty good about it—until your next-door neighbor proudly rolled *his* shiny new Cadillac into his driveway. Your Chevy is still exactly the same car, but suddenly you may not feel quite so proud of it. In fact, you may experience *egoistic relative deprivation,* a sense that you are doing less well than other individuals (Runciman, 1966).

Competition and fraternal deprivation Minorities are often perceived as having the potential to outpace the majority and thus as posing a competitive threat. Responses to that threat often aggravate intergroup conflict. This advertisement from the 1880s shows one response to perceived competition. Magic Washer cleaning liquid is offered as the patriotic alternative to stereotypic views of cheap Chinese labor.

Under many circumstances, however, the crucial comparison people make is not between themselves and other individuals, but between their group and other groups. *Fraternal relative deprivation* is the sense that one's group is not doing as well as other groups (Runciman, 1966). Like egoistic deprivation, fraternal deprivation has little to do with objective levels of adequacy or success. A group with little may be content if those around them

relative deprivation theory The theory that feelings of discontent arise from the belief that other individuals or other groups are better off.

also have little. Conversely, a group whose situation is improving may feel discontent if other groups seem to be improving at a faster rate. During the economic boom of the 1960s, for example, most people in the United States achieved substantial economic gains. Yet the 1960s were also a period of some of the worst racial violence in U.S. history, in part because African Americans saw their economic situation lagging behind that of Whites (Sears & McConahay, 1973).

When comparisons are based on a group's relative success or failure, its members may feel deprived even over issues that are of no personal concern. For example, many childless Whites are opposed to achieving school desegregation through forced busing. Since these people are not worried about their own children, their opposition probably reflects their fear that Blacks as a group are surpassing Whites (Bobo, 1988; Sears & Kinder, 1985). Thus, fraternal deprivation is much more likely to cause intergroup conflict than is egoistic deprivation. Feelings of fraternal deprivation have been found to be directly related to conflicts between unemployed youths and the authorities in Australia (Walker & Mann, 1987), gay and lesbian groups and straight groups in Toronto (Birt & Dion, 1987), French and English speakers in Canada (Guimond & Dube-Simard, 1983), and Muslims and Hindus in India (Tripathi & Srivasta, 1981).

The Special Competitiveness of Groups

Groups are generally more competitive than individuals because group members strive for positive social identity by competing against out-groups and because they demand loyalty from one another in a conflict. Also, compared with individuals, groups are more willing to reciprocate the competitiveness they anticipate receiving from other groups, and they are more willing to exploit out-groups for the in-group's benefit.

Nabith Berri, chief of one militia group in conflict-torn Lebanon, once stated, "When we deal with each other individually, we can be civilized . . . but when we deal with each other as groups, we are like savage tribes in the Middle Ages" (*Indianapolis Star,* 1989). Research evidence confirms Berri's observation: groups usually are much more competitive than individuals. For example, subjects allocating valuable points to themselves and to others like their opponents less and make more competitive choices when playing in teams of two or three than they do when playing alone (McCallum and others, 1985; Insko and others, 1987, 1988). In fact, anything that increases a group's feeling of identity can boost its competitiveness. To demonstrate this point, one group of researchers gave young members of informal handball teams bright orange jerseys to wear—emphasizing their identity as a group. This symbol of group solidarity was enough to increase their aggressiveness relative to their opponents who wore their usual street clothes (Rehm and others, 1987).

In a display of supercompetitiveness, groups sometimes give up absolute gain in order to dominate their rivals (Brewer, 1979). For example, a typical research dilemma offers a choice between two alternatives. Choice *A* gives each group 15 points. Choice *B* gives only 12 points to the in-group but gives the out-group even less, 9 points. A group that chooses *A* gets an absolute maximum amount, so making this choice suggests it cares about obtaining the best for its group regardless of what anyone else gets. But if the group chooses *B*, it will make a smaller profit but have an edge over the out-group. When people maximize their advantage over the out-group at the expense of the in-group's profits, it is a clear sign of a group's supercompetitiveness: doing better than others has become more important than doing well.

The idea that group members strive to outdo others to obtain a positive social identity was discussed in Chapter 6, especially pages 239 to 241.

When group meets group, the competition is fiercer than when individual meets individual. This is true for at least four reasons.

Groups Often Value Respect over Riches. In late 1992 when it appeared that Ford's Taurus model might outsell Honda's Accord, the long-time best seller in the United States, Ford dealers put on an all-out sales push. More than a battle for a few percentage points of the automobile market, this was a struggle to be "Number One." In this kind of situation, social competition and the effort to outdo one's opponent can overshadow competition for material resources (Insko & Schopler, 1987).

The human price of war Victories and defeats are often measured in terms of material resources gained and lost. But the human cost of war goes far beyond such measures, as can be seen in the faces of these young Bosnian soldiers weeping over the grave of one of their comrades. Similar experiences, of course, occur on both sides of the battlelines.

Chester Insko and his colleagues (1992) documented this power of respect over riches in their studies of resource-allocation choices. In these studies, subjects choose among several alternative ways to distribute points worth a small amount of money to their own group and to another group. Groups of subjects initially choose alternatives that maximize the in-group's profit, and they pay little or no attention to the out-group's relative position.

As the play continues, however, the players' choices become more competitive—maximizing the advantage of the in-group over the out-group. And, of course, as soon as one side makes a competitive choice, the other retaliates.

Similar shifts occur in organizational and international conflicts. As Ford and Honda focused on becoming Number One, the battle for profits that originally sparked the competition seemed to fade into the background. If companies focus completely on becoming Number One, sales at deeply discounted prices may even wipe out any profits! Similarly, nations begin wars knowing that either victory or defeat will exact an enormous cost in physical pain, economic ruin, and ecological devastation. Yet they sound the war drums anyway, accepting these losses in exchange for the chance of victory over their opponent. When competition for riches turns into competition for respect, winning becomes everything.

When Conflict Arises, Groups Close Ranks. In situations of conflict, groups demand loyalty, solidarity, and strict adherence to group norms. Group members usually respond, presenting a united front. This tight discipline permits no interaction or empathy with the out-group, which widens the gap between the groups, making further conflict almost inevitable.

Leaders sometimes take advantage of the unifying effect of conflict to strengthen their hold on power. In a demonstration of this process, Jacob Rabbie and Frits Bekkers (1978) simulated a labor-management conflict in their laboratory at the University of Utrecht in The Netherlands. Subjects took the role of a union leader who could be removed from power by an election at any stage during the negotiations. Some students were in an unstable leadership position; only two negative votes would have removed them from office. Others held more stable positions—only a unanimous negative vote could have deposed them. Leaders whose jobs were shaky behaved more competitively in their negotiations with management, apparently to prove themselves and strengthen their position in the eyes of the group.

Rabbie and Bekkers' findings reflect a process that has operated throughout history. A grim roster of leaders have taken their nations into wars and other misadventures to shore up power that was threatened by political rivals, economic troubles, or declining prestige. When his leadership position in Yugoslavia was weakened by the fall of Communism in Eastern Europe and the resulting breakup of the country, Slobodan Milosevic stirred up Serbian nationalistic sentiment and masterminded invasions of Croatia and Bosnia aimed at "ethnic cleansing." His policies seem to have achieved their goal: in late 1992, even as the conflicts he set in motion raged on, Milosevic was overwhelmingly reelected president over a "peace" candidate, Milan Panic.

People Expect Groups to Be Supercompetitive, So They React in Kind. Increased group loyalty and a passion for victory are not the only reasons groups act more competitively than individuals. People also *expect* groups to be more competitively cutthroat. In one study illustrating this point, Rick Hoyle and his colleagues (1989) asked college students to imagine an interaction between two individuals or between two groups. Sure enough, subjects thought that group interaction would be more competitive and more abrasive than one-on-one interactions.

Subjects in a second study believed they would actually interact with others as part of an experiment on how people behave in everyday social encounters. Some subjects expected to participate as individuals whereas others were told they would be part of a three-person team. Half the subjects in each of these conditions expected to interact with an individual, whereas the rest were led to believe they would interact with another three-person team. Before any contact actually took place, all subjects were asked to describe what they thought would occur during the interaction. Once again, regardless of whether they anticipated acting alone or as members of a group, subjects expected a group to be a tougher opponent than an individual would be (Hoyle and others, 1989). This expectation has a self-fulfilling quality. If you think your opponents will act competitively, you will probably try to beat them to it, either to deter them or at least to defend yourself. A recent study confirms this prediction as well (Insko and others, 1990).

Why does an expectation often elicit behavior that confirms it? To review the ways self-fulfilling prophecies produce behavior that corresponds with our expectations see Chapter 3, pages 103 to 105, and Chapter 5, pages 202 to 203.

Groups Offer Social Support for Competitiveness. Groups seem to offer a rich soil for greed-motivated behavior. Taking advantage of others, playing hardball with competitors, putting our own self-interest above others' good—these and similar actions ranked high on the "don't do" list that parents, teachers, or religious figures taught to most of us. But in a group, competing with or even exploiting out-groups can be rationalized as a form of group loyalty—a motive that fits well with people's general tendency to look out for "me and mine." The result is that groups often act more aggressively than individuals even when they do not expect or receive equally competitive treatment from an opponent (Schopler and others, 1993).

Group membership has many effects on the cognitive and social processes underlying conflict. As we have seen, these effects usually operate to make conflict between groups worse than conflict between individuals.

Conflict Escalation: Going from Bad to Worse

Once conflict catches fire the flames spread quickly. Persuasion, promises, and verbal sparring are replaced by attempted coercion, threats, and physical assault. And as new issues and disagreements come to light and inhibitions about breaking the peace dissolve, the arena of conflict broadens. Social competition may displace material competition as conflict escalates. The Rattlers and Eagles certainly followed this pattern. Their initial name calling soon moved on to flag burning and brawling accompanied by food fights and midnight cabin raids.

What causes this pattern of escalating conflict? By now our answer should be familiar: the same social and cognitive processes responsible for other forms of social behavior play a role in conflict situations, too. Those processes—which can affect even the most well-intentioned individuals and groups—intensify conflict and cause opinions to harden.

Intensifying Conflict: Communication and Interaction That Make Things Worse

> *Once conflict starts, poor communication can make it worse. In-group interaction hardens in-group opinion, threats are directed at the out-group, each group retaliates more and more harshly, and other parties choose up sides. All of these processes tend to escalate the conflict.*

We all know the tried and true way to settle disputes: talk it out, spend some time together, try to get along better. But the solution is not always that easy. When conflict heads the agenda, opportunities for communication and interaction may make things worse, not better.

Talking to the In-Group: Polarization and Commitment. Discussion won't help if the only people you talk to are those who take your side. Talking things over with like-minded others pushes group members toward extreme views, a process called *group polarization*. As a result of group discussion, then, people may see their group's position as even more valid and valuable, and they may become even more firmly attached to it.

Why group polarization occurs and the many ways in which group discussion can make the majority opinion more extreme were discussed in Chapter 9, pages 368 to 371.

During discussions we also become more committed to our views. As we explain and defend them, we marshal the best evidence, cite the strongest precedents, and organize every shred of support we can muster. We may pound the table for emphasis as we pick holes in the opposition's reasoning, seize on their slightest hesitations, and counter their every argument. These actions are unlikely to convince the opponents, but they can strengthen our own confidence and commitment (Hovland and others, 1953). As group members see themselves getting worked up, they conclude that they must care a lot about the issues. At the same time, dissonance reduction processes ensure that their private attitudes line up with public positions—even if at first those public positions were just argued for effect without being fully believed. The very public nature of advocacy constitutes a commitment, which makes it even more difficult for group members to back down or change their mind.

To remind yourselves of the ways that self-perception processes and dissonance reduction can bring attitudes into lockstep with actions, review Chapter 8, pages 314 to 323.

Of course, the same processes are also at work in the other group, so positions harden into extreme opposition. As in-group views are confirmed and out-group arguments demolished, each group's position becomes entrenched at the extreme and each group's commitment intensifies (Staw & Ross, 1987). Now the battle lines between groups are drawn even more clearly.

Talking to the Out-Group: Back Off, or Else! As positions harden, groups find it increasingly difficult to communicate productively. At this point persuasion and discussion often give way to attempted coercion and threats. Most people believe threats increase their bargaining power and their chances of getting their way (Falbo & Peplau, 1980; Rothbart & Hallmark, 1988). Of course, since most people believe this, neither group has an advantage. Each is thinking exactly the same thing—cursing the other's unwillingness to listen to reason, deciding that the language of force is the only language the opponent can understand. The reality, unfortunately, is that threats provoke counterthreats, diminish people's willingness to compromise, and in the end, generate hostility.

To see how counterproductive threats can be, consider the findings from a study by Morton Deutsch and Robert Krauss (1960). They asked pairs of female subjects to imagine themselves as owners of two rival trucking companies, named Acme and Bolt, whose profits were based on the speed with which they carried merchandise over roads to specific destinations. For each completed trip, the "owner" earned a flat rate minus operating expenses proportional to the time her trucks spent on the road. To make the most profit, each player needed to take the short central road rather than the long and winding bypass (see Figure 14.2). As the map shows, a potential source of conflict is built into the game: one section of the central road is only one lane wide. If both players reach this section at the same time, one must back up and let the other proceed. This problem was not insurmountable, however. Subjects soon worked out a cooperative solution: they took turns making deliveries along the central road, each earning close to the maximum profit from the experimenter.

Figure 14.2 Routes to conflict

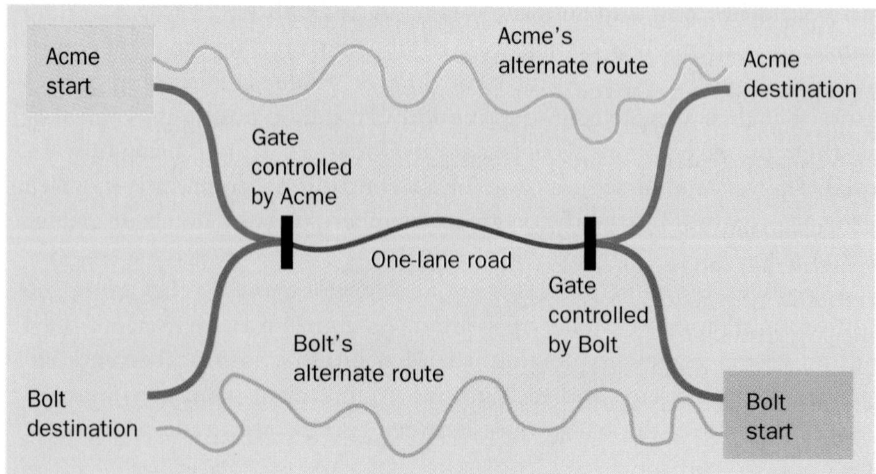

In this study, each subject had to move her company's trucks from a starting point to a destination. Subjects could save time and earn more money by going over the central road, but conflict arose because only one truck could pass through the one-lane section at a time. When one or both parties controlled gates on the central road and threatened to close them, the trucks had to take a long alternate route, losing money. (Adapted from Deutsch & Krauss, 1960.)

So far, so good. But then researchers introduced conditions that allowed the players to control a threat: a gate on the central road. By closing the gate, a player could force the opponent's truck to back up and take the bypass, costing extra time and lowering profits. In the *unilateral threat* condition, Acme controlled the only gate at one end of the one-lane stretch of road. In the *bilateral threat* condition, each company controlled a gate. As before, the companies were free to communicate to try to solve their differences.

How did the would-be trucking company operators react? When Acme could threaten Bolt, Bolt suffered quite a large loss, because the company could not make trips on the roads whenever it wanted to. Acme lost money, too: her trucks waited on the road during confrontations. When both players could use threats matters were even worse. The players consistently lost money as gate closures forced both to travel longer routes. And whether the threat was unilateral or bilateral, players' communications focused on the use and consequences of threat rather than on ways of cooperating to resolve the conflict.

It may have occurred to you that nothing in the rules of the trucking game *forced* the players to threaten one another. They could have ignored the gates and worked together, contentedly taking turns and happily making money. But the evidence indicates that the mere availability of a potential threat appears to be enough to bring about its use. Once people have coercive means at their disposal, they shift from reward-seeking to socially competitive behavior.

The irony is that, as we said earlier, threats usually are counterproductive. The threatened group may assume aggression is inevitable no matter how it responds. And if it responds with a counterthreat, the first group's belief in the opponent's hostility and unwillingness to compromise will be confirmed (North and others, 1964). Further, concerns over prestige and fears of losing face may make groups cling to their views more firmly, resolutely refusing to give in even when the potential costs are very high (Kaplowitz, 1990). Finally, when threats dominate communication, as they did when players controlled gates in the trucking game, they crowd out messages about cooperative solutions (Knudson and others, 1980). Communication can effectively deter and resolve conflict only when threats are not permitted (Smith & Anderson, 1975) or when opponents learn to avoid making threats that spark retaliation (Lawler and others, 1988).

Threat and Deterrence in International Affairs. What can laboratory research tell us about policies of deterrence between nations? A policy of *deterrence* is a political strategy in which one side threatens to use force in the hope of preventing an adversary's use of force (Morgan, 1983). Its central principle is that dangers arise when a potential aggressor believes its opponents are weak or vulnerable (Jervis, 1976). Proponents of these policies follow the maxim that "if you want peace, prepare for war." The lesson of history, however, suggests that if you prepare for war, you get war (Lebow &

Stein, 1987). An analysis of two thousand years of international relations suggests that attempting to deter war by threats usually makes war more, not less, likely (Naroll and others, 1974). Groups that stockpile resources in an effort at deterrence are often perceived as attempting to acquire an offensive edge in preparation for aggression. As a result, they often face escalating conflict from others who fear them (Hornstein, 1975). Speeches proclaiming defensive intentions are unlikely to persuade adversaries who feel threatened by an arms buildup.

Thus, deterrence, like other uses of threats, can backfire, eliciting counterthreats and escalation. This does not mean that it is wise for groups to neglect their defenses. As we have seen, intergroup conflict can stem from greed, and a group without power may appear easy prey for strong aggressors who have little fear of retaliation. Such large differences in power leave the door open for those who would impose deadly "final solutions" to group conflict. Research indicates that groups roughly equal in power and ability use threats and coercion less often and achieve agreements more often than do parties with unequal power (Hornstein, 1975; Lawler and others, 1988). But even equality in power and command of threats cannot guarantee an absence of conflict: recall that in the Acme-Bolt trucking game, the parties fared worst when they both controlled gates they could use as threats.

The multiple effects of the norm of reciprocity are discussed in more detail in Chapter 10, especially pages 410 to 415.

Reciprocity and Conflict Escalation: Do unto Others, Only More So. The Old Testament admonition "an eye for an eye and a tooth for a tooth" was intended to curb revenge for hurts and injuries received. But in an atmosphere of threats and counterthreats, the norm of reciprocity—do unto others as they have done unto you—intensifies conflict more often than it dampens it (Tedeschi and others, 1977; Tedeschi and others, 1974). In laboratory simulations of international conflict, for example, other groups follow suit when one group stockpiles arms, and an arms race usually results (Kramer, 1989).

Of course, if conflict followed the norm of reciprocity *perfectly*, there would be no escalation. A mild threat would elicit a mild threat in return, and conflict would never get any worse. Unfortunately, conflicts tend to spiral upward, suggesting that norms governing pay-back of negative actions might differ from those that generate reciprocal positive behavior (Carroll, 1987; Milburn, 1977). According to George Youngs (1986), conflict escalates because aggression is often met with reciprocity plus a kicker: parties retaliate with more than they received. To test his hypothesis, Youngs set up a competitive game in which women players could use threats to influence their opponent's actions. The opponent's reactions supported his hypothesis—their counterthreats were usually larger than the threats that provoked them. Youngs suspects that parties intensify threats to deter further aggression. If this was the strategy, it was unsuccessful. As threat was answered by bigger threat, the intensity of conflict escalated.

Coalition Formation: Escalation as Others Choose Sides. Conflicts often begin as one-on-one confrontations, but as positions harden, the participants—particularly the weaker side—may call on outside parties for help. *Coalition formation* occurs when two or more parties pool their resources to obtain a mutual goal they probably could not achieve alone (Komorita & Meek, 1978). Coalition formation tends to polarize multiple parties into two opposing sides (Mack & Snyder, 1957). When groups are in conflict, coalition formation is usually seen as a threatening action that, like most threats, only intensifies competition. Those excluded from the coalition may react with fear and anger, and they often form their own coalitions. As unaffiliated groups ally with one side or the other, differences become polarized and the dangerous allure of consensus convinces each side that it is right.

These events may remind you of what happens when groupthink interferes with group decision making. To see the many parallels, reread the discussion of groupthink processes in Chapter 9, pages 381 to 385.

For all these reasons, the formation of coalitions and alliances between nations usually increases the possibility of armed hostility (Wright, 1965). This point—as well as the failure of threats and deterrence—is illustrated by the beginning of the First World War. The scene was set when Austrian Archduke Francis Ferdinand was assassinated by a Serbian nationalist; leaders of the Austro-Hungarian empire retaliated by attacking Serbia. Even then, the conflict might have remained relatively localized, but the two parties' powerful allies stepped in. Serbia's ally Russia, viewing the Austrian attack as a pretext for a German-Austrian conquest of Europe, responded with military mobilization. Germany, feeling endangered, threatened war if Russia did not halt its mobilization. Russia's rejection of this demand led Germany to declare war, first on Russia and then on Russia's ally, France. The escalating hostilities finally drew another ally, Great Britain, into the war (Holsti & North, 1965; North and others, 1964).

Perceptions in Conflict: What Else Could You Expect From Them?

> *As escalation continues, the in-group sees the out-group as totally evil and sees itself in unrealistically positive terms. Because the same biases characterize each group, each group's image of itself and its opponent tends to be similar. Emotion and arousal make these biases even worse.*

As conflict escalates, groups' views of themselves and of their opponents change—and not for the better. These conflict-driven perceptions have little basis in reality, but they affect the group's understanding of what is happening and why. This skewed understanding in turn becomes a guide for group behavior (White, 1965, 1977, 1984). When perceptions are negative, distrust and suspicion casts every action in the worst possible light. And self-fulfilling prophecies exert their own pressure: if one side expects the other to be hostile and devious, a vicious cycle can begin in which the other is *made* to be more hostile and devious.

Polarized Perceptions of In-Group and Out-Group. If mere categorization—with no hint of conflict or competition—can make people evaluate their own group more positively than the out-group, imagine how much stronger perceptual biases become in the midst of bloody conflict. In fact, groups enmeshed in conflict tend to develop three blind spots in their thinking.

When ethnic conflict divides families We are used to thinking about the group-level consequences of ethnic conflict—competition between groups for material goods, power, status, self-determination. But the costs of intergroup conflict are felt at an individual level too. This young boy, his family divided by ethnic warfare in the former Yugoslavia presses his hands against his father's through the window of the bus that is evacuating him and the rest of his family.

1. *The in-group can do no wrong.* Biased perceptions cause members of the in-group to see their group as righteous and morally superior. Its every intention seems pure hearted, its every action justifiable. Not surprisingly, groups in conflict almost always invoke religion to support their view. Leaders of warring parties in the Middle East have characterized their struggles as holy wars, and both the Germans and the Allies in the two World Wars were confident that God was on *their* side. Abraham Lincoln spoke to this issue in his Second Inaugural Address, delivered at the height of the Civil War. Since the North was fighting slavery, wasn't God on its side? "Lincoln's conclusion was that God might not be on either side: 'The Almighty has his own purposes.' He later wrote to a political ally about that speech: '. . . I believe it is not immediately popular. Men are not flattered by being shown that there has been a difference of purpose between the Almighty and them'" (Safire, 1992).

2. *The out-group can do no right.* In contrast, the out-group is now seen as evil, even diabolical. In the recent war in the former Yugoslavia, Bosnian Muslim refugees spoke bitterly of Serbian former neighbors and friends who had turned informers or even taken up arms in the drive for "ethnic cleansing." The Serbians saw their opponents as equally despicable, insisting that their invasion of Bosnia was justified because of reports that Serbian babies were being fed to the lions in the Sarajevo zoo (Lane and others, 1993). Perceptions like these dehumanize the enemy, supporting the idea that they are capable of doing anything to win—and therefore justifying any action taken against them.

3. *The in-group is all powerful.* The in-group soon sees itself as having might as well as right on its side, leading to a preoccupation with appearing powerful, prestigious, tough, and courageous. This aggressive posturing, or what journalist Ross Barnet (1971) termed the "hairy chest syndrome," has dangerous side effects. The focus on winning may crowd out consideration of the merits or morals of in-group actions. The boasts of power may be seen as threats that deserve a response in kind (Lebow & Stein, 1987). Finally, the overconfident in-group may fall for its own rhetoric, just as it hopes the enemy will. U.S. policy in Vietnam offered many examples of overconfidence, as military and political leaders repeatedly promised that the next minor escalation, the next 25,000 troops, would be enough to do the job.

Biased Attributions for Behavior. Groups in conflict frequently attribute identical behaviors by the in-group and the out-group to diametrically opposed causes. One study carried out during the Cold War contrasted American college students' responses to similar military actions supposedly carried out by the United States or the Soviets (Oskamp & Hartry, 1968). Students considered, for example, the sending of aircraft carriers to patrol international waters off the coast of the other country. Subjects who thought the United States had taken the actions against the Soviet Union saw them as more positive and more justifiable than did those who thought the Soviets had acted against the United States. Research has discovered three ways attributions for in-group and out-group actions are biased.

1. *In-group motives are positive; out-group motives are negative.* An in-group action is correct and justified—a protection of our rights, a measured defense against their hostile intentions. When the out-group carries out exactly the same action, it is seen as provocative—a revelation of aggression. We offer concessions, but they attempt to lure us with ploys. We are steadfast and courageous, but they are unyielding, irrational, stubborn, and blinded by ideology.

If this pattern of attributions for behavior seems familiar, you're right. They are group-serving attributions, which were discussed in Chapter 6, pages 231 to 232.

2. *Situations dictate in-group actions; character flaws prompt out-group actions.* People see their own group's actions as reasonable responses to difficult situations—the need to defend oneself from attack, to restrain internal unrest, to stand up for principle against compromise and corruption. Out-

group actions, however, seem to be evidence of their flawed characters—their military moves reflect aggressiveness; their harassment of dissidents reflects inhumanity, intolerance, and insecurity; their rejection of compromise reflects stubbornness and irrationality.

In particular, we often fail to recognize how often fear motivates out-group actions (White, 1987). During the Cold War, fear of powerful Soviet forces largely motivated the U.S. arms buildup. Failing to understand this motivation, however, the Soviets took the buildup as threatening, and they responded with increased military production of their own. The U.S. side similarly reacted to their increase but not to the underlying Soviet fear. And so the cycle continued.

3. *Powerful leaders dictate out-group actions.* Although the combatants often cast the other side as uniformly negative, a more complex pattern of perceptions sometimes develops, particularly in international conflicts. In such cases, the ordinary rank-and-file out-group members are not seen as intrinsically evil themselves but as duped and inflamed by evil leaders. Ralph White (1965) coined the term the *blacktop illusion* for this phenomenon. Such views are seductive. If the majority of the enemy population has no quarrel with us, our position must be right, our cause just, and our victory inevitable. The blacktop illusion has the added benefit of providing a convenient scapegoat—a powerful individual who is easier to vilify and condemn than are the ordinary people who bear the brunt of war and conflict. Thus, during the Persian Gulf War, the U.S. public generally regarded Iraqi leader Saddam Hussein as crazy, villainous, and even demonic, but they often expressed sympathy toward the Iraqi population he governed.

Mirror-Image Thinking. Whatever their differences, the two parties in a conflict usually have one thing in common—the biased perceptions and interpretations that each of them has about the other. Urie Bronfenbrenner (1961) termed these reciprocal misperceptions *mirror-image thinking*. The Russian-speaking Bronfenbrenner first noticed this phenomenon during a trip through the Soviet Union in 1961. In conversations with ordinary citizens, he found that Soviet citizens had the same extremely negative view of the United States that Americans had of the Soviet Union. Each side believed that the other side was aggressively seeking military superiority and that they could not be trusted.

The same phenomenon arises in laboratory studies of conflict. In one study, researchers had students play the role of citizens of "Takonia" or "Navalia"—two fictitious nations in a conflict. The students' task was to rate the effectiveness of various actions designed to resolve the conflict (Rothbart & Hallmark, 1988). As Figure 14.3 shows, subjects thought coercive actions would be more effective than conciliatory actions when carried out by their side. But in rating coercion by the other nation, the same subjects believed it would be much less effective than acts of conciliation. This finding suggests that in real intergroup conflict groups apply the very types of policies that they would never accept if directed against themselves.

Figure 14.3 Mirror-image perceptions: Strong-arm them, be nice to us

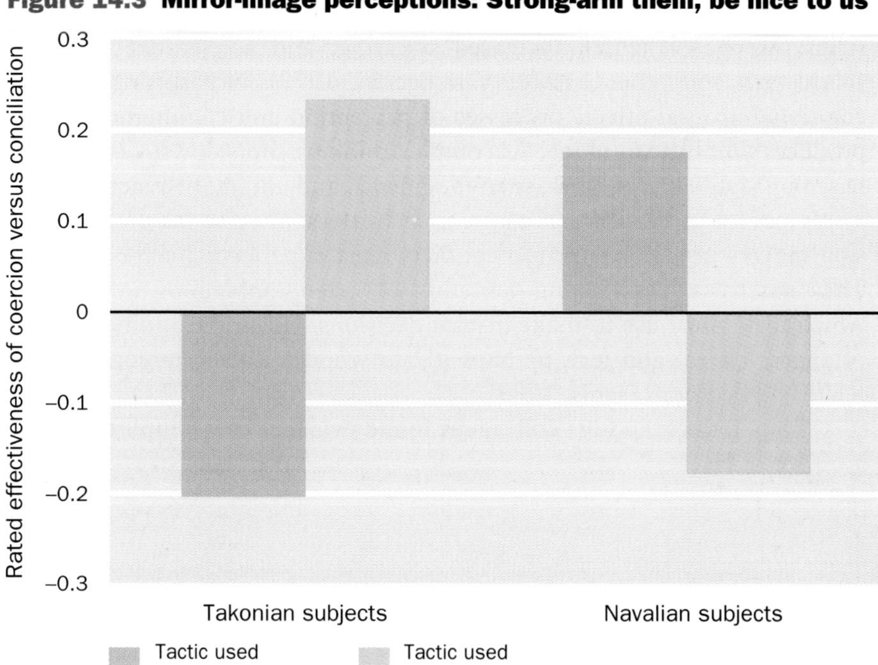

In this study, subjects were asked to play the role of a citizen of either "Takonia" or "Navalia" in a fictitious conflict. Subjects rated coercive tactics as much more effective than conciliation (shown by positive values on the scale) when they used them against their adversary. In contrast they rated coercion as less effective than conciliation (negative values) when their adversary used them. (Data from Rothbart and Hallmark, 1988.)

Mirror-Image Thinking in International Conflicts. Mirror-image thinking often plays a role in international conflicts, as Ralph White (1977) discovered in his in-depth studies of the Arab-Israeli conflict in the Middle East. In the wars of 1956 and 1967, the Arabs believed the Israelis attacked without cause, whereas the Israelis felt Arab threats and provocations had forced them to act. In the wars of 1948 and 1973, the Israelis saw the Arabs' initial attacks as aggression, while the Arabs felt they were forced to respond to Israel's expansionist policies. Similar misperceptions were reported in the conflict in the former Yugoslavia. As journalists described concentration camps in which Serbian forces imprisoned thousands of their enemies under brutal conditions, Serbians countered with claims that six thousand Serbians had died in Croatian and Muslim camps (McAllister, 1992). And while Muslims generally saw themselves as the victims of aggressive Serbian "ethnic cleansing" policies, Serbians viewed themselves as victims of what they perceived as Muslim attempts to control areas in which Serbs had lived for centuries. In their own eyes, the Serbs sought only what other people had: self-government in a unified nation (Lane and others, 1993). Thus in the real world of international conflict as well as in laboratory studies, reciprocal biases produce mirror-image thinking that justifies and escalates conflict.

The Impact of Emotion and Arousal: More Heat, Less Light. As conflict rises, people experience tension, anxiety, anger, frustration, and fear. Even participants in competitive games in the laboratory show obvious signs of stress: nervous laughter, increased sweating, and accelerated heart rate (Blascovich and others, 1978; Van Egeren, 1979). Not surprisingly, this emotional arousal affects processes of perception and communication and produces simplistic thinking. As complex thinking shuts down, decisions are based on simple stereotypes, snap judgments, and automatic reactions.

Recall from Chapter 5, pages 197 to 199, that these were just the circumstances that cause people to rely more on stereotypic views of others. And as Chapter 12, pages 532 to 533, discussed, these conditions also increase aggression.

If laboratory studies can generate such stress, imagine the pressure decision makers in real intergroup conflicts must experience (Milburn, 1977). They receive overwhelming amounts of often ambiguous information, which they must use to make instant decisions. Given the additional stress of anger, hatred, and fear, perhaps it's no wonder leaders in conflict often make bad decisions (Janis, 1989).

Philip Tetlock and his colleagues found evidence of a simplistic pattern

Figure 14.4 Simplistic thinking appears when conflict escalates

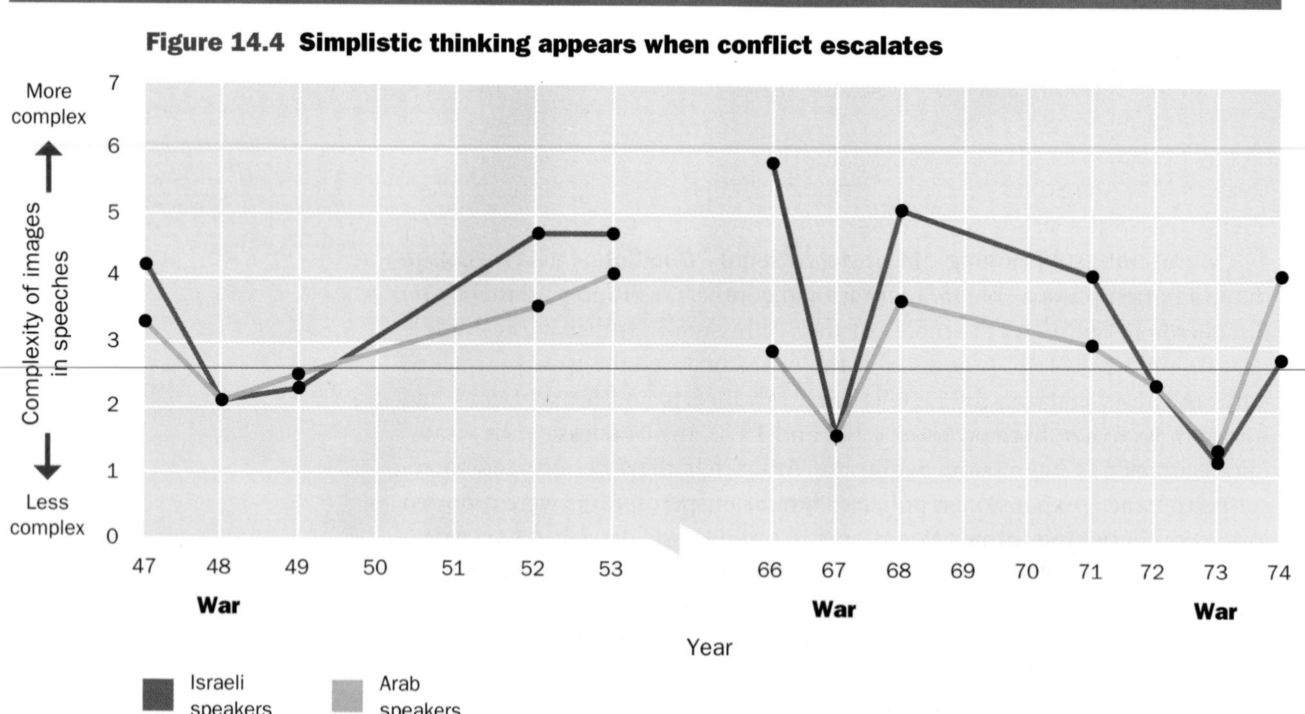

This study tracked the degree of complex thinking in verbal images of the opponent used in speeches by Arab and Israeli leaders in the united Nations. Note that the scores hit their lowest points in the years Arab-Israeli wars occurred. (Data from Suedfeld and others, 1977.).

Figure 14.5 Social and cognitive processes in conflict escalation

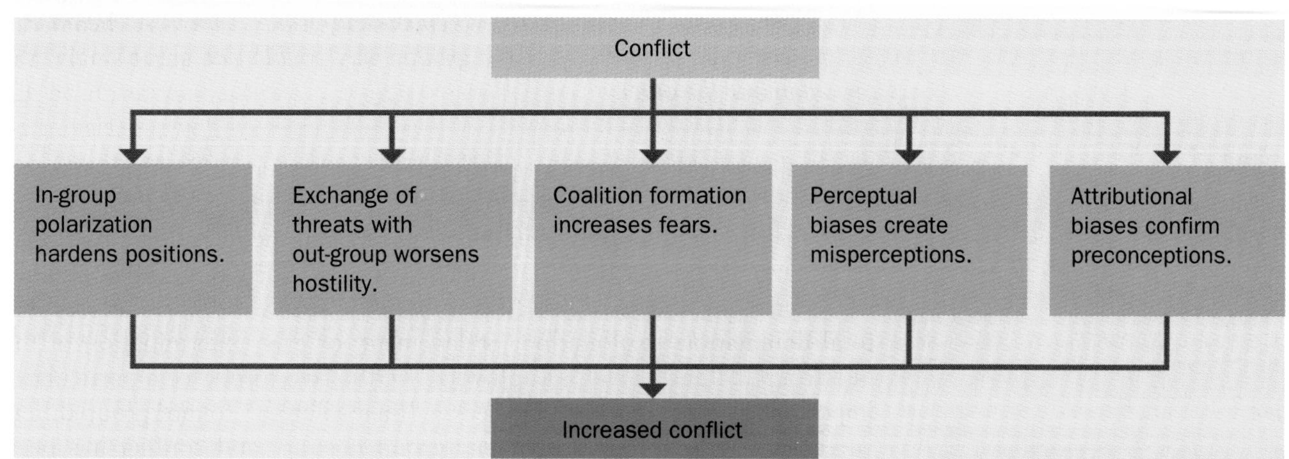

Conflict between groups sets in motion a series of social and cognitive processes. Unfortunately, these processes usually harden each side's position and reinforce mutual negative views.

of thinking when they analyzed U.S. and former Soviet leaders' portrayals of each other in several decades of public speeches (Suedfeld & Tetlock, 1977; Tetlock, 1988). During times of East-West crisis—the Berlin blockade, the Korean War, the Soviet invasion of Afghanistan—both sides' political statements reflected a simplistic dichotomy between the moral in-group and the diabolical out-group. The United States was seen as an imperialist aggressor and the Soviet Union an "evil empire." When tensions relaxed, each side's statements about the other became more complex, acknowledging areas of agreement and common interests as well as continuing disputes. Editorials appearing in major newspapers in the United States, Canada, and the Soviet Union also shifted between simpler and more complex images as the level of conflict changed (Suedfeld, 1992). A study of United Nations speeches, shown in Figure 14.4, showed a similar pattern of simplification in the images used in Arab-Israeli exchanges during years in which war occurred.

There is an important lesson in all of this. People tend to perceive members of out-groups negatively, and anxiety, emotion, and tension strengthen this tendency. In stressful conflict situations, we may leap to the erroneous conclusion that our opponents are ignorant, are willfully misinterpreting evidence, and are fools whose self-interest or pernicious ideology blinds them to the truth. Of course, our opponents are viewing us in the same way. As a result neither side understands the other's perceptions or intentions, and, as Figure 14.5 illustrates, conflict may continue to escalate.

"Final Solutions": Eliminating the Out-Group

Ultimately, conflict may escalate into an attempt at total domination or destruction of the out-group. When the out-group is morally excluded, power differences between the groups may enable one group to try to eliminate the other.

As conflicts escalate, intergroup attitudes may harden, and mutual misperceptions can become oversimplified and overwhelmingly negative. An initially realistic conflict over valuable resources can then become a battle for social supremacy in which the primary concern is defeating the opponent, not controlling the resource. And in extreme cases, the goal can become total domination, exploitation, enslavement, or even extermination of the out-group (Allport, 1954b; Kaplowitz, 1990). Two forces seem particularly important in pushing a group to seek a "final solution" to intergroup differences once the groundwork of intergroup hostility and conflict has been laid.

1. *Moral unconcern progresses to moral exclusion.* When we discussed moral unconcern in Chapter 6, we noted that perceptions of out-group differences and inferiority can make us indifferent to the plight of out-group members. Learning of their victimization or suffering, we shrug and go about our business. But however abhorrent moral unconcern is, it is essentially a passive response. Moral exclusion is a much more active and vicious reaction, which places out-group members outside the boundaries of moral principles. Out-groups are seen as less than human, and they can be treated in whatever way the in-group finds convenient or profitable.
2. *A difference in power between the groups translates desire into action.* Without power, no group can turn prejudice into discrimination, or discrimination into domination. But power gives a group the ability to attain its goals without fear of interference or retaliation, thereby increasing its ability and motivation to discriminate, dominate, and, eventually, eradicate a weaker opponent (Sachdev & Bourhis, 1985, 1991). As history shows, political repression, religious inquisitions, slavery, and genocide often follow (Opotow, 1990).

The effects of these two forces can be seen in the events culminating in the Holocaust in Nazi Germany. Many of the conditions that set the stage for a "final solution" were already in place. Germany had been defeated in the First World War and had suffered economic hardships in the 1930s. The situation was ripe for a *scapegoat*—an enemy who, by bearing the blame for Germany's defeat and material ills, could enhance in-group cohesion and solidify leaders' power. Nazi ideologists drew on centuries of European anti-Semitism to emphasize supposed distinctions between in-group Aryans (supposedly racially pure Germanic folk) and out-group Jews. Negative perceptions and attitudes toward Jews flourished, and German Jews were blamed for the nation's problems.

The two forces that make "final solutions" possible were also operating. First, the Nazis dehumanized the Jews, labeling them "worms" and "vermin," thereby excluding them from the sphere in which fair, just, or human treatment could be expected or demanded. Second, the Nazis held all the high cards, particularly after Hitler's election as chancellor. Their control over the media, government, and military enabled them to enforce rules about every aspect of their victims' social, political, religious, and economic life. Jews as a group held little political power within Germany, and their appeals to other nations for rescue went largely unanswered.

The Nazi Holocaust was unique in many respects, but the social psychological processes that allowed it to happen are not. They can be found whenever one powerful group oppresses a weaker opponent. They were at work when Serbian gunmen herded 57 Muslim residents of the village of Koritnik into a cellar and tossed in grenades, joking that the victims' screams "sounded just like a mosque" (McAllister, 1992). The same processes played a part in the mutual massacres of Muslims and Hindus in India in 1948, Turkey's massacres of Armenians early in this century, European settlers' conquest of Native Americans in the New World, and White Americans' and Europeans' capture of Africans for sale into slavery. When one group holds power over another and begins to dominate or exploit them, negative stereotypes shade into dehumanization, and moral exclusion of the out-group is not far behind. Ultimately, as the processes shown in Figure 14.6 operate, enslavement and genocide become acceptable actions justified by the superiority of the dominant group.

Figure 14.6 Two shifts in conflict

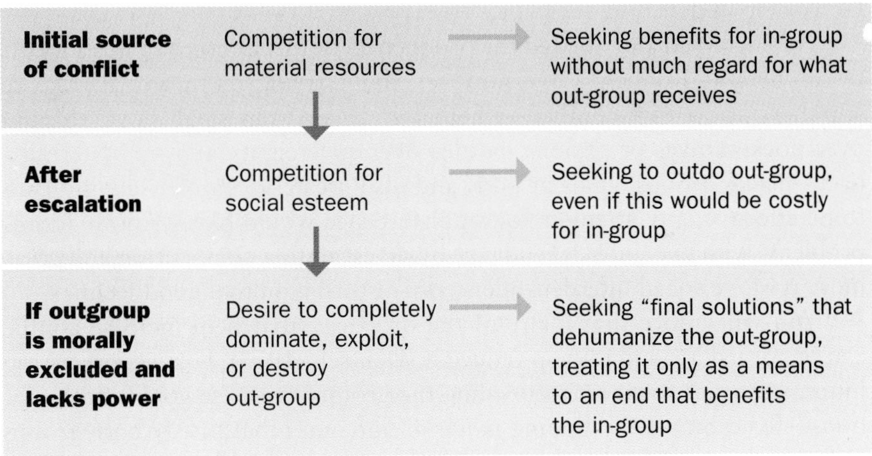

Initial source of conflict
Competition for material resources
Seeking benefits for in-group without much regard for what out-group receives
After escalation
Competition for social esteem
Seeking to outdo out-group, even if this would be costly for in-group
If outgroup is morally excluded and lacks power
Desire to completely dominate, exploit, or destroy out-group
Seeking "final solutions" that dehumanize the out-group, treating it only as a means to an end that benefits the in-group

Conflicts often begin with realistic competition over material resources. If escalation occurs, groups may turn from seeking to do well for themselves to seeking to outdo their opponents. Winning, not prospering, then becomes the goal. In a context where the out-group is morally excluded and the groups have differential power, further escalation may result in a final shift in which the goal changes from outdoing the out-group to completely dominating or eliminating it.

The social psychological study of intergroup conflict yields many significant lessons, but perhaps the most important is that each of us is psychologically capable of hatred and dehumanization of and violence toward out-group members. Many of the New England ship captains who transported Africans to slavery in the Americas were regular churchgoers, fine family men, and respected leaders within their own communities (Deutsch, 1990). And as we noted in Chapter 10, Nazi leaders claimed to be no more than ordinary citizens who cared about their families and did their job to protect them. Yet when groups are in conflict, social and cognitive processes—the same processes that sometimes produce empathy, bravery, altruism, and self-sacrifice—can conspire to produce extraordinary evil.

Resolving Intergroup Conflict

When we left the Rattlers and the Eagles at Robbers Cave State Park, they were thoroughly at odds with each other. Of course, their war did not spiral out of control like many international conflicts, but as childhood conflicts go, the hostility was pretty bad. Moreover, they displayed many of the earmarks of conflict discussed in the previous sections. The groups' negative feelings about each other escalated; "those guys" became, in the slang of the day, "bums," "bad guys," "those damn campers," and "stinkers." The groups felt powerful: as the athletic tournament began, each team was supremely confident of winning. Group norms were strictly enforced. Anyone wanting to be friends or even seen speaking with a member of the other team was branded a traitor and ruthlessly brought into line with threats of bodily harm or ostracism. And as competition heated up, the groups struggled to differentiate themselves from the hated out-group. When the Rattlers became known for their propensity to swear, for example, the Eagles decided to ban all profanity. Finally, each group believed in the righteousness of its cause—that God was on its side. Before setting out to raid the opponent's campsites, the Eagles held prayer meetings to ask for God's help in defeating their foe.

Having aided and abetted the production of this intergroup hostility, the researchers at Robbers Cave now set about trying to resolve it. The researchers knew that conflict—whether it arises from small boys' disputes over pocketknives or nations' battles over sovereignty and self-determination—places groups' goals at odds and also creates negative feelings. Thus, to be effective, any attempts to establish peace would have to both address problems with task interdependence by de-escalating competition and create more positive social interdependence by restoring mutual good feelings.

It's interesting that task and social interdependence, the main issues that must be solved to reduce intergroup conflict, are the same issues that must be handled for a single group to perform effectively. See Chapter 13, pages 563 to 585.

You will notice that many of the processes that help increase conflict can be turned around to help reduce it (Deutsch, 1973). Some conflict-resolution strategies focus on reconciling the groups' concrete goals and aspirations—for example, by finding material outcomes that satisfy both groups. Other strategies address the negative intergroup attitudes and interactions that both follow from and intensify conflict. Of course, the strategies often overlap. Solutions for concrete issues also leave the two parties feeling better about each other. And any approach that helps reduce hostility and negative assumptions about each others' motives will also help the parties discuss their real differences productively.

Communicating Peace: Conflict Resolution Through Negotiation

To resolve conflicts, the parties try to find mutually acceptable solutions, which requires understanding and trust. When direct discussion is unproductive, third parties can intervene to help the parties settle their conflict.

Types of Solutions. One approach to conflict resolution seeks solutions for the concrete disagreements that separate the groups. Sometimes one group dictates a solution—as when one nation overwhelms another by force, or one firm lowers prices until it drives its opponent out of business. In such cases, the conflict is resolved by an *imposed solution.* Imposed solutions are based on the assumption that mutual agreement and mutual benefit are impossible: what one party gains, the other must lose. Not surprisingly, those who lose are usually dissatisfied with the outcome, and such solutions are rarely successful in ending conflict (Burke, 1970). Discontent with the outcome may actually increase irritation over the original cause of conflict and make later aggression even more likely. Historians often point to the galling terms of defeat imposed on Germany after the First World War as one of the factors that contributed to the rise of the Nazis and Germany's later aggression.

Communicating to resolve conflict Unless parties in conflict communicate, the common interests that may provide a basis for integrative solutions may never be realized. With an historic handshake in September 1993, Israeli Prime Minister Yitzhak Rabin (left) and Palestine Liberation Organization Chairman Yasser Arafat conclude negotiations that have produced increased self-determination for Palestinians in Israel's occupied territories. Although great difficulties remain, there is hope for peace in a region long torn by ethnic and religious differences.

Most conflicts, however, are settled in more moderate ways as groups abandon the goal of completely vanquishing their opponents. Perhaps the mounting costs of conflict become clear, or the perceived chance of victory fades, or tempers finally cool and emotions are reined in (Kriesberg, 1982). Under these conditions, most opponents turn to *distributive solutions,* which involve mutual compromise or concessions that carve up a fixed-size pie. Examples of such solutions include international treaties that divide territory under dispute or union-management contracts that set workers' raises at a point midway between union demands and management's proposals (Fisher & Ury, 1981). Compromise and concession mean that all parties must give up something they wanted, but the loss may be tolerable, particularly when compared to the cost of continued conflict.

Calvin and Hobbes by Bill Watterson

Reprinted with permission.

Integrative solutions are the best solutions because one side's gain is not necessarily the other's loss. These solutions are often termed *win-win solutions* because both sides can benefit simultaneously (Pruitt & Rubin, 1986). Imagine, for example, a resolution in which labor and management agree to split the increased profits from a new way of organizing production so that both sides come out ahead (Pruitt & Lewis, 1977; Kimmel and others, 1980). Dean Pruitt (1986) suggests several strategies that can lead to integrative solutions. One is log-rolling, in which each party gives up on issues that it considers less important but that the other group views as crucial. Although each party gets only some of its demands, it wins on the issues it considers most important. In an industry where employment is dropping as a result of foreign competition, for example, the union may accept small pay raises to get guarantees of job security. Management's concessions on job security enable it to maintain wage scales that allow competitive pricing. Another strategy that leads to integrative solutions is cost cutting, which consists of giving one party what it wants in a way that minimizes the costs to the other party. For example, if the union wanted company-paid health insurance, and the company could take advantage of a state tax break by offering such coverage, a cost-cutting solution would have been found.

Finding an integrative solution generally requires creative thinking and an understanding of each party's interests, values, goals, and costs. Identifying an integrative solution is more difficult than locating some halfway point between the parties' demands. Integrative solutions attempt to satisfy the parties' underlying motives, rather than their explicit demands (Fisher & Ury, 1981). A story is told of two library patrons who fell to quarreling over whether a window should be open or closed. Hearing the commotion, the librarian asked the patrons what they really wanted. When it turned out that one wanted some fresh air and the other wanted no draft, the librarian satisfied them both by opening a window in the next room. The point is that two parties' interests may be compatible even when their stated positions are not.

Some real-world situations may be similar. For example, Israel captured the Golan Heights region from Syria in 1967. Syria demands the return of this land and Israel refuses; neither party will accept a division of the territory between them. Some diplomats have suggested that an integrative solution might be possible, based on an analysis of the two parties' underlying needs rather than their contradictory claims to the same piece of landscape. Syria's main interest appears to be its national honor: international recognition of its sovereignty over the Golan Heights might satisfy it. Israel's overriding concern is military security: an ironclad guarantee that Syria could never mass troops and guns on the Golan might suffice. Both parties' most basic needs might be satisfied by a solution that restored the Golan Heights to Syria but guaranteed international monitoring to ensure that arms would never be emplaced there. Compared with solutions based on compromise, integrative solutions result in better outcomes for both parties, are more enduring, and produce better interparty relationships (Pruitt, 1986; Thompson, 1993).

Achieving Solutions: The Negotiation Process. Finding a solution to a conflict—particularly an integrative solution—requires the parties to communicate. **Negotiation** is reciprocal communication designed to reach agreement in situations in which some interests are shared and some are in opposition (Fisher & Ury, 1981; Rubin & Brown, 1975). Diplomatic negotiations have successfully resolved international disputes over arms control, territory, and trade. Of course, not all negotiation is large scale and formal. We all negotiate with others virtually every day: when we discuss what movie to see with our friends, split up the work with our co-workers, or debate bedtime with our children.

The fundamental goal of negotiation is to help each party understand how the other interprets and evaluates the issues. Unfortunately, parties in conflicts often misperceive each other's position and goals, usually exaggerating their disagreement (Thompson, 1990). In one study demonstrating this point, 85 percent of the participants failed to realize—even after a period of negotiations—that they and their opponents agreed perfectly on one issue in contention (Thompson & Hastie, 1990a). These biased perceptions

negotiation The process by which parties in conflict communicate and influence each other to reach agreement when they have partially opposing preferences.

of adversaries lower the chances of an integrative solution. When one side proposes a solution, the other side automatically views it less favorably, reasoning that "if it's good for them it must be bad for us." This obstacle to integrative solutions is termed *reactive devaluation* (Ross & Nisbett, 1990).

One study demonstrated reactive devaluation in the context of a conflict between Stanford University administrators and student groups demanding the university's divestment of stock holdings linked to South Africa (Stillinger and others, 1989). Two possible compromises were proposed: one for divestiture only of those stocks specifically linked to the South African military or police; the other for setting a deadline for total divestiture two years in the future. When students were told, truthfully, that the university was considering both proposals, they rated them as nearly equally desirable. But when they were told that the university was about to enact one of the two proposals, they rated it less satisfactory than the unchosen alternative. Apparently, when one party in a conflict takes a position, it triggers a search for hidden motives by the other party.

Building Trust. One of the priorities in negotiation is building trust so that parties will abandon their search for negative motives within each other's proposals. This is not easily accomplished because a history of bitter conflict is a poor foundation for trust. Even a sincere offer may be seen as a trick, a subterfuge designed to lull the opponent into a false sense of security. In such situations, trust must be built up by repeated displays of consistency between words and deeds (Lindskold, 1978). The impact of trustworthy behavior is increased if the parties repeatedly and explicitly refer to the concepts of trust, cooperation, and fairness (Swingle & Santi, 1972).

Another approach to building trust involves prenegotiation workshop meetings between members of the opposing sides. By providing a controlled environment, these meetings help individuals to develop trust, share perspectives, disabuse each other of false impressions, and explore each other's goals and values (Burton, 1969; Kelman, 1978). Although nothing is binding on the warring parties, their increased knowledge of the other side's perspectives and interpretations can lay the groundwork for productive negotiations and, perhaps, the discovery of integrative solutions. Research shows that negotiators who first meet with opposition representatives are less likely to see negotiation as a competitive win-lose enterprise than are negotiators who confer only with their own supporters (Druckman & Zechmeister, 1973).

graduated and reciprocated initiatives in tension reduction (GRIT) A process in which one party makes a concession to induce the other to reciprocate in order to reduce tension and de-escalate conflict.

Trust and the Norm of Reciprocity. During the height of the Cold War, Charles Osgood (1962) and Amitai Etzioni (1962) independently suggested that reciprocal concessions could both build trust and reduce intergroup tensions. Osgood advised world governments to use **graduated and reciprocated initiatives in tension reduction (GRIT)** to de-escalate conflicts.

The GRIT process begins when one side states its intention to reduce the conflict and makes a small concession to its opponent. The norm of reciprocity pushes the opposing group to make a small concession of its own or risk public condemnation. Of course, the party offering the first concession must walk a fine line between strength and weakness because total cooperation is often interpreted as an opportunity for exploitation (Reychler, 1979). If the opponent reciprocates with a concession, the first group follows with a slightly more significant concession. Again the opponent reciprocates with a greater concession, and a feeling of trust gradually builds as tensions wind down. Simulations of international negotiations in the laboratory have confirmed that reciprocal concessions may be effective in reducing international tensions (Lindskold, 1986).

Remember from Chapter 10, pages 413 to 415, that just as we feel obligated to return a favor for a favor, we feel obligated to follow a concession with a concession.

GRIT and International Conflicts. The tactics recommended in the GRIT strategy have been used successfully in international relations. In June 1963 President John F. Kennedy, calling attention to the dangers of nuclear war, announced a unilateral halt to American atmospheric tests of nuclear weapons and promised not to resume testing unless another country did so first. Within two months, Soviet Premier Nikita Khrushchev ended the production of Soviet strategic bombers, agreed to the emergency communication hot line between Moscow and Washington, and signed a treaty limiting nuclear testing. Similarly, in 1977 Egyptian President Anwar Sadat's dramatic initiative of traveling to Jerusalem led to the Camp David peace talks and a treaty normalizing relations between Israel and Egypt. Cases like these suggest that GRIT shows promise in reducing international tensions (Druckman, 1990; Etzioni, 1967).

More recently, the foreign policy initiatives of former Soviet leader Mikhail Gorbachev are credited with de-escalating Cold War tensions between the United States and the Soviet Union. In the mid-1980s, Gorbachev initiated a series of meetings with then-president Ronald Reagan; the meetings culminated in a treaty eliminating intermediate-range nuclear weapons. Gorbachev later completed the withdrawal of Soviet troops from Afghanistan and normalized relations with China. These initiatives brought about massive political changes and the collapse of the old Communist order in Eastern Europe—and ultimately of the Soviet Union itself. Although historians will debate the complex causes of this web of connected events for decades to come, Gorbachev's conciliatory gestures undoubtedly made a major contribution to the reduction of world tensions.

Settling on Solutions. Because the goal of negotiation is to bridge the parties' divergent perceptions of the issues, negotiators usually try to break conflicts into sets of small, manageable issues. For example, a labor-management dispute may be structured as a series of negotiable issues, such as wage rates, payment of medical benefits, changes in grievance procedures, and so on. The two sides can then discuss these issues in concrete and realistic terms, exchanging offers and counteroffers. By concentrating on specific issues, negotiation can reverse the process of escalation that occurred during the commitment and coalition formation phases of the conflict. This reversal occurs in two ways. First, when individual group members successfully negotiate one issue with an out-group member, their liking for the out-group increases, perhaps making other issues easier to settle (Thompson, 1993). Second, when issues are narrow and specific, groups have a better chance of accurately perceiving each other's position rather than assuming the worst about it. Accurate perceptions of the other side's views and interests are the best hope for success in negotiation (Thompson & Hastie, 1990a, 1990b). Negotiators sometimes use a procedure called *role reversal* to check on the accuracy of opponents' perceptions. In role reversal, each side states the *other* side's position and demands as clearly and objectively as it can. As misperceptions are revealed they can be corrected (Deutsch, 1993).

What negotiation strategies are likely to result in a positive outcome for groups? Negotiators who demand more usually get more (Deutsch, 1980; Thompson, 1990). Tough bargaining may lower the other side's expectations, making them willing to settle for less (Yukl, 1974). But being tough sometimes backfires. A demanding and inflexible bargainer can create a deadlock, not only increasing irritation but also prolonging the negotiations (Druckman, 1973). Failure to reach an agreement or rejection of reasonable proposals could further increase intergroup tensions.

Negotiation has a better chance of success when authority is delegated to a group representative, usually a skilled negotiator. This strategy maximizes efficiency because skilled negotiators know conflict-resolution strategies, are familiar with the background of the dispute, and can keep their emotions under control while pursuing the best solution. Appointing a single group representative also reduces the number of different perspectives and claims that need to be considered. And the strategy has an additional advantage: the negotiator can delay making a commitment until he or she consults the group, which allows time to consider the options carefully.

But relying on group representatives has disadvantages as well. The other side may refuse to bargain with someone who lacks the authority to make the final decision. And for their part, negotiators—knowing that they may be rejected if they are seen as having failed the group (Blake & Mouton, 1979)—may not consider all possible options or may present themselves as so tough that negotiations become hopelessly deadlocked (Thompson, 1990). To insulate themselves from their constituents' constant evaluation and the resulting polarization into hard-line positions, negotiators often choose closed-door meetings, which they find more effective than those conducted in public (Druckman, 1973).

Cultural Perspectives on Negotiation. Pervasive differences among cultures influence the way people negotiate just as they influence other types of social interaction (Adler, 1991; Casse, 1982). Negotiators from the United States prefer making small gains on the way to larger agreements and mixing competition and cooperation in the form of mutual concessions. In contrast, Russian negotiators generally start with extreme positions, make few concessions, and view their opponents' concessions as signs of weakness that should be exploited rather than reciprocated (Adler, 1991). (Perhaps the impact of Mikhail Gorbachev's initiatives, described earlier, stemmed in part from their very unexpectedness.) Similarly, the Chinese approach to negotiation has been described as a tough offensive posture characterized by a lack of reciprocal concessions and an unwillingness to begin with small issues and move to larger ones. Perhaps it's not surprising that deadlocks frequently occur when U.S. and Chinese negotiators sit down at the bargaining table (Druckman & Mahoney, 1977). Training in cultural styles and expectations for negotiation could be a valuable preparation for those who bargain with members of other cultures.

Mediation and Arbitration: Bringing in Third Parties. Even if people share the same culture, direct communication is not always the best way to resolve conflicts. When opponents are too angry to discuss issues rationally or negotiators run out of ideas for resolving an impasse, third-party intervention may offer the best hope for a solution. The United Nations Security Council, baseball labor arbitrators, divorce mediators, moderators at a debate, and parents intervening in their children's squabbles are all third parties attempting to inhibit, regulate, or help resolve conflicts. Some negotiations involve *mediators* who help the opponents focus their discussion on the issues and reach a voluntary agreement. In *arbitration,* the third party has the power to hand down a decision after hearing the disputants present their arguments and information.

Third-party intervention has several advantages. First, mediators or arbitrators can arrange meeting agendas, times, and places so that these details don't themselves become sources of conflict (Raven & Rubin, 1976). Second, skillful intervention—mediation in particular—can improve intergroup relationships. In one case, third parties were called in to mediate a dispute between public housing tenants and private homeowners in a small Canadian community. As a result of their work, intergroup attitudes improved, as did understanding of the complexity of each side's position (Fisher & White, 1976). The third advantage of third-party intervention is that, because outsiders bring fresh ideas, they may be able to offer more creative integrative solutions than those proposed by people deeply enmeshed in the conflict (Fisher & Ury, 1981). Finally, a skilled third party can leave room for graceful retreat and face saving when disputants lock themselves into positions they themselves realize are untenable (Pruitt, 1981). Third-party intervention may allow both sides to accept concessions without embarrassment. By doing so, it is more likely to lead to a mutually acceptable outcome than is unaided negotiation (Rubin, 1980).

Mediators and arbitrators must, of course, win the trust of the parties in the dispute. Parties in conflicts bring their biased perceptions to the bargaining table whether they deal with each other directly or through an impartial third party. Consider what happens when a mediator proposes a compromise solution or offers an interpretation of events that lies between the views of the two parties. Because each party sees its view of reality as objectively correct, it may interpret this movement away from the "correct" position as evidence of the mediator's bias—or at least his or her lack of understanding of the issues. One study demonstrating this point found that supporters of both sides in a conflict considered news coverage to be biased against them (Vallone and others, 1985). It's always possible that third parties who independently arrive at moderate views of the issues will be attacked by all sides.

Intergroup Cooperation: Solving Disputes by Working Together

Conflict resolution can also be facilitated by having groups cooperate toward shared goals that can be attained only if both groups work together. Under the proper conditions, cooperative intergroup interaction reduces conflict.

After an athletic contest that marked the height of the Robbers Cave conflict, the researchers decided to see whether joint participation in some pleasant activity could reduce hostilities. They arranged for the boys to have meals at the same time and to watch a movie together. If you recall our discussion in Chapter 5 of the conditions under which contact improves intergroup attitudes, you will not be surprised that the group contact did not help. Rather than providing the opportunity for consistently friendly interaction that disconfirmed stereotypes—the key to changing negative group perceptions—this kind of contact increased hostilities. The boys found that the shared meals provided perfect opportunities for food fights.

Superordinate Goals. When simple contact failed, the researchers tried a different strategy. They engaged the groups in the pursuit of **superordinate goals,** which are goals that can be attained only if groups work coopera-

Joining together to attain superordinate goals Korean small business owners were the target of African-American rage during the 1993 Los Angeles riots. In the riots' aftermath, many members of the two groups joined together in the realization that only by working together could they overcome their much greater common enemies of poverty and powerlessness.

Figure 14.7 Cooperation cures conflict

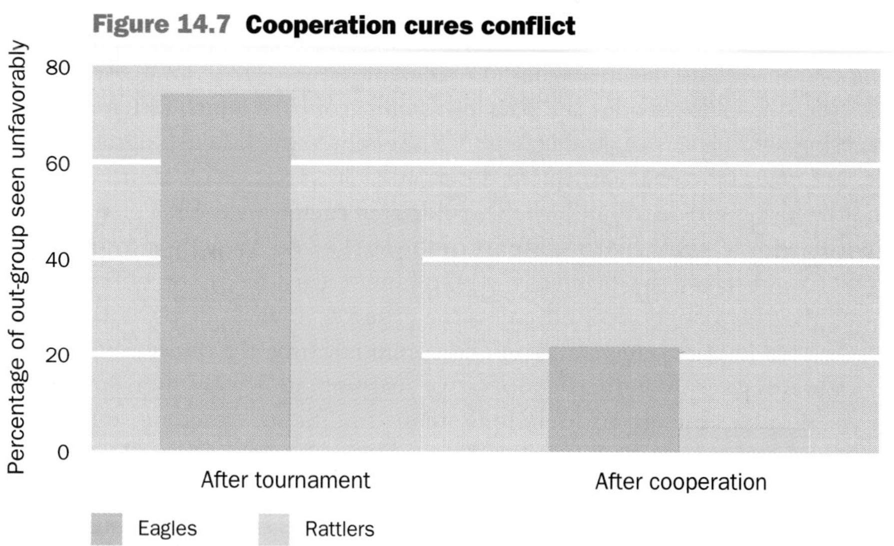

In the Robbers Cave experiment, hostility between Eagles and Rattlers reached a peak right after an athletic tournament. Researchers then arranged for the two groups to work together to achieve a series of superordinate goals that neither could attain alone. As the boys cooperated, intergroup hostility greatly declined. (Data from Sherif & Sherif, 1953.)

tively as a team. Examples of superordinate goals in political life are cooperation between agricultural and urban interests to increase water supplies for all, or between nations to eliminate greenhouse gases from the atmosphere to stop global warming. At Robbers Cave the superordinate goals were a series of "problems" that could be solved only if the teams worked together. For example, the staff staged a breakdown of the water supply, and the boys worked together to trace the water pipeline back into the hills. A movie was too expensive for either group alone to rent, so all the boys pooled their funds to pay the rental fee. Finally, after finding that the camp truck had broken down, they figured out how to restart the truck by pulling on a rope attached to its bumper. In contrast to the earlier competitive tug-of-war contests, the boys literally had to pull together, and—thanks to the driver's carefully calibrated foot pressure on the brake—it took the efforts of all the boys from both groups to get the truck moving.

Superordinate goals improved intergroup relationships, but not overnight. After repairing the water supply, the two groups mingled good-naturedly, but they capped the day off with a food fight. They rented the movie with pooled resources, but the two groups sat on opposite sides of the dining hall to watch it. After six days of cooperation, however, their previous hostilities were greatly decreased, as can be seen in Figure 14.7. In fact, when it was time to leave they asked if they could travel home together on one bus. As the boys took their seats on the bus, the camp staff noticed that a Rattler was just as likely to sit next to an Eagle as to another Rattler (Sherif & Sherif, 1953). Superordinate goals have had similar success in eliminating other forms of experimentally induced conflict (Diab, 1970).

superordinate goals Shared goals that can be attained only if groups work together.

Superordinate Goals in the Classroom. Can working toward superordinate goals reduce racial and ethnic antagonism among students? Research shows that they can. The **jigsaw classroom technique** developed by Elliot Aronson and his colleagues (1978; Blaney and others, 1977; Aronson & Osherow, 1980) divides children into small groups in which different ethnic groups and levels of academic ability are represented. Like a jigsaw puzzle, the material to be learned for a particular lesson is divided into pieces, and the pieces are distributed to the children in each group. Each child is responsible for learning his or her part of the lesson and teaching it to the rest of the group. Thus, the group as a whole cannot learn the lesson unless each group member cooperates and unless the group as a whole helps each member succeed in both understanding and communicating the information.

Studies show that such cooperative learning strategies often produce more positive intergroup relations than traditional teaching methods (Johnson and others, 1984). Children taught in jigsaw classrooms in the United States and in Israel feel more liked and more supported than those in ordinary classrooms. They also develop more out-group friendships, are more aware of feelings and thoughts of peers, and have greater self-esteem (Johnson and others, 1981; Sharan & Sharan, 1976; Slavin, 1980).

Why Does Intergroup Cooperation Work? Intergroup cooperation is not a fool-proof cure for conflict. But when the right conditions exist, intergroup cooperation undermines many processes that contribute to conflict and it encourages positive interactions that can ultimately reduce prejudice (Allport, 1954b). What are those conditions?

1. *Cooperation should be for a valued common goal, which eliminates competition for material and social resources.* Rather than battling for pocketknives or bragging rights, the campers at Robbers Cave pooled their talents and resources to reach mutually desired goals. Rather than competing to learn the most, or to be the first to answer the teacher's questions, children in jigsaw classrooms pool their efforts for joint gain.

2. *Cooperation should provide repeated opportunities to disconfirm out-group stereotypes.* Remember that intergroup conflict arises from group differences as well as from competition over resources. As we saw at Robbers Cave, it took several bouts of cooperation to bring the Rattlers and Eagles together. Similar results are found in laboratory studies: a single cooperative episode often has quite limited effects (Wilder & Thompson, 1980; Lockhart & Elliot, 1981). When groups have a history of bitter intergroup conflict, it is not surprising that building a friendly and egalitarian social climate and breaking down ingrained stereotypes takes time.

3. *Cooperation should produce successful results.* If groups fail while working together, each is likely to blame the other, and hostility may

jigsaw classroom technique A procedure in which groups of diverse students cooperate in teaching one another individual pieces of the material to be learned.

even increase (Worchel, 1979; Worchel & Norvell, 1980). Residual distrust between the groups means that each finds the other a highly salient scapegoat on which to place the blame. In contrast, success helps the intergroup climate. Children in jigsaw classrooms see classmates of varying backgrounds and abilities confidently and correctly teaching them material and contributing to the team's success. In this setting, the bias that leads people to attribute others' behavior to their internal characteristics now helps the children perceive each other not as failures but as successful people.

The kind of cooperation that works In the small Israeli village of Neve Shalom/Wahat al-Salaam (Hebrew and Arabic for "oasis of peace") Palestinian, Israeli, and Bedouin villagers have organized a wool festival designed to invigorate their community's economy. Before the festival, Arab and Jewish children work together to wash the sheep in local streams. This kind of cooperation—involving successful pursuit of shared goals through personal contact that disconfirms stereotypes—is the best hope for breaking down the barriers of dislike and distrust that fuel group conflict.

4. *Cooperation should take place between equals, at least for the task at hand.* The Rattlers and the Eagles were all equally capable of pulling the bus and donating to the film fund. True cooperation is not possible in jigsaw classrooms if children from different groups enter the situation with very different levels of preparation or access to resources. Thus, teachers in these classrooms try to assign tasks that all children are equally able to master.

5. *Cooperation should be supported and promoted by social norms.* The goal of peaceable and respectful coexistence needs official institutional endorsement (Allport, 1954b; Amir, 1969). A few instances of cooperation cannot overwhelm intergroup hostility that is culturally ingrained

and institutionally supported. Thus, for example, brief programs that bring together Catholic and Protestant children in Northern Ireland will not change intergroup perceptions if armed conflict continues and sectarian leaders on both sides insist on separate schools (Trew, 1986).

Intergroup cooperation resolves conflicts because it eliminates negative task interdependence between the groups by making the out-group a source of rewards rather than punishments. Cooperation also resolves problems of social interdependence by fusing the warring parties into one new and improved in-group (Gaertner and others, 1989, 1990). Figure 14.8 portrays this idea. As "we" and "they" become just "we," the new, larger group membership can be a source of self-esteem and a positive social identity (Feshbach & Singer, 1957; Turner, 1981a). Even more importantly, "we" feelings decrease competition. In an experimental demonstration of this point, Roderick Kramer (1989) had small groups of subjects play a game simulating an arms race. To create in-group feelings, some subjects were reminded that all the groups had some features in common. Compared with subjects not receiving the reminder, those with "we" feelings were much less likely to stockpile weapons. Similarly, in a study in which two groups of subjects drew from a common resource pool, each took large amounts and quickly depleted the resource (Kramer & Brewer, 1984). However, when subjects were reminded of their joint membership in a larger shared group, both groups cooperated more and used less of the resource.

Forming a new and more inclusive in-group works best in solving intergroup conflict if the original groups are permitted to retain some measure of distinctiveness rather than merging completely (Condor & Brown, 1988). For example, each group might perform distinct roles and tasks that contribute to the overall good (Brown & Wade, 1987; Brown and others, 1986; Deschamps & Brown, 1983). In this way, each group maintains its own cultural distinctiveness and its positive identity, while cooperating toward a greater goal improves its view of other groups (Taylor & Simard, 1979). The real ideal of a multicultural society is a tossed salad, not a melting pot. Every group's contribution is valued and respected for itself rather than as an indistinguishable part of a uniform whole. Cultural differences then become opportunities for learning and mutual enrichment rather than bases for conflict (Deutsch, 1993).

Intergroup cooperation for superordinate goals holds the promise of true conflict *resolution,* rather than conflict *management* (Cohen & Arnone, 1988). Conflict resolution turns groups' basic strivings for mastery and connectedness toward positive ends. Previously hostile groups find ways to enhance their identities by cooperating—for example, in creating a truly multicultural society—rather than by outdoing one another. New symbols are created that reflect pride and respect for both sides, and the groups' old symbols of intransigence and hatred are allowed to slip into history. Just as conflict can build on itself and escalate, each step toward conflict resolution—whether aimed at task or social interdependence—can help to further reduce conflict, as Figure 14.8 shows. Peaceful relations will ultimately be

Figure 14.8 Processes in conflict resolution

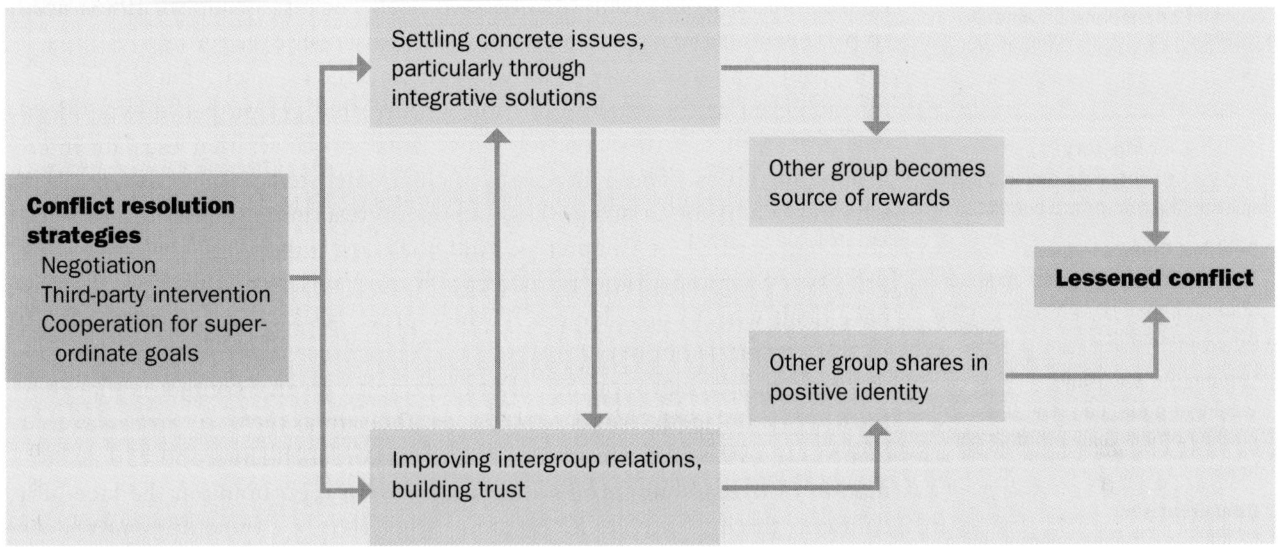

Just as social and cognitive processes can help escalate conflict, the processes involved in conflict resolution can build on themselves. Interventions that either help the groups settle the concrete issues in dispute or improve their feelings about each other can set the tone for further reductions in conflict.

possible when the world community finds ways to accommodate the needs of groups and nations not only for physical security and material resources, but also for positive and distinctive identities.

Concluding Comments

It's sometimes hard to remember that intergroup conflict can have value as a legitimate means of initiating change and overturning injustice. As we saw in Chapter 9, diversity and difference, constant formulation and reformulation, are vital ingredients in the formation of a sound consensus. Similarly, competition, challenge, and debate are sometimes necessary in overcoming inequality, righting wrongs, and establishing groups' legitimate need for respect and material well-being.

Unfortunately, however, conflicts between nations and other political, socioeconomic, ethnic, and religious groups often get out of hand. The damage that results—from chronic waste of human potential to possible global devastation from nuclear war—make intergroup conflict one of the most serious challenges to the world community. A social psychological understanding of conflict and conflict resolution hints at ways to address this challenge.

Chapter 14 Themes

Construction of reality
Conflict is often driven by the parties' mutual perception of each other.

Pervasiveness of Social Influence
Conflict or cooperation among groups dramatically influences group members' thoughts and behavior.

Striving for Mastery
Striving for concrete rewards frequently triggers group conflict.

Seeking Connectedness
The desire to view group membership in a positive light often sets off group conflict.

Valuing Me and Mine
Valuing a group can lead to downgrading others, exacerbating conflicts.

Conservatisim
Conflict is often self-perpetuating.

This chapter has tried to show that intergroup hostility does not develop because the social and cognitive processes regulating human behavior go strangely awry. Rather, it is governed by those *same* processes. Social conflict arises from group membership itself because group members need to perceive their social and material superiority over other groups. Although one group's intention may be only to gain an edge for itself, that edge is usually achieved at the expense of other groups that get pushed down. Social categorization sets the stage for many other processes that escalate intergroup hostilities. These processes include the stereotyping discussed in Chapter 5 and the in-group bias, out-group discrimination, and moral exclusion described in Chapter 6. And they are aided and abetted by the processes of competition, misperception, and miscommunication that we have dealt with in this chapter. As these processes kick in one by one, conflict often spirals out of control.

The challenge groups face in attempting to resolve conflict is that they must work on many fronts at once, to undermine the very processes that contribute to hostilities in the first place. Interdependent cooperation, formation of overarching group allegiances—even regrouping in the face of a common threat—provide a common rather than a competitive means for obtaining social identity. Overt conflict is halted, and erstwhile enemies become fellow in-group members who can contribute to, rather than detract from, positive group identity. Successful cooperation also allows sharing resources with others, creates constructive intergroup contacts that break down negative stereotypes, and builds trust. Activating the norm of reciprocity for concessions, rather than for retaliation, initiates a mutual reduction of tension, distrust, and hostility.

Understanding the social psychological processes underlying group conflict offers no miracles—no quick-fix techniques for eliminating conflict. What it does offer is the reassurance that conflict, like any other form of human interaction, is the product of common and comprehensible processes. It suggests alternatives to the use of force and violence and a means of regulating, reversing, or even resolving conflict through negotiation. More fundamentally, it offers strategies aimed at restoring and maintaining positive and peaceable relations between groups. If we understand how they work, the processes that built the walls of intergroup separation can be harnessed to tear them down.

Summary

The Genesis of Intergroup Conflict Much conflict stems from **competition** for valued material resources, as **realistic conflict theory** emphasizes. Conflict can also stem from competition for social rewards like respect and esteem. **Relative deprivation theory** holds that social comparisons between groups contribute to people's assessments of how well they are doing, and these comparisons can spur intergroup conflict.

Groups are generally more competitive than individuals because group members strive for positive social identity by competing against out-groups and because they demand loyalty from one another in a conflict. Also, compared with individuals, groups are more willing to reciprocate the competitiveness they anticipate receiving from other groups, and they are more willing to exploit out-groups for the in-group's benefit.

Conflict Escalation: Going from Bad to Worse Once conflict starts, poor communication can make it worse. In-group interaction hardens in-group opinion. As threats are directed toward the out-group, each group retaliates more and more harshly, and other parties choose sides. All of these processes tend to escalate the conflict.

As escalation continues, the in-group sees the out-group as totally evil and sees itself in unrealistically positive terms. Because the same biases characterize both groups, each group's image of itself and its opponent tends to be similar. Emotion and arousal strengthen these biases even more.

Ultimately, conflict may escalate into an attempt at total domination or destruction of the out-group. When the out-group is morally excluded, power differences between the groups may enable one group to try to eliminate the other.

Resolving Intergroup Conflict To resolve conflicts, the parties try to find mutually acceptable solutions, which requires understanding and trust. When direct **negotiation** is unproductive, the parties can try the approach of **graduated and reciprocated initiatives in tension reduction (GRIT)**. Or third parties can intervene to help the parties settle their conflicts.

Conflicts may also be resolved when groups cooperate toward **superordinate goals** that can be attained only when both groups work together. Under the proper conditions, cooperative intergroup interaction, such as that produced by the **jigsaw classroom technique**, reduces conflict. Cooperation must involve a valued common goal, provide repeated opportunities to disconfirm out-group stereotypes, produce successful results, and be supported and promoted by social norms.

Chapter 14 Overview

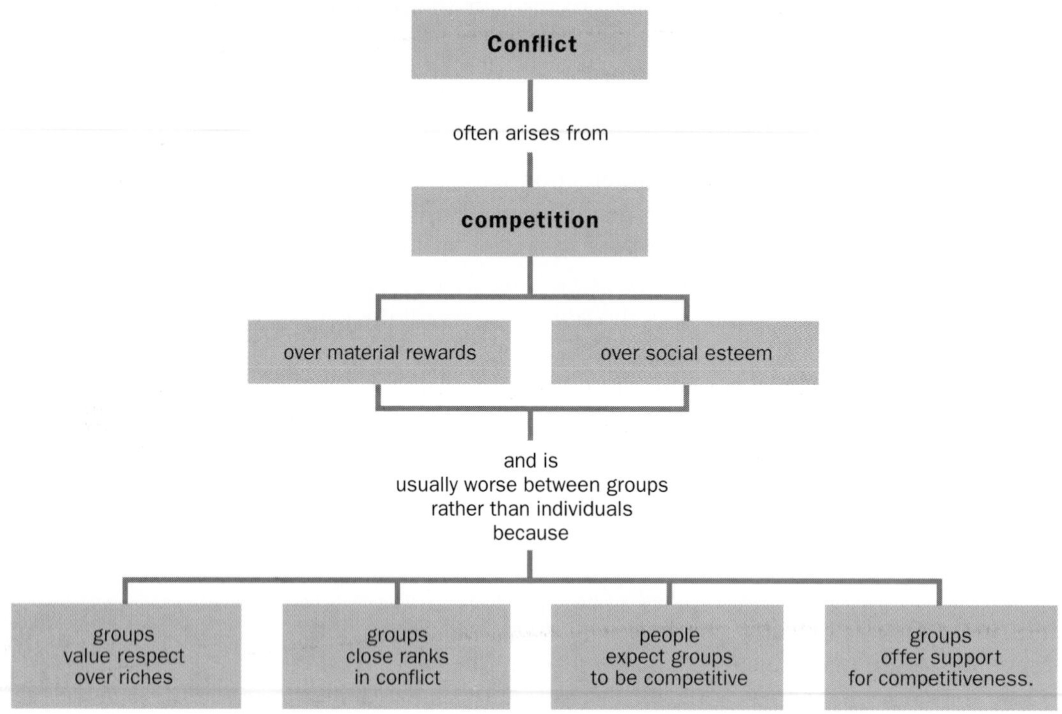

Conflict
often arises from
competition
over material rewards
over social esteem
and is
usually worse between groups
rather than individuals
because
groups
value respect
over riches
groups
close ranks
in conflict
people
expect groups
to be competitive
groups
offer support
for competitiveness.

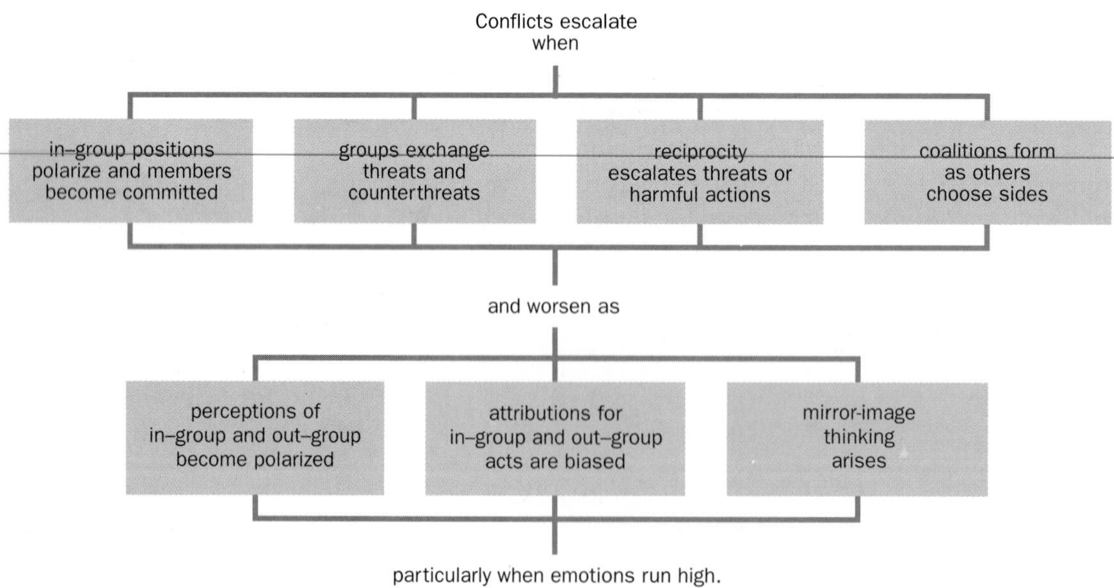

Conflicts escalate
when
in-group positions
polarize and members
become committed
groups exchange
threats and
counterthreats
reciprocity
escalates threats or
harmful actions
coalitions form
as others
choose sides
and worsen as
perceptions of
in-group and out-group
become polarized
attributions for
in-group and out-group
acts are biased
mirror-image
thinking
arises
particularly when emotions run high.

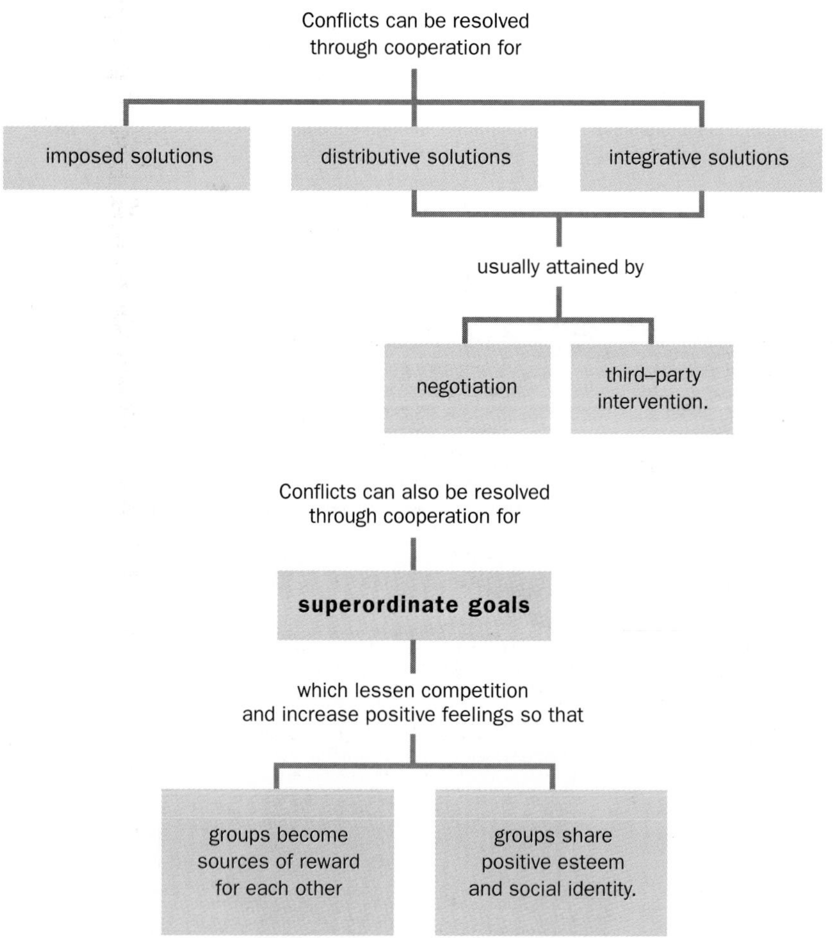

Conflicts can be resolved
through cooperation for
imposed solutions
distributive solutions
integrative solutions
usually attained by
negotiation
third–party
intervention.
Conflicts can also be resolved
through cooperation for
superordinate goals
which lessen competition
and increase positive feelings so that
groups become
sources of reward
for each other
groups share
positive esteem
and social identity.

Epilogue

Now that we are at the end of our journey, we hope you have come to appreciate the incredible diversity of behavior that social psychologists study. We also hope you noticed a few key ideas coming up again and again as we described such diverse topics as impression formation, intergroup conflict, close relationships, and attitude change. In fact, just as a limited number of chemical elements can be combined to form millions of different substances, so a set of basic principles can be seen to underlie all social behavior. It is this orderliness underlying diversity that makes social psychology a unified field instead of a random collection of interesting topics.

Core Principles of Social Psychology

The principles we highlighted throughout this text are those we see as most important for understanding the findings and theories of social psychology. Let's take a final look at how we can use these principles to help understand the wide range of social behavior we encounter in everyday life.

- Whether we are alone or with others, we construct social reality as we form impressions of other people and groups (Chapters 3 and 5) and as we act in ways that reflect our own attitudes and group norms (Chapters 8 and 10). This is why we so often react to unexpected, unusual, or ambiguous events by immediately turning to others and asking, "Do you smell gas?" or "Was that an earthquake?" or "So what have *you* heard about Bill?"
- The pervasive effects of social influence are evident when we conform to the opinions of important groups (Chapter 9) and cooperate or compete with others (Chapters 13 and 14). Next time you find yourself caught up in the latest clothing fad, realize that you just said something your dad always used to say, or feel uncomfortable about expressing your political views, you may remind yourself of the power and pervasiveness of social influence.

- Our strivings for mastery explain why we want to form accurate opinions and attitudes about ourselves and others (Chapters 4 and 7) and why we are capable of helping or harming others in order to gain rewards (Chapter 12). This principle offers insights into why we work so hard to find out what instructors want in test answers; why group efforts are often so much more successful than any one person's efforts; and why we spend so much time trying to work out who we really are.
- We seek connectedness with others when we conform to group norms (Chapter 9) and when we form close relationships (Chapter 11). This principle explains why many people feel empty and incomplete when they lack intimate relationships, why the support of a good friend seems to make daily hassles as well as big crises easier to cope with, and why our memberships in groups and our relationships with others are some of the most important aspects of human life.
- Our desire to value me and mine is evident in our efforts to feel good about ourselves as individuals and as members of groups (Chapters 4 and 6). It also helps explain why we aggress against out-group members while often behaving with kindness and altruism toward members of the in-group (Chapters 12 and 14). Perhaps understanding the me-and-mine principle will alert you to the moments when your group puts others down just to make yourselves feel better. It may also help explain why news of an earthquake in a nearby state elicits more donations than news of a similar tragedy in some distant place.
- The processing principle of accessibility is responsible for our using easily grasped information to form our impressions of other people and our attitudes (Chapters 3 and 7) and for the times we find ourselves conforming to accessible norms (Chapters 6 and 10). After staring blankly at the rows of breakfast cereal in the supermarket, have you ever just grabbed the first one you could remember hearing about? Or realized that you'd felt compelled to exchange gifts with someone you don't really like? Accessibility may have been at work.
- The principle of conservatism accounts for the persistence of first impressions and stereotypes (Chapters 3 and 5) and also for the difficulties minorities experience in swaying a majority's opinion (Chapter 9). If conservatism were not such a powerful influence on our thinking, advertisers wouldn't have to spend so much money trying to persuade us, and friends wouldn't have to work so hard to change our mistaken snap judgments.
- Finally, the principle of superficial versus extensive processing operates when we decide how much thought to devote to understanding a member of a stereotyped group (Chapter 5) or to acting in accordance with our attitudes (Chapter 8). Understanding this principle helps explain why we often make snap judgments when the stakes are low but give considerable thought to matters of importance.

Of course, these are just a few examples of the principles at work. We hope that as you review or reread the chapters, you will think of others. We also hope these principles will help you take a fresh look at events in your own lives. Perhaps you now see why making a good first impression at a job interview is important (conservatism), why you feel so good when your favorite team wins (me and mine), or why the whole world looks bleak when you're feeling low (accessibility). You may be better able to understand why people care so much about the majority point of view (connectedness) and how the majority's opinion can sometimes be changed by minority dissent (systematic processing). If these ideas help you make sense of the world in which you live, our goals for this book have been achieved.

How the Principles Interrelate

Although we have described the eight principles separately so that you can see how they operate, we do not mean to suggest that they are unrelated to each other. They operate together, usually in a harmonious fashion.

Part of the reason we construct reality, for example, is because we want to master the environment, and part of the reason we influence others and accept social influence is because we seek connectedness. Social influence is important because we want to construct an appropriate and correct reality, and we need other people to do so. Accessibility helps us make judgments quickly and efficiently, which in turn helps us to master the environment we construct. It also means that we pay most attention to those closest to us, which helps us achieve connectedness and makes possible the give and take of social influence. The principle of conservatism, on the other hand, helps maintain a stable view of the world—how would we be able to master the environment or form relationships with others if our views of them changed from minute to minute? Superficial versus systematic processing is the moderating principle, the fulcrum that keeps us balanced between the stability of conservatism and the flux of accessibility. For example, receiving unexpected or inconsistent information from those connected to us makes us think hard, opening the way for change.

Although the principles usually operate together to produce positive outcomes, they sometimes can result in conflicts and paradoxes. For example, the shortcuts we use to make inferences are often efficient routes to the right answer, but they sometimes lead us astray (Chapter 3). Relying on social consensus often helps people master the environment and achieve connectedness, but it also can lead to mindless acceptance of a dangerous status quo (Chapter 9). Thus, depending on the circumstances, the same motives and processes produce useful and valuable outcomes or misleading and destructive ones. In fact, almost every aspect of social behavior has an up side and a down side, whether that behavior is adherence to norms like obedience and reciprocity (Chapter 10) or the biased thinking we use to elevate our self-esteem, sometimes at the expense of disparaging other people and groups (Chapters 4 and 6).

These examples of ways in which the principles work with and against one another are not a complete list. We hope you have found other meaningful interrelationships that link different types and forms of social behavior.

An Invitation to Social Psychology

When you first picked up this textbook, you probably expected it to tell you how much social psychologists know. Were you surprised to discover how many things we *don't* know? Our understanding of social behavior still has many gaping holes and many unresolved issues because research in social psychology—like research in all fields of human knowledge—has been shaped by its historical development and social context. In the late 1800s, when researchers were just beginning to ask social psychological questions, nobody could have written down the list of principles we just presented and used them to guide research. (Correspondingly, twenty years from now, the set of principles that social psychologists think are most important may have changed again.) Instead, as we have said, specific events have inspired and guided researchers' questions. The most important events for North American social psychology were the Nazi domination of Europe and the Second World War, which gave rise to research areas involving persuasion, prejudice, obedience to authority, and conformity.

As research traditions grew up around socially significant and culturally relevant issues, other areas were relatively neglected. For instance, the social effects of drug abuse, heterogeneity in the work force, and variations in family composition were not widespread enough to gain scientists' attention fifty years ago. Many important issues involving group identification, kin and friend relationships, and social stability and change have been neglected, perhaps because so much social psychological research to date has been done in the individually-oriented United States. As social psychology becomes a global enterprise, questions of concern outside the West may come to the fore. For example, the issue of social change is of particular importance to social psychologists in developing countries, who underscore that social psychology should be even more active as a positive force in bringing about and guiding such change. And though much is known about how people form and change attitudes on the basis of information, much less is known about the impact of values, ethics, and religious convictions on people's social behavior. These are just a few of the many areas in which social psychology needs to grow and develop.

We mention these gaps in knowledge and opportunities for development because we want you to understand that social psychology is a young science. One unfortunate characteristic that is almost inherent in the nature of textbooks is that they convey the impression that everything worth learning has already been learned: that all the *i's* have been dotted, all the *t's* have been crossed, and everyone agrees about everything. How boring social psychology would be if this were true. But it is not true; social psychologists are well aware of how much we still need to know about human social behavior. We guarantee that as you read these words, whatever the day or time, somewhere social psychologists are in their offices, laboratories, schools, businesses, hospitals, or out on the streets planning or carrying out research or reporting new findings. If that idea appeals to you and if you find yourself interested in the topics and issues social psychologists study, we invite you to consider becoming a social psychologist. You could help to shape the future of our science and contribute to what we know about the endlessly fascinating forms of human social behavior.

Glossary

A

accessibility The ease and rapidity with which a cognitive representation comes to mind and is used. (p. 75)

accessibility principle The processing principle that the information that is most readily available generally has the most impact on thoughts, feelings, and behavior. (p. 22)

actor–observer differences in attribution The tendency to attribute our own behaviors to situational causes while seeing others' acts as due to their inner characteristics. (p. 120)

aggression Behavior intended to harm someone else. (p. 503)

altruism Behavior intended to help someone else without any prospect of personal rewards for the helper. (p. 503)

association A link between two or more cognitive representations. (p. 75)

attachment styles People's basic securely attached, avoidant, or anxious orientation toward others in close relationships. (p. 472)

attitude A cognitive representation that summarizes an individual's evaluation of a particular person, group, thing, action, or idea. (p. 266)

B

BIRG (bask in reflected glory) A way of boosting positive mood and self-esteem by identifying oneself with the accomplishments or good qualities of fellow in-group members. (p. 229)

C

causal attribution A judgment about the cause of a behavior or other event. (p. 85)

classical conditioning The process by which a previously neutral object, after repeated pairings with an emotion or other response, comes to elicit that response. (p. 188)

close relationship A relationship involving strong and frequent interdependence in many domains of life. (p. 462)

cognitive appraisal An individual's interpretation of a self-relevant event or situation that directs emotional responses and behavior. (p. 139)

cognitive dissonance An unpleasant state caused by people's awareness of inconsistency among various beliefs or attitudes. (p. 319)

cognitive processes The ways our minds work: how our memories, perceptions, thoughts, emotions, and motives influence our understanding of the world and guide our actions. (p. 5)

cognitive representation A body of knowledge that an individual has stored in memory. (p. 68)

collective A number of people who are in the same place but have minimal direct interaction and minimal interdependence. (p. 556)

commitment The combined forces that hold the partners together in an enduring relationship. (p. 469)

communal relationship A relationship in which people reward their partner out of direct concern and to show caring. (p. 467)

competition A type of interdependence in which one party's gains result from another party's losses. (p. 601)

conflict The perceived incompatibility of goals between two or more parties. (p. 600)

conformity The convergence of individuals' thoughts, feelings, or behavior toward a group norm. (p. 357)

conservatism The processing principle that individuals' and groups' views of the world are slow to change and prone to perpetuate themselves. (p. 21)

construct validity The extent to which the independent and dependent variables used in research correspond to the theoretical constructs under investigation. (p. 34)

construction of reality The axiom that each person's view of reality is a construction, shaped both by cognitive processes—the ways our minds work—and by social processes—input from others either actually present or imagined. (p. 19)

constructs Abstract and general concepts that are used in scientific theories and that are not directly observable. (p. 32)

contact hypothesis The theory that certain types of direct contact between members of hostile groups will reduce prejudice. (p. 205)

coping strategies Efforts undertaken to reduce negative consequences of self-threatening events. (p. 151)

CORF (cut off reflected failure) The act of criticizing or distancing oneself from an in-group member who is viewed negatively. (p. 253)

correspondence bias The tendency to infer an actor's personal characteristics from observed behaviors even when the inference is unjustified because other possible causes of the behavior exist. (p. 83)

correspondent inference The process of characterizing someone as having a personality trait that corresponds to his or her observed behavior. (p. 81)

D

debriefing Informing research participants—as soon as possible after the completion of their participation in research—about the purposes, procedures, and scientific value of the study, and answering any questions participants may have. (p. 59)

demand characteristics Cues in a research setting that lead participants to make inferences about what researchers expect or desire and that therefore bias how the participants act. (p. 35)

dependent variable A concrete measurement of a construct that is thought to be influenced by other constructs. (p. 34)

diffusion of responsibility A reduction in the normative pressure to help others that each individual feels when other potential helpers are also present. (p. 520)

discrimination Any positive or negative behavior that is directed toward a social group and its members. (p. 170)

door-in-the-face technique A technique in which the influencer makes an initial request so large that it will be rejected, and follows it with a smaller request that looks like a concession, making it more likely that the other person will concede in turn. (p. 413)

E

elaboration The generation of favorable or unfavorable reactions to the content of a message. (p. 280)

empathy-altruism model The theory that concern for the victim's suffering motivates people to help others even though there is no reward. (p. 514)

exchange relationship A relationship in which people exchange rewards following the principle of equity. (p. 467)

experimental research A research design in which researchers randomly assign subjects to different groups and manipulate one or more independent variables. (p. 41)

external validity The extent to which research results can be generalized to other appropriate people, times, and settings. (p. 43)

F

face-to-face group Two or more individuals who interact and influence each other. (p. 352)

false consensus effect The tendency to overestimate others' agreement with one's own opinions, characteristics, and behaviors. (p. 359)

foot-in-the-door technique A technique for increasing compliance with a large request by first asking people to go along with a smaller request. (p. 315)

G

graduated and reciprocated initiatives in tension reduction (GRIT) A process in which one party makes a concession to induce the other to reciprocate in order to reduce tension and de-escalate conflict. (p. 628)

group polarization The exaggeration during group interaction of a group's initial position or preference. (p. 370)

groupthink Group decision making that is impaired by the drive to reach consensus regardless of how the consensus is formed. (p. 381)

I

independent variable A concrete manipulation or measurement of a construct that is thought to influence other constructs. (p. 34)

informed consent Consent voluntarily given by a research participant who decides to participate in a study after being told what will be involved in participation. (p. 58)

interdependence A situation in which each person's thoughts, emotions, and behaviors influence those of one or more other people. (p. 462)

internal validity The extent to which it can be concluded that changes in the independent variable actually caused changes in the dependent variable in a research study. (p. 40)

intimacy Psychological closeness in a relationship, involving extensive self-disclosure and mutual feelings of understanding, caring, and acceptance. (p. 468)

J

jigsaw classroom technique A procedure in which groups of diverse students cooperate in teaching one another individual pieces of the material to be learned. (p. 632)

L

leadership A process in which group members are permitted to influence and motivate others to help attain group goals. (p. 576)

low-ball technique A technique in which the influencer secures agreement with a request but then increases the cost of honoring the commitment. (p. 417)

M

mere exposure effect People's tendency to evaluate objects they have seen before more positively than they evaluate comparable novel objects. (p. 301)

minimal intergroup situation A research situation in which people are categorized, on an arbitrary or trivial basis, into groups that have no history, no conflicts of interest, and no stereotypes. (p. 239)

moral exclusion The view that out-group members are outside the boundary of moral principles, often leading to their oppression, exploitation, or genocide. (p. 244)

moral unconcern The view that out-group members are expendable individuals whose suffering can be ignored. (p. 244)

N

negative-state relief model The theory that people help others in order to reduce their own feelings of distress caused by the victim's suffering. (p. 513)

negotiation The process by which parties in conflict communicate and influence each other to reach agreement when they have partially opposing preferences. (p. 625)

nonexperimental research A research design in which both the independent and dependent variables are measured. (p. 40)

norm of equity The shared view that demands that the rewards obtained by the partners in a relationship should be proportional to their inputs. (p. 458)

norm of obedience to authority The shared view that people should obey those with legitimate authority. (p. 424)

norm of social commitment The shared view that people are required to honor their agreements and obligations. (p. 416)

norm of social reciprocity The shared view that we are obligated to return to others the goods, services, and concessions they offer to us. (p. 410)

O

out-group homogeneity effect The tendency to see the outgroup as relatively more homogeneous and less diverse than the in-group. (p. 235)

P

persuasion The process of forming, reinforcing, or changing attitudes by means of communication. (p. 266)

persuasion heuristic A simple rule that allows people to evaluate an object based on superficial cues. (p. 275)

pervasiveness of social influence The axiom that other people influence virtually all of our thoughts, feelings, and behavior, whether those others are physically present or not. (p. 19)

prejudice Positive or negative evaluation of a social group and its members. (p. 170)

private conformity Private acceptance of group norms. (p. 357)

prosocial behavior Behavior intended to help someone else. (p. 503)

public conformity Overt behavior consistent with group norms that are not privately accepted. (p. 357)

R

random assignment The procedure of assigning subjects to different experimental groups so that every subject has exactly the same chance as every other subject of being in any given group. (p. 41)

reactance The motive to protect or restore a threatened sense of behavioral freedom. (p. 433)

realistic conflict theory The theory that intergroup hostility arises from competition among groups for scarce but valued material resources. (p. 601)

reference group Those people accepted as an appropriate source of information for a judgment because they share the attributes relevant for making that judgment. (p. 361)

relative deprivation theory The theory that feelings of discontent arise from the belief that other individuals or other groups are better off. (p. 605)

replication Conducting new studies in an effort to provide evidence for the same theoretically predicted relations found in prior research. (p. 52)

S

salience The ability of a cue to attract attention in its context. (p. 74)

seeking connectedness The motivational principle that people seek support, liking, and acceptance from the people and groups they care about and value. (p. 21)

self-awareness A state of heightened awareness of the self, including our internal standards and whether we measure up to them. (p. 136)

self-categorization The process of seeing oneself as a member of a social group. (p. 221)

self-complexity The number and diversity of the self-aspects that people develop for different roles, activities, and relationships. (p. 123)

self-concept The totality of an individual's knowledge about his or her personal qualities. (p. 114)

self-discrepancy theory The theory that people evaluate themselves against internal "ideal" and "ought" standards, producing specific emotional consequences. (p. 134)

self-enhancing bias Any tendency to gather or interpret information concerning the self in a way that leads to overly positive evaluations. (p. 130)

self-esteem An individual's positive or negative evaluation of himself or herself. (p. 128)

self-expression A motive for choosing behaviors that are intended to reflect and express the self-concept. (p. 143)

self-fulfilling prophecy The process by which one person's expectations about another become reality by eliciting behaviors that confirm the expectations. (p. 103)

self-monitoring A personality characteristic defined as the degree to which people are sensitive to the demands of social situations and shape their behaviors accordingly. (p. 146)

self-perception theory The theory that we make inferences about our personal characteristics on the basis of our overt behaviors when internal cues are weak or ambiguous. (p. 115)

self-presentation A motive for choosing behaviors intended to create in observers a desired impression of the self. (p. 144)

social categorization The process of identifying individual people as members of a social group because they share certain features that are typical of the group. (p. 175)

social change In general, the goal of altering the political, economic, and social institutions of society. In social psychology, the strategy of improving the overall societal situation of a group held in low esteem. (p. 255)

social comparison theory The theory that people learn about and evaluate their personal qualities by comparing themselves to others. (p. 118)

social desirability response bias People's tendency to act in ways that they believe others find acceptable and approve of. (p. 37)

social dilemma A form of interdependence in which the most rewarding short-term action for each individual will, if chosen by all individuals, produce a long-term negative outcome for the entire group. (p. 585)

social facilitation The finding that in the presence of others highly accessible responses become more likely and less accessible responses become less likely. (p. 558)

social group Two or more people who share some common characteristic that is socially meaningful for themselves or for others. (p. 173)

social identity Those aspects of the self-concept that derive from an individual's knowledge and feelings about the group memberships he or she shares with others. (p. 220)

social identity theory The theory that people's motivation to derive positive self-esteem from their group memberships is one driving force behind in-group bias. (p. 240)

social interdependence Reliance on other members of the group for feelings of connectedness, social and emotional rewards, and a positive social identity. (p. 563)

social learning theory The theory that much social behavior is learned through observing and imitating others. (p. 519)

social loafing The tendency to exert less effort on a task when an individual's efforts are an unidentifiable part of a group than when the same task is performed alone. (p. 569)

social mobility In general, the process of moving from one position in a hierarchy to another. In social psychology, the strategy of individual escape, either physical or psychological, from a group held in low esteem. (p. 253)

social norms Generally accepted ways of thinking, feeling, or behaving that people in a group agree on and endorse as right and proper. (p. 189)

social processes The ways in which our thoughts, feelings, and actions are affected by input from the people and groups around us. (p. 5)

social psychology The scientific study of the effects of social and cognitive processes on the way individuals perceive, influence, and relate to others. (p. 3)

social support Emotional and physical coping resources provided by other people. (p. 475)

stereotype A cognitive representation or impression of a social group that people form by associating particular characteristics and emotions with the group. (p. 170)

striving for mastery The motivational principle that people seek to understand and predict events in the social world in order to obtain rewards. (p. 20)

subtype A narrower and more specific social group that is included within a broad social group like *men, women, Latinos, or Whites*. (p. 206)

superficial processing Relying on accessible information to make inferences or judgments, while expending little effort in processing. (p. 98)

superficiality versus depth The processing principle that people ordinarily put little effort into dealing with information but at times are motivated to consider information in more depth. (p. 22)

superordinate goals Shared goals that can be attained only if groups work together. (p. 631)

symbolic prejudice Hatred for out-groups that arises, together with the exaltation of in-group symbols, in response to perceived threat. (p. 242)

systematic processing Giving thorough, effortful consideration to a wide range of information relevant to a judgment. (p. 100)

T

task interdependence Reliance on other members of a group for mastery of material outcomes that arise from the group's task. (p. 563)

theory A statement that satisfies three requirements: It is about constructs; it describes causal relations; and it is general in scope, although the range of generality differs for different theories. (p. 31)

theory of planned behavior The theory that attitudes, perceived social norms, and perceived control combine to influence behavior. (p. 440)

V

valuing "me and mine" The motivational principle that people desire to see themselves, and other people and groups connected to themselves, in a positive light. (p. 21)

References

Aboud, F. E. (1976). Self-evaluation: Information-seeking strategies for interethnic social comparisons. *Journal of Cross-Cultural Psychology, 7,* 289–300.

Aboud, F. E., & Taylor, D. M. (1971). Ethnic and role stereotypes: Their relative importance in person perception. *Journal of Social Psychology, 85,* 17–27.

Abrams, J. (1991, August 31). Survey cites racism in housing. *Santa Barbara News Press,* p. A5.

Abramson, L. Y., Seligman, M. E. P., & Teasdale, J. (1978). Learned helplessness in humans: Critique and reformulation. *Journal of Abnormal Psychology, 87,* 49–74.

Adams, G. R., & Shea, J. A. (1981). Talking and loving: A cross-lagged panel investigation. *Basic and Applied Social Psychology, 2,* 81–88.

Adams, J. S. (1965). Inequity in social exchange. In L. Berkowitz (Ed.), *Advances in experimental social psychology* (Vol. 2, pp. 267–299). New York: Academic Press.

Adelmann, P. K., & Zajonc, R. B. (1989). Facial efference and the experience of emotion. *Annual Review of Psychology, 40,* 249–280.

Adler, N. J. (1991). *International dimensions of organizational behavior* (2nd ed.). Boston: PWS-Kent Publishing Co.

Adorno, T. W., Frenkel-Brunswik, E., Levinson, D. J., & Sanford, R. N. (1950). *The authoritarian personality.* New York: Harper.

Ailes, R. (1988). *You are the message.* New York: Doubleday.

Ainsworth, M., Blehar, M., Waters, E., & Wall, S. (1978). *Patterns of attachment.* Hillsdale, NJ: Erlbaum.

Ajzen, I. (1991). The theory of planned behavior. *Organizational Behavior and Human Decision Processes, 50,* 179–211.

Ajzen, I., & Fishbein, M. (1977). Attitude-behavior relations: A theoretical analysis and review of empirical research. *Psychological Bulletin, 84,* 888–918.

Ajzen, I., & Fishbein, M. (1980). *Understanding attitudes and predicting social behavior.* Englewood Cliffs, NJ: Prentice-Hall.

Ajzen, I., & Madden, T. J. (1986). Prediction of goal-directed behavior: Attitudes, intentions, and perceived behavioral control. *Journal of Experimental Social Psychology, 22,* 453–474.

Alagna, S. W., & Reddy, D. M. (1984). Predictors of proficient technique and successful lesion detection in breast self-examination. *Health Psychology, 3,* 113–127.

Alcock, J. E., Carment, D. W., & Sadava, S. W. (1988). *A textbook of social psychology.* Scarborough, Ontario: Prentice-Hall.

Alexander, R. D. (1987). *The biology of moral systems.* New York: Aldine de Gruyter.

Allen, B. P. (1988). Dramaturgical quality. *Journal of Social Psychology, 128,* 181–190.

Allen, K. M., Blascovich, J., Tomaka, J., & Kelsey, R. M. (1991). Presence of human friends and pet dogs as moderators of autonomic responses to stress in women. *Journal of Personality and Social Psychology, 61,* 582–589.

Allen, V. L. (1965). Situational factors in conformity. In L. Berkowitz (Ed.), *Advances in experimental social psychology* (Vol. 8, pp. 133–175). New York: Academic Press.

Allen, V. L. (1975). Social support for nonconformity. In L. Berkowitz (Ed.), *Advances in experimental social psychology* (Vol. 18, pp. 2–43). New York: Academic Press.

Allen, V. L., & Bragg, B. W. (1965). *The generalization of nonconformity within a homogeneous content dimension.* Unpublished manuscript (cited in Allen, 1975).

Allen, V. L., & Wilder, D. A. (1972). *Social support in absentia: Effect of an absentee partner on conformity.* Unpublished manuscript (cited in Allen 1975).

Allen, V. L., & Wilder, D. A. (1979). Group categorization and belief similarity. *Small Group Behavior,* 10, 73–80.

Allison, S. T., & Messick, D. M. (1985). The group attribution error. *Journal of Experimental Social Psychology, 21,* 563–579.

Allison, S. T., & Messick, D. M. (1990). Social decision heuristics in the use of shared resources. *Journal of Behavioral Decision Making, 3,* 195–204.

Allison, S. T., Messick, D. M., & Goethals, G. R. (1989). On being better but not smarter than others: The Muhammad Ali effect. *Social Cognition, 7,* 275–295.

Allison, S. T., Mackie, D. M., Muller, M. M., & Worth, L. T. (1993). Sequential correspondence biases and perceptions of change: The Castro studies revisited. *Personality and Social Psychology Bulletin, 19,* 151–157.

Alloy, L. B., & Abramson, L. Y. (1979). Judgment of contingency in depressed and nondepressed students: Sadder but wiser? *Journal of Experimental Psychology: General, 108,* 441–485.

Alloy, L. B., & Ahrens, A. H. (1987). Depression and pessimism for the future: Biased use of statistically relevant information in predictions for self versus others. *Journal of Personality and Social Psychology, 52,* 366–378.

Allport, F. H. (1924). *Social psychology.* Boston: Houghton Mifflin.

Allport, G. W. (1935). Attitudes. In G. Murchison (Ed.), *Handbook of social psychology.* Worcester, MA: Clark University Press.

Allport, G. W. (1954a). The historical background of modern social psychology. In G. Lindzey (Ed.), *Handbook of social psychology* (Vol. 1, pp. 3–56). Cambridge, MA: Addison-Wesley.

Allport, G. W. (1954b). *The nature of prejudice.* New York: Addison-Wesley.

Allport, G. W. (1958). *The nature of prejudice.* Garden City, NY: Doubleday Anchor.

Altman, I., & Taylor, D. A. (1973). *Social penetration.* New York: Holt, Rinehart, Winston.

Amir, Y. (1969). Contact hypothesis in ethnic relations. *Psychological Bulletin, 71,* 319–342.

Andersen, S. M. (1984). Self-knowledge and social inference: II. The diagnosticity of cognitive/affective and behavioral data. *Journal of Personality and Social Psychology, 46,* 294–307.

Andersen, S. M., & Cole, S. W. (1990). "Do I know you?" The role of significant others in general social perception. *Journal of Personality and Social Psychology, 59,* 384–399.

Andersen, S. M., & Klatzky, R. L. (1987). Traits and social stereotypes: Levels of categorization in person perception. *Journal of Personality and Social Psychology, 53,* 235–246.

Andersen, S. M., & Ross, L. (1984). Self-knowledge and social inference: I. The impact of cognitive/affective and behavioral data. *Journal of Personality and Social Psychology, 46,* 280–293.

Anderson, C. A. (1987). Temperature and aggression: Effects on quarterly, yearly, and city rates of violent and nonviolent crime. *Journal of Personality and Social Psychology, 52,* 1161–1173.

Anderson, C. A., & Anderson, D. C. (1984). Ambient temperature and violent crime: Tests of the linear and curvilinear hypotheses. *Journal of Personality and Social Psychology, 46,* 91–97.

Anderson, C. A., & Godfrey, S. S. (1987). Thoughts about actions: The effects of specificity and availability of imagined behavioral scripts on expectations about oneself and others. *Social Cognition, 5* (Special issue: Cognition and action), 238–258.

Anderson, C. A., Jennings, D. L., & Arnoult, L. H. (1988). Validity and utility of the attributional style construct at a moderate level of specificity. *Journal of Personality and Social Psychology, 55,* 979–990.

Anderson, N. H. (1981). *Foundations of information integration theory.* New York: Academic Press.

Andreoli, V., & Worchel, S. (1978). Effects of media, communicator, and message position on attitude change. *Public Opinion Quarterly, 42,* 59–70.

Angier, N. (1990, October 16). Marriage is lifesaver for men after 45. *The New York Times.*

Angier, N. (1990, December 13). Anger can ruin more than your day. *The New York Times.*

Anthony, T., Copper, C., & Mullen, B. (1992). Cross-racial facial identification: A social cognitive integration. *Personality and Social Psychology Bulletin, 18,* 296–301.

Archer, D., Iratani, B., Kimes, D. B., & Barrios, M. (1983). Face-ism: Five studies of sex differences in facial prominence. *Journal of Personality and Social Psychology, 45,* 725–735.

Archer, R. L. (1980). Self-disclosure. In D. M. Wegner & R. R. Vallacher (Eds.), *The self in social psychology* (pp. 183–205). New York: Oxford University Press.

Archer, R. L., Berg, J. H., & Runge, T. E. (1980). Active and passive observers: Attraction to self-disclosing others. *Journal of Experimental Social Psychology, 16,* 130–145.

Ardrey, R. (1966). *The territorial imperative.* New York: Atheneum.

Arendt, H. (1965). *Eichmann in Jerusalem: A report on the banality of evil.* New York: Viking Press.

Arkin, R. M. (1981). Self-presentation styles. In J. T. Tedeschi (Ed.), *Impression management theory and social psychological research* (pp. 311–333). New York: Academic Press.

Arnold, M. B. (1960). *Emotion and personality.* New York: Columbia University Press.

Aron, A., & Aron, E. N. (1991). Love and sexuality. In K. McKinney & S. Sprecher (Eds.), *Sexuality in close relationships* (pp. 25–48). Hillsdale, NJ: Erlbaum.

Aron, A., Aron, E. N., Tudor, M., & Nelson, G. (1991). Close relationships as including other in the self. *Journal of Personality and Social Psychology, 60,* 241–253.

Aronson, E., Blaney, N., Stephan, C., Sikes, J., & Snapp, M. (1978). *The jigsaw classroom.* Beverly Hills, CA: Sage Publications.

Aronson, E., & Carlsmith, J. M. (1963). Effect of severity of threat on the devaluation of forbidden behavior. *Journal of Abnormal and Social Psychology, 66,* 584–588.

Aronson, E., & Mills, J. (1959). The effect of severity of initiation on liking for a group. *Journal of Abnormal and Social Psychology, 59,* 177–181.

Aronson, E., & Osherow, N. (1980). Cooperation, prosocial behavior, and academic performance: Experiments in the desegregated classroom. In L. Bickman (Ed.), *Applied social psychology annual* (vol. 1, pp. 163–196). Beverly Hills, CA: Sage Publications.

Aronson, E., & Worchel, S. (1966). Similarity versus liking as determinants of interpersonal attractiveness. *Psychonomic Science, 5,* 157–158.

Asch, S. E. (1946). Forming impressions of personality. *Journal of Abnormal and Social Psychology, 41,* 258–290.

Asch, S. E. (1951). Effects of group pressure upon the modification and distortion of judgment. In H. Guetzkow (Ed.), *Groups, leadership, and men* (pp. 177–190). Pittsburgh: Carnegie Press.

Asch, S. E. (1955). Studies of independence and conformity: A minority of one against a unanimous majority. *Psychology Monographs, 70,* 1–70.

Asch, S. E. (1956). Opinions and social pressure. *Scientific American, 193*(5) 31–35.

Asch, S. E., & Zukier, H. (1984). Thinking about persons. *Journal of Personality and Social Psychology, 46,* 1230–1240.

Ashley, J. H. (1976). *Hospitals, paternalism, and the role of the nurse.* New York: Teachers College Press.

Ashmore, R. D. (1981). Sex stereotypes and implicit personality theory. In D. L. Hamilton (Ed.), *Cognitive processes in stereotyping and intergroup behavior* (pp. 37–81). Hillsdale, NJ: Erlbaum.

Ashmore, R. D., & Del Boca, F. K. (1981). Conceptual approaches to stereotypes and stereotyping. In D. L. Hamilton (Ed.), *Cognitive processes in stereotyping and intergroup behavior* (pp. 1–36). Hillsdale, NJ: Erlbaum.

Askenasy, H. (1978). *Are we all Nazis?* Secaucus, NJ: Lyle Stuart.

Astin, A. W., Green, K. C., Korn, W. S., & Schalit, M. (1987). *The American freshman: National norms for Fall 1987.* Los Angeles, CA: Higher Education Research Institute, University of California at Los Angeles.

Atkinson, J., & Huston, T. L. (1984). Sex-role orientation and division of labor early in marriage. *Journal of Personality and Social Psychology, 46,* 330–345.

Ault, C. R. (1985). Concept mapping as a study strategy in earth science. *Journal of College Science Teaching, 15,* 38–44.

Axsom, D., & Cooper, J. (1985). Cognitive dissonance and psychotherapy: The role of effort justification in inducing weight loss. *Journal of Experimental Psychology, 21,* 149–160.

Axsom, D., Yates, S., & Chaiken, S. (1987). Audience response as a heuristic cue in persuasion. *Journal of Personality and Social Psychology, 53,* 30–40.

Bakan, D. (1966). *The duality of human existence.* Boston: Beacon Press.

Baker, J. N. (1991, November 25). Battling the bias. *Newsweek,* p. 25.

Baker, J. N., Annin, P., Barrett, T., & Gordon, J. (1991, November 25). Battling the bias: Can gays and cops come to new terms? *Newsweek,* p. 25.

Baker, S. M., & Petty, R. E. (in press). Majority and minor ity influence: Source-position imbalance as a determinant of message scrutiny. *Journal of Personality and Social Psychology.*

Baldwin, M. W. (1992). Relational schemas and the processing of social information. *Psychological Bulletin, 112,* 461–484.

Baldwin, M. W., Carrell, S. E., & Lopez, D. F. (1990). Priming relationship schemas: My advisor and the Pope are watching me from the back of my mind. *Journal of Experimental Social Psychology, 26,* 435–454.

Bales, R. F. (1953). The equilibrium problem in small groups. In T. Parsons, R. F. Bales, & E. A. Shils (Eds.), *Working papers in the theory of action.* Glencoe, IL: Free Press.

Bales, R. F., Cohen, S. P., & Williamson, S. A. (1979). *SYMLOG: A system for the multiple level observation of groups.* New York: Free Press.

Bales, R. F., & Slater, P. E. (1955). Role differentiation. In T. Parsons, R. F. Bales, and others (Eds.), *The family, socialization, and interaction process* (pp. 259–306). Glencoe, IL: Free Press.

Bandura, A. (1973). *Aggression: A social learning analysis.* Englewood Cliffs, NJ: Prentice-Hall.

Bandura, A. (1977a). Self-efficacy: Toward a unifying theory of behavioral change. *Psychological Review, 84,* 191–215.

Bandura, A. (1977b). *Social learning theory.* Englewood Cliffs, NJ: Prentice-Hall.

Bandura, A. (1982). Self-efficacy: Mechanism in human agency. *American Psychologist, 37,* 122–147.

Bandura, A. (1986). The explanatory and predictive scope of self-efficacy theory. *Journal of Social and Clinical Psychology, 4* (Special issue: Self-efficacy theory in contemporary psychology), 359–373.

Bandura, A. (1990). Selective activation and disengagement of moral control. *Journal of Social Issues, 46*(1), 27–46.

Bandura, A., Ross, D., & Ross, S. A. (1961). Transmission of aggression through imitation of aggressive models. *Journal of Abnormal and Social Psychology, 63,* 575–582.

Bandura, A., Ross, D., & Ross, S. A. (1963). Imitation of film-mediated aggressive models. *Journal of Abnormal and Social Psychology, 66,* 3–11.

Banner, L. W. (1983). *American beauty.* Chicago: University of Chicago Press.

Bard, M., & Sangrey, D. (1979). *The crime victim's book.* New York: Basic Books.

Bargh, J., Chaiken, S., Govender, D., & Pratto, F. (1992). The generality of the automatic attitude activation effect. *Journal of Personality and Social Psychology, 62,* 893–912.

Bargh, J. A. (1989). Conditional automaticity: Varieties of automatic influence in social perception and cognition. In J. S. Uleman & J. A. Bargh (Eds.), *Unintended thought: Limits of awareness, intention, and control* (pp. 3–51). New York: Guilford Press.

Bargh, J. A., Bond, R. N., Lombardi, W. J., & Tota, M. E. (1986). The additive nature of chronic and temporary sources of construct accessibility. *Journal of Personality and Social Psychology, 50,* 869–878.

Bargh, J. A., & Gollwitzer, P. M. (in press). Environmental control of goal-directed action: Automatic and strategic contingencies between situations and behavior. In W. J. Arnold & D. Levine (Eds.), *Nebraska Symposium on Motivation.* Lincoln: University of Nebraska Press.

Bargh, J. A., & Pietromonaco, P. (1982). Automatic information processing and social perception: The influence of trait information presented outside of conscious awareness on impression formation. *Journal of Personality and Social Psychology, 43,* 437–449.

Bargh, J. A., & Thein, R. D. (1985). Individual construct accessibility, person memory, and the recall-judgment link: The case of information overload. *Journal of Personality and Social Psychology, 49,* 1129–1146.

Barnet, R. (1971, November). The game of nations. *Harper's, 243,* 53–59.

Baron, R. A. (1971). Aggression as a function of magnitude of victim's pain cues, level of prior anger arousal, and aggressor-victim similarity. *Journal of Personality and Social Psychology, 18,* 48–54.

Baron, R. A. (1972). Aggression as a function of ambient temperature and prior anger arousal. *Journal of Personality and Social Psychology, 21,* 183–189.

Baron, R. A. (1983a). The control of human aggression: An optimistic perspective. *Journal of Social and Clinical Psychology, 1,* 97–119.

Baron, R. A. (1983b). The control of human aggression: A strategy based on incompatible responses. In R. G. Geen & E. Donnerstein (Eds.), *Aggression: Theoretical and empirical reviews* (Vol. 2, pp. 173–190). New York: Academic Press.

Baron, R. A., Baron, P., & Miller, N. (1973). The relation between distraction and persuasion. *Psychological Bulletin, 80,* 310–323.

Baron, R. A., & Kepner, C. R. (1970). Model's behavior and attraction toward the model as determinants of adult aggressive behavior. *Journal of Personality and Social Psychology, 14,* 335–344.

Baron, R. S. (1986). Distraction-conflict theory: Progress and problems. In L. Berkowitz (Ed.), *Advances in experimental social psychology* (Vol. 19, pp. 1–40). New York: Academic Press.

Baron, R. S., & Roper, G. (1976). Reaffirmation of social comparison views of choice shift: Averaging and extremitization in an auto-kinetic situation. *Journal of Personality and Social Psychology, 35,* 521–530.

Bartis, S., Szymanski, K., & Harkins, S. G. (1988). Evaluation and performance: A two-edged knife. *Personality and Social Psychology Bulletin, 14,* 242–251.

Bass, B. M. (1985). *Leadership and performance beyond expectations.* New York: Free Press.

Batson, C. D. (1975). Rational processing or rationalization?: The effect of disconfirming information on a stated religious belief. *Journal of Personality and Social Psychology, 32,* 176–184.

Batson, C. D., Batson, J. G., Slingsby, J. K., Harrell, K. L., Peekna, H. M., & Todd, R. M. (1991). Empathic joy and the empathy-altruism hypothesis. *Journal of Personality and Social Psychology, 61,* 413–426.

Batson, C. D., Coke, J. S., Jasnoski, M. L., & Hanson, M. (1978). Buying kindness: Effect of an extrinsic incentive for helping on perceived altruism. *Personality and Social Psychology Bulletin, 4,* 86–91.

Batson, C. D., Duncan, B. D., Ackerman, P., Buckley, T., & Birch, K. (1981). Is empathic emotion a source of altruistic motivation? *Journal of Personality and Social Psychology, 40,* 290–302.

Batson, C. D., Dyck, J. L., Brandt, J. R., & Batson, J. G. (1988). Five studies testing two new egoistic alternatives to the empathy-altruism hypothesis. *Journal of Personality and Social Psychology, 55,* 52–77.

Batson, C. D., Fultz, J., Schoenrade, P. A., & Paduano, A. (1987). Critical self-reflection and self-perceived altruism: When self-reward fails. *Journal of Personality and Social Psychology, 53,* 594–602.

Baumeister, R. F. (1982). A self-presentational view of social phenomena. *Psychological Bulletin, 91,* 3–26.

Baumeister, R. F. (1991). *Escaping the self: Alcoholism, spirituality, masochism, and other flights from the burden of selfhood.* New York: Basic Books.

Baumeister, R. F., Chesner, S. P., Senders, P. S., & Tice, D. M. (1988). Who's in charge here? Group leaders do lend help in emergencies. *Personality and Social Psychology Bulletin, 14,* 17–22.

Baumeister, R. F., Hutton, D. G., & Tice, D. M. (1989). Cognitive processes during deliberate self-presentation: How self-presenters alter and misinterpret the behavior of their interaction partners. *Journal of Experimental Social Psychology, 25,* 59–78.

Baumeister, R. F., & Showers, C. J. (1986). A review of paradoxical performance effects: Choking under pressure in sports and mental tests. *European Journal of Social Psyochology, 16,* 361–383.

Baumeister, R. F., & Wotman, S. R. (1992). *Breaking hearts: The two sides of unrequited love.* New York: Guilford Press.

Baumgardner, A. H., & Brownlee, E. A. (1987). Strategic failure in social interaction: Evidence for expectancy disconfirmation process. *Journal of Personality and Social Psychology, 52,* 525–535.

Baumrind, D. (1964). Some thoughts on the ethics of research after reading Milgram's "Behavioral Study of Obedience." *American Psychologist, 19,* 421–423.

Baxter, L. A. (1986). Gender differences in the heterosexual relationship rules embedded in break-up accounts. *Journal of Social and Personal Relationships, 1,* 29–48.

Baxter, T. L., & Goldberg, L. R. (1987). Perceived behavioral consistency underlying trait attributions to oneself and another: An extension of the actor-observer effect. *Personality and Social Psychology Bulletin, 13,* 437–447.

Bechtold, A., Naccarato, M. E., & Zanna, M. P. (1986). *Need for structure and the prejudice-discrimination link.* Unpublished paper presented at the annual meeting of the Canadian Psychological Association, Toronto.

Beck, A. T. (1976). *Cognitive therapy and emotional disorders.* New York: International Universities Press.

Becker, B. J. (1986). Influence again: Another look at studies of gender differences in social influence. In J. S. Hyde & M. Linn (Eds.), *The psychology of gender: Advances through meta-analysis* (pp. 178–209). Baltimore: Johns Hopkins University Press.

Beggan, J. K. (1992). On the social nature of nonsocial perception: The mere ownership effect. *Journal of Personality and Social Psychology, 62,* 229–237.

Belch, G. E. (1981). An examination of comparative and noncomparative television commercials: The effects of claim variation and repetition on cognitive response and message acceptance. *Journal of Marketing Research, 18,* 333–349.

Bell, D. A. (1973). Racism in American courts: Cause for Black disruption or despair? *California Law Review, 761,* 165–203.

Bellah, R. N., Madsen, R., Sullivan, W. M., Swidler, A., & Tipton, S. M. (1985). *Habits of the heart: Individualism and commitment in American life.* Berkeley, CA: University of California Press.

Belmore, S. M., & Hubbard, M. L. (1987). The role of advance expectancies in person memory. *Journal of Personality and Social Psychology, 53,* 61–70.

Belsky, J. (1990). Children and marriage. In F. D. Fincham & T. N. Bradbury (Eds.), *The psychology of marriage: Basic issues and applications* (pp. 172–200). New York: Guilford.

Bem, D. J. (1963). An experimental analysis of self-persuasion. *Journal of Experimental Social Psychology, 1,* 199–218.

Bem, D. J. (1967). Self-perception: An alternative interpretation of cognitive dissonance phenomena. *Psychological Review, 74,* 183–200.

Bem, D. J. (1972). Self-perception theory. In L. Berkowitz (Ed.), *Advances in experimental social psychology* (Vol. 6). New York: Academic Press.

Bem, S. (1981). Gender schema theory: A cognitive account of sex typing. *Psychological Review, 88,* 354–364.

Benning, V., & Bennett, P. (1992, September 16). Reconciling principles, racial identity. *The Boston Globe,* pp. 1, 8.

Benson, P. L., Dehority, J., Garman, L., Hanson, E., Hochschwender, M., Lebod, C., Rohr, R., & Sullivan, J. (1980). Intrapersonal correlates of nonspontaneous helping behavior. *Journal of Social Psychology, 110,* 87–95.

Benson, P. L., Karabenic, S. A., & Lerner, R. A. (1976). Pretty pleases: The effects of physical attractiveness on race, sex, and receiving help. *Journal of Experimental Social Psychology, 12,* 409–415.

Bentler, P. M., & Speckart, G. (1979). Models of attitude-behavior relations. *Psychological Review, 86,* 452–464.

Berg, J. H. (1984). The development of friendship between roommates. *Journal of Personality and Social Psychology, 46,* 346–356.

Berg, J. H., & Archer, R. L. (1980). Disclosure or concern: A second look at liking for the norm-breaker. *Journal of Personality, 48,* 245–257.

Berg, J. H., & McQuinn, R. D. (1986). Attraction and exchange in continuing and noncontinuing dating relationships. *Journal of Personality and Social Psychology, 50,* 942–952.

Berglas, S., & Jones, E. E. (1978). Drug choice as a self-handicapping strategy in response to noncontingent success. *Journal of Personality and Social Psychology, 36,* 405–417.

Berk, R. A., & Newton, P. J. (1985). Does arrest really deter wife battery? *American Sociological Review, 50,* 253–262.

Berkman, L. F., Leo-Summers, C., & Horwitz, R. I. (1992). Emotional support and survival after myocardial infarction: A prospective population-based study of the elderly. *Annals of Internal Medicine, 117,* 1003–1009.

Berkman, L. F., & Syme, S. L. (1979). Social networks, host resistance, and mortality: A nine year follow-up of Alameda county residents. *American Journal of Epidemiology, 109,* 186–204.

Berkowitz, L. (1965). The concept of aggressive drive: Some additional considerations. In L. Berkowitz (Ed.), *Advances in experimental social psychology* (Vol. 2, pp. 301–329). New York: Academic Press.

Berkowitz, L. (1972). Social norms, feelings, and other factors affecting helping behavior and altruism. In L. Berkowitz (Ed.), *Advances in experimental social psychology* (Vol. 6, pp. 63–108). New York: Academic Press.

Berkowitz, L. (1984). Some effects of thoughts on anti- and prosocial influences of media events: A cognitive-neoassociationist analysis. *Psychological Bulletin, 95,* 410–427.

Berkowitz, L. (1989). The frustration-aggression hypothesis: An examination and reformulation. *Psychological Bulletin, 106,* 59–73.

Berkowitz, L. (1993). *Aggression: Its causes, consequences, and control.* New York: McGraw-Hill.

Berkowitz, L., & Daniels, L. R. (1963). Responsibility and dependency. *Journal of Abnormal and Social Psychology, 66,* 429–436.

Berkowitz, L., & Donnerstein, E. (1982). External validity is more than skin deep: Some answers to the criticisms of laboratory experiments. *American Psychologist, 37,* 245–257.

Berkowitz, L., & LePage, A. (1967). Weapons as aggression-eliciting stimuli. *Journal of Personality and Social Psychology, 7,* 202–207.

Bernard, J. (1973). *The future of marriage.* New York: Bantam.

Bernstein, M., & Crosby, F. (1980). An experimental examination of relative deprivation theory. *Journal of Experimental Social Psychology, 16,* 442–456.

Berry, D. S., & Brownlow, S. (1989). Were the physiognomists right? Personality correlates of facial babyishness. *Personality and Social Psychology Bulletin, 15,* 266–279.

Berry, D. S., & McArthur, L. Z. (1985). Some components and consequences of a babyface. *Journal of Personality and Social Psychology, 48,* 312–323.

Berscheid, E. (1983). Emotion. In H. H. Kelley, E. Berscheid, A. Christensen, J. H. Harvey, T. L. Huston, G. Levinger, E. McClintock, L. A. Peplau, & D. R. Peterson (Eds.), *Close relationships* (pp. 110–168). San Francisco, CA: Freeman.

Berscheid, E. (1988). Some comments on love's anatomy: Or, whatever happened to old-fashioned lust? In R. Sternberg & M. Barnes (Eds.), *The psychology of love* (pp. 359–374). New Haven, CT: Yale University Press.

Berscheid, E., Snyder, M., & Omoto, A. M. (1989). The Relationship Closeness Inventory: Assessing the closeness of interpersonal relationships. *Journal of Personality and Social Psychology, 57,* 792–807.

Berscheid, E., & Walster, G. W. (1978). *Interpersonal attraction* (2nd ed.). Reading, MA: Addison-Wesley.

Bickman, L. (1974). The social power of a uniform. *Journal of Applied Social Psychology, 4,* 47–61.

Bickman, L. (1979). Interpersonal influence and the reporting of a crime. *Personality and Social Psychology Bulletin, 5,* 32–35.

Bickman, L., & Rosenbaum, D. P. (1977). Crime reporting as a function of bystander encouragement, surveillance, and credibility. *Journal of Personality and Social Psychology, 35,* 577–586.

Biernat, M., & Wortman, C. (1991). Sharing of home responsibilities between professionally employed women and their husbands. *Journal of Personality and Social Psychology, 60,* 844–860.

Billig, M. (1976). *Social psychology and intergroup relations.* New York: Academic Press.

Billig, M., & Tajfel, H. (1973). Social categorization and similarity in intergroup behavior. *European Journal of Social Psychology, 3,* 27–52.

Binning, J. F., Goldstein, M. A., Garcia, M. F., & Scatteregia, J. H. (1988). Effects of preinterview impressions on questioning strategies in same- and opposite-sex employment interviews. *Journal of Applied Psychology, 73,* 30–37.

Birchler, G. R., & Webb, L. J. (1977). Discriminating interaction behavior in happy and unhappy marriages. *Journal of Consulting and Clinical Psychology, 45,* 494–495.

Bird, A. (1977). Team structure and success as related to cohesiveness and leadership. *Journal of Social Psychology, 103,* 217–223.

Birt, C. M., & Dion, K. L. (1987). Relative deprivation theory and responses to deprivation in a gay male and lesbian sample. *British Journal of Social Psychology, 26,* 139–145.

Blake, R. R., & Mouton, J. S. (1979). Intergroup problem solving in organizations: From theory to practice. In W. G. Austin & S. Worchel (Eds.), *The social psychology of intergroup relations* (pp. 19–32). Monterey, CA: Brooks/Cole.

Blake, R. R., & Mouton, J. S. (1980). *The versatile manager: A Grid profile.* Homewood, IL: Dow Jones-Irwin.

Blake, R. R., & Mouton, J. S. (1984). *Solving costly organizational conflicts.* San Francisco, CA: Jossey Bass.

Blanchard, F. A., & Cook, S. W. (1976). Effects of helping a less competent member of a cooperating interracial group on the development of interpersonal attraction. *Journal of Personality and Social Psychology, 34,* 1245–1255.

Blaney, N. T., Stephan, C., Rosenfield, D., Aronson, E., & Sikes, J. (1977). Interdependence in the classroom: A field study. *Journal of Educational Psychology, 69,* 121–128.

Blascovich, J., Nash, R. F., & Ginsburg, G. P. (1978). Heartrate and competitive decision making. *Personality and Social Psychology Bulletin, 4,* 115–118.

Bless, H., Bohner, G., Schwarz, N., & Strach, F. (1990). Mood and persuasion: A cognitive responses analysis. *Personality and Social Psychology Bulletin, 16,* 331–345.

Block, J. (1973). Conceptions of sex role: Some cross-cultural and longitudinal perspectives. *American Psychologist, 28,* 512–526.

Blumstein, P., & Schwartz, P. (1983). *American couples: Money, work, sex.* New York: William Morrow.

Bobo, L. (1983). Whites' opposition to busing: Symbolic racism or realistic group conflict? *Journal of Personality and Social Psychology, 45,* 1196–1210.

Bobo, L. (1988). Group conflict, prejudice, and the paradox of contemporary racial attitudes. In P. A. Katz & D. A. Taylor (Eds.), *Eliminating racism: Profiles in controversy* (pp. 85–114). New York: Plenum.

Bodenhausen, G. V. (1990). Stereotypes as judgmental heuristics: Evidence of circadian variations in discrimination. *Psychological Science, 1,* 319–322.

Bodenhausen, G. V., & Kramer, G. P. (1990). Affective states and the heuristic use of stereotypes in social judgment. Cited in Bodenhausen, G. V. (1993). *Emotions, arousal and stereotyping judgments: A heuristic model of affect and stereotyping.* In D. M. Mackie & D. L. Hamilton (Eds.), *Affect, cognition, and stereotyping: Interactive processes in group perception* (pp. 13–37). San Diego, CA: Academic Press.

Bodenhausen, G. V., & Lichtenstein, M. (1987). Social stereotypes and information-processing strategies: The impact of task complexity. *Journal of Personality and Social Psychology, 52,* 871–880.

Bohlen, C. (1992, October 20). Irate Russians demonize traders from Caucasus. *The New York Times,* p. A3.

Bond, C. F., & Titus, L. J. (1983). Social facilitation: A meta-analysis of 241 studies. *Psychological Bulletin, 94,* 265–292.

Bond, C. F., Jr., & Brockett, D. R. (1987). A social context–personality index theory of memory for acquaintances. *Journal of Personality and Social Psychology, 52,* 1110–1121.

Bond, M. H. (1988). *The cross-cultural challenge to social psychology.* Newbury Park, CA: Sage Publications.

Booth-Kewley, S., & Friedman, H. S. (1987). Psychological predictors of heart disease: A quantitative review. *Psychological Bulletin, 101,* 343–362.

Borgida, E., & Campbell, B. (1982). Belief relevance and attitude-behavior consistency: The moderating role of personal experience. *Journal of Personality and Social Psychology, 42,* 239–247.

Bornstein, R. F., Kale, A. R., & Cornell, K. R. (1990). Boredom as a limiting condition on the mere exposure effect. *Journal of Personality and Social Psychology, 58,* 791–800.

Bornstein, R. F., Leone, D. R., & Galley, D. J. (1987). The generalizability of subliminal mere exposure effects: Influence of stimuli perceived without awareness on social behavior. *Journal of Personality and Social Psychology, 53,* 1070–1079.

Boswell, T. E. (1986). Discrimination and Chinese immigration. *American Sociological Review, 51,* 352–371.

Bothwell, R. K., Brigham, J. C., & Malpass, R. S. (1989). Cross-racial identification. *Personality and Social Psychology Bulletin, 15,* 19–25.

Bourhis, R. Y., Giles, H., Leyens, J. P., & Tajfel, H. (1978). Psychological distinctiveness: Language divergence in Belgium. In H. Giles & R. St. Clair (Eds.), *Language and social psychology* (pp. 158–185). Oxford: Blackwell.

Boyanowsky, E. O., & Griffiths, C. T. (1982). Weapons and eye contact as instigators or inhibitors of aggressive arousal in police-citizen interaction. *Journal of Applied Social Psychology, 12,* 398–407.

Bradbury, T. N., & Fincham, F. D. (1990). Attributions in marriage: Review and critique. *Psychological Bulletin, 107,* 3–33.

Branscombe, N. R., Wann, D. L., Noel, J. G., & Coleman, J. (1993). In-group or out-group extremity: Importance of the threatened social identity. *Personality and Social Psychology Bulletin, 19,* 381–388.

Brawley, L. R., Carron, A. V., & Widmeyer, W. N. (1987). Assessing the cohesion of teams: Validity of the Group Environment Questionnaire. *Journal of Sport Psychology, 9,* 275–294.

Brawley, L. R., Carron, A. V., & Widmeyer, W. N. (1988). Exploring the relationship between cohesion and group resistance to disruption. *Journal of Sport and Exercise Psychology, 10,* 199–213.

Bray, R. M., Johnson, D., & Chilstrom, J. T., Jr., (1982). Social influence by group members with minority opinions: A comparison of Hollander and Moscovici. *Journal of Personality and Social Psychology, 43,* 78–88.

Brean, H. (1958, March 31). What hidden sell is all about. *Life,* 104–114.

Breckler, S. J., & Wiggins, E. C. (1989). Affect versus evaluation in the structure of attitudes. *Journal of Experimental Social Psychology, 25,* 253–271.

Brehm, J. W. (1956). Post-decision changes in desirability of alternatives. *Journal of Abnormal and Social Psychology, 52,* 384–389.

Brehm, J. W. (1966). *A theory of psychological reactance.* New York: Academic Press.

Bretschneider, J. G., & McCoy, N. L. (1988). Sexual interest and behavior in healthy 80- to 102-year-olds. *Archives of Sexual Behavior, 17,* 188–195.

Brewer, M. B. (1979). In-group bias in the minimal intergroup situation: A cognitive-motivational analysis. *Psychological Bulletin, 86,* 307–324.

Brewer, M. B. (1988). A dual process model of impression formation. In T. Srull & R. Wyer (Eds.), *Advances in social cognition* (Vol. 1, pp. 177–183). Hillsdale, NJ: Erlbaum.

Brewer, M. B. (1991). The social self: On being the same and different at the same time. *Personality and Social Psychology Bulletin, 17,* 475–482.

Brewer, M. B., & Campbell, D. T. (1976). *Ethnocentrism and intergroup attitudes: East African evidence.* New York: Halstead Press.

Brewer, M. B., Dull, V., & Lui, L. (1981). Perceptions of the elderly: Stereotypes as prototypes. *Journal of Personality and Social Psychology, 41,* 656–670.

Brewer, M. B., & Kramer, R. M. (1986). Choice behavior in social dilemmas: Effects of social identity, group size, and decision framing. *Journal of Personality and Social Psychology, 50,* 543–549.

Brewer, M. B., & Miller, N. (1984). Beyond the contact hypothesis: Theoretical perspectives on desegregation. In N. Miller & M. B. Brewer (Eds.), *Groups in contact: The psychology of desegregation* (pp. 281–302). New York: Academic Press.

Brewer, M. B., & Silver, M. (1978). Ingroup bias as a function of task characteristics. *European Journal of Social Psychology, 8,* 393–400.

Brickman, P., Coates, D., & Janoff-Bulman, R. (1978). Lottery winners and accident victims: Is happiness relative? *Journal of Personality and Social Psychology, 36,* 917–927.

Brickner, M. A., Harkins, S. G., & Ostrom, T. M. (1986). Effects of personal involvement: Thought-provoking implications for social loafing. *Journal of Personality and Social Psychology, 51,* 763–770.

Brigham, J. C. (1971). Ethnic stereotypes. *Psychological Bulletin, 76,* 15–33.

Briscoe, C., & LaMaster, S. U. (1991). Meaningful learning in college biology through concept mapping. *The American Biology Teacher, 53,* 214–219.

Bronfenbrenner, U. (1961). The mirror image in Soviet-American relations: A social psychologist's report. *Journal of Social Issues, 17*(3), 45–56.

Brown, J. D. (1986). Evaluations of self and others: Self-enhancing biases in social judgment. *Social Cognition, 4,* 353–376.

Brown, J. D., & Smart, S. A. (1991). The self and social conduct: Linking self-representations to prosocial behavior. *Journal of Personality and Social Psychology, 60,* 368–375.

Brown, R., Condor, S., Matthews, A., Wade, G., & Williams, J. A. (1986). Explaining intergroup differentiation in an industrial organization. *Journal of Occupational Psychology, 59,* 273–286.

Brown, R., & Fish, D. (1983). The psychological causality implicit in language. *Cognition, 14,* 237–273.

Brown, R., & Smith, A. (1989). Perceptions of and by minority groups: The case of women in academia. *European Journal of Social Psychology, 19,* 61–75.

Brown, R., & Wade, G. (1987). Superordinate goals and intergroup behavior: The effects of role ambiguity and status on intergroup attitudes and task performance. *European Journal of Social Psychology, 17,* 131–142.

Bruner, J. (1957). On perceptual readiness. *Psychological Review, 64,* 123–152.

Bruner, J. (1986). *Actual minds, possible worlds.* New York: Plenum.

Bryan, J. H., & Test, M. A. (1967). Models and helping: Naturalistic studies in aiding behavior. *Journal of Personality and Social Psychology, 10,* 222–226.

Buck, R., & Ginsburg, B. (1991). Spontaneous communication and altruism: The communicative gene hypothesis. In M. S. Clark (Ed.), *Prosocial behavior* (pp. 149–175). Newbury Park, CA: Sage Publications.

Budescu, D. V., Rapoport, A., & Suleiman, R. (1990). Resource dilemmas with environmental uncertainty and asymmetric players. European *Journal of Social Psychology, 20,* 475–487.

Bulman, R., & Wortman, C. (1977). Attributions of blame and coping in the "real world": Severe accident victims respond to their lot. *Journal of Personality and Social Psychology, 35,* 351–363.

Burger, J. M. (1986). Increasing compliance by improving the deal: The that's-not-all technique. *Journal of Personality and Social Psychology, 51,* 277–283.

Burger, J. M., & Burns, L. (1988). The illusion of unique invulnerability and the use of effective contraception. *Personality and Social Psychology Bulletin, 14,* 264–270.

Burke, P. J. (1967). The development of task and social-emotional role differentiation. *Sociometry, 30,* 379–392.

Burke, R. J. (1970). Methods of resolving superior-subordinate conflict; The constructive use of subordinate differences and disagreements. *Organizational Behavior and Human Performance, 5,* 393–411.

Burnstein, E., & Vinokur, A. (1977). Persuasive argumentation and social comparison as determinants of attitude polarization. *Journal of Experimental Social Psychology, 13,* 315–332.

Burton, J. W. (1969). *Conflict and communication.* New York: Free Press.

Bushman, B. J., & Cooper, H. M. (1990). Effects of alcohol on human aggression: An integrative research review. *Psychological Bulletin, 107,* 341–354.

Bushman, B. J., & Geen, R. G. (1990). Role of cognitive-emotional mediators and individual differences in the effects of media violence on aggression. *Journal of Personality and Social Psychology, 58,* 156–163.

Buss, A. (1961). *The psychology of aggression.* New York: Wiley.

Byrne, D. (1971). *The attraction paradigm.* New York: Academic Press.

Byrne, D., & Murnen, S. K. (1988). Maintaining loving relationships. In R. J. Sternberg & M. L. Barnes (Eds.), *The psychology of love* (pp. 293–310). New Haven: Yale University Press.

Cacioppo, J. T., & Petty, R. E. (1979). Attitudes and cognitive responses: An electro-physiological approach. *Journal of Personality and Social Psychology, 37,* 2181–2199.

Cacioppo, J. T., & Petty, R. E. (1982). The need for cognition. *Journal of Personality and Social Psychology, 42,* 116–131.

Cacioppo, J. T., & Petty, R. E. (1984). The need for cognition: Relationship to attitudinal processes. In R. McGlynn, J. Maddux, C. Stoltenberg, & J. Harvey (Eds.), *Social perception in clinical and counseling psychology* (pp. 113–139). Lubbock, TX: Texas Tech Press.

Cacioppo, J. T., Petty, R. E., Losch, M. E., & Kim, H. S. (1986). Electromyographic activity over facial muscle regions can differentiate the valence and intensity of affective reactions. *Journal of Personality and Social Psychology, 50,* 260–268.

Cacioppo, J. T., Petty, R. E., & Morris, K. J. (1983). Effects of need for cognition on message evaluation, recall, and persuasion. *Journal of Personality and Social Psychology, 45,* 805–818.

Cacioppo, J. T., Petty, R. E., & Sidera, J. (1982). The effects of a salient self-schema on the evaluation of proattitudinal editorials: Top-down versus bottom-up message processing. *Journal of Experimental Social Psychology, 18,* 324–338.

Campbell, A., Converse, P. E., & Rodgers, W. L. (1976). *The quality of American life.* New York: Russell Sage Foundation.

Campbell, D. T. (1963). Social attitudes and other acquired behavioral dispositions. In S. Koch (Ed.), *Psychology: A study of a science* (Vol. 6, pp. 94–172). New York: McGraw-Hill.

Campbell, D. T. (1965). Ethnocentric and other altruistic motives. In D. Levine (Ed.), *Nebraska Symposium on Motivation* (Vol. 13, pp. 283–312). Lincoln: University of Nebraska Press.

Campbell, D. T. (1967). Stereotypes and the perception of group differences. *American Psychologist, 22,* 817–829.

Campbell, J. D., & Fairey, P. (1985). Effects of self-esteem, hypothetical explanations, and verbalization of expectancies on future performance. *Journal of Personality and Social Psychology, 48,* 1097–1111.

Cantor, N., & Kihlstrom, J. F. (1987). *Personality and social intelligence.* Englewood Cliffs, NJ: Prentice-Hall.

Cantor, N., & Malley, J. (1991). Life tasks, personal needs, and close relationships. In G. Fletcher & F. Fincham (Eds.), *Cognition in close relationships* (pp. 101–126). Hillsdale, NJ: Erlbaum.

Caporael, L. R., & Brewer, M. B. (1991). Reviving evolutionary psychology: Biology meets society. *Journal of Social Issues, 47*(3), 187–195.

Caporael, L. R., Dawes, R. M., Orbell, J. M., & Van de Kragt, A. J. C. (1989). Selfishness examined: Cooperation in the absence of egoistic incentives. *Behavioral and Brain Sciences, 12,* 683–699.

Carli, L. (1990). Gender, language, and influence. *Journal of Personality and Social Psychology, 59,* 941–951.

Carli, L. L., & Leonard, J. B. (1989). The effect of hindsight on victim derogation. *Journal of Social and Clinical Psychology, 8,* 331–343.

Carlson, M., Marcus-Newhall, A., & Miller, N. (1989). Evidence for a general construct of aggression. *Personality and Social Psychology Bulletin, 15,* 377–389.

Carlson, M., Marcus-Newhall, A., & Miller, N. (1990). Effects of situational aggression cues: A quantitative review. *Journal of Personality and Social Psychology, 58,* 622–633.

Carlson, M., & Miller, N. (1987). Explanation of the relation between negative mood and helping. *Psychological Bulletin, 102,* 91–108.

Carlson, M., & Miller, N. (1988). Bad experiences and aggression. *Sociology and Social Research, 72,* 155–158.

Carlston, D. E., & Skowronski, J. J. (1986). Trait memory and behavior memory: The effects of alternative pathways on impression judgment response times. *Journal of Personality and Social Psychology, 50,* 5–13.

Carroll, J. W. (1987). Indefinite terminating points and the iterated Prisoner's Dilemma. *Theory and Decision, 22,* 247–256.

Carter, S. (1991). *Reflections of an affirmative action baby.* New York: Basic Books.

Cartwright, D. (1979). Contemporary social psychology in historical perspective. *Social Psychology Quarterly, 42,* 82–93.

Cartwright, D., & Zander, A. (1960). Group cohesiveness: Introduction. In D. Cartwright & A. Zander (Eds.), *Group dynamics: Research and theory* (2nd ed., pp. 69–94). Evanston, IL: Row, Peterson.

Carver, C. S. (1975). Physical aggression as a function of objective self-awareness and attitudes toward punishment. *Journal of Experimental Social Psychology, 11,* 510–519.

Carver, C. S., Ganellen, R. J., Froming, W. J., & Chambers, W. (1983). Modeling: An analysis in terms of category accessibility. *Journal of Experimental Social Psychology, 19,* 403–421.

Carver, C. S., & Scheier, M. F. (1981). *Attention and self-regulation: A control theory approach to human behavior.* New York: Springer-Verlag.

Carver, C. S., & Scheier, M. F. (1990). Origins and functions of positive and negative affect: A control-process view. *Psychological Review, 97,* 19–35.

Cary, L. (1992, June 29). As plain as Black and White. *Newsweek,* p. 53.

Cash, T. F., Gillen, B., & Burns, D. S. (1977). Sexism and beautyism in personnel consultant decision making. *Journal of Applied Psychology, 62,* 301–310.

Cash, T. F., & Kilcullen, R. N. (1985). The eye of the beholder: Susceptibility to sexism and beautyism in the evaluation of managerial applicants. *Journal of Applied Social Psychology, 15,* 591–605.

Casse, P. (1982). *Training for the multicultural manager: A practical and cross-cultural approach to the management of people.* Washington, DC: Society for Intercultural Education, Training, and Research.

Cate, R. M., & Lloyd, S. A. (1988). Courtship. In S. Duck (Ed.), *Handbook of personal relationships: Theory, relationships, and interventions* (pp. 409–427). Chichester, England: Wiley.

Celis, W. (1993, October 25). Give science more life, a panel urges teachers. *The New York Times,* p. A8.

Chacko, T. I. (1982). Women and equal employment opportunity: Some unintended effects. *Journal of Applied Psychology, 67,* 119–123.

Chaiken, S. (1979). Communicator physical attractiveness and persuasion. *Journal of Personality and Social Psychology, 37,* 1387–1397.

Chaiken, S. (1980). Heuristic versus systematic information processing and the use of source versus message cues in persuasion. *Journal of Personality and Social Psychology, 39,* 752–756.

Chaiken, S. (1987). The heuristic model of persuasion. In M. P. Zanna, J. M. Olson, & C. P. Herman (Eds.), *Social influence: The Ontario Symposium* (Vol. 5, pp. 3–40). Hillsdale, NJ: Erlbaum.

Chaiken, S., & Baldwin, M. W. (1981). Affective-cognitive consistency and the effect of salient behavioral information on the self-perception of attitudes. *Journal of Personality and Social Psychology, 41,* 1–12.

Chaiken S., & Eagly, A. H. (1976). Communication modality as a determinant of message persuasiveness and message comprehensibility. *Journal of Personality and Social Psychology, 34,* 605–614.

Chaiken, S., Liberman, A., & Eagly, A. H. (1989). Heuristic and systematic information processing: Within and beyond the persuasion context. In J. S. Uleman & J. A. Bargh (Eds.), *Unintended thought: Limits of awareness, intention, and control* (pp. 212–252). New York: Guilford.

Chandra, F. (1973). The effects of group pressure on perception: A cross-cultural conformity study. *International Journal of Psychology, 8,* 37–39.

Charters, W. W., & Newcomb, T. M. (1958). Some attitudinal effects of experimentally increased salience of a membership group. In E. E. Maccoby, T. M. Newcomb, & E. L. Hartley (Eds.), *Readings in social psychology* (pp. 276–281). New York: Holt.

Cherlin, A. J., Furstenberg, F. F., Jr., Chase-Lansdale, L., Kiernan, K. E., Robins, P. K., Morrison, D. R., & Teitler, J. O. (1991). Longitudinal studies of effects of divorce on children in Great Britain and the United States. *Science, 252,* 1386–1389.

Cialdini, R. B. (1984). Principles of automatic influence. In J. Jacoby & G. S. Craig (Eds.), *Personal selling* (pp. 1–27). Lexington, MA: Lexington Books.

Cialdini, R. B. (1993). *Influence: Science and practice* (3rd ed.). New York: HarperCollins.

Cialdini, R. B., & Ascani, K. (1976). Test of a concession procedure for inducing verbal, behavioral, and further compliance with a request to donate blood. *Journal of Applied Psychology, 61,* 295–300.

Cialdini, R. B., Borden, R. J., Thorne, A., Walker, M. R., Freeman, S., & Sloan, L. R. (1976). Basking in reflected glory: Three (football) field studies. *Journal of Personality and Social Psychology, 34,* 366–375.

Cialdini, R. B., Cacioppo, J. T., Bassett, R., & Miller, J. A. (1978). Low-ball procedure for producing compliance: Commitment then cost. *Journal of Personality and Social Psychology, 36,* 463–476.

Cialdini, R. B., Darby, B. L., & Vincent, J. E. (1973). Transgression and altruism: A case for hedonism. *Journal of Experimental Social Psychology, 9,* 502–516.

Cialdini, R. B., & De Nicholas, M. E. (1989). Self-presentation by association. *Journal of Personality and Social Psychology, 57,* 626–631.

Cialdini, R. B., & Kenrick, D. T. (1976). Altruism as hedonism: A social development perspective on the relationship of negative mood state and helping. *Journal of Personality and Social Psychology, 34,* 907–914.

Cialdini, R. B., Reno, R. R., & Kallgren, C. A. (1990). A focus theory of normative conduct: Recycling the concept of norms to reduce littering in public places. *Journal of Personality and Social Psychology, 58,* 1015–1026.

Cialdini, R. B., & Schroeder, D. A. (1976). Increasing compliance by legitimizing paltry contributions: When even a penny helps. *Journal of Personality and Social Psychology, 34,* 599–604.

Cialdini, R. B., Vincent, J. E., Lewis, S. K., Catalan, J., Wheeler, D., & Darby, B. L. (1975). Reciprocal concessions procedure for inducing compliance: The door-in-the-face technique. *Journal of Personality and Social Psychology, 31,* 206–215.

Clark, K. B. (1965). *Dark ghetto: Dilemmas of social power.* New York: Harper & Row.

Clark, L. F., & Collins, J. E. (1993). Remembering old flames: How the past affects assessments of the present. *Personality and Social Psychology Bulletin, 19,* 399–408.

Clark, M. S., & Mills, J. (1979). Interpersonal attraction in exchange and communal relationships. *Journal of Personality and Social Psychology, 37,* 12–24.

Clark, M. S., & Taraban, C. (1991). Reactions to and willingness to express emotion in communal and exchange relationships. *Journal of Experimental Social Psychology, 27,* 324–336.

Clark, N. K., Stephenson, G. M., & Kniveton, B. H. (1990). Social remembering: Quantitative aspects of individual and collaborative remembering by police officers and students. *British Journal of Psychology, 81,* 73–94.

Clark, R. D., & Word, L. E. (1972). Why don't bystanders help? Because of ambiguity. *Journal of Personality and Social Psychology, 24,* 392–400.

Clifford, M. M. (1975). Physical attractiveness and academic performance. *Child Study Journal, 5,* 201–209.

Cline, V. B., Croft, R. G., & Courrier, S. (1973). Desensitization of children to television violence. *Journal of Personality and Social Psychology, 27,* 360–365.

Clines, F. X. (1982, January 14). Plane hits bridge over the Potomac: 12 dead, 50 missing. *The New York Times,* pp. A1, B6.

Coch, L., & French, J. R. P., Jr. (1948). Overcoming resistance to change. *Human Relations, 1,* 512–532.

Codol, J. P. (1975). On the so-called "superior conformity of the self" behavior: Twenty experimental investigations. *European Journal of Social Psychology, 5,* 457–501.

Cohen, A. (1957). Need for cognition and order of communication as determinants of opinion change. In C. Hovland (Ed.), *The order of presentation in persuasion.* New Haven, CT: Yale University Press.

Cohen, F. (1984). Coping. In J. D. Matarazzo, S. M. Weiss, J. A. Herd, N. E. Miller, & S. M. Weiss (Eds.), *Behavioral health* (pp. 261–274). New York: Wiley.

Cohen, S. P., & Arnone, H. C. (1988). Conflict resolution as the alternative to terrorism. *Journal of Social Issues, 44*(2), 175–190.

Colasanto, D. (1989, November). Americans show commitment to helping those in need. *Gallup Report,* No. 290, 17–24.

Collins, N. L., & Read, S. J. (1990). Adult attachment, working models, and relationship quality in dating couples. *Journal of Personality and Social Psychology, 58,* 644–663.

Condon, J. W., & Crano, W. D. (1988). Inferred evaluation and the relation between attitude similarity and interpersonal attraction. *Journal of Personality and Social Psychology, 54,* 789–797.

Condor, S., & Brown, R. (1988). Psychological processes in intergroup conflict. In W. Stroebe, A. W. Kruglanski, D. Bar-Tal, & M. Hewstone (Eds.), *The social psychology of intergroup conflict* (pp. 3–26). New York: Springer-Verlag.

Cook, S. W. (1971). *The effect of unintended interracial contact upon racial interaction and attitude change.* (Final report, Project No. 5-1320). Washington, DC: U.S. Department of Health, Education, and Welfare, Office of Education.

Cook, S. W. (1985). Experimenting on social issues: The case of school desegregation. *American Psychologist, 40,* 452–460.

Cook, T. D., & Campbell, D. T. (1979). *Quasi-experimentation.* Chicago: Rand McNally.

Cook, T. D., & Flay, B. (1978). The temporal persistence of experimentally induced attitude change: An evaluative review. In L. Berkowitz (Ed.), *Advances in experimental social psychology* (Vol. 11, pp. 1–57). New York: Academic Press.

Cooley, D. H. (1902). *Human nature and the social order.* New York: Scribners.

Cooper, H. (1990). Meta-analysis and the integrative research review. In C. Hendrick & M. S. Clark (Eds.), *Review of personality and social psychology* (Vol. 11, pp. 142–163). Newbury Park, CA: Sage Publications.

Cooper, H., & Good, T. (1983). *Pygmalion grows up: Studies in the expectation communication process.* New York: Longman.

Cooper, J., & Brehm, J. W. (1971). Prechoice awareness of relative deprivation as a determinant of cognitive dissonance. *Journal of Experimental Social Psychology, 7,* 571–581.

Cooper, J., & Fazio, R. H. (1984). A new look at dissonance theory. In L. Berkowitz (Ed.), *Advances in experimental social psychology* (Vol. 17, 229–266). New York: Academic Press.

Cooper, J., Zanna, M. P., & Taves, P. A. (1978). Arousal as a necessary condition for attitude change following induced compliance. *Journal of Personality and Social Psychology, 36,* 1101–1106.

Cooper, W. H. (1981). Ubiquitous halo. *Psychological Bulletin, 90,* 218–224.

Copper, C., Mullen, B., Asuncion, A., Gibbons, P., Goethals, G. R., Riordan, C., Schroeder, D., Tice, D., & Worth, L. (in press). Bias in the media: The subtle effects of a newscaster's smile. In B. Laczek (Ed.), *Media effects.*

Corey, S. M. (1937). Professed attitudes and actual behavior. *Journal of Educational Psychology, 28,* 271–280.

Cosmides, L. (1989). The logic of social exchange: Has natural selection shaped how humans reason? Studies with the Wason selection task. *Cognition, 31,* 187–276.

Courtney, A. E., & Whipple, T. W. (1983). *Sex stereotyping in advertising.* Lexington, MA: Lexington Books.

Cousins, S. (1989). Culture and selfhood in Japan and the U.S. *Journal of Personality and Social Psychology, 56,* 124–131.

Cowley, G. (1991, December 23). I'd toddle a mile for a Camel. *Newsweek,* p. 70.

Cramer, R. E., McMaster, M. R., & Bartell, P. A. (1988). Subject competence and minimization of the bystander effect. *Journal of Applied Social Psychology, 18,* 1133–1148.

Crano, W. D., Gorenflo, D. W., & Shackelford, S. L. (1988). Overjustification, assumed consensus, and attitude change: Further investigation of the incentive-aroused ambivalence hypothesis. *Journal of Personality and Social Psychology, 55,* 12–22.

Crocker, J., Hannah, D. B., & Weber, R. (1983). Person memory and causal attributions. *Journal of Personality and Social Psychology, 44,* 55–66.

Crocker, J., & Major, B. (1989). Social stigma and self-esteem: The self-protective properties of stigma. *Psychological Review, 96,* 608–630.

Crocker, J., Thompson, L. L., McGraw, K. M., & Ingerman, C. (1987). Downward comparison, prejudice, and evaluations of others: Effects of self-esteem and threat. *Journal of Personality and Social Psychology, 52,* 907–916.

Crocker, J., Voelkl, K., Testa, M., & Major, B. (1991). Social stigma: The affective consequences of attributional ambiguity. *Journal of Personality and Social Psychology, 60,* 218–228.

Crosby, F. (1976). A model of egoistic relative deprivation. *Psychological Review, 83,* 85–113.

Crosby, F., Bromley, S., & Saxe, L. (1980). Recent unobtrusive studies of Black and White discrimination and prejudice: *A literature review. Psychological Bulletin, 87,* 546–563.

Crosby, F. J., Pufall, A., Snyder, R. C., O'Connell, M., & Whalen, P. (1989). The denial of personal disadvantage among you, me, and all the other ostriches. In M. Crawford & M. Gentry (Eds.), *Gender and thought: Psychological perspectives* (pp. 79–99). New York: Springer-Verlag.

Croyle, R., & Cooper, J. (1983). Dissonance arousal: Physiological evidence. *Journal of Personality and Social Psychology, 45,* 782–791.

Crutchfield, R. S. (1955). Conformity and character. *American Psychologist, 10,* 191–198.

Csikszentmihalyi, M., & Figurski, T. J. (1982). Self-awareness and aversive experience in everyday life. *Journal of Personality, 50,* 15–28.

Cutrona, C. E. (1982). Transition to college: Loneliness and the process of social adjustment. In L. A. Peplau & D. Perlman (Eds.), *Loneliness* (pp. 291–309). New York: Wiley Interscience.

Darke, S. (1988). Effects of anxiety on inferential reasoning task performance. *Journal of Personality and Social Psychology, 55,* 499–505.

Darley, J. M., & Batson, C. D. (1973). From Jerusalem to Jericho: A study of situational and dispositional variables in helping behavior. *Journal of Personality and Social Psychology, 27,* 100–108.

Darley, J. M., & Fazio, R. H. (1980). Expectancy confirmation processes arising in the social interaction sequence. *American Psychologist, 35,* 867–881.

Darley, J. M., & Gross, P. H. (1983). A hypothesis-confirming bias in labelling effects. *Journal of Personality and Social Psychology, 44,* 20–33.

Darley, J. M., & Latané, B. (1968). Bystander intervention in emergencies: Diffusion of responsibility. *Journal of Personality and Social Psychology, 8,* 377–383.

Darwin, C. (1909). *The descent of man.* New York: Appleton.

Davidson, A. R., & Jaccard, J. J. (1979). Variables that moderate the attitude-behavior relation: Results of a longitudinal survey. *Journal of Personality and Social Psychology, 37,* 1364–1376.

Davidson, A. R., Yantis, S., Norwood, M., & Monano, D. E. (1985). Amount of information about the attitude object and attitude-behavior consistency. *Journal of Personality and Social Psychology, 49,* 1184–1198.

Davis, K., & Newstrom, J. W. (1985). *Human behavior at work: Organizational behavior* (7th ed.). New York: McGraw-Hill.

Davis, K. E., & Jones, E. E. (1960). Changes in interpersonal perception as a means of reducing cognitive dissonance. *Journal of Abnormal and Social Psychology, 61,* 402–410.

Davis, N. M., & Cohen, M. R. (1981). *Medication errors: Causes and prevention.* Philadelphia: G.F. Stickley Co.

Dawes, R. M., & Smith, T. L. (1985). Attitude and opinion measurement. In G. Lindzey & E. Aronson (Eds.), *The handbook of social psychology* (3rd ed., Vol. 1, pp. 509–566). New York: Random House.

DeAngelis, T. (1993, January). The pen's might may aid those searching for a job. *APA Monitor,* p. 25.

Deaux, K., & Emswiller, T. (1974). Explanations of successful performance on sex-linked tasks: What is skill for the male is luck for the female. *Journal of Personality and Social Psychology, 29,* 80–85.

Deaux, K., & Lewis, L. L. (1983). Components of gender stereotypes. *Psychological Documents, 13,* 25–34.

Deaux, K., & Lewis, L. L. (1984). Structure of gender stereotypes: Interrelationships among components and gender label. *Journal of Personality and Social Psychology, 46,* 991–1004.

Deaux, K. K., & Hanna, R. (1984). Courtship in the personals column: The influence of gender and sexual orientation. *Sex Roles, 11,* 363–375.

DeBono, K. G. (1987). Investigating the social-adjustive and value-expressive functions of attitudes: Implications for persuasion processes. *Journal of Personality and Social Psychology, 52,* 279–287.

DeBono, K. G., & Harnish, R. (1988). Source expertise, source attractiveness, and the processing of persuasive information: A functional approach. *Journal of Personality and Social Psychology, 55,* 541–546.

Deci, E. L. (1971). Effects of externally mediated rewards on intrinsic motivation. *Journal of Personality and Social Psychology, 18,* 105–115.

Deci, E. L. (1975). *Intrinsic motivation.* New York: Plenum.

Deci, E. L., & Ryan, R. M. (1987). The support of autonomy and the control of behavior. *Journal of Personality and Social Psychology, 53* (Special issue: Integrating personality and social psychology), 1024–1037.

DeJong, W. (1979). An examination of self-perception mediation on the foot-in-the-door effect. *Journal of Personality and Social Psychology, 37,* 2221–2239.

DeLamater, J., & MacCorquodale, P. (1979). *Premarital sexuality: Attitudes, relationships, behavior.* Madison, WI: University of Wisconsin Press.

Dembroski, T. M., & Costa, P. T. (1987). Coronary prone behavior: Components of the Type A pattern and hostility. *Journal of Personality, 55* (Special issue: Personality and physical health), 211–235.

Denmark, F., Russo, N. F., Frieze, I. H., & Sechzer, J. A. (1988). Guidelines for avoiding sexism in psychological research. *American Psychologist, 43,* 582–585.

Denmark, F. L., Shaw, J. S., & Ciali, S. O. (1985). The relationship among sex roles, living arrangements, and the division of household responsibilities. *Sex Roles, 12,* 617–625.

Department of the Army. (1956). *The law of land warfare* (Field Manual No. 27-10). Washington, DC: U.S. Government Printing Office.

DePaulo, B. M., Lassiter, G. D., & Stone, J. I. (1982). Attentional determinants of success at detecting deception and truth. *Personality and Social Psychology Bulletin, 8,* 273–279.

De Rivera, J. (1977). *A structural theory of the emotions.* New York: International Universities Press.

Derlega, V. J., Wilson, M., & Chaikin, A. L. (1976). Friendship and disclosure reciprocity. *Journal of Personality and Social Psychology, 34,* 578–587.

Derlega, V. J., Winstead, B. A., Wong, P. T. P., & Hunter, S. (1985). Gender effects in an initial encounter: A case where men exceed women in disclosure. *Journal of Social and Personal Relationships, 2,* 25–44.

Deschamps, J. C., & Brown, R. (1983). Superordinate goals and intergroup conflict. *British Journal of Social Psychology, 22,* 189–195.

Desforges, D. M., Lord, C. G., Ramsey, S. L., Mason, J. A., Van Leeuwen, M. D., West, S. C., & Lepper, M. R. (1991). Effects of structured cooperative contact on changing negative attitudes toward stigmatized social groups. *Journal of Personality and Social Psychology, 60,* 531–544.

Desmond, E. W. (1987, November 30). Out in the open. *Time,* pp. 80–90.

Deutsch, M. (1949). An experimental study of the effects of cooperation and competition upon group process. *Human Relations, 2,* 199–231.

Deutsch, M. (1973). *The resolution of conflict.* New Haven, CT: Yale University Press.

Deutsch, M. (1980). Fifty years of conflict. In L. Festinger (Ed.), *Retrospections on social psychology* (pp. 46–77). New York: Oxford University Press.

Deutsch, M. (1990). Psychological roots of moral exclusion. *Journal of Social Issues, 46*(1), 21–25.

Deutsch, M. (1993). Educating for a peaceful world. *American Psychologist, 48,* 510–517.

Deutsch, M., & Collins, M. E. (1951). *Interracial housing: A psychological evaluation of a social experiment.* Minneapolis, MN: University of Minnesota Press.

Deutsch, M., & Gerard, H. B. (1955). A study of normative and informational social influence upon individual judgment. *Journal of Abnormal and Social Psychology, 51,* 629–636.

Deutsch, M., & Krauss, R. M. (1960). The effect of threat upon interpersonal bargaining. *Journal of Abnormal and Social Psychology, 61,* 181–189.

Devine, P. G. (1989). Stereotypes and prejudice: Their automatic and controlled components. *Journal of Personality and Social Psychology, 56,* 5–18.

Devine, P. G., & Baker, S. M. (1991). Measurement of racial stereotypes subtyping. *Personality and Social Psychology Bulletin, 17,* 44–50.

Devine, P. G., & Monteith, M. J. (1993). The role of discrepancy-associated affect in prejudice reduction. In D. M. Mackie & D. L. Hamilton (Eds.), *Affect, cognition, and stereotyping* (pp. 317–344). San Diego, CA: Academic Press.

Diab, L. N. (1970). A study of intragroup and intergroup relations among experimentally produced small groups. *Genetic Psychology Monographs, 82,* 49–82.

Diehl, M., & Stroebe, W. (1991). Productivity loss in idea-generating groups: Tracking down the blocking effect. *Journal of Personality and Social Psychology, 61,* 392–403.

Diener, E. (1980). Deindividuation: The absence of self-awareness and self-regulation in group members. In P. Paulus (Ed.), *The psychology of group influence* (pp. 209–242). Hillsdale, NJ: Erlbaum.

Diener, E., & Crandall, R. (1979). An evaluation of the Jamaican anticrime program. *Journal of Applied Social Psychology, 9,* 135–146.

Diener, E., & Wallbom, M. (1976). Effects of self-awareness on antinormative behavior. *Journal of Research in Personality, 10,* 107–111.

Dietrich, D. M., & Berkowitz, L. (1989). *The role of the self in dissonance-motivated behavior.* Unpublished paper, University of Wisconsin, Madison. Cited in Eagly & Chaiken.

Dijker, A. J. M. (1987). Emotional reactions to ethnic minorities. *European Journal of Social Psychology, 47,* 1105–1117.

Dindia, K., & Allen, M. (1992). Sex differences in self-disclosure: A meta-analysis. *Psychological Bulletin, 112,* 106–122.

Dion, K. K., & Berscheid, E. (1974). Physical attractiveness and peer perception among children. *Sociometry, 37,* 1–12.

Dion, K. K., Berscheid, E., & Walster, E. (1972). What is beautiful is good. *Journal of Personality and Social Psychology, 24,* 285–290.

Dion, K. L., & Dion, K. K. (1988). Romantic love: Individual and cultural perspectives. In R. Sternberg & M. Barnes (Eds.), *The psychology of love* (pp. 264–289). New Haven, CT: Yale University Press.

Dobzhansky, T. (1973). *Genetic diversity and human equality.* New York: Basic Books.

Dodge, K., & Coie, J. D. (1987). Social information-processing factors in reactive and proactive aggression in children's peer groups. *Journal of Personality and Social Psychology, 53,* 1146–1158.

Dodge, K. A., Bates, J. E., & Pettit, G. S. (1990). Mechanisms of the cycle of violence. *Science, 250,* 1678–1683.

Dodge, K. A., & Crick, N. R. (1990). Social information-processing bases of aggressive behavior in children. Special issue: Illustrating the value of basic research. *Personality and Social Psychology Bulletin, 16,* 8–22.

Dodge, K. A., & Newman, J. P. (1981). Biased decision-making processes in aggressive boys. *Journal of Abnormal Psychology, 90,* 375–379.

Dodge, K. A., Pettit, G. S., McClaskey, C. L., & Brown, M. (1986). Social competence in children. *Monographs of the Society for Research in Child Development, 51* (2, Serial No. 213).

Dodge, K. A., & Somberg, D. R. (1987). Hostile attributional biases among aggressive boys are exacerbated under conditions of threat to the self. *Child Development, 58,* 213–224.

Doise, W. (1978). *Groups and individuals: Explanations in social psychology.* Cambridge: Cambridge University Press.

Doise, W., & Sinclair, A. (1973). The categorization process in intergroup relations. *European Journal of Social Psychology, 3,* 145–157.

Doise, W., & Weinberger, M. (1973). Representations masculines dans differentes situations de rencontre mixtes. *Bulletin de Psychologie, 26,* 649–657.

Dollard, J., Doob, L. W., Miller, M. E., Mowrer, O. H., & Sears, R. R. (1939). *Frustration and aggression.* New Haven: Yale University Press.

Donnerstein, E., & Donnerstein, M. (1976). Research in the control of interracial aggression. In R. G. Geen & E. C. O'Neal (Eds.), *Perspectives on aggression* (pp. 133–168). New York: Academic Press.

Donnerstein, E., Linz, D., & Penrod, S. (1987). *The question of pornography: Research findings and policy implications.* New York: Free Press.

Donnerstein, E. I., & Linz, D. G. (1986). The question of pornography. *Psychology Today, 20*(12), 56–59.

Dovidio, J. F., Allen, J. L., & Schroeder, D. A. (1990). Specificity of empathy-induced helping: Evidence for altruistic motivation. *Journal of Personality and Social Psychology, 59,* 249–260.

Dovidio, J. F., & Gaertner, S. L. (Eds.) (1986). *Prejudice, discrimination, and racism.* Orlando, FL: Academic Press.

Dovidio, J. F., & Gaertner, S. L. (1993). Stereotypes and evaluative intergroup bias. In D. M. Mackie & D. L. Hamilton (Eds.), *Affect, cognition, and stereotyping: Interactive processes in group perception* (pp. 167–193). San Diego, CA: Academic Press.

Dovidio, J. F., Piliavin, J. A., Gaertner, S. L., Schroeder, D. A., & Clark, R. D. (1991). The arousal: cost-reward model and the process of intervention: A review of the evidence. In M. S. Clark (Ed.), *Prosocial behavior* (pp. 86–118). Newbury Park, CA: Sage Publications.

Downs, A. C., & Lyons, P. M. (1991). Natural observations of the links between attractiveness and initial legal judgments. *Personality and Social Psychology Bulletin, 17,* 541–547.

Drigotas, S. M., & Rusbult, C. E. (1992). Should I stay or should I go? A dependence model of breakups. *Journal of Personality and Social Psychology, 62,* 62–87.

Driscoll, R., Davis, K. W., & Lipetz, M. E. (1972). Parental interference and romantic love. *Journal of Personality and Social Psychology, 24,* 1–10.

Druckman, D. (1973). Social psychology in international negotiations. In R. F. Kidd & M. J. Saks (Eds.), *Advances in applied social psychology* (Vol. 2, pp. 51–82). Hillsdale, NJ: Erlbaum.

Druckman, D. (1990). The social psychology of arms control and reciprocation. *Political Psychology, 11,* 553–581.

Druckman, D., & Mahoney, R. (1977). Processes and consequences of international negotiations. *Journal of Social Issues, 33*(1), 60–87.

Druckman, D., & Zechmeister, K. (1973). Conflict of interest and value dissensus: Propositions on the sociology of conflict. *Human Relations, 26,* 449–466.

Dubrovsky, V. J., Kiesler, S., & Sethna, B. N. (1991). The equalization phenomenon: Status effects in computer-mediated and face-to-face decision-making groups. *Human Computer Interaction, 6,* 119–146.

Duke, L., & Morin, R. (1992, March 8). Focusing on race: Candid dialogue, elusive answers. *The Washington Post,* p. A35.

Duncan, B. L. (1976). Differential social perception and attribution of intergroup violence: Testing the lower limits of stereotyping of blacks. *Journal of Personality and Social Psychology, 34,* 590–598.

Dunning, D., Meyerowitz, J. A., & Holzberg, A. D. (1989). Ambiguity and self-evaluation: The role of idiosyncratic trait definitions in self-serving assessments of ability. *Journal of Personality and Social Psychology, 57,* 1082–1090.

Durkheim, E. (1898). *The rules of sociological method.* New York: Free Press.

Duval, S., Duval, V. H., & Neely, R. (1979). Self-focus, felt responsibility, and helping behavior. *Journal of Personality and Social Psychology, 37,* 1769–1778.

Duval, S., & Wicklund, R. A. (1972). *A theory of objective self-awareness.* New York: Academic Press.

Dweck, C. S. (1986). Motivational processes affecting learning. *American Psychologist, 41,* 1040–1048.

Eagly, A. H. (1987). *Sex differences in social behavior: A social-role interpretation.* Hillsdale, NJ: Erlbaum.

Eagly, A. H., Ashmore, R. D., Makhijani, M. G., & Longo, L. C. (1991). What is beautiful is good, but . . . : A meta-analytic review of research on the physical attractiveness stereotype. *Psychological Bulletin, 110,* 109–128.

Eagly, A. H., & Carli, L. L. (1981). Sex of researchers and sex-typed communications as determinants of sex differences in influenceability: A meta-analysis of social influence studies. *Psychological Bulletin, 90,* 1–20.

Eagly, A. H., & Chaiken, S. (1993). *The psychology of attitudes.* San Diego, CA: Harcourt Brace Jovanovich.

Eagly, A. H., Chaiken, S., & Wood, W. (1981). An attributional analysis of persuasion. In J. H. Harvey, W. J. Ickes, & R. F. Kidd (Eds.), *New directions in attribution research* (Vol. 3, pp. 37–62). Hillsdale, NJ: Erlbaum.

Eagly, A. H., & Crowley, M. (1986). Gender and helping behavior: A meta-analytic review of the social psychological literature. *Psychological Bulletin, 100,* 283–308.

Eagly, A. H., & Johnson, B. T. (1990). Gender and leadership style: A meta-analysis. *Psychological Bulletin, 108,* 233–256.

Eagly, A. H., & Karau, S. J. (1991). Gender and the emergence of leaders: A meta-analysis. *Journal of Personality and Social Psychology, 60,* 685–710.

Eagly, A. H., Karau, S. J., & Makhijani, M. G. (1994). *Gender and the effectiveness of leaders: A meta-analysis.* Unpublished paper, Purdue University.

Eagly, A. H., & Makhijani, M. (1991). What is beautiful is good, but . . . : A meta-analytic review of research on the physical attractiveness stereotype. *Psychological Bulletin, 110,* 109–128.

Eagly, A. H., Makhijani, M. G., & Klonsky, B. G. (1992). Gender and the evaluation of leaders: A meta-analysis. *Psychological Bulletin, 111,* 3–22.

Eagly, A. H., & Mladinic, A. (1989). Gender stereotypes and attitudes toward women and men. *Personality and Social Psychology Bulletin, 15,* 543–558.

Eagly, A. H., & Steffen, V. J. (1984). Gender stereotypes stem from the distribution of women and men into social roles. *Journal of Personality and Social Psychology, 46,* 735–754.

Eagly, A. H., Wood, W., & Chaiken, S. (1978). Causal inferences about communicators and their effect on opinion change. *Journal of Personality and Social Psychology, 36,* 424–435.

Earley, P. C. (1989). Social loafing and collectivism: A comparison of the United States and the People's Republic of China. *Administrative Science Quarterly, 34,* 565–581.

Easterbrook, J. A. (1959). The effect of emotion on cue utilization and the organization of behavior. *Psychological Review, 66,* 183–201.

Ebbesen, E. B., Kjos, G. L., & Konecni, V. J. (1976). Spatial ecology: Its effects on the choice of friends and enemies. *Journal of Experimental Social Psychology, 12,* 505–518.

Ebbesen, E. B., & Konecni, V. J. (1975). Decision making and information integration in the courts: The setting of bail. *Journal of Personality and Social Psychology, 32,* 805–821.

Edney, J. J. (1980). The commons problem: Alternative perspectives. *American Psychologist, 35,* 131–150.

Eibl-Eibesfeldt, I. (1979). *The biology of peace and war: Men, animals, and aggression.* New York: Viking.

Eisenberg, N. (1991). Meta-analytic contributions to the literature on prosocial behavior. *Personality and Social Psychology Bulletin, 17,* 273–282.

Eisenberg, N., & Fabes, R. A. (1991). Prosocial behavior and empathy: A multimethod developmental perspective. In M. S. Clark (Ed.), *Prosocial behavior* (pp. 34–61). Newbury Park, CA: Sage Publications.

Eisenberger, R., Cotterell, N., & Marvel, J. (1987). Reciprocation ideology. *Journal of Personality and Social Psychology, 53,* 743–750.

Eisenger, R., & Mills, J. (1968). Perception of the sincerity and competence of a communicator as a function of the extremity of his position. *Journal of Experimental Social Psychology, 4,* 224–232.

Eisenstat, R. A. (1990). Compressor team start-up. In J. R. Hackman (Ed.), *Groups that work (and those that don't)* (pp. 411–426). San Francisco: Jossey-Bass.

Eiser, J. R., & Sutton, S. R. (1977). Smoking as a subjectively rational choice. *Addictive Behaviors, 2,* 129–134.

Eiser, J. R., & van der Pligt, J. (1986). Smoking cessation and smokers' perceptions of their addiction. *Journal of Social and Clinical Psychology, 4,* 60–70.

Eiser, J. R., van der Pligt, J., Raw, M., & Sutton, S. R. (1985). Trying to stop smoking: Effects of perceived addiction, attributions for failure and expectancy of success. *Journal of Behavioral Medicine, 8,* 321–341.

Ekman, P. (1973). Universal facial expressions in emotion. *Studia Psychologica, 15,* 140–147.

Ekman, P. (1992). Facial expressions of emotion: New findings, new questions. *Psychological Science, 3,* 34–38.

Ekman, P., & Friesen, W. V. (1974). Detecting deception from the body or face. *Journal of Personality and Social Psychology, 29,* 288–298.

Ekman, P., Friesen, W. V., & Ellsworth, P. (1972). *Emotion in the human face.* Elmsford, NY: Pergamon Press.

Ekman, P., Friesen, W. V., O'Sullivan, M., Chan, A., Diacoyanni-Tarlatzis, I., Heider, K., Krause, R., LeCompte, W. A., Pitcairn, T., Ricci-Bitti, P. E., Scherer, K., Tomita, M., & Tzavaras, A. (1987). Universals and cultural differences in the judgments of facial expressions of emotion. *Journal of Personality and Social Psychology, 53,* 712–717.

Ekman, P., & O'Sullivan, M. (1991). Who can catch a liar? *American Psychologist, 46,* 913–920.

Elkin, R. A., & Leippe, M. R. (1986). Physiological arousal, dissonance, and attitude change: Evidence for a dissonance arousal link and a "don't remind me" effect. *Journal of Personality and Social Psychology, 51,* 55–56.

Ellis, A., & Grieger, R. (1977). *Handbook of rational-emotive therapy.* New York: Springer.

Ellsworth, P., & Carlsmith, J. M. (1973). Eye contact and gaze aversion in an aggressive encounter. *Journal of Personality and Social Psychology, 28,* 280–292.

Ennis, R., & Zanna, M. P. (1991). *Norms and aggressive attitudes in hockey.* Unpublished paper presented at Canadian Psychological Association convention, Ottawa.

Epstein, R., & Komorita S. S. (1966). Childhood prejudice as a function of parental ethnocentrism, punitiveness, and outgroup characteristics. *Journal of Personality and Social Psychology, 3,* 259–64.

Epstein, S. (1992). Coping ability, negative self-evaluation, and overgeneralization: Experiment and theory. *Journal of Personality and Social Psychology, 62,* 826–836.

Epstein, Y. M., Suedfeld, P., & Silverstein, S. J. (1973). The experimental contract: Subjects' expectations of and reactions to some behaviors of experimenters. *American Psychologist, 28,* 212–221.

Erickson, B., Lind, E. A., Johnson, B. C., & O'Barr, W. M. (1978). Speech style and impression formation in a court setting: The effects of powerful and powerless speech. *Journal of Experimental Social Psychology, 14,* 266–279.

Esser, J. K., & Lindoerfer, J. S. (1989). Groupthink and the space shuttle *Challenger* accident: Toward a quantitative case analysis. *Journal of Behavioral Decision Making, 2,* 167–177.

Esses, V. M., Haddock, G., & Zanna, M. P. (1993). Values, stereotypes, and emotions as determinants of intergroup attitudes. In D. M. Mackie & D. L. Hamilton (Eds.), *Affect, cognition, and stereotyping: Interactive processes in group perception* (pp. 137–166). San Diego, CA: Academic Press.

Ethical Principles of Psychologists and Code of Conduct. (1992). Washington, DC: American Psychological Association.

Etzioni, A. (1962). *The hard way to peace.* New York: Collier.

Etzioni, A. (1967). The Kennedy experiment. *Western Political Quarterly, 20,* 361–380.

Evans, G. W. (1979). Behavioral and physiological consequences of crowding in humans. *Journal of Applied Social Psychology, 9,* 27–46.

Falbo, T., & Peplau, L. A. (1980). Power strategies in intimate relationships. *Journal of Personality and Social Psychology, 38,* 618–628.

Fay, R. E., Turner, C. F., Klassen, A. D., & Gagnon, J. H. (1989). Prevalence and patterns of same-gender sexual contact among men. *Science, 243,* 338–348.

Fazio, R. H. (1986). How do attitudes guide behavior? In R. M. Sorrentino & E. T. Higgins (Eds.), *Handbook of motivation and cognition: Foundations of social behavior* (Vol. 1, pp. 204–243). New York: Guilford Press.

Fazio, R. H. (1989). On the power and functionality of attitudes: The role of attitude accessibility. In A. R. Pratkanis, S. J. Breckler, & A. G. Greenwald (Eds.), *Attitude structure and function* (pp. 153–179). Hillsdale, NJ: Erlbaum.

Fazio, R. H. (1990). Multiple processes by which attitudes guide behavior: The MODE model as an integrative framework. In M. P. Zanna (Ed.), *Advances in experimental social psychology* (Vol. 23, pp. 75–109). New York: Academic Press.

Fazio, R. H., Blascovich, J., & Driscoll, D. M. (1992). On the functional value of attitudes: The influence of accessible attitudes upon the ease and quality of decision making. *Personality and Social Psychology Bulletin, 18,* 388–401.

Fazio, R. H., Chen, J., McDonel, E., & Sherman, S. J. (1982). Attitude accessibility, attitude-behavior consistency, and the strength of the object-evaluation association. *Journal of Experimental Social Psychology, 18,* 339–357.

Fazio, R. H., Effrein, E. A., & Falender, V. J. (1981). Self-perceptions following social interactions. *Journal of Personality and Social Psychology, 41,* 232–242.

Fazio, R. H., & Zanna, M. P. (1981). Direct experience and attitude-behavior consistency. In L. Berkowitz (Ed.), *Advances in experimental social psychology* (Vol. 14, pp. 161–202). San Diego, CA: Academic Press.

Fazio, R. H., Zanna, M. P., & Cooper, J. (1977). Dissonance and self-perception: An integrative view of each theory's proper domain of application. *Journal of Experimental Social Psychology, 13,* 464–479.

Feather, N. T. (1969). Attitude and selective recall. *Journal of Personality and Social Psychology, 12,* 310–319.

Fein, S., & Hilton, J. L. (1992). Attitudes toward groups and behavioral intentions toward individual group members: The impact of nondiagnostic information. *Journal of Experimental Social Psychology, 28,* 101–124.

Fein, S., Hilton, J. L., & Miller, D. T. (1990). Suspicion of ulterior motivation and the correspondence bias. *Journal of Personality and Social Psychology, 58,* 753–764.

Feingold, A. (1990). Gender differences in effects of physical attractiveness on romantic attraction: A comparison across five research paradigms. *Journal of Personality and Social Psychology, 59,* 981–993.

Feingold, A. (1992). Good-looking people are not what we think. *Psychological Bulletin, 111,* 304–341.

Felson, R. B. (1989). Parents and the reflected appraisal process: A longitudinal analysis. *Journal of Personality and Social Psychology, 56,* 965–971.

Fenigstein, A., Scheier, M. F., & Buss, A. H. (1975). Public and private self-consciousness: Assessment and theory. *Journal of Consulting and Clinical Psychology, 43,* 522–527.

Feshbach, N. (1980). *The child as "psychologist" and "economist": Two curricula.* Paper presented at the American Psychological Association convention.

Feshbach, N., & Feshbach, S. (1982). Empathy training and the regulation of aggression: Potentialities and limitations. *Academic Psychology Bulletin, 4,* 399–413.

Feshbach, S., & Singer, R. (1957). The effects of personality and shared threats upon social prejudice. *Journal of Abnormal and Social Psychology, 54,* 411–416.

Festinger, L. (1950). Informal social communication. *Psychological Review, 57,* 271–282.

Festinger, L. (1954). A theory of social comparison processes. *Human Relations, 7,* 117–140.

Festinger, L. (1957). *A theory of cognitive dissonance.* Stanford, CA: Stanford University Press.

Festinger, L., & Carlsmith, J. M. (1959). Cognitive consequences of forced compliance. *Journal of Abnormal and Social Psychology, 58,* 203–210.

Festinger, L., Pepitone, A., & Newcomb, T. (1952). Some consequences of de-individuation in a group. *Journal of Abnormal and Social Psychology, 58,* 203–210.

Festinger, L., Schacter, S., & Back, K. (1950). *Social pressures in informal groups: A study of human factors in housing.* Stanford, CA: Stanford University Press.

Fiedler, F. (1964). A contingency model of leadership effectiveness. In L. Berkowitz (Ed.), *Advances in experimental social psychology* (Vol. 1, pp. 149–190). New York: Academic Press.

Fincham, F., & O'Leary, K. D. (1983). Causal inferences for spouse behavior in maritally distressed and nondistressed couples. *Journal of Clinical and Social Psychology, 1,* 42–57.

Fincham, F. D., & Bradbury, T. N. (1987). Cognitive processes and conflict in close relationships: An attribution-efficacy model. *Journal of Personality and Social Psychology, 53,* 1106–1118.

Fishbein, M., & Ajzen, I. (1975). *Belief, attitude, intention, and behavior: An introduction to theory and research.* Reading, MA: Addison-Wesley.

Fisher, J. D., & Fisher, W. A. (1992). Changing AIDS-risk behavior. *Psychological Bulletin, 111,* 455–474.

Fisher, J. D., Nadler, A., & Whitcher-Alagner, S. (1982). Recipient reactions to aid. *Psychological Bulletin, 91,* 27–54.

Fisher, R., & Ury, W. L. (1981). *Getting to yes: Negotiating agreement without giving in.* Boston: Houghton Mifflin.

Fisher, R., & White, J. H. (1976). Intergroup conflicts resolved by outside consultants. *Journal of Community Development, 7,* 88–98.

Fiske, A. P. (1991). The cultural relativity of selfish individualism. In M. S. Clark (Ed.), *Prosocial behavior* (pp. 176–214). Newbury Park, CA: Sage Publications.

Fiske, A. P. (1992). The four elementary forms of sociality: Framework for a unified theory of social relations. *Psychological Review, 99,* 689–724.

Fiske, S. T. (1993). Social cognition and social perception. *Annual Review of Psychology, 44,* 155–194.

Fiske, S. T., Bersoff, D. N., Borgida, E., Deaux, K., & Heilman, M. E. (1991). Social science research on trial: Use of sex stereotyping research in *Price Waterhouse* v. *Hopkins. American Psychologist, 46,* 1049–1060.

Fiske, S. T., & Neuberg, S. L. (1990). A continuum of impression formation, from category-based to individuating processes: Influences of information and motivation on attention and interpretation. In M. P. Zanna (Ed.), *Advances in experimental social psychology* (Vol. 23, pp. 1–74). New York: Academic Press.

Fiske, S. T., & Pavelchak, M. A. (1986). Category-based versus piecemeal-based affective responses: Developments in schema-triggered affect. In R. M. Sorrentino & E. T. Higgins (Eds.), *Handbook of motivation and cognition: Foundations of social behavior* (Vol. 1, pp. 167–203). New York: Guilford Press.

Fiske, S. T., & Stevens, L. E. (1993). What's so special about sex? Gender stereotyping and discrimination. In S. Oskamp & M. Costanzo (Eds.), *Gender issues in contemporary society* (pp. 173–196). Newbury Park, CA: Sage Publications.

Flay, B. R., Ryan, K. B., Best, J. A., Brown, K. S., Kersell, M. W., d'Avernas, J. R., & Zanna, M. P. (1985). Are social-psychological smoking prevention programs effective? The Waterlook study. *Journal of Behavioral Medicine, 8,* 37–59.

Fleming, I., Baum, A., & Weiss, L. (1987). Social density and perceived control as mediators of crowding stress in high-density residential neighborhoods. *Journal of Personality and Social Psychology, 52,* 899–906.

Fletcher, G., & Haig, B. (1990). *The layperson as "naive scientist": An appropriate model for personality and social psychology?* Unpublished paper, University of Canterbury, Christchurch, New Zealand.

Fletcher, G. J. O., & Fincham, F. D. (1991). Attribution processes in close relationships. In G. Fletcher & F. Fincham (Eds.), *Cognition in close relationships* (pp. 7–36). Hillsdale, NJ: Erlbaum.

Flier on school jewelry has manipulative ring to it. (1993, September 11). *Lafayette Journal and Courier,* Lafayette, Indiana, p. A2.

Flink, C., & Park, B. (1991). Increasing consensus in trait judgments through outcome dependency. *Journal of Experimental Social Psychology, 27,* 453–467.

Foersterling, F. (1986). Attributional conceptions in clinical psychology. *American Psychologist, 41,* 275–285.

Folkman, S. (1984). Personal control and stress and coping processes: A theoretical analysis. *Journal of Personality and Social Psychology, 46,* 839–852.

Ford, C. S., & Beach, F. A. (1951). *Patterns of sexual behavior.* New York: Harper & Row.

Forsyth, D. R. (1990). *Group dynamics* (2nd ed.). Pacific Grove, CA: Brooks/Cole.

Forsyth, D. R., Schlenker, B. R., Leary, M. R., & McCown, N. E. (1985). Self-presentational determinants of sex differences in leadership behavior. *Small Group Behavior, 16,* 197–210.

Foushee, H. C. (1984). Dyads and triads at 35,000 feet: Factors affecting group process and aircrew performance. *American Psychologist, 39,* 885–893.

Foushee, H. C., & Manos, K. L. (1981). Information transfer within the cockpit: Problems in intracockpit communications. In C. E. Billings & E. S. Cheaney (Eds.), *Information transfer problems in the aviation system.* NASA Report No. TP-1875. Moffett Field, CA: NASA-Ames Research Center.

Frable, D. E. S. (1989). Sex typing and gender ideology: Two facets of the individual's gender psychology that go together. *Journal of Personality and Social Psychology, 56,* 95–108.

Frank, M. G., & Gilovich, T. (1988). The dark side of self- and social perception: Black uniforms and aggression in professional sports. *Journal of Personality and Social Psychology, 54,* 74–85.

Frankenhaeuser, M., & Johansson, G. (1986). Stress at work: Psychobiological and psychosocial aspects. *International Review of Applied Psychology, 35* (Special issue: Occupational and life stress and the family), 287–299.

Freedman, J. L., & Fraser, S. C. (1966). Compliance without pressure: The foot-in-the-door technique. *Journal of Personality and Social Psychology, 4,* 195–202.

Freedman, J. L., & Sears, D. O. (1965). Warning, distraction and resistance to influence. *Journal of Personality and Social Psychology, 1,* 262–266.

Freiberg, P. (1991, January). Surprise—most bosses are incompetent. *APA Monitor,* p. 23.

Freiberg, P. (1991, April). Self-esteem gender gap widens in adolescence. *APA Monitor,* p. 29.

Frenkel, O. J., & Doob, A. N. (1976). Post-decision dissonance at the polling booth. *Canadian Journal of Behavioral Science, 8,* 347–350.

Freund, T., Kruglanski, A. W., & Shpitzajzen, A. (1985). The freezing and unfreezing of impression primacy: Effects of need for structure and the fear of invalidity. *Personality and Social Psychology Bulletin, 11,* 479–487.

Frey, D. (1986). Recent research on selective exposure to information. In L. Berkowitz (Ed.), *Advances in experimental social psychology* (Vol. 19, pp. 41–80). New York: Academic Press.

Friedman, H. S., Riggio, R. E., & Casella, D. F. (1988). Nonverbal skill, personal charisma, and initial attraction. *Personality and Social Psychology Bulletin, 14,* 203–211.

Friedman, P. (1978). *Their brothers' keepers.* New York: Holocaust Library.

Frijda, N. H. (1986). *The emotions.* Cambridge: Cambridge University Press.

Frijda, N. H., Kuipers, P., & ter Schure, E. (1989). Relations among emotion, appraisal, and emotional action readiness. *Journal of Personality and Social Psychology, 57,* 212–228.

Froming, W. J., Walker, G. R., & Lopyan, K. J. (1982). Public and private self-awareness: When personal attitudes conflict with societal expectations. *Journal of Experimental Social Psychology, 18,* 476–487.

Fukada, H. (1986). Psychological processes mediating the persuasion-inhibiting effect of forewarning in fear-arousing communication. *Psychological Reports, 58,* 87–90.

Fuller, R. G., & Sheehy-Skeffington, A. (1974). Effects of group laughter on responses to humorous materials: A replication and extension. *Psychological Reports, 35,* 531–534.

Funder, D. C., & Colvin, C. R. (1988). Friends and strangers: Acquaintanceship, agreement, and the accuracy of personality judgments. *Journal of Personality and Social Psychology, 55,* 149–158.

Furnham, A., & Gunter, B. (1984). Just world beliefs and attitudes towards the poor. *British Journal of Social Psychology, 23,* 265–269.

Furnham, A. F. (1982). Explanations for unemployment in Britain. *European Journal of Social Psychology, 12,* 335–352.

Gabor, A. (1992, January 26). Take this job and love it. *The New York Times,* p. 1F.

Gabrenya, W. K., Wang, Y., & Latané, B. (1985). Social loafing on an optimizing task: Cross-cultural differences among Chinese and Americans. *Journal of Cross Cultural Psychology, 16,* 223–242.

Gaertner, S. L., Mann, J. A., Dovidio, J. F., Murrell, A. J., & Pomare, M. (1990). How does cooperation reduce intergroup bias? *Journal of Personality and Social Psychology, 59,* 692–704.

Gaertner, S. L., Mann, J., Murrell, A., & Dovidio, J. F. (1989). Reducing intergroup bias: The benefits of recategorization. *Journal of Personality and Social Psychology, 57,* 239–249.

Galizio, M., & Hendrick, C. (1972). Effect of music accompaniment on attitudes. *Journal of Applied Social Psychology, 2,* 350–359.

Gallup Organization. (1990). *Giving and volunteering in the United States.* Washington, DC: Independent Sector.

Gamson, W. A., Fireman, B., & Rytina, S. (1982). *Encounters with unjust authority.* Homewood, IL: Dorsey Press.

Gardner, R. C., Lalone, R. N., Nero, A. M., & Young M. Y. (1988). Ethnic stereotypes: Implications of measurement strategy. *Social Cognition, 6,* 40–60.

Geen, R. (1990). *Human aggression.* Pacific Grove, CA: Brooks/Cole.

Geen, R., Rakosky, J. J., & Pigg, R. (1972). Awareness of arousal and its relation to aggression. *British Journal of Social and Clinical Psychology, 11,* 115–121.

Geen, R., & Quanty, M. B. (1977). The catharsis of aggression: An evaluation of a hypothesis. In L. Berkowitz (Ed.), *Advances in experimental social psychology* (Vol. 10, pp. 1–37). New York: Academic Press.

Geen, R. G. (1991). Social motivation. *Annual Review of Psychology, 42,* 377–391.

Geis, F. L., Brown, V., Jennings, J., & Porter, N. (1984). TV commercials as achievement scripts for women. *Sex Roles, 10,* 513–525.

Gelles, R. J. (1972). *The violent home: A study of physical aggression between husband and wife.* Beverly Hills, CA: Sage Publications.

Gelles, R. J., & Cornell, L. P. (1985). *Intimate violence in families.* Beverly Hills, CA: Sage Publications.

Gerard, H. B., & Rabbie, J. M. (1961). Fear and social comparison. *Journal of Abnormal and Social Psychology, 62,* 586–592.

Gerbner, G., Gross, L., Morgan, M., & Signorielli, N. (1986). Living with television: The dynamics of the cultivation process. In J. Bryant & D. Zillmann (Eds.), *Perspectives on media effects* (pp. 17–40). Hillsdale, NJ: Erlbaum.

Gergen, K. J. (1965). Interaction goals and personalistic feedback as factors affecting the presentation of self. *Journal of Personality and Social Psychology, 1,* 413–424.

Gergen, K. J., & Gergen, M. M. (1988). Narrative and the self as relationship. In L. Berkowitz (Ed.), *Advances in experimental social psychology* (Vol. 21, pp. 17–56). San Diego, CA: Academic Press.

Gersick, C. J. G. (1990). The students. In J. R. Hackman (Ed.), *Groups that work (and those that don't)* (pp. 89–111). San Francisco: Jossey-Bass.

Gibbons, F. X. (1978). Sexual standards and reactions to pornography: Enhancing behavioral consistency through self-focused attention. *Journal of Personality and Social Psychology, 36,* 976–987.

Gibbons, F. X., & Wicklund, R. A. (1982). Self-focused attention and helping behavior. *Journal of Personality and Social Psychology, 43,* 462–474.

Gilbert, D. T. (1991). How mental systems believe. *American Psychologist, 46,* 107–119.

Gilbert, D. T., & Jones, E. E. (1986). Perceiver-induced constraint: Interpretations of self-generated reality. *Journal of Personality and Social Psychology, 50,* 269–280.

Gilbert, D. T., & Krull, D. S. (1988). Seeing less and knowing more: The benefits of perceptual ignorance. *Journal of Personality and Social Psychology, 54,* 193–202.

Gilbert, D. T., Krull, D. S., & Malone, P. S. (1990). Unbelieving the unbelievable: Some problems in the rejection of false information. *Journal of Personality and Social Psychology, 59,* 601–613.

Gilbert, D. T., & Osborne, R. E. (1989). Thinking backward: Some curable and incurable consequences of cognitive busyness. *Journal of Personality and Social Psychology, 57,* 940–949.

Gilbert, D. T., Pelham, B. W., & Krull, D. S. (1988). On cognitive busyness: When person perceivers meet persons perceived. *Journal of Personality and Social Psychology, 54,* 733–740.

Gilovich, T. (1990). Differential construal and the false consensus effect. *Journal of Personality and Social Psychology, 59,* 623–634.

Ginossar, Z., & Trope, Y. (1987). Problem solving in judgment under uncertainty. *Journal of Personality and Social Psychology, 52,* 464–474.

Gioia, D. A., & Sims, H. P. (1985). Self-serving bias and actor-observer differences in organizations: An empirical analysis. *Journal of Applied Social Psychology, 15,* 547–563.

Glass, D. C. (1964). Changes in liking as a means of reducing cognitive discrepancies between self-esteem and aggression. *Journal of Personality, 32,* 491–549.

Globe and Mail (Toronto). (1993, August 4). P. A18.

Godfrey, D. K., Jones, E. E., & Lord, C. G. (1986). Self-promotion is not ingratiating. *Journal of Personality and Social Psychology, 50,* 106–115.

Goethals, G. R., Cooper, J., & Nacify, A. (1979). Role of foreseen, foreseeable, and unforeseeable behavioral consequences in the arousal of cognitive dissonance. *Journal of Personality and Social Psychology, 37,* 1179–1185.

Goethals, G. R., Messick, D. M., & Allison, S. T. (1991). The uniqueness bias: Studies of constructive social comparison. In J. Suls & T. A. Wills (Eds.), *Social comparison: Contemporary theory and research* (pp. 149–176). Hillsdale, NJ: Erlbaum.

Goethals, G. R., & Nelson, R. E. (1973). Similarity in the influence process: The belief-value distinction. *Journal of Personality and Social Psychology, 25,* 117–122.

Goffman, E. (1959). *The presentation of self in everyday life.* Garden City, NY: Doubleday.

Goldin, C. (1990). *Understanding the gender gap.* New York: Oxford University Press.

Goldstein, A. G., & Chance, J. E. (1985). Effects of training on Japanese face recognition: Reduction of the other-race effect. *Bulletin of the Psychonomic Society, 23,* 211–214.

Goldstein, J. H. (1982). Sports violence. *National Forum,* 62(1), 9–11.

Goleman, D. (1990, October 18). Support groups may do more in cancer than relieve the mind. *The New York Times.*

Goleman, D. (1992, December 15). New light on how stress erodes health. *The New York Times,* pp. B5, B9.

Gollwitzer, P. M. (1990). Action phases and mindset. In E. T. Higgins & R. M. Sorrentino (Eds.), *Handbook of motivation and cognition: Foundations of social behavior* (Vol. 2, pp. 53–92). New York: Guilford Press.

Goodman, M. (1952). *Race awareness in young children.* Cambridge, MA: Addison-Wesley.

Goranson, R. E., & Berkowitz, L. (1966). Reciprocity and responsibility reactions to prior help. *Journal of Personality and Social Psychology, 3,* 227–232.

Gorenflo, D. W., & Crano, W. D. (1989). Judgmental subjectivity/objectivity and locus of choice in social comparison. *Journal of Personality and Social Psychology, 57,* 605–614.

Gorer, G. (1968). Man has no "killer" instinct. In M. F. A. Montagu (Ed.), *Man and aggression* (pp. 27–36). New York: Oxford University Press.

Gorn, G. (1982). The effects of music in advertising on choice behavior: A classical conditioning approach. *Journal of Marketing Research, 46,* 94–101.

Gottman, J., Notarius, C., Markman, H., Bank, S., Yoppi, S., & Rubin, M. (1976). Behavior exchange theory and marital decision making. *Journal of Personality and Social Psychology, 34,* 14–23.

Gottman, J. M. (1979). *Marital interaction: Experimental investigations.* New York: Academic Press.

Gould, S. J. (1978). Morton's ranking of races by cranial capacity. *Science, 200,* 503–509.

Gould, S. J. (1981). *The mismeasure of man.* New York: Norton.

Gould, S. J. (1991). *Bully for Brontosaurus.* New York: W. W. Norton & Co.

Gouldner, A. W. (1960). The norm of reciprocity: A preliminary statement. *American Sociological Review, 25,* 161–178.

Gray, J. D., & Silver, R. C. (1990). Opposite sides of the same coin: Former spouses' divergent perspectives in coping with their divorce. *Journal of Personality and Social Psychology, 59,* 1180–1191.

Greenberg, J., & Pyszczynski, T. (1985). The effect of an overheard ethnic slur on evaluations of the target: How to spread a social disease. *Journal of Experimental Social Psychology, 21,* 61–72.

Greenberg, M. S., & Westcott, D. R. (1983). Indebtedness as a mediator of reactions to aid. In J. D. Fisher, A. Nadler, & B. M. DePaulo (Eds.), *New directions in helping. Volume 1: Recipient reactions to aid* (pp. 85–112). New York: Academic Press.

Greene, G. (1980). *Ways of escape.* New York: Simon & Schuster.

Greenwald, A. G. (1968). Cognitive learning, cognitive response to persuasion, and attitude change. In A. Greenwald, T. Brock, & T. Ostrom (Eds.), *Psychological foundations of attitudes* (pp. 148–170). New York: Academic Press.

Greenwald, A. G. (1980). The totalitarian ego: Fabrication and revision of personal history. *American Psychologist, 35,* 603–618.

Greenwald, A. G., Pratkanis, A. R., Leippe, M. R., & Baumgardener, M. H. (1986). Under what conditions does theory obstruct research progress? *Psychological Review, 93,* 216–229.

Greenwald, A. G., Spangenberg, E. R., Pratkanis, A. R., & Eskenazi, J. (1991). Double-blind tests of subliminal self-help audiotapes. *Psychological Science, 2,* 119–122.

Greenwell, J., & Dengerink, H. A. (1973). The role of perceived versus actual attack in human physical aggression. *Journal of Personality and Social Psychology, 26,* 66–71.

Greer, C. (1991, April 28). We must take a stand. *Parade,* pp. 4–6.

Gross, A. E., & Latané, J. G. (1974). Receiving help, reciprocation, and interpersonal attraction. *Journal of Applied Social Psychology, 4,* 210–223.

Gruder, C. L., Cook, T. D., Hennigan, K. M., Flay, B. R., Alessis, C., & Halamaj, J. (1978). Empirical tests of the absolute sleeper effect predicted from the discounting cue hypothesis. *Journal of Personality and Social Psychology, 36,* 1061–1074.

Guerin, B. (1986). The effects of mere presence on a motor task. *Journal of Social Psychology, 126,* 399–401.

Guimond, S., & Dube-Simard, L. (1983). Relative deprivation theory and Quebec Nationalist Movement: The cognitive-emotion distinction and the personal-group deprivation issue. *Journal of Personality and Social Psychology, 44,* 526–535.

Gurr, T. (1970). *Why men rebel.* Princeton, NJ: Princeton University Press.

Hacker, H. M. (1951). Women as a minority group. *Social Forces, 30,* 60–69.

Hackman, J. R. (1987). The design of work teams. In J. Lorsch (Ed.), *Handbook of organizational behavior* (pp. 315–342). Englewood Cliffs, NJ: Prentice-Hall.

Haines, H., & Vaughan, G. M. (1979). Was 1898 a "great date" in the history of experimental social psychology? *Journal of the History of Behavioral Sciences, 15,* 323–332.

Halberstam, D. (1972). *The best and the brightest.* New York: Random House.

Hall, E. G., & Hardy, C. J. (1991). Ready, aim, fire . . . Relaxation strategies for enhancing pistol marksmanship. *Perceptual and Motor Skills, 72,* 775–786.

Hamilton, D. L. (1981). Stereotyping and intergroup behavior: Some thoughts on the cognitive approach. In D. L. Hamilton (Ed.), *Cognitive processes in stereotyping and intergroup behavior* (pp. 333–354). Hillsdale, NJ: Erlbaum.

Hamilton, D. L., & Bishop, G. D. (1976). Attitudinal and behavioral effects of initial integration of White suburban neighborhoods. *Journal of Social Issues, 32,* 47–67.

Hamilton, D. L., Driscoll, D., & Worth, L. T. (1989). Cognitive organization of impressions: Effects of incongruency in complex representations. *Journal of Personality and Social Psychology, 57,* 925–939.

Hamilton, D. L., & Gifford, R. K. (1976). Illusory correlation in interpersonal perception: A cognitive basis for stereotypic judgments. *Journal of Experimental Social Psychology, 12,* 392–407.

Hamilton, D. L., Katz, L. B., & Leirer, V. (1980). Organizational processes in impression formation. In R. Hastie, T. M. Ostrom, E. B. Ebbesen, R. S. Wyer, D. L. Hamilton, & D. E. Carlston (Eds.), *Person memory* (pp. 121–153). Hillsdale, NJ: Erlbaum.

Hamilton, D. L., & Mackie, D. M. (1990). Specificity and generality in the nature and use of stereotypes. In T. Srull & R. S. Wyer, Jr. (Eds), *Advances in social cognition: Content and process specificity in the effects of prior experiences* (Vol. 3, pp. 99–110). Hillsdale, NJ: Erlbaum.

Hamilton, D. L., & Rose, T. L., (1980). Illusory correlation and the maintenance of stereotypic beliefs. *Journal of Personality and Social Psychology, 39,* 832–845.

Hamilton, D. L., & Sherman, S. J. (1989). Illusory correlations: Implications for stereotype theory and research. In D. Bar-Tal, C. F. Graumann, A. W. Kruglanski, & W. Stroebe (Eds.), *Stereotypes and prejudice: Changing conceptions* (pp. 59–82). New York: Springer-Verlag.

Hamilton, D. L., Stroessner, S. J., & Mackie, D. M. (1993). The influence of affect on stereotyping: The case of illusory correlations. In D. M. Mackie and D. L. Hamilton (Eds.), *Affect, cognition, and stereotyping: Interactive processes in group perception* (pp. 39–61). San Diego, CA: Academic Press.

Hamilton, D. L., & Trolier, T. L. (1986). Stereotypes and stereotyping: An overview of the cognitive approach. In J. F. Dovidio & S. L. Gaertner (Eds.), *Prejudice, discrimination, and racism* (pp. 127–163). Orlando, FL: Academic Press.

Hamilton, W. D. (1964). The genetical evolution of social behavior, I & II. *Journal of Theoretical Biology, 7,* 1–52.

Hammer, J. (1992, January 27). Business as usual. *Newsweek,* pp. 38–40.

Hammond, K. R. (1948). Measuring attitudes by error-choice: An indirect method. *Journal of Abnormal and Social Psychology, 43,* 38–48.

Han, S., & Shavitt, S. (1993). *Persuasion and culture: Advertising appeals in individualistic and collectivistic societies.* Unpublished manuscript, University of Illinois.

Haney, C., Banks, C., & Zimbardo, P. (1973). Interpersonal dynamics in a simulated prison. *International Journal of Criminology and Penology, 1,* 69–97.

Hansen, C. H., & Hansen, R. D. (1988). Finding the face in the crowd: An anger superiority effect. *Journal of Personality and Social Psychology, 54,* 917–924.

Hansson, R. O., Strobe, M. S., & Stroebe, W. (1988). In conclusion: Current themes in bereavement and widowhood research. *Journal of Social Issues, 44*(3), 207–216.

Harackiewicz, J. M. (1979). The effects of reward contingency and performance feedback on intrinsic motivation. *Journal of Personality and Social Psychology, 37,* 1352–1363.

Hardy, C., & Latané, B. (1986). Social loafing on a cheering task. *Social Science, 71,* 165–172.

Hare-Mustin, R. T., & Marecek, J. (1988). The meaning of difference: Gender theory, postmodernism, and psychology. *American Psychologist, 43,* 455–464.

Harkins, S. G., & Petty, R. E. (1983). Social context effects in persuasion: The effects of multiple sources and multiple targets. In P. Paulus (Ed.), *Basic group processes* (pp. 149–175). New York: Springer-Verlag.

Harkins, S. G., & Petty, R. E. (1987). Information utility and the multiple source effect. *Journal of Personality and Social Psychology, 52,* 260–268.

Harkins, S. G., & Szymanski, K. (1989). Social loafing and group evaluation. *Journal of Personality and Social Psychology, 56,* 934–941.

Harper, C. R., Kidera, G. J., & Cullen, J. F. (1971). Study of simulated airline pilot incapacitation: Phase II, subtle or partial loss of function. *Aerospace Medicine, 42,* 946–948.

Harris, M. B., Benson, S. M., & Hall, C. L. (1975). The effects of confession on altruism. *Journal of Social Psychology, 96,* 187–192.

Harris, M. J. (1991). Controversy and cumulation: Meta-analysis and research on interpersonal expectancy effects. *Personality and Social Psychology Bulletin, 17,* 316–322.

Harris, M. J., & Rosenthal, R. (1985). Mediation of interpersonal expectancy effects: 31 meta-analyses. *Psychological Bulletin, 97,* 363–386.

Harvey, J. H., Wells, G. L., & Alvarez, M. D. (1978). Attribution in the context of conflict and separation in close relationships. In J. H. Harvey, W. Ickes, & R. F. Kidd (Eds.), *New directions in attribution research* (Vol. 2, pp. 235–260). Hillsdale, NJ: Erlbaum.

Hastie, R. (1984). Causes and effects of causal attribution. *Journal of Personality and Social Psychology, 46,* 44–56.

Hastie, R., & Kumar, P. A. (1979). Person memory: Personality traits as organizing principles in memory for behaviors. *Journal of Personality and Social Psychology, 37,* 25–38.

Hastie, R., Penrod, S. D., & Pennington, N. (1983). *Inside the jury.* Cambridge, MA: Harvard University Press.

Hastorf, A., & Cantril, H. (1954). They saw a game: A case study. *Journal of Abnormal and Social Psychology, 49,* 129–134.

Hatfield, E. (1982). What do men and women want from love and sex? In E. R. Allgeier & N. B. McCormick (Eds.), *Changing boundaries: Gender roles and sexual behavior* (pp. 106–134). Palo Alto, CA: Mayfield.

Hatfield, E. (1988). Passionate and companionate love. In R. Sternberg & M. Barnes (Eds.), *The psychology of love* (pp. 191–217). New Haven, CT: Yale University Press.

Hatfield, E., & Rapson, R. L. (1993). *Love, sex, and intimacy.* New York: HarperCollins.

Hatfield, E., Sprecher, S., Pillemer, J. T., Greenberger, D., & Wexler, P. (1989). Gender differences in what is desired in the sexual relationship. *Journal of Psychology and Human Sexuality, 1,* 39–52.

Hatfield, E., Traupmann, J., Sprecher, S., Utne, M., & Hay, J. (1985). Equity and intimate relations: Recent research. In W. Ickes (Ed.), *Compatible and incompatible relationships* (pp. 91–118). New York: Springer-Verlag.

Hatfield, E., Walster, G. W., & Berscheid, E. (1978). *Equity:Theory and research.* Boston: Allyn & Bacon.

Haugtvedt, C. P., & Petty, R. E. (1992). Personality and persuasion: Need for cognition moderates the persistence and resistance of attitude changes. *Journal of Personality and Social Psychology, 63,* 308–319.

Hays, R. B. (1984). The development and maintenance of friendship. *Journal of Social and Personal Relationships, 1,* 75–98.

Hazan, C., & Shaver, P. (1987). Romantic love conceptualized as an attachment process. *Journal of Personality and Social Psychology, 52,* 511–524.

Hazan, C., & Shaver, P. (1990). Love and work: An attachment-theoretical perspective. *Journal of Personality and Social Psychology, 59,* 270–280.

Hearold, S. (1986). A synthesis of 1043 effects of television on social behavior. In G. Comstock (Ed.), *Public communications and behavior* (Vol. 1, pp. 65–133). New York: Academic Press.

Heider, F. (1944). Social perception and phenomenal causality. *Psychological Review, 51,* 358–374.

Heider, F. (1958). *The psychology of interpersonal relations.* New York: Wiley.

Heilman, M. E., Simon, M. C., & Repper, D. P. (1987). Intentionally favored, unintentionally harmed? Impact of sex-based preferential selection on self-perceptions and self-evaluations. *Journal of Applied Psychology, 72,* 62–68.

Heilman, M. E., & Stopeck, M. H. (1985). Attractiveness and corporate success: Different causal attributions for males and females. *Journal of Applied Psychology, 70,* 379–388.

Hendrick, S., Hendrick, C., & Adler, N. L. (1988). Romantic relationships: Love, satisfaction, and staying together. *Journal of Personality and Social Psychology, 54,* 980–988.

Hendrick, S., Hendrick, C., Slapion-Foote, M. J., & Foote, F. H. (1985). Gender differences in sexual attitudes. *Journal of Personality and Social Psychology, 48,* 1630–1642.

Hepworth, J. T., & West, S. G. (1988). Lynchings and the economy: A time-series reanalysis of Hovland and Sears (1940). *Journal of Personality and Social Psychology, 55,* 239–247.

Herr, P. M., Sherman, S. J., & Fazio, R. H. (1983). On the consequences of priming: Assimilation and contrast effects. *Journal of Experimental Social Psychology, 19,* 323–340.

Hersey, P., & Blanchard, K. H. (1982). *Management of organizational behavior* (4th ed.). Englewood Cliffs, NJ: Prentice-Hall.

Hewstone, M., Jaspars, J., & Lalljee, M. (1982). Social representations, social attribution and social identity: The intergroup images of "public" and "comprehensive" schoolboys. *European Journal of Social Psychology, 12,* 241–269.

Heymann, T. (1989). *On an average day.* New York: Fawcett Columbine.

Higgins, E. T. (1987). Self-discrepancy: A theory relating self and affect. *Psychological Review, 94,* 319–340.

Higgins, E. T. (1989). Knowledge accessibility and activation: Subjectivity and suffering from unconscious sources. In J. S. Uleman & J. A. Bargh (Eds.), *Unintended thought: The limits of awareness, intention, and control* (pp. 75–123). New York: Guilford Press.

Higgins, E. T., & Bargh, J. A. (1987). Social cognition and social perception. *Annual Review of Psychology, 38,* 369–425.

Higgins, E. T., Bargh, J. A., & Lombardi, W. (1985). The nature of priming effects on categorization. *Journal of Experimental Psychology: Learning, Memory, and Cognition, 11,* 59–69.

Higgins, E. T., & King, G. A. (1981). Accessibility of social constructs: Information-processing consequences of individual and contextual variability. In N. Cantor & J. F. Kihlstrom (Eds.), *Personality, cognition, and social interaction* (pp. 69–122). Hillsdale, NJ: Erlbaum.

Higgins, E. T., King, G. A., & Mavin, G. H. (1982). Individual construct accessibility and subjective impressions and recall. *Journal of Personality and Social Psychology, 43,* 35–47.

Higgins, E. T., & McCann, C. D. (1984). Social encoding and subsequent attitudes, impressions, and memory: "Context-driven" and motivational aspects of processing. *Journal of Personality and Social Psychology, 47,* 26–39.

Higgins, E. T., & Rholes, W. S. (1978). Saying is believing: Effects of message modification on memory and liking for the person described. *Journal of Experimental Social Psychology, 14,* 363–378.

Higgins, E. T., Rholes, W. S., & Jones, C. R. (1977). Category accessibility and impression formation. *Journal of Experimental Social Psychology, 13,* 141–154.

Hill, C. T., Rubin, Z., & Peplau, L. A. (1976). Breakups before marriage: The end of 103 affairs. *Journal of Social Issues, 32*(1), 147–168.

Hillery, J. M., & Fugita, S. S. (1975). Group size effects in employment testing. *Educational and Psychological Measurement, 35,* 745–750.

Hilton, J. L., & Darley, J. M. (1985). Constructing other persons: A limit on the effect. *Journal of Experimental Social Psychology, 21,* 1–18.

Hinsz, V. B., & Davis, J. H. (1984). Persuasive arguments theory, group polarization, and choice shifts. *Personality and Social Psychology Bulletin, 10,* 260–268.

Hiroto, D. S. (1974). Locus of control and learned helplessness. *Journal of Experimental Psychology, 102,* 187–193.

Hirschman, R. S., & Leventhal, H. (1984). Preventing smoking behavior in schoolchildren: An initial test of a cognitive-development program. *Journal of Applied Social Psychology, 19,* 559–583.

Hoelter, J. W. (1985). The structure of self-conception: Conceptualization and measurement. *Journal of Personality and Social Psychology, 49,* 1392–1407.

Hoffman, C., & Hurst, N. (1990) Gender stereotypes: perception or rationalization? *Journal of Personality and Social Psychology, 58,* 197–208.

Hoffman, M. L. (1981). Is altruism part of human nature? *Journal of Personality and Social Psychology, 40,* 121–137.

Hoffman, M. L. (1986). Affect, cognition, motivation. In R. M. Sorrentino & E. T. Higgins (Eds.), *Handbook of motivation and cognition: Foundations of social behavior* (Vol. 1, pp. 244–280). New York: Guilford Press.

Hofling, C. K., Brotzman, E., Dalrymple, S., Graves, N., & Pierce, C. M. (1966). An experimental study in nurse-physician relationships. *Journal of Nervous and Mental Disease, 143,* 171–180.

Hogg, M. (1987). Social identity and group cohesiveness. In J. C. Turner, M. A. Hogg, P. J. Oakes, S. D. Reicher, & M. S. Wetherell (Eds.), *Rediscovering the social group: A self-categorization theory* (pp. 89–116). Oxford: Blackwell.

Hogg, M. A. (1987). Social identity and group cohesiveness. In J. C. Turner, M. A. Hogg, P. J. Oakes, S. D. Reicher, & M. S. Wetherell, *Rediscovering the social group* (pp. 89–116). Oxford: Blackwell.

Hogg, M. A., & Abrams, D. (1988). *Social identifications.* London: Routledge.

Hogg, M. A., Cooper-Shaw, L., & Holzworth, D. W. (1993). Group prototypicality and depersonalized attraction in small interactive groups. *Personality and Social Psychology Bulletin, 19,* 452–465.

Hogg, M. A., & Hardie, E. A. (1991). Social attraction, personal attraction, and self-categorization: A field study. *Personality and Social Psychology Bulletin, 17,* 175–180.

Holland, D. C., & Eisenhart, M. A. (1990). *Educated in romance: Women, achievement, and college culture.* Chicago, IL: University of Chicago Press.

Hollander, E. P. (1958). Conformity, status, and idiosyncrasy credit. *Psychological Review, 65,* 117–127.

Hollander, E. P. (1985). Leadership and power. In G. Lindsey & E. Aronson (Eds.), *The handbook of social psychology* (3rd ed., Vol. 2, pp. 485–537). New York: Random House.

Holsti, O. R., & North, R. (1965). The history of human conflict. In E. B. McNeil (Ed.), *The nature of human conflict* (pp. 155–171). Englewood Cliffs, NJ: Prentice-Hall.

Holtgraves, T., & Srull, T. K. (1989). The effects of positive self-descriptions on impressions: General principles and individual differences. *Personality and Social Psychology Bulletin, 15,* 452–462.

Hooker, E. (1957). The adjustment of the male overt homosexual. *Journal of Projective Techniques, 21,* 18–31.

Hoover, C. W., Wood, E. E., & Knowles, E. S. (1983). Forms of social awareness and helping. *Journal of Experimental Social Psychology, 19,* 577–590.

Hornstein, H. A. (1975). Social psychology as social intervention. In M. Deutsch & H. A. Hornstein (Eds.), *Applying social psychology: Implications for research, practice, and training* (pp. 211–234). Hillsdale, NJ: Erlbaum.

Horowitz, M. J. (1987). *States of mind.* New York: Plenum.

Horwitz, M., & Rabbie, J. M. (1982). Individuality and membership in the intergroup system. In H. Tajfel (Ed.), *Social identity and intergroup relations* (pp. 241–274). New York: Cambridge University Press.

Hosey, G. R., Wood, M., Thompson, R. J., & Druck, P. L. (1985). Social facilitation in a "non-social" animal, the centipede *Lithobius forficatus. Behavioural Processes, 10,* 1–2.

Hovland, C. I., Janis, I. L., & Kelley, H. H. (1953). Communication and persuasion: *Psychological studies of opinion change.* New Haven, CT: Yale University Press.

Hovland, C. I., Lumsdaine, A., & Sheffield, F. (1949). *Experiments on mass communication.* Princeton, NJ: Princeton University Press.

Hovland, C. I., & Weiss, W. (1951). The influence of source-credibility on communication effectiveness. *Public Opinion Quarterly, 15,* 635–650.

Howard, L. (1990, July 9). Periscope. *Newsweek,* p. 7.

Hoyle, R. H., Pinkley, R. L., & Insko, C. A. (1989). Perceptions of social behavior: Evidence of differing expectations for interpersonal and intergroup interaction. *Personality and Social Psychology Bulletin, 15,* 365–376.

Hsu, F. L. K. (1983). *Rugged individualism reconsidered.* Knoxville, TN: University of Tennessee Press.

Huesmann, L. R. (1986). Psychological processes promoting the relation between exposure to media violence and aggressive behavior by the viewer. *Journal of Social Issues, 42*(3), 125–139.

Huesmann, L. R., & Eron, L. D. (1984). Cognitive processes and the persistence of aggressive behavior. *Aggressive Behavior, 10,* 243–251.

Huesmann, L. R., & Eron, L. D. (1986). *Television and the aggressive child: A cross-national comparison.* Hillsdale, NJ: Erlbaum.

Huesmann, L. R., Eron, L. D., Klein, R., Brice, P., & Fischer, P. (1983). Mitigating the imitation of aggressive behaviors by changing children's attitudes about media violence. *Journal of Personality and Social Psychology, 44,* 899–910.

Huesmann, L. R., Eron, L. D., & Yarmel, P. W. (1987). Intellectual functioning and aggression. *Journal of Personality and Social Psychology, 52,* 232–240.

Huff, C., Sproull, L., & Kiesler, S. (1989). Computer communication and organizational commitment: Tracing the relationship in a city government. *Journal of Applied Social Psychology, 19,* 1371–1391.

Hull, J. G. (1981). A self-awareness model of the causes and effects of alcohol consumption. *Journal of Abnormal Psychology, 90,* 586–600.

Hull, J. G., & Young, R. D. (1983). Self-consciousness, self-esteem, and success-failure as determinants of alcohol consumption in male social drinkers. *Journal of Personality and Social Psychology, 44,* 1097–1109.

Hull, J. G., Young, R. D., & Jouriles, E. (1986). Applications of the self-awareness model of alcohol consumption: Predicting patterns of use and abuse. *Journal of Personality and Social Psychology, 51,* 790–796.

Humphrey, R. (1985). How work roles influence perception: Structural-cognitive processes and organizational behavior. *American Sociological Review, 50,* 242–252.

Hunt, W. A., Matarazzo, J. D., Weiss, S. M., & Gentry, W. D. (1979). Associative learning, habit and health behavior. *Journal of Behavioral Medicine, 2,* 111–124.

Hunter, C. E., & Ross, M. W. (1991). Determinants of health-care workers' attitudes toward people with AIDS. *Journal of Applied Social Psychology, 21,* 947–956.

Hyde, J. S. (1979). *Understanding human sexuality.* New York: McGraw-Hill.

Hyman, H. H., & Singer, E. (Eds.). (1968). *Readings in reference group theory and research.* New York: Free Press.

Ikard, F. F., Green, D. E., & Horn, D. (1969). A scale to differentiate between types of smoking as related to the management of affect. *International Journal of the Addictions, 4,* 649–659.

Indianapolis Star. (1989, September 12).

Insko, C. A. (1981). Balance theory and phenomenology. In R. Petty, T. Ostrom, & T. Brock (Eds.), *Cognitive responses and persuasion.* Hillsdale, NJ: Erlbaum.

Insko, C. A., Hoyle, R. H., Pinkley, R. L., Hong, G-Y., Slim, R. M., Dalton, B., Lin, Y-H. W., Ruffin, P. P., Dardis, G. J., Bernthal, P. R., & Schopler, J. (1988). Individual-group discontinuity: The role of a consensus rule. *Journal of Experimental Social Psychology, 24,* 505–519.

Insko, C. A., Pinkley, R. L., Hoyle, R. H., & Dalton, B. (1987). Individual versus group discontinuity: The role of intergroup contact. *Journal of Experimental Social Psychology, 23,* 250–267.

Insko, C. A., & Schopler, J. (1987). Categorization, competition, and collectivity. In C. Hendrick (Ed.), *Group processes* (Vol. 8, pp. 213–251). New York: Sage Publications.

Insko, C. A., Schopler, J., Hoyle, R. H., Dardis, G. J., & Graetz, K. A. (1990). Individual-group discontinuity as a function of fear and greed. *Journal of Personality and Social Psychology, 58,* 68–79.

Insko, C. A., Schopler, J., Kennedy, J. F., Dahl, K. R., Graetz, K. A., & Drigotas, S. M. (1992). Individual-group discontinuity from the differing perspectives of Campbell's Realistic Group Conflict Theory and Tajfel and Turner's Social Identity Theory. *Social Psychology Quarterly, 55,* 272–291.

Insko, C. A., Thompson, V. D., Stroebe, W., Shaud, K. F., Pinner, B. E., & Layton, B. D. (1973). Implied evaluation and the similarity-attraction effect. *Journal of Personality and Social Psychology, 25,* 297–308.

Insko, C. A., & Wilson, M. (1977). Interpersonal attraction as a function of social interaction. *Journal of Personality and Social Psychology, 35,* 903–911.

Insko, S. A., Dreenan, S., Soloman, M. R., Smith, R., & Wade, T. J. (1983). Conformity as a function of the consistency of positive self-evaluation with being liked and being right. *Journal of Experimental Social Psychology, 19,* 341–358.

Isen, A. (1970). Success, failure, attention, and reaction to others: The warm glow of success. *Journal of Personality and Social Psychology, 15,* 294–301.

Isen, A., & Levin, P. F. (1972). Effect of feeling good on helping: Cookies and kindness. *Journal of Personality and Social Psychology, 21,* 384–388.

Isen, A., & Simmonds, S. F. (1978). The effect of feeling good on a helping task that is incompatible with good mood. *Social Psychology, 41,* 345–349.

Isen, A. M. (1984). Toward understanding the role of affect in cognition. In R. S. Wyer & T. K. Srull (Eds.), *Handbook of social cognition* (Vol. 3, pp. 179–236). Hillsdale, NJ: Erlbaum.

Isen, A. M. (1987). Positive affect, cognitive processes, and social behavior. In L. Berkowitz (Ed.), *Advances in experimental social psychology* (Vol. 20, pp. 203–253). New York: Academic Press.

Isen, A. M., & Levin, P. F. (1972). The effect of feeling good on helping: Cookies and kindness. *Journal of Personality and Social Psychology, 21,* 384–388.

Islam, M. R., & Hewstone, M. (1993). Intergroup attributions and affective consequences in majority and minority groups. *Journal of Personality and Social Psychology, 64,* 936–950.

Isozaki, M. (1984). The effects of discussion on polarization of judgment. *Japanese Psychological Research, 26,* 187–198.

Jackman, M. R., & Senter, M. S. (1981). Beliefs about race, gender, and social class: Different therefore unequal. In D. J. Treiman & R. V. Robinson (Eds.), *Research in stratification and mobility* (Vol. 2). Greenwich, CT: JAI Press.

Jackson, L. A., & Sullivan, L. A. (1989). Cognition and affect in evaluations of stereotyped group members. *Journal of Social Psychology, 129,* 659–672.

Jacoby, J. (1984). Some social psychological perspectives on closing. In J. Jacoby & C. S. Craig (Eds.), *Personal selling* (pp. 73–92). Lexington, MA: Lexington Books.

Jacoby, J., & Hoyer, W. D. (1989). The comprehension/miscomprehension of print communication: Selected findings. *Journal of Consumer Research, 15,* 434–443.

Jacoby, J., Hoyer, W. D., & Sheluga, D. A. (1980). *Miscomprehension of televised communications.* New York: American Association of Advertising Agencies.

James, W. (1884). What is an emotion? *Mind, 9,* 188–205.

James, W. (1890). *Psychology.* New York: Holt.

Jamieson, D. W., & Zanna, M. P. (1983). *The lie detector expectation procedure: Ensuring veracious self-reports of attitude.* Paper presented to the Canadian Psychological Association, Winnipeg.

Janis, I. (1972). *Victims of groupthink.* Boston: Houghton Mifflin.

Janis, I. (1982). *Groupthink* (2nd ed.). Boston: Houghton Mifflin.

Janis, I. (1989). *Crucial decisions: Leadership in policymaking and crisis management.* New York: Free Press.

Janis, I. L., & Feshbach, S. (1953). Effects of fear-arousing communication. *Journal of Abnormal Social Psychology, 48,* 78–92.

Janis, I. L., Kaye, D., & Kirschner, P. (1965). Facilitating effects of "eating while reading" on responsiveness to persuasive communications. *Journal of Personality and Social Psychology, 1,* 181–186.

Janis, I. L., & Mann, L. (1965). Effectiveness of emotional role-playing in modifying smoking habits and attitudes. *Journal of Experimental Research in Personality, 1,* 84–90.

Janis, I. L., & Rife, D. (1959). Persuasibility and emotional disorder. In C. Hovland & I. Janis (Eds.), *Personality and persuasibility.* New Haven, CT: Yale University Press.

Janis, I. L., & Terwilliger, R. (1962). An experimental study of psychological resistances to fear-arousing communication. *Journal of Abnormal and Social Psychology, 65,* 403–410.

Jason, L. A., Greiner, B. J., Naylor, K., Johnson, S. P., & Van Egeren, L. (1991). A large-scale, short-term, media-based weight loss program. *American Journal of Health Promotion, 5,* 432–437.

Jason, L. A., Reichler, A., Easton, J., Neal, A., & Wilson, M. (1984). Female harassment after ending a relationship: A preliminary study. *Alternative Lifestyles, 6,* 259–269.

Jennings, J., Geis, F. L., & Brown, V. (1980). Influence of television commercials on women's self-confidence and independent judgment. *Journal of Personality and Social Psychology, 38,* 203–210.

Jepson, C., & Chaiken S. (1990). Chronic issue-specific fear inhibits systematic processing of persuasive communications. *Journal of Social Behavior and Personality, 2,* 61–84.

Jervis, R. (1976). *Perception and misperception in international politics.* Princeton, NJ: Princeton University Press.

Johnson, D. W., Johnson, R. T., & Maruyama, G. (1984). Goal interdependence and interpersonal attraction in heterogeneous classrooms: A meta-analysis. In N. Miller & M. Brewer (Eds.), *Groups in contact: The psychology of desegregation* (pp. 187–212). New York: Academic Press.

Johnson, D. W., Maruyama, G., Johnson, R. T., Nelson, D., & Skon, L. (1981). Effects of cooperative, competitive, and individualistic goal structures on achievement: A meta-analysis. *Psychological Bulletin, 89,* 47–62.

Johnson, E. J., & Tversky, A. (1983). Affect, generalization, and the perception of risk. *Journal of Personality and Social Psychology, 45,* 20-31.

Johnson, M. P., & Ewens, W. (1971). Power relations and affective style as determinants of confidence in impression formation in a game situation. *Journal of Experimental Social Psychology, 7,* 98–110.

Johnson, R. D., & Downing, L. L. (1979). Deindividuation and valence of cues: Effects on prosocial and antisocial behavior. *Journal of Personality and Social Psychology, 37,* 1532–1538.

Johnston, J., & Ettema, J. (1986). Using television to best advantage: Research for prosocial television. In J. Bryant & D. Zillman (Eds.), *Perspectives on media effects* (pp. 143–164). Hillsdale, NJ: Erlbaum.

Johnston, L., & Hewstone, M. (1992). Cognitive models of stereotype change. 3. Subtyping and the perceived typicality of disconfirming group members. *Journal of Experimental Social Psychology, 28,* 360–386.

Jones, E. E. (1985). Major developments in social psychology during the last five decades. In G. Lindzey & E. Aronson (Eds.), *Handbook of social psychology* (3rd ed.; Vol. 1, pp. 47–107). New York: Random House.

Jones, E. E. (1990a). Constrained behavior and self-concept change. In J. M. Olson & M. P. Zanna (Eds.), *Self-inference processes: The Ontario Symposium* (Vol. 6, pp. 69–86). Hillsdale, NJ: Erlbaum.

Jones, E. E. (1990b). *Interpersonal perception.* New York: Freeman.

Jones, E. E., Brenner, K., & Knight, J. G. (1990). When failure elevates self-esteem. *Personality and Social Psychology Bulletin, 16,* 200–209.

Jones, E. E., & Davis, K. E. (1965). A theory of correspondent inferences: From acts to dispositions. In L. Berkowitz (Ed.), *Advances in experimental social psychology* (Vol. 2, pp. 219–266). New York: Academic Press.

Jones, E. E., & Gerard, H. B. (1967). *Foundations of social psychology.* New York: Wiley.

Jones, E. E., & Harris, V. A. (1967). The attribution of attitudes. *Journal of Experimental Social Psychology, 3,* 1–24.

Jones, E. E., & Nisbett, R. E. (1972). The actor and the observer: Divergent perceptions of the causes of behavior. In E. E. Jones, D. E. Kanouse, H. H. Kelley, R. E. Nisbett, S. Valins, & B. Weiner (Eds.), *Attribution: Perceiving the causes of behavior* (pp. 79–94). Morristown, NJ: General Learning Press.

Jones, E. E., & Pittman, T. S. (1982). Toward a general theory of strategic self-presentation. In J. Suls (Ed.), *Psychological perspectives on the self* (Vol. 1, pp. 231–262). Hillsdale, NJ: Erlbaum.

Jones, E. E., Rhodewalt, F., Berglas, S., & Skelton, J. A. (1981). Effects of strategic self-presentation on subsequent self-esteem. *Journal of Personality and Social Psychology, 41,* 407–421.

Jones, E. E., Rock, L., Shaver, K. G., Goethals, G. R., & Ward, L. M. (1968). Pattern of performance and ability attribution: An unexpected primacy effect. *Journal of Personality and Social Psychology, 10,* 317–340.

Jones, E. E., & Wortman, C. (1973). *Ingratiation: An attributional approach.* Morristown, NJ: General Learning Press.

Jones, J. M. (1992). Understanding the mental health consequences of race: Contributions of basic social psychological processes. In D. N. Ruble, P. R. Costanzo, & M. E. Oliveri (Eds.), *The social psychology of mental health* (pp. 199–240). New York: Guilford Press.

Jones, R. A., & Brehm, J. W. (1970). Persuasiveness of one-sided and two-sided communications as a function of the awareness that there are two sides. *Journal of Experimental Social Psychology, 6,* 47–56.

Josephs, R. A., Larrick, R. P., Steele, C. M., & Nisbett, R. E. (1992). Protecting the self from the negative consequences of risky decisions. *Journal of Personality and Social Psychology, 62,* 26–37.

Jost, J. T., & Banaji, M. R. (1993). *The role of stereotyping in system-justification and the production of false consciousness.* Unpublished paper, Yale University.

Judd, C. M., & Kulik, J. A. (1980). Schematic effects of social attitudes on information processing and recall. *Journal of Personality and Social Psychology, 38,* 569–578.

Judd, C. M., & Park, B. (1988). Out-group homogeneity: Judgments of variability at the individual and group levels. *Journal of Personality and Social Psychology, 54,* 778–788.

Judd, C. M., Smith, E. R., & Kidder, L. H. (1991). *Research methods in social relations* (6th ed.). Fort Worth, TX: Holt, Rinehart, & Winston.

Kahle, L. R., & Berman, J. (1979). Attitudes cause behaviors: A cross-lagged panel analysis. *Journal of Personality and Social Psychology, 37,* 315–321.

Kahneman, D., & Miller, D. T. (1986). Norm theory: Comparing reality to its alternatives. *Psychological Review, 93,* 136–153.

Kahneman, D., & Tversky, A. (1973). On the psychology of prediction. *Psychological Review, 80,* 237–251.

Kalin, R., & Berry, J. W. (1982). The social ecology of ethnic attitudes in Canada. *Canadian Journal of Behavioral Science, 14,* 97–109.

Kallgren, C. A., & Wood, W. (1986). Access to attitude-relevant information in memory as a determinant of attitude-behavior consistency. *Journal of Experimental Social Psychology, 22,* 328–338.

Kalven, H., Jr., & Zeisel, H. (1966). *The American jury.* London: University of Chicago Press.

Kandel, D. B. (1978). Similarity in real-life adolescent friendship pairs. *Journal of Personality and Social Psychology, 36,* 306–312.

Kanter, R. (1977). *Men and women of the corporation.* New York: Basic Books.

Kantrowitz, B. (1991, August 5). The right to fight. *Newsweek,* p. 23.

Kaplan, M. F., & Miller, C. E. (1987). Group decision making and normative versus informational influence: Effects of type of issue and assigned decision rule. *Journal of Personality and Social Psychology, 53,* 306–313.

Kaplowitz, N. (1990). National self-images, perception of enemies, and conflict strategies: Psychopolitical dimensions of international relations. *Political Psychology, 11,* 39–82.

Karabenick, S. A., Lerner, R. M., & Beecher, M. D. (1973). Relation of political affiliation to helping behavior on election day, November 7, 1972. *Journal of Social Psychology, 91,* 223–227.

Karau, S. J., & Williams, K. D. (in press). Social loafing: A meta-analytic review and theoretical integration. *Journal of Personality and Social Psychology, 65,* 681–706.

Karlin, R. A., Rosen, L., & Epstein, Y. (1979). Three into two doesn't go: A follow-up of the effects of overcrowded dormitory rooms. *Personality and Social Psychology Bulletin, 5,* 391–395.

Kassin, S. M., & Wrightsman, L. S. (1985). *The psychology of evidence and trial procedure.* Beverly Hills, CA: Sage Publications.

Katz, D. (1960). The functional approach to the study of attitudes. *Public Opinion Quarterly, 24,* 163–204.

Katz, D. (1965). Nationalism and strategies of international conflict resolution. In H. C. Kelman (Ed.), *International behavior: A social-psychological analysis* (pp. 354–390). New York: Holt, Rinehart & Winston.

Katz, D., & Braly, K. W. (1933). Racial stereotypes of 100 college students. *Journal of Abnormal and Social Psychology, 28,* 280–290.

Katz, I., & Hass, R. G. (1988). Racial ambivalence and American value conflict: Correlational and priming studies of dual cognitive structures. *Journal of Personality and Social Psychology, 55,* 893–905.

Keller, R. T. (1986). Predictors of the performance of project groups in R & D organizations. *Academy of Management Journal, 29,* 715–726.

Kelley, H. H. (1950). The warm-cold variable in first impressions of persons. *Journal of Personality, 18,* 431–439.

Kelley, H. H. (1952). Two functions of reference groups. In G. E. Swanson, T. M. Newcomb, & E. L. Hartley (Eds.), *Readings in social psychology* (pp. 410–414). New York: Henry Holt.

Kelley, H. H. (1967). Attribution theory in social psychology. In D. Levine (Ed.), *Nebraska Symposium on Motivation* (Vol. 15, pp. 192–241). Lincoln: University of Nebraska Press.

Kelley, H. H. (1972). Attribution in social interaction. In E. E. Jones, D. E. Kanouse, H. H. Kelley, R. E. Nisbett, S. Valins, & B. Weiner (Eds.), *Attribution: Perceiving the causes of behavior* (pp. 1–26). Morristown, NJ: General Learning Press.

Kelley, H. H. (1979). *Personal relationships: Their structures and processes.* Hillsdale, NJ: Erlbaum.

Kelley, H. H., Berscheid, E., Christensen, A., Harvey, J. H., Huston, T. L., Levinger, G., McClintock, E., Peplau, L. A., & Peterson, D. R. (Eds.). (1983). *Close relationships.* San Francisco: Freeman.

Kelly, D. (1990). Victim participation in the criminal justice system. In A. J. Lurigio, W. G. Skogan, & R. C. Davis (Eds.), *Victims of crime: Problems, policies, and programs* (pp. 172–187). Newbury Park, CA: Sage Publications.

Kelman, H. C. (1961). Processes of opinion change. *Public Opinion Quarterly, 25,* 57–78.

Kelman, H. C. (1978). Israelis and Palestinians: Psychological prerequisites for mutual acceptance. *International Security, 3,* 162–186.

Kelman, H. C., & Hamilton, V. L. (1989). Crimes of obedience: *Toward a social psychology of authority and responsibility.* New Haven, CT: Yale University Press.

Kelman, H. C., & Hovland, C. I. (1953). "Reinstatement" of the communicator in delayed measurement of opinion change. *Journal of Abnormal and Social Psychology, 48,* 327–335.

Kelman, H. C., & Lawrence, L. (1972). Assignment of responsibility in the case of Lt. Calley: Preliminary report on a national survey. *Journal of Social Issues, 28*(19), 177–212.

Kennedy, P. (1991, July 9). Can we still be shocked? *Lafayette Journal & Courier,* Lafayette, Indiana, p. B1.

Kenny, D. A. (1991). A general model of consensus and accuracy in interpersonal perception. *Psychological Review, 98,* 155–163.

Kenny, D. A. (in press). Using the social relations model to understand relationships. In R. Gilmour (Ed.), *Theories for the study of relationships.* Hillsdale, NJ: Erlbaum.

Kenrick, D. T., Groth, G. E., Trost, M. R., & Sadalla, E. K. (1993). Integrating evolutionary and social exchange perspectives on relationships: Effects of gender, self-appraisal, and involvement level on mate selection criteria. *Journal of Personality and Social Psychology, 64,* 951–969.

Kerr, N. L. (1992). Efficacy as a causal and moderating variable in social dilemmas. In W. Liebrand, D. Messick, & H. Wilke (Eds.), *A social psychological approach to social dilemmas* (pp. 59–80). New York: Pergamon Press.

Kerr, N. L., & Bruun, S. (1983). The dispensability of member effort and group motivation losses: Free rider effects. *Journal of Personality and Social Psychology, 44,* 78–94.

Kerr, N. L., & Kaufman-Gilliland, C. M. (1993). *Communication, commitment, and cooperation in social dilemmas.* Unpublished paper, Michigan State University.

Kerr, N. L., MacCoun, R. J., Hansen, C. H., & Hymes, J. A. (1987). Gaining and losing social support: Momentum in decision making groups. *Journal of Experimental Social Psychology, 23,* 119–145.

Kerr, S., & Jermier, J. M. (1978). Substitutes for leadership: Their meaning and measurement. *Organizational Behavior and Human Performance, 22,* 375–403.

Kiecolt-Glaser, J. K., Fisher, L. D., Ogrocki, P., Stout, J., Speicher, C. E., & Glaser, R. (1987). Marital quality, marital disruption, and immune function. *Psychosomatic Medicine, 49,* 13–34.

Kiecolt-Glaser, J. K., & Glaser, R. (1988). Psychological influences on immunity: Implications for AIDS. *American Psychologist, 43* (Special issue: Psychology and AIDS), 892–898.

Kiesler, C. A. (1971). *The psychology of commitment.* New York: Academic Press.

Kiesler, C. A., & Kiesler, S. (1964). Role of forewarning in persuasive communications. *Journal of Abnormal and Social Psychology, 68,* 547–549.

Kiesler, C. A., & Kiesler, S. B. (1969). *Conformity.* Reading, MA: Addison-Wesley.

Kiesler, S., & Sproull, L. (1992). Group decision making and communication technology. *Organizational Behavior and Human Decision Processes, 52,* 96–123.

Kiesler, S. B., & Mathog, R. (1968). The distraction hypothesis in attitude change. *Psychological Reports, 23,* 1123–1133.

Kim, H-S., & Baron, R. S. (1988). Exercise and the illusory correlation: Does arousal heighten stereotypic processing? *Journal of Experimental Social Psychology, 24,* 366–380.

Kimmel, M. J., Pruitt, P. G., Maganau, J. M., Konar-Goldband, E., & Carnevale, P. J. D. (1980). Effects of trust, aspiration, and gender on negotiation tactics. *Journal of Personality and Social Psychology, 38,* 9–22.

Kinder, D. R. (1986). The continuing American dilemma: White resistance to racial change forty years after Myrdal. *Journal of Social Issues, 42*(2), 151–171.

Kinder, D. R., & Sears, D. O. (1985). Public opinion and political action. In G. Lindzey & E. Aronson (Eds.), *Handbook of social psychology* (Vol. 2, pp. 659–742). New York: Random House.

King, M. L. (1967). *Where do we go from here? Chaos or community.* New York: Harper & Row.

Klama, J. [pseudonym for John Durant, Peter Klopfer, and Susan Oyama] (1988). *Aggression: The myth of the beast within.* New York: John Wiley & Sons.

Kleck, R. E., & Strenta, A. (1980). Perceptions of the impact of negatively valued physical characteristics on social interaction. *Journal of Personality and Social Psychology, 39,* 861–873.

Klein, M. W. (1969). Violence in American juvenile gangs. In D. Mulvihill & M. Tumin (Eds.), *Crimes of violence: A staff report submitted to the National Commission on the Causes and Prevention of Violence* (Vol. 13, pp. 1427–1460). Washington, DC: U.S. Government Printing Office.

Klein, S. B., & Loftus, J. (1993). The mental representation of trait and autobiographical knowledge about the self. In T. K. Srull & R. S. Wyer (Eds.), *Advances in social cognition* (Vol. 5, pp. 1–50). Hillsdale, NJ: Erlbaum.

Klein, W. M., & Kunda, Z. (in press). *Organizational Behavior and Human Decision Processes.*

Klein, W. M., & Kunda, Z. (1992). Motivated person perception: Constructing justifications for desired beliefs. *Journal of Experimental Social Psychology, 28,* 145–168.

Kleinfield, N. R. (1993, Jan. 5). No superstar, just a working model: A "great smile" and a six-figure income. *The New York Times,* pp. B1, B4.

Kleinke, C. L., Meeker, F. B., & LaFong, C. (1974). Effects of gaze, touch, and use of name on evaluation of engaged couples. *Journal of Research in Personality, 7,* 368–373.

Klentz, B., Beaman, A. L., Mapelli, S. D., & Ullrich, J. R. (1987). Perceived physical attractiveness of supporters and nonsupporters of the women's movement: An attitude-similarity-mediated error (ASME). *Personality and Social Psychology Bulletin, 13,* 513–523.

Klineberg, O. (1986). SPSSI and race relations in the 1950's and after. *Journal of Social Issues, 42*(4), 53–60.

Kluegel, J. R., & Smith, E. R. (1986). *Beliefs about inequality: Americans' views of what is and what ought to be.* Hawthorne, NY: Aldine de Gruyter.

Knapp, M. L. (1978). *Nonverbal communication in human interaction.* New York: Holt, Rinehart, Winston.

Knight, P. A., & Weiss, H. M. (1980). *Benefits of suffering: Communicator suffering, benefiting, and influence.* Paper presented at the American Psychological convention.

Knight-Ridder Newspapers. (1991, October 13). Whites' IDs of Blacks in crime cases often wrong, studies show. *Columbus Dispatch.*

Knox, R. E., & Inkster, J. A. (1968). Postdecision dissonance at post time. *Journal of Personality and Social Psychology, 8,* 319–323.

Knudson, R. M., Sommers, A. A., & Golding, S. L. (1980). Interpersonal perception and mode of resolution in marital conflict. *Journal of Personality and Social Psychology, 38,* 751–763.

Kobak, R. R., & Hazan, C. (1991). Attachment in marriage: Effects of security and accuracy of working models. *Journal of Personality and Social Psychology, 60,* 861–869.

Komorita, S. S., & Meek, D. D. (1978). Generality and validity of some theories of coalition formation. *Journal of Personality and Social Psychology, 36,* 392–404.

Korte, C., Ypma, I., & Toppen, A. (1975). Helpfulness in Dutch society as a function of urbanization and environmental input level. *Journal of Personality and Social Psychology, 32,* 996–1003.

Kotkin, J. (1986, February). The "SMART-TEAM" at Compaq Computer. *Inc.,* pp. 48–56.

Kramer, R. M. (1989). Windows of vulnerability or cognitive illusions? Cognitive processes and the nuclear arms race. *Journal of Experimental Social Psychology, 25,* 79–84.

Kramer, R. M., & Brewer, M. B. (1984). Effects of group identity on resource use in a simulated commons dilemma. *Journal of Personality and Social Psychology, 46,* 1044–1057.

Krauss, R. M., Freedman, J. L., & Whitcup, M. (1978). Field and laboratory studies of littering. *Journal of Experimental Social Psychology, 14,* 109–122.

Kraut, R. E. (1973). Effects of social labeling on giving to charity. *Journal of Experimental Social Psychology, 9,* 551–562.

Kravitz, D. A., & Martin, B. (1986). Ringelmann rediscovered: The original article. *Journal of Personality and Social Psychology, 50,* 936–941.

Krebs, D., & Miller, D. (1985). Altruism and aggression. In G. Lindzey & E. Aronson (Eds.), *Handbook of social psychology* (3rd ed., Vol. 2, pp. 1–72). New York: Random House.

Krebs, D. L. (1970). Altruism—an examination of the concept and review of the literature. *Psychological Bulletin, 73,* 258–303.

Kriesberg, L. (1982). *Social conflict* (2nd ed.). Englewood Cliffs, NJ: Prentice-Hall.

Krosnick, J. A. (1988). The role of attitude importance in social evaluation: A study of political preferences, presidential candidates evaluations, and voting behavior. *Journal of Personality and Social Psychology, 55,* 196–210.

Krueger, J., & Rothbart, M. (1990). Contrast and accentuation effects in category learning. *Journal of Personality and Social Psychology, 59,* 651–663.

Kruglanski, A., & Mackie, D. M. (1990). Majority and minority influence: A judgmental process integration. In W. Stroebe & M. Hewstone (Eds.), *Advances in European social psychology* (Vol. 1, pp. 229–262). Chichester, England: John Wiley & Sons.

Kruglanski, A. W. (1975). The human subject in the psychology experiment: Fact and artifact. In L. Berkowitz (Ed.), *Advances in experimental social psychology* (Vol. 8, pp. 101–147). New York: Academic Press.

Kruglanski, A. W. (1988). *Lay epistemics and human knowledge: Cognitive and motivational biases.* New York: Plenum Press.

Kruglanski, A. W., & Freund, T. (1983). The freezing and unfreezing of lay-inferences: Effects on impressional primacy, ethnic stereotyping, and numerical anchoring. *Journal of Experimental Social Psychology, 19,* 448–468.

Kuhn, M. H., & McPartland, T. (1954). An empirical investigation of self attitudes. *American Sociological Review, 19,* 68–76.

Kulka, R. A., & Kessler, J. B. (1978). Is justice really blind? The influence of litigan physical attractiveness on juridical judgment. *Journal of Applied Social Psychology, 8,* 366–381.

Kunda, Z. (1987). Motivated inference: Self-serving generation and evaluation of causal theories. *Journal of Personality and Social Psychology, 53,* 636–647.

Kunda, Z. (1990). The case for motivated reasoning. *Psychological Bulletin, 108,* 480–498.

Kunst-Wilson, W. R., & Zajonc, R. B. (1980). Affective discrimination of stimuli that cannot be recognized. *Science, 207,* 557–558.

Kurdek, L. A. (1991). Sexuality in homosexual and heterosexual couples. In K. McKinney & S. Sprecher (Eds.), *Sexuality in close relationships* (pp. 177–192). Hillsdale, NJ: Erlbaum.

Kurland, J. A. (1979). Paternity, mother's brother, and human sociality. In N. A. Chagnon & W. Irons (Eds.), *Evolutionary biology and human social behavior: An anthropological perspective* (pp. 145–180). North Scituate, MA: Duxbury Press.

Lagerquist, R. (1992, August 15). Band's not pretty, but the money's lovely. *Santa Barbara News Press,* p. B3.

Lalonde, R. N. (1992). The dynamics of group differentiation in the face of defeat. *Personality and Social Psychology Bulletin, 18,* 336–342.

Lambert, W. E., & Taylor, D. M. (1986). *Cultural and racial diversity in the lives of urban Americans: The Hamtramck/Pontiac study.* Unpublished monograph, McGill University, Montreal, Canada.

Lane, C., Stanger, T., & Post, T. (1993, April 19). The ghosts of Serbia. *Newsweek,* pp. 30–31.

Langer, E. J. (1975). The illusion of control. *Journal of Personality and Social Psychology, 32,* 311–328.

Langer, E. J., Blank, A., & Chanowitz, B. (1978). The mindlessness of ostensibly thoughtful action. *Journal of Personality and Social Psychology, 36,* 635–642.

Langer, E. J., & Rodin, J. (1976). The effects of choice and enhanced personal responsibility for the aged: A field experiment in an institutional setting. *Journal of Personality and Social Psychology, 34,* 191–198.

Lanzetta, J. T., & Roby, T. B. (1960). The relationship between certain group process variables and group problem-solving efficiency. *Journal of Social Psychology, 52,* 135–148.

LaPiere, R. T. (1936). Type-rationalizations of group antipathy. *Social Forces, 15,* 232–237.

LaPrelle, J., Hoyle, R. H., Insko, C. A., & Bernthal, P. (1990). Interpersonal attraction and descriptions of the traits of others: Ideal similarity, self similarity, and liking. *Journal of Research in Personality, 24,* 216–240.

Larwood, L., & Whittaker, W. (1977). Managerial myopia: Self-serving biases in organizational planning. *Journal of Applied Psychology, 62,* 194–198.

Lassiter, G. D., & Irvine, A. A. (1986). Videotaped confessions: The impact of camera point of view on judgments of coercion. *Journal of Applied Social Psychology, 16,* 268–276.

Latané, B., & Dabbs, J. M. (1975). Sex, group size, and helping in three cities. *Sociometry, 38,* 180–194.

Latané, B., & Darley, J. M. (1970). *The unresponsive bystander: Why doesn't he help?* New York: Appleton-Crofts.

Latané, B., Nida, S. A., & Wilson, D. W. (1981). The effects of group size on helping behavior. In J. P. Rushton & R. M. Sorrentino (Eds.), *Altruism and helping behavior* (pp. 287–313). Hillsdale, NJ: Erlbaum.

Latané, B., Williams, K., & Harkins, S. (1979). Many hands make light the work: The causes and consequences of social loafing. *Journal of Personality and Social Psychology, 37,* 822–832.

Latané, B., & Wolf, S. (1981). The social impact of majorities and minorities. *Psychological Review, 88,* 438–453.

Laughlin, P. R. (1980). Social combination processes of cooperative problem solving groups on verbal intellective tasks. In M. Fishbein (Ed.), *Progress in social psychology* (pp. 127–155). Hillsdale, NJ: Erlbaum.

Laughlin, P. R., VanderStoep, S. W., & Hollingshead, A. B. (1991). Collective versus individual induction: Recognition of truth, rejection of error, and collective information processing. *Journal of Personality and Social Psychology, 61,* 50–67.

Lawler, E. J., Ford, R. S., & Bleger, M. A. (1988). Coercive capability in conflict: A test of bilateral deterrence versus conflict spiral theory. *Social Psychology Quarterly, 51,* 93–107.

Lazarus, R. S. (1984). On the primacy of cognition. *American Psychologist, 39,* 124–129.

Leary, M. R., Barners, B. D., & Griebel, C. (1986). Cognitive, affective, and attributional effects of potential threats to self-esteem. *Journal of Social and Clinical Psychology, 4,* 461–474.

LeBon, G. (1908). *The crowd.* London: Unwin.

Lebow, R. N., & Stein, J. G. (1987). Beyond deterrence. *Journal of Social Issues, 43*(4), 5–71.

Lee, M. T., & Ofshe, R. (1981). The impact of behavioral style and status characteristics on social influence: A test of two competing theories. *Social Psychology Quarterly, 44,* 73–82.

Leigh, B. C. (1989). Reasons for having and avoiding sex: Gender, sexual orientation, and relationship to sexual behavior. *Journal of Sex Research, 26,* 199–209.

Lemaine, G. (1974). Social differentiation and social originality. *European Journal of Social Psychology, 4,* 17–52.

Lemyre, L., & Smith, P. M. (1985). Intergroup discrimination and self-esteem in the minimal group paradigm. *Journal of Personality and Social Psychology, 49,* 660–670.

Lepper, M. R., Greene, D., & Nisbett, R. E. (1973). Undermining children's intrinsic interest with extrinsic reward: A test of the "overjustification" hypothesis. *Journal of Personality and Social Psychology, 28,* 129–137.

Lerner, M. J. (1980). *The belief in a just world: A fundamental delusion.* New York: Plenum.

Lerner, M. J., & Miller, D. T. (1978). Just-world research and the attribution process: Looking back and ahead. *Psychological Bulletin, 85,* 1030–1051.

Lerner, M. J., & Simmons, C. H. (1966). Observers' reaction to the "innocent victim": Compassion or rejection? *Journal of Personality and Social Psychology, 4,* 203–210.

Levenson, R. W., & Gottman, J. M. (1985). Six physiological and affective predictors of change in relationship satisfaction. *Journal of Personality and Social Psychology, 49,* 85–94.

Leventhal, H. (1970). Findings and theory in the study of fear communications. In L. Berkowitz (Ed.), *Advances in experimental social psychology* (Vol. 5, pp. 119–186). New York: Academic Press.

Leventhal, H., Singer, R. P., & Jones, F. (1965). Effects of fear and specificity of recommendations upon attitudes and behavior. *Journal of Personality and Social Psychology, 2,* 20–29.

Levine, J. M. (1980). Reaction to opinion deviance in small groups. In P. B. Paulus (Ed.), *Psychology of group influence* (pp. 375–429). Hillsdale, NJ: Erlbaum.

Levine, J. M., & Moreland, R. L. (1991). Culture and socialization in work groups. In L. B. Resnick, J. M. Levine, & S. D. Teasley (Eds.), *Perspectives on socially shared cognition* (pp. 257–279). Washington, DC: American Psychological Association.

LeVine, R. A., & Campbell, D. T. (1972). *Ethnocentrism: Theories of conflict, ethnic attitudes and group behavior.* New York: Wiley.

Levinger, G., & Schneider, D. (1969). Test of the "risk is a value" hypothesis. *Journal of Personality and Social Psychology, 11,* 165–169.

Levy, M. B., & Davis, K. E. (1988). Lovestyles and attachment styles compared: Their relations to each other and to various relationship characteristics. *Journal of Social and Personal Relationships, 5,* 439–471.

Lewicki, P. (1984). Self-schema and social information processing. *Journal of Personality and Social Psychology, 47,* 1177–1190.

Lewicki, P. (1985). Nonconscious biasing effects of single instances on subsequent judgments. *Journal of Personality and Social Psychology, 48,* 563–574.

Lewicki, P. (1986). *Nonconscious social information processing.* Hillsdale, NJ: Erlbaum.

Lewin, K. (1936). *Principles of topological psychology.* New York: McGraw-Hill.

Lewin, K. (1943). Forces behind food habits and methods of change. *Bulletin of the National Research Council, 108,* 35–65.

Lewin, K. (1947). Group decision and social change. In T. M. Newcomb & E. L. Hartley (Eds.), *Readings in social psychology* (pp. 330–344). New York: Henry Holt & Co.

Lewin, K. (1948). *Solving social conflicts.* New York: Harper & Brothers.

Lewin, K. (1951). Problems of research in social psychology. In D. Cartwright (Ed.), *Field theory in social science* (pp. 155–169). New York: Harper & Row.

Lewin, T. (1991, January 17). Women found to be frequent victims of assaults by intimates. *The New York Times,* p. A12.

Lewin, T. (1992, January 8). Study points to increase in tolerance of ethnicity. *The New York Times,* p. A10.

Lewis, M., & Brooks-Gunn, J. (1979). *Social cognition and the acquisition of self.* New York: Plenum.

Leyens, J.-P., & Fraczek, A. (1983). Aggression as an interpersonal phenomenon. In H. Tajfel (Ed.), *The social dimension* (Vol. 1, pp. 184–203). Cambridge: Cambridge University Press.

Liberman, A., de La Hoz, V., & Chaiken, S. (1988). *Prior attitudes as heuristic information.* Paper presented at Western Psychological Association, Burlingame, CA.

Lieberman, S. (1956). The effects of changes in roles on the attitudes of role occupants. *Human Relations, 9,* 385–402.

Liebert, R. M., & Sprafkin, J. (1988). *The early window: Effects of television on children and youth* (3rd ed.). New York: Pergamon Press.

Liebrand, W. B., Jansen, R. W., Rijken, V. M., & Suhre, C. J. (1986). Might over morality: Social values and the perception of other players in experimental games. *Journal of Experimental Social Psychology, 22,* 203–215.

Liebrand, W. B., & Van Run, G. J. (1985). The effects of social motives on behavior in social dilemmas in two cultures. *Journal of Experimental Social Psychology, 21,* 86–102.

Life (1988, Spring). What we believe, pp. 69–70.

Linder, D. E., Cooper, J., & Jones, E. E. (1967). Decision freedom as a determinant of the role of incentive magnitude in attitude change. *Journal of Personality and Social Psychology, 6,* 245–254.

Lindskold, S. (1978). Trust development, the GRIT proposal and the effects of conciliatory acts on conflict and cooperation. *Psychological Bulletin, 85,* 772–793.

Lindskold, S. (1986). GRIT: Reducing distrust through carefully introduced conciliation. In S. Worchel & W. G. Austin (Eds.), *Psychology of intergroup relations* (2nd ed., pp. 305–322). Chicago: Nelson Hall.

Lingle, J. H., & Ostrom, T. M. (1979). Retrieval selectivity in memory-based impression judgments. *Journal of Personality and Social Psychology, 37,* 180–194.

Linville, P. W. (1985). Self-complexity and affective extremity: Don't put all of your eggs in one cognitive basket. *Social Cognition, 3* (Special issue: Depression), 94–120.

Linville, P. W. (1987). Self-complexity as a cognitive buffer against stress-related illness and depression. *Journal of Personality and Social Psychology, 52,* 663–676.

Linville, P. W., & Fischer, G. W. (1991). Preferences for separating or combining events. *Journal of Personality and Social Psychology, 60,* 5–23.

Linville, P. W., Fisher, G. W., & Salovey, P. (1989). Perceived distributions of the characteristics of ingroup and outgroup members. *Journal of Personality and Social Psychology, 57,* 165–188.

Linz, D., Donnerstein, E., & Penrod, S. (1987). The findings and recommendations of the Attorney General's Commission on Pornography: Do the psychological "facts" fit the political fury? *American Psychologist, 42,* 946–953.

Lippmann, W. (1922). *Public opinion.* New York: Harcourt Brace.

Lipsitz, A., Kallmeyer, K., Ferguson, M., & Abas, A. (1989). Counting on blood donors: Increasing the impact of reminder calls. *Journal of Applied Social Psychology, 19,* 1057–1067.

Liska, A. E. (1984). A critical examination of the causal structure of the Fishbein/Ajzen attitude-behavior model. *Social Psychology Quarterly, 47,* 61–74.

Littlepage, G. E. (1991). Effects of group size and task characteristics on group performance: A test of Steiner's model. *Personality and Social Psychology Bulletin, 17,* 449–456.

Lloyd, S., Cate, R., & Henton, J. (1982). Equity and rewards as predictors of satisfaction in casual and intimate relationships. *Journal of Psychology, 110,* 43–48.

Lockhart, W. H., & Elliot, R. (1981). Changes in the attitudes of young offenders in an integrated assessment centre. In J. Harbison & J. Harbison (Eds.), *A society under stress.* Somerset: Open Books.

Loewenstein, G. F., Thompson, L., & Bazerman, M. H. (1989). Social utility and decision making in interpersonal contexts. *Journal of Personality and Social Psychology, 57,* 426–441.

Loftin, C., McDowall, D., Wiersema, B., & Cottey, T. J. (1991). Effects of restrictive licensing of handguns on homicide and suicide in the District of Columbia. *New England Journal of Medicine, 325,* 1615–1620.

Loftus, E. F. (1974). The incredible eyewitness. *Psychology Today, 8*(7), 116–119.

Lombardi, W. J., Higgins, E. T., & Bargh, J. A. (1987). The role of consciousness in priming effects on categorization: Assimilation versus contrast as a function of awareness of the priming task. *Personality and Social Psychology Bulletin, 13,* 411–429.

Lord, C. G., Lepper, M. R., & Mackie, D. (1984). Attitude prototypes as determinants of attitude-behavior consistency. *Journal of Personality and Social Psychology, 46,* 1254–1266.

Lord, C. G., Lepper, M. R., & Preston, E. (1984). Considering the opposite: A corrective strategy for social judgment. *Journal of Personality and Social Psychology, 47,* 1231–1243.

Lord, C. G., Ross, L., & Lepper, M. (1979). Biased assimilation and attitude polarization: The effects of prior theories on subsequently considered evidence. *Journal of Personality and Social Psychology, 37,* 2098–2109.

Lord, C. G., & Saenz, D. S. (1985). Memory deficits and memory surfeits: Differential cognitive consequences of tokenism for tokens and observers. *Journal of Personality and Social Psychology, 49,* 918–926.

Lord, R. G., De Vader, C. L., & Alliger, G. M. (1986). A meta-analysis of the relation between personality traits and leadership perceptions: An application of validity generalization procedures. *Journal of Applied Psychology, 71,* 402–410.

Lorenz, K. (1966). *On aggression.* New York: Harcourt Brace Jovanovich.

Lortie-Lusier, M. (1987). Minority influence and idiosyncrasy credit: A new comparison of the Moscovici and Hollander theories of innovation. *European Journal of Social Psychology, 17,* 431–446.

Losch, M. E., & Cacioppo, J. T. (1990). Cognitive dissonance may enhance sympathetic tonus, but attitudes are changed to reduce negative affect rather than arousal. *Journal of Experimental Social Psychology, 26,* 289–304.

Luhtanen, R., Blaine, B., & Crocker, J. (1991). *Personal and collective self-esteem and depression in African-American and White students.* Unpublished paper presented at Eastern Psychological Association, New York.

Luhtanen, R., & Crocker, J. (1992). A collective self-esteem scale: Self-evaluation of one's social identity. *Personality and Social Psychology Bulletin, 18,* 302–318.

Luthans, F., Paul, R., & Baker, D. (1981). An experimental analysis of the impact of contingent reinforcement on salespersons' performance behavior. *Journal of Applied Psychology, 66,* 314–323.

Lykken, D. T. (1985). The probity of the polygraph. In S. Kassin & L. Wrightsman (Eds.), *The psychology of evidence and trial procedure* (pp. 95–123). Beverly Hills, CA: Sage Publications.

Lynn, M., & Oldenquist, A. (1986). Egoistic and nonegoistic motives in social dilemmas. *American Psychologist, 41,* 529–534.

Maass, A., & Clark, R. D., III. (1983). Internalization versus compliance: Differential processes underlying minority influence and conformity. *European Journal of Social Psychology, 13,* 197–215.

Maass, A., Clark, R. D., III, & Haberkorn, G. (1982). The effects of differential ascribed category membership and norms on minority influence. *European Journal of Social Psychology, 12,* 89–104.

Maass, A., Salvi, D., Arcuri, L., & Semin, G. (1989). Language use in intergroup contexts: The linguistic intergroup bias. *Journal of Personality and Social Psychology, 57,* 981–993.

Maccoby, E. E. (1980). *Social development: Psychological growth and the parent-child relationship.* New York: Harcourt Brace Jovanovich.

MacCoun, R. J., & Kerr, N. L. (1988). Asymmetric influence in mock jury deliberations: Jurors' bias for leniency. *Journal of Personality and Social Psychology, 54,* 21–33.

Mack, R. W., & Snyder, R. C. (1957). The analysis of social conflict—Toward an overview and synthesis. *Journal of Conflict Resolution, 1,* 212–248.

Mackie, D. (1984). Social comparison in high- and low-status groups. *Journal of Cross-Cultural Psychology, 15,* 379–398.

Mackie, D. (1986). Social identification effects in group polarization. *Journal of Personality and Social Psychology, 50,* 720–728.

Mackie, D. (1987). Systematic and nonsystematic processing of majority and minority persuasive communications. *Journal of Personality and Social Psychology, 53,* 41–52.

Mackie, D. M., & Goethals, G. R. (1987). Individual and group goals. In C. Hendrick (Ed.), *Group processes* (pp. 144–166). Beverly Hills, CA: Sage Publications.

Mackie, D. M., & Hamilton, D. L. (Eds.) (1993). *Affect, cognition, and stereotyping: Interactive processes in group perception.* San Diego, CA: Academic Press.

Mackie, D. M., Sherman, J. W., & Worth, L. T. (1993). On-line and memory-based processes in group variability judgments. *Social Cognition* (Vol. 2, pp. 44–69).

Mackie, D. M., & Worth, L. T. (1989). Cognitive deficits and the mediation of positive affect in persuasion. *Journal of Personality and Social Psychology, 57,* 27–40.

Mackie, D. M., Worth, L. T., & Asuncion, A. G. (1990). The processing of persuasive ingroup messages. *Journal of Personality and Social Psychology, 58,* 812–822.

MacLachlan, J., & Siegel, M. H. (1980). Reducing the costs of TV commercials by use of time compressions. *Journal of Marketing Research, 17,* 52–57.

Maddux, J. E., & Rogers, R. W. (1980). Effects of source expertness, physical attractiveness, and supporting arguments on persuasion: A case of brains over beauty. *Journal of Personality and Social Psychology, 38,* 235–244.

Magnusson, S. (1981). *The flying Scotsman.* London: Quartet Books.

Magura, S., Saddiqi, Q., Shapiro, J., Grossman, J. I., Lipton, D. S., Marion, I. J., Weisenfeld, L., Amann, K. R., & Koger, J. (1991). Outcomes of an AIDS prevention program for methadone patients. *International Journal of the Addictions, 26,* 629–655.

Maheswaran, D., & Chaiken, S. (1991). Promoting systematic processing in low motivation settings: The effect of incongruent information on processing and judgment. *Journal of Personality and Social Psychology, 61,* 13–25.

Malcolm X. (1966). *The autobiography of Malcolm X.* New York: Grove Press.

Manis, M., Nelson, T. E., & Shedler, J. (1988). Stereotypes and social judgment: Extremity, assimilation and contrast. *Journal of Personality and Social Psychology, 55,* 28–36.

Mann, L., & Janis, I. L. (1968). A follow-up study on the long-term effects of emotional role playing. *Journal of Personality and Social Psychology, 44,* 657–671.

Manstead, A. S. R., Plevin, C. E., & Smart, J. L. (1984). Predicting mothers' choice of infant-feeding method. *British Journal of Social Psychology, 23,* 223–231.

Manstead, A. S. R., Proffitt, C., & Smart, J. L. (1983). Predicting and understanding mothers' infant-feeding intentions and behavior: Testing the theory of reasoned action. *Journal of Personality and Social Psychology, 44,* 657–671.

Maquet, J. J. (1961). *The promise of inequality in Ruanda: A study of political relations in a central African community.* London: Oxford University Press.

Marks, M. L. (1986, March). The question of quality circles. *Psychology Today, 20,* 36–46.

Marks, M. L., Mirvis, P. H., Hackett, E. J., & Grady, J. F., Jr. (1986). Employee participation in a quality control circle program: Impact on quality of work life, productivity, and absenteeism. *Journal of Applied Psychology, 71,* 61–69.

Markus, H. (1977). Self-schemata and processing information about the self. *Journal of Personality and Social Psychology, 35,* 63–78.

Markus, H., & Kitayama, S. (1991). Culture and the self: Implications for cognition, emotion, and motivation. *Psychological Review, 98,* 224–253.

Markus, H., & Nurius, P. (1986). Possible selves. *American Psychologist, 41,* 954–969.

Markus, H., & Wurf, E. (1987). The dynamic self-concept: A social psychological perspective. *Annual Review of Psychology, 38,* 299–337.

Marques, J. M., & Yzerbyt, V. Y. (1988). The black sheep effect: Judgmental extremity towards ingroup members in inter- and intra-group situations. *European Journal of Social Psychology, 18,* 287–292.

Marques, J. M., Yzerbyt, V. Y., & Rijsman, J. B. (1988). Context effects on intergroup discrimination: In-group bias as a function of experimenter's provenance. *British Journal of Social Psychology, 27,* 301–318.

Martin, C. L. (1987). A ratio measure of sex stereotyping. *Journal of Personality and Social Psychology, 52,* 489–499.

Martin, L. L. (1986). Set/reset: Use and disuse of concepts in impression formation. *Journal of Personality and Social Psychology, 51,* 493–504.

Martin, L. L., Seta, J. J., & Crelia, R. A. (1990). Assimilation and contrast as a function of people's willingness and ability to expend effort in forming an impression. *Journal of Personality and Social Psychology, 59,* 38–49.

Martin, L. L., Ward, D. W., Achee, J. W., & Wyer, R. S. (1993). Mood as input: People have to interpret the motivational implications of their moods. *Journal of Personality and Social Psychology, 64,* 317–326.

Martin, S. E. (1982). *Breaking and entering: Policewomen on patrol.* Berkeley, CA: University of California Press.

Martineau, P. (1957). *Motivation in advertising.* New York: McGraw-Hill.

Mashberg, T. (1993, July 5). Diverse Muslim community thrives in Jersey City. *The Boston Globe,* pp. 1, 8.

Mathes, E. W., Adams, H. E., & Davies, R. M. (1985). Jealousy: Loss of relationship rewards, loss of self-esteem, depression, anxiety, and anger. *Journal of Personality and Social Psychology, 48,* 1552–1561.

Matsuda, N. (1985). Strong, quasi-, and weak conformity among Japanese in the modified Asch procedure. *Journal of Cross-Cultural Psychology, 16,* 83–97.

May, R. B. (1976, December 30). Business bulletin. *Wall Street Journal,* p. 1.

Mayadas, N., & Glasser, P. (1985). Termination: A neglected aspect of social group work. In M. Sundel, P. Glasser, R. Sarri, & R. Vinter (Eds.), *Individual change through small groups* (2nd ed., pp. 251–261). New York: Free Press.

McAdams, D. P. (1985). *Power, intimacy, and the life story: Personological inquiries into identity.* Homewood, IL: Dorsey Press.

McAdams, D. P., & Bryant, F. B. (1987). Intimacy motivation and subjective mental health in a nationwide sample. *Journal of Personality, 55,* 395–414.

McAdams, D. P., & Vaillant, G. E. (1982). Intimacy motivation and psychosocial adjustment: A longitudinal study. *Journal of Personality Assessment, 46,* 586–593.

McAlister, A., Perry, C., Killen, J., Slinkard, L. A., & Maccoby, N. (1980). Pilot study of smoking, alcohol and drug abuse prevention. *American Journal of Public Health, 70,* 719–721.

McAllister, J. F. O. (1992, August 17). Atrocity and outrage. *Time,* pp. 21–24.

McArthur, L. A. (1972). The how and what of why: Some determinants and consequences of causal attribution. *Journal of Personality and Social Psychology, 22,* 171–193.

McArthur, L. Z. (1981). What grabs you? The role of attention in impression formation and causal attribution. In E. T. Higgins, C. P. Herman, & M. P. Zanna (Eds.), *Social cognition: The Ontario Symposium* (Vol. 1, pp. 201–246). Hillsdale, NJ: Erlbaum.

McArthur, L. Z., & Berry, D. S. (1987). Cross-cultural agreement in perceptions of babyfaced adults. *Journal of Cross Cultural Psychology, 18,* 165–192.

McArthur, L. Z., & Post, D. L. (1977). Figural emphasis and person perception. *Journal of Experimental Social Psychology, 13,* 520–535.

McCain, G., Cox, V. C., & Paulus, P. B. (1980). *The effect of prison crowding on inmate behavior.* Washington, DC: National Institute of Justice.

McCallum, D. M., Harring, K., Gilmore, R., Drenan S., Chase, J. P., Insko, C. A., & Thibaut, J. (1985). Competition and cooperation between groups and between individuals. *Journal of Experimental Social Psychology, 21,* 301–320.

McClintock, C. G., & Liebrand, W. B. (1988). Role of interdependence structure, individual value orientation, and another's strategy in social decision making: A transformational analysis. *Journal of Personality and Social Psychology, 55,* 396–409.

McConnell, J. D. (1968). Effect of pricing on perception of product quality. *Journal of Applied Psychology, 52,* 331–334.

McCrae, R. R., & Costa, P. T. (1988). Psychological resilience among widowed men and women: A 10-year follow-up of a national sample. *Journal of Social Issues, 44(3),* 129–142.

McDougall, W. (1908). *An introduction to social psychology.* London: Methuen.

McFall, R. M. (1977). Parameters of self-monitoring. In R. B. Stuart (Ed.), *Behavioral self-management: Strategies, techniques, and outcomes* (pp. 196–214). New York: Brunner/Mazel.

McGill, A. L. (1989). Context effects in judgments of causation. *Journal of Personality and Social Psychology, 57,* 189–200.

McGrath, J. E. (1984). *Groups: Interaction and performance.* Englewood Cliffs, NJ: Prentice-Hall.

McGrath, J. E., Kelly, J. R., & Rhodes, J. E. (1993). A feminist perspective on research methodology: Some metatheoretical issues, contrasts, and choices. In S. Oskamp & M. Costanzo (Eds.), *Gender issues in contemporary society* (pp. 19–37). Newbury Park, CA: Sage Publications.

McGuire, T. W., Kiesler, S., & Siegel, J. (1987). Group and computer-mediated discussion effects in risk decision making. *Journal of Personality and Social Psychology, 52,* 917–930.

McGuire, W. J. (1964). Inducing resistance to persuasion: Some contemporary approaches. In L. Berkowitz (Ed.), *Advances in experimental social psychology* (Vol. 1, pp. 192–229). New York: Academic Press.

McGuire, W. J. (1969). The nature of attitudes and attitude change. In G. Lindzey & E. Aronson (Eds.), *Handbook of social psychology* (2nd ed., Vol. 3, pp. 136–314). Reading, MA: Addison-Wesley.

McGuire, W. J. (1985). Attitudes and attitude change. In G. Lindzey & E. Aronson (Eds.), *Handbook of social psychology* (3rd ed., Vol. 2, pp. 233–346). New York: Random House.

McGuire, W. J., & McGuire, C. V. (1981). The spontaneous-self-concept as affected by personal distinctiveness. In M. D. Lynch, A. A. Norem-Hebeisen, & K. J. Gergen (Eds.), *Self-concept: Advances in theory and research* (pp. 147–171). Cambridge, MA: Ballinger.

McGuire, W. J., McGuire, C. V., Child, P., & Fujioka, T. (1978). Salience of ethnicity in the spontaneous self-concept as a function of one's ethnic distinctiveness in the social environment. *Journal of Personality and Social Psychology, 36,* 511–520.

McGuire, W. J., McGuire, C. V., & Winton, W. (1979). Effects of household sex composition on the salience of one's gender in the spontaneous self-concept. *Journal of Experimental Social Psychology, 15,* 77–90.

McGuire, W. J., & Padawer-Singer, A. (1978). Trait salience in the spontaneous self-concept. *Journal of Personality and Social Psychology, 33,* 743–754.

McLachlan, A. (1986). The effects of two forms of decision reappraisal on the perception of pertinent arguments. *British Journal of Social Psychology, 25,* 129–138.

McMillen, D. L., & Austin, J. B. (1971). Effect of positive feedback on compliance following transgression. *Psychonomic Science, 24,* 59–61.

Mead, G. H. (1934). *Mind, self, and society.* Chicago: University of Chicago Press.

Meeus, W. H., & Raaijmakers, Q. A. W. (1986). Administrative obedience: Carrying out orders to use psychological-administrative violence. *European Journal of Social Psychology, 16,* 311–324.

Mehrabian, A. (1972). *Nonverbal communication.* Chicago: Aldine.

Merikle, P. M. (1988). Subliminal auditory messages: An evaluation. *Psychology and Marketing, 5,* 355–372.

Merton, R. (1948). The self-fulfilling prophecy. *Antioch Review, 8,* 193–210.

Messick, D. M. (1974). When a little "group interest" goes a long way: A note on social motives and union joining. *Organizational Behavior and Human Performance, 12,* 331–334.

Messick, D. M., & Brewer, M. B. (1983). Solving social dilemmas: A review. In L. Wheeler & P. Shaver (Eds.), *Review of personality and social psychology* (Vol. 4, pp. 11–44). Beverly Hills, CA: Sage Publications.

Messick, D. M., Wilke, H., Brewer, M. B., Kramer, R. M., Zemke, P. E., & Lui, L. (1983). Individual adaptations and structural change as solutions to social dilemmas. *Journal of Personality and Social Psychology, 44,* 294–309.

Michaels, J. W., Blommel, J. M., Brocato, R. M., Linkous, R. A., & Rowe, J. S. (1982). Social facilitation and inhibition in a natural setting. *Replications in Social Psychology, 2,* 21–24.

Mikula, G. (1980). *Justice and social interaction.* New York: Springer-Verlag.

Milburn, T. W. (1977). The nature of threat. *Journal of Social Issues, 33*(1), 126–139.

Milgram, S. (1963). The behavioral study of obedience. *Journal of Abnormal and Social Psychology, 67,* 467–472.

Milgram, S. (1964). Issues in the study of obedience: A reply to Baumrind. *American Psychologist, 19,* 848–852.

Milgram, S. (1974). *Obedience to authority.* New York: Harper & Row.

Milgram, S. (1977, October). Subjects' reactions: The neglected factor in the ethics of experimentation. *Hastings Center Report,* pp. 19–23.

Millar, M. G., Millar, K. U., & Tesser, A. (1988). The effects of helping and focus of attention on mood states. *Personality and Social Psychology Bulletin, 14,* 536–543.

Millar, M. G., & Tesser, A. (1986). Thought-induced attitude change: The effects of schema structure and commitment. *Journal of Personality and Social Psychology, 51,* 259–269.

Miller, D. T., & McFarland, C. (1987). Pluralistic ignorance: When similarity is interpreted as dissimilarity. *Journal of Personality and Social Psychology, 53,* 298–305.

Miller, D. T., & Ross, M. (1975). Self-serving biases in the attribution of causality: Fact or fiction? *Psychological Bulletin, 82,* 213–225.

Miller, D. T., & Turnbull, W. (1986). Expectancies and interpersonal processes. *Annual Review of Psychology, 37,* 233–256.

Miller, G. A., Galanter, E., & Pribram, K. H. (1960). *Plans and the structure of behavior.* New York: Holt.

Miller, J. G. (1984). Culture and the development of everyday social explanation. *Journal of Personality and Social Psychology, 46,* 961–978.

Miller, J. G., Bersoff, D. M., & Harwood, R. L. (1990). Perceptions of social responsibility in India and the United States: Moral imperatives or personal decisions? *Journal of Personality and Social Psychology, 58,* 33–47.

Miller, L. E., & Grush, J. E. (1986). Individual differences in attitudinal versus normative determination of behavior. *Journal of Experimental Social Psychology, 22,* 190–202.

Miller, N., & Brewer, M. B. (1986). Categorization effects on ingroup and outgroup perception. In J. F. Dovidio & S. L. Gaertner (Eds.), *Prejudice, discrimination, and racism* (pp. 209–230). Orlando, FL: Academic Press.

Miller, N., Maruyama, G., Beaber, R. J., & Valone, K. (1976). Speed of speech and persuasion. *Journal of Personality and Social Psychology, 34,* 615–624.

Miller, N. E. (1941). The frustration-aggression hypothesis. *Psychological Review, 48,* 337–342.

Miller, P. A., & Eisenberg, N. (1988). The relation of empathy to aggressive and externalizing/antisocial behavior. *Psychological Bulletin, 103,* 324–344.

Miller, R. L., Brickman, P., & Bolen, D. (1975). Attribution versus persuasion as a means for modifying behavior. *Journal of Personality and Social Psychology, 31,* 430–441.

Miller, R. L., Seligman, C., Clark, N. T., & Bush, M. (1976). Perceptual contrast versus reciprocal concessions as mediators of induced compliance. *Canadian Journal of Behavioral Science, 8,* 401–409.

Miller, S. M., & Mangan, C. E. (1983). Interacting effects of information and coping style in adapting to gynecologic stress: Should the doctor tell all? *Journal of Personality and Social Psychology, 45,* 223–236.

Millett, K. (1970). *Sexual politics.* Garden City, NY: Doubleday.

Mintzberg, H. (1980). *The nature of managerial work* (2nd ed.). Englewood Cliffs, NJ: Prentice-Hall.

Mischel, W., Ebbessen, E. B., & Zeiss, A. M. (1973). Selective attention to the self: Situational and dispositional determinants. *Journal of Personality and Social Psychology, 27,* 129–142.

Moghaddam, F. M., Taylor, D. M., & Wright, S. C. (1993). *Social psychology in cross-cultural perspective.* New York: W. H. Freeman & Company.

Montepare, J. M., & Zebrowitz-McArthur, L. (1987). Perceptions of adults with childlike voices in two cultures. *Journal of Experimental Social Psychology, 23,* 331–349.

Montepare, J. M., & Zebrowitz-McArthur, L. (1988). Impressions of people created by age-related qualities of their gaits. *Journal of Personality and Social Psychology, 55,* 547–556.

Mook, D. G. (1980). In defense of external invalidity. *American Psychologist, 38,* 379–388.

Moore, D. L., Hausknecht, D., & Thamodaran, K. (1986). Time compression, response opportunity, and persuasion. *Journal of Consumer Research, 13,* 85–99.

Moreland, R. L. (1987). The formation of small groups. In C. Hendrick (Ed.), *Group processes* (pp. 80–110). Beverly Hills, CA: Sage Publications.

Moreland, R. L., & Beach, S. R. (1992). Exposure effects in the classroom: The development of affinity among students. *Journal of Experimental Social Psychology, 28,* 255–276.

Moreland, R. L., & Levine, J. M. (1988). Group dynamics over time: Development and socialization in small groups. In J. E. McGrath (Ed.), *The social psychology of time: New perspectives* (pp. 151–181). Newbury Park, CA: Sage Publications.

Moretti, S., & Shaw, B. (1989). Automatic and dysfunctional cognitive processes in depression. In J. S. Uleman & J. A. Bargh (Eds.), *Unintended thought: The limits of awareness, intention, and control* (pp. 383–421). New York: Guilford Press.

Morgan, M. (1982). Television and adolescents' sex role stereotypes: A longitudinal study. *Journal of Personality and Social Psychology, 43,* 947–955.

Morgan, P. M. (1983). *Deterrence: A conceptual analysis.* Beverly Hills, CA: Sage Publications.

Moriarty, T. (1975). Crime, commitment, and the responsive bystander: Two field experiments. *Journal of Personality and Social Psychology, 31,* 370–376.

Morton, T. L. (1978). Intimacy and reciprocity of exchange: A comparison of spouses and strangers. *Journal of Personality and Social Psychology, 36,* 72–81.

Moscovici, S. (1976). *Social influence and social change.* London: Academic Press.

Moscovici, S. (1980). Toward a theory of conversion behavior. In L. Berkowitz (Ed.), *Advances in experimental social psychology* (Vol. 13, pp. 209–239). New York: Academic Press.

Moscovici, S., & Lage, E. (1976). Studies in social influence. III: Majority versus minority influence in a group. *European Journal of Social Psychology, 6,* 149–174.

Moscovici, S., Lage, S., & Naffrechoux, M. (1969). Influence of a consistent minority on the responses of a majority in a color perception task. *Sociometry, 32,* 365–380.

Moscovici, S., & Personnaz, B. (1980). Studies in social influence. V: Minority influence and conversion behavior in a perceptual task. *Journal of Experimental Social Psychology, 16*, 270–282.

Moscovici, S., & Zavalloni, M. (1969). The group as a polarizer of attitudes. *Journal of Personality and Social Psychology, 12*, 125–135.

Moskos, C. C., Jr. (1969). Why men fight: American combat soldiers in Vietnam. *Transaction, 7*(1), 13–23.

Moskowitz, D. S., & Schwartzman, A. E. (1989). Painting group portraits: Studying life outcomes for aggressive and withdrawn children. *Journal of Personality, 57*, 723–746.

Mowen, J. C., & Cialdini, R. B. (1980). On implementing the door-in-the-face compliance technique in a business context. *Journal of Marketing Research, 17*, 253–258.

Mugny, G. (1975). Negotiations, image of the other, and the process of minority influence. *European Journal of Social Psychology, 5*, 209–228.

Mugny, G. (1982). *The power of minorities.* London: Academic Press.

Mugny, G., & Papastamous, S. (1980). When rigidity does not fail: Individualization and psychologization as resistances to the diffusion of minority innovations. *European Journal of Social Psychology, 10*, 43–62.

Mullen, B. (1987). Self-attention theory: The effects of group composition on the individual. In B. Mullen & G. R. Goethals (Eds.), *Theories of group behavior* (pp. 125–146). New York: Springer-Verlag.

Mullen, B. (1991). Group composition, salience, and cognitive representations: The phenomenology of being in a group. *Journal of Experimental Social Psychology, 27*, 297–323.

Mullen, B., Atkins, J. L., Champion, D. S., Edwards, C., Hardy, D., Story, J. E., & Vanderklok, M. (1985). The false consensus effect: A meta-analysis of 115 hypothesis tests. *Journal of Experimental Social Psychology, 21*, 262–283.

Mullen, B., Brown, R., & Smith, C. (1992). Ingroup bias as a function of salience, relevance, and status: An integration. *European Journal of Social Psychology, 22*, 103–122.

Mullen, B., Futrell, D., Stairs, D., Tice, D., Baumeister, R., Dawson, K., Riordan, C., Radloff, C., Goethals, G., Kennedy, J., & Rosenfeld, P. (1986). Newscasters' facial expressions and voting behavior of viewers: Can a smile elect a president? *Journal of Personality and Social Psychology, 51*, 291–295.

Mullen, B., & Hu, L. (1989). Perceptions of ingroup and outgroup variability: A meta-analytic integration. *Basic and Applied Social Psychology, 10*, 233–252.

Mullen, B., & Riordan, C. A. (1988). Self-serving attributions for performance in naturalistic settings: A meta-analytic review. *Journal of Applied Social Psychology, 18*, 3–22.

Muller, J. (1991, July 9). Subliminal ads debunked. *Santa Barbara News Press*, p. B6.

Murphy, S., & Zajonc, R. (1993). Affect, cognition, and awareness: Affective priming with optimal and suboptimal stimulus exposures. *Journal of Personality and Social Psychology, 64*, 723–740.

Murphy, S. M. (1990). Models of imagery in sport psychology: A review. *Journal of Mental Imagery, 14*, 153–172.

Mydans, S. (1992, March 4). New unease for Japanese-Americans. *The New York Times*, p. A8.

Mydans, S. (1992, May 7). Revelers facing the music, or the looter as everyman. *The New York Times*, p. A11.

Myers, D. G., & Bishop, G. D. (1971). The enhancement of dominant attitudes in group discussion. *Journal of Personality and Social Psychology, 20*, 386–391.

Myers, D. G., & Kaplan, M. F. (1976). Group-induced polarization in simulated juries. *Personality and Social Psychology Bulletin, 2*, 63–66.

Myers, D. G., & Lamm, H. (1976). The group polarization phenomenon. *Psychological Bulletin, 83*, 602–627.

Nadler, A., & Fisher, J. D. (1986). The role of threat to self-esteem and perceived control in recipient reactions to help: Theory development and empirical validation. In L. Berkowitz (Ed.), *Advances in experimental social psychology* (Vol. 19, pp. 81–122). New York: Academic Press.

Naroll, R., Bullough, V. L., & Naroll, F. (1974). *Military deterrence in history: A pilot cross-historical survey.* Albany: State University of New York Press.

Natale, J. A. (1988). Are you open to suggestion? *Psychology Today, 22*(9), 28–30.

Neisser, U. (1967). *Cognitive psychology.* New York: Appleton-Century-Crofts.

Nelan, B. W. (1991, August 1). Racism. *Time*, pp. 36–38.

Nemeth, C. (1977). Interactions between jurors as a function of majority vs. unanimity decision rules. *Journal of Applied Social Psychology, 7*, 38–56.

Nemeth, C. (1986). Differential contributions of majority and minority influence. *Psychological Review, 93*, 1–10.

Nemeth, C., & Chiles, C. (1988). Modelling courage: The role of dissent in fostering independence. *European Journal of Social Psychology, 18*, 275–280.

Nemeth, C., Mayseless, O., Sherman, J. W., & Brown, Y. (1990). Exposure to dissent and recall of information. *Journal of Personality and Social Psychology, 58*, 429–437.

Nemeth, C., & Wachtler, J. (1974). Creating the perceptions of consistency and confidence: A necessary condition for minority influence. *Sociometry, 37*, 529–540.

Nemeth, C., & Wachtler, J. (1983). Consistency and the modification of judgments. *Journal of Experimental Social Psychology, 9,* 65–79.

Nemeth, C., Wachtler, J., & Endicott, J. (1977). Increasing the size of the minority: Some gains and losses. *European Journal of Social Psychology, 7,* 15–27.

Nettles, E. J., & Loevinger, J. (1983). Sex role expectations and ego level in relation to problem marriages. *Journal of Personality and Social Psychology, 45,* 676–687.

Neuberg, S. L. (1989a). Behavioral implications of information presented outside of conscious awareness: The effects of subliminal presentation of trait information on behavior in the prisoner's dilemma game. *Social Cognition, 6,* 53–64.

Neuberg, S. L. (1989b). The goal of forming accurate impressions during social interactions: Attenuating the impact of negative expectancies. *Journal of Personality and Social Psychology, 56,* 374–386.

Neuberg, S. L., & Fiske, S. T. (1987). Motivational influences on impression formation: Outcome dependency, accuracy-driven attention, and individuating processes. *Journal of Personality and Social Psychology, 53,* 431–444.

Newcomb, T. M. (1961). *The acquaintance process.* New York: Holt, Rinehart, & Winston.

Newell, D., McKillop, P., & Monroe, S. (1986, January 20). Arab-bashing in America. *Newsweek,* p. 21.

Newsweek. (1990a, June 25). Perspectives, p. 15.

Newsweek. (1990b, May 21). Perspectives, p. 17.

Newsweek Poll (1990, September 10). The golden door. *Newsweek,* p. 48.

Newsweek Poll (1991, August 5). Opinion watch: On the front lines? *Newsweek,* pp. 23, 27.

Newsweek. (1992, June 8). A mother's guiding message, p. 27.

Newsweek. (1992, October 5). Tailhook: Throwing down the gantlet, p. 58.

The New York Times. (1991, January 10). Poll finds Whites use stereotypes, p. B10.

The New York Times. (1992a, March 25). Plenty of fish in sea? Not anymore, p. A8.

The New York Times. (1992b, May 6). A juror describes the ordeal of deliberations, p. A13.

The New York Times. (1992c, June 28). Turning the tables: A reverse questionnaire, p. F23.

The New York Times. (1992d, July 17). California case puts spotlight on jury coercion and peer pressure, p. A23.

Niedenthal, P. M. (1990). Implicit perception of affective information. *Journal of Experimental Social Psychology, 26,* 505–527.

Nields, D. (1991, May 27). The dirt on Shakespeare. *Newsweek,* p. 8.

Nigra, G. N., Hill, D. E., Gelbein, M. E., & Clark, C. L. (1988). Changes in the facial prominence of women and men over the last decade. *Psychology of Women Quarterly, 12,* 225–235.

Nisbett, R. E., & Wilson, T. D. (1977). Telling more than we can know: Verbal reports on mental processes. *Psychological Review, 84,* 231–259.

Nolen-Hoeksema, S., Girgus, J. S., & Seligman, M. E. P. (1986). Learned helplessness in children: A longitudinal study of depression, achievement, and explanatory style. *Journal of Personality and Social Psychology, 51,* 435–442.

Noller, P. (1980). Misunderstandings in marital communication: A study of couples' nonverbal communication. *Journal of Personality and Social Psychology, 39,* 1135–1148.

Noller, P., & Ruzzene, M. (1991). Communication in marriage: The influence of affect and cognition. In G. Fletcher & F. Fincham (Eds.), *Cognition in close relationships* (pp. 203–234. Hillsdale, NJ: Erlbaum.

North, R. C., Brody, R. A., & Holsti, O. R. (1964). Some empirical data on the conflict spiral. Peace *Research Society International Papers, 1,* 1–14.

Nosanchuk, T. A., & Lightstone, J. (1974). Canned laughter and public and private conformity. *Journal of Personality and Social Psychology, 29,* 153–156.

O'Connell, L. (1984). An exploration of exchange in three relationships: Kinship, friendship, and the marketplace. *Journal of Social and Personal Relationships, 1,* 333–345.

Ogilvy, D. (1983). *Ogilvy on advertising.* New York: Vintage Books.

Ohbuchi, K., & Kambara, T. (1985). Attacker's intent and awareness of outcome, impression management, and retaliation. *Journal of Experimental Social Psychology, 21,* 321-330.

O'Leary, A. (1990). Stress, emotion, and human immune function. *Psychological Bulletin, 108,* 363–382.

Oliner, S. P., & Oliner, P. M. (1988). *The altruistic personality.* New York: Free Press.

Oliver, M. B., & Hyde, J. S. (1993). Gender differences in sexuality: A meta-analysis. *Psychological Bulletin, 114,* 29–51.

Olson, J. M. (1990). Self-inference processes in emotion. In J. M. Olson & M. P. Zanna (Eds.), *Self-inference processes: The Ontario Symposium* (Vol. 6, pp. 17–42). Hillsdale, NJ: Erlbaum.

Olweus, D. (1979). Stability of aggressive reaction patterns in males: A review. *Psychological Bulletin, 86,* 852–875.

Olzak, S., & Nagel, J. (1986). *Competitive ethnic relations.* Orlando, FL: Academic Press.

Omi, M. (1989). In living color: Race and American culture. In I. Agnus & S. Jhally (Eds.), *Cultural politics in contemporary America* (pp. 111–122). New York: Routledge.

Opotow, S. (1990). Moral exclusion and injustice: An introduction. *Journal of Social Issues, 46*(1), 1–20.

Orbell, J. M., Van-de Kragt, A. J., and Dawes, R. M. (1988). Explaining discussion-induced cooperation. *Journal of Personality and Social Psychology, 54,* 811–819.

O'Reilly, C. A., & Caldwell, D. F. (1985). The impact of normative social influence and cohesiveness on task perceptions and attitudes: A social-information processing approach. *Journal of Occupational Psychology, 59,* 193–206.

Orne, M. T. (1962). On the social psychology of the psychological experiment: With particular reference to demand characteristics and their implications. *American Psychologist, 17,* 776–783.

Osborn, A. F. (1953). *Applied imagination.* New York: Scribners.

Osgood, C. E. (1962). *An alternative to war or surrender.* Urbana, IL: University of Illinois Press.

Oskamp, S., & Hartry, A. (1968). A factor-analytic study of the double standard in attitudes toward U.S. and Russian actions. *Behavioral Science, 13,* 178–188.

Ostrom, T. M. (1969). The relationship between the affective, behavioral, and cognitive components of attitude. *Journal of Experimental Social Psychology, 5,* 12–30.

Owens, G., & Ford, J. G. (1978). Further consideration of the "What is good is beautiful" finding. *Social Psychology, 41,* 73–75.

Oyama, S. (1991). Bodies and minds: Dualism in evolutionary theory. *Journal of Social Issues, 47*(3), 27–42.

Packard, V. (1971). *The hidden persuaders.* New York: D. McKay Company.

Paichelier, G. (1976). Norms and attitude change I: Polarization and styles of behavior. *European Journal of Social Psychology, 6,* 405–427.

Pallak, M. S., Cook, D. A., & Sullivan, J. J. (1980). Commitment and energy conservation. In L. Bickman (Ed.), *Applied social psychology annual* (Vol. 1, pp. 235–254). Beverly Hills, CA: Sage Publications.

Pallak, S. R. (1983). Salience of a communicator's physical attractiveness and persuasion: A heuristic versus systematic processing interpretation. *Social Cognition, 2,* 156–168.

Palmer, E. L., & Dorr, A. (1980). *Children and the faces of television: Teaching, violence, selling.* New York: Academic Press.

Pandey, J., & Singh, A. K. (1986). Attribution and evaluation of manipulative social behavior. *Journal of Social Psychology, 126,* 735–744.

Park, B. (1986). A method for studying the development of impressions of real people. *Journal of Personality and Social Psychology, 51,* 907–917.

Park, B., & Judd, C. M. (1990). Measures and models of perceived group variability. *Journal of Personality and Social Psychology, 59,* 173–191.

Park, B., & Rothbart, M. (1982). Perception of out-group homogeneity and levels of social categorization: Memory for the subordinate attributes of in-group and out-group members. *Journal of Personality and Social Psychology, 42,* 1051–1068.

Parke, R. D., Berkowitz, L., Leyens, J.-P., West, S. G., & Sebastian, R. J. (1977). Some effects of violent and nonviolent movies on the behavior of juvenile delinquents. In L. Berkowitz (Ed.), *Advances in experimental social psychology* (Vol. 10, pp. 135–172). New York: Academic Press.

Patchen, M., Davidson, J. D., Hofmann, G., & Brown, W. R. (1977). Determinants of students' interracial behavior and opinion change. *Sociology of Education, 50, 55–75.*

Paternoster, R. (1983). Race of victim and location of crime: The decision to seek the death penalty in South Carolina. *Journal of Criminal Law and Criminology, 74,* 754–785.

Patterson, G. R., Littman, R. A., & Bricker, W. (1967). Assertive behavior in children: A step toward a theory of aggression. *Monographs of the Society for Research in Child Development* (No. 113), 32, 5.

Paulus, P. B. (1988). *Prison crowding: A psychological perspective.* New York: Springer-Verlag.

Paulus, P. B., Annis, A. B., Seta, J. J., Schkade, J. K., & Matthews, R. W. (1976). Density does affect task performance. *Journal of Personality and Social Psychology, 34,* 248–253.

Pelham, B. (1991). On confidence and consequence: The certainty and importance of self-knowledge. *Journal of Personality and Social Psychology, 60,* 518–530.

Pendleton, M. G., & Bateson, C. D. (1979). Self-presentation and the door-in-the-face technique for inducing compliance. *Personality and Social Psychology Bulletin, 5,* 77–81.

Pennebaker, J. W. (1989). Confession, inhibition, and disease. In L. Berkowitz (Ed.), *Advances in experimental social psychology* (Vol. 22, pp. 211–244). San Diego, CA: Academic Press.

Pennebaker, J. W. (1990). *Opening up: The healing power of confiding in others.* New York: Morrow.

Pennebaker, J. W., Kiecolt-Glaser, J. K., & Glaser, R. (1988). Disclosure of traumas and immune function: Health implications for psychotherapy. *Journal of Consulting and Clinical Psychology, 56,* 239–245.

Peplau, L. A., & Conrad, E. (1989). Beyond nonsexist research: The perils of feminist methods in psychology. *Psychology of Women Quarterly, 13,* 379–400.

Peplau, L. A., Rubin, Z., and Hill, C. T. (1977). Sexual intimacy in dating relationships. *Journal of Social Issues, 33,* 86–109.

Perdue, C. W., Dovidio, J. F., Gurtman, M. B., & Tyler, R. B. (1990). Us and them: Social categorization and the process of intergroup bias. *Journal of Personality and Social Psychology, 59,* 475–486.

Perry, D. G., Perry, L. C., & Rasmussen, P. (1986). Cognitive social learning mediators of aggression. *Child Development, 57,* 700–711.

Peterson, D. R. (1979). Assessing interpersonal relationships by means of interaction records. *Behavioral Assessment, 1,* 221–236.

Peterson, D. R. (1983). Conflict. In H. H. Kelley, E. Berscheid, A. Christensen, J. H. Harvey, T. L. Huston, G. Levinger, E. McClintock, L. A. Peplau, & D. R. Peterson (Eds.), *Close relationships* (pp. 360–396). San Francisco, CA: Freeman.

Peterson, R. A. (1977). Consumer perceptions as a function of product, color, price, and nutritional labeling. In W. D. Perrault (Ed.), *Advances in consumer research* (pp. 61–62). Atlanta, GA: Association for Consumer Research.

Pettigrew, T. F. (1958). Personality and sociocultural factors in intergroup attitudes: A cross-national comparison. *Journal of Conflict Resolution, 2,* 29–42.

Pettigrew, T. F. (1968). Race relations: Social and psychological aspects. In D. L. Sills (Ed.), *The international encyclopedia of the social sciences* (Vol. 13, pp. 277–282). New York: Macmillan Company.

Pettigrew, T. F. (1979). The ultimate attribution error: Extending Allport's cognitive analysis of prejudice. *Personality and Social Psychology Bulletin, 5,* 461–476.

Pettigrew, T. F. (1980). Prejudice. In S. Thernstrom (Ed.), *Harvard encyclopedia of American ethnic groups.* Cambridge, MA: Harvard University Press.

Pettigrew, T. F., & Martin, J. (1987). Shaping the organizational context for Black American inclusion. *Journal of Social Issues, 43,* 41–78.

Petty, R. E., & Cacioppo, J. T. (1977). Forewarning, cognitive responding, and resistance to persuasion. *Journal of Personality and Social Psychology, 35,* 645–655.

Petty, R. E., & Cacioppo, J. T. (1979). Effects of forewarning of persuasive intent and involvement on cognitive responses and persuasion. *Personality and Social Psychology Bulletin, 5,* 173–176.

Petty, R. E., & Cacioppo, J. T. (1981). *Attitudes and persuasion: Classic and contemporary approaches.* Dubuque, IA: Wm. C. Brown.

Petty, R. E., & Cacioppo, J. T. (1984). The effects of involvement on responses to argument quantity and quality: Central and peripheral routes to persuasion. *Journal of Personality and Social Psychology, 46,* 69–81.

Petty, R. E., & Cacioppo, J. T. (1986). *Communication and persuasion: Central and peripheral routes to attitude change.* New York: Springer-Verlag.

Petty, R. E., Cacioppo, J. T., & Goldman, R. (1981). Personal involvement as a determinant of argument-based persuasion. *Journal of Personality and Social Psychology, 41,* 847–855.

Petty, R. E., Cacioppo, J. T., Haugtvedt, C., & Heesacker, M. (1986). *Consequences of the route to persuasion: Persistence and resistance of attitude changes.* Unpublished manuscript, University of Missouri, Columbia, MO.

Petty, R. E., Cacioppo, J. T., & Schumann, D. (1983). Central and peripheral routes to advertising effectiveness: The moderating role of involvement. *Journal of Consumer Research, 10,* 134–148.

Petty, R. E., Schumann, D. W., Richman, S. A., & Strathman, A. J. (1993). Positive mood and persuasion: Different roles for affect under high- and low-elaboration conditions. *Journal of Personality and Social Psychology, 64,* 5–20.

Petty, R. E., Wells, G. L., & Brock, T. C. (1976). Distraction can enhance or reduce yielding to propaganda: Thought disruption versus effort justification. *Journal of Personality and Social Psychology, 34,* 874–884.

Pfau, M., & Burgoon, M. (1988). Inoculation in political campaign communication. *Human Communication Research, 15,* 91–111.

Pfau, M., Kenski, H. C., Nitz, M., & Sorensen, J. (1990). Efficacy of inoculation strategies in promoting resistance to political attack messages: Application to direct mail. *Communication Monographs, 57,* 25–43.

Phillips, A. P., & Dipboye, R. L. (1989). Correlational tests of predictions from a process model of the interview. *Journal of Applied Psychology, 74,* 41–52.

Phillips, D. P. (1983). The impact of mass media violence on U.S. homicides. *American Sociological Review, 48,* 560–568.

Piliavin, J. A., Callero, P. L., & Evans, D. E. (1982). Addiction to altruism? Opponent-process theory and habitual blood donation. *Journal of Personality and Social Psychology, 43,* 1200–1213.

Pines, A. M., Aronson, E. & Kafry, D. (1981). *Burnout: From tedium to personal growth.* New York: Freeman.

Pittman, T. S. (1975). Attribution of arousal as a mediator of dissonance reduction. *Journal of Experimental Social Psychology, 11,* 53–63.

Platz, S. J., & Hosch, H. M. (1988). Cross-racial/ethnic eyewitness identification: A field study. *Journal of Applied Social Psychology, 18,* 972–984.

Pleck, J. (1981). *The myth of masculinity.* Cambridge, MA: MIT Press.

Pranulis, M., Dabbs, J., & Johnson, J. (1975). General anesthesia and the patient's attempts at control. *Social Behavior and Personality, 3,* 49–54.

Pratkanis, A. R. (1984). *Attitudes and memory: The heuristic and schematic functions of attitudes.* Unpublished doctoral dissertation, Ohio State University, Columbus, OH.

Pratkanis, A. R. (1989). The attitude heuristic and selective fact identification. *British Journal of Social Psychology, 28,* 257–263.

Pratkanis, A. R., Greenwald, A. G., Leippe, M. R., & Baumgardner, M. H. (1988). In search of reliable persuasion effects: III. The sleeper effect is dead: Long live the sleeper effect. *Journal of Personality and Social Psychology, 54,* 203–218.

Prentice, D. A. (1990). Familiarity and differences in self- and other-representations. *Journal of Personality and Social Psychology, 59,* 369–383.

Prentice, D. A., & Miller, D. T. (1993). Pluralistic ignorance and alcohol use on campus: Some consequences of misperceiving the social norm. *Journal of Personality and Social Psychology, 64,* 243–256.

President's Commission on Law Enforcement and Administration of Justice (1967). *The challenge of crime in a free society.* Washington, DC: U.S. Government Printing Office.

Presidential Commission on the Space Shuttle Challenger Accident (1986, June 6). (W. Rodgers, Chair). *Report to the President.* Washington, DC: U.S. Government Printing Office.

President's Task Force on Victims of Crime. (1982). *Final report.* Washington, DC: U.S. Government Printing Office.

Price, J. M., & Dodge, K. A. (1989). Reactive and proactive aggression in childhood: Relations to peer status and social context dimensions. *Journal of Abnormal Child Psychology, 17,* 455–471.

Price, V. (1989). Social identification and public opinion: Effects of communicating group conflict. *Public Opinion Quarterly, 53,* 197–224.

Pruitt, D. G. (1981). *Negotiation behavior.* New York: Academic Press.

Pruitt, D. G. (1986). Achieving integrative agreements in negotiation. In R. K. White (Ed.), *Psychology and the prevention of nuclear war* (pp. 463–478). New York: New York University Press.

Pruitt, D. G., & Lewis, S. A. (1977). The psychology of integrative bargaining. In D. Druckman (Ed.), *Negotiations: A social-psychological analysis* (pp. 161–192). New York: Halstead.

Pruitt, D. G., & Rubin, J. Z. (1986). *Social conflict: Escalation, stalemate, and settlement.* New York: Random House.

Pryor, J. B., & Merluzzi, T. V. (1985). The role of expertise in processing social interaction scripts. *Journal of Experimental Social Psychology, 21,* 362–379.

Pyszczynski, T., & Greenberg, J. (1987). Self-regulatory perseveration and the depressive self-focusing style: A self-awareness theory of reactive depression. *Psychological Bulletin, 102,* 122–138.

Pyszczynski, T., Greenberg, J., & Holt, K. (1985). Maintaining consistency between self-serving beliefs and available data: A bias in information evaluation. *Personality and Social Psychology Bulletin, 11,* 179–190.

Quattrone, G. A., & Jones, E. E. (1980). The perception of variability within ingroups and outgroups: Implications for the law of small numbers. *Journal of Personality and Social Psychology, 38,* 141–152.

Quigley-Fernandez, B., & Tedeschi, J. T. (1978). The bogus pipeline as lie detector: Two validity studies. *Journal of Personality and Social Psychology, 36,* 247–256.

Quindlen, A. (1992, May 27). No closet space. *The New York Times,* p. A11.

Rabbie, J. M., & Bekkers, F. (1978). Threatened leadership and intergroup competition. *European Journal of Social Psychology, 8,* 9–20.

Radin, C. (1992, September 9). Colleges compete for high-achieving Black students. *The Boston Globe,* pp. 1, 19.

Rank, S. J., & Jacobsen, C. K. (1977). Hospital nurses' compliance with medication overdose orders: A failure to replicate. *Journal of Health and Social Behavior, 18,* 188–193.

Rapoport, A., & Eshed-Levy, D. (1989). Provision of step-level public goods: Effects of greed and fear of being gypped. *Organizational Behavior and Human Decision Processes, 44,* 325–344.

Rappaport, A., & Bornstein, G. (1987). Intergroup competition for the provision of binary public goods. *Psychological Review, 94,* 291–299.

Rasinski, K. A., Crocker, J., & Hastie, R. (1985). Another look at sex stereotypes and social judgments: An analysis of the social perceiver's use of subjective probabilities. *Journal of Personality and Social Psychology, 49,* 317–326.

Raven, B. H., & Rubin, J. Z. (1976). *Social psychology: People in groups.* New York: Wiley.

Razran, G. (1950). Ethnic dislikes and stereotypes: A laboratory study. *Journal of Abnormal and Social Psychology, 45,* 7–27.

Redfern, D. (1979). *Individual level and group level determinants of nurses' compliance with physicians' inappropriate medical orders.* Paper presented at the annual meeting of the American Psychological Association, New York.

Reeder, G. D., & Brewer, M. B. (1979). A schematic model of dispositional attribution in interpersonal perception. *Psychological Review, 86,* 61–79.

Regan, D. T. (1971). Effects of a favor and liking on compliance. *Journal of Experimental Social Psychology, 7,* 627–639.

Regan, D. T., & Kilduff, M. (1988). Optimism about elections: Dissonance reduction at the ballot box. *Political Psychology, 9,* 101–107.

Rehm, J., Steinleitner, J., & Lilli, W. (1987). Wearing uniforms and aggression: A field experiment. *European Journal of Social Psychology, 17,* 357–360.

Reicher, S. D. (1987). Crowd behavior as social action. In J. C. Turner, M. A. Hogg, P. J. Oakes, S. D. Reicher, & M. S. Wetherell (Eds.), *Rediscovering the social group: A self-categorization theory* (pp. 171–202). Oxford: Blackwell.

Reid, F. J. M. (1983). Polarizing effects of intergroup comparison. *European Journal of Social Psychology, 13,* 103–106.

Reis, H. T. (1986). Gender effects in social participation: Intimacy, loneliness, and the conduct of social interaction. In R. Gilmour & S. Duck (Eds.), *The emerging field of personal relationships* (pp. 91–108). Hillsdale, NJ: Erlbaum.

Reis, H. T., Senchak, M., & Solomon, B. (1985). Sex differences in the intimacy of social interaction. *Journal of Personality and Social Psychology, 48,* 1204–1217.

Reis, H. T., & Shaver, P. (1988). Intimacy as an interpersonal process. In S. Duck (Ed.), *Handbook of personal relationships: Theory, relationships, and interventions* (pp. 367–389). Chichester, England: Wiley.

Reisenzein, R. (1983). The Schacter theory of emotion: Two decades later. *Psychological Bulletin, 94,* 239–264.

Reisenzein, R. (1986). A structural equation analysis of Weiner's attribution-affect model of helping behavior. *Journal of Personality and Social Psychology, 50,* 1123–1133.

Reiss, I. L. (1986). A sociological journey into sexuality. *Journal of Marriage and the Family, 48,* 233–242.

Reiss, I. L., & Lee, G. R. (1988). *Family systems in America* (4th ed.). New York: Holt, Rinehart, & Winston.

Reychler, L. (1979). The effectiveness of a pacifist strategy in conflict resolution: An experimental study. *Journal of Conflict Resolution, 23,* 288–260.

Rhodewalt, F., & Agustsdottir, S. (1986). Effects of self-presentation on the phenomenal self. *Journal of Personality and Social Psychology, 50,* 47–55.

Rholes, W. S., & Pryor, J. B. (1982). Cognitive accessibility and causal attributions. *Personality and Social Psychology Bulletin, 8,* 719–727.

Ridgeway, J. (1991, April 28). A meeting with haters. *Parade,* p. 5.

Ringelmann, M. (1913). Recherches sur les moteurs animés: Travail de l'homme. *Annales de l'Institut National Agronomique,* 2e série, tom 12, 1–40.

Robberson, M. R., & Rogers, R. W. (1988). Beyond fear appeals: Negative and positive persuasive appeals to health and self-esteem. *Journal of Applied Social Psychology, 18,* 277–287.

Robertson, I. (1980). *Social problems* (2nd ed.). New York: Random House.

Robinson, J., & McArthur, L. Z. (1982). Impact of salient vocal qualities on causal attribution for a speaker's behavior. *Journal of Personality and Social Psychology, 43,* 236–247.

Robinson, R., & Bell, W. (1978). Equality, success, and social justice in England and the United States. *American Sociological Review, 43,* 125–143.

Rodin, J. (1985). The application of social psychology. In G. Lindzey & E. Aronson (Eds.), *Handbook of social psychology* (3rd ed.; Vol. 2, pp. 805–882). New York: Random House.

Rodin, J., & Langer, E. J. (1977). Long-term effects of a control-relevant intervention with the institutionalized aged. *Journal of Personality and Social Psychology, 35,* 897–902.

Rodin, J., & Salovey, P. (1989). Health psychology. *Annual Review of Psychology, 40,* 533–579.

Rodin, J., Solomon, S., & Metcalf, J. (1978). Role of control in mediating perceptions of density. *Journal of Personality and Social Psychology, 36,* 988–999.

Rodin, M. J. (1987). Who is memorable to whom: A study of cognitive disregard. *Social Cognition, 5,* 144–165.

Roethlisberger, F. J., & Dickson, W. J. (1939). *Management and the worker.* Cambridge, MA: Harvard University Press.

Rofé, Y. (1984). Stress and affiliation: Activity theory. *Psychological Review, 91,* 235–250.

Rogers, R. W. (1983). Cognitive and physiological processes in fear appeals and attitude change: A revised theory of protection motivation. In J. T. Cacioppo & R. E. Petty (Eds.), *Social psychophysiology: A sourcebook.* New York: Guilford Press.

Rogers, R. W., Deckner, C. W., & Mewborn, C. R. (1978). An expectancy-value theory approach to the long-term modification of smoking behavior. *Journal of Clinical Psychology, 34,* 562–566.

Rogers, R. W., & Mewborn, R. (1976). Fear appeals and attitude change: Effects of a threat's noxiousness, probability of occurrence, and the efficacy of coping responses. *Journal of Personality and Social Psychology, 34,* 54–61.

Rogers, R. W., & Prentice-Dunn, S. (1981). Deindividuation and anger-mediated interracial aggression: Unmasking regressive racism. *Journal of Personality and Social Psychology, 41,* 63–73.

Rogers, T. B. (1981). A model of the self as an aspect of the human information processing system. In N. Cantor & J. F. Kihlstrom (Eds.), *Personality, cognition, and social interaction* (pp. 193–214). Hillsdale, NJ: Erlbaum.

Rohrer, J. H., Baron, S. H., Hoffman, E. L., & Schwander, D. V. (1954). The stability of autokinetic judgments. *Journal of Abnormal and Social Psychology, 49,* 595–597.

Ronis, D. L., & Kaiser, M. K. (1989). Correlates of breast self-examination in a sample of college women: Analyses of linear structural relations. *Journal of Applied Social Psychology, 19,* 1068–1084.

Rook, K. S. (1987). Social support versus companionship: Effects on life stress, loneliness, and evaluations by others. *Journal of Personality and Social Psychology, 52,* 1132–1147.

Rook, K. S., & Peplau, L. A. (1982). Perspectives on helping the lonely. In L. A. Peplau & D. Perlman (Eds.), *Loneliness* (pp. 351–378). New York: Wiley Interscience.

Rook, K. S., & Pietromonaco, P. (1987). Close relationship: Ties that heal or ties that bind? In W. H. Jones & D. Perlman (Eds.), *Advances in personal relationships* (Vol. 1, pp. 1–35). Greenwich, CT: JAI Press.

Roseman, I. J., Spindel, M. S., & Jose, P. E. (1990). Appraisals of emotion-eliciting events: Testing a theory of discrete emotions. *Journal of Personality and Social Psychology, 59,* 899–915.

Rosenbaum, M. E. (1986). The repulsion hypothesis: On the nondevelopment of relationships. *Journal of Personality and Social Psychology, 51,* 1156–1166.

Rosenberg, M. (1956). Cognitive structure and attitudinal affect. *Journal of Abnormal and Social Psychology, 53,* 367–372.

Rosenberg, M. (1965). *Society and the adolescent self-image.* Princeton, NJ: Princeton University Press.

Rosenberg, M. (1969). The conditions and consequences of evaluation apprehension. In R. Rosenthal & R. L. Rosnow (Eds.), *Artifact in behavioral research* (pp. 279–349). New York: Academic Press.

Rosenberg, M. (1979). *Conceiving the self.* New York: Basic Books.

Rosenberg, M., & Simmons, R. B. (1971). *Black & White self-esteem: The urban school child.* Washington, DC: The American Sociological Association.

Rosenberg, S., Nelson, C., & Vivekananthan, P. S. (1968). A multidimensional approach to the structure of personality impressions. *Journal of Personality and Social Psychology, 9,* 283–294.

Rosenfeld, P., Giacalone, R., & Tedeschi, J. T. (1984). Cognitive dissonance and impression management explanations for effort justification. *Personality and Social Psychology Bulletin, 10,* 394–401.

Rosenfield, D., and Stephan, W. G. (1981). Intergroup relations among children. In S. Brehm, S. Kassin, & F. Gibbons (Eds.), *Developmental social psychology* (pp. 271–297). New York: Oxford University Press.

Rosenhan, D. (1970). The natural socialization of altruistic autonomy. In J. Macaulay & L. Berkowitz (Eds.), *Altruism and helping behavior* (pp. 251–268). New York: Academic Press.

Rosenhan, D. L. (1973). On being sane in insane places. *Science, 179,* 250–258.

Rosenthal, R. (1969). Interpersonal expectations: Effects of the experimenter's hypothesis. In R. Rosenthal & R. L. Rosnow (Eds.), *Artifact in behavioral research* (pp. 181–277). New York: Academic Press.

Rosenthal, R. (1985). From unconscious experimenter bias to teacher expectancy effects. In J. B. Dusek, V. C. Hall, & W. J. Meyer (Eds.), *Teacher expectancies* (pp. 37–65). Hillsdale, NJ: Erlbaum.

Rosenthal, R. (1991). Meta-analysis: A review. *Psychosomatic Medicine, 53,* 247–271.

Rosenthal, R., & Fode, K. L. (1963). Three experiments in experimenter bias. *Psychological Reports, 12,* 491–511.

Rosenthal, R., & Jacobson, L. (1968). *Pygmalion in the classroom.* New York: Holt, Rinehart, & Winston.

Rosnow, R. L., & Fine, G. A. (1976). *Rumor and gossip: The social psychology of hearsay.* New York: Elsevier.

Ross, E. A. (1908). *Social psychology: An outline and source book.* New York: Macmillan.

Ross, L., Lepper, M. R., & Hubbard, M. (1975). Perseverance in self-perception and social perception: Biased attributional processes in the debriefing paradigm. *Journal of Personality and Social Psychology, 32,* 880–892.

Ross, L., & Nisbett, R. E. (1990). *The person and the situation: Perspectives of social psychology.* New York: McGraw-Hill.

Ross, M. (1989). The relation of implicit theories to the construction of personal histories. *Psychological Review, 96,* 341–357.

Ross, M., & Conway, M. (1986). Remembering one's own past: The construction of personal histories. In R. Sorrentino & E. T. Higgins (Eds.), *Handbook of motivation and cognition* (pp. 122–144). New York: Guilford Press.

Ross, M., McFarland, C., & Fletcher, G. J. O. (1981). The effect of attitude on recall of past histories. *Journal of Personality and Social Psychology, 40,* 627–634.

Ross, M., & Sicoly, F. (1979). Egocentric biases in availability and attribution. *Journal of Personality and Social Psychology, 37,* 322–336.

Ross, S. I., & Jackson, J. M. (1991). Teachers' expectations for Black males' and Black females' academic achievement. *Personality and Social Psychology Bulletin, 17,* 78–82.

Rossiter, M. W. (1982). *Women scientists in America.* Baltimore, MD: Johns Hopkins University Press.

Rothbart, M. (1981). Memory processes and social beliefs. In D. L. Hamilton (Ed.), *Cognitive processes in stereotyping and intergroup behavior* (pp. 145–182). Hillsdale, NJ: Erlbaum.

Rothbart, M., Dawes, R., & Park. B. (1984). Stereotyping and sampling biases in intergroup perception. In J. R. Eiser (Ed.), *Attitudinal judgment* (pp. 109–134). New York: Springer-Verlag.

Rothbart, M., Evans, M., & Fulero, S. (1979). Recall for confirming events: Memory processes and the maintenance of social stereotyping. *Journal of Experimental Social Psychology, 15,* 343–355.

Rothbart, M., Fulero, S., Jensen, C., Howard, J., & Birrel, P. (1978). From individual to group impressions: Availability heuristics in stereotype formation. *Journal of Experimental Social Psychology, 14,* 237–255.

Rothbart, M., & Hallmark, W. (1988). In-group–out-group differences in the perceived efficacy of coercion and conciliation in resolving social conflict. *Journal of Personality and Social Psychology, 55,* 248–257.

Rothbart, M., & John, O. P. (1985). Social categorization and behavioral episodes: A cognitive analysis of the effects of intergroup contact. *Journal of Social Issues, 41,* 81–104.

Rothenberg, R. (1991, July 23). Blacks are found to be still scarce in advertisements in major magazines. *The New York Times,* p. A7.

Ruback, R. B., & Pandey, J. (1991). Crowding, perceived control, and relative power: An analysis of households in India. *Journal of Applied Social Psychology, 21,* 315–344.

Rubenstein, C. M., Shaver, P., & Peplau, L. A. (1979). Loneliness. *Human Nature, 2,* 58–65.

Rubin, B. (1987). *Third World coup makers, strongmen, and populist tyrants.* New York: McGraw-Hill.

Rubin, J. Z. (1980). Experimental research on third-party intervention in conflict: Toward some generalizations. *Psychological Bulletin, 87,* 379–391.

Rubin, J. Z., & Brown, B. R. (1975). *The social psychology of bargaining and negotiation.* New York: Academic Press.

Rubin, Z., Hill, C. T., Peplau, L. A., & Dunkel-Schetter, C. (1980). Self-disclosure in dating couples: Sex roles and the ethic of openness. *Journal of Marriage and the Family, 42,* 305–317.

Rule, B. G., Taylor, B. R., & Dobbs, A. R. (1987). Priming effects of heat on aggressive thoughts. *Social Cognition, 5,* 131–143.

Runciman, W. G. (1966). *Relative deprivation and social justice.* Berkeley, CA: University of California Press.

Rusbult, C. E. (1983). A longitudinal test of the investment model: The development (and deterioration) of satisfaction and commitment in heterosexual involvements. *Journal of Personality and Social Psychology, 45,* 101–117.

Rusbult, C. E., Verette, J., Whitney, G. A., Slovik, L. F., & Lipkus, I. (1991). Accommodation processes in close relationships: Theory and preliminary empirical evidence. *Journal of Personality and Social Psychology, 60,* 53–78.

Rushton, J. P. (1975). Generosity in children: Immediate and long-term effects of modeling, preaching, and moral judgment. *Journal of Personality and Social Psychology, 31,* 459–466.

Ruskin, J. (1907/1963). *The seven lamps of architecture.* London: Everyman's Library.

Rutter, D. R., & Robinson, B. (1981). An experimental analysis of teaching by telephone. In G. M. Stephenson & J. H. Davis (Eds.), *Progress in applied social psychology* (pp. 345–373). New York: Wiley.

Ryan, R. M., & Grolnick, W. S. (1986). Origins and pawns in the classroom: Self-report and projective assessments of individual differences in children's perceptions. *Journal of Personality and Social Psychology, 50,* 550–558.

Ryen, A. H., & Kahn, A. (1975). The effects of intergroup orientation on group attitudes and proxemic behavior. *Journal of Personality and Social Psychology, 31,* 302–310.

Sachdev, I., & Bourhis, R. Y. (1985). Social categorization and power differentials in group relations. *European Journal of Social Psychology, 15,* 415–434.

Sachdev, I., & Bourhis, R. Y. (1991). Power and status differentials in minority and majority group relations. *European Journal of Social Psychology, 21,* 1–24.

Safire, W. (1992, August 27). God bless us. *The New York Times,* p. A15.

Sagar, H. A., & Schofield, J. W. (1980). Racial and behavioral cues in Black and White children's perceptions of ambiguously aggressive acts. *Journal of Personality and Social Psychology, 39,* 590–598.

Salancik, G. R., & Conway, M. (1975). Attitude inference from salient and relevant cognitive content about behavior. *Journal of Personality and Social Psychology, 32,* 829–840.

Salovey, P., & Rodin, J. (1984). Some antecedents and consequences of social-comparison jealousy. *Journal of Personality and Social Psychology, 47,* 780–792.

Salovey, P., & Rodin, J. (1989). Envy and jealousy in close relationships. In C. Hendrick (Ed.), *Close relationships* (pp. 221–246). Beverly Hills, CA: Sage Publications.

Samuelson, C. D., Messick, D. M., Rutte, C. G., & Wilke, H. (1984). Individual and structural solutions to resource dilemmas in two cultures. *Journal of Personality and Social Psychology, 47,* 94–104.

Sande, G. N., Goethals, G. R., & Radloff, C. E. (1988). Perceiving one's own traits and others': The multifaceted self. *Journal of Personality and Social Psychology, 54,* 13–20.

Sanitioso, R., Kunda, Z., & Fong, G. T. (1990). Motivated recruitment of autobiographical memory. *Journal of Personality and Social Psychology, 59,* 229–241.

Sanna, L. J., & Shotland, R. L. (1990). Valence of anticipated evaluation and social facilitation. *Journal of Experimental Social Psychology, 26,* 82–92.

Santa Barbara News Press. (1990, December 25). East Germans open homes to Soviet army troops.

Santa Barbara News Press. (1992, March 12). One-day nerd surprised by some reactions, p. A5.

Sarason, B. R., Shearin, E. N., Pierce, G. R., & Sarason, I. G. (1987). Interrelations of social support measures: Theoretical and practical implications. *Journal of Personality and Social Psychology, 52,* 813–832.

Sato, K. (1987). Distribution of the cost of maintaining common resources. *Journal of Experimental Social Psychology, 23,* 19–31.

Sattler, D. N., & Kerr, N. L. (1991). Might versus morality explored: Motivational and cognitive bases for social motives. *Journal of Personality and Social Psychology, 60,* 756–765.

Saxe, L., Dougherty, D., & Cross, T. (1985). The validity of polygraph testing: Scientific analysis and public controversy. *American Psychologist, 40,* 355–366.

Schachter, S. (1951). Deviation, rejection, and communication. *Journal of Abnormal and Social Psychology, 46,* 190–207.

Schachter, S. (1959). *The psychology of affiliation.* Stanford, CA: Stanford University Press.

Schachter, S., Ellertson, N., McBride, D., & Gregory, D. (1951). An experimental study of cohesiveness and productivity. *Human Relations, 4,* 229–238.

Schachter, S., & Singer, J. (1962). Cognitive, social, and physiological determinants of the emotional state. *Psychological Review, 69,* 379–399.

Schaller, M., & Cialdini, R. B. (1988). The economics of empathic helping: Support for a mood management motive. *Journal of Experimental Social Psychology, 24,* 163–181.

Schaller, M., & Cialdini, R. B. (1990). Happiness, sadness, and helping: A motivational integration. In E. T. Higgins & R. M. Sorrentino (Eds.), *Handbook of motivation and cognition* (Vol. 2, pp. 265–296). New York: Guilford.

Scheier, M. F., & Carver, C. S. (1977). Self-focused attention and the experience of emotion: Attraction, repulsion, elation, and depression. *Journal of Personality and Social Psychology, 35,* 625–636.

Schein, E. H. (1956). The Chinese indoctrination program for prisoners of war: A study of attempted brainwashing. *Psychiatry, 19,* 149–172.

Scher, S., & Cooper, J. (1989). Motivational basis of dissonance: The singular role of behavioral consequences. *Journal of Personality and Social Psychology, 56,* 899–906.

Scherer, K. R. (1988). Cognitive antecedents of emotion. In V. Hamilton, G. H. Bower, & N. H. Frijda (Eds.), *Cognitive perspectives on emotion and motivation* (pp. 89–126). Dordrecht, The Netherlands: Kluwer.

Schiller, J. C. F. (1882). *Essays, esthetical and philosophical, including the dissertation on the "Connexions between the animal and the spiritual in man."* London: Bell.

Schlenker, B. R. (1982). Translating actions into attitudes: An identity-analytic approach to the explanation of social conduct. In L. Berkowitz (Ed.), *Advances in experimental social psychology* (Vol. 15, pp. 193–247). New York: Academic Press.

Schlenker, B. R. (1985). Identity and self-identification. In B. R. Schlenker (Ed.), *The self and social life* (pp. 65–100). New York: McGraw-Hill.

Schlenker, B. R., & Forsyth, D. R. (1977). On the ethics of psychological research. *Journal of Experimental Social Psychology, 13,* 369–396.

Schmalz, J. (1992, October 11). Gay politics goes mainstream. *The New York Times Magazine,* pp. 18–21, 29, 41.

Schmidt, G., & Weiner, B. (1988). An attribution-affect-action theory of behavior: Replications of judgments of help-giving. *Personality and Social Psychology Bulletin, 14,* 610–621.

Schmidt, W. E. (1990, December 13). White men get better deals on cars, study finds. *The New York Times.*

Schmitt, B. H., Gilovich, T., Goore, N., & Joseph, L. (1986). Mere presence and social facilitation: One more time. *Journal of Experimental Social Psychology, 22,* 242–248.

Schmutte, G. T., & Taylor, S. P. (1980). Physical aggression as a function of alcohol and pain feedback. *Journal of Social Psychology, 110,* 235–244.

Schneider, D. J. (1973). Implicit personality theory: A review. *Psychological Bulletin, 79,* 294–309.

Schoeneman, T. J., & Rubanowitz, D. E. (1985). Attributions in the advice columns: Actors and observers, causes and reasons. *Personality and Social Psychology Bulletin, 11,* 315–325.

Schoenrade, P. A., Batson, C. D., & Brandt, J. R. (1986). Attachment, accountability, and motivation to benefit another not in distress. *Journal of Personality and Social Psychology, 51,* 557–563.

Schofield, J. (1978). School desegregation and intergroup relations. In D. Bar-Tal & L. Saxe (Eds.), *Social psychology of education: Theory and research* (pp. 329–364). New York: Wiley.

Schofield, J. W. (1982). *Black and White in school: Trust, tension, or tolerance?* New York: Yaeger.

Schopler, J., Insko, C. A., Graetz, K. A., Drigotas, S., Smith, V. A., & Dahl, K. (1993). Individual-group discontinuity: Further evidence for mediation by fear and greed. *Personality and Social Psychology Bulletin, 19,* 419–431.

Schuman, H., & Johnson, M. P. (1976). Attitudes and behavior. *Annual Review of Sociology, 2,* 161–207.

Schuster, J. R. (1985, May). Compensation plan design. *Management Review, 74,* 21–25.

Schwartz, S. H. (1977). Normative influences on altruism. In L. Berkowitz (Ed.), *Advances in experimental social psychology* (Vol. 10, pp. 221–279). New York: Academic Press.

Schwartz, S. H., & Gottlieb, A. (1980). Bystander anonymity and reaction to emergencies. *Journal of Personality and Social Psychology, 39,* 418–430.

Schwarz, N., Bless, H., & Bohner, G. (1991). Mood and persuasion: Affective states influence processing of persuasive communications. In M. P. Zanna (Ed.), *Advances in experimental social psychology* (Vol. 24, pp. 161–199). San Diego, CA: Academic Press.

Schwarz, N., & Clore, G. L. (1983). Mood, misattribution, and judgments of well-being: Informative and directive functions of affective states. *Journal of Personality and Social Psychology, 45,* 513–523.

Schwarz, N., & Clore, G. L. (1988). How do I feel about it? Informative functions of affective states. In K. Fiedler & J. Forgas (Eds.), *Affect, cognition, and social behavior* (pp. 44–62). Toronto: Hogrefe.

Schwarzer, R., & Leppin, A. (1989). Social support and health: A meta-analysis. *Psychology and Health, 3,* 1–15.

Schwarzwald, J., Bizman, A., & Raz, M. (1983). The foot-in-the-door paradigm: Effects of second request size on donation probability and donor generosity. *Personality and Social Psychology Bulletin, 9,* 69–79.

Schwarzwald, J., Raz, M., & Zvibel, M. (1979). The efficacy of the door-in-the-face technique when established behavioral customs exist. *Journal of Applied Social Psychology, 9,* 576–586.

Sears, D. O. (1988). Symbolic racism. In P. Katz & D. Taylor (Eds.), *Eliminating racism: Profiles in controversy* (pp. 53–84). New York: Plenum.

Sears, D. O., & Allen, H. M., Jr. (1984). The trajectory of local desegregation controversies and Whites' opposition to busing. In N. Miller & M. Brewer (Eds.), *Groups in contact: The psychology of desegregation* (pp. 123–151). New York: Academic Press.

Sears, D. O., & Kinder, D. R. (1985). Whites' opposition to busing: On conceptualizing and operationalizing group conflict. *Journal of Personality and Social Psychology, 48,* 1141–1147.

Sears, D. O., & McConahay, J. B. (1973). *The politics of violence: The new urban blacks and the Watts riot.* Boston: Houghton Mifflin.

Seashore, S. E. (1954). *Group cohesiveness in the industrial work group.* Ann Arbor, MI: Institute for Social Research.

Sedek, G., & Kofta, M. (1990). When cognitive exertion does not yield cognitive gain: Toward an informational explanation of learned helplessness. *Journal of Personality and Social Psychology, 58,* 729–743.

Sedikides, C. (1990). Effects of fortuitously activated constructs versus activated communication goals on person impressions. *Journal of Personality and Social Psychology, 58,* 397–408.

Segal, H. A. (1954). Initial psychiatric findings of recently repatriated prisoners of war. *American Journal of Psychiatry, 61,* 358–363.

Segal, M. W. (1974). Alphabet and attraction: An unobtrusive measure of the effect of propinquity in a field setting. *Journal of Personality and Social Psychology, 30,* 654–657.

Seligman, C. L., Becker, J., & Darley, J. M. (1981). Encouraging residential energy conservation through feedback. In A. Baum & J. Singer (Eds.), *Advances in environmental psychology* (Vol. 3, pp. 53–91). Hillsdale, NJ: Erlbaum.

Seligman, M. E. P. (1975). *On depression, development, and death.* San Francisco: Freeman.

Seligman, M. E. P., & Maier, S. F. (1967). Failure to escape traumatic shock. *Journal of Experimental Psychology, 74,* 1–9.

Senneker, P., & Hendrick, C. (1983). Androgyny and helping behavior. *Journal of Personality and Social Psychology, 45,* 916–925.

Shanab, M. E., & Yahra, K. A. (1977). A behavioral study of obedience in children. *Journal of Personality and Social Psychology, 35,* 530–536.

Shanab, M. E., & Yahra, K. A. (1978). A cross-cultural study of obedience. *Bulletin of the Psychonomic Society, 11,* 267–269.

Sharan, S., & Sharan, Y. (1976). *Small group teaching.* Englewood Cliffs, NJ: Educational Technology.

Shaver, P., & Hazan, C. (1985). Incompatibility, loneliness, and "limerence." In W. Ickes (Ed.), *Compatible and incompatible relationships* (pp. 163–186). New York: Springer-Verlag.

Shaver, P., & Hazan, C. (1988). A biased overview of the study of love. *Journal of Social and Personal Relationships, 5,* 473–501.

Shaver, P., Hazan, C., & Bradshaw, D. (1988). Love as attachment: The integration of three behavioral systems. In R. Sternberg & M. Barnes (Eds.), *The psychology of love* (pp. 68–99). New Haven, CT: Yale University Press.

Shaver, P., Schwartz, J., Kirson, D., & O'Connor, C. (1987). Emotion knowledge: Further exploration of a prototype approach. *Journal of Personality and Social Psychology, 52,* 1061–1086.

Shavitt, S. (1990). The role of attitude objects in attitude functions. *Journal of Experimental Social Psychology, 26,* 124–148.

Shaw, M. E. (1954). Some effects of unequal distribution of information upon group performance in various communication nets. *Journal of Abnormal and Social Psychology, 49,* 547–553.

Shaw, M. E. (1976). Group dynamics: *The psychology of small group behavior* (2nd ed.). New York: McGraw-Hill.

Sheppard, B. M., Hartwick, J., & Warshaw, P. (1988). The theory of reasoned action: A meta-analysis of past research with recommendations for modifications and future research. *Journal of Consumer Research, 15,* 325–343.

Sherif, C. W. (1979). Bias in psychology. In J. A. Sherman & E. T. Beck (Eds.), *The prism of sex: Essays in the sociology of knowledge* (pp. 93–133). Madison, WI: University of Wisconsin Press.

Sherif, M. (1936). *The psychology of social norms.* New York: Harper.

Sherif, M. (1966). *In common predicament: Social psychology of intergroup conflict and cooperation.* Boston: Houghton Mifflin.

Sherif, M., Harvey, O. J., White, B. J., Hood, W. E., & Sherif, C. W. (1961). *Intergroup conflict and cooperation: The Robbers Cave experiment.* Norman, OK: University of Oklahoma Press/Book Exchange.

Sherif, M., & Sherif, C. W. (1953). *Groups in harmony and tension.* New York: Harper.

Sherman, L. W., & Berk, R. A. (1984). The specific deterrent effects of arrest for domestic assault. *American Sociological Review, 49,* 261–272.

Sherman, P. W. (1977). Nepotism and the evolution of alarm calls. *Science, 197,* 1246–1253.

Sherman, S. J. (1980). On the self-erasing nature of errors of prediction. *Journal of Personality and Social Psychology, 39,* 211–221.

Sherman, S. J., Chassin, L., Presson, C. C., & Agostinelli, G. (1984). The role of the evaluation and similarity principles in the false consensus effect. *Journal of Personality and Social Psychology, 47,* 1244–1262.

Sherrod, D. (1974). Crowding, perceived control, and behavioral aftereffects. *Journal of Applied Social Psychology, 4,* 171–186.

Shils, E. A., & Janowitz, M. (1948). Cohesion and disintegration in the Wehrmacht in World War II. *Public Opinion Quarterly, 12,* 280–315.

Shopland, D. R., & Brown, C. (1987). Toward the 1990 objectives for smoking: Measuring the progress with 1985 NHIS data. *Public Health Reports, 102,* 68–73.

Shotland, R. L., & Heinold, W. D. (1985). Bystander response to arterial bleeding: Helping skills, the decision-making process, and differentiating the helping response. *Journal of Personality and Social Psychology, 49,* 347–356.

Shotland, R. L., & Straw, M. K. (1976). Bystander response to an assault: When a man attacks a woman. *Journal of Personality and Social Psychology, 34,* 990–999.

Siegel, M. (1983). Crime and violence in America: The victims. *American Psychologist, 38,* 1267–1273.

Silka, L. (1989). *Intuitive judgments of change.* New York: Springer-Verlag.

Silver, M., & Geller, D. (1978). On the irrelevance of evil: The organization and individual action. *Journal of Social Issues, 34,* 125–136.

Silverstein, L. (1965). *Defense of the poor in criminal cases in American state courts.* Chicago: American Bar Foundation.

Simmel, G. (1950). *The sociology of Georg Simmel.* New York: Free Press.

Simmonds, D. B. (1985). The nature of the organizational grapevine. *Supervisory Management, 30,* 39–42.

Simon, B., & Brown, R. (1987). Perceived homogeneity in minority-majority contexts. *Journal of Personality and Social Psychology, 53,* 703–711.

Simon, B., & Hamilton, D. L. (in press). Self-stereotyping and social context: The effects of relative in-group size and in-group status. *Journal of Personality and Social Psychology.*

Simon, H. A. (1990). A mechanism for social selection and successful altruism. *Science, 250,* 1665–1668.

Simons, M. (1992, March 17). North-South chasm is threatening search for environmental solutions. *The New York Times*, p. A5.

Simpson, J. A. (1987). The dissolution of romantic relationships: Factors involved in relationship stability and emotional distress. *Journal of Personality and Social Psychology, 53*, 683–692.

Simpson, J. A. (1990). Influence of attachment styles on romantic relationships. *Journal of Personality and Social Psychology, 59*, 971–980.

Simpson, J. A., Campbell, B., & Berscheid, E. (1986). The association between romantic love and marriage: Kephart (1967) twice revisited. *Personality and Social Psychology Bulletin, 12*, 363–372.

Simpson, J. A., & Gangestad, S. W. (1991). Personality and sexuality: Empirical relations and an integrative theoretical model. In K. McKinney & S. Sprecher (Eds.), *Sexuality in close relationships* (pp. 71–92). Hillsdale, NJ: Erlbaum.

Simpson, J. A., Gangestad, S. W., & Lerma, M. (1990). Perception of physical attractiveness: Mechanisms involved in the maintenance of romantic relationships. *Journal of Personality and Social Psychology, 59*, 1192–1201.

Simpson, J. A., Rholes, W. S., & Nelligan, J. S. (1992). Support seeking and support giving within couples in an anxiety-provoking situation: The role of attachment styles. *Journal of Personality and Social Psychology, 62*, 434–446.

Sinclair, R. C., Mark, M. M., & Clore, G. L. (1991). *Mood, misattribution, and persuasion: The informational impact of mood on processing strategy.* Unpublished manuscript, University of Alberta, Canada.

Singer, J. L., & Singer, D. G. (1981). *Television, imagination, and aggression: A study of preschoolers.* Hillsdale, NJ: Erlbaum.

Singleton, R., Jr. (1979). Another look at the conformity explanation of group-induced shifts in choice. *Human Relations, 32*, 37–56.

Skaalvik, E. M. (1986). Sex differences in global self-esteem. *Scandinavian Journal of Educational Research, 30*, 167–179.

Skinner, M., & Stephenson, G. M. (1987). The effects of intergroup comparison on the polarization of opinions. *Current Psychological Research, 1*, 49–61.

Skitka, L. J., McMurray, P. J., & Burroughs, T. E. (1991). Willingness to provide post-war aid to Iraq and Kuwait: An application of the contingency model of distributive justice. *Contemporary Social Psychology, 15*, 179–188.

Skowronski, J. J., & Carlston, D. E. (1989). Negativity and extremity biases in impression formation: A review of explanations. *Psychological Bulletin, 105*, 131–142.

Slavin, R. E. (1980). Cooperative learning. *Review of Educational Research, 50*, 315–342.

Smith, E. R. (1977). Single-sex colleges and sex-typing. *Journal of Social Issues, 33*, 197–199.

Smith, E. R. (1991). Illusory correlation in a simulated exemplar-based memory. *Journal of Experimental Social Psychology, 27*, 107–123.

Smith, E. R. (1993). Social identity and social emotions: Toward new conceptualizations of prejudice. In D. M. Mackie & D. L. Hamilton (Eds.), *Affect, cognition, and stereotyping: Interactive processes in group perception* (pp. 297–315). San Diego, CA: Academic Press.

Smith, E. R., & Kluegel, J. R. (1982). Cognitive and social bases of emotional experience: Outcome, attribution, and affect. *Journal of Personality and Social Psychology, 43*, 1129–1141.

Smith, E. R., & Miller, F. D. (1979). Salience and the cognitive mediation of attribution. *Journal of Personality and Social Psychology, 37*, 2240–2252.

Smith, E. R., & Zárate, M. A. (1992). Exemplar-based model of social judgment. *Psychological Review, 99*, 3–21.

Smith, L. (1949). *Killers of the dream.* New York: W. W. Norton.

Smith, M. B., Bruner, J. S., & White, R. W. (1956). *Opinions and personality.* New York: Wiley.

Smith, P. B., & Bond, M. H. (1993). *Across cultures.* Boston, MA: Allyn & Bacon.

Smith, P. B., & Tayeb, M. (1989). Organizational structure and processes. In M. Bond (Ed.), *The cross-cultural challenge to social psychology* (pp. 153–164). Newbury Park, CA: Sage Publications.

Smith, R. E., Vanderbilt, K., & Callen, M. B. (1973). Social comparison and bystander intervention in emergencies. *Journal of Applied Social Psychology, 3*, 186–196.

Smith, S. S., & Richardson, D. (1983). Amelioration of deception and harm in psychological research: The important role of debriefing. *Journal of Personality and Social Psychology, 44*, 1075–1082.

Smith, T. W. (1990). Report: The sexual revolution? *Public Opinion Quarterly, 54*, 415–435.

Smith, W. P., & Anderson, A. J. (1975). Threats, communication, and bargaining. *Journal of Personality and Social Psychology, 32*, 76–82.

Smyth, M. M., & Fuller, R. G. C. (1972). *Across cultures.* Boston, MA: Allyn & Bacon.

Snyder, C. R., & Higgins, R. L. (1988). Excuses: Their effective role in the negotiation of reality. *Psychological Bulletin, 104*, 23–35.

Snyder, C. R., Lassegard, M. A., & Ford, C. E. (1986). Distancing after group success and failure: Basking in reflected glory and cutting off reflected failure. *Journal of Personality and Social Psychology, 51*, 382–388.

Snyder, C. R., Smith, T. W., Augelli, R. W., & Ingram, R. E. (1985). On the self-serving function of social anxiety: Shyness as a self-handicapping strategy. *Journal of Personality and Social Psychology, 48,* 970–980.

Snyder, M. (1974). The self-monitoring of expressive behavior. *Journal of Personality and Social Psychology, 30,* 526–537.

Snyder, M. (1982). When believing means doing: Creating links between attitudes and behavior. In M. Zanna, E. T. Higgins, & C. P. Herman (Eds.), *Consistency in social behavior: The Ontario Symposium* (Vol. 2, pp. 105–130). Hillsdale, NJ: Erlbaum.

Snyder, M., Berscheid, E., & Glick, P. (1985). Focusing on the exterior and the interior: Two investigations of the initiation of personal relationships. *Journal of Personality and Social Psychology, 48,* 1427–1439.

Snyder, M., Berscheid, E., & Matwuchuk, A. (1988). Orientations toward personnel selection: Differential reliance on appearance and personality. *Journal of Personality and Social Psychology, 54,* 972–979.

Snyder, M., & DeBono, K. G. (1985). Appeals to image and claims about quality: Understanding the psychology of advertising. *Journal of Personality and Social Psychology, 49,* 586–597.

Snyder, M., & Gangestad, S. (1982). Choosing social situations: Two investigations of self-monitoring processes. *Journal of Personality and Social Psychology, 43,* 123–135.

Snyder, M., & Kendzierski, D. (1982). Acting on one's attitudes: Procedures for linking attitude and behavior. *Journal of Experimental Social Psychology, 18,* 165–183.

Snyder, M., & Omoto, A. M. (1992). Volunteerism and society's response to the HIV epidemic. *Current Directions in Psychological Science, 1,* 113–116.

Snyder, M., & Swann, W. B., Jr. (1976). When actions reflect attitudes: The politics of impression management. *Journal of Personality and Social Psychology, 34,* 1034–1042.

Snyder, M., & Swann, W. B. (1978). Behavioral confirmation in social interaction: From social perception to social reality. *Journal of Personality and Social Psychology, 36,* 1202–1212.

Snyder, M., Tanke, E. D., & Berscheid, E. (1977). Social perception and interpersonal behavior: On the self-fulfilling nature of social stereotypes. *Journal of Personality and Social Psychology, 35,* 656–666.

Solomon, H., Solomon, L. Z., Arnone, M. M., Maur, B. J., Reda, R. M., & Rother, E. O. (1981). Anonymity and helping. *Journal of Social Psychology, 113,* 37–43.

Sorrentino, R. M., & Field, N. (1986). Emergent leadership over time: The functional value of positive motivation. *Journal of Personality and Social Psychology, 50,* 1091–1099.

Spence, J. T., Deaux, K., and Helmreich, R. L. (1985). Sex roles in contemporary American society. In G. Lindzey & E. Aronson (Eds.), *Handbook of social psychology* (3rd ed., pp. 149–178). Hillsdale, NJ: Erlbaum.

Spinoza, B. (1930). The ethics. In J. Wild (Ed.), *Spinoza selections* (p. 249). (First published in 1677.)

Sprague, J., & Quadagno, D. (1989). Gender and sexual motivation: An exploration of two assumptions. *Journal of Psychology and Human Sexuality, 2,* 57–76.

Sprecher, S. (1987). The effects of self-disclosure given and received on affection for an intimate partner and stability of the relationship. *Journal of Social and Personal Relationships, 4,* 115–128.

Srull, T. K. (1981). Person memory: Some tests of associative storage and retrieval models. *Journal of Experimental Psychology: Human Learning and Memory, 7,* 440–463.

Srull, T. K., & Brand, J. F. (1983). Memory for information about persons: The effect of encoding operations upon subsequent retrieval. *Journal of Verbal Learning and Verbal Behavior, 22,* 219–230.

Srull, T. K., Lichtenstein, M., & Rothbart, M. (1985). Associative storage and retrieval processes in person memory. *Journal of Experimental Psychology: Learning, Memory, and Cognition, 11,* 316–345.

Srull, T. K., & Wyer, R. S. (1980). Category accessibility and social perception: Some implications for the study of person memory and interpersonal judgment. *Journal of Personality and Social Psychology, 38,* 841–856.

Stangor, C., Lynch, L., Duan, C., & Glass, B. (1992). Categorization of individuals on the basis of multiple social features. *Journal of Personality and Social Psychology, 62,* 207–218.

Stanley, A. (1992, November 17). President will be old enough to be (gasp!) me, many say. *New York Times.*

Stasser, G., & Stewart, D. (1992). Discovery of hidden profiles by decision-making groups: Solving a problem versus making a judgment. *Journal of Personality and Social Psychology, 63,* 426–434.

Stasser, G., Taylor, L. A., & Hanna, C. (1989). Information sampling in structured and unstructured discussions of three- and six-person groups. *Journal of Personality and Social Psychology, 57,* 67–78.

Staub, E. (1978). *Positive social behavior and morality.* New York: Academic Press.

Staub, E. (1990). Moral exclusion, personal goal theory, and extreme destructiveness. *Journal of Social Issues, 46*(1), 47–64.

Staw, B. M. (1974). Attitudinal and behavioral consequences of changing a major organizational reward: A natural field experiment. *Journal of Personality and Social Psychology, 29,* 742–751.

Staw, B. M., & Ross, J. (1987). Behavior in escalation situations: Antecedents, prototypes, and solutions. *Research in Organizational Behavior, 9,* 39–78.

Steele, C. M. (1975). Name calling and compliance. *Journal of Personality and Social Psychology, 31,* 361–369.

Steele, C. M. (1988). The psychology of self-affirmation: Sustaining the integrity of the self. In L. Berkowitz (Ed.), *Advances in experimental social psychology* (Vol. 21, pp. 261–302). San Diego, CA: Academic Press.

Steele, C. M. (1992, April). Race and the schooling of Black Americans. *Atlantic, 269*(4), pp. 68–78.

Steele, C. M., & Josephs, R. A. (1990). Alcohol myopia: Its prized and dangerous effects. *American Psychologist, 45,* 921–933.

Steele, C. M., & Liu, T. J. (1983). Dissonance processes as self-affirmation. *Journal of Personality and Social Psychology, 45,* 5–19.

Steele, C. M., & Southwick, L. (1985). Alcohol and social behavior I: The psychology of drunken excess. *Journal of Personality and Social Psychology, 48,* 18–34.

Steele, C. M., Southwick, L. L., & Critchlow, B. (1981). Dissonance and alcohol: Drinking your troubles away. *Journal of Personality and Social Psychology, 41,* 831–846.

Steele, C. M., Spencer, S. J., & Lynch, M. (1993). Self-image resilience and dissonance: The role of affirmational resources. *Journal of Personality and Social Psychology, 64,* 885–896.

Stein, A. K., & Friedrich, L. K. (1972). Television content and young children's behavior. In J. Murray, E. Rubenstein, & C. Comstock (Eds.), *Television and social learning.* Washington, DC: U.S. Government Printing Office.

Stein, L. (1967). The doctor-nurse game. *Archives of General Psychiatry, 16,* 699–703.

Steiner, I. (1972). *Group process and productivity.* New York: Academic Press.

Stephan, C. W., & Stephan, W. G. (1984). The role of ignorance in intergroup relations. In N. Miller & M. Brewer (Eds.), *Groups in contact: The psychology of desegregation* (pp. 229–255). New York: Academic Press.

Stephan, W. G. (1987). The contact hypothesis in intergroup relations. In C. Hendrick (Ed.), *Review of personality and social psychology,* (Vol. 9, pp. 13–40). Newbury Park, CA: Sage.

Stephan, W. G., & Rosenfield, D. (1978). Effects of desegregation on racial attitudes. *Journal of Personality and Social Psychology, 36,* 795–804.

Stephan, W. G., & Stephan, C. W. (1985). Intergroup anxiety. *Journal of Social Issues, 41,* 157–175.

Stern, P. C. (1992). Psychological dimensions of global environmental change. *Annual Review of Psychology, 43,* 269–302.

Sternberg, L. (1990). *From velleity to specific plans: How planning affects attitude, intention, behavior relations.* Unpublished Ph.D. dissertation, Purdue University.

Sternberg, R. J. (1986). A triangular theory of love. *Psychological Review, 93,* 119–135.

Sternberg, R. J. (1988). Triangulating love. In R. J. Sternberg & M. L. Barnes (Eds.), *The psychology of love* (pp. 119–138). New Haven: Yale University Press.

Sternberg, R. J., & Grajek, S. (1984). The nature of love. *Journal of Personality and Social Psychology, 47,* 312–329.

Sterngold, J. (1992, May 21). Japan cuts back on fingerprinting. *The New York Times,* p. A4.

Sternthal, B., Dholakia, R., & Leavitt, C. (1978). The persuasive effect of source credibility: A test of cognitive response analysis. *Journal of Consumer Research, 4,* 252–260.

Stewart, J. E. (1985). Appearance and punishment: The attraction-leniency effect in the courtroom. *Journal of Social Psychology, 125,* 373–378.

Stillinger, C., Epelbaum, M., Keltner, D., & Ross, L. (1989). *The reactive devaluation barrier to conflict resolution.* Unpublished manuscript, Stanford University.

Stogdill, R. M. (1963). *Handbook for the leader behavior description questionnaire—Form XII.* Columbus, OH: Ohio State University.

Stoltzfus, N. (1992, September). Dissent in Nazi Germany. *Atlantic Monthly,* pp. 87–94.

Stoner, J. A. (1961). *A comparison of individual and group decisions involving risk.* Unpublished master's thesis, Massachusetts Institute of Technology, Cambridge, MA.

Storms, M. D. (1973). Videotape and the attribution process: Reversing actors' and observers' points of view. *Journal of Personality and Social Psychology, 27,* 165–175.

Stouffer, S. A., Suchman, E. A., DeVinney, L. C., Star, S. A., & Williams, R. M., Jr. (1949). *The American soldier: Adjustment during army life* (Vol. 1). Princeton, NJ: Princeton University Press.

Strack, F., Martin, L. L., & Stepper, S. (1988). Inhibiting and facilitating conditions of the human smile: A nonobtrusive test of the facial feedback hypothesis. *Journal of Personality and Social Psychology, 54,* 768–777.

Strack, F., Schwarz, N., Bless, H., Kubler, A., & Wanke, M. (1989). *Remember the priming events! Episodic cues may determine assimilation versus contrast effects.* Unpublished paper, University of Mannheim.

Strauman, T. J., & Higgins, E. T. (1988). Self-discrepancies as predictors of vulnerability to distinct syndromes of chronic emotional distress. *Journal of Personality, 56,* 685–707.

Strauman, T. J., Lemieux, A. M., & Coe, C. L. (1993). Self-discrepancy and natural killer cell activity: Immunological consequences of negative self-evaluation. *Journal of Personality and Social Psychology, 64,* 1042–1052.

Straus, M. A., & Gelles, R. J. (1986). Societal change and change in family violence from 1975 to 1985 as revealed by two national surveys. *Journal of Marriage and the Family, 48,* 465–479.

Straus, M. A., Gelles, R. J., & Steinmetz, S. K. (1980). *Behind closed doors: Violence in the American family.* New York: Anchor Press.

Streufert, S., & Streufert, S. C. (1986). The development of internation conflict. In S. Worchel & W. G. Austin (Eds.), *Psychology of intergroup relations* (2nd ed., pp. 134–152). Chicago: Nelson-Hall.

Stroebe, W., & Diehl, M. (1991). You can't beat good experiments with correlational evidence: Mullen, Johnson, and Sala's meta-analytic misinterpretations. *Journal of Basic and Applied Social Psychology, 12,* 25–32.

Stroebe, W., & Stroebe, M. S. (1986). Beyond marriage: The impact of partner loss on health. In R. Gilmour & S. Duck (Eds.), *The emerging field of personal relationships* (pp. 203–224). Hillsdale, NJ: Erlbaum.

Stroebe, W., Stroebe, M. S., & Domittner, G. (1988). Individual and situational differences in recovery from bereavement: A risk group identified. *Journal of Social Issues, 44*(3), 143–158.

Stroessner, S. J., & Mackie, D. M. (1992). The impact of induced affect on the perception of variability in social groups. *Personality and Social Psychology Bulletin, 18,* 546–554.

Strube, M. J., & Garcia, J. E. (1981). A meta-analytic investigation of Fiedler's contingency model of leadership effectiveness. *Psychological Bulletin, 90,* 307–321.

Strube, M. J., Keller, N. R., Oxenberg, J., & Lapidot, D. (1989). Actual and perceived group performance as a function of group composition: The moderating role of the Type A and B behavior patterns. *Journal of Applied Social Psychology, 19,* 140–158.

Struch, N., & Schwartz, S. H. (1989). Intergroup aggression: Its predictors and distinctness from in-group bias. *Journal of Personality and Social Psychology, 56,* 364–373.

Stryker, S. (1980). *Symbolic interactionism.* Menlo Park, CA: Benjamin/Cummings.

Suedfeld, P. (1992). Bilateral relations between countries and the complexity of newspaper editorials. *Political Psychology, 13,* 601–632.

Suedfeld, P., & Tetlock, P. (1977). Integrative complexity of communications in international crises. *Journal of Conflict Resolution, 21,* 169–184.

Sugarman, D. B., & Hotaling, G. T. (1989). Violent men in intimate relationships: An analysis of risk markers. *Journal of Applied Social Psychology, 19,* 1034–1048.

Suls, J., & Fletcher, B. (1985). The relative efficacy of avoidant and nonavoidant coping strategies: A meta-analysis. *Health Psychology, 4,* 249–288.

Sumner, W. G. (1906). *Folkways.* New York: Ginn.

Surra, C. A., & Bohman, T. (1991). The development of close relationships: A cognitive perspective. In G. Fletcher & F. Fincham (Eds.), *Cognition in close relationships* (pp. 281–306.). Hillsdale, NJ: Erlbaum.

Surra, C. A., & Longstreth, M. (1990). Similarity of outcomes, interdependence, and conflict in dating relationships. *Journal of Personality and Social Psychology, 59,* 501–516.

Svenson, O. (1981). Are we all less risky and more skillful than our fellow drivers? *Acta Psychologica, 47,* 143–148.

Swann, W. B., & Ely, R. J. (1984). A battle of wills: Self-verification versus behavioral confirmation. *Journal of Personality and Social Psychology, 46,* 1287–1302.

Swann, W. B., & Hill, C. A. (1982). When our identities are mistaken: Reaffirming self-conceptions through social interaction. *Journal of Personality and Social Psychology, 43,* 59–66.

Swann, W. B., Hixon, J. G., & de la Ronde, C. (1992). Embracing the bitter "truth": Negative self-concepts and marital commitment. *Psychological Science, 3,* 118–121.

Swann, W. B., & Read, S. J. (1981). Acquiring self-knowledge: The search for feedback that fits. *Journal of Personality and Social Psychology, 41,* 1119–1128.

Swartley, W. M. (1983). *Slavery, Sabbath, war, and women.* Scottsdale, PA: Herald Press.

Sweeney, P. D., & Gruber, K. L. (1984). Selective exposure: Voter information preferences and the Watergate affair. *Journal of Personality and Social Psychology, 46,* 1208–1221.

Swingle, P. G., & Santi, A. (1972). Communication in non-zero sum games. *Journal of Personality and Social Psychology, 23,* 54–63.

Szybillo, G. J., & Heslin, R. (1973). Resistance to persuasion: Inoculation theory in a marketing context. *Journal of Marketing Research, 10,* 396–403.

Tait, R., & Silver, R. C. (1989). Coming to terms with major negative life events. In J. S. Uleman & J. A. Bargh (Eds.), *Unintended thought: Limits of awareness, intention, and control* (pp. 351–382). New York: Guilford Press.

Tajfel, H. (1972). La categorization sociale. In S. Moscovici (Ed.), *Introduction a la psychologie sociale* (Vol. 1, pp. 272–302). Paris: Larousse.

Tajfel, H. (1978). *Differentiation between social groups: Studies in the social psychology of intergroup relations.* London: Academic Press.

Tajfel, H., Billig, M. G., Bundy, R. P., & Flament, C. (1971). Social categorization and intergroup behavior. *European Journal of Social Psychology, 1,* 149–178.

Tajfel, H., Sheikh, A. A., & Gardner, R. C. (1964). Content of stereotypes and the inference of similarity between members of stereotyped groups. *Acta Psychologica, 22,* 191–201.

Tajfel, H., & Turner, J. C. (1979). An integrative theory of intergroup conflict. In W. G. Austin & S. Worchel (Eds.), *The social psychology of intergroup relations* (pp. 33–47). Monterey, CA: Brooks/Cole.

Tajfel, H., & Wilkes, A. L. (1963). Classification and quantitative judgment. *British Journal of Psychology, 54,* 101–114.

Tannen, D. (1990). *You just don't understand.* New York: Ballantine Books.

Taylor, D. A., & Moriarty, B. F. (1987) In-group bias as a function of competition and race. *Journal of Conflict Resolution, 31,* 192–199.

Taylor, D. M., Doria, J., & Tyler, J. K. (1983). Group performance and cohesiveness: An attribution analysis. *Journal of Social Psychology, 119,* 187–198.

Taylor, D. M., & Jaggi, V. (1974). Ethnocentrism and causal attribution in a south Indian context. *Journal of Cross-Cultural Psychology, 5,* 162–171.

Taylor, D. M., & Simard, L. M. (1979). Ethnic identity and intergroup relations. In D. J. Lee (Ed.), *Emerging ethnic boundaries* (pp. 155–174). Ottawa, Canada: University of Ottawa Press.

Taylor, D. M., Wright, S. C., Moghaddam, F. M., & Lalonde, R. N. (1990). The personal/group discrimination discrepancy: Perceiving my group, but not myself, to be a target for discrimination. *Personality and Social Psychology Bulletin, 16,* 254–262.

Taylor, S. E. (1975). On inferring one's attitude from one's behavior: Some delimiting conditions. *Journal of Personality and Social Psychology, 31,* 126–131.

Taylor, S. E. (1981). A categorization approach to stereotyping. In D. L. Hamilton (Ed.), *Cognitive processes in stereotyping and intergroup behavior* (pp. 83–114). Hillsdale, NJ: Erlbaum.

Taylor, S. E. (1983). Adjustment to threatening events: A theory of cognitive adaptation. *American Psychologist, 38,* 1161–1173.

Taylor, S. E., & Brown, J. D. (1988). Illusion and well-being: A social psychological perspective on mental health. *Psychological Bulletin, 103,* 193–210.

Taylor, S. E., Falke, R. L., Shoptaw, S. J., & Lichtman, R. R. (1986). Social support, support groups, and the cancer patient. *Journal of Consulting and Clinical Psychology, 54,* 608–615.

Taylor, S. E., & Fiske, S. T. (1975). Point of view and perceptions of causality. *Journal of Personality and Social Psychology, 32,* 439–445.

Taylor, S. E., Fiske, S. T., Etcoff, N. L., & Ruderman, A. J. (1978). Categorical and contextual bases of person memory and stereotyping. *Journal of Personality and Social Psychology, 36,* 778–793.

Taylor, S. E., & Lobel, M. (1989). Social comparison activity under threat: Downward evaluation and upward contacts. *Psychological Review, 96,* 569–575.

Taylor, S. P., Gammon, C. B., & Capasso, D. R. (1976). Aggression as a function of alcohol and threat. *Journal of Personality and Social Psychology, 34,* 938–941.

Tedeschi, J. T. (Ed.) (1981). *Impression management theory and social psychological research.* New York: Academic Press.

Tedeschi, J. T., Gaes, G. G., & Rivera, A. N. (1977). Aggression and the use of coercive power. *Journal of Social Issues, 33*(1), 101–125.

Tedeschi, J. T., Smith, R. B., III, & Brown, R. C. (1974). A reinterpretation of research on aggression. *Psychological Bulletin, 81,* 540–563.

Telch, M. J., Killen, J. D., McAlister, A. L., Perry, C. L., & Maccoby, N. (1981). *Long-term follow-up of a pilot program on smoking prevention with adolescents.* Paper presented at the American Psychological Association convention.

Tempest, R. (1990, June 27). French official loses job after rent-a-crowd caper. *Los Angeles Times,* pp. A1, A16.

Terkel, S. (1992). *Race.* New York: New Press.

Terry, D. (1991, February 4). Project tenants see island of safety washing away. *The New York Times,* pp. A1, B4.

Terry, D. (1993, April 11). Fear and ghosts: The world of Marcus, 19. *The New York Times,* pp. A1, A11.

Tesser, A. (1978). Self-generated attitude change. In L. Berkowitz (Ed.), *Advances in experimental social psychology* (Vol. 11, pp. 288–338). New York: Academic Press.

Tesser, A. (1988). Toward a self-evaluation maintenance model of social behavior. In L. Berkowitz (Ed.), *Advances in experimental social psychology* (Vol. 21, pp. 181–227). San Diego, CA: Academic Press.

Tesser, A. (1993). The importance of heritability in psychological research: The case of attitudes. *Psychological Review, 100,* 129–142.

Tesser, A., & Collins, J. E. (1988). Emotion in social reflection and comparison situations: Intuitive, systematic, and exploratory approaches. *Journal of Personality and Social Psychology, 55,* 695–709.

Tesser, A., & Cornell, D. P. (1991). On the confluence of self processes. *Journal of Experimental Social Psychology, 27,* 501–526.

Tetlock, P. E. (1983). Accountability and complexity of thought. *Journal of Personality and Social Psychology, 45,* 74–83.

Tetlock, P. E. (1985). Accountability: The neglected social context of judgment and choice. *Research in Organizational Behavior, 7,* 297–332.

Tetlock, P. E. (1988). Monitoring the integrative complexity of American and Soviet policy rhetoric: What can be learned? *Journal of Social Issues, 44*(2), 101–131.

Tetlock, P. E. (1989). The selfishness-altruism debate: In defense of agnosticism. *Behavioral and Brain Sciences, 12,* 723–724.

Tetlock, R. E. (1985). Integrative complexity of American and Soviet foreign policy rhetoric: A time-series analysis. *Journal of Personality and Social Psychology, 49,* 1565–1585.

Thibaut, J. J., & Kelley, H. H. (1959). *The social psychology of groups.* New York: Wiley.

Thompson, L. (1990). Negotiation behavior and outcomes: Empirical evidence and theoretical issues. *Psychological Bulletin, 108,* 515–532.

Thompson, L. (1993). The impact of negotiation on intergroup relations. *Journal of Experimental Social Psychology, 29,* 304–325.

Thompson, L., & Hastie, R. (1990a). Judgment tasks and biases in negotiation. In B. H. Sheppard, M. H. Bazerman, & R. J. Lewicki (Eds.), *Research in negotiation in organizations* (Vol. 2, pp. 31–54). Greenwich, CT: JAI Press.

Thompson, L., & Hastie, R. (1990b). Social perception in negotiation. *Organizational Behavior and Human Decision Processes, 47,* 98–123.

Thompson, W. C., Cowan, C. L., & Rosenhan, D. L. (1980). Focus of attention mediates the impact of negative affect on altruism. *Journal of Personality and Social Psychology, 38,* 291–300.

Thompson, W. C., Fong, G. T., & Rosenhan, D. L. (1981). Inadmissible evidence and juror verdicts. *Journal of Personality and Social Psychology, 40,* 453–463.

Thoresen, C. E., & Low, K. G. (1990). Women and the Type A behavior pattern: Review and commentary. *Journal of Social Behavior and Personality, 5,* 117–133.

Tilker, H. A. (1970). Socially responsible behavior as a function of observer responsibility and victim feedback. *Journal of Personality and Social Psychology, 49,* 420–428.

Tindale, R. S., & Davis, J. H. (1983). Group decision making and jury verdicts. In H. H. Blumberg, A. P. Hare, V. Kent, & M. F. Davies (Eds.), *Small groups and social interaction* (Vol. 2, pp. 9–38). New York: Wiley.

Tindale, R. S., Davis, J. H., Vollrath, D. A., Nagao, D. H., & Hinsz, V. B. (1990). Asymmetrical social influence in freely interacting groups: A test of three models. *Journal of Personality and Social Psychology, 58,* 438–449.

Tobias, S. (1990). *They're not dumb, they're different.* Tucson, AZ: Research Corporation.

Toi, M., & Batson, C. D. (1982). More evidence that empathy is a source of altruistic motivation. *Journal of Personality and Social Psychology, 43,* 281–292.

Tourangeau, R., & Rasinski, K. A. (1988). Cognitive processes underlying context effects in attitude measurement. *Psychological Bulletin, 103,* 299–314.

Trafimow, D., Triandis, H. C., & Goto, S. G. (1991). Some tests of the distinction between the private self and the collective self. *Journal of Personality and Social Psychology, 60,* 649–655.

Trew, K. (1986). Catholic-Protestant contact in Northern Ireland. In M. Hewstone & R. Brown (Eds), *Contact and conflict in intergroup encounters* (pp. 93–106). London: Blackwell.

Triandis, H. C. (1977). *Interpersonal behavior.* Monterey, CA: Brooks/Cole.

Triandis, H. C. (1980). Values, attitudes, and interpersonal behavior. In H. Howe & M. Page (Eds.), *Nebraska Symposium on Motivation* (Vol. 27, pp. 195–260). Lincoln: University of Nebraska Press.

Triandis, H. C., Bontempo, R., Villareal, M. J., Asai, M., & Lucca, N. (1988). Individualism and collectivism: Cross-cultural perspectives on self-ingroup relationships. *Journal of Personality and Social Psychology, 54,* 323–338.

Trimble, J. E. (1988). Stereotypical images, American Indians, and prejudice. In P. A. Katz & D. A. Taylor (Eds.), *Eliminating racism: Profiles in controversy* (pp. 181–202). New York: Plenum Press.

Tripathi, R. C., & Srivasta, R. (1981). Relative deprivation and intergroup attitudes. *European Journal of Social Psychology, 11,* 313–318.

Triplett, N. (1898). The dynamogenic factors in pacemaking and competition. *American Journal of Psychology, 9,* 507–533.

Tripp, C. A. (1975). *The homosexual matrix.* New York: McGraw-Hill.

Trivers, R. L. (1971). The evolution of reciprocal altruism. *Quarterly Review of Biology, 46,* 35–57.

Trope, Y. (1986). Identification and inferential processes in dispositional attribution. *Psychological Review, 93,* 239–257.

Trope, Y., Bassok, M., & Alon, E. (1984). The questions lay interviewers ask. *Journal of Personality, 52,* 90–106.

Trope, Y., & Mackie, D. M. (1987). Sensitivity to alternatives in social hypothesis-testing. *Journal of Experimental Social Psychology, 23,* 445–459.

Trost, M. R., Cialdini, R. B., & Maas, A. (1989). Effects of an international conflict simulation of perceptions of the Soviet Union: A FIREBREAKS backfire. *Journal of Social Issues, 45,* 139–158.

Tuckman, B. W. (1965). Developmental sequences in small groups. *Psychological Bulletin, 63,* 384–399.

Turnbull, W., Miller, D. T., & McFarland, C. (1990). Population-distinctiveness, identity, and bonding. In J. M. Olson & M. P. Zanna (Eds.), *Self-inference processes: The Ontario Symposium* (Vol. 6, pp. 115–133). Hillsdale, NJ: Erlbaum.

Turner, C. W., Simons, L. S., Berkowitz, L., & Frodi, A. (1977). The stimulating and inhibiting effects of weapons on aggressive behavior. *Aggressive Behavior, 3,* 355–378.

Turner, J. C. (1980). Fairness or discrimination in intergroup behavior? A reply to Braithwaite, Doyle, and Lightbrown. *European Journal of Social Psychology, 10,* 131–147.

Turner, J. C. (1981a). The experimental social psychology of intergroup behavior. In J. C. Turner & H. Giles (Eds.), *Intergroup behavior* (pp. 66–101). Chicago, IL: University of Chicago Press.

Turner, J. C. (1981b). Towards a cognitive redefinition of the social group. *Cahiers de Psychologie Cognitive, 1,* 93–118.

Turner, J. C. (1982). Towards a cognitive redefinition of the social group. In H. Tajfel (Ed.), *Social identity and intergroup relations.* Cambridge: Cambridge University Press.

Turner, J. C. (1991). *Social influence.* Pacific Grove, CA: Brooks/Cole.

Turner, J. C., Hogg, M. A., Oakes, P. J., Reicher, S. D., & Wetherell, M. S. (1987). *Rediscovering the social group: A self-categorization theory.* Oxford: Blackwell.

Turner, J. C., Sachdev, I., & Hogg, M. A. (1983). Social categorization, interpersonal attraction, and group formation. *British Journal of Social Psychology, 22,* 227–239.

Tushman, M. L. (1978). Technical communication in research and development laboratories: The impact of project work characteristics. *Academy of Management Journal, 21,* 624–645.

Tyler, T. R., & Lind, E. A. (1990). Intrinsic versus community-based justice models: When does group membership matter? *Journal of Social Issues, 46*(1), 83–94.

Uleman, J. S., & Bargh, J. A. (1989). *Unintended thought: Limits of awareness, intention, and control.* New York: Guilford Press.

U.S. Census Bureau. (1986). *Statistical Abstract of the United States: 1987.* Washington, DC: U.S. Government Printing Office.

U.S. Health Care Financing Administration. (1982). Cited in Cialdini, R. B. (1988). *Influence: Science and practice* (2nd ed., p. 208). Glenview, IL: Scott, Foresman & Co.

Vachon, M. L., Rogers, J., Lyall, W. A., Lancee, W. J., Sheldon, A. R., & Freeman, S. J. J. (1982). Predictors and correlates of adaptation to conjugal bereavement. *American Journal of Psychiatry, 139,* 998–1002.

Vallacher, R. R., & Wegner, D. M. (1987). What do people think they're doing? Action identification and human behavior. *Psychological Review, 94,* 3–15.

Vallone, R. P., Ross, L., & Lepper, M. R. (1985). The hostile media phenomenon: Biased perception and perceptions of media bias in coverage of the Beirut massacre. *Journal of Personality and Social Psychology, 49,* 577–585.

Vanbeselaere, N. (1991). The different effects of simple and crossed categorization: A result of the category differentiation process or of differential category salience? In W. Stroebe & M. Hewstone (Eds.), *European review of social psychology* (Vol. 2, pp. 247–278). Chichester, England: John Wiley & Sons.

Van Egeren, L. F. (1979). Cardiovascular changes during social competition in a mixed-motive game. *Journal of Personality and Social Psychology, 37,* 858–864.

Van Gyn, G. H., Wenger, H. A., & Gaul, C. A. (1990). Imagery as a method of enhancing transfer from training to performance. *Journal of Sport and Exercise Psychology, 12,* 366–375.

Vanman, E. J., & Miller, N. (1993). Applications of emotion theory and research to stereotyping and intergroup relations. In D. M. Mackie & D. L. Hamilton (Eds.), *Affect, cognition, and stereotyping: Interactive processes in group perception* (pp. 213–238). New York: Academic Press.

Vanneman, R. D., & Pettigrew, T. F. (1972). Race and relative deprivation in the urban United States. *Race, 13,* 461–486.

Van Yperen, N. W., & Buunk, B. P. (1991). Sex-role attitudes, social comparison, and satisfaction with relationships. *Social Psychology Quarterly, 54,* 169–180.

Veroff, J., Douvan, E., & Kukla, R. A. (1981). *The inner American: A self-portrait from 1957 to 1976.* New York: Basic Books.

Vroom, V. H. (1976). Leadership. In M. D. Dunnette (Ed.),

Handbook of industrial and organizational psychology (pp. 1527–1552). Chicago: Rand McNally.

Waldman, S. (1991, May 6). Watering the grass roots: How to buy a "spontaneous" popular uprising. *Newsweek,* p. 35.

Walker, I., & Mann, L. (1987). Unemployment, relative deprivation, and social protest. *Personality and Social Psychology Bulletin, 13,* 275–283.

Walster, E., Aronson, V., Abrahams, D., & Rottman, L. (1966). The importance of physical attractiveness in dating behavior. *Journal of Personality and Social Psychology, 4,* 508–516.

Walster, E., & Festinger, L. (1962). The effectiveness of "overheard" persuasive communications. *Journal of Abnormal and Social Psychology, 65,* 395–402.

Walster, E., Walster, G. W., & Berscheid, E. (1978). *Equity: Theory and research.* Boston, MA: Allyn & Bacon.

Walton, R. E., Dutton, J. M., & Cafferty, T. P. (1969). Organizational context and interdepartmental conflict. *Administrative Sciences Quarterly, 14,* 522–542.

Walzer, M. (1970). *Obligations.* Cambridge, MA: Harvard University Press.

Watson, D., & Pennebaker, J. W. (1989). Health complaints, stress, and distress: Exploring the central role of negative affectivity. *Psychological Review, 96,* 234–254.

Weber, R., & Crocker, J. (1983). Cognitive processes in the revision of stereotypic beliefs. *Journal of Personality and Social Psychology, 45,* 961–977.

Wech, C. E., Lundstrum, R. H., & Moore, A. (1989). Bogus-pipeline effects on self-reported college student drug use, problems, and attitudes. *The International Journal of the Addictions, 24,* 1003–1010.

Wegner, D., & Schaefer, D. (1978). The concentration of responsibility: An objective self-awareness analysis of group size effects in helping situations. *Journal of Personality and Social Psychology, 36,* 147–155.

Wegner, D. M., & Vallacher, R. R. (1986). Action identification. In R. M. Sorrentino & E. T. Higgins (Eds.), *Handbook of motivation and cognition: Foundations of social behavior* (Vol. 1, pp. 550–582). New York: Guilford Press.

Weigel, R. H., Loomis, J. W., & Soja, M. J. (1980). Race relations on prime-time television. *Journal of Personality and Social Pyschology, 39,* 884–893.

Weiner, B. (1985). An attributional theory of achievement motivation and emotion. *Psychological Review, 92,* 548–573.

Weinstein, N. D. (1980). Unrealistic optimism about future life events. *Journal of Personality and Social Psychology, 39,* 806–820.

Weinstein, N. D. (1987). Unrealistic optimism about susceptibility to health problems: Conclusions from a community-wide sample. *Journal of Behavioral Medicine, 10,* 481–500.

Weir, W. (1984). Another look at subliminal "facts." *Advertising Age, 46.*

Weiss, R. S. (1976). The emotional impact of marital separation. *Journal of Social Issues, 32*(1), 135–146.

Weldon, E., & Mustari, E. L. (1988). Felt dispensability in groups of coactors: The effects of shared responsibility and explicit anonymity on cognitive effort. *Organizational Behavior and Human Decision Processes, 41,* 330–351.

Wellesley College Center for Research on Women. (1992). *How schools shortchange girls: The AAUW Report.* Washington, DC: American Association of University Women Educational Foundation.

Wells, G. L., & Gavanski, I. (1989). Mental simulation of causality. *Journal of Personality and Social Psychology, 56,* 161–169.

Wells, G. L., & Murray, D. M. (1984). Eyewitness confidence. In G. L. Wells & E. F. Loftus (Eds.), *Eyewitness testimony: Psychological perspectives.* New York: Cambridge University Press.

Wells, G. L., & Petty, R. E. (1980). The effects of overt head-movements on persuasion: Compatibility and incompatibility of responses. *Basic and Applied Social Psychology, 1,* 219–230.

Wetherell, M. S. (1987). Social identity and group polarization. In J. C. Turner, M. A. Hogg, P. J. Oakes, S. D. Reicher, & M. S. Wetherell (Eds.), *Rediscovering the social group: A self-categorization theory* (pp. 142–170). Oxford: Blackwell.

Wheeler, L. (1974). Social comparison and selective affiliation. In T. Huston (Ed.), *Foundations of interpersonal attraction* (pp. 309–329). New York: Academic Press.

Wheeler, L., Reis, H. T., & Nezlek, J. (1983). Loneliness, social interaction, and sex roles. *Journal of Personality and Social Psychology, 45,* 943–953.

White, G. L. (1981). A model of romantic jealousy. *Motivation and emotion, 5,* 295–310.

White, G. L., Fishbein, S., & Rutstein, J. (1981). Passionate love: The misattribution of arousal. *Journal of Personality and Social Psychology, 41,* 56–62.

White, R. W. (1959). Motivation reconsidered: The concept of competence. *Psychological Review, 66,* 297–333.

White, R. K. (1965). Images in the context of international conflict: Soviet perceptions of the U.S. and the U.S.S.R. In H. C. Kelman (Ed.), *International behavior: A social-psychological analysis* (pp. 236–276). New York: Holt, Rinehart & Winston.

White, R. K. (1971, November). Selective inattention. *Psychology Today,* pp. 47–50, 78–84.

White, R. K. (1977). Misperception in the Arab-Israeli conflict. *Journal of Social Issues, 33,* 190–221.

White, R. K. (1984). *Fearful warriors: A psychological profile in U.S.-Soviet relations.* New York: Free Press.

White, R. K. (1987). Underestimating and overestimating others' fear. *Journal of Social Issues, 43*(4), 105–110.

Wicker, A. W. (1969). Attitudes versus actions: The relationship of verbal and overt behavioral responses to attitude objects. *Journal of Social Issues, 25,* 41–78.

Wicklund, R. A., & Brehm, J. W. (1976). *Perspectives on cognitive dissonance.* Hillsdale, NJ: Erlbaum.

Wilder, D. (1977). Perception of groups, size of opposition, and social influence. *Journal of Experimental Social Psychology, 13,* 253–268.

Wilder, D. A. (1981). Perceiving persons as a group: Categorization and intergroup relations. In D. L. Hamilton (Ed.), *Cognitive processes in stereotyping and intergroup behavior* (pp. 213–258). Hillsdale, NJ: Erlbaum.

Wilder, D. A. (1984). Intergroup contact: The typical member and the exception to the rule. *Journal of Experimental Social Psychology, 20,* 177–194.

Wilder, D. A. (1986). Social categorization: Implications for creation and reduction of intergroup bias. In L. Berkowitz (Ed.), *Advances in experimental social psychology* (Vol. 19, pp. 291–355). New York: Academic Press.

Wilder, D. A. (1990). Some determinants of the persuasive power of in-groups and out-groups: Organization of information and attribution of independence. *Journal of Personality and Social Psychology, 59,* 1202–1213.

Wilder, D. A., & Shapiro, P. N. (1984). Role of out-group cues in determining social identity. *Journal of Personality and Social Psychology, 47,* 342–348.

Wilder, D. A., & Shapiro, P. N. (1988). Role of competition-induced anxiety in limiting the beneficial impact of positive behavior by out-group members. *Journal of Personality and Social Psychology, 56,* 60–69.

Wilder, D. A., & Shapiro, P. (1991). Facilitation of outgroup stereotypes by enhanced ingroup identity. *Journal of Experimental Social Psychology, 27,* 431–452.

Wilder, D. A., & Thompson, J. E. (1980). Intergroup contact with independent manipulations of in-group and out-group interaction. *Journal of Personality and Social Psychology, 38,* 589–603.

Wilke, W. L., & Farris, P. W. (1975). *Consumer information processing: Perspective and implications for advertising.* Cambridge, MA: Marketing Science Institute.

Wilkerson, I. (1992, June 21). The tallest fence: Feelings on race in a White neighborhood. *The New York Times,* pp. A1, A12.

Williams, E. (1977). Experimental comparisons of face-to-face and mediated communication: A review. *Psychological Bulletin, 84,* 963–976.

Williams, J. E., & Best, D. L. (1982). *Measuring sex stereotypes: A thirty-nation study.* Beverly Hills, CA: Sage Publications.

Williams, K. D., Harkins, S., & Latané, B. (1981). Identifiability as a deterrent to social loafing: Two cheering experiments. *Journal of Personality and Social Psychology, 40,* 303–311.

Williams, K. D., & Karau, S. J. (1991). Social loafing and social compensation: The effects of expectations of co-worker performance. *Journal of Personality and Social Psychology, 61,* 570–581.

Williams, L. (1991, April 30). When Blacks shop, bias often accompanies sale. *The New York Times,* pp. A1, A9.

Williams, L. (1991, November 30). In a 90's quest for Black identity, intense doubts and disagreement. *The New York Times,* pp. A1, A7.

Williams, L. (1992, December 15). Scrambling to manage a diverse work force. *The New York Times,* pp. A1, C2.

Williamson, G. M., & Clark, M. S. (1989). Providing help and desired relationship type as determinants of changes in moods and self-evaluations. *Journal of Personality and Social Psychology, 56,* 722–734.

Willis, R. (1986, March). Harley Davidson comes roaring back. *Management Review, 75,* 20–27.

Wills, T. A. (1991). Social support and interpersonal relations. In M. S. Clark (Ed.), *Prosocial behavior* (pp. 265–289). Beverly Hills, CA: Sage Publications.

Wilson, D. K., Kaplan, R. M., & Schneiderman, L. J. (1987). Framing of decisions and selections of alternatives in health care. *Social Behavior, 2,* 51–59.

Wilson, D. K., Purdon, S. E., & Wallston, K. A. (1988). Compliance to health recommendations: A theoretical overview of message framing. *Health Education Research, 3,* 161–171.

Wilson, T. D., & Dunn, D. S. (1986). Effects of introspection on attitude-behavior consistency. Analyzing reasons versus focusing on feelings. *Journal of Experimental Social Psychology, 22,* 249–263.

Wilson, T. D., Laser, P. S., & Stone, J. I. (1982). Judging the predictors of one's own mood: Accuracy and the use of shared theories. *Journal of Experimental Social Psychology, 18,* 537–549.

Wilson, T. D., & Linville, P. W. (1982). Improving the academic performance of college freshmen: Attribution therapy revisited. *Journal of Personality and Social Psychology, 42,* 367–376.

Wilson, T. D., Lisle, D. J., Schooler, J. W., Hodges, S. D., Klaaren, K. J., & LaFleur, S. J. (1993). Introspecting about reasons can reduce post-choice satisfaction. *Personality and Social Psychology Bulletin, 19,* 331–339.

Witteman, P. A. (1990, April 30). Vietnam: Fifteen years later. *Time,* pp. 19–21.

Wolfgang, M., & Strohm, R. B. (1956). The relationship between alcohol and criminal homicide. *Quarterly Journal of Studies on Alcohol, 17,* 411–425.

Wood, J. V. (1989). Theory and research concerning social comparisons of personal attributes. *Psychological Bulletin, 106,* 231–248.

Wood, J. V., Taylor, S. E., & Lichtman, R. R. (1985). Social comparison in adjustment to breast cancer. *Journal of Personality and Social Psychology, 49,* 1169–1183.

Wood, W. (1982). Retrieval of attitude-relevant information from memory: Effects on susceptibility to persuasion and on intrinsic motivation. *Journal of Personality and Social Psychology, 42,* 798–810.

Wood, W. (1987). Meta-analytic review of sex differences in group performance. *Psychological Bulletin, 102,* 53–71.

Wood, W., Kallgren, C., & Preisler, R. (1985). Access to attitude relevant information in memory as a determinant of persuasion. *Journal of Experimental Social Psychology, 21,* 73–85.

Worchel, S., Lee, J., & Adewole, A. (1975). Effects of supply and demand on ratings of object value. *Journal of Personality and Social Psychology, 32,* 906–914.

Worchel, S. (1979). Cooperation and the reduction of intergroup conflict: Some determining factors. In W. G. Austin & S. Worchel (Eds.), *The social psychology of intergroup conflict* (pp. 262–273). Monterey, CA: Brooks/Cole.

Worchel, S., & Norvell, N. (1980). Effect of perceived environmental conditions during cooperation on intergroup attraction. *Journal of Personality and Social Psychology, 38,* 764–772.

Word, C. O., Zanna, M. P., & Cooper, J. (1974). The nonverbal mediation of self-fulfilling prophecies in interracial interaction. *Journal of Experimental Social Psychology, 10,* 109–120.

Worringham, C. J., & Messick, D. M. (1983). Social facilitation of running: An unobtrusive study. *Journal of Social Psychology, 121,* 23–29.

Worth, L. T., & Mackie, D. M. (1987). Cognitive mediation of positive affect in persuasion. *Social Cognition, 5,* 76–94.

Worth, L. T., Smith, J., & Mackie, D. M. (1992). Gender schematicity and preference for gene-typed products. *Psychology and Marketing, 9,* 17–30.

Wortman, C., Adesman, P., Herman, E., & Greenberg, R. (1976). Self-disclosure: An attributional perspective. *Journal of Personality and Social Psychology, 33,* 184–191.

Wright, J. C., & Mischel, W. (1987). A conditional approach to dispositional constructs: The local predictability of social behavior. *Journal of Personality and Social Psychology, 53,* 1159–1177.

Wright, P. H. (1982). Men's friendships, women's friendships and the alleged inferiority of the latter. *Sex Roles, 8,* 1–20.

Wright, Q. (1965). Escalation of international conflicts. *Journal of Conflict Resolution, 9,* 434–449.

Wyer, R. S., Budesheim, T. L., & Lambert, A. J. (1990). Cognitive representation of conversations about persons. *Journal of Personality and Social Psychology, 58,* 218–238.

Wyer, R. S., & Srull, T. K. (1989). *Memory and cognition in its social context.* Hillsdale, NJ: Erlbaum.

Yalom, I. D. (1985). *The theory and practice of group psychotherapy.* New York: Basic Books.

Yamagishi, T. (1986). The provision of a sanctioning system as a public good. *Journal of Personality and Social Psychology, 51,* 110–116.

Yamagishi, T. (1988). The provision of a sanctioning system in the United States and Japan. *Social Psychology Quarterly, 51,* 265–271.

Younger, J. C., Walker, L., & Arrowood, A. J. (1977). Postdecision dissonance at the fair. *Personality and Social Psychology Bulletin, 3,* 247–287.

Youngs, G. A., Jr. (1986). Patterns of threat and punishment reciprocity in a conflict setting. *Journal of Personality and Social Psychology, 51,* 541–546.

Yukl, G. (1974). Effects of the opponent's initial offer, concession magnitude, and concession frequency on bargaining behavior. *Journal of Personality and Social Psychology, 30,* 323–335.

Zaccaro, S. J. (1984). Social loafing: The role of task attractiveness. *Personality and Social Psychology Bulletin, 10,* 99–106.

Zajonc, R. B. (1965). Social facilitation. *Science, 149,* 269–274.

Zajonc, R. B. (1968). Attitudinal effects of mere exposure. *Journal of Personality and Social Psychology, 9,* Monograph Suppl. No. 2, part 2.

Zajonc, R. B., & Sales, S. M. (1966). Social facilitation of dominant and subordinate responses. *Journal of Experimental Social Psychology, 2,* 160–168.

Zanna, M. P., Kiesler, C. A., & Pilkonis, P. A. (1970). Positive and negative attitudinal affect established by classical conditioning. *Journal of Personality and Social Psychology, 14,* 321–328.

Zanna, M. P., & Rempel, J. K. (1988). Attitudes: A new look at an old concept. In D. Bar-Tal & A. Kruglanski (Eds.), *The social psychology of knowledge* (pp. 315–334). New York: Cambridge University Press.

Zárate, M. A., & Smith, E. R. (1990). Person categorization and stereotyping. *Social Cognition, 8,* 161–185.

Zastrow, C. (1988). *Social problems: Issues and solutions* (2nd ed.). Chicago: Nelson-Hall.

Zillmann, D. (1971). Excitation transfer in communication-mediated aggressive behavior. *Journal of Experimental Social Psychology, 7,* 419–434.

Zillmann, D. (1978). Attribution and misattribution of excitatory reactions. In J. H. Harvey, W. J. Ickes, & R. F. Kidd (Eds.), *New directions in attribution research* (Vol. 2, pp. 335–368). Hillsdale, NJ: Erlbaum.

Zillmann, D. (1979). *Hostility and aggression.* Hillsdale, NJ: Erlbaum.

Zillmann, D. (1982). Transfer of excitation in emotional behavior. In J. T. Cacioppo & R. E. Petty (Eds.), *Social psychophysiology* (pp. 215–240). New York: Guilford Press.

Zillmann, D., & Cantor, J. R. (1976). Effect of timing of information about mitigating circumstances on emotional responses to provocation and retaliatory behavior. *Journal of Experimental Social Psychology, 12,* 38–55.

Zillmann, D., Katcher, A. H., & Milavsky, B. (1972). Excitation transfer from physical exercise to subsequent aggressive behavior. *Journal of Experimental Social Psychology, 8,* 247–259.

Zimbardo, P. G. (1970). The human choice: Individuation, reason, and order versus deindividuation, impulse, and chaos. In W. J. Arnold & D. Levine (Eds.), *Nebraska Symposium on Motivation 1969* (Vol. 17, pp. 237–307). Lincoln: University of Nebraska Press.

Zimbardo, P. G. (1977). *Shyness.* New York: Jove.

Zimbardo, P. G., Banks, W. C., Haney, C., & Jaffe, D. (1973, April 8). The mind is a formidable jailer: A Pirandellian prison. *The New York Times Magazine,* pp. 38–60.

Zuckerman, M. (1979). *Sensation seeking: Beyond the optimal level of arousal.* Hillsdale, NJ: Erlbaum.

Zuckerman, M., DePaulo, B. M., & Rosenthal, R. (1981). Verbal and nonverbal communication of deception. In L. Berkowitz (Ed.), *Advances in experimental social psychology* (Vol. 14, pp. 1–59). New York: Academic Press.

Illustration Credits

Chapter 1 Opener Joel Gordon; **p. 3** Joel Gordon; **p. 6** Catherine Karnow/Woodfin Camp & Associates; **p. 9** Bill Bachmann/Stock, Boston; **p. 13** UPI/Bettmann Archive; **p. 16** Spencer Grant/Photo Researchers; **p. 18** Ted Mathias/AP/Wide World Photos; **p. 23** Ann States/Saba

Chapter 2 Opener Fujifotos/The Image Works; **p. 35 (left and right)** From "Social Psychology," Fig. 11-18a (p. 258) and Fig. 11-11 (p. 249), Copyright 1969, Muzafer Sherif and Carolyn W. Sherif, published by Harper & Row, Publishers, Inc.; **p. 38** Treë; **p. 41** Peter Byron/Monkmeyer; **p. 47** Treë; **p. 49 (left)** Fujifotos/The Image Works; **(right)** K. B. Kaplan/The Picture Cube; **p. 56 and p. 57 (left and right)** Philip G. Zimbardo, Stanford University

Chapter 3 Opener Treë; **p. 68 and p. 69** Treë; **p. 72** Busacca/Tisman/Retna Ltd.; **p. 76** R. Bossu/Sygma; **p. 77 and p. 78** Neal Simpson/Empics Ltd./Woodfin Camp & Associates; **p. 87** Larry Downing/Woodfin Camp & Associates; **p. 99** Treë; **p. 101** F. Lee Corkran/Sygma

Chapter 4 Opener Richard Hutchings/Photo Researchers; **p. 116** Robert McElroy/Woodfin Camp & Associates; **p. 118** Tom McCarthy/The Picture Cube; **p. 121** Reuters/Bettmann Archive; **p. 128** Haruyoshi Yamaguchi/Sygma; **p. 149** John Sotomayer/New York Times Pictures; **p. 159** Tony Duffy/Allsport USA

Chapter 5 Opener Robert W. Ginn/The Picture Cube; **p. 170** Susan Greenwood/New York Times Pictures; **p. 174** Bill Anderson/Monkmeyer; **p. 183** Joseph Pepe DeChiazza/New York Times Pictures; **p. 189** Eric Pasquier/Sygma; **p. 197** Courtesy Master Lock Company; **p. 204** James D. Denham; **p. 206** Goldberg/Sygma

Chapter 6 Opener Mikki Ansin/The Picture Cube; **p. 222** Gene Peach/The Picture Cube; **p. 225** Courtesy Saturn Corporation; **p. 228** Courtesy Zupnik Cinema Group II/GGR; **p. 229** Rashid/Monkmeyer; **p. 243** P. Chauvel/Sygma; **p. 246** AP/Wide World Photos; **p. 252** Peter Glass/Monkmeyer

Chapter 7 Opener Joan Liftin/Actuality; **p. 267** Elsa Peterson/Design Conceptions; **p. 281** Courtesy Save The Children Federation; **p. 293** Pat Farley/Monkmeyer; **p. 297** MADD, Minnesota State Office and Clarity Coverdale Rueff, Minneapolis

Chapter 8 Opener Ivan Massar/Positive Images; **p. 313** Marty Heitner/Impact Visuals; **p. 327** Richard Kalvar/Magnum Photos; **p. 340** Treë

Chapter 9 Opener Dominique Buisson/Agence Vandystadt/Photo Researchers; **p. 353** Gary Rogers/The Image Bank; **p. 356** William Vandivert/*Scientific American;* **p. 363** Art Seitz/Sygma; **p. 370** Marilyn Humphries/Impact Visuals; **p. 372** Rick Scott/The Picture Cube; **p. 377** Peter Southwick/Stock, Boston; **p. 392** Photofest

Chapter 10 Opener Bob Daemmrich/The Image Works; **p. 406** Ted Thai/*Time* Magazine; **p. 408** S. Franklin/Sygma; **p. 410** Bob Daemmrich/The Image Works; **p. 421 and 422** ©1965 Stanley Milgram. From the film "Obedience," dist. by Pennsylvania State U, PCR; **p. 430** John Paul Filo; **p. 437** Reuters/Bettmann Archive

Chapter 11 Opener Eric Millette/The Picture Cube; **p. 451** The Granger Collection; **p. 453** Frank Siteman/The Picture Cube; **p. 477** Joel Gordon; **p. 484** James D. Wilson/Woodfin Camp & Associates; **p. 487 (left)** The Granger Collection; **(right)** © Kinuko Y. Craft; **p. 491** Steve Wewerka/Impact Visuals

Chapter 12 Opener Randy Taylor/Gamma-Liaison; **p. 504 (top)** Bruce Coleman/Bruce Coleman, Inc.; **(bottom)** L. & D. Klein/Photo Researchers; **p. 507** Jeffrey D. Scott/Impact Visuals; **p. 509** Ricky Flores/Impact Visuals; **p. 511** Eli Reed/Magnum Photos; **p. 516** Jerry Howard/Positive Images; **p. 527** Steve McCurry/Magnum Photos; **p. 531** Serge de Sazo/Rapho/Photo Researchers; **p. 535** B. Daemmrich/The Image Works; **p. 541** Jeffrey D. Scott/Impact Visuals

Chapter 13 Opener Juliet Stone/Boston Urban Gardeners; **p. 557** Jerry Howard/Postive Images; **p. 561** John Beiver/*Sports Illustrated;* **p. 563** Lars Bahl/Impact Visuals; **p. 568** Paul Bocuse/Stock, Boston; **p. 584** Laura Pedrick/New York Times Pictures; **p. 588** Rick Friedman/New York Times Pictures

Chapter 14 Opener Jay Ullal/Stern/Black Star; **p. 604** The Granger Collection; **p. 606** Reuters/Bettmann Archive; **p. 614** AP/Wide World Photos; **p. 623** Reuters/Bettmann Archive; **p. 630** Allan Tannenbaum/Sygma; **p. 633** Gary Langley

Epilogue Opener Joel Gordon

Name Index

Subject Index

	Chapter 8 **Attitudes and Behavior**	Chapter 9 **Groups, Norms, and Conformity**	Chapter 10 **Norms and Behavior**
Construction of Reality	Our actions are guided by the attitudes we have constructed toward the world.	Individuals and groups construct consensus about what is true and good.	Every situation can be interpreted in multiple ways, making different norms applicable.
Pervasive Social Influence	Both our attitudes and our behavior are shaped by other people and by our social surroundings.	This construction process involves conformity and mutual influence among group members.	Social norms influence our actions, even when we are not physically in the group.
Striving for Mastery		Conformity helps us to hold valid opinions because the convergence of many opinions often means correctness.	Following norms helps us to obtain rewards from others.
Seeking Connectedness		Conformity helps us feel connected to and valued by other group members.	Following norms helps us to feel like good group members.
Valuing Me and Mine			
Conservatism		Positions supported by a majority in a group usually attract more supporters and do not readily change.	
Accessibility	Attitudes can guide behavior only when they come to mind.		Increasing the accessibility of norms increases their impact on behavior.
Superficiality Versus Depth	The effect of behavior on attitudes, and also the effect of attitudes on behavior, can reflect either superficial processing or more thoughtful systematic processing.	People process the opinions of other group members either in superficial ways or with careful consideration.	Resisting the effects of norms sometimes requires extensive thought.